TIMELINES
WORLD
of
HISTORY

JOHN B TEEPLE

DK PUBLISHING

LONDON • NEW YORK • MUNICH • MELBOURNE • DELHI

www.dk.com

LONDON, NEW YORK, MUNICH, MELBOURNE, DELHI

DORLING KINDERSLEY LIMITED

Senior Editor Debra Clapson
Art Editor Karen Gregory
Editorial Contributors Ailsa Heritage, Elizabeth Wyse,
Thomas Cussans, Ferdie McDonald, Catherine Day
Designer Heather Dunleavy

Publisher Andrew Heritage
Senior Project Manager David Roberts
Senior Managing Art Editor Philip Lord

Picture Research Franziska Marking
Picture librarians Jonathan Brooks, Mark Dennis,
Sarah Mills, Hayley Smith
Digital maps created by Rob Stokes
Project cartographer Iowerth Watkins
Systems Coordinator Philip Rowles
Production Wendy Penn, Louise Daly
Jacket design Chris Drew

DORLING KINDERSLEY INDIA LIMITED
Project Editor Dipali Singh
Editor Glenda Fernandes
Project designer Romi Chakraborty
Designer Elizabeth Thomas
DTP Narender Kumar
DTP Coordinator Pankaj Sharma
Managing Editor Ira Pande
Managing Art Editor Shuka Jain

First American Edition, 2002
Reprinted (with revisions) 2003, 2006
06 07 08 09 10 10 9 8 7 6 5 4 3

Published in the United States by
DK Publishing, Inc.
375 Hudson Street
New York, New York 10014

A Cataloging-in-Publication record for this book
is available from the Library of Congress

ISBN: 0-7566-1703-0

Color reproduction by GRB, Italy
Printed and bound by Tien Wah Press, Singapore

For our complete catalog visit
www.dk.com

Foreword

When the astronauts took that first photography of the earth from space – and it became obvious that there was indeed only "one world" – my mind returned fifty years, watching my great uncle, Floyd O. Pease, work on his world history. I was eight at the time and had to stretch to see to the top of the table where he hand-printed information in columns, each representing a country, opposite dates in the margins. "Unc" had been a civil engineer (the first at the Panama Canal) and had helped build railroads in Brazil and Persia. But in retirement he was devoted to world history. When I retired, I remembered the format he had used and it seemed to me this was the way to present the story of that "one world" as seen by the astronauts.

This project began some fifteen years ago as a self-study, to learn a little more about my abode before I left it. Friends began to make nice comments and other professionals were encouraging. Lincoln Bloomfield at MIT deserves the credit for keeping this author motivated. The manuscript attempts to separate the data of world history – what happened, by whom, and when – from interpretation, those generalizations which purport to tell what history "means." If the reader can gain half the pleasure from this book as the author did compiling it, the hours spend will have been amply justified.

I can still see that eight-year-old peering over the edge of the table watching "Unc" write. It is Floyd Pease's book as much as mine. All of the authors whose works appear in the references deserve thanks, as well as influences I can no longer trace.

This work has been prepared with two major objectives. The first is to provide a reference work which looks at the world as an outsider – as though standing on the moon, a possibility which is no longer the stuff of fantasy. From this vantage point there is no country or civilization at its center. The second aim has been the attempt to separate fact from interpretation. History began as a written record with chronicles celebrating the victories of leaders and generals – written by the ancients' "press corps." The general was always honorable, the enemy barbarous, and the country of origin of the writer the epitome of civilization. A look at the bookshelves in a moderate sized library shows this historical tradition is still very much alive. Most of the books you will see in the history section concern ours wars, and there are many more volumes describing ourselves than devoted to others. Even our "world histories" rarely look east of the Urals or south of the Mediterranean. We still see ourselves as the "best hope of the future" and our enemies are, of course, barbarians.

This volume attempts in its format and coverage to avoid this alliance between history and patriotism. The chronological arrangement presents factual data, who, what, where and when and why. Insofar as references permitted, equal time is given to all areas and eras. While the focus is on political and military leaders, there are also included references to literature and the arts.

John B. Teeple

Publisher's Note

John B. Teeple passed away in Spring 2002, tragically never seeing his labors come to publication. The manuscript, nurtured by Paul Fargis of the Stonesong Press, New York, was passed to us in Fall 2000. It was in many ways a publisher's dream, a mind-expanding labor of love; as we worked to find a way of presenting the material to the public, often hard editorial and design decisions had to be made; the sheer size of the manuscript necessitated judicious cutting, checking, and redrafting. A team of consulting editors were brought in to handle this, working alongside designers, picture researchers and cartographers.

In the absence of final discussions and approval from the author we hope that we have developed a book which reflects the manner and spirit of his original aspirations.

CONTENTS

How to Use The Book

TIMELINES OF WORLD HISTORY begins with the origins of life on Earth and concludes at the outset of the 3rd millennium. Each section of the book is built around a sequence of timelines, illustrated with contemporary images, and supported by detailed introductory and map spreads. The timeline entries are organized, date-by-date, into geographic regions, creating a vivid picture of what was happening simultaneously across the globe at any given time. The emergence of historic figures, military and political upheavals, the rise and fall of civilizations, the movements of people, and the spread of ideas and technologies are all dated and succinctly described.

Timelines

The timelines cover successfully shorter time spans as the book progresses. From 10,000–5000 BCE the spans vary according to historical and archaeological information; from 500 BCE–300 CE each spread covers 50 years; from 300–1000 CE, 25 years; from 1000–1800 CE, 10 years; and finally, the period from 1800 to 2005 is covered in five-year intervals.

Sidebars feature additional chronologies, or detailed captions, which examine the significant people, pivotal developments, or events of the time span.

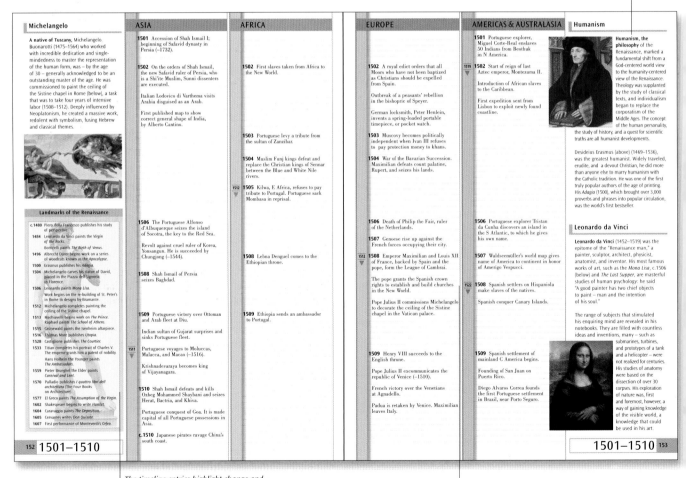

Michelangelo

A native of Tuscany, Michelangelo Buonarotti (1475–1564) who worked with incredible dedication and single-mindedness to master the representation of the human form, was – by the age of 30 – generally acknowledged to be an outstanding master of the age. He was commissioned to paint the ceiling of the Sistine chapel in Rome (below), a task that was to take four years of intensive labor (1508–1512). Deeply influenced by Neoplatonism, he created a massive work, redolent with symbolism, fusing Hebrew and classical themes.

Landmarks of the Renaissance

c.1480 Piero della Francesca publishes his study of perspective.
1484 Leonardo da Vinci paints the *Virgin of the Rocks*.
    Botticelli paints *The Birth of Venus*.
1496 Albrecht Dürer begins work on a series of woodcuts known as the *Apocalypse*.
1500 Erasmus publishes his *Adagia*.
1504 Michelangelo carves his statue of David, placed in the Piazza del Signoria in Florence.
1506 Leonardo paints *Mona Lisa*.
    Work begins on the re-building of St. Peter's in Rome to designs by Bramante.
1512 Michelangelo completes painting the ceiling of the Sistine chapel.
1513 Machiavelli begins work on *The Prince*.
    Raphael paints *The School of Athens*.
1515 Grünewald paints the Isenheim altarpiece.
1516 Thomas More publishes *Utopia*.
1528 Castiglione publishes *The Courtier*.
1533 Titian completes his portrait of Charles V. The emperor grants him a patent of nobility.
    Hans Holbein the Younger paints *The Ambassadors*.
1559 Pieter Brueghel the Elder paints *Carnival and Lent*.
1570 Palladio publishes *I quattro libri dell' architettura* (The Four Books on Architecture).
1577 El Greco paints *The Assumption of the Virgin*.
1602 Shakespeare begins to write *Hamlet*.
1604 Caravaggio paints *The Deposition*.
1605 Cervantes writes *Don Quixote*.
1607 First performance of Monteverdi's *Orfeo*.

ASIA

1501 Accession of Shah Ismail I; beginning of Safavid dynasty in Persia (–1732).

1502 On the orders of Shah Ismail, the new Safavid ruler of Persia, who is a Shi'ite Muslim, Sunni dissenters are executed.

Italian Lodovico di Varthema visits Arabia disguised as an Arab.

First published map to show correct general shape of India, by Alberto Cantino.

1506 The Portuguese Alfonso d'Albuquerque seizes the island of Socotra, the key to the Red Sea.

Revolt against cruel ruler of Korea, Yonsangun. He is succeeded by Chungjong (–1544).

1508 Shah Ismail of Persia seizes Baghdad.

1509 Portuguese victory over Ottoman and Arab fleet at Diu.

Indian sultan of Gujarat surprises and sinks Portuguese fleet.

1511 Portuguese voyages to Moluccas, Malacca, and Macao (–1516).

Krishnadevaraya becomes king of Vijayanagara.

1510 Shah Ismail defeats and kills Ozbeg Mohammed Shaybani and seizes Herat, Bactria, and Khiva.

Portuguese conquest of Goa. It is made capital of all Portuguese possessions in Asia.

c.1510 Japanese pirates ravage China's south coast.

AFRICA

1502 First slaves taken from Africa to the New World.

1503 Portuguese levy a tribute from the sultan of Zanzibar.

1504 Muslim Funj kings defeat and replace the Christian kings of Sennar between the Blue and White Nile rivers.

1512 1505 Kilwa, E Africa, refuses to pay tribute to Portugal. Portuguese sack Mombasa in reprisal.

1508 Lebna Denguel comes to the Ethiopian throne.

1509 Ethiopia sends an ambassador to Portugal.

EUROPE

1502 A royal edict orders that all Moors who have not been baptized as Christians should be expelled from Spain.

Outbreak of a peasants' rebellion in the bishopric of Speyer.

German locksmith, Peter Henlein, invents a spring-loaded portable timepiece, or pocket watch.

1503 Muscovy becomes politically independent when Ivan III refuses to pay protection money to khans.

1504 War of the Bavarian Succession. Maximilian defeats count palatine, Rupert, and seizes his lands.

1506 Death of Philip the Fair, ruler of the Netherlands.

1507 Genoese rise up against the French forces occupying their city.

1512 1508 Emperor Maximilian and Louis XII of France, backed by Spain and the pope, form the League of Cambrai.

The pope grants the Spanish crown rights to establish and build churches in the New World.

Pope Julius II commissions Michelangelo to decorate the ceiling of the Sistine chapel in the Vatican palace.

1509 Henry VIII succeeds to the English throne.

Pope Julius II excommunicates the republic of Venice (–1510).

French victory over the Venetians at Agnadello.

Padua is retaken by Venice. Maximilian leaves Italy.

AMERICAS & AUSTRALASIA

1501 Portuguese explorer, Miguel Corte-Real enslaves 50 Indians from Beothuk in N America.

1519 1502 Start of reign of last Aztec emperor, Montezuma II.

Introduction of African slaves to the Caribbean.

First expedition sent from Lisbon to exploit newly found coastline.

1506 Portuguese explorer Tristan da Cunha discovers an island in the S Atlantic, to which he gives his own name.

1507 Waldseemüller's world map gives name of America to continent in honor of Amerigo Vespucci.

1522 1508 Spanish settlers on Hispaniola make slaves of the natives.

Spanish conquer Canary Islands.

1509 Spanish settlement of mainland C America begins.

Founding of San Juan on Puerto Rico.

Diego Alvares Correa founds the first Portuguese settlement in Brazil, near Porto Seguro.

Humanism

Humanism, the philosophy of the Renaissance, marked a fundamental shift from a God-centered world view to the humanity-centered view of the Renaissance. Theology was supplanted by the study of classical texts, and individualism began to replace the corporatism of the Middle Ages. The concept of the human personality, the study of history, and a quest for scientific truths are all humanist developments.

Desideius Erasmus (above) (1469–1536), was the greatest humanist. Widely traveled, erudite, and a devout Christian, he did more than anyone else to marry humanism with the Catholic tradition. He was one of the first truly popular authors of the age of printing. His *Adagia* (1500), which brought over 3,000 proverbs and phrases into popular circulation, was the world's first bestseller.

Leonardo da Vinci

Leonardo da Vinci (1452–1519) was the epitome of the "Renaissance man," a painter, sculptor, architect, physicist, anatomist, and inventor. His most famous works of art, such as the *Mona Lisa*, c.1506 (below) and *The Last Supper*, are masterful studies of human psychology: he said "A good painter has two chief objects to paint – man and the intention of his soul."

The range of subjects that stimulated his enquiring mind are revealed in his notebooks. They are filled with countless ideas and inventions, many – such as submarines, turbines, and prototypes of a tank and a helicopter – were not realized for centuries. His studies of anatomy were based on the dissection of over 30 corpses. His exploration of nature was, first and foremost, however, a way of gaining knowledge of the visible world, a knowledge that could be used in his art.

152 **1501–1510**

1501–1510 153

The timeline entries highlight change and continuity in different societies and cultures across the world. Each geographical region is color-coded throughout.

Many events are cross-referenced to other relevant dates, allowing the reader to navigate through time.

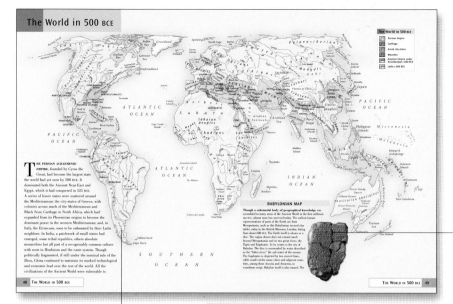

The world maps are complemented by maps or views of the world produced at the time.

13 full-colour maps build up a continual narrative of the changing map of the world.

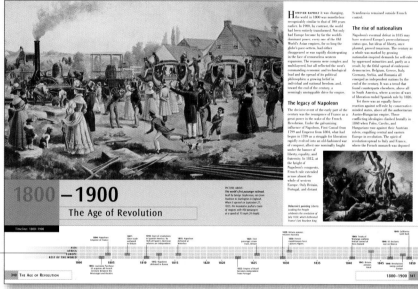

Quick reference timelines give an instant overview of the most important events of the period.

World Overviews and World Maps

Each timeline section opens with a World Overview: an introduction that sets the period under discussion in its historical context. At the end of the timeline section a detailed World Map summarizes the global situation at the close of the period. These maps portray the changing map of the world and its cultures from ancient times to the modern world, accompanied by summaries of regional developments.

Concordance

The final section of the book comprises an extensive, encyclopedic reference to world history. It features all the major events and episodes, brief biographies of key historical figures, lists of major rulers and leaders, and individual chronologies of each of the world's nations. This section also acts as an index and glossary to the main body of the book.

The Prehistoric World

THE EARTH HAS EXISTED for over 4.6 billion years. It was probably formed when small fragments of material, known as planetesimals, coalesced in space, creating an enormous release of energy. During the ensuing 100-million-year meltdown the Earth's interior assumed its present form, and by 4 billion years ago, an early atmosphere and the first water appeared on the planet. At this point, microscopic life began to appear. These organisms were able to survive extreme temperatures and an atmosphere that was, as yet, devoid of oxygen. As continents emerged and the chemistry of the oceans stabilized, more complex lifeforms evolved; by c.360 million years ago the first amphibians had crawled onto the land. Despite environmental conditions that underwent dramatic changes, and periodic mass extinctions, terrestrial life continued to expand. It was not until 65 million years ago, with the extinction of the dinosaurs, that recognizably modern animals began to evolve.

CONTINENTAL DRIFT

The Earth's surface is in constant motion, a complex, moving jigsaw of interlocking tectonic plates. Beneath the Earth's crust lies a partially molten layer – the mantle. Heat sources within the mantle set up huge convection currents. The overlying crust is made up of a series of rigid plates, in which the continents are embedded, that move in response to the currents in the mantle. Where plates are moving toward each other, one will be pushed, or subducted, beneath the other, and driven down into the mantle. It is at these destructive plate boundaries that most of the Earth's geological activity – volcanoes and earthquakes – occurs. The continents have moved over the Earth over geological time and continue to do so – our present world map is merely a snapshot in time.

2: DEVONIAN PERIOD (408–362 million years ago)
The continents of Gondwanaland and Laurentia are drifting northward.

3: CARBONIFEROUS PERIOD (362–290 million years ago)
The Earth is dominated by three continents; Laurentia, Angaraland, and Gondwanaland.

4: JURASSIC PERIOD (208–145 million years ago)
The supercontinent of Pangea begins to break up causing an overall rise in sea levels.

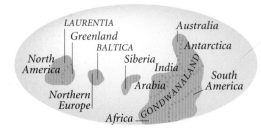

1: CAMBRIAN PERIOD
(570–510 million years ago).
Most continents are in topical latitudes.
The supercontinent of Gondwanaland reaches the South Pole.

5: TERTIARY PERIOD
(65-2 million years ago)
Although the world's geography is becoming more recognizable, major events such as the creation of the Himalayan mountain chain, are still to occur during this period.

The Fossil Record

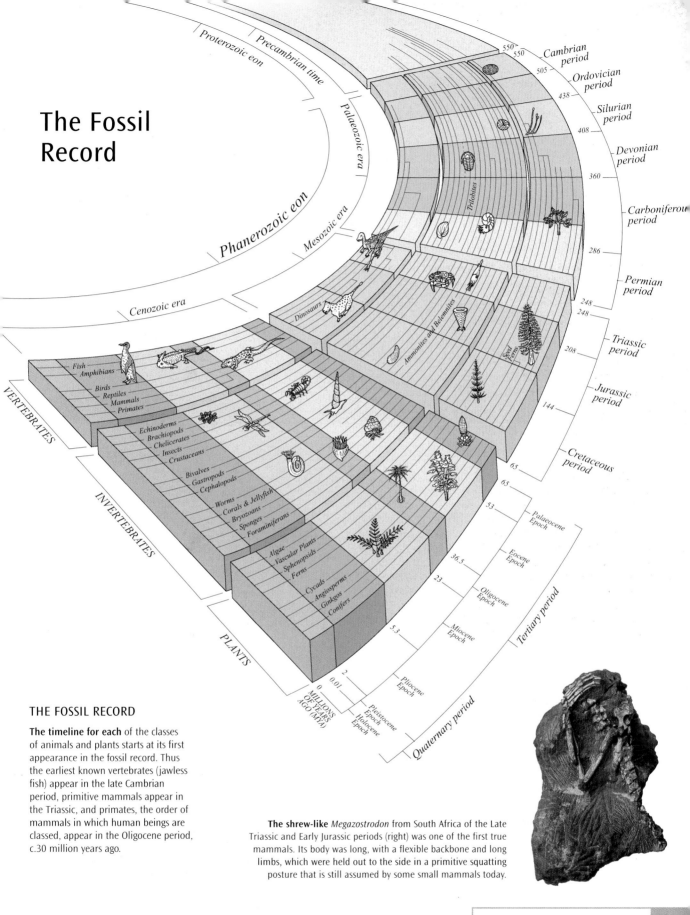

Proterozoic eon — Precambrian time
Palaeozoic era
Phanerozoic eon
Mesozoic era
Cenozoic era

550   Cambrian period
505   Ordovician period
438   Silurian period
408   Devonian period
360   Carboniferous period
286   Permian period
248   Triassic period
208   Jurassic period
144   Cretaceous period
65   Palaeocene Epoch
53   Eocene Epoch
36.5   Oligocene Epoch
23   Miocene Epoch
5.3   Pliocene Epoch
2   Pleistocene Epoch
0.01   Holocene Epoch
Tertiary period
Quaternary period

Trilobites
Dinosaurs
Ammonites and Belemnites
Seed ferns

MILLIONS OF YEARS AGO (MYA)

VERTEBRATES
Fish
Amphibians
Birds
Reptiles
Mammals
Primates

INVERTEBRATES
Echinoderms
Brachiopods
Chelicerates
Insects
Crustaceans
Bivalves
Gastropods
Cephalopods
Worms
Corals & Jellyfish
Bryozoans
Sponges
Foraminiferans

PLANTS
Algae
Vascular Plants
Sphenopsids
Ferns
Cycads
Angiosperms
Ginkgos
Conifers

THE FOSSIL RECORD

The timeline for each of the classes of animals and plants starts at its first appearance in the fossil record. Thus the earliest known vertebrates (jawless fish) appear in the late Cambrian period, primitive mammals appear in the Triassic, and primates, the order of mammals in which human beings are classed, appear in the Oligocene period, c.30 million years ago.

The shrew-like *Megazostrodon* from South Africa of the Late Triassic and Early Jurassic periods (right) was one of the first true mammals. Its body was long, with a flexible backbone and long limbs, which were held out to the side in a primitive squatting posture that is still assumed by some small mammals today.

Early Humanity

T HE FUNDAMENTAL evolutionary adaptation that distinguished early hominids from their primate ancestors was bipedal walking. The earliest evidence of bipedalism, deduced from the remains of an *australopithecine*, or southern ape, found on the shores of Lake Rudolf in east Africa, dates to c.4.2 million years ago. The *australopithecines* combined human and ape characteristics and evolved into several different species. They may have been ancestral to the earliest species of *Homo* (man), which emerged some 2.5 million years ago. *Homo Habilis* was distinguished by a larger brain, as well as the ability to make tools. These new skills marked the first step in human cultural development, enabling early hominids to exploit a much wider range of food and resources. From c.1.7 million years ago, hominids began to move out of Africa, adapting to a range of environments in Asia, Europe, and the Middle East. The first anatomically modern humans, with their superior tool technology and ability to colonize marginal environments, emerged in southern Africa about 100,000 years ago.

Tool Technology

The first stone tools, which appeared about 2.5 million years ago, were the key to early humans' cultural development. The earliest tools were fashioned by using a stone to chip flakes off another stone, creating a series of sharp, irregular edges. Tools could be used for butchering animals, working hides, cutting firewood, building shelters, preparing plants for eating. As tools became more sophisticated, humans became increasingly effective hunters of big game, expanding their range of habitable environments. These chipped stone handaxes (above) from Hoxne, in eastern England, date to at least 10,000 years ago.

Neanderthals

The Neanderthals emerged some 120,000 years ago in Western Eurasia and Europe. A separate and distinct branch of the Homo genus, their brains were the same size as modern humans, but they were distinguished by their strong, sturdy skeletons, with a projecting jaw, nose and brow ridge. The Neanderthals were the first type of human known to have buried their dead (left), and there is evidence that they engaged in a range of ritual behaviour. They manufactured fine flaked tools, which were used for hunting, butchering, food preparation, and woodworking. They were able to adapt to a range of environments, from the temperate shores of the Mediterranean to glacial northern Europe.

Human Ancestors

The first *australopithecine* fossil was found in 1925 in a cave called Taung in South Africa. A child's skull, (right) the fossil was estimated to be c.2.5 million years old. Since then, at least seven species of *australopithecine* have been identified, and older remains have been found, dating to c.4.2 million years ago. Most scientists agree that the oldest species, *Australopithecus afarensis*, whose most famous representative is the 3.4-million-year-old skeleton of "Lucy,"

was the crossing line from ape to human. Though – like an ape – it had a small brain, long arms and short legs, it walked upright, as fossilized footprints, at least 4 million years old, from Lateolil in Tanzania testify.

Human evolution

c.4.2 million years ago: *Australopithecus anamensis*: limited remains of bipedal hominid found on shores of Lake Rudolf

c.3 million years ago: *Australopithecus africanus*: notable for powerful build of upper body

c.2.5 million years ago: *Homo habilis*: large brain in relation to body size. Average male height, 1.32 m

c.2 million years ago: *Australopithecus robustus*: hand bones indicate anatomical ability to make stone tools

c.900,000 years ago: Earliest evidence of hominids in Asia

c.1 million years ago: Earliest evidence of the use of fire

c.120,000 years ago: Neanderthals: short-limbed, thick-bodied. Average male height, 1.65 m

c.800,000 years ago: Archaic *Homo sapiens*; Average male height, 1.75 m

c.35,000 years ago: First fully modern humans in Europe; disappearance of Neanderthals

4,000,000 BP	3,000,000 BP	2,000,000 BP	1,000,000 BP	present

c.3.4 million years ago: *Australopithecus afarensis*: based on find of "Lucy" skeleton at Hadar, Ethiopia. Average male height, 1.5 m

c.2.6 million years ago: *Australopithecus boisei* with massive chewing muscles. Earliest finds of stone stools

c.1.8 million years ago: *Homo erectus*: distinguished by long limbs. Average male height, 1.77 m

c.850,000 years ago: Hominids reach Europe from Africa

c.100,000 years ago: *Homo sapiens* (anatomically modern humans): earliest evidence in Africa

Sea of Japan

PACIFIC OCEAN

Tropic of Cancer

Zhoukoudian
Xujiayao Dingcun
Langtandong
Yunxian Maba
Lantian Changyang
Changwu Tongzi
Tham Khuyen

China
ASIA
Yangtze
South China Sea
Borneo

Yellow River
Gobi
Altai Mountains

Lena
Arctic Circle
Yenisey

ARCTIC OCEAN
Siberia
Ob'
Ural Mountains

Lake Baikal

Yuanmou
Earliest evidence of hominids in mainland Asia dates to 1.7 million years ago

Mekong
Irrawaddy

AUSTRALIA

Malay Peninsula
Kedungbrubus
Trinil
Sangiran
Java
Sumatra

Earliest evidence of hominids in maritime Asia dates to 1.3 million years ago

Lake Balkhash
Tien Shan
Plateau of Tibet
Himalayas
Ganges

Bay of Bengal

Barents Sea

Syr Darya
Amu Darya
Aral Sea
Teshik Tash

Thar Desert
Indus
India
Narmada

Equator

Scale varies with perspective
13,340 km
(8290 miles)
20,040 km
(12,450 miles)

Volga
Caspian Sea
Iranian Plateau
Arabian Sea

INDIAN OCEAN

Scandinavia

EUROPE
It is thought that early humanoids arrived in Europe from Africa c.850,000 years ago

Dzhruchula
Caucasus
Black Sea
Kiik-Koba
Staroselye
Shanidar
Zagros Mountains
Persian Gulf

Bilzingsleben
Šipka
Neanderthal
Mauer
Kalna Cave
Steinheim
Biache
Spy
La Chapelle-aux-Saints
Hortus
St Césaire
Saccopastore
Circeo
Pezetxiki
La Ferrassie
Arago
Montmaurin
Atapuerca
Cova Negra

Tigris
Euphrates

Kebana
Amud
Zuttiyen
Es-Skhul
Qafzeh
Tabun
Petralona
Danube
Anatolia

Arabian Peninsula

The emergence of modern humans

◇ finds of *Australopithecus*
◆ finds of *Homo habilis*
◆ finds of *Homo erectus*
◆ finds of archaic *Homo sapiens*
◇ finds of Neanderthals
◇ finds of modern *Homo sapiens* (over 50,000 years old)

Forbes Quarry
Taforalt
El Guettar
Mughuret el-'Aliya
Dar es-Soltan
Thomas Quarry
Sidi Abderrahman
Jebel Irhoud

Mediterranean Sea
Nile
Red Sea

Hajj Creiem
Haua Fteah

Bir Tarfawi
Nazlet Khatir
Bir Sahara
Singa

Dire Dawa
Lake Tana
Ethiopian Highlands
Ileret

Sahara
Tibesti
Ahaggar

AFRICA

Omo
Nariokotome
Limited remains of first hominid, *Australopithecus anamensis*, date to c.4.2 million years ago
Chesowanja
Matupi

Koobi Fora
Lake Rudolph
Lothagam
Olduvai Gorge
Laetolil
Great Rift Valley
Lake Victoria
Malema
Lake Nyasa

Madagascar
Mozambique Channel

Tropic of Cancer
Lake Chad
Niger

Congo Basin
Congo

Lake Tanganyika
Zambezi

Makapansgat
Cave of Hearths
Sterkfontein
Swartkrans
Taung

Kromdraai
Border Cave
Howieson's Poort
Klasies River Mouth
Site of some of the earliest known anatomically modern humans dating to c.100,000 years ago
Florisbad
Die Kelders

ATLANTIC OCEAN

Equator
Tropic of Capricorn
Orange River
Langebaan

The World to 10,000 BCE

c.25,000 years ago: Humans cross the Bering land bridge, created by lower sea levels during the last Ice Age.

25,000 years ago: Stylized female figurines found throughout Europe

17,000 years ago: Cave painting at Lascaux

c.27,000 years ago: Last Neanderthals die out

20,000 years ago: Terracotta figurine from Algeria

c.10,000 years ago: Clovis point tool technology: evidence of large scale big-game hunting in North America

c.11,000 years ago: Evidence of substantial village settlement

BY 100,000 YEARS AGO, fully modern humans had evolved in Africa. With a large brain, refined tool-making capability, and the ability to form cohesive social groups, *Homo sapiens sapiens* was well equipped to colonize the globe. The last Ice Age reached a peak between 20,000 and 10,000 years ago. Confronted with harsh climatic conditions, humans were forced to be inventive and flexible; the refinement of stone tool technology, the building of shelters, and the use of clothing all reflect these imperatives. It was during this period too that complex social structures began to emerge, evident in remains of communal graves and organized settlements. The development of ritual and abstract expression is reflected in cave paintings, personal ornaments, and carved Venus figurines, which were traded over great distances. When temperatures rose at the end of the Ice Age, plants and animals became more abundant. As growing populations competed for resources, people began to experiment with the domestication of plants and animals, and the transition to agriculture was under way.

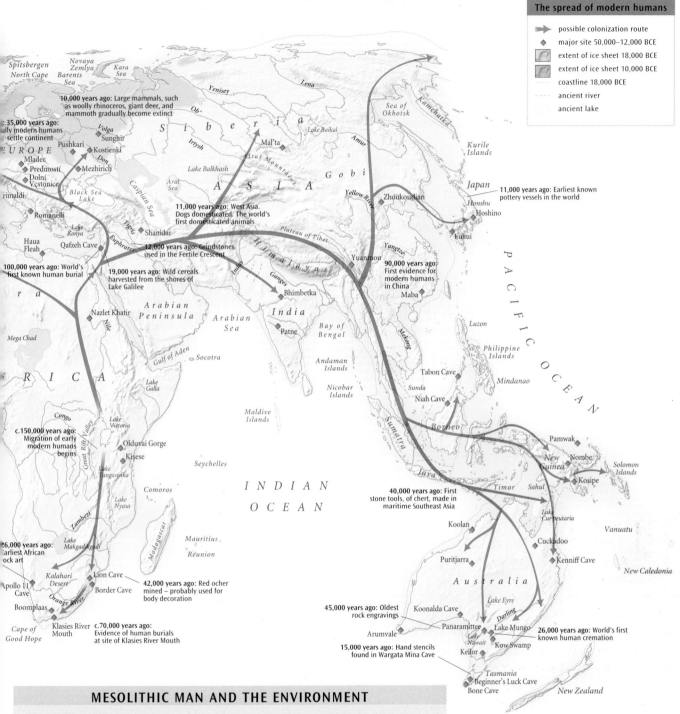

The spread of modern humans

➤ possible colonization route
◆ major site 50,000–12,000 BCE
extent of ice sheet 18,000 BCE
extent of ice sheet 10,000 BCE
.... coastline 18,000 BCE
– – – ancient river
ancient lake

Spitsbergen
North Cape

Novaya Zemlya

Kara Sea

Barents Sea

10,000 years ago: Large mammals, such as woolly rhinoceros, giant deer, and mammoth gradually become extinct

Yenisey

Ob'

Lena

Sea of Okhotsk

Kamchatka

c.35,000 years ago: fully modern humans settle continent

EUROPE

Volga
Sunghir
Pushkari
Kostienki
Mladec
Predmostí
Dolní
Vçstonice
Irtysh
Mezhirich
Don

S i b e r i a

Lake Baikal

Mal'ta

Altai Mountains

Amur

Kurile Islands

rimaldi

Lake Balkhash

A S I A

G o b i

Yellow River

Zhoukoudian

Japan

11,000 years ago: Earliest known pottery vessels in the world

Black Sea Lake

Caspian Sea

Aral Sea

Honshu

Hoshino

Romanelli

Lake Konya

Tigris

Shanidar

Qafzeh Cave

11,000 years ago: West Asia. Dogs domesticated. The world's first domesticated animals

Fukui

Haua Fleah

12,000 years ago: Grindstones used in the Fertile Crescent

Euphrates

Plateau of Tibet

Yangtze

Yuanmou

90,000 years ago: First evidence for modern humans in China

100,000 years ago: World's first known human burial

19,000 years ago: Wild cereals harvested from the shores of Lake Galilee

Indus

H i m a l a y a s

Ganges

Bhimbetka

Maba

P A C I F I C   O C E A N

r a

Nazlet Khatir

Nile

A r a b i a n   P e n i n s u l a

Arabian Sea

I n d i a

Patne

Bay of Bengal

Luzon

Mega Chad

Gulf of Aden

Socotra

Lake Galla

Maldive Islands

Andaman Islands

Nicobar Islands

Philippine Islands

Mindanao

Tabon Cave

R I C A

Congo

Great Rift Valley

Lake Victoria

Olduvai Gorge

Kisese

c.150,000 years ago: Migration of early modern humans begins

Lake Tanganyika

Seychelles

Sumatra

Sunda

Niah Cave

Borneo

Pamwak

Lake Nyasa

Comoros

I N D I A N

O C E A N

Java

Timor

New Guinea

Nombe

Solomon Islands

Kosipe

Zambezi

Madagascar

Mauritius

Réunion

Sahul

40,000 years ago: First stone tools, of chert, made in maritime Southeast Asia

Koolan

Lake Carpeutaria

Vanuatu

c.26,000 years ago: Earliest African rock art

Lake Makgadikgadi

Lion Cave

42,000 years ago: Red ocher mined – probably used for body decoration

Cuckadoo

Apollo 11 Cave

Kalahari Desert

Border Cave

Puritjarra

Kenniff Cave

New Caledonia

Boomplaas

Orange River

A u s t r a l i a

Cape of Good Hope

Klasies River Mouth

c.70,000 years ago: Evidence of human burials at site of Klasies River Mouth

45,000 years ago: Oldest rock engravings

Koonalda Cave

Lake Eyre

Darling

Panaramittee

Lake Mungo

26,000 years ago: World's first known human cremation

Arumvale

15,000 years ago: Hand stencils found in Wargata Mina Cave

Lake Nawait

Kow Swamp

Keilor

Tasmania

Beginner's Luck Cave

Bone Cave

New Zealand

S O U T H E R N

O C E A N

MESOLITHIC MAN AND THE ENVIRONMENT

The hunters of the late Ice Age and its aftermath adapted to many different environments, using a range of tools and weapons: spear-throwers, bows and arrows, harpoons, boomerangs. They were able to follow animal herds, or live in semi-permanent camps where they could exploit the potential of seasonal migrations. By 9000 BCE, intense hunting had led to the near-extinction of large mammals, such as mastodons and mammoths. Intimate knowledge of the environment was a vital survival strategy. Precious water and food sources may have become centers of cultic activity, as this rock painting from Kalhotia in central India (right), which represents cascades of water, seems to indicate.

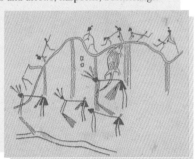

The First Farmers

The domestication of animals as a source of food, clothing, and transportation was typically followed by the development of strains of wild grasses to produce a surplus of cereal crops. This constituted a major development in human history, known as the Agricultural Revolution, and inaugurated firstly pastoralism, and then a sedentary lifestyle. These innovations occurred at different times in various parts of the world, a chronology often determined by levels of population, and by the relative abundance of game animals and collectable wild vegetables and fruits.

The Establishment of Sedentary Agriculture

c.9000	Near East, Mesopotamia, Anatolia
7000	Yellow river basin, N China
c.7000	SE Europe
6000	S C Asia (Uzbekistan, Afghanistan)
6000	Andes
c.6000	Baluchistan
5500	N Mediterranean coast
5000	Nile Valley
c.5000	C Europe
c.4750	C America
c.4500	Ganges floodplain, E India
4000	Mainland SE Asia
4000	NW Europe
c.4000	Sub-Saharan Africa
c.3500	Ukraine, European Russia
c.2500	Maritime SE Asia
2000	N America (Mississippi basin)
2000	Amazon basin
1500	Melanesia
c.1000	Caribbean
c.1000	Southern Africa
c.500 CE	Japan

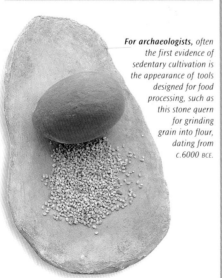

For archaeologists, often the first evidence of sedentary cultivation is the appearance of tools designed for food processing, such as this stone quern for grinding grain into flour, dating from c.6000 BCE.

ASIA

c.10,000 Earliest known pottery vessels in the world in use, from Honshu, Japan.

c.9000 Einkorn wheat grown in N Syria: first evidence of true cultivation.

Limestone caves in C China give evidence of hunting, fishing, and gathering way of life.

Evidence of sheep domestication, N Mesopotamia.

c.8500 Earliest Chinese pottery.

 c.5000

7000 First Chinese agricultural communities in Yellow river basin.

c.7000 Broomcorn and foxtail millets domesticated on N China plain.

Foundation of Çatal Hüyük, Anatolia, the largest Neolithic site in the Near East.

Goat established as main domesticated animal, SW Asia.

Pig domesticated in Anatolia.

c.6500 Small-scale copper smelting at Çatal Hüyük.

"Jomon" pottery spreads throughout S Japanese archipelago.

First pottery in the Near East.

 c.5000

c.6000 Painted pottery, and copper and lead smelting at Hassuna in N Mesopotamia.

Pottery in grave goods from Mehrgarh, C Asia, indicates trade with C India; first pottery in mainland SE Asia.

Farming in Baluchistan; barley is main crop.

c.5500 World's earliest irrigation system, at Choga Mami, Mesopotamia.

AFRICA

c.8500 Saharan rock art depicts wide array of wild animals: elephants, giraffes, hippopotamuses, rhinoceroses, long since extinct in the region.

Finely crafted stone spearheads, arrowheads, and cutting tools in use in Sahara region.

c.7500 Characteristic "wavy-line" pottery – made by dragging a catfish spine across the wet clay – of the Sahara and its southern fringes is produced.

c.6500 Cattle successfully domesticated in N Africa, Sahara region.

c.6000 Agriculture and pastoralism, especially along the Nile river.

 c.4100 Native millet domesticated and cultivated in Sahel region.

10,000–5000 BCE

EUROPE

c.10,000 Retreat of glaciers; temperate deciduous woodland spreads northward. Rich array of marine and land resources.

Large mammals, such as wooly rhinoceros, giant deer, and mammoth gradually become extinct.

c.8300 Retreat of glaciers causes flooding of many lowland areas. New resources available to Mesolithic hunters.

c.8000 Hunter-gatherers move into Scandinavia, including the ancestral Saarni of Lapland.

c.7000 Farming spreads from Anatolia to SE Europe.

c.6500 Rising postglacial sea levels separate British Isles from the rest of the European continent.

c.6200 Farming spreads along the Mediterranean to S Italy and Sicily.

c.5000

c.6000 Farming starts to spread along west coast of the Mediterranean.

c.5500 Bandkeramik pottery produced by farmers of C Europe.

c.5400 Emergence of agricultural villages in C Europe heralds beginning of European Neolithic Period and beginning of forest clearance.

AMERICAS & AUSTRALASIA

c.10,000 Melting of ice sheets in N America leads to rapidly changing environments. Retreat of ice sheets opens up more land suitable for human habitation.

Clovis point tool technology; evidence of large-scale big-game hunting in N America.

Large game, plants, fish, shellfish form hunters' diet in N and C America.

First humanlike figures in Australian rock art.

Land bridge connecting Australia and Tasmania starts to disappear.

c.9500 Colonists reach Patagonia and southern regions of S America.

c.8500 Evidence of grasses, squash, beans, peppers, and potatoes in use in Andes.

c.4500

c.8000 Growing use of plant resources in N and C America evident in finds of food-processing equipment such as grindstones.

Rising sea level covers New Guinea land bridge (–6000).

c.7500 Earliest known cemetery in N America: Sloan burial site.

Evidence of drainage and cultivation in the highlands of New Guinea.

Manioc cultivation in Amazon Basin.

c.6000 Corn (maize) is cultivated in Ecuador.

c.4500

Migrations from SE Asia give rise to Austronesian culture.

c.5500 Evidence that squash, avocados, and chilis form part of the diet of the peoples of C America.

c.4750

c.5400 Camelid (llamas, alpacas) herding in Andes.

Big game hunters in N America

Sophisticated hunting techniques were developed at an early stage in North America. A finely knapped variety of stone, producing extremely sharp, flat spearheads, arrow points, cutting and skinning tools known collectively as Clovis Points (*left*), has been found widely across the Great Plains and Rockies. There is also evidence, dating from c.8000 BCE, of highly organized mass kills, such as near Casper, Wyoming, where some 20 hunters trapped and slaughtered 75 bison, which were butchered and presumably preserved by drying as pemmican (a compressed dried meat-and-berry cake).

The Development of Pottery

The discovery of fired pottery technology occurred at very different times around the world, but the impact of the discovery was uniform. The ability to store, cook, preserve, and transport foodstuffs in secure, cleanable containers is a major adjunct to the revolution in agriculture, encouraging sedentary life and long-distance trade. The craft nature of pottery manufacture provoked artistic expression in its decoration, and the durability of pottery has made it one of the stable benchmarks for archaeologists.

Japanese pottery, the earliest known in the world, is remarkable for its simplicity of form. Later "Jomon" pottery is notable for its corded decoration.

The Invention of Pottery

c.11,000	Jomon, Japan
c.8500	Xianrendong, China
c.7500	Nile Valley, Sahara, Africa
c.6500	Tell Sotto, Near East
c.6500	Mehrgarh, S Asia
5500	Bandkeramik, C Europe
c.2200	Ecuador, S America
c.1500	Chiapa de Corzo, C America

The World in 5000 BCE

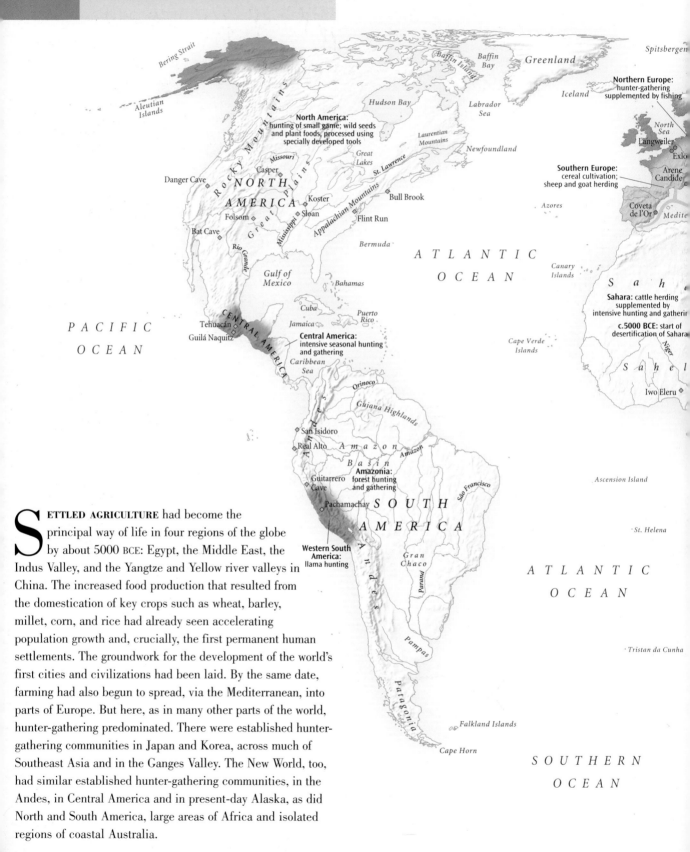

Northern Europe:
hunter-gathering
supplemented by fishing

Spitsbergen

Greenland

*Baffin
Bay*

Baffin Island

Iceland

*North
Sea*

Langweiler

Exlo

*Labrador
Sea*

North America:
hunting of small game; wild seeds
and plant foods, processed using
specially developed tools

Southern Europe:
cereal cultivation;
sheep and goat herding

Arene
Candide

Bering Strait

*Aleutian
Islands*

Rocky Mountains

Hudson Bay

*Laurentian
Mountains*

Newfoundland

Azores

Coveta
de l'Or

Medite

Danger Cave

Casper

**NORTH
AMERICA**

Missouri

Koster

St. Lawrence

*Great
Lakes*

Appalachian Mountains

Bull Brook

*ATLANTIC

OCEAN*

*Canary
Islands*

S a h a

Folsom

Sloan

Flint Run

Bat Cave

Great Plains

Mississippi

Rio Grande

Bermuda

Sahara: cattle herding
supplemented by
intensive hunting and gathering

*PACIFIC

OCEAN*

*Gulf of
Mexico*

Bahamas

*Cape Verde
Islands*

c.5000 BCE: start of
desertification of Sahara

S a h e l

Tehuacán

CENTRAL AMERICA

Cuba

Jamaica

*Puerto
Rico*

Niger

Guilá Naquitz

Central America:
intensive seasonal hunting
and gathering

*Caribbean
Sea*

Iwo Eleru

Orinoco

Guiana Highlands

San Isidoro

Andes

Real Alto

A m a z o n

Amazon

Ascension Island

B a s i n

Amazonia:
forest hunting
and gathering

Guitarrero
Cave

São Francisco

Pachamachay

**S O U T H

A M E R I C A**

**Western South
America:**
llama hunting

*Gran
Chaco*

*ATLANTIC

OCEAN*

St. Helena

Paraná

Tristan da Cunha

Andes

Pampas

Patagonia

Falkland Islands

Cape Horn

*SOUTHERN

OCEAN*

SETTLED AGRICULTURE had become the
principal way of life in four regions of the globe
by about 5000 BCE: Egypt, the Middle East, the
Indus Valley, and the Yangtze and Yellow river valleys in
China. The increased food production that resulted from
the domestication of key crops such as wheat, barley,
millet, corn, and rice had already seen accelerating
population growth and, crucially, the first permanent human
settlements. The groundwork for the development of the world's
first cities and civilizations had been laid. By the same date,
farming had also begun to spread, via the Mediterranean, into
parts of Europe. But here, as in many other parts of the world,
hunter-gathering predominated. There were established hunter-
gathering communities in Japan and Korea, across much of
Southeast Asia and in the Ganges Valley. The New World, too,
had similar established hunter-gathering communities, in the
Andes, in Central America and in present-day Alaska, as did
North and South America, large areas of Africa and isolated
regions of coastal Australia.

The World in 5000 BCE

- intensive hunting and gathering
- centers of agricultural development
- secondary areas of settled agriculture
- spread of farming
- early agricultural settlements and pre-urban sites 6000–5000 BCE
- hunter-gatherer sites

Novaya Zemlya
North Cape *Barents Sea* *Kara Sea*
Kamchatka
Bering Strait
Yenisey *Ob'* *Lena*
Ural Mts *S i b e r i a* *Sea of Okhotsk*
Volga *Irtysh* *Amur* *Manchuria* *Kurile Islands*
EUROPE *A S I A* *Gobi* *Hokkaido* *Honshu*
Pantic Steppes: horse hunting
Danube *Lake Baikal*
Lepenski Vir *Altai Mountains* *Yellow River* *Nitaro Cave* *Japan*
Karanovo *Black Sea* *Çayönü* *Lake Balkhash*
Varna *Caspian Sea* *Aral Sea* *Tien Shan* *Takla Makan*
Northern China: millet cultivation; evidence of domesticated pigs and dogs
Cishan *Korea* *Kami-Kuroiwa* *Kyushu*
Japan and Korea: hunting and gathering supplemented by fishing
Tell Halaf *Nineveh* *Hallan Çemi* *Beishouling* *Banpo* *Fukui Cave*
Çatal Hüyük *Tepe Gawra* *Peiligang* *Songze*
Frankhthi *Tell Brak* *Hassuna* *Plateau of Tibet* *Majiabang*
Abu Hureyra *Samarra* *Choga Mami* **Yangtze Delta and Yellow River:** early wet rice cultivation *Hemudu*
Yarim Tepe *Nippur* *Ali Kosh* *Mehrgarh* *Bengdoushan*
southern Anatolia: farming villages trade in flint, obsidian, timber, shells, and copper
Jericho *Eridu* *Warka* *Himalayas* *TAIWAN*
Faiyum *Beidha* *Ur* **Southern Mesopotamia:** populations on arid plains dependent on irrigation agriculture
a *Nile Valley:* wheat and barley cultivation
Naqada **Near East:** domestication of wild wheat and barley c.9000 BCE *Ganges* *Chopani-Mando* *Padah-lin* *Nam Tun* *PACIFIC OCEAN*
Nabta *Arabian Peninsula* **Indus Valley:** wheat and barley cultivation; cattle, sheep, and goat herding *Hoa Binh*
Esh Shaheinab *Khartoum* **Ganges Valley:** intensive forest hunting and gathering *Spirit Cave* *Musang Cave*
Lake Chad *Red Sea* *Gulf of Aden* *Gobedra* *Socotra* *Luzon*
A F R I C A *Mandheera* *Ban Kao Caves* *Philippine Islands*
Maldive Islands *Andaman Islands* *Mindanao*
Melka Kunture *Nicobar Islands* *Gua Cha* *Niah Cave* *South China Sea*
Mainland Southeast Asia: intensive hunter-gathering *Borneo*
Ishango *Congo Basin* *Lake Victoria* **Maritime Southeast Asia:** hunter-gatherers exploit rich marine resources
Kalambo Falls *Lake Tanganyika* *Seychelles* *Sumatra* *Java* *Gua Lawa* *New Guinea*
Makwe *Lake Nyasa* *Comoros* *Timor*
Okavango *Zambezi* *Madagascar* *Mauritius* *Réunion* **New Guinea:** upland drainage to encourage growth of wild taro
Okavango Delta *Amadzimba* *I N D I A N   O C E A N* *Ingaladdi Shelter*
Namib Desert *Kalahari Desert* *Millstream* **Australia:** hunter-gatherers settle along major rivers *Kenniff Cave*
Orange River *A U S T R A L I A* *Great Dividing Range*
Nelson Bay Cave *Orchestra Shell Cave* *Lake Eyre* *Darling*
Cape of Good Hope *Mount Burr* *Currarong* *Tasman Sea*
Wilson's Promontory *Tasmania* *New Zealand*

5000 –2500 BCE
The Advent of Agriculture

PICTURE ABOVE:
Ur was the capital of a
south Mesopotamian
empire toward the end of
the 3rd millennium. The
Royal Standard of Ur,
from the Royal Graves,
shows the Sumerian ruler
at war and in peacetime.

Timeline: 5000-2500

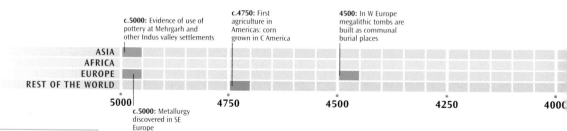

c.5000: Evidence of use of pottery at Mehrgarh and other Indus valley settlements

c.4750: First agriculture in Americas: corn grown in C America

4500: In W Europe megalithic tombs are built as communal burial places

	5000		4750	4500	4250	4000
ASIA						
AFRICA						
EUROPE						
REST OF THE WORLD						

c.5000: Metallurgy discovered in SE Europe

THE TRANSITION from hunter-gathering to farming, which took place in the Middle East in about 9000 BCE, was a development that was to transform the face of the globe. Increasing crop yields led to food surpluses, enabling people to live in large, settled communities. Surplus food supplies also meant that a growing number of people were able to dedicate themselves to other activities, such as pottery-making, metallurgy, and trade. Trading contacts between peoples, communal ventures such as irrigation and construction, and the emergence of an elite class of specialists were developments that would ultimately pave the way for the emergence of the first cities.

Agriculture developed independently in several different parts of the world, in a subtropical belt stretching from Central America to China, spreading rapidly to neighboring regions. In Central and South America the transition from hunting to agriculture was slow and farming villages were only gradually established, while in many other regions hunter-gathering remained the mainstay of the economy.

The Fertile Crescent

The last Ice Age had created unusually moist conditions in which wild cereals flourished. In the Middle East, people began to gather and transplant the wild cereals, improving nature by selecting and propagating beneficial traits.

By this process, they developed cereals with large grains and a seed head that did not shatter on ripening. By c.7000 BCE, wheat and barley were being cultivated from Anatolia to Pakistan, and the process of domesticating animals, mainly goat and sheep, had also begun.

Both the Tigris and Euphrates flood in winter, and an elaborate system of irrigation channels was dug to transport water to the parched plains where wheat and barley were grown. In Egypt and Pakistan, on the other hand, agriculture was dependent on the annual flooding of the Nile and Indus rivers. When the floodwaters retreated, they deposited a covering of extremely fertile alluvial silt. Irrigation channels could be dug to divert the water to fields, while embankments and dikes controlled the floodwaters.

The First Cities

Intensive agriculture supported larger populations. As farming became more ambitious, divisions of labor became more complex. Social hierarchies developed, and a ruling class began to emerge that was responsible for organizing local production and long-distance trade – vital for ensuring the supply of raw materials for a growing number of specialized craftsmen.

By the 5th millennium, cities had begun to emerge in Mesopotamia. Each was governed by a priestly elite, which ruled from a focal temple complex. The city was the center of an agricultural hinterland, which was controlled and administered by the city temple. Stocks of surplus agricultural produce were stored in temple warehouses, where an accurate tally was kept of supplies. Initially, goods were represented by clay counting tokens. These were eventually sealed in clay envelopes, and marked on the outside with signs indicating their contents – the first written symbols (late fourth millennium BCE).

In Egypt, on the other hand, a group of small towns had grown in prosperity. In 3100 BCE, King Narmer, a ruler from the southern Nile, conquered the Nile delta, creating a unified state and becoming the first pharaoh. Egypt was a theocratic state, ruled by a divine king, and belief in the afterlife was a fundamental tenet. The pyramids were elaborate burial monuments constructed for the pharaohs between 2550 and 2470 BCE.

Monument-builders

Farming spread to southeastern Europe in the seventh millennium BCE. As it became established across the continent, trading contacts were established, and communities increased in size. Remains of great megalithic tombs in western Europe testify to the early Europeans' building skills. From c.3200 BCE, the peoples of England and western France began to build monuments of standing stones, many of them arranged to be illuminated by the Sun on significant days.

TRANSPORTATION

Much of the early trade between Mesopotamia, Egypt, and the Nile valley was maritime. All of these civilizations were based on rivers and waterways and shallow-draught boats, made of reeds or timber, plied their way along the rivers and on coast-hugging voyages around the Persian Gulf and Arabian Sea. The timber boats of the Nile, depicted carrying columns of granite and alabaster, are known from tomb reliefs, models, and burials. The invention of the wheel in Mesopotamia in c.3500 BCE heralded a transportation revolution. Carts and wagons, drawn by oxen or onagers (a kind of wild ass) could be used to carry bulky produce overland, a development that encouraged trading links, leading to the spread of urban civilizations. For longer distances, pack animals were used to carry merchandise; the domestication of the camel, in Arabia and Central Asia, and the ass, in Egypt, greatly increased the trading spheres of early civilizations.

Some of the earliest vessels with sails were developed in Egypt, where the Nile river offered the most effective means of transportation.

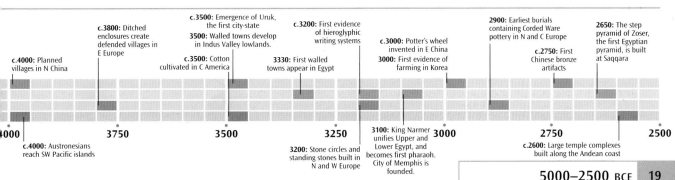

c.4000: Planned villages in N China

c.4000: Austronesians reach SW Pacific islands

c.3800: Ditched enclosures create defended villages in E Europe

c.3500: Emergence of Uruk, the first city-state
3500: Walled towns develop in Indus Valley lowlands.
c.3500: Cotton cultivated in C America

3330: First walled towns appear in Egypt

c.3200: First evidence of hieroglyphic writing systems

3200: Stone circles and standing stones built in N and W Europe

3100: King Narmer unifies Upper and Lower Egypt, and becomes first pharaoh. City of Memphis is founded.

c.3000: Potter's wheel invented in E China
3000: First evidence of farming in Korea

2900: Earliest burials containing Corded Ware pottery in N and C Europe

c.2750: First Chinese bronze artifacts

c.2600: Large temple complexes built along the Andean coast

2650: The step pyramid of Zoser, the first Egyptian pyramid, is built at Saqqara

4000   3750   3500   3250   3000   2750   2500

Terra-cotta figurines with swollen abdomens were found at Çatal Hüyük suggesting a thriving earth-mother cult. Plaster shrines in many houses, featuring bovine heads and horns, also suggest a parallel bull-worshiping practice.

Çatal Hüyük

Although only about one fifth of the isolated site of Çatal Hüyük, set in a fertile volcanic plain in central Anatolia, has been excavated, it is clear it was a thriving agricultural community, had fairly extensive trading links, and supported some industry, specializing in blades and weapons, textiles, molded and carved figurines, pottery, and early copper-smelting. Wall paintings show the town sited beneath a neighboring volcano and display hunting and farming actvities; bull-worship shrines and figurines indicate a similarly wide array of local cults.

Çatal Hüyük was built of sundried brick, the houses decorated with wall-paintings and plaster sculptures, and jammed together without streets or alleys, the interiors only accessible by wooden ladders from flat roofs.

ASIA

c.5000 Jade imported into N Manchuria from C Asia or Siberia.

Evidence of use of pottery vessels at Mehrgarh and other Indus Valley settlements.

Copper first used in Mesopotamia.

c.3500 Irrigation supports large population in Mesopotamia.

Wetrice farming near east coast of China.

Hunting and fishing villages in Yangtze river delta begin cultivating rice.

Millet, dogs, and pigs widely domesticated in the Yellow river basin.

Yangshao culture in Yellow river basin (–3000).

c.3500 **c.4500** Introduction of irrigation techniques in Indus Valley increases size and prosperity of farming settlements.

First use of sail, Mesopotamia.

Rice cultivated south of Ganges river in India; pottery made with corded decoration.

Horse domesticated in C Asia.

2600 **c.4000** Use of plow in Mesopotamia.

c.3500 Planned villages in N China, with distinct residential, workshop, and burial areas.

AFRICA

c.4100 Sorghum and rice cultivated in Sudan.

c.4000 Agriculture in W Africa at Taruga.

Plants domesticated in sub-Saharan Africa.

Use of sail in Egypt.

Desiccation of Sahara begins (–3000). N African populations expand east and south.

EUROPE

c.5000 Cereal-farming villages established in W Europe.

Agriculture well established in S France and in the Netherlands.

Gold and copper artifacts produced in SE Europe, first European metallurgy.

c.4500 Large cemeteries, for example on the western coast of the Black Sea, contain rich burials with elaborate gold jewelry.

 c.3200 In W Europe, megalithic (large stone) chamber tombs, built as communal burial places.

 c.3500 Evidence of cattle being used as draft animals in E Europe.

c.4000 Farming villages of the Cucuteni-Tripolye group appear in S Ukraine.

 c.3000 Copper mines being exploited in Bulgaria and Yugoslavia.

Flint intensively mined in N and W Europe.

c.3800 Ditched enclosures around settlements in C Europe create defended villages.

AMERICAS & AUSTRALASIA

c.5000 Corn cultivation begins in Tehuacán Valley, C America.

Bottlegourd cultivation in Mississippi basin.

  c.4750 First evidence of animal domestication in C America.

c.4500 Cultivation of corn in eastern N America.

c.3000 Evidence of agriculture in south-central Andes.

c.4000 Austronesians reach SW Pacific islands.

When do the first towns appear?

The emergence of the first towns appears to be linked to the development of crop domestication and sedentary agriculture. The appearance of the first towns also heralds the beginnings of craft products, significantly pottery and metallurgy, organized religion, and the beginnings of long distance trade. Towns developed at very different times across the world.

Palestine	Jericho	9th century BCE
Anatolia	Çatal Hüyük	c.7000 BCE
	Troy	c.3000 BCE
E Asia	Chengziyai	2500 BCE
S Asia	Kot Diji	3000 BCE
SE Europe	Karanovo	6000 BCE
C Europe	Magdalen	2000 BCE
SW Europe	Cortes de Navarra	800 BCE
N Europe	Hedeby	750 CE
Africa	Jenne jeno	c.600 BCE
C America	San Jose Mogote	1200 BCE
S America	Caral	2600 BCE
N America	Cahokia	c.900 CE

Australasia/Oceania There is no evidence of town development in the region before European settlement in the 18th century CE.

Metallurgy (9500–3750 BCE)

Copper and tin, later combined to form bronze, were most accessible in ore form and were thus the first of many metals to be worked by metalsmiths. Gold and iron soon followed. The chemistry of copper-working was discovered variously in widely separated regions in Eurasia. The use of bronze, a stronger and more durable alloy, usually emerged within a short period.

Iron metallurgy emerged in Southwest Asia, where it was first smelted c.2000 BCE, while cast iron evolved separately in East Asia. In sub-Saharan Africa there is no evidence of metalworking before the first millennium BCE; in the Americas, only gold was worked widely before European contact in the 13th century CE.

This pair of horned bulls, fashioned from sheet gold, are from a rich set of grave goods unearthed at a cemetery in Varna in Southeast Europe. They date from the late 5th millennium BCE.

The 203-foot (62-m) high Step Pyramid of Zoser marks an unprecedented leap forward in the history of world architecture.

Egyptian Pyramids

The prototype of the pyramid was the *mastaba*, a low, flat-topped rectangular mudbrick structure with a shaft descending to the burial chamber far below it. In c.2650, the 3rd-dynasty King Zoser employed his architect, the high priest Imhotep to undertake for the first time the construction of a *mastaba* entirely of stone. Within a century, the first true – and largest – pyramids were built. The Great Pyramid of Khufu in Giza was constructed during the 4th dynasty and incorporates an estimated 2.5 million blocks of stone weighing on average around 2.8 tons (2.5 tonnes) and reaching an elevation of 482 feet (147 m).

Work on the Giza pyramids probably took place during the summertime Nile flood, when agricultural laborers could not work the land, and the high Nile tides facilitated the movement of granite blocks by barge. The blocks were then rolled up earthwork ramps which increased in height and gradient as successive layers were added. The ramps were removed when the pyramid was complete.

The Sphinx, built c.2500 stands guard over the pyramids in Giza, and their attendant Queens' pyramids, temples, and tombs. It is the earliest known monumental sculpture.

3750–2500 BCE

ASIA

3650 Earliest vehicle burials found in C Russia; ox-drawn wagons in use.

c.2500 **c.3500** Uruk period; emergence of first city-states in S Mesopotamia. Uruk may have been the first city in the world.

c.2500 Indus Valley lowlands settled by farmers; walled towns develop.

Ceremonial complexes built in Mesopotamia as centers of early cities.

First Chinese cities, with walls and rammed-earth platforms.

Evidence of trade in luxury items in China; increased social stratification.

c.3400 Sumerians use clay counting tokens and first written symbols.

c.3250 Pictographic clay tablets from Tell Brak, N Mesopotamia, used for temple accounts; earliest evidence of writing.

c.3200 Evidence of use of wheeled transportation in Sumer.

Wheeled carts buried in tombs of rulers of Ur and Kish.

3100 Sumerian trading post at Habuba Kabira, Syria. Sumerian merchants have their own quarters in Persian city of Godin Tepe.

Development of cuneiform script in Mesopotamia. Experiments with bronzeworking.

c.3000 First evidence of farming (millet cultivation) in Korea.

Longshan culture in NE China (–2000); first jade-working.

First agricultural settlements in SE Asia.

Potter's wheel invented during formative phase of Longshan culture of E China.

Sheep and cattle domesticated in N China; water buffalo in S China; use of plowshare.

c.2750 First Chinese bronze artifacts.

c.2700 Silk weaving practiced in China.

2600 Evidence for use of the plow in Indus Valley.

AFRICA

c.3300 First walled towns in Egypt: Hieraconpolis and Naqada.

c.2500 **c.3200** Earliest hieroglyphic script in Egypt.

c.3100 King Narmer unifies Upper and Lower Egypt, and becomes first pharaoh.

Early urban communities emerge in the Nile Delta. Memphis is founded as the capital city of the new, unified Egyptian state.

Hieroglyphic writing appears on Egyptian stone monuments.

c.3000 The Egyptian state ruled by 1st–3rd dynasty.

c.2650 Start of great period of pyramid building in Egypt; construction of Step Pyramid of Zoser at Saqqara.

c.2150 **c.2575** Old Kingdom Egypt ruled by 4th–6th dynasties.

c.2540 Construction of Great Pyramid of Khufu, the largest of the Egyptian pyramids, at Giza.

Writing

c.3500 New farming methods: animals used for traction, wool, and milk.

Stone circles and alignments, henges, and menhirs appear throughout NW Europe.

First wheeled vehicles in C Europe.

c.3200 Stone circles and rows of standing stones built throughout N and W Europe.

c.2500 ▽

c.3000 Copper-working begins in S France.

Walled citadels built in Mediterranean Europe for the powerful elite.

2900 Appearance of Corded Ware pottery and stone battleaxes in burials in N Europe.

c.3500 Cotton cultivated in C America; used to make fishing nets and textiles.

Llama used as a pack animal and for other products in Peru.

c.3400 Farming villages established in Tehuacán Valley, C America.

c.3000 Cotton cultivated in C Andes. Large village settlements begin to appear.

c.2600 Large temple complexes built in villages along the Andean coast.

Writing developed in different ways, and took different forms, around the world. Most early scripts were pictographic, hieroglyphic, or cuneiform, as here, *left*, where the unique pictoform lettering was impressed on a slab of clay using a pointed triangular stylus. The Roman alphabet has its roots in Egyptian script as used in the Levant before 2000 BCE, and passed via the Greeks and Phoenicians into Europe.

The first Mesopotamian cuneiform tablets appear to record trading transactions, a form of accounting, also used on "cylinder" seals.

The development of writing	
c.3400	Mesopotamia: cuneiform/pictographic/syllabic
c.3200	Egypt: hieroglyphic/ideographic
c.3000	E China: pictographic/ideographic
c.2500	Indus Valley: pictographic
c.2000	Crete: hieroglyphic
c.1750	Crete: Linear A (pictographic)
c.1600	Crete: Linear B (syllabic)
c.600	C America: pictographic
c.100	Egypt: Coptic script
c.250 CE	NW Europe: runic

Megalithic Europe

As agriculture spread through Europe a variety of Megalithic monuments were built. These range in date from c.3500–1500 BCE, and include often circular arrangements of standing stones (as in Carnac in northwest France, (*below*), or Stonehenge, southwest England, or, in the case of Seahenge on the East Anglian coast in England, wooden monoliths). These were probably ceremonial centers, often associated with stonebuilt tombs (as in West Kennet, southwest England) and barrow burials. Quarrying, mining, and the logistically-complicated transportation of bulk materials over long distances, and decorated pottery, suggest a sophisticated social structure.

The World in 2500 BCE

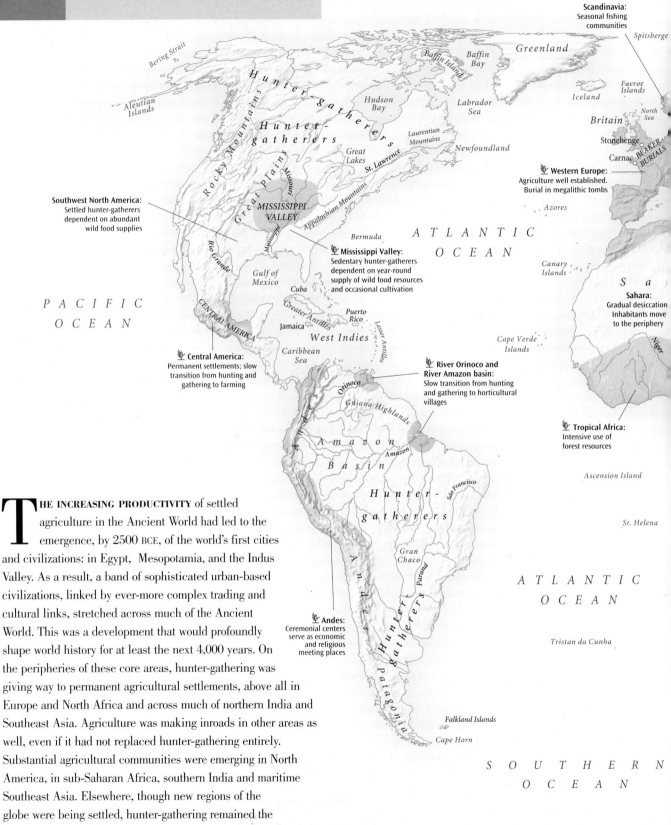

Scandinavia:
Seasonal fishing communities

Western Europe:
Agriculture well established. Burial in megalithic tombs

Sahara:
Gradual desiccation Inhabitants move to the periphery

Tropical Africa:
Intensive use of forest resources

Southwest North America:
Settled hunter-gatherers dependent on abundant wild food supplies

Mississippi Valley:
Sedentary hunter-gatherers dependent on year-round supply of wild food resources and occasional cultivation

Central America:
Permanent settlements; slow transition from hunting and gathering to farming

River Orinoco and River Amazon basin:
Slow transition from hunting and gathering to horticultural villages

Andes:
Ceremonial centers serve as economic and religious meeting places

THE INCREASING PRODUCTIVITY of settled agriculture in the Ancient World had led to the emergence, by 2500 BCE, of the world's first cities and civilizations: in Egypt, Mesopotamia, and the Indus Valley. As a result, a band of sophisticated urban-based civilizations, linked by ever-more complex trading and cultural links, stretched across much of the Ancient World. This was a development that would profoundly shape world history for at least the next 4,000 years. On the peripheries of these core areas, hunter-gathering was giving way to permanent agricultural settlements, above all in Europe and North Africa and across much of northern India and Southeast Asia. Agriculture was making inroads in other areas as well, even if it had not replaced hunter-gathering entirely. Substantial agricultural communities were emerging in North America, in sub-Saharan Africa, southern India and maritime Southeast Asia. Elsewhere, though new regions of the globe were being settled, hunter-gathering remained the dominant way of life.

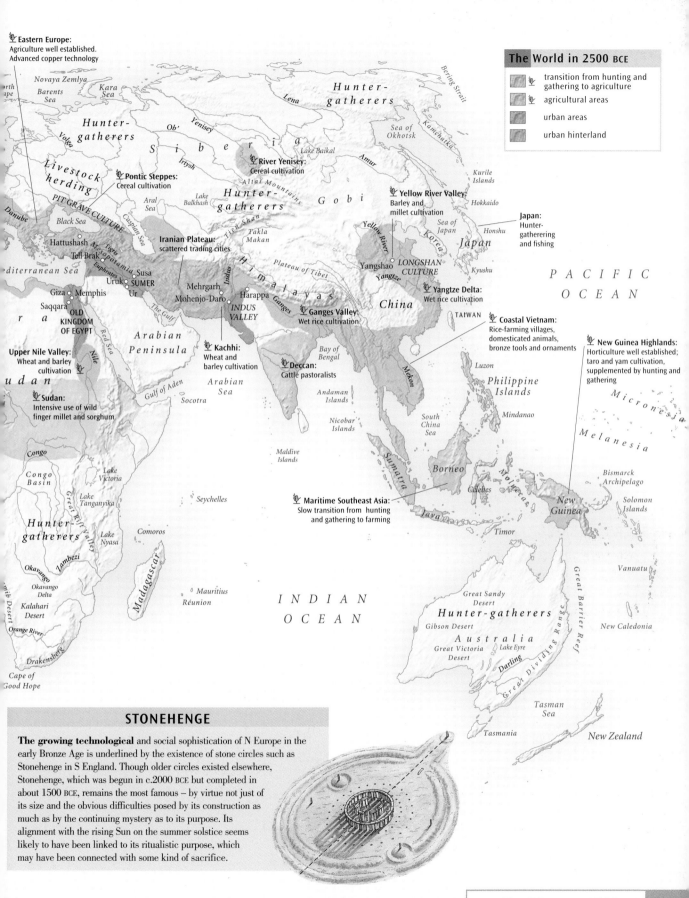

Eastern Europe:
Agriculture well established.
Advanced copper technology

Novaya Zemlya

Barents Sea

Kara Sea

Hunter-gatherers

Pontic Steppes:
Cereal cultivation

Lena

Hunter-gatherers

River Yenisey:
Cereal cultivation

Sea of Okhotsk

Kamchatka

Ob' *Yenisey*

S i b e r i a

Irtysh

Livestock herding

PIT GRAVE CULTURE

Volga

Black Sea

Aral Sea

Lake Balkhash

Hunter-gatherers

Altai Mountains

Lake Baikal

G o b i

Amur

Kurile Islands

Hokkaido

Yellow River Valley:
Barley and
millet cultivation

Japan:
Hunter-
gatherering
and fishing

Danube

Caspian Sea

Mediterranean Sea

Hattushash

Tell Brak

Mesopotamia

Tigris

Euphrates

Susa

Uruk

SUMER

Ur

Giza *Memphis*

Saqqara

OLD KINGDOM OF EGYPT

ra

Iranian Plateau:
scattered trading cities

Tien Shan

Takla Makan

Plateau of Tibet

H i m a l a y a s

Mehrgarh

Mohenjo-Daro

Indus

Harappa

INDUS VALLEY

Ganges

Ganges Valley:
Wet rice cultivation

Yellow River

Yangshao

Yangtze

LONGSHAN CULTURE

Sea of Japan

Korea

Honshu

Japan

Kyushu

China

Yangtze Delta:
Wet rice cultivation

P A C I F I C   O C E A N

TAIWAN

Kachhi:
Wheat and
barley cultivation

Coastal Vietnam:
Rice-farming villages,
domesticated animals,
bronze tools and ornaments

New Guinea Highlands:
Horticulture well established;
taro and yam cultivation,
supplemented by hunting and
gathering

Upper Nile Valley:
Wheat and barley
cultivation

Arabian Peninsula

Red Sea

Nile

Deccan:
Cattle pastoralists

Bay of Bengal

Luzon

Philippine Islands

Mekong

M i c r o n e s i a

sudan

Sudan:
Intensive use of wild
finger millet and sorghum

Gulf of Aden

Socotra

Arabian Sea

Andaman Islands

Mindanao

South China Sea

M e l a n e s i a

Congo

Congo Basin

Lake Victoria

Great Rift Valley

Nicobar Islands

Maldive Islands

Maritime Southeast Asia:
Slow transition from hunting
and gathering to farming

Sumatra

Borneo

Celebes

Moluccas

Bismarck Archipelago

New Guinea

Solomon Islands

Hunter-gatherers

Lake Tanganyika

Lake Nyasa

Comoros

Seychelles

Java

Timor

Vanuatu

Okavango

Zambezi

Madagascar

Mauritius

Réunion

I N D I A N
O C E A N

Great Sandy Desert

Hunter-gatherers

A u s t r a l i a

New Caledonia

Okavango Delta

Kalahari Desert

Orange River

Gibson Desert

Great Victoria Desert

Lake Eyre

Darling

Great Dividing Range

Great Barrier Reef

Drakensberg

Cape of Good Hope

Tasman Sea

Tasmania

New Zealand

STONEHENGE

The growing technological and social sophistication of N Europe in the
early Bronze Age is underlined by the existence of stone circles such as
Stonehenge in S England. Though older circles existed elsewhere,
Stonehenge, which was begun in c.2000 BCE but completed in
about 1500 BCE, remains the most famous – by virtue not just of
its size and the obvious difficulties posed by its construction as
much as by the continuing mystery as to its purpose. Its
alignment with the rising Sun on the summer solstice seems
likely to have been linked to its ritualistic purpose, which
may have been connected with some kind of sacrifice.

2500–1000 BCE
The First Cities

Timeline: 2500-1000 BCE

2500: City-states present throughout Mesopotamia and Levant

c.2500: First domesticated animals and pottery in island SE Asia

2300: City-states of S Mesopotamia temporarily united under Sargon of Agade

2040: Egypt reunited under Middle Kingdom pharaohs after a period of dominance by nobles

c.2000: Minoan civilization becomes established on the island of Crete

c.2000: Fortified settlements appear in C and E Europe

c.1900: First Chinese city founded at Erlitou on Yellow river

	2500	2400	2300	2200	2100	2000	1900
ASIA							
AFRICA							
EUROPE							
REST OF THE WORLD							

c.2300: Bronze technology reaches Europe

c.2000: Large-scale cultivation in Peru

By 2500 BCE, urban civilization stretched in a great arc from the Eastern Mediterranean to the Indus Valley, and along the Yellow river in China. Nevertheless, urbanism only flourished on a tiny portion of the Earth's surface; most people still lived as hunter-gatherers, or as subsistence farmers. The whole of Polynesia remained unpeopled; the colonization of the Pacific, which was to take over 2,000 years, was only just beginning in 1500 BCE. At La Venta in Mexico and El Aspero in Peru, large-scale ceremonial centers, which would require the cooperation of several communities, indicate that states were beginning to form.

Old World civilizations

In the Middle East, a plethora of city-states were locked in contact and conflict. Demand for raw materials had created an extensive trade network, but there was a constant struggle for political and economic hegemony. In Syria, a number of city-states, such as Mari and Ebla, emerged in the latter half of the 3rd millennium. Centered on religious complexes and palaces, they have yielded large archives of clay tablets recording economic transactions, taxation, and tribute. In the 18th century BCE, Babylon gained temporary control over the region. The Babylonians were famous for their expertise in mathematics, astronomy, and astrology. They also produced a written law code and the first written literature.

In about 2000 BCE, the powerful Hittite state emerged in western Anatolia, based on the citadel of Hattushash, which was fortified by a 4-mile (6-km) long perimeter wall. The Hittites' ambition to gain control of the coastal cities of the Levant, and their lucrative trade, brought them into conflict with New Kingdom Egypt. By 1560 BCE, Egypt had reached the height of its power, controlling an empire that stretched from Syria to Nubia, with its rich gold deposits. The royal tombs from the Valley of the Kings reveal stupendous wealth – even a minor king, such as Tutankhamun, was buried with a panoply of valuable grave goods. Egypt was noted for its jewelry, carved ivory, glassware, pottery, and linens.

By 2500 BCE, Indus valley civilization – centered on the cities of Mohenjo Daro and Harappa, had reached its peak. Like Egypt, Indus civilization was based on the annual flooding of the river, which brought fertility to the parched land. The Indus peoples lived in planned cities with wells, piped water supply, drains, and baths. The Indus script has not yet been deciphered, but it is evident from finds of seals, used for securing bales of merchandise, that the Indus peoples were in contact with Mesopotamia. Indus civilization began to collapse in about 2000 BCE, possibly as the result of a shift in the course of the Indus river.

The Shang civilization developed separately from the other urban areas of the Old World in about 1800 BCE. Many features of later Chinese civilization were already present: a hierarchical society; rule by a powerful royal dynasty; ancestor worship. A complex writing system, used to record divinations, had already evolved, and many traditional Chinese crafts – bronze-working, stone- and jade-carving, and lacquerware, also developed during this period.

Bronze Age Europe

The first palace-centered state in Europe developed at Knossos in Crete, c.2000 BCE. Palaces served as royal households, economic centers, and a ritual and ceremonial focus. Cretan civilization was abruptly destroyed by a volcanic eruption in c.1450 BCE. By this time, the more warlike Mycenaeans were emerging as the major power in mainland Greece.

The discovery that metals can be extracted from rock, hammered, smelted, and molded was made separately in different parts of the world. Beaten copper was used as early as 9,000 years ago in parts of Central Asia, but it was not until about 7000 BCE that it was discovered that metal could be cast when molten. Bronze, an alloy of copper and tin, was discovered in western Asia in c.4000 BCE, and the knowledge spread through the Old World between 3000 and 2000 BCE. Bronze was probably discovered separately in East Asia. Throughout this period early metal-smiths produced a great profusion of fine bronze. Around 1500 BCE, iron-smelting was discovered in western Asia. Over the next 1,000 years, iron-working spread all over the Old World, and iron was used to make tools and weapons – bronze was restricted to ornamental use.

Wheeled bronze model of a horse drawing a gold-plated disk, found in the Trundholm bog in Denmark (c.1650 BCE). The disk probably represents the sun, which was worshiped by the peoples of Scandinavia.

Each of their small kingdoms was dominated by a fortified palace or citadel. Craftsmen used bronze to make swords and armor, and war chariots were in use. The Mycenaeans were enterprising sailors and traders, but conflict was endemic, and by c.1150 BCE all the Mycenaean towns had been sacked and abandoned.

Elsewhere in Europe, population growth was placing pressure on the land; boundaries were being laid out, and farming settlements were enclosed and defended. In many regions, large burial mounds contained rich grave goods, an indication of wealth and status.

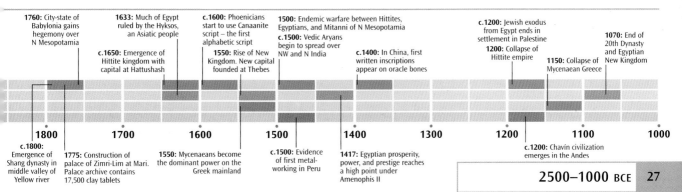

1760: City-state of Babylonia gains hegemony over N Mesopotamia

1633: Much of Egypt ruled by the Hyksos, an Asiatic people

c.1650: Emergence of Hittite kingdom with capital at Hattushash

c.1600: Phoenicians start to use Canaanite script – the first alphabetic script

1550: Rise of New Kingdom. New capital founded at Thebes

1500: Endemic warfare between Hittites, Egyptians, and Mitanni of N Mesopotamia

c.1500: Vedic Aryans begin to spread over NW and N India

1400: In China, first written inscriptions appear on oracle bones

c.1200: Jewish exodus from Egypt ends in settlement in Palestine

1200: Collapse of Hittite empire

1150: Collapse of Mycenaean Greece

1070: End of 20th Dynasty and Egyptian New Kingdom

1800 1700 1600 1500 1400 1300 1200 1100 1000

c.1800: Emergence of Shang dynasty in middle valley of Yellow river

1775: Construction of palace of Zimri-Lim at Mari. Palace archive contains 17,500 clay tablets

1550: Mycenaeans become the dominant power on the Greek mainland

c.1500: Evidence of first metal-working in Peru

1417: Egyptian prosperity, power, and prestige reaches a high point under Amenophis II

c.1200: Chavín civilization emerges in the Andes

Mohenjo-Daro

With Harappa, and the recently discovered remains of an unnamed city in the Gulf of Khambhat, Mohenjo-Daro was one of the principal centers of Harappan, or Indus, civilization. These cities date from c.2500 BCE. Covering an area of over 148 acres (60 ha), Mohenjo-Daro may have had a population of up to 55,000. The city was arranged around a citadel (*below*) and both areas were built on a regular grid plan, with paved streets and underground sewage drains. The lower residential area was divided into nine districts, with mudbrick housing ranging from luxurious private homes to low-rise tenement blocks. The Indus civilization came to an end c.2000 BCE, for unclear reasons, although a shift in the course of the Indus river at this time probably contributed to the decline of Mohenjo-Daro.

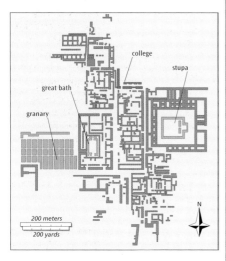

A bust of a bearded man found in Mohenjo-Daro (c.2100 BCE), combining both naturalistic and stylized features, probably representing a priest-king.

The groundplan of the citadel at Mohenjo-Daro, the most heavily excavated area of the site and built on a raised mound, reveals a regular grid street pattern and a careful arrangement of municipal buildings for public, sacred, and administrative use.

c.2500 Rich array of grave goods at Royal Graves at Ur indicate extensive trade links.

First domesticated animals and pottery in island SE Asia.

c.1900 Banshan culture of W China produces boldly painted burial urns.

Earliest syllabic script used in Sumerian literature.

Emergence of cities in Levant and N Mesopotamia, each focused on a palace complex.

City of Ur in S Mesopotamia is a major center of trade and manufacture.

The city of Ebla in W Mesopotamia begins to trade with Mediterranean peoples.

Four-wheeled wagon in use in Mesopotamia.

c.2000 Cities begin to appear in the Indus Valley. Mohenjo-Daro and Harappa may have had population of c.40,000.

Indus Valley civilization marks seals with inscriptions.

Indus Valley trading colony of Shortughai, 621 miles (1,000 km) from Harappa, supplies tin and lapis lazuli.

Harappan Bronze Age civilization centered on Indus plain until c.2000 BCE.

Earliest known woven cotton cloth found at Mohenjo-Daro.

Bronze metallurgy in SE Asia.

c.2400 Foundation of Akkadian dynasty in S Mesopotamia.

c.2340 Sargon I founds and rules city of Agade.

c.2300 City-states of S Mesopotamia temporarily united under Sargon of Agade to form first world empire.

c.1763 **2150** Gutians conquer Sumer, ruling it until 2050.

c.2100 Construction of Ziggurat at Ur in Sumer.

c.2500 Egyptian calendar pioneers division of day into 24 units.

c.2150 Series of floods brings famine and discontent in Egypt.

Collapse of the Egyptian Old Kingdom.

c.2134 First Intermediate Period in Egypt.

1783 **c.2040** Egypt reunited under Middle Kingdom pharaohs after period of dominance by nobles. New capital is founded at El-Lisht.

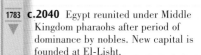

c.2500 Copper-working reaches British Isles. Bell Beaker pottery found in individual burials in W Europe.

c.2500 Evidence of long-distance trade throughout S America, mainly of valuables.

 c.1750 Masonry building and temple architecture in S America at sites such as Aspero and Kotosh.

Dingo introduced to Australia, probably from SE Asia.

Crop yields improve in S America due to selection and hybridization; appearance of large permanent villages.

Loom-weaving, grinding, and polishing of stones, and irrigation in S America.

The European Bronze Age was a period of great cultural and technological innovation. Beginning in the palace cultures of Minoan Crete and Mycenaean Greece, bronze technology spread rapidly with sedentary agriculture, initially along major river valleys such as the Danube and the Rhine. Villages developed and soon towns, based on trade, began to flourish. Tin resources in eastern Europe, essential for bronze manufacture, were traded over long distances in exchange for other valuable commodities, such as Baltic amber, metal ores, and salt. Barrow burials of rich chieftains contain an extensive range of prized goods. Agriculturally marginal lands and forests were cleared for cultivation to feed a growing population, but with increasing trade and pressure on valuable resources, the development of hill forts (from c.2200 BCE) and other defended sites reflect growing conflict and competition for control of resources and trade.

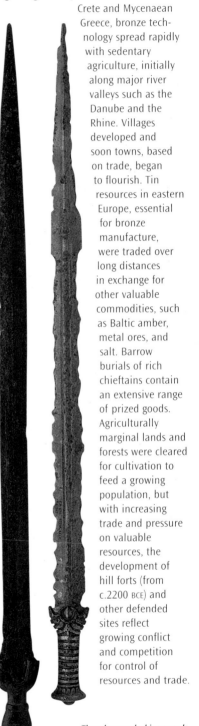

c.2300 Beginning of European Bronze Age; bronze objects begin to appear in tombs.

c.2000
c.2200 Defensive enclosures built in S Britain as communities compete for land and resources.

c.2200 Earliest pottery in S America.

These bronze slashing swords, made toward the end of the second millennium BCE, illustrate considerable cultural sophistication in their style and decoration while indicating growing aggression and militarism.

Mesopotamia – Cradle of Civilization

Mesopotamia is the fertile valley of the Tigris and Euphrates – the eastern arc of the Fertile Crescent. Organized farming emerged by 6000, and the world's earliest known irrigation system appeared in Choga Mami by c.5500. There is evidence of the use of the sail by c.4500, and the first city-state developed in Sumer by c.3500.

c.3500	Sumer is first organized state (–2500).
c.3250	First pictographic script in use.
3100	Evidence of first cuneiform writing.
2500	Earliest syllabic script in Sumerian literature.
	Palace-based cities develop in C Mesopotamia.
	Four-wheeled war chariot in use.
2300	First Sumerian empire under Sargon of Agade, stretching from Persian Gulf to E Mediterrranean (–2230).
2112	Third dynasty of Ur, renaissance of Sumerian empire (–2004).
c.1800	Shamshi-Adad founds first Assyrian state.
1795	Hammurabi founds first Babylonian dynasty (–1750)
1650	Formation of Hittite empire in C Anatolia, with capital at Hattushash.
1595	Babylon sacked by Hittites from C Anatolia.
1500	Mitanni dominant in N Mesopotamia, extend control to Mediterranean coast.
c.1200	Collapse of Hittite empire.
c.950	Foundation of Assyrian empire.

Hammurabi's Law Code c.1750

The Babylonian ruler Hammurabi was among the first to publish administrative laws. This basalt pillar depicts him receiving the instruction to promulgate his royal laws and codes from a Babylonian god. Below this scene the laws are inscribed, making this one of the earliest examples of the use of writing in public administrative art.

2000–1500 BCE

ASIA

c.2000 First cities established in Anatolia.

Collapse of Indus Valley civilization.

c.1950 Foundation of Assyrian trading colonies in Anatolia, i.e. Kanesh.

c.1900 First known Shang city in Erlitou on Yellow river in China.

c.1850 Light carts pulled by horses in western steppes.

c.1800 Two-wheeled war chariots and battering ram in use in Near East.

Beginnings of Shang state in China.

c.1775 Construction of palace of Zimri-Lim at Mari. Palace archive contained 17,500 clay tablets.

c.1750 Hammurabi writes his Law Code, the first in world history.

c.1763 Hammurabi of Babylon conquers all of Sumer. Founds first Babylonian dynasty (1795).

c.1400 **c.1700** First bronze vessels cast in Shang China.

c.1650 Anatolian city-states unite as Hittite empire, with Hattushash as capital.

c.1550 Arrival of Indo-Aryans in India.

c.1600 Phoenicians start to use Canaanite script – the first alphabetic script.

Kassites conquer most of Mesopotamia.

c.1500 **1595** Hittites sack Babylon.

c.1500 **c.1550** Aryans overwhelm Indus Valley civilization and settle N India.

AFRICA

c.1990 El-Lisht becomes the New Egyptian capital.

c.1965 Nubia is conquered by Egypt; frontier at Second Cataract.

c.1800 Horse introduced to Egypt.

1783 Fall of the Middle Kingdom in Egypt.

c.1640 Second Intermediate Period in Egypt.

1633 Much of Egypt ruled by the Hyksos, an Asiatic people.

c.1570 Egyptian rulers buried in rockcut tombs in the Valley of the Kings.

c.1350 **1550** Rise of New Kingdom in Egypt. New capital founded at Thebes, which becomes center of Egyptian empire.

New Kingdom ruled by 18–20th dynasties (–1085).

c.1550 Deir-el-Medina founded in Egypt – village of craftsmen who built Egyptian royal tombs.

EUROPE

c.2000 Fortified settlements begin to appear in E and C Europe, a sign of increased social and economic pressure.

Minoan civilization becomes established on island of Crete; palace of Knossos is built.

Appearance of Egyptian-influenced hieroglyphic script in Crete.

Stonehenge is erected.

Use of sail in the Aegean.

c.1900 Potter's wheel introduced to Crete.

c.1800 Finds of wooden plows in Scandinavian bogs. Bronze artifacts suggest sun worship.

c.1750 Linear A script comes into use on Crete.

1600 Linear B script comes into use on Crete.

c.1600 Mycenae becomes center of Aegean civilization.

c.1550 Mycenaeans become dominant power on Greek mainland.

AMERICAS & AUSTRALASIA

c.2000 Large-scale cultivation of corn (maize) in Peru.

Austronesians settle New Caledonia.

Early Inuit culture – Arctic Small Tool Tradition – found from Siberia to Greenland.

Melanesia begins to be settled by immigrants from Indonesia.

c.1800 Cultivation of sunflowers and gourds in eastern N America. Long-distance trade networks established.

Ceremonial center of La Florida built in Peru.

c.1750 Massive ceremonial architecture at Sechin Alto, Peru.

Northern areas of Greenland settled.

c.1600 Earliest datable examples of Lapita pottery in Bismarck archipelago.

Minoan Civilization c.2000–c.1450

Around 2000, Europe's first advanced civilization, the Minoans, developed on the island of Crete. This colorful fresco of a priest-king adorned a wall at Knossos, one of the extensive, palace-based cities that characterize the culture. After a volcanic eruption c.1450 on neighboring Thera, the civilization came to an abrupt end. Knossos was rebuilt, but it was under Greek-speaking rulers, and Minoan culture gave way to Mycenaean Greece as the dominant force in the eastern Mediterranean.

The pottery vessels produced by the Lapita people were decorated with designs made by stamping the unfired clay with a toothlike implement.

The Lapita people

The gradual migration of Austronesian-speakers from Maritime Southeast Asia into Melanesia (reached c.2000 BCE), Micronesia (c.1500–c.1000 BCE) and into Polynesia (Samoa by c.1000, the Marquesas Islands by c.200 BCE) depended on considerable navigational skills. This dispersal is one of the most remarkable demographic shifts in premodern times. Their progress has been traced through finds of distinctly decorated Lapita pottery.

2000–1500 BCE 31

The enormous wealth amassed from foreign tribute during the New Kingdom was channeled into massive building projects in and around Thebes. Karnak, one of the largest temple complexes in the world, was largely completed during the 18th dynasty but added to during the reign of Ramses II, whose colossal statue (above) stands in the Temple of Amun, dedicated to the king of the gods.

Monumental Architecture

The Egyptians were among the first civilizations to attempt to reflect political and regal power through elaborate architectural complexes. Many of those that remain are to be found in the New Kingdom tombs of the 18th Dynasty in the Valley of the Kings at Thebes; architecturally sophisticated and ambitious in scale (as at the tomb of Queen Hatshepsut), these probably reflect a more general trend in Egyptian architecture as an expression of imperial power and stature. The hierarchical and highly organized nature of Ancient Egyptian society is apparent in the logistical solutions which had to be reached in order to create such monuments.

1500–1000 BCE

ASIA

c.1500 Period of endemic warfare between Hittites, Egyptians, and Mitanni of N Mesopotamia as they compete for control of Levantine city-states.

Vedic Aryans begin to spread over much of northwest and north of Indian subcontinent.

In India, composition of hymns of *Rig Veda* begins (completed c.900 BCE.)

Evidence of bronze-working in NE Thailand and Vietnam.

c.1400 Anyang succeeds Zhengzhou as the Shang capital.

First written inscriptions appear on Shang oracle bones, which were used in a process of divination in China.

c.1000 ▼ Pastoral nomadism on the Steppes – cattle herded from horseback.

Development of first alphabets in Sinai and Levant.

c.1285 Hittites meet the Egyptians in battle in Kadesh.

1200 Collapse of the Hittite empire.

c.1200 Jewish exodus from Egypt and settlement in Palestine.

Bronze industry established in C Steppes.

Teachings of Zoroaster.

Levantine states collapse due to maritime raids.

Wheeled chariots spread to China from C Asia.

c.1100 Syria and Palestine settled by nomadic tribes.

c.1000 **c.1030** Aryans in India expand down the Ganges valley.

1027 Western Zhou dynasty supplants Shang in China.

c.1020 Saul becomes first king of the Israelites.

c.1006 David succeeds as king of the Israelites.

AFRICA

c.1500 Copper worked in the Saharan region.

1417 Egyptian prosperity, power, and prestige reach their high point under Amenophis III.

1350 Pharaoh Akhenaton introduces sun worship in Egypt.

c.1350 Short-lived Egyptian capital founded in El-Amarna.

c.1285 Battle of Kadesh: Egypt versus the Hittites.

c.1245 Ramses II moves Egyptian capital to new city, Pi-Ramesse.

c.1200 Chariot rock carvings in the Sahara.

1166 Death of Ramses III, Egypt's last great pharaoh.

945 ▼ **1070** End of 20th dynasty and Egyptian New Kingdom.

EUROPE

c.1450 Mycenaen Greece at height of power and prosperity, linked by trading networks from the Levant to Sicily.

Destruction of Minoan palaces of Crete. Mycenaeans take control of island.

c.1250 Defenses strengthened at several Mycenaean palaces, suggesting troubled conditions.

c.1200 New Urnfield culture emerges in Danube area. Named after tradition of placing cremated ashes in urns in large communal burial fields.

c.1150 Collapse of Mycenaean Greece.

c.1100 Mycenaean palaces and towns sacked or abandoned.

 c.1000
Expansion of the Phoenicians in the Mediterranean (–700).

Earliest fortified hilltop sites in W Europe.

AMERICAS & AUSTRALASIA

c.1500 Evidence of first metalworking in Peru.

 c.1000
Lapita colonists start to colonize the Pacific Ocean, reaching Tonga and Samoa by c.1000 BCE.

Earliest evidence of colonization of Fiji – by makers of incised Lapita pottery.

First pottery in C America.

c.1300 Cerro Sechin is earliest C Andean site.

 c.1000
Colonization of Tonga.

c.850 **c.1200** Chavín civilization emerges in the Andes.

Olmec civilization emerges.

c.1100 Establishment of Poverty Point in present-day Louisiana, an early nonagrarian settlement.

The Olmec c.1200–800 BCE

The first great pre-Columbian culture of Mesoamerica emerged in the coastal lowlands southwest of Yucatán around 1200. The Olmec people founded a number of ceremonial centers, notably in San Lorenzo and La Venta and also developed a wide trading network in commodities such as obsidian, jade, and basalt. Their cultural influence spread northwestward to the Valley of Mexico and southeastward to parts of Central America; later Mesoamerican native religions and iconography can be traced back to Olmec beginnings.

In San Lorenzo, the Olmec sculpted remarkable stone monuments, including colossal stone heads with characteristic flat faces, thickened lips, and helmetlike headgear. This head (*above*) which stands over 13 feet (2 m) tall and weighs many tons, was sculpted in basalt obtained from the Tuxtla mountains and transported overland and by raft to San Lorenzo.

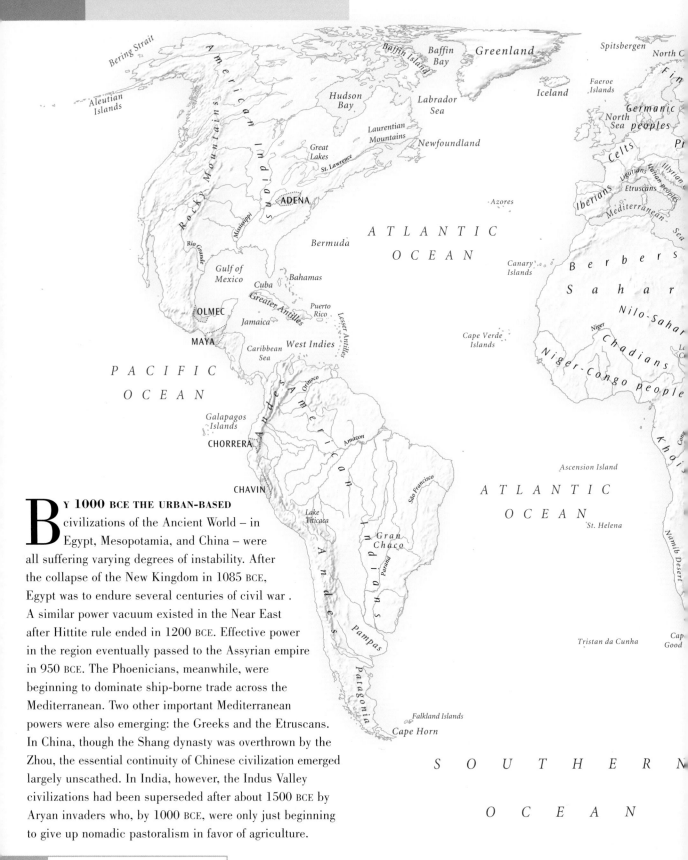

Bering Strait

American Mountains

Aleutian Islands

Rocky Mountains

Adena

Indians

Baffin Island
Baffin Bay
Greenland

Spitsbergen
North C

Faeroe Islands
Iceland

Fin

Germanic
North Sea peoples

Celts
Pr

Hudson Bay

Labrador Sea

Newfoundland

Laurentian Mountains

Great Lakes
St. Lawrence

Azores

Iberians
Liguirians
Etruscans
Illyrian
Hellenic peoples
Mediterranean Sea

Mississippi

Rio Grande

Gulf of Mexico

Bermuda

Bahamas
Cuba
Greater Antilles
Puerto Rico
Jamaica

OLMEC
MAYA

Caribbean Sea
West Indies
Lesser Antilles

Canary Islands

Berbers

Sahar

Nilo-Sahar

Niger

Chadians

Le C

Cape Verde Islands

Niger-Congo people

ATLANTIC OCEAN

PACIFIC OCEAN

Galapagos Islands

CHORRERA

Andes Mountains
South America

Orinoco

Amazon

Khai

Congo

Ascension Island

ATLANTIC OCEAN

St. Helena

Namib Desert

CHAVIN

Lake Titicaca

São Francisco

Gran Chaco

Paraná

Andes

Pampas

Patagonia

Falkland Islands
Cape Horn

Tristan da Cunha

Cap Good

SOUTHERN

OCEAN

BY 1000 BCE THE URBAN-BASED
civilizations of the Ancient World – in
Egypt, Mesopotamia, and China – were
all suffering varying degrees of instability. After
the collapse of the New Kingdom in 1085 BCE,
Egypt was to endure several centuries of civil war .
A similar power vacuum existed in the Near East
after Hittite rule ended in 1200 BCE. Effective power
in the region eventually passed to the Assyrian empire
in 950 BCE. The Phoenicians, meanwhile, were
beginning to dominate ship-borne trade across the
Mediterranean. Two other important Mediterranean
powers were also emerging: the Greeks and the Etruscans.
In China, though the Shang dynasty was overthrown by the
Zhou, the essential continuity of Chinese civilization emerged
largely unscathed. In India, however, the Indus Valley
civilizations had been superseded after about 1500 BCE by
Aryan invaders who, by 1000 BCE, were only just beginning
to give up nomadic pastoralism in favor of agriculture.

EGYPTIAN VIEW OF THE HEAVENS

The ceilings of royal tombs and temples, such as this one in the Osireion of Seti I at Abydos, were often decorated with a depiction of the heavens. During the Old Kingdom, the belief was established that the sky goddess, Nut, spread her star-studded body over the Earth, and that humans could be reborn as stars. Astronomers used a kind of astrolabe to take sightings of the Orion and Great Bear constellations in order to orientate temples with great accuracy. By the Middle Kingdom, they had developed calendars consisting of 36 columns listing 36 groups of stars ("decans"), each of which rose above the horizon at dawn for ten days of the year, although this calendar slipped by 10 days every 40 years. Many New Kingdom tombs were painted with star grids allowing the measurement of specified stars' transits through the sky.

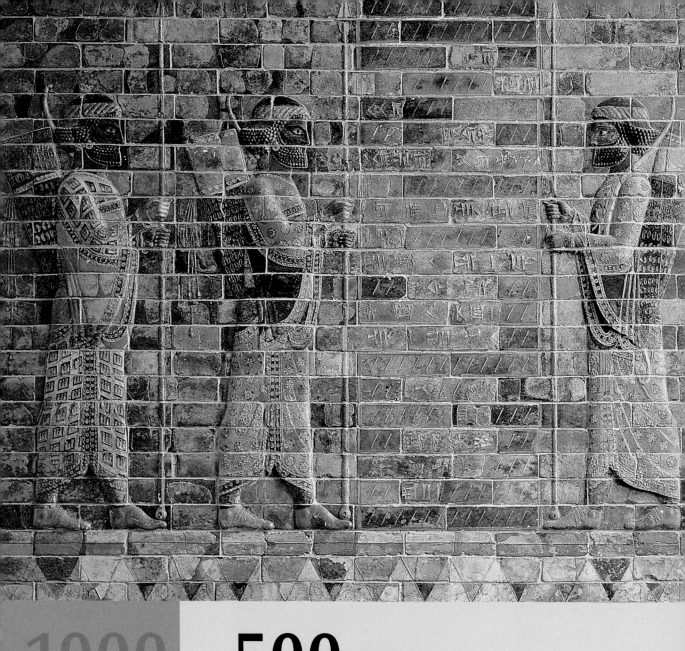

1000–500 BCE
Early Civilizations

c.1000: Colonists from mainland Greece settle W Asia Minor and E Aegean islands

c.1000: King David unites Israel and Judaea, with capital at Jerusalem.

c.1000: Aryans in India begin shift from pastoral to agricultural lifestyle

c.950: Foundation of the Assyrian empire

	1000	975	950	925	90
ASIA					
AFRICA					
EUROPE					
REST OF THE WORLD					

945: Civil war in Egypt leads to division into small states

c.1000: Lapita colonists reach Samoa and Tonga
c.1000: Adena culture develops in E North America

As cities reached an unprecedented size and trade and manufacture flourished, the age of Empire began. From 1000 BCE, iron was in general use throughout Eurasia; it was used to make more effective agricultural implements, which increased yields, leading to ever-expanding populations. It was also used in the manufacture of a range of weaponry, reflecting the militarism of early civilizations. However, the empires of the Old World came under increasing threat from fast-moving mounted tribes of pastoralists, such as the Scythians, who were sweeping across Central Asia, southern Russia, and Siberia. During the first millennium BCE, the three most important centers of civilization – the Near East, Egypt, and China – all underwent periods of instability and destructive wars were fought to gain control of their rich resources.

Empires of the New World

The early civilizations of the Americas were more isolated than those of the Old World, and lacked many of the technologies that had spread rapidly between the empires of Eurasia and North Africa. The city-states and empires of Central and South America had no iron metallurgy – agricultural implements and weapons were made of stone, wood, and bone. Nor did they ever develop the wheel, although in Mexico wheeled ceramic toys were made for the amusement of children. In any case they had no horses, donkeys, or oxen to pull wheeled vehicles. The only beasts of burden that could be domesticated were the llamas of the Andes. Similarly, the Americas had no large

herbivores, such as Eurasia's sheep, goats, pigs, and cattle that could be domesticated and raised for food. Apart from llamas, the only other animals domesticated by the Andean civilizations of South America were guinea pigs and dogs. In North and Central America the only animals successfully domesticated were dogs and turkeys.

The Americas also lacked wild grasses with large seeds such as rice, or the wheat and barley cultivated by the farmers of the Fertile Crescent. The one cereal that became a high-yielding crop capable of supporting large populations was corn, the staple of Central America. It also grew in the Andes region, where potatoes provided a second dependable crop.

Despite these disadvantages, a series of civilizations emerged, remarkable for their social organization and artistic achievements. The first of these was the Olmec civilization of Mexico, which began to emerge in c.1200 BCE. It established a system of religious beliefs and values that were adopted by many subsequent civilizations of Central America. The Olmec homeland lay in the marshy lowlands of Veracruz and Tabasco. The Olmecs were famous for their monumental stone sculptures, which depicted fearsome supernatural beings, eagles, snakes, and sharks. At their city of La Venta, they constructed a 111-foot- (34-m-) high pyramid, and a series of plazas laid out in the shape of a jaguar mask – felines occupied an important place in New World iconography.

In Peru, Chavín culture, the earliest Andean civilization, emerged c.1200 BCE. The site of Chavín de Huantar, with its temple complexes, stone platforms, and monumental

Carved ceremonial adze from the Olmec center of La Venta. It is made of jade, which was much prized by the Olmecs.

PICTURE ABOVE:
Polychrome glazed brick frieze depicting archers of the royal bodyguard from the palace of the Achaemenid king Darius at Susa (522–486 BCE). The sumptuous palace was built by craftsmen from Egypt, Babylon, Greece, and Asia Minor.

900: Kingdom of Urartu established in Armenia. Resists Assyrian expansion

c.900: Foundation of Nubian kingdom of Cush

c.850: Earliest villages on Rome's Palatine Hill

814: Foundation of Phoenician colony of Carthage

c.800: Rise of Etruscan city-states in C Italy

c.800: First phase of Celtic Iron Age

771: Zhou period ends with collapse of centralized power

900   875   850   825   800   775   750

900: End of dark ages in Greece

c.900: Olmec city of San Lorenzo is destroyed. Its leading role is taken over by La Venta
c.900: Chorrera-style pottery vessels are found widely distributed in N South America

c.850: Chavín cult, based on the worship of part-human, part-animal supernatural beings, reaches its height in Peru

776: First pan-Hellenic athletics festival held at Sanctuary of Zeus, Olympia

The Assyrian and Babylonian empires 950–539 BCE

- Assyrian empire (934–912)
- Assyrian empire at maximum extent, 663
- New Babylonian empire (625–539)
- ✕ Assyrian victory
- ✕ Babylonian victory
- -- present-day coastline/river
- ◇ royal capital

statues, peaked between 850 and 200 BCE. The religious cult of Chavín spread its influence peacefully throughout Peru. Chavín designs typically combine humans and animals such as jaguars, snakes, and eagles, and feature snarling mouths, curved fangs, and serpentine hair.

In North America, however, there were no large, organized, stratified societies like the Olmec or the Chavín. Agriculture on a scale that would create sufficient food surpluses was not possible with the plants and animals available. Hunter-gathering remained the normal way of life, although in the eastern United States horticulture – sunflowers, squashes, and a range of vegetables – made a valuable contribution to the diet. The Adena culture of the Ohio valley, which flourished from c.700 BCE, was the most striking example of a more settled, horticultural society. Its people cooperated to construct large burial mounds and earthworks.

Empires of the Near East

The Assyrians were based in the northern valley of the Tigris river. During the 9th century BCE, Assyrian armies began a relentless advance against the patchwork of warring states that occupied the Middle East, conquering Syria, Phoenicia, Israel, and Judaea. Even once-mighty Egypt fell under Assyrian attack. These nations, once subjugated, were forced to pay tribute; failure to do so was met with the utmost ruthlessness. The Assyrians' military supremacy was reinforced by a number of innovations, which included the use of mail armor, armored charioteers, and the effective

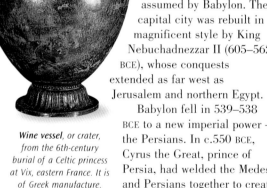

Wine vessel, or crater, from the 6th-century burial of a Celtic princess at Vix, eastern France. It is of Greek manufacture.

implementation of siege warfare. But, at the end of the 7th century, Assyria's enemies joined forces to overthrow the empire, sacking and destroying the Assyrian cities of Nineveh and Nimrud in 612 BCE. For a time Assyria's position as the dominant state of Mesopotamia was assumed by Babylon. The capital city was rebuilt in magnificent style by King Nebuchadnezzar II (605–562 BCE), whose conquests extended as far west as Jerusalem and northern Egypt.

Babylon fell in 539–538 BCE to a new imperial power – the Persians. In c.550 BCE, Cyrus the Great, prince of Persia, had welded the Medes and Persians together to create

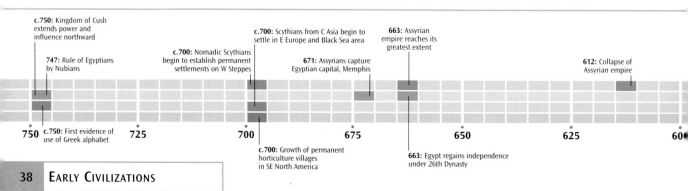

c.750: Kingdom of Cush extends power and influence northward

747: Rule of Egyptians by Nubians

c.700: Nomadic Scythians begin to establish permanent settlements on W Steppes

c.700: Scythians from C Asia begin to settle in E Europe and Black Sea area

671: Assyrians capture Egyptian capital, Memphis

663: Assyrian empire reaches its greatest extent

612: Collapse of Assyrian empire

c.750: First evidence of use of Greek alphabet

c.700: Growth of permanent horticulture villages in SE North America

663: Egypt regains independence under 26th Dynasty

750 | 725 | 700 | 675 | 650 | 625 | 600

the Achaemenid empire. This was the largest empire the world had yet seen, stretching from the Nile to the Indus, and centered on a series of imposing palace complexes at Persepolis, Pasargadae, and Susa. Persia was remarkable for its stable currency, administrative control through regional governors (satraps), fair taxes, and tolerance of other forms of religion.

Iron Age Europe

In the rugged, mountainous terrain of Greece, isolated communities began to form city-states. Bereft of land and resources, each city-state, or polis, sent out colonists to found Greek settlements along the shores of the Mediterranean, from Spain to the Black Sea. Many of the cities of central Greece began as small settlements huddled beneath a naturally defensible hilly outcrop, or acropolis. As prosperity increased, fine buildings – an expression of civic pride – were erected. The cities, with their temples, amphitheaters, and agoras (markets), reflected the central concerns of Greek life: government, religion, physical fitness, trade, theater. Each polis minted its own coins, proclaiming the unique identity of the city.

In Italy, the indigenous peoples of Tuscany, the Etruscans, founded a series of cities from c.800 BCE, such as Cerveteri and Tarquinii. Central Italy was rich in copper and tin deposits, and the Etruscans traded as far afield as North Africa, the Danube, and the Rhine. They were famous for their skill in metalwork, their paintings, and their pottery. Further north, iron metallurgy had spread throughout Europe, and by the 8th century BCE, rich Celtic burials from Hallstatt in Austria begin to indicate the emergence of a new warrior aristocracy. By the 6th century BCE, Europe north and west of the Alps was coming into contact with the Greek colonies of the western Mediterranean

along the coast of Spain and southern France, and the Rhône-Saône corridor had become a major trading route.

Early Asian Civilizations

In China, the Western Zhou period perpetuated the Shang legacy, but in 770 BCE the capital moved to Luoyang, marking the beginning of the Eastern Zhou era. This was a time of endemic warfare, as many small states struggled for supremacy. But it was also a period of innovation; the development of iron metallurgy greatly increased the productivity of the land. As a result, towns and cities proliferated. Armies and bureaucracies expanded, undermining the traditional domination of the landed aristocracy, and offering unprecedented opportunities to commoners.

In India, the Ganges plain was settled between 1000 and 600 BCE by Aryans,

nomadic warriors and pastoralists from the northwest, who gradually adopted a sedentary life. By 600 BCE, 16 small states had developed across northern India, ranging from tribal republics to absolute monarchies. Whatever their political differences, they shared the Hindu pantheon of gods and all were subject to the authority of the Brahman priesthood and the caste system.

Against this background the Buddha was born in c.563 BCE. A wealthy prince, he resolved to become an ascetic at the age of 29. He sought spiritual enlightenment through good conduct, acquired many disciples, and founded a religious order. The sixth century BCE saw the emergence of another important Indian religion, Jainism. Both Buddhism and Jainism were reactions against the rigid hierarchical structure of the Hindu religion as practised by the Brahmans and rapidly gained new adherents.

THE BABYLONIAN LEGACY

Precise knowledge of the movement of the sun, moon, and stars dates back to Babylonian times – the earliest recorded astronomical observations are found on Babylonian tablets dated to c.2000 BCE. The Babylonians were able to predict solar and lunar eclipses, plot the path of the sun, and measure the length of the year. They could also predict the path of Venus, Mercury, Mars, Jupiter, and Saturn through the night sky.

This bronze model of the solar system is from Lake Sevan in Armenia. It dates back to the 10th–9th century BCE.

The Babylonians were keen astrologers as well as astronomers, and, following earlier traditions, mapped the constellations that lay in the path of the sun (the zodiac), dividing it into twelve equal parts, or signs. They created a calendar that was based on twelve lunar months; an extra, 13th month, was added to ensure that the calendar kept in step with the seasons. The Babylonians were also innovative mathematicians. They devised a system of counting with a base of 60; numbers up to 60 were represented by two different marks symbolizing tens and units. This sexagesimal system is still evident in our divisions of hours and minutes.

A Babylonian mathematical text, with cuneiform numbers, dating to 500 BCE.

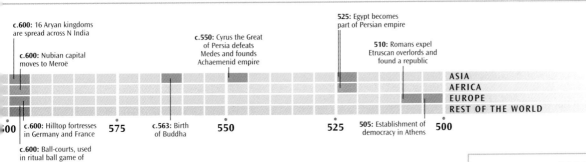

c.600: 16 Aryan kingdoms are spread across N India

c.600: Nubian capital moves to Meroë

c.550: Cyrus the Great of Persia defeats Medes and founds Achaemenid empire

525: Egypt becomes part of Persian empire

510: Romans expel Etruscan overlords and found a republic

ASIA
AFRICA
EUROPE
REST OF THE WORLD

00

c.600: Hilltop fortresses in Germany and France

575

c.563: Birth of Buddha

550

525

505: Establishment of democracy in Athens

500

c.600: Ball-courts, used in ritual ball game of C American civilizations, found in Olmec centers

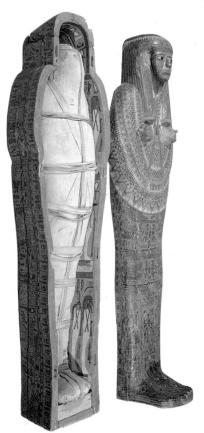

Mummy cases were made of narrow, pegged planks, plastered and painted to give a smooth finish. The exterior of this case is emblazoned with colorful hieroglyphs of spells designed to protect the deceased on the journey to the afterlife.

Mummification in Egypt

The ancient Egyptians regarded life after death quite literally, ensuring the deceased had food, everyday items, and luxury goods at their burial. Central to this tradition was the preservation of the mortal body after death. The Egyptians developed a sophisticated system of mummification for the wealthy and powerful which, aided by an exceptionally arid climate, provides archaeologists with many valuable insights into daily life in ancient Egypt.

One of the earliest surviving mummies is that of the noble Ranefer (c.2500) from Maidum in Lower Egypt; his internal organs were wrapped in linen and placed in a recess. The body cavity was packed with linen soaked in resin, and the entire body wrapped in resin-soaked bandages, with molded and painted bandages over the face. The practice developed with elaborately decorated coffins, and continued through the Ptolemaic period (304–30 BCE) but declined during Roman imperial rule (30BCE–395 CE).

ASIA

c.1000 Chinese bronze casting reaches level of craftsmanship unrivaled elsewhere at this period.

King David unites Israel and Judaea, with its capital city at Jerusalem.

Phoenicians become the major maritime power in the Levant region. They develop an alphabetic script (the basis of all modern European scripts).

Nomadic economy established on the steppes based on rearing horses, sheep, and cattle.

c.800 ▼ Aryans begin shift from pastoral to agricultural lifestyle and establish a number of small states in India.

Iron technology starts to diffuse over much of India.

Western Zhou sponsor exploration and recording of China's geography.

Wet rice cultivation introduced to Korea from China.

Bronze technology reaches Korea from N China.

c.965 Accession of Solomon as king of Israel.

951 Megiddo becomes important royal fortress and administrative center in Israel.

c.950 Foundation of the Assyrian empire.

c.926 Death of Solomon; nation divides into Israel and Judah.

900 Establishment of kingdom of Urartu in Armenia; resists Assyrian expansion and lasts until its destruction by Assyrians in 714.

c.900 Composition of later Vedas, Brahmanas, and Upanishads begins in India.

744 ▼ **880** Nimrud becomes capital of Assyria.

AFRICA

945 Civil war in Egypt. By mid-8th century, Egypt is divided into several small states.

c.750 ▼ **c.900** Foundation of Nubian kingdom of Cush.

c.1000 Colonists begin to migrate from Greece to Asia Minor and E Aegean.

Ironworking reaches C Europe from the Near East.

Phoenicians take alphabet to Malta, Sardinia, and Spain (–700).

c.800 Etruscans arrive in Italy.

c.800 900 End of Dark Ages in Greece.

c.900 Phoenicians sail westward in search of metals and found colonies near rich metal deposits.

c.1000 Adena culture develops in middle Ohio river valley in eastern N America.

Development of large-scale societies in S Andes.

Long-distance trade in Australia of raw materials and ornaments.

Lapita settlers well-established on Tonga and Samoa.

Distinct Polynesian culture starts to emerge in Fiji, Tonga, and Samoa.

c.900 San Lorenzo in C America is destroyed. Its leading role is taken over by La Venta.

Chorrera-style pottery vessels are found widely distributed in northern S America.

Judaism

Although there is little archaeological evidence to support the Hebraic texts of the Old Testament, it is clear that a a group of Semitic tribes united to form a kingdom in Palestine, known as Judaea, around 1000 BCE under David (reigned c.1006–965 BCE). David defeated the "Philistines" and moved the capital from Hebron to Jerusalem (Zion, the "City of David") where he brought the Ark of the Covenant, said to contain the Ten Commandments.

The kingdom prospered under his second son Solomon (reigned 965–926 BCE) achieving its widest limit, and a period of great temple and palace construction. After Solomon's death the kingdom divided into Israel and Judaea and went into decline, dwarfed by its neighbors in Egypt and Assyria.

The Jewish candelabra (menorah) *symbolizes the eternal light (ner tamid) which burned in the first Temple of Soloman.*

The Shang: masters of bronze

The Shang dynasty was feudal and martial in structure and espoused ancestor worship. Remains of their cities and graves contain many fine examples of sophisticated bronze casting, including exquisite vessels, created primarily for ritual sacrifices to the ancestors and associated ceremonies, and oracle bones inscribed with the first Chinese writing.

Shang vessels were often decorated wtih the sylized heads of animals.

1000–850 BCE 41

The Assyrian empire

By 950 BCE Assyria had reemerged as the dominant power in Mesopotamia, based around Nimrud (from 880) and (from 705) Nineveh. Rapid expansion was achieved under Shalmaneser III (858–824), but preeminence was only achieved with the conquest of Urartu (714) during the reign of Sargon II and Babylon (689) under Sennacherib.

The Assyrian empire reached its greatest extent after the conquest of Egypt (669), reaching from the Nile valley to Oman under Ashurbanipal (668–626). Assyrian kings plowed the proceeds of their military conquests into the building of vast temples and palaces at Nimrud and Nineveh. Booty acquired during the campaigns, like this ivory sphinx (*above*) enriched many palace furnishings. Assyria was defeated by a coalition of Babylonian and Medean forces at Carchemish in 612.

Chavín culture

The Andean city of Chavín de Huantar became politically and culturally dominant in Peru between c.850 and 200 BCE. The Chavín are distinguished by the sophistication of their architecture and monumental sculpture, and by technological achievements such as canal building, although their mastery of textiles, pottery, and goldwork form their greatest legacy.

The Chavín shared a love of animal imagery with many other culture in Central and South America.

ASIA

c.840 Rise of Urartu.

817 Traditional date of birth of early Jain teacher, Parshvanatha.

c.800 Rise of urban culture in Ganges valley.

Aryans expand to the south in India.

771 Decline of Zhou central administration in China.

Eastern Zhou establish new capital at Luoyang; beginning of "Spring and Autumn" period.

Western Zhou period in China ends with collapse of centralized power.

c.750 Amos, first great prophet in Israel.

744 Accession of Tiglath-Pileser III of Assyria.

722 Accession of Sargon II; Israel conquered by Assyrians, becomes an Assyrian province (–21).

c.650 "Annals" period (–481); China in loose confederation under nominal control of Eastern Zhou.

710 Khorsabad replaces Nimrud as capital of Assyria.

612 **705** Capital of Assyria moves to Nineveh.

701 Assyrians invade Judah.

AFRICA

814 Foundation of Phoenician colony of Carthage.

c.670 **c.800** First ironworking in sub-Saharan Africa.

c.750 Kingdom of Cush extends power and influence northward.

663 **747** Rule of Egypt by Nubians.

c.850 Earliest village on Rome's Palatine Hill.

c.850 Chavín cult, based on the worship of part-human, part-animal supernatural beings, reaches its height in Peru.

Florescence of Chavín de Huantar; Chavín style widely disseminated.

c.800 First phase of Celtic Iron Age named after cemetery at Hallstatt in Austria.

c.700 ▽

Emergence of Etruscan city-states in C Italy.

Greeks adopt Phoenician alphabet.

c.800 Evidence that Maya beginning to spread northward into Yucatan peninsula.

Evidence of writing in the Americas (Zapotec).

Corn cultivated on Amazon floodplain.

776 First pan-Hellenic athletics festival held at the Sanctuary of Zeus, Olympia.

616 ▽ **753** Traditional date for founding of Rome by Romulus.

750 First evidence of use of Greek alphabet.

c.750 Homer's *Iliad* and Hesiod's poetry first written down.

733 Corinth founds the colony of Syracuse; start of Greek colonization of Mediterranean.

Greek art

In addition to architecture and sculpture, the Ancient Greeks were particularly talented ceramacists, inventive in both form and decoration. The abundance and resilience of their pottery means that this medium remains one of the most important sources for historians and archaeologists. Painted Greek pottery dating from as early as the mid-8th century BCE, such as the funerary Dipylon vase (*above*) show enormous sophistication, and the beginnings of the figurative narrative tradition that was later to dominate Greek ceramic decoration.

850–700 BCE

The Etruscans

Etruscan civilization flourished in the fortified hilltop towns of Tuscany between 800 and 300 BCE. Its wealth was based on agriculture and rich deposits of copper and iron. Much
of our knowledge of the Etruscans is derived from tomb paintings (*above*) which depict evocative scenes of feasting, hunting, dancing, and wrestling, while their gravegoods are a testament to their skills in bronze-working and sculpture. Etruscan imagery greatly influenced later Roman pastoral art and

Early Rome

Founded in the 8th century BCE, Rome was by the 7th century a small town under Etruscan domination; the principal remains are cemeteries and funerary "hut urns" (*below*) which give an insight into the style of architecture that must have characterized the community. These artifacts remain unique to Rome, and mark the beginning of Rome's emergence from Etruscan culture.

ASIA

c.700 Nomadic Scythians begin to establish permanent settlements on western steppes.

689 Babylon destroyed by Assyrian king, Sennacherib.

669 Assyrian king, Esarhaddon, conquers N Egypt.

c.663 Assyrian empire reaches greatest extent with sack of Thebes in Egypt.

c.660 Jimmu, legendary first emperor in Japan.

650 First coins in Lydia in Asia Minor.

c.650 Introduction of iron technology to China. Silk painting, lacquerwork, and ceramics become highly skilled.

612 Nineveh and Nimrud are sacked by Babylonians and Medes; end of Assyrian empire.

597

605 Nebuchadnezzar II succeeds to throne of Babylon.

Birth of Lao-tzu, traditional founder of Taoism (–520).

604 Nebuchadnezzar II rebuilds Babylon.

AFRICA

671 Assyrian king, Esarhaddon, captures Egyptian capital, Memphis.

c.600

c.670 Introduction of ironworking in Egypt.

525

663 Egypt regains independence under 26th dynasty, which rules from Sais in the Nile delta until 525.

c.700 Scythians from C Asia begin to settle in E Europe and Black Sea area.

Beginning of Archaic Period in Greece; rise of city-states.

First peristyle Greek temples.

c.530 Start of Etruscan expansion to the south of Italy.

c.690 Etruscan script developed from Greek.

c.700 Start of Adena culture in the upper Ohio valley.

Growth of permanent horticulture villages in southeastern N America.

This Roman bronze copy of Discobolus by *Myron of Elerutherae (mid-5th century BCE), possibly designed for a frieze, reflects the Greek admiration of human physical beauty and dynamism.*

The Olympic Games

One of the most vital legacies of Ancient Greece, the games in honor of the supreme God Zeus were traditionally initiated in 776 BCE and continued every four years until they were abolished by the Roman emperor Theodosius I at the end of the 4th century CE, due largely to increasing professional competitiveness. The Games were revived in 896 CE in an attempt to encourage international cooperation.

Adena culture

Settlements in the upper Ohio valley centered on burial mounds and extensive earthworks, dating from c.700 BCE, provide evidence of one of the earliest cultural groupings of North America. Our knowledge of the Adena is, however, largely based on their gravegoods, including jewelry, often made from traded copper, carved tablets, decorated human skulls (*left*), and tubular pipes – evidence of the early use of tobacco.

c.650 Rise of "tyrants" in many Greek cities.

510
616 Traditional date for accession of Tarquin I, Etruscan king of Rome.

700–600 BCE

The first Chinese coins, introduced c.500 BCE, were miniature bronze hoes or spades (below), copies of the tools that had previously been used for barter.

The first coins

As trading networks expanded barter, depending on face-to-face negotiation, became increasingly inconvenient. The need to establish an acceptable system equivalent to fiscal values led to the invention of coinage, metal bullion of a certain value stamped and guaranteed by local authorities.

The first coins for commercial exchange were minted in China in the 6th century BCE, and usually took the form of tools such as axes and blades. Independently, the first European coins were developed by the Lydians of Western Anatolia in the 7th century BCE, but widespread usage for trade did not develop until the 5th century BCE. The emergence of currency is often linked with the development of accurate measuring and weighing systems, and of exact calendrical records.

Early Greek coins carried stamped designs, many derived from the animal world. minim veniam, quis nostrud minim veniam, quis nostrud exerci tation minim veniam, quis nostrud exerci tat.

ASIA

c.600 Sixteen Aryan kingdoms are spread across N India.

Use of elephants in India in warfare.

Rise to dominance of Magadha which emerges as preeminent state in India.

Emergence of Hinduism in late sixth to early fifth century.

Ujjayini and Kausambi develop as earliest post-Harappan cities in India.

597 Nebuchadnezzar captures Jerusalem.

587 Jerusalem and Temple destroyed by Nebuchadnezzar; Jews exiled to Babylon.

c.483

c.563 Birth of Buddha, who forsakes life of a nobleman to seek enlightenment through asceticism and good conduct.

550 Rise of states around Red Sea and Gulf of Aden; frankincense and myrrh exported from S Arabia to E Mediterranean.

551 Zoroastrianism becomes official religion of Persia.

Birth of Confucius (−479), author of the *Analects*, which provides central philosophy for Chinese way of life.

c.550 Cyrus the Great of Persia defeats Medes and founds Achaemenid empire.

Manufacture of cast iron in China.

c.540 Deutero-Isaiah, Hebrew prophet, active during exile in Babylon.

Birth of Mahavira, founder of Jain religion (−468).

539 Cyrus the Great takes Babylon, and Babylonian empire, without bloodshed.

538 Jews return from exile.

525 Cambyses II of Persia conquers Egypt and advances to Nubia and Libya.

486

521 Persian empire reaches greatest extent under Darius the Great.

c.520 Darius I of Persia completes canal connecting Nile with the Red Sea.

AFRICA

c.600 Nubian capital moves to Meroë.

c.500 First known ironworking in Nok region.

525 Egypt becomes part of Persian empire.

600 Foundation of Greek colony of Massalia. Trade between Greeks and Celts.

Rome becomes an urban center.

c.600 Defensive hilltop fortresses built throughout S Germany and E France.

Central lowlands of N Europe settled.

First Greek coins.

c.600 Olmec jade artifacts, often used as offerings in ritual "cache" deposits, traded as far afield as southern C America.

Ball courts, used in ritual ball game of C American civilizations, found in Olmec centers.

Beginnings of Paracas culture in S Peru, famed for brightly colored textiles woven with Chavín-style images.

c.480

586 Beginnings of Greek rationalist philosophy.

c.530 Etruscan influence at its height; extends as far south as Neapolis (Naples).

Pythagoras, Greek mathematician and mystic, active.

510 Romans expel Etruscan overlords and establish a republic.

Temple of Jupiter Optimus Maximus, Rome.

505 Establishment of democracy in Athens.

The wealth and power of the Achaemenid empire was reflected in the reliefs of tribute peoples on the walls of the palace at Persepolis, the royal residence.

The Achaemenid empire

The unification under Cyrus the Great of the Medes and the Persians created the Achaemenid Persian empire, which grew into the largest state the world had yet seen. Eastern Anatolia and Babylon were rapidly conquered and, under two of Cyrus's greatest successors, Darius I the Great and Xerxes I, the empire was extended further and organized into 20 provinces, or satrapies. Taxes were levied and ambitious building programs undertaken, including the construction of a 1,500-mile (2,400-km) Royal Road from Susa in modern Iran to Ephesus in Turkey.

However, both rulers failed to conquer Greece and, weakened from without by raiding and from within by ambitious satraps, the empire was finally conquered by the Macedonian general Alexander the Great, following his decisive victory on the Issus in 333 BCE.

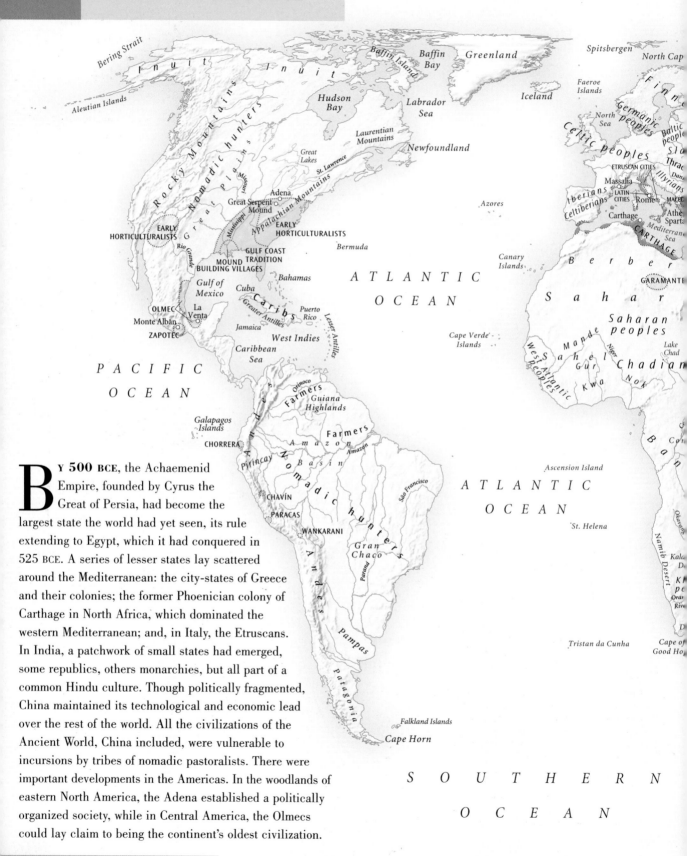

BY **500** BCE, the Achaemenid Empire, founded by Cyrus the Great of Persia, had become the largest state the world had yet seen, its rule extending to Egypt, which it had conquered in 525 BCE. A series of lesser states lay scattered around the Mediterranean: the city-states of Greece and their colonies; the former Phoenician colony of Carthage in North Africa, which dominated the western Mediterranean; and, in Italy, the Etruscans. In India, a patchwork of small states had emerged, some republics, others monarchies, but all part of a common Hindu culture. Though politically fragmented, China maintained its technological and economic lead over the rest of the world. All the civilizations of the Ancient World, China included, were vulnerable to incursions by tribes of nomadic pastoralists. There were important developments in the Americas. In the woodlands of eastern North America, the Adena established a politically organized society, while in Central America, the Olmecs could lay claim to being the continent's oldest civilization.

	Persian Empire
	Carthage
	Greek city-states
	Macedon
	Assyrian Empire under Assurbanipal c.660 BCE
	Lydia c.600 BCE

vaya Zemlya

ents

Kara Sea

Yenisey

P a l a e o s i b e r i a n s

Lena

Bering Strait

Sea of Okhotsk

Kamchatka

Kurile Islands

S a m o y e d s

Ural Mts

Ob'

Volga

T u r k s

T u n g u s

brians

Irtysh

Altai Mountains

Lake Baikal

Amur

M o n g o l s

Hokkaido

S c y t h i a n s

Don

Caspian Sea

Aral Sea

Lake Balkhash

Tien Shan

T o c h a r i

G o b i

Yellow River

Sea of Japan

Ainu

Honshu

Japanese

J a p a n

ack Sea

ERSIAN

dis

Ephesus

etus

amascus

Nineveh

Nimrud

Ecbatana

Bactra

GANDHARA

Takla Makan

Plateau of Tibet

T i b e t a n s

Taxila

Himalayas

Zhengzhou

Wu

ZHOU CHINA

Kyushu

East China Sea

E M P I R E

is

Jerusalem

Babylon

Tigris

Susa

Persepolis

INDIAN STATES

Indus

Ganges

KOSALA

Kapilavastu VAJJI CONFEDERATION

Yangtze

S i n i t i c p e o p l e s

YUE

P A C I F I C O C E A N

emphis

Thebes

Nile

Red Sea

The Gulf

Thar Desert

VATSA *Pataliputra*

AVANTI

MAGADHA

Taiwan

S e m i t e s

Arabian Peninsula

Arabian Sea

INDIAN STATES

Bay of Bengal

M o n - K h m e r p e o p l e s

Mekong

C h a m s

South China Sea

Luzon

M i c r o n e s i a

CUSH

Meroe

Naga

SABA

DAAMAT

Gulf of Aden

Socotra

D r a v i d i a n s

Andaman Islands

Philippine Islands

Mindanao

M e l a n e s i a

Fur

C u s h i t e s

N i l o t i c p e o p l e s

sin

Lake Victoria

Maldive Islands

Nicobar Islands

M a l a y s

Sumatra

Borneo

Celebes

Moluccas

Bismarck Archipelago

P a p u a n s

M e l a n e s i a n s

Solomon Islands

Lake Tanganyika

Seychelles

Comoros

Lake Nyasa

Zambezi

Madagascar

Mauritius

Réunion

I N D I A N O C E A N

Java

Timor

New Guinea

Vanuatu

Fiji

New Caledonia

vango

Great Sandy Desert

Gibson Desert

A u s t r a l i a n A b o r i g i n e s

Simpson Desert

Great Barrier Reef

Great Dividing Range

Great Victoria Desert

Lake Eyre

Darling

Tasman Sea

BABYLONIAN MAP

Though a substantial body of geographical knowledge was assembled in many areas of the Ancient World in the first millennium BCE, almost none has survived today. The earliest known representations of parts of the Earth are from Mesopotamia, such as this Babylonian incised clay tablet, today in the British Museum, London, dating from about 600 BCE. The Earth itself is shown as a disc. The region shown does not extend much beyond Mesopotamia and its two great rivers, the Tigris and Euphrates. At its center is the city of Babylon. The disc is surrounded by water described as the "bitter river," the salt water of the oceans. The Euphrates is depicted by two curved lines, while small circles name cities and adjacent countries, among them Assyria and Armenia, in cuneiform script. Babylon itself is also named.

Tasmania

New Zealand

500 BCE –1 CE
The Early Classical Age

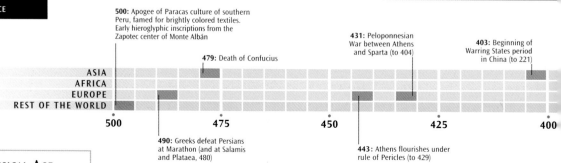

500: Apogee of Paracas culture of southern Peru, famed for brightly colored textiles. Early hieroglyphic inscriptions from the Zapotec center of Monte Albán

479: Death of Confucius

431: Peloponnesian War between Athens and Sparta (to 404)

403: Beginning of Warring States period in China (to 221)

ASIA				
AFRICA				
EUROPE				
REST OF THE WORLD				

| 500 | 475 | 450 | 425 | 400 |

490: Greeks defeat Persians at Marathon (and at Salamis and Plataea, 480)

443: Athens flourishes under rule of Pericles (to 429)

THE WORLD IN 500 BCE consisted of a number of more or less isolated centers of civilization across much of Eurasia, chiefly the city-states of Greece, their neighbor, the immense Achaemenid Persian Empire, and, far to the east, Zhou China, already recognizably "Chinese" in terms of culture, economy, and political organization. At the same time, other, smaller states were beginning to emerge, principally in northern Europe, Africa, the Americas, and India. However, much of the rest of the world's population still consisted of nomadic pastoralists, who ranged over vast areas of eastern Europe, Central Asia, and Siberia.

By 1 CE, the imperial successors of these early Eurasian empires had dramatically increased in size and influence and accounted for more than half the world's population of 250 million. A broad belt of civilized states now extended across Eurasia, from the Atlantic to the Pacific Ocean, linked by a series of increasingly important trade routes, including the Silk Road that allowed the luxuries of China to reach Europe across Central Asia and a number of well-traveled sea routes that crisscrossed the Indian Ocean.

In the west, there was Rome, a hugely powerful empire built on conquest and trade that embraced almost the whole of western Europe as well as much of the ancient Near East and North Africa. To the east there was Han China, centralized, bureaucratic, technologically unchallenged, and increasingly prosperous. Between them, from west to east, stretched the Parthian empire in Persia and, in India, the inheritors of the Mauryan empire that, from 321 BCE onwards, had united India for the first time (see box, p.53).

Han China

The processes that brought about this burst of empire building were never less than varied. China, for example, had undergone a period of rapid technological and cultural advance from as early as the 8th century BCE. The teachings of Confucius (551–479 BCE) had established a model for good government, civic responsibility, and strategies for avoiding social conflict. Nevertheless, conflict remained endemic during what came to be known as the Warring States period (403–221 BCE).

The eventual success of the Qin dynasty in forcibly uniting China in 221 BCE under Shi Huangdi, who took the title "First Emperor," proved short-lived. By 206 BCE the Han dynasty under Gao Zu had taken power. Han China was

PICTURE ABOVE:
The Acropolis in Athens is the best-known symbol of Classical Greek civilization. The main temple, the Parthenon, was dedicated to the city's patron goddess, Athena Parthenos. It was begun on the orders of Pericles in 447 BCE.

The Great Wall of China was created by Shi Huangdi, who linked a number of existing defensive walls. Under the Han the wall played a crucial role in excluding the Xiongnu and other warrior nomads from the empire.

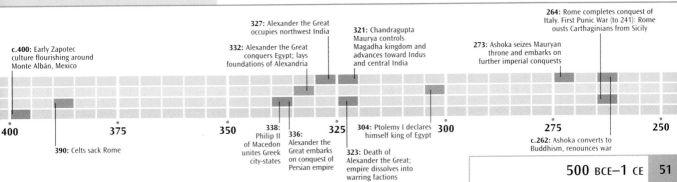

c.400: Early Zapotec culture flourishing around Monte Albán, Mexico

390: Celts sack Rome

332: Alexander the Great conquers Egypt; lays foundations of Alexandria

327: Alexander the Great occupies northwest India

338: Philip II of Macedon unites Greek city-states

336: Alexander the Great embarks on conquest of Persian empire

323: Death of Alexander the Great; empire dissolves into warring factions

321: Chandragupta Maurya controls Magadha kingdom and advances toward Indus and central India

304: Ptolemy I declares himself king of Egypt

273: Ashoka seizes Mauryan throne and embarks on further imperial conquests

c.262: Ashoka converts to Buddhism, renounces war

264: Rome completes conquest of Italy. First Punic War (to 241): Rome ousts Carthaginians from Sicily

400   375   350   325   300   275   250

easily the most powerful and influential cultural, political, and economic force in Asia. It was also, by Chinese standards, exceptionally expansionist. The country's borders were dramatically expanded far into Central Asia, in the process opening up the Silk Road, as well as south into Champa (Vietnam) and east into Korea. A new Great Wall was also built to protect the northern border against the Xiongnu and other steppe nomads. Though the Han bureaucracy was structured on the Confucian principles of discipline and obedience, it was also during this period that Buddhism started to take root in China. By 2 CE, when the first imperial census was undertaken, the population had risen to over 57 million.

The Greek world

The cultural vibrancy of China was echoed in the Greek world. From the 5th century BCE onward, Greece, above all Athens, enjoyed a period of exceptional cultural and political innovation. Its legacy to western civilization – in architecture, literature, science, philosophy, and political thought, above

all in the ideal of democracy – is hard to overstate. Yet whatever these achievements, or those of exporting Greek culture across the Mediterranean through a network of Greek colonies, Greece itself remained politically fragmented. The threat of Persian invasion between 490 and 480 BCE briefly united the Greek city-states, but victory over the Persians was followed by renewed conflict between them. The most powerful state of this period was Athens. Though the city itself had been sacked by the Persians in 480, Athens possessed a powerful navy of galleys and became the dominant force in a confederation of Greek city-states, known as the Delian League. The city was rebuilt and enjoyed a cultural "golden age", under the rule of Pericles (443–429 BCE). But Athenian imperialism bred resentment both among its allies and its rivals, notably the militaristic Spartans. The resulting struggle, the Peloponnesian War (431–404 BCE), was as protracted as it was inconclusive.

The empire of Alexander

Greece was plunged into disarray until, in 338 BCE, Philip II of Macedon united it under his bloodthirsty rule. When Philip

was assassinated in his throne passed to his 20-year-old son Alexander. In a 13-year rule of almost non-stop conquest, Alexander took Greek armies to Egypt, Mesopotamia, the Hindu Kush, and the western borders of India, in the process overthrowing the military superpower of Achaemenid Persia. Alexander's audacity and dazzling military success created a cosmopolitan Greek world across the whole of western Asia whose effects were felt for centuries. But Alexander's empire itself scarcely survived his early death in 323. Feuding among his generals saw it split broadly in three: Ptolemaic Egypt, Antigonid Macedonia, and Seleucid Persia.

The rise of Rome

The real inheritor of Greece was Rome. From obscure beginnings in the 7th century BCE, by 264 Rome had overcome the Etruscan city-states to the north and the Greek colonies to the south to emerge as the most powerful state in Italy. As yet it all Rome's territories were on the Italian mainland. The island of Sicily was controlled by Greek colonies and the North African Phoenician state of Carthage. Rome's decision to intervene in Sicily in 264 brought it into conflict with Carthage, a significant naval power that controlled most of the trade of the western Mediterranean. The First Punic War obliged Rome to build a navy for the first time. Thanks to its effectiveness, Rome eventually acquired control of Sicily in 241.

The Second Punic War (218–202 BCE) was fought on an altogether different scale. The Carthaginian general Hannibal famously crossed the Alps with his elephants and won a succession of spectacular victories. Rome's infant empire and the city of Rome itself were in danger of annihilation. However, by avoiding battle with Hannibal in Italy and carrying the war to Spain and North

Alexander the Great leads his army to victory over the vastly superior forces of Darius, king of Persia, at the battle of Issus (333 BCE), in this detail from a mosaic at Pompeii. Alexander was only 23 years old.

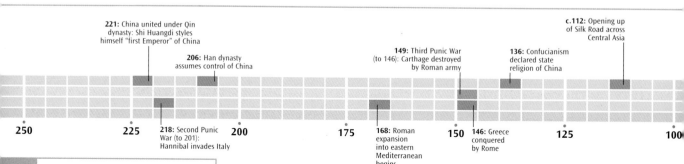

221: China united under Qin dynasty: Shi Huangdi styles himself "first Emperor" of China

206: Han dynasty assumes control of China

149: Third Punic War (to 146): Carthage destroyed by Roman army

136: Confucianism declared state religion of China

c.112: Opening up of Silk Road across Central Asia

250 · 225 · 200 · 175 · 150 · 125 · 100

218: Second Punic War (to 201): Hannibal invades Italy

168: Roman expansion into eastern Mediterranean begins

146: Greece conquered by Rome

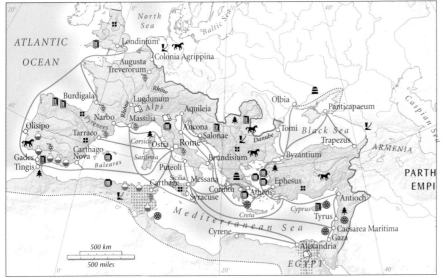

In the course of the first century BCE the Romans imposed their rule on all the lands surrounding the Mediterranean, which they called *Mare Nostrum* (Our Sea). The map shows the major trade routes at the beginning of the 2nd century CE, when the empire had reached its greatest extent. Vast grain shipments from Sicily, Egypt, and North Africa were needed to feed the population of Rome.

Africa instead, the Romans were able to defeat their formidable enemy. The city of Carthage was finally razed to the ground in 146 after an epic 95-year struggle.

Rome, which now controlled the western Mediterranean, then embarked on a further dramatic surge of expansion. Within less than a century, North Africa, most of Iberia, southern Gaul, Macedon, Greece, and Asia Minor had all been added to its empire.

The Roman Empire

Having grown so rapidly, it was perhaps no surprise that Rome's traditional republican system of government struggled to cope with its huge new empire. By the 1st century BCE, a successful Roman general could equip, feed, and pay a large army out of the booty he gained in battle and the tribute and taxes imposed on newly conquered territories, without reference to the consuls and senators in Rome. The rivalry between ambitious generals sparked off a series of civil wars. The victory of Julius Caesar, conqueror of Gaul, over his rival Pompey, victor of campaigns in the Near East and Iberia, led to his being appointed dictator for life.

Caesar's assassination in 44 BCE led to a further civil war between Octavian, great-nephew of Julius Caesar, and Mark Antony, who was supported by the ruler of Ptolemaic Egypt, Cleopatra. For a time the empire was in serious danger of dividing, but in 31 BCE, Octavian won a decisive victory over Antony at Actium and became undisputed master of Rome. The system of government he put in place paid lipservice to old Roman traditions, but power now lay firmly in his own hands. In 27 BCE the senate bestowed on him the title Augustus. Despite occasional wars over the succession, the empire was reunited, and the reforms of Augustus ushered in two centuries of stability and prosperity.

THE MAURYAN EMPIRE

By about 600 BCE, the Ganges plain of northeast India was dominated by 16 distinct political units, which, over the next century, all came under the control of the state of Magadha. By the time of the Nanda dynasty (c.365–321 BCE), the extent of the Magadhan empire was already substantial. The succeeding Mauryan empire (321–181 BCE), however, was the first to achieve pan-Indian status and its political and cultural influence extended well beyond the sub-continent. When the Mauryan leader Ashoka converted to Buddhism in about 262 BCE, he foreswore war. Following the decline of the empire, northwest India suffered a series of invasions by peoples from northeast Asia, propelled into migration by the expansion of Han China.

Ashoka's rule is still remembered as a golden age. The four beautifully carved lions that decorate the top of one of the pillars on which his principles and edicts were inscribed were chosen as the emblem of the modern state of India.

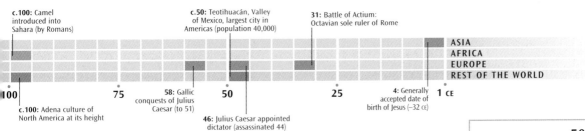

c.100: Camel introduced into Sahara (by Romans)

c.50: Teotihuacán, Valley of Mexico, largest city in Americas (population 40,000)

31: Battle of Actium: Octavian sole ruler of Rome

ASIA
AFRICA
EUROPE
REST OF THE WORLD

100 — 75 — 58: Gallic conquests of Julius Caesar (to 51) — 50 — 25 — 4: Generally accepted date of birth of Jesus (–32 CE) — 1 CE

c.100: Adena culture of North America at its height

46: Julius Caesar appointed dictator (assassinated 44)

The Zapotecs

The Zapotec civilization of southern Pacific Mexico was centered on Monte Albán, set above the Oaxaca valley. The city dominated the region for about 1,000 years. Hieroglyphic inscriptions of calendrical notations found in the city are the earliest examples of writing known to us in the

Americas. Carved stele in Monte Albán show contorted human figures (*left*), known as *Los Danzantes* (the Dancers); they may represent the vanquished enemies of the Zapotecs.

Nok culture

The earliest evidence of ironworking south of the Sahara is found in Nok, the center of a culture which focused on the confluence of the Niger and Benue rivers. Iron technology probably spread there from north of the Sahara, which was at this time beginning to change from grassland to desert. The Nok peoples also produced unique terra-cotta portrait sculptures, with elaborate hairstyles and facial decoration, rendered in a highly individualized manner. From Nok, iron technology spread south along the Atlantic coast and east toward the Great Rift Valley.

ASIA

c.500 Hebrews evolve use of seven-day week.

Building of the Persian Royal Road.

Rice cultivation spreads to Japan from China.

Scylax reaches Indus, returning via Red Sea in 6th century.

Codes of religious laws (*Dharmashastra*) composed in India (–300).

Caste system introduced in India.

Iron casting used to manufacture huge quantities of tools and weapons in China.

Bronze coinage introduced in China

Sinhalese, Aryan peoples, reach Ceylon.

Iron introduced to SE Asia.

Dong Son drums produced in N Vietnam.

490 Persian expedition to Greece is defeated by Athenians at Marathon.

c.483 Death of Buddha.

486 Darius I of Persia is succeeded by his son Xerxes, who invades Greece in 480 with huge army, but is defeated at Salamis, Plataea, and Mycale.

479 Death of Confucius, who developed a humanistic ethical system.

c.460 Parchment replaces clay tablets in Achaemenid administration documents.

458 Qin domain in China partitioned (–424).

AFRICA

c.500 Ironworking in the Great Lakes region.

Foundation of kingdom of Daamat, the first state of the Ethiopian Highlands.

Period of Nok culture in N Nigeria (–200 CE).

Iron-using Bantus begin to spread from Niger to E African lakes region and down west coast of Africa.

EUROPE

c.500 Rich burial at Vix, France, includes Greek and Etruscan imports.

496 Rome defeats Latins at battle of Lake Regillus.

490 Greeks defeat Persians at Marathon.

480 Vast Persian army under Xerxes sent to Greece; defeated at Salamis, Plataea, and Mycale.

c.480 Period of Classical Greek culture.

c.450 **478** Foundation of Confederacy of Delos, later transformed into Athenian empire.

AMERICAS & AUSTRALASIA

c.500 Cultural influence of Chavín begins to weaken in western S America.

Early hieroglyphic inscriptions from the Zapotec center of Monte Albán.

On Samoa, Lapita style of pottery is replaced by plain, undecorated bowls.

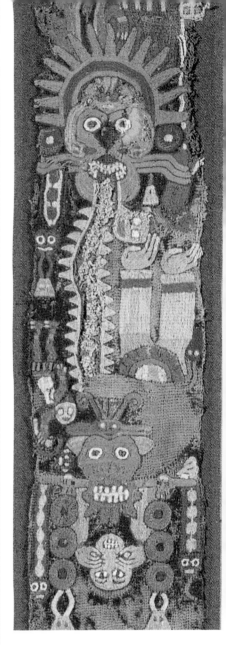

Paracas culture

Paracas culture flourished in southern Peru c.600–350 BCE. Large cemeteries in the Paracas region contained thousands of mummified bodies wrapped in richly woven and highly colored woolen textiles (*above*). The motif of a large-eyed deity, the Occulate Being, frequently appears and shows a strong stylistic and iconographic affinity with the principal Chavín deity, known as the Smiling God. The cult center Chavín de Huantar, lying about 500 miles (805 km) to the north of the Paracas region, remained the most influential center in the Andes in the last millennium BCE.

The Parthenon

The leading Peloponnesian city-state of Athens was at its political and cultural peak in the 5th century BCE. Following the sack of the city by the Persians (480 BCE) and their subsequent defeat, a huge program of public building was inaugurated. The city's leading temple, the Parthenon, was adorned with elaborate sculpted friezes (*below*) depicting the Panathenaic procession in honor of Athena, the patron deity of the city. Removed from the ruins of the Parthenon by the Englishman Lord Elgin at the beginning of the 19th century, they were purchased for the British nation in 1816 and are now in the British Museum in London. They remain outstanding examples of Greek heroic naturalism in art.

captioncaptioncaptioncaptioncaptioncaptioncaptioncaptio ncaptioncaptioncaptioncaptioncaptioncaptioncaptioncapti

Pericles

Pericles (c.495–429 BCE) was an Athenian general who rose to become uncrowned king of Athens during its "Golden Age" (c.443–429 BCE). A political radical, he was responsible for establishing full democracy in Athens and the foundation of the Delian league, which launched the Athenian empire. His opposition to the threat posed in Sparta was imstrumental in provoking the Peloponnesian Wars.

ASIA

c.450 Burials at Pazyryk and Noin Ula in Siberia give insight into life of steppe nomads.

c.410 Xenophon leads army of 10,000 Greek mercenaries from Babylon to Black Sea.

403 "Warring States" period in China (–221).

AFRICA

c.450 Earliest evidence of metallurgy in sub-Saharan Africa.

450–400 BCE

EUROPE

c.450 Celtic (La Tène) culture emerges in W and C Europe. Burials include chariots and weapons.

Athens, the center of the most powerful Greek city-state, reaches its peak.

c.400
Celts expand into British Isles and to east and south.

448 Construction of Parthenon in Athens begins.

443 Athens flourishes under rule of Pericles (–429).

432 Completion of Parthenon in Athens.

431 Peloponnesian Wars between Athens and Sparta (–404).

AMERICAS & AUSTRALASIA

c.400 Emergence of Moche civilization in Peru.

Steppe nomads

Lying north of the belt of civilized states stretching from the Mediterranean to China was the domain of groups of pastoral nomads – often referred to by classical writers as the Scythians. Elaborate burial goods reveal a sophisticated mobile culture. Tombs in the Altai mountains contain leather goods, finely carved wooden artifacts, furs, textiles, and tattooed bodies. Steppe chieftains may have acted as middlemen in trade between China and the west. These groups posed a constant threat to the sedentary civilizations of Eurasia, frequently mounting damaging campaigns against China and Persia.

A stag is gripped in the jaws of a griffin in this wooden carving made by the peoples of the Altai region. Mythical combat was a recurrent theme in their art.

Sparta

The imperial aspirations of Athens and her allies in the Delian League inevitably caused resentment among other Greek city-states. The city of Sparta formed an alliance to counter Athens, which led to the Peloponnesian Wars. The militaristic Spartan society – embodied in this bronze of a soldier – was ruled by kings, with an underclass of serfs. Following a series of largely successful land campaigns, Sparta reached a truce with Athens (421 BCE) but an Athenian expedition to Sicily (415–413 BCE) ended in a further Spartan victory at Syracuse, and their capture of the Athenian navy. Following this, the Athenian empire went into decline.

The Mahabharata

Work began on the composition of the two major epics of Sanskrit literature, the *Mahabharata* and the *Ramayana*, in about 400 BCE. The *Mahabharata* is a compilation of both legendary and didactic material, traditionally ascribed to the sage, Vyasa. The poem is an invaluable source of information about the evolution of Hinduism in India between 400 BCE–200 CE. It is built around a central narrative – the heroic struggle for supremacy between two groups of cousins, the Kauravas and Pandavas, that culminates in a series of battles on the field of Kurukshetra (north of modern Delhi) illustrated above.

ASIA

400 Ironworking introduced to Korea.

c.400 Start of Hindu diffusion to S India and Sri Lanka.

Composition and compilation of the epics, *Mahabharata* and *Ramayana*, begins in India.

The Indian scholar Panini assembles a Sanskrit grammar, formulating 4,000 grammatical rules.

c.377 Mausolus, satrap (governor) of Caria, SW Anatolia. Best known for his monumental tomb, the Mausoleum, one of the Seven Wonders of the Ancient World.

370 The satraps of Persian empire are in revolt.

c.360 Warfare in China is now dominated by the crossbow, a deadly device that uses a pressure-sensitive trigger to fire an arrow.

338

358 In Persia, Artaxerxes III succeeds Artaxerxes II, and ends the satraps' revolt. Fearing possible rivals, he has his whole family massacred.

325

356 Shang Yang, chancellor of the W Chinese Qin state, introduces wide-ranging reforms; he increases the power of centralized government and introduces a rigorous penal code.

AFRICA

c.400 Beginnings of ironworking in Ethiopian highlands.

310

W Mediterranean dominated by Carthage; massive new defenses constructed.

c.380 Farming and the use of iron metallurgy is being spread by Bantu-speaking people in the W Zambezi region.

c.370 Ironworking cultures are beginning to penetrate the forest belt running along the W African coastal hinterland.

342

359 Nectanebo II ascends to the Egyptian throne, and is immediately forced to put down a revolt.

c.400 Celtic settlement of N Italy.

399 The Athenian philosopher Socrates is condemned to death by his fellow citizens, accused of corrupting the youth of the city.

396 Etruscan city of Veii taken by Rome.

390 Celts sack Rome.

386 Sparta and Persia sign a peace treaty recognizing Persian rights to cities in Asia and Cyprus and Athenian rights to the islands of Skyros, Imbros, and Lemnos.

385 Plato returns to his native Athens to open his own academy.

384 Plato writes his philosophical dialogue, *The Symposium*.

380 Construction of massive Servian Wall greatly improves the defenses of Rome.

378 Exiled Theban democrats lead an uprising, murdering members of the pro-Spartan ruling party. The Spartan garrison abandons the city of Thebes.

370 New laws are passed in Rome, allowing plebeians to be elected as consul (senior magistrate).

c.370 Eudoxus of Cnidus develops theories to explain the movements of planets, and assesses the length of the year as 365 and a quarter days.

367 End of the reign of Dionysius, tyrant of Syracuse, who freed the slaves, made peace with Carthage, and turned Syracuse into one of the most important cities in S Italy.

362 Battle of Mantinea marks final eclipse of Spartan power. The Peloponnesian regions gain autonomy, and Thebes becomes the dominant power in Greece.

359 Philip II starts rise to power, and begins to extend Macedonian territory; becomes king of Macedonia.

357 Chios, Rhodes, and Cos leave the Athenian alliance.

356 Birth of Philip II's son, Alexander.

Philip of Macedon signs a pact with the Chalcidian league, naming Athens as the common enemy.

c.400 Great temple complex at Chavín de Huantar (Peru), with cult objects.

Early Zapotec culture flourishing around city of Monte Albán.

Olmec site of La Venta is destroyed. Final phase of Olmec civilization.

*A **mosaic from** the Roman town of Pompeii depicts Plato conversing with his pupils. He argued that true philosophy is live and interactive, involving the animated exchange of ideas.*

Greek philosophy

Traditionally, Greek philosophy began as cosmology, an attempt to explain the universe in a way that would make it intelligible. By the time Socrates was teaching, in 5th-century Athens, a new tradition had also been established, which saw philosophy as a route to self-understanding, a quest for enlightenment.

Plato (c.427–c.347), like Socrates, devoted his life to philosophy. He rejected prose, or verse exposition of his ideas, and favored the dialogue form as a way of presenting stimulating philosophical arguments. He founded the Academy in Athens, which became a lively center for metaphysical and ethical teaching. Aristotle (384–322) set up his own philosophical school, the Lyceum. Unlike Plato, Aristotle adhered to the tradition that upholds study of the natural world, and a systematic explanation of it, as philosophy's natural challenge.

Aristotle's fascination with the natural world took him into the realms of theoretical physics and empirical biology.

Pella, the capital of the Macedonian kingdom, was Alexander's birthplace. The Lion Hunt mosaic, from the Palace of Pella, may depict Hephaestion, Alexander's favorite companion.

Alexander the Great

Alexander succeeded to the Macedonian throne after the assassination of his father, Philip, in 336 BCE. In just ten years, this ruthless and charismatic commander led his victorious Greek armies to Mesopotamia, Egypt, Afghanistan, and India, and forced Achaemenid Persia, the most powerful empire in the world, into submission.

In 334 BCE, Alexander crossed the Hellespont, liberating the old Greek cities of Asia Minor. After a brief sojourn in Egypt, where he founded the great city of Alexandria, he pushed on into Persia, confronted the mighty Persian army, conquered Babylon, Susa, and Persepolis, and pursued the fleeing Persian emperor, Darius III, to the Caspian Gates. His relentless advance to the Hindu Kush, Sind, and Punjab was only halted when his army refused to go further.

Alexander died in Babylon aged only 32. His audacious military adventure had created a truly cosmopolitan civilization. The ideals of Greek civilization had penetrated far to the east, and in many parts of West Asia Greek remained the official language until the 8th and 9th centuries CE.

Alexander was exceptionally tough and resourceful, with great reserves of courage and stamina.

ASIA

338 Artaxerxes III is poisoned to death by his favorite eunuch.

333 Persian king, Darius III is defeated at Issus by Alexander the Great.

331 Decisive defeat of the Persians at battle of Gaugamela by Alexander. His victory at Gaugamela brings Achaemenid Persian empire to an end.

330 Alexander's army pillages the royal city of Persepolis. Darius, the Persian king, is assassinated by rebels.

327 Alexander secures the conquest of Bactria and Sogdiana.

326 Alexander reaches Taxila, but is prevented from advancing further by a revolt of his troops.

325 The prince of Qin takes the title of Wang (king), a claim to be the legitimate ruler of all of China.

Nearchus, admiral of Alexander's fleet, sails from the Indus to the Persian Gulf.

324 Alexander arranges for 90 of his Graeco-Macedonian companions to marry daughters of the Medean and Persian nobility.

321 Chandragupta Maurya founds Mauryan empire, with its capital at Pataliputra.

320 Chandragupta Maurya controls Magadha kingdom and advances toward Indus and C India.

286 **318** Qin forces advance into Szechwan.

c.315 The *Song of Songs*, a collection of love poems, appears in Palestine.

278 **312** Seleucus gains control of Persia, Syria, and much of Asia Minor; takes Babylon, founds the Seleucid dynasty.

297 **302** Chandragupta Maurya signs a peace treaty with Seleucus, ruler of Babylon.

301 Antigonus defeated and killed by Seleucus and Lysimachus at Ipsus.

AFRICA

342 After 60 years of rebellion, Egypt is invaded and is once again under the oppressive rule of the Persians.

332 Alexander the Great of Macedonia conquers Egypt, beginning Greek domination.

285 **331** Alexander founds the city of Alexandria in N Egypt.

310 In response to a Carthaginian siege of Syracuse, troops from Sicily land in Carthage, and negotiate a peace treaty.

c.300 **308** The last royal burial of the Cush king, Natasen, takes place at Napata. Future burials will take place in Meroë.

285 **304** Ptolemy I declares himself king of Egypt. The Ptolemies take pharaonic titles and worship Egyptian deities.

348 Philip of Macedon gains control of the Chalcidice peninsula.

346 War in C Greece ends in uneasy peace between Philip and Athens.

342 Philip of Macedon is master of Thrace; one of conquered cities renamed Philippopolis.

339 Carthage withdraws its support of the Greek tyrants in Sicily.

Start of the Fourth Sacred War between Athens and Macedonia. An alliance between Athens and Thebes saves the Athenians from disaster.

338 Battle of Chaeronea; Philip of Macedon defeats Greek states and Macedonia gains control of Greece.

Rome dissolves the Latin League, and unites Latium. Campania (S Italy) incorporated into the Roman state.

336 Philip is assassinated; succeeded by his son, Alexander.

Alexander embarks on conquest of the Persian empire. He will eventually control an empire that extends from the Mediterranean to the Himalayas (–323).

332 Zeno of Cyprus founds the Stoic school of philosophy in Athens, based on the doctrine that virtue is the only good.

327 Second Samnite War against Samnites in central Apennines, Italy. Romans are defeated (–321).

323 Death of Alexander. On his death, his empire disintegrates among warring factions.

321 Athens is defeated on land and sea by Antipater, the regent of Macedon. Peace terms entail the end of Athenian democracy.

315 Olympias, mother of Alexander, is murdered.

311 Alexander's successors agree on division of empire: Antigonus (Asia), Cassander (Macedon/Greece), Lysimachus (Thrace), Seleucus (N Syria), Ptolemy (Egypt).

310 Alexander IV, son of Alexander the Great and last member of the dynasty, dies.

307 Athenian independence struggle fails: Athens falls under Macedonian control.

306 Ptolemy I of Egypt is defeated off Salamis, Cyprus, by Greeks under the command of Demetrius.

c.350 Beginnings of Nazca culture in S Peru.

c.300 Hopewell culture established in eastern woodlands of N America. Chiefdoms and long-distance trade networks evolve.

356 Birth of Alexander the Great.

334 Alexander crosses the Hellespont to Asia.

333 Alexander travels through C Turkey; the battle of Issus.

332 Siege of Tyre, siege of Gaza. Alexander crosses into Egypt.

331 Foundation of Alexandria. Alexander travels through Syria and N Iraq and captures Babylon and Susa.

330 Persian campaigns; the fall of Persepolis. Alexander reaches Afghanistan.

329 Alexander advances to Kabul, crosses the Hindu Kush to Balkh, crosses the Oxus river, reaches Samarkand.

328 Campaigns in Sogdiana and Bactria.

327 Alexander marries Roxana, daughter of Oxyartes of Sogdiana, in Balkh. After six months in Kabul Valley, he marches up the Kunar Valley into Swat.

326 Siege of Aornos (Pir Sar). Alexander crosses the Indus river, arrives at Taxila. Advances to the Beas river but, after fighting in the Punjab, the army refuses to go on.

325 Reaches the Indus delta, crosses the Makran desert to reach Hormuz.

324 Alexander marches into Persia. His beloved friend, Hephaestion, dies after a drinking bout in Hamadan.

323 Alexander arrives in Babylon, falls ill, and dies.

Roman roads

The Appian Way (*above*) was opened in 312 BCE. It ran for 132 miles (212 km) through rocky coastal terrain, linking Rome with the southern city of Capua. It provided a secure route south, less vulnerable to attack by the Samnite tribesmen of southern Italy. Roman roads are among the empire's most durable monuments. Meticulously surveyed and engineered, they were straight and direct, wherever possible, and were regularly marked with milestones. Roads were often constructed for military uses, as well as for speedy communications: they were used by the *cursus publicus*, or imperial courier service, and by authorized officials. They soon became major trading highways, heavily used for the local transportation of bulk goods.

Ashoka built a total of eight stupas on the hilltop of Sanchi including the Great Stupa. A great number of stupas and other religious structures were added over the succeeding centuries.

Emperor Ashoka

The third king of the Mauryan dynasty, Ashoka of India (reigned 273–232 BCE) became the world's first Buddhist monarch. In the eighth year of his reign, Ashoka conquered Kalinga (modern Orissa). Shocked by the horrors of the Kalinga War, in which 100,000 were slain, Ashoka renounced armed conquest, and became a Buddhist convert. He resolved to live according to Buddhist precepts, and to establish a state based on "universal order."

Across his vast empire, which encompassed all of India Afghansistan, Ashoka ordered that inscriptions should be carved on rocks and pillars, announcing his conversion to Buddhism, and pledging that his empire would be ruled through principles of "kindness, liberality, truthfulness, and purity." One of the most famous Buddhist monuments built by Ashoka is the Great *Stupa* (ritual center of a monastery) at Sanchi (*above*).

301–250 BCE

ASIA

300 City of Antioch founded by Seleucus I.

c.300 Mencius continues Confucian teaching (–300).

297 Chandragupta, the first man to unite the Indian subcontinent, abdicates in favor of his son, Bindusara.

287 The northern states of China begin to build sections of a "Great Wall" to protect themselves against barbarian invasions.

286 Beginning of an era of Qin expansion in China.

281 Lysimachus defeated by Seleucus at Corupedium.

276 Ptolemaic empire expands into Syria during war with Seleucids (–272).

Pergamum in Asia Minor is saved from attack by Gallic forces.

278 The Seleucid Hellenistic kingdom is now established in Babylonia and Syria.

274 First Syrian War between Ptolemy II and Antiochus I (–271).

273 Reign of Ashoka (–232) in India; he seizes throne and embarks on further imperial conquests.

270 Seleucus II subdues Gallic forces who settled in Asia Minor after their attack on Delphi.

263 Eumenes, the ruler of Pergamum, establishes it as an independent power, and begins an ambitious building program.

c.246 **262** Ashoka converts to Buddhism and promulgates Buddhism as state religion.

257 State of Au Lac established in Red river basin; succeeded by Nam Viet in 207.

256 Qin takes Luoyang area in China.

247 Qin puts an end to the royal house of the Zhou.

254 A six-year war between the Seleucids and Ptolemies over possession of Syria is concluded by a marriage alliance.

AFRICA

c.300 Development of the pre-Roman Berber states in N Africa.

Capital of Napata moved to Meroë; the kingdom expands.

c.290 The Alexandrian mathematician, Euclid, sets out the principles of geometry in his *Elements*.

285 Ptolemy I of Egypt abdicates in favor of his son.

c.200 **c.260** Theocritus, Greek poet and creator of pastoral poetry celebrates pastoral life in Alexandria in his *idylls*.

238 **255** Roman invasion of Carthaginian territory in N Africa ends in defeat.

c.300 Appearance of Celtic coinage and formation of the first Celtic states in Europe.

298 Start of Third Samnite War (–290). Following a Roman defeat of Gauls and Samnites at the battle of Sentinum, Roman territory extends from the Bay of Naples to the Adriatic.

294 Demetrius Poliorcetes seizes the throne of Macedonia.

292 Menander, one of Greece's most prolific playwrights, dies at the age of 50.

283 The Romans massacre or disperse the Gallic people known as the Senones.

281 The Achaean League, with its elected federal assembly and council, controls the whole of the Peloponnese.

Seleucus Nicator, the last surviving general of those appointed by Alexander, and ruler of Syria, dies in Macedonia.

280 Pyrrhus, king of Epirus, sends troops to the Greek cities of S Italy to help in the struggle against Rome, but is defeated (–275).

279 Celtic peoples attack Macedonia and N Greece, but are repelled.

272 Tarentum, the leading Greek city in S Italy, falls to the Romans.

Celts sack Delphi, N Greece.

264 Two Roman legions arrive in the Carthaginian-held seaport of Messana, Sicily, but encounter scant resistance. Outbreak of First Punic War.

First gladiatorial combat in Rome.

262 Romans capture Agrigentum in Sicily.

After a long siege, Athens falls to Antigonus Gonatas, the Macedonian ruler who is extending his authority over much of Greece.

260 Roman naval victory over Carthaginians at Mylae.

256 Romans win huge naval battle over Carathaginians off Ecnomus.

255 Failure of Roman invasion of N Africa.

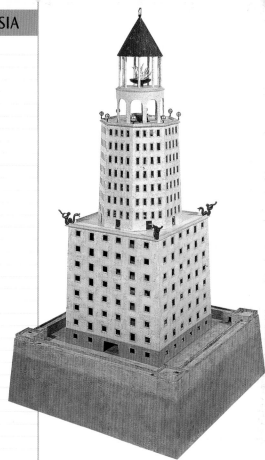

Lighthouse at Pharos

One of the Seven Wonders of the World, the Pharos (lighthouse) of Alexandria was built around 280 BCE by Sostratus of Cnidus possibly for Ptolemy I of Egypt, though it was finished during the reign of his son, Ptolemy II. Constructed on the island of Pharos, in the harbor of Alexandria, it is said to have been more than 350 feet (107 m) high. The lighthouse was built in three stages: the base was square, the middle octagonal, while the top – where a fire burned all night – was cylindrical. Some reports say that it was surmounted by a huge statue, representing either Alexander the Great or Ptolemy I in the form of the sun god Helios.

Within a century of its foundation, Alexandria had become the greatest city in the world, famed as a center of Greek scholarship and learning. Its celebrated library is alleged to have contained nearly half a million book-rolls, while a further 42,000 were housed in a second library attached to the temple of Serapis. Scholars, such as Archimedes, the philosopher Plotinus, and geographers Ptolemy and Eratosthenes, studied at the Mouseion, the great research institute founded by the Ptolemaic dynasty.

ASIA

c.250 Bactrian kingdom becomes independent from Seleucid empire.

Arsaces I founds the Arsacid, or Parthian dynasty.

King Zheng (later Shi Huangdi) becomes ruler of Qin domain.

c.246 King Tissa of Sri Lanka converts to Buddhism.

c.240 Parthian state secedes from Seleucid empire.

232 Death of Ashoka. Start of disintegration of Mauryan empire.

230 Campaigns of Shi Huangdi begin.

223 Accession of Antiochus III to Selucid throne.

177

221 Great Wall of China built as protection against northern nomadic incursions.

The first emperor (Shi Huangdi) unites China under Qin dynasty (–206).

Qin empire established, organized into 36 commanderies.

General disarmament, standardization of weights, measures, and axle widths to facilitate commerce in China.

217 Egyptian hoplites, led by Ptolemy IV Philopator, crush the Seleucid army under Antiochus III at Raphia, Palestine.

213 Proscription of nonscientific books; standardization and simplification of Chinese script.

212 Antiochus III campaigns in the east in an unsuccessful attempt to capture Bactria and Parthia.

210 Death of Shi Huangdi leads to revolts throughout Qin empire. He is entombed with vast terra-cotta army.

206 End of the Qin dynasty.

200

Liu Bang proclaims himself emperor of a new dynasty, the Han.

188

202 After signing a treaty with Philip V of Macedonia, Antiochus III, the Seleucid king, seizes Syria, held by the Egyptians.

AFRICA

c.240 Callimachus, the African scholar-poet who wrote over 800 volumes of verse, dies in Alexandria.

238 Revolt by Carthaginian mercenaries, led by Matho and Spendius.

237 Hamilcar, the Carthaginian general defeated by Rome in Sicily, embarks for Spain.

202 Hannibal defeated at Zama. Carthage now overshadowed by Rome.

167

201 Masinissa unites the kingdoms of Massyli and Massaesyli, called Numidia by Romans.

c.200 Alexandria is now the scientific capital of the Hellenistic world, famous for its museum, university, and library.

Cattle-herding peoples are spreading toward the southernmost tip of Africa.

China's first empire

The rule of China was divided between three kingdoms during the Warring States Period. By 221 BCE, the Qin king had defeated all his rivals to become the first Chinese emperor, known as Qin Shi Huangdi. As emperor, he strove to unite all the Chinese people under his rule, by creating a strong, disciplined army, firmly implementing laws, and introducing a unified system of weights, measures, writing, and currency. He died in the eleventh year of his reign and was buried, as befitted his achievements, in a vast manmade mountain near the capital, Xianyang. In death he was guarded by an entire army of more than 7,000 uniformed, brilliantly painted terra-cotta warriors (*above*).

EUROPE

250 The whole Italian peninsula is under control of Rome.

243 The Peloponnese is liberated from Macedonian dominion by Aratus of Sicyon.

241 Following a Roman victory at the Aegadian Islands, Rome emerges from 23 years of war with Carthage as a major sea power. Rome now controls Sicily.

238 Romans occupy Corsica and Sardinia.

236 Spain becomes part of the Carthaginian empire.

229 Thessalians, Athenians, and Achaeans revolt against Macedonian rule.

226 Agreement on Iberus river (Ebro) as limit of Carthage's expansion in Iberian peninsula.

225 Sparta intervenes in conflict between Macedonia and the Greek cities.

A powerful army of Gallic tribes is defeated by Roman legions at Telamon, N Italy.

224 A plan is agreed between Macedonia and the Achaean League to ensure that they can peacefully coexist.

222 Antigonus III Doson, the Macedonian king, and the Achaean League defeat Sparta.

221 Accession of Philip V of Macedon.

218 Siege of Saguntum begins Second Punic War (−201). Carthaginians led by Hannibal, invade Italy.

212 Rome becomes involved in Greece in First Macedonian War, when Philip V of Macedon allies with Carthage.

211 Romans capture the city of Syracuse, Sicily, a Carthaginian ally.

209 Romans take Tarentum, S Italy.

207 Hasdrubal's attempt to reinforce Hannibal in Italy ends in defeat.

206 Scipio Africanus concludes successful campaign in Iberia.

205 At the peace of Phoenice, Rome, and Macedonia agree to share the protectorate of Illyria.

202 Decisive Roman victory at Zama.

201 Carthage bows to Roman victory, accepting terms of surrender.

AMERICAS & AUSTRALASIA

c.250 Many small coastal cultures, such as the Guangala, flourish in present-day Ecuador.

c.200 El Mirador, the largest early Maya city flourishes. Sites, such as Becan, fortified.

Hannibal (247–c.183 BCE)

The son of the great Carthaginian general, Hamilcar Barca, Hannibal was a superlative military leader. He led the Carthaginian attack on Saguntum in Spain, which precipitated the First Punic War. In 218, with 20,000 infantry, 6,000 cavalry, and 38 elephants, he led his army across the Pyrenees, through southern Gaul (patrolled by warlike tribes), across the Alps, and into Roman Italy. Between 218 and 216, Hannibal inflicted a series of crushing defeats on the Romans, culminating in the battle of Cannae. But Rome gradually managed to gain control over his overstretched and under-provisioned army. The war was eventually carried over to African soil. Hannibal was recalled from Italy, but defeated at the battle of Zama (202). Hannibal went into exile and c.183 he ended his own life, rather than surrender to the Romans.

The Punic Wars

Roman expansion into southern Italy brought it into conflict with Carthage, the other major Mediterranean power. The Carthaginians proved unable to break the Roman hold of the Italian peninsula, and Rome became the regional superpower.

264 Italian mercenaries at Messana call for Roman help against Carthaginians. Start of First Punic War (−241).

262 Roman victories at Agrigentum and at sea (Mylae).

255 Roman expedition to Africa ends in disaster.

249 Carthaginians defeat Romans at sea, at Drepanum.

247 Hamilcar Barca begins Carthaginian offensive in Sicily.

241 Roman victory in sea battle off the Aegadian Islands brings war to an end.

218 Carthaginian general Hannibal crosses Alps to invade Italy, starting the Second Punic War (−201).

217 Hannibal defeats Romans at Lake Trasimene.

216 Hannibal defeats Romans at Cannae.

215 Romans mount counterattack in Spain.

212 Romans besiege Syracuse, a Carthaginian ally.

211 Hannibal marches on Rome; Capua and Syracuse fall. Scipio Africanus defeats Hasdrubal in Spain.

204 Scipio invades Africa.

203 Hannibal recalled from Italy to defend Carthage.

202 Scipio defeats Hannibal at battle of Zama; Carthage overshadowed by Rome.

The Rosetta Stone

This piece of black basalt was found near the town of Rosetta, northeast of Alexandria in Egypt. It was inscribed by the priests of Memphis, and summarizes the benefactions of Ptolemy V Epiphanes (205–180 BCE). The stone is inscribed in both Egyptian and Greek, and in three writing systems – hieroglyphics, demotic (a cursive form of Egyptian hieroglyphics), and the Greek alphabet. The stone was to prove crucial in Egyptologist Jean-Francçois Champollion's decipherment of Egyptian hieroglyphic writing in the early 19th century.

Pergamum

The capital of the Attalid dynasty, Pergamum in western Asia Minor, was a wealthy and imposing city. Its library was second only to Alexandria's, and it is famous for the new school of spectacular baroque architecture that developed there. The most grandiose monument of the 2nd century BCE is the Great Altar of Pergamum (*above*). The relief frieze is both a bold and minutely detailed depiction of a battle between gods and giants.

ASIA

200 Chinese emperor Liu Bang sets up his capital at Chang'an.

c.200 Bactrian Greeks establish small kingdoms in E Anatolia.

191 In China, the most rigorous Qin laws are abolished.

190 Seleucids give up their claim to Thrace, and evacuate Asia Minor as far as the Taurus Mountains.

c.190 Establishment of several Greek kingdoms in northwestern S Asia. Buddhism adopted in Indo-Greek kingdoms, rise of Gandhara art.

188 Seleucid ruler Antiochus III concludes a peace treaty with the Romans at Apamea in Phrygia, effectively ending Seleucid influence in the Mediterranean.

c.181 End of Mauryan and start of Shunga dynasty in N India.

177 Advance of Xiongnu nomads into the Henan region of N China.

146 **171** Mithridates I becomes king of Persia.

167 Antiochus IV, the Seleucid king of Syria, dedicates the temple of Jerusalem to Olympian Zeus.

142 **165** Judas Maccabaeus, leader of a revolt against the Hellenization of Judaea, enters Jerusalem, purifies the temple, and reestablishes Judaism.

First official examination for selection of Chinese civil servants.

160 The city of Pergamum, ruled by King Eumenes II, rivals Athens for architectural magnificence. It is a renowned cultural center.

145 **150** Demetrius, king of Syria, dies in battle against Alexander Balas, a pretender to the Seleucid throne.

AFRICA

c.200 Settlement now established in Jenne, on the inland Niger delta.

The 25-year rule of King Arkamani at Meroë is at an end. During his reign he promoted friendly relations with the Ptolemaic pharaohs of Egypt.

c.180 Under Ptolemy VI Philometor, Egypt is beset with internal disputes and fiscal and military crises.

167 Masinissa, king of Numidia, takes possession of the emporia of Syrtis on north coast of Africa from the Romans.

146 **151** Masinissa invades Carthage, which is still recovering from the Punic Wars, and achieves a military victory.

EUROPE

200 Second Macedonian War (–197).

197 Defeated by the Romans at Cynoscephalae, Philip V of Macedon sues for peace. Macedonia is stripped of its possessions in European Greece and Asia Minor.

196 Rome declares the freedom of the Greeks at the Isthmus of Corinth.

194 The last Roman soldiers leave Greek soil, taking many works of art with them.

192 War with Seleucid king, Antiochus (–189); Roman victories at Thermopylae and Magnesia.

184 The Roman censor, Marcus Porcius Cato (the Elder), attacks Rome's decadence.

c.180 Romans subjugate Italian Celts between the Apennines and the Alps.

179 Perseus succeeds his father, Philip V, as king of Macedon. He raises a coalition to mount an assault on Rome, by restoring power to pro-Macedonian factions in Greek cities.

172 Third Macedonian War (–167).

168 Roman expansion into E Mediterranean begins. Romans crush Macedonians at Pydna.

167 The Romans declare Delos a free port. The tiny Aegean island becomes a pivot of east–west trade routes.

155 Athens sends representatives of its three great schools of philosophy – the Academy, the Stoa Poikile, and the Lyceum – on a mission to Rome.

Romans invade Dalmatia, E Adriatic, and destroy the capital, Delminium.

AMERICAS & AUSTRALASIA

200 Regional cultures begin to appear in C Andes.

c.200 Nazca Lines carved into the surface of the S Peruvian desert.

c.50 Small communities in Mexico's Teotihuacán valley are merging. The people follow the cult of the rain god, Tlaloc.

Marquesas Islands settled by Lapita colonists.

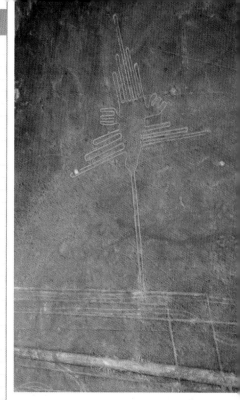

This aerial view shows Nazca lines etched into the shape of a hummingbird. Some of these images can be up to 328 feet (100 m) across.

Nazca culture

Based on the south coast of Peru, the Nazca people continued the fine textile-working traditions of Paracas culture. Over approximately 700 years (c.350 BCE– 400 CE), their pottery working reached artistic heights. Up to 14 different colored slips were used to create the rich polychrome designs that were painted on the pottery before it was fired. They have left few traces of major public buildings; the enigmatic Nazca lines are their most famous legacy. These straight, geometric, or figurative designs were etched, over large distances, on the surface of the Peruvian desert. It is thought that the designs may have represented offerings to mountain and sky gods.

Nazca pot showing a farmer, holding plants.

The Parthian empire

The Parthians were Iranian nomads from east of the Caspian Sea who, from about 240 BCE, spread west into Mesopotamia, consolidating their control of the region by 123 BCE, under the rule of King Mithridates II. They founded their capital at the city of Ctesiphon on the Tigris river. The Parthian conquerors left local administrators and rulers in place, and styled their own ruler "the king of kings," because he governed so many smaller kingdoms.

The ancient religion of Mesopotamia was replaced by Oriental mystery cults and Iranian cults. Parthian art and architecture was expressionistic and stylized. The frequent portrayal of the "flying gallop" (*top*) in sculpture and painting reflects the importance of armored cavalry and mounted archers in the Parthian armies. It was these military innovations that led to Parthian victories against Rome in the 1st century BCE.

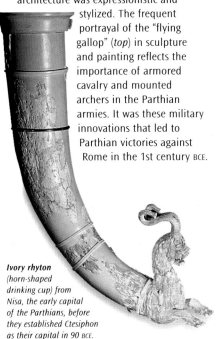

Ivory rhyton (horn-shaped drinking cup) from Nisa, the early capital of the Parthians, before they established Ctesiphon as their capital in 90 BCE.

ASIA

146 Mithridates I lays foundations of the Parthian empire, after gaining control of Media, Babylon, Elam and parts of Bactria.

c.146 Eudoxus of Cyzicus sails from Black Sea to W Africa.

Scythian warriors invade Bactria (Afghanistan).

145 Demetrius II kills Alexander Balas, the pretender to the Seleucid throne, and becomes king.

142 Jews liberate Jerusalem, and make it their capital.

141 Parthians control Mesopotamia, following capture of the old Selucid capital, Seleucia-on-the-Tigris.

Han emperor, Wudi expands Han power into C Asia.

138 Embassy of Zhang Qian to Xiongnu and C Asia (–126).

136 Confucianism becomes state religion of China.

131 Roman army sent to Pergamum to quell unrest that follows a slave revolt, led by Aristonicus, the pretender to the throne.

130 Graeco-Bactrian kingdom falls to the Kushans.

129 Romans regain control of Pergamum, creating the province of Asia.

c.125 A Scythian tribe, known as the Shakas, invade the Punjab.

123 Accession of Mithridates II the Great. Parthian empire reaches greatest extent.

120 Eudoxus is the first Greek to reach India from Egypt.

119 State monopoly on ironworking established in China.

c.110 Opening up of Silk Road across C Asia.

111 Annam falls to Han empire.

Chinese Han empire conquers and incorporates N Vietnam.

108 Chinese Han take military control of Korea; occupy N Korea.

101 Chinese conquests of the Tarim basin and Ferghana make them masters of C Asia.

AFRICA

149 Rome intervenes in the dispute between Numidia and Carthage: the Third Punic War (–146).

146 Rome conquers Carthage.

Destruction of Carthage; Rome creates province of Africa from former Carthaginian possessions.

118 Jugurtha assassinates his cousin, who is also heir, to become king of Numidia.

116 Cleopatra III rules Egypt jointly with her son, Ptolemy IX.

112 Romans at war with Jugurtha, king of Numidia.

107 Alexander, governor of Cyprus, expels his brother Ptolemy IX from the Egyptian throne.

105 Jugurtha defeated by Roman general, Gaius Marius.

c.100 Khoisan herding culture has now spread to the far south coast of Africa.

148 Roman victory in Fourth Macedonian War.

146 Roman army destroys conquered city of Corinth. Greece comes under Roman rule, and N Africa a Roman province.

140 The Roman general Fabius is defeated in Spain by a rebel force led by Viriathus. He secures a favorable peace with Rome.

139 Defeat of Lusitani.

133 Pergamum bequeathed to Rome.

Romans take Iberian city of Numantia.

Liberal social reforms of tribune Tiberius Gracchus lead to his murder.

132 Slaves' revolt in Sicily ends with mass crucifixion.

125 Fregellae, a Latin colony in C Italy, revolts against Rome. The rebellion is brutally suppressed.

123 Romans suppress attacks by the Celto-Ligurian tribe, the Salluvii, on the Roman province of Gallia Transalpina (Provence).

107 Rome's new model army offers military training for working-class recruits.

105 The Cimbri and Teutoni, Germanic tribes in E Gaul, win a victory over the Romans at Arausio (Orange).

102 Romans decisively defeat Cimbri and Teutoni at Aquae Sextiae (Aix-en-Provence).

101 A second slave revolt in Sicily is quelled by Roman forces.

100 Civil unrest amongst Roman nobility when new social laws, including a reduction in the price of corn for the poorest people, are introduced.

c.100 Development of Celtic oppida in W Europe – fortified settlements.

c.150 Great Serpent Mound in Ohio, N America; a 1,312-foot (405-m) -long earthen effigy mound is built.

The Celts

The Celts was the collective name given by the Greeks and Romans to the peoples of Europe north of the Alps. The oldest archaeological evidence of Celtic culture comes from the site of Hallstatt, near Salzburg, Austria (c.800 BCE). Here, graves of chieftains display swords made using the new iron technology, as well as bronze and pottery. This wealthy warrior elite controlled trade routes along the Rhône, Seine, and Rhine rivers, eventually trading with Greek cities. In the 5th century BCE, the center of Celtic power moved northward and westward. This change is associated with the La Tène culture, with its distinctive art style of abstract designs and stylized birds and animals (*left*). From about 400 BCE, diverse Celtic warbands began to appear in Greece and Roman Italy. They sacked and pillaged Etruscan towns and Rome itself, causing widespread havoc, until they were eventually subdued by imperial forces in the 1st century BCE.

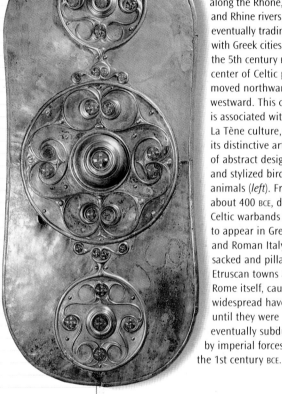

Roman Revolts

136 Sicilian slave wars (–132).

133 Celtoiberian stronghold of Numantia, N Spain, destroyed, after 70 years of intermittent warfare.

131 Revolt by pretender to throne of Pergamum, Asia Minor, suppressed.

126 Revolts in Sardinia (–122).

123 Attacks by the Celto-Ligurian tribe, the Salluvii, on Massilia suppressed.

115 Revolts in Sardinia (–111).

114 Scordisi defeat a Roman army and invade Macedonia.

105 Movements of Teutoni and Cimbri throughout S Gaul. Decisive defeat of Romans at Orange.

104 Sicilian slave wars (–101).

102 Romans defeat Teutoni at Aix-en-Provence.

101 Cimbri defeated at Vercellae.

73 Revolt by the gladiator, Spartacus

Petra

In the 1st millennium BCE, the Red Sea became a major trading corridor. The kingdom of Nabataea, with Petra as its capital, controlled the overland caravan trade between southern Arabia and the Roman Empire. This trade was based on frankincense, myrrh, and aromatic gums, all in great demand in the Near East, for incense, cosmetics, and perfumes. The desert city of Petra (*above*) reached its period of greatest prosperity from 100 BCE to 150 CE. It was carved out of the sandstone mountains that lay to the northeast of the Red Sea. The fine Hellenistic facades of its major public buildings reflect the close trading contacts between Petra and the Hellenistic world.

Two Centuries of Roman Conquest

In the course of just a century, Rome became a dominant military and political power in the eastern Mediterranean. Meanwhile, their campaigns in Europe culminated in 51 BCE, when seven years of bitter fighting were rewarded with the prize of Gaul.

241	Sicilia.
238	Corsica and Sardinia.
197	Hispania Ulterior, Hispania Citerior.
146	Macedonia, Achaea, Africa.
140	Epirus.
133	Asia.
121	Gallia Narbonensis, Baleares Insulae.
101	Cilicia.
74	Bithynia, Lycia, Cyrene.
67	Creta.
64	Syria.
58	Cyprus.
51	Gallia.

ASIA

c.100 Indian influences spread to SE Asia via maritime trade routes.

Composition of 700-verse *Bhagavad Gita*, Vedic religious text, India (–100 CE).

99 Insurrections in the eastern part of Han China.

98 Chinese establish a state monopoly on alcohol.

c.30

90 Bactrian kingdom of Gandhara falls to Scythians (Shakas).

Ctesiphon established as Parthian capital.

88 Mithridates, the king of Pontus, attacks Bithynia and the Roman province of Asia.

Mithridates II, king of Parthia, is killed by Scythian invaders sweeping westward.

83 Outbreak of Second Mithridatic War (–81).

74 Bithynia is organized as a Roman province. Mithridates, king of Pontus, invades Bithynia once again.

73 Following a Roman occupation of Pontus, Mithridates flees to Armenia.

70 Attacks by Tigranes, king of Armenia, lead to a Parthian collapse.

66 Roman general, Pompey vanquishes Mithridates, king of Pontus, and Tigranes, king of Armenia, who has been attempting to annex Cappadocia and Syria.

c.64 Birth of Strabo, author of the famous *Geographica* at Amasia, N Asia Minor.

40

63 Pompey captures Jerusalem and annexes Judaea.

60 Oldest watermills in the world, in Asia Minor.

55 Xiongnu confederacy breaks up; southern group becomes tributary of Han China.

53 A Roman expeditionary force, led by Crassus, is wiped out by Parthian cavalry at Carrhae in the Mesopotamian desert.

AFRICA

100 Rise of Axum.

c.100 Camel introduced into Sahara by the Romans.

98 Ptolemy Apion, ruler of Cyrenaica, bequeaths his territories to Rome.

96 Romans, accompanied by their Berber allies, the Garamantes, make an expedition into the Sahara.

30

74 Cyrenaica is organized as a Roman province.

59 Ptolemy XII king of Egypt, is named "friend and ally" of the Roman people, but is expelled from Egypt by the Alexandrians.

55 Ptolemy XII is restored to the Egyptian throne, helped by a large bribe to the Roman consul, Aulus Gabinius.

Pompey's victories in Spain and the Near East ensured that he had a loyal following amongst soldiers and ordinary people, but he met his match in Julius Caesar.

c.100 Language and culture of Etruscans in terminal decline.

c.100 Adena culture of N America at its height.

91 Tribune Marcus Livius Drusus, a liberal reformer, is assassinated in Rome. The Social War (–89); Rome defeats rebellious Italian allies, but grants concessions.

89 Roman citizenship extended to all Italians.

88 Sulla becomes consul, marches on Rome, and purges his opponents, led by Marius.

87 Sulla controls much of Greece, and lays siege to Athens and Piraeus (–86).

86 Marius allies with newly elected consul, Cinna against Sulla. Marches on Rome and brutal massacre follows.

82 Sulla returns to Rome, where he presides over a reign of terror.

77 Following the senate's rejections of his liberal reforms, Marcus Aemilius Lepidus marches on Rome with an Etruscan army. He is halted by Pompey.

73 A revolt led by a gladiator, Spartacus, devastates S Italy (–71).

67 Roman general Pompey leads a successful campaign against piracy in the E Mediterranean.

63 Statesman and orator, Cicero is elected consul. He denounces Catiline, former governor of Africa, as a conspirator.

62 The rebel Catiline is slain in battle at Pistoria, Italy.

61 Julius Caesar forms a triumvirate with Pompey and Crassus.

49 ▼

58 Gallic conquests of Julius Caesar (–50).

55 Caesar invades Britain, but withdraws. He makes a further attempt the following year.

54 Revolts by the Gallic Eburones and Belgic Nervii against Caesar are suppressed.

52 Vercingetorix leads a revolt in Gaul, but is defeated.

43 ▼

50 New forum under construction in Rome.

Sulla and Pompey

The Roman general, Lucius Cornelius Sulla distinguished himself in the Social War of 91–89 BCE against Rome's former Italian allies. But, in 82 BCE, he returned from wars in the east to wreak vengeance on his political enemies at home. He unleashed a reign of terror on the Roman world, and had himself made a dictator with absolute power. In 77 BCE he resigned the dictatorship, dying soon afterward. One of Sulla's protégés, Gnaeus Pompeius Magnus (Pompey) first rose to prominence at the head of three legions, which fought successfully in Sicily and Africa. In 70 BCE, at the age of 36, Pompey was elected consul, one of the two chief magistrates of Rome. In 64 BCE, he imposed a general settlement on the Near East, creating the Roman province of Syria. In 49 BCE, Pompey was charged with defending Italy against Julius Caesar, a former ally. Defeated at Pharsalus in Greece, he was pursued by Caesar to Egypt and treacherously murdered by the Egyptian king.

Sulla's military successes in the Social War of 91–89 BCE and his defeat of King Mithridates of Pontus were undermined by his bloodthirsty persecution of his enemies when he returned to Rome.

The Portland Vase, made in the early 1st century CE, is the finest surviving example of Roman cameo glass, glassware that is decorated with figures and forms of colored glass carved in relief against a background of contrasting color.

Luxury in Rome

By the time of Rome's first emperor, Augustus, wealthier Roman citizens were living lives of unparalleled luxury. Their homes were decorated with mosaics, sculptures, and wall-paintings. The nouveaux riches even displayed their culture by hanging reproductions of Greek old masters. Furniture was ornate, made of elaborately carved and sculpted bronze, marble, and wood. While the diet of the masses was frugal, extraordinarily lavish banquets were served by the wealthy – a wide array of game-birds, meats, and seafood were served in complex sauces. Tables were laden with the best silver and tableware, decorated with repoussé reliefs of plants and mythological scenes.

Profligate spending was much criticized; frequently connections were made between excessive luxury and moral and social collapse. Augustus even tried to set legal limits to luxury, although with little success. As Roman control extended beyond Italy, a much wider array of goods became available to the Romans. In addition, conquest made them wealthy, enabling them to bring back to Rome the finest art objects, sculptures, and paintings their new territories could offer.

ASIA

c.50 Powerful Satavahana dynasty arises in Deccan, lasts until 250 CE.

47 At Zela, Caesar defeats Pharnaces, son of Mithridates king of Pontus, who had earlier invaded Bithynia.

40 Herod the Great becomes king of Judaea, which remains a loyal client kingdom of Rome.

Parthian troops invade Syria, and capture Jerusalem.

39 Marcus Antonius (Antony) inflicts two crushing defeats on the Parthians in Cilicia.

37 Romans drive Parthian invaders out of Jerusalem. Herod becomes king.

Antony marries Cleopatra, queen of Egypt, at Antioch.

36 Following a defeat by the Parthians, Antony retreats to Armenia.

c.30 Shakas overrun Indo-Greek kingdoms of Indus Valley.

25 Aelius Gallus explores W Arabia (–24).

c.25 Buddhist canon committed to writing for first time in Sinhala in Ceylon (Sri Lanka).

20 Settlement with Parthians, who return captured Roman standards.

19 Herod rebuilds temple at Jerusalem.

14 Peasant revolts in Han China.

4 Generally accepted date of birth of Christ in Bethlehem.

Death of Herod; kingdom divided between his three sons.

c.1 The Silk Road in C Asia is a trade route linking China with SW Asia.

AFRICA

48 Following defeat at Pharsalus, Pompey flees to Egypt where he is killed on the orders of the Egyptian king, Ptolemy XIII.

47 Caesar is besieged in Alexandria by an Egyptian force. He is relieved by an army from Asia.

46 Foundation of Roman colony of Carthage.

Supporters of Pompey, hiding with King Juba of Numidia, are killed in a battle with Caesar's troops at Thapsus.

Kingdom of Numidia is added to Roman province of Africa, after suicide of King Juba.

44 Cleopatra murders Ptolemy XIV, coruler of Egypt.

33 King Bocchus II of the Mauri bequeaths his kingdom to the Roman Empire.

31 Octavian defeats Antony at the battle of Actium.

30 Antony and Cleopatra commit suicide. Annexation of Egypt by Rome.

25 Frontiers between Egypt and Ethiopia are secured.

23 Romans invade the Meroë kingdom of Cush, sacking its capital, Napata.

Julius Caesar

49 Caesar crosses the Rubicon river into Italy, and Pompey, his former ally, leaves for Greece.

48 Ceasar defeats Pompey at the battle of Pharsalus, Greece.

47 Caesar campaigns against republicans in Asia, Africa, and Spain.

46 Julian calendrical reforms; "Year of Confusion" is 445 days long.

Julius Caesar appointed dictator.

44 Caesar is murdered by conspirators. Marcus Antonius (Antony) controls Rome.

43 Octavian seizes the consulate. Second triumvirate – Antony, Octavian, Lepidus – cemented by marriage of Antony to Octavian's sister.

In Gaul, the Roman colony of Lugdunum (Lyons) is founded. Roman soldiers are being settled throughout Gaul.

42 Republicans defeated at the battle of Philippi; Brutus and Cassius commit suicide.

40 Peace treaty at Brundisium divides Roman world between Octavian and Antony.

36 Campaigns against Sextus Pompeius, son of Pompey, in Sicily.

32 Final breach between Antony and Octavian.

31 Octavian defeats Antony and Cleopatra at the naval battle of Actium, consolidating control of E Mediterranean.

29 Publication of Virgil's *Georgics* confirms that he is the foremost poet of the age.

27 Assuming the title Augustus, Octavian becomes first Roman emperor (–14).

Agrippa completes the conquest of NW Spain (–19).

15 Roman conquest of Noricum and Raetia is complete.

12 Augustus becomes Pontifex Maximus. Worship of Augustus as a god has spread throughout the empire.

Romans conquer Germany as far as the Elbe river (–9).

c.100 c.50 Teotihuacán in valley of Mexico is largest city in the Americas, with population of 40,000.

A rising star of the Roman political world, Caesar was appointed governor of northern Italy and southern France in 59 BCE. He immediately embarked on a six-year campaign of conquest in Gaul, and by 53 BCE the triumphant Caesar was ready to seize supreme power in Rome itself. In command of a powerful army, Caesar was able to rout his enemies between 49 and 45 BCE, stamping out all opposition. He had himself declared perpetual dictator in February 46 BCE but two years later he was assassinated by a group of nobles in the Senate house on March 15, the Ides of March.

Julius Caesar was an immensely gifted soldier, writer, orator, and politician. But he was both unscrupulous and ambitious. During his last years, he ruled as king in all but name.

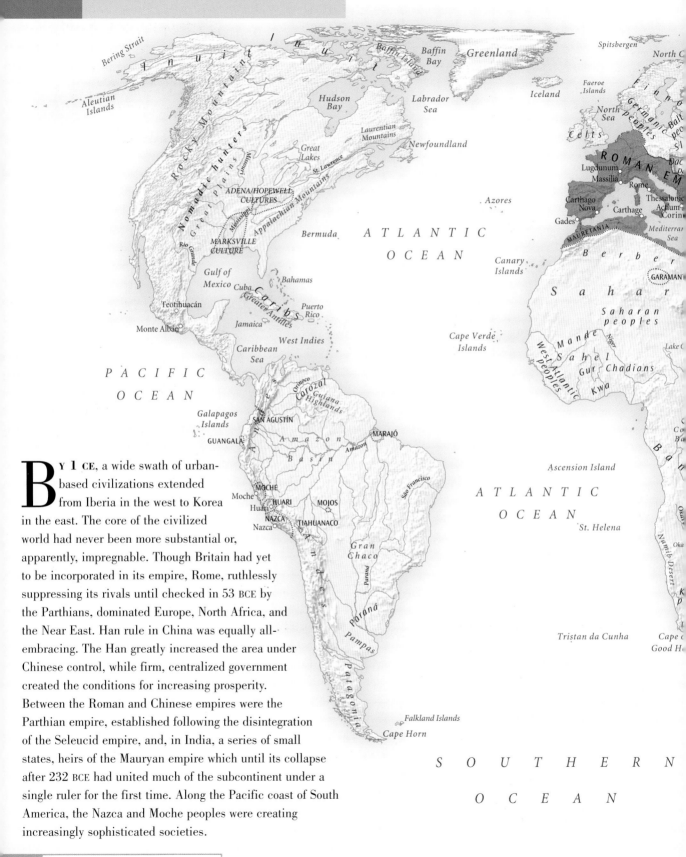

BY 1 CE, a wide swath of urban-based civilizations extended from Iberia in the west to Korea in the east. The core of the civilized world had never been more substantial or, apparently, impregnable. Though Britain had yet to be incorporated in its empire, Rome, ruthlessly suppressing its rivals until checked in 53 BCE by the Parthians, dominated Europe, North Africa, and the Near East. Han rule in China was equally all-embracing. The Han greatly increased the area under Chinese control, while firm, centralized government created the conditions for increasing prosperity. Between the Roman and Chinese empires were the Parthian empire, established following the disintegration of the Seleucid empire, and, in India, a series of small states, heirs of the Mauryan empire which until its collapse after 232 BCE had united much of the subcontinent under a single ruler for the first time. Along the Pacific coast of South America, the Nazca and Moche peoples were creating increasingly sophisticated societies.

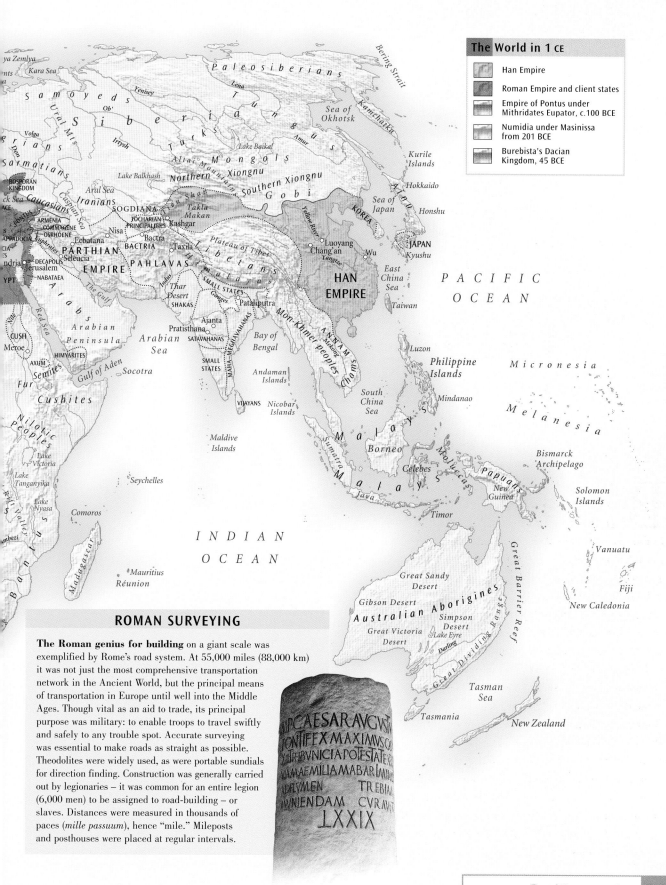

The World in 1 CE

- Han Empire
- Roman Empire and client states
- Empire of Pontus under Mithridates Eupator, c.100 BCE
- Numidia under Masinissa from 201 BCE
- Burebista's Dacian Kingdom, 45 BCE

Map labels:

ya Zemlya · Kara Sea · Samoyeds · Ural Mts · Volga · Don · Irtysh · Ob' · Yenisey · Lena · Siberia · Tungus · Paleosiberians · Bering Strait · Sea of Okhotsk · Kamchatka · Kurile Islands · Ainu · Hokkaido · Honshu · Sea of Japan · KOREA · JAPAN · Kyushu · Lake Baikal · Amur · Altai Mountains · Mongols · Northern Xiongnu · Southern Xiongnu · Gobi · Yellow River · Luoyang · Chang'an · Wu · Yangtze · HAN EMPIRE · East China Sea · Taiwan · PACIFIC OCEAN · Turks · Sarmatians · Iranians · Caspian Sea · Aral Sea · Lake Balkhash · SOGDIANA · Tien Shan · Takla Makan · Kashgar · Nisa · Bactra · BACTRIA · Taxila · TOCHARIAN PRINCIPALITIES · Plateau of Tibet · Tibetans · Himalayas · Indus · Ganges · Pataliputra · SMALL STATES · BOSPORAN KINGDOM · Black Sea · Caucasians · PONTUS · ARMENIA · COMMAGENE · OSRHOENE · CAPPADOCIA · APPADOCIA · Euphrates · Ecbatana · PARTHIAN EMPIRE · Seleucia · PAHLAVAS · DECAPOLIS · Jerusalem · NABATAEA · EGYPT · andria · Arabs · The Gulf · Arabian Peninsula · Thar Desert · SHAKAS · Ajanta · Pratisthana · SATAVAHANAS · MAHAVAHANAS · MEGHAVAHANAS · SMALL STATES · VIJAYANS · Andaman Islands · Nicobar Islands · Mon-Khmer peoples · ANNAM · Chams · Mekong · Bay of Bengal · Luzon · Philippine Islands · Mindanao · Micronesia · Melanesia · South China Sea · Malays · Borneo · Celebes · Moluccas · Papuans · New Guinea · Bismarck Archipelago · Solomon Islands · Sumatra · Java · Timor · Vanuatu · Fiji · New Caledonia · Nile · Red Sea · CUSH · Meroe · HIMYARITES · AXUM · Semites · Gulf of Aden · Socotra · Fur · Cushites · Nilotic Peoples · Lake Victoria · Lake Tanganyika · Lake Nyasa · Rift Valley · Zambezi · Bantu · Comoros · Madagascar · Mauritius · Réunion · Seychelles · Maldive Islands · INDIAN OCEAN · Australian Aborigines · Great Sandy Desert · Gibson Desert · Great Victoria Desert · Simpson Desert · Lake Eyre · Darling · Great Dividing Range · Great Barrier Reef · Tasman Sea · Tasmania · New Zealand

ROMAN SURVEYING

The Roman genius for building on a giant scale was exemplified by Rome's road system. At 55,000 miles (88,000 km) it was not just the most comprehensive transportation network in the Ancient World, but the principal means of transportation in Europe until well into the Middle Ages. Though vital as an aid to trade, its principal purpose was military: to enable troops to travel swiftly and safely to any trouble spot. Accurate surveying was essential to make roads as straight as possible. Theodolites were widely used, as were portable sundials for direction finding. Construction was generally carried out by legionaries – it was common for an entire legion (6,000 men) to be assigned to road-building – or slaves. Distances were measured in thousands of paces (*mille passuum*), hence "mile." Mileposts and posthouses were placed at regular intervals.

1 –500 CE
The Later Classical Age

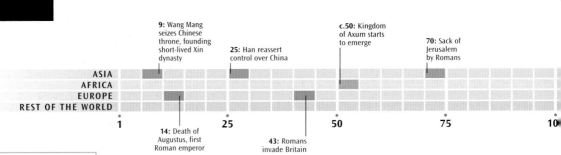

9: Wang Mang seizes Chinese throne, founding short-lived Xin dynasty

25: Han reassert control over China

c.50: Kingdom of Axum starts to emerge

70: Sack of Jerusalem by Romans

ASIA
AFRICA
EUROPE
REST OF THE WORLD

1   25   50   75   10

14: Death of Augustus, first Roman emperor

43: Romans invade Britain

PICTURE ABOVE:
Rome's empire depended on the strength and loyalty of its armies. This 2nd-century relief shows officers and soldiers of the Praetorian Guard, the emperor's (usually) loyal bodyguard and the only miltary unit stationed in Rome.

TWO GREAT CIVILIZATIONS dominated the world in 1 CE, the Roman and the Chinese Han empires. By 500 CE, the Han empire had disappeared to be replaced by three aggressively competing kingdoms while the Roman Empire had been reduced to just the eastern half of the territories it ruled at its height. Other organized states still existed, chiefly in the Middle East and India. Japan, too, had begun to emerge as a significant power in the Far East. But whereas in 1 CE there had been a great swath of stable, centralized Eurasian empires, by 500 CE only the Sassanian empire in Persia could claim to be a major imperial power.

At much the same time, a parallel process, begun several centuries earlier, was now gathering pace. In many parts of the globe world religions were emerging to take the place of local cults and beliefs: Christianity in the west, Hinduism in the Indian subcontinent, Buddhism across Central Asia and China.

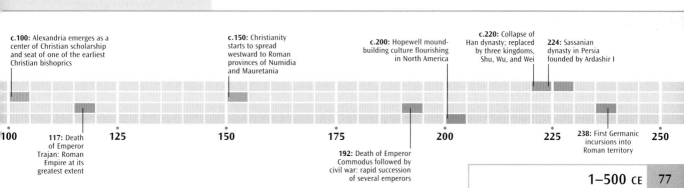

The nimble "horses of heaven" from Ferghana in Central Asia were prized by the Han as cavalry horses in their wars against the Xiongnu.

Although it was only in the Roman empire that a new religion, Christianity, adopted by the Romans as their official religion in 391, had a direct impact on political developments, the emergence of these religions on a global scale was a genuinely new development in world history and one that would shape the future attitudes of empires and states.

Conflict in Asia

The collapse of the Han Empire was sudden and violent. Beset by internal revolts, unable to collect taxes and increasingly reliant on mercenaries from steppe tribes to the north and east, in 220 Han authority disintegrated. Regional warlords carved out new kingdoms for themselves, leading to almost 300 years of chaos and a decline in traditional Confucian values. Almost all the Han's territorial gains, in Korea, Vietnam, and in Central Asia, were lost.

As much as the Romans, the Han also fell victim to the incursions of the steppe peoples across their borders, who from the 3rd century, above all in Central Asia, were becoming increasingly organized and militaristic – not least following the invention of the stirrup in about 300, which greatly increased the efficiency of their cavalry. Opportunistic campaigns were launched against more sedentary peoples to the south, disrupting states across Eurasia. Even the Sassanian empire, founded in about 224 by Ardashir I following his uprising against the Parthian rulers of Persia, and the most stable power in Late Antiquity, was threatened when in 350 and 400 Hun attacks were launched against it.

Decline of the Romans

The disintegration of the Roman Empire was slow. At its peak early in the 2nd century CE under Trajan (98–117), the Roman Empire stretched from Britain, invaded in 43 CE, in the northwest to Armenia, Assyria, and Mesopotamia, seized from the Parthians at the end of Trajan's reign, in the southeast. Trajan's successor, Hadrian, chose to abandon these last three provinces and adopted a policy of strengthening the defences of the empire's existing borders rather than

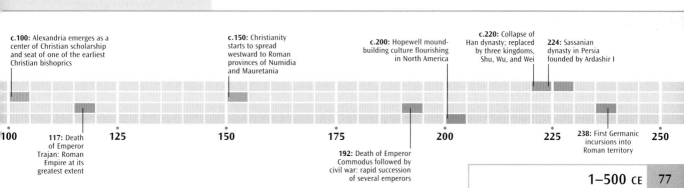

c.100: Alexandria emerges as a center of Christian scholarship and seat of one of the earliest Christian bishoprics

c.150: Christianity starts to spread westward to Roman provinces of Numidia and Mauretania

c.200: Hopewell mound-building culture flourishing in North America

c.220: Collapse of Han dynasty; replaced by three kingdoms, Shu, Wu, and Wei

224: Sassanian dynasty in Persia founded by Ardashir I

100

117: Death of Emperor Trajan: Roman Empire at its greatest extent

125

150

175

192: Death of Emperor Commodus followed by civil war: rapid succession of several emperors

200

225

238: First Germanic incursions into Roman territory

250

attempting any further conquests. Under Hadrian a standing army of 300,000 legionaries was sufficient for the task. The most vulnerable frontier lay along the Rhine and Danube rivers, which served as a barrier against invasion by Germanic tribes from the northeast. Local insurrections were dealt with swiftly and savagely. The Second Jewish Revolt of 132–135 CE, for example, ended in the expulsion of the Jews from Jerusalem on pain of death, and the rebuilding of the city as the Roman Aelia Capitolina.

During the largely peaceful reign of Hadrian, Rome ruled over some 50 million people in 5,000 administrative units. Yet within 80 years this seemingly impregnable edifice was being undermined by conflicts over the imperial succession which, in turn, fatally weakened central authority, leading to civil war, economic breakdown, and revolts by the army. At the same time, the empire's resources were being increasingly stretched by the need to repel incursions across its immense frontiers, above all by Germanic tribes.

Diocletian (284–305) attempted to prevent the haemorrhage by the division of the empire into four smaller units. The process of dividing up the empire was continued by Constantine (307–337), who built a magnificent new eastern capital at Byzantium (Constantinople). It was Constantine, too, who shaped the future of Europe by embracing Christianity and granting freedom of worship to Christians throughout the empire.

For a time Christianity had to compete with traditional pagan deities and various eastern cults until Theodosius, the last man to rule over a united empire, made it the state religion in 391. On the death of Theodosius in 395 the empire definitively split into its western and eastern halves. Though the latter, through many vicissitudes, would endure for almost 1,000 years as the Byzantine empire, in

476 what remained of the West Roman Empire precipitately disintegrated under the immense pressures of the Germanic peoples who had poured across its frontiers throughout the 4th and 5th centuries. Many of these – the Goths, for example, who helped the Romans defeat the Huns – were originally invited in as allies by the Romans, but when the Romans were unable to meet their demands for reward in the form of lands and money, turned against them.

Germanic kingdoms

In 492, the Ostrogothic king, Theodoric, having defeated his rival, Odoacer, at Ravenna, made the city the capital of the new Ostrogothic kingdom of Italy. Elsewhere, the map of western Europe was as comprehensively redrawn. The Sueves and the Visigoths had settled in Iberia, the Franks in much of France and Germany, the Burgundians in southeast France, the Saxons in Britain. Most of Rome's former North African provinces were ruled by the Vandals.

Despite the reputation of these peoples as the barbarous destroyers of Roman civilization, their ambition was to enjoy the culture, prosperity, and material comforts of the Roman way of life. Their leaders were quick to adopt the Christian religion and some made politically advantageous marriages with Byzantine princesses. However, disputes over the succession frequently led to further periods of civil war and the structures the Romans had built up over the centuries for administering justice and collecting taxes

soon crumbled, as did the physical structures, such as roads and aqueducts, on which their cities and towns depended.

Flourishing economies

Elsewhere, other powers prospered. The Red Sea kingdom of Axum had emerged as a major trading center as early as 50 CE, its wealth based on control of seaborne trade between India and Rome. From the 4th century, it would also become a key outpost of Christianity in Africa. In West Africa, trans-Saharan trade was being revolutionized by the introduction of the camel for transportation. Berber nomads from North Africa dominated the trade, bringing West African gold and ivory from the southern Sahara to the Mediterranean.

The Gupta empire

In India, the Gupta dynasty also grew in power and influence after about 320. By the end of the 4th century, the Guptas dominated north India, ushering in a "golden age" of Sanskrit literature, poetry, sculpture, and architecture. Although the dynasty presided over a resurgence of Hinduism at the expense of Buddhism, this was nevertheless a period of great religious toleration. The Gupta

This Indian ivory was part of an eclectic hoard discovered at Begram in the Hindu Kush. It lay alongside Roman glassware, Greco-Roman statuary, and Chinese lacquerware, striking evidence of the extent of trade across Eurasia.

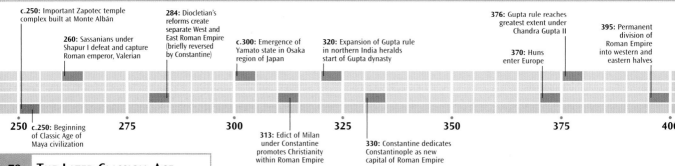

c.250: Important Zapotec temple complex built at Monte Albán

260: Sassanians under Shapur I defeat and capture Roman emperor, Valerian

284: Diocletian's reforms create separate West and East Roman Empire (briefly reversed by Constantine)

c.300: Emergence of Yamato state in Osaka region of Japan

320: Expansion of Gupta rule in northern India heralds start of Gupta dynasty

376: Gupta rule reaches greatest extent under Chandra Gupta II

370: Huns enter Europe

395: Permanent division of Roman Empire into western and eastern halves

250   275   300   325   350   375   400

c.250: Beginning of Classic Age of Maya civilization

313: Edict of Milan under Constantine promotes Christianity within Roman Empire

330: Constantine dedicates Constantinople as new capital of Roman Empire

THE EXPANDING WORLD VIEW

Though there is no direct evidence of first-hand contact between Rome and Han China, developing trade links helped build an increasingly detailed picture of the world, or at any rate of Eurasia and North Africa. As early as 20 CE the Greek geographer Strabo gave a detailed description of the known world in his 20-volume *Geography*. Building on this tradition, in 150 CE the Alexandrian geographer Ptolemy published his own *Geography*, which was to influence cartographers for the next 1,500 years. Though none of his own maps survived – if indeed he made any – Greek, Roman, Arab, and medieval European geographers and map-makers all blindly followed the authority of Ptolemy. The *Geography* gives instructions for drawing maps of what he believed to be the entire inhabited world, together with the longitudes and latitudes of some 8,000 locations in Europe, Africa, and Asia.

Medieval and Renaissance reconstructions reveal the extent of Ptolemy's information. China (Sinae) and Chang'an (Sera Metropolis) were both known to him, as was Ceylon (Taprobane). He also used lines of latitude and longitude. His *Geography* was still a standard source when Columbus sailed to the Americas in 1492.

empire came to an end in c.480 following a series of invasions of northern India by the Hephthalites (White Huns).

Although Buddhism lost adherents in its homeland of northern India during this period, it became widely diffused across other parts of Asia. As well as putting down firm roots in Sri Lanka and parts of Southeast Asia, Buddhism was carried through China, where it became a state religion, to Korea, eventually reaching Japan in c.550 CE.

New World cultures

Perhaps the most notable advances in the spread of civilization were in Central America where two distinct cultures emerged: in Mexico after about 1 CE; and on the Yucatán peninsula, which from about 200 became the site of a flourishing Maya civilization. City-states controlled both areas. In the Maya area, these were small, multicity regional polities or autonomous cities. Mexico, by contrast, was dominated by a series of empires, of which the most important was centered on Teotihuacán. By 500, the city's population may have been as much as 500,000. The Later, or Classic, Maya civilization can also lay claim to having been the first fully literate culture of the Americas, developing a hieroglyphic writing system. It also used a complex calendrical system, dating back to the Mayan year zero, 3114 BCE.

In South America, the most significant civilizations continued to be found in the Andes and along the coast of Peru. The largest of these, the Moche, creators of magnificent figurative pottery, emerged in the 1st century CE. To the south of the Moche lay the heartland of the mysterious Nazca, whose vast stylized drawings on the surface of the desert were designed to be viewed from the sky.

The decorative styles of Teotihuacán, as in this mosaic mask of turquoise and coral with obsidian and shells used for the eyes – influenced later Central American cultures such as the Toltecs and the Aztecs.

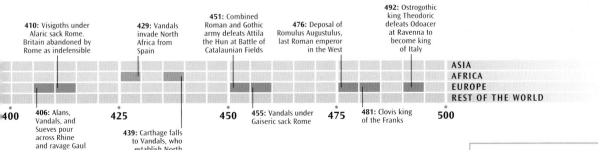

410: Visigoths under Alaric sack Rome. Britain abandoned by Rome as indefensible

429: Vandals invade North Africa from Spain

451: Combined Roman and Gothic army defeats Attila the Hun at Battle of Catalaunian Fields

476: Deposal of Romulus Augustulus, last Roman emperor in the West

492: Ostrogothic king Theodoric defeats Odoacer at Ravenna to become king of Italy

ASIA
AFRICA
EUROPE
REST OF THE WORLD

400

406: Alans, Vandals, and Sueves pour across Rhine and ravage Gaul

425

439: Carthage falls to Vandals, who establish North African Kingdom

450

455: Vandals under Gaiseric sack Rome

475

481: Clovis king of the Franks

500

The realistic and sensitive modeling of the features on this stirrup-spouted portrait vessel reveals the great skill of the Moche craftsman.

Moche culture

The Moche people of northern Peru, who flourished in the first six centuries CE built some of the largest monuments in South America. The Temple of the Sun at Moche was built of adobe brick, and was 130 feet (40 m) high and 1,150 feet (350 m) long. The Moche expanded their territory by force, building roads, fortifications, and elaborate irrigation channels. Their leaders were buried in great splendor, with goldwork, textiles, and pottery. High and low relief pots were hand-modeled and decorated with scenes from everyday life, ritual ceremonies, and mythology.

ASIA

c.1 Kushans invade NW India.

Funan, precursor of Cambodia, arises as first Hinduized state of SE Asia in 1st century CE.

Buddhism starts to spread to many coastal localities of mainland SE Asia during 1st century CE.

2 First census of Chinese population.

6 Judaea is placed under Roman military procurator.

12 Artabanus II becomes king of Parthia, following his victory over the Pahlavas, a tribe of warrior horsemen related to the Scythians.

14 Hippalus sails through Red Sea to the Indus (–37).

17 Cappadocia and Antiochus, in Asia Minor, are annexed to Rome.

The prolific poet, Ovid, dies in exile following his banishment by Augustus.

18 Artaxias (Zeno) is installed on the Armenian throne.

19 Germanicus, conqueror of the German armies, dies in Syria. Tiberius is implicated in his death.

23 Rebellions and insurrections sweep away Wang Mang's interregnum Xin dynasty in China.

25 In Gandhara, the Buddha is represented for the first time in human form.

A new Chinese dynasty, known as the Eastern Han, is established. The capital at Luoyang is reinstated.

c.29 Crucifixion of Christ.

35 Artabanus III of Persia is overthrown by his cousin, with Rome's support.

36 Artabanus III, restored to the throne, is recognized as king of Parthia, and accepts the Armenian protectorate.

43 Chinese crush a revolt, led by sisters Trung Trac and Trung Nhu, in Vietnam.

44 Judaea is annexed to the Roman Empire.

47 Journeys of St. Paul (–57).

48 Eastern Han emperor, Guang Wudi reestablishes Chinese dominion over the peoples of inner Mongolia.

AFRICA

c.1 Sheep herded by Khoisans in S Africa.

9 The ruler of Cush, King Nakatamani, is renovating cities and founding temples and palaces.

17 Revolt by Numidians against Romans, led by King Tacfarinas (–24).

40 King Ptolemy of Mauretania, a Moorish kingdom in NW Africa, is assassinated by Caligula during a visit to Rome. Following his murder, the Mauri rise up against Rome.

41 Interracial violence in Alexandria between Greek and Jewish inhabitants.

42 The Romans suppress the Mauri revolt and pacify Mauretania.

44 Client kingdom of Mauretania annexed by Rome.

c.50 Kingdom of Axum starts to emerge.

EUROPE	AMERICAS & AUSTRALASIA

EUROPE

4 Tiberius adopted son of Augsustus becomes tribune and adopts his nephew, Germanicus.

6 Planned conquest of C Europe abandoned after rebellion in the Balkans (–9).

9 Three Roman legions wiped out by Germans. Roman frontier pulled back to the Rhine.

New province of Pannonia secures Danube frontier.

14 Emperor Augustus dies, succeeded by his stepson Tiberius (–37).

17 Germanicus, adopted son of Tiberius, wins a great victory over the Germans.

21 A revolt among the Gallic tribes, the Treveri and Aedui, is swiftly suppressed.

26 Tiberius retires to island of Capri. The most powerful man in Rome is now Sejanus, corrupt prefect of the praetorian guard, who is killed in 31 CE.

37 Reign of Gaius Caligula (–41), great-nephew of Tiberius. He proceeds to squander money, while having many of his relatives murdered.

41 Caligula assassinated. Reign of Caligula's uncle, Claudius (–54).

43 Roman invasion of Britain under Aulus Plautius.

46 The kingdom of Thrace becomes a province of Rome.

48 Noblemen from Gaul are given access to the senate.

AMERICAS & AUSTRALASIA

c.290

c.1 Moche culture is flourishing. The Moche, famous for their gold and pottery, substantial buildings, and irrigation works, dominate N Peru.

Maya complexes start to appear at sites such as El Mirador.

Hieroglyphic writing and the use of the "Long Count" calendar is developing in the Maya area of SE Mexico.

Basketmaker II Period in southwest N America. Hamlets contain up to 11 circular houses.

c.40 The Arawak people have migrated down the Orinoco river, and are settling in many W Indian islands.

Ara Pacis Augustae

Augustus asserted that he had found Rome a city of brick and left it a city of marble. Augustus' ambitious building program proclaimed Rome's renewed power and confidence. The Altar of Augustan Peace (*above*, 13 BCE) used its sculpted relief panels as propaganda. It borrowed from Greek forms to illustrate the essential values that Augustus stood for: solemnity, family life, humanity, and peace.

Emperor Augustus (27 BCE–14 CE)

Augustus claimed to have restored the Roman republic; in fact, he ruled with absolute authority under the cloak of republican forms. He transformed Rome into a capital worthy of a great empire, concentrating on public works. Monumental depictions of the emperor emphasize his sense of command and self-confidence.

Augustus is portrayed in full dress uniform.

Pompeii

The provincial town of Pompeii in southern Italy lay in the shadow of Mount Vesuvius, surrounded by a fertile hinterland. Wealthy citizens lived in luxurious townhouses, richly decorated with wall paintings that advertized the wealth, refinement, and status of the erstwhile inhabitants. These houses were focused around the atrium, an open hall, and the colonnaded garden. They stood in close proximity

A mosaic from Pompeii depicts a poet or princess. Houses were lavishly decorated with colored stuccowork, mosaic pavements, and wall paintings.

to the rabbit warren of tiny apartments or *tabernae* (shops) occupied by the poor.

On August 24, 79 CE Vesuvius erupted, ejecting a mushroom-shaped cloud of volcanic debris. These fragments of pumice stone showered Pompeii, forming a layer 10 feet (3 m) thick, but were not lethal to the inhabitants, many of whom escaped. The eyewitness Pliny described the scene: "A dark and horrible cloud was coming up behind us as we were fleeing, spreading over the earth like a flood." Within 12 hours a thick, asphyxiating cloud of ash and poisonous gases suffocated the remaining inhabitants. Their bodies left imprints in the volcanic ash, which hardened around them, preserving the town and its people intact.

The bodies of the victims of Vesuvius have been recovered by pouring plaster into the imprints they left in the volcanic ash. Many were found, frozen in self-protective postures, in the cellars and bedrooms in which they took refuge.

51–100 CE

ASIA

53 Vologeses, king of Parthia, challenges Rome by putting his brother, Tiridates on the Armenian throne.

57 An ambassador from the king of Nu (Japan), arrives at Luoyang, capital of China, and is recognized by the Han emperor.

58 Armenia becomes a Roman protectorate.

60 Establishment of Kushan empire.

c.60 Mark, one of the disciples of Jesus of Nazareth, begins his account of the life of Christ.

Kushans, under Kujula Kadphises, unite Yuezhi tribes and advance into N India.

63 Peace of Rhandeia; Tiridates returns to Armenian throne.

65 First evidence of Buddhism in China.

66 Start of First Jewish Revolt against Roman rule (–70).

67 Roman emperor Vespasian invades Judaea; recovers Galilee.

70 Romans suppress Jewish Revolt and destroy temple in Jerusalem. Province of Judaea established.

73 Peak of Han military success. Chinese now control western oasis states.

73 Romans take Masada.

132 ▼ **75** A general uprising in the Tarim basin area is suppressed by the Han army.

78 Kushan king, Vima Kadphises, ruler of N India, sends a delegation to Rome to arrange a surprise attack on the Parthians.

c.80 The apostle Luke begins to write his gospel.

87 Embassy from the Indian Kushans arrives in Luoyang.

88 Abolition of Chinese state monopolies on iron and salt.

c.90 Shakas invade northwest S Asia.

125 ▼ **91** Han defeat Xiongnu in China, forcing them westward.

c.150 ▼ **99** Indian embassy to court of Trajan in Rome, probably to announce Kushan conquests.

Kushan emperor, Kanishka propagates Buddhism over much of C Asia in late 1st century CE.

AFRICA

60 Nero sends expedition to explore Meroë (Sudan).

69 Romans defeat powerful Saharan kingdom of Garamantes, but do not absorb it into empire.

c.70 Pottery typical of early iron-users is now being made as far south as Maputo, in Mozambique.

100 Roman colonies are established at Thamugadi (Timgad) and Lambaesis, Numidia, N Africa. Trajan bases the only African legion at Thamugadi.

c.150 ▼ **c.100** Alexandria emerges as a center of Christian scholarship, seat of one of the earliest Christian bishoprics.

EUROPE

51 Romans capture Caractacus, the leader of British resistance to Roman occupation.

52 Paul of Tarsus arrives in Corinth, and embarks on his Christian evangelization of Greece.

54 After his murder by his wife Agrippina, Claudius is succeeded by his stepson, Nero.

59 Agrippina is assassinated on her son's orders.

60 Revolt of Iceni in Britain under Boudicca. Crushed in 61.

c.62–68 Probable martyrdom of St. Paul by Nero (37–68).

Rome is devastated by fire. Christians are made scapegoats.

65 A conspiracy to assassinate Nero is discovered. The plotters, including the writers Seneca and Petronius, are forced to commit suicide.

67 Nero orders the construction of a canal through the isthmus of Corinth.

68 Uprisings against Nero in Spain and Gaul. Nero, out of favor with the senate, commits suicide.

69 Year of the Four Emperors. Danubian armies lead an invasion of Italy in support of their candidate, Vespasian, who is adopted as emperor (–79).

74 Vespasian gives town dwellers the same civil rights as citizens.

79 Vesuvius erupts, destroying Pompeii and Herculaneum.

85 Spanish poet Martial publishes a collection of pithy, satirical epigrams.

Roman forces under Agricola defeat Caledonians and circumnavigate British Isles.

Emperor Domitian repulses a Dacian invasion of Moesia.

89 Domitian is defeated by Dacia (Romania) and its allies, is forced to sign a humiliating treaty with the Dacian king.

Domitian banishes the philosophers from Rome.

96 Domitian, who has been conducting a reign of terror in Rome, is assassinated.

98 Trajan, Spanish-born governor of lower Germany, becomes emperor. He institutes many liberal reforms.

AMERICAS & AUSTRALASIA

100 Emergence of the Anasazi, Hohokam and Mogollon cultures in southwest of N America.

c.100 City of Teotihuacán begins to expand; 90 percent of local population move to the city.

The Pyramids of the Sun and Moon are under construction at Teotihuacán, Mexico.

Masada

The impregnable mountain-top fortress of Masada, in southeastern Israel, was fortified by King Herod as a secure palace, complete with heated baths, storerooms, and a synagogue. At the beginning of the Jewish Revolt against Roman rule (66–70) the Zealots, a Jewish sect strongly opposed to domination by Rome, took over the fort. In 70, Roman forces besieged the site, which could only be approached by the precipitous Snake Path, eventually manoeuvring their siege engines up a purpose-built ramp. The siege ended in 73, but the Zealots preferred death to enslavement and the conquerers found that the defenders had taken their own lives.

Roman Literature

The outstanding literature of imperial Rome ranges from epic poetry to natural history, encyclopedias, satire, treatises, and political polemics.

(Arranged in order of birth dates)

100–44 BCE Julius Caesar; *Gallic War; Civil Wars.*

c.99–55 BCE Lucretius; *The Nature of Things* (philosophical poem).

86–35 BCE Sallust; *The Jugurthine War, The Catiline Conspiracy.*

c.85–54 BCE Catullus; poems and epigrams.

70–19 BCE Virgil; *Georgics, Eclogues, Aeneid.*

65–8 BCE Horace; *Odes, Carmen, Saeculare.*

64 BCE–21 CE Strabo; *Geography.*

43 BCE–18 CE Ovid; *The Art of Love, Metamorphoses.*

39–65 CE Lucan; *Pharsalia* (heroic poem).

34–c.98 CE Josephus; *History of the Jewish Wars, Jewish Antiquities.*

23–79 CE Pliny the Elder; *Natural History.*

40–104 CE Martial; *Epigrams.*

c.55–117 CE Tacitus; *Annals; Histories; Agricola; Germania.*

61–119 CE Pliny the Younger; *Panegyric of Trajan,* letters.

c.45–125 CE Plutarch; *Parallel Lives.*

60–c.130 CE Juvenal; *Satires.*

A Chinese worker lifts a mesh screen covered with a thin layer of pulp that will drain and dry to form a sheet of paper.

The invention of paper: 105 CE

Cai Lun, a eunuch serving in China's imperial court, invented paper by soaking and pounding flat the bark of trees, rag, hemp, and old fishing nets. Solid ink was rubbed onto an inkstone with water, then a brush was used to apply the liquid ink to the paper. With this innovation, the Chinese were able to discard expensive bamboo blocks and silk and adopt a cheap, and easily transportable, writing medium.

Roman Imperial Conquests (50 BCE–117 CE)

On his accession, Augustus greatly expanded the empire, rationalizing imperial frontiers through his conquests in the Alps and Balkans. His successors consolidated these major gains

(Showing date of conquest or annexation by Rome)

46 BCE	Numidia
33 BCE	Dalmatia
30 BCE	Aegyptus
29 BCE	Moesia Superior
25 BCE	Galatia
15 BCE	Raetia
15 BCE	Noricum
9 BCE	Pannonia Superior, Pannonia Inferior
6 CE	Judaea
17 CE	Cappadocia
43 CE	Britannia (south)
44 CE	Mauretania
46 CE	Thracia
74 CE	Lycia, Rhodus
78 CE	Britannia (north)
83 CE	Germania Inferior, Germania Superior
106 CE	Arabia
105 CE	Dacia
114 CE	Armenia (–117), Assyria (–117)
115 CE	Mesopotamia (–117)

ASIA

c.102 Death of the greatest Kushan ruler, Kanishka.

105 Paper is invented in Han China.

106 The kingdom of Nabataea, with its capital at Petra, is invaded, annexed, and becomes the Roman province of Arabia.

c.110 A grand Buddhist council is held in Kashmir. Buddhism is divided into two branches: Mahayana and Hinayana.

114 Emperor Trajan annexes Armenia, takes Seleucia, and reaches Persian Gulf (–117).

117 Death of Trajan; Rome gives up his conquests in Mesopotamia.

Trajan's heir, Hadrian, abandons Mesopotamia and Assyria.

120 An embassy from the Shan kingdom of Burma offers the Han court, based at Luoyang, dancers and tumblers from East Roman Empire.

125 Gautamiputra Satakarni, king of the Andhra dynasty of E Deccan, destroys the Shaka kingdom of Maharashtra.

132 Second Jewish Revolt (–135), led by Bar Cochba, precipitates diaspora. Jerusalem refounded as Roman city, Aelia Capitolina.

154 **134** Alans, nomadic pastoralists from SE Russia, attack Cappadocia, but are repulsed.

135 Hadrian proceeds with building of Aelia Capitolina on ruins of Jerusalem.

The Chinese repel a Kushan attempt to conquer the Tarim basin.

c.150 Kushans become Persian vassals.

Han have reestablished their dominion over C Asia.

AFRICA

132 **115** Revolt of Jewish community in Cyrenaica (NE Libya) against Roman administration.

128 Hadrian reviews the troops stationed in the province of N Africa.

130 In Egypt, Hadrian founds the city of Antinoopolis in memory of his lover, Antinous

c.150 Christianity starts to spread westward to Roman provinces of Numidia and Mauretania.

Ptolemy of Alexandria writes his *Geography*; publishes first World Atlas.

In Nigeria, the Nok Iron Age culture reaches its apogee, producing exquisite terra-cotta sculptures.

101 Trajan invades Dacia (Romania), forcing King Decebalus into an alliance (–102).

105 Following Decebalus's siege of the Roman garrisons, Trajan recaptures the capital. Dacia becomes a Roman province (–106).

113 Completion of Trajan's magnificent new Forum in Rome.

117 Roman Empire at maximum extent on death of Trajan in this year.

118 Hadrian subdues an uprising in Moesia by the Roxolani, a Sarmatian tribe.

165

122 Hadrian's Wall built as defensive frontier in N Britain (–128).

c.125 Death of Plutarch, writer, moralist, and politician. His most famous work, *Parallel Lives*, comprises biographies of key historical figures.

127 Hadrian returns to Rome after seven years of touring the provinces.

c.130 Hadrian has a palatial villa erected at Tivoli.

138 Hadrian is succeeded by Titus Antoninus Pius, whom he has adopted.

142 Anti-Roman revolt amongst Brigantes of Britain (–143).

161

147 Antoninus celebrates the 900th anniversary of Rome's foundation.

Trajan's Column

Erected in 113, Trajan's Column was part of a great Forum and market in Rome. The column presents a narrative of Trajan's two Dacian wars (101–02 and 105–06), shown in the form of a continuous, spiraling relief, some 650 feet (200 m) long. The reliefs are a vivid, and accurate, depiction of the Roman army – marching, engineering, building, worshiping. Scenes showing the Romans striking camp and assaulting fortifications have revealed much to later historians about Roman warfare. Throughout, Trajan himself is presented as a modest, comradely soldier and is depicted reviewing his troops, receiving embassies, making sacrifices, or in contemplative mood.

Gandhara Buddha

The Gandharan style of Buddhist art developed in what is now northwestern Pakistan and eastern Afghanistan between the 1st century BCE and 7th century CE. Part of the Kushan empire, Gandhara maintained close contact with Rome, and incorporated many Roman motifs, including scrolls, cherubs, and centaurs, into its Buddhist art, although the iconography remains Indian. Gandharan art depicted the Buddha for the first time, representing him as a youthful Apollo-like figure.

Sculpture of the Buddha represented in the Gandharan style, which is clearly influenced by Graeco-Roman art.

Early Christianity

The 2nd century was a time of persecution for the Christians of the Roman empire. Many became martyrs, or were forced to recant their faith. Yet, despite their understandable wariness of pagan persecutors, they used symbols to identify themselves. The cross commemorated Christ's crucifixion; the fish became a symbol of Christ – the letters of the Greek word *ichthus* (fish) make up the initials of his title: *Jesou Christos Theou Uios Soter* (Jesus Christ, Son of God, Savior).

Stone slab engraved with fish and cross from Egypt.

Han China

The Han ruled China for over 400 years, establishing an authoritarian, centralized regime. They extended Chinese control into Central Asia, establishing a domain that was by far the greatest the world had yet seen. Their military garrisons, or commanderies, were established throughout the empire, protecting the great trans-Asian trade routes that underpinned their economic stability. By 2 CE, an imperial census revealed a Chinese population of over 57 million, mainly concentrated in the north.

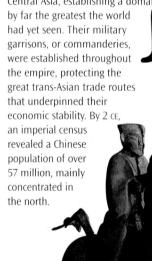

This bronze model of a mounted guard was found among the goods in the grave of a high-ranking officer of the Han period.

151–200 CE

ASIA

154 Kingdoms of Bosporus and Black Sea turn to Rome for protection against Alans from the Caucasus.

155 Inconclusive peace following Parthians' attempt to conquer Armenia.

159 Han imperial family feuds hand effective power to court eunuchs.

162 Parthians install king on Armenian throne and launch attack on Syria.

163 Parthians are expelled from Armenia. New capital founded at Valarshapat.

165 The governor of Syria, Avidius Cassius sacks Seleucia and Ctesiphon.

166 Roman coemperor Verus makes peace with Parthians.

Embassy of Syrian merchants arrives in China.

168 Following the death of Emperor Huandi, palace eunuchs reassert their power. Han empire is in decline.

184 Revolt of the Yellow Turbans, an insurgent group, in China.

c.220 ▼ **189** General Dong Zhuo ends the rule of the eunuchs and takes power in China.

c.192 Establishment of Lin-yi Champa, longest-lived Hinduized state of SE Asia.

193 Roman army in the east proclaims Pescennius Niger, governor of Syria, emperor.

194 Pescennius Niger is defeated and executed; Syria is divided into two provinces.

195 Xiongnu nomads are settled in N China, where they present a continuing threat.

216 ▼ **197** Septimius Severus sails down Euphrates to invade Parthian empire.

198 N Mesopotamia made Roman province.

c.200 Cities appear for first time on Deccan plateau in India.

India's trading links with classical western world and China at their height.

End of Chinese occupation of Korea; growth of native Korean states of Koguryo, Paekche, Silla.

AFRICA

160 Rome's crippling tax demands are destroying the Egyptian economy.

297 ▼ **173** Avidius Cassius is made governor of the East Roman Empire. He crushes the insurrections of shepherd brigands (*boukoloi*) in Egypt.

c.190 Iron-using cultures have spread as far south as the Limpopo valley, Zimbabwe, and Botswana.

c.200 The first human settlements have been established on the island of Madagascar.

Ghana, a state in the savannah region, is gaining wealth and power through contacts with Berber traders.

160 The *limes* (fortified frontier) of the Rhine is extended beyond the Neckar valley.

161 Accession of Marcus Aurelius as Roman emperor.

Marcus Aurelius makes his adoptive brother Lucius Verus coemperor, the first time that two emperors have shared the throne.

165 In Britain, Romans abandon the Antonine Wall (built in 143), and retreat to Hadrian's Wall.

166 German tribes pour across the Danube and invade N Italy.

167 Rome is ravaged by plague.

175 Marcus Aurelius imposes peace on the Sarmatian Iazyges in the Danube region.

177 In the Balkans, the Quadi and Marcomanni declare war on the Roman Empire.

179 Decisive victory over Germanic Marcommani at Vindobona on the Danube.

238

c.180 A Germanic people from S Scandinavia, the Goths, are settling on the shores of the Black Sea.

187 The Chatti, a Germanic tribe which has been threatening the Black Forest area of Germany, is conquered.

192 Emperor Commodus, the son of Marcus Aurelius is assassinated. A civil war follows, as four emperors now contend for power.

193 Septimius Severus, a respected soldier, is declared emperor by the army in Illyricum. He makes an uncontested entry into Rome.

196 Clodius Albinus, governor of Britain, is declared emperor by his army, and crosses to Gaul.

211

197 At the battle of Lugdunum (Lyons), Septimius Severus defeats Clodius Albinus, reuniting the Roman Empire.

Britain is divided into two provinces.

c.200 Teotihuancán in Mexico is now the largest city in the Americas.

Hopewell moundbuilding culture flourishes in N America.

290

The Maya city of Tikal in C America rises to importance.

An ivory openwork plaque from India, one of the treasures of the Begram hoard.

The Silk Road

Chinese silk first appeared in the Mediterranean region during the 6th century BCE, marking the beginning of 1,500 years of overland trade across Asia. Much of this trade was carried along the Silk Road, a collection of caravan routes that connected the isolated oasis towns that lie scattered across the barren deserts of Central Asia, linking China with West Asia and Europe.

Chinese silk was much sought after in Rome; Pliny the Elder complained about the lavish and decadent use of the new material. Other Chinese exports include spices, lacquerware, and bronze. The west, in turn, probably exported a variety of goods – coins, ivory, precious stones, glass vessels – to Asia. At the city of Begram, situated to the north of Kabul in Afghanistan, archaeologists excavated a storehouse of diverse objects from China, India, and the Mediterranean, dating to the 1st–2nd centuries CE a testament to the diversity and range of Silk Road trade.

Hopewell culture

The Hopewell culture of North America's eastern woodlands (a zone that centers on Ohio), flourished between c.300 BCE–500 CE. The chief archaeological remains are extensive earthworks, consisting of large enclosures containing burials, linked by long causeways. These burials were accompanied by large collections of grave goods, including flint and obsidian spearthrowers, knives, and polished axes. Beautifully crafted Hopewell effigy pipes, such as this frog pipe, reveal the importance of ceremonial tobacco-smoking among the native peoples of North America.

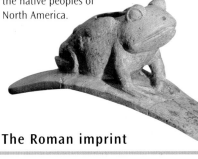

The Roman imprint

When the Romans took command of Egypt in 30 BCE, the Greek community continued to flourish, and Greek remained the official language of the government. The Romans continued the Egyptian tradition of mummification. Instead of placing a mask over the face, as had been the earlier practice, the Romans inserted a portrait board, painted in melted wax paint. These naturalistic portraits were painted from life, and are reminiscent of portraits from Pompeii and Herculaneum, although many sitters have Egyptian attributes, including jewelry and clothing.

ASIA

279 ▼
216 Romans invade Parthia and attack Arbela.

219 A Hebrew edition of the *Mishna*, a collection of sayings and teachings drawn from the Torah, is published.

c.220 Collapse of Han dynasty; replaced by three kingdoms: Shu, Wu, and Wei.

224 Parthia falls to the Sassanians under Ardashir I who founds a new dynasty.

229 There are three emperors reigning in China.

230 Ardashir invades Syria.

253 ▼
232 Romans expel Ardashir from Mesopotamia and Cappadocia.

238 Carrhae and Nisibis fall to Persian king, Ardashir.

242 The Kushans confront the Sassanians in Bactria.

247 Queen Himiko of Yamatai, Japan, goes to war with the king of nearby Kunukoku. Civil war follows.

265 ▼
249 Following a palace coup, the Wei dynasty of China exists only in name.

c.250 Lodestone compass used in China.

AFRICA

238 Gordian, governor of Africa, is proclaimed emperor by rebels. He dies after defeat by Numidians, following a "reign" of just 22 days.

c.300 ▼
c.250 Axum is growing into a powerful kingdom under the rule of King Aphilas.

EUROPE

202 An edict is issued against Christianity in the Roman Empire.

210 The Romans make peace with the Scots.

211 Septimius Severus dies of natural causes at Eburacum (York).

212 Caracalla murders his cosuccessor Geta, and unleashes bloody repression in Rome. He grants Roman citizenship to virtually all free inhabitants of the Empire.

222 During an anti-Christian popular rising in Rome, Pope Callistus is killed.

235 A period of 50 years of military anarchy begins (–285). There are nearly 20 Roman emperors.

253 ▼ **c.235** Raids by Germanic Alemanni league against upper Rhine and Black Forest frontiers.

267 ▼ **238** Goths and Carpi cross the Danube and invade the province of Moesia. Rome pays them tribute.

242 The Cimmerian Bosporus (S Russia) falls under the domination of Ostrogoths.

c.250 Period of civil wars and runaway inflation in Roman Empire.

AMERICAS & AUSTRALASIA

c.250 Tiahuanaco becomes a large town, both an economic and cult center.

Beginnings of Classic Maya civilization.

Roman Emperors

(Some brief reigns omitted. Co-rule is indicated by overlapping dates)

27 BCE–14 CE	Augustus
14–37	Tiberius
37–41	Caligula
41–54	Claudius
54–68	Nero
68–69	Galba
69	Otho
69	Vitellius
69–79	Vespasian
79–81	Titus
81–96	Domitian
96–98	Nerva
98–117	Trajan
117–138	Hadrian
138–161	Titus Antoninus Pius
161–180	Marcus Aurelius
180–192	Commodus
193	Pertinax
193	Didus Julianus
193–211	Septimius Severus
211(198)–217	Caracalla
209–211	Geta
217–218	Macrinus
218–222	Elagabalus
222–235	Alexander Severus
235–238	Maximin
237–238	Gordian I
238–244	Gordian III
244–249	Philipp ("Arabs")
249–251	Decius
251–253	Gallus
253–259	Valerian
259(255)–268	Gallien
268–270	Claudius II
270–275	Aurelian
276–282	Probus
281–283	Carus
284–305	Diocletian and the Tetrarchy
303–313	Constantine and the Later Tetrarchy
313–324	Joint rule of Constantine and Licinius
324–337	Constantine

Emperor Septimius Severus was a martial leader, who fought wars in Britain and the East. In Italy, however, his reign was characterized by economic decline.

This iron Bactrian plaque, plated in sheet gold with turquoise gems, and depicting a horseman, is typical of the intricate, but very portable, art of the steppe peoples.

Steppe warriors

The steppe peoples of Central Asia and Mongolia formed hierarchical societies, with warrior chiefs and tribesmen. Warfare was an endemic feature of steppe life, and these redoubtable warriors were skilled horsemen, highly mobile, and adept with reflex bows, swords, and lances. Between the 3rd and 6th centuries CE, they began to organize themselves into military confederations. Lacking in natural resources, they preyed on the settled civilizations to the south, wreaking havoc and destruction.

Early Christianity

c.29	Crucifixion of Jesus Christ.
47	St. Paul embarks on his missionary travels.
51	St. Paul's mission to Europe.
58	St. Paul's *Letter to the Corinthians*.
64	Fire of Rome; Emperor Nero begins persecution of Christians.
c.60	Gospel according to St. Mark.
c.62–8	Martyrdom of St. Paul.
64	St. Peter executed.
70	Jerusalem destroyed.
85	Gospels according to St. John and St. Matthew.
112	Martyrdom of Ignatius, bishop of Antioch.
156	Martyrdom of Polycarp, bishop of Smyrna.
165	Martyrdom of Justin; philosopher and Christian convert.
c.200	Bishop of Rome gains prominent position as pope.
300	Armenia is converted to Christianity, the first state to accept Christianity as a state religion.
304	Edicts of Diocletian provide for arrests of "church leaders," destruction of churches, and confiscation of books and sacred vessels.
c.310	The hermit, Antony of Egypt, founds tradition of desert hermits and monks.
313	Edict of Milan; Constantine grants Christians freedom of worship.
318	Arian heresy teaches that Son of God was not coequal and coessential with the Father.
321	Recognition of Sunday as day of rest.
325	Council of Nicaea, Bithynia, asserts that Christ is "of one substance with the Father."
329	Basilican Church of St. Peter's built in Rome.
341	Bible translated into Gothic.

253 Sassanians defeat Romans and take Antioch.

260 At Edessa, Sassanians under Shapur I defeat and capture Roman emperor, Valerian.

265 Western Jin take over Wei state in China.

267 Odenathus, prince of Palmyra and a long-standing ally of Rome, is murdered, apparently on the emperor's orders.

269 **270** Zenobia, widow of Odenathus of Palmyra, gains control of most of Asia Minor.

271 Zenobia declares herself empress and breaks with the Roman Empire.

272 Aurelian reoccupies Anatolia and takes Queen Zenobia prisoner.

273 A revolt in Palmyra, Syria, is suppressed by Aurelian.

275 Aurelian is murdered at Byzantium, the result of a military plot.

277 Mani, the Persian founder of Manichaeism, a religious sect relating to Christianity, is crucified by Sassanians.

279 Jewish scholars based in Tiberias issue a collection of Jewish laws, doctrines, and legends, called the *Talmud*.

280 Western Jin conquer S China.

Sima Yao, leader of the Jin dynasty, unites China.

304 **291** Steppe peoples from beyond the Great Wall allowed to settle within Chinese empire.

296 Sassanians occupy Armenia and defeat Roman emperor, Galerius.

298 Treaty of Nisibis affirms Roman supremacy over Armenia and ensures peace for next 40 years.

300 Armenia is converted to Christianity, the first state to accept Christianity as a state religion.

c.300 The *Kama Sutra*, or "Aphorisms on Love," is written by Vatsyayana in Benares, India.

Rice cultivation in Japan reaches N Honshu.

Emergence of Yamato state in Japan.

258 Cyprianus, the bishop of Carthage, is martyred.

269 Zenobia of Palmyra conquers Egypt.

271 Roman troops are sent to Egypt. Aurelian loses his general, Probus, in a battle for control of the country.

310 **c.280** Pappus of Alexandria publishes his *Mathematical Collection*, and describes five machines in use: cogwheel, pulley, lever, screw, and wedge.

297 A second revolt in Egypt is put down by Emperor Diocletian. He begins reorganization of local government in N Africa.

320 **c.300** Bantu cereal cultivators in SE Africa begin to herd cattle.

Axumites start minting their own coinage.

EUROPE

253 Franks and Alemanni invade Gaul.

304

257 Edict issued forbidding Christian worship.

258 Alemanni and Suevi conquer N Italy, but are defeated at Milan.

260 Gallic empire established by Postumus.

267 Goths pillage Thrace, Macedonia, and Greece.

271 Romans evacuate Dacia.

Emperor Aurelian orders Rome's fortification with new walls.

273 Roman Empire reunited by Aurelian (end of Gallic empire).

274 Mithras admitted into pantheons of Roman Empire.

275 Gaul is pillaged by Franks and Alemanni.

277 Final pacification of Gaul.

306

284 Diocletian divides empire into Eastern and Western halves.

287 Carausius, admiral of the Channel fleet, seizes control of Britain and N Gaul.

293 Diocletian establishes Tetrarchy and twelve dioceses.

296 The province of Britain is recovered by Emperor Constantius Chlorus.

AMERICAS & AUSTRALASIA

c.290 Moche elite are buried in richly furnished graves at Sipán, accompanied by attendants, and adorned with gold and silver jewelry.

292 Stela 29, found at Tikal, has a "Long Count" date of 292. One of the earliest objects inscribed with the fully developed Maya calendar.

c.300 Settlement of Rapa Nui (Easter Island).

Yayoi Japan

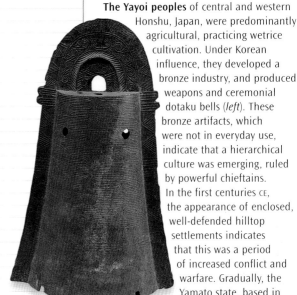

The Yayoi peoples of central and western Honshu, Japan, were predominantly agricultural, practicing wetrice cultivation. Under Korean influence, they developed a bronze industry, and produced weapons and ceremonial dotaku bells (*left*). These bronze artifacts, which were not in everyday use, indicate that a hierarchical culture was emerging, ruled by powerful chieftains. In the first centuries CE, the appearance of enclosed, well-defended hilltop settlements indicates that this was a period of increased conflict and warfare. Gradually, the Yamato state, based in the Kinai region, began to extend its hegemony over much of Japan, dominating the region between 300–700.

Sassanian Persia

In about 224 CE, the last Parthian king was overthrown by Ardashir, a leading member of the Sassanian dynasty from Fars, Persia. He founded a dynasty that ruled Persia for over 400 years. His son, Shapur I (240–272) expanded the empire's borders to include modern Iran, Iraq, parts of Afghanistan, Pakistan, and Central Asia. Sassanian Persia became a major threat to Roman interests in Asia, and the two powers were frequently in conflict. In the 4th century, the Sassanians were confronted by unrest amongst the nomadic peoples on their northern and eastern borders. In 637, the Sassanian capital, Ctesiphon, fell to an Arab Islamic army, and the Sassanian dynasty came to an end.

This cameo depicts the capture of the Emperor Valerian by Shapur I, following the great Persian victory against the Romans near Edessa in 260.

The Maya

The Maya civilization was the only truly literate culture in pre-Columbian North America. From about 250, substantial cities were constructed in the lowland and highland zones of Guatemala, Belize, Honduras, Yucatán, and eastern Mexico. Maya cities, such as Tikal, Palenque, and Copan, typically included multistory palaces, temple-topped pyramids, and astronomical observatories, all grouped around a central plaza. Ruled by different dynasties, the conflict between these distinctive kingdoms is depicted on wall paintings and reliefs.

The large resident populations of the Maya cities grew corn, beans, squash, and manioc as their staple foods, and traded in goods such as obsidian, jade, cacao, and copal.

Maya vases usually show events in the lives of kings, often as here, involving sacrifice.

Maya Civilization

600 BCE	Middle Formative Period: In the lowlands of Guatemala, early settlers build platforms.
c.300 BCE	Temple platforms built at early Maya sites, such as Uaxactún, Tikal, El Mirador.
c.250 CE	Classic Period (–900). New World's most brilliant civilization flourishes in forested lowlands of N Guatemala and the Yucatán peninsula.
292	One of the earliest examples of a stela bearing a "Long Count" date; Stela 29 at Tikal.
375	First recorded royal accession in a Maya city. "Curl Snout" becomes king of Tikal.
426	Copán dynasty founded by K'inich Yax K'uk' Mo' (–437).
c.600	Construction of city of Palenque, Chiapas, Mexico. Jade-ornamented burial of ruler-priest dates to 7th century.
c.780	Murals at Bonampak, E Mexico. Abandoned soon after completion.
c.790	A period of cultural paralysis. Many sites are abandoned.
889	The date inscribed on one of the last monuments from the C Maya region.
c.900	Postclassic Maya (–1500). Period of decline. Natural resources can no longer support Maya populations.
1200	City of Chichén Itzá abandoned.
1328	The new city of Mayapán, N Yucatán, becomes Maya capital. City is destroyed by civil wars.

ASIA

304 Xiongnu invade China, inaugurating a century of civil war in north.

"Sixteen Kingdoms" period in China (–439).

337 **309** Accession of Shapur II. Persian borders are threatened by nomads.

311 Luoyang is sacked by Xiongnu mercenaries.

317 In China, Western Jin collapses, following capture of Chang'an by the Xiongnu.

317 Beginning of Eastern Jin dynasty.

c.335 **320** Expansion of Gupta family from Magadha, heralds start of Gupta dynasty; India's "Golden Age."

AFRICA

310 In Alexandria, the Greek mathematician Diophantus publishes *Arithmetika*, which introduces the concept of algebra.

311 A serious rift in the African church, the Donatist schism; Donatists are extremists who hold that anyone who has sacrificed to Roman gods should not be readmitted to church.

336 **318** Arius, the priest of Alexandria, puts forward his doctrine which denies Christ's fully divine nature.

350 **320** Accession of Axumite king, Ezana (–350).

323 Egyptian monastic tradition; foundation of monastery of Tabennisi in the desert.

Imperial Rome

Successive emperors sought to make their mark on Rome, leaving a legacy of fine buildings and public monuments – forums, arenas, temples, palaces. Rome was a huge conurbation, with a population of over one million. The squalor of the overcrowded slums and tenements contrasted with the magnificent public buildings. Following Constantine's conversion, Rome emerged as a great center of Christian culture.

304 Persecution of Christians by Roman emperor, Diocletian (284–305).

305 Abdication of Diocletian.

306 Period of conflict as different candidates compete for imperial control.

Maxentius is elevated to the throne by the praetorian guard and people of Rome. He takes control of Italy, Spain, and Africa.

308 Maxentius is declared a public enemy, and Licinius is proclaimed rightful emperor of the West.

312 Battle of Milvian Bridge, just north of Rome; Constantine defeats rival, Maxentius. Western Roman Empire briefly united under Constantine's rule.

331

313 Edict of Milan under Constantine confirms freedom of religious observance.

Licinius unifies the whole of the Eastern Empire under his rule.

337

324 After inflicting defeats on Licinius, Constantine becomes sole ruler.

Constantine founds a new imperial capital at Byzantium. The city is to be called "Constantinople."

325 Council of Nicaea assembled by Constantine.

Map: Imperial Rome

N

1000 meters
1000 yards

Tiberis

Camp of the Praetorian Guard

Mausoleum of Augustus

Mausoleum of Hadrian

Ara Pacis

CAMPUS MARTIUS

Quirinal Hill

Temple of Hadrian

Viminal Hill

Baths of Diocletian

Stadium of Domitian

Temple of Serapis

Baths of Constantine

Forum Romanum
Imperial Fora

Anio Vetus

Pantheon

Temple of Trajan

Esquiline Hill

Aqua Traiana

Capitoline Hill

SUBURA

Baths of Titus

Baths of Trajan

Theater of Marcellus

Via Aurelia

Palatine Hill

Colosseum

Temple of Venus and Rome

Aqua Claudia

Aqua Marcia

Temple of Jupiter
Temple of Saturn
Temple of Vesta

Imperial palace

Temple of Claudius

Circus Maximus

Cachan Hill

Aventine Hill

Aqua Appia

Emporium (warehouses)

Mons Testaceus

Baths of Caracalla

Tiberis

Aqua Antoninian

Imperial Rome c.300 CE

- temple
- stadium or theater
- baths
- other important buildings
- built-up area within city wall
- city gate
- aqueduct
- city wall in Republican era 4th century BCE
- wall of Aurelian 271

Constantine (reigned 306–337)

Constantine was a successful military commander, who introduced many administrative reforms, but he will chiefly be remembered for his conversion to Christianity, which he actively promoted as the Roman state religion. When he dedicated a new imperial capital at Constantinople on the Bosporus, he dealt a further blow to Rome's status as the imperial capital.

The great complex of rock-carved temples and monasteries near the village of Ajanta in western India is famous for its colorful, fresco-type paintings depicting Buddhist legends and divinities, many of which were painted during the Gupta period.

Imperial Guptas (300–550)

Over the course of the 4th century, the Gupta dynasty, based in Magadha, extended its control over the whole of northern India. The Guptas, who established their capital at Pataliputra, held sway over many tributary states by virtue of marital and military alliances. This was the "Golden Age" of Indian civilization, an era of peace and stability which led to a great flowering of Indian literature, architecture, sculpture, painting, and science. But Gupta rule was shattered by the invasion of White Huns (Hephthalites), nomads from Central Asia, in the 5th and 6th centuries.

ASIA

375 ▼

335 Consecration of the church of the Holy Sepulchre in Jerusalem. It becomes Christianity's greatest shrine.

c.335 In India, Chandragupta I is succeeded by Samudragupta, who sets about creating an empire in the Ganges plain.

359 ▼

337 Shapur II embarks on new warfare against Romans.

341 Thousands of Christians are persecuted and executed in Seleucia.

348 Battle of Singara between Romans and Persians ends indecisively.

350 White Huns (Hephthalites) invade Persia and India.

c.350 Black Huns invade Persia and India.

Invention of stirrup in China.

AFRICA

333 Ezana of Axum is converted to Christianity.

356 ▼

336 Athanasius, patriarch of Alexandria, is condemned by council of Tyre for his uncompromising attitude to Arian and Meletian sects. He is exiled.

346 A compromise is reached between the Eastern and Western churches. Athanasius is restored to his see.

350 Meroë, capital of Cush (Sudan), is destroyed by Ethiopian forces under the Axumite king, Ezana.

EUROPE

329 St. Peter's basilica, Rome, is completed.

331 Constantine confiscates treasures from pagan temples, vigorously promoting Christianity.

336 Death of Alexandrian priest, Arius, at Constantinople. The Arian heresy regards Jesus Christ as a demigod, less divine than God.

337 Constantine dies; his three sons take control of the Roman Empire.

340 Constans defeats his brother at Aquileia in N Italy, uniting the Western Empire under his rule.

343 A joint imperial council, held at Serdíca (Sofia) in Thrace, fails to heal the rift between the Eastern and Western Empires.

350 Constans is murdered in a *coup d'etat* by the military commander Magnentius, who takes control of the Western Empire.

c.350 Ulfilas, the first Gothic bishop, translates the Bible into his people's vernacular.

AMERICAS & AUSTRALASIA

Teotihuacán

In c.400, Teotihuacán, in the central valley of Mexico, northeast of modern Mexico City, was the sixth largest city in the world, with a population of c.250,000. From the 1st century, country dwellers had been persuaded to move to the city, where residences, workshops, palaces, and temples were laid out on a rectangular grid pattern.

The city's iconography, with its symbolism of water, sun, and weather spread throughout the south-central Andes. The Temple of the Sun (*below*), one of the largest manmade constructions in pre-Columbian America, was said to mark the birthplace of the sun and moon. This site of great ritual importance became a major pilgrimage center for the peoples of Mesoamerica.

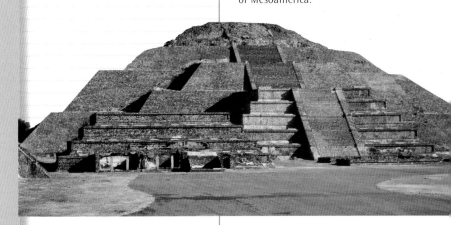

The Huns

A nomadic people from Mongolia, the Huns became a formidable force from as early as the 3rd century BCE. Their warlike reputation was well-founded. These superbly skilled horsemen lived and fought in the saddle, covering great distances across the barren steppes of Central Asia. Their portable bronze cauldrons (*below*) used for cooking, have been found all over Asia. Their main weapon was the reflex bow, which they were able to fire accurately while traveling at great speed.

The Hun's continual raids across the borders of Han China, prompted the Chinese to build the Great Wall, a 4,000-mile- (6,400-km-) long barrier against invasion, which was nevertheless frequently breached by the Huns. From about 350 CE, the Huns began to move westward, invading southern Russia, India, and the Sassanian empire.

Like other barbarian groups before them, the Huns were displaced and pushed westward by more successful rivals. Their arrival in the west in the late 4th century precipitated a major crisis. They overran Ostrogothic territory, defeated the Alans, and then turned on the Visigoths. These barbarian groups turned to Rome for protection. Entering the empire as *foederati* (confederates), they served against other barbarians under the command of their own chiefs. The last great Hunnish assault on the west, in 440, all but delivered the final *coup de grâce* to the Roman Empire. It was just a matter of time before the final collapse.

ASIA

351 Foundation of Chinese Jin kingdom at Chang'an.

359 Sassanian king, Shapur II invades Syria and captures Roman town of Amida.

Council of the Eastern church held at Seleucia is persuaded to accept a pro-Arian creed.

360 Persians capture Singara and Bezabde, Mesopotamia, from Romans.

361 Wang Xizhi who established the Chinese art of fine calligraphy, dies.

362 The pagan Roman emperor, Julian, campaigns to restore pagan worship in the Eastern Empire.

363 Emperor Julian invades Persia, but dies at Ctesiphon. The pagan revival ends.

Under terms of a peace treaty, Emperor Jovian surrenders territory to the Persians.

 c.390

369 Shapur II occupies the pro-Roman kingdom of Armenia.

A Japanese expeditionary force establishes a colony in Mimana, in S Korea.

 376

373 Fu Jian, king of the Former Jin, occupies Sichuan, Yunnan, and part of Guizhou.

375 Samudragupta dies, leaving an empire dominating N and C India.

AFRICA

356 Athanasius, former patriarch of Alexandria, takes refuge in the Egyptian desert after being expelled from Alexandria by the pro-Arian emperor, Constantius II.

The stirrup

353 Constantius II becomes sole emperor.

355 Alemanni, a Germanic tribe, wreak havoc in Gaul.

357 Julian, made Caesar by his cousin Constantius II, defeats the Alemanni at Strasbourg and drives them back, beyond the Rhine.

360 In Constantinople, a council ratifies pro-Arian alterations to the Nicene creed.

361 Julian becomes sole emperor.

381

364 Division of Eastern and Western Empires between Valentinian and Valens is matched by a true division between resources and armies.

368 A long series of campaigns against Alemanni on Rhine frontier ends in Roman victory.

378

369 Visigoths are forced to accept an unfavorable treaty on the Rhine frontier.

420

c.370 Huns begin to invade E Europe.

372 Martin, bishop of Tours, establishes one of the first hermit communities in the west.

c.375 In Ukraine, nomadic Huns, moving east from C Asia, defeat the Ostrogoths.

375 "Curly Snout" becomes king of Maya city of Tikal.

The stirrup was a vitally important innovation in mounted warfare, enabling the rider to keep his seat while executing complex manoeuvres, such as firing a bow or lassoing an enemy. The nomadic Scythians may have used leather stirrups as early as 400 BCE, although these were probably just an aid for mounting. There is evidence that crude rope loops, a kind of rudimentary stirrup, were used in India in the late 2nd century BCE. But the first rigid, metal stirrups appeared in China c.350 CE – metal-sheathed wooden examples have been found at the site of Wanbaoting, in northeastern China.

From here the invention spread rapidly across Asia and into Europe. Stirrups have been found in 4th-century graves from Silla Korea. The Byzantine heavy cavalry adopted the stirrup in the 7th century, and stirrups are found in Frankish graves from the mid-8th century, the beginning of the emergence of the armed, and mounted, medieval knight.

This Chinese ceramic figurine of a hunter attacked by a lion demonstrates one of the advantages of the stirrup as the rider turns to deal with his aggressor.

351–375 CE

Axum (100 BCE–600 CE)

The early inhabitants of Ethiopia were skilled agriculturalists and traders. They evolved their own language, Ge'ez, from which modern Amharic is descended, and their own Ge'ez script.

By the 1st century CE, these farmers and traders developed their own powerful state based inland at Axum. The Red Sea port of Adulis became the most important ivory market in northeastern Africa, diverting much of this trade from the inland kingdom of Meroë. In the 4th century, the Axumites began to carve tall, solid stone stelae (*above*), used to mark the tombs of their rulers. At about this time, Axum was converted to Christianity by scholars from Alexandria and developed a distinctive Axumite church.

376–400 CE

ASIA

375 Beginning of reign of Chandragupta II (–415) ; Gupta rule reaches its greatest extent.

376 Fu Jian, ruler of the Former Jin, extends his control to C Asia, uniting all of N China.

383 Fu Jian is decisively defeated at the battle of the Fei river in C Anhui.

384 Buddhism reaches Korea.

386 Toba Wei reunify N China, intermarry with Chinese, and adopt Chinese culture.

387 Foundation of Northern Wei dynasty by the Toba people of Mongolian origin. The capital is at Pingcheng (Datong). Beginning of north–south division in China.

c.390 Theodosius and Shapur agree to a treaty on the partition of Armenia between the Persian and Roman empires.

393 Invaders from Yamato, Japan, overrun Silla and Paekche in Korea.

395 Eastern Roman Empire left to Arcadius. Definitive division of Roman Empire.

399 Yezdegerd succeeds to the Persian throne. He is tolerant of Christianity and builds up good relations with the Romans.

Chinese monk and pilgrim, Fa Xian, embarks on an epic journey to India to study Buddhism; travels through S Asia (–415).

AFRICA

385 Copper-mining and smelting has begun at Kansanshi, on the Congo-Zambia border.

c.397 Berber prince, Gildo begins a major rebellion against the Roman emperor, Honorius.

376 Goths petition Emperor Valens to settle within Roman Empire.

378 Visigoths under Alaric defeat Roman force under Emperor Valens at battle of Adrianopolis.

379 Theodosius becomes new Eastern emperor. He takes charge of the war against the Goths.

381 At an ecumenical council in Constantinople, Arianism is finally condemned.

402

382 The Roman imperial court is moved to Milan.

383 Theodosius signs a peace treaty with the Visigoths, giving them land and autonomy in exchange for military service.

387 Maximus, proclaimed emperor by troops in Britain, invades Italy. He is defeated, and executed at Aquileia (–388).

390 Theodosius performs public penance for his massacre of thousands of rebellious citizens in Thessalonica.

391 Theodosius makes Christianity religion of the Roman Empire. All pagan ritual is banned.

392 Valentinian II, Augustus of Italy and Illyricum, is murdered by his Frankish military commander, who proclaims Eugenius emperor.

394 Theodosius defeats and kills Eugenius, becoming new sole emperor.

395 Theodosius dies; definitive division of empire into East and West. West Roman Empire left to child emperor, Honorius.

401

Alaric, Visigothic leader, seeks homeland within Roman Empire.

c.378 Maya city of Tikal invades the city of Uaxactún.

c.400 Intensive building at Teotihuacán in Mexico

Early Christianity

By the end of the 4th century, Christian churches were clustered around the Mediterranean. The Christian church modeled itself on the empire; dioceses mirrored the administrative divisions of Diocletian. The bishops of Rome, the see of St. Peter, shared rank and power with those of Antioch and Alexandria.

Rome itself had become a major Christian center. The chief focus of Christian Rome was the basilica of St. Peter, founded by Constantine. The catacombs of Rome, an intricate network of underground passages outside the city, are rich in Christian remains. Here, Christians gathered for funerals and anniversaries, building underground shrines for devotions to saints and martyrs. Christian sarcophagi were decorated with narrative iconography, such as scenes from the Old Testament or the life of Christ. The sarcophagus (*above*), is from Syracuse in Sicily, another important center of early Christianity, and is decorated with a narrative relief of Adam and Eve.

Sassanian silverware

Sassanian stuccos, ivories, and silverwork all demonstrate a revival in Near Eastern artistic traditions in the early centuries CE. A number of Sassanian motifs, such as vine scrolls, peacocks, palms, and winged crowns found their way into the Byzantine artistic repertoire. In turn, Sassanian artisans drew on pagan classical imagery, a legacy of their long exposure to Graeco-Roman culture.

Coin of Emperor Honorius

Honorius was Western emperor from 395–423, coruling with his brother Arcadius, the Eastern emperor. He succeeded his father, Theodosius I, while he was still a child, and his reign was notable for his lack of achievements. He was said to only recognize "Roma" as the name of his pet chicken. He ruled under the "protectorate" of the half-Vandal general Stilicho. However, Stilicho proved incapable of resisting the attacks of Alaric the Visigoth, who besieged, captured, and sacked Rome in 410.

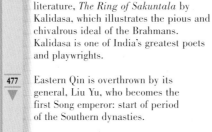

411 Death of Gu Kaizhi, first famous painter in Chinese history.

415 Greek mathematician and philosopher, Hypatia, is tortured to death by a mob of Christian zealots in Alexandria.

420 Publication of masterpiece of Indian literature, *The Ring of Sakuntala* by Kalidasa, which illustrates the pious and chivalrous ideal of the Brahmans. Kalidasa is one of India's greatest poets and playwrights.

477 ▼ Eastern Qin is overthrown by its general, Liu Yu, who becomes the first Song emperor: start of period of the Southern dynasties.

Nanjing is reinstated as capital of N China.

502 ▼ **422** Peace treaty concluded between Emperor Theodosius II and King Varahran of the Persians, which aims to end hostilities between Persians and Christians for the next 100 years.

401 Visigoths from the Balkans, led by Alaric, invade N Italy.

402 Visigoths are forced out of Italy after their defeat by the Roman army, led by the Vandal commander, Stilicho.

Imperial Roman court moved to Ravenna.

404 The patriarch John Chrysostom is banished from Constantinople, following outspoken attacks on the empress.

Vulgate (Latin version of the Bible) completed.

406 On December 31, hordes of Vandals, Alans, and Sueves cross the frozen Rhine into the Roman Empire.

407 The usurper Constantine III, who has been declared emperor by the army, leaves Britain for Gaul, which is being ravaged by barbarian invaders.

408 Constantine extends his authority into Spain.

409 Vandals, Sueves, and Alans cross the Pyrenees.

410 Visigoths, under Alaric, capture and sack Rome.

411 Constantine is besieged at Arelate (Arles), and captured by forces loyal to Emperor Honorius.

c.411 Sueves establish kingdom in NW Iberia.

413 Burgundians conclude a treaty with the Roman Empire, allowing them to settle on former imperial land beside the Rhine.

414 New leader, Athaulf, sets up Visigothic state at Narbo (Narbonne), which expands into Iberia.

418 Visigoths settle in Aquitaine.

420 Huns build capital on the Tisza (Theiss) river on Hungarian plains.

c.420 Moche culture, based in the Chicama and Moche valleys of Peru, now extends from the Andes to the Pacific. The Temple of the Sun, in the Moche valley, is built with 50 million bricks.

422 Eastern emperor, Theodosius II agrees to pay an annual tribute to the Huns in order to buy peace.

A page from the Lichfield Gospels (720–730 CE) in the Vulgate version. Jerome's Vulgate version of the Bible set a standard for the King James version in English, some 1,200 years later.

The Latin Bible

By the 5th century, the church had agreed upon which books from the Old Testament and writings from the time of Jesus should constitute the Bible. Latin was rapidly replacing Greek as the language of western Christendom. The Bible had already been translated into the so-called Old Latin version, but hardly any two manuscripts agreed in their readings.

Jerome, one of the most learned men of his day, was born in Strido, Dalmatia (present-day Croatia) in about 342 CE. He studied in Rome under the leading grammarian, Donatus. He spent some time living as a desert hermit in Syria, where he learnt Hebrew from a Jewish rabbi, then went on to study under the great theologian, Gregory of Nazianzus, in Cappadocia (Turkey). Jerome, fluent in Greek, Hebrew, and Aramaic, was given the task of producing a reliable, consistent, Latin translation of the Bible. His so-called Vulgate version (a reference to its being in the common tongue), was completed in about 404. He revised and corrected Old Latin and Greek versions of many of the scriptures, and made some independent translations from the Hebrew. His work on the Old Testament alone took him 15 years to complete. It was a breathtaking achievement.

Barbarian Invasions and Migrations

In the 5th century, the Roman Empire was subjected to a wave of invasions by Germanic peoples. Driven by famine, population pressure, land-hunger, and the prospect of a better standard of living, their aim was to share in the fruits of empire, not to destroy it. The only invaders bent purely on destruction and plunder were the Huns.

At first, the Romans were able to contain the new arrivals, recruiting them into their depleted army, and allowing them to retain their own leaders and laws. But when they began to oppose the settlement of large groups or refused to reward them for their their way across the empire, leading to its eventual collapse.

350	White Huns (Hephthalites) invade Persia and India.
c.370	First appearance of Huns in E Europe
	Huns overwhelm Alans
376	Goths petition Emperor Valens to settle within Roman Empire.
378	Goths defeat Valens at battle of Adrianopolis.
395	Alaric, Visigothic leader, seeks homeland within Roman Empire.
406	Vandals, Sueves, and Alans cross Rhine.
409	Vandals, Sueves, and Alans cross Pyrenees.
410	Visigoths, under Alaric, sack Rome.
	Death of Alaric; Visigoths abandon plan to invade Africa.
c.410	Romans abandon Britain
c.411	Sueves establish kingdom in NW Iberia.
414	New Visigothic leader, Athaulf marries Galla Placidia, daughter of the late Emperor Theodosius. She had been captured during the sack of Rome.
	Athaulf sets up state at Narbo (Narbonne), which expands into Iberia.
418	Visigoths settle in Aquitaine.
420	Huns build capital on the river Tisza (Theiss) in Hungary.
429	Vandals cross Strait of Gibraltar.
430	City of Hippo taken by Vandals.
439	Vandals reach city of Carthage.
c.444	Attila becomes king of the Huns.
451	Attila invades Gaul; defeated at the Catalaunian Fields.
452	Attila persuaded to leave Roman Empire.
453	Ostrogoths embark on bloody campaigns against the Eastern empire.
	On death of Attila, Empire of the Huns collapses
455	Sack of Rome by Vandal king, Gaiseric.
457	Jutes, Angles, and Saxons cross to British Isles.
474	Rome recognizes Vandal kingdom.
476	Deposition of last Western emperor in Rome; Odoacer becomes ruler of Italy.
492	Ostrogothic king, Theodoric defeats Odoacer at Ravenna to become king of Italy.
507	Franks defeat Visigoths and drive them out of Aquitaine.
533	Beginning of reconquest of Italy by East Roman Empire

ASIA

439 Northern (Toba) Wei dominate N China (–543). The northern and southern courts stand in direct conflict. Beginning of the period of the Southern and Northern dynasties.

440 A great center of Buddhist studies is founded on the plain of the Ganges at Nalanda.

477

444 Taoism is made the official religion of the Northern Wei empire, following the conversion of the emperor.

446 Rebellion of Buddhist monastery at Chang'an against Taoist reforms. Wei emperor orders execution of every monk in the empire. Officials delay the executions and many monks escape.

450 Death of the famous minister Cui Hao, principal architect of the administrative reforms of the Northern Wei empire.

467

c.450 Hephthalites attack northeastern borders of Sassanian empire.

477

Buddhism reaches Java and other islands of SE Asia.

In India, composition of early *Puranas* and near-final form of *Mahabharata*, the world's longest epic poem (5th century).

Development of Indian architecture in stone.

AFRICA

c.426 Berber Christians continue to defy Roman authority, and refuse to accept the official Roman church.

429 Nomadic Vandals invade N Africa from Spain.

430 St. Augustine, bishop of Hippo, dies while his town is under siege by the Vandals.

439 Fall of Carthage. Vandals set up N African kingdom.

474

442 The Vandal king, Gaiseric, signs a peace treaty with Emperor Valentinian III, and is granted full rights as a ruler over most of the Roman provinces of Africa.

c.480 **428** Nestorius, the patriarch of Constantinople, preaches a new doctrine which emphasizes the distinction beween Christ's divine and human natures. The pope immediately condemns Nestorianism as heresy.

429 **429** Vandals cross Strait of Gibraltar.

Angles, Saxons, and Jutes expel Picts and Scots from S England.

431 Pope Celestine sends his deacon, Palladius to Ireland as its first bishop.

434 The armies of Theodosius II are defeated by the Huns in Thrace.

435 Foundation of Constantinople university.

480 **436** Burgundians are defeated by Huns, who are fighting for the empire as mercenaries.

The last Roman troops leave Britain.

438 The *Theodosian Code* of imperial laws is published, the first law code for over a century.

453 **c.444** Attila becomes king of the Huns.

446 Burgundians are granted imperial land in the Geneva area, and become allies of Rome.

447 Huns, led by Attila, cross the Danube to invade Thrace, forcing the Romans to pay them a heavier tribute.

484 **449** The doctrine of Monophysitism is accepted at a meeting of the council of Ephesus. The Monophysites teach that the incarnate Christ is of a single, divine nature.

c.500 **450** Teotihuacán influence found in Maya territory over 60 miles (100 km) away. Maya settlements and cities, such as Kaminaljuyú, are set out in the Teotihuacán style.

c.450 Flourishing of Nazca people, famous for lines and giant figures drawn in desert.

Founding Fathers

St. Augustine (*above*) (354–430) was bishop of Hippo in North Africa for 34 years, and was regarded by later generations as an exemplary prelate. He saw his chief role as shepherd to his church, responsible for the instruction, through preaching, of his flock. He lived an austere life, dedicated to teaching and writing. He was a penetrating theologian, most famously in *The City of God*, which sets out to show that the fall of Rome in 410 was not caused by the abandonment of pagan religion. His *Confessions* is one of the world's great autobiographies.

In another part of Europe, St. Patrick (*below*) (born c.385) was bringing Christianity to the remote land of Ireland. Born in England, St. Patrick began his Christian mission to Ireland in 432. He traveled through wild and dangerous country, preaching the gospel, and baptizing converts. By 444 he had established an episcopal see at Armagh, and had almost single-handedly brought into being the monastic structure of the Irish church.

536 **c.451** The Ethiopian kingdom of Axum reaches its apogee.

454 The kingdom of Axum decides to give its support to the Coptic patriarch of Alexandria, who follows the Monophysite doctrine.

495 **467** Following the death of Skanda Gupta (455–467), the Gupta empire begins to break up under pressure from the Hephthalite Huns, who have conquered much of W India.

Yungang cave

The magnificent Buddhist cave temples of Yungang were created in the late 5th century near the city of Datong in northern China. They are among the earliest remaining examples of the first major flowering of Buddhist art in China. Some of the caves, carved out of a ridge of soft sandstone, are no more than niches designed to hold colossal figures of the Buddha (*above*) up to 45 feet (14 m) tall, while others contained chapels. The earliest caves were constructed as an act of propitiation by the Northern Wei rulers, who had persecuted Buddhists during the period, 446–52. The predominant sculptural style is dominated by the Buddhist art of India – a uniquely Chinese style only emerged with the later construction of the cave-temples at Longmen.

475 Completion of keyhole tomb of Emperor Nintoku (died 421), the largest keyhole tomb in Japan.

EUROPE

451 Attila the Hun invades Gaul. In the battle of Catalaunian Fields, Romans and Goths defeat Attila.

Council of Chalcedon; Orthodox Church denounces Monophysite sects, such as Copts and Nestorians.

452 Following their invasion of Italy, the Huns attack a series of cities, including Padua and Verona. They are persuaded by Pope Leo to withdraw.

City of Venice founded by refugees from Attila's Huns.

492

453 Ostrogoths embark on bloody campaigns against East Roman Empire.

Death of Attila, followed by retreat of Huns.

454 The Huns' Germanic vassals, inspired by Ardaric, king of the Gepids, rebel against them, and the Hun empire begins to disintegrate.

455 Sack of Rome by Vandal king, Gaiseric; Vandals plunder Rome.

Accession of Avitus as Roman emperor of the West.

456 Emperor Avitus is defeated in battle at Placentia, N Italy, and is forced to abdicate by the rebel general Ricimer, an Arian barbarian from the Suevian tribe, who aims to rule through a puppet emperor, Majorian (–461).

476

The powerful Suevian king, Rechiarus is defeated and killed by the Visigoths, who begin to gain dominance in Spain.

461 Ricimer deposes and kills Majorian. He appoints Libius Severus as puppet emperor (–465).

468 The Western forces are defeated by the Vandals, who conquer the island of Sicily.

473 Julius Nepos, backed by Byzantine emperor Leo I, marches on Rome and proclaims himself emperor of the West.

474 Rome recognizes Vandal kingdom.

475 Western emperor, Julius Nepos grants Euric, king of the Visigoths, legal tenure. The Visigoths control SW Gaul and most of Spain.

AMERICAS & AUSTRALASIA

Keyhole tomb of Nintoku

By about 300, the plain of Osaka in southeastern Japan was the political center of the Yamato state, which controlled much of the country until about 700. Among the many ancient burial mounds in the Osaka area is the massive keyhole-shaped tomb, attributed to the 15th Yamato emperor, Nintoku, completed in about 475. It measures 1,590 feet (485 m) in length and occupies some 80 acres (32 hectares). It is surrounded by three moats and by a number of ancillary tombs, some also keyhole-shaped.

A Vandal noble

At Christmas 406 a vast horde of Vandals, Sueves, and Alans crossed the frozen River Rhine into the empire. They swept through Gaul and Spain, and Vandals crossed to North Africa, sacking Carthage in 439. In Gaul, barbarian settlement took place on the basis on hospitalitas, a sharing of land between the Roman landowner and his barbarian "guest."

In Spain and Africa, the barbarian arrival was much more violent and disruptive. The Vandal settlement of North Africa inevitably involved the widespread dispossession of Roman landowners. The Vandals themselves were more than capable of appreciating the comforts of Roman civilization, as this mosaic of a Vandal landowner, leaving his villa on horseback, demonstrates.

Classis

From 476 Ostrogothic kings ruled Italy from the city of Ravenna, which had been chosen by Honorius, the Western emperor, as his capital in 404. Located on flat, marshy land, Ravenna was linked to the mainland by a raised causeway, and was nearly impregnable. From the harbor at Classis (*above*) there were direct sea links to Constantinople. The cultural and social life of Ravenna is demonstrated by the rich array of 5th-century mosaics that adorn the city.

The Copts

Early Christians in Egypt adopted the doctrine of Monophysitism, which emphasized the divine nature of Christ, denying that he could also have been a human being. In 451, at the Council of Chalcedon, the Roman church denounced this doctrine as a heresy, and Monophysites were expelled from the church. The bulk of the Egyptian population nevertheless adhered to the Monophysite doctrine, replacing the Greek of the official church with their own Coptic language.

Under Byzantine rule, Coptic Christians wove fine textiles, decorated with the cross and other Christian imagery.

ASIA

477 The Liu Song dynasty collapses when general Xiao Daocheng has the emperor killed and makes himself regent.

538 Buddhism becomes China's state religion.

c.477 Kasyapa, the parricide, builds his palace at Sigiriya, Ceylon.

478 The first Shinto shrine appears in Japan.

502 **479** Rule of S China passes to the Qi dynasty.

480 Hephthalites from beyond the Oxus river begin the overthrow of the Gupta empire.

c.480 Nestorianism, the Christian doctrine that emphasizes the distinction between Christ's divine and human natures, reaches India.

484 Hephthalites defeat and kill Sassanian ruler, but the empire survives.

489 Nestorian Christians expelled from Egypt and settle in Persia.

Northern Wei rulers, restored to Buddhism, honor their religion by commissioning a huge cave temple at Yungang, N Shanxi province.

491 The Armenian Church secedes from Byzantium and Rome.

493 Northern Wei capital moved to rebuilt city of Luoyang.

495 Work begins on the Buddhist caves of Longmen near the Wei capital, Luoyang.

Death of Kasyapa, self-appointed god-king of Sigiriya in Ceylon.

c.500 Development of esoteric Tantric Buddhist literature.

AFRICA

534 **477** Huneric succeeds his father, Gaiseric, as Vandal king of N Africa. He is an Arian Christian, and embarks on a policy of violent persecution of the Catholics.

c.550 **c.500** Arrival of the Bantu in S Africa, with iron and domesticated cattle.

A dynasty of Hagha kings begins to rule Ghana, W Africa. Their camel caravans trade gold and salt across the Sahara to N Africa.

EUROPE

476 Child emperor, Romulus Augustulus, last Roman emperor in the West, deposed by Odoacer, "king of Italy." Odoacer becomes ruler of Italy; end of Western Empire.

507
The Visigothic king, Euric, conquers the remainder of S Gaul, reaching the Italian frontier.

480 Gundobad becomes king of the Burgundians. Their kingdom extends over E Gaul, with two capitals, at Lyon and Geneva.

511 **c.481** Accession of Frankish king, Clovis I.

484 Despite attempts to reconcile the conflict between Chalcedonian Monophysites and Catholics, a schism splits the churches of Constantinople and Rome.

486 Clovis conquers much of N Gaul.

526 **492** Conquest of Italy by Ostrogothic king, Theodoric; he defeats Odoacer at Ravenna to become king of Italy.

c.500 Clovis is converted to Christianity. He becomes the only orthodox Catholic Christian sovereign – the kings of the Visigoths, Vandals, Burgundians, and Ostrogoths are all Aryans.

568
Lombards occupy the area north of the Danube.

AMERICAS & AUSTRALASIA

c.500 The Basketmaker III phase begins in southwest N America. Large villages, with up to 50 houses, are agricultural centers.

c.700
Teotihuacán, in C Mexico, is the sixth largest city in the world, with a population of c.200,000.

Large cemeteries of the Paracas culture, on south coast of Peru, contain mummified bodies.

c.600
Tiahuanaco civilization, centered on Lake Titicaca in Bolivia, begins to emerge as a strong regional power, based on its control of trade routes. Its influence extends to Argentina and Chile, and is evident in pottery and architecture at secondary centers.

c.600
Huari civilization, based in Ayachucho valley of C Andes is expanding, through conquest, into N and S Peru.

Kasyapa

Kasyapa (447–495) usurped power in Ceylon in c.477, believing himself to be the god-king. He built a palace fortress at Sigiriya, precipitously sited on the top of a sheer pillar of rock, which rises some 1,144 feet (349 m) above sea level. The summit was reached by walkways that clung to the rock-face. Overhanging boulders were decorated with wall paintings, such as this depiction of an aerial maiden (*above*). Visitors began the final ascent to the palace complex through the open jaws and throat (*giriya*) of a monumental lion (*sinha*), hence the name Sigiriya.

The World in 500 CE

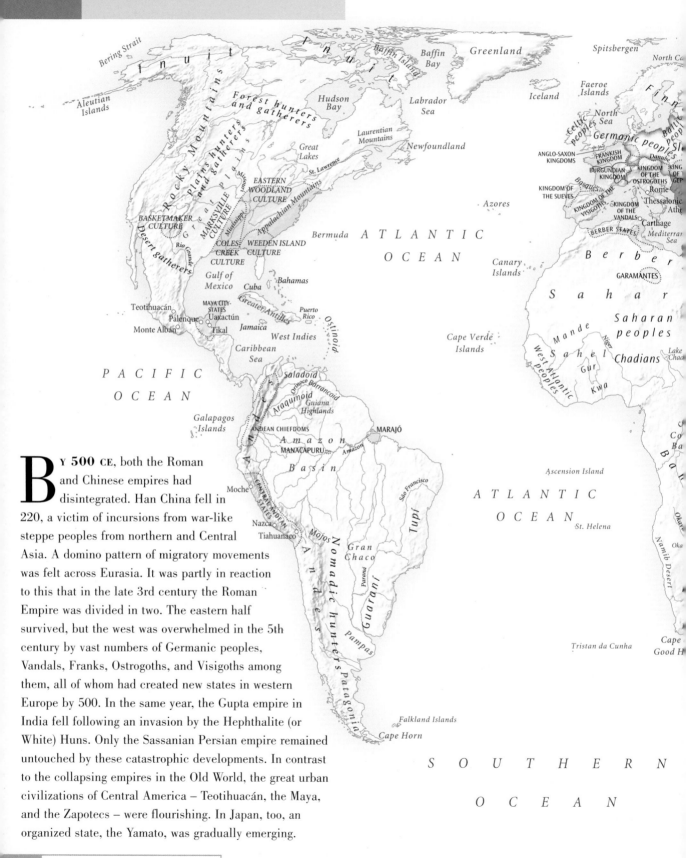

BY **500** CE, both the Roman and Chinese empires had disintegrated. Han China fell in 220, a victim of incursions from war-like steppe peoples from northern and Central Asia. A domino pattern of migratory movements was felt across Eurasia. It was partly in reaction to this that in the late 3rd century the Roman Empire was divided in two. The eastern half survived, but the west was overwhelmed in the 5th century by vast numbers of Germanic peoples, Vandals, Franks, Ostrogoths, and Visigoths among them, all of whom had created new states in western Europe by 500. In the same year, the Gupta empire in India fell following an invasion by the Hephthalite (or White) Huns. Only the Sassanian Persian empire remained untouched by these catastrophic developments. In contrast to the collapsing empires in the Old World, the great urban civilizations of Central America – Teotihuacán, the Maya, and the Zapotecs – were flourishing. In Japan, too, an organized state, the Yamato, was gradually emerging.

The World in 500 CE

- East Roman Empire
- Empire of the Ostrogoths under Ermanaric, 370 CE
- Hun Empire under Attila, 450 CE

Novaya Zemlya
Kara Sea
Paleosiberians
Bering Strait
Yenisey
Lena
Sea of Okhotsk
Kamchatka
Samoyeds
S i b e r i a
Tungus
Ob'
Lake Baikal
Amur
Volga
Ural
Msteppes
Irtysh
Altai Mountains
Turkic peoples
Aral Sea
Lake Balkhash
Gobi
Kurile Islands
Hokkaido
Ainu
Alans
Tien Shan
Takla Makan
EMPIRE OF THE RUANRUAN
Yellow R.
Sea of Japan
Honshu
Caucasian Peoples
Caspian Sea
EMPIRE OF THE HEPHTHALITES
TUYUHUN
TOBA
KOGURYO
PAEKCHE
SILLA
JAPAN
LAZICA
ARMENIA
Edessa
Ecbatana
Bactra
Chang'an
Luoyang
Kyushu
EAST ROMAN EMPIRE
Ctesiphon
Susa
Taxila
Tibetans
Plateau of Tibet
Nanjing
Jerusalem
Alexandria
SASSANIAN EMPIRE
Himalayas
Yangtze
East China Sea
PACIFIC OCEAN
LAKHMIDS
The Gulf
Thar Desert
Ganges
QI EMPIRE
Taiwan
GHASSANIDS
Ayodhya
Pataliputra
NUBIA
Arabian Peninsula
Arabian Sea
GUPTA EMPIRE
Ujjain
CANDRA
KURIA
Red Sea
VAKATAKAS
EASTERN GANGAS
Bay of Bengal
CHAMPA
Medang
Luzon
Philippine Islands
Micronesia
Soba
Axum
HIMYARITES
Socotra
SMALL STATES
CHENLA
Mindanao
ALWA
AXUM
Gulf of Aden
KADAMBAS
Andaman Islands
FUNAN
Vyadhapura
Melanesia
Fur
Cushites
KALABHRAS
Sigiriya
MON AND MALAY STATES
South China Sea
Nilotic peoples
LAMBAKANNAS
Ceylon
Nicobar Islands
Bismarck Archipelago
Lake Victoria
Maldive Islands
M
GANTOLI
Borneo
Celebes
Moluccas
Papuans
New Guinea
Solomon Islands
Lake Tanganyika
Seychelles
Sumatra
TARUMA
Java
Timor
Melanesia
Vanuatu
Lake Nyasa
Comoros
INDIAN OCEAN
Fiji
New Caledonia
Bantus
Malays
Madagascar
Mauritius
Réunion
Great Sandy Desert
Great Barrier Reef
Gibson Desert
Australian Aborigines
Simpson Desert
Lake Eyre
Great Victoria Desert
Darling
Great Dividing Range
Tasman Sea
Tasmania
New Zealand

MOSAIC MAP OF JERUSALEM

With the conversion of the Roman Emperor Constantine in 312 CE, the spread of Christianity was greatly accelerated. Within 80 years it had become the majority religion of the Roman Empire with an elaborate hierarchy closely identified with the Roman state. By the 5th century, even many of the Germanic peoples invading the West Roman Empire had been converted to Christianity. One consequence was that many of the sites associated with the life of Christ became major centers of pilgrimage and sources of relics, Jerusalem, site of Christ's Passion, above all. The city was depicted in great detail in this 6th-century mosaic found at Madaba in Jordan. Its bird's eye view indicates all the important churches and pilgrimage sites in the city.

500–1000 CE

Successors to the Classical Age

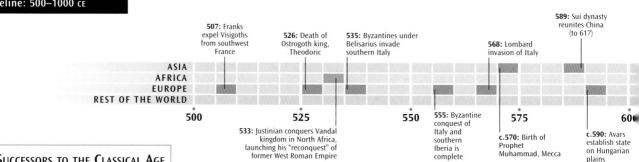

507: Franks expel Visigoths from southwest France

526: Death of Ostrogoth king, Theodoric

535: Byzantines under Belisarius invade southern Italy

568: Lombard invasion of Italy

589: Sui dynasty reunites China (to 617)

ASIA			
AFRICA			
EUROPE			
REST OF THE WORLD			
500	525	550	575	600

533: Justinian conquers Vandal kingdom in North Africa, launching his "reconquest" of former West Roman Empire

555: Byzantine conquest of Italy and southern Iberia is complete

c.570: Birth of Prophet Muhammad, Mecca

c.590: Avars establish state on Hungarian plains

THOUGH NEW STATES emerged to take the place of Rome in western Europe almost as soon as the West Roman Empire finally collapsed in 476 – the Ostrogoths in Italy, the Vandals, Sueves, and Visigoths in the Iberian Peninsula, and the Franks and Burgundians in France and western Germany – Europe remained politically fragile. There were continuing incursions of nomadic peoples from the east – Lombards, Avars, Slavs, Magyars, and Bulgars – and, from the late 8th century, raids by the Vikings of Scandinavia, which reached as far south as the Mediterranean and the Black Sea. At the same time, however much they sought to emulate Roman traditions, almost all the new states were politically immature; shifting frontiers and short-lived kingdoms were a feature of almost the whole period.

The East Roman (Byzantine) Empire, eager to reassert its authority in the West, was also a source of instability. In 533, the Emperor Justinian (527–65) undertook a series of ambitious campaigns to reconquer the West. The Vandals were driven from North Africa and, two years later, the slow business of expelling the Ostrogoths from Italy began. Twenty years of almost continuous warfare inflicted far more damage on the cities and towns of Roman Italy than the original invasion by the Ostrogoths had in the previous century.

The Byzantine reconquest was finally completed in 555, but in 568, Italy was attacked by new Germanic invaders, the Lombards, who established their capital at Pavia in northern Italy. A 200-year conflict followed, during

which the invaders never gained complete control of the peninsula. The Byzantines held on to their stronghold at Ravenna until 751. When it fell, the Pope in Rome, nominally a representative of Byzantine rule, took a hand, inviting the Frankish leader Pepin III to come to his aid. The Frankish invasion of northern Italy (753–756) did not crush Lombard power completely, but following a second appeal to Pepin's son, Charlemagne, the Lombards were finally conquered by the Franks in 774.

Charlemagne

The most successful of all the new states established after the fall of Rome was the Kingdom of the Franks. By 600, its authority extended over the whole of France and well into Germany. After the accession of Charlemagne in 771, it was extended yet further, becoming almost a pan-European empire. Charlemagne's coronation as Holy Roman emperor in 800 underlined not just the extent of his domains but amounted to an ambitious attempt to recreate the central authority of imperial Rome. It also highlighted the central and growing role of the Church in Europe: it was the Pope himself who crowned Charlemagne. Though clashes between later Holy Roman emperors and popes would come to dominate medieval politics, the authority of the Church had become a central fact of life in Europe.

The Vikings

On the periphery of Christian Europe, however, there were still pagan peoples who presented a serious threat to its stability. Not

Charlemagne, king of the Franks, extended his rule over much of western Europe, driving the Lombards from northern Italy and subduing the pagan Saxons.

PICTURE ABOVE:
***The Dome of the Rock** in Jerusalem (688–691) is the oldest surviving Islamic place of worship. The architecture with its dome, arcades, and mosaics owes much to the Byzantines, from whom the Arabs captured the city in 638.*

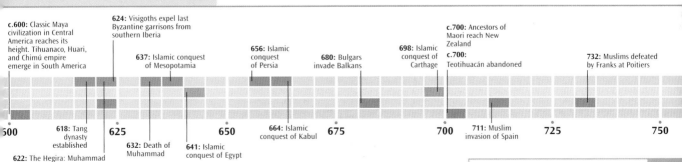

c.600: Classic Maya civilization in Central America reaches its height. Tihuanaco, Huari, and Chimú empire emerge in South America

624: Visigoths expel last Byzantine garrisons from southern Iberia

637: Islamic conquest of Mesopotamia

656: Islamic conquest of Persia

680: Bulgars invade Balkans

698: Islamic conquest of Carthage

c.700: Ancestors of Maori reach New Zealand

c.700: Teotihuacán abandoned

732: Muslims defeated by Franks at Poitiers

500

618: Tang dynasty established

625

650

664: Islamic conquest of Kabul

675

700

711: Muslim invasion of Spain

725

750

632: Death of Muhammad

641: Islamic conquest of Egypt

622: The Hegira: Muhammad and his followers move to Medina; start of Islamic era

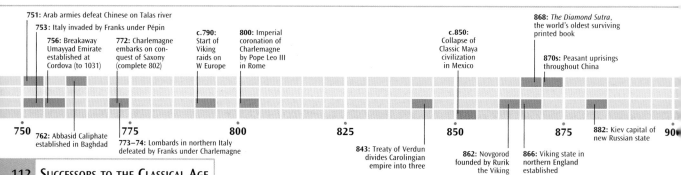

This bronze and iron chieftain's helmet (7th century CE) was found in a boat grave at Vendel, Upplands, in Sweden. The Vendel period is the name given to the era 550–800, before the great Vikings raids and voyages of exploration.

even Charlemagne's empire was immune to the raids of the Scandinavian Vikings. In the late 8th century, seafaring warriors from Denmark and Norway began plundering the coasts of England, Scotland, and Ireland. In the following century their raids extended to France, Spain, and Italy. Epic voyages of exploration established settlements in Iceland and Greenland, while Swedish Vikings traded and plundered along the rivers of Russia, reaching the Black Sea and Constantinople.

As they adopted a more settled way of life, the Vikings abandoned their pagan deities and accepted Christianity. The same was true of the Magyars, who terrorized Germany with frequent raids in the 9th and 10th centuries. Following their defeat by the German King Otto I in 955, they were largely confined to their homeland of Hungary, which became a Christian kingdom in the year 1000.

The rise of Islam

The spread of Christianity from its main centers at Constantinople and Rome to outlying parts of Europe was a slow, gradual process that met with determined opposition. In contrast, the wide diffusion of the new religion of Islam, beginning in the 7th century, was accomplished in an astonishingly short period of time. The aggressive expansion of Islam after the death of its founder, the Prophet Muhammad, in 632 was a decisive

development of the medieval period. Within less than 30 years of his death, Arab armies, erupting from their heartland in the Arabian peninsula, fired by their belief in *jihad* (holy war), had overrun the Byzantine possessions of Egypt, Libya, and Syria, and conquered the once-mighty Sassanian Empire in Persia. By the early 8th century, they had reached India in the east and Spain in the west. In 732, an Arab army penetrated as far as Poitiers in central France. In 751, an Arab force confronted the Chinese in Central Asia.

With the establishment of the Abbasid Caliphate in Baghdad in 762, the Muslim realm was second only to that of Tang China both in extent and in cultural sophistication. But just as Charlemagne's empire broke into its constituent elements after his death in 814, so the Abbasid Caliphate, which under Harun al-Rashid (786–809) had reached the height of its power as well as becoming a brilliant center of learning and culture, struggled to maintain its control over the vast Islamic world.

In the 9th and 10th centuries many local Islamic dynasties ruled with little or no regard for the authority of the caliph in Baghdad. The Ummayad dynasty had ruled in Spain since 756, having fled there after their defeat by the Abbasids. In the 10th century, following the decline of Abbasid power, they reasserted their claim to be the true caliphs (successors of Muhammad). The Shi'ite Fatimids of North Africa also claimed to be the true caliphs, their claim resting on the fact that they were descended from Muhammad's daughter, Fatima. In 969 they conquered Egypt, establishing their capital at Cairo, which gradually came to rival Baghdad as the center of the Islamic world. Another Shi'ite dynasty, the Persian Buwayhids, actually conquered

Baghdad in 945. They allowed the Abbasid caliph to retain his title, but effectively ruled in his name. Other powerful Islamic dynasties included the Samanids in Transoxiana and the Ghaznavids in Afghanistan. Despite this political fragmentation, the Islamic world, still expanding aggressively, remained a major player on the world stage.

Tang China

By the early 7th century China, after the chaos following the disintegration of Han power in 220, had recovered much of its former vigor and unity. Briefly reunited by the Sui dynasty in 589, in 618 China was taken over by the Tang. Chinese territory was again extended into Central Asia – allowing the Silk Road to be reestablished – and protectorates set up as far away as eastern Persia. The prosperity and stability of Tang China was reflected in its great cities such as the capital, Chang'an, which in the 8th century was the largest in the world with a population of about one million.

Tang rule in China lasted only until the late 9th century, undone by the recurring problem of peasant revolts and depredations along the northern frontier by warlike steppe peoples. In 881, China fragmented again into as many as ten separate states.

Other Asian states

During the Tang period, Chinese forms of government were copied in neighboring countries, above all Korea and Japan. In the latter, increasing Chinese influence after the 6th century began the transformation of Japan from a clan-based society into an imperial state. The simultaneous introduction of Buddhism to Japan had an equally profound impact on the culture and society of the country. Japan's imperialist ambitions on the

751: Arab armies defeat Chinese on Talas river
753: Italy invaded by Franks under Pépin
756: Breakaway Umayyad Emirate established at Cordova (to 1031)
772: Charlemagne embarks on conquest of Saxony (complete 802)
c.790: Start of Viking raids on W Europe
800: Imperial coronation of Charlemagne by Pope Leo III in Rome
c.850: Collapse of Classic Maya civilization in Mexico
868: *The Diamond Sutra,* the world's oldest surviving printed book
870s: Peasant uprisings throughout China

750 **775** **800** **825** **850** **875** **900**

762: Abbasid Caliphate established in Baghdad
773–74: Lombards in northern Italy defeated by Franks under Charlemagne
843: Treaty of Verdun divides Carolingian empire into three
862: Novgorod founded by Rurik the Viking
866: Viking state in northern England established
882: Kiev capital of new Russian state

mainland, where it entered into alliances with the warring Korean states, were thwarted by the invention of Tang forces on the side of Silla, which by the mid-7th century had won control of the entire Korean peninsula.

Buddhism also continued to spread in Southeast Asia, usually in conjunction with Hinduism. This happened both on the mainland and in the Indonesian archipelago, which was dominated by the maritime empire of Srivijaya. During this period, India itself was divided into a multitude of small states.

American empires

At this time, both the dominant civilizations in Central America were in decline. The great Mexican city of Teotihuacán was abandoned in c.700 – the vacuum was partly filled by the Toltecs – while from the middle of the 9th century the Classic Maya civilization began to disintegrate. By 900, the Maya had effectively disappeared. In South America, by contrast, three important empires, precursors of the Inca, had emerged: those centered on Tihuanaco and Huari, and, on the coast of northern Peru, the smaller Chimú empire with its capital at Chan Chan.

Polynesian migrations

In concentrating on the rise and fall of continental civilizations, it is easy to overlook the achievements of the Polynesians, who by the year 1000 had colonized all the inhabitable islands of the Pacific Ocean. Their last major discovery was New Zealand (Aotearoa), which was reached by colonists from the Cook Islands in about 1000 CE.

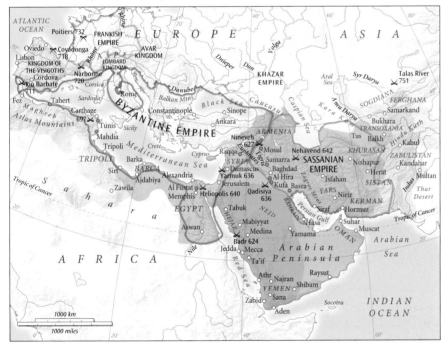

In theory all Muslims lands came under the authority of the caliph (successor) of Muhammad. The caliphate was often in dispute and the capital was transferred from Medina to Damascus to Baghdad. The Muslim world was a remarkably homogenous society, rich and powerful from its control of Eurasian trade by land and sea.

The growth of the Islamic world

Muslim lands by 634	Byzantine Empire c.610
Muslim lands by 656	Sassanian Empire c.610
Muslim lands by 756	Frankish Empire c.610
• new city founded by Muslims	
✘ Muslim victory, with date	
✗ Muslim defeat, with date	

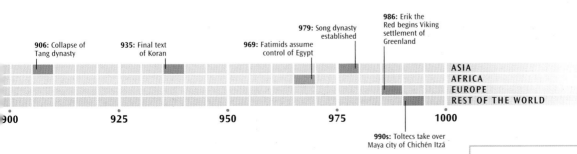

906: Collapse of Tang dynasty

935: Final text of Koran

969: Fatimids assume control of Egypt

979: Song dynasty established

986: Erik the Red begins Viking settlement of Greenland

ASIA
AFRICA
EUROPE
REST OF THE WORLD

900   925   950   975   1000

990s: Toltecs take over Maya city of Chichén Itzá

Japanese tomb models

In Japan, unglazed terra-cotta sculptures (*haniwa*) were placed on, and around, the tomb mounds of the elite (c.250–500 CE). They originated as barrel-shaped cylinders (*haniwa* means "circle of clay"), but by the 4th century had evolved into a wide range of sculptural forms, from warriors to dogs, horses, and birds. The keyhole-shaped tomb of Nintoku was surrounded by some 23,000 *haniwa* warriors. Human figures averaged 3 feet (90 cm) in height, and were decorated with red, white, and blue pigmentation. The eyes, noses, and mouths were hollow. They were mass-produced in the 6th century, but the introduction of Buddhism and, with it, the practice of cremation, led to a decline in both tomb-building and the production of *haniwa*.

ASIA

c.501 Rise of Indianized Mon state of Dvaravati in what is now Thailand.

Wall paintings in Buddhist cave-temples at Ajanta, N India.

548 ▼

502 Xiao Yan marches on Nanjing, forcing the Qi rulers to cede their power. He founds the Liang dynasty.

Persians declare war on the Eastern Empire, sacking the town of Amida in N Mesopotamia.

506 After a Roman counteroffensive, peace is reestablished between Persia and the Eastern Empire.

554 ▼

512 Four provinces in S Korea, known as Mimana, are ceded to the state of Paekche, based in SW Korea.

518 Sung Yun is sent on a mission to India by Empress Wu of the Wei.

524 Invasion of Wei by Ruanruan and Turks.

525 Insurrections of soldiers and nomads begin to break out on the northern frontier of the Wei empire.

AFRICA

525 Ethiopians win back Yemen from the Jewish prince, Dhu Nuwas, and reestablish Christianity. They build many churches.

543 ▼

c.525 Monophysite Christian missionaries introduce their distinctive doctrine and monastic tradition to Nubia.

502 Bulgars, a Mongolian people, ravage Thrace (N Greece), unopposed by the Eastern Empire.

506 Alaric II, the king of the Visigoths, publishes a code of laws, the *Breviary of Alaric*.

507 Visigoths defeated by Franks at the battle of Vouillé and driven out of Aquitaine.

541

508 Ostrogoths occupy Provence.

Clovis, the Frankish king, receives imperial recognition of his rule over Gaul.

510 Theodoric, the Ostrogothic king, controls a kingdom that extends from Gaul to Illyricum (Yugoslavia).

537

511 Death of Frankish king, Clovis; his kingdom divided between four sons.

516 Burgundian kingdom adopts Catholicism.

534

518 Accession of new Byzantine emperor, Justin I. He reestablishes orthodoxy and relations with Rome, bringing the 35-year schism between the Eastern and Western churches to an end.

524 The Roman scholar and senator, Boethius, is accused of treasonable contacts with the Eastern emperor, imprisoned and executed. During his imprisonment he writes *De consolatione philosophiae*.

Lydenburg heads

The use of iron technology had been gradually spreading southward throughout the African continent from the middle of the 1st millennium BCE. The new technology was introduced by farmers, ancestors of the present-day Bantu people. By the 5th century CE, ironworking had reached Zimbabwe, and from there it spread to eastern Botswana and the Transvaal highveld of South Africa. At Lydenburg, in east Transvaal, archaeologists discovered hollow ceramic heads, dating to about 500, which were probably used as ceremonial or religious masks. The sophistication of the craftsmanship indicates the development of a settled and well-organized society.

The Byzantine Empire (–800)

Under Emperor Justinian, the Eastern Roman empire turned its back on the Roman world. Justinian and his successors sought to unify the empire, improve its government, and establish both social and ethnic unity. The church served the political authorities, and a single dogma was imposed on the state. Frequently, the extreme control imposed by the state, especially on conquered Christian peoples, led to violent conflict.

330	Constantine makes Byzantium his capital.
527	Reign of Justinian (–565).
529	Suppression of the Platonic Academy in Athens.
532	Nika insurrection in Constantinople.
534	Publication of Justinian's code of civil laws.
537	Completion of construction of Hagia Sophia cathedral in Constantinople.
717	Siege of Constantinople by the Arabs.
726	Iconoclastic controversy (–843).

Hagia Sophia

The cathedral Hagia Sophia, which stands on the main hill in Constantinople, was completed in 537. It was built, under the direction of Justinian I, in the amazingly short time of about six years. The architects were Anthemius of Tralles and Isidore of Miletus. The cathedral is the archetype of the eastern three-naved domed basilica. The crown, which rises 180 feet (55 m) above the ground, floods the building with light. Daylight enters through windows commemorating the 40 martyrs. Magnificent Byzantine mosaics adorn the upper galleries.

ASIA

529 In Korea, the southern states of Mimana are under threat from Silla, a powerful kingdom based in SE Korea.

530 Following a five-year war, the Byzantines defeat the Persians at the battle of Dara.

531 Beginning of reign of Sassanian ruler, Khosrau I Anushirvan.

628 ▼ **532** After a seven-year war, the Persian king, Khosrau, signs a "treaty of eternal peace" with Justinian.

535 The Northern Wei dynasty splits into Eastern and Western halves.

645 ▼ **538** Buddhism reaches Japan from Korea.

560 ▼ **540** Khosrau resumes war with Byzantines, invading Syria, and sacking Antioch.

544 Proclamation in Vietnam of the kingdom of Viet.

548 General Hou Jing heads a rebellion against his Liang masters in S China and leads his troops to Nanjing, which is sacked (–549).

c.550 Western migrations of Turkish tribes (Avars) begins.

Khmer state of Chenla overthrows its former suzerain, Funan.

AFRICA

572 ▼ **531** Byzantine emperor, Justinian, tries to recruit Axum in his fight against Persia.

534 Byzantine forces, led by Belisarius, conquer the Vandal kingdom. Much of N Africa is now controlled by Byzantines.

536 Axum severs its links with Rome, the result of Roman persecution of the Coptic Church.

540 Cush, to the south of Egypt, is divided into three Nubian kingdoms: Nobatia, Alodia, and Mukuria (Dongola).

c.540 Ethiopian monks begin to translate the Bible into their own language.

543 The Nubian kingdom of Nobatia is converted to Christianity by Coptic missionaries.

547 Byzantines crush the rebellious Berber tribes of N Africa.

569 ▼ **550** The Nubian kingdom of Alodia is converted to Coptic Christianity.

c.550 Farming communities in the Drakensberg mountains (S Africa) make pots, intricate ceramics, and terra-cotta heads.

526 Death of Theodoric; succeeded by grandson with daughter as regent.

Dionysius Exiguus, a Scythian monk, publishes *Easter Tables*, aimed at settling the controversy about the date of Easter. He also proposes the AD system of dating from the birth of Christ.

527 Justinian I, nephew of Justin I becomes Byzantine emperor.

529 Regulation of monasticism in Europe under St. Benedict, who founds the monastery of Monte Cassino.

558 ▼

531 Frankish kingdom absorbs Burgundy.

Thuringia is conquered by the Franks.

532 A popular revolt against Justinian's rule leads to massacre of 30,000 rebels by imperial troops (the Nika insurrection).

554 ▼

533 Beginning of reconquest of Italy by East Roman Empire.

East Roman Empire conquers Vandal kingdom.

534 The kingdom of the Burgundians is annexed by the Franks.

Final revisions of Justinian's *Codex*, produces a unified code of statutes, valid for the whole Roman world.

535 Byzantine general, Belisarius invades S Italy.

536 Belisarius takes Rome.

537 Ostrogothic leader, Vitgis lays siege to Rome (−538).

540 Byzantines take Ravenna.

A Bulgar horde ravages Thrace and Macedonia, reaching the walls of Constantinople.

541 Franks attack the Visigothic kingdom in N Spain. They are driven back at Saragossa.

542 Bubonic plague kills many thousands of people in Constantinople, and spreads to Italy.

552 ▼

546 Ostrogothic king, Totila, captures Rome after a year's siege. It is immediately recaptured by Belisarius.

547 Death of King Maelgwyn of Gwynedd (Wales) prompts renewed German advances on W British Isles.

550 Belisarius is recalled from Italy; Totila recaptures Rome.

Theodoric the Great

At the age of seven, Theodoric the Great (493–526) king of the Ostrogoths was sent as a hostage to the court of Emperor Zeno at Constantinople. With the emperor's consent, he set out, with some 100,000 followers, to drive Odoacer out of Italy and restore imperial control. He succeeded and soon proved how swiftly he could come to terms with his new artistic and political heritage. He set up a capital at Ravenna, which he enriched with remarkable monuments. On his death in 526 he was buried, in true Roman fashion, in an imposing mausoleum (*above*).

Emperor Justinian

Justinian I was Byzantine emperor from 527 to 565. He is portrayed here, flanked by Archbishop Maximian and Byzantine priests and bodyguards, in a mosaic from the Church of San Vitale at Ravenna. The mosaic was completed soon after Justinian recaptured Ravenna in 540, symbolizing his success in restoring imperial authority in the West. However, Justinian's most lasting achievement was his codification of Roman law (*Codex Justinianus*, 534), which outlasted his imperial conquests, and became the basis for many centuries of subsequent western legislation.

The Visigoths

The Visigoths arrived in the Roman Empire from Romania in the 4th century CE. After rampaging through Greece and Italy in the early 5th century, they finally settled in Spain and France where they set up kingdoms. In 475, their leader Euric, declared himself an independent king. He codified laws issued by himself, and fragments of his law code, written in Latin, still survive. Under his rule, the Visigothic domain extended from the Loire to the Pyrenees, and included much of Spain.

This Visigothic cross dates from the 6th century. Although Christian, the Visigoths were Arians (they denied the Trinity). This changed in 589 when King Reccared (586–601) converted to the orthodox Catholicism of his Hispano-Roman subjects.

Lombards

In 568–9 the Lombards, a Germanic tribe from Pannonia (modern Hungary), invaded Italy. Although they were already partly Romanized, they lacked the political coherence of the Ostrogoths, and never conquered all of Italy. Their king, Algoin (c.560–72) was murdered, his successor Cleph (572–574) was also murdered. A decade of fragmentation followed, with local duchies but no king. Faced, in 584, with a Frankish invasion from beyond the Alps, the Lombards united and elected Authari king (583–590). He succeeded in uniting the northern duchies into a single kingdom, but it was not long before Lombard rule again fragmented.

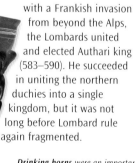

Drinking horns were an important element of Germanic warrior tradition. They were used at the feasts hosted by warrior lords to reward their followers.

ASIA

551 Some 250,000 people lose their lives in an earthquake in Beirut.

552 Northern Qi dynasty (–577).

Mutinous general, Hou Jing is driven from Nanjing. Gao Yang deposes the last emperor of the Northern Qi, gaining control of most of N China.

554 Yamato supports Paekche against Silla (Korea).

557 Yu Wenjue sets up the Northern Zhou dynasty (–581), having deposed the last emperor of the Western Wei.

560 Khosrau, king of the Persians, allies with the western Turks to defeat the Hephthalites.

589 ▼

c.560 The Turks found two states. One is based in Mongolia (eastern Turks), the other in Dzungaria (western Turks).

570 The Korean kingdom of Koguryo sends its first embassy to Japan.

610 ▼

c.570 Birth of Prophet Muhammad in Mecca.

572 Persians expel the Axumites from Yemen, driving them back to Ethiopia.

574 The Northern Zhou take measures against the Buddhist clergy.

AFRICA

552 Catholicism is reestablished in Alexandria (Egypt), but Coptic resistance remains strong.

569 The Nubian kingdom of Makuria (Dongola) is converted to Christianity.

c.570 Sef ibn Dhi Yazan founds the first Bornu kingdom of Kanem.

552 A huge Byzantine force defeats and kills Totila, king of the Ostrogoths, at the battle of Busta Gallorum.

553 Monks smuggle silkworms from China to Constantinople; start of Byzantine silk industry.

554 Frankish invasion defeated; Italy under Byzantine control.

Justinian's troops occupy S Spain; Córdoba is their capital.

555 Byzantines complete reconquest of Italy and south coast of Visigothic Iberia.

557 An earthquake damages the cathedral of Hagia Sophia, Constantinople.

558 Chlotar I, sole king of the Franks.

561 Death of Chlotar I; kingdom divided between his four sons.

563 The Irish missionary, St. Columba begins to spread Christianity in Scotland.

565 Justinian dies after a reign of 38 years. He leaves his nephew an empire at its territorial peak.

567 Visigoths drive the Byzantines from W Spain.

Lombards and Avars combine to crush the Gepids in Hungary.

568 Lombards invade Italy.

590

572 After a three-year siege, Pavia falls to the Lombards, who have overrun N Italy.

613
573 Beginning of major civil wars between the Franks.

585
Visigoths recapture Córdoba in Spain from the Byzantines.

St. Columba

Born in c.521, in Ireland, Columba was the abbot and missionary credited with converting Scotland to Christianity. Columba was ordained priest in about 551. He founded churches and two famous monasteries, in Derry and Durrow, in his native Ireland, before moving with 12 disciples to Scotland. On the island of Iona, they erected a church and monastery (c.563). It was the monastery at Iona that became the springboard for Columba's tireless mission.

Columba spent the last years of his life (he died in 597) at Iona, where he was revered as a saint. He, his associates, and his successors did more to spread the gospel than any other contemporary group in Britain.

The Maya calendar

The Maya excelled at astronomical observation, and evolved a numerical system based on units of 20, which included the concept of zero. Numbers were notated by a series of horizontal bars, dots, and a stylized shell for zero. The Maya kept three major calendars. The Solar Year calendar consisted of 365 days and 18 named months of 20 days each, with five extra days added at the year's end. Eras were counted in 52-year-long Calendar Rounds. The third calendar was the Long Count, used for dates which fell outside the Calendar Round. The current cycle is thought to begin on September 8, 3114 BCE, and is expressed in units of time ranging from 400 years to single days.

Monte Albán

The Zapotec culture of Mesoamerica was centered on Monte Albán, in Mexico. Initial construction at the site began in the 8th century BCE. It contains pyramids, plazas, and underground passageways, and about 170 tombs. The great plaza, *above*, which sits on the highest hill, is flanked by four temple platforms. It is evident that this complex city must have been governed by an elite group, capable of mobilizing the huge workforce required to construct its elaborate buildings. Monte Albán reached its zenith c.600 CE. Little is known about its subsequent decline, when it lost its political prominence and its structures began to decay.

576–600 CE

ASIA

581 The last emperor of the Northern Zhou is overthrown by his own general, Yang Jian. Foundation of the Sui dynasty.

616

585 Construction of great walls in N China begins.

589 The western Turks, based in Dzungaria, take control of the Silk Road.

Khosrau II of Persia is deposed by a military revolt, and flees to Constantinople.

General Yang Jian attacks the Yan capital, takes the south, and reunites China under the Sui dynasty.

605

591 The Byzantine emperor restores Khosrau II to the Persian throne in exchange for territorial concessions.

592 In Japan, conflict between Soga clans, who support Buddhism, and the Mononobe, who worship indigenous deities, leads to the execution of the emperor.

595 First record of Indian mathematicians using the decimal system.

c.600 Florescence of architecture and sculpture in India.

Book printing in China.

Yamato controls Japan south of C Honshu.

AFRICA

c.600 Trans-Saharan trade is dominated by Sanhaja and Tuareg Berbers.

The ancient kingdom of Ghana, the first state known in Africa, founded.

Cattle and ironworking widespread in S Africa.

EUROPE

c.580 Avars, nomads from the steppes, establish state on Hungarian plains.

582 Byzantine emperor, Tiberius II surrenders Sirmium to the Avars, and agrees to pay them tribute to safeguard the rest of the Balkans.

585 Visigoths conquer Sueves in NW Spain.

589 Following the death of the Arian Visigothic king, Leovigild, the council of Toledo decrees that Spain is a Catholic country.

590 Slavs begin to settle in the Balkans. They recognize Avar supremacy.

Papacy of Gregory the Great, who negotiates with Lombards to save Rome (–604).

Lombards in Italy survive combined attacks by Byzantine and Frankish forces.

592 Byzantine emperor Maurice begins warfare against the Avars and Slavs, who have ravaged the Balkans and threaten Constantinople.

597 Mission of St. Augustine, papal missionary, to England. He converts the king of Kent to Christianity. Also begins conversion of Anglo-Saxon kings to Roman Christianity.

598 Byzantines agree to a treaty conceding N Italy to the Lombards.

AMERICAS & AUSTRALASIA

c.600 Hohokam culture emerges in southwest N America. It shows signs of Mexican influence.

In Peru, Huari leaders conquer territory stretching 560 miles (900 km) along Andean coast. Expansion leads to Moche collapse.

The ceremonial center, Monte Albán in Mexico reaches its zenith.

Tiahuanaco, Bolivia, the highest ancient city in the Andes, has a peak population of c.35,000.

Maya civilization in C America reaches its height.

The Ponce monolith stands inside the Kalasasaya, the main temple enclosure at Tiahuanaco. The mask-like face is characteristic of Tiahuanaco art.

Tiahuanaco

Tiahuanaco, located high in the Andes was a major pilgrimage center, occupied by up to 40,000 people. The cult center consisted of monumental gateways, stone-built temples, sunken courtyards, and monolithic sculptures up to 25 feet (7.6 m) high. Statues and reliefs of an anthropomorphic figure, depicted frontally, and holding a staff may be early representations of Viracocha, the Creator God of later Andean cultures. By c.500 CE, Tiahuanaco was the center of a large state, administered by government officials at regional centers, who supervized public works carried out as a labor tax by the inhabitants.

Polychrome painted vessel in the form of a jaguar, an important motif in many S American religions. It may have contained oil, used for anointing during religious ceremonies.

Sutton Hoo

In c.624, an Anglo-Saxon ruler was buried in a ship at Sutton Hoo, in eastern England. Although the timbers have rotted away, it is evident that the ship was a mastless, clinker-built rowing boat, over 80 feet (24 m) long. The burial was filled with a rich array of grave goods, many of Swedish origin. There were 41 items of solid gold, as well as imported silverware, including a Byzantine dish. Silver and bronze bowls, cups, and spoons from the Near East reveal the extent of the kingdom's trading contacts. Among the most impressive items are the king's personal equipment, including a sword, shield, and Swedish-style helmet (*above*).

Bronze Buddha, Thailand

In Suvarnabhumi, or the "Land of Gold" as Southeast Asia was known by its neighbors from as early as the 1st millennium BCE, demand for oriental products from the Roman Empire had encouraged Indian merchants to travel there. In Thailand, many small commercial settlements became Hindu–Buddhist kingdoms. Indians intermarried with the local population, and both religions flourished. This early representation of the Buddha, from Thailand, shows the strong influence of Indian forms on the artists of Southeast Asia.

ASIA

605 Persians under Khosrau II resume war against the Byzantines.

Sui emperor Yangdi expands and reorganizes the Confucian system of civil service examinations.

606 Harsha of Thanesar founds last native empire in N India (dies 647).

607 First record of Japanese diplomatic mission to China.

Tibet unified (–842).

608 The Persian army, having seized Armenia and Syria, marches into Asia Minor.

Pulakesin II Chalukya becomes ruler of the Deccan (–642).

610 Muhammad, a member of the Quraysh tribe, begins to preach in Mecca, Arabia. He calls for an end to idols and demons, and conversion to the ways of one god, Allah.

Emperor Yangdi completes a grand canal which links the Yangtze with Chang'an.

611 Arabs invade Mesopotamia.

614 Persian armies capture Jerusalem and overrun Asia Minor (–626).

616 In China, rebellion breaks out against Yangdi, leading to the collapse of the Sui dynasty (–617).

618 Li Yuan founds the Tang dynasty in China (–906).

619 Tang introduce system of three taxes: taxes on grain, compulsory labor, and deliveries of cloth.

632 ▼ **622** Start of the Islamic era marked by the Hegira (Muhammad's flight to Medina with his followers).

AFRICA

615 Muslim refugees from Arabia are given refuge in Axum (Ethiopia).

619 Persians complete their conquest of Egypt.

620 Oldest Chinese coins found on the east coast of Africa.

625 First Islamic Arab invasion of Makuria.

602 Following a mutiny among Byzantine troops in the Balkans, the centurion Phocas becomes emperor.

603 Lombards of Italy convert to Roman Catholicism.

Northumbrians defeat Scots at Degsastan.

610 Constantinople is attacked by Heraclius, son of the governor of Africa. Phocas is seized and executed. The empire is on the brink of collapse.

613 Chlothar II, king of all Gaul (–629); civil wars end.

614 Chlothar II issues the Edict of Paris, an attempt to eradicate corruption. He appoints mayors of the palace to act as chief ministers for Neustria, Austrasia, and Burgundy.

627 ▼ **616** Northumbrians defeat Britons at Chester.

c.640 ▼ **617** Slavs migrating south appear at walls of Constantinople.

628 ▼ **622** Emperor Heraclius launches a counterattack on the Persians.

624 Visigoths expel last Byzantine garrisons from S Iberia.

c.624 The gold treasure of an Anglo-Saxon king is buried in a ship grave at Sutton Hoo, Suffolk.

Tang tomb guardian

The Tang dynasty united China in 618, creating a vast empire of c.60 million people, which extended into Central Asia. Tang civilization has left a wealth of paintings, sculptures, ceramics, textiles, and written documents. Tomb guardians (*above*) were made in such numbers that attempts were made, through legislation, to limit their number and size. They were generally earthenware, made in molds, and slip-painted or glazed. This hybrid figure, half-human, half beast, was one of a pair that guarded a tomb chamber.

The Advance of Islam (622–850)

By 750 Islam had spread, through conquest and trade, from its Arabian homeland to Persia, the Middle East and Central Asia, and North Africa. The Islamic religion was founded by the prophet Muhammad in about 622. Islam means "submission." A devout Muslim must submit to the will of Allah (God) and fulfil the five duties known as the Pillars of Islam: profession of the Shahada (creed); formal prayer five times daily; alms-giving; fasting during the lunar month of Ramadan; and Haj – a pilgrimage to Mecca.

622	Beginning of Islamic calendar; marked by Hegira of Mohammed.
632	Death of Muhammad; succession of Abu Bakr (–634).
633	Muslim conquest of Syria, Palestine, and Iraq (–640).
634	Caliphate of 'Umar (–644).
637	Conquest of Mesopotamia.
642	Conquest of Egypt.
644	Caliphate of 'Uthman (–646).
656	Imamate of 'Ali (–661).
651	Muslim conquest of W Persia.
661	Umayyad caliphate (–750).
664	Conquest of Kabul.
692	Construction of Dome of the Rock mosque, Jerusalem.
711	Invasion of Iberian peninsula.
718	Christians halt Arab advance at battle of Covadonga, Spain.
732	Arab armies halted at Poitiers.
750	Abbasid caliphate established.
751	Arab armies defeat Chinese at Talas river.
756	Breakaway Umayyad emirate established at Córdoba (–1031).
762	Baghdad becomes Abbasid capital.
800	Reign of the Aghlabids in Tunisia, Algeria, and Sicily (–909).
819	Reign of the Samanids in Khurasan and Transoxiania (–1005).
836	Abbasid capital moves to Samarra.

***Mohammed at the Ka'ba in Mecca,** the temple that Muslims believe was built by Abraham and his son Ishmael, which is the spiritual center of the Islamic world. Depictions of Mohammed are rare, as figurative representation is generally proscribed by Islamic law.*

626–650 CE

ASIA

626 In China, Li Yuan's son, Li Shimin kills his brothers and forces his father to abdicate. Tang court adopts Buddhism.

627 Byzantine emperor Heraclius, allied with the Mongolian Khazars, annihilates Persian army at Nineveh.

628 Defeat of Sassanians by Heraclius; they sue for peace, and make territorial concessions to the Byzantines.

Muhammad and his followers make pilgrimage from Medina to Mecca.

629 Chinese monk, Zuanzang brings back sacred Sanskrit texts from India.

630 Having defeated the Meccans, Muhammad takes control of Mecca.

Tang Chinese defeat the eastern Turks. First Japanese embassy at the Tang court.

632 Death of Muhammad; succession of Abu Bakr (–634). Era of Arab expansion begins.

633 Muslims begin conquest of Syria and Mesopotamia.

634 'Umar appointed caliph (–644).

636 Byzantine army routed by Muslims on Yarmuk river. *659*

637 Arab conquest of Mesopotamia; Sassanian capital, Ctesiphon, captured.

Arabs defeat Persians at Al Qadisiya; Jerusalem seized.

640 Tang armies reach Turfan in C Asia.

641 Nestorian Christianity reaches China from Persia.

642 Arabs crush Sassanians at Nehavend; Sassanian empire falls.

644 Death of 'Umar; 'Uthman appointed caliph. *656*

Tang offensive, by land and sea, against Koguryo in Korea. *668*

645 The Soga family's control of Japan's imperial throne ends with the murder of Soga Iruka in a *coup d'etat*.

Buddhism reaches Tibet. *685*

646 In Japan, Taika reforms initiated under Prince Shotoku. All private land is brought under public ownership.

647 Death of Harsha of Kanauj, who united India under his rule for 41 years.

c.650 Hindu empire established in Sumatra, Indonesia.

AFRICA

634 Arab Muslims take the Ethiopian town of Massawa on the Red Sea from the Axumites.

641 Arab conquest of Lower Egypt begins.

642 Egypt surrenders to Arabs, who advance south to Nubia. They found the new Islamic capital of Cairo. *652*

Arabs capture Alexandria, the last Byzantine outpost in Egypt.

643 Arab forces reach Cyrenaica and Tripolitania.

646 Gregory, the governor of Carthage, rebels against Emperor Constans II.

647 Arabs raid the Byzantine province of Africa, remove the usurper Gregory, and effectively end the African rebellion. *670*

EUROPE

626 Constantinople is attacked by a combined force of Persians and Avars. The Avar fleet is destroyed, and the city is saved.

627 King Edwin of Northumbria is converted to Christianity.

629 Chlothar II, king of Gaul, dies; succeeded by son, Dagobert I.

Visigoths complete the recovery of S Spain from the Byzantines.

635 Emperor Heraclius forms an alliance with Kuvrat, the Bulgar king, aimed at keeping the Avars out of Constantinople.

667
639 Death of Dagobert; kingdom divided between two sons.

c.640 Slavs establish an independent Bohemian kingdom, led by Samo, a Frankish merchant.

655
642 Oswald, the Christian king of Northumbria is killed by Penda, the pagan king of Mercia, at Maserfelth.

652
643 *Edict of Rothari*: first book of Lombard law.

655
649 Arabs conquer Cyprus.

675
c.650 Khazars conquer the Great Bulgarian empire in S Russia.

AMERICAS & AUSTRALASIA

650 Settlement of Xochicalco and Cacaxtla in C America.

c.650 Easter Islanders start to build *ahus*, sacred stone platforms.

Throne of Dagobert

The Frankish Merovingian dynasty was founded by Clovis (ruled c.481–511). By the middle of the 6th century, the Merovingians had gained control of nearly all of Roman Gaul, as well as conquering much of Central Europe. The Frankish practice of subdividing the kingdom among heirs meant that very few rulers reigned over all the Frankish lands. Dagobert I, sole king from 629 to 639, was an exception. His throne is a powerful emblem of the continuity of the French kingdom, which lasted until the Revolution in 1790.

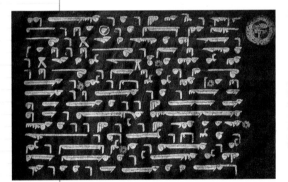

The Koran

Muslims believe that the Koran contains the word of God as revealed to Mohammed by the Angel Gabriel. Mohammed's companions established the text in its present form in about 650. Its pages contain not only religious injunctions, but also social guidance for the faithful, including instructions about hygiene, inheritance, dowries, and marriage, as well as discussions about commerce, law and order, and war and peace. This sacred text of Islam is written in Arabic. Muslim authorities believe that the Koran cannot be translated without losing its divine authority. Infinite care was taken over individual manuscript copies of the text, such as this example in gold on black *kufic* script, produced at Kairouan in Tunisia.

Hindu Cambodia

This statue of Uma (Light), consort of Shiva, is from 7th-century Cambodia. Southeast Asia was receptive to many important aspects of Indian civilization, which arrived as a result of commercial links with the subcontinent: the Hindu religion, Indian concepts of kingship and law, Indian styles of art and architecture. Local rulers were happy to accept Indian ideas of kingship, which served to strengthen their own position in fast-developing hierarchical societies.

655 Yazdegerd III, the last Sassanid king, who fled from Persia after its defeat by Arabs, is assassinated. Arabs take Kabul and Kandahar.

656 Murder of Caliph 'Uthman in Medina; first civil war. 'Ali, son-in-law of Muhammad, gains control of caliphate (–661).

651 Arabs overrun Persia.

657 Indian mathematician, Brahmagupta, establishes the rules of calculation by introducing the concept of zero.

Tang Chinese and Uighurs inflict a serious defeat on the western Turks.

659 A truce is reached between the Byzantines and the Arab commander in Syria.

660 Tang forces support Silla (Korea) in destruction of Paekche.

c.660 Tang forces in India and C Asia.

678 **661** Start of Umayyad caliphate (–750). Damascus is center of Islamic empire.

Caliph 'Ali is assassinated in Kufa, Mesopotamia.

Chinese administration in Kashmir, C Asia, and on the borders of E Persia.

698 **668** Tang forces destroy Koguryo (Korea); refugees flee to Manchuria.

The king of Silla recaptures the kingdoms of Koguryo and Paekche with the help of China; takes control of Korean peninsula, which is united under Silla dynasty. Manchuria and Korea are now under Chinese control.

670 The khanate of Orkhon, an E Turkish empire, is reestablished after its destruction by the Chinese.

692 Tibetans take control of the Tarim basin.

651 Nubia again invaded by Arabian Muslims.

652 Christian Nubians and Arabs in Egypt agree that Aswan, on the Nile, should mark southern limit of Arab expansion.

670 Arabs complete their conquest of N Africa. Their control extends from Egypt to E Algeria.

Foundation of city of Kairouan in Tunisia.

Crown of King Recceswinth

652 Airpert, successor to the Lombard king Rothari, is baptized a Catholic at Pavia.

653 Recceswinth, king of the Lombards, draws up a legal code, the *Liber Judiciorum*, based on Roman law. It applies alike to all subjects, both Hispano-Romans and Goths.

654 Arabs invade Rhodes, and pillage the island.

655 Byzantines are defeated in a major sea battle with the Arabs off the coast of Asia Minor. The Arab fleet now commands the E Mediterranean.

679 Northumbrians defeat Mercians at Winwaed.

c.700 657 Pacal becomes king of the Maya religious center, Palenque.

The resplendent votive gold crown of King Recceswinth (reigned 649–72), Visigothic ruler of Spain, reflects the close relationship between this Germanic ruler and the Church of Rome. The Visigoths had been among the first of the Germanic peoples to reject the Arian heresy, and embrace Roman Catholicism. Their faith is reflected in the numerous basilicas they built and in the intricately wrought, bejeweled, cruciform brooches that are characteristic Visigothic artifacts.

Large hoards of gold ornaments, such as these intricate earrings, were found in the Silla tombs by archaeologists in the 20th century.

663 Byzantine emperor, Constans II invades Italy and sacks Rome.

687 664 Synod of Whitby. "Roman" Christianity adopted instead of "Celtic."

The British Isles are ravaged by plague.

687 667 The death of Childeric II leads to anarchy in the Frankish kingdom.

668 Emperor Constans II is assassinated during a mutiny at Syracuse (Sicily).

674 Arabs besiege Constantinople, but fail to take it (–678).

675 Bulgarians settle areas south of Danube and found the first (eastern) Bulgarian empire.

Silla Korea

Between 57 BCE and 668 CE, Korea was ruled by three kingdoms: Koguryo in the north; Paekche in the southwest; Silla in the southeast. Eventually Silla was to conquer the other two kingdoms, controlling Korea until the 9th century. All three societies were hierarchical, ruled by a hereditary aristocracy. The elite were buried in monumental tombs, with rich grave goods. The Silla tombs, which consisted of a wooden chamber and coffin covered with a mound of stones and earth, were inaccessible to looters.

The architects at Palenque used plaster to give exterior walls a smooth finish. Interior walls were embellished with stucco bas-reliefs.

Palenque

During the Late Classic Period (600–900), Maya civilization underwent a period of vigorous expansion, when several major cities were rebuilt and elaborated. The beautiful city of Palenque lies on the floodplain of the Usumacinta river, which drains into the Gulf of Mexico. The graceful pyramids and palaces have mansard-style roofs, and are decorated with stucco reliefs of rulers, gods, and ceremonies and terra-cotta images. One of the best preserved structures is the Temple of the Inscriptions, so-called because of its Mayan hieroglyphic reliefs. In 1952 a crypt was discovered underneath the temple containing, within the sarcophagus, the body of an unusually tall man, thought to be Pacal, ruler of Palenque.

Jade death-mask of Pacal, the 7th-century Maya ruler buried at Palenque. His burial contained the richest offering of jade ever found in a Maya tomb.

ASIA

678 Yazid, the governor of Damascus, is elected caliph, strengthening the Umayyads' dynastic ambitions.

680 Al-Husayn, the son of 'Ali (the prophet's son-in-law) is killed in combat at Kerbela, Mesopotamia. A dissident group, the Shi'ites, claim that the rights of interpreting the Koran belong solely to Muhammad's descendants. They proclaim al-Husayn a martyr.

Tibetan incursions into NW China and C Asia grow more frequent.

682 Abdullah ibn Zubayr is acclaimed as caliph in Arabia, Mesopotamia, and Egypt. He is supported by the people of Mecca and Medina.

683 Turkish khan, Qutlugh, sacks the Chinese region of Zhan Yu.

 705

Chinese emperor, Gaozong dies. His concubine, Wu Zhao, usurps the throne, founding the Zhou dynasty.

684 Umayyads defeat the Qays tribe, who support ibn Zubayr's claim to the caliphate, at Marj Rahit, Syria.

685 'Abd al-Malik becomes caliph of the Umayyads. They are Sunnites, and believe that doctrinal authority passes from caliph to caliph.

710

Buddhism becomes the state religion of Japan.

690 Caliph Abd al-Malik defeats Mus'ab, governor of Mesopotamia and brother of rebel, ibn Zubayr, on the Tigris river.

The Malayan kingdom of Srivijaya conquers Malayu, sets up a capital at Palembang (Sumatra) and adopts Buddhism.

692 Dome of the Rock mosque completed in Jerusalem.

China recaptures the Tarim basin from Tibet.

693 Armenia falls to the Arabs.

 705

Umayyads crush the ibn Zubayr rebellion, capturing Mecca. 'Abd al-Malik becomes master of the Umayyad empire.

695 First Arabic coinage.

696 Arabic becomes the official language of the Umayyad empire.

698 Pohai empire formed in Manchuria by Koguryo refugees.

c.700 Wooden temple pagodas built at Nara, Japan.

AFRICA

678 Arab armies, led by Uqba ibn Nafi, reach the Atlantic coast of N Africa.

c.690 The state of Gao is founded on the upper Niger, W Africa.

698 Arabs occupy Carthage, bringing Byzantine rule of N Africa to an end. They found city of Tunis nearby.

Arabs suppress a revolt by Berbers in the Aures mountains of N Africa.

742

c.700 The kingdom of Ghana in W Africa is becoming more powerful. It controls trans-Saharan trade routes, especially in gold.

750

Madagascar settled by Malays from SE Asia.

EUROPE

678 Byzantines defend Constantinople from Arab attack, using "Greek fire" – an explosive mixture of sulphur, rock salt, resin, and petroleum. Arabs and Byzantines sign a peace treaty.

679 Mercians conquer Lindsey from Northumbrians.

680 In Spain, Count Ervig overthrows Wamba, king of the Visigoths, and makes concessions to the rebellious aristocrats.

681 Having defeated the Byzantines, the Bulgars found a new state on the delta of the Danube.

682 Wilfrid converts the Saxons of Sussex (S England) to Christianity.

685 Last great king of Northumbria killed by Picts at Nechtansmere.

687 The Isle of Wight is the last area of Anglo-Saxon England to be converted to Christianity.

715 Pepin II, mayor of Austrasia, wins a victory over his Neustrian rival at the battle of Tertry. The Franks are now united under one king.

690 The Northumbrian monk, Willibrord preaches the gospel to the heathen Frisians.

Slavs, based in Macedonia and Thrace, are defeated by Byzantine emperor, Justinian II.

692 An episcopal council asserts that the patriarch of Constantinople is equal to the pope. The council votes for many church reforms, including allowing priests to marry. The pope rejects the new measures.

693 Byzantines break their treaty with the Arabs, but are crushed in battle at Sebastea.

711 **694** In Toledo, Spain, the Visigothic council decrees the enslavement of all Spanish Jews and confiscation of their property.

705 **695** Justinian II is overthrown by the general, Leontius. He takes refuge with the Bulgars of the Crimea.

697 Venice elects its first leader, or doge. The city has become one of the world's great trading centers.

700 Greek, instead of Latin, is the official language of the Eastern Roman empire.

c.700 The *Lindisfarne Gospels*, the finest of all Anglo-Saxon manuscripts, are produced in N England.

AMERICAS & AUSTRALASIA

c.700 In N America, new innovations, such as bows and arrows and hoes, transform Native American society.

Domination of southwest N America by Hohokam, Mogollon, and Anasazi cultures. They produce high-quality ceramics.

The city of Teotihuacán, Mexico, is destroyed by fire and deserted by its inhabitants.

The ceremonial center of Monte Albán, Mexico, is abandoned.

c.850 Maya civilization reaches new heights. The Temple of Inscriptions and Temple of the Cross are under construction at Palenque, an important Maya religious center. The Maya city of Tikal is being rebuilt.

N Peru is dominated by the Chimú state, with its capital at Chan Chan.

850 Polynesian ancestors of Maori reach Aotearoa, the North Island of New Zealand.

Manuscript illumination

During this period, the art of manuscript illumination flourished in Northumbria, following the revival of learning initiated there by the foundation of monasteries at Lindisfarne, Wearmouth, and Jarrow. These monasteries were in the Irish tradition, and Irish monks introduced their English counterparts to the ancient Celtic forms of curvilinear lines and spirals, which were to characterize their work.

The Lindisfarne Gospels (above) show the fusion of Irish, classical, and Byzantine elements of manuscript illumination.

Christianity in Europe (400–850)

The sack of Rome in 410 shocked the civilized world. But the arrival of the barbarians did not signal the end of the Christian religion. Over the next few centuries, intrepid missionaries took Christianity to the farthest, and most isolated, corners of Europe.

404	Vulgate Bible translated by St Jerome.
410	Sack of Rome by the Goths.
432	St. Patrick arrives in Ireland.
c.500	Clovis, king of the Franks, baptized.
526	Dionysius Exiguus creates *Anno Domini* system of dating.
529	Benedict establishes a monastery at Monte Cassino. Regulates monasticism in Europe.
563	St. Columba founds a monastery at Iona.
590	Gregory the Great becomes pope.
597	St. Augustine begins conversion of Anglo-Saxon kings to Roman Christianity.
604	First church of St. Paul built in London.
637	Jerusalem captured by Muslims.
653	Conversion of Lombards of Italy to Christianity.
664	Synod of Whitby: "Roman" Christianity adopted in England.
c.725	Willibrord leads first Christian mission to Scandinavia.
722	Boniface made bishop of all Germany.
793	Sack of Lindisfarne monastery by Vikings.

Arab invasions

The inexorable advance of the Arab armies took them as far east as Sind, which they conquered in 711, and which has remained Muslim ever since. To the west, they invaded Spain defeating the Visigoths and driving the Christians to take refuge in the mountains of the northeast.

This Persian miniature depicts the Arab cavalry in action. Mounted on dromedary camels they were able to cover great distances rapidly without stopping for food and water.

The cosmopolitan Tang

At its greatest extent, Tang control penetrated far beyond the borders of modern China into Central Asia. Tang China was a truly cosmopolitan society, with sizeable foreign communities, including Turks, Persians, Arabs, Sogdians, and Japanese. Glazed pottery models of pack-camels (*below*) are a reflection of China's extensive trade links, along the Silk Road, with Central Asia, the Near East, and Europe.

701–725 CE

ASIA

701 In Japan, the Taiho code covering civil and criminal matters is issued.

705 Walid succeeds his father, Abd al-Malik as Umayyad caliph. Work starts on the construction of the Great Mosque in Damascus.

Empress Wu of China is deposed in a *coup d'etat*.

741 **710** Nara period in Japan (–794). Establishment of new capital at Nara, imperial court, and Japanese Buddhism.

c.750 **711** Arabs invade India, led by Mohammed ibn al-Kassim, conquering Sind and part of the Punjab.

751 **712** Arabs occupy Samarkand, which becomes a center of Arab learning.

The accession of the Tang emperor, Xuanzong to the Chinese throne brings an end to a period of instability.

725 In China, state stud farms put 420,000 horses at the government's disposal.

c.725 Chinese capital, Chang'an, is the largest city in the world.

AFRICA

705 Rebuilding of the 5th-century cathedral at Faras in Christian Nubia begins.

c.725 Rock art is widespread throughout E and S Africa.

705 Constantinople attacked by Tervel, the Bulgar khan, who restores the exiled Justinian II to the Byzantine throne.

710 Rebel leader, Roderic, is elected king of the Visigoths; the kingdom remains divided by internal unrest.

711 Repressive government by Justinian II provokes a revolt in the Crimea, supported by Turkish Khazars. The rebels march on Constantinople, and kill the emperor in battle in N Asia Minor.

Islamic armies led by Tariq cross the Strait of Gibraltar and rapidly conquer Visigothic Spain.

Spanish Jews are liberated by the Arab invaders.

712 Liutprand becomes Lombard king; tries to unite Italy.

715 On the death of Pepin II, an illegitimate son, Charles Martel, overcomes other claimants to become mayor of the Austrasian palace, the effective power behind the Frankish throne.

716 Ethelbald fights way to crown of Mercia; kingdom dominates all England south of Humber.

Charles Martel defeats his Neustrian rivals at the battle of Amblève.

Arabs conquer Lisbon.

717 Constantinople is besieged by an Arab army of 80,000 men.

718 Christian victory at battle of Covadonga halts Muslim advance in Iberian peninsula.

Byzantine emperor, Leo III, raises the Arab siege of Constantinople, blocking further Arab expansion.

719 The pope sends the West Saxon monk, Winfrid as a missionary to Germany. He is renamed Boniface.

721 Arabs attack the Franks, but are defeated outside Toulouse by Duke Eudo.

722 Boniface ordained as bishop of Germany.

725 *De temporum ratione* ("On the reckoning of time") published by the Northumbrian monk Bede, disseminates the AD system of dating throughout Europe.

St. Anne fresco, Nubia

In the 5th and 6th centuries, Monophysite Christian missionaries from Egypt pushed southward into Nubia. The kingdom of Nobatia, which lay between the first and third cataracts of the Nile, had its capital at Faras. In the 8th century, the cathedral of St. Anne was built on an existing 5th-century foundation. The cathedral walls were decorated with frescoes depicting kings, religious scenes, and saints. The distinctive Christian civilization of Nubia long outlasted the Arab invasion of Egypt in the 7th century.

Great Mosque, Damascus

The Great Mosque at Damascus was one of the great imperial mosques of the Umayyad dynasty. The mosque was built between 705 and 715 on the site of a former Christian church. The courtyard served as an extension of the covered prayer area, and was a model for a number of other mosques within the caliphate.

Celtic chalice from Ardagh,
County Limerick, a striking
illustration of the richness and
sophistication of Irish
monastic culture.

Northern Christianity

Bede, an English monk and scholar
of European renown, stood at the heart
of the cultural florescence of N Europe.
His *Ecclesiastical History of the English
People* (completed 731) was informative,
well researched and wonderfully
readable, earning him a reputation
as the father of English history. His
Bible commentaries were circulated
to monasteries throughout Europe and
were much admired for their illuminating
insights. From the confines of the
monastery at Jarrow, Bede helped to
keep learning and literature alive.

Many monks from the British Isles
preferred to take on a more active role,
traveling to pagan Europe, where they
founded monasteries and set about
converting the pagan population. A
contemporary of Bede's, Boniface may
have been one of the Christian church's
most successful missionaries. He was
born in Devon, England, in about 675, and
commissioned by the pope for missionary
work in pagan Germany. From his base in
the Low Countries, he founded bishoprics
in Hesse, Thuringia, and Bavaria. He
eventually became archbishop of Mainz,
which gave him authority over the church
throughout
Germany.

*A 12th-century
manuscript of
Bede's* Life and
Miracles of St.
Cuthbert. *Bede's
works continued
to be reproduced
and illuminated
in the Middle Ages.*

726–750 CE

ASIA

733 In China, the number of imperial civil
servants rises to 17,680.

739 Arab invaders of Asia Minor are
defeated by Byzantine forces at the battle
of Akroinon.

741 In a Shi'ite revolt at Kufa,
Mesopotamia, Zayd, grandson of the
Shi'ite martyr al-Husayn, is killed.

The Japanese government decrees that
Buddhist temples shall be established
throughout the nation.

756 **742** In China, under the rule of Xuanzong,
measures are taken against Buddhism in
favor of Taoism.

780 **745** Foundation of Uighur empire (–840).

751 Chinese counteroffensive against the
Arabs in Transoxiana and the region south
of Lake Balkhash begins.

747 At Khurasan in Persia, Abu Moslem leads
an Abbasid revolt against the Umayyads. The
Abbasids are a clan descended from the
prophet's uncle, al-'Abbas.

754 **749** The last Umayyad caliph, Marwan, is
defeated by Abbasids at the battle of the
Zab, Syria. The Abbasids now gain
spiritual and political control of most of
the Muslim world.

c.750 Muslim merchants establish Islam
in Kerala, SW India.

Apogee of Pala dynasty, the last major
Buddhist state in S Asia.

AFRICA

737 Christians invade Egypt from the
south to protect the patriarch of
Alexandria, who has been imprisoned by
the caliph, Marwan II of Egypt.

740 Muslims from Arabia and Persia are
trading on the E African coast.

742 Arabs suppress a revolt of Kharajites
and Berbers in N Africa.

745 Nubians and Ethiopians invade
Egypt and temporarily occupy Cairo.
The caliph capitulates.

c.750 Arabs from N Africa have begun to
cross the Sahara in large numbers to trade
in gold with W African kingdoms.

726 Iconoclast Period; Byzantine emperor, Leo III bans the worship of religious images (–843). His decrees meet with violent popular opposition.

727 Following the pope's condemnation of iconoclasm, Byzantine Italy breaks with the Eastern Empire.

728 The Lombard king, Liutprand, occupies all the imperial territories in Italy, except Ravenna.

730 Charles Martel, effective ruler of the Franks, launches raids across the Rhine on the Saxons.

731 The devout monk and scholar, Bede, completes his *Ecclesiastical History* at Jarrow Abbey, N England.

Pope Gregory III excommunicates the supporters of iconoclasm.

732 Frankish leader, Charles Martel defeats Arab armies at battle of Poitiers.

733 Emperor Leo III withdraws all the Balkans, Sicily, and Calabria (S Italy) from the jurisdiction of the pope, putting them under the control of the church at Constantinople.

739 Alfonso is king of the Christian territory of Asturias, Spain. He makes frequent raids on Arab-held territory.

741 Following the death of effective Frankish ruler, Charles Martel, his mayoral power is divided between his sons, Pepin III and Carloman.

742 King Liutprand of the Lombards subjects the independent Italian duchies of Spoleto and Benevento to his rule.

Constantinople is seized by rebel opponents of iconoclasm. Emperor Constantine V storms the capital, regains control, and intensifies his persecution of image-worshipers.

c.745 An outbreak of bubonic plague spreads from Constantinople throughout Europe.

746 Greeks defeat the Arabs to regain control of Cyprus.

747 Following Carloman's abdication, Pepin III becomes the sole effective head of the Frankish kingdom.

c.750 The Sacred Cenote at Chichén Itzá, Yucatán, is used for ritual offerings. It is in continuous use for 1,000 years.

First true towns appear in Mississippi valley.

Martel's victory at the Battle of Poitiers has often been regarded as decisive for world history, since it preserved Western Europe from Muslim conquest and Islamization

Charles Martel

The ruler of the Franks, Charles Martel ("the hammer") never took the title of king, being known simply as the mayor of the Austrasian palace. Charles Martel pursued an expansionist policy. He expanded his power base into Central Europe, subjugated Burgundy and Provence, and defeated the Frisians, Bavarians, and Saxons in a series of campaigns from 724 to 738. At the battle of Poitiers (732) he repelled the Arab advance north of the Pyrenees. On good terms with the pope, he also took responsibility for the safety of the English missionary Boniface as he spread the gospel in southern Germany. He was succeeded by his sons, Pepin III the Short and Carloman.

Micronesian shell map

During the first millennium CE, Polynesians completed their colonization of the islands of the Pacific Ocean, making them the most widespread ethnic group in the world. Since less than one percent of their territory was dry land, they are also regarded as the world's greatest navigators. They traveled in partially open double-hulled canoes, carrying settlers, livestock, and plant seeds.

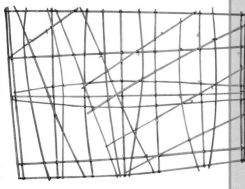

The Polynesians navigated using observations of the currents and stars. They traditionally used shell and cowrie maps to represent the position of islands, and their relationship to currents and swells.

The Lombard kingdom

The Lombard kingdom of Italy, based at Pavia, owed its political foundations to the 6th-century king, Aigulf, who organized its central government with the help of Roman administrators. King Rothari (636–642) produced, in his Edict of 643, a law code that set out the basis of Lombard custom. Liutprand (712–744) revised Rothari's law code, introducing some Roman law into the Lombard system. He conquered the southern duchies of Spoleto and Benevento, bringing Spoleto firmly into Pavia's domain. During his reign, Liutprand was the dominant military force in Italy, reasserting Lombard power, and opposing Byzantine rule.

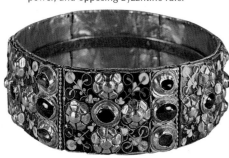

Originally an armlet, or possibly a votive crown, the Iron Crown of Lombardy consists of six hinged gold plates, reinforced by an interior ring of iron. It is decorated with jewels and translucent enamel and is apparently of Byzantine workmanship.

ASIA

751 Battle of Samarkand; China loses dominion of C Asia to the Arabs.

Defeat of Chinese by Arab forces at battle of Talas river. Islamic influence spreads throughout C Asia.

752 Arabs learn the technique of paper-making from the Chinese, and establish the first paper mill in the Arab world.

754 Al-Mansur, brother to the first Abbasid caliph, succeeds him.

755 Revolt in Khurasan, Persia, against the Umayyads.

Rebel Mongol general, An Lushan captures Luoyang, and enthrones himself as emperor of a new Xia dynasty.

756 On the death of the imperial concubine, Emperor Xuanzong abdicates. An Lushan seizes Chang'an, and declares himself emperor.

757 An Lushan is assassinated, his rebellion suppressed.

760 Indian system of numerals is adopted by the Abbasid dynasty.

Construction of the Hindu temple of Kailasa at Ellora, India.

786 **762** Baghdad becomes the capital of the Abbasid dynasty.

Shi'ite revolt against the Abbasids in Mesopotamia.

787 **763** Tang China is invaded by Tibetans.

840 Uighurs of C Asia sack the Chinese city of Luoyang and massacre the inhabitants.

775 The kingdom of Srivijaya conquers the whole of the Malayan peninsula.

AFRICA

761 Ibn Rustam founds the Rustamid dynasty at Tahert, Algeria.

751 Pepin III, the Frankish mayor of the palace, takes the title of king for himself, founding the royal Carolingian dynasty.

Ravenna, the last Byzantine possession in N Italy, falls to the Lombards under Aistulf; end of Byzantine rule.

753 Italy invaded by Pepin (–756).

754 Under Lombard attack, Pope Stephen II appeals for Frankish aid. The Lombard king, Aistulf submits.

755 Emperor Constantine V embarks on a campaign against the Bulgars.

756 Breakaway Umayyad emirate established at Córdoba by Umayyad prince, 'Abd al-Rahman (–1031); claims status of caliphate in 928.

After renewed attack by the Lombards, Pepin intervenes in N Italy. The pope is given control over a larger papal state under Carolingian protection.

757 King Aethelbald of Mercia is murdered by his bodyguard, and succeeded by Offa, the most powerful of the Mercian kings.

759 Franks recapture Narbonne, S France, from the Arabs.

764 Bulgars are forced to sign a peace treaty with the Byzantine emperor.

768 Pepin III and the Carolingians establish firm control over the Aquitaine area. On Pepin III's death, his dominions pass to his sons, Charles (Charlemagne) and Carloman.

769 The laity lose the right to participate in papal elections.

771 Following his brother's death, Charlemagne becomes the sole ruler of the Frankish empire.

772 Charlemagne embarks on conquest of Saxony; subdues it and converts it to Christianity (–802).

Pope Hadrian appeals for Charlemagne's help against the Lombard king.

774 Conquest of Lombards by Charlemagne who absorbs the Lombard kingdom into Frankish empire. N Italy comes under Frankish rule.

The three-story wooden pagoda of Yakushi-ji in the Nara vicinity was constructed in 730 and dedicated to the Buddha of healing.

Buddhist Japan

Buddhism, founded in India, arrived in Japan via China and Korea and was adopted by the Japanese court in the mid-6th century. Different sects evolved and were adopted over the centuries. In 741, a decree was promulgated ordering the construction of a network of Buddhist monasteries and nunneries near every provincial capital.

The centralized, bureaucratic government of the Nara period (710–794) was based in the capital Nara, which was modeled on the great Chinese Tang dynasty capital Chang'an. The city is estimated to have housed a population of 200,000, the majority of them court functionaries. Avidly absorbing ideas from mainland East Asia, the city became the grand diocese of Buddhism and the Far Eastern destination of the Silk Road. Nara artisans produced refined Buddhist sculpture and built grand Buddhist temples.

On the upper terraces of the Borobudur temple, 72 bell-shaped stupas contain statues of the Buddha.

Borobudur

The powerful Buddhist kingdoms of Southeast Asia began to construct monumental temple complexes from the early 9th century. In Java, the temple of Borobudur was built between c.778 and 850. This massive temple is centered on the square base of the stupa mound, with five square or circular terraces surrounding it to form a three-dimensional *mandala*, or cosmic diagram. Each of the terraces represents the individual stages toward perfection in a person's life. A series of reliefs on the terrace wall represent the ascending stages of enlightenment toward *nirvana* (spiritual enlightenment).

ASIA

778 Arab army is defeated by Byzantines at battle of Germanikeia, Asia Minor.

780 Alp Qutlug, emperor of the Uighurs, adopts Manichaeism as the state religion.

c.780 New form of ascetic mysticism, Sufism, appears in Islamic world.

781 Christianity spreads to the Chinese court.

Dezong, the Chinese emperor, fails to bring rebellious local warlords under his authority. He is forced to accept a degree of regional autonomy.

809 **786** Harun al-Rashid becomes caliph. Under him, Baghdad becomes a center of arts and learning.

821 **787** Peace treaty concluded between Tang and Tibetans. Tang are allied with Uighurs and Nanzhao against the Tibetans.

790 Tang have now lost all territory west of W Kansu.

794 Heian Period in Japan (–1185); transition from Chinese influence to warrior lords.

Emperor Kammu moves the Japanese capital from Nara to Kyoto.

797 Controversy at Lhasa between Chinese and Indian monks.

800 Harun al-Rashid sends an embassy to the court of Charlemagne.

Rajput kingdom in India established, extending from Bihar to Sutlej river.

c.800 Arab ships probably sailing as far as China.

820 Shankaracharya, Shaivite philosopher in the early 9th century, founds five major monasteries in India.

Kamban composes S Indian version of the *Ramayana* in the 9th century.

Collapse of Buddhism in Afghanistan in wake of Muslim conquest (9th–10th century).

AFRICA

c.788 Idris, Arab chief, becomes ruler in Morocco. He builds a new capital, Fez.

789 Idrisids establish power in NW Africa.

828 **791** Idris is murdered, apparently by a poisoned toothpick sent by Caliph Harun al-Rashid of Baghdad.

817 **800** Reign of the Aghlabid dynasty in Tunisia, Algeria, and Sicily. Caliph's authority now only extends as far west as Egypt.

Establishment of trading colonies such as Manda and Kilwa on east coast.

c.825 **c.800** Emergence of trading towns on E African coast.

EUROPE

810 ▼

777 Telerig, khan of the Bulgars, converts to Christianity and becomes an ally of the Eastern Empire.

778 Charlemagne's forces invade Umayyad Spain, but meet heavy resistance at Saragossa.

Roland, Charlemagne's general, is killed in a Basque ambush in the Pyrenees.

782 Charlemagne makes Saxony a Frankish province, imposing Christianity on the inhabitants.

Alcuin of York (735–804) organizes education in Carolingian empire.

784 Construction of the Great Mosque of Córdoba begins.

832 ▼

787 At the second council of Nicaea, iconoclasm is condemned, and the veneration of images is restored in the Eastern Empire.

788 Charlemagne annexes Bavaria.

c.789 First recorded Viking raid on England; first raids on Ireland and Scotland recorded in 795.

Charlemagne issues the *Admonitio Generalis* (General Reminder), a declaration of his plans to encourage learning throughout his domains; the "Carolingian Renaissance."

c.790 Beginnings of Viking raids on W Europe.

793 Vikings plunder island monastery of Lindisfarne off northeast coast of England.

802 ▼

795 First recorded Viking raid on isle of Iona.

Charlemagne creates a frontier province, or "march," between the Frankish and Arab empires.

796 Anglo-Saxon king, Offa, dies after completing a massive 150-mile- (240-km-) long dike, marking the border between his kingdom and Welsh territories.

800 The pope crowns Charlemagne Holy Roman Emperor at St. Peter's.

c.800 Romanesque style of architecture develops in Frankish empire.

AMERICAS & AUSTRALASIA

800 Mimbres pottery starts to be made by Mogollon.

City of Huari in the Andes abandoned.

c.800 First use of bows and arrows in the Mississippi valley, N America. Big-game hunting is now more efficient.

Dorset culture in NE Greenland and Canada. Inuit people live by sea-ice hunting.

Charlemagne (c.742–814)

Charles the Great, or Charlemagne, was crowned emperor by the pope at St. Peter's basilica, Rome, on Christmas Day, 800 (*below*) It was an outstanding achievement.

Charlemagne had secured the legitimacy of the Carolingian dynasty, established his rule in Gaul, and extended his control from the Elbe to the Ebro, and from the North Sea to Rome. Charlemagne was a dedicated patron of the arts and learning. The scholars at his court in Aachen rescued classical Latin learning from oblivion, and developed a new script, Carolingian minuscule, which became a model for lower case type in the Renaissance.

Harun al-Rashid

The luxury of the court of the Abbasid caliph, Harun al-Rashid (786–809) was memorably evoked in the *Arabian Nights*, an anonymous collection of 1001 tales written at a later date in Arabic. Untold wealth had flowed into the new capital of Baghdad since its foundation in 762. Harun ruled from a vast palace, filled with eunuchs, concubines, entertainers, and servants. He ate off gold and silver tableware, studded with gems. He was a connoisseur of music and poetry and surrounded himself with outstanding artists. The great wealth of his court earned Harun a place in Arabic legend.

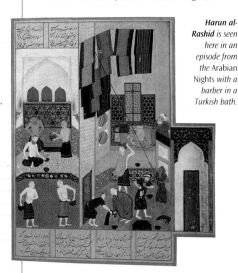

Harun al-Rashid is seen here in an episode from the Arabian Nights with a barber in a Turkish bath.

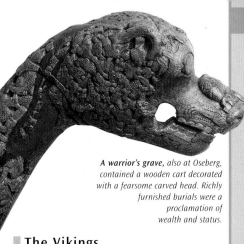

A warrior's grave, also at Oseberg, contained a wooden cart decorated with a fearsome carved head. Richly furnished burials were a proclamation of wealth and status.

The Vikings

The peace established in western Europe by strong rulers such as Charlemagne and Offa, was rudely shattered by the Viking invasions. Groups of pagan Vikings, probably led by warlords who had been supplanted by more powerful kings, left their Scandinavian homeland and embarked on a series of lightning raids. Traveling in fast, seaworthy ships they harried river ports and coastal settlements, attacking and plundering monasteries and towns, taking captives for ransom or slave markets. The first wave of Viking attacks were dominated by raiders; subsequently Vikings were motivated by conquest and colonization. By the 9th century, they ruled kingdoms in England, Ireland, and Normandy, adopting Christianity and settling in commercial towns. Their long-distance trade network extended from the Byzantine empire and the Islamic world to Russia.

This exquisitely decorated ship was discovered in the burial mound of a Viking queen at Oseberg. It dates to c.800, and was probably a ceremonial, rather than a practical, vessel.

802 Angkorian dynasty founded by King Jayavarman II.

Founding of Khmer state of Kambujadesha by Devaraya II, with capital at Angkor.

807 Harun al-Rashid grants the Franks a decree protecting the holy places in Jerusalem.

809 Death of Harun al-Rashid; start of Abbasid civil war.

832 **813** Al-Amin, son of Harun al-Rashid, is killed in a siege of Baghdad, led by his brother al-Ma'mun, who becomes caliph.

827 **817** Ziyadat Allah becomes the third Aghlabid king of Ifriqiyah (Tunisia).

819 Reign of the Samanid dynasty in Khurasan and Transoxiana.

820 Death of radical Hindu philosopher, Shankaracharya.

c.820 Persian mathematician, Musa al-Chwarazmi develops system of algebra.

821 Ratification of a Sino–Tibetan treaty recognizing the independence of Tibet.

c.825 Rashtrakuta dynasty rules over S India and Sri Lanka.

c.825 Market towns on east coast of Africa (N Kenya, Zanzibar, Kilwa, and Comoro Islands) are engaged in overseas trade with Arabs and Persians.

EUROPE

802 Irene, the first Byzantine empress, is exiled by the finance minister Nicephorus, who puts himself on the throne.

Vikings dominate Ireland.

805 Frankish army, led by Charlemagne's son Pepin, overcomes Mongolian Avars of Pannonia (Hungary).

806 Viking raiders sack the monastery of Iona, Scotland, for the third time.

810 Charlemagne sends his son, Pepin, to attack pro-Byzantine Venice, but with limited success.

Krum, king of Bulgaria, defeats and kills Emperor Nicephorus I.

811 Following the deaths of his two brothers, Louis is Charlemagne's sole surviving heir.

812 Byzantine emperor, Michael formally recognizes Charlemagne as emperor of the west. The Franks concede Venice and Dalmatia to the Byzantines.

814 Accession of Charlemagne's son, Louis the Pious, as emperor on Charlemagne's death.

Omurtag, the Bulgar khan, concludes a treaty with the Byzantines, gaining territory in the Balkans.

816 Byzantines make peace with the Bulgars after prolonged military campaigns.

820 Emperor Leo V is assassinated in Hagia Sophia by supporters of the commander of the guards, who becomes Emperor Michael II.

825 King Egbert of Wessex wins a decisive victory over King Beornred of Mercia at Ellendun.

c.825 First Viking settlement in the Faeroes.

Irish monks probably first to discover Iceland.

AMERICAS & AUSTRALASIA

Viking coin hoard

This 9th-century hoard from Hon, Norway contains Byzantine, Carolingian, Arab, and Anglo-Saxon coins. Europe and the Middle East were becoming increasingly prosperous at this time. It was the lure of these rich pickings that initially turned the Scandinavians to piracy, plunder, and, eventually, trade. Scandinavia was a source of luxury goods such as walrus ivory, furs, and amber.

Viking Invasions

Viking raids affected the whole coastline of western Europe, North Africa, and the Mediterranean. Vikings even sailed down the great navigable rivers of Russia to attack Constantinople. They were intrepid explorers, founding colonies in Iceland and Greenland and discovering, but not settling in, North America.

c.570	Danes raid Frisia.
c.600	Kingdoms develop in Denmark, Norway, and Sweden.
c.700	Viking ship burial at Vendel.
793	Vikings attack and plunder monastery at Lindisfarne, Northumbria.
795	First recorded Viking raids on Ireland and Scotland.
799	Vikings raid Aquitaine.
800	Charlemagne organizes defences against Vikings.
c.825	Irish monks driven out of Faeroes by Vikings.
826	Danish king, Harald Klak baptized at Mainz. First mission of Christian monk, Ansgar to Denmark.
832	Armagh, N Ireland, raided three times in one month.
839	Swedish traders reach Constantinople.
841	Viking base established at Dublin.
843	Frisia under intermittent Viking control (–885).
844	First Viking raid on Spain.
845	Paris and Hamburg sacked. First *danegeld* (tribute) paid by Franks.
850	Vikings overwinter for first time in England.

Great Mosque of Al-Mutawakkil

The Great Mosque, or Friday Mosque, at Samarra, built by the caliph al-Mutawakkil (847–861) in 848–852 was, for many centuries, the largest mosque in the world. As the Muslim world expanded across Eurasia, its progress was marked by ambitious architectural projects – new cities, forts, universities, libraries and, most notably, mosques.

The walls of the mosque enclosure, measuring 787 feet (240 m) by 492 feet (150 m), comprised tall brick walls strengthened by semicircular buttresses. An outer enclosure comprised 41 acre (17 hectares). The minaret, which is one of the few standing remains of the city, rises 165 feet (50 m) above the floodplain of the nearby Tigris river. It is also built of brick, and is notable for its remarkable spiral form. This unique structure may have been derived from the ancient Mesopotamian ziggurat. Sixteen doorways led to the interior of the mosque, where a hypostyle hall of hundreds of square brick pillars supported a flat wooden roof. The interior was decorated with marble and glass mosaics.

ASIA

832 Caliph al-Ma'mun of Baghdad founds a scholarly "House of Wisdom" to support efforts to translate ancient Greek wisdom into Arabic.

c.833 Abbasid trade connections have now been established with India, China, Africa, and Europe.

862 ▼ **836** Baghdad terrorized by Turkish slave troops; Abbasid caliph, al-Mu'tasim builds new capital at Samarra.

863 ▼ **838** Arabs take control of Amorium, one of the main Byzantine cities in Asia Minor.

Babak, leader of a religious and social revolutionary movement in NW Persia, is executed at Samarra.

840 Attacks by Kirghiz Turks lead to the collapse of the C Asian empire of the Uighur Turks.

845 In China, Buddhism and foreign religions are proscribed. Land is recovered from the church.

847 Caliph al-Mutawakkil tries to restore Abbasid authority, supported by the orthodox Sunnis.

848 Work begins on the Great Mosque in Samarra; largest to date in Muslim world.

c.850 Beginning of Arabic translation of key Greek scientific and philosophical texts.

Arab navigators, Wahab and Abu Sa'id, travel to S China and take home tea, rice, porcelain, and brandy (distilled rice wine).

Arab navigators perfect the astrolabe.

Arabian goatherd, Kaldi, supposedly discovers coffee.

Buddhism begins to decline in N India, replaced by Jainism and Hinduism.

Cholas, under King Vijayalaya, gain power and dominance in Tamil Nadu, India.

Collapse of Tibetan power.

Japanese painter, Kaneoka produces religious and secular paintings with strong Chinese influence.

AFRICA

827 The Aghlabids of Tunisia launch an expedition to capture Sicily from the Byzantines.

828 King Idris II of Morocco dies; his kingdom is divided between his sons.

835 Dogoun, the first king of the Saifawa dynasty of Kanem-Bornu, W Africa, dies at his capital, Njimi.

c.850 Citadel of Great Zimbabwe, SE Africa, built.

Elaborate chief's burial at Igbo-Ukwu, Nigeria reveals rich ceremonial culture.

827 Crete and Sicily occupied by Saracen (Arab) raiders.

831 Frankish missionary in Denmark, Anskar, is appointed bishop of Hamburg, and given responsibility for all the northern peoples.

832 Theophilus, the Byzantine emperor, resumes a violent campaign against icons.

833 Carolingian emperor, Louis the Pious, is deserted by his army and imprisoned by his son, Lothair.

834 Louis the Pious is rescued by loyalists and reinstated as emperor.

839 Swedes travel through Russia to establish trade links with Constantinople.

King Egbert of Wessex dies, leaving a strong kingdom in S England.

855 ▼

840 Death of Carolingian emperor, Louis the Pious; Lothair succeeds to the Carolingian throne, but inheritance disputes continue.

English defenders repulse a Viking raid on Southampton.

841 Vikings establish settlement at Dublin.

Charles the Bald and Louis the German, sons of Louis the Pious, defeat their elder brother, Lothair, at Fontenay.

842 On the death of Emperor Theophilus, his wife, Theodora, restores image worship in the Byzantine empire.

Having sacked the monastery of Noirmoutier, the Vikings overwinter on occupied territory for the first time.

843 Treaty of Verdun divides Carolingian empire into three. Eastern and western parts roughly correspond to Germany and France.

Kenneth Mac Alpin unites kingdom of Scotia and becomes first king of Scotland (–c.858).

844 Vikings raid as far as Toulouse.

845 Vikings sack Paris; exact tribute from Franks.

846 Death of Mojmir, prince of Moravia, who united for the first time the Slav tribes of Bohemia, Moravia, Slovakia, and Pannonia, to form Greater Moravia.

c.850 Shetlands come under direct Viking rule.

Yiddish develops among Jewish settlers in C Europe.

850 Abandonment of Cacaxtla.

c.850 Sican culture, centered on Baton Grande, is developing in N Peru.

Settlement of New Zealand by tropical Polynesian colonists, ancestors of the Maori, is complete.

Collapse of Classic Maya culture in Mesoamerica, Mexico's southern lowlands.

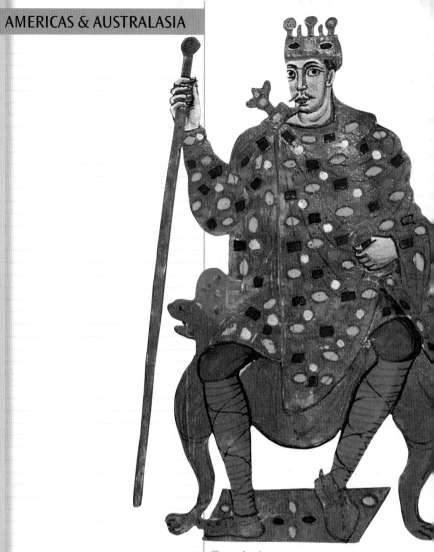

Lothair I

The unified Frankish empire of Charlemagne did not long survive his death. The Frankish custom of partible inheritance, by which an inheritance was divided between male heirs, soon led to disunity and fragmentation. Lothair I (795–855) was a grandson of Charlemagne. In 817, his father Louis the Pious, Charlemagne's successor, declared that on his death the empire would be split up among his heirs. This caused a wave of resentment among his children, who waged civil war – with their father – and amongst themselves – between 830 and 843.

In 843 the Treaty of Verdun resolved the dispute. Lothair, the eldest son, retained the imperial title and, with it, the Middle Realm of the Frankish empire – from the North Sea to Italy. This was flanked by "East Francia," under Louis the German, and "West Francia," under Charles the Bald.

Printing in China

The oldest extant printed book in the world is the *Diamond Sutra* (*below*) from Dunhuang in northwest China, dating from 868. Dunhuang was remote from the center of imperial Tang power, although it lay at the eastern end of the Silk Road, joining East Asia to West Asia and Europe; the discovery in a sealed cave of a wealth of documents dating from this period remains unique, although it does not necessarily mean that Dunhuang was in itself unique.

The documents found here include government archives, contracts, legal deeds, formal template letters, local histories, and educational primers. They reveal a highly organized and bureaucratic society. Although many documents are manuscript, the presence of printed books and sheets indicates that these were first developed to replicate educational primers, Buddhist texts, dictionaries, and almanacs.

The first printed documents were created by carving blocks of lettering and illustrations, and printing the offset image on scrolls. Printing itself was a logical development from the use of seals and cylinder seals, and duplication through rubbing. Bound books with folded pages, more convenient for storage and access, developed in China over the following two centuries.

The Diamond Sutra is made from seven rolls of paper pasted together and double-folded into book form.

ASIA

c.855 Ko Fuang temple, Shanxi, oldest surviving Chinese wooden building.

856 Death of theologian Ahmad ibn Muhammad ibn Hanbal; one of the four central rites of Islam based on his writings.

858 Ascendancy of Fujiwara clan in Japan (–1160).

860 Zaidi imams rise to power in Yemen; rule intermittently (–1281).

c.860 Rus Vikings besiege Constantinople.

Foundation of city of Angkor Thom, Cambodia.

862 Qubba al-Sulaybiya mausoleum, Samarra; first monumental Islamic tomb.

863 Byzantines annihilate Arab forces to stem Muslim advance in Anatolia.

890
c.866 Fujiwara clan gaining dominance in Japan.

867 Founding of Saffarid dynasty in E Persia (–1495).

868 The *Diamond Sutra*, world's oldest surviving printed work (China).

Death of al-Jahiz, Muslim writer on history, sex, and literature.

c.868 First printed newspaper, China.

869 Revolt of black slaves in S Iraq.

870 Peasant uprisings throughout Tang China.

c.873 Invention of concept of zero by Arab mathematicians.

874 Muslim Samanid dynasty established in Transoxiana (–1005).

c.875 Famine and unrest disrupt Tang China.

AFRICA

876
868 Ahmad ibn-Tulun founds the Tulunid dynasty in Egypt (–905); control spreads to Syria. Tulunid dynasty rules Egypt, Levant, and Syria, with capital at Fustat, Cairo.

851 Major earthquake in Rome.

Danish forces enter Thames estuary and march on Canterbury.

855 Death of Frankish ruler Lothair; kingdom divided between his three sons, with Louis II (the German) taking Italy and title of emperor (–875).

860 Viking raids on Iberia begin.

Death of Kenneth Mac Alpin, first ruler of united kingdom of Scotland.

c.860 Vikings land on Iceland; first trip round Iceland by Gardar Svavarsson.

Brothers Ingolf and Hjerleif reconnoiter East Fjords in late 860s.

862 Foundation of Novgorod, C Russia, by Rus under Rurik the Viking.

Magyars launch first raid on W Europe, attacking forces of Frankish emperor Louis II (the German).

863 Saints Cyril and Methodius sent as Orthodox Christian missionaries to Moravia.

Cyrillic alphabet created in E Europe.

866 Vikings take York, England.

Boris of Bulgaria converted to Christianity.

867 Basil I, founder of Macedonian dynasty (–886).

869 Slavs of Moravia converted to Christianity.

870 Danes invade East Anglia, killing St. Edmund, its last English king.

Treaty of Mersen: Frankish successors divide Lotharingia between France and Germany.

c.870 Otfrid, first known German poet.

871 Accession of Alfred (the Great), king of Wessex; forced to pay tribute to the Danes, he then musters coalition army and halts Danish advance in England.

874 Viking "Great Army" creates kingdom of York.

Danes retain control of Mercia (north-central England).

875 Frankish ascendant Charles the Bald, crowned Holy Roman emperor by Pope John VIII (–877).

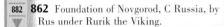

St. Cyril and St. Methodius

The threat to European Christendom posed initially by the 5th-century Germanic invasions, and by the 7th century by the rapid rise of Islam, forced Christianity on to the defensive. Monastic foundations consolidated Christian learning and thought, and it was from these that the first wave of revivalist Christian missionaries emerged in the 7th century.

The split between Roman Catholic and Byzantine, or Eastern Orthodox, Christianity saw Central and Eastern Europe transformed into a competitive arena for accumulating converts. The Byzantine missionaries Cyril (825–69) and Methodius (827–84) *above*, were sent by the Byzantine emperor Michael III to the kingdom of the Khazars, northeast of the Black Sea, in 863–864. They translated the scriptures into a language known as Old Bulgarian, or Old Church Slavonic, developing as they did the Cyrillic alphabet, which is still used in Russia and Bulgaria today.

Major Christian Missionaries

563	Columba, Ireland to Iona
c.590	Columba, Ireland to Burgundy and Italy
596	Augustine, Rome to Canterbury
635	Aidan, Iona to Lindisfarne
678	Wilfrid, Northumbria to Low Countries
690	Willibrord, Northumbria to Rhineland
716	Boniface, London to Low Countries
739	Boniface, Rome to Bavaria
788	Boniface, Low Countries to Thuringia
788	Willihod, Low Countries to Bremen
863	Cyril and Methodius, Constantinople to Serbia
864	Cyril and Methodius, Constantinople to Hungary
875	Cyril and Methodius, Constantinople to Kiev

Ibn Tulun mosque, Cairo

Built by Ahmad ibn Tulun, the governor of Egypt under the Abbasids in 876–879 this structure introduced Mesopotamian architectural forms to North Africa. Enclosed in a grand, colonnaded courtyard, with an original minaret (rebuilt in the 13th century), the mosque itself is a hypostyle building of massive piers supporting arches, surmounted by a timber roof. The fountain pavilion (*above*) in the center of the courtyard dates from the 13th century.

Abbasid Caliphs

750–754	Abu-l-Abbas al-Saffah
754–775	Al-Mansur
775–785	Al-Mahdi
785–786	Al-Hadi
786–809	Harun al-Rashid
809–813	Al-Amin
813–833	Al-Ma'mun
833–842	Al-Mu'tasim
842–847	Al-Wathiq
847–861	Al-Mutawakkil
861–862	Al-Muntasir
862–866	Al-Musta'in
866–869	Al-Mu'tazz
869–870	Al-Muhtadi
870–892	Al-Mu'tamid
892–902	Al-Mu'tadid
902–908	Al-Muktafi
908–932	Al-Muqtadir
932–934	Al-Qahir
934–940	Al-Radi
940–944	Al Muttaqi
944–946	Al-Mustakfi
946–974	Al-Muti'
974–991	Al-Ta'i
991–1031	Al-Qadir
1031–1075	Al-Qa'im
1075–1094	Aal-Muqtadi
1094–1118	Al-Mustazhir
1118–1135	Al-Mustarshid
1135–1136	Al-Rashid II
1136–1160	Al-Muqtafi
1160–1170	Al-Mustanjid
1170–1180	Al-Mustadi
1180–1225	Al-Nasir
1226–1242	Al-Mustansir
1242–1258	Al-Musta'sim

ASIA

878 Beginning of celestial observations by Arab astronomer, al-Battani (–929).

879 Nepal gains independence from Tibet.

885 Foundation of Armenian state.

886 Chola dynasty rules much of S India.

889 Khmer king, Indravarman I, begins construction of Angkor, Cambodia.

905 ▼

c.890 Renaissance of Japanese arts, notably in poetry and landscape painting; significant Chinese (Taoist/Buddhist) influence.

Taketori Monogatari, earliest Japanese narrative work of literature.

892 Capital of Abbasid caliphate shifts back from Samarra to Baghdad.

894 Shi'ite Qarmatians establish power base in C Arabia.

Political and cultural relations between China and Japan begin to decline.

899 Abbasid campaign against Egypt (–905).

c.900 Beginning of golden age of Hindu temple-building in India; emergence of cult of the god-king and of pilgrimage as a central expression of Hindu observation.

Gurjara-Pratiharas dominate N India.

First maps of Japan, showing provinces.

Japanese language and institutions revivified to counter Chinese influence.

AFRICA

905 ▼

876 Mosque of Ibn Tulun, Cairo, based on Great Mosque at Samarra.

c.880 Falasha Jews settle in Ethiopia.

890 Kingdom of Songhay conquers trading state of Gao.

908 ▼

c.900 Arab *dhows* (sailing ships) begin to ply the coastal routes of E Africa, as far south as Sofala.

Arab merchants trading from Kilwa and Manda on C African east coast.

EUROPE

877 Danes colonize S Northumbria (England).

878 Alfred of England defeats Danes at Edington.

880 Foundation of Benedictine monastery at Montserrat, Catalonia.

882 Kiev replaces Novgorod as capital of Viking Rus state.

885 Saxon ruler, Alfred the Great, reconquers London from Vikings.

Vikings sail up Seine and besiege Paris.

889 Fragmentation of Frankish empire in W Europe caused by dynastic rivalries.

891 King Arnulf of Germany defeats Vikings and expels them from his realm.

Anglo Saxon Chronicle, source of much early British history, begun (–1154).

910 ▼

895 Alfred of England musters fleet to oppose Danes; origins of English Royal Navy.

911 ▼

896 Danish raiders besiege Paris.

906 ▼

Magyars start to settle in Danube basin; set up state in Hungary.

898 Magyars invade Italy and sack Pavia (–899).

c.899 Varangians develop north–south riverine trade route linking Baltic and Black seas.

c.900 Bulgaria becomes part of Orthodox church.

Norwegians settle in Scotland and NW England.

Harald Fairhair unites Norway.

Greenland first sighted by Viking seamen.

Foundation of school of medicine at Salerno, Italy.

Invention of horse collar and harness (Europe); greatly increases plowing and load-carrying capacity.

Earliest surviving musical manuscripts.

916 ▼

Aghlabid Arab invasion of Sicily completed.

AMERICAS & AUSTRALASIA

900 Abandonment of the Toltec city of Xochicalco.

Rise to power of Toltecs as classic Maya sites collapse.

c.900 Advanced Thule culture among Inuit of Alaska.

Topiltzin, the Toltec religious leader, founds capital at Tula.

Sedentary Hohokam agriculturists of N American Southwest using irrigation.

Anasazi agriculturalists of N American southwest build pueblo settlements.

Chichén Itzá becomes center of Maya culture.

The Classic Maya

The Mayan ceremonial center of Edzná, in the Puuc region of the Yucatan peninsula in Mexico, reached its height during the 9th century, but was abandoned some time after 900. The temple at Edzná, is a fine example of a Classic Maya site, built in the Puuc style. Its five-storied central temple was constructed as a series of terraced, windowed floors, fronted by a processional unclimbable stairway. The northern Maya Puuc sites often exhibit an intense architectural and sculptural decoration, but also retain a simplicity and purity of architectural style which influenced 20th century architects such as Frank Lloyd Wright.

The Alfred Jewel

A superb example of the wealth and cultural sophistication of Anglo-Saxon England, this gold-wrought medallion dating from the reign of Alfred the Great (871–899) suggests a possible motive for the successive attempts to invade England by the Danes during the 9th century, and the ultimately successful conquest by the Normans a century and a half later. The jewel takes its name from an inscription in Old English on the gold frame which reads "Alfred had me made."

Prambanan temple, Java

The spread of Hindu-Buddhist culture
into Maritime Southeast Asia during
the last centuries of the first millennium
CE is best exemplified in the architecture
of the administrative and cultural center
of Prambanam, in Java, and the earlier
temple complex at nearby Borobodur.

Follwing a period of Buddhist
dominance in central Java from about
780 to 830 CE, during which no important
Hindu monuments were built, Hinduism
experienced a resurgence, culminating
in the construction of a vast complex
dedicated to Siva at Prambanan, called
Loro Jonggrang. The complex has eight
shrines, of which the three main ones are
dedicated to Siva, Vishnu and Brahma
(all are manifestations of God in Hindu).
The main temple of Shiva (*above*) rises to
a height of 130 feet (40 m). The shrines
were deserted within a century, maybe
because of a natural catastrophe such as
earthquake, and the center of the
kingdom was moved to eastern Java.

ASIA

938

c.905 *Kokinshu*, earliest known anthology
of Japanese poetry.

906 End of Chinese Tang dynasty.

907 Beginning of "Five Dynasties and Ten
Kingdoms" period in China (–960).

916 Foundation of Siberian Khitan empire
in Mongolia.

926

918 Foundation of state of Koryo (Korea).

AFRICA

901 Berber revolt against
Aghlabids (–911).

905 Suppression of Tulunid dynasty in
Egypt; return of Abbasid governors who
take over Egypt.

908 Permanent Arab trading settlements
in Somalia.

935

909 Shi'ite Fatimids expel Aghlabids from
Tunis; extend power to Egypt, Syria, and
proclaim Fatimid caliphate (–1171).

925 Gulf Arabs colonize Zanzibar.

EUROPE

933 ▼

906 Magyars destroy Moravia; begin systematic campaign to dominate Germany.

930 ▼

910 Foundation of Benedictine abbey at Cluny, France.

937 ▼

Edward of Wessex defeats Danes at Tettenhall.

911 Vikings found duchy of Normandy.

Oleg of Kiev enters commercial pact with Constantinople.

Rollo the Viking granted dukedom of Normandy; origins of Norman powerbase.

912 Apogee of Umayyad caliphate at Córdoba (–961).

916 Danes renew attacks on Ireland.

Arabs expelled from C Italy.

919 Henry of Saxony elected king of eastern kingdom of the Franks (Germany).

End of Carolingian (Frankish) dynasty in France.

Monastic Foundations pre-900

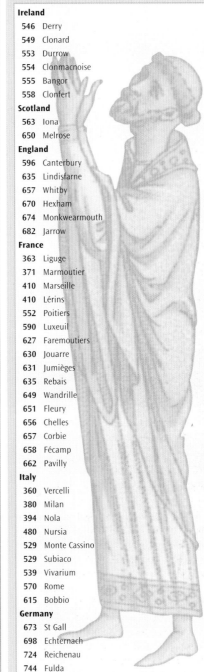

Ireland
- 546 Derry
- 549 Clonard
- 553 Durrow
- 554 Clonmacnoise
- 555 Bangor
- 558 Clonfert

Scotland
- 563 Iona
- 650 Melrose

England
- 596 Canterbury
- 635 Lindisfarne
- 657 Whitby
- 670 Hexham
- 674 Monkwearmouth
- 682 Jarrow

France
- 363 Liguge
- 371 Marmoutier
- 410 Marseille
- 410 Lérins
- 552 Poitiers
- 590 Luxeuil
- 627 Faremoutiers
- 630 Jouarre
- 631 Jumièges
- 635 Rebais
- 649 Wandrille
- 651 Fleury
- 656 Chelles
- 657 Corbie
- 658 Fécamp
- 662 Pavilly

Italy
- 360 Vercelli
- 380 Milan
- 394 Nola
- 480 Nursia
- 529 Monte Cassino
- 529 Subiaco
- 539 Vivarium
- 570 Rome
- 615 Bobbio

Germany
- 673 St Gall
- 698 Echternach
- 724 Reichenau
- 744 Fulda

Benedict (c.480–547) wrote the rule that became the accepted guide to leading a monastic life. Benedict's rule sets out the division of the day into eight liturgical offices, manual work, and spiritual reading. Its influence spread far from its Italian base. By the 10th century, Benedictine monasteries, including Cluny in France, left, had been founded all over Europe. Well-planned monasteries resembled villages, with infirmaries, workshops, storerooms, cellars, dairies, breweries, bakeries, schools, and guesthouses. The dominant feature of all monasteries was the church, where monks would assemble to sing their daily offices. Monasteries were centers of civilized life in a frequently unstable and wartorn society.

Pueblo Bonito

Several overlapping cultures settled the American Southwest during the 1st millennium CE, including the Hohokam, Mogollon and Anasazi. All three peoples built multistory "pueblos" – storehouses and dwellings of stone or adobe, sometimes with ball courts and low platform mounds.

One of the largest and most complex pueblos – Pueblo Bonito in Chaco Canyon (*below*) – was constructed between 900 and 1150 and may have been an administrative or religious center. It had a population of some 1200, living in over 800 rooms within D-shaped outer walls some 37 feet (12 m) high. The close-knit agricultural community there paid careful attention to changes in the weather. Fields were tended while domestic chores were performed on the pueblo's terraces. Rituals were performed in the *kivas*, or ceremonial rooms, the people asking the gods for rain to safeguard crops and ensure prosperity. The settlement lay at the hub of a road network passing through the canyon, and was probably a trading and distribution center for food and exotic goods.

ASIA

926 Manchuria and N Korea annexed to Khitan empire.

932 Shi'ite Buwayhids (Buyids) establish powerbase in Persia, Iraq; rule in name of Abbasid caliphate (–1082).

935 Text of Koran reaches final form.

c.935 Tsurayuki, Japanese diarist and traveler, active (–946).

936 Caliphs of Baghdad lose effective power; caliphate under control of Turkish troops.

Abbasid caliphate relinquishes administrative powers; Buwayhids take effective control of caliphate.

938 Mongol Khitans invade N China; establish new capital at Yanqing (later Peking/Beijing).

939 Nam Viet throws off Chinese rule.

968 Annamese win independence from China; foundation of kingdom of Dai Viet.

967 **940** Beginning of Taira revolt against imperial rule, starting long period of civil war in Japan (–1185).

941 Kievan Rus defeated at Constantinople.

945 Persian Buwayhids capture Baghdad; decline of Abbasid caliphate as a political power, but caliph allowed to reign as figurehead.

Hamdanids establish powerbase in Syria and Lebanon (–1004).

947 Khitans invade N China, establishing Liao dynasty at Beijing.

950 Death of philosopher, al-Farabi.

c.950 Invention of gunpowder in China.

AFRICA

931 Caliphate of Córdoba wrests Morocco from Fatimids.

935 Fatimid armies defeated in Egypt by Muhammad ibn Tughj.

969 **943** Caliph of Baghdad confirms control of Egypt to Muhammad ibn Tughj for 30 years.

945 Malayo-Indonesian raid from Madagascar is launched on E African coast at Sofala.

972 **947** Foundation of Zirid dynasty in Algeria.

c.950 Emergence of small kingdom of Igbo-Ukwu near Niger delta.

928 Ruler of Córdoba, 'Abd-al Rahman III, claims the caliphate.

c.930 Viking settlement of Iceland complete.

Cluniac Benedictine monastic reform extended over France and Lorraine by Odo of Cluny.

955 ▼

933 Henry I of Germany defeats Magyars at Riade.

936 Henry I of Germany is succeeded by his son, Otto I; Bohemians rebel (made tributary in 950).

Córdoba palace complex of Madinat al-Zahra begun.

954 ▼

937 Battle of Brunanburh; Athelstan of Wessex defeats alliance of Danes, Scots, and Strathclyde Britons.

945 Cumberland and Westmoreland (the Lake District) annexed from England by Scots.

c.950 Lapps enter Norway.

940 Sack of Zapotec capital at Monte Albán, Mesoamerica.

c.950 Flourishing pueblo culture in American Southwest.

Viking raids on Ireland

Few parts of the Christian west were safe from Viking attacks in the 9th and 10th centuries. Norwegians first attacked and settled the Shetland and Orkney islands, northern Scotland, and the Hebrides, and moved down from these bases into the Irish Sea, settling the regions around Dublin (941) and the southeast of Ireland, in Wexford and Kilkenny. Irish monasteries were often built with distinctive round towers, such as these at Glendalough, which served as lookout posts and refuges.

Bronze of Vishnu, India

Despite the decline of the Gupta dynasty in the 6th century CE, when their northern Indian centers were overrun by the Hunas (Huns, Hephthalites), their establishment of a rich Hindu culture throughout South and Southeast Asia persisted. Bronze relief sculptures such as this (*left*) demonstrate the vitality of Hindu culture, despite the vicissitudes of political power which characterize early medieval India.

Song Taizu

Zhao Kuangyin was a Chinese general who was created emperor (Taizu) by his own troops and founded the Song dynasty, reigning from 960–76. He extended imperial rule to the south, reunifiying the Chinese empire. He created a strong professional army, placing the best military units in the palace army, under his direct control. Regional forces were placed under civilian control, and officers constantly circulated to avoid the emergence of local power groups.

The Jelling Stone

Stone slabs, inscribed with pictures and runic characters, often memorials to particular individuals are found in burial sites throughout the Viking world. The Jelling Stone (a modern copy of which is pictured here) was erected by Harald Bluetooth, king of Denmark at the royal burial place of Jelling in Jutland, in memory of his parents, King Gorm and Queen Thyre. The stone is a three-sided pyramid, two sides bearing pictures and the third, a long inscription. Its carvings depict ornamental animal forms, sophisticated interlacing linear patterns, and a Christian theme (the Crucifixion) – Harald was converted to Christianity around 960 CE.

ASIA

956 Al-Mas'udi's major historical/geographical work, *The Meadows of Gold*.

960 Northern Song dynasty founded in N China, capital at Kaifeng.

Nine embassies from Srivijaya attend Chinese court (–988).

c.960 Samanids of Bukhara invade Afghanistan.

Period of artistic splendor in China, watercolorists, poets, and Hi-Khio, Chinese drama in which central character sings (–1119).

c.963 Al Sufi's *Book of the Fixed Stars* contains earliest description of a nebula.

967 Fujiwara clan begin unification of Japan.

968 Dinh Bo Linh founds Dinh empire in Dai Viet (N Vietnam).

969 Byzantines gain Antioch from Arabs.

Rockets using gunpowder first used in combat (China).

970 Fatimids establish control of Damascus.

Paper money introduced by Chinese government.

974 Song dynasty unites China; capital at Luoyang.

975 Southern Tang empire submits to Northern Song; China united under Song, end of "Five Dynasties and Ten Kingdoms" period.

AFRICA

957 Kilwa sultanate founded on east coast of Africa.

969 Fatimids assume control of Egypt; foundation of Cairo as their capital.

972 Zirid dynasty, of Berber origin, rule Tunisia and E Algeria, based at Kairouan (–1148).

973 Fatimids of Egypt establish Sanhaja Berber dynasty of the Zirids in Ifriqiyah (Tunisia).

Direct commerce between Fatimid Egypt and Italy established.

975 Christian kingdom of Axum overrun.

1008

954 Expulsion of Eric Bloodaxe, last Danish king of York.

955 Otto I of Germany defeats Magyars decisively at Lechfeld, and halts expansion of Hungary.

959 England united under Edgar.

960 Polish state founded by Mieszko I.

c.960 King of Denmark converts to Christianity, prohibits paganism.

Foundation of Augsburg cathedral.

961 Byzantines recover Crete from Arabs.

962 Otto I of Germany crowned emperor by John XII; spends later years in Italy.

963 First monasteries built on Mount Athos, which becomes the center for Orthodox monasticism.

965 Byzantines recover Cyprus from Arabs.

1002

968 Foundation of university of Córdoba.

972 Foundation of Hungarian state under Duke Geisa.

c.973 Christianity established in Bohemia; foundation of bishopric of Prague.

975 Arithmetical notation in use, adopted from Arab world.

The al-Azhar mosque was the first major Fatimid building at Cairo, and became the leading Shi'ite university for many centuries. The dome and minaret were added in 1469.

The Fatimids

The Fatimids emerged in North Africa in the early 10th century, directly challenging centralized Abbasid authority. In 969 their general Jawhar conquered Egypt with a force of 10,000 men and built a new city north of the ancient settlement of Fustat, encircled by fortified walls and containing palaces, great mosques, and plazas. They called their new city al-Qahira, "The Victorious," a name later corrupted by European tongues to "Cairo."

Under the caliph al-Aziz (975–996), Egypt became the richest and most stable region in the Islamic world, and the heart of a revived Eurasian trading network. The zenith of Fatimid power was reached during the caliphate of al-Mustansir (1036–94), although high taxation and regional unrest led to a half century of steady decline.

Otto II

This representation of the Holy Roman emperor Otto II (973–983) receiving homage from the subject nations of his empire reflects the Western Empire's debt to its Byzantine counterpart. The Holy Roman emperors were portrayed as God's representatives on earth, which caused frequent clashes with the papacy, although the Ottonian dynasty oversaw the establishment of Christian states in Poland, Bohemia, and Hungary.

Vladimir I

The prince of Novgorod and grand duke of Kiev, Vladimir I (956–1015) converted to Christianity in 988, and is regarded as the father of the Orthodox Russian church. A dissolute and brutal man prior to his baptism, he was later noted for his acts of charity and tolerance. He married Anna, the sister of the Byzantine emperor Basil II, cementing the relationship between the two empires, and was later canonized.

ASIA

c.1000

977 Founding of Ghaznavid dynasty that takes power in Afghanistan.

Byzantine forces threaten to take Jerusalem.

Chinese *Great Encyclopedia of 1000 volumes* begun (completed c.984). Original destroyed during Boxer Rebellion (1900–01).

979 Song dynasty establishes power and completes unification of C and S China (–1279).

983 Locks invented when constructing Grand Canal, China.

986 Khitans (Liao dynasty) rebuild Beijing.

992 Establishment of Qarakhanid dynasty in Transoxiana (–1211).

993 Khitans force Koryo to recognize them as overlords of Korea.

999 Earliest Yamato-e paintings showing indigenous Japanese style, free of Chinese influence.

1000 Tibetan Tanguts found Xixia state.

c.1000 Seljuk Turks invade Transoxiana.

First Muslim raids into N India, led by Sultan Mahmud of Ghazni, ruler of the Ghaznivid dynasty; he conquers NW India.

Cholas occupy Ceylon.

Development of Song landscape painting (China).

Spinning wheel in use, S Asia; Chinese develop silk-reeling devices.

Cholas gain control of Deccan region of India.

Le dynasty assumes power in Dai Viet.

AFRICA

c.988 Foundation of Al-Azhar university, Cairo.

990 Al Hakim mosque, Cairo, built.

992 Ghana captures Berber town of Awdaghost, gaining control of southern portion of trans-Saharan trade route.

c.1000 Arab merchants begin to set up trading states in Ethiopian Highlands.

Islam begins to spread in sub-Saharan Africa, borne by overland and coastal trade.

Evidence of iron technology in Great Zimbabwe.

EUROPE

976 Fire destroys Doge's palace in Venice; rebuilt over next five centuries.

Decline of Arab power in Iberia (–1009).

980 Renewed Danish raids on England.

Effective end of Viking dynasty at Dublin.

Otto II, Holy Roman emperor, campaigns against Arabs in Italy (–983).

982 Emperor Otto II defeated by Arabs in Italy.

983 Great Slav Rebellion against eastward migration of German settlers.

986 Beginning of Bulgarian expansion in SE Europe.

Erik the Red, Norwegian navigator and explorer, begins settlement of Greenland.

Norse traders found three settlements on Greenland.

987 French Capetian dynasty founded.

988 Conversion of Vladimir of Kiev to Christianity; Orthodox church established in Russia.

990 Ottonian campaign against Bohemians.

994 London besieged by Danes and Norwegians.

996 Start of war between Byzantines, led by emperor Basil II, and Bulgaria.

1000 Hungary officially becomes a Christian state.

Poland joins Catholic church.

Viking raids on Normandy.

c.1000 Sacrificial graves in Lapland contain metal goods from NW England and Russia.

AMERICAS & AUSTRALASIA

987 Toltec high priest and followers expelled from Tula by rival cult that favors human sacrifice.

c.990 Exiled Toltecs take over Maya city of Chichén Itzá.

999 Topiltzan founds new Maya kingdom of Chichén Itzá.

1000 Start of Mississippian culture in N America.

Almost all Pacific islands inhabited.

c.1000 Voyages from Greenland to Newfoundland and coast of N America.

Leif Ericson, son of Eric the Red, sets sail from Greenland and reaches N America.

Cree and other groups of N America trade furs with southern peoples for grain.

Iroquois peoples in northeast N America living in villages, cultivating beans and corn.

Development of Southern Cult, S Mississippi, centered on Grand Village.

Thule Eskimos begin to migrate to E Arctic.

Sicán culture flourishes around El Purgatorio in N Peru.

Collapse of Andean states of Tiahuanaco and Huari.

Incas found Cuzco, S Peru.

Maya civilization in Yucatan peninsula at its height with distinctive art and architecture, and a calendar based on astronomical studies.

Toltec incursions into Maya territory.

Tairona culture of Colombia is now flourishing.

Molds used in pottery-making, C America.

First carvings and stone statues, Easter Island.

Demise of the Coclé culture in Panama, which had emerged some 500 years ago.

Great Mosque of Córdoba

Founded in 784, and completed in 988, this magnificent mosque was commissioned by the Umayyad ruler 'Abd ar-Rahman I. It was added to and extended over the following 200 years, to make one of the largest sacred buildings in the Islamic world.

The mosque, built on the site of a Visigothic church, comprises a massive rectangular prayer-hall of 19 aisles, the saddleback roof supported by arcades of almost-capitaled marble columns (*above*). A formal courtyard of orange trees complements the prayer hall. In the 13th century, following the Reconquista, the mosque became a place of Christian worship and in 1526 a cathedral was built in the center of the prayer hall, creating a unique architectural and religious complex.

The World in 1000 CE

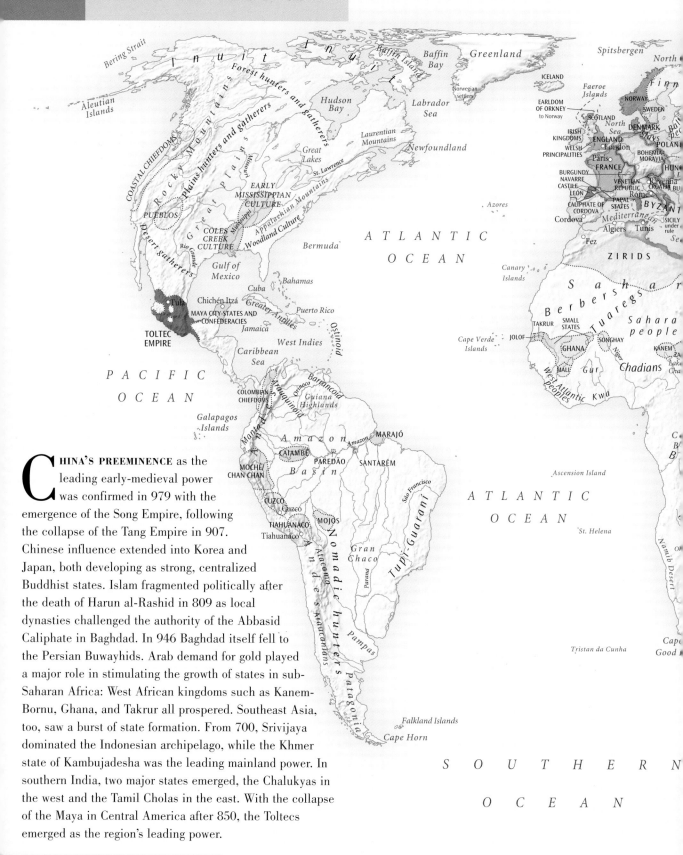

CHINA'S PREEMINENCE as the leading early-medieval power was confirmed in 979 with the emergence of the Song Empire, following the collapse of the Tang Empire in 907. Chinese influence extended into Korea and Japan, both developing as strong, centralized Buddhist states. Islam fragmented politically after the death of Harun al-Rashid in 809 as local dynasties challenged the authority of the Abbasid Caliphate in Baghdad. In 946 Baghdad itself fell to the Persian Buwayhids. Arab demand for gold played a major role in stimulating the growth of states in sub-Saharan Africa: West African kingdoms such as Kanem-Bornu, Ghana, and Takrur all prospered. Southeast Asia, too, saw a burst of state formation. From 700, Srivijaya dominated the Indonesian archipelago, while the Khmer state of Kambujadesha was the leading mainland power. In southern India, two major states emerged, the Chalukyas in the west and the Tamil Cholas in the east. With the collapse of the Maya in Central America after 850, the Toltecs emerged as the region's leading power.

The World in 1000

	Song Empire
	Byzantine Empire
	Denmark and possessions
	Toltec Empire
	Kievan Rus and possessions
	Abbasid Caliphate under Harun al-Rashid, 786 CE
	Tibet c.800 CE
	Empire of the Franks under Charlemagne, 814 CE
	Holy Roman Empire

ya Zemlya
Kara Sea
Ugrians peoples
Ural Mts
Volga Bulgar VOLGA BULGARIA
Don
Turkic peoples
Sea
KIEVAN RUS
Tmutarakan
GEORGIAN STATES
antinople SMALL STATES
ARMENIA
IRE
ioch DANIDS
lem
Cairo
QARMATIANS
IMIDS
Mecca
Red Sea
KURIA
YEMEN
Gulf of Aden
ALODIA
ETHIOPIA
DAMOT
SHOA
Nilotic peoples
Cushites
Lake Victoria
Manda
Lake Tanganyika
Zanzibar
Kilwa
Lake Nyasa
Comoros
anzi
Malays Madagascar
Seychelles
Mauritius
Réunion

PALEOSIBERIANS
Kara Sea
Lena
Samoyeds
Siberia
Ob'
Irtysh
Tungus
Yenisey
Mongols
Amur
Lake Baikal
Altai Mountains
Lake Balkhash
KHITAN EMPIRE
Gobi
Linhuang
QARAKHANIDS
Tien Shan
Uighurs
Tanguts
Aral Sea
Oxus
Samarkand
Takla Makan
Dunhuang
Yellow River
GHAZNAVIDS
Ghazni
KASHMIR
HINDU SHAHIS
QARMATIS
Plateau of Tibet
Chang'an
Yangtze
TIBET
Himalayas
SONG EMPIRE
Kaifeng
Kaesong
KORYO
JAPAN
Kyoto
Kyushu
Honshu
Hokkaido
Sea of Japan
Kurile Islands
Kamchatka
Bering Strait
Sea of Okhotsk
BUWAYHIDS
Baghdad
Samarra
Caspian Sea
Euphrates
Tigris
Thar Desert
GURJARA PRATIHARAS
CHAHAMANAS
PARAMARAS
CHANDELLAS
KALACURIS
CHAULUKYAS
ABHIRAS
Godavari
Kalyani
Krishna
EASTERN CHALUKYAS
CHALUKYAS
SMALL STATES
CHOLAS
Ceylon
LAMBAKANNAS
Andaman Islands
Nicobar Islands
BHAUMAS
PALAS
Ganges
ARAKAN
PAGAN
Thais
PEGU
THATON
HARIPUNJAYA
DVARAVATI
ANNAM
CHAMPA
KHMER
Mekong
Angkor
South China Sea
Luzon
Mindanao
Philippine Islands
TAIWAN
East China Sea
PACIFIC OCEAN
MICRONESIA
MELANESIA
NANZHAO
Bay of Bengal
Maldive Islands
SRIVIJAYA
Borneo
Palembang
Celebes
Malay Peninsula
Malays
EAST JAVA KINGDOM
Borobudur
Java
Timor
Moluccas
New Guinea
Papuans
Bismarck Archipelago
Solomon Islands
Melanesians
Vanuatu
Fiji
New Caledonia
INDIAN OCEAN
Great Sandy Desert
Gibson Desert
Australian Aborigines
Great Victoria Desert
Simpson Desert
Lake Eyre
Darling
Great Dividing Range
Great Barrier Reef
Tasman Sea
Tasmania
Maoris
New Zealand

ARAB STAR MAPS

By the 9th century, Arab science, building on Graeco-Roman, Persian, and Indian foundations, was making notable advances on many fronts. The Caliph al Ma'mun (813–33), for example, had the world's first observatory built in Baghdad. A tradition of practical astronomy was rapidly established. As well as making significant contributions to direction-finding – the astrolabe, an accurate measurement of the size of the Earth, a world map – the Arabs charted and named stars and constellations. Stars such as Aldebaran, Rigel, and Rasalgethi are still known by their Arab names. The illustration (*right*) is of the constellation of Andromeda and comes from *The Book of the Fixed Stars*, compiled by Abd-al-Rahman ibn Umar al-Sufi in the 10th century.

1000–1200

The Early Middle Ages

c.1000: First Muslim raids into N India, led by Mahmud of Ghazni

1005: Song China becomes subject state of northern Liao kingdom, with capital at Beijing

1031: Beginning of Christian reconquest of Spain

	1000	1010	1020	1030	10
ASIA					
AFRICA					
EUROPE					
REST OF THE WORLD					

c. 1000: Leif Ericson reaches N America from Greenland. Start of Mississippian culture

1016: England, Denmark, and Norway united under Canute

T HE WORLD'S TWO DOMINANT CIVILIZATIONS in 1000 were Song China and the Islamic world. Both not only ruled over vast areas but, in terms of trade and prosperity, learning and technology, and, most importantly of all, cultural unity, they were far in advance of any of the fledgling civilizations in other parts of the world. Yet both China and the Islamic world had recently endured serious threats to the fabric of their society – as they would continue to over the next 200 years. It is a remarkable tribute to the underlying stability of both civilizations that by 1200 they were if anything stronger and more firmly established than ever.

In contrast to these two long-established civilizations, medieval Europe was poor, backward, and politically divided. In spite of this, it was able to issue a strong military challenge to the Islamic world.

Threats to Song China

The Song had emerged in northern China in 960 and by 979 had successfully reunited the country, ending the chaos which followed the fragmentation of the Tang Empire 80 years before. Yet they were continually threatened by their steppeland neighbors to the north and west, the Liao in Manchuria, and the Xixia. By the early 12th century, a further threat arose, the Jin, vassals of the Liao. The Jin state, established in 1126, came to occupy much of the former northern heartland of China.

The inevitable consequence was not just that the political and economic center of gravity in China was shifted south, but that Song China became more inward-looking and defensively minded. Yet even so, it remained exceptionally prosperous. Population and trade, boosted by much improved agriculture, increased dramatically while the new capital, Hangzhou, rapidly became the world's greatest city. Reforms in education and the civil service were paralleled by the appearance of a new and hugely wealthy merchant class. In science and technology this was a period of exceptional achievements, among them the discovery of the formula for gunpowder, the development of movable type, and the appearance of the world's first paper money.

The Islamic world

Although for China, however prosperous, this was nonetheless still a period of political and territorial retrenchment, Islam on the other hand continued its formidable expansion. By 1000, Islam already occupied a larger area than any previous civilization, one which stretched from Iberia to northern India with trading outposts established as far east as the Malay peninsula. But this

PICTURE ABOVE:
Monks give their blessing to a group of departing Crusaders. The Crusades were fought in the name of Christianity, but the conquest of Islamic territories in the Holy Land was essentially an extension of European feudalism.

Song China was the most advanced civilization of the age. This detail is from a scroll depicting all the various activities taking place in the bustling city of Kaifeng.

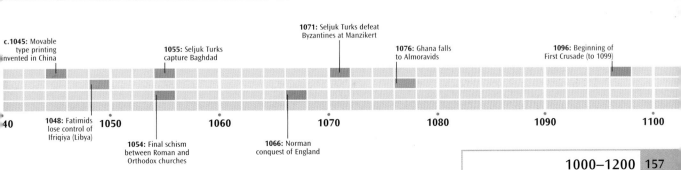

c.1045: Movable type printing invented in China

1048: Fatimids lose control of Ifriqiya (Libya)

1054: Final schism between Roman and Orthodox churches

1055: Seljuk Turks capture Baghdad

1066: Norman conquest of England

1071: Seljuk Turks defeat Byzantines at Manzikert

1076: Ghana falls to Almoravids

1096: Beginning of First Crusade (to 1099)

40   1050   1060   1070   1080   1090   1100

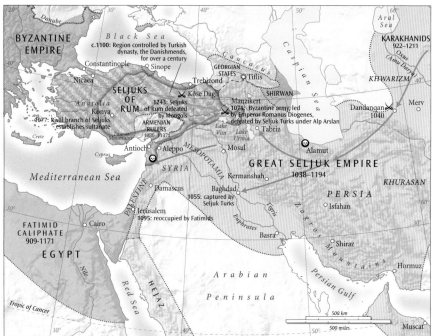

In the 11th century, the Seljuk Turks swept westward, converting to Islam en route. They reached Baghdad in 1055, where they ruled in the name of the Abbasid caliphs. Victory at Manzikert (1071) threatened the very existence of the Byzantine empire, but by the end of the century their own empire was beginning to fragment.

very size made the exercise of central authority impossible and rival dynasties and factions continually competed for power, chief among them the Berbers in North Africa, the Fatimids and, later, the Ayyubids in Egypt, and the Ghaznavids in eastern Persia and Afghanistan, beneficiaries not just of their own relentless aggression but of the political fragility of northern India. But the most important of the new Islamic dynasties were the Seljuk Turks, who, from their homelands in Central Asia, swept westward in the 11th century, capturing Baghdad in 1055. Their continued westward thrust then brought them into contact with the eastern border of the Christian Byzantine empire in Anatolia. Decisively defeated by the Seljuks in 1071, within 25 years the Byzantines had been pushed back all the way to Constantinople. The Seljuks meanwhile continued their whirlwind conquests to the south in Syria and Palestine, where they defeated the forces of the Egyptian Fatimids and took the cities of Damascus and Jerusalem.

The Crusades

Despite increasing contact through trade, relations between the Byzantine empire and the Christian kingdoms of western Europe during the 11th century had been poor. The latter owed allegiance to the Roman rather than the Eastern Orthodox Church, and there had been a definitive schism between the two churches in 1054. These differences were put aside in 1095, when the Byzantine emperor sent a desperate appeal to the Pope for military aid against the Seljuks. In response, Pope Urban II launched an impassioned plea for Latin Christendom to go to the rescue of the beleaguered Christians of the Byzantine empire. This signalled the start of the Crusades, an extraordinary period in European history which would continue for over 200 years.

The First Crusade was undeniably lucky. By the time the Crusaders, led by minor nobles from France, Flanders, and the Rhineland, reached the Holy Land, the Seljuks had ceased to be a major force in the region. Against all the odds, the Crusaders captured Jerusalem in 1099 and established a number of small states that they were able, for a time, to defend against Muslim counterattacks.

In the second half of the 12th century, opposition to the invaders became better organized under leaders such as Nur al-Din and Saladin, founder of the Ayyubid dynasty in Egypt. Further Crusader armies were sent to assist the Christian principalities, but none of these subsequent Crusades enjoyed the success of the first. Finally, in 1302, the Crusaders were driven from their last remaining stronghold in the Near East. The long-term consequence of the Crusades was a conflict between Islam

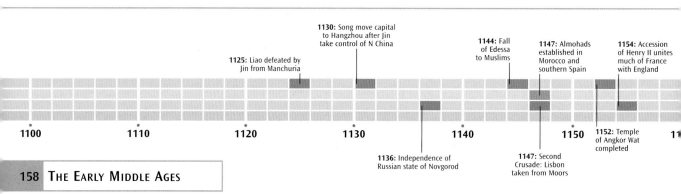

1125: Liao defeated by Jin from Manchuria

1130: Song move capital to Hangzhou after Jin take control of N China

1144: Fall of Edessa to Muslims

1147: Almohads established in Morocco and southern Spain

1154: Accession of Henry II unites much of France with England

1136: Independence of Russian state of Novgorod

1147: Second Crusade: Lisbon taken from Moors

1152: Temple of Angkor Wat completed

1100 1110 1120 1130 1140 1150 11

and the west that in some senses can be said to endure even today. The meeting point of Christian west and Muslim east was to prove one of the world's great pressure points.

In Europe itself, the period saw a steady increase in political stability and prosperity. This was partly a matter of state formation, partly of the overarching and growing influence of the Church. In 1000, for example, both Poland and Hungary converted to Christianity while in 1031 the Christian reconquest of Spain began. Though conflict between the Church and Europe's rulers was to prove a persistent cause of political instability, nonetheless, however falteringly at first, from the 12th century Europe enjoyed a significant period of cultural reawakening. In part, this was the result of increased contact with the Arabs of the Mediterranean and southern Spain, guardians of much of the Ancient world's knowledge, as European traders expanded southward. But from the 11th century it was also encouraged by the activities of a number of new monastic orders, the Cistercians, the Franciscans, and the Dominicans, who encouraged a renewed interest in scholarship. The new confidence of Christian Europe is dramatically expressed in the soaring Gothic cathedrals that first appeared in northern France in the 12th century. The new Gothic style of architecture spread rapidly to the Low Countries, Germany, Britain, and Spain.

New trading networks

European trade increased significantly in the 12th century. The two wealthiest trading centers were the textile-producing regions of Flanders and northern Italy. Arab control of Mediterranean shipping routes had been weakened by the Norman conquest of Sicily in 1047 and suffered a further setback with the onset of the Crusades. The Italian maritime republics of Venice, Genoa, and Amalfi, which provided much of the shipping for transporting men and supplies to the Holy Land, all profited from this new business opportunity to extend their trading links with the Byzantine empire and the east.

Expansion in the Americas

The most significant developments in North America occurred with the growth of the continent's first true towns, along the fertile Mississippi Valley. By about 1050, the population of the largest, Cahokia, was more than 10,000. The cultures of the southwest, the Hohokam, Mogollon, and Anasazi, had also adopted a settled way of life in their pueblos – impressive villages and multistory cliff-dwellings of adobe mud-brick. To contend with the harsh, semiarid environment, the Hohokam developed irrigation systems that captured seasonal rainfall.

North American towns and villages paled, however, in comparison with the major centers of Central America, where the Toltec civilization dominated the region until the arrival of the Aztecs in

The Toltecs dominated Central America *from the 10th to the 12th century CE. These statues of warriors stand at Tula, the Toltec capital, the hub of an extensive trading network with a population of 60,000.*

about 1200. Equally impressive was the powerful Chimú empire in the Andes, which rose to prominence in the 11th century and expanded rapidly by military conquest. Its subject territories were linked by an advanced road system and kept under strict centralized economic control. Its institutions formed the basis for the later empire of the Incas.

JAPAN

Just as much as its vastly bigger neighbor, China, Japan by the 7th century had developed as a highly stratified imperial society. Yet by the 10th century, the country had become embroiled in bitter civil wars as provincial governors, tasked with quelling regional unrest, instead engaged in a series of struggles for supremacy. The most successful were the Fujiwara. But by 1061, Fujiwara ascendancy was decisively challenged by the Minamoto. This uneasy rivalry continued until 1160, when the Taira clan usurped them both. However, Taira supremacy was almost immediately challenged by a Minamoto regalvanized by the charismatic general Minamoto Yorimoto, who by 1185 had eliminated practically all potential rivals. The Kamakura Shogunate established by Minamoto, even if it remained nominally answerable to the emperor, ensured the continuation of Japan's distinctive military-based society until its overthrow in 1333.

Minamoto Yoritomo, the first shogun, who imposed order on Japan's warring clans.

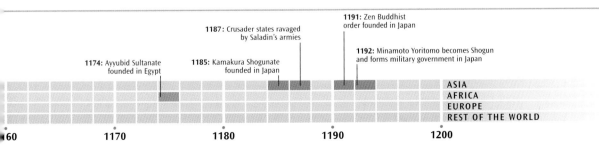

1174: Ayyubid Sultanate founded in Egypt

1185: Kamakura Shogunate founded in Japan

1187: Crusader states ravaged by Saladin's armies

1191: Zen Buddhist order founded in Japan

1192: Minamoto Yoritomo becomes Shogun and forms military government in Japan

ASIA
AFRICA
EUROPE
REST OF THE WORLD

1160   1170   1180   1190   1200

Chichén Itzá was built by the Toltecs as a ritual center, arranged around a typical stepped pyramid dedicated to the god Quetzalcoatl.

The Toltecs

Following the collapse of Teotihuácan and the decline of the Classic Maya, central Mexico was occupied by the Toltecs, a warrior people from northwest Mexico. By 1000 CE the influence of the Toltecs had spread over a large region of Meso-america. Their capital was at Tula, in the modern state of Hidalgo, Mexico. The city reached a peak population of 60,000 inhabitants, with an equal number in the immediate hinterland. The Toltecs were traders, trading as far south as Costa Rica and north into the desert. Their architecure and sculpture reflects their militaristic society, and their worship involved the ritual appeasement of their gods through human sacrifice.

This figure of a coyote warrior from Tula is decorated with mother of pearl. Toltec society was dominated by knightly orders of eagles, jaguars, and coyotes.

ASIA

c.1001 Murasaki Shikibu, Japanese noblewoman, writes the world's first novel, *The Tale of Genji*.

1005 Al-Sufi's *Geography*; (now in St. Petersburg) probably oldest extant illustrated Arabic manuscript.

Song China becomes subject state of northern Liao kingdom, with capital at Beijing.

1008 Firdausi begins *Shah Nameh*, national epic verse history of Persia (–1020).

1009 Desecration of the Church of the Holy Sepulchre, Jerusalem, by Muslims.

c.1010 Upperclass Chinese begin binding girls' feet.

Emergence of warrior bands (*bushidan*) in Japanese provinces.

AFRICA

1001 Coronation of Stephen I who unites Hungary.

1002 Massacre of St. Brice's Day; Danish settlers in England slaughtered on Ethelred II's orders.

Umayyad caliphate in Spain disintegrates into rival states.

1003 Danes under Sweyn I invade England.

1004 Foundation of the cathedral of Bamberg.

1008 English fleet built by Ethelred II to repel Danish attacks.

1009 Foundation of Mainz cathedral.

c.1010 Chess introduced to Europe from Asia.

Murasaki Shikibu

Widely acknowledged as a masterpiece of Japanese literature, the long narrative the *Tale of Genji* was written in the first decade of the 10th century by Murasaki Shikibu (died c.1014). Little is known of her life, but she was married to a minor member of the Fujiwara clan. After her husband's death, she entered the service of Shoshi, one of the mistresses of the emperor Ichijo, whose court produced several talented poets and writers. The narrative tells of the life of a brilliant prince, and reflects in great detail the ideal qualities of courtly life in Heian Japan.

Song porcelain

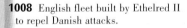

Under the Song dynasty (960–1279) China reached its greatest heights of civilization. Advances in science and technology preciptiated a minor industrial revolution and the world's first mechanized industry was developed. In the decorative arts the Song dynasty marked a high point in Chinese pottery. Fine porcelain and stoneware was produced in many regional centers, where mass-production techniques were developed to meet the heavy international demands for such products. Highly inventive and sophisticated in form, Song porcelain is often very restrained in color and decoration, and finely glazed.

Chola craftsmen excelled in using bronze as a medium for creating exquisite statues of Hindu gods and goddesses. This remarkable bronze is in the form of a folding lotus flower.

The Chola dynasty

The Tamil Cholas emerged in southwest India some time in the 9th century. Centered on their capital Thanjavur (Tanjore) under Rajaraja (985–1014) and his son, Rajendra I (1014–1044) the Cholas conquered much of southern India and Ceylon, and established a maritime trading empire which extended across Southeast Asia to the Malay peninsula. The Cholas presided over a flowering of Hindu culture and elaborately carved temple complexes spread throughout the area. By the 13th century the kingdom was in decline, and the dynasty ended in 1279.

The Brihadeshwara temple at the Chola capital of Thanjavur (Tanjore) is one of several elaborate Dravidian edifices in the city, dating from the 11th century.

1014 Rajendra I becomes ruler of the Cholas of SE India.

1015 Ghaznavid army invades Kashmir, but forced to retreat.

1015 Hammadids, offshoot of Zirids, rule E Algeria (–1152).

1018 Ghaznavids sack Kanauj, N India, shatter unity of Hindu Pratihara states; proceed to occupy much of N India.

Rajendra I conquers Ceylon.

1019 Mahmud of Ghazni founds the Great Mosque at Ghazni, his capital.

1020 Death of Ibn Sina (Avicenna), leading Persian philosopher.

King Canute

Norway and Sweden came under Danish control under Sweyn I (Sven Forkbeard, died 1014) who also became king of England in 1013. Sweyn's son, Canute (Cnut) the Great (c.995–1035, reigned 1016–35) thus ruled a large, but short-lived, Anglo-Scandinavian empire, which disintegrated upon his death. Initially, he shared the kingdom of England with Edmund II, but assumed total control on Edmund's death in 1016, inheriting the Danish throne in 1019, and invading Scotland in 1027. It was this legacy which led to the Scandinavian claim to the English throne upon the death of Edward the Confessor in 1065. Canute proved an effective ruler who brought internal peace and prosperity to the land. He became a strong supporter and a generous donor to the church, and his journey to Rome was inspired by religious as well as diplomatic motives.

1013 Renewed Danish invasion of England.

1014 Henry II becomes Holy Roman emperor (–1024).

1016 Accession of Canute unites England, Denmark, and Norway.

1017 First Russian stone-built church.

1018 Byzantine emperor Basil II (the Bulgar Slayer) conquers Bulgaria; orders Bulgarian army to be blinded as defeated Bulgars submit to Byzantine empire.

Malcolm II of Scotland defeats English at Carham.

Council of Pavia enforces celibacy of the clergy.

1019 Arabs attack Narbonne, S France.

c.1020 Kievan Rus at height of its power (–1054).

c.1020 Maya center of Uxmal abandoned.

Henry II of Germany

Born in Bavaria in 973, Henry succeeded to the German throne in 1002, and became Holy Roman emperor in 1014. He concentrated on consolidating the power of the monarchy and the reorganization and reform of the Church. He and his wife, Cunegund, were patrons of Benedictine monasticism, and among his foundations was the see of Bamberg, which became a major ecclesiastical and educational center. Rumors of Henry's celibate marriage were probably promoted by his supporters after his death; nevertheless the couple were canonized in 1146 and 1200 respectively.

1021 Cholas invade Bengal.

1023 Ghaznavids invade Transoxiana.

1024 Ghaznavids sack Hindu religious center of Somnath.

1025 Cholas raid Pegu (Burma) and Srivijaya (Indonesia).

c.1025 Conquest of the Punjab by Ghaznavids.

Apogee of Tamil Chola dynasty.

Avicenna's *Book of Healing*.

c.1027 Birth of Omar Khayyam, Persian mathematician and poet, author of the *Rubaiyat* (–c.1123).

Shinto

Shinto is Japan's oldest religion, the "way of the gods." Based on a cycle of rituals, customs, and pilgrimages to shrines, Shinto celebrates a host of superior or supernatural deities (*kami*) which preside over all things in nature, be they living, dead or inaminate.

The religion was formalized in texts created in the 8th century ce, such as the *Kojiki* (712 CE) and the *Nohvigi* (720 CE). Shinto syncretized with Buddhism at the same time, to create a unique admixture of the two religions, and was codified in the Yengishiki, completed in the 10th century.

Shinto shrines (*jinja,*) such as the one pictured above at Hakata in Kyushu, are often located in places of natural beauty, on rocks, offshore islands, and waterfalls. They feature a *torii* or sacred gateway, which marks the entrance to the sacred precincts of a shrine and a *shimenawa*, a rope made of twisted rice straw, which is hung over entrances within shrine precincts to separate sacred and secular places.

1040

1030 Tower of Victory built by Mahmud of Ghazni, Muslim conqueror of N India. At his death Ghaznavid empire reaches from Ganges valley to C Persia.

EUROPE

1021 Epidemic of St. Vitus' Dance.

1025 Death of great Byzantine emperor, Basil II (the Bulgar Slayer).

Byzantine empire reaches greatest extent under Constantine VIII.

1027 Norman forces operating in S Italy.

Conrad II becomes Holy Roman emperor.

1037

1028 Sancho III, king of Navarre, conquers Castile.

AMERICAS & AUSTRALASIA

Parsvanatha temple, Khajurako

The Hindu temples at Khajurako were erected by the Chaidellas who ruled central India from the 9th to the 11th centuries. Among the many ornate carvings on the soaring, mountain-like structures are reliefs of couples and trios in erotic postures, which may reflect Tantric practices or idealized representations of courtly love. Although their significance is not clear, these sculptures display an intensity and vitality which reflect the high point of classical Hindu art and architecture.

Basil II, the Bulgar Slayer

The Byzantine emperor Basil II (reigned 976–1025) earned his soubriquet after his 15-year war against the Bulgarian empire culminated in his victory at the Belasica mountains in 1015; some 15,000 prisoners were blinded and sent home in groups of one hundred, each group led by a one-eyed man. The Bulgarian czar Samuel died of shock and Bulgaria was annexed to Byzantium in 1018.

The Bulgarians cower before Basil II.

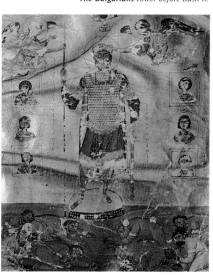

Dom St. Kilian at Würtzburg is Germany's fourth largest Romanesque cathedral. Begun in 1045, it was the crowning architectural gem of the capital of medieval Franconia.

Würtzburg cathedral

This splendid Romanesque church dominates the old center of Würtzburg on the banks of the Main river in northwestern Bavaria, southern Germany. When building commenced in 1045, the city already had a long history as an important religious center. The earliest surviving record tells us that St. Boniface established a bishopric there in 741.

Würtzburg was then the capital of the medieval Franconia, which had been settled by the Franks in the 6th century. By the time of the cathedral's completion in 1188, Würtzburg's bishops held authority over the whole of eastern Franconia. Several important councils were held at Würtzburg, including that of 1180 when the Duchy of Franconia was taken from Henry the Lion and given to Otto of Wittelsbach, whose family was to remain one of Germany's most important ruling families until 1918. Würtzburg cathedral is named after St. Kilian, an Irish monk who came to the city in 686 and died a martyr.

1034 Genoa and Pisa take control of port of Bône, Tunisia.

1035 Foundation of Xixia empire in W China.

1038 Seljuks conquer Khorasan and found the first major Turkish Muslim dynasty and empire (–1194).

1055 ▼ **c.1040** Seljuk Turks defeat Ghaznavids, halting their western expansion; conquer Afghanistan and E Persia.

1031 Beginning of Christian reconquest of Spain.

End of caliphate of Córdoba.

1035 Canute the Great divides northern empire between his three sons.

Magnus restores Norwegian independence.

William I becomes duke of Normandy.

1043

1037 Ferdinand I of Castile annexes León, asserts leadership of Christian kingdoms in Spain.

1040 Macbeth king of Scotland (–1057), after murdering Duncan.

c.1040 Death of Guido d'Arezzo, musician and teacher.

c.1040 Tiahuanaco-style pottery-making spreads to Ayacucho, Peru.

Coclé warrior art *often featured fierce or repellent animals, such as this gold pendant of two sylized bats.*

Coclé culture, Panama

Panama's earliest-known inhabitants were the Coclé and Cueva cultures. Named after an archaeological site in southwestern Panama, the Coclé civilization arose at the beginning of the 6th century and lasted for 500 years. The excavation of magificent gravegoods shows that they achieved high levels of sophistication in pottery and gold-working, while the discovery of artifacts belived to be Coclé as far north as Yucatan suggests a well-organized trade network.

Monastery of the Caves, Kiev

Christianity was introduced to Kiev in 988. By the following century, the city, with a population of 50,000, had become one of the largest and most cultured in the Christian world. Its great monastery, Pecherska Lavra, *below* – so-called after the caves (*pechera* in Ukrainian) nearby in which monks lived, worshiped and were buried – was founded in 1051. It became a place of pilgrimage and, by the 12th century, was the center of Orthodox Christianity in Europe.

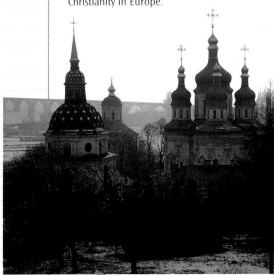

Invention of movable type

The art and science of printing originated in China, with the key factor being the invention of movable type in the 11th century. Wood block printing on paper had already been practiced since the 6th century and the world's first known book had been produced in China in 868. However, it was between the years 1041 and 1048 that Pi Sheng, a Chinese alchemist, invented the idea of movable type.

He made an amalgam of clay and glue, formed it into blocks and carved each one with a single element of a character. The blocks, or "type," were then fired to harden them. To form a text they were arranged side by side, face up, on an iron plate that had been coated with resin, wax, turpentine and burned paper ash and held in place by an iron band. The iron plate was then heated gently to melt the mixture. When it solidified, the type remained fixed to the plate and the text could be printed. The type could easily be removed by reheating the plate and therefore reused an infinite number of times. The complex nature of Chinese script meant that characters were usually made up of several pieces of type – often as many as 20. Pi Sheng used clay rather than wood for his type as clay would be more resistant to shrinking, cracking or distorting when exposed to moisture or the heat used to fix it to the plate.

However, in about 1313 a magistrate named Wang Chen succesfully ordered his craftsmen to carve 60,000 characters on movable wooden blocks which were used to print a history of technology. The characters were sorted according to a rhyming system and stored in revolving cases.

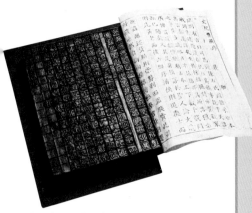

This modern replica of Chinese movable type demonstrates the kind of wooden blocks used by Wang Chen, where each block is carved with one character.

ASIA

1044 Anawratha creates first Burmese state, centered on Pegu.

c.1045 Movable type printing invented in China.

1048 Death of al-Biruni, Arab physician, astronomer, chemist, physicist, historian, and geographer.

c.1050 Construction of Jain temple complex at Mount Abu, India.

Burmese conquer Mon tribes of Irrawaddy delta.

Sima Guang's *History of China*, covers c.500 BCE–1000 CE.

Purely Japanese style of sculpture emerges.

AFRICA

1041 Zirids of Ifriqiyah gain independence.

1055

1042 Berber Almoravids, fundamentalist Muslim reformers, invade Morocco.

1048 Fatimids lose control of Ifriqiyah (Libya).

1050 King of Takrur converts to Islam.

c.1050 Military rivalry in Egypt; Fatimids seize control (–1121).

Thriving Indian Ocean trade network, extending to Mapungubwe, S Africa.

1042 End of Danish rule in England.

Edward the Confessor accedes to English throne (–1066).

1043 Magnus of Norway defeats Slavs.

Settlement on current site of Copenhagen.

Cahokia mounds

A large number of mounds extend over the North American settlement of Cahokia, which lies in a fertile valley close to the confluence of the Mississippi, Missouri, and Illinois rivers. Serving as temple-platforms or burial mounds, the first of these structures was raised in about 1050 and building continued for 300 years. It is known that by 1230 there were 120 mounds covering some 3,700 acres (1,500 hectares), making Cahokia the largest of the early settlements north of Mexico. The population in Cahokia and the surrounding region, the American Bottoms, is estimated to have reached 38,000 in the 12th and 13th centuries.

 1047 Normans conquer S Italy and Sicily (–1090).

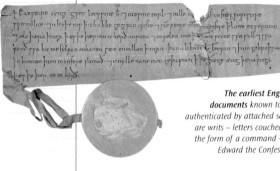

The earliest English documents known to be authenticated by attached seals are writs – letters couched in the form of a command – of Edward the Confessor.

Edward the Confessor

1050 Cahokia is center of Mississippian culture in N America with population of c.10,000.

Pueblos built for defensive purposes by Anasazi in southwest N America.

c.1050 Astrolabe in use, derived from the Arabs.

Foundation of Norwegian capital of Christiania (Oslo).

c.1050 Settlements of moundbuilders in Mississippi valley in N America expand to become true towns; growth of urban culture and large ceremonial centers in Mississippi basin (–c.1250).

Edward (reigned 1042–66) was the son of Ethelred II the Unready and Emma of Normandy, where he fled when the Danes occupied England in 1016 on Ethelred's death. Edward was eventually invited back in 1041 by Hardicanute, his half-brother, and succeeded to the English throne in 1042. Though an ineffectual and unpopular king, allowing huge powers to Godwin, Earl of Wessex, and lands and favors to Normans, he founded the new Westminster Abbey and was canonized in 1161 for his piety.

Pagan, Burma

On a vast plain beside the Irawaddy river, Pagan in central Burma (Myanmar) is one of the world's great religious sites and was the capital of Burma's first supreme king, Anawrahta (1044–77). He introduced Theravada Buddhism to his people and encouraged the building of pagodas and temples. By the 13th century, several thousand stood within an area of 5 sq miles (41 sq km), 2,000 of which still survive today – a complex rivaled only by Angkor Wat in Cambodia, which flourished at the same time.

Rural life in Byzantium

The economic decline of the Greek and Roman worlds in the 5th and 6th centuries had led to a reduction in population. Cities had decayed and many had shrunk to villages. Thereafter, however, local rural economies flourished and, by the 10th century, agricultural surpluses were supporting an urban revival, particularly south of the Black Sea. Monasteries represented a huge economic force, as they maintained vast estates and thousands of dependent peasants. By the 12th century Constantinople's Pantokrator Monastery, for example, was producing 44 million pounds (20 million kilograms) of grain each year.

Illumination from a 10th-century Byzantine manuscript showing Byzantine peasants disguised as the swineherds of the biblical parable of the prodigal son.

1051 Minamoto clan gain control of N and E Honshu in Japan (–1087).

1052 Seljuk Turks take Isfahan.

1054 Chinese record observation of supernova in Taurus.

1055 Seljuk Turks invade and capture Baghdad.

1062 ▽

1054 Commercial links between Egypt and Italy develop rapidly after rift with Constantinople.

1055 Awdaghost in central W Africa overrun by Almoravids.

1062 **1056** Almoravids conquer N Africa.
▽

The Great Schism, 1054

The most serious dispute within the Christian church occurred in 1054 and resulted in the permanent separation of the Eastern Greek-speaking (Orthodox) church centered on Constantinople, and the Western Latin-speaking church centred on Rome. The rift had its roots in the division of the Roman Empire in 330 into East and West. The main issue was the Eastern Church's refusal to accept the Western doctrine that the Holy Spirit came not from the

Byzantine miniature of the 11th century showing the patriarch of Constantinople with representatives of the Greek and Roman clergy.

Father alone, but from Father and Son. Other differences included the East allowing married clergy whereas the West enforced celibacy, and territorial disputes between missionaries. In 1054 Patriarch Michael Cerularius and Pope Leo XI excommunicated each another. Despite efforts made in 1274 and 1438 the schism was never healed.

1052 Foundation of Westminster Abbey, London.

1061
1053 Pope Leo IX raises army to expel Normans from S Italy; papal forces defeated at Civitate; foundation of Norman empire in S Italy (–1090).

1054 Final schism between Roman and Orthodox churches.

Yaroslav, prince of Kiev dies; beginning of decline of Kievan Rus.

Odda's Chapel

This tiny Saxon chapel in the village of Deerhurst in Gloucestershire has survived the centuries remarkably intact, even though it was assimilated into a medieval timber-framed farmhouse. It was built by Odda, Earl of Hwicce, who was a kinsman of Edward the Confessor and a captain in the king's fleet. Odda dedicated it to the memory of his half-brother, Elfric, who died in 1053. Although a private chapel, it was built at a time of great church building, as the Saxons in the 10th century invented the concept of the parish church – previously priests had traveled to villages from the large minsters.

1056 Almoravids take control of S Iberia (–1147).

1057 Macbeth of Scotland murdered by Malcolm, who accedes to Scottish throne (–1058).

Halley's Comet

The earliest depiction of Halley's Comet is in the Bayeux Tapestry, completed c.1092. This 230-foot (70-m-) -long embroidery tells the story of the Battle of Hastings in 1066. Although this took place on September 25, the comet, shown in the scene *above*, actually appeared on 24 April and was probably included in the tapestry because it had come to be regarded as a portent of the Norman defeat of Harold II of England.

It was the English astronomer Edmund Halley (1656–1742) who was the first to predict the return of a comet. From his study of orbits, he realized that the bright comet of 1682 must be the same object as that recorded in 1607 and 1531. It now bears his name and its 76-year cycle shows that it must have been the comet seen in 1066.

Pisa cathedral

Designed by the architect Giovanni Giudice di Buscheto and built between 1064 and 1180, Pisa's Duomo is one of Italy's finest Romanesque buildings. Faced in white and red marble and decorated with glass, marble, and majolica mosaics, it illustrates Pisa's medieval wealth, the color in the decoration reflecting the city-state's trading links with the Arab world. At that time, Pisa had a large port and its powerful navy ensured its dominance of the western Mediterranean.

ASIA

1062 Seljuk Turks invade Syria and E Anatolia.

1063 Alp Arslan becomes ruler of Seljuk Turks (–1071).

1064 Seljuk Turks invade Christian state of Armenia.

Wang Jian *Island of the Immortals*, early Chinese painting on silk.

1065 Nizamiyeh academy founded in Baghdad.

1067 Wang Anshi campaigns against corruption in Chinese army and government; introduction of unsuccessful land reforms.

1068 Nationalization of agricultural production and distribution in China.

1071 **1069** Seljuks take Iconium (Konya).
▼

AFRICA

1076 **1062** Berber Almoravids establish capital
▼ at Marrakesh, Morocco.

c.1070 Islam established in sub-Saharan W Africa.

EUROPE	AMERICAS & AUSTRALASIA	The Norman conquest

EUROPE

1071 ▼
1061 Normans invade Sicily.

1063 Foundation of St Mark's, Venice.

1064 Ferdinand of Castile captures Coimbra (Portugal).

1072 ▼
1065 Death of Ferdinand of Castile.

Earliest known stained glass in Europe, at Augsburg cathedral, Germany.

1066 ▼
Battle of Hastings; Norman conquest of England.

1072 ▼
1068 William I of England crushes northern revolt under Edwin and Morcar.

1070 English bribe Danish invasion fleet to retire. Collapse of resistance to Norman invasion, led by Hereward the Wake.

AMERICAS & AUSTRALASIA

The Norman conquest

England in the mid-11th century already had strong ties with Normandy through royal marriages, and Edward the Confessor had showered many favors on Normans. However, when he died, the English chose Harold, the second son of Godwin, Earl of the West Saxons as king. Godwin had led rebellions against Norman influence, but the Normans finally obtained supreme control when William, Duke of Normandy, invaded and defeated Harold at Hastings in 1066. Although many of the English ruling class were killed in battle or in rebellions in 1068–70, and although Norman feudalism was introduced and Norman French became the language of the elite, greatly influencing the development of the English language, the English judicial and administrative systems largely survived.

The Norman Conquest

1066

5 Jan:	Death of Edward the Confessor, King of England; Harold assumes throne.
Apr:	Harold's fleet drives off Tostig; guards English Channel until September.
	Raids along south coast of England by Harold's exiled brother, Tostig.
Aug–Sept:	William of Normandy assembles fleet and army at Dives-sur-Mer.
Sept 25:	Harold defeats his brother, Tostig, and Harald Hardrada of Norway at Stamford Bridge.
Sept 28:	William lands at Pevensey.
Oct 14:	Battle of Hastings; Harold defeated and killed.
Dec 25:	William crowned in London.
1067	Founding of Tower of London as Norman base; Bayeux Tapestry, celebrating Norman victory in England, begun.

One of the 58 scenes in the Bayeux Tapestry, which is believed to have been commissioned by William the Conqueror's half-brother, Odo, Bishop of Bayeux.

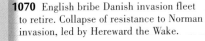

ASIA

1071 Seljuk Turks, under Seljuk leader, Alp Arslan, defeat Byzantines at battle of Manzikert.

Revival of Islam under Seljuk Turks.

1076 Seljuk Turks capture Damascus and Jerusalem.

1077 Seljuk province established in Anatolia with capital first at Nicaea and then Iconium (Konya); dynasty comes to be known as the Seljuks of Rum (Rome).

Seljuk governors in Oxus region establish separate state of Khwarizm Shah (–1231).

Chola merchants of India send embassy to China.

1084 ▼

AFRICA

1076 Ghana falls to Almoravids.

King of Ghana converts to Islam.

The humiliation of Henry IV

As the German king and Holy Roman emperor, Henry VI tried to break the power of the Saxons. He defeated them at Hohenburg in 1075, but his later vengeance on them provoked the anger of Pope Gregory VII, sparking a huge duel between pope and emperor. One issue was over who should appoint bishops. Henry deposed the pope, but in 1077 he had to beg for absolution in sackcloth at Canossa in Italy to regain his vassals' waning support.

The Seljuk Turks

In about 1038, a group of nomadic Turkish tribes dominated by the Seljuks swept out of Central Asia. In 1055 they occupied Baghdad and went on to conquer Armenia. Alarmed by the approaching threat, the Byzantines marched east from Constantinople under Emperor Romanus Diogenes, but they suffered a crushing defeat at Manzikert in 1071. This drove the Byzantines out of Asia Minor and ultimately provoked the Crusades.

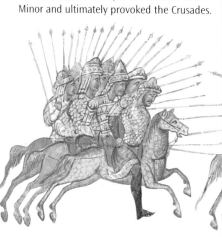

1071 Normans capture the last Byzantine possessions in Italy: Bari, and Brindisi.

1072 Alfonso VI becomes king of León and Castile.

William I of England invades Scotland.

c.1072 Normans seize Palermo and Amalfi in Italy, effectively gaining control of C Mediterranean maritime trade routes.

1073 Gregory VII becomes pope; beginning of conflict between papacy and Holy Roman Empire.

1075 Pope Gregory VII declares absolute authority of the papacy.

c.1075 Development of the Nordic saga, associated with Viking colonization of Iceland.

1077 German king, Henry IV, forced to seek absolution from Pope Gregory VII.

1078 Foundation of Santiago de Compostela cathedral in N Spain; becomes major pilgrimage center.

1079 Newcastle founded as Norman base in N England.

Birth of Abelard, theologian and philosopher (–1142).

The architecture and decoration of St. Mark's Basilica in Venice owes its splendor to Byzantine influence. Its design was inspired by the Church of the Apostles in Constantinople.

Byzantine art

Byzantine craftsmen invested all of their work, whether wood carvings, jewelry, cloth, or architecture with lavish decoration and, wherever possible, gold embellishment. However, their two most remarkable contributions were new architectural forms and mosaics. In architecture, they realized that curved or multifaceted surfaces reflected the sun's rays throughout the day and so introduced the idea of crowning a polygonal building with a dome. They took the art of mosaics to new heights, making *tesserae* of glass and gold and using them on walls and ceilings rather than on floors. They also developed icon painting and made the gilt iconostasis an enduring feature of Orthodox churches.

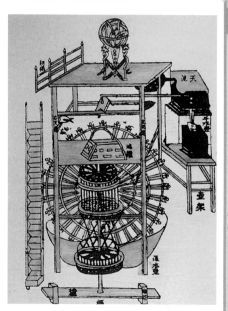

Song technology

A remarkable mechanical clock was built in China during the Song dynasty by the inventor Su Sung and his colleagues in 1090. His complex, 23-foot- (7-m-) tall mechanism was powered by a water-driven escapement. It incorporated an armillary sphere with a rotating celestial globe, and five doors through which viewers could watch statues ringing bells, striking gongs, or holding tablets showing the hour.

Seljuk architecture

The Seljuk Turks, who held power in Mesopotamia, Persia, and Asia Minor from the mid-11th to the mid-13th centuries, were great builders. Their architectural forms and intricate abstract designs, such as this splendid, 11th-century glazed tile-work dome in Isfahan's Friday Mosque, had a lasting influence on Islamic art. They excelled in ceramics decorated in luster and overglazed enamel colors with leaf gilding.

ASIA

c.1082 Earliest known Japanese roll paintings illustrating scenes from novels, deeds of great men, legends, and religious scenes.

1083 Printed mathematical textbooks and tables in use in China.

c.1083 Toba, Japanese artist, portrays priests and bureaucrats using birds and animals.

1094

1084 Fall of Antioch to Seljuks.

1086 Minamoto clan under Yoshiie suppresses rival clans to take control of Japan.

1090 Shia Ismailis (Alamut) Assassins, emerge as major force in N Persia (–1256).

Hasan ibn al-Sabbah founds Assassin sect in Syria.

Water-powered mechanical clock built for Chinese Song court.

AFRICA

1087 Pisans and Genoans gain trading privileges in N Africa, creating a dominant trading network in W Mediterranean.

EUROPE

1081 Venetians negotiate trading treaty with Constantinople.

1083 Emperor Henry IV besieges Rome (–1084).

1094

1084 Rome submits to Emperor Henry IV, who installs an antipope, Clement III.

1091

Normans attack Rome; widespread destruction, Henry IV retreats.

1085 Civil war in Ireland.

1094

Christian forces under Alfonso VI of León capture Toledo, the greatest city the Christians have captured in the Reconquest.

1086 The Domesday Book compiled by Normans to provide detailed survey of English landownership and agricultural resources.

Carthusian Order founded by Bruno of Cologne.

Almoravids enter Spain.

1087 St. Paul's, London, burnt down; rebuilt (completed, 1284).

1090 Turkish tribes enter Europe, settling between Balkan mountains and the Danube.

AMERICAS & AUSTRALASIA

c.1085 Thule Eskimo culture, having crossed Bering Strait, now extends across N Siberia, N American Arctic, and Greenland.

The Domesday Book

Commissioned by William the Conqueror and compiled during 1085–86, this great survey of England was a comprehensive census of all landholdings and livestock in the kingdom. It was designed as a basis for determining taxation with new accuracy, especially for military purposes, and was the most complete and efficient survey ever taken in medieval history. It took just two years to complete, during which royal officials visited every village in each "hundred" (the sub-division of a shire) twice. To further ensure accuracy and comparability of information, the officials were provided with standard questionnaires. The returns for each county were then rearranged under the names of the king and his chief tenants, reflecting the feudal organization of the land that the Normans had imposed on England.

The information was then compiled into two volumes by the king's clerks in Winchester. The final document covered the whole country except a few northern areas, although the records for London and Winchester have not survived. Organized by county, it lists all England's manors, the names of their holders both in 1066, the year of the Norman Conquest, and in 1086, their size, number of workers, mills, fishponds, other assets and their monetary value.

Mesa Verde

The Anasazi people were the largest of the three prehistoric tribes inhabiting South-Western North America, roughly today's Utah and Colorado. Their society reached its peak between 900 and 1100. In the 11th century, they left the river valleys and open upland that they had inhabited up to then and began building on well-defended sites, such as this one at Mesa Verde, (*mesa* in Spanish meaning table or flat-topped hill). Here, for example, they built apartment dwellings, storehouses, and watchtowers in rock shelters high in the canyon cliffs.

El Cid

Rodrigo Díaz de Vivar (1043–99) was a noble of the court of Fernando I of Castile, but was exiled after involvement in the fratricidal disputes of the king's sons. He then fought for the Moors, (when he gained the name El Cid, meaning "lord" in Arabic), but later changed sides again, capturing Valencia for the Christians and becoming its ruler. His exploits in the Reconquest of Spain are immortalized in an epic poem written in 1180.

ASIA

1092 Seljuk vizier Nizam al-Mulk murdered by Ismaili Assassin.

1094 Seljuk dynasty of Syria founded with capital at Aleppo.

1096 First Crusade; establishment of Latin kingdoms in Levant. Attacks on Jewish communities by Crusaders and their supporters.

1097 Crusaders defeat Turks at Dorylaeum.

1098 Crusaders take Antioch.

1104

Byzantines recover control of Smyrna, Ephesus, and Sardis from Seljuk Turks.

1099 Jerusalem captured by Crusaders.

Fatimids regain control of Jerusalem from Seljuk Turks.

Crusaders defeat Fatimids of Egypt at Ascalon.

Crusaders rebuild Church of the Holy Sepulchre, Jerusalem.

1100 Creation of Frankish feudal kingdom of Jerusalem under Godfrey of Bouillon, who dies and is succeeded immediately by Baldwin.

Arabs expelled from Tiflis.

AFRICA

c.1100 Rise to prominence of Zimbabwe, centered on stone-built city of Great Zimbabwe (–c.1600).

1091 Completion of Norman conquest of Sicily; Norman king, Roger of Sicily takes control of the island, establishing a cultured and powerful court.

1101 ▼

c.1091 Walcher of Malvern observes and records lunar eclipse in Italy.

1092 Foundation of Durham cathedral (completed 1133).

1094 Christian warlord, El Cid, takes Valencia in Spain from Almoravids.

Anti-pope Clement III deposed; Urban II takes office.

Welsh revolt against Normans.

1095 Byzantine empire appeals for aid to pope, who preaches in France to raise support.

Pope Urban II proclaims First Crusade.

1096 First wave of Crusaders departs. Attacks on Jewish communities by Crusaders and their supporters.

1098 Foundation of new Cistercian monastery at Cîteaux in France.

1100 Genoa, Pisa, and Venice in Italy granted trading privileges on Levant coast as a reward for transporting and supplying Crusader forces.

c.1100 *Chanson de Roland*, early example of French *Chansons de Geste*, epic poems forming the core of the Charlemagne legends.

Development of secular polyphonic music at school of Limoges, France.

Outbreak of leprosy in Europe.

Craftsmen's guilds begin to develop, mainly in European market towns.

c.1100 Anasazi people of southwest N America build fortified cliff dwellings at Mesa Verde and Chaco Canyon.

Beginnings of Inca state under Sinchi Roca, based at Cuzco.

Toltecs establish capital at Tula, Mexico.

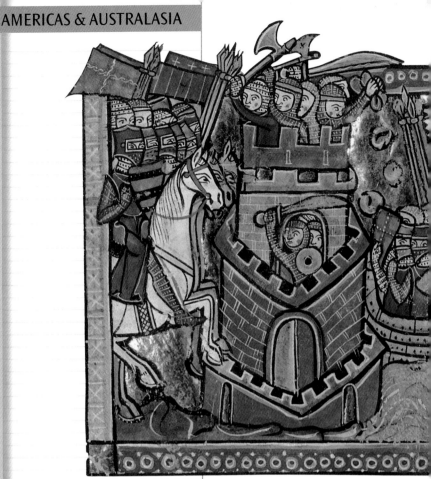

In 1098, the Christians captured Antioch, one of their first successes on the First Crusade. This heavily fortified city in the empire of the Seljuk Turks held out for seven months.

The First Crusade

Jerusalem was regarded as holy by Jews, Muslims, and Christians. Although it fell under Muslim control in 638, Christians and Jews were permitted to live there and Christian pilgrims were given safe passage under successive Arab dynasties. This equilibrium was destroyed in 1009 when caliph El-Hakim initiated a persecution of non-Muslims and destroyed the Church of the Holy Sepulchre. The situation worsened when the Seljuk Turks took the Holy City in 1071 and forbade Christians access to it.

Pope Urban II's response was to launch an appeal to liberate Jerusalem and the Holy Land from the Muslims, which he did at the Council of Clermont in 1095. His words "God wills it!" inspired 100,000 men and women from all over Europe to join the Christian armies. After consolidating their forces in Constantinople, they took Jerusalem in 1099 and set up a Christian state there, followed by others in Antioch, Edessa, and Tripoli.

The Samurai

Originally, the samurai were warriors belonging to Japan's aristocracy. In the 12th century, as a result of intensified clashes between the Taira and Minamoto clans, their power increased and they came to dominate all aspects of government, admitting members to their elite from other sections of society. The period of their greatest ascendency was known as the Kamakura culture (1185–1333) when feudalism was firmly established in Japan. The samurai regarded martial skills and the achievement of high ideals of bravery and stoicism, loyalty to their overlords *(bushido)* and duty as their greatest goals. They developed the cult of the sword, securing the privilege of wearing two, and the practice of ritual suicide by disembowelment *(seppuku)*. They lost their privileges only in 1871 when feudalism was abolished.

ASIA

c.1101 Career of Ramanuja, Indian Vaishnava philosopher, in late 11th–12th century.

1103 *Method of Architecture* published in China, illustrating buildings and building techniques.

1118 ▼

1104 Sustained warfare between Byzantines and Crusader principality of Antioch (–1108).

Seljuk Turks defeat Crusaders at Harran, Syria.

c.1108 Iso no Zenji, mother of Japanese drama, active.

1109 Japanese Taira and Minamoto clans unite to counter warrior monks.

AFRICA

1109 Crusaders take Tripoli.

c.1110 Onset of serious desiccation of Sahel region.

1101 Almoravids counterattack in Iberia, besieging Valencia for a year.

1102 Valencia relieved by Alfonso VI; city evacuated and razed.

Boleslav III of Poland conquers Pomerania, expands westwards.

Europe's oldest paper document dates from court of Roger of Sicily.

1104 Construction of Arsenal at Venice begun.

1105 Renewed German expansion eastward.

1106 Emperor Henry V campaigns against Bohemians.

Russian Orthodox abbot, Daniel, visits Holy Land.

English Normans defeat Normandy at Tinchebrai, reuniting England and Normandy (divided since death of William the Conqueror, 1087).

1108 Emperor Henry V's invasion of Hungary fails.

1109 Emperor Henry V's invasion of Poland fails.

War between France and England (–1113).

1110 Basil, leader of heretical Bogomil sect, burnt in Constantinople.

Earliest evidence of a miracle play performed in England. One of three principal kinds of vernacular drama of the European Middle Ages (along with the mystery play and the morality play), the miracle play presents a real or fictitious account of the life, miracles, or martyrdom of a saint.

The Cistercians

This monastic order was founded in 1098 at Cîteaux (Cistercium) in France by St. Robert of Molesme, a Benedictine who felt his abbey had strayed from the Rule of St. Benedict. After St. Bernard joined and founded Clairvaux in 1115, Cistercian abbeys were built all over Europe, including Fountains in England (*above*), until there were 530 by 1200. The Cistercians' development of farming, and of wool production in England, greatly advanced 12th-century European economic growth.

Arabic literature

Entertainment for the masses, as well as for a more sophisticated audience, formed an important part of the *adab* (nonreligious) literature of the Abbasid period. Addressed to the latter were the so-called *maqamat*, dramatic anecdotes narrated by a witty but unscrupulous rogue which poke fun at all levels of society. This illustration is taken from the *maqamat* by al-Hariri of Basra (1054–1122), which relates the adventures of Abu Zaid who traveled the Muslim world earning a living from his wits.

GVROPA MVNDI PARS QVARTA

The Medieval World

This map, the Liber Floribus of Lambert of Ardres (c.1120) is an early attempt to represent a world view. Europe and Africa are shown as occupying half the globe, Asia occupies the other half. In the Middle Ages geographical knowledge was vague, maps were rare and inaccurate, and transportation was difficult, slow, and unsafe. Roads were impassable in bad weather, mountain passes were closed by snow, and bandits lurked in the forests. Many people strayed no more than a few miles from their home villages in their lifetimes.

Despite this, a great number of people – merchants, knights, priests, scholars, pilgrims, actors – traveled the length and breadth of Europe. Horses, requiring an abundant diet of grain, oats, and barley, were far beyond the means of most ordinary people. Most people were reduced to traveling on foot, and probably could travel no more than 15–20 miles (24–32 km) a day, although lightweight two-wheeled carts (drawn by oxen or mules) were used for short journeys.

Carrying goods (and even people) by riverboat was much cheaper and quicker than traveling by road, despite the frequent tolls imposed by landowners. The cheapest, and quickest, form of transportation was by sea. However, the seas were far from safe. Pirate raids, especially in the Mediterranean were common, storms were a hazard, while calm weather could bring insufferable delays.

ASIA

1111 Death of Muslim theologian, al-Ghazali.

1113 Foundation of Knights of the Hospital of St. John (Hospitallers) to care for pilgrims in Holy Land.

Accession of Suryavarman II, powerful warrior king of the Khmer.

1115 Jurchen of Manchuria ally with Song to crush Khitan (Liao) dynasty in N China; replaced by Jin dynasty.

1125 ▼

c.1115 Renaissance of Byzantine arts under patronage of emperor, Alexius Comnenus, notably icon painting, mosaics, and gold-working.

c.1118 Crusading order known as the "Knights of the Temple of Solomon of Jerusalem," or Knights Templar, led by two French knights, Hugh of Payens and Geoffrey of St. Omer, founded in Jerusalem to protect pilgrimage routes to Holy Land.

1129 ▼

c.1120 Playing cards in use in China.

AFRICA

The Medieval knight

Medieval knights were mounted warriors, many of whom were feudal vassals, granted lands as fiefs from the lords in whose armies they served. As the knighthood evolved, ideals of behavior emerged that promoted a code of personal honor, loyalty to superiors, and respect for the teachings of the Church.

The knightly ideal reached its apogee during the Crusades, when the knights of Europe were brought together, under the auspices of the Church, to achieve a common purpose – the liberation of the Holy Land. During the Crusades, the first orders of knights emerged: The Knights Templar (c.1118) and the Knights of St. John (c.1130). Organized on monastic lines, and religious in their purpose, these crusading orders soon amassed great wealth and political power. By the 14th century, the gradual end of the Crusades, the emergence of mercenary armies of foot-soldiers with new skills such as archery, and the gradual erosion of feudalism all led to the decline of the traditional knighthood.

1113 Building of St. Nicholas, Novgorod; early use of onion domes.

1114 Almoravid assault on Toledo in Spain fails, as does attack on Barcelona by Almoravid governor of Saragossa, defeated near Martorell.

1115 Bernard founds Cistercian daughter house at Clairvaux.

Florence establishes free republic.

1115 Chaco Canyon in Southwest N America a thriving trade center, probably an entrepot between C and N America.

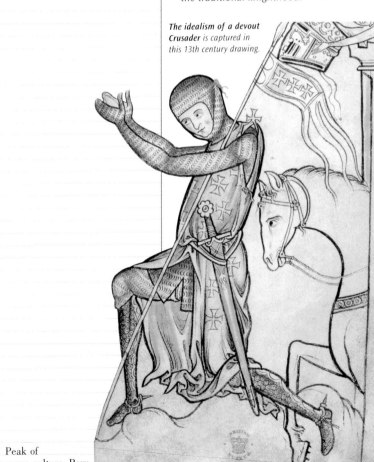

The idealism of a devout Crusader is captured in this 13th century drawing.

1125

1118 Alfonso VI retakes Saragossa in Spain from Almoravids; makes it his capital.

c.1120 Peak of Lambayeque culture, Peru.

Cotton garments widely used in Andes.

Flemish weavers use horizontal two-bar looms, mounted in a frame connected to a foot-operated treadle. These looms arrived in Europe from East Asia in the 12th century.

The textile industry

Sheep farming on the chalky soils and marshes of Flanders supplied wool for a fast-growing textile industry that, by the 12th century, was an important factor in the growth of cities such as Arras, Douai, Lille, Tournai, Bruges, Ypres, and Ghent. Cloth merchants from these towns joined together to form the Flemish Hanse, a trade association. As the cloth trade expanded, the Flemish economy became increasingly dependent on imports of English wool. The raw material was bought by drapers, who had it treated by spinners, weavers, fullers, and dyers. The finished cloth was then exported to the Rhineland, Italy, France, and the Baltic.

The Almohads

In the 1140s, 'Abd al-Mu'min united the North African Berbers in a *jihad* against the Almoravid rulers of Morocco, who they condemned for their corruption and loss of piety. They founded the Almohad state, taking Marrakesh from the Almoravids in 1147, and went on to conquer all of Morocco and Muslim Spain. By 1163, the Almohads controlled all of NE Africa, from the Atlantic coast to Libya.

Almohad battle banners proclaimed that they were fighting for stricter observance of Muslim law.

1121 Great mosque of Isfahan rebuilt with four *iwans* (porch like vaults, opening onto a central courtyard).

1122 Capture of Beijing by the Jin.

1123 The Venetian fleet, fighting in support of the Crusaders, defeats the Egyptian fleet off Ascalon.

1124 Capture of important port of Tyre by Crusaders.

1125 Liao defeated by Jin from Manchuria.

1126 Death of Persian mathematician and astrologer, Omar Khayyam. He also had a prolific career as a poet, and is celebrated for his *rubaiyats*, quatrains celebrating the melancholy pleasures of life.

Jin soldiers capture Kaifeng, the capital of the Song dynasty, seizing two Song emperors and looting the imperial treasury.

1127 Zangid dynasty of Seljuk governors control Syria and Mesopotamia (–1222); initiate Muslim counteroffensive against Crusaders.

Confronted by Jin attacks, the Song take refuge south of the Yangtze. Beginning of the Southern Song.

1128 The church council approves the crusading order, the Knight's Templar.

1144 Zangi, governor of Mosul, occupies Aleppo.

1129 Crusaders attack Jerusalem.

1138 **1130** Song capital moves to Hangzhou.

1132 **1128** Almohad religious revival order starts takeover of Almoravid dominions in N Africa and Iberia (1130–1269).

1121 Bishop Eirik visits N America from Greenland.

1122 At the Diet of Worms Henry V, the German king, renounces the right to invest bishops.

1124 Henry V of Germany invades France, with the support of his father-in-law, Henry I of England, but retires when the majority of French magnates rally to Louis VI.

1133

1125 When Emperor Henry V dies without an heir, Lothair is chosen to succeed him, but civil war ensues.

Venetians occupy Cephalonia (Ionian Sea). Byzantine emperor, John II Comnenus, restores their trading privileges.

Venetians occupy Chios, and pillage Rhodes, Samos, and Lesbos.

Alfonso VI raids S Spain (–1126).

Beginnings of troubador music in France.

1126 Birth of Muslim philosopher, Averroës (Ibn Rushd), in Córdoba.

1127 Conrad III, the brother of Frederick of Hohenstaufen, becomes king of Italy.

Succession disputes in Flanders, following the murder of Count Charles; the Flemings eventually accept Thierry of Alsace.

1138

1128 Geoffrey V of Anjou marries Matilda, daughter of Henry, king of England, and widow of Henry V of Germany.

Byzantine emperor John II Comnenus defeats Magyar invaders on the Danube, near Haram.

1139

Having defeated his mother, Teresa, at the battle of São Mamede, Afonso Henriques gains control of Portugal.

1147

1130 The Norman, Roger II, is crowned king of Sicily.

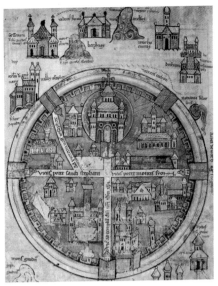

A 12th-century map of Jerusalem, the Holy City. It is depicted as a circle to emphasize both its perfection and its position at the center of the known world.

Crusader states

The crusading expeditions of the early 12th century secured the Levantine coast for Latin settlers, who dedicated themselves to the defense of the Holy Land. They occupied a stretch of coast some 600 miles (966 km) long, isolated from the interior by mountain ranges. Eventually four Crusader states were established: Jerusalem, Tripoli, Edessa, and Antioch. Muslim occupants were driven out of existing towns, which were adapted to the Crusaders' needs – mosques, for example, were turned into churches. The Crusader states were run on feudal principles, ruled by feudal lords who had complete jurisdiction over their own vassals, who provided military service when required. However, there were never enough permanent settlers to ensure that their hold on the territory was secure.

Crusader states (1098–1230)

1098	Crusaders take Antioch.
1099	Godfrey of Bouillon elected king of Jerusalem.
1124	Capture of port of Tyre.
1144	Edessa lost to Zangi, governor of Mosul.
1151	Last Christian stronghold in county of Edessa falls to Nur al-Din.
1187	Crusader states ravaged by Saladin's army (–1188).
1191	Richard I the Lion-heart wins back Jaffa, but fails to recapture Jerusalem (–1192).
1225	Emperor Frederick II inherits kingdom of Jerusalem.
1229	Frederick negotiates settlement that wins back control over Jerusalem.

Krak des Chevaliers

The Crusaders began to build castles as soon as they arrived in the east. Krak des Chevaliers in modern Syria (*above*) was built in 1131 by the Crusading Order of the Knights of St. John (Hospitallers). Built to withstand sieges, it had two concentric towered walls that were separated by a wide moat. It stood on a natural rocky outcrop, which was inaccessible and gave commanding views of the surrounding countryside. It could garrison 2,000 men. The castle was held by the Knights of St. John until 1271, when it was captured by the Mamluk sultan, Baybars I.

Roger II of Sicily

Roger II was crowned king of Sicily in 1130. He was the son of Roger I, count of Sicily, a Norman noble who had won the island from the Muslims. His court was based on the Norman feudal system, but his Byzantine administration included Greeks, Arabs, and many other races. This silk mantle of Roger II was made in 1133 by Muslim weavers based at the royal workshop in Palermo.

1132 Emperor Gao Zong of the Southern Song takes up residence in Hangzhou.

1135 Jin withdraw to the north, leaving puppet regimes in C China.

1136 The castle of Bethgibelin in S Palestine is granted to the Knights Hospitallers.

1137 Antioch becomes a vassal of Byzantium.

1162

1138 Peace treaty between the Song and the Jin.

1146

1132 The Almohad, 'Abd al-Mu'min, is recognized as caliph.

1134 Death of Gijimasu (1095–1134), the third ruler of the Hausa city-state of Kano in Nigeria.

c.1139 Igbo culture flourishes on Niger river. An elaborate tomb, containing regalia and bronze-work ornaments, may be the burial place of the Eze Nri, or religious leader.

1132 Palatine chapel at Palermo in Sicily; unique blend of Romanesque, Byzantine, and Islamic architectural elements.

1133 Lothair III of Saxony is crowned emperor.

Muslim craftsmen weave Roger II's coronation robe in Sicily.

1135 Almohads control the Iberian peninsula.

1144

Death of Henry I of England. Crown is passed to his nephew, Stephen of Blois.

1136 Lothair III invades S Italy, and conquers Apulia.

Independence of Russian state of Novgorod.

1137 Union of Aragon and Catalonia.

In Paris, Abbot Suger begins the construction of the church of St. Denis in the Gothic style.

1138 Conrad III of Hohenstaufen succeeds Lothair III of Saxony, beginning the Hohenstaufen dynasty. He immediately seizes Saxony and Bavaria, precipitating a civil war.

On the death of Boleslav III, king of Poland for 28 years, the kingdom is divided into four principalities.

David I of Scotland invades England on behalf of Matilda, King Henry's daughter, and is defeated at the battle of the Standard.

1139 The Anacletus Schism, which arose when rival groups of cardinals elected two different popes in 1130, is settled by a Lateran council.

1143

Afonso I of Portugal defeats the Almohads at Ourique and assumes title of king.

Civil war breaks out in England over the disputed royal succession.

1140 Peter Abelard, the celebrated French philosopher and teacher, is condemned for heresy by the council of Sens.

The empire and the papacy

In the 11th century, it became an established practice for the Holy Roman emperor to appoint bishops and invest them with the powers of office. But when, in 1057, the Milanese rose up against their bishop, who had been appointed by the emperor, they precipitated a long struggle between church reformers, frequently monastic leaders, and the bishops.

The pope rejected the principle that kings could dispense ecclesiastical office. Eventually, in 1122, a compromise was reached: kings could be present at episcopal elections, but did not have the decisive vote. Kingship, as depicted in this 12th-century Cistercian manuscript (*above*) was seen as subordinate to the church, administering justice and maintaining order at its direction.

St. James the Apostle, brother of St. John the Evangelist, is the patron saint of Spain. Pilgrims wore cockleshell badges to indicate that they had visited the shrine of St. James at Santiago de Compostela.

Pilgrimages

The magnificent cathedral in Santiago de Compostela, Spain, became a major pilgrimage center in the 11th and 12th centuries. The cathedral's crypt houses the remains of St. James the Apostle and pilgrimages to his shrine became increasingly popular as a way of gaining remission for sins. Many roads converged on Santiago, and travelers followed special guides that listed wayside inns, abbeys, and churches where they could rest and pray.

The other great pilgrimage center was Rome, and a spate of church-building in the 11th and 12th centuries helped to enhance the appearance of the Holy See. The main pilgrimage routes ran from France or the Rhineland towns, crossing the Alps by the Mont-Cenis or St. Bernard passes into northern Italy. These routes became the busiest in Europe in the 11th and 12th centuries.

ASIA

1151 ▼ **1144** Crusaders lose Edessa to Zangi, governor of Mosul.

1145 Construction of the Friday mosque at Isfahan.

1147 Second Crusade; Emperor Conrad defeated by Turks at Dorylaeum.

1148 Second Crusade ends in humiliating failure, when Crusaders abandon the siege of Damascus and retreat.

1154 ▼ **1149** Nur al-Din kills Raymond of Poitiers, the prince of Antioch, near Apamea.

Dedication of new church of the Holy Sepulchre in Jerusalem.

c.1150 Rise of anticaste Virashaiva (Lingayat) sect in S India.

AFRICA

1146 The Almohad caliph, 'Abd al-Mu'min conquers much of Morocco.

1184 ▼ **1147** Marrakesh, capital of the Almoravid empire, falls to the Almohads under 'Abd al-Mu'min.

1159 ▼ **1148** Roger II of Sicily takes Sousse and Sfax in Tunis.

1150 Tsaraki dan Gimimasu, the ruler of the Kano, has completed the city's walls, which will guarantee the continued existence of this Nigerian city-state.

c.1150 In Ethiopia, the founder of the Zagwe dynasty seizes the throne from the descendants of the Axumite line of kings. The Zagwe kings will inaugurate a more aggressively expansionist era.

The culture of the Yoruba people flourishes in W Africa.

1141 England has fallen into anarchy as Matilda, daughter of the late King Henry, and her cousin Stephen fight for the throne. Stephen is captured at the battle of Lincoln.

1143 Romans declare their independence of the pope.

Foundation of Lübeck.

Afonso of Portugal is recognized as king by Alfonso VII of Castile.

1144 Geoffrey of Anjou secures Normandy in the civil war that follows Henry I's death in 1135.

1146 Bernard of Clairvaux preaches the Second Crusade.

1147 Second Crusade ; Lisbon taken from Moors by Christians.

Roger II of Sicily takes the Greek island of Corfu from the Byzantines, and pillages Corinth, Athens, and Thebes.

1148 Pope extends Crusade to Spain. Crusaders take Almería and Lisbon.

Papal bull *Divina dispensatione* authorizes German crusades against the Wends, a Slavic people of NE Germany.

1150 Byzantine forces attempt to recapture Italy.

c.1150 A university is founded in Paris.

c.1150 Anasazi dominate Southwest N America, forming a pueblo culture. Their most famous site is Mesa Verde.

Maoris begin to settle river mouth areas in the north of New Zealand's South Island, such as Wairau Bar.

The Cathars

In the 12th century, heresy took hold in the lands of the counts of Toulouse, in southwest France. The Cathars, based in the area between Albi, Carcassonne, and Toulouse, followed the Albigensian heresy. They believed that the material world was intrinsically evil, and only an elite of "perfects" could aspire to a life of purity. The Cathars gained a considerable following among peasants, who revered the "perfects," and the elite classes, who approved of the movement's anticlerical bias. The Cathars were forced to defend their faith from mountain fortresses such as Peyrepertuse (*above*) when marauding knights under Simon de Montfort conducted a ferocious, and successful, campaign against them in 1209.

Norwegian Christianity

The wooden stave churches of Norway date from the 11th century, when Christianity began to spread across the country. Most of the 500 or 600 stave churches eventually constructed date from the 12th century. The church at Borgund (*left*) built in about 1150, is one of about 24 surviving examples. Its double-sloped roofs are coated with shell like wooden shingles. It is carved with elaborate dragons and other legendary motifs, giving it an almost Oriental appearance.

Eleanor of Aquitaine

Eleanor (c.1122–1204) was perhaps the most powerful woman in 12th-century Europe. She was the daughter, and heiress, of William X, duke of Aquitaine. She married Louis VII, king of France, but the marriage was subsequently annulled. She then married the grandson of Henry I of England, who became King Henry II in 1154. Imprisoned by her husband when she became involved in a revolt by her four sons, she supported her son, Richard the Lion-heart when he became king, keeping the kingdom intact, and fending off the conspiracies of his brother and the king of France.

Angkor Wat

The Hindu temple of Angkor Wat was commissioned by the Khmer king, Suryavarman II as his funeral temple. The temple was surrounded by a moat, and galleries decorated by bas-relief scenes from Hindu mythology. The central temple pyramid, dedicated to Vishnu, consists of five bell-shaped towers. It forms part of the monumental city of Angkor, planned to reflect the structure of the world according to Hindu cosmology. The entire city is moated, and centers on a pyramidal temple that represents sacred Mount Meru in the Himalayas. The whole complex is a symbol of the harmony between the human and divine worlds.

ASIA

1151 Last Christian stronghold in county of Edessa falls to Nur al-Din.

The Jin transfer their main capital to Beijing.

1152 Baldwin III, king of Jerusalem, besieges the citadel and exiles his mother and coruler, Melisande, to Nablus.

Alauddin of Ghur sacks Ghazni (Afghanistan), and drives out the last Ghaznavid ruler.

c.1180 The largest, and most magnificent, Hindu temple in Asia is completed at Angkor Wat, the Khmer capital.

1153 Baldwin III takes Ascalon, the last Fatimid possession in Palestine.

1154 Nur al-Din seizes Damascus.

1180 **1156** Wars between two Japanese clans; the Taira and the Minamoto.

c.1160 Taira clan gain political control in Japan.

AFRICA

1159 Arabs retake the lands in Tunis conquered by Roger of Sicily, and expel the Normans from N Africa.

EUROPE

1151 Henry (later Henry II, king of England) succeeds Geoffrey as count of Anjou.

1152 Frederick Barbarossa becomes king of Germany (–1190).

Eleanor of Aquitaine's marriage to Louis VII is dissolved. She marries Henry of Anjou.

1153 Bernard, who preached the Second Crusade, dies at the monastery of Clairvaux, where he has been abbot since 1115.

1154 King Stephen of England dies at Dover.

Succession of Henry of Anjou (Henry II) to English crown.

Muhammad al-Idrisi's *Geography* is published in Palermo, Sicily.

Roger II dies at Palermo and is succeeded by his son, William (the Bad).

Building of Chartres cathedral, France.

1155 Arnold of Brescia, an idealistic priest who preached the joys of purity and poverty, and founded the Arnoldist movement, is burnt for heresy.

Frederick I Barbarossa is chosen as Holy Roman emperor (–1190).

1156 With the backing of the pope, the Byzantines invade Apulia and Sicily revolts. William of Sicily crushes the revolt and defeats the Byzantines at Brindisi.

Sack of Cyprus by Reginald of Châtillon, the prince of Antioch.

1157 The realms of Castile and Leon are ruled separately by the two sons of Afonso VII.

1173

Henry II of England regains control of Northumbria.

Erik of Sweden conquers Finland.

1158 Emperor Frederick I Barbarossa grants imperial protection to university of Bologna.

1159 The election of Pope Alexander III, following the death of Adrian IV, creates a schism.

John of Salisbury produces *Policraticus*, a work of political observation that draws heavily on classical sources.

1167

1160 Emperor Frederick I Barbarossa violently crushes the rebellious cities of N Italy.

AMERICAS & AUSTRALASIA

The Great Age of Cathedral Building

Asterisks indicate beginning of construction; all other dates are for completion/consecration

1078	Santiago de Compostela
1105	Angoulême
1122	Piacenza
1124	Rochester
1137	Mainz
1145	Norwich
1147	Lisbon
1154	Chartres
1184	Modena
1187	Verona
1199	Siena*
1220	Brussels*
1221	Burgos*
1227	Toledo*
1237	Bamberg
1248	Cologne*
1258	Salisbury
1269	Amiens
1270	Westminster Abbey
1296	Florence*
1311	Rheims

The cathedrals of Europe

A great number of cathedrals were built throughout Europe in the 11th and 12th centuries in the early Gothic style. Gothic architecture is characterized by the ribbed vault, pointed arch, and flying buttress. The Gothic achievement was to use already established engineering expertize to create far more ambitious buildings. Flying buttresses made it possible to build taller buildings and to open up wall spaces to create larger windows.

Richly colored stained glass produced novel lighting effects. The Gothic emphasis on large areas of glazing set in the upper parts of the church was widely adopted. Decorative features were simple; the elaborate figured carving of Romanesque buildings was abandoned in favor of simplified versions of the classical Corinthian capital.

The soaring height of Chartres cathedral in France was achieved through innovative use of flying buttresses. The use of window tracery – decorative ribwork subdividing the window openings – was much copied.

Thomas Becket

On December 29, 1170, four knights of the royal household stabbed the Archbishop of Canterbury, Thomas Becket, to death in the north transept of his own cathedral. Becket had fought hard to uphold ecclesiastical privileges, and this was the culmination of a long dispute between the archbishop and King Henry II. When Henry cried "Will no one rid me of this turbulent priest?" his words were taken literally, a deed that shocked all Christendom.

Becket was subsequently canonized, and came to symbolize resistance to the oppressive authority of the state. In fact, despite the tragedy, Henry's grip on his vast empire, which stretched from the Scottish border to the Pyrenees, remained secure. His wealth rivaled even that of the Holy Roman emperor.

Nur al-Din

An able general and just ruler, who united the military tribes of Syria, Nur al-Din (1118–1174) laid the foundations that led to the achievements of Saladin. He waged many military campaigns against the Crusaders in an attempt to expel them from Syria and Palestine, capturing Edessa in 1151, taking Damascus in 1154, and annexing Egypt (1169–71).

ASIA

1161 Chinese invention of gunpowder.

1162 Song forces defeat the Jin armies at the battle of Caishi in Anhui.

1163 Amalric becomes king of Jerusalem (–1174).

Iplici mosque at Konya, probably the first to have a campanile (tower) minaret.

A Jewish synagogue is built in Kaifeng, China.

Xiaozong becomes Song emperor (–1190).

c.1167 Birth of Genghis Khan, founder of the Mongol empire.

1170 Zenith of Srivijaya kingdom of Java.

AFRICA

1163 First expedition to Egypt by Amalric, king of Jerusalem; the start of an ambitious campaign to capture Egypt.

1164 Amalric's second expedition to Egypt.

1166 Saladin begins construction of Cairo citadel.

1167 Amalric's third expedition to Egypt.

1168 Amalric's fourth expedition to Egypt.

1171

1169 Saladin becomes vizier of the Fatimid caliphate of Cairo.

Amalric's fifth expedition to Egypt.

Muslim ruler Nur al-Din annexes Egypt in stages (–1171).

1162 Emperor Frederick I Barbarossa seizes and destroys Milan.

1166 Revolt of the Serbians under Stefan Nemanja.

1167 The Lombard League formed to oppose Emperor Frederick I Barbarossa in N Italy. The League opposes Frederick Barbarossa's attempt to abolish liberties of Italian communes.

Frederick I seizes Rome. Pope Alexander III leaves the city.

Foundation of Oxford university.

1168 Henry the Lion marries Matilda, daughter of Henry II of England.

Bogolyubsky sacks Kiev and assumes title of grand prince.

1169 English conquest of Ireland begins (–1172).

1170 The Lombard League forms an alliance with the pope.

Thomas Becket, the Archbishop of Canterbury, is murdered at Canterbury cathedral by four knights of the royal household, the climax to a prolonged quarrel between King Henry II and Becket.

Appearance of Chrétien de Troyes' *Lancelot*, a romance of courtly love.

c.1170 Toltec capital at Tula is overthrown by Chichimec nomads from the northern desert.

Emperor Frederick I

Frederick Barbarossa (1123–1190) was the German emperor who challenged papal authority and established German predominance over much of Europe. He was elected king in 1152 and immediately challenged the authority of the pope. Crowned emperor in 1155, he embarked on a protracted series of military campaigns against the Lombard leagues. In 1177, Barbarossa eventually recognized Alexander III as the true pope, and was publicly reconciled to him. Within the empire, Barbarossa became involved in violent struggles with the most powerful prince, Henry the Lion, duke of Bavaria, who was eventually stripped of his possessions. An enthusiastic supporter of the ideals of knighthood and chivalry, Barbarossa embarked on the Third Crusade in 1190, but died before he reached the Holy Land.

Herati ewer

In the Islamic world, metalworking was a leading art form, a vehicle for creative and elaborate decoration, as can be seen in the inlaid brass ewer (*below*), made in about 1180. The great centers for the production of high-quality metalwork were in the cities of Khurasan, such as Herat, where metal-working techniques and designs were inherited from the Sassanian era. Bronze and brass were cast using the lost-wax method. Repoussé was a highly skilled technique of hammering out brass sheets from within the object to create a raised decorative surface.

Ife culture

The Ife culture of the Yoruba people flourished in the forested areas to the west of the Niger between the 11th and 15th centuries. Ife was the capital city, and many later Yoruba kings claimed their descent from Ife as a way of establishing legitimacy. Ife was famous for its naturalistic ritual bronze heads, cast using the lost-wax method, which may have spread from the north, along with Saharan copper. The forest was a rich source of iron ore and wood for smelting.

1171–1180

ASIA

1173 Saladin seizes Aden.

Reign of Hoysala king, Ballala III (–1220) in S India. Hoysala expansion supplants Chola power.

1174 Baldwin IV, aged only 13, succeeds Amalric as king of Jerusalem (–1186). A struggle over the regency ensues.

Nur al-Din is succeeded by an 11-year-old child, plunging the Muslim world into disunity. Saladin occupies Damascus.

1186 **1175** Muhammad of Ghur founds the first Muslim empire in India.

1176 Seljuk Turks crush the Byzantine army at Myriocephalum.

Saladin conquers Syria.

1177 Saladin is defeated by Baldwin IV of Jerusalem at Ramleh.

Persian poet, Farid al-Din Attar completes *Mantiq al-Tayr* (The Conference of Birds).

1183 **1180** Baldwin IV of Jerusalem and Saladin agree a truce.

1185 Campaigns of Minamoto Yoritomo in Japan (–1185).

c.1180 Angkor empire of Cambodia has reached its greatest extent.

AFRICA

1171 Saladin, a Mesopotamian Kurd, overthrows the Fatimid caliphate in Egypt, and reestablishes Sunnism, becoming the effective sovereign of Egypt.

1174 Founding of Ayyubid sultanate in Egypt (–1260).

The Crusades (1050–1350)

The Crusades were holy wars fought against the enemies of Christendom, who included Muslims, Slavs, Orthodox Christians, and heretics. Crusades were waged in the Near East, North Africa, Eastern Europe, Spain, the Baltic, and even within Western Europe itself. It was believed that they were authorized by Christ himself, speaking through his mouthpiece, the pope. Warriors who joined the Crusades were rewarded with papal indulgences. Those who reached the Holy Land were endowed with land and attempted to recreate the society of feudal Europe by establishing Crusader states on foreign soil.

EUROPE

1171 King Louis VII of France grants river-merchants' guild a monopoly of river trade.

Byzantine emperor, Manuel I Comnenus orders the arrest of all Venetians within the empire and seizure of their property.

1172 Construction of Great mosque at Seville, intended to be the largest in the world, and the Giralda, a great square minaret.

1181 **1173** Henry II of England quells French-backed rebellion by his sons (–1174).

1174 Construction of campanile ("Leaning Tower") of Pisa.

1175 Manuel I Comnenus restores Venetian trading privileges.

1183 **1176** Emperor Frederick I Barbarossa concludes peace terms with the pope at Anagni.

1177 Frederick I Barbarossa finally succumbs to papal authority, accepting Alexander III as the one and only pontiff.

1189 **1178** Frederick I Barbarossa crowned king of Burgundy.

1180 First windmills with vertical sails in Europe.

1185 Louis VII of France is succeeded by his son, Philip II Augustus (–1223).

AMERICAS & AUSTRALASIA

c.1175 Fire, famine, and anarchy complete the destruction of Tula, and the whole of Toltec civilization.

1179 Maya city of Chichén Itzá is sacked and burned by Hunac Ceel, the ruthless and ambitious Mayapán king.

The Crusades

1071	Seljuk Turks defeat Byzantines at the battle of Manzikert.
1095	Byzantine empire pleads for papal support. Pope preaches for a Crusade in France.
	First Crusade (–1099). First wave of Crusaders depart.
1098	Crusaders take Antioch; foundation of Crusader states in Levant begins.
1099	Capture of Jerusalem.
1118	Crusading order of Knights Templar founded.
c.1130	Hospital of St. John of Jerusalem (the Hospitallers) becomes military order.
1147	Second Crusade; Emperor Conrad defeated by Turks at Dorylaeum. Castles become vital for Crusader states' survival.
1148	Crusader army abandons siege of Damascus.
1187	Saladin defeats Christians at Hattin.
1189	Third Crusade (–1192).
1191	Richard I the Lion-heart of England wins back some of the territory taken by Saladin.
1202	Fourth Crusade (–1204); Crusaders take Constantinople, but never reach Jerusalem. New Crusader states are established in Greece.
1209	Crusades begin against the Cathar sect in southern France.
1212	Children's Crusade.
1217	Fifth Crusade (–1221).
1219	Crusaders take Damietta (Egypt), but are ejected in 1221.
1229	Through diplomacy, Emperor Frederick II regains control of Jerusalem.
1248	First Crusade of Louis IX of France (–1254). He is defeated at Mansurah, Egypt, captured and ransomed.
1270	Second Crusade of Louis IX; death of Louis IX outside walls of Tunis.
1291	Loss of Acre.
c.1302	Last Christian territory in Levant falls to Mamluks.
1306	Hospitallers make Rhodes their headquarters.

The Templars were a military order based in Jerusalem. They were entrusted with the defense of large stretches of territory in the Holy Land.

Kilwa

The city-state of Kilwa was created by uniting Mafia Island, a prosperous trading center south of Zanzibar in East Africa, with Kilwa, well known for its iron smelting industry and cowrie shell trade. Much of Kilwa's prosperity was based on the fact that its rulers were able to break the control that the Muslim merchants of Mogadishu wielded over the East African gold trade. The merchants of Kilwa sent ships south to Sofala where they traded for gold with the peoples of the interior. Much of the weatlth brought by this trade is reflected in the fine stone buildings that adorn the capital, Kilwa Kisiwani, including the great mosque (*above*).

Paper money

In 9th-century China, certificates of deposit, issued in favor of merchants by the representatives of their provincial government in the capital, were known as "flying money." These were the precursors of banknotes, which were first printed by the state in Sichuan in 1024. Paper currency became the principal kind of money used in China in the 12th and 13th centuries. Its use reduced the reliance on minted coins, but compulsory rates of exchange contributed to economic chaos in the years leading up to the Mongol invasions.

This 14th-century Chinese banknote is the largest ever issued. It measured 9 x 13 inches (22.8 x 33 cm) and represented 1,000 coins.

ASIA

1183 Reginald of Châtillon launches an attack aimed at Mecca.

Saladin conquers Syria and becomes sultan.

1185 Taira clan eliminated in Japan.

Start of Kamakura shogunate.

1192

1186 Muhammad of Ghur deposes the Ghaznavids by taking the Punjab and Lahore. The end of Buddhism in N India.

Mosul recognizes the overlordship of Saladin.

1187 Saladin defeats Christians at Hattin; recaptures Jerusalem and takes Acre.

Crusader states ravaged by Saladin's armies (–1188).

1188 Saladin conquers Latin kingdoms in Levant.

Crusader states reduced to coastal enclaves by Saladin.

The mosque at Rabat, like Seville, is intended to be the largest in the world.

Nizami's *Layla and Majnun*, a Persian recasting of the perennially popular pre-Islamic love story in verse.

1191 **1189** Start of Third Crusade.

1192 Yoritomo destroys Fujiwara rising in N Honshu.

1190 Emperor Frederick I Barbarossa drowns in Anatolia on way to the Holy Land.

AFRICA

1184 Completion of citadel at Cairo.

1203 Abu Yusuf Ya'qub al-Mansur succeeds to the Almohad throne.

1188 Death of Sultan Ali bin Hasan, the ruler of the powerful city-state and trading center of Kilwa, E Africa.

EUROPE

1181 In England, Henry II's sons revolt against the king.

1182 In Constantinople, a revolt led by Andronicus Comnenus against the dowager empress Mary of Antioch prompts a massacre of Italians. Andronicus and Alexius rule jointly.

1183 Peace of Constance ends the conflict between the emperor Frederick and the Lombard League.

1184 King Magnus V of Norway is defeated by his rival, Sverre.

A church council at Verona condemns all heretics.

1185 Byzantine emperor Andronicus is killed in a rebellion.

Treaty of Boves: Philip II Augustus substantially increases French crown lands at the expense of Count Philip of Flanders.

Bulgarians brothers Ivan and Peter Asen launch a revolt to throw off Byzantine sovereignty. They defeat the Byzantines and force Constantinople to recognize Bulgarian independence.

1186 Thessalonica is sacked by Normans.

1189 Philip II Augustus, Henry II of England, and Frederick I Barbarossa assemble troops for the Third Crusade.

Henry II of England is succeeded by Richard the Lion-heart (–1199).

Silves (Portugal) is captured by Christian forces.

1190 Emperor Frederick I Barbarossa, embarks on a crusade to the Holy Land.

Teutonic knights are established for the defense of the Holy Land.

Anti-Semitic riots leads to massacre of more than 500 Jews in York, England.

Bulgarians defeat Emperor Isaac II at Stara Zagora.

1235

1191

1190

AMERICAS & AUSTRALASIA

Saladin

The founder of the Ayyubid dynasty, Saladin (1137/8–1193) is a celebrated Muslim hero. Born into a powerful Kurdish family, he grew up in Syria. In 1169 he was appointed commander of Syrian troops in Egypt, charged with defending Egypt from attacks by Latin Christians. He also became the vizier of the Fatimid caliphate, which he abolished in 1171, announcing a popular return to Sunni Islam in Egypt.

Between 1174 and 1186, he dedicated himself to the task of uniting the Muslim territories of Syria, northern Mesopotamia, Palestine, and Egypt under his rule, a task he achieved by using a combination of skillful diplomacy and military force. Dedicated to the idea of *jihad*, or holy war, he embarked on the reconquest of the Holy Land in 1187, a campaign that culminated in his capture of Jerusalem itself, after 88 years of Frankish rule.

The Third Crusade, launched to recapture Jerusalem, only succeeded in leaving the Crusaders with a foothold in the Levant. Saladin died shortly afterward. The dynasty he founded lasted until 1250.

In July 1187, Saladin crushed the 20,000-strong Crusader army at the battle of Hattin. Three months later, he took possession of the ultimate prize – Jerusalem, at that point defended by only a handful of men. Saladin agreed to allow the inhabitants to leave after paying a ransom.

Rock-cut churches, Lalibela

The Zagwe king of Ethiopia, Lalibela, ruled between c.1200 and 1250. During his reign the monks in the region of the capital, Adefa, began the construction of a remarkable series of churches, which were carved out of the solid rock. Eleven such churches have been found in the mountains near Adefa, many named after famous sites in Jerusalem, such as Golgotha, perhaps as a way of developing a sense of connection between the Ethiopian Church and Old Testament Jerusalem. These unique churches are a tribute to the strength and fervor of Christianity in 13th-century Ethiopia.

The Delhi sultanate

Between 1175 and 1206, the Afghan Ghurids, led by Muhammad of Ghur (brother of the Ghurid sultan) and his lieutenant Qutb-ud-Din Aibak, conducted a series of campaigns against the Rajputs of northern India. Their victories led to the establishment, in 1206, of the Delhi sultanate. No break was made with the traditions of the later Hindu Period; the Delhi sultans were paramount rulers, but never sought sovereignty over their conquered territory. Begun in 1199, the Qutb Minar minaret in Delhi (*below*) became the symbol of Muslim rule in northern India.

ASIA

1191 Crusaders recover Acre.

Richard I the Lion-heart of England wins back Jaffa, but fails to reach Jerusalem (–1192).

Zen Buddhist order founded in Japan.

1204

1192 Richard the Lion-heart makes treaty with Saladin.

1206

Afghan Ghurids under Muhammad of Ghur defeat Rajputs; seize Delhi and much of N India (–1193).

Minamoto Yoritomo becomes shogun and forms military government in Japan.

1193 Death of Saladin. Civil war amongst his heirs.

1194 Khwarizm Shah defeats the Seljuks in Iran.

1197 Arabs destroy the Buddhist monastery of Nalanda, India.

1200 Sultan Al-Malik al-Adil, who has succeeded his brother Saladin, restores the unity of Ayyubid possessions and annexes Mesopotamia.

c.1200 Muslim Sufi saint, Khwajah Mu'inud-Din Chishtip, founds first Sufi order in subcontinent.

Height of Khmer Empire of Cambodia, under reign of Jayavarman VII.

AFRICA

1196 Marinids take control of Morocco (–1485).

1198 Death of Averroës – the greatest Moorish philosopher and scientist of his day – in Marrakesh.

1200 Emergence of Hausa city-states, which come to dominate sub-Saharan trade.

1270

c.1200 King Lalibela of Ethiopia begins construction of rock-cut churches.

EUROPE

1191 On the Third Crusade, Richard the Lion-heart seizes Cyprus.

Henry VI, son of Frederick I Barbarossa, is crowned emperor in Rome.

1204
1192 Edicts against Cathars by rulers of Montpellier and Aragon.

1205
1193 Philip II Augustus seizes the Vexin, part of English territory in France.

Richard the Lion-heart is taken prisoner in Vienna and given up to the emperor, Henry VI.

1194 Richard the Lion-heart is freed after paying a large ransom. He crushes Philip II Augustus at Fréteval, and reconquers his French fiefs. They sign the truce of Verneuil.

Emperor Henry VI of Germany conquers Sicily and is crowned king of Sicily.

1198 On his election as pope, Innocent III calls for a new crusade.

1201
Otto of Brunswick is crowned king by the Welf faction. His rival, Philip of Swabia, leader of the Hohenstaufen faction, has also been elected king by his supporters. Civil war is inevitable.

1201
1199 Death of Richard the Lion-heart in Châlus, France. Accession of John, youngest son of Henry II, as king of England (–1216).

c.1200 Bishopric of Riga established in Baltic Europe.

Silver coins, notably the *grosso*, introduced in N Italy.

Paris undergoes improvements; streets are paved.

AMERICAS & AUSTRALASIA

c.1200 Entry of Aztecs into valley of Mexico.

Construction of Moundville in Alabama by the Mississippian culture; it flourishes until 1300.

Peak of importance of Chaco Canyon.

c.1300
Incas, led by Manco Capac, enter and settle in Andean valley near Cusco.

Expansion of Chimú state.

Chimú civilization

The Chimú civilization dominated the northern coast of Peru between c.700 and 1476, when the area was conquered by the Incas, who learned much from their predecessors. The Chimú capital at Chan Chan was the center of the state which stretched 995 miles (1,600 km) along the Peruvian coast. At its heart lies ten royal compounds, or *ciudadelas*, each belonging to a successive Chimú king, and serving as their final burial place. Chimú society was governed by hereditary kings and a ruling elite. Newly conquered territory was ruled by provincial governors, and emphasis on an efficient road network and ambitious irrigation schemes ensured that the kingdom was well run. The Chimú were skilled metalworkers – this *tumi*, or ceremonial knife (*above*), is made from cast and hammered gold.

The World in 1200

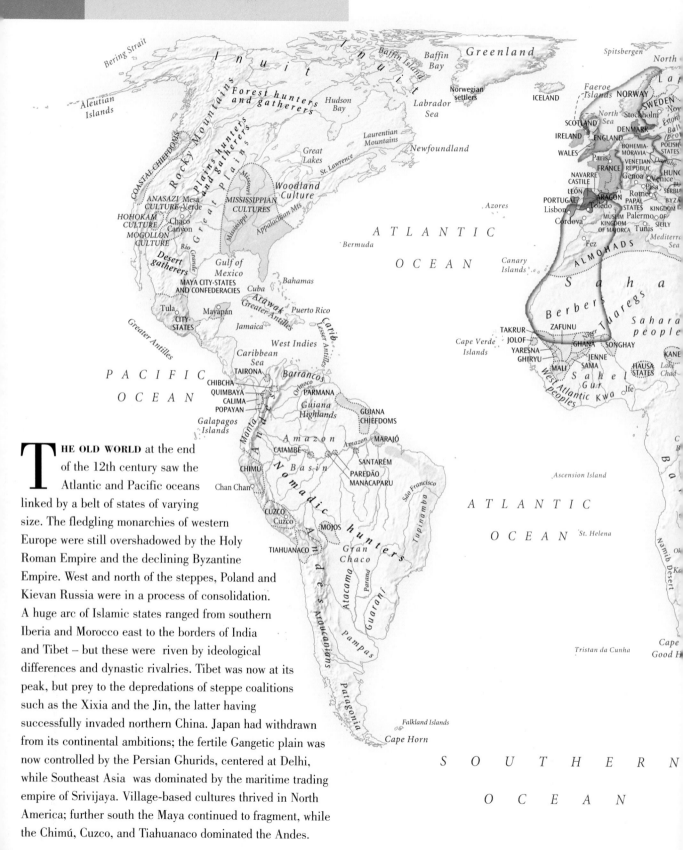

THE OLD WORLD at the end of the 12th century saw the Atlantic and Pacific oceans linked by a belt of states of varying size. The fledgling monarchies of western Europe were still overshadowed by the Holy Roman Empire and the declining Byzantine Empire. West and north of the steppes, Poland and Kievan Russia were in a process of consolidation. A huge arc of Islamic states ranged from southern Iberia and Morocco east to the borders of India and Tibet – but these were riven by ideological differences and dynastic rivalries. Tibet was now at its peak, but prey to the depredations of steppe coalitions such as the Xixia and the Jin, the latter having successfully invaded northern China. Japan had withdrawn from its continental ambitions; the fertile Gangetic plain was now controlled by the Persian Ghurids, centered at Delhi, while Southeast Asia was dominated by the maritime trading empire of Srivijaya. Village-based cultures thrived in North America; further south the Maya continued to fragment, while the Chimú, Cuzco, and Tiahuanaco dominated the Andes.

The World in 1200

- Byzantine Empire
- England and possessions
- Holy Roman Empire
- Almoravid Empire 1120
- Great Seljuk Empire 1071
- possessions of Canute 1028–1035

AL-IDRISI'S WORLD MAP

In 1154 al-Idrisi, a Moroccan prince, was commissioned by Roger II of Sicily to prepare a map of the world. Following the Ptolemaic system, al-Idrisi divided the inhabited world into six "climes" and then drew 10 arbitrary north–south meridians, producing 16 regional maps. These maps were then combined to produce a world map that was engraved on a silver disc (now lost). The Arabic text of the *Book of Roger*, as al-Idrisi's geography is usually known, provides descriptions of the cities, rivers, mountains, and routes of each clime. Al-Idrisi cites accounts by travelers and merchants but does not appear to have enquired of any with practical knowledge of the sea. In keeping with Islamic tradition, the map is oriented with the south at the top.

aquesta carauana es partida de linpi
te sarra panar adreatayo

iachon

camill

fugur

fiacur

sungir

febur

1200 –1400
The High Middle Ages

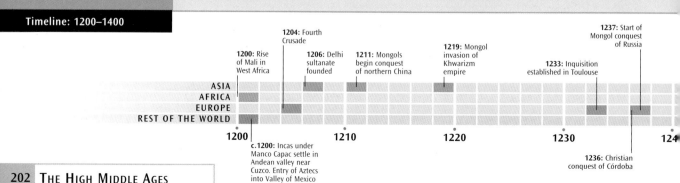

Timeline: 1200–1400

1200: Rise of Mali in West Africa

1204: Fourth Crusade

1206: Delhi sultanate founded

1211: Mongols begin conquest of northern China

1219: Mongol invasion of Khwarizm empire

1233: Inquisition established in Toulouse

1237: Start of Mongol conquest of Russia

	1200		1210		1220		1230		124
ASIA									
AFRICA									
EUROPE									
REST OF THE WORLD									

c.1200: Incas under Manco Capac settle in Andean valley near Cuzco. Entry of Aztecs into Valley of Mexico

1236: Christian conquest of Córdoba

PICTURE ABOVE:
Caravan routes across
Central Asia thrived in the
climate of law and order
imposed by Mongol rule. This
illustration from the Catalan
Atlas of 1375 shows a group
of European merchants
riding along the Silk Road.

DURING THE THIRTEENTH CENTURY
Eurasia was engulfed by one of the most remarkable phenomena of world history: the sudden and terrifying invasions of the Mongols, nomadic herdsmen from the steppes north of China. The fortified cities of the great urban civilizations of China and the Islamic world proved no defence against their ferocity and inspired tactics. Their first leader was Genghis Khan, a military genius who rose to become leader of a federation of Mongol tribes in 1206. In less than 20 years the Mongols shattered the Muslim states of Central Asia, overran northern China, and made a lightning raid on Russia. Genghis's son Ögödei then destroyed the Jin and the Khwarizm empires and began the conquest of Song China, while simultaneously directing the invasion of Hungary and Poland, thousands of miles to the west. The defeat of the Song was completed by 1279 by Kublai Khan, who became emperor of China. Kublai's brother, Hülegü, had meanwhile destroyed the Abbasid Caliphate, sacking the great Islamic city of Baghdad in 1258. Only defeat by the Mamluks in Syria in 1260 prevented a Mongol conquest of Egypt. Their two attempted invasions of Japan were also unsuccessful, both failing when their fleets were struck by gales, the "divine wind" (*kamikaze*) to the Japanese.

By the time of Kublai Khan's death in 1294, the Mongol world had been divided into four great khanates that stretched from the Black Sea to Korea. The scale

Genghis Khan receives homage from the leaders of other Mongol tribes. White horsetails flying from his tent indicated that the Mongols were temporarily at peace. Black ones meant they were at war.

and speed of these conquests remain unmatched in any era. Yet whatever the immensity of the Mongol achievement, their empires were to disappear almost as rapidly as they had been created.

The Mongols and Islam

Despite the fall of the Abbasid caliphate, the cultural unity of the Islamic world managed to survive the Mongol onslaught largely intact. The Mongol conquerors of Central Asia, the rulers of the Il-Khanate and the Golden Horde, soon converted to Islam. A further burst of conquest by Timur, who carved out a huge empire in Central Asia after 1370, briefly revived the great age of Mongol conquest, but his campaigns, he claimed, were all waged in the name of Islam. In the 15th century the Mongols became divided and weakened and most of their territories were lost.

Whatever the initial reverses suffered by the Islamic world at the hands of the Mongols, for most of the period Islam retained its early vigor and continued its aggressive expansion. In India the sultanate of Delhi was founded in 1206 by Qutb ud-Din, leader of the Islamic raiders who had terrorized northern India for the past 30 years – by 1335 it dominated almost the whole of the subcontinent. In Africa the Islamic Mali empire grew by about 1300 to control the lucrative trans-Saharan caravan trade in gold, slaves, and salt, using its profits to maintain a powerful army that dominated West Africa. On the other side of Africa,

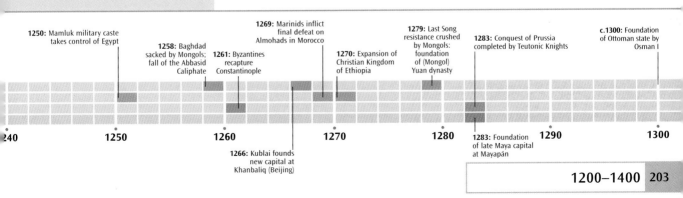

1250: Mamluk military caste takes control of Egypt

1258: Baghdad sacked by Mongols; fall of the Abbasid Caliphate

1261: Byzantines recapture Constantinople

1269: Marinids inflict final defeat on Almohads in Morocco

1270: Expansion of Christian Kingdom of Ethiopia

1279: Last Song resistance crushed by Mongols; foundation of (Mongol) Yuan dynasty

1283: Conquest of Prussia completed by Teutonic Knights

c.1300: Foundation of Ottoman state by Osman I

1266: Kublai founds new capital at Khanbaliq (Beijing)

1283: Foundation of late Maya capital at Mayapán

240   1250   1260   1270   1280   1290   1300

groups of increasingly important Islamic Swahili city-states had appeared to exploit complex trading links across the whole of the Indian Ocean. Islam did not reach central and southern Africa, but the trade it generated led to the establishment of wealthy inland states such as the kingdom of Great Zimbabwe.

Ming China and Japan

The Yuan dynasty founded by Kublai Khan was unable to sustain Mongol rule in China for long. In the first half of the 14th century, the Chinese were hit by plague, floods, and famine, causing widespread suffering and resentment of their Mongol rulers. Decades of increasingly violent uprisings ended in 1368 with the establishment of the Ming dynasty. For the first time in over 400 years, China was under the control of a unified native dynasty determined to restore traditional Chinese virtues. That the country was to grow even more prosperous under the Ming is testimony to the enduring sophistication of Chinese culture and technology. The Great Wall was rebuilt as a defense against the Mongols, Tatars, and other tribespeople to the north, while the Grand Canal, which connected Hangzhou on the Yangtze with Beijing in the north, facilitated trade between the two most heavily populated regions of the empire.

Japan meanwhile, which was under the exacting militaristic hegemony of the Kamakura Shogunate until 1333, was then to be riven by a further period of internecine warfare between rival warlords for well over 100 years.

Trade and the Black Death

However short-lived the ascendancy of the Mongols, one crucial consequence of their trans-Asian empires was that large-scale contact between east and west was revived for the first time since the collapse of the expansionist Tang Empire in 907. This brought renewed trade between China and Europe along the Silk Road, as well as making possible the extraordinary journeys of a number of travelers from the west, among them the Venetian Marco Polo and the Moroccan Muslim scholar Ibn Battuta, both of whom visited China during the reign of Kublai Khan. Unfortunately it also resulted in the long-distance transmission of disease. In the 14th century, epidemics of bubonic plague, carried by rat fleas, swept across the Old World from China to western Europe, weakening states throughout Eurasia and North Africa, and causing widespread social and economic disruption. Europe, where the terrifying plague became known as the "Black Death," was particularly badly affected.

Late medieval Europe

In the early 13th century, the population of Europe was expanding and German settlers were migrating to the east in search of new lands. This led to clashes with Slavic peoples and with the pagan Prussians, Livonians, and Lithuanians on the Baltic. Crusades were launched to subdue the Baltic region, spearheaded by the Knights of the Teutonic Order.

Following the incursions of the Mongols, a number of powerful states were established on the eastern periphery of the continent. Bohemia, fabulously wealthy from its silver mines, at one point stretched from the Adriatic to the Baltic, but its expansion was halted by the Habsburgs of Austria, whose gradual rise

The conquests of Osman I (1258–1324) formed the nucleus of the Ottoman Empire. The name of the dynasty he founded is derived from the Arabic form of his name. He captured the major Byzantine cities of Bursa and Nicaea (Iznik) in western Anatolia.

to become the dominant power in central Europe dates from this period. For the time being, however, Austria was just one of many small German dukedoms and principalities. In the 14th century, the kingdoms of Poland and Lithuania were the most extensive in the region, uniting in 1386 to form the largest state in Christendom. In the west, too, Christian Europe was expanding. The Muslim Almohad empire in Spain was being pushed steadily southward by the kingdoms of Leon, Castile, and Aragon.

Despite this aggressive expansion, the 14th century saw social unrest across much of the continent. This was compounded by climate change, the so-called "Little Ice Age," which disrupted harvests and trade and brought famine and economic decline in its wake. At the same time, dynastic struggles in England, France, Germany, and Italy brought further upheaval. English claims to the throne of France led to the 100 Years' War, a bitter, though intermittent, conflict that would not be resolved until the mid-15th century. The effects of the Black Death on a continent already thus weakened – within two years of the

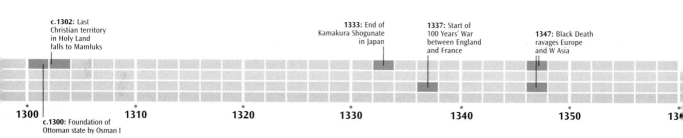

c.1302: Last Christian territory in Holy Land falls to Mamluks

1333: End of Kamakura Shogunate in Japan

1337: Start of 100 Years' War between England and France

1347: Black Death ravages Europe and W Asia

1300   1310   1320   1330   1340   1350   13

c.1300: Foundation of Ottoman state by Osman I

plague's first appearance, in 1347, Europe had lost a third of its population – were little short of devastating.

The rise of the Ottomans

By now, Europe also faced another major threat to its security in the shape of the Turkish Ottoman Empire. Founded in c.1300 by Osman I, over the next 100 years the Ottomans developed into an astonishingly dynamic military force that expanded its initially insignificant powerbase in western Anatolia north and west into the Balkans at an extraordinary rate. Victory over the Serbs and their allies at Kosovo in 1389 confirmed the Ottomans as the dominant power in the region. In order to maintain sufficient numbers of troops to police their expanding empire, the Ottomans used to impose a levy of young Christian boys on the lands they had conquered. The boys were taken from their parents and trained to become part of an elite force known as the janissaries (literally, new troops).

The Ottomans received what might have been a fatal blow to their empire when they were defeated by Timur in 1402 and the emperor, Bayezid I, was captured, but his successors soon restored Ottoman fortunes and by the mid-15th century, they were poised to become a major world power and a permanent threat to Europe's southeastern frontiers.

American empires

Two other major empires were also beginning to take shape on the other side of the world: that of the Aztecs, who had arrived in Central America in about 1200; and, in the Andes, that of the Incas, whose aggressive empire-building after 1400 was to create an expansionist and highly sophisticated society dependent on forced labor.

THE VENETIAN REPUBLIC

The era of the Crusades provided splendid new business opportunities for the maritime republics of Italy – Venice, Genoa, Pisa, and Amalfi. Venice, the most powerful of the four, strengthened its hold on the valuable eastern shipping routes, profiting from the trade in silks, sugar, spices, and gems from India and the east and furs from the Black Sea. Most of these valuable commodities were shipped through Constantinople, so Venice depended on good relations with the Byzantine Empire. In 1171, urged on by the Genoese, the Byzantine emperor had all the Venetian merchants in the city arrested and confiscated their goods. But Venice had its revenge. When in 1204 the Fourth Crusade sacked Constantinople, Venice gained even more power and influence, not to mention the works of art it carried back to adorn its own churches. Though nominally a republic, Venice was in effect an oligarchy, ruled by the city's richest families. In 1380 Venice defeated its main rival, Genoa, becoming the undisputed mistress of the eastern Mediterranean, but its empire and trading interests were gradually lost to the Ottomans.

Marco Polo sets off with his father and uncle from Venice, the wealthiest city in western Europe, on his first journey in 1271.

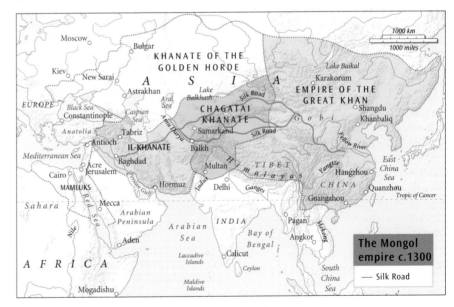

The Mongol empire c.1300
— Silk Road

Until the end of the 13th century, political unity was maintained in the Mongol world, despite sporadic outbreaks of fighting among rivals for supreme power. But after the death of Genghis's grandson Kublai in 1294 the empire began to break up internally as subject peoples asserted their independence.

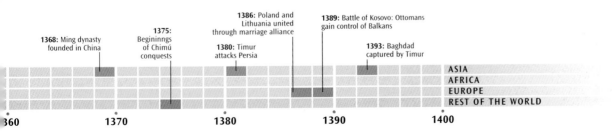

1368: Ming dynasty founded in China

1375: Begininngs of Chimú conquests

1386: Poland and Lithuania united through marriage alliance

1380: Timur attacks Persia

1389: Battle of Kosovo: Ottomans gain control of Balkans

1393: Baghdad captured by Timur

ASIA
AFRICA
EUROPE
REST OF THE WORLD

360   1370   1380   1390   1400

The Fourth Crusade

Although the destination of the Fourth
Crusade (declared in 1198) was Egypt,
when part of the force arrived in Venice
they were unable to pay back a loan that
had been raised to fund the Crusade.
The deposed Byzantine emperor Alexius IV
had fled to the west for aid, and pleaded
with the Crusaders to restore him to
power, in exchange for 200,000 marks. The
Crusaders agreed to storm Constantinople
in 1203, *above*, restoring the emperor. In
January 1204, confronted by a rising tide of
anti-western feeling, they decided to take
the city for themselves. In April, after three
terrible days of pillaging, violence, and
desecration, Constantinople was theirs.

Pope Innocent III

Innocent III (1160–1216) is widely
regarded as the pope who brought
the medieval church to new heights of
prestige and power. He asserted the
power of the papacy in the political
arena, in particular the succession disputes
within the Holy Roman Empire and Anglo-
French conflicts. At the Fourth Lateran
Council (1215), he laid down some of the
fundamental tenets of Catholic belief and
practice. At the same time, he gave his
approval to apostolic poverty and itinerant
preaching, supporting the foundation of
mendicant orders such as the Franciscans.

ASIA

1201 Tartars are crushed by Mongol
warrior, Temujin.

1203 The Hindu temple of Nataraja
is completed at Chidambaram, S India,
the finest temple yet built by the
Chola empire.

1217

1204 Fourth Crusade never reaches Holy
Land; Crusaders take Constantinople.

1206 Citadel of Damascus is completed.

Mongols united by Temujin, who is
proclaimed Genghis Khan and comes to
power in Mongolia. *The Great Yasa*, law
code of the Mongols, promulgated by
Genghis Khan. Mongols begin conquest
of C Asia.

c.1215

After the murder of the last Ghurid sultan,
breakaway Mamluk (Slave) dynasty, under
Qutb-ud-Din Aibak, establishes Delhi
sultanate (–1555).

1215

1208 Genghis Khan conquers Turkestan.

1209 Construction of citadel at Aleppo,
Syria, begins.

AFRICA

1204 Death of controversial Jewish lawyer
and philosopher, Maimonides, at Cairo.

1201–1210

EUROPE

1201 Otto IV is recognized as emperor by Pope Innocent III.

King Philip of France confiscates French fiefs of King John of England. War ensues, and John's army wins a great victory at Mirebeau.

1203 Almohads begin conquest of Balearic Islands, W Mediterranean.

Brittany revolts against King John of England.

1204 Constantinople captured by Latin crusaders diverted from Fourth Crusade.

Sack of Constantinople; Venetian gains in the Adriatic and Greece.

Peter of Castelnau and Armand Amalric, abbot of Cîteaux, are dispatched to wipe out Cathar heresy in Languedoc.

 1214 The whole of the duchy of Normandy, apart from Channel Islands, is now in French hands.

1205 Philip II Augustus of France conquers Anjou.

Crusader Othon de la Roche founds duchy of Athens.

1208 Crusade against Cathars, or Albigensians, in S France.

 1213 **1209** Following a dispute with Pope Innocent III over his nomination for archbishop of Canterbury, King John of England is excommunicated.

1213 Simon de Montfort, crusading against the Cathars, sacks Béziers; thousands are killed.

Recognized as emperor after the murder of his rival, Philip of Swabia, Otto IV is crowned by the pope.

University of Cambridge is founded by disaffected Oxford scholars.

1210 Pope Innocent III approves the foundation of the order of Franciscan friars, named after their leader, St. Francis of Assisi, and dedicated to removing poverty.

AMERICAS & AUSTRALASIA

Born in 1181, St. Francis was the son of a wealthy cloth merchant. Troubled by the contrasts between wealth and poverty that surrounded him, he experienced a profound conversion when he forced himself to touch a leper. He transformed himself into a street beggar, and his resulting estrangement from his father led to a dramatic, public repudiation of his wealthy background. From that point onward, he devoted himself to helping the poor and the sick. His austere lifestyle and love of nature attracted some 5,000 disciples, and the religious order he founded, the Friars Minor (later called the Franciscans), received the recognition of Pope Innocent III in 1210. Franciscan friars could own no possessions, either individually or communally. They wandered freely among the people, helping the poor and sick, supporting themselves by working, and by begging for food.

St. Francis preaches to the birds. A century after the death of St. Francis of Assisi in 1226, the Italian artist Giotto was commissioned to paint scenes commemorating his life.

1201–1210

Magna Carta

In 1203, King John of England suffered a series of humiliating defeats at the hands of the king of France, and withdrew from his French possessions. Inflation and economic hardship caused resentment against him among the English nobility. He clashed with Pope Innocent III and was excommunicated in 1209. When he failed to recapture his lost lands in 1214, England descended into revolt and anarchy.

In June 1215, the rebels – disaffected members of the nobility – captured London, forcing John to accept the terms laid out in a document which became known as the Magna Carta. Essentially a peace treaty between king and nobles, the Magna Carta both guarantees the barons their feudal privileges, and promises that the king will maintain the nation's laws. He promises to administer an equitable legal system; everyone will be entitled to the judgement of his peers and justice shall be available to all free men.

ASIA

1211 Mongols begin conquest of Jin empire, N China.

1215 Mongols, under command of Genghis Khan, capture Beijing.

c.1215 Islamic architecture spreads to India.

1217 Crusaders arrive in Palestine on Fifth Crusade.

1218 Genghis Khan occupies Kashgar and the Tarim basin. Korea acknowledges its vassal status.

Genghis Khan conquers Persia.

1227

1219 Genghis Khan attacks Khwarizm in Mongol invasion of Khwarizm Shah empire.

Minamoto line ends; Hojo clan act as regents for Fujiwara shogun.

1220 Mongol invasion of Transoxania.

c.1220 Zhao Rugua publishes account of travels in SE Asia.

AFRICA

1218 Fifth Crusade lands in Egypt.

1221

1219 The port of Damietta, Egypt, falls to the Crusaders after a siege.

c.1224

c.1220 Southern Soninke chiefdom of Sosso takes over most of former Ghana, as well as their southern neighbors, the Malinke. Soninke farmers and traders disperse from Kumbi-Saleh, settling woodland savannah to south and west.

EUROPE	AMERICAS & AUSTRALASIA	

High Gothic architecture

The smiling angel sculpture at the Gothic cathedral of Rheims in France is a tranquil reflection of the expansive spirit of optimism that characterized High Gothic architecture. High Gothic religious buildings combined light, color, and dramatic perspectives. Spires and arches seemed to defy gravity: in 1270, at Beauvais cathedral, engineering expertise enabled the construction of a vault that stood 147 feet (48 m) high. But it collapsed in 1284 and architects subsequently became more interested in creating visual effects through decoration than achieving great height.

Genghis Khan

Born in about 1167, Temujin (later Genghis Khan) was the son of the chief of the Mangkhol tribe, who lived on the harsh steppes of Mongolia. Gradually, he established his authority over many Turkish and Mongol tribes until, in 1206, he was proclaimed "supreme ruler." First, he turned his fierce nomadic warriors on China, capturing Beijing in 1215. Then he waged a devastating campaign in the Islamic empire of Khwarizm Shah, which stretched from the Caspian Sea to the Pamir mountains. In 1220, he sacked Bukhara, massacring its 30,000 defenders. He is pictured here preaching a sermon to the surviving population. In 1226, he invaded China again, but died soon afterward, having extended his rule from the Pacific Ocean to the Caspian Sea.

1212 With papal backing, Frederick II of Hohenstaufen is crowned king of Germany.

Children's Crusade, led by 12-year-old Stephen of Cloyes, leaves France for Jerusalem.

Crusade proclaimed in Spain. Battle of Las Navas de Tolosa; defeat of Almohads by Christians in Iberia.

Venetians occupy Crete.

Golden Bull establishes kingdom of Bohemia.

1213 Pope Innocent III proclaims Fifth Crusade.

King John submits to the papal nuncio, offering to make England and Ireland papal fiefs.

King Peter of Aragon dies in siege of Muret, leaving Simon de Montfort in control of S France.

1214 Defeat of English and German allies at Bouvines. King John loses English fiefs in N France.

1215 Fourth Lateran Council. Dominic petitions pope to found new order of friars.

King John of Englande seals the *Magna Carta* – the Great Charter of Liberties – at Runnymede.

1216 King John of England is succeeded by his nine-year-old son, Henry.

1217 Severe famine in E and C Europe.

1218 Simon de Montfort killed outside Toulouse.

Dannebrogen, the oldest national flag in the world, is adopted by Denmark.

1219 Danes invade N Estonia.

1220 Frederick II is crowned Holy Roman emperor after promising to go to the aid of the Fifth Crusade.

First chapter of the Dominican order of friars.

Citizens of Paris granted right to collect import duty.

Jousting

In the 12th century, holding a sham battle, or mêlée, became a general sport and entertainment for skilled, but landless, knights. These gatherings of armed men easily disintegrated into actual conflict and rebellion, and, in the 13th century, they gave way to highly formalized "jousting," or combat between two armed, and mounted, knights.

At first, jousting carried real risks of injury or death. By the 14th century, it had become a sport; two armored horsemen charged each other with leveled lances, each attempting to unhorse the other. Complete with colorful livery and banners, elaborate armor, and a well-dressed and excited crowd, jousting was a thrilling spectacle for the European nobility.

In a 13th-century illumination, the young Louis IX is enthroned beside his mother, Blanche of Castile, during the period when she acted as a regent.

Blanche of Castile

The granddaughter of Eleanor of Aquitaine, Blanche of Castile (1188–1252) married Louis VIII of France. She served as a regent from 1226 to 1234 when her son, Louis IX, was a minor, and again, between 1248 and 1252 when her son was away on crusade. It was common practice among the women of the social elite to take over the administrative aspects of property when their male relatives were away at war.

ASIA

1221 Sultan Khalil, Saladin's nephew and successor, offers to surrender Palestine to the Crusaders if the Egyptian port of Damietta is restored.

1225 Emperor Frederick II inherits kingdom of Jerusalem.

Iltutmish, the sultan of Delhi, repulses attacks by the Mongols.

1227 Death of Genghis Khan.

End of the empire of the Western Xia.

1253 Japanese monk Dogen introduces Zen Buddhism to Japan. It is adopted by many powerful *samurai* warriors.

Japanese potter Toshiro, after four years traveling in China, introduces porcelain manufacture to Japan.

1244 **1229** Emperor Frederick II arrives in Jerusalem; regains control of the city through diplomatic negotiations with the sultan of Egypt, al-Kamil.

Ögödei elected great khan.

Rasulids control Yemen (–1454).

AFRICA

1221 Trapped in the marshes of the Nile delta, the Crusaders are forced to withdraw from their siege of Damietta.

1235 **c.1224** Sosso establish state in W Africa under leadership of Sumanguru. They attack the northern Soninke of Ghana, sacking their capital.

1228 Start of collapse of Almohad empire in N Africa.

1244 Abu Zakariyya Yahya founds the Hafsid dynasty, and establishes a capital at Tunis (–1574).

Foundations of universities

1223 Mongols invade Russia. Battle at Kalka river.

Philip II Augustus of France is succeeded as king by his son, Louis VIII.

1224 Latin kingdom of Salonica conquered by despotate of Epirus.

1226 Louis VIII is succeeded by Louis IX of France, with his mother, Blanche of Castile, acting as a regent.

Golden Bull of Rimini gives grand master of Teutonic knights the status of an imperial prince.

Teutonic knights invited to crusade in Prussia.

Creation of the Golden Horde, Mongol state in S Russia (–1502.)

1227 Crusade proclaimed against heretics in Bosnia.

Jousting tournaments become popular among the aristocrats of Europe.

1228 Papal invasion of Emperor Frederick II's territory in S Italy (–1230).

James I of Aragon resolves on a major offensive against the Muslims in Majorca.

1229 Civil war in Cyprus (–1233) between Frederick II's Cypriot knights and John of Beirut.

1230 Establishment of Nasrid kingdom of Granada, Muslim stronghold in S Spain (–1492).

James I of Aragon captures Palma, and overcomes Muslim resistance in Majorca.

Ferdinand III of Castile becomes king of Leon, unifying the two kingdoms.

The 12th-century Renaissance established the important principle that secular learning had value. Universities emerged as a form of academic guild, founded to protect the interests of both faculties and students. Universities usually had four faculties: arts, theology, medicine, civil and church law. Instruction was in Latin, the universal language of medieval Europe. Following in the footsteps of the earliest universities, at Bologna, Paris, and Oxford, which became great centers of intellectual life in the 13th century, a growing number of universities were founded throughout Europe. Most were founded on the initiative of rulers, and many became centers of an emerging sense of national identity.

All Souls College, Oxford, England, founded in 1438. The various colleges of Oxford were originally endowed as boarding houses for impoverished scholars.

European University Foundations

1088	Bologna
c.1150	Paris
1167	Oxford
c.1178	Palencia
1188	Reggio
1204	Piacenza
1209	Cambridge
1218–19	Salamanca
1222	Padua
1224	Naples
1228	Vercelli
1229	Toulouse
c.1237	Valladolid
1248	Piacenza
1254	Seville
1255	Arezzo
1289	Montpellier
1290	Lisbon
1300	Lérida
1303	Rome
	Avignon
1306	Orléans
1308	Perugia
	Coimbra
1318	Treviso
1332	Cahors
1337	Angers
1339	Grenoble
1343	Pisa
1347	Prague
1350	Perpignan

Frederick II

Emperor Frederick II was a maverick monarch who pitted himself against the powers of successive popes. He paid little attention to his German realm, concentrating instead on the reorganization of Sicily and northern Italy, which brought him into direct conflict with the Vatican. His vacillations about embarking on a crusade to Jerusalem in 1227 incurred the wrath of Pope Gregory IX, who excommunicated him twice. His negotiated settlement with the Muslims did little to redeem his reputation in the eyes of the pope.

Frederick II was an enthusiastic falconer. He is portrayed above with a falcon in the dedicatory picture that accompanies his famous work, De arte venadi cum avibus, *"The art of hunting with birds."*

The Hohenstaufens and the Papacy

The aspirations of the Holy Roman emperors to universal authority were blocked by the papacy and by the city-based communes of northern Italy.

1167	Lombard League formed to oppose Emperor Frederick I Barbarossa in N Italy.
1194	Emperor Henry VI crowned king of Sicily.
1198	Accession of Pope Innocent III.
1220	Frederick II becomes emperor.
1237	Frederick II defeats the Italian communes at Cortenuova.
1245	Innocent IV excommunicates Frederick.
1250	Death of Frederick.
1268	Charles of Anjou defeats Conradin, Frederick's grandson, at Tagliacozzo.
1282	Sicilian Vespers; Charles of Anjou defeated by Aragonese.
1305	Pope Clement V takes up residency at Avignon under French supervision.

ASIA

1231 Mongols reconquer resurgent empire of the Khwarizm Shah.

1232 Ibn al-'Arabi writes *The Bezels of Wisdom*, a learned work that defines the doctrine of Sufism.

1233 Death of the Arab historian, Ibn al-Athir.

Mongols take Jin capital, Kaifeng.

1234 Mongols take Jin empire.

1243 ▼ **1235** Walled city built at Karakorum as fixed Mongol capital.

1236 The founder of the Sufi order, the famous ascetic Khwajah Mu'inud-Din Chishtip, dies in Rajasthan.

First issue of paper money in the Mongol realm.

1243 ▼ **1237** Huand Khatun mosque, mausoleum, *madarsa*, and baths at Kayseri, C Turkey; a major complex endowed by Seljuk noblewoman.

1244 ▼ **1239** A new crusade obtains restitution of a part of the kingdom of Jerusalem from the sultans of Damascus and Egypt.

Mongols entrust the collection of taxes in N China to Muslims from C Asia.

1240 Sultana Raziyya, the first woman to rule a Muslim state, is killed by Turkish-backed Hindu troops while trying to regain control of Delhi.

c.1240 *The Secret History of the Mongols*, written by an anonymous author, tells the story of Genghis Khan.

AFRICA

1235 The Berber kingdom of the 'Abd al-Wadids is founded at Tlemcen in the Maghreb.

Sundiata, a Malinke survivor of the Sosso raids, leads a Malinke army against the Sosso of Sumanguru, who are defeated at the battle of Kirinia (near modern Bamako).

c.1250 ▼ **c.1240** Sundiata takes control of all the Soninke peoples, including much of former Ghana. The beginning of the empire of Mali.

1231 John of Brienne's crusade to Constantinople.

1233 Inquisition established in Toulouse.

1234 Henry, the viceregent of the empire, revolts against his father Frederick, and allies with the Lombard League.

Prussia becomes a papal fief.

1235 Viceregent Henry is deposed, and imprisoned by his father.

 1280

Bulgarians under Ivan Asen II ally with John III Vatatzes of Nicaea. They conquer Thrace and besiege Constantinople. They are defeated by John of Brienne.

1236 Christian reconquest of Córdoba, taken by Ferdinand III of Castile and Leon.

 1245 **1237** Frederick II defeats Italian communes at Cortenuova.

Start of Mongol conquest and invasion of Russia.

Opening of St. Gotthard pass through Alps.

1238 James I of Aragon retakes Valencia from the Arabs.

Mongols take Vladimir, Yaroslavl, and Rostov.

1239 Crusade of Theobald of Champagne, and Richard of Cornwall embarks for Jerusalem (–1241).

 1241 **1240** Mongols take Kiev.

Islamic trade

Extensive trade networks crisscrossed the Islamic world. Overland trade was by camel caravans; the caravan routes through Central Asia and China can still be traced today through remains of *caravanserais* – road stations that provided food and rest for

travelers. Arabs, sailing in *dhows*, also ruled the seas at this time, plying the routes that crossed the Indian Ocean. A variety of goods were traded: spices and ceramics from the Far East; gold, ivory, and slaves from Africa; amber, furs, and wax from the Baltic. But overland routes were vulnerable, and the sudden onslaught of Mongols from the steppes disrupted Central Asian trade.

In this 13th-century Arab manuscript, two Muslim merchants are depicted mounted on camels. By 1200 the message of the Prophet had already been spread, by merchants and missionaries, from the Atlantic to the Himalayas.

Windmills

Although wind power had been harnessed in both Persia and China for grinding corn and raising water, windmills were not used in Europe until the 13th century. The mills of northern Europe differed from earlier versions in that the shaft turned horizontally rather than vertically, and the sails were turned so that they kept facing the wind. At first, European windmills were only used for grinding corn. It was not until the 15th century that their power was exploited for tasks such as land drainage.

In the 14th century, village mills were built by the lord of the manor, who leased the mill to a miller. He then charged the peasants a toll (a proportion of their grain) for his service.

Sukhothai

Originally a distant outpost of the Angkor-based Khmer empire, Sukhothai gained its independence in the 13th century and became the capital of the first independent Thai state. Under the leadership of the kingdom's third ruler, King Ramkhamhaeng (reigned 1279–1298), the city came to dominate Thailand's central plains. A benevolent monarch, his kingdom was prosperous and well-governed.

The seated Buddha (*above*) is from Wat Mahathat, the spiritual center of the Sukhothai kingdom, founded by Si Intharathit (c.1240–1270), the first king. The Sukhothai Period is noted for its sculpture, in particular bronze sculptures of the Buddha. Celadon ware (stoneware decorated with glazes), influenced by Chinese wares, was made in Sukhothai and exported throughout Southeast Asia. The influence of Sukhothai began to wane in the 14th century, and in 1438, the town was conquered and incorporated into the Ayutthaya kingdom.

ASIA

1253

1243 Seljuk Turks are wiped out by the Mongols, who have advanced to Sivas.

1244 After sacking Jerusalem, the nomadic Khwarizmian Turks join with Egypt to rout the Latins at Gaza.

1256

c.1245 The "Assassins," a rebel Isma'ili Muslim sect, carry out ruthless murders for its cause against Islamic orthodoxy. They establish new headquarters at Jabal Ansariyah, Syria.

1247 Khwarizmian Turks retake Tiberias and Ascalon.

1251

1250 Mamluks seize power from Ayyubids; take over Syria, Egypt, and Hejaz (–1517).

Louis IX in Palestine (–1254).

c.1250 Thai state established in Sukhothai.

AFRICA

1244 The suzerainty of Abu Zakariyya Yahya, the Hafsid monarch, over Tunis is recognized by Seville, Ceuta, Tlemcen, and Meknes.

1248 Louis IX of France disembarks in Egypt and takes Damietta.

1250 Mamluk military caste from Caucasus takes over Egypt.

First of Louis IX's crusades; invasion of Egypt ends in defeat at Mansurah (–1254). Louis is captured; hands over the keys to the Egyptian city of Damietta, having paid a ransom of one million dinars.

c.1250 Building of stone mosques in Swahili city-states.

1255 Mali empire at its apogee.

Construction of stone enclosures in SE Africa, including building at Great Zimbabwe.

Emergence of empire of Benin (Nigeria).

Burials from Sanga, Zaire, contain pottery, metal implements, and copper jewelry; the metal was mined some 185 miles (300 km) to the south.

EUROPE

1241 Mongols invade Poland and Hungary.

1242 At Lake Peipus, Alexander Nevsky, prince of Novgorod, launches a successful counteroffensive against the Teutonic knights, bringing their planned invasion of Russia to a halt.

Mongols withdraw from Hungary and Dalmatia, cross the Carpathians, and return to Lower Volga.

Batu, grandson of Genghis Khan, establishes his warriors – the "Golden Horde" – on the Lower Volga.

1243 Death of Conrad IV. Interregnum in Holy Roman Empire (–1273).

1245 A council at Lyons condemns and deposes Frederick II. Innocent IV excommunicates him and calls for a crusade against him.

Italian merchants granted own courts to settle trading disputes at Champagne fairs.

1246 Henry Raspe of Thuringia is elected antiking by the Rhenish prelates. He defeats Conrad IV, the son of Frederick II, at the battle of Nidda.

Seville expels its Tunisian ruler, Abu Zakariyya Yahya. Ferdinand III of Castile besieges the city.

 1248 Seville surrenders to Ferdinand III. Most of the Muslim inhabitants flee to Granada.

 Genoese take the island of Rhodes.

1249 After a century of warfare, Sweden conquers Finland.

1250 Following the death of Emperor Frederick II, rebellions break out in N Italy against the feudal lords.

AMERICAS & AUSTRALASIA

1250 The Southern Cult, a widespread religion over much of southeast N America, reaches its height.

Burial of Roy Mata, a powerful Melanesian ruler, on the island of Retoka. He is interred with 40 sacrificial victims.

c.1250 Start of decline of important Mississippian site at Cahokia.

Settlement of Mexican people in C America.

Beginnings of intensive valley irrigation schemes in the Hawaiian islands.

St. Alexander Nevsky

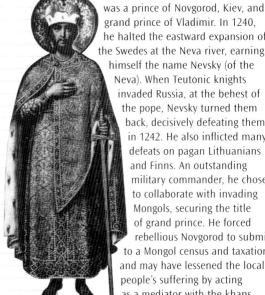

Alexander Yaroslavich (c.1220–1263) was a prince of Novgorod, Kiev, and grand prince of Vladimir. In 1240, he halted the eastward expansion of the Swedes at the Neva river, earning himself the name Nevsky (of the Neva). When Teutonic knights invaded Russia, at the behest of the pope, Nevsky turned them back, decisively defeating them in 1242. He also inflicted many defeats on pagan Lithuanians and Finns. An outstanding military commander, he chose to collaborate with invading Mongols, securing the title of grand prince. He forced rebellious Novgorod to submit to a Mongol census and taxation, and may have lessened the local people's suffering by acting as a mediator with the khans.

The Crusades of Louis IX

Louis IX, king of France, led two disastrous crusades. On the first expedition, (1248–54) his forces took the Egyptian fort of Damietta. However, their attempts to penetrate inland Egypt were unsuccessful, and they were surrounded at Sharamsah. Louis was forced to surrender and pay a huge ransom. Louis took the cross again in 1267, with Tunis at his target. From the outset his crusade was poorly supported. The fleet landed in Tunis in July 1270, and was immediately struck down by disease. Louis died on August 25, and the crusade ended with a negotiated treaty. Here his coffin is being loaded on a ship to be carried back to France.

Hülegü Khan

The Mongol ruler who subdued Persia and founded the Il-Khanate, Hülegü (c.1217–1265) is notorious for his bloodthirsty sack of Baghdad. A grandson of Genghis Khan, he was commissioned to extend Mongol power in Islamic areas. He captured Alamut, the fortress of the militant Assassins, in 1256, then went on to defeat the caliph's army. The last Abbasid caliph was captured, rolled in a carpet, and trampled to death by galloping horses.

In 1258, Hülegü seized and largely destroyed Baghdad, reputedly murdering around 800,000 of its inhabitants. He went on to capture Syria, but was decisively defeated by an Egyptian army in 1260. He returned to Persia, settling in the province of Azerbaijan.

The Mongol Invasions

c.1167	Birth of Genghis Khan in Mongolia.
1206	Mongol tribes confirm Genghis as khan, or ruler.
1211	Mongol troops enter Jin China.
1215	Beijing is besieged and falls to Genghis Khan.
1219	Genghis attacks Khwarizm.
1227	Death of Genghis; his son Ögödei succeeds.
1234	Combined actions of Mongols and Song bring about end of Jin.
1242	Batu founds Golden Horde.
1257	Mongol incursions into Vietnam.
1258	Sack of Baghdad.
1264	Kublai elected great khan.
1266	Beijing becomes the Mongol capital.
1274	First attempts by Mongols to invade Japan.
1279	Kublai recognized as ruler of all China.
1281	Second attempt by Mongols to invade Japan is turned back.
1288	Vietnam recognizes Mongol suzerainty.
1294	Death of Kublai Khan.
1351	Anti-Mongol insurrections spread through China.
1368	Mongols driven from China by Ming forces.

ASIA

1251 Mamluks defeat Syrians at al-'Abbasa.

1253 French Franciscan friar William of Rubrouck crosses Asia to Karakorum (–1255). He intends to conclude an anti-Muslim alliance with the Mongols.

Mongol armies reach Sichuan and Yunnan.

In Japan, the Buddhist monk Nichieren denounces traditional Buddhism, establishing his own sect based on the Lotus *sutra*.

1256 Hülegü crosses Oxus (Amu Darya).

Assassins' stronghold at Alamut falls to Hülegü (–1257).

Hülegü founds the Mongol Il-khanate dynasty of Persia.

Civil war in Acre (–1258

1257 First Mongol expedition to Annam (Vietnam).

Sa'di's *Gulistan*, major popular classic of Persian literature.

1258 Mongol sack of Baghdad and fall of Abbasid caliphate.

1259 Great khan Möngke dies.

1265 ▼ **1260** Hülegü invades Syria.

Mamluks defeat Mongols at Ain Jalut, north of Jerusalem; take Aleppo and Damascus.

1264 ▼ Kublai Khan succeeds his brother, Möngke, as ruler of the empire founded by their grandfather, Genghis Khan. Civil war ensues.

Antioch and Cilician Armenia ally with the Mongols.

AFRICA

1255 Death of Sundiata, founder of the empire of Mali.

1260 Manse Ule, the king of Mali, who is based at Timbuktu, embarks on a pilgrimage to Mecca.

1263 ▼ Assassination of Qutuz, sultan of Egypt. Baybars becomes sultan (–1277).

Castilian crusade temporarily occupies Salé in Morocco.

1252 The first gold florin is struck in Florence.

1254 King Ottokar II of Bohemia, Rudolf of Habsburg, and Otto of Brandenburg lead a crusade to Prussia. The city of Königsberg is founded.

1255 The Roman inquisition authorizes the use of physical torture in cases of heresy.

Prague and Stockholm become towns.

1257 Foundation of Sorbonne; it soon becomes most famous college of Paris university.

1264

1258 Led by Simon de Montfort, the rebellious English barons wrest various concessions, known as the Provisions of Oxford, from Henry III. They include the institution of a parliament that meets three times a year.

1259 Treaty of Paris; Louis IX cedes territory to Henry III of England, who gives up all claims to the Plantagenet fiefs of Normandy, Anjou, Touraine, Maine, and Poitou, becoming Louis' vassal.

Byzantine Nicaean forces at Pelagonia, Greece, rout the allied western Christian armies of Michael II of Epirus and the Frankish prince of Achaea, William of Villehardouin.

1260 Ottokar II of Bohemia defeats Bela IV of Hungary.

1262

At the battle of Montaperti, the Florentine Guelfs, who support papal power, are crushed by the Tuscan Ghibellines, who support the emperor.

The Livonian Teutonic knights are defeated by the Lithuanians at Durben.

The siege of Hezhou

The Mongols were experts in siege warfare, undermining cities' defenders with a range of strategies: bombardment with rocks and firebombs, starvation, and even flooding. They also employed ingenious tactics to fool their enemies, for example, feigning retreat in order to lure the defenders out into the open, or using smokescreens to conceal their positions. Perhaps their most effective tool was their fearsome reputation; the Mongols used the severed heads of the vanquished to ornament beacons warning enemies of the fate that awaited them. At the siege of Hezhou (1258–59) (*above*) the Mongols tried, unsuccessfully, to cross the Yangtze river on a pontoon of boats.

Mongol military tactics

The Mongol horseman, mounted on his sturdy pony, was a formidable foe. Disc-shaped stirrups gave the rider a steady platform, allowing him to fire his bow in any direction, even when riding at speed. The Mongols were hardy and adaptable. They achieved the only successful winter invasion of Russia in history, riding along the frozen rivers, which they used as roads. They crossed Asia in vast numbers, traveling with women, children, captives, slaves, herds of cattle, and spare horses. Each cavalryman traveled with as many as four replacement mounts.

The proportions of Kamakura's Great Buddha are distorted so tht it seems balanced to those in front of it.

Kamakura culture, Japan

After a period of civil strife in Japan, the shogunate of Minamoto Yoritomo was founded in 1192. Its power center was located at the seaside village of Kamakura, on the Pacific coast of Honshu island. Power had shifted from a civil aristocracy to a provincial warrior class. Courtly Heian culture was replaced by a politically effective system based on new bureaucratic methods, military power, and the security offered by *samurai* warriors.

This new ethos, which valued the warrior values of strength, discipline, and austerity found resonance in the precepts of Zen Buddhism. Japanese sculpture reached its apogee during the Kamakura Period; the 44-foot- (13.5-m-) high bronze statue of the Great Buddha (*above*), dating to the mid-13th century, is one of the finest surviving examples.

1261–1270

ASIA

1263 Baybars, sultan of Egypt, destroys Nazareth.

1264 Kublai defeats rival for title of great khan, ending civil war.

1265 Death of Hülegü.

Baybars takes Caesarea and Arsur.

1271 **1266** Kublai founds new capital at Khanbaliq (Beijing).

1271 **1268** Mamluks, led by Baybars, capture Antioch and Jaffa from Crusaders.

1269 Aragonese crusade arrives in Acre.

Adoption of the script invented by the Tibetan lama, 'Phags-pa, to transcribe Mongol.

AFRICA

1269 Marinids inflict final defeat on Almohads in Morocco.

1270 Death of Louis IX outside walls of Tunis.

Expansion of Christian kingdom of Ethiopia.

c.1290 Beginning of Solomonid dynasty in Ethiopia, founded by Yekuno Amlak.

EUROPE

1261 Michael VIII Palaeologus, emperor of Nicaea, recaptures Constantinople and restores Byzantine empire.

Michael VIII Palaeologus signs a treaty promising the Genoese all the trading privileges within the empire enjoyed by the Venetians.

1262 Supported by Pope Urban IV, the Guelfs return to power in Tuscany.

1274
William of Villehardouin cedes part of Morea (the Peloponnese) to Michael VIII Palaeologus.

1263 Venetians defeat the Genoese in a sea battle off Settepozzi.

1264 Louis IX intervenes in the dispute between the English barons and Henry III, and annuls the Provisions of Oxford.

1265 Simon de Montfort, leader of the dissident English barons, dies at the battle of Evesham.

The Crusade of Charles of Anjou, younger brother of Louis IX of France, leaves France.

1266 Norway cedes the Hebrides and the Isle of Man to Scotland.

1282
Charles of Anjou is invested with the crown of Sicily by the pope, Clement IV, having defeated and killed King Manfred of Sicily at Benevento.

1268 The last Hohenstaufen, Frederick's grandson Conradin, invades Italy, but is defeated by Charles of Anjou at the battle of Tagliacozzo.

1278
1270 Charles of Anjou becomes master of Tuscany.

1270
French crusade, led by Louis IX, departs for Tunis.

AMERICAS & AUSTRALASIA

A 14th-century manuscript shows Mamluk cavalrymen exercising their horses.

The Mamluks

In 1250, the Ayyubid sultanate of Egypt was overthrown by the Mamluks, originally slaves employed as soldiers by Muslim rulers. The Mamluks founded a military aristocracy, which produced strong generals and an efficient army.

This was demonstrated in 1260, when a Mamluk army defeated and turned back the Mongol onslaught at Ain Jalut in Palestine. Baybars, a Turkish slave, seized power and made himself sultan. He was a great military leader, who led his army in the reconquest of some of the most important Christian strongholds in Palestine. He also presided over a wealthy and well-governed empire, reflected in its fine architecture and infrastructure.

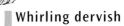

Whirling dervish

The greatest Sufi mystic and poet in the Persian language, Jalal ad-Din ar-Rumi (c.1207–73) grew up in the Anatolian city of Konya. He is credited with founding the so-called "whirling dervishes," a mystical Islamic fraternity who earned their nickname from the rotating dance that they use to attain a state of mystical transcendence. It is probable that Jalal ad-Din composed most of his poetry in a state of ecstasy, induced by the music of the flute or the drum, and he accompanied the recitation of his verses with the whirling dance that became central to his disciples' ritual.

The Welsh wars

Although English kings claimed over-lordship of Wales, there was piecemeal conflict between the numerous Welsh princes and the Anglo-Norman marcher lords throughout the 12th century. But in the 13th century the prince of Gwynedd, Llywelyn ap Gruffudd managed, by force and diplomacy, to bring all the other Welsh dynasties under his authority.

In 1277, Edward I of England led his army to the Welsh border, annexing Wales in 1284. He then embarked on a massive program of castle-building. Harlech Castle (*above*), perched on a prominent cliff, was one of a chain of castles that protected Edward's conquests.

The magnetic compass

The Chinese had long known that a floating magnetized needle always points in the same direction. From about 1100, Chinese sailors were able to exploit this knowledge – this 13th-century boxed compass is an early Chinese example. By the 13th century, the magnetic compass was in widespread use among the Arab navigators of the Indian Ocean. European written sources refer to the principles of the compass as early as 1190.

ASIA

1271 Marco Polo travels throughout Asia, returning by ship through Persian Gulf (–1295).

Mamluk sultan Baybars takes Chastel Blanc, Krak des Chevaliers, and Montfort.

Prince Edward of England launches attack on Caco, Palestine. He survives an assassination attempt.

Kublai Khan crushes last Song resistance.

1272 Crusaders, led by Edward of England, reach a truce with Sultan Baybars at Caesarea.

1273 Death of the Persian poet and mystic, Jalal ad-Din ar-Rumi.

1281 **1274** First Mongol attempt to invade Japan; Mongol invasion defeated.

1292 **1275** Marco Polo reaches Kublai's summer palace at Shangdu (Xanadu).

1276 Mongol armies enter Hangzhou.

1277 Baybars dies in Damascus. He is revered throughout the Near East for his defeat of advancing Mongols, and leaves the Mamluk army the most powerful in the Near East.

1286 Maria of Antioch sells crown of Jerusalem to Charles of Anjou. Kingdom divided between those who will or will not recognize Charles of Anjou.

Civil war in the county of Tripoli (–1283).

1279 Foundation of Yuan (Mongol) dynasty by Kublai Khan. Yuan take over Southern Song.

Construction of the northern section of China's Grand Canal (–1294).

1283 **c.1280** Mongol invasions destroy Pagan in Burma and eclipse Dai Viet.

AFRICA

1279 Accession of Qalawun to the sultanate of Egypt (–1290).

Marco Polo (1254–1324)

1271 Departure of Marco Polo for China.

Philip III, the new king of France, inherits Poitou, the Auvergne, and the county of Toulouse. N and S France are unified.

1273 Rudolf of Habsburg is elected emperor, putting an end to the interregnum which began with the death of Conrad IV in 1243.

Foundation of Alhambra palace at Granada.

1274 Death of Thomas Aquinas. His *Summa Theologica* defines Christian dogma.

A general council at Lyons regulates the election of the pope.

Michael VIII Palaeologus is granted papal protection at the council of Lyons.

1275 Principality of Achaea inherited by Philip of Anjou; rules from Naples.

Establishment of Peruzzi trading company in Florence.

1276 Hereford wall map designed by Richard of Haldingham and Lafford.

Publication of *Il Compasso da Navigare*, a collection of verbal descriptions of key routes.

1277 Edward I of England begins campaigns against Wales.

Genoese begin annual convoys to Bruges and other Channel ports.

1278 Backed by Ladislas IV of Hungary, the emperor Rudolf I defeats his rival, Ottokar II of Bohemia.

Charles of Anjou takes over the government of Achaia.

1280 Rebellion of Flemish textile workers against their exploiters.

End of Asen dynasty in Bulgaria, which becomes subject to Serbs, Greeks, and Mongols.

By the reign of Möngke, it was said that a virgin with a pot of gold on her head could walk unmolested across the Mongol empire. The Mongol conquests brought long periods of peace and security, when travelers could make their way across the overland routes of Central Asia.

In c.1275, a young Venetian named Marco Polo arrived, with his two uncles, at the court of Kublai Khan, at Shangdu. He became a great favorite of the khan, who employed Marco on a number of diplomatic missions. He traveled in Persia and India on the khan's business, and became fluent in Mongolian and Persian. An acute observer, his accounts of his travels, *Il Milione*, were dismissed as fantastic and unreliable, but stimulated further exploration.

Marco Polo, with elephants and camels, arrives at Hormuz, in the Gulf of Persia.

The Mongol Peace

Following their conquests, the Mongol imposition of law and order ensured that routes across Central Asia were safe.

1235	Walled city built at Karakorum as fixed Mongol capital.
1246	John of Piano Carpini almost reaches Karakorum.
1251	Rule of Möngke; Silk Road routes across Central Asia are now secure.
1253	William of Rubrouck reaches Karakorum.
1264	Kublai defeats rival for the title of great khan, ending civil war.
1266	Kublai founds new capital at Khanbaliq (Beijing).
1275	Marco Polo reaches Kublai's summer palace at Shangdu (Xanadu).
1292	Marco Polo given task of escorting Mongol princess to Hormuz.
1325	Ibn Battuta, a Muslim legal scholar from Morocco, begins his travels.
1341	Mission of John of Marignolli to Beijing.
1345	Ibn Battuta visits Souteast Asia and China.

The Japanese defeat of Kublai's armies in 1274 (30,000 troops) and 1281 (140,000 troops), the largest amphibious invasion forces of premodern times, were recorded in this illustrated scroll.

Divine wind

In 1274, the first Mongol invasion of Japan was turned back by a great storm. In 1281, a much larger invasion, manned by subject Koreans and Chinese, arrived. The fleet was immediately hemmed in on a narrow beachhead near Hakata. For two months, *samurai* warriors battled with the invaders.

In August 1281, a violent typhoon destroyed much of the Mongol fleet at anchor, forcing them to turn back. The *samurai* slaughtered any remaining troops. The Japanese attributed their double deliverance to a "divine wind" or *kamikaze.*

ASIA

1281 Second attempted Mongol invasion of Japan fails; Mongols defeated.

Death of leader of the Golden Horde, Khan Mangu Temir.

1283 Mongol expeditions against Annam and Champa.

Death of the cosmographer al-Qazwini, author of *Ajaib al-Makhluqat* (Wonders of Creation).

1286 Kingdom of Jerusalem reunited under Henry of Cyprus.

1297 **1287** Crusade of Alice of Blois lands in Acre.

Kublai Khan sends a fresh expedition to Annam.

Mongol expedition to Pagan (Burma).

1294 **1288** Kublai Khan gives up attempt to subdue Annam and Champa.

1291 **1289** Qalawun, the sultan of Egypt, captures Tripoli, leaving Acre as the only remaining Christian stronghold.

Foundation of the Islamic Academy of Beijing.

1296 **1290** Kaikobad, sultan of Delhi, murdered; succeeded by Jalaluddin Firuz Khalji.

AFRICA

1291 **1290** Death of Sultan Qalawun. Accession of Al-Ashraf Kalil to the sultanate of Egypt.

c.1290 Beginning of a period of civil war in Ethiopia over dynastic succession.

EUROPE

1281 The bible of the tradition of "courtly love," the *Roman de la Rose*, is updated and revised by Jean de Meun.

1282 Llywelyn, the prince of Wales, dies near Builth while rebelling against Edward of England.

The Sicilian Vespers. The Sicilian population, encouraged by the emperor Michael VIII Palaeologus, rebels against French rule. Charles of Anjou is defeated by the Aragonese.

1283 Conquest of Prussia completed by Teutonic knights.

1296 Pope Martin IV deposes Peter III of Aragon, who has captured Sicily. He appoints Charles, count of Valois, in his place. He calls for a crusade to conquer Aragon for Charles.

1296 **1284** Edward I annexes Wales.

1291 Genoa destroys the Pisan navy at Meloria. Genoa is now Venice's main rival.

First gold ducats minted in Venice.

1285 Charles of Anjou dies after losing Sicily.

1294 Philip IV the Fair is king of France (–1314).

1290 English expel the Jewish community.

Invention of spectacles in Italy.

AMERICAS & AUSTRALASIA

1283 Foundation of late Maya capital at Mayapán.

The agricultural year

Illuminated Books of Hours, which assemble prayers for appropriate times of the day, are frequently illustrated with the month-by-month activities of the medieval peasant.

Winter was a time for mending tools, repairing fences and gathering wood. Animals were slaughtered in December and salted, smoked, or cured. In spring, fields were plowed, ready for the spring-sowing of oats, peas, and beans. Trees were pruned, and sheep and cattle were turned out to graze. In June, the hay was scythed, tossed with pitchforks, and raked into haycocks. Peas and beans were harvested. In the fall, grain was harvested, threshed, and winnowed by being tossed in the air and caught in straw baskets. This process allowed the wind to blow away the chaff, leaving just the grain.

Fall crops were sown in freshly plowed fields. Fruit was picked from the orchards, grapes were harvested, and timber was collected from the nearby woodland. In November, pigs were turned out into the woods to eat acorns, fattening them up before the winter slaughters began.

A manuscript illustration for October shows a peasant sowing seeds in a plowed field.

Hanging scroll, ink on paper, Landscape after Rain, attributed to Kao K'o-kung, c.1300.

Chinese landscapes

The Chinese landscape paintings of the 12th and 13th centuries are contemplative and meditative pieces. These restrained and austere works emerged from a revered tradition of great landscape masters. The Mongol invasion of China did not destroy the cultural traditions that had flourished under the Song dynasty. During the period of Mongol occupation, styles and standards of landscape painting developed that were to dominate Chinese art for many centuries. Drama and vernacular literature flourished anew.

1291–1300

1291 Acre, the last Christian bridgehead into Palestine, falls to a Muslim army, led by al-Ashraf Khalil (son of Qalawun) sultan of Egypt, after a siege of 53 days.

1292 Marco Polo leaves China and is given task of escorting Mongol princess to Hormuz.

1293 A Mongol expedition to Java ends in failure.

1294 Kublai Khan, the conqueror of Asia, dies.

1295 Conversion of sultan of Achin (Sumatra) to Islam, which spreads over much of the East Indies.

Conversion of the Il-Khan, Ghazan to Islam.

1296 Jalaluddin Firuz Khalji, sultan of Delhi, founds a dynasty and extends his power over much of India (–1316)

1297 Burmese become vassals of the Chinese Mongols.

1299 Mongols defeat Mamluks near Homs.

c.1300 Ottoman state founded by Osman I. Beginning of Ottoman dynasty (–1924) and first phase of expansion.

c.1300 Kanuri empire moves capital from Kanem to Borno.

Emergence of empire of Benin (Nigeria).

Muslim merchants, mainly of Arab origin, begin to penetrate the Ethiopian highlands, setting up small kingdoms, and trading in slaves and ivory. The kingdom of Ifat becomes the dominant Muslim state.

1291 The three forest cantons – Uri, Schwyz, and Unterwalden – sign a pact; the beginning of the Swiss Confederation.

Genoese open sea route through Strait of Gibraltar to Bruges.

Knights of St. John of Jerusalem settle in Cyprus.

1293 The "Ordinances of Justice," passed in Florence, exclude magnate families from participation in government.

1294 War breaks out between Edward of England and Philip the Fair of France over Gascony.

Conflict begins between Philip the Fair and Pope Boniface VIII.

Death of Roger Bacon, the English philosopher and scientist (born 1214).

1295 Foundation of oligarchic grand council (*Maggior Consiglio*) of Venice.

Formation of a Franco-Scottish alliance.

1296 Frederick, the brother of James of Aragon, becomes king of Sicily.

Edward I of England invades Scotland; the Castle of Dunbar surrenders.

1304 ▼

1297 The pope gives Corsica and Sardinia to James II, the king of Aragon.

A Scottish rebellion, led by William Wallace, defeats the English at Stirling.

1305 ▼

1298 Albert I of Austria defeats and kills his rival, Adolf of Nassau, the elected king of Germany, at the battle of Göllheim, near Worms.

1299 Battle of Cape Orlando, NE Sicily. Angevin naval victory over the Aragonese.

1300 Trade fairs established at Bruges, Antwerp, Lyons, and Geneva.

c.1300 Venetians improve Brenner Pass. Now suitable for vehicles.

c.1300 The pueblo villages of Mesa Verde and the Canyon de Chelly in Arizona, southeast N America, are deserted by Anasazi and Hohokam Indians, possibly because of adverse climatic conditions.

Inca tribe base themselves in the valley of the Peruvian Andes, and found a capital at Cuzco (now Cusco).

New Zealand Maoris hunt the giant moa bird and other indigenous fauna to extinction.

The June Fair was held at Lendit, near Paris. It began with the blessing of trade (below). The innkeeper's stall, on the far right, is already doing a roaring trade.

Medieval fairs

In the 12th century, when the bulk of trade was carried overland, merchants and traders from all over Europe took part in the Champagne fairs in France. These six annual events were held in Troyes, Provins, Bar-sur-Aube, and Lagny, over the year. The Champagne region, to the south of Paris, became the crossroads of Europe, the meeting place of Mediterranean and Nordic Europe. Here, Italian merchants bought Flemish woolen textiles, and traded them for Italian silks and spices imported from the Far East.

This was all to change in the 14th century, when the Genoese and Venetians opened a direct sea route to northern Europe. This new route, and the introduction of heavy merchant ships, meant that bulk goods, such as wood, metal, wine, and oil, could be rapidly and efficiently transported all over Europe.

The Teutonic Knights

The eastward migration of Germans from c.1100 transformed E Europe and the Baltic, introducing German language and law, and trading networks such as the Hanseatic League. In 1226, at the height of the Crusades, the Teutonic Knights were invited to subdue pagan Prussia. Completed in 1309, this process saw the Order, from its headquarters in Marienburg (*above*), take over the lands of the Sword Brothers, and Livonia and Estonia, although their eastward expansion was halted when they were defeated by Russia at the "Battle on the Ice" at Lake Peipus (1242).

Rapa Nui (Easter Island)

Rapa Nui (Easter Island) was first colonized around 300 CE, and a culture appears to have developed in relative isolation. The population grew to around 7000, and the once palm-forested island was gradually denuded, resulting in increasing competition for limited resources. The culture collapsed around 1700. The island is famous for its giant stone statues, of which there are more than 600. The statues were made to stand on stone platforms, altars sacred to the island's various clans. Many had topknots of carved tufa (*above*).

1301 Ottoman Turks defeat Byzantine army at Baphaion.

1302 Malik Kafur, a former Hindu slave, conquers S India.

c.1302 Last Christian territory in Levant falls to Mamluks.

1336 **1303** Mongol invasion army defeated at Damascus.

Catalonian merchants gain control of W Mediterranean trade with Constantinople.

1304 Ikhan Ghazan, Mongol ruler of Persia, dies; succeeded by his brother, Uljaitu.

An 18-year-old Franciscan missionary, Oderico da Pordenose sets out to retrace Marco Polo's journey to China.

1301 Death of Andras III of Hungary brings the Arpad dynasty to an end. A civil war errupts.

1302 Papal bull *Unam Sanctam* declares supreme papal authority.

Battle of Courtrai; Flemings defeat French.

End of War of the Sicilian Vespers.

First meeting of Estates General in France.

Eviction of French from Bordeaux; establishment of trade links with England.

Bartolommeo da Varignana writes first formal record of a postmortem.

1303 Edward I of England grants trading privileges to foreign merchants.

1304 Edward I of England completes conquest of Scotland.

Birth of Petrarch, Italian scholar and poet (–1374).

1305 Pope Clement V takes up residency at Avignon, which becomes papal seat under French supervision (–1377).

Execution of William Wallace, Scottish nationalist leader.

Robert Bruce rebels against English rule in Scotland.

1306 Hospitallers conquer Rhodes and make it their headquarters (–1310).

Philip IV expels Jews from France.

1307 Robert Bruce defeats the English at Loudon Hill.

Composition of Dante's *La Divina Commedia* begun.

1308 Philip IV of France builds first indoor tennis court.

Edward II of England marries Isabella of Spain.

1309 Teutonic Order's subjugation of Prussia complete.

Grand master of the Teutonic Order transfers official residence from Venice to Marienburg, Prussia; launch of crusade against Lithuanians.

Union of Aragon and Valencia.

Foundation of Doge's palace, Venice.

1334 ▽

1312 ▽

Giotto di Bondone

The Florentine painter, Giotto is regarded as one of the founders of modern painting, in that he broke away from the stylized and stereotyped forms of Italo-Byzantine art, giving his figures a solidity and naturalism, painting scenes with a freshness and passion hitherto largely absent in devotional art.

Among Giotto's most significant achievements were the ambitious fresco cycles he created, depicting scenes from the lives of saints Joachim and Anna, the Virgin Mary, and the life and Passion of Christ, in the Arena chapel, Padua, *above* (completed between 1306–06). Before this he had created a fresco cycle depicting the life of St. Francis in the Upper Church at Assisi (recently restored after an earthquake); in the 1320s he decorated four chapels in Santa Croce, Florence. He also worked in Rome and Naples, and he and his near contemporary Cimabue were both sufficiently admired to be mentioned by Dante. He was appointed supervisor of Florence Cathedral, and designed the campanile (bell-tower) though this was subsequently altered.

Robert Bruce (1274–1329)

King of Scotland from 1306, Robert Bruce emerged heroic from the war of Scottish independence. He had joined William Wallace in 1297 to resist Edward I's invasion, and was appointed one of the four guardians of Scotland 1298. From 1306–14 he transformed Scottish resistance from a guerrilla campaign into a coordinated national movement, which culminated in his decisive victory over the English at Bannockburn (1314). The Anglo-Scottish war persisted until 1328, but he was recognized as king by Pope John XXII in 1323. He forced Edward III to agree to the Treaty of Northampton whereby Scottish sovereignty was acknowledged by England.

William Tell

A legendary figure, whose exploits, including the marksman's test (*above*), were described by Johannes von Muller in his *History of Switzerland* (1786), Tell nevertheless represents the Swiss struggle for independence, especially in the defense of the Forest Cantons against Austria. In 1291 Uri, Schwyz, and Unterwalden united to proclaim autonomy, and defeated the Habsburgs at Morgarten. Joined by neighboring regions and cities, they resisted campaigns by the Habsburgs and Burgundy over the next 200 years, winning the Swabian war (1499) and establishing *de facto* independence.

ASIA

1311 Delhi sultanate captures Madura, Pandya capital.

1312 Delhi sultanate conquers N Deccan (India).

1313 Özbeg, khan of the Golden Horde, converts to Islam.

1314 Rashid al-Din's *Jami' al-tawarikh*, Persian history of Mongol conquest.

1318 Delhi sultanate invades kingdom of Maharashtra, C India.

1320 Murder of Delhi sultan, Tughluq dynasty assumes control as Muhammad ibn Tughluq succeeds to sultanate of Delhi.

Outbreak of plague in Yunnan province in China.

Mongol armies help spread plague throughout China (–1330).

1321

1330

AFRICA

The cannon

Gunpowder, used in China from the 11th century, came to Europe by the mid-13th century, probably via Muslim traders. The first primitive cannons appear in illustrations from c.1320, and within 20 years they were widely used in sieges and defensive actions. The first cannons were made from iron or bronze rods either welded together or bound by iron hoops, and fired stone, iron or, later, lead balls.

After c.1370 the ability to cast cannons in single tubes made them stronger, and capable of firing ammunition of about 800 pounds (360 kg). Siege guns were remarkably heavy, and transported by water or on wheeled carriages, having special mounts built for them when in use. By the early 15th century the role of the more powerful cannon was primarily in siege warfare, although medium sized firearms and even hand-held culverins were in use on the battlefield.

1311 Scottish armies raid N England.

Completion of Rheims Cathedral, France.

Earliest known example of Portolan chart.

1312 Order of Knights Templar accused of heresy and dissolved by papal decree, its property transferred to Knights Hospitaller.

Robert Bruce attempts invasion of England.

Treaty of Vienne; Lyons formally annexed to France.

c.1313 Berthold Schwarz invents first European cannon.

1314 English defeated by Scots at Bannockburn.

Hereford *Mappa Mundi* (wall map).

Completion of first cathedral of St. Paul's, London.

1315 Battle of Morgarten; defeat of Habsburgs by the Swiss.

Famine ravages N Europe (–1317).

c.1315 Lyons silk industry developed by Italian immigrants.

1316 Edward Bruce, brother of Robert, becomes king of Ireland.

Anatomia by Mondino of Luzzi; first textbook of anatomy based on dissection.

1317 Salic law bars women from succession to French throne.

Suppression of Knights Templar in Spain.

Hansa granted exclusive trading privileges in England by Edward II.

Papacy outlaws alchemy.

1318 Edward Bruce killed in Ireland.

1319 Unification of Norway and Sweden.

1320 Reunification of Poland.

Peace of Paris between France and Flanders.

Flanders loses wool monopoly to Brabant; start of decline of Champagne fairs.

The earliest metal cannons in Europe were forged, but these were superceded by much larger ones cast using the technology initially developed for making church bells.

Mansa Musa

The Islamic empire of Mali in West Africa controlled the trans-Saharan caravan trade from c.1200. It used the profits to maintain a powerful army, dominating its neighbors. Gold and slaves went north in exchange for salt, textiles, horses, and manufactured goods. Tales of the wealth of Mali spread to Europe, especially after an ostentatious pilgrimage to Mecca by one of Mali's most powerful rulers, Mansa Musa in 1324–25. This illustration, showing Mansa Musa on his throne, is from the Catalan Atlas, produced in Aragon in 1375.

No Theater

One of several classical Japanese theatrical forms, No drama emerged in the pre-Edo period, and was derived from a blend of traditions to form masked musical dance drama. Most No pieces center on an encounter between a troubled spirit (*shite*) and a bystander or priest (*waki*), as a result of which the *shite* may find spiritual relief. The drama is presented in dance, which moves from the stately to a controlled intensity, reflected in the accompanying music. Stylized masks (*above*) with a spiritual or mystic significance are used to denote characters.

ASIA

1321 Delhi Sultanate achieves greatest extent.

1322 Death of Zhao Mengfu, Chinese painter and calligrapher.

1325 First pilgrimage to Mecca by Ibn Battuta, Arab geographer, historian and traveler.

Death of Amir Khusrau, Indian Muslim mystic poet, aged 95. He has become known as the "Parrot of India."

c.1325 Development of No drama in Japan.

1326 Ottomans capture Byzantine city of Bursa and make it their capital.

1330 Plague reaches NE China.

Majapahit empire in SE Asia at greatest extent under Gaja Mada.

1340

AFRICA

1324 Pilgrimage to Mecca by Mansa Musa, ruler of Mali (–1325).

EUROPE

1321 Death of Italian poet Dante.

1322 English parliament decrees that all laws require consent of both parliament and the throne.

Scottish barons assert independence in Declaration of Arbroath.

University of Florence founded.

1324 Outbreak of warfare between France and England in Gascony.

German refutation of papal supremacy results in excommunication of emperor, Louis IV.

Moors recapture Baza from Castile.

York Minster completed, England.

1325 Completion of Siena Cathedral, Italy.

1326 France under Charles IV recovers Gascony from English.

First use of cannon in warfare by Florentine army.

1327 Murder of English king, Edward II, following his deposition by parliament.

1328 Foundation of Valois dynasty by Philip VI.

Scottish independence confirmed by Treaty of Northampton.

Beginning of Muscovite expansion under Ivan I.

Invention of sawmill.

1329 Death of Robert Bruce; succeeded by his five-year-old son, David II.

c.1330 Apogee of English longbow technology.

AMERICAS & AUSTRALASIA

c.1325 Foundation of Tenochtitlán on island in Lake Texcoco, Mesoamerica. Beginning of rise of the Aztecs.

Tenochtitlán

The Aztecs were originally a farming people from western Mexico who were forced – perhaps because of drought or warfare – to migrate to the Valley of Mexico in the early 14th century. They settled on two marshy islands in the south of Lake Texcoco.

In the 1320s they began to build a city from stone, Tenochtitlán, on one of the islands. The city was linked to the mainland by a series of causeways and surrounded by agricultural *chinampas*, reclaimed swamp land protected by dikes, which provided an immediate source of food. Several crops of beans, squash, and corn were harvested annually, producing an agricultural surplus which sustained both the city dwellers and the standing Aztec army. Surrounding the city, on the shores of the lake, were regional centers such as Texcoco, numerous villages and ceremonial centers, salt-making centers and quarries.

According to Aztec legend, the war god gave priest-leaders a sign, an eagle on a cactus, to show them where to built Tenochtitlán. This codex shows the city with this symbol at its crossroads.

Papal palace, Avignon

During the early years of the 14th century, a period of warfare, famine, pestilence, and scandal disrupted the stability of the Church. In 1305, the French king, Philip IV, seeking to secure his domination of the papacy, pressured the French pope, Clement V, to move the seat of the papacy from Rome to Avignon, where it remained until 1377. In 1334, a new palace (*above*) was begun.

While Avignon removed the papacy from the political turmoil and conflict in Rome, it did assure that the papacy was under effective French control – all seven popes in office during the Avignon period were Frenchmen, while of the 134 cardinals appointed, no fewer than 111 were French. The English, Germans, and Italians were resentful of French power, and the authority of the Avignon popes was not accepted in all countries, while Rome itself suffered severely from the loss of papal revenues. Latin Christendom was effectively divided against itself.

ASIA

 1333

1331 Dispute over imperial succession leads to civil war against Hojo regency in Japan.

1333 Accession of last Mongol emperor in China provokes period of civil war.

Decline of Minamoto (Kamakura shogunate) rule in Japan. Emperor Go-Daigo overthrows Hojo clan, and captures Kamakura.

1334 Ibn Battuta serves as *qazi* (judge) in Delhi (–1341).

1335 Demotte's *Shah Nama*, fine example of Persian illuminated manuscript.

Rebellions against Mongol rule in China.

1336 Birth of Timur (Tamerlane).

 1370

Hindu kingdom of Vijayanagara founded in S India; rebellion against Tughluqs marks beginning of Vijayanagara empire.

1338 Ottomans reach the Bosporus.

c.1350

Foundation of Ashikaga shogunate in Japan.

 1346

1340 Black Death (bubonic plague) breaks out in Asia.

AFRICA

1331 Ibn Battuta's voyage to the Swahili cities of E Africa.

1332 Ewostatewos founds Ethiopian monastic movement.

c.1340 Building of Great Mosque of Jenne, Mali.

Islam in Africa

1331 Serbia becomes dominant power in the Balkans.

1332 English parliament provisionally divided into two houses for the first time.

Luzern joins union of Swiss cantons and cities.

Denmark cedes Scania (Skåne) to Sweden.

1333 Accession of Casimir the Great of Poland; he abandons war against Teutonic Knights.

Edward III defeats Scots at Halidon Hill.

Gibraltar retaken from Castile by Moors.

Accession of Yusuf I as caliph of Granada; Granada reaches peak of Islamic civilization in Iberia.

1334 Papal palace at Avignon begun.

1335 First striking clock in a public space, Milan, Italy.

1337 Start of Hundred Years' War (–1453); Scots ally with French against England.

Philip VI of France confiscates Guyenne; Edward III claims kingdom of France.

Death of Giotto (born c.1266) innovative Italian painter in naturalistic/classical manner.

First scientific weather forecasts, Oxford, England.

1338 Lorenzetti's *Allegory of Good and Bad Government* frescoes, town hall, Siena, Italy; early Renaissance masterpiece.

First light cannon mounted on English ships.

1339 Swiss defeat Burgundians at Laupen.

1340 English defeat French fleet at battle of Sluys off Flemish coast, gaining command of sea links to France.

Bankruptcy of Peruzzis throughout the decade; economic chaos compounded by arrival of Black Death in 1347.

Alfonso XI of Castile defeats Moors at Salado river.

First European paper mill built at Fabriano, Italy.

From as early as the 8th century, Arab travelers were reporting on the fabled gold of West Africa. By the end of the 9th century Islamic influence was beginning to penetrate the sub-Saharan regions, carried by Berber nomads who had converted to Islam.

In the savannah country of the upper Niger river lay the mighty empire of Mali, whose wealth was based on rich deposits of gold. Most of the rulers had converted to Islam, some even made pilgrimages to Mecca, but the they never fully rejected their traditional religion – if they had done so they would have lost the support of the peasant farmers, the large majority of whom were pagan.

In Morocco, the former desert nomads were corrupted by the wealth and power of the settled existence introduced by Arab traders. Their loss of piety provoked a *jihad* amongst the Berbers of north Africa, who founded the Almohad state, and set about unifying the whole of the Maghrib. At this time, immigrant Arab nomads began to introduce Arabic language and culture into rural areas. One consequence was that literacy spread throughout northern and western Africa. Mosques, such as Jenne (*below*) and Timbuktu, became important centers of learning.

The Hundred Years' War (1337–1453)

1337 War between England and France over Gascony – outbreak of the Hundred Years' War.

1346 Battle of Crécy; English defeat the French. Henry of Lancaster campaigns successfully from Bordeaux.

1347 English capture Calais, gain bridgehead in France.

1356 Battle of Poitiers; Anglo-Gascon force defeats French, French king captured.

1360 Treaty of Brétigny between England and France.

1369 Renewal of Hundred Years' War.

1369-81 French restrict English in France to Calais, Bordeaux, and Bayonne.

1372 English fleet destroyed by Franco-Castilian fleet off La Rochelle.

1377 Franco-Castilian fleet raids south coast of England.

1396 Treaty of Leulinghen ends second phase of Hundred Years' War.

1415 Henry V of England captures Harfleur and defeats French at Agincourt.

1419 Henry V conquers Normandy.

1420 Treaty of Troyes makes Henry V heir to French throne.

1421 Henry campaigns around Paris.

1422 Death of Henry V.

1423 Anglo-Burgundian army destroys Franco-Scottish army at Verneuil.

1429 Joan of Arc inspires French recovery; Charles VII crowned at Rheims.

1435 Burgundy defects from English alliance.

1442 French expedition to Gascony.

1444 Anglo-French Truce of Tours.

1448 French occupy Maine.

1449 English break truce; renewal of war leading to French conquest of Normandy.

1450 French recover Gascony.

1453 Hundred Years' War ends with final French recovery of Bordeaux.

The Battle of Crécy, fought in northern France in 1346, was one of the great battles of the Hundred Years' War. Edward III's English force of 10,000 archers and 4,000 other men defeated Philip VI of France, whose army was made up of 12,000 men-at-arms and a large contingent of other troops. The tactics of the English archers and the efficiency of their longbows contributed to the fame of this English weapon.

ASIA

1343 Capital temple city of Vijayanagara empire, India, founded by Harihara.

Ibn Battuta visits SE Asia and China (–1346).

Majapahit empire completes conquest of Bali (Indonesia).

1345 Ottomans annex emirate of Karasi, empire reaches Dardanelles.

1346 Plague reaches Kaffa, Crimea, on coast of Black Sea.

1349 ▶

1347 Black Death reaches Baghdad and Constantinople.

1349 First Chinese settlement at Singapore; beginning of Chinese settlement of SE Asia.

1378 ▼

1350 Founding of Ayutthaya, capital of new kingdom of Siam; campaigns against Cambodia.

c.1350 Ashikaga shoguns dominant in Japan.

Majapahit empire, Java, at its height; exercises sway over most of E Indies.

AFRICA

1344 Ethiopia at its height at death of ruler, Amde Tseyon.

1347 Marinids take Tunis.

The Black Death

1341 Italian poet, scholar and humanist, Petrarch, is crowned Poet Laureate in Rome.

1342 Accession of Louis the Great of Hungary.

1343 Treaty of Kalisz: Poland cedes Pomerelia and Kulm to Teutonic Knights.

c.1345 Aragonese conquer Mallorca from Moors.

1346 English defeat French at battle of Crécy.

Denmark sells Estonia to Teutonic Knights.

1347 English capture Calais from France.

Foundation of Prague University, first to be established east of the Rhine. Truce between England and France (–1355).

Black Death reaches Europe, appearing first in Kaffa on the Crimean peninsula.

Boccaccio's *Decameron* (–1353).

1348 Black Death reaches Greece, Italy, France, Spain, Britain, and N Africa.

1349 Black Death arrives in C Europe; estimated to have killed one-third of population of England.

Widespread persecution of Jews in Germany.

1350 Rivalry between Venice and Genoa at its peak for control of E Mediterranean maritime trade.

English replaces French in English schools.

Prague becomes Holy Roman Empire's imperial capital. Emperor Charles IV plans to transform the city into the "Rome of the North."

c.1350 *Sir Gawain and the Green Knight*, masterpiece of Middle English.

School of icon painting flourishing at Novgorod (–c.1450).

Italian majolica ware develops.

1350 War between Inca and Chimú states.

c.1350 Collapse of Pueblo cultures in N American Southwest, possibly due to warfare or climatic change.

Classic Maori Period begins on North Island, New Zealand; settlements within earthwork fortifications.

One of the greatest calamities in European history began in 1347 when bubonic plague struck, brought to Italy, it is thought, by a group of Genoese returning home through Sicily and Pisa from Kaffa in the Crimea. Their fortress there had been besieged by

Any house where one of the occupants had fallen victim to the plague was marked with a warning cross. However, no preventative measures to halt contagion proved effective.

Mongol invaders who had suddenly begun to die of a disease that caused black, blood-oozing swellings and immense pain. The epidemic had begun in the foothills of the Himalayas in India in the 13th century and had spread rapidly along trade routes, reaching China in the 1330s and striking the Byzantine empire with great ferocity in 1347. By 1351, it had spread over most of Europe. The only areas which escaped were Milan, Poland, Belgium, eastern Germany and part of southwest France.

The plague was carried by parasites living in the stomachs of fleas that favored house rats and humans as their hosts. As it was thought that cats and dogs were the source of infection, these were killed, which in fact aggravated the epidemic as rats then multiplied faster than ever. About 20 million people died – about one third of the population. As a result, a Europe that had been suffering the consequences of over-population became underpopulated. Abandoned fields and labor shortages meant that economic recovery took a century to come into effect.

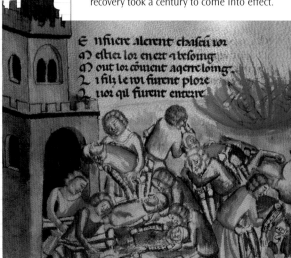

When the Black Death struck a town, it did so with such ferocity and speed that burying people in mass graves was the only way of coping with the huge daily death toll.

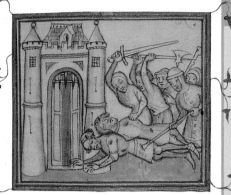

Étienne Marcel

The Hundred Years' War had begun badly for for the French, with defeats at Poitiers and Crécy, and the capture of King John II in 1358. In the king's absence, the peasants, crushed by taxation, agitated for reforms and much of the area around Beauvais rose up in rebellion. In Paris, the merchant's provost, Étienne Marcel, led a municipal movement demanding greater autonomy. He instigated the murder of the Dauphin's two marshals, in an attempt to intimidate the Dauphin into accepting rule by the Council of the Estates. This unprecedented violence led to a backlash from the nobles who suppressed the revolts, and murdered Marcel.

The Hanseatic League

Hanses were associations of merchants who acted together to secure their commercial interests and protect the transportation of their goods. The Hanseatic League first appeared in 1360, when the city of Lübeck organized a meeting among the Hanseatic towns. For more than 100 years, the Hanseatic League, which eventually included more than 60 towns, dominated trade in northeastern and central Europe. Close political ties and affiliations were formed between the various Hanse towns. There was no formal constitution, but a body of law and custom accumulated, with Lübeck acting as the home for the League's General Assemblies.

Miniature showing the Hanse town of Hamburg.

1351 Massive flooding of Yellow river in China.

White Lotus rebellion in N China.

1353 Mongol Persian empire of Il-Khanate collapses.

Black Death recurs in China.

1354

1354 First phase of Ottoman imperial expansion in Anatolia. They take the Gallipoli peninsula and continue in Thrace.

1356 Korea lapses into disorder. The Koryo kings are little more than satellites ofthe Mongol imperial family.

1352 Ibn Battuta travels trans-Saharan trade routes.

1358 Ibn Battuta travels in Mali.

1351 Zurich joins the Swiss League.

Black Death reaches much of N Europe.

Tennis becomes a popular open air game in England.

1352 Black Death reaches Russia.

Foundation of Antwerp Cathedral, largest church in Belgium.

1353 Berne joins Swiss League.

1354 Peace concluded by Venice with Genoa, after over 50 years of warfare over trade supremacy.

c.1354 Ottomans capture Gallipoli, their first foothold in Europe.

1355 Edward III and his son Edward, the Black Prince, resume open war with France.

1356 Battle of Poitiers, English defeat the French.

Holy Roman emperor Charles IV issues Golden Bull, abolishing papal involvement in imperial elections.

Provost of merchants, Étienne Marcel, takes over running of Paris and orders building of new city wall.

1358 Suppression of Jacquerie peasant revolt, a popular uprising against nobility in France.

Louis of Hungary gains Dalmatia following Genoese defeat of Venice.

Peace treaty between Habsburgs and Swiss League.

1359 Treaty of London guaranteeing English lands in France rejected; Edward III invades N France.

1360 Treaty of Brétigny ends first phase of Hundred Years' War; England retains control of lands south of Loire river, Calais, and Ponthieu; peace lasts nine years, but bands of mercenaries, the Great Companies, ravage SE France.

Formation of Hanseatic League, N European trading network.

Scania (Skåne) recovered from Sweden by Denmark.

Franc introduced in France.

Emperor Stefan Dušan

Medieval Serbia reached its apogee under the fearsome Stefan Dušan (1331–55), who de-throned his own father to become king. Dušan conquered Albania, Montenegro, and Macedonia, even penetrating as far south as Thessaly in Greece. He presided over the promulgation of a law code and oversaw the building of many churches and monasteries. Dušan's ambitions to conquer Constantinople were never realized; in 1389, his successor, the last Serbian king, fell at the battle of Kosovo.

The Golden Bull

In 1356, the German emperor Charles IV (reigned 1346–78) promulgated the Golden Bull, a constitutional document which consisted of a series of decrees laying down the procedure for the election of the emperor. Disputed elections had previously erupted into civil war, and the stability of the monarchy was precariously dependent on the cooperation of the territorial princes, especially the prince-electors.

Great Zimbabwe

The royal enclosure at Great Zimbabwe (*above*) is the largest ancient structure in sub-Saharan Africa. It is the most spectacular of many similar, smaller *mazimbabwe* (*zimbabwe* meaning "stone house"). This remarkable city formed the heart of the rich and powerful Shona empire that existed between the Zambezi and Limpopo rivers in south central Africa from the 9th to the 15th century. Its rulers owed their wealth to the export of cattle and, from 1200, locally mined gold and copper.

Vijayanagara empire

In 1336 this powerful new Hindu kingdom was established in the Krishna valley and grew to cover, at its maximum extent in 1370, the entire southern half of the Indian subcontinent. Its capital (modern Hampi), similarly called Vijayanagara, "City of Victory," was an impressive temple city and had massive fortifications and a royal palace (*above*). It withstood repeated attacks by the Muslim Bahamani kingdom to the north, but eventually fell after a severe defeat in 1565.

1368 Establishment of the Ming dynasty in China (–1644). Mongols driven from Peking.

Ashikaga Yoshimitsu assumes shogunate in Japan.

The Diwan by Hafiz, masterpiece of Persian poetry.

1369 Timur establishes capital of his empire at Samarkand.

1380 ▼

1370 Beginning of Timur's conquests; Timurid successors rule his empire to 1506.

Vijayanagara empire reaches greatest extent in S India.

1364 Norman navigators reach mouth of Senegal river.

EUROPE

1361 Capture of Edirne (Adrianople) by the Ottoman Turks.

War between Hanseatic League and Denmark.

Black Death recurs in England.

1364 University of Cracow founded.

Crete revolts against Venetian rule.

1366 English parliament refuses to pay taxes to Roman papacy.

English theologian John Wyclif questions papal supremacy.

El Tránsito synagogue in Toledo completed.

Statutes of Kilkenny ban Anglo-Irish marriage, Irish language, and Irish laws.

1367 Coalition forces of Pedro the Cruel and Edward, the Black Prince, defeat Henry of Trastámara at Nájera, Spain.

1368 Casimir III of Poland issues central law code.

1369 Peace between England and Scotland (–1384).

Henry of Trastámara defeats Pedro the Cruel of Castile.

French attempt to restrict English to Calais, Bayonne, and Bordeaux; renewal of hostilities in Hundred Years' War.

Geoffrey Chaucer writes *Book of the Duchess*; his writing becomes basis for standard English.

1370 After death of Casimir III of Poland, Louis of Hungary assumes Polish throne.

Edward, the Black Prince sacks Limoges, in France.

Defeat of Denmark by Hanseatic League. Peace of Stralsund assures freedom of trade in the Baltic.

Teutonic Order defeats Lithuanians at Rudau.

The Bastille, Paris, built.

Steel crossbow introduced.

c.1370 Development of decorated and flamboyant styles of Gothic architecture in NW Europe.

Piers Plowman, major Middle English poem, attributed to Langland.

Emergence of legend of Robin Hood in England.

AMERICAS & AUSTRALASIA

1365 Aztecs employed as mercenaries by Tezozomac of Atzcapotzalco.

1370 Chimú conquers Sican state, C Andes.

c.1370 Michancamon, Chimú leader, captured by Incas.

The Conquests of Timur (Tamerlane)

1370 Beginning of conquests of Timur.

1380 Timur launches series of attacks on Persia.

1384 Herat rebels; Timur suppresses ruling dynasty.

1387 Isfahan rebels; in reprisal Timur kills 70,000, building towers with their skulls.

1388 Timur wages war against Mongol khanate of the Golden Horde.

1392 Timur campaigns in Persia.

1393 Timur captures Baghdad.

1395 Timur invades large parts of S Russia. Timur sacks New Sarai, capital of Golden Horde.

1398 Timur takes Delhi.

1400 Sack of Aleppo and Damascus.

1401 Timur sacks Baghdad for second time.

1402 Timur defeats Ottomans at Ankara.

1405 Death of Timur.

Zhu Yuanzhang

A man of humble origins, Zhu Yuanzhang became a rebel leader during the upheavals that accompanied the decline of the Mongol Yuan dynasty in China in the 14th century. Also known as Taizu, he overcame his rivals and installed his capital at Nanjing in 1356. In 1368 his forces drove out the remaining Mongols, enabling him to establish himself as the founder of the Ming Dynasty – the first time in over 400 years that China had come under the unified control of a native dynasty.

He initiated an aggressive foreign policy which extended the empire over Annam in Vietnam, and Mongolia, and it was under the Ming that the Great Wall, originally built in 221 BCE, was rebuilt and extended to it present size.

A decorated window in the Alhambra. The palace's splendid interiors are attributed to Yusef I (died 1354). After the expulsion of the Moors in 1492, much of the interior was effaced and the furniture was ruined or removed.

Granada

The Islamic city of Granada in Spain, situated on the slopes of the Sierra Nevada, rose to prominence after the disintegration of the caliphate of Córdoba in 1031. As the Christian reconquest of Iberia began to gain momentum, Muslim refugees started to flee to the city of the kingdom of Granada, swelling the population of the city to 50,000.

The city reached its peak of prosperity during the rule of the Nasrid dynasty (1230–1492), which conquered Granada in 1238. For the following two centuries Granada remained the only Islamic state in Iberia. The Nasrids were patrons of learning and the arts, and their capital attracted many learned Muslims. The greatest monuments of this golden age are the Alhambra, a palace-fortress, and the Generalife, a summer retreat. The Alhambra, built between 1238 and 1358, is richly decorated in an ornate Arabasque style, with colored tiles, geometric figures, and floral motifs. Its graceful arches, shady arcades, and delicately wrought columns are the culmination of Islamic architecture in Iberia.

1372 *Kitab hayyat al-hayyawan* by al-Damiri, encyclopedic collection of tales, traditions, and scientific observations concerning animals.

Chinese campaigns across Gobi force Mongol armies to retreat to the steppes.

1374 Death of Ni Zan, leading Chinese landscape painter.

1375 Little Armenian capital, Sis, captured by Mamluks, ending country's independence.

1377 Death of Ibn Battuta, Arab geographer, historian, and traveler.

Malays found Malacca at key position on Strait of Malacca.

1378 Foundation of Ak Koyunlu, state based on Turkoman tribesmen in E Anatolia, Azerbaijan, and the Zagros mountains (–1508).

1395 Sukhothai becomes vassal of Siam and is gradually absorbed.

1379 Timur marches on Urgench.

1384 **1380** Timur launches series of attacks on Persia; beginning of his campaigns in C Asia.

First Malayan metrical verse.

c.1380 Foundation of Janissary corps by Ottomans.

EUROPE

1371 Ottomans defeat Serbs at Maritsa river.

1372 Franco-Castilian fleet defeats English off La Rochelle.

1373 John of Gaunt leads English invasion of France.

Dutch invent form of lock to control water levels on canals.

1374 Truce between France and England; English restricted to Calais, Bayonne, and Bordeaux.

Peace between Castile and Aragon.

1375 Peace of Bruges between England and France; English restricted to Calais and coastal areas of Gascony.

c.1375 Creation of the Catalan Atlas by Majorcan cartographers, first attempt to create an atlas based on known trade routes.

1377 Court of Lions and Alhambra palace in Granada built; masterpiece of Moorish architecture in Iberia.

1378 Beginning of Great Schism in Catholic church, with popes in both Rome and Avignon (–1417).

Renewal of Hundred Years' War, with England campaigning against Franco-Scottish alliance.

Greek artist, Theophanes, travels to Novgorod; beginning of Greek influence in Russian art and architecture.

1379 Introduction of poll tax in England, to help fund wars.

1380 Decisive Muscovite victory over Golden Horde at Kulikovo.

Union of Norway and Denmark.

Foundation of international banking system by Hans Fugger at Augsburg, Germany.

John Wyclif translates the Bible into vernacular.

Death of Christian mystic, Catherine of Siena.

c.1380 Rise of Lollards in England, religious reformers inspired by John Wyclif.

AMERICAS & AUSTRALASIA

1375 Chimú begin conquest of C Andes.

c.1380 First phase of Aztec expansion in Mexico.

The Southern Cult

The first true towns in North America, characterized by temple-mounds, plazas, and wooden stockades, emerged in the Middle Mississippi valley c.700. By the 12th and 13th centuries, a group of artifacts, found in mortuary mounds as far apart as Mississippi, Minnesota, and Oklahoma, testify to the existence of a widespread religion, known as the Southern Cult. Ritual objects are decorated with recurring motifs: human eyes, flying winged figures, and elaborate sunbursts. Pottery vessels in the shape of effigy heads (*above*) may be representations of ancestors.

The Janissary corps

The Janissaries were an elite corps within the standing army of the Ottoman Empire, which evolved in the late 14th century. The Janissary corps was originally staffed by Christian youths from the conquered Balkan provinces, who were drafted into military service, and forcibly converted to Islam. They were subject to strict discipline, and celibacy was enforced. Widely respected for their military prowess, the Janissaries became a powerful political force within the Ottoman state, and by the 17th and 18th centuries were responsible for engineering a series of palace coups.

Wat Tyler's revolt

This was the first mass popular uprising in English history. It was led by Walter Tyler, a former soldier, who captained thousands of angry peasants from Kent and eastern England on a march to London to demand higher wages and the repeal of the new poll tax. They captured Canterbury and the Tower of London and burnt the Savoy Palace, but when the 14-year-old King Richard II met the rebels, a quarrel broke out and Tyler was killed. Within a month the rebellion fizzled out and all concessions to the peasants were rescinded.

Wells Cathedral clock

The invention of mechanical clocks c.1280 was one indication of the revival of technological development in Europe in the later Middle Ages. Among the earliest to survive is this one, dating from about 1386. The mechanism is now in the Science Museum, London. It was installed in the north transept of Wells Cathedral and would not have been visible to the general public, serving instead, as most early clocks, to alert the clergy to the times of religious services. The original face inside the cathedral is the oldest clockface in the world. It has a 24-hour dial and shows the motion of the sun and moon.

1381–1390

ASIA

1384 Herat rebels; Timur suppresses ruling dynasty.

1385 Death of the revered Chinese artist, Ni Zan, painter of austerely beautiful landscapes.

1387 Isfahan rebels; in reprisal, Timur kills 70,000, building towers with their skulls.

Timur conquers Shiraz and Isfahan; begins campaigns against Armenia and Georgia.

1389 Bayezid succeeds his father, Murat, as sultan of the Ottomans.

Death of the poet and Muslim mystic, Shams al-din Muhammad, known as Hafiz. He was master of the Persian *ghazal*, a lyrical short poem, infused with mysticism.

AFRICA

1381 Black Death recurs in Egypt.

1382 In Egypt, the Mamluk dynasty of the Bahrites is replaced by that of the Burjites.

1390 Formation of the kingdom of Kongo.

1381 Venice defeats Genoa, gains upper hand in Mediterranean trade.

Wat Tyler's peasant revolt in England; collapses upon his death.

1382 Tax riot brutally suppressed in Paris; municipal government suspended.

Ottomans under Murat take Sofia in Bulgaria.

1383 Collapse of Maillotin revolt in Paris against high taxes raised for war against England.

1384 Anglo-Scottish warfare resumes.

1385 Portuguese victory at battle of Aljubarrota against Castile secures Portuguese independence.

Foundation of St. Giles Cathedral, Edinburgh (–1495).

Anglo-French hostilities resume.

Foundation of Heidelberg University.

1386 Swiss Confederation defeats Habsburgs under emperor, Leopold III, at Sempach; Leopold III killed.

Union of Poland and Lithuania through royal marriage; becomes largest state in Europe.

Ottomans capture Salonica, following three-year siege, effectively securing all Byzantine lands beyond Constantinople.

Geoffrey Chaucer begins *The Canterbury Tales* (–c.1400).

Foundation of Milan Cathedral, unique Italian Gothic style in marble.

1387 Lithuania converts to Christianity.

Medici Bank founded in Florence.

1388 Swiss victory at Naifels forces Habsburgs to negotiate.

Scots defeat English at Otterburn.

Persecution of Lollard church reformers in England.

First Urban Sanitary Act (England).

1389 Treaty of Zurich recognizes Swiss territories.

Battle of Kosovo; Ottomans gain control of the Balkans; decisive victory of Ottomans over Serbs and Bosnians.

Golden Horde recaptures Moscow.

1414

Geoffrey Chaucer

In the *Canterbury Tales*, Geoffrey Chaucer produced one of the greatest poetic works in the English language. However, he was not only a brilliant writer, but also served Edward III, Richard II, and Henry IV as a civil servant. Born in 1342 or 1343 into a wealthy family of London vintners, Geoffrey grew up at court and learnt Latin and Italian. He fought in France, was captured and then ransomed and thereafter was sent on several royal diplomatic missions around Europe, including one to Italy, where he was deeply influenced by the works of Dante, Petrarch, and Boccaccio.

In 1369 he wrote his first work, the *Book of the Duchess*, an elegy for Blanche, wife of John of Gaunt. The *Canterbury Tales* was written in the 1390s and remained unfinished at his death in 1400. Its tale of a group of pilgrims who engage in a story-telling contest provided Chaucer with the opportunity to write in a masterly variety of literary genres.

1381–1390

Timur

After making himself ruler of Samarkand Timur "Leng" ("the Lame"), or Tamerlane, created an empire that stretched from the Ganges in India to the shores of the Red and Black seas. Born in 1336, Timur was a Muslim of Turkic origin who claimed descent from Genghis Khan and determined to recreate his great ancestor's empire. He was a gifted general with an army of superb horsemen. He died in 1405 on the way to conquer China.

Timur is shown here leading his army through the Hindu Kush in 1398 before sacking Delhi.

Inca *quipus*

The Incas never developed writing, but had an accounting system that was standardized throughout their empire. Information such as statistics, lists, and even historical records were stored on a string-and-knot device called a *quipu*. It consisted of a long cord, or set of cords, from which hung 48 strings, with subsidiary strings attached to them. The strings

were colored according to the type of information, (such as land, ceremonies, taxes, harvests, and the organization of warfare), and knots represented numbers. *Quipu* interpreters were expected to memorize extra details.

ASIA

1392 Further campaigns of Timur (Tamerlane) in Persia (–1394).

Foundation of Yi dynasty in Korea, ending Mongol Chinese domination.

In Japan, the rival southern and northern courts of the divided imperial family are reunited after fifty years of strife.

1393 Sack and capture of Baghdad by Timur.

1394 Golden Pavilion, Kyoto, built by Yoshimitsu.

1395 Sack of New Sarai, capital of Golden Horde, by Timur.

Thais invade Khmer kingdom, which is then relocated to Phnom Penh.

1398 Timur's invasion of India; sack of Delhi leads to fall of Tughluq dynasty.

1401 **1400** Timur attacks Ottoman territories and invades Syria; sacks Aleppo and Damascus.

c.1400 Collapse of Khmer kingdom leads to turmoil in mainland SE Asia.

AFRICA

c.1400 Songhay establishes independence from Mali.

Gold trade centered on Sofala and the Zambezi valley in E Africa develops.

Naturalistic bronze castings, using lost-wax technique, being produced at Benin, Nigeria.

City of Great Zimbabwe reaches final form.

EUROPE

1391 Massacre of Jews in Spain.

1392 Trading relations between Hanseatic League and Novgorod established.

Muscovy annexes Nizhniy Novgorod and Suzdal.

1393 Ottoman conquest of Bulgaria; Bayezid annexes Bulgaria to Ottoman Empire.

1394 Habsburgs and Swiss Confederation agree to a 20-year truce; Swiss Confederation now comprises eight cantons.

Jews expelled from France by decree of Charles VI.

Richard II of England campaigns in Ireland.

1395 Timur takes Astrakhan, SW Russia.

1396 Treaty of Leulinghen ends second phase of Hundred Years' War; 28-year truce agreed. Richard II marries Isabelle of France.

Defeat of Crusader army at Nicopolis, Bulgaria, by Bayezid, the Turkish sultan.

1397 Union of Kalmar; Norway, Denmark, and Sweden united.

c.1397 Medici family found the Medici banking house in Florence.

1398 Jan Hus (1369–1415) begins lecturing at Prague university; develops Hussite church reformist movement, influenced by John Wyclif.

1399 Richard II of England's second Irish campaign; he is later deposed, and Henry IV assumes throne (–1413).

Mongol victory over Lithuanians at Vorskla river, Ukraine.

1400 Richard II of England dies, possibly murdered, at Pontefract Castle.

Rebellion of Welsh against English rule, under Owen Glendower.

c.1400 Visconti family dominates N Italy.

Three-masted caravel developed by Portuguese; becomes the major long-distance trading vessel.

Flags used to convey messages at sea.

Leprosy eradicated in Europe.

AMERICAS & AUSTRALASIA

The Ming dynasty

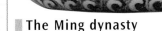

Following the death of the first Ming emperor, Zhu Yuanzhang, in 1398, his fourth son, Chengzu, usurped the imperial throne, calling himself Yunglo. He had been governor of Peking and now made it his capital, employing 200,000 workmen to demolish the mud houses and rebuild in stone and brick, creating what is today called the Forbidden City. Ming expansionism reached its apogee under his leadership. To improve internal communications and take advantage of the growing global trade network, he extended the Grand Canal from Peking to Hangzhou 1,000 miles (1,600 km) away.

Under the Ming dynasty, porcelain became one of China's most successful exports. Blue-and-white wares, such as the vase *above*, were made in vast quantities at the imperial factory. They were highly prized for their artistry of form and decoration, and reached an appreciative European aristocracy through Middle-Eastern intermediaries.

The World in 1400

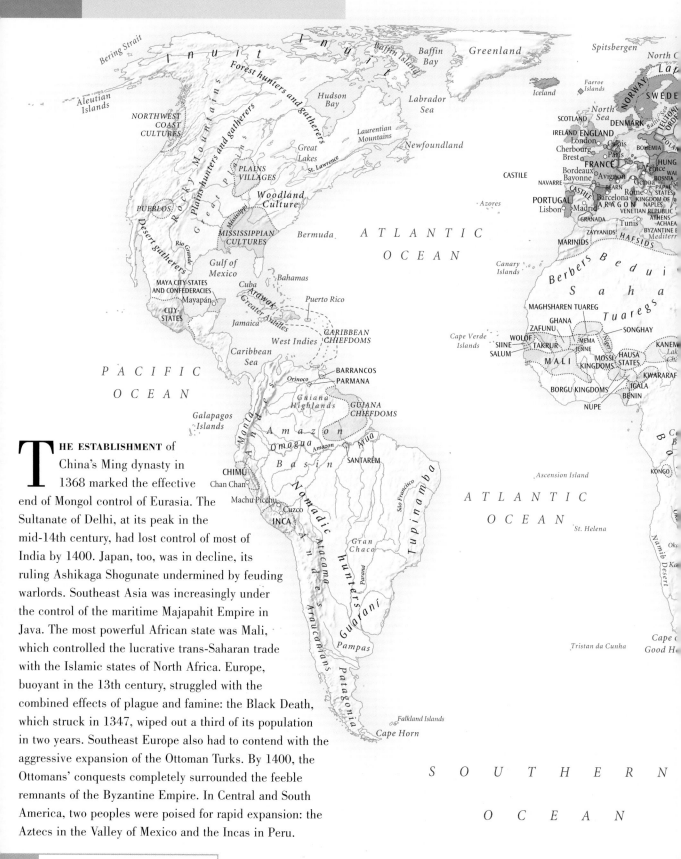

THE ESTABLISHMENT of China's Ming dynasty in 1368 marked the effective end of Mongol control of Eurasia. The Sultanate of Delhi, at its peak in the mid-14th century, had lost control of most of India by 1400. Japan, too, was in decline, its ruling Ashikaga Shogunate undermined by feuding warlords. Southeast Asia was increasingly under the control of the maritime Majapahit Empire in Java. The most powerful African state was Mali, which controlled the lucrative trans-Saharan trade with the Islamic states of North Africa. Europe, buoyant in the 13th century, struggled with the combined effects of plague and famine: the Black Death, which struck in 1347, wiped out a third of its population in two years. Southeast Europe also had to contend with the aggressive expansion of the Ottoman Turks. By 1400, the Ottomans' conquests completely surrounded the feeble remnants of the Byzantine Empire. In Central and South America, two peoples were poised for rapid expansion: the Aztecs in the Valley of Mexico and the Incas in Peru.

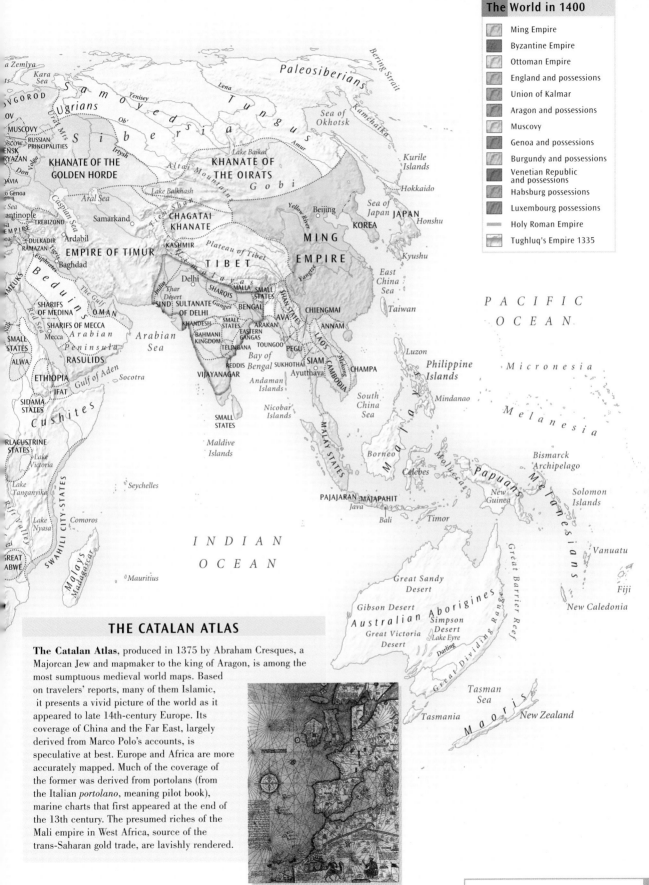

The World in 1400

- Ming Empire
- Byzantine Empire
- Ottoman Empire
- England and possessions
- Union of Kalmar
- Aragon and possessions
- Muscovy
- Genoa and possessions
- Burgundy and possessions
- Venetian Republic and possessions
- Habsburg possessions
- Luxembourg possessions
- Holy Roman Empire
- Tughluq's Empire 1335

a Zemlya
Kara Sea
OVGOROD
Ugrians
Samoyedsia
MUSCOVY
OSCOW
RUSSIAN
ENSK
PRINCIPALITIES
RYAZAN
Ob'
Yenisey
Lena
Tungus
Paleosiberians
Bering Strait
AVIA
Don
Volga
Ural Mts.
Irtysh
Siberia
Altai Mountains
Amur
Sea of Okhotsk
Kamchatka
KHANATE OF THE GOLDEN HORDE
Lake Baikal
KHANATE OF THE OIRATS
Gobi
Kurile Islands
Genoa
Aral Sea
Lake Balkhash
Hokkaido
ea
Caspian Sea
Tien Shan
Yellow River
Beijing
Sea of Japan
JAPAN
antinople
TREBIZOND
Samarkand
CHAGATAI KHANATE
Honshu
a
DULKADIR
Ardabil
KASHMIR
Plateau of Tibet
MING
KOREA
RAMAZAN
Tigris
EMPIRE OF TIMUR
Himalayas
Kyushu
AVIA
Baghdad
Euphrates
TIBET
Yangtze
EMPIRE
East China Sea
MLUKS
Beduins
Delhi
Thar Desert
MALLA
SHAROIS
SMALL STATES
SHAN STATES
CHIENGMAI
Taiwan
The Gulf
SIND
SULTANATE OF DELHI
Ganges
BENGAL
AVA
ANNAM
PACIFIC OCEAN
SHARIFS OF MEDINA
OMAN
KHANDESH
SMALL STATES
ARAKAN
LAOS
Luzon
SHARIFS OF MECCA
Arabian Peninsula
Arabian Sea
BAHMANI KINGDOM
EASTERN GANGAS
TOUNGOO
Philippine Islands
Micronesia
SMALL STATES
Mecca
Red Sea
TELINGANA
TELINGANA
SUKHOTHAI
PEGU
SIAM
CAMBODIA
CHAMPA
Mindanao
ALWA
RASULIDS
REDDIS
VIJAYANAGAR
Andaman Islands
Ayutthaya
South China Sea
Melanesia
ETHIOPIA
Gulf of Aden
Socotra
Nicobar Islands
Mekong
IFAT
SIDAMA STATES
Cushites
Maldive Islands
SMALL STATES
Borneo
Celebes
Malay States
Moluccas
Papuans
Bismarck Archipelago
RLACUSTRINE STATES
Lake Victoria
Seychelles
New Guinea
Solomon Islands
Melanesians
Lake Tanganyika
SWAHILI CITY-STATES
Comoros
INDIAN OCEAN
Java
PAJAJARAN
MAJAPAHIT
Vanuatu
Lake Nyasa
Mauritius
Bali
Timor
Fiji
GREAT ABWE
Malays
Madagascar
Great Sandy Desert
Australian Aborigines
Great Barrier Reef
New Caledonia
Gibson Desert
Simpson Desert
Great Dividing Range
Great Victoria Desert
Lake Eyre
Darling
Tasman Sea
Tasmania
Maoris
New Zealand

THE CATALAN ATLAS

The Catalan Atlas, produced in 1375 by Abraham Cresques, a Majorcan Jew and mapmaker to the king of Aragon, is among the most sumptuous medieval world maps. Based on travelers' reports, many of them Islamic, it presents a vivid picture of the world as it appeared to late 14th-century Europe. Its coverage of China and the Far East, largely derived from Marco Polo's accounts, is speculative at best. Europe and Africa are more accurately mapped. Much of the coverage of the former was derived from portolans (from the Italian *portolano*, meaning pilot book), marine charts that first appeared at the end of the 13th century. The presumed riches of the Mali empire in West Africa, source of the trans-Saharan gold trade, are lavishly rendered.

1400–1600

The Renaissance

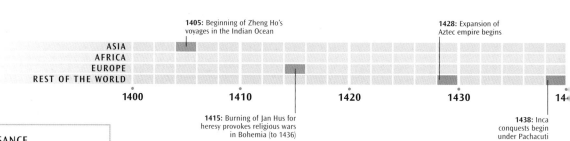

1405: Beginning of Zheng Ho's voyages in the Indian Ocean

1428: Expansion of Aztec empire begins

ASIA				
AFRICA				
EUROPE				
REST OF THE WORLD				
1400	**1410**	**1420**	**1430**	**14**

1415: Burning of Jan Hus for heresy provokes religious wars in Bohemia (to 1436)

1438: Inca conquests begin under Pachacuti

THE TWO CENTURIES between 1400 and 1600 were an era of crucial change, especially for Europe. The period known as the Renaissance saw radical developments in philosophy, culture, and the spirit of scientific enquiry, initially in Italy, then in all the Christian kingdoms of western Europe. Wider familiarity with classical art, literature, and philosophy combined with the sudden availability of printed books to challenge the old certainties of medieval thought with a new spirit of Humanism.

One consequence of this intellectual activity was the questioning of the traditional beliefs of the Catholic Church. The Protestant Reformation, a reaction to the doctrines and authority of the Church of Rome, split Europe in two. The criticisms levelled by the German Martin Luther, initially, in 1517, at the greed and corruption of the Church, sparked off a period of intense theological debate. As the new ideas spread, peasants rose in protest at the tithes paid to the Church, while many rulers, especially the princes of the small north German states, rejected the authority of the Pope. They were joined by the kings of Sweden, Denmark, and England. From 1562 France was wracked by religious civil wars, while in the

Suleyman the Magnificent extended Ottoman rule far into southeastern Europe. In this miniature, he is seen receiving homage from his many Christian vassals.

Netherlands, the northern provinces, which had embraced Protestantism, rose against their Spanish rulers in 1565.

This process of questioning religious and moral values was paralleled by a second, even more rapid development, the expansion of Europe's maritime powers and the first steps in the creation of a worldwide greater European empire. Within 30 years of Columbus's first crossing of the Atlantic in 1492, Magellan's expedition had circumnavigated the globe. Europe's lead in the exploration of the world would shift the global balance of power in its favor.

The Ottomans

To a large extent, it was the new empires in the Old World that sparked Europe's expansionary burst, above all the Islamic empires in Asia and North Africa. The most important in the 15th and early 16th centuries was the Turkish Ottoman

This mural from Isfahan shows a man and a girl taking refreshment in a garden. Figurative art flourished at the cultured Safavid court in the reign of Shah Abbas I.

PICTURE ABOVE:
The mythological figures of Botticelli's Primavera *(c.1478) are a magnificent example of the secular art of the Florentine Renaissance. Painters of the period were inspired by Greek and Roman sculpture and also by classical texts.*

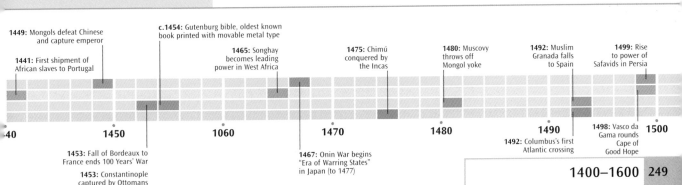

1441: First shipment of African slaves to Portugal

1449: Mongols defeat Chinese and capture emperor

c.1454: Gutenburg bible, oldest known book printed with movable metal type

1465: Songhay becomes leading power in West Africa

1475: Chimú conquered by the Incas

1480: Muscovy throws off Mongol yoke

1492: Muslim Granada falls to Spain

1499: Rise to power of Safavids in Persia

40 — 1450 — 1060 — 1470 — 1480 — 1490 — 1500

1453: Fall of Bordeaux to France ends 100 Years' War

1453: Constantinople captured by Ottomans

1467: Onin War begins "Era of Warring States" in Japan (to 1477)

1492: Columbus's first Atlantic crossing

1498: Vasco da Gama rounds Cape of Good Hope

Empire. As it grew, so the overland routes to the lucrative markets of Central Asia and the Far East were blocked to Europeans. In response, the Portuguese in particular attempted to outflank the Ottomans by pioneering a new sea route around Africa to India and the Spice Islands of the Indonesian archipelago.

But the Ottoman Empire was more than just an inconvenience to European sailors and merchants. Aggressively expansionist, it was an active threat to Christian Europe as a whole. The capture of Constantinople by the Ottomans in 1453 marked the end of the Byzantine empire. It had outlived the Roman Empire by nearly a thousand years, serving for much of that time as a bulwark against Muslim expansion into Europe. Having made Constantinople their capital, the Ottomans followed up this success with sustained victories in Europe, the Near East, and North Africa.

Under Selim I (1512–20), Ottoman armies conquered Syria and Palestine and overthrew the Mamluk rulers of Egypt. With command of the Red Sea, they were able to take control of the Hejaz and the two holy cities of Islam, Mecca and Medina. Selim's son, Suleyman I (the Magnificent), set his sights on Christian Europe, conquering Hungary in 1526 and laying siege to Vienna in 1529.

Ottoman domination of the Middle East was completed by their capture of Baghdad in 1534 and their navy established supremacy in the eastern Mediterranean. Though checked by a combined Spanish-Italian fleet at Lepanto in 1571, the Ottomans, rich, populous and well-organized, remained a major threat to Europe, in particular to the Habsburg empire, until the 19th century.

Persia and India

The Ottomans were a threat, too, to their new neighbor to the east, the Persian Safavid empire, which arose and spread rapidly around 1500 under Shah Ismail I. Conflict between the Shi'ite Safavids and the Sunni Ottomans would continue until the Safavid decline in the 17th century. The Safavid empire was important, too, for an exceptional cultural flowering, a process matched by its equally sophisticated neighbor to the east, the Mughal empire, founded by Babur in 1526 when he swept aside the disintegrating sultanate of Delhi. By 1600, the Mughals controlled the whole of north and central India.

European trade with Asia

But, however powerful, none of the Islamic empires was able to prevent the arrival of the Portuguese in the Indian Ocean. Vasco da Gama, who reached India in 1498, and the mariners who followed him exploited local Arab knowledge to master its long-established trade routes. By 1600, the Portuguese had established settlements on the east coast of Africa, the west coast of India, in

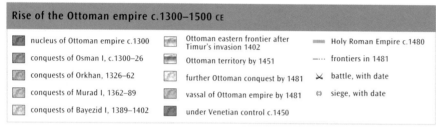

Rise of the Ottoman empire c.1300–1500 CE

- nucleus of Ottoman empire c.1300
- conquests of Osman I, c.1300–26
- conquests of Orkhan, 1326–62
- conquests of Murad I, 1362–89
- conquests of Bayezid I, 1389–1402
- Ottoman eastern frontier after Timur's invasion 1402
- Ottoman territory by 1451
- further Ottoman conquest by 1481
- vassal of Ottoman empire by 1481
- under Venetian control c.1450
- Holy Roman Empire c.1480
- frontiers in 1481
- battle, with date
- siege, with date

The Ottoman state, founded by Osman I at the end of the 13th century, grew rapidly at the expense of the Byzantine empire and the Christian states of the Balkans. In 1453 the Ottomans captured Constantinople, which they made their capital. They remained the dominant force in the Islamic world until World War I.

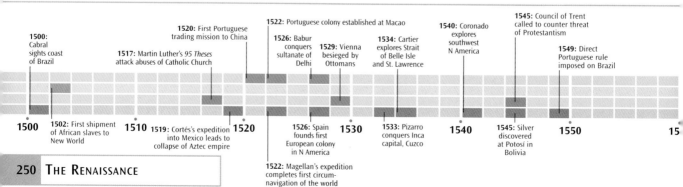

1500: Cabral sights coast of Brazil

1502: First shipment of African slaves to New World

1517: Martin Luther's *95 Theses* attack abuses of Catholic Church

1519: Cortés's expedition into Mexico leads to collapse of Aztec empire

1520: First Portuguese trading mission to China

1522: Portuguese colony established at Macao

1522: Magellan's expedition completes first circumnavigation of the world

1526: Babur conquers sultanate of Delhi

1526: Spain founds first European colony in N America

1529: Vienna besieged by Ottomans

1533: Pizarro conquers Inca capital, Cuzco

1534: Cartier explores Strait of Belle Isle and St. Lawrence

1540: Coronado explores southwest N America

1545: Silver discovered at Potosí in Bolivia

1545: Council of Trent called to counter threat of Protestantism

1549: Direct Portuguese rule imposed on Brazil

1500 1510 1520 1530 1540 1550 15

Sri Lanka, the Malay states and the Moluccas (the Spice Islands), and at Macao on the coast of Ming China.

Ironically, in the early 15th century, before the Portuguese reached the Indian Ocean, Ming China had seemed set to become a major force in the region, sponsoring a series of epic trading voyages across it, before, in 1433, suddenly abandoning its maritime ventures. The Ming were happy to take advantage of the Europeans' global trading network. Buoyed by huge inflows of silver from the New World, their economy boomed. Japan, too, shortly to be consolidated under the virtual dictatorship of Oda Nobunaga in 1582, benefited from trading contacts with the Portuguese when in 1570 Nagasaki was opened to foreign trade.

The New World

Empire building was not restricted to the Old World. The New World also laid claim to two spectacular empires: that of the Aztecs, which by 1520 dominated central Mexico; and that of the Incas, which in less than a century had become the preeminent state in South America. Yet, however well established, both collapsed in a matter of years to the invading Spanish, the Aztecs between 1519 and 1521, the Incas between 1531 and 1532. The Spanish conquests were accomplished by tiny forces, vastly outnumbered by the armies of the indigenous peoples. Their success was due to a number of factors. Guns, armor, and horses played their part, but more important was the ability of the Spanish conquistadores to exploit the local political situation. In Mexico, Hernán Cortés formed an alliance with tribes subject to the Aztecs that welcomed the chance of release from Aztec oppression. Francisco Pizarro arrived in Peru at a moment when the Inca had been

seriously weakened by civil war and an epidemic of a European disease (probably smallpox) to which they had no resistance.

In place of the Aztec and Inca empires, the Spanish created two huge colonial domains, the Viceroyalties of New Spain and of Peru. Their production of gold and above all silver made Spain a world power, a process reinforced by its capture of the Philippines in 1565, which allowed Spain to create a global trading network, shipping silver from the Americas to the Philippines to pay for silk and spices from China and the East.

Expansion within Europe

Europe itself was not immune to empire building. In western Europe this mostly took the form of state consolidation, especially in France, England, and Spain, where in 1492 the last Islamic foothold had been prised loose. The first half of the 16th century was marked by the intense rivalry between Francis I of France (1515–47) and Charles V, Holy Roman Emperor (1519–58) and king of Spain (1516–56). The emperor had inherited the Low Countries and the Austrian Habsburg lands as well as Spain and its extensive possessions in Italy. Throughout his reign, the French king devoted most of his energies to trying to limit Habsburg power in Europe, even forming an alliance against Charles with the Ottoman Turks. Though Francis failed in his ambitions during his lifetime, the united European empire of the Habsburgs did not survive long after his death. In 1555 Charles announced his abdication, leaving Spain and the Low Countries to his son Philip II and his Austrian possessions to his brother Ferdinand.

The wars between Francis I and Charles V were all fought against the tumultuous background of the Reformation. To the east, Russia was untouched by these events and there the

THE EUROPEAN DISCOVERY OF NORTH AMERICA

The rapid European discoveries in the Caribbean and Central America were echoed further north by the almost equally swift exploration and mapping of the eastern seaboard of North America. Only five years after Columbus's first Atlantic crossing, the Italian John Cabot, reached Newfoundland, a feat repeated by Portuguese explorers three years later. But the key voyage was made by another Italian, Giovanni Verrazano, in 1524. His north-south voyage from Florida to Newfoundland established for the first time that Columbus's and Cabot's discoveries were only the extremities of a continuous landmass. This unexpected discovery provoked disappointment rather than excitement. Like almost all his contemporaries, Verrazano had been hoping to find an easily sailed route to the riches of the East. That North America could be an exploitable asset in its own right was a realization that grew only very slowly.

The world's oldest known globe, made by Martin Behaim of Nuremberg. Produced just before Columbus's first voyage in 1492, it shows no trace of the Americas.

sudden expansion of the small principality of Muscovy under the first czar, Ivan III, in the late 15th century was a case of genuine empire building. It continued in the 16th century, so that by 1556, with the defeat of the Khanate of Astrakhan, Russia had become a major power.

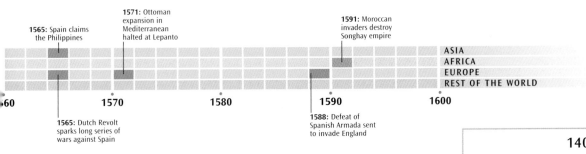

1565: Spain claims the Philippines

1571: Ottoman expansion in Mediterranean halted at Lepanto

1591: Moroccan invaders destroy Songhay empire

ASIA
AFRICA
EUROPE
REST OF THE WORLD

60   1570   1580   1590   1600

1565: Dutch Revolt sparks long series of wars against Spain

1588: Defeat of Spanish Armada sent to invade England

Donatello's David

The artists of the Renaissance, immersed in humanist ideals, began to experiment with the rendition of the human body in a wholly natural condition, which contrasted strongly with the stylized images of medieval art. The Florentine sculptor Donatello (1386 –1466) had a profound influence on Renaissance painters. His bronze statue of a virtually nude David was the first freestanding nude sculpture since antiquity. It is a fine example of the combination of Christian and pagan elements in Renaissance art. The figure is from the Old Testament, but the rendition is heavily influenced by classical Greek sculpture.

Stonemasons and sculptors

The Renaissance architects rejected the Gothic style in favor of a classical-influenced style, with arches, columns, capitals, and a feeling of ordered simplicity. Filippo Brunelleschi (1377–1466) pioneered Renaissance architecture when he used classical principles to construct the vast dome that crowned the new cathedral in Florence. In the late 14th and 15th centuries, the wealthy city-states of the Italian peninsula vied with each other in their quest for ever-more magnificent churches and public buildings, ensuring that stonemasons and sculptors (*below*) were in great demand.

ASIA

1401 Sack of Baghdad by Timur for the second time.

1402 Ottomans defeated by Timur at Ankara.

1403 *Yongluo Dadian*, Chinese encyclopedia, completed.

1404 Opening of trade relations between Ming China and Japan.

1405 The Registan, Samarkand, built by Timur, one of the glories of his capital.

Death of Timur, while leading an expedition against Ming China.

1433 Beginning of Chinese admiral Zheng He's seven voyages in the Indian Ocean (–1433).

1406 Building of Timur's mausoleum, Samarkand.

1427 Occupation of Annam in Vietnam by Ming China.

1424 **1409** Beginning of a series of unsuccessful Ming campaigns against the Mongols (–1424).

AFRICA

1402 Castilian navigators and settlers reach the Canaries.

1406 Major Arab diplomat and historian, ibn Khaldun, completes *Muqaddima*, the first attempt in any language to elucidate the laws governing the rise and fall of civilizations.

Death of ibn Khaldun.

1410 Death of Kanajeji, king of Kano, during whose rule the Hausa came to dominate sub-Saharan trade and politics; Hausa cavalry equipped with iron weaponry and armor.

EUROPE

1401 Formal union by marriage, of Poland and Lithuania. Becomes largest state in Europe, and solid bastion against Mongol attacks from east.

1402 The reformer Jan Hus begins to preach in Bethlehem chapel in Prague.

Henry of Castile sends an expedition to conquer the Canary Islands.

1405 Florence conquers Pisa, establishing access to the sea.

1406 Republic of Genoa takes control of Corsica.

Giacomo d'Angelo translates Ptolemy's *Geography*; beginning of formal cartography in Europe.

1408 Donatello's *David*, early masterpiece of Florentine Renaissance sculpture.

1409 Trading agreement between England and Hanseatic League.

1410 Ferdinand, regent of Castile, takes Antequera; becomes king of Aragon.

Battle of Tannenberg; Polish defeat of Teutonic Order.

Italian architect/inventor, Brunelleschi, experiments with coiled springs to develop mechanical clock.

AMERICAS & AUSTRALASIA

1410 Under the leadership of Viracocha Inca, the Inca empire in Peru is expanding and the hierarchical structure of its society is growing more formalized.

The voyages of Zheng He (1405–1433)

Zheng He was a Chinese admiral and diplomat selected by the emperor to help extend the Chinese maritime and commercial influence throughout the regions bordering the Indian Ocean.

1405–1407	To Java, Sumatra, Ceylon, Calicut
1407–1409	To Thailand, Cochin, Calicut, Champa
1409–1411	To Champa, Java, Malacca, Ceylon, Calicut
1413–1415	To Ceylon, Maldives, Persian Gulf
1417–1419	To Persian Gulf, Aden, Mogadishu
1421–1422	To Aden, Dhofar, Thailand
1431–1433	To Andaman Islands, Chittagong, Persian Gulf, Jeddah, Malindi, Ceylon

Medieval chronicles

During the Middle Ages there was a great explosion of history-writing, from the lives of saints to sophisticated treatises, chronicles of war, and collections of stories and legends. All these works share a uniquely medieval world view; no distinction is made between past and present, local and cosmopolitan, human and miraculous. It is therefore impossible to read most of these works as accurate history in the conventional sense.

Chronicles of war were popular in later medieval Europe, and their authors became internationally famous. Jean Froissart (1337–1410) and Jean Wavrin (1400–1471) were both Frenchmen, who traveled freely across national borders to collect information about war. Froissart's accounts are full of praise for chivalric deeds and are highly romanticized. Wavrin presented his magnificently illuminated *Chronique d'Angleterre* to King Edward IV of England.

The main subject of Froissart's Chronicles was the "honorable adventures and feats of arms" of the Hundred Years' War. This scene depicts an unsuccessful French expedition to North Africa in 1390.

Calendar page for June from Les Très Riches Heures *by the Limbourg brothers – one of the very few great medieval works of art created for a private patron. The brothers were among the first to render specific landscape scenes with accuracy.*

Books of Hours

The peoples of the Middle Ages measured time primarily by the annual march of the seasons and the daily progress of the sun. In Christian Europe, the sense of time was intimately bound up with the rites and festivals of the Christian year, and with the agricultural cycle. From the 10th century, wealthy people commissioned illuminated books (Books of Hours) of prayers that could be offered up at the appropriate hours of the day (matins, vespers, and so on). The Books of Hours usually began with a calendar which helped the reader follow the succession of Christian feasts throughout the year.

Les Très Riches Heures of Jean, Duc de Berry, commissioned in the early 15th century, is one of the finest examples of this artform. It contains a calendar section in which each month is accompanied by a miniature illustrating appropriately seasonal scenes.

The great feasts of the liturgical year – Christmas, Easter, Ascension, Pentecost, and All Saints – were celebrated with special services, banquets, and other festivities. In many ways, holy days mirrored the agricultural cycle. Most religious holidays avoided the busiest months of the agricultural year (June–September), and were clustered around the more leisurely days of winter.

1414 Paramesvara, prince of Palembang, converts to Islam.

1415 Portuguese capture Ceuta in Morocco, beginning of Portuguese overseas empire.

An embassy from Malindi in E Africa (coast of Kenya) is sent to China.

1418 Madeira discovered and settled by Portuguese under Prince Henry the Navigator. They plant sugarcane from Sicily.

1419 Sejong becomes king of Korea; florescence of Korean arts, and suppression of Japanese pirate raids on Korean coast (–1451).

1420 Ming move capital to Peking (Beijing); probably largest city in the world at this time.

1411 Aragon and Portugal reach peace after over 30 years of warfare.

c.1411 Trinity icons, Zagorsk monastery, completed by Andrei Rublev; apogee of Russian icon painting.

Trigger for cannon developed in Germany.

1413 Henry V accedes to English throne upon death of his father (–1422); begins to build fleet, inaugurating a new phase of Hundred Years' War.

1414 Medicis become papal bankers.

Heretical Lollard rebellion crushed in England.

c.1414 *De Imitatione Christi* (Imitation of Christ) by Thomas à Kempis, major work of medieval theology.

1415 Henry V invades France; campaigns in NW France, with major English victory at Agincourt.

Jan Hus burned for heresy at Constance.

1417 End of the Great Schism in the Catholic church.

1419 Defenestration of Prague; Catholics murdered by Hussites, German bürgermeister thrown from window by Czech crowds. Beginning of Hussite wars in Bohemia (–1436).

Henry V captures Rouen, most of Normandy under English control.

Prince Henry the Navigator founds observatory and school of navigation at Sagres, S Portugal.

1420 Treaty of Troyes; Henry V marries Catherine of France.

c.1420 Brunelleschi develops frame for accurately drawing in perspective. Begins construction of dome of Florence cathedral, largest vaulted span in Europe (completed 1434.)

c.1420 Chimú conquer Lambayeque culture, N Peru.

In Eastern Christian tradition, icons were venerated representations of sacred events or people in mural painting, wood, or mosaic. The most sophisticated work originated in Constantinople, where artists adhered to long traditions of austere lines, dark colors, and established patterns. But in the 13th and 14th centuries, Russian icons, especially from Novgorod, used a lighter palette of colors; faces were softened, and composition was simplified.

The Holy Trinity (c.1410) by the great icon painter, Andrei Rublev (c.1370–1430). Rublev made use of a technique called sfumato, a soft blending of light and shade.

Jan Hus (c.1370–1415)

Jan Hus was dean of the philosophy faculty at the University of Prague. An ardent critic of the misdeeds of the clergy, his teachings anticipated the Lutheran reformation by a century. His passionate support for church reform, together with his Bohemian nationalism, brought him into conflict with the church authorities. At the Council of Constance he was found guilty of heresy and burned at the stake.

Tommaso Masaccio (1401–1428)

Renaissance painting was revolutionized by the work of the Florentine artist Masaccio. His use of the newfound principles of perspective, as well as the solemn grandeur and simplicity of his figures was a new, and surprising, artistic departure. His use of the technique known as *chiaroscuro*, which conveys the reflection of light from three-dimensional surfaces, helps give his work an extraordinary sense of depth. Masaccio's paintings showing the expulsion of Adam and Eve from the Garden of Eve (*above*) are masterpieces of psychological insight. By placing his figures within a classical frame, he heightens the sensation of perspective, at the same time linking both Christian and classical references. His influence was far-reaching; Michelangelo sketched Masaccio's works in order to learn his techniques.

ASIA

1424 End of long Ming campaign against Mongols (against 1409).

1427 Ming forces expelled from Annam, N Vietnam.

AFRICA

1427 The Ethiopian emperor, Yeshaq sends envoys to Aragon in Spain to forge an alliance against Islam.

1430 Sultans of Kilwa begin grand building program.

EUROPE

1421 Henry V campaigns in region of Paris.

Patents introduced in Italy.

La Belle Dame Sans Merci by Alain Chartier, ironic apogee of chivalric poetry.

More than 100,000 people die in the Netherlands as the sea spills into low-lyig land, forming the Zuider Zee.

1422 Lisbon becomes the seat of Portugal's government.

1423 Beginning of 30-year war between Milan and Florence.

1424 Mamluks begin a series of unsuccessful attempts to invade Cyprus (–1426).

James I of Scotland, newly freed by the English after 18 years in captivity, is crowned King of Scotland.

1425 Power struggles lead to civil war in Muscovy (–1450).

c.1425 Masaccio begins to paint in naturalistic style, using perspective; birth of Florentine Renaissance painting.

1428 Peace agreed between Milan and Venice.

1429 English siege of Orléans relieved by Joan of Arc, who leads French recovery in the Hundred Years' War and recaptures Rheims.

1430 Ottomans take Salonica from Venice.

c.1430 Plate armor begins to replace chain mail.

Emergence of Modern English from Middle English.

AMERICAS & AUSTRALASIA

1425 Maya under Quicab dominate highland Guatemala.

1428 Expansion of Aztec empire begins. Aztecs conquer Atzcapotzalco, becoming the dominant state in C Mexico, consolidated by alliance with Texcoco and Tlacopan. Itzcóatl becomes ruler of Aztec empire.

In this 15th-century miniature, the Duke of Orléans, captured at Agincourt in 1415, is shown imprisoned in the Tower, where he was held for 25 years.

The Tower of London

Begun by William the Conqueror in the 11th century, the central keep of the Tower of London – known as the White Tower – was begun in about 1078 and built of white limestone from Caen in Normandy. During the 13th and 14th centuries the fortifications were extended beyond the city wall, and over the following centuries the Tower served as a royal residence, a prison, and a place of execution. The 13th-century watergate, the main approach from the Thames river, is known as Traitor's Gate, since it was the route by which many prisoners were brought into captivity.

Temple of Heaven, Peking

The Ming capital at Peking (Beijing), begun c.1400, was designed to make a statement of imperial power and majesty. Within the walled outer city was the Imperial City, enclosed within its own 5-mile- (8-km-) long wall. It in turn enclosed the walls of the Forbidden City, open only to those on official business, which was dominated by palaces, throne halls, court-yards, and terraces. The Temple of Heaven, *left*, located in the outer city, consists of three main buildings: the Hall of Prayer for Good Harvests, the Imperial Vault of Heaven and the circular Mound Altar.

Joan of Arc (c.1412–1431)

Canonized in 1920, the French national heroine, Joan of Arc, led a divinely inspired campaign to "drive the English out of France" during the Hundred Years' War. In the 1420s, the throne of France was being disputed between the Valois dauphin, Charles, and Henry VI of England, who, with the support of Philip, Duke of Burgundy, was occupying northern France. In 1427, the year of Joan's divine calling and five years after the king's death, Charles had not yet been crowned because Reims, the traditional place of crownings, was in English-held territory.

Born c.1412, Joan was a peasant girl from Domrémy in Lorraine. Claiming to have heard the voices of saints Michael, Margaret, and Catherine, she persuaded the religious authorities and the dauphin by her piousness and dignity to engage the English at Orléans rather than Poitiers. Armed as a soldier, she led the French in a string of victories culminating in Charles's coronation at Reims in 1429. However, his troops failed to take Paris and Joan was captured by the English at Compiègne in 1430. In 1431 she was tried in Rouen as a heretic and burned at the stake. Charles later ordered an enquiry into the verdict, which was revoked in 1456.

ASIA

1433 Ming China bans construction of oceangoing junks to limit trade with the west; beginning of Chinese isolationism.

Completion of Zheng He's seven voyages in the Indian Ocean.

1434 Capital of the Khymer kingdom in SE Asia moves from Angkor to Phnom Penh.

1438 Death of Mamluk sultan, al-Zahiri; beginning of Mamluk decline.

1439 Poggio Bracciolini records Asian journeys of Niccolò Conti.

1440 Widespread agrarian rebellions in China.

AFRICA

1431 Ming admiral Zheng He reaches Malindi on E African coast; trades silk and bullion for lions, rhinos, and myrrh.

1433 Tuaregs from NW Sahara regain Timbuktu from Mali, gaining control of sub-Saharan trade routes.

1434 Portuguese navigator, Gil Eanes, passes Cape Bojador, W Africa.

1441 ▼

1436 Portuguese navigators begin exploration of W African coast.

Monumental funerary mosque for Qait Bey built in Cairo (–1480).

EUROPE

1431 Joan of Arc burned for heresy by English at Rouen, France.

Henry VI of England crowned king of France in Paris.

Truce between England and Scotland.

Hussites win a series of victories against German troops attempting to suppress them.

1432 Portuguese discover an uninhabited archipelago in the N Atlantic, which they name the Azores.

1434 Battle of Lipany; victory of moderate Hussites over extremists.

Riksdag, Swedish parliament, convenes for first time.

Cosimo de Medici becomes ruler of Florence; Florentine republic emerging as major center of the arts.

1435 Congress of Arras; Burgundy, an English ally, makes terms with France.

Alliance of Burgundy and England collapses.

Treaty of Arras confirms Charles VII as king of France.

c.1435 Bruges in Flanders emerges as commercial and artistic capital of NW Europe.

1437 Emperor Sigismund appointed king of Bohemia.

c.1437 Counterpoint in music developed by John Dunstable.

1439 Greek and Roman churches agree to unite, recognizing the pope as leader of the church.

1440 Eton college, England, founded.

c.1440 Quadrant developed in Europe.

AMERICAS & AUSTRALASIA

1438 Incas rise to power as Pachacuti becomes ruler of Inca empire, which under his rule achieves greatest extent, dominating the C Andes (–1471). Beginning of period of aggressive Inca conquests as Incas defeat Chanca, attack Lake Titicaca basin, and establish an upland empire.

1440 Motecuhzoma I becomes ruler of Aztec empire.

Timbuktu

This West African city was founded by the Tuareg nomads in 1100 as a trading post. When it was assimilated by the Islamic Mali empire in the 1300s, it prospered on the trans-Saharan trade in gold and salt and became a university city of great mosques. Although the Tuareg regained it in 1433, they ruled from the desert and its prosperity survived.

Il Duomo, Florence

Europe's fourth largest cathedral is topped by a spectacular dome designed by the Florentine architect Filippo Brunelleschi. Completed in 1434, this has an outer shell supported by a thicker inner shell and was built without scaffolding. The Baptistry, where Dante was baptized and which may date from the 4th century, is famous for its bronze doors (1401–52) by Lorenzo Ghiberti. The campanile was designed by Giotto in 1334.

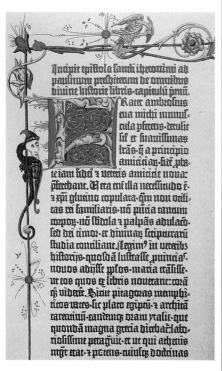

The Bible published by Johannes Gutenberg in 1456 was in Latin (Vulgate). At least 163 Vulgate editions of the Bible were published in the 15th century; the Gutenberg is one of the finest.

The printing revolution

The advent of movable metal type in Europe was a revolutionary advance in mass communications. The new technology was pioneered by Johannes Gutenberg of Mainz in Germany, who published a papal proclamation in 1454. Just two years later, he published his first Bible. By 1520, there were more than 200 different printed editions of the Bible in existence. Many of these were in the vernacular, ranging from German to Catalan, Dutch, and Czech.

As printing technology spread throughout Europe, the price of books fell, and literacy became more widespread. Ideas began to travel rapidly, encouraging cross-cultural exchange. Laws and ordinances became available to a wider public, political decrees were publicly aired, propaganda and news were more widely available.

Printing was intimately connected with the Reformation (*see pages 274–5*). Dissenting views were published in pamphlet form, and disseminated widely. Between 1518 and 1523, as many as 500,000 publications circulated in Germany. Many were in the vernacular, rather than in Latin, which meant that they were available to almost everyone.

1443 Great Library at Herat, Persia founded.

1445 Conversion of Malacca (Malaysia) to Islam.

1447 Persia, Afghanistan, and N India regain independence following death of Timur.

Death of Shah Rukh (son of Timur).

1449 Death of Ulugh Beg, Timur's grandson, ruler and astronomer, author of accurate set of astronomical tables.

Mongols defeat Chinese and capture Ming emperor.

Yoshimasa, eighth shogun of Japan, during whose reign imperial court goes into decline.

c.1450 Islam spreads over much of East Indies.

Apogee of Ming enamel-working.

1441 First shipment of African slaves to Portugal.

Act of Union signed between Church of Ethiopia and Church of Rome.

1442 Al-Maqrizi writes detailed topographical survey of Egypt.

1444 Portuguese navigators reach Cape Verde.

c.1450 Beginning of decline of Great Zimbabwe, probably due to hyperinflation.

Mwenemutapa (Mutapa) empire founded, S Africa. Eclipse of Great Zimbabwe by Mutapa empire.

Songhay empire, C W Africa, reaches greatest extent; Islamic university founded at Timbuktu.

1441 Foundation of King's College, Cambridge by Henry VI.

Death of Jan van Eyck, leading exponent of early oil Renaissance painting in NW Europe.

1442 Hospitallers repel attacks on Rhodes by Mamluks (–1444).

Alfonso V of Aragon conquers Naples, and is crowned king.

1443 Albania proclaims independence after governor George Kastrioti converts to Christianity.

Epirus captured by Ottomans.

1444 Ottomans defeat crusade of Varna; death of Ladislas III of Poland and Hungary.

c.1445 Johannes Gutenberg introduces printing press in Germany, using movable type.

1448 Accession of Constantine X, the last East Roman (Byzantine) emperor.

Ottomans under Murad II win decisive victory over Hungary at Kosovo.

1449 Truce of Tours broken by English: last phase of Hundred Years' War sees France retake Rouen and reconquer Normandy (–1450).

1450 Alliance of Florence, Naples, and Milan dominates N and C Italy, isolating the papal states.

Francesco Sforza assumes dukedom of Milan; begins to build cultural and political powerbase.

Norway accepts Act of Union with Denmark; Sweden in state of civil war.

Foundation of Barcelona University.

c.1450 Nicholas of Cusa (Germany) develops concave lens to correct short-sightedness.

Gold in use for filling teeth.

1445 Incas establish presence on Pacific seaboard.

c.1450 Population crash in Middle Mississippi area, N America, possibly due to disease.

An Aztec priest is shown removing the heart from a sacrificial victim. During the last decades of Aztec rule at least 15,000 humans a year were sacrificed. The Aztecs believed that their deities had to be fed human blood to prevent the end of the world. Sacrifice also terrorized the Aztecs' neighbors.

The rise of the Aztecs

In 1428, the Aztec king, Itzcóatl, formed an alliance with the two adjacent states of Texcoco and Tlacopan and overthrew their powerful neighbors the Tapenecs. Before long the Aztecs controlled a vast empire, with a population of 10 million people. The great city of Tenochtitlán, which by now contained hundreds of temples, three huge pyramids, a royal palace, and two vast markets was the absolute center of the empire and a holy place. Complex irrigation works and land reclamation schemes created a fertile hinterland. But the Aztec homeland lacked many natural resources, and it seems likely that the Aztecs turned to conquest to obtain important commodities such as corn, metals, and jade.

The Aztec empire was ruled by a priest-king, elected by a council of nobles, priests, and warriors. A large professional army was dedicated to conquest and obtaining tribute from surrounding territories. Conquered lands also provided the Aztecs with a plentiful supply of human beings destined for sacrifice in Tenochtitlán. When the Spanish arrived in 1519, disaffected native groups rallied to the colonists' cause, and within two years the mighty Aztec empire had fallen and the capital renamed Mexico.

Sandro Botticelli (1444–1510)

Born Alessandro di Mariano Filipepi, Sandro Botticelli trained under the great Florentine painter Fra Filippo Lippi and then spent most of his life in Florence, working under the patronage of Lorenzo de' Medici. However, he did spend some time in Rome where he helped decorate the Sistine Chapel. In common with other Renaissance artists, he turned to the classical myths for inspiration. The above detail of *Primavera* (Spring) shows the Three Graces from his masterpiece depicting the story of the nymph Chloris.

Topkapi Palace, Constantinople

After his conquest of Constantinople in 1453 the Ottoman sultan Mehmet II began rebuilding the wrecked city. The most splendid new building was the the Topkapi Palace, designed as his private residence and seat of government. Built between 1454 and 1472, it was conceived as a series of pavilions, or "kiosks," set in four huge courtyards. One of the most important was the Çinili Kiosk (Pavilion of the Tiles) pictured *above*.

ASIA

1451 First Pathan (Afghan) dynasty, the Lodi, established at Delhi.

1453 With fall of Constantinople to Ottoman Turks, first Asian dynasty to rule in Europe becomes established.

c.1460 Ming establish porcelain factory to create exports for the west.

AFRICA

1460 Sunni Ali, king of Songhay (–1490).

EUROPE	AMERICAS & AUSTRALASIA	The fall of Constantinople

EUROPE

1452 Lorenzo Ghiberti completes *Gates of Paradise* bronze relief doors of the baptistery, Florence Cathedral.

1453 Fall of Bordeaux to France ends Hundred Years' War. England loses all territory in France except Calais.

Constantinople falls to Ottomans, ending Eastern Roman Empire.

Ottomans convert cathedral of Hagia Sophia, Constantinople, into a mosque.

1454 Peace of Lodi ends wars in Italy.

Beginning of Thirteen Years' War between Poland and Teutonic Order.

Foundatation of Topkapi Place at Constantinople.

1455 Civil war in England between Yorkist and Lancastrian rival dynastic houses, the Wars of the Roses (–1485).

Completion of Palazzo Venezia in Rome, archetypal Renaissance palace.

1456 Hungarians defeat the Ottomans at Belgrade.

Ottomans capture Athens.

Vlad the Impaler, king of Romania (–1477). His brutality gave rise to the legend of Dracula.

Le Petit Testament by François Villon, leading early French poet and criminal.

Alessandro Botticelli, leading Florentine painter, completes *Primavera*.

1457 Christian of Denmark and Norway crowned king of Sweden.

Teutonic Knights lose Marienburg to the Poles; relocate headquarters to Königsberg.

1459 Annexation of Serbia by the Turks.

1460 Schleswig-Holstein comes under Danish control at Treaty of Ribe.

Major Yorkist defeat at Wakefield, England; Richard, duke of York, killed in battle.

Ottomans complete conquest of the Peloponnese.

AMERICAS & AUSTRALASIA

The fall of Constantinople

After a 54-day siege, the cannon of Sultan Mehmet II succeeded in tearing a huge hole in the great, double city walls built by Theodosius II between 412 and 422 to protect Constantinople. Stretching 4 miles (6.5 km) and fortified with 192 towers and 11 gates, they had remained unbreached until Mehmet II's 100,000-strong army burst through on May 29, 1453. Mehmet II had come to the throne in 1451 as sultan of the Ottoman state, which, since its foundation in c.1300, had expanded by 1362 to occupy all Byzantine lands except the city-state of Constantinople and a small area to its west.

Once inside the city, the Turks met fierce resistance from the Byzantines, who were led in person by Emperor Constantine XI. He was killed in the fighting and within hours the city fell, marking the end of the Byzantine empire.

Known as "the Conqueror," Mehmet II was an enlightened and cultured leader as well as a gifted military tactician. He made Constantinople his capital, repopulating it with a mixture of force and encouragement and turning it into a cosmopolitan city of Muslims, Jews, and Christians.

The fall of Constantinople removed the major Christian stronghold barring Islam's spread to the west.

White stone-glazed Thai figurine from the time of the reign of King Trailok.

1461 Ottomans take Christian city of Trebizond, N Anatolia.

1465 Beginning of Songhay expansion under Sunni Ali. Songhay begins raids on Mali and replaces Mali as major power in sub-Saharan W Africa.

1467 Onin war begins "Era of Warring States" in Japan (–1477).

1468 Ottomans conquer Karaman.

1468 Songhay under Sunni Ali expels Tuaregs from Timbuktu.

King Trailok

Trailok, eighth king of Siam (Thailand) (1448–1488), was an energetic leader who reformed the administration and established a centralized political system that lasted until the late 19th century. He formalized the division of responsibilities among government departments. He also stabilized the structure of Siamese society by assigning all his subjects a numerical rank – this was expressed in terms of units of land, with the lowliest freeman being assigned a rank of 10 acres (4 ha). In 1468, he issued a law that clarified the succession to the throne.

Trailok's reign was beset by warfare with the kingdom of Lan Na, in the north. As his empire expanded, Trailok moved his capital north to P'itsanulok. He also extended Siamese influence southward into the Malay peninsula.

1470 Russian trading mission, led by Afanasii Nikitin, arrives in Bidar, N India.

1470 Portuguese start trading on Gold Coast of W Africa.

1461–1470

EUROPE

1461 Yorkists defeat Lancastrians at Towton, W England; Henry VI of England deposed, replaced by Edward IV.

Gunpowder manufactured in England.

1462 Ivan III the Great assumes power in Muscovy (–1505); beginning of Muscovite expansion and campaigns against Tartars.

1466 Second Treaty of Toruń; Prussia becomes a fief of Poland; Teutonic Order loses control of W Prussia.

1469 Marriage of Ferdinand II of Aragon and Isabella of Castile; unification of kingdoms to form kingdom of Spain.

Lorenzo de Medici the Magnificent assumes control of republic of Florence.

Translation of works of Plato into Italian by Marsilio Ficino.

1470 Henry VI briefly restored to English throne (–1471).

Ottomans recapture Negroponte from Venice.

Astrolabe widely used by European navigators as means of establishing latitude.

First printing press established in France, at Sorbonne, Paris.

AMERICAS & AUSTRALASIA

1473 **1469** Axayacatl assumes control of Aztec empire (–1481).

1471 **c.1470** Conquest of Chimú empire by the Incas.

Yi Korea (1392–1910)

When the Mongol empire collapsed in 1353, a new Korean dynasty, the Yi, arose. China considered Korea a client state, and Chinese cultural influences were very strong during this period. The Yi administration was modeled on Chinese bureaucracy, and Buddhism was displaced by the puritanical state religion of Neo-Confucianism. Following state redistribution of land, a new rural aristocracy was created, called the *yangban*. Although Korea's economic development was hampered by the country's mountainous landscape, a very distinctive Korean culture emerged. The 15th century was a brilliant period in Korean history, and the Confucian state placed a high value on education and learning.

Stone statues of civil and military officers, some over *6 feet (1.8 m) in height, were erected in front of the tombs of members of the Korean royal family at Chim Jon, near Seoul.*

Wars of the Roses

Fought between the Houses of Lancaster and York for the English throne, both claimed the right throught descent from the sons of Edward III. The Lancastrian victors started the Tudor dynasty.

1452	Richard of York tries to remove Henry VI's favorite, Somerset. Lancastrian army at Northampton cuts off York at Ludlow.
1455	Battle of St. Albans: York defeats royal army.
1461	Young Duke of York proclaimed King Edward IV. Battle of Towton: Yorkist victory. End of first period of Wars of the Roses.
1469	Second period of Wars of the Roses (–71).
1471	Battles of Barnet and Tewkesbury: Yorkist victories.
1483	Third period in Wars of the Roses (–87).
1485	Battle of Bosworth: Richard III defeated by Henry Tudor.
1485	Accession of Henry VII to English throne: start of Tudor dynasty.

Porcelain

During the Ming dynasty, the Chinese economy became more commercialized. Porcelain, silk, tea, and lacquerware were exported to East and Southeast Asia in exchange for silver. Merchants became increasingly prominent, and despite the disdain of the Confucian scholar-gentry for their activities, were able to grow rich, buy land, and live in style – perhaps even becoming patrons of the arts.

Local workshops began to produce porcelain, paper, and art objects in large numbers, for sale in local, and national, markets. Some workshops employed several hundred workers, the first step in the process of industrialization. A cluster of porcelain workshops in the central Yangtze valley produced fine porcelain for the imperial household, as well as more everyday objects for the domestic market. A huge network of canals linked the workshops with the populous south. Chinese porcelain was also exported to the west. There have been many finds of 15th-century Chinese porcelain along the east coast of Africa. Subsequently, Spanish colonists in Manila transported Chinese porcelain across the Pacific to the Americas and Europe.

ASIA

1471 Annamites expand to south by invading Hindu state of Champa in S Vietnam. Final collapse of Champa.

c.1471 Ottoman domains now stretch unbroken from Taurus Mountains to Adriatic Sea.

Final decline of Khmer civilization.

1472 Persians halt Ottoman eastward expansion at Otlukbeli.

Birth of Neo-Confucian philosopher, Wang Yangming.

1473 Venetians destroy Smyrna.

1480 Invention of Islamic spherical astrolabe.

AFRICA

1471 Portuguese gain Tangiers from Moors.

Portuguese navigators reach Gulf of Guinea.

1472 Fernão do Pó, Portuguese navigator, discovers and claims island of Fernando Po off W Africa.

EUROPE

1472 First publication of the *Etymologies* by Bishop Isodore of Seville.

Earliest printed sheet music, Bologna, Italy.

1473 Cyprus comes under Venetian control.

1474 Habsburgs recognize independence of Swiss League.

Treaty of Utrecht grants Hanseatic League major trading advantages in England.

Novgorod incorporated into grand duchy of Muscovy.

1475 Burgundy at height of its power under Charles the Bold.

Publication of Ptolemy's *Geography*.

1476 Swiss defeat Burgundians under Charles the Bold at Grandson and Murten.

William Caxton begins printing at Westminster, London.

1477 Battle of Nancy; Charles the Bold killed. Habsburgs acquire former Burgundian lands, including the Netherlands and Franche-Comté.

1479 Peace of Constantinople, Venice cedes Lemnos and coastal Albania to the Ottomans.

Treaty of Alcáçovas permits Portuguese importation of slaves into Spain.

Union of Castile and Aragon.

1480 Ferdinand and Isabella of Spain authorize papacy to instigate Inquisition against heresy.

Muscovy throws off Mongol yoke; Ivan the Great stops paying tribute to Tartars (Golden Horde).

c.1480 Giovanni Bellini, leading painter of Renaissance Venice, active.

Leonardo da Vinci begins mechanical and scientific experiments.

AMERICAS & AUSTRALASIA

1471 Topa Inca assumes Inca throne (–1493); during his reign, further expansion is halted by Amazon jungle.

1473 Aztecs under Axayacatl defeat neighboring state of Tlatelolco and annex it.

1476 Incas conquer south coast of Peru.

1480 Civil war in N Maya states.

The Moscow Kremlin

At the heart of the city of Moscow, the Kremlin (fortified city) is a symbol of Russian power and authority. It was built toward the end of the 15th century by Italian builders who came to Moscow at the invitation of the Grand Duke Ivan III, "the Great."

The outer, crenellated walls of the Kremlin are of red brick, and contain 20 towers, many designed by the Italian architect Pietro Solario in the 1490s. The Kremlin walls enclose an imposing open square, surrounded by cathedrals and a grand ducal residence. The oldest, the Cathedral of the Dormition, was built between 1475–79 in the Italian-Byzantine style.

The Cathedral of the Annunciation, with its cluster of golden roofs and domes, was built between 1484 and 1489 by craftsmen from Pskov. The Archangel cathedral was rebuilt in 1505–08, and contains the remains of the Russian czars, with the exception of Boris Godunov. The oldest palace, the Palace of the Facets – named after the diamond-cut stones of its facade – was built between 1497–89, and was occupied by Ivan's household.

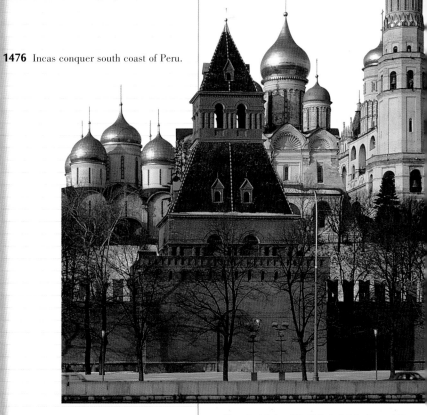

The entire interior of the Cathedral of the Annunciation, (above) *is painted with frescoes. The cathedral also contains a number of 15th-century icons by Russia's foremost icon painters, Andrei Rublev and Theophanes the Greek.*

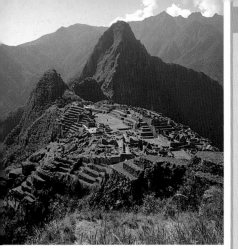

The Inca

The centralized Inca empire of the Peruvian Andes dominated the region in the 15th century. The success of the empire depended on a highly organized bureaucracy, an excellent communications network, and tight government controls on agricultural and industrial production. Well-engineered roads, built as a labor tax by peasants, facilitated the movement of troops, products, and communications.

The spectacular fortress city of Machu Picchu (*above*) is perched at an altitude of 7,710 feet (2,350 m) high in the Andes, west of Cusco. In the center, land was flattened for the construction of temples and plazas. This area was surrounded by thatched houses and terraced gardens, linked by more than 3,000 steps.

Benin

The forest kingdom of Benin was founded in western Nigeria in the 11th–12th centuries. The most famous religious and political leader, or *oba*, Ewuare the Great (reigned c.1440–80), described as a great warrior and magician, established a hereditary succession. He rebuilt the capital (present-day Benin City), surrounding it with moats and extensive earthworks. Benin is renowned for its brass heads and sculptures, which depict *obas*, chieftains, traders, court ceremonials, and even, as this statue represents, the newly arrived Portuguese soldiers.

ASIA

1481 Death of Mehmet the Conqueror. He has taken most of Serbia, Albania, Herzegovina, much of Bosnia and Greece, and subdued Anatolia.
He is succeeded by his son, Bayezid II.

Italian artist, Gentile Bellini, is active in Istanbul.

Revolts in rural Japan against punitive taxation and high interest rates.

1487 Portuguese Pero de Covilhã sails through Red Sea to India (–1489).

1488 Ming emperors set out to rebuild 1,700-year-old Great Wall.

First major uprising of Ikko Buddhists in Japan.

1489 Yusuf Adil Shah, a former slave, becomes ruler of Bijapur, India.

1490 Mausoleum of Timur (Tamerlane) is erected at Samarkand.

AFRICA

c.1481 The Mossi people, from savannah country south of the Niger bend, raid the weakening Mali empire, reaching as far as Walata.

Portuguese build Fort São Jorge da Mina (Elmina) on the Gold Coast.

1483 Portuguese explorer, Diogo Cão, sails around mouth of Congo river, setting up a stone column to mark his arrival.

1484 Diogo Cão lands in Angola.

1485 Four Portuguese Catholic missionaries arrive in the Kongo kingdom (Angola).

c.1485 End of the reign of Matope over Shona Mutapa state. Wide-ranging tribute demands indicate the power of Mutapa.

1487 Portuguese explorer Bartolomeu Dias rounds the Cape of Good Hope.

1492 **c.1489** The armies of the Songhay empire, under Sunni Ali, raid deep into Mossi territory.

EUROPE

1481 John II succeeds his father as king of Portugal. His accession gives a boost to voyages of exploration.

Beginning of Spanish war against Granada.

Ottoman Turks in Otranto, S Italy, surrender after occupying it for one year.

1482 Treaty of Arras: Burgundy and Picardy are absorbed into France.

1483 Edward IV of England dies. The two boy princes, Edward V and Richard of York, disappear; they are believed to have been murdered in the Tower of London by their uncle and successor, Richard III.

The Spanish Inquisition formally established by the union of the Inquisitions of Aragon and Castile.

Pope Sixtus IV celebrates the first mass in the Sistine chapel.

1484 Ottoman Turks capture Akkerman at the mouth of the Dniester.

The first European manual of navigation and nautical almanac is prepared at the request of King John II of Portugal.

1485 At Bosworth the victory of Henry Tudor (Henry VII) over Richard III establishes the Tudor dynasty.

1486 Christopher Columbus persuades Queen Isabella of Spain to sponsor his expedition to discover a western route to the Indies.

The publication in Rome of *Malleus Maleficarum*, an encyclopedia of witchcraft, indicates that the papacy is lending its support to the growing practice of persecuting and burning witches.

1487 Jakob Fugger, a rich merchant from Augsburg, secures the right to mine silver in the Tyrol.

1488 Uprising among disaffected tradesmen in Flanders. Maximilian I, King of the Romans, is forced to agree to give up his regency of the Low Countries.

1489 Venetians purchase Cyprus, ending several centuries of Frankish sovereignty.

1490 Anglo-Spanish alliance against France is supported by Maximilian I of Austria.

Accession of Ladislas II, King of Bohemia, to the Hungarian throne; Polish Jagiellon dynasty now controls Poland, Bohemia, and Hungary.

(margin markers: 1492, 1508, 1492, 1494)

AMERICAS & AUSTRALASIA

A money-changer and his wife, by Reymers Waele. Following the discovery of the New World, Europe was flooded with great quantities of precious metals and the circulation of wealth rapidly accelerated.

1487 Inauguration of great pyramid temple honoring Huitzilopochtli at Tenochtitlán. 20,000 people are ritually sacrificed there.

Money and banking

The banking system began to evolve when merchants, unwilling to carry large sums of money when they traveled, began to leave money on deposit with money-changers in exchange for a receipt.

Bills of Exchange, which emerged in the 14th century, were a response to increasingly complex trading transactions. The Bill was a letter in which one person instructed another, in a different city, to pay a certain amount of money, in a specified currency, to a third party.

In time, great merchant families were beginning to rely on trade in money itself (the "bank"), exploiting currency fluctuations and interest rates, for their greatest profits. Banks first appeared in Lombardy in northern Italy; by 1472, Florence had 33 banking houses.

Soon, banks could be found in all the major cities. Rich banking families, such as the Medici and Strozzi in Italy, and the Fuggers and Weschlers in the Holy Roman Empire, wielded great political and economic influence. Kings were in their debt and artists vied for their patronage.

Christopher Columbus

Cristóforo Colombo (c.1446–1505) was a Genoese sailor who sought the patronage of Ferdinand and Isabella of Spain. In 1492, he and a total crew of only 90 men set sail in three tiny ships, intent on proving that

it was possible to reach the Indies by sailing west from Europe. Land was sighted 33 days later, and Columbus claimed the new territory – the Bahamas – for Spain. He crossed the Atlantic three more times, landing on the South American mainland in 1496. The colony he founded in Hispaniola was beset by revolts by the Spanish settlers and incursions by the natives, and he finally returned to Spain, rich but disillusioned, in 1504.

Navigation

The great voyages of discovery in the 15th and 16th centuries tested mariners' navigational skills to the limit. Portuguese cartographers were pioneers in the field, creating portulans, or maritime charts, which included important innovations such as a scale of latitude worked out from observation of the sun and stars. But sailing into the unknown required new skills; portulans and compasses were inadequate.

Navigators now had to understand the workings of the cosmos, as well as the fundamentals of astronomy. By using instruments such as the astrolabe, quadrant, and arablest, they were able to reckon the position of the stars as a way of checking latitude and hence taking their own bearings. European navigators were indebted to the Arabs and Chinese; the astrolabe (shown here) was a kind of map of the sky, showing the position of the sun and stars. It had been invented by Arabs as early as the 10th century.

ASIA

1491 Ottomans and Mamluks reach a peace agreement after six years of war. Cilicia in Anatolia is placed under Egyptian control.

1494 Death of Behzad, one of the greatest painters of Persian miniatures.

1498 Portuguese explorer Vasco da Gama arrives on the Malabar coast of W India, the first European to discover a sea route to India around the Cape of Good Hope.

1501 ▼

1499 Rise to power of Safavids in Persia.

1500 Shaybanid dynasty, of Mongol descent, assumes control of Transoxania (–1598).

1510 ▼

Cabral creates the first Portuguese trading posts in W India.

AFRICA

1491 A Portuguese embassy is sent to Nkuma, the king of Kongo (Angola).

Portuguese envoy Pero da Covilhã completes a journey that takes him as far south as Sofala, SE Africa.

1492 Death of Sunni Ali, the W African ruler who transformed the small kingdom of Gao into the huge Songhay empire.

1512 ▼

1493 Muhammad Ture succeeds Sunni Ali as ruler of Songhay, founding the Askiya dynasty. He consolidates Ali's conquests and uses Islam to unite his far-flung empire.

1509 ▼

1494 Pero da Covilhã reaches Ethiopia and is detained by the emperor.

1498 Vasco da Gama rounds the Cape of Good Hope, *en route* to India.

1505 ▼

1500 Portuguese trading posts are set up along the E African coast.

Sheikh Masfarma ben Uthman writes *A History of Bornu* (N Nigeria, Niger, and Chad).

c.1500 Empire of Benin stretches from the Niger delta to the coastal lagoon of Lagos.

EUROPE

1491 French occupation effectively ends the independence of Brittany.

1492 Treaty of Étaples between Charles VIII of France and Henry VII of England averts an English invasion.

Ferdinand and Isabella take Granada, the last Muslim kingdom in Spain.

 In Spain, a royal edict is issued decreeing the expulsion of Jews.

Death of Lorenzo de Medici, the tyrannical ruler of Florence, a patron of arts and learning.

1493 Under the Treaty of Barcelona, Charles VIII returns Cerdagne and Roussillon to Ferdinand of Aragon.

 1494 Treaty of Tordesillas divides western hemisphere between Spain and Portugal.

 Philip the Fair, son of the emperor Maximilian I, becomes ruler of the Low Countries.

Dominican friar Savonarola sets up a form of religious dictatorship in Florence.

A new, highly infectious, sexually transmitted disease, known as the "French pox," has arrived in Europe.

 1495 Venice, Milan, Spain, the pope, and the emperor set up a holy league against Charles VIII of France who has seized Naples.

French forces are defeated by the alliance at Fornovo, N Italy.

1496 Ottoman forces invade Montenegro.

1497 King John of Denmark invades Sweden and reunites Norway, Sweden, and Denmark under his rule.

1498 Savonarola dies at the stake.

1499 Swiss victory in Swabian War; Treaty of Basle confirms independence of the Swiss Confederation from imperial authority.

Louis XII, now king of France, claims his right of succession to the duchy of Milan. The French, led by the mercenary Trivulzio, seize Milan.

Ottomans at war with Venice (–1503).

1500 Milanese rebel against Trivulzio's rule.

France invades Italy; defeated at battle of Cerignola.

AMERICAS & AUSTRALASIA

1492 Christopher Columbus, in search of Asia, lands on the Bahamas on his first expedition.

Columbus lands on Cuba and Hispaniola (Santo Domingo).

1493 Accession of Inca ruler Huayna Capac.

1495 Columbus orders the Indians in Hispaniola to pay tribute to the king of Spain.

1496 Columbus establishes first Spanish settlement in W hemisphere.

1497 Genoese explorer John Cabot, who is sponsored by the English, reaches Newfoundland after a journey lasting 35 days.

1498 Columbus, on third voyage, anchors off coast near Trinidad.

Columbus is first European to sight S American mainland.

1499 Italian explorer Amerigo Vespucci explores northeast S America.

Revolt by Spanish settlers and natives against the poor administration of Columbus in Hispaniola.

1500 Pedro Álvares Cabral sights Brazilian coast on voyage to India; reaches Brazil and sails on to India.

Cabral claims Brazil for Portugal; Pinzón discovers mouth of the Amazon.

Protracted military campaigns at northern and southern extremes of Inca empire lead to establishment of second capital at Tomebamba.

c.1500 Inuit peoples are found throughout Arctic region.

1502	
1508	
1506	
1511	

European Voyages of Discovery

1481 Start of voyage of Portuguese explorer, Diogo Cão, to Congo and Angola.

1488 Portuguese navigator and explorer, Bartolomeu Dias, enters Indian Ocean, having rounded the Cape of Good Hope.

1492 First epic voyage of Christopher Columbus (–1493), sponsored by Spain. He discovers Bahamas, Cuba, and Hispaniola.

1497 John Cabot, sponsored by England, rediscovers Newfoundland, first reached by Norse explorers in the 11th century.

Italian navigator, Amerigo Vespucci, sails to the Gulf of Mexico and the Florida coast.

Voyage of Vasco da Gama (–1499). First Portuguese voyage to India.

1498 Columbus discovers Trinidad and the coast of Venezuela.

1499 Spanish *conquistador* Alonso de Ojeda, and Vespucci reach the coast of Guiana (–1500) They give the first report of the Amazon.

1500 Portuguese navigator, Pedro Álvares Cabral, sights the coast of Brazil.

1502 Columbus explores coast of Honduras and Nicaragua.

1508 Expedition of Sebastian Cabot in search of the Northwest Passage.

1509 Portuguese reach Malacca, in the East Indies.

1513 Spanish *conquistador* Juan Ponce de León explores the coast of Florida.

1519 Portuguese explorer Ferdinand Magellan embarks on first circumnavigation of the world (–1521). Having crossed the Pacific, Magellan is killed in the Philippines (1521).

1523 Francisco Pizarro of Spain explores west coast of S America. Conquest of Peru begins (–1532).

1534 Jacques Cartier of France explores St. Lawrence river and sights Montreal.

1539 Spanish explorer Hernando de Soto explores southeast N America.

1540 Spanish explorer Francisco Vázquez de Coronado explores the Colorado river, Grand Canyon, and New Mexico.

1540 Spanish *conquistador* Francisco de Orellana discovers the source of the Amazon.

1578 English navigator Martin Frobisher discovers Frobisher Bay and Hudson Strait (Canada).

1577 Francis Drake is the first Englishman to circumnavigate the globe.

1594 Dutchman William Barents discovers Novaya Zemlya, Barents Island, and the Barents Sea.

1595 Sir Walter Raleigh journeys up the Orinoco river in search of El Dorado.

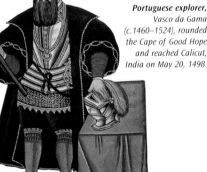

Portuguese explorer, Vasco da Gama (c.1460–1524), rounded the Cape of Good Hope and reached Calicut, India on May 20, 1498.

Michelangelo

A native of Tuscany, Michelangelo Buonarroti (1475–1564), who worked with incredible dedication and single-mindedness to master the representation of the human form, was – by the age of 30 – generally acknowledged to be an outstanding master of the age. He was commissioned to paint the ceiling of the Sistine chapel in Rome (*below*), a task that was to take four years of intensive labor (1508–1512). Deeply influenced by Neoplatonism, he created a massive work, redolent with symbolism, fusing Hebrew and classical themes.

Landmarks of the Renaissance

c.1480	Piero della Francesca publishes his study of perspective.
1484	Leonardo da Vinci paints the *Virgin of the Rocks*.
	Botticelli paints *The Birth of Venus*.
1496	Albrecht Dürer begins work on a series of woodcuts known as the *Apocalypse*.
1500	Erasmus publishes his *Adagia*.
1504	Michelangelo carves his statue of David, placed in the Piazza della Signoria in Florence.
1506	Leonardo paints *Mona Lisa*.
	Work begins on the rebuilding of St. Peter's in Rome to designs by Bramante.
1512	Michelangelo completes painting the ceiling of the Sistine chapel.
1513	Machiavelli begins work on *The Prince*. Raphael paints *The School of Athens*.
1515	Grünewald paints the Isenheim altarpiece.
1516	Thomas More publishes *Utopia*.
1528	Castiglione publishes *The Courtier*.
1533	Titian completes his portrait of Charles V. The emperor grants him a patent of nobility.
	Hans Holbein the Younger paints *The Ambassadors*.
1559	Pieter Brueghel the Elder paints *Carnival and Lent*.
1570	Palladio publishes *I quattro libri dell' architettura* (The Four Books on Architecture).
1577	El Greco paints *The Assumption of the Virgin*.
1601	Shakespeare begins to write *Hamlet*.
1604	Caravaggio paints *The Deposition*.
1605	Cervantes writes *Don Quixote*.
1607	First performance of Monteverdi's *Orfeo*.

ASIA

1501 Accession of Shah Ismail I; beginning of Safavid dynasty in Persia (–1732).

1502 On the orders of Shah Ismail, the new Safavid ruler of Persia and a Shi'ite Muslim, Sunni dissenters are executed.

Italian Lodovico di Varthema visits Arabia disguised as an Arab.

First published map to show correct general shape of India, by Alberto Cantino.

1506 The Portuguese Afonso de Albuquerque seizes the island of Socotra, the key to the Red Sea.

Revolt against cruel ruler of Korea, Yonsangun. He is succeeded by Chungjong (–1544).

1508 Shah Ismail I of Persia seizes Baghdad.

1509 Portuguese victory over Ottoman and Arab fleet at Diu.

Indian sultan of Gujarat surprises and sinks Portuguese fleet.

1511 Portuguese voyages to Moluccas, Malacca, and Macao (–1516).

Krishna Deva Raya becomes king of Vijayanagara.

1510 Shah Ismail I defeats and kills Ozbeg Mohammed Shaybani and seizes Herat, Bactria, and Khiva.

Portuguese conquest of Goa. It is made capital of all Portuguese possessions in Asia.

c.1510 Japanese pirates ravage China's south coast.

AFRICA

1502 First slaves taken from Africa to the New World.

1503 Portuguese levy a tribute from the sultan of Zanzibar.

1504 Muslim Funj kings defeat and replace the Christian kings of Sennar between the Blue and White Nile rivers.

1512 **1505** Kilwa, E Africa, refuses to pay tribute to Portugal. Portuguese sack Mombasa in reprisal.

1508 Lebna Dengal comes to the Ethiopian throne.

1509 Ethiopia sends an ambassador to Portugal.

Humanism

1502 A royal edict orders that all Moors who have not been baptized as Christians should be expelled from Spain.

Outbreak of a peasants' rebellion in the bishopric of Speyer in Germany.

German locksmith, Peter Henlein, invents a spring-loaded portable timepiece, or pocket watch.

1503 Muscovy becomes politically independent when Ivan III refuses to pay protection money to khans.

1504 War of the Bavarian Succession. Maximilian I defeats count palatine, Rupert, and seizes his lands.

1506 Death of Philip the Fair, ruler of the Netherlands.

1507 Genoese rise up against the French forces occupying their city.

1512
1508 Emperor Maximilian I and Louis XII of France, backed by Spain and Pope Julius II, form the League of Cambrai.

Pope Julius II grants the Spanish crown rights to establish and build churches in the New World.

Pope Julius II commissions Michelangelo to decorate the ceiling of the Sistine chapel in the Vatican palace.

1509 Henry VIII succeeds to the English throne.

Pope Julius II excommunicates the republic of Venice (–1510).

French victory over the Venetians at Agnadello.

Padua is retaken by Venice. Maximilian I leaves Italy.

1501 Portuguese explorer Miguel Corte-Real enslaves 50 Beothuk Indians.

1519
1502 Start of reign of last Aztec emperor, Montezuma II.

Introduction of African slaves to the Caribbean.

First expedition sent from Lisbon to exploit newly found coastline.

1506 Portuguese explorer Tristan da Cunha discovers an island in the S Atlantic, to which he gives his own name.

1507 Waldseemüller's world map gives name of America to continent in honor of Amerigo Vespucci.

1522
1508 Spanish settlers on Hispaniola make slaves of the natives.

Spanish conquer Canary Islands.

1509 Spanish settlement of mainland C America begins.

Founding of San Juan on Puerto Rico.

Diego Alvaros Correa founds the first Portuguese settlement in Brazil, near Pôrto Seguro.

Humanism, the **philosophy** of the Renaissance, marked a fundamental shift from a God-centered world view to the humanity-centered view of the Renaissance. Theology was supplanted by the study of classical texts, and individualism began to replace the corporatism of the Middle Ages. The concept of the human personality, the study of history, and the quest for scientific truths are all humanist developments.

Desiderius Erasmus (*above*) (1469–1536), was the greatest humanist. Widely traveled, erudite, and a devout Christian, he did more than anyone else to marry humanism with the Catholic tradition. He was one of the first truly popular authors of the age of printing. His *Adagia* (1500), which brought over 3,000 proverbs and phrases into popular circulation, was the world's first bestseller.

Leonardo da Vinci

Leonardo da Vinci (1452–1519) was the epitome of the "Renaissance man," a painter, sculptor, architect, physicist, anatomist, and inventor. His most famous paintings, such as *The Last Supper* (1498), and the *Mona Lisa*, (c.1506) (*below*), are masterful studies of human psychology: he said "A good painter has two chief objects to paint – man and the intention of his soul."

The range of subjects that stimulated his enquiring mind are revealed in his many notebooks. They are filled with countless ideas and inventions, and many – such as submarines, turbines, and prototypes of a tank and a helicopter – being so radical and ahead of their time were not realized for centuries. His studies of anatomy were based on the dissection of over 30 corpses. However, his exploration of nature was, first and foremost, a way of gaining knowledge of the visible world, a knowledge that could be used in his art.

Martin Luther

The Reformation (see box, right) was spearheaded by Martin Luther (*above*) (1483–1546), whose teachings emphasized the importance of the Bible, and rejected prayers to saints, veneration of relics, sales of indulgences, and pilgrimages.

The new Protestant religion spread rapidly through northern Europe, sometimes adopted because of political and economic expediency, rather than through zealous belief. A more austere form of Protestantism emerged in the Swiss Reformed tradition under the guidance of Ulrich Zwingli and John Calvin. Throughout northern Europe, bitter divisions over religious belief ultimately led to civil war and social upheaval.

Iznik pottery

In the 15th century, the Ottoman town of Iznik, in western Anatolia, became a center for high-quality glazed ceramic production. Based originally on Iranian blue-and-white ware, the designers at Iznik experimented with a range of styles, designs, and colors. The palette was widened; "Damascus" ware produced at Iznik used sage green, manganese purple, and blue. The potters of Iznik were able to produce higher temperatures in their kilns than their competitors, and were thus able to produce larger and finer pieces. By the mid-16th century, Iznik had become a major center of production of ceramic tiles for the building industry.

ASIA

1511 Civil war in the Ottoman Empire.

Portuguese explorer Afonso de Albuquerque occupies Malacca on the Malayan peninsula. The Portuguese now control the main strategic positions along the spice route.

1512 Forced abdication of Ottoman sultan, Bayezid. Accession of Selim I who is raised to power by the Janissaries. Selim executes his brothers, potential rivals for the throne.

Portuguese explorer Francisco Serrão makes his way to the Moluccas.

Tax revolt by peasants in Sichuan.

1514 Ottomans crush the Safavid Persians at Çaldiran.

1515 Syria is overrun by the Turks; mutiny of the Janissaries.

`1526` Babur, king of Kabul, invades N India; conquers Punjab, occupies Delhi.

Confucian scholar Wang Yangming reforms the Chinese state.

1516 Ottomans conquer Syria, Egypt, the Hejaz, and Yemen (–1516).

1517 Selim I orders construction of Ottoman fleet at Suez; Portuguese attack on Jedda repulsed.

Selim is now the guardian of the holy places of Mecca and Medina after downfall of Mamluk Egypt.

First Portuguese trading mission to China.

`1526` **1520** Accession of Suleyman the Magnificent as Ottoman sultan (–1566).

A Portuguese ambassador arrives in Beijing.

AFRICA

`1525` **1511** Sa'di dynasty comes to power in Morocco (–1659).

A Spanish force occupies the island of Peñón, off Morocco in the W Mediterranean.

`1528` **1512** Askiya Muhammad the Great, the king of Songhay, conquers the Hausa states of Katsina, Zaria, and Kano.

Portuguese abandon Kilwa, E Africa.

1515 Barbary pirates, 'Aruj and Khayr al-Din Barbarossa, install their fleet at Algiers, challenging the Spanish forces occupying Peñón.

`1524` **1517** Downfall of Mamluk Egypt; Sultan Selim makes his entry into Cairo. The Ottomans are masters of Egypt.

Moroccan explorer Leo Africanus completes an expedition to Timbuktu, Gao, Katsina, Kano, and Lake Chad.

1518 Spaniards take Tlemcen; 'Aruj is killed during the fighting.

`1529` **1519** Khayr al-Din Barbarossa repulses a Spanish offensive on Algiers.

c.1520 Portuguese ambassadors reside at the court of Lebna Dengal, king of Ethiopia.

EUROPE

1511 Pope Julius II recruits England as a member of his Holy League against France.

1512 French forces heavily defeat the armies of the Holy League at the battle of Ravenna.

Emperor Maximilian I severs his alliance with Louis XII of France.

The army of King Ferdinand II occupies the entire kingdom of Navarre.

1513 Swiss foot-soldiers rout French at Novara, near Milan.

French are defeated at Guinegatte by the combined forces of the emperor Maximilian I and King Henry VIII of England.

English forces defeat the Scots at Flodden and James IV of Scotland is killed.

Niccolò Machiavelli writes *The Prince*, a remarkable study of political power.

A new edition of Ptolemy's *Geographia* shows the newly discovered western lands as two continents, situated between Europe and Asia.

1514 The astronomer, Nicolaus Copernicus, proposes that the earth revolves around the sun.

1522

1515 French invasion of Italy and victory at Marignano. French occupy Milan.

Francis I of France makes his peace with Pope Leo X.

An alliance is forged between the Habsburg and Jagiellon dynasties by the Holy Roman emperor Maximilian I and Vladislav II of Bohemia.

1516 Charles of Habsburg is crowned king of Spain.

Francis I of France agrees the Concordat of Bologna with the papacy.

New World territory assigned to Portugal by the Treaty of Tordesillas (of 1494) is divided into 15 hereditary fiefdoms.

1519 Charles I of Spain is elected Holy Roman emperor, and takes the name Charles V.

1520 Meeting of Henry VIII of England and Francis I of France at the Field of the Cloth of Gold. An alliance is formed between England and France.

The Laws of Burgos give New World natives legal protection against abuse and authorize Negro slavery.

AMERICAS & AUSTRALASIA

1511 Juan de Esquival undertakes the conquest of Jamaica.

Led by Diego Velázquez, the Spanish take control of the island of Cuba.

1521 **1513** Juan Ponce de León traces coast of Florida and claims Florida for Spain.

1514 New World natives in Spanish-held territory are forced to convert to Christianity under threat of enslavement or death.

Spanish priest Bartolomé de las Casas shocks his compatriots with his eyewitness accounts of the depraved behavior of Spanish colonists in Cuba.

1515 Spanish found the city of Havana in Cuba.

1517 Córdoba leads expedition to Mexico.

1518 Grijalva lands on Veracruz coast.

1519 Envoys of the Aztec leader Montezuma II attend the first Easter mass to be celebrated in C America.

Spanish explorer Hernán Cortés lands at Veracruz with a force of 500 men. He marches on the Aztec capital Tenochtitlán. Montezuma II surrenders without a fight.

1521 **1520** Cortés is driven from Tenochtitlán by the Aztec leader, Cuauhtémoc.

Death of Aztec emperor, Montezuma II.

1521 Spanish explorer Ferdinand Magellan overwinters at Puerto San Julián, southeast S America, in preparation for his circumnavigation of the globe. He discovers the strait that now bears his name, and enters the Pacific.

The Reformation

The fragile unity of western Christendom was shattered by the Reformation, a doctrinal revolution that targeted the spiritual complacency, material wealth, and abuses of power of the Roman Catholic church.

1483	Martin Luther is born in Eisleben, Germany (d. 1546)
1484	Ulrich Zwingli is born near Glarus, Switzerland.
1506	Zwingli is made parish priest at Glarus.
1507	Martin Luther is ordained a priest.
1509	Birth of John Calvin at Noyon, France. (dies 1564).
1517	Luther produces his *95 Theses*, intended to stimulate debate about church abuses.
1518	Luther presents his arguments to an imperial diet in Augsburg.
1519	Luther is summoned to Rome to answer a charge of heresy.
1519	Zwingli begins preaching sermons critical of the church. He develops his own evangelical teaching.
1521	Luther is excommunicated by papal bull. Charles V declares Luther to be an outlaw.
1523	First disputation held in Zurich. Zwingli prepares *67 Articles* relating to religious doctrine and practice for discussion.
1524	In support of Zwingli's arguments, the Zurich city council orders the removal of all religious images from churches.
1526	Zwingli rejects belief in transubstantiation, insisting that bread and wine at the eucharist are symbolic. This brings him into conflict with the Lutherans.
1529	Luther and Zwingli meet at the colloquy of Marburg, but are unable to agree over eucharistic teaching.
1531	Zwingli dies at the battle of Kappel.
1534	Luther publishes his translation of the entire Bible into German.
1535	Calvin completes the first edition of the *Institutes of the Christian Religion*.
1536	Calvin stays in Geneva to assist in the consolidation of the Reformation there. He proposes his doctrine of predetermination.
1541	The city of Geneva accepts Calvin's proposals for church reform.
1543	Luther publishes an intemperate attack on Jews and their beliefs, *On Jews and their Lies*, and argues for their expulsion from Germany.
1549	Increasing numbers of French Huguenot refugees flee to Protestant Geneva.
1555	Refugees in Geneva are granted citizen status. Riots in protest are suppressed, marking the triumph of Calvin over opponents in the city.

The Schlosskapelle in Hartenfels Castle, in Torgau, Germany (right) was built in 1543–44 and consecrated by Martin Luther. It is generally considered to be the first church built specifically for the Lutheran community.

The siege of Vienna

Under Suleyman the Magnificent

(1520–1566), the conquest of Europe became the main focus of Ottoman attention. In the eastern Mediterranean, naval pressure was increased with the sieges of Corfu (1537) and Reggio (1543). But the most important theater was the Danube valley. In 1526, Ottoman armies invaded Hungary; at the battle of Mohács the Hungarian feudal cavalry was devastated by the Ottomans' superior forces.

In 1529, Ottoman armies advanced to besiege Vienna (*right*). The city withstood the siege for six weeks, when the onset of winter and the Ottomans' extended supply lines forced them to retreat. Vienna was not besieged again until 1683, but the Ottoman armies continued to maintain pressure on the frontiers of Habsburg territory.

The battle of Pavia

The election of Charles V as Holy Roman emperor in 1519 confirmed French fears of Habsburg hegemony. Francis I of France declared war in 1521, and northern Italy became the main theater of conflict. The French suffered a major defeat at the battle of Bicocca (1522). In 1525, the French were once again defeated at Pavia in Lombardy. The French siege lines were broken by a Spanish relief army, and cut to pieces by pikemen and arquebus fire. Francis I was captured and forced to agree to terms, signing the Treaty of Madrid. In 1526, however, he once again renewed hostilities.

ASIA

1521 Portuguese navigator, Ferdinand Magellan, who has sailed across the Pacific Ocean, is killed in a tribal skirmish in the Philippines.

1523 Ibrahim becomes Ottoman grand vizier.

Japanese pirates repulsed from Chinese mainland.

1524 Shah Ismail of Persia is succeeded by his ten-year-old son, Tahmasp.

Vasco da Gama becomes viceroy of Goa, but dies only three months after his arrival.

Hojo Ujitsuna attacks and captures Edo castles. Followers of the Nichiren sect of Buddhism are expelled from Edo.

1525 Ottomans again defeat Portuguese fleet in Red Sea.

1526 At Panipat, N India, an army led by Babur annihilates the Indian army of the sultan of Delhi. Establishment of Mughal empire.

1527 Emperor Babur defeats the Rajputs at the battle of Khanua, eliminating the main rivals to Mughal power in N India.

1534 ▼ **1528** Safavids take Baghdad from Kurdish usurper.

Portuguese reach Bengal.

1529 Babur defeats the Afghan chiefs of Bihar and Bengal at Ghagra. His power now stretches from Kabul to Bengal.

Monks from the Tendai monasteries on Mount Hiei, northwest of Kyoto, massacre followers of the Nichiren sect of Buddhism.

1535 ▼ **1530** Humayun succeeds Babur as emperor of Delhi.

AFRICA

1524 A rebellion by Ahmed Pasha of Egypt against Ottoman rule is suppressed.

1541 ▼ **1525** The Sa'di dynasty, claiming descent from the prophet's son-in-law Ali, establish their capital at Marrakesh.

c.1527 Muslims conquer Christian Nubia after a seven-year war.

1528 Askiya Muhammad, ruler of the Songhay empire, is deposed by his son.

Mombasa revolts against Portuguese rule.

1531 ▼ **1529** Ahmad Grañ ("the left-handed"), leader of the Muslim state of Adal, leads jihad against Christian Ethiopia.

Algiers is captured by the knights of Malta.

1533 ▼ Khayr al-Din Barbarossa completes his conquest of Algeria in the name of the Ottoman sultan.

1530 Chicukyo, the Munhumutapa or king who has ruled the S Zambezi escarpment for 30 years, is killed during a civil war.

EUROPE

1521 Imperial forces invade Champagne, France.

Ottoman forces take Belgrade.

1522 Rhodes, former base of the Knights of St. John of Jerusalem, falls to the Ottomans under Suleyman after a six-month siege.

French are defeated by imperial troops at Bicocca, Italy, and are forced to surrender Milan.

Lithuania cedes Smolensk to Moscow, ending a ten-year dispute.

1523 Rebellion in Denmark. Christian II flees the country and Frederick, duke of Schleswig-Holstein, is elected king.

The architect of Swedish independence, Gustav Vasa, is elected king of Sweden by the diet, the Swedish parliament.

1524 Led by the theologian Thomas Münzer, peasants in S Germany rebel, demanding the abolition of feudal dues, serfdom, and tithes (–1525).

1525 French army decisively defeated at Pavia, N Italy, by imperial forces. Francis I captured.

Albert von Brandenburg declares that Prussia is a Protestant state.

The hereditary territories of Austria, Hungary, and Bohemia are reunited under the Habsburgs.

The Roman Mass is banned by local magistrates in Zurich.

1526 The League of Torgau is joined by most of the Protestant states of the German empire.

1532 Ottoman invasion of Hungary; Ottoman victory at battle of Mohács.

First translations of the New Testament into English begin to appear.

1527 German mercenaries sack and burn Rome.

1532 **1529** At diet of Speyer, Holy Roman emperor Charles V attempts to reach compromise with Lutheran princes.

Ottoman Turks capture Buda. Their siege of Vienna is repulsed.

Peace of Cambrai; France renounces its rights in Italy, Flanders, and Artois. Charles V renounces any claims to Burgundy.

1533 The pope refuses to annul Henry VIII of England's marriage with Catherine of Aragon.

AMERICAS & AUSTRALASIA

1521 Tenochtitlán falls to Spanish and their Indian allies.

Juan Ponce de León, the Spanish governor of Puerto Rico, sets out for Florida with 200 prospective colonists. He is wounded by natives and the attempt is abandoned.

1522 First American slave revolt in Hispaniola.

Cortés becomes captain-general and governor of New Spain.

Spanish found Mexico City on the ruins of Tenochtitlán.

Spanish launch a series of expeditions against the Zapotec highlanders.

1524 Italian explorer, Giovanni da Verrazano sails up Atlantic coast as far as Nova Scotia.

Cuauhtémoc, the last Aztec king, is hanged by the Spanish on a charge of treason.

Verrazano explores Atlantic coast of N America.

1532 **1525** The Inca ruler Huayna Capac dies, leaving two rival claimants to the throne; civil war ensues.

1526 Jorge de Meneses is first European to sight New Guinea.

Dominican monks arrive in Mexico.

1528 Cabeza de Vaca explores Gulf of Mexico and southwest.

Charles V grants lands around Coro to German bankers, the Welsers.

1530 Portuguese begin to colonize Brazil.

Magellan's circumnavigation

In 1519, **Ferdinand Magellan,** a Portuguese explorer sponsored by Spain, embarked on a momentous journey to find a western route to Asia. In October 1520, his fleet of five ships sailed down the eastern coast of South America. Over the course of 38 days they negotiated the hazardous passage round Cape Horn and, on November 28, 1520, entered the Pacific Ocean.

Now with only three ships, they embarked on the first recorded crossing of the Pacific, reaching Guam on March 6, 1521. The fleet then sailed on to Cebu in the Philippines, where Magellan and his men became embroiled in a conflict between local rulers. Magellan was killed on April 27. Only one of his ships, the *Victoria,* returned to Europe, completing the first circumnavigation of the globe.

Cortés captures Tenochtitlán

In 1519, **Hernán Cortés,** the mayor of Havana, led a 600-strong colonizing expedition to Mexico. The invaders, armed with swords, guns, and crossbows, soon overcame the local Indians, who decided to join the Spanish and overthrow their Aztec oppressors. When Cortés, now at the head of a strong army, reached the capital of Tenochtitlán, he was welcomed into the city, where he proceeded to take the Aztec leader, Montezuma, captive. Recalled to Veracruz to repel an Indian attack, he lost the initiative and the Aztecs rose against their captors. Cortés returned, again supported by Indian allies, and – in 1521 – after desperate fighting, Tenochtitlán finally fell (*below*).

1521–1530

Biological diffusions

The most dramatic effect of the European colonization of the New World was the disastrous decline in native populations. By 1510, for example, nearly 90 percent of the Amerindians in Hispaniola were dead. Although warfare, famine, and ruthless exploitation were responsible for many deaths, by far the greatest killers were European diseases, such as smallpox and measles (*above*), to which the natives had no immunity.

On a more positive note, Europeans introduced new plants and animals to the Americas, which hitherto had exploited a very narrow range of draft and domestic animals. With the Europeans came horses, sheep, cattle, pigs, dogs, chickens, wheat, sugarcane, onions, citrus fruits, and bananas. A wide range of foods was also taken back to Europe, including corn, tomatoes, potatoes, peanuts, chili peppers, and cocoa.

Francisco Pizarro

Pizarro (1476–1541), the Spanish *conquistador* who conquered the Inca empire, was 48 years old when he arrived in South America. Motivated by consuming worldly ambition and religious zeal, he reached the highlands of Peru in 1532. He was accompanied by just 180 men, but they were well equipped with armor, steel weapons, and horses. Atahualpa, the Inca leader, was encamped with an army of over 40,000 men near the town of Cajamarca. During negotiations, Pizarro captured Atahualpa, and demanded a vast ransom for his release. When the ransom had been paid, Pizarro had him murdered, setting the seal on the Spanish conquest of Peru. The murder of the "divine Inca" broke the resistance of the Inca people, and civil war and disease soon led to their submission.

1531–1540

ASIA

1534 Suleyman retakes Baghdad from Safavids.

Ottoman armies capture Tabriz in NW Persia.

1545 ▼

1535 Mughal emperor Humayun leads a raid into Gujarat, storming the fortress of Champaner.

Waldseemüller's map improves on shape of India.

1538 Khadim Suleyman Pasha, the Ottoman governor of Egypt, sends a fleet to attack India. The Turks fail to take Diu in Gujarat and return home.

1546 ▼

Ottomans subjugate Yemen and Aden and occupy port of Basra on Persian Gulf.

1539 Death of Guru Nanak, poet, mystic, and founder of the Sikh religion.

1540 Afghan chief, Sher Sur Shah defeats the Mughal emperor, Humayun, at Kanauj. Sher Khan Sur becomes ruler of N India.

Portuguese start to trade with Cochin China (Vietnam).

AFRICA

1531 Portugal sends troops to assist Ethiopia against the Muslims.

Portuguese begin to trade at the Muslim port of Sena on the lower Zambezi, Mozambique.

1533 Süleyman the Magnificent appoints Khayr al-Din Barbarossa commander of Algiers.

1534 Khayr al-Din Barbarossa wins back Tunis from its Moorish king, an ally of Spain.

1541 ▼

1535 Emperor Charles V captures Tunis from Barbarossa.

Portuguese penetrate Zambezi valley to Muslim market at Tete.

1536 Khayr al-Din Barbarossa recaptures Bizerta, N Africa.

1543 ▼

1540 Portuguese come to the aid of Ethiopia against *jihad* leader Ahmad Grañ.

EUROPE

1531 German Protestants form the League of Schmalkalden to resist the power of the emperor, Charles V.

Charles V prohibits the adoption of Protestant doctrine in the Netherlands.

Civil war in Switzerland over religion. Protestants are defeated at Kapel.

1532 Francis I of France secures an alliance with Bavaria, Saxony, and Hesse against the Habsburg king of the Romans, Ferdinand.

Peace of Nuremberg grants German Protestant princes freedom of worship.

Süleyman the Magnificent is defeated at Güns, Hungary.

Sahib Giray founds the khanate of Crimea under Ottoman protection.

1533 Henry VIII of England marries Anne Boleyn. Henry is excommunicated.

Ottomans sign a peace treaty with Ferdinand of Habsburg – Hungarian rule is divided between Ferdinand and the Ottoman puppet, John Zápolyai.

1534 Act of Supremacy: Henry VIII of England breaks with Rome.

Francis I of France signs the Treaty of Augsburg, an alliance with the Protestant princes against Charles V.

Christian III, a Protestant, becomes king of Denmark after defeating Catholic supporters of his brother, John.

1536 An Act of Union brings together Wales and England under one administration.

Henry VIII crushes the "Pilgrimage of Grace," a religious and social rebellion in N England.

Anne Boleyn, wife of Henry VIII of England, is beheaded, a victim of court intrigues and her own arrogance.

1537 An alliance of French and Turks attack Charles V's forces in the Mediterranean.

1538 Ottoman navy defeats combined Venetian, Spanish, and papal armada at Preveza.

1539 Emperor Charles V puts down a rebellion in Ghent, and strips the town of its privileges.

1540 Over the past four years, more than 550 monasteries in England have been dissolved. Their treasures have passed into the king's hands.

AMERICAS & AUSTRALASIA

1531 Hernán Cortés returns to New Spain as captain-general.

1532 Francisco Pizarro conquers the Inca empire (–1533).

First captaincies granted for purposes of settlement.

1533 Francisco Pizarro captures Inca capital, Cusco; orders the execution of the Inca chief, Atahualpa.

1534 French explorer Jacques Cartier explores Strait of Belle Isle and St. Lawrence, laying the basis for later French claims to Canada.

Inca leader Manco Capac II leads an uprising against Pizarro.

1535 Francisco Pizarro founds the city of Lima.

1536 Diego de Almagro, the governor of New Toledo, reaches Chile.

1537 Antonio de Mendoza, the viceroy of New Spain, establishes the territorial limits of the estates distributed to Spanish conquerors.

Manco Capac II establishes a new Inca state at Vilcabamba.

1539 Hernando de Soto leads expedition into southeastern N America; begins exploration (–1543).

The first printing press in the New World is established in Mexico City.

1540 Spaniard Hernando de Alvaro sails up the Rio Grande, southwestern N America, to the Indian village of Taos.

Coronado leads expedition into southwestern N America.

Valdivia crosses Atacama desert to extend Spanish conquests to south.

Religious Orders

1524 Foundation of the Theatine Order by Tommaso de Vio and Gian Pietro Carafa. The Theatines are an order of priests dedicated to performing works of charity, preaching, and administering sacraments.

1528 Foundation of the Capuchins by Matteo da Bascio. They strictly follow the rule of St. Francis.

1533 Barnabite Order established in Milan by Antonio Maria Zaccaria. The Order also receives papal approval for a female Order, the Angelic Sisters of St. Paul the Converted (the Angelics).

1534 Establishment of the Jesuit Order (Society of Jesus) by Ignatius Loyola.

Establishment of the Somascans by Jerome Emiliani. The main focus of the Order is care of orphans and establishment of schools.

1535 Foundation of the Ursulines. Dedicated to works of charity and education, the Ursulines initially live in the community, but from the 1560s, convents are established.

1542 Bernadino Ochino, vicar-general of the Capuchins, leaves the Order and becomes a Protestant.

1551 Jesuits establish the Gregorian university in Rome.

1568 John of the Cross founds the first monastery of barefoot Carmelites in Spain. Teresa de Ávila establishes the Order of Carmelite Nuns.

1582 Establishment of the Camillans, by Camillus of Lellis. The Order is devoted to helping the sick, in mind and body.

1597 Establishment of the Poor Clerics Regular of the Mother of God of the Pious Schools (Piarists or Scolopi) by José de Calasanz. The Order is devoted to providing free education for poor boys.

The Jesuits

St. Ignatius of Loyola (1491–1556), the son of a Basque nobleman, was the founder of the Society of Jesus, or Jesuits. Injured in battle in 1521, he dedicated his life to the Virgin Mary. He distilled his religious experience into *Spiritual Exercises*, a handbook to develop self-mastery and spiritual discipline. In 1540, he received papal approval for his new order. Although traditional monastic vows were required, Jesuits were exempt from many typical monastic duties. Their main purpose was to spread the Catholic faith. The Jesuits launched a program to build new schools, which combined the best humanist teaching with traditional Catholic beliefs.

Henry VIII (1509–1547)

The marriage of Henry VIII of England with Catherine of Aragon had produced only one daughter, Mary. Henry, fearful of succession disputes, and infatuated with Anne Boleyn, one of the ladies of the court, requested a papal annulment. When the pope was unresponsive, Henry bullied the English clergy into recognizing him as head of the English church, and eventually a convocation of the clergy declared the marriage null and void.

The crown then proceeded to seize papal authority and property. The king received the right to make church appointments, and to act as the final authority on all ecclesiastical legislation. Between 1536 and 1540 the crown dissolved the monasteries and confiscated their properties. Henry did not adhere to Protestant dogma, and during his reign the English church remained, despite its break with Rome, essentially Catholic.

The Six Wives of Henry VIII

1509	Henry marries Catherine of Aragon.
1529	Negotiations for a divorce between Henry and Catherine of Aragon fail. The couple separate in 1531.
1533	**Jan**: Henry marries Anne Boleyn; birth of Princess Elizabeth.
	May: Archbishop of Canterbury annuls Henry's marriage to Catherine of Aragon.
1534	Act of Supremacy is passed by parliament, establishing Henry as supreme head of the church in England.
1536	**May 19**: Execution of Anne Boleyn.
	May 30: Henry marries Jane Seymour.
1537	Birth of Prince Edward; Jane Seymour dies 12 days later.
1540	**Jan 1**: Henry marries Anne of Cleves. Marriage is unconsummated, and he divorces "the Flemish mare" on July 9.
	July 28: Henry marries Catherine Howard, a maid of honor to Anne of Cleves.
1542	Catherine Howard is executed for adultery.
1543	Henry marries twice-widowed Catherine Parr. She survives him.

1541–1550

ASIA

1542 Spanish Jesuit Francis Xavier arrives in Goa on a mission to spread the gospel.

1543 A Portuguese ship is wrecked off Tanegashima Island, Japan.

1545 Humayun, the Mughal emperor, captures Kandahar.

1546 Ottomans retake Basra after revolt.

Ottomans capture Yemen, the gateway to the Red Sea.

Portuguese rout the Indian army at Diu.

1555 **1547** Humayun, the Mughal emperor, ousts his Afghan supplanters to regain his Indian lands. He captures Kabul.

1551 **1549** Jesuit Francis Xavier preaches Christianity in Kagoshima, Japan.

1550 Work begins on the construction of the Suleymaniye mosque in Istanbul, designed by the architect Sinan (–1557).

Beijing is besieged for a week by the Mongols.

AFRICA

1553 **1541** Portuguese are driven out of Agadir, Morocco, by the Sa'di rulers.

Spanish Jesuit Francis Xavier begins a mission to Mozambique, Malindi, and Socotra.

Emperor Charles V launches an unsuccessful expedition against Algiers.

1543 Death of Ahmad Grañ, shot by a Portuguese musketeer.

1544 Portuguese trading posts are opened at the former Muslim port of Quelimane and at Maputo Bay.

1554 **1546** Songhay destroys Mali empire.

1548 Jesuits begin a mission in the Kongo.

1549 Portuguese are driven out of Arzila, their last stronghold in Morocco.

c.1550 The Nupe defeat the Yoruba of the Oyo kingdom (Nigeria).

Importance of slave trade starts to outweigh trade in gold.

EUROPE

1541 Following a victory at Pest, Hungary is made a Turkish province.

1542 Francis I of France reopens hostilities with Emperor Charles V, who has forged an alliance with Henry VIII of England.

English defeat the Scots at the battle of Solway Moss.

1543 Francis I, king of France, attacks Charles V in the Netherlands and N Spain.

The imperial city of Nice, S France, is bombarded by the joint forces of the Berber corsair, Khayr al-Din Barbarossa, and Francis I of France.

1544 An imperial army is defeated by French forces at the battle of Ceresole, Italy.

1551 ▼ The Treaty of Crépy. Francis I promises emperor Charles V his support against the Protestants.

Treaty of Speyer grants the Netherlands full rights of trade and passage in the Baltic.

Following a major witch hunt, 52 witches are executed in Denmark.

1545 Start of council of Trent, which defines modern Catholicism.

Massacre of the Waldensian Protestants in Provence, S France.

1546 Francis I of France and Henry VIII of England sign the peace of Ardres. Boulogne will remain in English hands for eight years.

1555 ▼ **1547** Charles V's forces defeat the Protestant League of Schmalkalden at the battle of Mühlberg.

1558 ▼ In Scotland, the Protestant reformer John Knox is captured by royalist forces and exiled. English forces defeat Scots at battle of Pinkie.

Michelangelo is commissioned to direct work on the building of St. Peter's basilica, Rome.

1549 Renewed war between England and France.

The Act of Uniformity imposes the use of the Protestant Book of Common Prayer in English churches.

1550 English surrender Boulogne to the French. English troops withdraw from Scotland.

Maurice of Saxony lays siege to Magdeburg, the center of Protestant opposition.

AMERICAS & AUSTRALASIA

1541 The explorer Hernando de Soto reaches the Mississippi river.

Jacques Cartier founds a French colony in Canada.

Francisco Pizarro is assassinated in Lima.

Pedro de Valdivia founds Santiago.

1542 Diego el Monzo Almagro, the self-proclaimed governor of Peru, is defeated at the battle of Chupas by forces loyal to the Spanish crown.

Spanish explorer Juan Rodríguez Cabrillo is the first European in California.

Spanish conquistador Francisco de Orellana sails length of the Amazon.

1543 Spanish discover oil in Texas.

1545 Discovery of silver at Potosí; opening of vast silver mine there.

1552 ▼ Bartolomé de las Casas, the bishop of Chiapas, is a champion of Indian rights.

Spanish gain control of the Maya region after crushing a revolt by the Maya people.

1549 Portuguese royal government established in Brazil; direct royal rule imposed from new capital at Bahia.

1550 Spanish crown forbids new expeditions against indigenous peoples; ban lasts ten years.

First Jesuits reach Brazil.

This detail from a map of South America by John Rotz in 1542 shows Native Americans carrying logs of brazil wood for trade with Europeans.

Exploring South America

In the early 1500s, Portuguese and Spanish explorers probed all the navigable eastern river estuaries of South America in the hope of finding a route to the Far East. The Atlantic coastline was consequently well mapped, and knowledge of the area increased when Portuguese traders began to arrive in the area seeking trade with the Native Americans in brazil wood, which they coveted for its valuable red dye. The well-engineered Inca roads that crossed the Andes were soon followed by the *conquistadors*. But, for the most part, the inhospitable interior remained unexplored; expeditions were turned back by impassable terrain or hostile native peoples.

The Potosí silver mine

In the 1540s, Spanish colonists discovered Cerro Rico, the fabulous mountain of silver, at Potosí in the Andes. They embarked on an intensive program of exploitation, and by 1570 Potosí had a population of 120,000, nearly the same as Paris at that time. New technology was introduced by German miners, including a water-powered stamp mill and a mercury amalgamation process that purified the silver. Silver became Spanish South America's most important export, flooding the European markets. By the 1590s, more than 10 million ounces a year of silver were exported from the New World.

Akbar's Mughal armies honed their combat skills by participating in organized tiger-hunts. This Mughal miniature depicts the moment when the men close in on their victims.

Mughal India

Akbar (1542–1605) was an outstanding ruler, able to build on the achievements of his grandfather Babur, who had made himself the master of northern India and proclaimed the Mughal dynasty. Upon his accession in 1556, Akbar was immediately challenged by Hindu forces, defeating them at the battle of Panipat. In 1562 he married a Rajput princess, and embarked on a lifelong campaign to create a new, inclusive empire, that would integrate India's various cultural and religious heritages.

A gracious ruler, he could also be ruthless; in 1568, when the Rajputs opposed him, he sacked their capital, and massacred its defenders. Thereafter, he invited loyal Rajputs to play a strong role in the imperial army. Akbar's military conquests included Gujarat, Bengal, and most of Afghanistan. Akbar patronized Persian, Urdu, and Hindu art and literature, and his court became a center of art and civilization. In later life, he rejected orthodox Islam in favor of a more mystical universal faith.

ASIA

1551 Spanish Jesuit Francis Xavier leaves for China, having introduced Christianity into Japan.

1552 Portuguese repulse the Ottomans at Hormuz.

Foundation of Portuguese colony at Macao.

Francis Xavier dies of exhaustion near Canton.

1553 War of Safavid Persia with Ottomans (–1555).

1554 Ottomans capture Bahrain.

1555 Ottomans and the Persians sign the peace of Amasya.

Mughal emperor Humayun reoccupies Delhi and Agra after defeating an Afghan claimant to the throne.

Earthquake in NW China claims some 830,000 victims.

1563 ▼ Japanese pirates besiege Nanjing, China.

1556 The Russian army under Ivan IV seizes the khanate of Astrakhan, reaching the Caspian Sea.

Mughal emperor Humayun dies, and is succeeded by his son, Akbar. Reign of Akbar marked by territorial expansion and cordial Hindu–Muslim relations (–1605).

Akbar defeats Afghans at battle of Panipat.

1568 ▼ **1558** Akbar conquers Gwalior.

1559 Ottoman sultan Selim defeats his brother Bayezid at the battle of Konya.

1567 ▼ **1560** Reunification of Japan, a land of warring nobles, begins.

AFRICA

1551 Ottomans capture Tripoli.

1553 The Sa'di defeat the last of their enemies and establish themselves as rulers of all Morocco.

1554 Katsina in Nigeria regains its independence from Songhay.

1555 The emperor of Ethiopia, Galwdewos, is victorious in the Ethiopian–Galla war.

1557 Muhammad al-Mahdi, the effective founder of the Sa'di kingdom of Morocco, is assassinated.

EUROPE

1551 Henry II of France resumes the war against Emperor Charles V and disavows the council of Trent. He allies with Maurice of Saxony.

1552 Maurice of Saxony takes Augsburg.

A French army occupies the three bishoprics of Metz, Verdun, and Toul.

1553 French forces invade Tuscany and are defeated by an imperial army at the battle of Marciano.

Mary Tudor, a Roman Catholic, succeeds the Protestant king of England, Edward VI. Roman Catholic bishops are restored.

1554 Sir Thomas Wyatt leads a Protestant rebellion in Kent. He surrenders to government forces.

In London, the Muscovy Company is formed to trade in furs and wood with Russia.

1555 At the peace of Augsburg, Lutheran princes win right to choose their religion.

French forces occupying Siena surrender to an imperial army after a 15-month siege.

Persecution of Protestants begins in England.

1557 In support of her husband Philip II of Spain, Queen Mary I of England declares war on France. Spanish troops defeat the French at St Quentin.

1558 A French army takes Calais from the English.

French forces suffer a resounding defeat at the hands of the Spanish at Gravelines.

In Scotland, John Knox publishes his *First Blast of the Trumpet against the Monstrous Regiment of Women*, attacking female monarchs.

Ivan the Terrible of Russia invades Lithuania, seizing several Baltic towns.

1559 Spain, England, and France sign the peace of Cateau-Cambrésis, ending the Habsburg–Valois wars. Henry II of France accepts treaty; Habsburgs victorious.

1560 King Gustav I of Sweden abdicates in favor of his son after 43 years on the throne.

On the death of King Henry II of France, his widow Catherine de Medici becomes regent.

AMERICAS & AUSTRALASIA

c.1570

c.1551 Jesuit missionaries in Brazil set new standards for the treatment of Indians in New World colonies.

1552 Dominican monk, Bartolomé de las Casas, issues a savage condemnation of Spanish rule in the New World.

1555 Some 600 French settlers found short-lived colony of France Antarctique at Rio de Janeiro.

The Spanish settlement at Havana, Cuba, is attacked by the French.

A Basque fleet captures the French fort at St. John's Fishery, Newfoundland.

1559 Spaniard Tristán de Luna y Arellano founds a settlement in Mobile Bay, Alabama.

1560 Portuguese begin sugarcane cultivation in Brazil.

El Dorado

Persistent rumors spoke of El Dorado, a land of fabulous wealth, located in northwestern South America. The great wealth revealed by the conquests of Aztec Mexico and Inca Peru, as well as local Indians' tales, all served to bolster the myth. Indians reported that a chief was ritually dusted with powdered gold, then washed in a lake into which many fine artifacts were then thrown. The mythical land was named after this "gilded" man, "*dorado*" in Spanish. Throughout the 1530s and 1540s, a succession of expeditions searched in vain; three parties, led by Jiménez de Quesada, Nikolaus Federmann, and Sebastián de Benalcázar, converged on the gold-rich civilization of the Muisca, located in the Colombian tableland. The rich array of gold artifacts they found only served to stimulate their imaginations. The fruitless search then shifted to the east, and it was speculated that El Dorado was located in the Guiana Highlands. Expeditions to find the mythical land continued into the 17th century.

Ivan the Terrible

In 1547, at the age of 16, Ivan IV (1533–84) was crowned "Caesar (czar) of all the Russians." At first he was an able ruler. He established a new law code, forged trade links with western Europe, and convened Russia's first consultative assembly.

By the late 1550s, however, he was becoming increasingly paranoid and unstable, and a reign of terror ensued. In 1565 he created the *oprichina*, or "private domain," an area around Moscow administered by the czar, and terrorized by a secret police force. He imprisoned and executed *boyars* (nobles) who opposed him, and confiscated their estates. Vast numbers of oppressed people fled to newly acquired lands along the Don and Volga rivers, where they could be free of Ivan's arbitrary rule. These refugees were known as Cossacks.

The Dutch Revolt (1565–1648)

The opposition of a Calvinist minority against Spanish rule in the Netherlands eventually secured the independence of seven northern Netherlands provinces, known as the Dutch Republic. The southern Netherlands (modern Belgium) remained Catholic.

1565	Riots in the Netherlands against Philip II's unpopular fiscal and religious policies.
1568	Raids by Dutch "Sea Beggars" on Spanish naval transports and bases (–1572).
1574	Dutch capture Middelburg and force Spanish to retreat from siege of Leiden.
1576	Unpaid Spanish army mutinies in Antwerp and sacks city.
1579	Catholic nobility in the south sign Treaty of Arras with Philip II.
1585	The duke of Parma captures the rebel town of Antwerp. English side with the rebels.
1590	Dutch rebels make major gains in northeast.
1600	Victory of United Provinces at Nieuwpoort.
1609	A 12-year truce negotiated with Spain.
1621	War resumes.
1625	Spanish troops capture Breda.
1629	Dutch capture 'sHertogenbosch.
1639	Battle of the Downs; Spanish fleet defeated by Dutch.
1648	Peace of Münster; Spain acknowledges Dutch United Provinces as sovereign independent state.

Elizabeth I

Elizabeth I ascended the throne of England in 1558 and ruled for 44 years. A well-educated and astute woman, she created an atmosphere conducive to brilliant cultural achievements and assiduously cultivated a glorious image of her rule. The works of William Shakespeare and Edmund Spenser reflect this self-confident mood. Spenser exalted, in *The Faerie Queene*, "the most excellent and glorious person of our sovereigne the queen, and her kingdom in Fairy Land." Her cult was fed by poets of genius, by her frequent travels around the land, which made her visible to her people, and by her great skill at handling parliament. By the time her youthful glamor had faded, she had acquired an aura of majesty, which was enhanced by her longevity and sheer powers of survival.

1561–1570

ASIA

1563 Ming generals have finally asserted control over Japanese pirates.

Burmese king Bayinnaung invades Siam (Thailand).

1565 At the battle of Talikota the capital of the Hindu empire of Vijayanagara is captured and sacked by the united forces of the five Deccan sultanates.

1585 ▼

Spanish fleet claims Philippines in name of King Philip II.

1566 Suleyman succeeded by Selim II.

1571 ▼

1567 In Japan, the powerful nobleman Oda Nobunaga puts down resistance from the Saito family and takes the town of Inabayama (Gifu).

1572 ▼

1568 Mughal emperor Akbar captures the fortress of Chitor.

In Japan, the Christian nobleman Omura Sumitada gives permission for foreign traders to establish posts at a small fishing village called Fukae (Nagasaki).

1569 Akbar captures the fortress of Ranthambhor, bringing Rajput power to an end.

1570 Portuguese ships begin trading in Nagasaki.

c.1570 First imports of silver from America reach China.

AFRICA

1561 Father da Silveira, the Portuguese Christian envoy to the Mwenemutapa court in SE Africa, is killed at court – probably at the instigation of the Muslim imam.

1562 Englishman John Hawkins begins trading slaves across the Atlantic. He leaves Sierra Leone with a shipment of 300 slaves, sailing to Hispaniola.

1565 King Afonso II of Kongo is assassinated during mass.

1575 ▼

1570 Establishment of Portuguese colony in Angola.

Portuguese slave trading on the Zambezi river leads to the Zimba War among the Chewa to the north.

EUROPE

1561 Collapse of Teutonic Order in Livonia; region partitioned into Russian, Swedish, and Polish–Lithuanian spheres of interest.

The reformer John Knox sets out a new Calvinist Scottish church constitution.

1562 In France, the massacre of a Protestant Huguenot congregation at Vassy sets off a religious war.

The English sign a treaty with Louis de Bourbon, prince of Condé and leader of the Huguenots, entitling them to occupy Le Havre.

After inconclusive skirmishes, Ottomans gain Transylvania.

1563 War of the Three Crowns breaks out between Sweden and Denmark (–1570).

The port of Le Havre is seized from the English by Catholic troops.

The 39 Articles of the Protestant Church of England are published.

In London, a quarter of the population dies in an epidemic of bubonic plague.

1565 Beginning of Ivan IV's "reign of terror" in Russia.

A statute in London empowers the Royal College of Physicians to carry out dissections of the human body, hitherto regarded as taboo.

1566 An outbreak of Calvinist iconoclasm in the Netherlands triggers the Dutch revolt.

Turks take possession of the Aegean island of Chios.

1567 Mary, Queen of Scots, is defeated by the Protestant nobility, imprisoned, and forced to abdicate.

Spanish troops are sent to the Netherlands to help crush the Calvinist revolt.

1568 In Spain, Moors who have converted to Christianity revolt.

Raids by Dutch "Sea Beggars" on Spanish naval transports and bases.

1569 French royalist forces defeat the Huguenots at the battle of Jarnac.

The grand duchy of Lithuania unites with Poland; new state stretches from the Baltic to the Dneister.

Mercator's new projection used for the first time in a world map.

AMERICAS & AUSTRALASIA

1562 War and disease kill much of the Indian population in Brazil (–1563).

1564 Frenchman René Ludonnière lands in Florida with a party of 300 to set up the post of Fort Caroline.

1565 Spanish massacre French colonists in Florida and found St. Augustine, the first permanent European settlement in the future US.

A Portuguese colony is established at Rio de Janeiro.

1567 Álvaro de Mendaña explores Solomon Islands (–1569).

1568 A French force led by Dominique de Corgues avenges the Spanish massacre of French troops in 1565; they burn down the San Mateo fort.

French occupy N Maranhão.

Spanish ships trap the English sailors John Hawkins and Francis Drake in the West Indies on a slaving voyage. Two English ships are lost in the attack.

c.1570 Jesuit missions established in southeast N America (Florida) and in the Southwest.

Iroquois Indians in northeast N America form a league of tribes.

Baltic wars

In 1563, Sweden and Denmark went to war for supremacy in the Baltic region. The first modern naval war ensued, as the two countries competed for control of the maritime invasion routes. The Danes were supported by the semiindependent German city of Lübeck. Seven major naval battles were fought between 1563 and 1570, including the battle of Öland in 1564 (*above*), in which the Swedes lost their new flagship, the *Mars*. By 1568, both sides were exhausted, and a truce was agreed in 1570 without any territorial gains on either side.

The colonization of Florida

The first European to reach Florida was the Spanish explorer, Juan Ponce de León, who established a colony near modern Fort Myers, but was mortally wounded in a battle with Calusa Indians in 1521. Two successive expeditions, by Pánfilo de Narváez (1528) and Hernando de Soto (1539) failed to gain a foothold in the region.

In 1564 a group of French Huguenots established Fort Caroline on the banks of the St. John's river. The Spanish saw the French presence as a threat to their sea route between Cuba and Spain. In 1565 an expedition commanded by Pedro Menéndez de Avilés founded the fort at St. Augustine (*above*), and massacred most of the French colony.

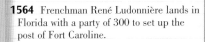

St Bartholomew's Day massacre

The massacre of French Huguenots on August 24, 1572 was the worst atrocity of the French wars of religion. One of the Huguenot leaders, Admiral Gaspard de Coligny, had persuaded the king, Charles IX, to intervene to help the Dutch in their struggle against their Spanish overlords.

Catherine de Medici, mother of King Charles IX, feared a Franco-Spanish war, and was alarmed by the growing power of the Huguenots, reflected in the marriage between Henry of Navarre, a prominent Huguenot, and the king's sister, Marguerite of Valois. With Catherine's approval, an assassination plot was hatched, in which Coligny was wounded. Fearing reprisals, Catherine persuaded the king to approve the execution of Protestant leaders on trumped-up charges that they were plotting his overthrow.

At dawn on August 24, following the murder of Coligny and his associates, militant Catholics began to slaughter Protestants. About 3,000 died in Paris alone, perhaps as many as 20,000 were killed in all of France.

PARIS

ASIA

1571 The Spaniard López de Legazpi founds the city of Manila.

1581 Oda Nobunaga destroys the rebellious Ikko sect, based near Nara, Japan.

1572 Mughal emperor Akbar abolishes the *jizya* tax on non-Muslims.

Mughal forces overrun Gujarat.

1573 The Muromachi shogunate, founded in 1335, collapses when the shogun submits to Oda Nobunaga.

1584 Reign of Wanli in China (–1620). Period of great paintings and porcelain-making.

1574 Sultan Selim II, "the Sot," dies after a drinking bout. He is succeeded by his son, Murad III.

1575 Completion of the Selimiye mosque in Edirne, Anatolia, by Sinan.

1576 Mughal forces conquer Bengal, N India.

Foundation of new city of Fatehpur Sikri in C India, Akbar's new capital.

1578 Ottomans seek to dominate Georgia and other Caucasian principalities. War breaks out between Ottomans and Safavid Persia.

In China, the *Bencao Gangmu*, a celebrated treatise on the pharmacopoeia by Li Shizhen, is completed.

1582 **1579** Akbar invites Jesuits from the Portuguese colony at Goa to visit his court.

AFRICA

1571 Portuguese slave trading on the coast of Angola leads to the Jaga War in the interior.

After the unsuccessful attempts to convert the Mutapa of the Zambezi valley to Christianity, the Portuguese launch an invasion.

1573 Led by Don John of Austria, the Spanish seize Tunis and Bizerta from the Berbers.

1574 Ottomans recapture Tunis and Bizerta from the Spanish.

Portuguese force the ruler of Uteve in the Zambezi valley to pay tribute.

1575 Portuguese found the city of Luanda, Angola.

1577 Ethiopia conquers the sultanate of Harar.

1578 Portuguese sign a treaty with the Mutapa kingdom of the S Zambezi area.

Portuguese lead Christian crusade against Moors. They are decisively defeated by the Moroccans under Ahmad al-Mansur at Alcazar-el-Kebir.

1589 Accession of Ahmad al-Mansur as sultan of Morocco (–1603). His vigorous rule brings Morocco to the height of its power.

c.1580 In the kingdom of Songhay, dynastic disputes erupt into a series of civil wars.

EUROPE

1571 Battle of Lepanto; Ottoman navy defeated by united Christian fleet off Greek coast.

Pope Pius V orders the drawing up of an index of censored books.

1572 The "Sea Beggars" (Calvinist rebels against the duke of Alba's rule in the Netherlands) capture Briel.

St. Bartholomew's Day massacre; thousands of French Protestants (Huguenots) are massacred in Paris with the connivance of Catherine de Medici, the king's mother.

Danish astronomer Tycho Brahe sights a new star, undermining the concept of celestial stability.

1573 Henry of Anjou, brother of Charles IX, king of France, becomes the first elected king of Poland.

Catherine de Medici makes peace with the French Huguenots.

Spanish recapture Haarlem from the rebels.

Sister Teresa, prioress of the Convent of the Incarnation in Ávila, writes her mystical handbook, *The Way of Perfection*.

1574 Dutch capture Middelburg and force Spanish to retreat from siege of Leiden.

1575 At a conference in Breda, Requesens, the Spanish governor of the Netherlands, agrees to withdraw Spanish troops and officials.

Catholic forces under Henry, duke of Guise, defeat the Protestants at the battle of Dormans.

Supported by the Turks, Stephen Báthory, prince of Transylvania, is elected king of Poland.

1576 Ivan IV of Russia conquers most of Livonia, but his army is crushed by the Polish–Swedish alliance at Wenden (–1578).

Plague kills the great Venetian painter, Titian, who had become the most famous portrait painter in Europe.

1579 Union of Utrecht: the seven provinces of the Netherlands form the United Provinces to maintain peace and independence. Catholics in the south remain loyal to Spain.

Spanish make an unsuccessful attempt to land in Ireland.

1580 Philip II of Spain seizes Portuguese crown; union of Spanish and Portuguese crowns.

AMERICAS & AUSTRALASIA

1571 Spanish install an inquisitorial tribune in Mexico.

1572 In Peru, the Spanish capture Vilcabamba, the stronghold of the Inca rebels. Their leader, Tupac Amaru, is executed.

English sailor Francis Drake launches attacks on Spanish harbors and shipping in the Caribbean.

1573 Rules drawn up for planning Jesuit towns in S America.

New legislation in Brazil makes slavery a common practice.

1575 Friar Cristóbal de Molina compiles a collection of Inca hymns, *Tales and Ceremonies of the Incas*.

c.1575 Brazil becomes world's largest sugar producer.

1576 Following a siege by Indians, 287 colonists are evacuated from Santa Elena, Florida, which is destroyed.

Englishman Martin Frobisher explores Labrador and discovers Baffin Island.

An epidemic of plague kills 40 percent of the Indians in New Spain.

1577 Francis Drake circumnavigates the globe (–1580).

1578 An earthquake destroys the city of Santiago, Chile.

1579 Francis Drake discovers San Francisco Bay. He claims the surrounding land, which he calls New Albion, for Queen Elizabeth.

1580 Philip II of Spain becomes king of Portugal and its Brazilian empire.

Spanish trap and destroy a French vessel under Gilberto Gil in the mouth of St. John's river, Florida.

The battle of Lepanto

In 1571, under attack by Selim II's Ottoman forces, the Venetians of Cyprus appealed for help from Philip II of Spain. In May 1571, the fleet of the Holy League of Spain, Venice, and the papacy set sail for Cyprus. The opposing sides met at Lepanto, off the west coast of Greece. After four hours of fighting, the superior gunpower of the Christian fleet and the tenacity of the Spanish infantry inflicted a crushing defeat on the Ottomans; 113 galleys were sunk and 117 captured. Although the triumph was celebrated throughout Europe, the Christians were unable to consolidate their victory. By 1573, Venice had signed a peace treaty with the Ottoman empire, recognizing their conquest of Cyprus.

The French Wars of Religion (1562–1598)

1562 First civil war (–1563). Forces of duke of Guise attack a Huguenot congregation at Vassy. Huguenots rally by taking several towns.

1563 Edict of Amboise grants Huguenots limited rights of worship.

1567 Second civil war (–1568). Huguenots seize some cities and attempt to capture the king.

1568 Pacification of Longjumeau. Restores terms of Edict of Amboise.

Third civil war (–1570). Huguenots defeat the royal army at the battle of Arnay-le-Duc.

1570 Pacification of St. Germain restores Protestant rights of worship.

1572 Fourth civil war (–1573). Massacre of St. Bartholomew's Day (August 24). Several Huguenot communities refuse to accept royal authority.

1573 Edict of Boulogne limits Huguenot worship to towns of La Rochelle, Montauban, and Nîmes.

1574 Fifth civil war (–1576). Huguenots' military strength grows in S France.

1576 Peace of Monsieur (peace of Beaulieu). Huguenot worship is allowed in France, except in Paris region.

1577 Sixth civil war. Military skirmishes follow estates general's declaration of intention to impose Catholicism on France.

Peace of Bergerac restores Huguenot rights of worship.

1580 Seventh civil war. Peace of Fleix ends the conflict.

1585 Wars of the League (–1598). Catholic League is headed by Guise faction. Huguenots are aided by German and Swiss mercenaries.

1588 Day of the Barricades. Duke of Guise, leader of the League, enters Paris in triumph. He is assassinated on orders of King Henry III.

1589 Rebellion by League supporters. Henry III is mortally wounded.

1590 Henry of Navarre defeats League forces at the battle of Ivry.

1593 Henry of Navarre renounces his Huguenot beliefs, and is accepted as King Henry IV.

1598 Edict of Nantes restores Catholic worship to all parts of France. Huguenot worship is restricted.

Shah Abbas I

After a period of civil war in Persia, Abbas I became Shah in 1588. Shah Abbas, pictured here with one of his pages, was the Safavid dynasty most outstanding leader. He had the military strength to drive the Ottomans and their allies out of parts of western and northern Persia that they had occupied during earlier periods of civil disorder.

At the same time, he was an efficient administrator, who restored much of the imperial structure laid down centuries before by Cyrus and Darius. The road network was reinstated, cities grew and expanded, and new commercial links were established. Under his influence, Persia became the cultural center of the Islamic world. Architecture, painting, and literature flourished, and the restored capital city, Isfahan, was an outstanding example of the medieval Persian style.

Toyotomi Hideyoshi

In the 1570s, Japan's Ashikaga shogunate dissolved into chaotic civil war. Oda Nobunaga, a minor feudal lord, seized control of Kyoto in 1568. With the help of his ablest general, Toyotomi Hideyoshi (1537–1598), he ruthlessly broke the military power of the major Buddhist monasteries around the capital. When he was killed in 1582, Hideyoshi seized power. A peasant by birth, he consolidated Nobunaga's work. All non-*samurai* were disarmed to ensure that commoners were unable to challenge his authority. His reorganization of the tax system and redistribution of land ensured that the gulf between peasants and warriors widened. By the 1590s, he had succeeded in unifying most of Japan for the first time.

ASIA

1581 Russian Cossack Timofeyevich Yermak begins Russian conquest of Siberia (–1582).

Oda Nobunaga attacks Mount Koya, the headquarters of the Shingon Buddhist sect.

1582 Mughal emperor Akbar attempts to synthesize the world's great religions.

Jesuit missionary Matteo Ricci arrives in Macao. He begins to study Chinese language and civilization.

Japan sends its first Christian ambassador to the Vatican.

Oda Nobunaga, who has begun the process of unifying Japan, is killed in battle by Akechi Mitsuhide.

1583 Yunnan province is invaded by the Burmese.

1584 Construction work begins on the tomb of the Chinese emperor, Wanli (–1590).

The first Catholic catechism in Chinese is published.

1585 Spain establishes first permanent European settlement at Cebu, in the Philippines.

1586 Mughal emperor Akbar annexes the kingdom of Kashmir.

Toyotomi Hideyoshi takes the title of *Kanpaku* (civil dictator). He embarks on the unification of Japan.

1587 Toyotomi Hideyoshi brings the whole of Kyushu under his control.

An anti-Christian edict is issued in Japan. Christians are ordered out of the country.

1588 The feeble Mohammed Shah, sultan of Persia, hands over power to his 17-year-old son, Abbas.

Famine and pestilence sweep China, leading to depopulation and lawlessness.

1590 Persian ruler Shah Abbas I concludes a peace treaty with the Ottomans. Under its terms, the Turks extend their frontiers to the Caucasus and Caspian.

The town of Hyderabad is founded on the banks of the Musi river, India.

Toyotomi Hideyoshi completes the political unification of Japan. His political and administrative base is moved to Edo (Tokyo).

AFRICA

1587 Second Zimba War, caused by Portuguese slave trading on the Zambezi, breaks out between the Chewa peoples in Mozambique and Malawi.

1589 The sultan of Mombasa refuses to pay tribute to the Portuguese and the town is sacked.

1591 A Moroccan army, led by al-Mansur, sets out across the Sahara to invade the kingdom of Songhay.

1590 Oromo bands begin occupation of S Ethiopia.

Second Jaga War breaks out in Zaire, caused by Portuguese slave trading on the Angolan coast.

EUROPE

1581 Swedes recapture Estonia.

The Dutch estates general deposes Philip II as ruler of the seven provinces of the Netherlands; declares war by doing so.

1582 Russians resist the siege of Pskov by Polish–Lithuanian troops. After 25 years of conflict, the Russians agree to give up their claims to Lithuania.

The Julian calendar (46 BCE) is replaced by the Gregorian calendar, by papal decree. Ten days are removed from the 1582 calendar, bringing the spring equinox back to March 21.

1583 Troops of the United Provinces of the Netherlands blockade the port of Antwerp.

1585 Alessandro Farnese, governor of the Netherlands, has secured the submission of the S Netherlands, Flanders, and Brabant to the Spanish crown.

England allies with the United Provinces and sends an army to the Netherlands.

1586 El Greco paints *The Burial of the Count of Orgaz*. Its dramatic forms and colors confirm his growing reputation.

1593

1587 Poles elect a Swedish king, Sigismund Vasa.

Elizabeth I of England orders the execution of Mary, Queen of Scots, who has been found guilty of conspiracy to murder Elizabeth and promote a Spanish invasion.

Francis Drake attacks Cádiz, and pillages the Spanish coast.

1588 The Spanish Armada, an attempted invasion of England by Philip II of Spain, is defeated.

King Henry III of France is forced to flee Paris after Henry of Guise's triumphant entry into the city. The king orders the assassination of Henry, duke of Guise.

1589 English raid on Corunna and Portugal.

Henry III, the last Valois king of France, assassinated; Henry of Navarre succeeds him.

1590 The composer Claudio Monteverdi publishes a collection of madrigals.

AMERICAS & AUSTRALASIA

1581 Francisco Chamuscado claims southwest N America for Spain, naming it San Felipe del Nuevo Mexico.

1583 Sir Humphrey Gilbert takes possession of Newfoundland in the name of Queen Elizabeth of England.

1584 An English expedition to southeast N America claims the area for England, and names it Virginia after the Virgin Queen (Elizabeth I).

First English attempt to establish a colony at Roanoke, Virginia.

1585 Second English expedition to Roanoke Island, led by Sir Richard Grenville.

1586 Francis Drake makes a surprise attack on the fortified city of Santo Domingo, Hispaniola, forcing the governor to pay a ransom.

1596

Drake sacks Cartagena, Colombia.

English fend off an Indian attack on Roanoke, killing an Indian chief.

Sir Richard Grenville sets sail from Roanoke, leaving 20 settlers behind.

1587 Spanish evacuate Santa Elena, N Florida.

The first English child born in the New World is named Virginia.

John White, English explorer and artist arrives at Roanoke with 177 colonists.

1607

1588 Jesuit missionaries gather Guaraní Indians of Paraguay into mission towns and build a trade empire from sale of their produce.

1607

1590 John White returns from Europe with supplies to find the colony at Roanoke abandoned.

European Colonization (1455–1600)

1455	Portuguese confirmed in their African possessions by the papal bull *Romanus Pontifex*.
1471	Tangier is taken by Portugal.
1482	Construction of the Portuguese fort at Elmina on the Guinea coast.
1494	Treaty of Tordesillas establishes a demarcation line in the Atlantic between Spanish and Portuguese New World possessions.
1496	Spanish found Santo Domingo on Hispaniola, the first European town in the Americas.
1498	Spanish claims to newly discovered lands are recognized in the papal bull *Inter Caetera Eximiae Devotionis*.
1500	First Franciscan mission to the New World.
1507	First Portuguese landing in Ceylon.
1509	Portuguese naval victory at Diu against a combined Egyptian and Gujarati fleet confirms Portuguese dominance.
1510	Portuguese capture Goa, India.
1511	Portuguese trading post at Malacca established.
1512	Exploitation of labor in the New World is regulated by the Laws of Burgos (Spain).
1519	Beginning of Spanish conquest of Aztec empire by Hernán Cortés.
1532	Francisco Pizarro begins the conquest of Peru for Spain.
	First permanent Portuguese settlement in Brazil established.
1535	Foundation of Lima, Peru, marks beginning of Spanish colonization.
1536	Spanish conquest of Colombia begins.
1541	First Spanish settlement in Chile is established by Pedro de Valdivia.
1557	Portuguese establish trading post on Macao.
1570	Portuguese trading post in Nagasaki, Japan, is established.
1583	Establishment of Spanish colony at Buenos Aires.
1584	Short-lived English settlement at Roanoke is founded by Sir Walter Raleigh.
1600	English form East India Company.

All that remains of the English colony at Roanoke are the evocative sketches of John White (above), who was commissioned to depict life in the New World on the eve of the European colonization.

Fort Jesus, Mombasa

For centuries Arabians, Indonesians, Persians, and Indians had traded with the coastal communities of East Africa. By the 13th century, Arabs dominated the East African trade, and evolved the Swahili city-states, which grew wealthy on trade in ivory, gold, hides, and slaves. When the Portuguese arrived in 1497, the Swahili cities refused to accept their control. The Portuguese attacked the towns and forcibly subjugated the inhabitants, breaking the Islamic monopoly on trade in the region. They built fortresses at Sofala, Mozambique, Kilwa, and Mombasa. Fort Jesus, at Mombasa, (*below*) was the Portuguese powerbase throughout the 17th century.

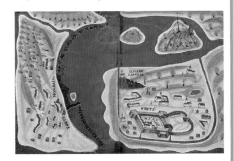

Feudal Japan

The Himeji castle at Hyogo in west Honshu (*below*) was the base for Toyotomi Hideyoshi's campaign to unify Japan in the 1570s and 1580s. Japan's network of regional power bases, often centered on castles, was viewed as a threat to control and unity by Hideyoshi and his successor, Tokugawa Ieyasu, who founded the Tokugawa shogunate in 1603. Both leaders aimed to reduce regional power by destroying local strongholds and prohibiting the use of arms by merchants, monks, and farmers. In addition, a policy of *shi-no-ko-sho* froze class distinctions, rigidly separating Japanese society into warriors, farmers, artisans, and tradesmen. The *samurai*, or warrior class, were based at castle towns, such as Hyogo, where they became bureaucrats.

ASIA

1592 Zaydi imams regain control of Yemen, and establish rule (–1962).

Mughal forces annex Orissa on the east coast of India.

Japanese invade Korea, capturing the castle at Pusan.

1593 Korean navy embarks on a damaging series of raids against Japanese supply ships. Guerrilla bands hound the Japanese invaders.

1594 Mughal troops under Emperor Akbar annex Baluchistan and Makran.

1595 The new Ottoman sultan, Mehmet III, enforces the "law of fratricide," which obliges a new sultan to execute his brothers and male heirs.

1601 Mughal troops annex Kandahar.

1605 Dutch begin colonization of East Indies.

1597 Shah Abbas of Persia drives back Turkish Ozbeg invaders.

Japanese under Hideyoshi launch a further expedition to Korea but are expelled by the Chinese.

Twenty-six Christians are crucified outside Nagasaki on the orders of Hideyoshi.

1598 Anthony and Robert Sherley travel to Persia, where they meet Shah Abbas.

Isfahan becomes imperial capital of Safavid Persia.

Toyotomi Hideyoshi dies, entrusting his dynasty to Tokugawa Ieyasu (–1616).

1612 **1600** English East India Company founded.

1603 Tokugawa Ieyasu defeats his enemies in battle. He is Japan's most powerful warlord.

AFRICA

1591 Moroccan troops under the command of Sultan Ahmad al-Mansur capture the Songhay city of Timbuktu, W Africa.

1592 English ships join in slave trade.

1603 Moroccans capture the Songhay capital, Gao.

1594 Portuguese complete the building of Fort Jesus in Mombasa, Kenya.

1607 **1597** Death of Sarsa Dengel, King of Ethiopia. He has established trading contacts with Ottoman Turks at Massawa. As many as 10,000 captives a year are sold to Turkish traders.

1598 The Bambara people from the Jenne region overthrow the last of the Mali kings and found the kingdom of Segu.

1600 The kingdom of Buganda, CE Africa, defeats an attack by the kingdom of Bunyoro.

c.1600 Kalunga Masula establishes the powerful Maravi empire (–1650) in the Zambezi valley and reinstates peaceful ivory-trading with the Portuguese.

Hausa city-states of W Africa flourishing.

Akan states of W Africa compete for access to goldfields and trade routes to the Atlantic coast.

EUROPE

1591 German Protestant princes form the League of Torgau.

Ivan the Terrible of Russia's nine-year-old son is murdered; the boyar Boris Godunov, the regent, is suspected.

Famous English playwright William Shakespeare is writing dramas for London's theaters.

1592 A peasant revolt in SW France against high taxes is savagely suppressed.

Completion of the Rialto Bridge, Venice.

1593 Start of Great Hungarian War against the Ottoman Turks (–1606).

Swedes impose the condition that Lutheranism remains the state religion on their new king, Sigismund of Poland, a Catholic (–1599).

King Henry IV of France abjures Protestantism and becomes a Catholic.

The English parliament enacts strict new laws against Protestant dissenters, such as Puritans.

1594 Ottoman Turks capture the Hungarian fortress of Raab.

Death of Giovanni da Palestrina, director of music at St. Peter's, Rome, and composer of over 100 masses and 600 motets.

1595 France declares war on Spain (–1598). Henry IV defeats the Spanish at Fontaine-Française and drives them out of Burgundy.

Turkish forces are defeated by Hungarians, led by Sigismund Bathory, at Giurgiu.

1596 An Anglo-Dutch fleet captures and sacks Cadiz, Spain.

Turks defeat Hungarians at Erlau and Mezokereztes.

1597 Danish astronomer, Tycho Brahe records 777 stars.

Dutch explorer, William Barents dies while on his third voyage to find a northeast passage to China.

1598 Rebellious Irish lord Hugh O'Neill defeats an English force at the battle of Yellow Ford.

1598 Boris Godunov is elected czar of Russia (–1605).

AMERICAS & AUSTRALASIA

1591 A Spanish fleet defeats the English off the Azores, C Atlantic.

1594 In Florida, Father Baltasar López holds a mass baptism of 80 Indians.

1595 Spain divides southeast N America into mission provinces.

1596 Francis Drake, English navigator and privateer, dies in the Caribbean.

1597 Simon Ferdinando, a Portuguese navigator working for the English crown, lands on the coast of Maine.

1598 The Marquis of la Roche founds a French colony on Sable Island, Canada.

1600 French found a fur-trading post at Tadoussac, on the St. Lawrence river, Canada.

Spanish are making a new spirit, rum, in their Caribbean sugar plantations.

c.1600 Classic Maori phase in N Island, New Zealand. Population increases, intertribal warfare, and construction of fortresses.

Statue-building culture of Easter Island begins to decline, as the island can no longer produce sufficient food or timber.

The kingdom of Kongo

The Portuguese arrived at the mouth of the Zaire river in the 1480s, and established contact with the kingdom of Kongo (present-day Zaire). As a result of Portuguese missionary activity, the local king adopted the name Alfonso I (1506–43) and embraced Christianity, promoting it as a royal religious cult, and made efforts to westernize his kingdom. When Kongo was attacked by nomadic warriors, known as the Jaga, in 1568, the Portuguese came to Kongo's aid, providing the military support it needed to drive them out. But Kongo was now a client state of Portuguese traders. In 1571, King Alvaro I was installed on the throne by the Portuguese (*above*). He became increasingly dependent on Portuguese military aid, which he paid for by exporting captives for the Atlantic slave trade. As the demand for slaves grew in the 17th century, the king's authority collapsed and Kongo disintegrated into rival factions.

The East India Company

Incorporated by royal charter on December 31, 1600, the English East India Company was formed for the exploitation of trade with East and Southeast Asia and India. Initially formed simply as a monopolistic commercial body, the company eventually became a political

The East India Company crest on an artifact from Thailand

instrument, acting as the agent for the English government's colonial policy in the 18th and 19th centuries. The company was originally formed to share in the profitable East Indian spice trade, which had been a Spanish and Portuguese monopoly. Following the defeat of the Spanish Armada in 1588, the English seized the opportunity to break the monopoly. The company's defeat of the Portuguese in India in 1612 enabled it to win concessions from the Mughals, allowing them to trade in spices, cotton, silk, and indigo. The opposition of the Dutch in the East Indies proved more troublesome.

The World in 1600

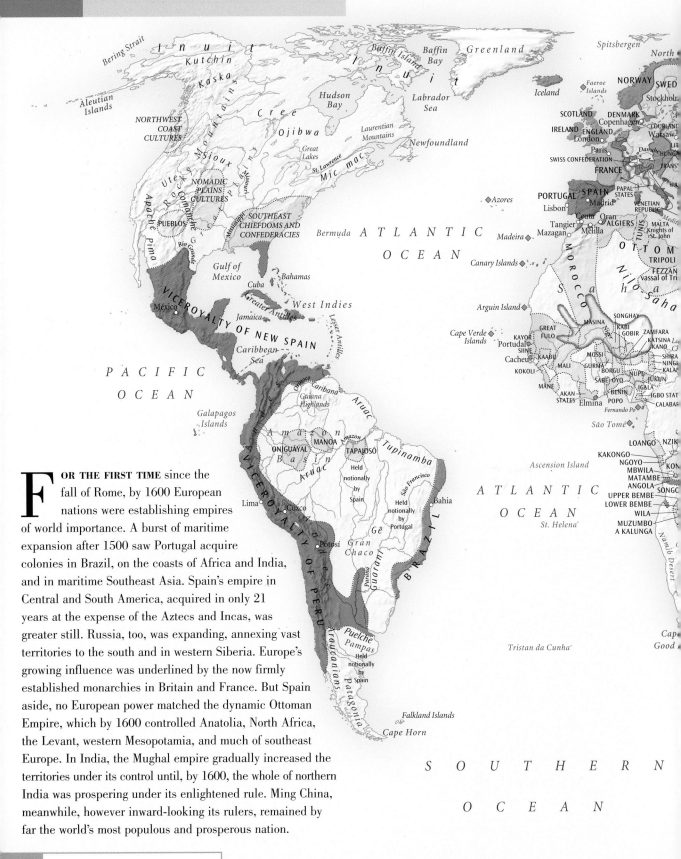

F**OR THE FIRST TIME** since the fall of Rome, by 1600 European nations were establishing empires of world importance. A burst of maritime expansion after 1500 saw Portugal acquire colonies in Brazil, on the coasts of Africa and India, and in maritime Southeast Asia. Spain's empire in Central and South America, acquired in only 21 years at the expense of the Aztecs and Incas, was greater still. Russia, too, was expanding, annexing vast territories to the south and in western Siberia. Europe's growing influence was underlined by the now firmly established monarchies in Britain and France. But Spain aside, no European power matched the dynamic Ottoman Empire, which by 1600 controlled Anatolia, North Africa, the Levant, western Mesopotamia, and much of southeast Europe. In India, the Mughal empire gradually increased the territories under its control until, by 1600, the whole of northern India was prospering under its enlightened rule. Ming China, meanwhile, however inward-looking its rulers, remained by far the world's most populous and prosperous nation.

The World in 1600

- Ming Empire
- Ottoman Empire
- ◆ Spain and possessions
- ◆ Portugal and possessions (ruled by Kings of Spain 1580–1640)
- England and possessions
- Austrian Habsburg territories
- France
- Denmark and possessions
- Venetian Republic and possessions
- United Provinces (fighting for independence from Spain)
- ◇ Dutch (United Provinces)
- Mughal Empire at Akbar's accession, 1556
- under Burmese control, 1575
- Songhay to 1590
- Holy Roman Empire

Map labels:

a Zemlya, Kara Sea, SSIAN, OSCOW, PIRE, VA, KHANATE OF CRIMEA, k Sea, antinople, Volga, Don, Caucasus, Caspian Sea, Ural Mts, Ob', Irtysh, Yenisey, Lena, Bering Strait, Kamchatka, Amur, Sea of Okhotsk, Kurile Islands, Hokkaido, Honshu, Sea of Japan, Kyushu, East China Sea, Taiwan, Macao

Paleosiberians, Samoyeds, Yakuts, Tungus, Buryats, Siberia, Turkic peoples, Aral Sea, Lake Balkhash, KHIVA, BUKHARA, CHAGATAI KHANATE, Altai Mountains, Takla Makan, MONGOLIA in disintegration, Gobi, MANCHURIA, Lake Baikal, Yellow River, Beijing, KOREA, JAPAN, MING EMPIRE, Yangtze

SAFAVID EMPIRE, Isfahan, Tigris, Euphrates, MPIRE, Beduins, Red Sea, The Gulf, Hormuz, Muscat, OMAN, Arabian Sea, Arabian Peninsula, Diu, Surat, Damão, Cambay, Bassein, Chaul, Bombay, GONDWANA, AHMADNAGAR, BIJAPUR, Goa, Bhatkal, Mangalore, Calicut, Cannanore, Negapatam, Cochin, Quilon, Colombo, Jaffna, Batticaloa, Galle, CEYLON, POLYGAR KINGDOMS, Masulipatam, GOLCONDA, BIDAR, Bay of Bengal, ARAKAN, BURMA, SHAN STATES, Mekong, LAOS, ANNAM, SIAM, CAMBODIA, CHAMPA, TRAN NINH, Plateau of Tibet, TIBET, Himalayas, Ganges, Indus, Thar Desert, Agra, MUGHAL EMPIRE, NEPALESE PRINCIPALITIES, BHUTAN, ASSAMESE STATES, Nile

FUNJ, Gulf of Aden, Socotra, AUSSA, ETHIOPIA, HARAR, ADAL, SMALL OROMO STATES, Cushites, ople, Lake Victoria, Mombasa, Lake Tanganyika, Lake Nyasa, MARAVI, LUNDU, TAPA, UA, Sofala, Inhambane, Delagoa Bay, zbezi, Mozambique, Madagascar, Malays, Comoros, Seychelles, Réunion, ◆ Mauritius

Maldive Islands, INDIAN OCEAN, Nicobar Islands, Andaman Islands, South China Sea, ATJEH, MALAY STATES, Malacca, SULTANATE OF JOHORE, MALAYS, BANTAM, MALAY STATES, CHERIBON, MATARAM, East Indies, Celebes, Moluccas, Area under Portuguese influence, Amboina, Timor, New Guinea, Papuans, BRUNEI, SULU, Mindanao, Luzon, PHILIPPINE ISLANDS

PACIFIC OCEAN, Micronesia, Scattered Spanish possessions, Melanesia, Bismarck Archipelago, Solomon Islands, Vanuatu, Fiji, New Caledonia, Melanesians

Great Sandy Desert, Gibson Desert, Great Victoria Desert, Australian Aborigines, Simpson Desert, Lake Eyre, Darling, Great Barrier Reef, Great Dividing Range, Tasman Sea, Tasmania, New Zealand, Maoris

THE NEW WORLD BY ABRAHAM ORTELIUS

Abraham Ortelius was an Antwerp map-seller whose *Theatrum Orbis Terrarum* of 1570 is considered the first modern atlas. He was not an original cartographer, but he traveled widely in search of reliable sources and his atlas sold well throughout Europe for nearly 40 years. His map of the New World was a summary of European explorers' knowledge of the Americas. The vast southern continent, Terra Australis, a relic of the classical geography of Ptolemy, featured on most maps of the period. It includes part of Terra del Fuego and part of New Guinea but the rest is pure conjecture. With his contemporary Gerardus Mercator, Ortelius helped shift the center of European cartography from Italy to the Low Countries.

1600–1800
The Expanding World

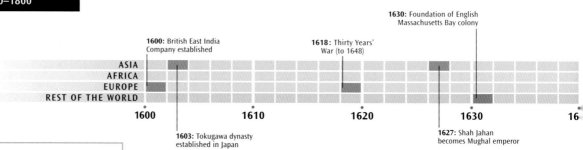

1630: Foundation of English Massachusetts Bay colony

1600: British East India Company established

1618: Thirty Years' War (to 1648)

ASIA
AFRICA
EUROPE
REST OF THE WORLD

1600   1610   1620   1630   16

1603: Tokugawa dynasty established in Japan

1627: Shah Jahan becomes Mughal emperor

B Y 1600, EUROPE'S VOYAGES of discovery over the preceding 150 years had created the world's first global trading network. It was a process that accelerated rapidly after 1600, as English, Dutch, and French mariners followed the Spanish and Portuguese onto the world's oceans. In addition to the expanding empires of Spain and Portugal in the Americas, France, Britain, and the Netherlands founded forts and trading posts across the globe: in North America, in India, and in the Far East, where the Dutch ousted the Portuguese to establish a stranglehold on the lucrative spice trade. Trade was very loosely regulated: piracy and commerce were often two sides of the same coin.

Global trade

For the most part, the goal of European expansion was trade, not conquest or settlement. Even though European explorers had been aware of Australia and New Zealand since about 1620, their lack of sophisticated societies, and hence opportunities for trade, made any attempt at exploiting these vast new lands seem a profitless exercise.

Two distinct trading areas, very different in character, emerged: the Atlantic and the Indian Ocean. The most valuable imports to Europe from across the Atlantic were sugar, grown on plantations in Brazil and the Caribbean, silver, and furs. Europe's demand for sugar generated an increasingly well-organized slave trade to provide labor for plantations. By the end of the 18th century, upwards of 12 million African slaves had

PICTURE ABOVE:
In China, skilled Qing artists rendered images such as this vivid portrayal of an archery contest on silk. Silk and porcelain produced to a quality unknown in the west were prized by European traders.

A group of African slaves is led to the coast by traders using a coffle, a device that secured slaves by the neck, leaving their legs free.

been shipped to the New World. Trade with the East, by contrast, yielded spices, such as pepper, nutmeg, and cinnamon, and luxury goods, such as silks, porcelain, and tea from China, which were paid for with silver.

Anxiously watching Europe's commerce-based expansion were the established empires of Eurasia: Russia, relentlessly expanding eastward; the Ottomans in the Middle East and Balkans; the Safavids in Persia; the Mughals in India; and, after the fall of the Ming in 1644, the Qing in China. With the exception of Russia, and at least until about 1700, they remained the technological, economic, and cultural equals of Europe.

European ascendancy

By the early 18th century, however, Europe was clearly drawing ahead. In part, this was the result of its increasing wealth, which allowed the funding of yet more ambitious trading ventures. But it was also

Harrison's chronometer was used by Captain James Cook on his second round-the-world voyage. At the end of the three-year-long expedition, the chronometer had lost only eight minutes of time.

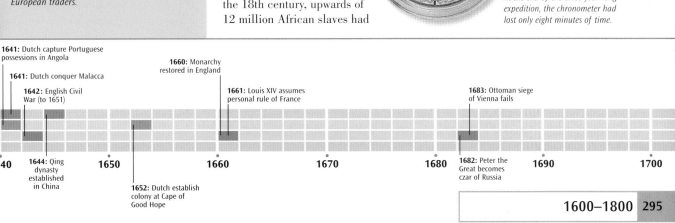

1641: Dutch capture Portuguese possessions in Angola

1641: Dutch conquer Malacca

1642: English Civil War (to 1651)

1660: Monarchy restored in England

1661: Louis XIV assumes personal rule of France

1683: Ottoman siege of Vienna fails

40   **1644:** Qing dynasty established in China   1650   1660   1670   1680   **1682:** Peter the Great becomes czar of Russia   1690   1700

1652: Dutch establish colony at Cape of Good Hope

the result of a European scientific revolution. Improvements in European technology – whether in ships, in arms, or in navigation – both helped underpin its overseas endeavors and led to the pursuit of knowledge as an end in itself, in turn increasing opportunities for trade. In the 17th century, the kings of France and England both founded scientific societies. With the aid of new scientific instruments, including telescopes, microscopes, barometers, and thermometers, European understanding of the physical world advanced at an unprecedented rate, culminating in the work of Isaac Newton. Captain Cook's three Pacific voyages in the second half of the 18th century, which revealed the true extent of the oceans for the first time, were motivated as much by scientific inquiry as by commercial gain.

Constitutional monarchy

In this era of intense scientific and philosophical speculation, the subject of politics was not forgotten. Many theories were advanced as to how the state should be governed, especially in England. In the mid-17th century, this led to a head-on clash between the king, Charles I, and his parliament over who ruled the country. Their irreconcilable differences provoked civil war (1642–46) and the execution of the king. This was followed by the Commonwealth when the country was ruled by the parliamentarian general, Oliver Cromwell. Although the Commonwealth collapsed folowing the death of Cromwell and the monarchy was restored in 1660, English monarchs would never again attempt to rule without the sanction of parliament.

The Age of Absolutism

At this point in history, these experiments with new forms of government were unique to England. In the great kingdoms

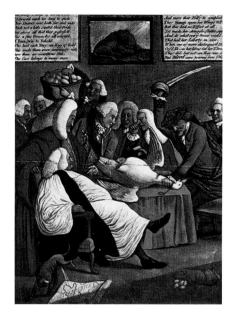

This cartoon, published in 1776, shows members of the British government killing their "golden goose" – the American colonies.

of Europe, power was increasingly concentrated in the hands of the monarch. Louis XIV of France embodied the ideal of the absolute monarch, choosing his own ministers and dismissing them as he thought fit, patronizing the arts and sciences, and building his magnificent palace at Versailles as a reflection of his own glory. Louis' example was followed by rulers such as Peter the Great and Catherine the Great of Russia and Frederick the Great of Prussia.

Colonial wars

One consequence of Europe's global activities was that struggles between European powers increasingly came to be played out on a world stage. This climaxed from the mid-18th century onward as Britain and France, by now the most powerful maritime nations in the world, sought to establish their dominance over each other.

In 1756 a powerful coalition, consisting of Austria, Russia, France, Sweden, and Saxony, was formed with the aim of destroying the growing power of Frederick the Great of Prussia. Prussia's only allies were Britain and Hanover. In what would become known as the Seven Years' War the Prussians managed to hold on to all their territory, but the British played only a very minor role in the campaigns fought in Germany; for them the conflict was an excuse for a maritime and colonial war against their traditional enemy France. British successes in North America and India enormously increased the lands under its control. In North America, the British won control of the whole of French Canada; in India they defeated a French and Mughal force to become masters of Bengal. Though British control of its American colonies would prove short-lived, its hegemony in India was clear. The French were at least partly revenged, however, by the help they provided to the colonists in North America in their successful fight for independence from Britain after 1776.

The Age of Revolution

The American War of Independence neatly encapsulates the paradox of European empire building in the 18th century. Though in Spain's New World empire conquest and commerce were seen as inseparable from the start, for most European powers the drawbacks of permanent settlement, not least the cost and difficulty of administering such distant territories, outweighed the advantages. Yet the British government persisted in taxing the American colonists and dictating who they could and could not trade with. At the same time rationalist philosophers of the "Enlightenment" increasingly held that individuals and nations should be able to live free from the tyranny of unjust rulers.

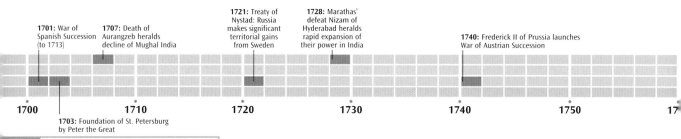

1701: War of Spanish Succession (to 1713)

1707: Death of Aurangzeb heralds decline of Mughal India

1721: Treaty of Nystad: Russia makes significant territorial gains from Sweden

1728: Marathas' defeat Nizam of Hyderabad heralds rapid expansion of their power in India

1740: Frederick II of Prussia launches War of Austrian Succession

1700   1710   1720   1730   1740   1750   17

1703: Foundation of St. Petersburg by Peter the Great

It was this desire for liberty that drove the American War of Independence, as well as the French Revolution in 1789. In France, the original principles of the revolution, Liberty, Equality, and Fraternity, were soon betrayed in an orgy of blood-letting, and republican rule was replaced by the empire of Napoleon. Yet, in spite of the apparent failure of the revolution, an entirely new political climate was being created which would have enormous consequences for the future of the western world.

China and Japan

The expansion of Europe's empires was mirrored by the rapid growth of China under the Qing in the 17th and 18th centuries. Following the collapse of the

Ming in 1644, the Qing, or Manchu, dynasty had gained control of China by the end of the 17th century. Successive campaigns, promoted in part by the threat of Russian, British, and French moves into Asia, established an enormous empire, which included Mongolia, Tibet, and Nepal, and an array of tributary states. By 1790, the population had leaped to 300 million. The economy was booming too, through trade in tea, porcelain, and silk with Russia and the west.

Japan, by contrast, under the rule of the Tokugawa Shogunate from 1603, remained resolutely inward-looking. By 1634, all Europeans had been expelled from the country, except for a tiny trading post on an island in Nagasaki harbor, where the Dutch were allowed to maintain a presence. European attempts

to reestablish trading links were consistently rebuffed as the country entered a 250-year period of isolation.

Ottoman decline

Meanwhile, the once irresistible Ottoman Empire, increasingly squeezed by Europe's imperial powers, began a slow decline. In the second half of the 17th century the Ottomans still presented a powerful threat to the Habsburg empire in southeastern Europe. Twice large armies marched on Vienna. However, after the siege of Vienna in 1683 had been relieved, the Habsburgs were able to drive back the Ottomans from Hungary and Transylvania. The Ottomans' military vigor and innovation declined and one by one, their empire's outlying territories were lost.

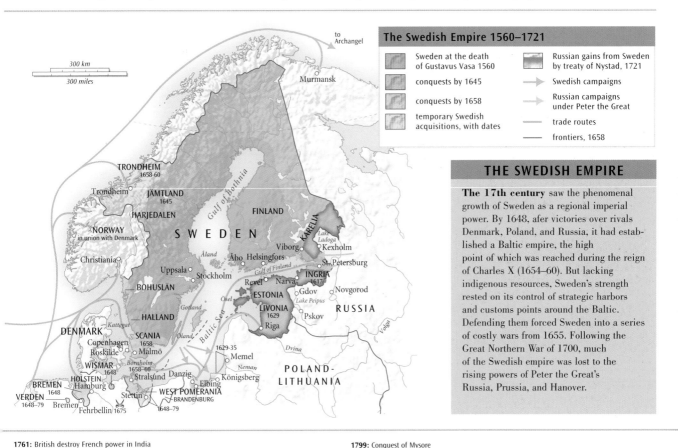

The Swedish Empire 1560–1721

- Sweden at the death of Gustavus Vasa 1560
- conquests by 1645
- conquests by 1658
- temporary Swedish acquisitions, with dates
- Russian gains from Sweden by treaty of Nystad, 1721
- Swedish campaigns
- Russian campaigns under Peter the Great
- trade routes
- frontiers, 1658

THE SWEDISH EMPIRE

The 17th century saw the phenomenal growth of Sweden as a regional imperial power. By 1648, afer victories over rivals Denmark, Poland, and Russia, it had established a Baltic empire, the high point of which was reached during the reign of Charles X (1654–60). But lacking indigenous resources, Sweden's strength rested on its control of strategic harbors and customs points around the Baltic. Defending them forced Sweden into a series of costly wars from 1655. Following the Great Northern War of 1700, much of the Swedish empire was lost to the rising powers of Peter the Great's Russia, Prussia, and Hanover.

1761: British destroy French power in India

1763: Treaty of Paris confirms British supremacy in N America

c.1770: European slave trade reaches peak

1776: American colonies declare independence from Britain

1789: French Revolution

1783: Russia annexes Crimea

1799: Conquest of Mysore confirms British supremacy in southern India

1795: Britain captures Cape of Good Hope from Dutch

ASIA
AFRICA
EUROPE
REST OF THE WORLD

760

1765: Bengal comes under British control

1770

1768: Cook's first Pacific voyage

1772: Poland partitioned between Prussia, Austria, and Russia

1780

1783: Britain acknowledges American independence

1790

1788: First British settlement at Botany Bay, Australia

1798: Napoleon invades Egypt

1800

William Shakespeare

William Shakespeare (1564–1616) exerted more influence on English literature and European drama than any other writer. The author of 38 plays and 154 sonnets, amongst them masterpieces such as *Hamlet* (1601) and *King Lear* (1605), his exuberant zest for language and sheer virtuosity is unmatched.

However, he was not an elitist, or academic, writer. Born in Stratford-upon-Avon, the son of a local burgess and tradesman, he spent much of his adult life as an actor-writer in the successful Lord Chamberlain's Company of players, based at London's Globe theater. The rich variety of his personal experience, reflected in his plays, is the key to their universal appeal.

Shakespeare was very much a man of his age, dedicated to exploring the intricacies of the individual character, his motivations, and the external forces that shape him. This focus on self-expression and individuality paralleled the expansion of education and literacy, the growth of cosmopolitan attitudes, and the influence of Calvinist theology, with its stress on relentless self-scrutiny.

William Shakespeare

The chronology of Shakespeare's plays is uncertain, and many dates are conjectural.

1589	*Henry VI (Parts I, II and III)*
1592–3	*Richard III, The Comedy of Errors*
1593–4	*Titus Andronicus, The Taming of the Shrew*
1594–5	*The Two Gentlemen of Verona, Love's Labor's Lost, Romeo and Juliet*
1595–6	*Richard II, A Midsummer Night's Dream*
1596–7	*King John, The Merchant of Venice*
1597–8	*Henry IV Part 1, Henry IV Part 2*
1598–9	*The Merry Wives of Windsor*
1598	*Much Ado About Nothing, Henry V*
1599–1600	*Julius Caesar, As you Like It*
1600–01	*Hamlet, The Merry Wives of Windsor*
1601–02	*Twelfth Night, Troilus and Cressida*
1602–03	*All's Well That Ends Well*
1604–05	*Measure for Measure, Othello*
1605–06	*King Lear, Macbeth*
1606–07	*Antony and Cleopatra*
1607–08	*Coriolanus, Timon of Athens*
1608–09	*Pericles*
1609–10	*Cymbeline*
1610–11	*The Winter's Tale*
1611–12	*The Tempest*
1612–13	*Henry VIII, The Two Noble Kinsmen*

ASIA

1601 Mughal emperor Akbar has now absorbed the Deccan kingdoms of Berar, Ahmadnagar, and Khandesh into his kingdom.

1602 Jesuit missionary Matteo Ricci is given permission to stay in Beijing.

1603 Safavid war with Ottomans; Shah Abbas retakes Tabriz in first year (–1619).

Tokugawa Ieyasu is appointed shogun, establishing Tokugawa dynasty in Japan. He builds a castle at Edo.

Beginnings of a new Japanese theatrical tradition, Kabuki.

1604 Shah Abbas of Persia conquers Erivan (Yerevan) Shirvan, and Kars.

1605 Akbar the Great dies, possibly poisoned. He is succeeded as Mughal emperor by his son, Jahangir.

The Golden Temple of Amritsar is completed. It is the holiest shrine of the Sikhs, who reject Muslim and Hindu orthodoxies.

1623 ▼ Dutch capture Amboina and take the Moluccas from the Portuguese.

1607 Mughal emperor Jahangir sends an envoy to meet the Portuguese at Goa.

AFRICA

1603 Death of Idris Aloma, the king of Bornu, W Africa. With the help of Turkish firearms he has won many campaigns in his 33-year reign.

1627 ▼ Death of the sultan of Morocco, Ahmad al-Mansur, known as the "Victorious." Morocco is weakened by dynastic disputes and divides into two rival sultanates, Fez and Marrakesh.

1607 Accession of Susenyos as king of Ethiopia (–1632). He gives official recognition to the Oromo in the south of his kingdom.

1610 Death of Ralambo, ruler of the Merina kingdom of Madagascar. During his 35-year reign he had extended his territory by conquest.

Establishment of the Dahomey kingdom, W Africa.

c.1610 Oromo are the dominant population in S Ethiopia, and are prominent among the Muslims of the Harar plateau.

EUROPE

1601 War between France and Savoy ends with French victory at Chambéry.

1602 Foundation of the Dutch East India Company.

Persecution of Protestants in Hungary and Bohemia.

1603 Death of Queen Elizabeth I of England. James VI of Scotland is her successor, uniting the English and Scottish thrones.

1604 Ostend falls to the Spanish after a two-year siege.

King James of Scotland and England condemns tobacco-smoking as "vile and stinking."

1605 Guy Fawkes, a Catholic conspirator, plots to blow up both houses of the English parliament.

"Time of Troubles" in Russia, which is threatened by Sweden and Poland.

Miguel de Cervantes' masterpiece, *Don Quixote de la Mancha*, appears in Spain.

1606 War between Habsburgs and Ottomans ends with the Treaty of Zsitvatorok.

1607 In Russia, a peasant uprising, led by Bolotnikov, a former serf enslaved by the Tartars, is suppressed.

Monteverdi's opera *Orfeo* is performed in Mantua.

1608 Formation of the Protestant Evangelical union at Anhausen, near Nördlingen. A Catholic League is formed in response (–1609).

1621 ▼ **1609** Spain and the Netherlands sign a truce.

In Spain, the Moriscos – former Muslims who have converted to Christianity – are expelled.

1611 ▼ Polish war with Russia (–1618).

1610 Death of the painter Caravaggio. He has been a fugitive for four years, following the murder of a man in a Roman brawl.

AMERICAS & AUSTRALASIA

1602 Dutch colonists found a settlement near the estuary of the Essequibo river, Guiana.

1603 Samuel de Champlain arrives in Canada to assess French colonization possibilities.

1604 Foundation of French colony of Acadia in present-day Nova Scotia (–1608).

1606 Luis Váez de Torres sails through the strait that now bears his name and proves New Guinea is an island.

A Portuguese expedition under Torres discovers a new continent in the southern seas (Australia).

1619 ▼ **1607** Foundation of first permanent English colony at Jamestown, Virginia, by John Smith; colonists complete James Fort here.

1614 ▼ John Smith, founder of the Jamestown colony, is captured by the Indian chief Powhatan. Smith's life is saved by the pleas of Powhatan's daughter, Pocahontas.

Jesuits found province of Paraguay around Asunción and first mission villages on Paraguay river.

1615 ▼ **1608** Champlain colonizes Québec for France.

A Spanish royal decree legalizes the slavery of the Chilean Indians.

1609 Champlain explores St. Lawrence river and eastern Great Lakes (–1613).

Champlain allies with Algonquins and initiates war with Iroquois.

English explorer, Henry Hudson, explores the Hudson river, northeast N America.

1611 ▼ **1610** Henry Hudson discovers Hudson Bay, E Canada.

It is announced that Santa Fe will be the new capital of the Spanish province of New Mexico.

New France

Great reserves of cod, and trade in furs had drawn the French to northern Canada in the early 16th century. In the 1530s, Jacques Cartier tried to establish a permanent settlement at Québec, but hostile natives and harsh conditions forced the French to abandon the colony.

In 1608, the explorer Samuel de Champlain established Québec as a base for trade with the Huron and Algonquin tribes. He was a tireless explorer of the Canadian interior, and did much to promote the colonial possibilities. A succession of trading forts was subsequently established along the Mississippi river.

But French attempts at colonization were half-hearted; colonial settlers in Nova Scotia and along the St. Lawrence river were thinly scattered, scraping together an existence as subsistence farmers. By the 18th century, the numerical superiority of the English would overwhelm the French settlers.

Jesuits in Japan

Initially welcomed to Buddhist Japan, the tide turned for Jesuit missionaries in the 1590s, when the shoguns issued a series of edicts forbidding Christianity. The rulers were suspicious of the alien faith; they were also alarmed when local feudal lords adopted the new religion as a badge of independence from the ruling elite.

The Japanese began to execute missionaries, often by crucifixion, torturing Japanese converts until they recanted or died. Although the Portuguese and Spanish were expelled, the Dutch – and the

profitable trade they brought – were allowed to remain. A small colony of Dutch people was confined to Deshima, an island in Nagasaki Bay, where the inhabitants became objects of local curiosity.

Science and Technology (c.1500–1630)

c.1500 European ships begin to use jib sails.

1502 Henlein invents the pocket watch.

1543 Copernicus publishes *De Revolutionibus*, in which he explores the heliocentric theory of the universe.

1547 Girolamo Cardano publishes *De Subilitate*, establishing the organic origin of fossils.

1569 Publication of Mercator's world map, which makes allowance for the curvature of the globe.

c.1570 Florentine potters produce soft-paste porcelain.

1571 Leonard Digges invents the theodolite.

1578 Tycho Brahe publishes *Nova Stella*.

1586 Invention of the mechanical loom, Danzig.

1589 Invention of the stocking knitting frame.

1592 In Holland a windmill is used for the first time to power a sawmill.

1592 Galileo develops the first thermometer.

1595 First *fluyt* merchant ships built in Holland.

1605 Invention of the flintlock musket.

1608 Invention of the telescope by Hans Lippershey.

1609 Kepler establishes the laws of planetary motion in *Astronomia Nova*.

1614 Napier publishes the first logarithmic tables.

1628 Harvey describes the circulation of blood in *On the Motion of the Heart*.

1630 Galileo establishes the movement of the earth round the sun in *Dialogue on the World Systems*.

The Danish astronomer Tycho Brahe (1564–1601) – shown seated in the right-hand corner – observed the heavens without a telescope, and was able to deduce the orbit of each planet.

Astronomy

The Renaissance was a time when great advances were made in the observation of the natural world. One of the most important was the discovery that the planets rotated round the sun, and the moon rotated round the earth. A major convert to this theory was the Polish astronomer Nicolaus Copernicus (1473–1543). In 1610, Galileo Galilei (1564–1642) made observations through a primitive telescope and accepted Copernicus's theories. His ideas brought him into direct conflict with the Catholic church, which taught that the earth was the center of the universe. He was arrested by the Inquisition, forced to recant, and his writings were suppressed.

ASIA

1611 Dutch found a trading post at Masulipatam, E India.

1612 The English East India Company establishes its first factory at Surat, W India.

The English East India Company establishes factories at Syriam, Prome, and Ava (Burma).

1614 Japanese shogun, Tokugawa Ieyasu, issues an edict suppressing Christianity.

1615 An English fleet defeats the Portuguese near Bombay.

Sir Thomas Roe, the first European ambassador to the Mughal court, is received by emperor Jahangir.

1625 In Ming China, conflict breaks out between the Donglin party, composed of civil servants and intellectuals, and the corrupt eunuch party (–1627).

The fortress of Osaka, held by Hideyori, falls to the army of Ieyasu after a six-month siege.

1616 Death of shogun Tokugawa Ieyasu. He is succeeded by his son, Tokugawa Hidetada.

Sultan Ahmed's mosque, also known as the "Blue mosque" is completed in Istanbul.

1617 Work is under way on the Royal mosque or Masjed-e Shah, the most striking building in the magnificent new Persian capital, Isfahan.

1622 **1618** Ottomans recognize the reconquest of Persia by Shah Abbas.

1619 Dutch found Batavia as the center of their trading empire in SE Asia.

William Baffin's map of the Mughal empire, the first by an English cartographer.

1620 The imperial palace of Katsura is built in Kyoto, Japan.

AFRICA

1612 Portuguese are exporting Angolans as slaves to Brazil at a rate of over 10,000 a year.

c.1612 Death of Kibinda Ilunga, the founder of the Lunda kingdom of S Zaire.

1615 Khoisan herders, taken to England to learn the language and culture, return to the Cape of Good Hope, S Africa.

1617 Dutch purchase Gorée Island, off Cape Verde, W Africa.

1619 African slaves taken to the English colony at Jamestown, N America.

1620 The English colony of Saldanha Bay, near the Cape of Good Hope, fails.

1611 Swedes enter Russia; the Poles occupy Moscow.

War between Denmark and Sweden over control of the Baltic.

A new English version of the Bible is published, authorized by King James.

1612 Russians force invading Poles to capitulate.

Rubens paints his *Descent from the Cross* for Notre Dame cathedral, Antwerp.

1613 A Swedish victory at Kalmar leads to the peace of Knäred. Sweden gives up Finland.

Systematic colonization of Ulster, N Ireland, by Protestants begins.

Mikhail Romanov is elected czar by the *zemsky sobor* (assembly of the land).

1614 Aristocratic uprising in France ends with the peace of St Menehould.

In Frankfurt, Vincent Fettmilch leads an attack on the Jewish ghetto.

Czar Mikhail Romanov defeats the Cossacks at Rostokino.

Scottish mathematician John Napier publishes logarithmic tables.

1633 **1616** Galileo is placed under arrest by the Inquisition for his astronomical theories.

Death of Cervantes and Shakespeare.

1617 Treaty of Stolbovo ends Swedish occupation of N Russia.

1618 French secretary of state, Richelieu, is ordered into exile at Avignon for conspiring with the queen mother, Marie de Medici.

Start of Thirty Years' War. Bohemian revolt against Habsburg authority sparks off the war.

Defenestration of Prague: a revolt against the pro-Catholic policy of the regents in Prague.

1619 Marie de Medici leads an uprising against her son, Louis XIII of France. Richelieu is recalled to defuse the revolt (–1620).

1621 **1620** Battle of the White Mountain; Habsburgs defeat Bohemians.

English dissenters set sail in the *Mayflower* for Virginia.

1611 Henry Hudson's crew mutinies and abandons him in icy waters with little prospect of survival.

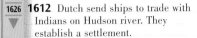

1626 **1612** Dutch send ships to trade with Indians on Hudson river. They establish a settlement.

Settlers in Virginia begin to cultivate tobacco.

1613 Dutch begin to settle in Paramaribo, Guiana.

After a guerilla war, a settlement of runaway slaves in the mountains of Mexico is granted freedom by the colonial government.

1614 Native American princess, Pocahontas, is married to a Jamestown settler.

1615 French explorer Samuel de Champlain discovers Lake Huron, Canada.

Franciscans arrive in Québec to start missionary work.

1616 Willem Schouten and Jakob Le Maire discover a route to the Pacific round Cape Horn.

Portuguese expel the French from St. Louis de Maragnan, ending French efforts to establish an Amazonian colony.

Dutch found the colony of Guiana.

1617 British set up a penal colony in Virginia.

1618 A smallpox epidemic rages throughout New England.

1619 The first general assembly in the provincial capital of Virginia, Jamestown, passes strict laws against drinking, gambling, and immorality. About 20 Africans are brought to the colony.

1620 Pilgrim fathers arrive at Plymouth.

Gorée

The island of Gorée lies to the south of the Cape Verde peninsula, Senegal. By the mid-15th century, the Senegambia region was being transformed by the arrival of the Portuguese, and subsequently other Europeans. Once the island's indigenous Lebu people had been displaced, the town of Gorée, founded by the Dutch in 1621, became a major slaving entrepôt.

Many trading forts were established along the West African coast in the 17th century, with permission from local African rulers, to whom the Europeans paid tribute. Local rulers provided slaves, mainly captured in warfare, for the Europeans in exchange for cotton, copper, tin, iron, brandy, and glass trinkets. The slaves were then dispatched, in terrible conditions, to the sugar plantations of the New World, at a profit to unscrupulous traders of as much as 800 percent.

Merchant shipping

The Dutch dominance of East India trade in the 17th century was a result of their maritime supremacy. The merchant ship that was operated by Dutch traders was the *fluyt*, a long, narrow ship with three masts, and a large amount of storage space beneath a single deck. These ships were easily and cheaply built, and could be sailed great distances without having to make landfall. In contrast, the designs of the fully-rigged and multimasted English merchantmen were ungainly, their storage capacity restricted by the necessity for large crews, who protected the ships against attack and piracy.

The Thirty Years' War

A bid by the Austrian Habsburgs to dominate Central Europe led to three decades of warfare, fought bitterly on German soil. Other European nations soon became embroiled in the conflict, which encompassed Sweden, Denmark, France, Spain, and the Netherlands. But the real victims were the German people; famine and marauding armies caused a catastrophic population loss – 40 percent perished in rural areas.

1618	Bohemian revolt against Habsburg authority starts war.
1620	Battle of the White Mountain; Imperialists (Habsburgs) defeat Bohemians.
1624	Cardinal Richelieu brings France into war against Imperialists; alliance of France, Holland, England, Sweden, Denmark, Savoy, and Venice against Habsburgs.
1625	Denmark invades Germany.
1626	Danish forces routed by Imperialists at battle of Lutter.
1629	Imperialists are triumphant in much of N Germany. Danes are forced out of the war by imperial armies.
1630	Swedish king, Gustavus Adolphus, invades N Europe.
1631	Habsburg army crushed by Gustavus Adolphus at Breitenfeld. City of Magdeburg sacked by imperial forces.
1632	Swedish victory at Lech; Gustavus occupies Augsburg, Munich, and S Bavaria. Gustavus Adolphus killed at Lützen.
1634	Battle of Nördlingen; Swedes routed by Imperialists.
1635	Peace of Prague strengthens the position of Habsburg emperor, Ferdinand II.
1636	Open war between France and Holy Roman Empire.
1639	French take Alsace.
1643	Battle of Rocroi; French forces annihilate Spanish army.
1644	Imperial armies defeated by French, Swedish, and Dutch (–1648).
1648	Peace of Westphalia.

The Thirty Years' War *provoked great advances in methods of mass destruction, and involved an unprecedented number of soldiers, over a million of whom died before it ceased.*

ASIA

1621 Japanese are forbidden to travel overseas, on pain of death.

 1622 Ottoman sultan Osman II is deposed and assassinated by his own guards.

Persians capture Kandahar from the Mughals.

Persian ruler Shah Abbas drives the Portuguese out of Hormuz Island.

Christians are crucified and beheaded in Japan.

1623 Shah Abbas takes Baghdad, Mosul, and Mesopotamia from the Ottomans.

Amboina massacre: agents of the Dutch East India Company in Amboina Island, SE Asia, seize and execute ten English traders.

1624 Spanish are forbidden access to any part of the Japanese archipelago.

Dutch establish trading posts on the coast of Taiwan.

1625 The first Manchu kings establish their capital at Mukden; they pose a threat to China's weakening Ming dynasty.

In China, persecution of the intellectual sect, Donglin, begins.

1626 Nurachi, the Manchu chieftain, dies in a failed assault on the Chinese town of Ningyuan.

1627 Shah Jahan becomes Mughal emperor.

Unrest among soldiers and peasants in Ming China.

1629 Death of Shah Abbas of Persia. He is succeeded by his grandson, Shah Safi.

AFRICA

1621 Nzinga, sister of the king of Mbundu (Angola), is sent as an envoy to Portugal.

The Mutapa state of the lower Zambezi valley is invaded by the Maravi empire, which stretches from the Zambezi to Mozambique.

1627 Queen of Mbundu, Nzinga, is victorious in a year-old war with Portugal.

Death of Sultan Zaydan marks the end of the Moroccan Sa'di dynasty.

1629 Following a Portuguese defeat, the Mutapa state is forced to make a humiliating treaty with Portugal.

EUROPE

1621 Huguenot rebellion in Provence, S France.

Catholic troops, led by Count Tilly, sack the university library at Heidelberg.

Hostilities are renewed between Spain and the Netherlands.

Swedish king Gustavus Adolphus seizes Riga from the Poles.

1622 Louis XIII of France lays siege to Montpellier, S France, and forces the rebellious Protestants to come to terms. La Rochelle and Montauban are the only remaining Protestant strongholds.

Spanish forces seize the key fortress town of Bergen op Zoom from the Dutch.

1623 Death of the English composer William Byrd, a master of polyphony.

1625 Plague ravages London.

The Dutch town of Breda surrenders to the Spanish who are poised to overrun the Netherlands.

1626 Following a plot against him, Cardinal Richelieu, chief minister of the French royal council, clamps down on the powers of the nobility.

Death of the great English statesman and philosopher Francis Bacon.

German harvest fails; country ravaged by famine, plague, and violence.

1627 Imperial forces, under the command of Albrecht von Wallenstein, overrun Denmark and Baltic coast.

French wrest control of a vital route through the Alps from Spain, countering the Habsburgs' growing influence.

1628 The Huguenot town of La Rochelle surrenders to royalist forces.

The Duke of Buckingham, chief ally of the English king Charles I, is assassinated. Charles I dissolves parliament.

1640 The great Flemish painter Rubens is sent on a diplomatic mission to Madrid, where he meets Spanish artist, Velázquez.

1629 War of the Mantuan Succession. Spaniards besiege Casale; imperialists besiege Mantua.

1634 **1630** Swedish king, Gustavus Adolphus, invades Pomerania and Mecklenburg, to counteract recent German military successes.

German astronomer Johannes Kepler, who devised three principles of planetary motion, dies.

AMERICAS & AUSTRALASIA

1621 English settlers in Massachusetts form an alliance with the chief of the Wampanoag Indians.

Elias Legardo is the first Jewish colonial settler in N America.

1622 An Indian attack in the James river area of Virginia leaves 240 colonists dead.

1623 Captain John Mason of Hampshire, England establishes the territory of New Hampshire, NE America, from land granted him by King James.

1624 The first English settlers in the Caribbean occupy the island of St. Christopher.

Dutch seize Bahia, capital of Brazil, from Spain.

1625 Dutch seize San Juan, on Puerto Rico.

Portuguese expelled from Maranhão.

1626 Salem is founded as the capital of Massachusetts.

Dutch acquire island of Manhattan from Canarsee Indians.

1627 The Company of New France gains a fur monopoly and land from Florida to the Arctic.

English settlers arrive in Barbados.

1634 **1628** The New England Company is established to promote trade and colonization in N America.

1629 The Dutch sailor Francisco Pelsaeir lands in NW Australia.

1630 Foundation of English Massachusetts Bay colony; Boston is founded as Massachusetts' capital.

1637 Beginning of Dutch conquest of Brazil. Dutch establish New Holland, covering much of NE Brazil.

c.1630 Intense Jesuit missionary activity in Paraguay region.

Gustavus Adolphus II

Gustavus Adolphus succeeded to the Swedish throne in 1611, at the age of 17. He was to lay the foundation of the modern Swedish state, and make it into a major European power. By combining tactical innovations, such as the introduction of an easily maneuverable light artillery, with a fine sense of strategy he transformed the art of early 17th-century warfare. Believing attack to be the best means of defence, he recovered Kalmar from Denmark in 1613, intervened in Muscovy's "Time of Troubles" (1605–17), and attacked Poland–Lithuania (1617–29), taking Riga in 1621. In 1630, he launched himself into the Thirty Years' War, in a bold bid to ensure the survival of German Protestantism against the onslaught of the Counter-Reformation. His death on the battlefield at Lützen in 1632 cut short a career that was still full of promise.

Isfahan

The golden age of Isfahan in southwest Iran, began in 1598, when Shah Abbas I made it the Safavid capital. He rebuilt it to create one of the most beautiful 17th-century cities in the world. The center of the city is dominated by the immense Meydan-e Shah (Royal square), and the striking Masjed-e Shah (Royal mosque), which is famous for its outer coating of glazed turquoise tiles with arabesque decorations (*below*). The city became an artistic and cultural center; the shah revered and patronized the work of many artists and craftsmen, and did much to encourage silk production, a royal monopoly. An accessible ruler, Shah Abbas was reputed to stroll around the Meydan in the early evenings, meeting his subjects, and examining the goods on sale on their stalls.

Shah Jahan

The son of the Mughal emperor Jahangir, Shah Jahan long nursed ambitions to rebel against his powerful mother, Nur Jahan, empress in all but name. In 1623 he openly rebelled and, when his father died in 1627, he had all his closest relatives killed and pensioned off his mother. He declared himself "Emperor of the World," and presided over the Mughal empire for three decades.

His rule was characterized by the lavish and opulent splendor of court life, and his greatest legacy is the Taj Mahal, an exquisite memorial built for a much-loved wife, Mumtaz Mahal. He ordered campaigns to reclaim Afghanistan, and restore Mughal dominance of Central Asia. He did not succeed, and warfare drained his already depleted treasury. His sons disputed the succession and conspired against each other. Eventually, Shah Jahan was imprisoned by his ambitious son Aurangzeb, who ascended to the throne in 1658.

ASIA

1632 Revolt by Turkish Janissaries; Sultan Murad IV purges traitors.

Mughal emperor Shah Jahan orders the destruction of Hindu temples.

1653 Shah Jahan begins the construction of the Taj Mahal at Agra, in memory of his wife, Mumtaz Mahal.

Portuguese are forced out of Bengal.

Closure of Japan by Tokugawa shoguns.

1634 English traders establish a factory in Canton.

Foreign residents in Japan are restricted to Deshima, a manmade island in Nagasaki harbor.

1635 Ottomans capture Erivan (Yerevan) from the Safavid Persians.

Druse emir, Fakhr ed-Din, who tried to liberate Lebanon from Ottoman occupation, is executed.

Introduction of the Sankin Kotai system; all *daimyo* (feudal lords) must spend alternate years in Edo, preventing the formation of regional powerbases.

1636 Ottoman Turks are driven out of Yemen by Zaydi imams.

1658 Dutch establish a commercial presence in Ceylon (Sri Lanka).

1644 Manchus establish Qing imperial rule at Mukden.

1637 Song Yingxing, a Chinese civil servant, publishes *Tiangong kaiwu* (The Creations of Nature and Man), which explains the latest ideas in agriculture and industry.

Hon'ami Koetsu, a Japanese artist who excelled in calligraphy, painting, and ceramics, dies.

Korean Yi rulers adopt a closed-borders policy; contact with the outside world is punishable by death.

1638 Ottomans recapture Baghdad from Safavid Persia.

A Christian rebellion at Shimabara, Japan, ends with the fall of Hara castle.

1639 Treaty of Qasr-i-Shirin between Ottomans and Safavids.

Russian explorers cross Siberia to reach the Pacific.

AFRICA

1631 War breaks out again between Mutapa and the Portuguese.

1632 Following a rebellion, Emperor Susenyos of Ethiopia is forced to abdicate. He has made Catholicism the state religion, but his son, Fasiladas, promises to restore Coptic Christianity.

1634 French establish a settlement at St. Louis, Senegal.

1635 Abd el-Krim founds a Muslim sultanate in Chad.

1636 King Fasiladas founds permanent capital at Gondar, Ethiopia.

1637 Dutch take Portuguese fort of Elmina.

French slave traders become established in Senegal.

1639 Dutch seize the Kongo kingdom from the Portuguese.

EUROPE

1631 Tilly, commander of the German Catholic League, sacks the Protestant town of Magdeburg. Gustavus Adolphus of Sweden crushes the Catholics at Breitenfeld.

1632 Treaty of Altmark marks the annexation of the coast of Lithuania by Sweden.

1633 The Inquisition in Rome condemns the astronomer Galileo, who rejects his former affirmation that the earth is the center of the universe.

Russians besiege Smolensk; Cossacks aid Poles in a successful defense.

Bernini finishes the *baldacchino* of St. Peter's basilica, Rome.

1634 Swedish influence in S Germany ends with defeat at the battle of Nördlingen.

1635 Peace of Prague; Habsburg forces are victorious in Germany.

Louis XIII of France finally declares war on Spain.

King Louis XIII grants letters patent to a new French academy.

1636 Death of Spain's most prolific playwright, Lope de Vega.

First performance of Pierre Corneille's tragedy *El Cid* in Paris.

1637 French peasant revolutionaries (*croquantes*) rebel in Périgord and Rouergue.

French forces drive back Spaniards, after invasion of Languedoc.

French philosopher René Descartes publishes his *Discours de la méthode*.

Tulip fever in Netherlands leads to unprecedented economic boom and collapse.

1643 ▼

1638 Presbyterians who object to Charles I's attempts to introduce Anglicanism to Scotland sign national covenant to preserve purity of the gospel. Outbreak of First Bishops' War.

1640 Death of Peter Paul Rubens.

1641 ▼

Portuguese uprising from Spanish domination. John IV is declared king.

AMERICAS & AUSTRALASIA

1631 Father Ruíz de Montoya descends Paraná river with 12,000 Indians to escape slave-raiders.

1634 The English colony of Maryland is founded by Lord Baltimore.

1635 English found the colony of Connecticut.

Samuel de Champlain, the explorer of Canada and founder of New France, dies.

French claim the Caribbean island of Guadeloupe.

1636 The Puritan, John Harvard, founds the first American university, at Cambridge, Massachusetts.

French take the Caribbean island of Martinique from the Spanish.

First English colonists settle Rhode Island.

1637 A Puritan force from the Connecticut river area attacks a Pequot village, massacring 500 Pequot Indians. This is the culmination of several years of war between settlers and Pequot Indians.

Dutchman Maurice of Nassau becomes governor of Brazil.

1655 ▼

1638 Swedes and Finns lay the foundation of a colony, New Sweden, in the Delaware estuary, northeast N America.

Christian Ethiopia

In the 16th century, the Catholic church renewed its interest in converting the Christians of Ethiopia, and Jesuit missionaries were dispatched. They met with some success; two emperors converted to Catholicism in the early 17th century. However, when the Jesuits demanded that the liturgy be brought into line with Rome, and the entire population re-baptized, a rebellion ensued, and traditional Ethiopian Christianity was restored in 1632.

Under Fasiladas (1632–67) a permanent capital was established at Gondar (*above*). Hitherto, the emperor had been itinerant, which had allowed him close contact with his people. Shut away in the inaccessible new capital, his influence ebbed, and by the mid-18th century Ethiopia had no effective central government.

Fort St. George

In 1639, the English East India Company obtained permission from the Aravidu *rajas*, the relics of the great Vijayanagara empire of southern India, to build a fort and factory in the fishing village of Madraspatan. This small English foothold on the Indian subcontinent was to become the city of Madras. The settlement, known as Fort St. George, soon became a magnet for local weavers of cotton fabrics and merchants, who settled around the trading post. By 1652, Fort St. George was recognized as a presidency, an administrative unit, and soon became a base from which the East India Company expanded its control.

1631–1640

The English Civil Wars (1642–51)

The conflict between monarchy and parliament had its origins in Charles I's belief in the Divine Rights of Kings, according to which the monarch is answerable only to God and not the will of the people.

1638 First Bishops' War: Scots oppose English ecclesiastical innovations.

1640 The short parliament refuses to vote King Charles funds; hostilities resume with the Second Bishops' War.

1642 Charles I forcibly enters parliament to seize opponents, who have already fled.

Hostilities begin when Charles raises the royal standard at Nottingham. The battle of Edgehill is indecisive.

1643 Parliament allies with the Scots in the Solemn League and Covenant.

1644 Parliamentarians inflict a defeat on the royalists at Marston Moor.

1645 Parliament creates the New Model Army under the command of Oliver Cromwell; victories at Naseby and Langport follow.

1646 Royalist stronghold at Oxford falls. Charles surrenders to the Scots at Newark; the end of the first civil war. An uneasy peace begins (–1648).

1648 Charles makes secret peace with Scots to establish Presbyterianism in England. Scots invade England. Royalists are defeated at battle of Preston.

1649 Charles I is executed. The monarchy and House of Lords is abolished, and England is declared a "Commonwealth or Free State."

Royalist risings in Ireland are brutally suppressed by Cromwell's forces (–1651).

1650 Scottish risings against parliamentarians. Cromwell defeats Scots at battle of Dunbar.

1651 Charles' son, Charles II, is defeated at the battle of Worcester by Cromwell's forces; end of the civil wars. Charles II flees to France.

Charles I and Oliver Cromwell

Charles I's imposition of a version of the Anglican liturgy and prayerbook on Scotland in 1637 ignited a rebellion. Charles I was forced to appeal to parliament for funds to combat the rebellious Scots, but was refused and confronted with a catalogue of recriminations. Charles fled London, and called his subjects to arms in 1642. The conflict between royalists and parliamentarians, commanded by Oliver Cromwell (*above*), dragged on for four years. Charles surrendered at Newark but refused to reach a compromise agreement with parliament, and was executed in 1649. Cromwell went on to subdue the Irish and Scots and ruled as a virtual dictator. The royalist cause revived on his death and, in 1660, Charles's son, Charles II, was restored to the throne.

ASIA

1641 Dutch capture Malacca from the Portuguese.

Revolt of Li Zicheng ousts Ming rulers of China (–1645).

Revolt of Zhang Xianzhong disrupts Ming control in C China (–1647).

1643 The Potala palace in Lhasa, Tibet, is completed; it is a winter palace and Tibet's largest Buddhist monastery.

1655

Russian pioneers reach the Amur river in Siberia.

1644 Qing dynasty, last of the Imperial dynasties in China, is established.

1645 Conflict between Mughals and Marathas in India. Hindu warriors led by Shivaji Bhonsle, who is creating a powerful state in W Deccan, begins (–1670).

German Jesuit Johann Schall becomes director of the Institute of Astronomy and Mathematics in Beijing.

Manchus make the Chinese wear the pigtail and Manchu clothes.

1646 Mughals capture provinces of Balkh and Badakhsan in N Afghanistan from the Ozbegs. They withdraw in the following year.

Manchus occupy Zhejiang, Fujian, and Sichuan.

1647 Canton is taken by the Manchus.

c.1647 Completion of *Atlas of India* by Sadiq Isfahani.

1648 Arabs capture Muscat from the Portuguese.

Ottoman sultan, Ibrahim, is deposed and murdered with the connivance of his mother.

The imperial Mughal court is moved to Shahjahanabad (Delhi).

1650 Dutch seize many Portuguese posts and become dominant mercantile power in SE and S Asia.

The English East India Company establishes a trading post at Hooghly, Bengal.

AFRICA

1654

1641 Dutch capture Portuguese possessions in Angola.

1642 Dutch capture the Portuguese fort of Axim on the Gold Coast.

1644 Dutch slave traders allied to Queen Nzinga of Angola take Luanda from the Portuguese.

The victors in the Torwa civil war move to a new capital at Danongome (Zimbabwe).

1645 Portuguese take slaves from Mozambique to Brazil for the first time.

1652

1648 Survivors from the Dutch ship *Haarlem*, wrecked in Table Bay, settle on the Cape of Good Hope.

1650 Portuguese recapture the coast of Angola from the Dutch. Queen Nzinga makes her peace with the Portuguese.

Sultan of Oman evicts the Portuguese from the Swahili ports, E Africa.

1655

c.1650 As the power of the Moroccan Sa'di dynasty wanes, several Berber tribes are vying for supremacy.

Wegbaja becomes king of Dahomey (Benin) and organizes it as a powerful, centralized state.

EUROPE

1641 France and Portugal form an alliance against Spain.

Parliamentarians draw up a "Grand Remonstrance" for King Charles, objecting to his authoritarian rule.

Gaelic Irish rebel against Protestant immigration in Ireland and slaughter English settlers.

1642 King Charles's declaration of war on parliament initiates a civil war in England between royalists (Cavaliers) and puritans (Roundheads).

1643 Louis XIV becomes king of France.

English Parliamentarians and Scottish Covenanters form alliance against Charles I.

French forces crush the Spanish at Rocroi.

Sweden invades Denmark.

1644 Oliver Cromwell, commander of Roundhead forces, crushes the royalists at the battle of Marston Moor, near York.

Imperial armies defeated by French, Swedish, and Dutch (–1648).

1645 The peace of Linz guarantees the religious freedom of Hungarians.

1648 Thirty Years' War ended by peace of Westphalia.

1652 Fronde uprising in Paris against growing authority of crown and rising taxes (–1649). Cardinal Mazarin, the chief minister, helps the royal family to escape.

The Dutch and Spanish sign the Treaty of Münster; the Spanish recognize the independence of seven Dutch provinces.

Royalist uprisings in Wales, Kent, and Essex. Charles gains support of Scots.

New laws in Russia deprive serfs of virtually all their civil rights.

The people of Moscow revolt against heavy taxation.

Ottoman Turks besiege Heraklion, Crete – part of their continuing conflict with Venice.

1654 Ukrainian Cossacks rise up against their Polish landlords.

1649 Execution of Charles I of England.

1650 Oliver Cromwell's forces subdue Scotland at the battle of Dunbar.

AMERICAS & AUSTRALASIA

1641 The general court of the Massachusetts Bay Colony establishes the *Body of Liberties*, a code of 100 laws.

Indians and Jesuits defeat slave-raiders from São Paulo on Uruguay river.

1642 Dutch settlers slaughter Indians of the lower Hudson valley, who are seeking refuge from Mohawk attacks.

French found Montréal.

Dutch explorer Abel Tasman, searching for a southern continent, finds Tasmania and New Zealand.

1652 **1643** The Puritan colonies of Plymouth, Massachusetts, Connecticut, and Newhaven unite to form the dominion of New England.

Dutch massacre of Algonquin Indians.

In Brazil, Portuguese settlers, supported by Tupí Indians, revolt against their Dutch masters.

Tasman discovers Tonga, and reaches Fiji and New Guinea.

1644 Tasman maps the north and west coasts of Australia.

1646 John Eliot, a pastor, starts preaching to the Algonquin Indians in their own tongue.

In Virginia, a war that has lasted for over two years ends when Chief Necotowance agrees to acknowledge that Indian lands are held by courtesy of the English crown.

1647 Catholic priests are banned from Massachusetts.

1653 **1648** Iroquois destroy French allies, the Huron (–1651).

Richard Bennett leads 400–600 Virginians to form the Puritan outpost of Providence (Annapolis).

1649 Maryland's new laws promoting religious tolerance attract many settlers.

1650 French Jesuits abandon the last of the Huron missions following Iroquois raids.

The siege of Oxford

Oxford was the royalist capital throughout the first phase of the English civil wars. The city was protected by garrisons at Banbury, Donnington Castle, and Wallingford, and by the royalist army. But in 1645, Charles I suffered a decisive defeat at Naseby, where his forces were overwhelmingly outnumbered. Nearly 5,000 royalists were captured there, and the royalist army virtually ceased to exist. Parliamentary pressure on Oxford increased. In 1646, a fort was built on Headington Hill, overlooking the city. For two weeks the parliamentary forces bombarded the city, which eventually surrendered when Charles gave himself up to the Scots in May 1646.

"The Miseries of War"

The 24 etchings created by the French artist, Jacques Callot (1592–1635) entitled *The Miseries of War* are a moving testament to the anarchy and suffering inflicted on the people of Germany between 1618 and 1648. As bands of half-starved, marauding soldiers roamed the devastated countryside, villagers were subjected to robbery, rape, violence, and summary justice. At the end of the war, Germany lay desolate. Whole cities, such as Magdeburg, were in ruins. The countryside was de-populated and despoiled; agriculture and trade had virtually ceased, replaced by famine, disease, and social disruption.

1641–1650

Witchcraft

The breakdown in social unity caused by the Wars of Religion may have contributed to a marked increase in the persecution of witches between 1580 and 1650. Persecuting witches was seen as a way of purging society of evil. It was also an effective way of finding scapegoats (such as Jews and homosexuals) in difficult times, when poverty, warfare, and rising crime were making people insecure. Most victims were female, since women were seen as more susceptible to the Devil's temptations. Confessions were frequently extracted by torture.

In 1634, the parish priest Urban Grandier was publicly burned. He was convicted of bewitching the nuns of Loudon.

Witches

1486	Publication of *Malleus Maleficarum*; a collection of contemporary beliefs about witchcraft.
1532	A law in the Holy Roman Empire decrees the death sentence for black magic.
1541	Four witches are burned in Wittenberg, with the approval of Martin Luther.
c.1580	A great upsurge of witch trials in Germany, Sweden, France, and England.
1590	James VI of Scotland takes an active role in the prosecution of witches.
1595	Nicholas Remy publishes *Demonlatreia*, a comprehensive account of witches.
1597	Publication of *Daemonologie* by James VI of Scotland.
1609	Basque witch trials (–1614).
1617	Diabolism is made a crime in Denmark.
1624	Witch-hunt in Bamberg, Germany (–1631). At least 300 people are executed.
1634	A priest, Urban Grandier, is charged with witchcraft and executed in Loudon, France.
1645	English witch trials; 19 people are executed (–1656).
1661	Scottish witch-hunt and trials (–1662).
1669	Swedish witch-hunt (–1676); about 200 people are executed.
1692	Salem witch trials in Massachusetts.
1714	Prosecutions for witchcraft are forbidden in Prussia.

ASIA

1653 The Taj Mahal in Agra is complete.

The Dalai Lama holds an investiture for the Manchu dynasty in Beijing.

1654 Kangxi becomes Qing emperor.

1655 Russian advances into Siberia are checked by Manchurian warriors on the banks of the Amur river.

1656 The new Ottoman grand vizier, Köprülü Mehmed, is charged with the reorganization of the empire and the reinstatement of order.

The Mughal prince, Aurangzeb, campaigning in the Deccan, raises the siege of Golconda, forcing the sultanate to pay an indemnity and to cede territory.

1669 ▼ **1658** Aurangzeb imprisons his father, Shah Jahan, and proclaims himself emperor. Mughal empire reaches maximum extent during his reign (–1707).

1661 ▼ Dutch take Jaffnapatam, Portugal's last possession in Ceylon (Sri Lanka).

1659 An Annamite (Vietnamese) invasion of Cambodia forces the English factors of the East India Company stationed there to flee the country.

c.1660 Gujaratis make earliest known Indian nautical charts.

AFRICA

1657 ▼ **1651** Swedes capture Carolusberg castle, a slave fort on the Gold Coast, W Africa, from the Dutch.

1666 ▼ **1652** A Dutch expeditionary force lands on the Cape of Good Hope, S Africa, to start building a supply station.

Manuza, king of the Mutapa empire in SE Africa, dies, and is succeeded by Kazuruku Musapa.

1662 ▼ **1654** Portuguese expel the Dutch by force from their conquests in Angola.

1655 The Sa'di dynasty of Morocco is overthrown.

1657 Danes drive out the Swedes from Carolusberg castle.

1659 The Dutch East India Company allows soldiers to set up as independent *boer* farmers on Khoisan land near Table Bay, S Africa. War breaks out between Dutch settlers and Khoisan herders.

1660 End of Khoisan war. Dutch claim "right of conquest," and *boers* continue to occupy Cape peninsula.

c.1660 Collapse of Mali empire.

1651 King Charles II, defeated by Oliver Cromwell at Worcester, flees to France.

1652 The Fronde rebels defeat loyalist forces commanded by the king's chief minister, Jules Mazarin, outside Paris. To popular acclaim, Louis XIV recovers Paris.

A rebellion takes place in Seville, S Spain, against the economic depression caused by the collapse of American trade.

Protective English laws challenge Dutch maritime supremacy. The English declare war on the Dutch.

Death of the English architect Inigo Jones, designer of the Banqueting Hall in London.

1653 Oliver Cromwell takes on dictatorial powers, with the title of "Lord Protector" (–1658).

In a naval battle near Portland, S England, the English defeat the Dutch.

A peasant uprising against high taxes and inflation is violently suppressed in Lucerne, Switzerland.

Peasant revolts break out in Croatia.

1654 The Peace of Westminster ends Anglo-Dutch conflict. England asserts its supremacy over the seas.

Archbishop of Armagh, Ireland, calculates the date of the Creation as 4004 BCE.

Ukraine comes under Russian domination.

1655 First Northern War (–1660). Warsaw and Cracow fall to the Swedes.

1656 In Madrid, Diego Velázquez paints *Las Meninas* (The Maids of Honor).

1657 Poland enlists support of Brandenburg. Swedes fall back on E Prussia, which becomes a fief of the Swedish crown.

Turks take the Aegean islands of Tenedos and Lemnos from the Venetians.

Dutch scientist Christiaan Huygens invents the pendulum clock.

1658 Spanish forces are defeated by an Anglo-French coalition at the battle of the Dunes. Dunkirk surrenders and is ceded to England.

1659 Franco-Spanish war ends with the Peace of the Pyrenees. It is sealed with a marriage agreement between Louis XIV and the Infanta.

1660 The English constitutional monarchy is restored with the return of Charles II.

1652 The royalist governor of Virginia, William Berkeley, submits to warships sent by the English parliament.

The colony of Massachusetts defies parliament and declares itself an independent commonwealth.

1653 Temporary French–Iroquois peace (–1661).

1654 English seize Jamaica from Spain.

Portuguese take Recife and regain control of Brazil.

A group of 23 Sephardic Jews, expelled by the Portuguese from Recife, Brazil, arrive in New Amsterdam (New York).

1655 Dutch capture Fort Christina and retake Fort Casimir from the Swedes, ending Swedish rule in N America.

1656 In Virginia, suffrage is extended to all free men, regardless of their religion.

1658 A French expedition sets out to explore the southern shores of Lake Superior.

The Cape Colony

During the 16th century, Dutch and English sailing ships began to pass around the Cape of Good Hope in South Africa, *en route* to the East Indies. Table Bay became a regular port of call, where ships could replenish their supplies with the help of local Khoisan herdsmen. At first, the Khoisan welcomed the trading opportunities offered by the European sailors, but there were soon conflicts about the prices the Khoisan charged for livestock.

The Dutch East India Company sought to regularize the situation by establishing a permanent settlement at Table Bay in 1652. In 1657, to meet the growing need for supplies, the Dutch commander allowed some of the soldiers at Table Bay to set up as independent *boers*, or farmers. Faced with an expansion of white settlement, the Khoisan united in opposition in 1659. They failed, despite several brave attempts, to overrun the Dutch settlement, and were forced to come to terms.

French drama's Great Age

The early decades of Louis XIV's reign mark one of the most fertile periods of French literature, when dramatists such as Corneille (1606–1684), Racine (1639–1699), and Molière (1622–1673) captivated court audiences, and thrived under royal patronage. Much of the drama written at this time reflects its court origins in its formal, stately verse, its choice of classical themes, and its emphasis on honor, virtue, and renunciation. By contrast, the racy dramas of Molière mocked the social pretensions of the bourgeoisie, although he wisely restrained himself from satirizing his aristocratic audiences.

1651–1660

Louis XIV (1638–1715)

The reign of Louis XIV of France (1643–1715) saw France become the ascendant absolutist state in Europe. Louis came to the throne aged five, and until 1651 the country was controlled by his mother and Cardinal Mazarin. During this period there was widespread rebellion by provincial nobles, the Fronde (1648–53), which was harshly suppressed. After 1661, Louis became his own first minister and emphasized the centrality of the French court. He appointed the able Colbert as superintendent of finances and, through Colbert's control of the economy and taxation, was able to build the palace of Versailles, and fight four costly wars, earning the soubriquet "The Sun King."

Optical instruments

The development of telescopes and microscopes greatly advanced human knowledge of both distant objects and those too small to see with naked eye during the 17th century. The refracting telescope, using a combination of lenses, was first used for observation of the moon and distant universe by Galileo in 1609. Newton's reflecting telescope (*below*), using lenses and mirrors, gave a still clearer picture of the stars and planets. In 1683, Anton van Leeuwenhoek made the first high-powered precision microscope.

ASIA

 1663

1661 Treaty between Portugal and Netherlands; Ceylon (Sri Lanka), Malacca, and Moluccas (Spice Islands) ceded to Dutch.

Widespread famine in S Asia following three-year drought.

Jesuit missionaries enter Tibet; first Jesuit mission to Lhasa.

1662 Bombay ceded to England by Portugal.

Dutch lose control of Formosa (Taiwan) to Chinese forces.

Takeda theater established in Osaka, Japan.

 1667

1663 Dutch complete expulsion of Portuguese from Ceylon.

Fireworks banned in Edo, Japan.

1667 Dutch conquest of sultanate of Macassar in Celebes (Indonesia).

1668 English crown grants Bombay to East India Company.

1669 Mughal emperor Aurangzeb outlaws freedom of worship in India, and orders destruction of all non-Islamic schools and temples.

Outbreak of cholera in China.

AFRICA

1664

1661 English capture of Fort James on the Gambia estuary marks beginning of rapid growth of transatlantic slave trade.

1662 Tangier ceded to England by Portugal upon marriage of Charles II and Catherine of Braganza.

1672

Royal Adventurers established under patronage of Charles II of England to begin trading in Africa.

1665

Portuguese defeat kingdom of Kongo at battle of Ambuila.

1664 English take control of Gorée and Guinea.

1665 Civil war breaks out in Kongo, seriously weakening the kingdom. Portuguese colonization of Angola (formerly Kongo) delayed by the local uprisings.

French colonize Bourbon Island (Réunion).

1666 Dutch settle Saldanha Bay near Cape of Good Hope.

1670 Omani Arabs raid E African coast as far south as Mozambique.

French establish trading station at Offa on Dahomey coast.

EUROPE

1661 Louis XIV becomes absolute ruler of France.

1662 Treaty of Paris; alliance between France and Netherlands.

Royal Society established under patronage of English crown.

1664 Second Anglo-Dutch War (–1667).

Establishment of French East India Company.

Ottomans occupy Hungary; Ottomans defeated at St. Gotthard by French and German armies.

Le Tartuffe by Molière; development of French satiric drama.

1665 Great Plague in London.

Discovery of principle of photosynthesis in plants by Robert Hooke.

1666 Great Fire of London.

Académie Française founded in Paris.

1667 War of Devolution; France invades Flanders (Spanish Netherlands).

Treaty of Aix-la-Chapelle ends War of Devolution between France and Spain.

Treaty of Andrusovo ends war between Poland and Russia; Smolensk and Kiev ceded to Russia.

Hand grenade developed in France.

1668 Treaty of Lisbon formalizes Spanish recognition of Portuguese independence.

Invention of reflecting telescope by Isaac Newton.

1669 Last formal meeting of Hanseatic League.

Ottomans capture Candia, Crete, effectively ending 25-year war with Venice.

Britannicus by Racine, development of French tragic drama.

Introduction of coffee-drinking to W Europe by Ottoman ambassador to Paris.

1670 Cossack uprising against Polish rule in Ukraine, suppressed by Jan Sobieski.

Champagne invented in France by Dom Perignon.

AMERICAS & AUSTRALASIA

1661 French–Iroquois War resumes in N America.

Quakers hold first annual meeting on Rhode Island.

Dutch renounce claims to Brazil.

1663 Brazil becomes viceroyalty.

The Bible translated into dialect of Massachusetts.

1664 English seizure of Dutch colony of New Amsterdam; renamed New York.

Dutch annex part of Guiana from English.

1665 Father Allouez explores Great Lakes (–1667), N America.

Colony of New Jersey founded.

1666 French capture Antigua and Montserrat.

Dutch form colony of Suriname.

1667 Virginia bans slaves from obtaining freedom by converting to Christianity.

1669 Robert Cavalier explores N American Midwest.

1670 Colony of South Carolina founded.

British establish colonies in Bahamas.

English Hudson Bay Company formed to trade in Canada.

Sack of Panama by English privateer, Henry Morgan.

Early settlers and traders in North America bartered with Indians to acquire furs for export to Europe.

The fur trade in North America

One of the most valuable natural assets of North America to be exploited by settlers was fur. European trappers and traders made use of the fur trade routes established by native peoples. In 1670, the British Hudson's Bay Company established fur "factories" to control the trade in Rupert's Land, around the bay. It was the search for furs that drove the French westward into Canada, and the Russians eastward into Alaska, establishing trading forts down the west coast of Canada.

The Great Fire of London

In 1665, London was struck by the bubonic plague, which killed up to 100,000 of the city's 400,000 inhabitants. The following year, the walled medieval city of narrow streets and closely built, multistoried timber housing fell prey to a further disaster. A fire, apparently starting in a baker's shop in Pudding Lane, and fanned by a strong dry wind had, within four days, consumed 13,000 houses, 52 company halls, and 87 churches. Nevertheless, the disaster provided the opportunity for rebuilding: by 1671 over 9,000 houses had been built and work had begun under Sir Christopher Wren on more than 50 churches.

Ceramic production in China

A major source of trading wealth for the Song and Ming dynasties had been the production of fine porcelain, or china. Under the Manchu Qing dynasty the porcelain industry became the first example of mass-production of high quality. This trade escalated to a point where oceangoing junks and Dutch East Indiamen would leave south Chinese ports with cargoes the individual value of which would ensure substantial fortunes for western investors.

European commerce with S Asia

Drawn initially by high-volume trade in spices and silks, western trading entrepreneurs soon realized the value of other Asian commodities, produced at a fraction of the cost of European goods. The English (1600) and Dutch (1602) East India companies rapidly expanded the trade, in South Asia, of textiles such as cotton and carpets, tobacco, perfumes, indigo, and basic staples such as rice, salt, and wheat. The Dutch built trading posts in India – such as Cranganur near Cochin (above). It was this intercontinental trade that formed the basis of the first commodity and stock markets in London and Amsterdam.

ASIA

1681

1671 Manchus (Qing) consolidate their control of China and introduce social laws, including the shaving of male heads except for a pigtail.

1674 Hindu Maratha kingdom founded. Maratha chieftain Shivaji crowned king; career marked by widespread conquests.

Pondicherry founded by François Martin as a base for French East India Company.

1681

Three Feudatories Rebellion in China (–1681); a final attempt by remaining Ming aristocracy to resist Manchus (Qing).

Start of pro-Ming revolts in S China; finally suppressed (–1681).

1699

1675 Gobind Singh increases Sikh militancy in N India.

c.1675 Development of *haiku* poetry in Japan.

1676 Afghans rebel against attempts by Mughals to occupy the country.

Intellectual history of the Ming period published in China.

S Chinese port of Amoy begins trading with westerners.

1679 War between Mughals and Rajputs in India (–1709).

First English ship navigates the Ganges.

Fleeing Manchus settle in Mekong delta.

1680 Qing establish factories to revive art and craft industries.

1688

1680 French establish trading stations (factories) in Siam (Thailand).

AFRICA

1671 Kingdom of Ndongo defeated at battle of Ngola by Portuguese who annex the territory to form the colony of Angola.

1698

1672 English Royal Africa Company founded.

1686

1674 French temporarily expelled from Madagascar.

1677 Dutch forts in Senegal seized by French.

c.1680 Foundation of Asante kingdom on W African Gold Coast.

EUROPE

1671 Spain allies with United Provinces against France.

Ottomans declare war on Poland.

Hungarian revolt.

German mathematician and philosopher, Gottfried Wilhelm Leibniz, develops first calculator.

1672 Third Anglo-Dutch War (–1674).

Treaty of Buczacz; Poland cedes Podolia and Ukraine to Ottomans.

Greatest extent of Ottoman Empire.

1673 *La Vida es Sueño* by Spanish playwright Pedro Calderón de la Barca.

1674 Treaty of Westminster ends Third Anglo-Dutch War.

French conquer Franche-Comté.

Jan Sobieski elected king of Poland (–1696).

1675 Brandenburg defeats Sweden at Fehrbellin.

Greenwich Observatory, London, built by Christopher Wren.

Dutchman Christiaan Huygens develops pocket watch with spring balance.

1676 Swedes defeat Danes at Lund.

1677 Swedes defeat Danes at Landskrona.

1678 *Pilgrim's Progress* by John Bunyan.

Chrysanthemums introduced to the Netherlands from Japan.

1679 Treaty of Nijmegen between France and Holy Roman Empire.

Act of Habeas Corpus introduced in England, making it illegal for anyone to be imprisoned without a court hearing.

AMERICAS & AUSTRALASIA

1673 Jolliet and Marquette explore Mississippi and Illinois rivers.

Needham and Arthur follow Occaneechee Path across Appalachians.

1674 Foundation of Manaus, 995 miles (1,601 km) from mouth of the Amazon.

Plantations in Québec become French royal colonies.

1675 Native American forces under "King Philip" wiped out by British.

Henry Morgan, becomes governor of Jamaica.

1676 Settlers defeat New England Indians.

First coffee house licenced in Boston.

1678 French explorer and missionary, Louis Hennepin, discovers Niagara Falls.

1679 English crown claims New Hampshire as a royal colony.

La Salle explores northern Midwest (Indiana).

1680 New Hampshire separated from Massachusetts.

Portugal outlaws enslavement of native Brazilians.

Spanish settlers and missionaries driven out of Rio Grande region by Pueblo peoples.

c.1680 Start of serious slump in economy of Spanish S America.

Aurangzeb, Mughal emperor

Son of the Islamic ruler Shah Jahan (1592–1658), Aurangzeb succeeded to the throne of Mughal India in 1658 after a bitter rivalry with his brothers. It took him some 30 years to consolidate power over both his Muslim and Hindu subjects, but under his rule the Mughal empire reached its greatest extent and Islamic culture and the arts in India achieved a high point of excellence.

Aurangzeb was an orthodox Sunni Muslim and his rejection of the traditional Islamic policy of tolerance toward Hindus led to the frequent destruction of Hindu shrines and idols. It particularly caused problems toward the end of his reign. Wars against the land-owning Rajputs, formerly close allies who controlled local politics in northern and western India (now Rajasthan), and against the Marathas of the Deccan led to the irrevocable decline of his empire. Aurangzeb is regarded as the last great Muslim ruler of India. His reign is noted as the apogee of Islamic culture in South Asia, his court producing poetry, calligraphy, and finely wrought miniature manuscript paintings of the highest quality.

The Ottoman siege of Vienna in 1683 marked the beginning of their greatest onslaught on the Habsburg Empire. Ringed by a huge enemy army, Vienna called on Poland and the papacy, which joined the German princes in a successful relief effort.

Habsburg-Ottoman conflict

The Ottomans first temporarily threatened Vienna in 1529; in many ways, their defeat at the hands of a central European alliance gave legitimacy to Habsburg rule in central Europe, whilst establishing Ottoman hegemony in southeast Europe.

When, in 1683, the Ottomans once again attacked the city, an anti-Ottoman alliance, led by the Polish king Jan Sobieski (reigned 1674–1696) began a sustained assault on Turkish holdings in mainland Europe which lasted for the next two centuries. The Habsburgs reconquered Hungary in 1699, and began a relentless tug of war process of recovery and defeat in the region, characterized as "Balkanization."

The Ottomans in Europe

c.1354	Ottomans occupy Gallipoli
1361	Ottomans take Adrianople
1389	Serbs defeated at Kosovo
1393	Occupation of Bulgaria; Wallachia becomes a tributary
1453	Constantinople falls to Ottomans
1458	Occupation of Peloponnese (–1460)
1459	Occupation of Serbia
1463	Occupation of Bosnia
1478	Occupation of Albania
1484	Ottomans occupy coastal Bessarabia
1504	Moldavia becomes tributary
1521	Ottomans take Belgrade
1526	Occupation of Jedisan, S Russia
1526	Ottoman victory at Mohács
1541	Occupation of Hungary; Transylvania becomes tributary
1672	Occupation of Podolia, SW Russia
1683	Ottomans unsuccessfully besiege Vienna

ASIA

1681 Kangxi, first Qing (Manchu) emperor, brings Ming resistance to an end, greatly extending Qing control in S China.

1683 Dutch merchants begin trading at Canton (Guangzhou).

1684 Buddhist-inspired reforms under Japanese shogun, Tsunayoshi, causes widespread economic hardship.

Dutch East India Company occupies sultanate of Bantam, S Sumatra.

1685 Mughal empire expels English East India Company from Surat.

Chinese ports opened to foreign trade.

French Jesuits establish first mission at Peking (Beijing).

English establish pepper trading center at Benkulen, Sumatra.

1686 French found trading post at Chandernagore, India.

1687 Mughals annex Golconda, S India.

1688 French provoke rebellion in Ayutthaya (Thailand) overthrowing King Narai.

Genroku Era in Japan: flowering of kabuki puppet theater, poetry, *ukiyo-e* painting, and narrative fiction (–1703).

Rapid growth of castle cities in Japan modeled on Edo and Osaka.

1689 Treaty of Nerchinsk between Russia and China; settles territorial dispute with Qing China. Treaty agrees upon Russian and Chinese spheres of influence in E Asia; acquisition of Amur and Ussuri regions by China from Russia. Russians withdraw from Amur basin.

1690 English found Fort William trading post at Calcutta.

Chinese forces defend Khalkha (Outer Mongolia) from Dzungar invasion.

AFRICA

c.1681 Changamire Dombo, king of Rozwi, conquers the Torwa of Butua (Zimbabwe) and establishes capital at Danongombe.

1682 Accession of Iyasu I in Ethiopia, last great king of Gondar Period.

First Danish settlement on Gold Coast.

1684 Sultan of Morocco takes Tangier from English.

Changamire Dombo defeats Portuguese at battle of Maungwe.

1686 France establishes Fort Dauphin and claims Madagascar.

1687 French Huguenots settle at Cape Colony.

c.1690 Aya kingdom of Whydah (Ouidah) on Dahomey coast emerges as principal supplier of slaves for Atlantic trade.

1681 Opening of Canal du Midi linking Bay of Biscay with the Mediterranean.

1682 English astronomer Edmund Halley observes Halley's comet.

1683 Failure of Ottoman siege of Vienna.

Invention of precision microscope by Anton van Leeuwenhoek.

1702

1685 Revocation of Edict of Nantes; beginning of persecution of Protestants in France; Huguenots flee.

Accession of Catholic king, James II (James VII of Scotland) to English throne (–1688).

1686 League of Augsburg formed to contain France's powers, includes Holy Roman Empire, Spain, and Sweden.

1697

1687 Ottomans defeated by Holy Roman Empire at battle of Mohács.

Venice regains Athens from Ottomans.

Principia Mathematica published by Isaac Newton includes full explanation of principle of gravity.

1688 Glorious Revolution in England; King James flees to France and constitutional monarchy restored under his daughter Mary and her husband, William of Orange.

1692

France launches war against League of Augsburg, which develops into War of the Grand Alliance after Netherlands and England join League.

France captures the Palatinate, Trier, Mainz, and Cologne from Holy Roman Empire; invades Franconia and Swabia.

1689 Exiled king, James of England, attempts invasion of Ireland; defeated by William of Orange at the battle of the Boyne (1690).

1699

Peter the Great becomes czar of Russia.

1690 *Essay Concerning Human Understanding* by John Locke establishes theories of empiricism and liberal democracy.

German instrument-maker Johann Christoph Denner invents clarinet.

c.1690 Turnip first cultivated in England; becomes basis of rotational mixed farming.

1693 **1682** Spanish begin settlement of Texas.

La Salle follows Mississippi to its mouth; claims Louisiana for France.

Quakers found Philadelphia.

1683 German immigration to Pennsylvania begins.

1685 French Huguenots settle in South Carolina.

Fur trade routes open up between Great Lakes and upper Ohio valley.

1700 French *Code Noir* restricts slavery in French Caribbean colonies.

1686 European War of the Grand Alliance spreads to N America, where it is known as King William's War; Iroquois and English ally against the French.

1699 **1688** William Dampier is first Englishman to visit Australia.

Mennonite radical Protestant sect becomes first religious group in American colonies to condemn slavery.

The popular appeal of Kabuki theater is here illustrated in the colored print of a popular playhouse, the audience picked out in vibrant caricature.

Japanese Kabuki theater

Although still highly formalized, Japanese Kabuki theater developed in the 17th century in response to the recondite formality of traditional No theater. It appeared first in Kyoto and then spread throughout Japan. Though founded by a woman, Izumo no Okuni, Kabuki, like the No, employs only male actors, even for female parts, but stresses action and conflict in the plot and avoids arcane literary references and symbolism. Kabuki is therefore flamboyant and colorful, with a large stage and cast. Elaborate make-up replaces the No masks.

The most popular Kabuki drama is *The Treasury of Loyal Retainers*. Kabuki reached its high point in the work of Monzaemon Chikamatsu (1653–1725), the first professional Japanese dramatist, who wrote over 30 Kabuki plays, both tragedies, such as *Shinju Ten no Amijima* (The Love Suicides of Amijima), and historical epics, such as the *Kokusenya-kassen* (The Battles of Coxinga). Chikamatsu, like Shakespeare in the west, remains a fundamental influence on Japanese drama.

Peter I, the Great (1672–1725)

Succeeding to the Russian throne at the age of ten in 1682, Peter took full control in 1689. Success in war against the Ottomans (1695–96) gave Russia access to the Black Sea, catapulting the state to superpower status. Peter toured the capitals of western Europe (1697–98) which exposed him to an array of innovative ideas concerning science, politics, and the military arts.

As a result, he introduced European technology to Russia, created a new army and navy, established strong trading relations with the west, and fundamentally reformed the government of Russia, limiting the power of the Church and the boyars in favor of constitutional administrative bodies.

War against Sweden, the Great Northern War (1700–21), won him access to the Baltic, and led him to relocate the Russian capital from Moscow to the new city, built on western models, at St. Petersburg on the Baltic coast. In the east, he promoted both campaigns against the Tartars and voyages of exploration, seeking (unsuccessfully) to establish a Northeast Passage, which began the expansion of Russia into Siberia and Asia.

ASIA

1691 Mughal empire in India reaches greatest extent.

S Cambodia organized into two provinces of Annam.

1692 Edict of Toleration introduced for Catholics in China.

1696 Suppression of Mongolia by Qing China (–1697).

1697 Start of conquest of Kamchatka; completed in 1732, it gives Russia 0control of Siberia.

Chinese occupy Outer (W) Mongolia.

1699 Uncut hair, the turban, and the dagger adopted as Sikh symbols.

c.1700 Probable commencement of Mughal military mapping.

AFRICA

1693 Changamire Dombo, king of Rozwi in Zimbabwe, expels Portuguese.

1695 Death of Changamire Dombo; Portuguese revive attempts to colonize SE Africa.

1698 Africa declared a free trade zone for British subjects.

Omani Arabs capture Mombasa, East Africa.

1699 Omani Arabs take control of island of Zanzibar, E Africa.

1700 English pirates establish base on Madagascar.

c.1700 Rise to prominence of Bantu kingdom of Buganda, E Africa.

Rapid increase in numbers of slaves sold annually to the Americas.

EUROPE	AMERICAS & AUSTRALASIA

EUROPE

1692 French fleet heavily defeated by Grand Alliance at La Hogue.

1697 ▼ **1693** French defeat Grand Alliance forces at Neerwinden.

1694 Foundation of Bank of England.

First dictionary of French language.

1695 End of press censorship in England.

1696 Russia captures Azov from Ottomans.

Window tax introduced in England.

1697 Treaty of Ryswick ends War of the Grand Alliance.

Holy Roman Empire troops under Eugene of Savoy defeat Ottomans at battle of Zenta.

1701 ▼ **1698** France, England, and the Netherlands agree upon a treaty to resolve problem of the Spanish Succession.

Isaac Newton calculates speed of sound.

London Stock Exchange founded.

Thomas Savery, English engineer, develops first steam pump for draining mines.

1699 Habsburgs recover Hungary from Ottomans.

Peace of Karlowitz confirms Austrian conquests.

1703 ▼ **c.1699** Peter the Great of Russia bans traditional dress, introduces western fashions, and reforms Russian calendar.

1710 ▼ **1700** Russia signs truce with Ottomans, retaining Azov but disbanding its Black Sea fleet.

Great Northern War.

Charles XII of Sweden invades Denmark and occupies Copenhagen.

c.1700 Great age of German baroque music – Buxtehude, Handel, Bach.

AMERICAS & AUSTRALASIA

1692 Salem witchcraft trials, New England.

1706 ▼ **1693** Juan Ponce de León completes reconquest of New Mexico for Spain.

Foundation of Kingston, Jamaica.

1695 Discovery of gold in Brazil; found in Minas Gerais region.

1697 Foundation of first Jesuit mission in Lower California, Mexico, at Loreto.

1699 Dampier explores New Guinea and New Britain (–1700).

Abenaki Indians and New England settlers reach peace settlement.

1700 First Baptist association established in the N American colonies, at Rhode Island.

The Selling of Joseph by Judge Samuel Sewall; first direct appeal for abolition of slavery in N America.

c.1700 Boston emerges as the principal port in the Atlantic slave trade.

J.S. Bach (1685–1750)

Taught from an early age by his father and then by his brother, the German composer and organist Johann Sebastian Bach developed a consummate mastery of Baroque polyphonic composition which remains enormously influential, and which defined both orchestral and chamber music as distinct art forms. He produced musical works in almost every form known at his time. Rarely published in his lifetime, his work was only recognized and publicized in the 19th century.

Portuguese South America

Following the Treaty of Tordesillas (1494), which divided the unconquered globe between Spain and Portugal, the latter began the aggressive exploitation of Brazil, the only sector of the American New World accorded to them. The first to recognize the economic advantages of transporting African slaves to the Americas, the Portuguese were also among the last European nations to abandon the trade, only abolishing slavery in Brazil in 1850.

Between 1550 and 1800, some 2.5 million African slaves were taken to Brazil, more than 70 percent of them to work for the sugar plantations and mills that underpinned the economy.

Every year the Asante people gathered for a festival in Kumasi, the capital, to celebrate the strength of the Asante nation.

1701 Start of Ashanti's rise to prominence under Osei Tutu.

Asante kingdom

The Asante were one of a number of Akan-speaking peoples of West Africa, centered on modern-day Togo, Ivory Coast (Côte d'Ivoire), and southern Ghana. They rose to prominence under Osei Tutu, who became chief of the small state of Kumasi in the 1670s. After persuading other small states to join him, he won independence from the suzerainty of the neighboring state of Denkyera and was subsequently crowned Asantehene, or King of the Asante.

Under his kingship, the Asante kingdom trebled in size and gained outlets to the sea. The Asante thereafter took an active part in developing the thriving slave trade, forcibly impressing native Africans from neighboring areas and dealing with Arab traders from the interior. The Asante licenced European slave "factories" on the coast, such as Elmina, where slaves were assembled before embarcation on the notorious Middle Passage to the Americas, earning the region the name the Slave Coast.

In addition to the immense fortunes accumulated by the Asante rulers and local chiefs, they also received firearms from the Europeans in payment for slaves, which enabled them to extend their lands further. The Asante kingdom reached its greatest extent around 1750. It finally broke up during wars with the British after Britain outlawed the slave trade in 1808.

1705 Foundation of Husaynid dynasty in Tunis (–1957).

1706 Shah Hussein founds *madrasa* at Isfahan.

1724 **1707** Death of Aurangzeb heralds decline of Mughal power in India.

Death of Shitao, leading Chinese landscape painter, poet, and calligrapher.

1708 Sikh leader, Gobind Singh, assassinated.

1711 **1709** Afghan uprising against Safavid Persians.

1710 Outbreak of war between Ottomans and Russia (–1711).

EUROPE

1701 War of the Spanish Succession (–1714).

Swedish forces invade Poland and occupy Warsaw and Cracow.

Act of Establishment excludes Catholics from English throne.

Jethro Tull invents seed drill (England).

1702 Camisards (French Protestants) revolt against persecution following repeal of Edict of Nantes; suppressed by Louis XIV.

Frederick IV of Denmark abolishes serfdom.

The Daily Courant, first daily newspaper in England.

1703 Portugal joins the Grand Alliance against France.

Foundation of St. Petersburg by Peter the Great.

1704 Grand Alliance forces under the Duke of Marlborough defeat French at Blenheim.

English occupy Gibraltar.

Opticks by Isaac Newton explores theories on light.

Newcomen collaborates with Savery to improve steam engine (England).

1705 *Trajectory of Planets* by English astronomer, Edmund Halley.

1707 Act of Union unites England and Scotland as Great Britain.

1708 Grand Alliance troops under Marlborough and Eugene of Savoy defeat French at Oudenaarde.

English seize Sardinia and Minorca from French.

1709 Grand Alliance troops defeat French at Malplaquet.

Charles XII of Sweden defeated by Russians at Poltava; seeks refuge in Ottoman Turkey.

Abraham Darby uses coke to smelt iron ore (England).

1710 Ottomans at war with Russia (–1711).

Meissen porcelain factory opens in Dresden, Germany.

AMERICAS & AUSTRALASIA

1701 French fort established at Detroit.

1702 Outbreak of war between English and French colonists in N America (–1713).

1703 Foundation of N American colony of Delaware by English.

1704 French massacre of English Puritan colony at Deerfield, Massachusetts; intensification of war.

English settlement at Bonavista, Newfoundland, seized by French and Native American forces.

Boston Newsletter, America's first weekly newspaper, published.

1706 Juan de Uribarri claims Colorado or Spain.

1708 French victory over English settlers at St. John's, Newfoundland, gives them control of the east coast of Canada.

1710 English forces take Port Royal in Acadia (Nova Scotia) from French.

The early 18th century in Europe saw the development of a highly decorative artistic style – rococo – which espoused an idyllic view of aristocratic dalliance and playful debauchery.

Meissen porcelain

The technique of creating finely glazed porcelain originated in China and was imitated in Europe with the opening of the Meissen factory in Germany in 1710. A chemist named Johann Böttger succeeded in developing a translucent glaze using local clay, and inaugurated one of the earliest commercial advances of the Industrial Revolution. Meissen porcelain reached a high point after 1731 in the modeling of the sculptor Johann Kändler; the figurine above dates from 1745.

The ronin (or "wave man") was a Samurai warrior with no particular allegiance to a feudal lord. They were much admired in popular culture as antiauthoritarian rebels.

The 47 ronin

The freelance ronin Samurai warriors emerged from the Japanese civil wars of the 14th and 15th centuries. They engaged in a major rebellion in 1651 and continued to instigate dissent into the 1700s. In 1701 a respected lord, Asano Naganori, was forced to kill himself for wounding an official who had insulted him. In revenge, 47 of his samurai became ronin and murdered the official, an act normally punished by execution. But because Confucionism taught that it is honorable to avenge a lord's violent death, they were allowed to commit suicide. The event later

King Frederick William held smoking parties, to which he invited Prussian army officers and other important figures. They were forced to sit smoking and discussing policy, although many of them actually disliked tobacco.

Frederick William I of Prussia

Frederick William I (1688–1740), was the son of Frederick I, who had crowned himself the first king of Prussia in 1701, building on the successes of a previous Frederick William, the Elector of Brandenburg. Known as the "Great Elector," the latter had effectively founded the Prussian state by freeing it from Polish suzerainty in 1660.

Frederick William I succeeded to the Prussian throne in 1713. He had taken part in the War of the Spanish Succession (1701–1714), during which he had gained a profound interest in military affairs. As king, he used his military experiences to reorganize Prussia's army. By the time of his death, it had increased in size from 38,000 to 83,000 men and had become the most efficient fighting force in Europe. He also gained Pomerania from Sweden in 1720 under the Treaty of Stockholm. His son, Frederick II, known as Frederick the Great, inherited a wealthy state and went on to make Prussia one of the major powers of Europe.

ASIA

1722

1711 Mirwais Neka of Afghanistan defeats Persians and establishes Afghan independence.

1713 French missionaries expelled from Tongking, N Vietnam.

1715 Japanese government severely restricts trade with the Dutch.

c.1715 Expansion of Burmese state; flowering of Burmese culture and arts.

1716 Qing emperor, Kangxi, repeals Edict of Toleration and bans Christian teaching in China.

Oirat Mongols invade Tibet, destroy Qing army, and sack Lhasa.

Start of Kyoho era in Japan.

1720 Qing forces from Gansu and Sichuan oust Mongols from Tibet and install acceptable Dalai Lama; Tibet becomes tributary state to China.

Yoshimune permits import of European books to Japan, leading to advances in science and medicine.

1728 **c.1720** Marathas start to expand over most of India.

AFRICA

1712 Bambara kingdom of Segu founded in W Africa, near Timbuktu, begins to take over territories of empire of Mali.

1713 Smallpox epidemic, introduced by European settlers, ravages Khoisan peoples of the Cape.

1717 Prussia sells its slaving stations to the Dutch.

1720 Dutch settlers reach Orange river from the Cape.

c.1730 Dutch occupy Portuguese settlement at Delagoa Bay (–1730).

EUROPE

1711 Completion of rebuilding of St. Paul's cathedral, London under direction of Christopher Wren.

 1725

1712 Seat of Russian government moves from Moscow to St. Petersburg.

University of Madrid founded.

Last execution for witchcraft in England.

 1727

1713 Treaty of Utrecht ends War of the Spanish Succession; confirms separation of French and Spanish crowns and recognizes Philip V of Spain.

1714 George I, the elector of Hanover, becomes first Hanoverian ruler of England (–1727).

Philip V of Spain revokes Catalonian political liberties.

German physicist, Gabriel Fahrenheit, devises temperature scale.

1717 Britain, France, and the Netherlands form Triple Alliance to contain expansionist plans of Philip V of Spain.

George Frederick Handel writes *Water Music* to entertain King George I of England's boating parties.

Opening of first Freemason's Lodge in London.

1718 Treaty of Passarowitz ends Austro-Turkish war.

Austria joins Triple Alliance, forming Quadruple Alliance, to uphold terms of Treaty of Utrecht.

Machine gun invented by James Puckle (England).

Introduction of banknotes in England.

1719 Spain declares war on France.

Frederick William of Prussia bans serfdom on crown lands.

Robinson Crusoe by Daniel Defoe.

1720 Treaty of The Hague between Spain and the Quadruple Alliance; Spain agrees to withdraw from Sicily and Sardinia.

Treaty of Stockholm ends war between Sweden and Prussia. Swedish power declines.

AMERICAS & AUSTRALASIA

1711 Jesuits banned from entering Minas Gerais region in Brazil.

 1713

Tuscarora War: Native Americans attack expanding European settlements on Roanoke and Chowan rivers (–1713).

French forces sack Rio de Janeiro during War of the Spanish Succession.

Allied British and Iroquois forces fail in campaign on French Canadian settlements at Montréal and Québec.

1712 Pennsylvania bans importation of slaves.

Early slave revolt in N America results in six suicides and 12 executions.

1713 Asiento agreement gives British control of slave trade to Spanish colonies for 30 years.

Treaty of Utrecht confirms British control of Newfoundland and Nova Scotia.

Troops from the Carolinas capture Tuscarora base at Fort Nahucke, forcing Native Americans to negotiate.

1715 Yamasee tribe, encouraged by Spaniards, massacre English settlers in South Carolina.

 1720

1716 Spain occupies parts of Texas in response to French westward expansion from Louisiana.

Frezier explores coasts of Chile and Peru.

1718 New Orleans founded by French.

Collegiate School of America transferred to New Haven, and named Yale University after its benefactor, Elihu Yale.

1720 First colonial settlements in Vermont.

Intermittent warfare between French and Spanish forces in Florida and Texas ends with Treaty of The Hague; Spanish possession of Texas confirmed.

British colony of Honduras established in C America.

The first known Newcomen engine was installed at a mine near Dudley Castle in Staffordshire, England, in 1712.

Newcomen's steam engine

The first steam-powered engine, built by the British engineer Thomas Newcomen (1663–1729) after he observed the inefficiency of horse-powered drainage pumps at the tin mines in Cornwall, should correctly be called an atmospheric engine. Designed to drain mines of flood water, steam filled the pumping engine, but atmospheric pressure pushed the piston as a spray of cold water condensed the steam. Newcomen went on to invent an automatic gear valve to control the device.

St. Paul's Cathedral, London

The architect Christopher Wren (1632–1723) had begun a survey of St. Paul's Cathedral (*left*) with a view to repairs in 1663. The Great Fire of London in 1666 laid open a broad field for his genius. He drew up elaborate designs for the rebuilding of the whole city, which were never realized. Nevertheless, his conceptions for rebuilding 50 city churches, culminating in the Baroque splendor of St. Paul's cathedral remain a remarkable legacy.

Slavery in the Americas

The transatlantic trade in human slaves, which prospered between the late 15th and early 19th centuries, proved one of the most significant – and devastating – demographic shifts in human history. Under appalling conditions, over 12 million people were transported, initially by the Spanish and Portuguese, but soon by the Dutch, French, and English, from the west coast of Africa to the Caribbean and the Americas to supply labor for the newly established plantations and mining concerns.

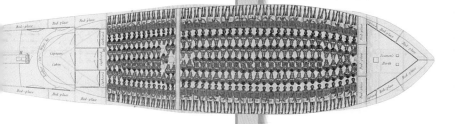

Conditions on slave ships on the terrible "Middle Passage" from the slave ports of West Africa to the New World were inhuman. Those that survived weeks, or even months, of suffocation, thirst, and sparse rations were sold to rich owners and put to work under cruel bailiffs.

The Atlantic Slave Trade

In 400 years, around 12.15 million slaves were delivered to the Americas, some 4–5 million losing their lives on the "Middle Passage."

1444	Portuguese import first West African slaves to Iberia.
1479	Treaty of Alcáçovas allows Portuguese to sell slaves in Spain
1502	Introduction of African slaves to the Caribbean.
1522	First American slave revolt in Hispaniola.
1619	First African slaves imported to Virginia, in North America
1685	*Code Noir* controls slave trade in French Caribbean colonies
1787	Abolition of slavery in North America; largely ignored by Southern states
	Foundation of Sierra Leone in Africa for freed slaves
1790	Zenith of Atlantic trade: c.70,000 slaves traded across Atlantic
1804	Foundation of independent state of Haiti
1807	Britain outlaws slave trade
1822	Freed slaves found colony of Liberia in West Africa
1825	More than 36 percent of all the New World slaves are in the southern US.
1863	Emancipation Proclamation frees slaves in North America; outbreak of American Civil war. The 13th amendment to the Constitution (passed 1865) ends slavery in full in the US.
1867	Last known arrival of a slave ship in Cuba.

ASIA

1726

1722 Subjugation of Afghans by Persia (–1736).

Last Safavid shah overthrown by Afghans.

1724 Oudh and Hyderabad establish independence from Mughal rule.

1733

c.1725 Major crop failures result in agrarian famine in Japan.

1726 Persians retake Isfahan from Afghans.

1727 Ottoman Turks and Persians form anti-Russian alliance.

Rajput ruler, Sawai Jai Singh II of Rajasthan, India, founds new capital at Jaipur, and builds Jantar Mantar observatory.

Treaty of Kyakhta fixes Sino-Russian border.

1728 Marathas defeat Nizam of Hyderabad and gain supremacy over Deccan; with subsequent territorial expansion.

1729 Qing emperor, Yongzheng, bans public sale of opium in China.

1730 End of Tulip Period of Ottoman rule, reduction in centralized militarism and increasing adoption of European culture.

Qing emperor, Yongzheng, imposes restrictions on slave trade in China.

c.1730 Revival of Shinto faith in Japan.

AFRICA

1721 French seize Mauritius from the Dutch.

1723 British Africa Company buys land on banks of Gambia river, W Africa.

King Agaja of Dahomey invades Allada.

1731

1724 Kingdom of Dahomey becomes principal supplier of slaves to European traders.

1729 Portuguese leave E Africa in wake of attacks from Oman.

1734

1730 Revival of ancient trading kingdom of Bornu in W Africa.

1744

Omani Arabs gain control of Mombasa from Portuguese.

c.1730 Emergence of Fulbe confederation of Futa Jallon.

Dutch abandon trading post on Maputo river at Delagoa Bay, SE Africa.

EUROPE

1721 Peace of Nystad; Sweden cedes Ingria, Livonia, and Karelia to Russia, ending the Second Northern War. Increases Russian power in the Baltic.

Robert Walpole becomes Britain's first prime minister (–1742).

Brandenburg Concertos by Johann Sebastian Bach.

1724 Longmans is Britain's first publishing house.

1725 Philip V of Spain and Emperor Charles VI sign Treaty of Vienna, agreeing to withdraw from the Quadruple Alliance.

Death of Peter I of Russia; succeeded by his second wife, Catherine (–1727).

Foundation of Academy of Sciences in St. Petersburg.

The Four Seasons by Antonio Vivaldi.

c.1725 Height of the European Grand Tour; Antonio Canaletto is only one of many Italian artists producing *verdute* paintings as souvenirs for rich visitors to Italy.

1726 *Gulliver's Travels* by Jonathan Swift.

English botanist and chemist, Stephen Hales, measures blood pressure for first time.

1727 Spain attacks British troops in Gibraltar, breaking terms of the Treaty of Utrecht.

1729 Treaty of Seville; Spain renounces its claims to Gibraltar.

1730 Wesley brothers found Methodism in Britain.

Townshend introduces crop rotation in England.

Height of Rococo Period in European art and architecture.

AMERICAS & AUSTRALASIA

1721 Jacob Roggeveen visits many Polynesian islands (–1722).

Swiss immigrants introduce the rifle to N America.

1722 Dutch navigators discover Easter Island, Samoa, and Society Islands.

1724 *Le Code Noir* (The Black Code) introduced in Louisiana, banning Jews and Catholics from the colony, and permitting slave-holders to cut off runaways' ears, hamstring, and brand them.

1726 Foundation of Montevideo, Uruguay.

1727 First coffee plantation in Brazil.

1728 Vitus Bering begins Russian exploration of Alaska; finds strait between N America and Asia.

1729 Chaussegros de Léry makes first proper survey of Allegheny and upper Ohio rivers in N America.

Natchez tribe massacre 300 soldiers and settlers at Fort Rosalie, Louisiana, in reaction to settlers' demands that they relinquish traditional worship centers and burial sites.

Foundation of Baltimore.

Gems identified as diamonds found at Minas Gerais, Brazil.

The Fulbe built elaborate temporary agricultural enclosures. This 17th-century illustration shows a Fulbe town on the Gambia river, with a plantation., and a corral for livestock.

The Fulbe

The Fulbe (or Fulani) are a primarily Muslim people scattered across many parts of West Africa, from the Atlantic coast of Gambia to Cameroon. The Fulani were originally pastoralists, their lives and organization dominated by the needs of their herds; today many practice sedentary agriculture or live in towns. They established enclosed settlements surrounded by earthworks or hedges to protect crops and enclose cattle, with an inner area fortified with stakes. European traders were impressed by the level of social organization among African peoples, but persistently represented them as disorganized tribal communities, incapable of self-government.

"Gulliver's Travels"

The Anglo-Irish journalist, clergyman, agitator, and pamphleteer Jonathan Swift (1667–1745) almost accidentally invented the novel with his account of the adventures of a ship's doctor, Lemuel Gulliver. This satirical narrative, published anonymously in 1726, was an instant success. It was aimed directly at current political and religious factions, but reveals a misanthropy and conservatism at odds with the contemporary British mood of scientific discovery and ethical liberalism.

Gin Lane (1747), a satirical engraving by Hogarth, comments on the deleterious effect of cheaply produced alcoholic spirit Geneva, or gin, widely available in England in the 18th century.

William Hogarth

Trained as a classical history painter, William Hogarth opened his own print shop in London in 1720. A practical, business-like artist with a keen eye for human foibles and frailties, he produced portraits and genre pieces of great originality. However, frustrated by the conventional strictures of established artistic practice, he resurrected the medieval morality tradition and produced highly popular series of satirical commentaries on contemporary life: *A Harlot's Progress* (1730–31), *A Rake's Progress* (1733–35), *Marriage a la Mode* (1743–45), and *Industry and Idleness* (1747).

Sack of Delhi

The declining power of the Mughal sultanate in northern India was dealt a serious blow in 1739 when Nadir Shah, the usurper of Safavid Persia, invaded northern India and sacked the Mughal capital, Delhi. He slaughtered many of the inhabitants, and stole the Koh-i-noor diamond and the Peacock Throne. Following the Indian campaign, Nadir Shah looked west, attacking the Ottoman Turks, but was assassinated by his own troops. In the wake of the sack of Delhi, the Maratha Confederacy acquired effective control of the Indian subcontinent.

ASIA

1733 Great Northern Expedition under Vitus Bering surveys northern coasts of Siberia (–1742).

Widespread food riots in Edo (Tokyo), Japan, in protest against high food prices enforced following famine.

1736 Nadir Shah becomes shah of Persia; formal end of Safavid dynasty in Persia.

1758 **1737** Hindu Marathas extend their power in N India.

Persians temporarily occupy S Afghanistan (–1747).

1739 Persians defeat Mughals and occupy Delhi.

1740 Mon kingdom of Pegu rebels against Burma, occupying Ava (–1752).

AFRICA

1747 **1731** Kingdom of Dahomey under suzerainty of the Oyo empire.

1734 Sultan of Bornu, W Africa, becomes overlord of neighboring Kanem to form major sub-Saharan trading state of Kanem-Bornu.

1735 French East India Company establishes sugar plantation industry in Mauritius and Réunion.

c.1740 Lunda kingdom begins, founded in C Africa.

1740

1731 Official residence for British prime ministers, 10 Downing Street, is built.

1732 Frederick William I of Prussia introduces conscription, building the fourth largest army in Europe.

Covent Garden Opera House opens in London.

1733 War of the Polish Succession (–1735).

John Kay invents flying shuttle loom; beginnings of English mass-textiles manufacturing industry in England.

Essay on Man by Alexander Pope and William Hogarth's *Rake's Progress* symbolize beginning of British radical humanism.

1734 Spain takes over kingdom of Naples.

1735 Treaty of Vienna ends War of the Polish Succession; Austria and Russia begin to dominate Polish affairs.

Russian Imperial Ballet School founded.

1736 Russians recover Azov from Ottomans and advance to Jassy.

Rubber first introduced from C America.

1737 End of Medici rule in Florence.

Swedish botanist, Carolus Linnaeus publishes *Genera Plantarum* in Holland; beginning of modern classification of plants.

1738 *Mass in B Minor* by J.S. Bach.

Cuckoo clocks manufactured in S Germany.

1739 Treaty of Belgrade ends Austro-Russian war with Ottoman Turkey; Ottomans regain control of N Serbia.

Treatise on Human Nature by David Hume.

Execution of highwayman Dick Turpin, at Tyburn (Marble Arch) in London.

1740 Accession of Frederick II (the Great) of Prussia (–1786); beginning of Prussian rise to dominance in NC Europe.

Prussia annexes Austrian Silesia, provoking War of the Austrian Succession (–1748).

1742

1731 The de la Vérendryes open the lower Saskatchewan fur trade (–1740).

1732 Georgia, the last of the Thirteen Colonies, founded.

The *Philadelphia Zeitung* published by Benjamin Franklin; first non-English newspaper published in British colonies.

1735 Expedition to Quito led by French scientist, La Condamine, to test sphericity of the earth.

French found first settlement in Indiana.

1739 Stono rebellion, a slave revolt, in South Carolina.

Anglo-Spanish naval war over trade in the New World.

Viceroyalty of New Granada established by the Spanish to defend Caribbean coast.

War of "Jenkin's Ear" between Britain and Spain; British sack Spanish trading city of Portobello, Panama.

The Mallet brothers reach Santa Fe overland from the eastern US.

Hostilities between Georgia and Spanish Florida (–1741).

French explorers reach Colorado.

Selective cross-breeding produced many breeds of sheep, pigs, and cows that gave higher yields of wool, meat, and dairy products.

Experimental agriculture

One significant aspect of the Enlightenment was the direct application of new ideas and discoveries on industry and agriculture. Farmers adopted a more scientific approach to agriculture to maximize their yields in response to the demands of a rapidly growing and increasingly urban population.

Inventors such as Jethro Tull (1674–1741) introduced horse-drawn implements such as the seed drill and harrow. Biologists and botanists experimented with crop rotation to preserve the fertility of farmland; fields once left fallow every second or third year could now be cropped continuously. Advances in zoology and genetics saw the development of highly productive new breeds of livestock such as Robert Bakewell's New Leicester long-wool sheep, and sturdier shire horses; John Ellmann developed short-wool sheep producing better lamb and mutton, while the Colling brothers developed short-horn cattle.

The Agricultural Revolution

A series of important innovations made England the most agriculturally productive and efficient nation in Europe.

1701	Englishman, Jethro Tull, invents the seed drill
1714	Jethro Tull introduces horseshoe to England from France
1730	Townshend introduces crop rotation in Norfolk, England
1745	Robert Bakewell of Leicestershire, England, begins improved methods of sheep breeding
c.1750	Enclosure in England leads to farmers practicing farming on a larger scale, mechanization, and extensive land drainage schemes
1778	Thomas Coke of Norfolk, England, begins experiments in new farming techniques and animal husbandry
1793	Board of Agriculture established in Britain, with Arthur Young as Secretary

Voltaire's **L'Encyclopédie** *was illustrated with fine engravings showing all sorts of craftsmen at work, such as the instrument makers in the illustration above. It was a massive work consisting of 28 volumes.*

The Enlightenment

Innovations in agriculture disrupted the traditional relationship between peasantry and the land. Many left the countryside to work in cities, swelling an increasingly politicized urban population. This was one of the main factors behind radical shifts in political thought and practice during the period.

The 18th-century "enlightened" writers, or *philosophes*, such as Voltaire and Diderot, appealed to human reason to challenge traditional assumptions about the Church, state, monarchy, education, and social institutions. "Man is born free, but everywhere he is in chains," wrote Jean-Jacques Rousseau in his *Social Contract* (1762), in which he sought to show how a democratic society could work. Some ideas stemmed from the work of the English philosopher John Locke (1632–1704), who had said that all men are equal and that the authority of government comes only from the consent of the governed.

The French philosopher Voltaire (1694–1778) played a leading role in the Enlightenment. He used drama, satire, and poetry to express his political views and opposition to the Catholic church. His major work, L'Encyclopédie, published between 1751 and 1772, was instrumental in spreading the new philosophic and scientific ideas.

ASIA

1741 Danish navigator Vitus Bering, working for the Russian crown, dies in the course of the Great Northern Expedition on an island off Kamchatka.

1743 Nizam of Hyderabad takes Arcot, S India, from the Marathas.

1744 Anglo-French War eclipses French power in S. Asia.

1745 Tokugawa rule in Japan enters decline due to corruption under Ieshige.

1751

1746 French occupy Madras; beginning of Anglo-French hostilities in S Asia.

c.1746 Intensive persecution of Christians in China (–1748).

1747 Foundation of kingdom of Afghanistan by Ahmad Khan Abdali.

1748 Punjab invaded by Afghans.

1749 Mysore starts to become major power in S India.

1754 **1750** French victory at Tanjore gives Dupleix, the French governor of Pondicherry, control of the Carnatic coast, SE India.

Qing China begins conquest of Tibet and Turkestan.

c.1750 Emergence of Wahhabi movement to purify Islam begins in Arabia.

1760 English East India Company's activities in China severely restricted.

AFRICA

1744 Governor of Mombasa declares his colony independent of Oman.

1747 Yoruba tribe conquers Dahomey (–1748); Oyo becomes main power in Niger delta.

c.1750 Afrikaans achieves its modern form in S Africa.

EUROPE

1741 Sweden declares war on Russia (–1743).

English physician William Brownrigg develops carbonated, or soda, water.

1742 Frederick of Prussia completes rapid conquest of Silesia.

Treaty of Berlin ends First Silesian War between Austria and Prussia.

Swedish astronomer Anders Celsius develops decimal temperature scale that bears his name, also known as centigrade.

Messiah by George Frederick Handel.

1743 Treaty of Åbo; Sweden cedes SE Finland to Russia.

1744 Prussians occupy Prague; beginning of Second Silesian War.

1745 Charles Edward Stuart (Bonnie Prince Charlie), grandson of James II and pretender to the British throne, leads Jacobite rebellion, defeating English army at Prestonpans.

German scientist Edward J von Kleist invents the Leyden Jar, an electric condenser.

Robert Bakewell introduces selective cross-breeding of sheep in Lancashire, England.

1746 Battle of Culloden: British forces brutally suppress Jacobite rebellion.

1747 English naval surgeon, James Lind, proves that citrus fruit (Vitamin C) can prevent scurvy.

1748 Peace of Aix-la-Chapelle ends War of the Austrian Succession.

c.1748 Platinum introduced to Europe from S America.

1749 Invention of sign language by Giacobbo Rodriguez Pereire.

1750 Thomas Gray's *Elegy Written in a Country Churchyard*; beginnings of English Romanticism.

Jean-Jacques Rousseau's *Discours sur les Sciences et les Arts*, arguing that civilization has corrupted mankind's natural instincts and freedom.

c.1750 Lancashire cotton mills start to supplant S Asian textile trade in W Europe.

AMERICAS & AUSTRALASIA

1741 Scots-Irish Presbyterians migrate to American colonies due to persecution in Ulster.

1742 Native American revolt against Spanish in Peru.

1743 King George's War between Britain and France in N America; British capture Louisbourg in Canada, French raid New York.

First settlements in South Dakota.

French explorers enter Rocky Mountains.

1745 French and Native American forces attack British settlements in New England.

1746 Foundation of Princeton University, New Jersey.

1748 First Lutheran synod in the colonies gathers in Philadelphia.

1749 Foundation of Halifax consolidates British control of Nova Scotia.

1750 Treaty of Madrid: defines boundary between Spanish colonies and Brazil; territory of seven Guaraní *reducciones* ceded to Portugal.

Portugal renounces claim to Colônia do Sacramento, Uruguay.

Jesuit Missions in China

By the end of the Ming dynasty in the 1640s, there were Jesuit, Franciscan, and Dominican missions in most of China's coastal provinces. Under the Qing emperors Kangxi, his son Yongzheng, and his grandson Qianlong, Christianity thrived. Kangxi appointed Jesuits to run the imperial board of astronomy, and in 1692 issued an Edict of Toleration. However, conflict over the observation of traditional ancestral rites by Chinese Christians brought a setback. The impact of Christianity on the Chinese is reflected in the appearance of Christian imagery on Qing porcelain (*below*).

Marquis of Pombal (1699–1782)

This outstanding Portuguese statesman did much to establish Portugal as a key western power. Initially ambassador to London and then Vienna, he became foreign secretary and did much to reorganize Portugal's colonies. Eventually becoming prime minister, he introduced elementary education, reorganized the army, encouraged overseas colonization, and set up the West India and Brazil trading companies. His alienation of the Catholic Inquisition brought his downfall with the accession of Mari I (1777).

The strong foundation of Portugal's overseas empire under the Marquis of Pombal meant that it was the last of the European empires to disintegrate, over two centuries later.

Robert Clive's first venture into military service was in India, where he soon proved himself an expert military tactician, winning a crucial battle for the English at Plassey.

The battle of Plassey

The massacre of British colonists in the "Black Hole of Calcutta" (1757) provided the British East India Company with the opportunity to launch a war of conquest and control. Under Robert Clive (1725–74) British forces retook Calcutta and captured the French colony at Chandernagore. His defeat of the Nawab of Bengal at the battle of Plassey left him effectively the sole ruler of Bengal and opened the way to the rapid expansion of British rule in India.

Conflict in North America

Conflict between Britain and France in North America at first mirrored the wars of Louis XIV in Europe in the 1690s; hostilities resumed in 1744–48, but the decisive struggle occurred in 1754–61. In 1755 British troops were repulsed at Fort Duquesne, but four years later General Wolfe's capture of Québec precipitated the surrender of Montreal. With the Treaty of Paris (1763) Britain became the dominant power in the New World.

The battle for Québec claimed the lives of both the British general James Wolfe (1727–1759), below, and, a day later, that of the French leader, the Marquis de Montcalm (1712–1759).

ASIA

1751 Robert Clive captures French city of Arcot, SE India; a turning point in Britain's struggle to control Indian trade.

Chinese invasion of Tibet.

Tibet, Dzungaria, and the Tarim basin overrun by Chinese.

1752 Clive captures Trichinopoly, SE India, from French.

1754 French–Indian War between France with Indian allies and Britain.

Joseph Dupleix, governor of French possessions in India, recalled to France.

Powerful Burmese dynasty established on capture of Ava by Alaungpaya.

1755 Alaungpaya founds Rangoon and reunites Burma.

1756 Calcutta captured from British by the nawab of Bengal; prisoners confined in the "Black Hole."

1757 Battle of Plassey. British victory over combined French and Mughal forces in N India establishes British power in Bengal; Robert Clive secures Bengal for East India Company.

Mughal control of Gujarat, NE India, ended by Maratha capture of Ahmedabad.

Ahmed Shah of Afghanistan occupies Delhi and the Punjab.

Expansion of Gurkha (Nepali) domains over much of Himalayas.

1758 British victorious over French at Fort St. David and Pondicherry in India.

Marathas occupy Punjab, NW India.

Campaigns by the Chinese Qing against Kalmyks (–1759).

1760 Canton (Guangzhou) becomes only port in China licenced to trade with Europeans.

Widespread peasant revolts in Japan.

AFRICA

1752 Sultanate of Darfur dominates Sahel, extending from Bornu in west to Nile valley in east.

1756 Tunisia occupied by the Bey of Algiers.

1757 Muhammad III becomes sultan of Morocco.

1758 British take Senegal in W Africa from French.

1760 Boers cross Orange river and begin settlement of S African interior.

EUROPE

1751 Denis Diderot begins publication of *L'Encyclopédie* (−1780).

Royal Worcester porcelain factory established in England.

1753 Thomas Chippendale opens his first furniture shop.

Foundation of British Museum in London.

1754 Joseph Black discovers carbon dioxide.

1755 Publication of Samuel Johnson's *Dictionary of the English Language*.

First Russian university opens in Moscow.

1756 Start of Seven Years' War in Europe; parallels conflict in N America (−1763).

Prussia faces coalition of Austria, Russia, and France in Seven Years' War.

French take Minorca from British.

Porcelain factory founded at Sèvres, France.

1757 Frederick II of Prussia defeats Austria at Leuthen.

1758 Prussians defeat invading Russian army at Zorndorf.

1759 French defeated at Minden by Prussians and British.

Jesuits expelled from Portugal.

John Harrison devises first accurate nautical chronometer, which allows navigators to correctly calculate longitude.

1760 Prussians defeat Austrians at Liegnitz and Torgau.

Austrian and Russian troops occupy Berlin, but Prussia survives.

Botanical gardens at Kew, London, founded.

Josiah Wedgwood begins to manufacture pottery in Staffordshire, England.

Laurence Sterne's *Tristram Shandy*.

c.1760 European Enlightenment embodied in works of Voltaire (1694–1778), Diderot (1715–84), Rousseau (1712–78), and Hume (1711–76).

AMERICAS & AUSTRALASIA

1751 Surveyors Mason and Dixon begin to accurately establish American territorial frontiers.

1752 John Finley realizes that the Cumberland Gap is a gateway to Kentucky lowlands.

Invention of lightning conductor by American polymath, Benjamin Franklin.

1753 French seize the Ohio valley.

1754 British and French renew warfare over control of N America.

French build Fort Duquesne in Ohio valley.

George II of England founds King's College, New York, now Columbia University.

French capture British Fort Necessity.

Guaraní War in protest at terms of Treaty of Madrid (−1755).

1755 British capture French Fort Beauséjour.

Braddock beaten back by French at Fort Duquesne.

First regular transatlantic passenger service begins between England and the colonies.

1756 French capture British Forts Oswego and William Henry (−1757).

1757 French abandon forts along Lake Champlain.

1758 French successfully repel British attack on Ticonderoga; British capture Fort Duquesne.

Louisbourg captured by British.

1759 British amphibious forces advance up the St. Lawrence river to capture Québec.

Expulsion of Jesuits from Brazil.

1760 End of French resistance in N America; Britain gains control of much of French America.

Cherokees held hostage at Fort St. George are executed in revenge for Indian attacks on frontier settlements.

Montreal surrenders to massed British forces.

Brandenburg Prussia

After the Peace of Westphalia in 1648, Germany consisted of some 300 small principalities, some Catholic, some Protestant. By the end of the 17th century Brandenburg had become the dominant Protestant state.

With the accession of Frederick II (the "Great") in 1740, Prussia's expansion continued, including the acquisition of the province of Silesia from the Habsburg Empire, a valuable gain as Silesia's mines and textile industries had made it one of the Habsburgs' wealthiest provinces. With additional territory from the partitions of Poland, by the end of the century Prussia had become one of Europe's great powers, with domains reaching from Memel and Königsberg in the east to East Frisia and Cleves, bordering the Netherlands, in the west.

These splendidly uniformed cavalry officers are representative of the highly-disciplined and efficient army which, by 1763, enabled Prussia to emerge as the dominant military force in 18th-century Europe.

Daniel Boone

The American frontiersman, explorer, and Indian fighter Daniel Boone was born in 1734 in Pennsylvania, but his family moved to the Carolina frontier when he was young. He first traveled from the Carolinas across the Cumberland Gap, a short route across the Appalachian mountains to Kentucky, in 1767 while on a hunting expedition. From 1769 he lived in the wilderness and explored much of Kentucky and Missouri with his brother.

In 1775 he pioneered and built a major trail (the Wilderness Road) across the Cumberland Gap for the Transylvania Company, opening Kentucky for new settlements, one of which was Boonesboro. This was originally a stockade to provide a focus for defense against the local Indian tribes. (He was twice taken prisoner.)

By the end of the Revolutionary War (1775–83) the newly formed United States could claim control of territories extending to the Mississippi, and the westward advance of the frontier was well under way.

Exploration of North America

By the late 17th century, European knowledge of the east coast of North America was quite detailed. It would take another two centuries before the interior of the continent could be mapped with confidence.

1528–1536	A.N. Cabeza de Vaca; Gulf coast and southwest.
1539–1542	H. de Soto; Appalachians and Mississippi.
1672	Jolliet and Marquette; Illinois river and Great Lakes.
1767–1771	Daniel Boone; Wilderness Road.
1804	Z. Pike; Upper Mississippi.
1804–1808	Lewis and Clarke; Missouri.
1805–1807	Z. Pike; Midwest/El Camino Real.
1806	J. Wilkinson; Arkansas river.
1807–1808	J. Colter; central Rockies.
1818–1821	D. Mackenzie; Cascades and northwest.
1842	J. Fremont; prairies and central Rockies.
1845	J. Fremont; California.
1869–1872	J. Powell; southern Rockies.

ASIA

1761 Mughal emperor and his Maratha allies defeated by Afghans at Panipat; Afghans briefly occupy Delhi. This defeat allows the British to extend their territorial penetration largely unopposed.

British destroy French power in India, following seizure of Pondicherry.

1765 Bengal comes under British control.

Manchu Chinese invade Burma (–1769).

1766 First Mysore War against British (–1769).

1767 Appointment of James Rennell as first surveyor-general of Bengal; beginning of Survey of India.

1769 French East India Company dissolved.

AFRICA

1769 Egypt declares independence from Ottoman Turkey.

c.1770 Peak years of European slave trade with Africa in this decade.

EUROPE

1761 Lomonosov identifies atmosphere on Saturn.

1762 Accession of German-born Catherine the Great of Russia after her husband's death (–1796).

Rousseau's *Du Contrat Social* argues for a more egalitarian society based on human rights.

Trevi fountain, Rome, completed.

Earl of Sandwich creates the first sandwich, seeking sustenance while at the gaming tables.

1763 Treaty of Paris ends Seven Years' War. France loses all territories in N America except New Orleans, and islands of St. Pierre, Miquelon, Martinique, and Guadeloupe; Florida ceded to Britain by Spain in exchange for British areas of Cuba.

Treaty of Hubertusburg allows Prussia to keep Silesia.

1764 Russia secures Polish crown for Stanislau Poniatowski.

Austrian prodigy Amadeus Mozart, aged eight, composes his first symphony.

German archaeologist, Johann Joachim Winckelmann, publishes *History of the Art of Antiquity*, provoking a widespread revival of classicism.

1765 James Hargreaves invents "Spinning Jenny" and increases output of spun cotton.

James Watt builds improved steam engine with separate condenser.

1766 English chemist, Henry Cavendish, discovers hydrogen.

1767 Jesuits expelled from Spain by Charles III.

1768 War between Russia and the Ottomans.

France purchases Corsica from Genoa.

Royal Academy of Arts founded under Sir Joshua Reynolds in London.

Swiss mathematician Leonhard Euler's first complete work on integral calculus (–1770).

1769 Russia invades Moldavia and Wallachia.

Richard Arkwright develops water-powered spinning frame.

1770 Ottoman fleet destroyed by Russians at Çesme.

AMERICAS & AUSTRALASIA

1762 France cedes all claims to territories west of the Mississippi (upper Louisiana) to Spain.

British capture Havana, Cuba.

1763 Treaty of Paris: France loses Canada to Britain and lands west of Mississippi to Spain.

Widespread Native American rebellion under Pontiac overruns many British forts on W frontier of colonies.

The Touro synagogue opens at Newport, Rhode Island; first major Jewish center in N America.

Rio de Janeiro becomes Brazilian capital.

1764 Sugar Act imposes tax on molasses brought from non-British colonies.

James Otis condemns Britain's "taxation without representation."

1765 British Stamp Act inspires the slogan "taxation without representation is tyranny."

1766 Invention of bifocal spectacles by Benjamin Franklin.

1767 Townshend Acts tax tea, paper, and other imports.

Boston revives the boycott of British imports.

Expulsion of Jesuits from all Spanish colonies.

1768 Wesley Chapel, the first Methodist center in the colonies, opened in New York.

Englishman Captain James Cook's first voyage; starts exploration of the Pacific.

1769 James Cook sails around New Zealand and up the E coast of Australia.

Spanish begin to settle in S California; foundation of mission at San Diego.

1770 British parliament repeals all duties imposed on colonies, except tea tax.

British soldiers shoot five colonists in "Boston Massacre."

James Cook discovers Botany Bay, Australia, and claims it for Britain.

Rococo

Although largely a style of decoration, developed in the Paris of the early 18th century, Rococo's influence soon spread throughout Europe. Pastel washes, gold stucco work, *grisailles*, flourishes, *cartouches*, and elaborate decorative designs developed from plant and shell forms found in nature. In southern Germany and Austria the style was adapted in many ornate churches built by the Asam brothers, while in Italy the supreme example of Rococo theatrical statuary was created at the Trevi Fountain (*above*) built between 1732 and 1762 by Nicola Salvi.

The battle of Panipat

The Marathas were a confederacy of states in central India that was attacked in the 1750s by the brilliant Afghan general Ahmad Shah Durrani (*below*). He had taken over control of the Afghan provinces when the Persian ruler Nadir Shah was assassinated, and had been crowned king in 1747, effectively founding the state of Afghanistan.

In 1761, Ahmad Shah won a great victory over a large Maratha army under the puppet Mughal emperor at Panipat north of Delhi. The Afghans proceeded to sack Delhi, but soon withdrew. Nevertheless, both Maratha and Mughal power in India was fatally weakened, and the British began to extend their territorial control west from Bengal into the interior.

The Revolutionary War 1775–1783

By the 1760s, the inhabitants of the British colonies had grown rapidly in population, wealth, and self confidence and were increasingly resistant to conventional methods of colonial control, such as taxation. In addition, the British government was perceived to be keeping all the fruits of victory against the French for itself, including the Canadian fur trade and the western lands.

In 1775, the first shots of the Revolutionary War were fired in Boston. Almost all of the early campaigns ended in stalemate. The American victory at Saratoga in 1777 convinced the French government to support the Americans with troops and ships. Later the Dutch and Spanish also joined against Britain. In 1781 George Washington forced General Cornwallis to surrender at Yorktown and the new nation was secure.

American War of Independence

The British forces tended to be superior in both numbers and weaponry, but the revolutionary patriots, who developed both a national army and state militias, gained support with every campaign as the struggle moved south.

1775	First shots of American revolution fired at Lexington
1775	Battle of Bunker Hill
1776	Declaration of Independence in Philadelphia
1776	British abandon Boston
1777	American troops under Washington defeat the British at Princeton
1777	British capture Fort Ticonderoga
1777	British troops defeated at Saratoga
1777	British occupy Philadelphia
1778	Battle of Monmouth: British evacuate Philadelphia
1779	Siege of Savannah
1780	Siege of Charleston
1781	French and American allies defeat the British at Yorktown
1782	Britain sues for peace
1783	Britain recognizes the independence of the American colonies

ASIA

1773 Revolt in Syria against Ottoman rule suppressed.

British East India Company gains monopoly of opium trade in Bengal.

Civil war in Vietnam (–1801).

Dissolution of the Jesuit order in China.

1774 First British mission to Tibet.

1775 First Anglo-Maratha War in India.

1776 Siam (Thailand) gains independence from Burma.

Trai Phum (Story of Three Worlds), Thai manuscript containing world's longest map 564 feet (172 m).

1780 Second Mysore War (–1783); alliance of Mysore and Marathas attack British holdings on Carnatic coast, SE India.

Bengal Gazette, India's first newspaper, published.

Japanese sumo wrestling begins to be performed in public.

1782

1785

AFRICA

1772 Scottish explorer, James Bruce, encounters the source of the Blue Nile.

1773 Revolt in Egypt against Ottoman rule suppressed.

1776 Abd el-Kader leads Muslims in holy war along the Senegal river.

Sultanate of Kilwa agrees to supply slaves to French sugar plantations on Réunion and Mauritius.

1778 African Association founded in London by Sir Joseph Banks.

1779 Boers and Bantu at war in S Africa (–1780).

Start of series of wars between Dutch settlers and Nguni.

British abandon colony of Senegambia, leaving Senegal region open to French colonists.

1780 Emergence of Buganda as a major power in C Africa.

c.1780 Masai peoples expand territories in E Africa.

EUROPE

1771 Russia conquers Crimea, destroying Ottoman fleet.

Encyclopaedia Britannica first published.

French chemist Antoine Lavoisier analyzes composition of air.

English scientist Joseph Priestley discovers that plants release oxygen.

1772 First partition of Poland by Russia, Prussia, and Austria. Prussian lands in the east now linked to Brandenburg.

Gustavus III of Sweden reestablishes absolute monarchy.

Pope Clement XIV suppresses the Jesuit order.

Scottish scientist Daniel Rutherford distinguishes between nitrogen and carbon dioxide.

1773 Peasant uprisings in SE Russia led by Pugachev.

Scottish architects Robert and James Adam publish *Works of Architecture*; instigate major revival of classicism in architecture and decorative arts.

1774 Accession of Louis XVI, last prerevolutionary king of France.

1776 Edward Gibbon's *Decline and Fall of the Roman Empire* begins publication (–1788).

Adam Smith's *The Wealth of Nations* published.

1777 War of Bavarian Succession (–1779).

James Watt develops first true steam engine.

1778 La Scala opera house in Milan inaugurated.

1779 First iron bridge constructed, Coalbrookdale, England.

The vélocipède, forerunner of the bicycle, introduced in Paris.

1780 Anglo-Dutch War (–1784).

Gordon Riots in England: hundreds killed in anti-Catholic uprisings.

AMERICAS & AUSTRALASIA

1772 Committees of Correspondence promote American identity.

James Cook's second voyage to the Pacific.

1773 Militants destroy shipments of tea in "Boston Tea Party," as a protest against British taxes.

James Cook crosses Antarctic Circle and circumnavigates continent (–1775).

1775 Start of American War of Independence (–1783).

Benjamin Franklin and Benjamin Rush form antislavery group in Philadelphia.

Thomas Paine's revolutionary pamphlet *Common Sense*.

1776 American Declaration of Independence.

New viceroyalty of Río de la Plata centered on Buenos Aires.

1777 Treaty of San Ildefonso confirms Spain's possession of Banda Oriental (Uruguay) and Portugal's possession of Amazon Basin. Pombal is dismissed.

1778 France enters war as American ally.

1779 Captain James Cook killed in Hawaii on third voyage.

1780 American troops brutally suppress Iroquois of the Mohawk river, central New York state.

Spain recaptures W Florida and the Bahamas from Britain.

The Declaration of Independence

The American colonists declared independence from British rule on July 4, 1776, when the Continental Congress renounced all allegiance to the British crown. Drawn up by a committee, but with the first draft written largely by the brilliant young Virginian Congressman Thomas Jefferson (1743–1826), the document was signed by representatives of all 13 British colonies. After independence, these would become the first 13 united, free and independent states. The declaration listed a range of grievances such as the British use of Indians against colonists, taxation without representation, and the denial of civil liberties.

Captain Cook

James Cook (1728–1779) was born the son of an agricultural laborer in Cleveland, Yorkshire. He began his maritime career in coastal and Baltic trading, but was soon engaged surveying Hudson Bay and Newfoundland. In 1768–1771, he sailed to the Pacific, circumnavigating New Zealand, exploring the east coast of Australia and rediscovering the Torres Strait between Australia and New Guinea. In 1772–1775 Cook explored the island groups of the central Pacific in the *Resolution*, a small ship originally built for carrying coal *(above)*. In 1776–80 he returned, discovering the Hawaiian islands and then navigating the Bering Strait and Aleutians. On his return to the Hawaiian islands he was unfortunately killed in a dispute with the islanders.

The Industrial Revolution

Britain's access to oceangoing trade, a wealth of mineral resources, especially coal and iron ore, and a rapidly growing urban population, gave it unique advantages over its continental neighbors as the Industrial Revolution developed. Britain also led the world in iron technology, producing the first iron bridge, ship and railroad, as well as the first efficient steel-making factory.

1709	Abraham Darby uses coke for pig-iron smelting (GB).
1733	John Kay invents the flying shuttle (GB).
1765	James Hargreaves invents the "Spinning Jenny" (GB).
	James Watt builds improved steam engine (GB).
1769	Arkwright's water-powered spinning frame (GB).
1781	Watt invents first rotative engine (GB).
1792	Invention of steam-powered loom (GB).
1793	Eli Whitney's cotton gin (US).
1812	First cylinder printing press introduced (GB).
1821	Electric motor and generator developed by Faraday (GB).
1825	First passenger steam railroad built by George Stevenson (GB).
1834	First mecanical reaper (US).
1838	First practical electric telegraph system (GB).
1840	Public postal system introduced (GB).
1847	First telegraph line (Germany).
1856	First commercial refrigeration unit (US).
	Bessemer furnace developed for mass production of steel (GB).
1859	First oil well drilled (US).
1863	Construction of first underground railroad (London, GB).
1869	First transcontinental railroad (US).
1876	Telephone system patented by Alexander Graham Bell (US).
1878	Gilchrist-Thomas method for steel production (GB).
	Internal combustion engine developed (Germany)
	First electric street lighting (London, GB)
1881	First electric trams (Berlin, Germany).

The bridge at Coalbrookedale *in Shropshire, England, was the first to be built of cast iron, a technology that was soon to be used not simply for bridge-building, but also for vaulting large architectural spans such as in railroad stations.*

ASIA

1781 British take over Dutch settlements in W Sumatra, Indonesia.

1782 Treaty ending First Anglo-Maratha War results in territorial losses for Marathas.

Siam (Thailand) reaches territorial apogee under Rama I.

1784 India Act: British government declares intention to directly control British territories in India.

1785 Burmese invasion of Siam.

1786 Start of Qajar dynasty in Persia.

British East India Company establish base at Penang, Malaya.

1788 Mughal emperors become puppets of Marathas.

Occupation of Delhi; Maratha territorial apogee.

Attempted invasion of Annam by Qing China.

AFRICA

1781 Massacre of the Xhosa by Boer settlers.

Portuguese regain control of Laurenço Marques, and recover control of Maputo Bay slave trade in the Indian Ocean.

1783 W African state of Oyo defeated by neighboring Borgu.

Portuguese establish trading fort at Cabinda, on north side of Congo estuary.

1786 Morocco agrees to cease raiding American ships in the Mediterranean in return for $10,000.

1800

1787 Settlement of first freed slaves from Britain at Freetown, Sierra Leone.

Sierra Leone acquired by British.

1788 British privy council begins investigation of slave trade.

EUROPE

1781 Joseph II renounces serfdom in Habsburg empire.

Immanuel Kant's *Critique of Pure Reason*.

1782 James Watt's rotative steam engine in use in factories.

Uranus discovered by William Herschel.

1783 Russia conquers and annexes Ottoman-controlled Crimea.

Montgolfier brothers; first manned flight in a hot air balloon.

John Macadam invents new road surfacing using tar and gravel.

1784 Uprisings in Dutch Netherlands.

1785 Power loom for clothmaking revolutionizes weaving.

Civil war in Netherlands; intervention by Prussian troops to restore order.

Mozart's *Marriage of Figaro*.

1786 Death of Frederick the Great of Prussia.

1787 Austro-Turkish War (–1791).

Catherine the Great of Russia launches second war with Ottoman Turkey (–1792).

1788 Sweden at war with Russia and Denmark.

1789 French Revolution begins.

1790 Revolt in Hungary.

c.1790 Apogee of European orchestral music: Mozart (1756–91), Haydn (1752–1809), and Beethoven (1770–1827).

1792

AMERICAS & AUSTRALASIA

1781 General George Washington defeats British at Yorktown.

1782 Native peoples in Peru, led by Tupac Amaru, revolt against Spanish rule; brutally suppressed.

1783 End of Revolutionary War. Treaty of Paris recognizes new United States; Britain accepts American independence via the treaty.

Spanish crown sponsors botanical expedition to S American colonies.

1788 First British settlement at Botany Bay in Australia.

First penal settlement established at Port Jackson (Sydney).

The "First Fleet" of convict settlers lands in New South Wales.

1789 George Washington becomes first president of the US (–1797).

Smallpox ravages aborigines of coastal New South Wales in Australia.

Mutiny on British vessel *Bounty*, on its way to collect breadfruit from the Pacific, focuses attention on conditions on naval vessels.

Mutineers from the *Bounty* settle on Pitcairn Island.

Tupac Amaru

Baptized José Gabriel Condorcanqui, but of Indian extraction, Tupac Amaru attempted to persuade the Spanish colonial government to provide better conditions for native Peruvians in the mines and mills. When this failed, he adopted the name of an Inca ancestor and led a rebellion (1780) which gained widespread support. Although he was captured and brutally executed, the revolt continued, culminating in the siege of La Paz (1782). It was eventually crushed, but reforms were finally introduced.

Here Tupac Amaru is seen surrounded by Spanish soliders. About 100,000 of his followers were killed in the revolt.

The "First Fleet"

The first British convicts were sent to penal settlements in Australia in 1788, transported there to relieve overcrowding in British prisons. The first colony was at Sydney Cove in New South Wales, but soon more were established at Norfolk Island (1788), Newcastle (1801), Hobart (1804), and Brisbane (1824). Free settlers did not appear until after 1813 when access to the interior had been won. When transportation ended in 1868, some 25,000 women and 137,000 men had been taken to Australia.

The treatment of native Aborigines was extremely callous, and many died from exposure to diseases imported by the settlers.

*The **Egyptian campaign**, and the many treasures looted at the time, sparked off a fascination with the mysterious monuments of Ancient Egypt, and laid the foundations of modern Egyptology.*

Napoleon invades Egypt

Revolutionary France's leading opponent, Great Britain, was effectively defended from direct attack by the supremacy of her navy. The French Republic, mindful of defeats earlier in the century, decided to attack British holdings in India, by way of Egypt, while developing other ambitious plans to recover her possessions in the Caribbean and North America.

An expeditionary force was sent, under the command of Napoleon Bonaparte, in July 1798. The force landed reasonably easily at Aboukir Bay near Alexandria, defeated the Egyptian army at the battle of the Pyramids, and began a campaign of systematic looting and suppression.

The following month, a British naval force under Nelson destroyed the French fleet at anchor (the battle of the Nile, August, 1798), leaving the French effectively stranded. The French proceeded up the Nile, reaching Aswan in February 1799, before turning north, crossing the Sinai peninsula and laying siege to Acre (March–May 1799), where once again the British intervened. Lacking supplies and succumbing to sickness, Napoleon finally withdrew to France.

1791–1800

1792 Colin Mackenzie completes first maps of the territories of Tipu Sultan (Hyderabad).

Qing China closes Tibet to visitors.

Chinese invasion of Nepal.

1793 British trade delegation to China rejected by Manchu court.

1795 British expedition to Ceylon (Sri Lanka) (–1796).

British take Malacca from Dutch.

1796 Outbreak of White Lotus rebellion which disrupts C China (–1804).

Edict of Peking bans import of opium to China.

British conquest of coastal Ceylon.

1798 Ceylon becomes a British colony.

1799 French army besieges Acre, Palestine.

British-led coalition defeats and partitions Mysore in India. British obtain the Carnatic coast; conquest of Mysore ends challenge to British power in S India.

1800 William Lambton commences triangulation of India.

c.1800 Extensive military and administrative mapping by Indian Marathas and Burmese.

1803

1795 British capture Cape of Good Hope and Cape Town from the Dutch.

1796 Scottish explorer Mungo Park travels up Niger river.

1798 Occupation of Egypt by Napoleon Bonaparte; defeat of Egyptians at battle of the Pyramids.

1804

Battle of the Nile: British fleet under Nelson defeats French at Aboukir Bay.

1799 Discovery of the Rosetta stone in Egypt; it contains parallel Greek and Egyptian texts, allowing historians to translate ancient Egyptian hieroglyphs.

1800 Asante slave rebels deported from Jamaica settle in Sierra Leone.

EUROPE

1791 Revolt in Poland.

William Wilberforce's motion for the abolition of slave trade succeeds in British parliament.

James Boswell's *Life of Samuel Johnson*.

1792 France declares war on Austria, Prussia, and Piedmont. Beginning of War of First Coalition.

Louis XVI overthrown.

French republic proclaimed.

Treaty of Jassy; Russia gains control of Black Sea coast from Ottoman Turks.

Denmark abolishes slave trade.

Edmund Cartwright develops the steam-powered loom.

1793 Second Partition of Poland.

Louis XVI of France executed.

1794 British defeat French at naval battle of Brest.

French invade Catalonia, NE Spain.

British invade Corsica.

1795 Third Partition of Poland.

1796 Napoleon's Italian campaign (–1797).

British surgeon Edward Jenner discovers smallpox vaccine (although previously in use in Turkey).

1798 Failed nationalist rebellion in Ireland led by Wolfe Tone.

1799 Coup brings Napoleon to power in France.

Prime minister William Pitt introduces income tax in Britain.

1800 French defeat Austrians at Marengo.

French revolutionary army under Napoleon invades Italy.

Sir William Herschel discovers infrared rays.

British invade Malta.

Italian Alessandro Volta invents the battery.

AMERICAS & AUSTRALASIA

1791 Vermont admitted to USA.

Slave revolt in Haiti led by Toussaint l'Ouverture.

1792 Kentucky admitted to USA.

Foundation of the White House, Washington (completed 1809).

Dollar introduced as currency of USA.

First British settlers land at Bay of Islands, New Zealand.

1793 Alexander Mackenzie completes first east–west crossing of Canada.

Eli Whitney invents the cotton gin, beginning of industrialization of cotton industry in American south.

1794 Battle of Fallen Timbers paves way for white settlement in the NW Territory.

1797 First Christian missionaries reach Tahiti.

1798 British navigators Flinders and Bass survey S Australian coast and island of Tasmania.

1800 Washington becomes home of US government.

Tahiti starts supplying Port Jackson (Sydney) with pigs.

Watercolors produced by the Le Sueur brothers reflect the popular enthusiasm for the Revolution.

The French Revolution

In 1789 political crises forced Louis XVI to summon the Estates-General, a parliament of nobles, clergy, and commoners. The third estate demanded reform, and declared a National assembly. Noble and clerical privileges were abolished, while provincial uprisings against landowners forced many into exile. The storming of the Bastille by a Parisian mob (July) precipitated full-scale revolution. The monarchy was abolished, the king imprisoned, and a republic declared. In January 1793 the king was executed as power shifted to the radical "Jacobins," inaugurating the "Terror," and executing all "enemies of the people." Resistance was crushed and it was not until 1799 that the Jacobins met the fate of their victims, and more moderate republican rule was restored under the Directory.

The French Revolution	
1789	**May 5**: Opening of the Estates-General
	Jul 14: Fall of the Bastille; beginning of the French Revolution
	Aug 26: Declaration of the Rights of Man
1791	**Oct 1**: Meeting of newly-elected legislative assembly in France
1792	**Aug 10**: Louis XVI overthrown
	Sept 22: French republic proclaimed
1793	**Jan 21**: Louis XVI executed
	May 31: Left-wing Jacobins take power; start of the Terror
1794	**Jul 27**: Fall of Robespierre and end of the Terror
1799	Directory overthrown and First Republic dissolved: Napoleon elected First Consul
1804	Napoleon crowned emperor: creation of First Empire

The World in 1800

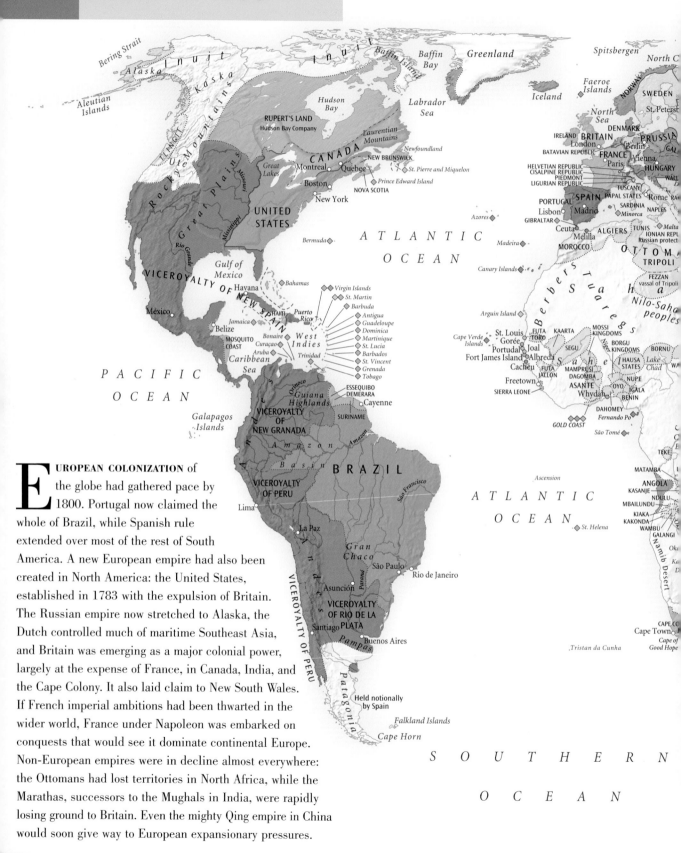

EUROPEAN COLONIZATION of the globe had gathered pace by 1800. Portugal now claimed the whole of Brazil, while Spanish rule extended over most of the rest of South America. A new European empire had also been created in North America: the United States, established in 1783 with the expulsion of Britain. The Russian empire now stretched to Alaska, the Dutch controlled much of maritime Southeast Asia, and Britain was emerging as a major colonial power, largely at the expense of France, in Canada, India, and the Cape Colony. It also laid claim to New South Wales. If French imperial ambitions had been thwarted in the wider world, France under Napoleon was embarked on conquests that would see it dominate continental Europe. Non-European empires were in decline almost everywhere: the Ottomans had lost territories in North Africa, while the Marathas, successors to the Mughals in India, were rapidly losing ground to Britain. Even the mighty Qing empire in China would soon give way to European expansionary pressures.

The World in 1800

- Qing Empire
- Persia and possessions
- Ottoman Empire
- Britain and possessions
- France and possessions
- Denmark and possessions
- Spain and possessions
- Portugal and possessions
- Netherlands and possessions
- Prussia and possessions
- Russian Empire
- Austrian Habsburg territories
- Holy Roman Empire
- Persia on death of Nadir Shah 1747
- French possessions lost during 18th century

CAPTAIN COOK'S MAP OF NEW ZEALAND

In the mid-18th century, the Pacific remained a geographical mystery. Though it had been sailed by Europeans since Magellan first crossed it in 1520–21, its true extent, as well as most of its landmasses, remained a matter of conjecture. It was Captain Cook in his three Pacific voyages between 1768 and 1779 who did most to settle these questions, in the process demolishing the widespread belief in a great southern landmass, *Terra Australis Incognita*, that had existed since the classical era. This map of New Zealand, made on Cook's first voyage, was typical of his methodical approach. Between October 1769 and March 1770, he systematically surveyed more than 2,400 miles (3,862 km) of coastline to produce the first accurate map of New Zealand.

1800 – 1900
The Age of Revolution

1804: Napoleon Emperor of France

1807: Slave trade outlawed in Britain

1810: Start of revolutions in Spanish America; by 1826 all Spain's American colonies are independent

1815: Napoleon defeated at Waterloo

ASIA																						
AFRICA																						
EUROPE																						
REST OF THE WORLD																						

1800   **1805**   **1810**   **1815**   **182**

1803: Louisiana Purchase: US acquires all French territory between the Mississippi and Rockies

1812: Napoleon defeated in Russia

HOWEVER RAPIDLY it was changing, the world in 1800 was nonetheless recognizably similar to that of 100 years earlier. In 1900, by contrast, the world had been entirely transformed. Not only had Europe become by far the world's dominant power, every one of the Old World's Asian empires, for so long the globe's pace-setters, had either disappeared or was rapidly disintegrating in the face of remorseless western expansion. The reasons were complex and multilayered, but all reflected the west's commanding economic and technological lead and the spread of its political philosophies: a growing belief in individual and national freedom; and, toward the end of the century, a seemingly unstoppable drive for empire.

The legacy of Napoleon

The decisive event of the early part of the century was the resurgence of France as a great power in the wake of the French Revolution. Under the galvanizing influence of Napoleon, First Consul from 1799 and Emperor from 1804, what had begun in 1789 as a struggle for liberation rapidly evolved into an old-fashioned war of conquest, albeit one nominally fought under the banner of liberty, equality, and fraternity. In 1812, at the height of Napoleon's conquests, French rule extended across almost the whole of western Europe. Only Britain, Portugal, and distant

PICTURE ABOVE:
The world's first passenger railroad, *built by George Stephenson, ran from Stockton to Darlington in England. When it opened on September 27, 1825, the locomotive pulled a train of wagons with 450 passengers at a speed of 15 mph (24 kmph).*

Scandinavia remained outside French control. But like so many empire-builders before him, Napoleon overreached himself. The ignominious retreat from Moscow in the winter of 1812 resulted in the virtual annihilation of the army of 450,000 men, with which he had begun the Russian campaign. This was a disaster from which even Napoleon could not hope to recover.

The rise of nationalism

Napoleon's eventual defeat in 1815 may have restored Europe's prerevolutionary status quo, but ideas of liberty, once planted, proved tenacious. The century as a whole was marked by growing nationalist-inspired demands for self-rule by oppressed minorities and, partly as a result, by the fitful spread of embryonic democracies. Belgium, Greece, Italy, Germany, Serbia, and Romania all emerged as independent nations by the end of the century.

The right to self-determination was a trend that found counterparts elsewhere, above all in South and Central America, where a series of wars of liberation ended Spanish rule by 1826. In the same period, Portugal lost Brazil, which

Delacroix's painting Liberty Leading the People *celebrates the revolution of July 1830, which dethroned France's last Bourbon king.*

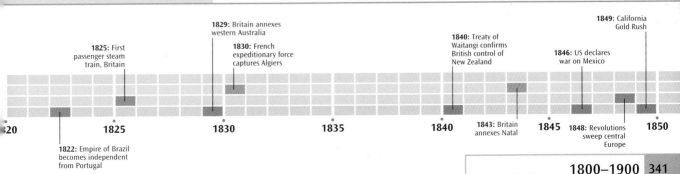

1825: First passenger steam train, Britain

1829: Britain annexes western Australia

1830: French expeditionary force captures Algiers

1840: Treaty of Waitangi confirms British control of New Zealand

1846: US declares war on Mexico

1849: California Gold Rush

1822: Empire of Brazil becomes independent from Portugal

1843: Britain annexes Natal

1848: Revolutions sweep central Europe

20   1825   1830   1835   1840   1845   1850

An Italian immigrant family arrives in the US in the late 19th century. In this period, when American industry was crying out for labor, only two percent of those who applied were refused entry.

became an independent empire in 1822, though it was still ruled by a branch of the Portuguese royal family. It eventually became a republic in 1889.

Revolution and reaction

Despite the widespread spirit of independence in Europe, there was an equally fierce reaction against self-rule by conservative-minded states, above all the authoritarian Austro-Hungarian empire. These conflicting ideologies clashed brutally in 1848 when Poles, Czechs, and Hungarians rose against their Austrian rulers, engulfing central and eastern Europe in revolution. The spirit of revolution spread to papal Rome and other states in Italy and to France, where the French monarch was deposed for the last time, to be replaced first by the Second Republic, and then by the Second Empire of Napoleon III.

Though the revolutionaries were defeated, they at least helped reinforce the climate of nationalistic fervor in which the later unifications of Italy and Germany took place. Ironically, the emergence of these two powerful new European states only added to the dominant influence of Europe's "Great Powers" – France, Austria, Germany, Italy, Britain, and Russia, the last still continuing its breakneck expansion south and east. These were the states that would subsequently line up against each other in the struggle for supremacy in Europe that culminated in the horrific slaughter of the First World War.

The American Civil War

Similar tensions between the principle of self-determination and power politics found a resonant echo in the United States, which since the early years of the century had combined an increasingly dynamic economy with rapid westward expansion. Yet the faultline between the industrialized North and the agricultural South, politically powerful yet dependent on slavery, became increasingly obvious. In the end, the issue provoked a bitter four-year civil war. The North's eventual triumph in 1865 was important not just in outlawing slavery but in underlining the superiority of industrial power, where the

North's lead was decisive. In the late 19th century the need for labor in the industrial cities of the North would be met by a flood of immigrants, mainly from southern and eastern Europe.

Industry and invention

In fact, by the middle of the century western technology and mass industrialization of a kind and on a scale unimaginable in 1800 were transforming the world. Until 1850, Britain had made the early pace. Thereafter, France, Belgium, Russia, and most significantly Germany and America proved ever more effective rivals. The range of inventions and the speed of development, the whole sparking rapid economic and population growth, were extraordinary.

The Industrial Revolution led to the appearance of huge new cities with poorly built housing, totally inadequate sanitation, and little or no concern for the health, social welfare, and education of the industrial workers and their children. Conditions were so barbaric that governments were forced to take action, but legislation to improve working and living conditions was usually too little and too late. Consequently, workers tried to take control of their own destiny by forming trades unions to fight for better pay and conditions. As industrial

The arrival of the US Commodore Perry *in Japan in 1853, depicted by a Japanese artist. The event marked the end of Japan's 250-year period of isolation from the west.*

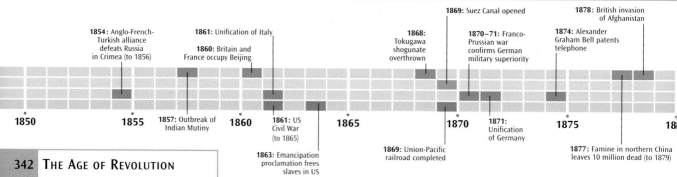

1854: Anglo-French-Turkish alliance defeats Russia in Crimea (to 1856)

1860: Britain and France occupy Beijing

1861: Unification of Italy

1868: Tokugawa shogunate overthrown

1869: Suez Canal opened

1870–71: Franco-Prussian war confirms German military superiority

1874: Alexander Graham Bell patents telephone

1878: British invasion of Afghanistan

1850

1855

1857: Outbreak of Indian Mutiny

1860

1861: US Civil War (to 1865)

1865

1870

1871: Unification of Germany

1875

18

1863: Emancipation proclamation frees slaves in US

1869: Union-Pacific railroad completed

1877: Famine in northern China leaves 10 million dead (to 1879)

societies became increasingly polarized, socialist and communist theorists declared that the whole basis of the capitalist economy was unjust. However, they would have to wait until the 20th century for a workers' revolution, which came, not as expected in a highly industrialized country such as Britain or Germany, but in relatively backward, agrarian Russia.

In the meantime, technological innovations such railroads, steamships, and the electric telegraph were creating a revolution in communications. This consolidated the global trade network, in which immense numbers of people and vast quantities of goods were moved across the globe, and stimulated the search for new raw materials and markets. In the process, there was an important shift in attitudes toward the overseas territories controlled by Europe's colonial powers.

Western imperialism

Where once the goal of the western powers had been trade rather than empire, after about 1870 empire in itself came to be seen as desirable. If the continent of Africa was the most fiercely contested prize, much of Southeast Asia

and Oceania was also appropriated. Even the United States, historically the champion of anticolonial movements, began to extend its territories across the Pacific to Hawaii and the Philippines.

Confronted with expansion and technological superiority on this scale, the empires of the Old World could offer only feeble resistance. The once-dynamic Ottoman Empire shrank dramatically, losing territories across North Africa and the Balkans. Japan, too, was powerless to resist western encroachment when 250 years of self-imposed isolation were ended in 1853 by the arrival of an American fleet demanding trading concessions. Japan, however, was able to adapt rapidly to the demands of modernization. By 1900, it was poised for a dramatic appearance on the world stage as an industrial and military power. In Qing China, by contrast, government complacency, resistance to modernization and an inability to counter mounting internal dissent played into the hands of the European powers, who competed to carve out "spheres of interest." By 1900, the Qing were a power in name only.

THE SCRAMBLE FOR AFRICA

Europe's African territories in 1880 amounted to no more than a handful of isolated colonies and trading forts scattered along its immense coasts. By 1900, almost the entire continent was under European control. This 20-year transformation was the most shameful example of Europe's empire-building in the 19th century. The process whereby Africa fell under European control varied from country to country: some European governments worked through commercial companies, occasionally Africans actually invited the Europeans in, but in most cases European control was a simple matter of armed conquest.

France ended up with most territory, chiefly in the north and west. But Britain and Germany also annexed enormous areas. Even Belgium, with no history of imperialism, gained vast areas around the Congo basin. Unusually, they became the private property of its king, Leopold II. One consequence of the "scramble" was that clashes between European powers for control of various regions could threaten major international incidents. In 1898 for example, Britain and France came close to war over their rival claims to Fashoda on the upper Nile.

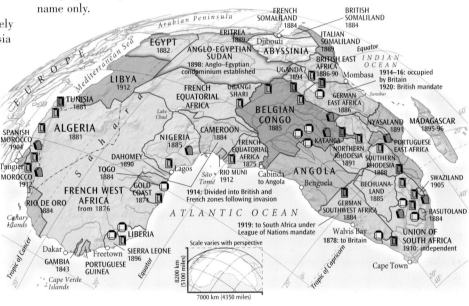

Imperialism in Africa, 1880–1920

Territory controlled by European nations by 1914	Important mineral deposits
Belgium	coal
Britain	copper
France	diamonds
Germany	gold
Italy	
Portugal	
Spain	
nominally Ottoman, under British control	
1882 date of taking control	
— borders in 1914	

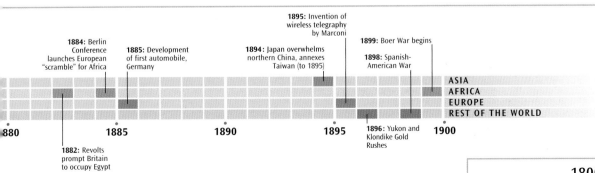

1884: Berlin Conference launches European "scramble" for Africa

1885: Development of first automobile, Germany

1894: Japan overwhelms northern China, annexes Taiwan (to 1895)

1895: Invention of wireless telegraphy by Marconi

1898: Spanish-American War

1899: Boer War begins

ASIA
AFRICA
EUROPE
REST OF THE WORLD

1880   1885   1890   1895   1900

1882: Revolts prompt Britain to occupy Egypt

1896: Yukon and Klondike Gold Rushes

Napoleon Bonaparte (1769–1821)

Napoleon established his military reputation with his bold, unexpected manuevers leading the French Revolutionary army against Austria in Italy. His expedition to Egypt was doomed, but he returned to stage a *coup d'etat* which made him ruler of France. As First Consul he reformed political administration, the legal system, the Church, and education. In 1804 he was declared Emperor. He defeated the Austrians at Austerlitz (1805) and by 1809 controlled central Europe, installing his family members as rulers. A war of attrition in Iberia, and the winter retreat from Moscow (1812) proved insupportable, and defeat at the hands of coalition armies in 1814 saw him imprisoned on Elba. He escaped to lead a final campaign, but after defeat at Waterloo (1815) he was exiled to St. Helena, where he died.

Campaigns of the Napoleonic Wars

Throughout almost his entire reign Napoleon was at war with one or more of the other major European powers – Britain, Austria, Russia, and Prussia – and their various allies.

1796–1797	Italian campaign
1798–1799	Egyptian campaign
1800	War of the Second Coalition
1805–1807	War of the Third Coalition
1808–1814	Peninsular War
1809	Austrian War
1812	Russian campaign
1813	War of Liberation from French rule
1814	Defense of France
1815	War of the 100 Days

ASIA

1801 Persia agrees trading pact with Britain.

1802 With French aid, Nguyen Anh unites and becomes emperor of Vietnam.

1803 Second Anglo-Maratha War results in British acquisition of Delhi.

Czar Alexander of Russia invades S Georgia.

1804 Russian envoy fails to agree on commercial treaty with Japan.

1805 Japanese doctor Seishu Hanaoka uses general anesthesia for the first time – for the treatment of breast cancer.

AFRICA

1806 **1803** Cape Colony restored to Dutch.

1807 **1804** Muslim Fulani leader, Usman dan Fodio declares *jihad* and conquers Hausa city-states.

Mohammad Ali becomes viceroy of Egypt.

EUROPE

1801 Peace of Lunéville between Austria and France.

Act of Union unites Britain and Ireland.

British fleet under Admiral Nelson destroys Danish fleet at Copenhagen.

British occupy Madeira.

Union Jack becomes flag of the United Kingdom.

Francesco Goya's *Naked Maja*.

Beethoven's *Moonlight Sonata*.

1802 Mar 27: Peace of Amiens between Britain and France (–1815).

Napoleon declares himself president of the Italian republic.

Piedmont annexed to France.

Napoleon introduces Legion of Honor.

1803 May 18: Britain declares war on France.

English engineer Richard Trevithick invents railroad locomotive.

Henry Shrapnel's fragmentation artillery shell adopted by British army.

1804 Dec 2: Napoleon becomes "emperor of the French" (–1815).

Revolt in Serbia.

Karageorges leads rebellion in Serbia against Ottoman rulers.

Napoleonic Code, innovative legal structure, introduced throughout France.

1805 Oct 19: Napoleon defeats Austrians at Ulm.

Oct 21: Nelson destroys Franco-Spanish fleet off Trafalgar.

Dec 2: Battle of Austerlitz: Napoleon defeats Russians and Austrians.

AMERICAS & AUSTRALASIA

1802 Issue of slavery divides American north and south.

First British and American sealing stations operate on E coast.

German explorer, botanist, and scientist, Alexander von Humboldt, climbs to record height on the mountain of Chimborazo; correctly attributes altitude sickness to lack of oxygen.

English naval officer, Matthew Flinders, circumnavigates Australia (–1803).

1803 France sells territory between the Mississippi and Rockies to the US government in Louisiana Purchase.

Ohio admitted to USA.

Russia occupies E Alaska.

"Incorrigible" convicts first transported to Van Diemen's Land (Tasmania).

British occupy St Lucia, Tobago, and Dutch Guiana.

1804 Foundation of independent Haitian state after slave rebellion overthrows French rule.

Sandalwood traders arrive in Fiji.

1805 US explorers Meriwether Lewis and William Clark explore new land acquired in the Louisiana Purchase and reach Pacific Ocean.

El Diario de México, first Mexican daily newspaper, published.

Toussaint l'Ouverture

Born into an African slave family in French Haiti, he led a slave revolt (1791) but did not declare Haiti independent. Recognized by the French Directory, he was appointed governor-general by the French (1797). He repulsed both British and French attemts to invade, and gained control of the whole island in 1801 When Napoleonic troops were sent to the island in 1802, Toussaint was forced to make terms with the French commander. He was subsequently betrayed, and died in prison in France.

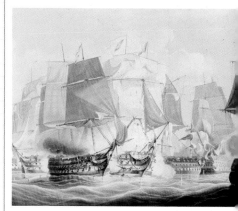

The Battle of Trafalgar (1805). Nelson divided his 27 ships into two columns to attack the rear of the enemy lines. Losses were heavy on both sides and Nelson himself was fatally wounded.

British sea power

Although Britain was continually involved in continental alliances designed initially to destroy Revolutionary France, and then to contain the imperial ambitions of Napoleon, it was its navy which proved most effective in sustaining pressure on the French. An attempted invasion of Ireland was thwarted (1797–98), as was a planned invasion of England (1804).

Under Horatio Nelson (1758–1805), the French expeditionary fleet was destroyed at Aboukir Bay, Egypt (1798), while his forces chased the French admiral Villeneuve to the Caribbean and back. Nelson also destroyed the Danish fleet at Copenhagen (1801), and blockaded the French southern port of Toulon for two years. British supremacy at sea was assured with his final victory at Trafalgar (1805).

The German poet and dramatist Wolfgang von Goethe *(1749–1832) was one of many artists and writers who found inspiration in the classical art and ruins of Rome.*

Romanticism

Imbued by the humanist and libertarian ideas of the Enlightenment, Romanticism found expression in all art forms from c.1775–1850. At its core lay the concept of the artist as hero – and hero worshiper – which took many forms: the emoter of the nostalgic grandeur of nature or the glories of the past; the intellectual and the naïve; the deifier of contemporaries such as Napoleon; the radical ideologist and rejecter of convention; the mystic searching for sensuality and heightened emotional states, or the quasi-scientist instinctively analyzing natural and psychological phenomena; the towering genius or the misunderstood soul starving in a garret. Romanticism transformed the artist from gifted artisan and observer to the bohemian mirror of the modern world, a legacy which reaches down to us today.

Romanticism	
1774	Goethe (1769–1832): *The Sorrows of Young Werther*
1786–1788	Goethe visits Rome
1831	Stendhal (1783–1842): *Le Rouge et le Noir*
1817	Géricault (1791–1824): *Raft of the Medusa*
from c.1820	English Romantic landscape school: Bonington (1801–1828); Constable (1776–1837); Turner (1775–1851)
1829	Delacroix (1798–1863): *Sardanapolis*
from c.1835	Art for Art's Sake movement: Gautier (1811–1872); Baudelaire (1821–1867)
1808	Kleist (1777–1811): *Michael Kohlhaas*
1831	Pushkin (1799–1837): *Boris Godunov*
1847	Emily Brontë (1818–1848): *Wuthering Heights*
1849–50	Chateaubriand (1768–1848): *Mémoires d'Outre-Tombe*
1876	Tchaikovsky (1840–1893): Swan Lake
1846	Berlioz (1803–1869): *The Damnation of Faust*
1838–39	Chopin (1810–1849): *Preludes*

1806–1810

ASIA

1812

1806 Wahhabis take Mecca.

1807 Revolt of the Janissaries leads to deposition of Ottoman sultan, Selim III; replaced by Mustapha IV.

First British Protestant mission to China lands at Canton (Guangzhou).

1810 Russia begins systematic expansion in Siberia and C Asia.

AFRICA

1806 Scottish explorer Mungo Park dies negotiating rapids on Niger.

British reoccupy Cape Colony.

1815

British construct major naval base at Simonstown, S Africa.

1807 Hausa kings replaced by Fulani emirs.

1808 Britain assumes control of Sierra Leone.

1811 **1810** Kingdom of Merina gains control of Madagascar.

Mauritius and Seychelles annexed by Britain.

EUROPE

1806 Oct 14: Defeat of Prussians by Napoleon at Jena/Auerstädt.

Abdication of Emperor Francis I; end of Holy Roman Empire.

Napoleon replaces Holy Roman Empire with Confederation of the Rhine.

Joseph Bonaparte, brother of Napoleon, installed as king of Naples, Italy.

Louis Bonaparte, brother of Napoleon, installed as king of Holland.

Sir Francis Beaufort devises scale to indicate wind strengths.

1807 Napoleon defeats Russians in battle of Eylau.

Peace treaty between Napoleon and Russia at Tilsit.

Napoleon defeats Prussia at Friedland.

Abolition of serfdom in Prussia.

Aboliton of slave trade by Britain.

William Wordsworth's *Poems* published.

1808 France invades Spain; outbreak of Peninsular War. British forces fight French in Spain (–1814).

Revolt against French in Madrid violently suppressed.

Several German principalities grant citizenship to Jews, which is reversed after fall of Napoleon.

Napoleon installs his brother Joseph as king of Spain.

French annex the Papal States.

Russia occupies Finland.

Beethoven's fifth and sixth symphonies.

Goethe's *Faust* Part 1.

1809 British defeated by French at Corunna.

1810 Napoleon marries Marie Louise, daughter of the emperor of Austria, intending to found a dynasty.

AMERICAS & AUSTRALASIA

1816

1807 Portuguese royal family flees to Brazil.

1811

1808 Independence movements in Spanish and Portuguese America; 13 new states created by 1828.

Importation of slaves into USA banned by federal government.

1809 Ecuador becomes part of republic of Colombia.

1810 Start of revolutions in Spanish America; by 1876 all Spanish colonies in S America have gained independence.

Father Miguel Hidalgo leads anti-Spanish revolution, *Grito de Dolores*, in Mexico; it is suppressed, and Hidalgo executed (–1811).

1817 Anti-Spanish revolution in Chile (–1814).

King Kamehameha I unites Hawaiian islands.

King Kamehameha I of Hawaii

Revered as the first ruler of a united Hawaii (1810), Kamehameha I emerged some 30 years after James Cook first visited the Sandwich (Hawaiian) islands, possibly gaining support in reaction to increasing European colonial interest in the central and south Pacific. Driven not by land-hunger, but by the proceeds of plant-gathering, prospecting, whaling and fishing rights, the Pacific was the world's last habitable area to attract western colonialists. By 1826 a treaty of friendship and commerce had been signed with the US.

New Zealand

The first European settlements in New Zealand were sealing and whaling stations, from c.1800. Relations with the Maori inhabitants were initially peaceful, encouraged by trade in metal axes and muskets. The results were disastrous, as intertribal warfare became more vicious, and the resulting migrations into conquered or safe territories disrupted the traditional social balance. European migration was limited during the "Musket Wars" (from 1815), but by 1837 the New Zealand Company had been founded to encourage colonization. The Treaty of Waitingi (1840), signed by over 500 Maori chiefs, gave sovereignty to Britain but control of the land to the Maoris. It became a major source of discontent during the 19th century.

This portrait of a tattooed Maori islander was drawn on James Cook's first voyage in 1769.

The Congress of Vienna was attended by five monarchs and the heads of 216 princely families.

Congress of Vienna, 1814

The Congress of Vienna met to share out the spoils of victory over Napoleon, though painful compromise was required to achieve a work-able balance of power. Political stability was reestablished by restoring the hereditary monarchs overthrown by Napoleon. France, though shorn of her recent conquests had a Bourbon again on the throne. But they ruled with too heavy a hand, and liberal, republican, and nationalist revolts began to break out, reaching a high point in 1848.

Mohammad Ali (1769–1849)

Born in Macedonia, Ali served in the Albanian militia, and was sent by the Ottomans to oppose Napoleon's invasion force in Egypt. After the French withdrawal he used his troops to support the Egyptian rulers from the conservative Mamluk military elite.

He was proclaimed viceroy of Egypt by his troops, a position confirmed by the Ottoman sultan. He began a brutal concerted effort to reform the army, massacring the Mamluks in Cairo (1811). He fought campaigns against the Arabian Wahhabis, annexed much of Sudan, and supported the Ottomans against the Greeks (1821–28), until the Egyptian navy was destroyed at Navarino.

1811–1815

ASIA

1811 During Napoleonic Wars, British take over French and Dutch possessions in SE and S Asia (–1815).

1816 British occupy Java.

1812 Swiss explorer, Johann Ludwig Burckhardt discovers Petra, ancient capital of Nabataea.

Egyptian forces retake Mecca and Medina.

1814 Burckhardt visits Mecca.

Eight Trigrams sect in China defeated in their attempt to mount a coup in royal palace, Peking (Beijing).

Dutch regain control of Sumatra and Java, in Indonesia.

1815 Victory in Anglo-Gurkha war extends British possessions into the Himalayas.

Final British defeat of the Marathas leads to effective British control of Indian subcontinent.

British annex Ceylonese kingdom of Kandy.

AFRICA

1811 British attempt to take control of Madagascar.

1815 British troops suppress rebellion by Boer farmers.

c.1815 Mfecane tribal wars in S Africa begin (–c.1830).

EUROPE

1811 Luddite rioters wreck new textile machinery in Derbyshire, England (–1812).

Friedrich Krupp founds ironworks at Essen: origins of Germany's leading armaments industry.

Canned food invented in France 0 by Nicolas Appert.

1812 Napoleon invades Russia.

Battle of Borodino.

French occupy Moscow, then retreat.

Treaty of Bucharest ends Russo-Turkish war.

Sweden cedes Finland to Russia.

Grimm brothers publish *Fairy Tales* in Germany.

Hydraulic jack invented by Joseph Bramah.

Elgin marbles go on display in London.

1813 Napoleon defeated by Allies at Leipzig (battle of the Nations).

British defeat French at Vitoria.

Jane Austen's *Pride and Prejudice*.

1814 Allies enter Paris; Napoleon abdicates.

Napoleon exiled to Elba.

Opening of Congress of Vienna.

George Stephenson constructs first efficient steam locomotive.

1815 New map of Europe drawn up at congress of Vienna.

Napoleon escapes from Elba; begins "hundred days" reign.

Napoleon is defeated by British and Prussians at Waterloo after escape from exile. Restoration of French monarchy after Waterloo.

Napoleon finally exiled to St. Helena (dies there, 1821).

Quadruple Alliance agrees to exile the Bonaparte dynasty from France for 20 years.

Renewed Serbian uprisings lead to independence from Ottoman Turkey (formalized, 1817).

English chemist Humphry Davy invents miner's safety lamp.

AMERICAS & AUSTRALASIA

1811 Annexation of W Florida.

Simón Bolívar starts fight to liberate Venezuela.

Paraguay declares independence from Spain.

1812 War of 1812. US foils British attempt to restrain US navy; Canada attacked by US forces.

Louisiana admitted to USA.

1813 Route found across Blue Mountains in Australia.

1814 British army burns down the White House, Washington.

Australia given its current name.

In ten years, Australian cutters have denuded Fiji of sandalwood reserves.

Samuel Marsden establishes mission in the Bay of Islands, New Zealand.

First British Protestant missionaries arrive in New Zealand.

1815 Reopening of European trade, following Napoleonic Wars and War of 1812, boosts cotton exports from N America.

General Morillo sent from Spain to reconquer Venezuela.

First kauri gum exported from New Zealand to Sydney.

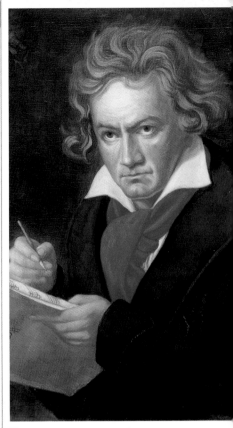

Ludwig van Beethoven

The German composer's vitality and range placed him at the forefront of contemporary music, and made him one of the acknowledged forefathers of 19th-century Romanticism. Driven by his ambitious alcoholic father, Beethoven performed as a child keyboard prodigy at Cologne (1778) and was sent to Vienna, possibly meeting Mozart, and being taught by Haydn.

By 1795 he had published his Opus 1 trios and Opus 2 piano sonatas. His early work was influenced by Mozart, and by 1802 he had published 3 piano concertos and two symphonies, but he was already suffering from the deafness and consequent depression which plagued the rest of his life.

Nevertheless, his middle period works show an heroic optimism; his 3rd symphony, *Eroica* (1804), was originally dedicated to Napoleon (it was withdrawn after his elevation to emperor) and he composed his only opera, *Fidelio* (completed 1814) toward the end of this period. By now he had abandoned public performances due to his deafness. His personal life included several unsuccessful romantic affairs, and an increasing irritation, unkemptness, and withdrawal from public life.

The Zulus

Under the leadership of Shaka (c.1787–1828), the Zulu were organized into a highly militarized kingdom. In 1810 Shaka was appointed by the Nguni leader, Dingiswayo, to train a force in northeast Natal. In 1816, he was instructed to take over the Zulu, who were then quite a small clan of some 1,500 individuals.

Within a year, Shaka's merciless attacks on neighboring clans had broken them completely. He incorporated their remaining members into the Zulu. In 1817 Dingiswayo was murdered and by the following year Shaka had established himself as supreme ruler of the region. He then continued crushing any rivals in Natal-Zululand in a series of wars which depopulated the southern interior, leaving it open to settlement by Afrikaners, who were seeking new pastures and an escape from the unwelcome imposition of British rule in the Cape. After Shaka's assassination by his half-brothers, Afrikaner migration north accelerated, notably in the "Great Trek" starting in 1836, defeating and dispersing the Zuluy and Nguni tribes in their path.

Shaka armed the Zulu with long-bladed, stabbing assegais, which forced them to fight at close quarters, bearing large body-protecting shields. Shield marking and headdresses distinguished different Zulu regiments.

ASIA

1821 ▼

1816 British trade mission expelled from China.

Sikkim accepts British control of its foreign relations.

Britain begins recruiting Gurkha soldiers from Nepal.

Java restored to Dutch control.

1818 Wahhabi resistance in Arabia crushed by Egyptian forces.

British army officer George Sadlier is first European to make east–west crossing of Arabian peninsula.

1823 ▼

Third Anglo-Maratha War in India ends in Maratha defeat. Britain annexes their state.

1820 Vietnamese emperor Minh Mang revives Confucianism and encourages persecution of Christians.

AFRICA

1816 Wool mills, flax mills, sugar refineries, indigo factories, and glassworks established in Egypt.

Inspired by Usman dan Fodio, Amadu Lobbo launches *jihad* in Masina.

Shaka becomes king of Zulus in S Africa.

British occupy Ascension Island.

1818 Shaka unites Zulu nation.

1821 ▼

1819 Shaka, leader of the Zulus, drives his enemies northward; Zulus defeat the Ndwandwe, becoming the dominant military force in the Natal region of S Africa.

1820 Nguni clans disperse to avoid Mfecane wars brought about by rise of Zulu empire.

Usman dan Fodio establishes Sokoto Fulani kingdom.

1825 ▼

Egypt conquers Sudan.

British settlers begin to arrive at the Cape (S Africa) in large numbers.

c.1820 Introduction of new crops by settlers to Africa, including cotton in Angola and cloves in Zanzibar.

EUROPE

1816 Emigration from SW Germany, following Napoleonic Wars (–1817).

French physician René Laënnec invents stethoscope.

1817 Greeks revolt against Ottoman Turkish rule.

James Parkinson identifies Parkinson's disease.

German Georg Handel's *Encyclopedia of the Physical Sciences*.

1818 John Nash begins replanning of central London, creating Regent's Park and Regent's Street.

Mary Shelley's *Frankenstein, or The Modern Prometheus*; John Keats' *Ode to a Nightingale*.

German philosopher Arthur Schopenhauer publishes *The Word as Will and Idea*.

Marc Brunel invents tunnelling engine in France.

1819 Carlsbad Decrees prohibit political meetings and censor press in German states.

Factory Act limits working time for children in England.

Peterloo Massacre; parliamentary reform meeting in Manchester, England, attacked by troops.

Lord Byron's *Don Juan*.

1820 Revolts in Spain, Portugal, Naples, Sicily, Piedmont, and the Balkans.

King Ferdinand VII of Spain restores the 1812 constitution to quell popular unrest.

John Constable's painting *Dedham Mill* exhibited.

Walter Scott's *Ivanhoe*.

AMERICAS & AUSTRALASIA

1816 Start of Russian exploration of Alaska.

Indiana admitted to USA.

Argentina (United Provinces of La Plata) declares war of independence from Spain.

Dom João, former prince regent of Portugal, declares himself King John VI of Brazil.

British ships reach Ryukyu Islands seeking trade with Japan, but are rebuffed.

1817 War between Seminole Indians and US troops.

Mississippi admitted to US.

Work begins on Erie Canal which will link New York to the Great Lakes via the Hudson river.

José de San Martín begins campaign for Chilean independence; wins a decisive victory over the Spanish and liberates Chile.

Bernardo O'Higgins becomes "supreme director" of Chile.

1818 Border between US and Canada agreed west of the Great Lakes as following 49th parallel.

Illinois admitted to US.

Chickasaw Indians sell territories within Tennessee to US government.

About 20,000 Irish emigrate to US as a result of famine.

Elisha Collier and Artemis Wheeler patent the revolver handgun in US; mass-produced by Samuel L. Colt from 1836.

Start of Maori "Musket Wars" in New Zealand.

1819 US purchases Florida from Spain.

Alabama admitted to US.

Simón Bolívar leads Colombia to independence from Spain.

The *Savannah* becomes the first steamship to cross the Atlantic.

1820 Missouri Compromise bans slavery north of 36°30´.

Maine, a free state, and Missouri, a slave state, admitted to USA.

Sir Stamford Raffles

A gifted colonial administrator and entrepreneur, Raffles was born the son of a sea-cook in Jamaica. He was given a clerkship in the East India House in 1795, and in 1805 was stationed at Penang in Malaya. In 1811 he accompanied an expedition against Java, whose administration he then reformed as lieutenant-governor. He was posted to Bengkulu in Sumatra from 1818–23, and established a defended post on the island of Singapore to counter Dutch influence in the area, a move that was to give Britain a commanding position in maritime Southeast Asian trade for the next 150 years. A keen naturalist, he was a founder of the London Zoo.

Industrial reform

The rapid rise in urbanism and industrialism in the last quarter of the 18th century introduced a new relationship between labor and capital. Changes in labor organization often caused unrest as craft-workers found their livelihood rendered obsolete by mechanization. Machine-wrecking became a form of resistance, notably with the Luddite riots in Britain (1811–12). The development of factories encouraged the birth of trades unions, initially limited to skilled craftsmen, but increasingly attracting less skilled workers. However, it was not until 1843 that Engels would publish *The Condition of the Working Class in England*.

The cotton-spinning town of New Lanark in Scotland was founded in 1785. In the 1900s, social reformer Robert Owen provided exemplary living conditions for workers there.

1816–1820

The age of steam

In the 1820s, the demand for better transportation, primarily for carrying coal from the English collieries to ports, was growing. The 25-mile (40-km) rail track between the coal-producing region of Darlington and the port of Stockton-on-Tees was built over a three-year period, and opened on September 27, 1825. George Stephenson, a mechanic who had been working on steam locomotives since 1813, designed a steam locomotive that could pull both passengers and freight. It was the beginning of the railroad revolution. In 1830, Stephenson's *Rocket* achieved speeds of 24 mph (39 kph) and by 1840, nearly 2,400 miles (3,862 km) of track had been laid in England alone.

Greek independence struggle

In 1821, the Greek Orthodox subjects of the Ottoman Turks rose up against their rulers in a rebellion organized by the *Phililkí Etaireía*, a secret society of Greek patriots. The Greek struggle for independence attracted the backing of Russia, motivated by religious affinities as well as territorial ambitions. When, in 1827, Britain and France also intervened, the Turkish fleet was destroyed at Navarino, and independence was secured. The Greeks' defiance of Turkey was an inspiration for liberals throughout Europe. The death of English Romantic poet, Lord Byron (*right*) at the siege of Missolonghi caused an outpouring of pro-Greek feelings.

ASIA

1821 A Chinese is killed in an attack on the landing party from *HMS Topaz* at Linding. The surrender of British sailors for punishment is refused.

1823 Lord Amherst is appointed governor-general of India.

| 1852 |
George Everest becomes superintendent of the Great Trigonometrical Survey.

| 1826 | **1824** War breaks out between Britain and Burma, following the Burmese occupation of Assam and Manipur, NE India. British naval forces seize Rangoon.

| 1826 | **1825** Persia rejects the Treaty of Gulistan, which cedes the Caucasus region to Russia, and attempts to retake Georgia.

China's balance of trade has fallen into deficit, following the East India Company's import of opium into China.

The Japanese shogun issues an edict calling for the expulsion of all foreign ships from Japanese waters.

Aristocrats in the ancient kingdom of Java, led by Prince Dipo Negoro, rise up against Dutch colonists.

AFRICA

1821 The W African enclave of the Gold Coast, formerly administered by British merchants, becomes a crown colony.

Mohammad Ali, the Egyptian pasha (viceroy), conquers the Funj sultanate of Sudan.

The Hlubi of Mpangazitha and the Ngwane of Matiwane flee the raids of Shaka Zulu. They cross the high passes of the Drakensberg, carrying the conflict of the Mfecane to the Sotho highveld.

1822 Freed black slaves found colony of Liberia.

1823 Sotho Mfecane raiders are defeated by the Tswana people at the battle of Dithakong.

European explorers, Dixon Denham and Hugh Clapperton, reach Lake Chad.

| 1827 | **1824** Moshoeshoe, the powerful leader of the Motlotheli clan, moves his people to the mountain stronghold of Thaba-Bosiu. From this secure capital, he builds up the powerful Sotho kingdom.

1825 Uthman Bey, the commander-in-chief of the Egyptian forces in Sudan, builds a citadel at Khartoum.

EUROPE

1821 A wave of nationalist revolts against Ottoman rule in Greece. The nationalist leader Alexander Ypsilantis invades Moldavia, seizing its capital, Jassy.

Revolution in Piedmont. Austrians and Sardinians defeat the Piedmontese at the battle of Novara, returning Piedmont to Sardinian rule.

German philosopher Georg Hegel publishes *The Philosophy of Right*.

English scientist Michael Faraday discovers electromagnetic rotation.

1822 Greek rebels declare the independence of Greece, and draw up a constitution.

Ottomans massacre thousands of Greek insurgents on the island of Chios. An Ottoman invasion disperses the newly established Greek government.

Rebels in Spain take King Ferdinand VII prisoner. At the congress of Verona, France is authorized to intervene and restore Ferdinand to the throne.

English Romantic poet Percy Bysshe Shelley is drowned off the Italian coast.

1823 Ottomans are forced to withdraw from the key fortress of Missolonghi, at the entrance to the Gulf of Corinth.

French forces defeat the Spanish rebels at the battle of Trocadero, and the Bourbon monarchy is restored.

British home secretary, Sir Robert Peel, introduces wide ranging reforms to the criminal law and penal system.

The game of rugby is invented at Rugby school, England.

Charles Macintosh invents waterproof fabric.

1824 Mohammad Ali, the pasha of Egypt, intervenes in the Greek war of independence on the Ottoman side, and captures Crete.

Ludwig van Beethoven composes his ninth symphony.

English Romantic poet, Lord Byron, dies at Missolonghi, and is mourned in Greece as a national hero.

1825 Decembrist uprising against Romanov autocracy in Russia by young army officers is crushed.

First passenger steam railroad from Stockton-on-Tees to Darlington in UK.

AMERICAS & AUSTRALASIA

1821 Czar Alexander declares that Russian influence in N America extends to Oregon. He closes Alaskan waters to foreigners.

Bolívar secures Venezuelan independence.

Peru declares itself independent of Spain.

Mexico gains independence from Spanish colonies.

El Salvador proclaims independence.

1822 California becomes part of the republic of Mexico.

Antonio José de Sucre secures the independence of Quito, Ecuador.

Brazil declares its independence from Portugal.

1823 The US recognizes new S American states.

In Mexico, an uprising led by Antonio de Santa Anna forces the emperor, Agustín de Iturbide to abdicate.

New South Wales becomes a crown colony.

1824 US signs a treaty with Russia, settling their border dispute.

Battle of Ayacucho; decisive victory of S American republicans over Spanish colonial forces.

Mexico declares itself a federal republic.

Spanish royalist troops withdraw from Peru. Peruvian independence is secured.

1825 Completion of the Erie Canal, linking the Great Lakes with New York City.

Creek Indians signs a treaty which cedes all their remaining land to Georgia.

Bolivia becomes independent of Peru, Uruguay of Brazil.

Joseph Smith founds the first Mormon church at Fayette, New York state.

Dutch annex W New Guinea.

Musket Wars at their peak in New Zealand; Christian missionaries attempt to mediate.

c.1825 Whaling and sealing stations on east coast of New Zealand.

South American Independence

1808	Rebellions against Spain begin in S America.
1810	Argentina becomes independent.
1811	Rebel state of New Granada (Venezuela, Colombia, and Ecuador) formed in opposition to Spanish rule.
	Paraguay declares independence.
1815	Spanish troops land in Colombia and embark on campaign of terror.
1817	San Martín defeats the Spanish army at Chacabuco in Chile.
1818	Chile declares independence.
	Simón Bolívar returns to S America from exile in the Caribbean.
1819	Simón Bolívar defeats the Spanish at Boyacá, Colombia. Republic of Greater Colombia (Ecuador, New Granada, and Venezuela) proclaimed.
1821	San Martín takes Lima. Peru declares independence.
	Venezuelan independence confirmed by Bolívar's defeat of Spanish forces at the battle of Carabobo.
1822	Pedro I, son of the Portuguese king becomes emperor of an independent Brazil.
	Quito, Ecuador, is liberated from Spain at the battle of Pichincha.
1824	Battle of Ayacucho; decisive victory of S American republicans over Spanish colonial forces.
1825	Bolívar founds the new state of Bolivia.
1828	Uruguay becomes fully independent.
1829	Venezuela breaks away from the republic of Gran Colombia.
1830	Republic of Gran Colombia separates into independent states.

Wars of liberation

Napoleon's invasion of 1808 cut off Spain from its empire. The colonies, left to fend for themselves until Ferdinand VII was restored in 1814, established ruling juntas. Following their taste of freedom, they were not prepared to accept a reimposition of royal government, and demanded autonomy. The South American wars of

liberation were fought between patriots and those who remained loyal to the Spanish crown. The Spanish were never able to send large forces to combat the rebels. José de San Martín (*left*) (1778–1850) led the freedom struggle in Peru and Argentina. He was joined by Bernardo O'Higgins, liberator of Chile, and Simón Bolívar, whose campaigns of 1818–1822 led to a triumphal progress through Venezuela to Ecuador, culminating in the creation of Bolivia, named in his honor. Within a decade Spain had been divested of an empire that it had ruled for 300 years, retaining only Cuba and Puerto Rico.

British India

Much of British rule in India was conducted through the sovereignty of the princely states, and the collaboration of their Indian rulers. The British left the structure of Indian society intact, although they did ban the practice of *sati* and slavery. Even the activities of Christian missionaries were strictly controlled by the East India Company. Peasants benefited from the British suppression of bandits and fairer taxation policies. On the other hand, the new commercialism, which emphasized profitable crops, such as indigo and cotton, placed the peasants under new pressures. The British enjoyed a life of great luxury (*right*), and unprecedented wealth and power. Gradually, however, their attitudes began to change, and their respect for Indian culture was replaced by an ethnocentric arrogance.

Japanese wood blocks

Japan's most famous woodblock printer was Hokusai (1760–1849), whose career spanned eight decades. The simple lines, freshness, and color of Hokusai's wood-block prints (*below*) which could be produced cheaply and duplicated in large numbers, found an appreciative audience in both Japan and the west. Europeans first encountered these prints when they arrived as wastepaper, used for wrapping porcelain and other exports. Soon they were valued and collected. Many of the Impressionists acknowledged their debt to Hokusai and his contemporaries, and produced work in their style.

ASIA

1826 Sultan Mahmud II annihilates the mutinous Janissaries, once the elite of the Ottoman army.

The Persian cavalry is routed by the Russians at the battle of Ganja in the Caucasus.

1852

British sign a peace treaty with the king of Ava, ending the Anglo-Burmese war.

Cholera epidemic begins in India. It will later spread to Europe.

Penang, Malacca, and Singapore are united to form the Straits Settlements.

1827 Ottomans refuse to accept an armistice in the war with Greece.

Russia seizes Yerevan from Persia.

The first English language paper in the Far East, the *Canton Register*, is published at Guangzhou (Canton.)

1828 Russia captures Teheran. Russia and Persia sign a peace treaty, by which Russia acquires Armenia.

1829 *Sati*, the practice of self-immolation by Hindu widows, is abolished in British India.

1830 Mysore added to Britain's Indian possessions.

Chinese census records 394,780,000 inhabitants.

AFRICA

1826 In W Africa, the leader of the Tukulor *jihad*, Al-Hajj 'Umar Tal, sets off on a lengthy pilgrimage to Mecca.

1827 Sotho leader, Moshoeshoe scatters the remnants of his Zulu enemy, driving them south into Thembuland.

1834

1828 In Cape Colony, Britain abolishes the Hottentot Code of 1809 that ties Khoisan servants to European masters as "apprentices," creating a labor shortage.

Shaka Zulu, the Zulu leader, is assassinated by his half-brother Dingane, who proclaims himself king.

Egyptian pasha, Mohammad Ali agrees to evacuate Egyptian forces from Greece.

1830 A French expeditionary force captures Algiers, and deposes the bey.

Some 20,000 slaves exported from C African ports to Brazil.

c.1830 Moshoeshoe, the Sotho ruler, invites missionaries from Cape Colony to settle in his kingdom.

1826 Civil war breaks out in Portugal as result of a constitutional dispute between King John VI's two heirs.

Missolonghi falls to Egyptian forces under Ibrahim Pasha.

Compulsory schooling, to the age of 14, is introduced in Prussia.

1827 Athens falls to the Ottomans.

In response to a joint demand by Britain, France, and Russia, the Ottomans refuse to accept an armistice in their war with Greece.

The Ottoman–Egyptian fleet is destroyed by British, French, and Russian forces at the battle of Navarino, Mediterranean Sea.

John Dalton presents the first formulation of atomic theory in his *New System of Chemical Philosophy*.

German physicist, Georg Ohm introduces a new law concerning the flow of electric current.

1828 Russia, in support of Greek independence, declares war on the Ottoman Empire.

Irish politician Daniel O'Connell is elected to the House of Commons, but his Catholicism makes him ineligible.

Russians take Varna, Bulgaria, from the Ottomans.

1829 In Britain, the Catholic Emancipation Act becomes law.

British parliament agrees on an act to create a police force for the metropolis.

Sultan Mahmud II signs a peace treaty with Czar Nicholas. He recognizes Greek and Serbian independence.

In Paris, Louis Braille invents a reading system for the blind.

1830 Revolution in Paris. King Charles X of France issues five ordinances limiting political and civil rights. French liberals, led by the marquis of Lafayette, seize Paris.

Charles X abdicates and Louis Philippe, the Duke of Orléans, is proclaimed king (–1848).

Belgian War of Independence (–1831). The Dutch bombard the Belgian city of Antwerp.

An anti-Russian insurrection breaks out in Warsaw.

1826 The first railroad in the US opens at Quincy, Massachusetts.

1827 Chief Red Bird, leader of an Indian uprising in Michigan, is captured, ending the Winnebago war.

Peru ends its union with Colombia and declares itself independent.

1828 Backed by the fledgling Democratic party, Andrew Jackson is elected US president.

Cherokee Indians cede their traditional lands in Arkansas to the US, and agree to migrate to lands west of the Mississippi.

Start of federalist/centralist wars in Mexico (–1859).

Uruguay becomes an independent republic.

1829 The Baltimore and Ohio railroad company opens the first passenger line in the US.

Juan Manuel de Rosas becomes *caudillo*, or dictator, of Buenos Aires for next 23 years.

Britain annexes western third of Australian continent.

Charles Sturt's journeys pave way for founding of colony of S Australia in 1836.

Venezuela breaks away from Gran Colombia (Great Colombia).

1830 The US Congress passes the Indian Removal Act.

The first wagon trains to cross the Rocky Mountains arrive in California.

Mexican colonization law bans future immigration into Texas.

Ecuador withdraws from Gran Colombia; death of Bolívar.

In Chile, the conservative party under Diego Portales is victorious in a civil war with the liberals.

Just 200 foreigners, mostly British, are permanently resident in New Zealand.

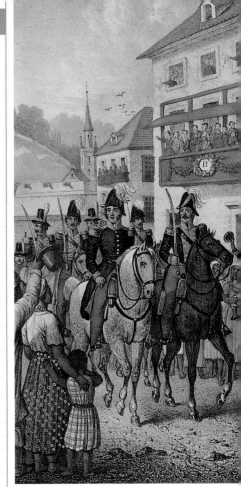

Bolívar enters Caracas in triumph in 1829 after putting down the uprising of his former lieutenant Antonio Páez.

Simón Bolívar

Born in Caracas, Venezuela, in 1783, Bolívar came from one of the oldest, and wealthiest, noble families in the city. His education was completed in Europe, where he absorbed the republican ideals of the French and American revolutions and the idea of independence for Hispanic America took root in his imagination.

His revolutionary career began with an abortive uprising in Caracas in 1810. In 1814, the charismatic Bolívar declared himself "liberator," and head of state of the new republic of Venezuela. In 1817, he staged a daring invasion of Colombia, and went on to complete the conquest of Ecuador and Peru (1824). His dream was to unite all of South America, except Brazil, Argentina, and Chile, into a single, great republic. But his dictatorial tendencies, and the brutality of his armies, led to dissent, and by his death in 1830, "Gran Colombia" had divided into separate countries.

The 19th Century Novel

From industrial Britain, to bourgeois France and agrarian Russia, the novels of the 19th century examine the harsh realities of exploitation and repression, as well as exploring individuals' quests for freedom.

Widely regarded as the greatest English novelist, Charles Dickens enjoyed worldwide fame. His unsparing appreciation of society and its shortcomings made him one of the greatest, and most compassionate, social commentators of his age. His career as a writer began with the stories and essays he wrote for magazines and newspapers, reprinted as Sketches by "Boz" (1836, right). His subsequent novels were widely read through serialization in newspapers and magazines.

356 **1831–1835**

ASIA

1831 Syria, part of the Ottoman Empire since 1516, is conquered by the Egyptians.

Holy war in NW India; Sikh forces of Ranjit Singh are defeated at Balakot.

1838

c.1831 10 million opium addicts in China.

1832 Russia offers Ottoman sultan Mahmud II assistance in his war with Egypt. Egyptian troops are now 50 miles (80 km) from Istanbul.

Ando Hiroshige (1797–1858), the master of Japanese color prints, publishes *Fifty-three Stages of the Tokaido.*

1839

1833 Treaty of Kutahya gives Egypt sovereignty over Syria and Cilicia. A truce is agreed between Egypt and the Ottoman Empire.

The East India Company ceases trading.

1837

Poor harvests bring famine to Japan. There are riots in several towns.

1839

1834 Sikhs, led by the Punjab ruler Ranjit Singh, capture Peshawar, the Muslim city in NW India.

British depose the rajah of Coorg, India.

Monopoly of China trade by East India Company abolished.

In Japan, a new senior councillor, Mizuno Tadakuni, is appointed to deal with the shogun's financial crisis.

1835 First tea plants ordered from China for India.

AFRICA

1831 The Shangane people, led by Soshangane, win a civil war among the Ngoni on the Save river, S Africa.

1834 British abolition of slavery in Cape Colony prompts many Boer farmers to move north in search of land outside British control.

Dutch-speaking hunting parties suffer disastrous defeat at the hands of the Ndebele of Mzilikazi in the Pretoria region of the Transvaal.

In Cape Colony, the British and the Xhosa clash in the "Sixth War" (–1835).

1848

1835 The Ngoni army of Zwangendaba heads north to spread the Mfecane wars to E Zambia and Malawi.

In N Africa, the emir of Mascara, 'Abd el-Kader, attacks and defeats French troops in the Macta pass.

c.1835 The Kololo of S Africa, led by Sebetwane, invade the Lozi kingdom on the upper Zambezi.

EUROPE

1831 Belgium becomes independent; Netherlands recognizes its independence.

Mass demonstrations in Swiss cities lead to an introduction of more liberal legislation.

Collapse of Polish revolt against Russia.

Italian republican activist, Giuseppe Mazzini, is exiled for a year.

Pushkin's *Eugene Onegin* is the first novel to take contemporary society as a subject of fiction.

1832 The Greek assembly elects king of Bavaria's son, Prince Otto, as king of Greece.

Duchy of Warsaw becomes part of Russia.

The Austrian government curtails the freedom of the press.

Papal bull *Mirai Vos*, condemns the freedom of the press.

Great Reform Act in Britain.

Cholera epidemic spreads through Europe. Cholera kills 31,000 people in Britain, reaching Scotland.

Death of German poet and dramatist, Goethe, whose greatest work is *Faust*.

1833 In Spain, a dispute over the succession of Queen Isabella leads to civil war. Supporters of the pretender, Don Carlos, are known as Carlists.

A customs treaty (*Zollverein*) is signed between Bavaria, Württemberg, Prussia, and Hesse-Darmstadt.

In Britain, tough new laws are passed to prevent the exploitation of children in textile factories.

The Greek church severs its links with Istanbul.

German physicist Carl Gauss invents the electromagnetic telegraph.

1834 An insurrection against the Bourbon monarchy of Louis Philippe is crushed in Paris.

Slavery is abolished throughout the British Empire.

A central proposal of a new British poor law is the establishment of workhouses.

1835 The first passenger service in mainland Europe, the Brussels–Malines rail line, is opened.

AMERICAS & AUSTRALASIA

1831 At least 200,000 people leave Ireland for Canada, many traveling to the US.

Southampton insurrection; slave revolt in Virginia led by Nat Turner.

English naturalist Charles Darwin sails on a surveying expedition in HMS *Beagle* to S America, New Zealand, and Australia.

Slave revolt in Jamaica.

1832 Chief Black Hawk and his tribe are massacred by US troops at the battle of Bad Axe river.

The Sauk chief Keokuk signs an agreement giving up his tribe's claims to lands east of the Mississippi ("the Trail of Tears.")

US artist George Catlin records scenes of Sioux and Mandan life.

Completion of the Rideau Canal between Ottawa and Kingston.

Infamous Port Arthur penal colony opened in Australia.

1833 US settlers agree to make Texas independent of Mexico.

British claim the Falkland Islands, S Atlantic, as crown territory.

US inventor Samuel Colt develops a new firearm – the revolver.

James Clark Ross reaches magnetic North Pole.

1834 Race riots erupt in Philadelphia. White rioters are condemned by a town meeting, and made to pay compensation to Black residents.

1835 Over 100 US troops are massacred by Seminole Indians resisting attempts to drive them out of Florida.

Texas revolution (–1836).

Juan Manuel de Rosas, the Argentinian dictator, embarks on a reign of terror.

British found Melbourne and Adelaide in Australia (–1836).

Reverend Peter Turner, a Wesleyan missionary, arrives on the island of Samoa.

China and the west

The rapidly expanding Qing economy of the 18th century had become prey to foreign ambitions. Trade missions from the west were met with disdain, but this was soon to change. By the early 1800s, China had fallen behind a confident, and resurgent, west. The power of the government was sapped by corruption and inefficiency, and the over-burdened peasantry turned to banditry and rebellion.

Westerners were quick to seize the opportunity. From the 1830s onward, western warehouses and shipping dominated the Canton waterfront (*above*). But patience was wearing thin. The British, in particular, wanted freer access to the huge Chinese markets, and diplomatic recognition as equals. Chinese resistance to these demands was simply seen as proof of their backwardness.

The Great Trek

In the 1830s and 1840s, several thousand Boer families trekked northward from Cape Colony, extending permanent white settlement into the interior of South Africa. The Boers sought freedom from British government controls, as well as access to vast stretches of new land. The British had introduced a new system of land tenure that led to ownership of land as private property, which poorer Boers could not afford. British-appointed magistrates, the use of English in schools and law courts, and the abolition of slavery, all served to alienate the Boers further. However, their aspirations to settle the fertile grasslands of the southeast *lowveld* brought them into conflict with the powerful Zulus.

Science and Technology (1831–1870)

1831	Chloroform simultaneously invented by Samuel Guthrie and Justus von Liebig.
	Michael Faraday carries out experiments demonstrating the discovery of electromagnetic induction.
1834	English mathematician Charles Babbage invents the principles of the "analytical engine" (modern computer).
	American inventor Cyrus Hall McCormick patents his reaping machine.
1837	Samuel Morse exhibits his electrical telegraph.
1838	The Daguerre-Niepce method of photography is presented in Paris.
1839	Tyre manufacturer Charles Goodyear discovers the process of "vulcanization."
	Swiss physicist Carl August Steinheil builds the first electric clock.
1841	Swiss embryologist Rudolf Albert von Kölliker describes the spermatozoa.
1842	US physicist Crawford W. Long uses ether to produce surgical anesthesia.
	First mechanical typesetter, the Pianotype machine, invented by Henry Bessemer.
1843	English physicist James Prescott Joule determines the amount of work required to produce a unit of heat.
1849	French physicist Armand Fizeau measures the speed of light.
1855	Austrian engineer Franz Köller invents tungsten steel.
1859	Charles Darwin proposes his theory of evolution.
1860	T. S. Mort (Sydney) builds the first machine-chilled cold storage unit.
1860	Lead acid battery invented by Gaston Planté.
1864	Louis Pasteur invents pasteurization (for wine).
1865	Gregor Mendel enunciates his law of heredity.
1865	Joseph Lister initiates antiseptic surgery by using carbolic acid on compound wounds.
1866	Alfred Nobel invents dynamite.
1869	Mendeleyev formulates his periodic law for the classification of the elements.

Photography

In 1826, **Joseph-Nicéphore Niepce** succeeded in capturing the first permanent photographic image – of an old barnyard in France – on a pewter plate after an exposure of eight hours. In 1838, his partner Louis Daguerre marketed a photographic system that required an exposure of 30 minutes onto copper plates covered by light-sensitive silver chloride. The so-called "daguerreotype" process rapidly spread throughout the world. Technical improvements in lenses, exposure times, and processing soon followed. By the mid-1800s, photography had transformed the way people saw the world.

"Still Life" daguerreotype by Louis Daguerre.

ASIA

1837 British concerns mount about increasing Russian influence in Afghanistan.

British prevent the Persians from occupying the town of Herat, Afghanistan.

Tokugawa Ieyoshi succeeds Ienari as Japanese shogun.

Abortive peasant uprising in Japan in protest against lack of famine relief.

1838 Ottoman–British trade treaty abolishes commercial monopolies throughout Ottoman Empire. Egyptian pasha, Mohammad Ali, is hostile to agreement and takes up arms.

Lin Zexu is appointed imperial commissioner in Canton, China. He is instructed to deal with a growing opium problem.

1839 The new Ottoman sultan, Mahmud Abdul-Medjid, confirms equal rights on all Ottoman subjects, and promises tax reforms; makes series of liberal *Tanzimat* decrees (–1861).

Sultan Mahmud II launches another offensive against pasha of Egypt, Mohammad Ali.

The Arabian port of Aden is annexed to British India.

The British army deposes the emir of Kabul, Dost Mohammed Khan, and starts an Afghan war (–1842).

1845

Ranjit Singh, who extended Sikh power to the borders of British India and Afghanistan, is dead.

British ships assemble off Canton and evacuate traders. British naval forces fire the first shots in the yet to be declared Opium War.

Commissioner Lin Zexu blockages foreign factories, forcing merchants to surrender their opium stocks.

1840 France, Britain, and Russia ally with the Ottoman Empire against Egypt. They occupy the Syria–Palestine coast, bombarding Beirut and Acre.

The formal beginning of the Opium War. British naval forces bombard Dinghai on Zoushan Island and occupy it.

British force the Qing court in Beijing into negotiations.

AFRICA

1841

1836 'Abd el-Kader, leader of the Algerians' resistance to French colonization, occupies the capital, Mascara.

Boers of Cape Colony begin to trek northeastward. They resent British "discrimination," and seek to occupy land outside British control.

The Rozvi kingdom of Zimbabwe suffers a serious defeat at the hands of Ngoni forces, led by a woman general, Nyamazana.

1837 Death of Muhammad Bello, ruler of the Sokoto empire. With a population of c.10 million people, Sokoto is the largest state in W Africa.

Death of al-Kanemi, religious leader of Borno in W Africa. He is succeeded by his son, Umar.

The Ndebele army fights a running battle with Boers and Griqua people in the Marico plains, S Africa.

1842

Thousands of Boer trekkers cross the Drakensberg mountains and settle in Natal.

The first groundnuts (called peanuts) are exported to America and Europe from Sierra Leone.

1838 Boers kill 3,000 Zulus at the battle of Blood river, Natal.

1840 The army of the Ndebele has marched north to the Zimbabwe grasslands, following their defeat by Boers in 1837.

Zulu king Dingane is killed in a civil war. His brother, Mpande succeeds him (–1872).

The great powers recognize the right of Mohammad Ali to the pashalik of Egypt. The Ottoman sultan recognizes the pashalik of Egypt as a hereditary position within Mohammad Ali's family.

Sayyid Sa'id, the sultan of Oman, moves his capital to Zanzibar, which becomes the largest slave market in E Africa.

EUROPE

1836 The British parliament introduces the Locomotive Act, limiting the speed of all trains to 5 mph (8 kmph).

1837 Princess Victoria becomes queen of Great Britain and Ireland.

First practical electric telegraph system produced by Cooke and Wheatstone.

1842 ▼

1838 Chartist movement in England (–1848). Chartism demands universal suffrage and vote by ballot.

1846 ▼

Anti-Corn Law League established in Manchester by Richard Cobden and friends.

Charles Dickens' serialized novel, *Oliver Twist*, depicts the life of London's poor with grim realism.

Launch of I. K. Brunel's *Great Western* steamship.

A new invention, the daguerreotype, produces exact images using a lens, copper plate, and light.

1839 The independence and neutrality of Belgium is finally guaranteed by the Treaty of London.

A Russian military expedition in C Asia fails to take the oasis town of Khiva.

Polish composer Frédéric Chopin publishes his 26 preludes.

First bicycle constructed by Scottish inventor, Kirkpatrick Macmillan.

Leipzig publisher Karl Baedeker starts to produce European travel guides.

1840 Cheap postal system introduced; one penny per letter to anywhere in Britain.

AMERICAS & AUSTRALASIA

1836 Republic of Texas is declared.

The Texan mission station, the Alamo, is besieged by 5,000 Mexican soldiers, and falls to Mexican troops.

Californian rebels proclaim the territory's freedom from Mexican rule.

Nature, a series of lectures in which Ralph Waldo Emerson develops the theory of the individual's potential for divinity, is published.

Arkansas becomes the 25th state of the US.

1845 ▼

1837 President Jackson recognizes the Lone Star republic of Texas. The US government notifies Texas that it will not be admitted to the union.

A smallpox epidemic in the Missouri river region kills 15,000 Indians.

Under a flag of truce, US forces seize the Indian Seminole chief, Osceola. They go on to rout Seminole Indians at Lake Okeechobee.

British troops suppress revolts in Lower and Upper Canada.

First Canadian railroad is constructed.

New Zealand Company founded.

1838 Rebel leader Robert Nelson declares himself president of the republic of Lower Canada. He is forced to flee from an advancing British army.

The *Sirius* is the first ship to cross the Atlantic by steam, a voyage that takes 15 days.

First game of baseball played at Beachville, Upper Canada.

1839 Confederation of Bolivia and Peru shattered at battle of Yungay by Chilean and Peruvian nationalists.

Indian leader Rafael Carrera seizes power in Guatemala.

An act uniting the British provinces of Upper and Lower Canada is passed.

Charles Goodyear discovers how to vulcanize rubber.

1840 James Clark Ross leads three Antarctic voyages (–1845).

Treaty of Waitangi; British takeover of New Zealand under the treaty. Start of influx of British settlers into New Zealand.

Transportation of felons from Britain to New South Wales ends.

The First Opium War (1839–42)

From 1810, the English East India Company encouraged the cultivation of opium as a cash crop for exchange on the Chinese market. There was a booming market for imported opium; its growing use in China was a symptom of the despair and decline of a once-proud nation. Attempts to ban the drug were unsuccessful, and European and American traders continued to profit from the trade.

In 1838, an imperial commissioner was sent to Canton to stop the opium traffic, and he ordered that stocks of the drug should be destroyed. The British used this incident as a pretext to declare war. They soon destroyed the Chinese navy, occupying Shanghai, and sailing up the Yangtze river to Nanjing. After three long years, the overwhelming superiority of western military technology was recognized by the Chinese, who signed the Treaty of Nanjing (1842).

The Treaty of Waitangi

European traders had first arrived in New Zealand in the 1790s, and had begun to trade with the Maoris, who had occupied the country for several centuries. When the first British colonists arrived in New Zealand in 1840, Britain dispatched a governor, Captain William Hobson. He negotiated an agreement with the Maori leaders, the Treaty of Waitangi, in which he granted them land rights and offered them British citizenship in exchange for recognition of British sovereignty. This unequal exchange soon led to resentment and, within three years, war.

1836–1840

Cotton plantations

In the southern states of the US, the profitable cultivation of cotton and tobacco was dependent on a system of plantation slavery that dated back to the 17th century. This anachronistic system survived into the 19th century because of the vast demand for cotton from the industrialized cotton mills of Lancashire in the UK, and New England, in the US.

In 1850, 347,000 southern families out of a total population of 6,000,000 were slave holders. The exploitation of unfree labor caused outrage and profound embarrassment to liberals outside the south. Throughout the 1840s and 1850s, a growing body of antislavery literature called for emancipation.

The Irish potato famine

Between 1845 and 1849, Ireland suffered from a devastating natural disaster, a potato blight that caused widespread famine, reducing its population by over a quarter,

This 1845 engraving shows an attack on a potato store.

and forcing over a million people to emigrate.

By the early 19th century, a large proportion of Ireland's population was totally dependent on the potato as a staple food. Conditions in the countryside were considerably worsened by English repression. Until 1829, Irish Catholics had not been allowed to buy land, and absentee landlords demanded high rents, which they enforced through the threat of eviction. As the potato blight took hold, starving families flocked to the towns, intent on emigration to North America. The English government's inadequate response to the tragedy caused bitterness and anglophobia.

ASIA

1841 British ships occupy island of Hong Kong and continue attacks along China's S coast, seeking a monopoly on China's lucrative opium trade.

A full-scale attack on Canton by British forces under General Gough. Troops, supported by 16 warships, enter the Yangtze river.

British army of occupation in Kabul, Afghanistan, comes under attack.

The sultan of Brunei, N Borneo, cedes Sarawak to James Brooke.

1842 A 16,500-strong Anglo-Indian force is massacred while retreating from Kabul.

Treaty of Nanjing; China cedes island of Hong Kong to Britain and opens five ports to foreign trade.

1843 In Arabia, the fortunes of Saud family restored by Faisal.

British troops capture the Sind area of NW India.

Dost Mohammed is restored to the leadership of Afghanistan.

Britain and China sign a diplomatic treaty. The port of Shanghai is opened to foreign trade.

Opium smoking in China is banned by imperial edict.

In China, Hong Xiuchuan experiences visions, and proclaims himself "King of the kingdom of Heaven."

1844 In India, British wage the southern Maratha campaign.

China and the US sign the Treaty of Wanaghiya, giving US nationals access to the five international ports.

In China, an imperial edict relaxes a ban on the Catholic church.

1846 ▼

The shogun of Japan refuses a demand by King William II of the Netherlands that Japanese ports should be opened to foreign trade.

1845 First Sikh War (–1846). The British army embarks on the conquest of Kashmir and Punjab.

China grants Belgium equal trading rights with Britain, France, and the US.

AFRICA

1841 A French expeditionary force drives the Algerian resistance leader, 'Abd el-Kader, into Morocco, where he seeks assistance.

1842 British troops move into Natal, S Africa, to cut off the inland Boer republic from the sea. They are besieged by Boers.

1843 British annex short-lived Boer republic of Natal; Boers forced to make second trek.

1847 ▼

1844 A French squadron bombards Tangiers, Morocco; attacks and defeats the army of 'Abd el-Kader.

Treaty of Tangiers; France and Morocco agree to end the conflict, and France withdraws from Morocco.

1850 ▼

The British governor of the Gold Coast (Ghana) forts makes a "bond" with the various Fante states of the coast.

1845 A French column surrenders at Sidi Brahim in the continuing Algerian war.

EUROPE

1841 The Straits Convention. The leading European powers agree that the Bosporus and Dardanelles should be closed to all nations' warships while the Ottoman Empire is at peace.

The first railroad to cross a frontier is completed between Strasbourg and Basle.

German philosopher Artur Schopenhauer publishes *The Two Fundamental Problems of Ethics*.

French writer, Victor Hugo is elected a member of the Académie Française.

English travel agent Thomas Cook arranges his first excursion.

1842 Riots and strikes against low wages in N England. The authorities blame the Chartist movement.

Lord Shaftesbury's Mines Act; underground employment of women and children prohibited.

The novelist, Nikolai Gogol, publishes *Dead Souls*, a somber and realistic portrayal of serfdom in Russia.

Nabucco, a new opera by Giuseppe Verdi, is premiered in Milan, to great acclaim.

1843 An uprising in Spain against the regent, General Espartero. General Narváez, the moderate leader that succeeds him, plans to reinstate the Spanish monarchy.

Richard Wagner's opera, *The Flying Dutchman*, is a great success, and he is given a conducting post at the Dresden opera.

Danish philosopher, Søren Kierkegaard, publishes *Either/Or, Fear and Trembling*, and *Repetition*.

Engels' *The Condition of the Working Class in England* is published.

1844 In Spain, a paramilitary police force, the *Guardia Civil*, is established to restore order.

1846
▼

In Silesia, a weavers' revolt is suppressed by the Prussian authorities.

Irish nationalist leader Daniel O'Connell is found guilty of conspiracy against British rule in Ireland.

British artist Joseph Mallord William Turner paints his dramatic work, *Rain, Steam and Speed*.

AMERICAS & AUSTRALASIA

1841 A group of 130 colonists cross the Rocky Mountains and arrive in Oregon by wagon train.

El Salvador declares its independence.

Edward Eyre is first European to cross Australia's Nullarbor plain.

New Zealand becomes a separate crown colony.

At least 35 whaling stations are established in Tasmania.

Edgar Allan Poe's *The Murders in the Rue Morgue* popularizes a new genre – the detective story.

1842 The Webster–Ashburton Treaty agrees the borders between the US and Canada.

Lt. John C. Fremont begins series of expeditions to map the American West and encourage settlement.

1843 Russian Orthodox church establishes mission schools for Alaskan Inuit.

1844 Haitian leader Boyer is ousted in a coup. Dominicans drive out Haitian forces and establish a republic.

Samuel Morse taps out the first telegraph message between two cities, Washington and Baltimore.

1847
▼

Joseph Smith, the leader of the Mormon sect, and his brother Hyrum, are killed by a mob in Carthage, Illinois. Brigham Young succeeds him as head of the Mormon church.

1845 Texas becomes the 38th state of the union.

1846
▼

Mexico severs relations with the US, following the US ratification of the annexation of Texas.

In Peru, Ramón Castilla seizes power and establishes a reformist dictatorship.

Northern War in New Zealand; started by Ngapuhi chiefs deprived of trade when capital moved from Russell to Auckland.

Maoris, led by Chief Hone-Heke, burn the small town of Kororareka in protest against European settlement of Maori lands.

The Age of Grand Opera

The 19th century saw the birth of "grand opera," an international style of large-scale theatrical spectacles, which used large casts, elaborate scenery, and costumes. These operas were frequently based on historical, or pseudohistorical, librettos.

1829	Rossini: *Guillaume Tell*, Paris Opera.
1830	Donizetti: *Anna Bolena*, Milan.
1835	Donizetti: *Lucia di Lammermoor*, Theatro San Carlo, Naples.
1836	Glinka: *A Life for the Tsar*, first Russian opera, St. Petersburg.
1843	Wagner: *Der Fliegende Holländer*, Dresden.
1846	Berlioz: *Damnation de Faust*, dramatic cantata, Paris.
1849	Meyerbeer: *Le Prophète*, Paris.
1851	Verdi: *Rigoletto*, Venice.
1852	Schumann: *Manfred*, Weimar.
1853	Verdi: *Il Trovatore*, Rome, and *La Traviata*, Venice.
1858	Offenbach: *Orphée aux Enfers*, Paris.
1859	Verdi: *Un Ballo in Maschera*, Rome.
1863	Berlioz: *Les Troyens*, Paris.
1865	Wagner: *Tristan und Isolde*, Munich.
1866	Offenbach: *La Vie Parisienne*, Paris. Smetana: *The Bartered Bride*, Prague.
1867	Gounod: *Roméo et Juliette*, Paris. Verdi: *Don Carlos*, Paris.
1868	Wagner: *Die Meistersinger von Nürnberg*, Munich.
1869	Wagner: *Das Rheingold*, Paris.
1870	Wagner: *Die Walküre*, Munich.

The exaggerated nationalism of the 19th century was frequently linked to racist doctrines. Richard Wagner (1813–1883) condemned "Jewish" influence in music. His famous cycle of four operas, Der Ring des Nibelungen (1848–1876), was a powerful celebration of German mythology.

Karl Marx

In 1848, the radical German socialist Karl Marx, together with his friend Friedrich Engels, wrote *The Communist Manifesto*. In this

seminal work, Marx described the history of humanity as a struggle for control of the technical means of production. He saw capitalism, based on waged labor, as a modern form of slavery. He argued that the contradiction between the prosperity of the few and poverty of the masses could no longer be ignored – the conditions were ripe for a socialist revolution. Marx's ultimate concern was for the creation of a just society, in which human beings would be free to realize their potential. His vision was to be the driving force behind many of the great social revolutions of the late 19th and 20th centuries.

Revolutions of 1848

Within the first few months of 1848, almost 50 revolutions erupted across Europe. A number of factors contributed to the disruption: rising food prices and industrial depression; simmering nationalist movements fueled discontent, especially in Italy and Germany; throughout Europe, the existing political order – in which monarchs appealed to divine right and tradition – seemed increasingly irrelevant in societies in which new commercial and industrial elites were gaining power.

The 1848 revolution in France (*above*) began in February, when rioting Parisians forced the proclamation of a republic. When the new republican government proved reluctant to enact reforms, the workers took up arms, and in the course of three days, 10,000 people were killed or wounded. An occupation army took control of Paris for four months.

ASIA

1846 East India Company's forces defeat the Sikhs at Sobraon and Aliwal.

Treaty of Lahore ends First Sikh War.

French monks visit Lhasa.

1853

Commodore Biddle arrives in Japan on an official mission from the US government. He asks for the opening of trade relations between Japan and the US, but is refused.

1847 Tu Duc, head of the Nguyen dynasty, succeeds to the throne of Annam, the biggest and most powerful state in SE Asia.

1848 Second Sikh War begins.

1849 Sikh forces are decisively defeated by the British at the battle of Gujarat. British annex Punjab.

Portuguese governor of Macao, Amaral, is assassinated because of his anti-Chinese policies.

1852

1850 In Persia, Sa'id 'Ali Mohammed, the founder of Babism, a new Islamic mystical movement, is executed on the orders of the shah, Naser od-Din.

Groups of pseudo-Christian "God worshipers" gather at Jintian, in Guangxi province, to stage a revolt. Start of the Taiping rebellion, led by Hong Xiuchuan (–1864).

AFRICA

1846 French and British bombard Tamatave, Madagascar, in protest against a government order making all foreigners subject to native law.

War of the Axe breaks out in Xhosa territory, S Africa, following moves by British sheep farmers to acquire more land (–1847).

Mai Ibrahim, the sultan of Bornu, and last in the Saifawa line, attempts to regain control of Bornu by organizing an invasion from the sultanate of Wadai. He is captured and executed.

1847 'Abd el-Kader is captured by French and exiled.

Liberia, the state founded by the American slave-trade abolitionists, declares its independence.

1848 Death of Zwangendaba, the Ngoni chief who led his people on a migration from Natal to W Tanzania. His people begin to break up into five smaller chiefdoms.

British take control of the southern highveld, S Africa.

1853
1849 David Livingstone reaches Lake Ngami.

1853
1850 Denmark sells off its Gold Coast possessions to Britain, and withdraws from African colonization.

1853
German explorer, Heinrich Barth, begins a journey of exploration into sub-Saharan Africa (–1855).

c.1850 Atlantic slave trade, including clandestine operations, begins to die out.

Swahili/Arab caravaneers cross Lake Tanganyika to collect ivory and slaves from E Zaire.

EUROPE

1846 Proindependence revolts in Galicia. The free republic of Cracow is annexed to Austrian-controlled Galicia.

King Christian VIII of Denmark lays claim to the independent duchies of Schleswig and Holstein.

Repeal of British corn laws.

Portuguese peasants revolt, and overthrow the dictatorial government of Costa-Cabral.

1847 "Reform banquets" are held in France, calling for universal suffrage and parliamentary reforms.

Sonderbund War in Switzerland. Conservative cantons refuse to dissolve union.

Siemens lays first telegraph line between Berlin and Frankfurt.

New novels published in England include *Vanity Fair* by William Thackeray, *Wuthering Heights* by Emily Brontë, *Jane Eyre* by Charlotte Brontë, and *Dombey and Sons* by Charles Dickens.

1848 Year of revolution in Europe. Rebellions throughout Europe are quickly suppressed. Revolutions lead to political crackdown and exodus of democrats from C Europe (–1849).

Partial or complete emancipation of Jews in Sweden, Denmark, Austria, and Greece.

Prussia invades Denmark over the Schleswig–Holstein question.

Denmark and Prussia sign a truce at Malmö, agreeing to evacuate Schleswig and Holstein.

The Austrian army invades Hungary.

Karl Marx and Friedrich Engels publish *The Communist Manifesto*.

A group of English painters, led by John Everett Millais, William Holman Hunt, and Dante Gabriel Rossetti, found the Pre-Raphaelite brotherhood.

1849 Russians and Ottomans sign the convention of Balta-Liman, agreeing on joint supervision of the Danubian principalities for seven years.

1850 Prussia and Denmark sign a peace treaty; Prussia withdraws from Schleswig and Holstein.

At the convention of Olmutz, Prussia agrees to acknowledge Austrian supremacy within the German Confederation.

AMERICAS & AUSTRALASIA

1846 Oregon settlement in the US.

US declares war on Mexico.

A US navy squadron formally claims California for the US. A pro-Mexican revolt in California is put down by US troops.

US troops defeat the Mexicans near Las Cruces, virtually completing the conquest of New Mexico.

1847 Final surrender of pro-Mexican protesters in California.

US troops win victories at the battles of Buena Vista and Cerro Gordo, and take possession of the stronghold at Vera Cruz.

Mexican War ends with the storming of Mexico City by US troops.

A group of Mormons led by Brigham Young founds a settlement on the banks of Great Salt Lake, Utah.

1848 California Gold Rush starts near Sutter's Mill on the Sacramento river.

Mexico cedes Texas and California to the US.

1849 California Gold Rush draws large numbers of migrants from Europe, Australia, Chile, and China.

US alone has 760 whaling ships operating in the Pacific.

1850 Effective end of slave trade in Brazil.

1855 ▼

The British parliament passes the Australian Colonies Government Act, giving the colonies self-government.

Nathaniel Hawthorne publishes *The Scarlet Letter*, a novel of adultery set in 17th-century Boston.

Migrant workers begin arriving in Hawaii from China, Japan, and the Philippines.

Copra becomes mainstay of trade on Society Islands.

1848 Jan: Revolt in Sicily. Provisional independent government proclaimed.

Revolt in Naples; a new constitution is promulgated.

Feb 22–24: Revolution in Paris. Proclamation of French second republic and universal male suffrage.

March: Uprisings in Munich, Vienna, Budapest, Venice, Cracow, Milan, Berlin.

Hungarian independence from Austria is declared.

Piedmontese declare war on Austria.

April: Abolition of serfdom in C Europe.

May: Prussian troops suppress Warsaw uprising.

The revolt in Naples collapses.

June 17: Rising in Prague crushed by Austrian general, Alfred Windischgrätz.

June 22–24: Insurrection in Paris crushed.

July: N Italy reconquered by Austrians.

Oct 31: Vienna bombarded into surrender.

Nov: New liberal constitution comes into force in France.

Dec: Louis-Napoléon Bonaparte elected president of French republic.

King Frederick William IV of Prussia dissolves the national assembly and grants a new constitution.

The Austrian army invades Hungary.

1849 Jan: Budapest surrenders to the Austrians.

Feb: Roman republic proclaimed.

March: German national assembly adopts a constitution that creates a federal state under a hereditary "Emperor of the Germans."

April: Pope Pius IX asks French forces to intervene against Roman republic, defended by Giuseppe Garibaldi.

Hungarians retake Budapest and declare independence from Austria.

May: Prussians suppress a revolt at Dresden.

French National Assembly is dissolved.

July: French troops suppress Roman republic.

Aug: Hungarian nationalists defeated.

Austrians recapture Vienna.

Venice surrenders to the Austrians.

The California Gold Rush

In 1848, gold was discovered at Sutter's Mill on the banks of the Sacramento river in California. Within a year, thousands of "Forty-niners" had flocked to the state, intent on making their fortune. The Gold Rush increased California's population from 14,000 in 1848 to 100,000 by the end of 1849. The majority of migrants were single men; only about half actually worked the gold mines, the rest hoped to profit from supplying the miners. Although most speculators came from the US, many came from Europe, Australia, and South America.

The Taiping rebellion

As Qing China became increasingly beset by a burgeoning population and growing poverty, the Taiping leader Hong Xiuchuan evolved an idiosyncratic version of Christianity, adopted from missionary teaching. He became a leader of a large, disaffected peasant group from the mountainous south of China. As the rebels marched north to Nanjing (*above*) they picked up massive support, capturing the city in 1853.

Although the rebels were turned back when they moved northward to Tianjin, they dominated the rich Yangtze valley. Sporadic conflict between the rebels and government forces continued until 1864, when the revolt was finally suppressed. As many as 50 million people died in the conflict and much of the fertile lower Yangtze valley was laid to waste.

The Crystal Palace

In 1851, the "Great Exhibition of the Works of Industry of all Nations," sponsored by the court and organized by the aristocracy, was a breathtaking celebration of Britain's imperial ascendancy. Exhibits were requested from all over the world, including machinery, crafts, fine arts, and wonders such as the Koh-i-Noor diamond. In all, over 100,000 exhibits were provided by 13,937 exhibitors. The palace of glass that housed the exhibition, designed by Joseph Paxton, was located in London's Hyde Park. The exhibition drew enormous crowds – over 2 million between May 1 and October 15.

ASIA

1851 Taiping rebels break out of the Qing military blockade and begin their march north into China.

1852 The Babis, a Shi'ite sect, are persecuted throughout Persia.

Second Anglo-Burmese War; British occupy Lower Burma.

Mount Everest, named after Sir George Everest, recognized as world's highest peak.

Taipings break the siege of Yong'an and arrive at Guilin, capital of Guangxi province.

1853 **1853** A dispute erupts between French and Russians over the protection of Christianity's holy places in Palestine.

East India Company annexes Nagpur.

India's first railroad, linking Bombay to Thana, opens.

Nian peasant rebellion around Kaifeng in China (–1868).

Small Sword Society captures Shanghai (–1855).

Taiping forces capture Nanjing.

A US squadron under Commodore Matthew Perry arrives off Edo (Tokyo) to demand that Japan opens up trade with the outside world.

1854 The "Red Turban" revolt breaks out in Guangdong province.

US and Japan sign the Treaty of Kanagawa, opening up the Japanese ports of Shimoda and Hakodate to US trade.

Under the Nagasaki Treaty with Japan, the British are awarded "most favored nation" status.

India's first cotton mill is established, in Bombay.

1855 Russians take the town of Kars from the Ottomans after a siege.

Treaty of Peshawar ends 12 years of war between Britain and Afghanistan.

1862 *Jihad* of Yunnan Muslims (–1873).

The Miao people rise up in rebellion in Guizhou province.

Russia and Japan sign a treaty of friendship at Shimoda.

Start of British trade with Siam.

AFRICA

1852 Al-Hajj 'Umar Tal conquers the Senegal valley.

1856 At the Sand river convention, the British recognize the independence of the Transvaal Boers.

Swahili traders from Zanzibar cross the African continent, and reach Benguela.

1853 Britain gives its Gold Coast colony a legislative council.

Livingstone crosses Africa; he encounters and names Victoria Falls.

Heinrich Barth arrives at Timbuktu.

1854 'Abbas, khedive of Egypt, is murdered near Cairo.

At the convention of Bloemfontein the British recognize the independence of the Orange Free State.

Al-Hajj 'Umar Tal, the Muslim preacher from Futa Toro (Senegal), leads a *jihad*, which captures the Bambara kingdom of Kaarta.

1859 Frenchman Ferdinand de Lesseps achieves a 99-year concession to build a canal linking the Red Sea and Mediterranean from Sa'id Pasha of Egypt.

In W Africa, quinine is used to treat malaria for the first time.

1865 **1855** Ras Kassa, who has reunified Gojjam, Begemdir, Tigrai, and Shoa, crowns himself Emperor Tewodros II of Ethiopia.

French annex Walo on the Senegal river.

c.1855 In E Africa, a Nyamwezi trader, Msiri, establishes a permanent inland base, with a capital at Bunyeka.

The Ovimbundu, in the hinterland of Benguela, organize trading caravans that penetrate as far as the upper Zambezi.

EUROPE

1851 Napoleon Bonaparte overthrows the French legislative assembly in a *coup d'etat* and dissolves the constitution. His actions are endorsed in a plebiscite.

An agreement is signed between Denmark and Russia guaranteeing the territorial integrity of Denmark.

Giuseppe Verdi's opera *Rigoletto* is performed for the first time.

Great Exhibition of Industry at Crystal Palace, London.

1852 Louis Napoléon is proclaimed emperor as Napoléon III.

Frenchman, Henri Giffard makes the first flight in a steam-driven balloon.

1853 In Milan, an uprising inspired by the nationalist Giuseppe Mazzini, ends in failure.

Ottomans sign a peace treaty with Prince Danilo of Montenegro.

Britain and France, opposed to Russian demands to take control of the holy places, assemble off the Dardanelles in support of the Ottoman Empire.

Russia invades Moldavia and Wallachia.

Russia refuses Ottoman demands to withdraw from Moldavia and Wallachia. The Ottomans declare war on Russia.

A Russian naval squadron destroys the Ottoman fleet at Sinope, Black Sea.

1854 Britain and France ally with the Ottomans and declare war on Russia.

Crimean War (–1856). Alliance of French, British, and Turks victorious against Russians in Crimea.

1857 ▼

Austrians occupy Moldavia and Wallachia.

In Spain, a liberal revolt ousts the authoritarian regent, Maria Christina. Her daughter, Isabella II, succeeds to the throne.

The papal bull, *Ineffabilis Deus*, proclaims that the Virgin Mary is free of original sin.

1855 British and French troops capture Sebastopol, the Russian naval base in the Black Sea (–1856).

AMERICAS & AUSTRALASIA

1851 José Justo de Urquiza leads a rebellion in Argentina.

An abortive Venezuelan-led uprising in Cuba attempts to overthrow the Spanish.

The former whaler Herman Melville publishes *Moby Dick*.

Americans invent the sewing machine. Isaac Singer's machine becomes the most popular.

Railroad tracks completed from Copiapó to port of Caldera in Chile.

Rich gold deposits found in S Australia; first gold strike at Bathurst, New South Wales.

1859 ▼

In Australia, Victoria is separated from New South Wales and becomes a distinct colony.

1852 José Justo de Urquiza defeats the Argentinian dictator, Juan Manuel de Rosas at the battle of Caseros.

Constitution Act divides New Zealand into six provinces.

1853 Gadsden Purchase (of land by US from Mexico to establish southern railroad to the Pacific).

Slave traffic to Brazil ceases.

Amelia Jenks Bloomer pioneers pants for women in the US.

The island of New Caledonia, off E Australia, is annexed by the French.

1854 Kansas and Nebraska are admitted to the union.

Brazil's first railroad opens between Guanabara Bay and Serra do Mar.

1855 Mexican dictator, Lope de Santa Anna, is ousted by liberals.

Ottawa becomes Canada's capital by royal decree.

The Panama railroad, which links the Atlantic and Pacific, is completed.

Henry Wadsworth Longfellow completes *The Song of Hiawatha*, a narrative poem about a young Ojibway Indian.

New South Wales and Victoria in Australia are granted parliaments.

The Crimean War

1853 **May:** The issue of the holy places causes conflict between Russia and Ottoman Empire.

July: Russia occupies Moldavia and Wallachia.

Sept: The British fleet is ordered to Istanbul.

Oct: Ottoman Empire declares war on Russia. Ottomans cross the Danube into Wallachia.

Nov: A Russian naval squadron destroys the Ottoman fleet at Sinope.

1854 **Jan:** British and French fleets enter the Black Sea to protect Ottoman shipping.

March: Britain and France declare war on Russia.

Sept: The allies land at Eupatoria, W Crimea. They defeat an inferior Russian force at the battle of Alma.

Oct: The allies lay siege to the Russian naval base at Sebastapol.

The allies win a victory over the Russians at Balaklava.

Nov: Russians are defeated by the allies at the battle of Inkerman.

A team of English nurses, led by Florence Nightingale, base themselves at Scutari hospital, Istanbul.

1855 **Jan:** Count Camillo Cavour, the prime minister of Piedmont, takes Piedmont into the Crimean War, alongside the allies.

Sept: Sebastopol, under siege for almost one year, capitulates to the allies.

1856 **March:** Britain, France, Russia, the Ottoman Empire, Piedmont, Austria, and Prussia sign the Treaty of Paris, ending the Crimean War and securing the neutrality of the Black Sea.

Battles in the Crimea

In 1854, Britain and France decided to assist the Ottoman government in its efforts to defend the Danubian principalities against Russian expansion, and to resist Russia's claims of protection over the Ottomans' Christian subjects. An Anglo-French fleet was dispatched to the Crimea. The campaign was largely static, centered on a series of sieges and dogged trench warfare, leading eventually to an allied victory at the siege of Sebastopol in 1855. Although the allies possessed technological superiority, they were hampered by the problems of supplying large armies at a considerable distance. The war was the first to be covered by newspaper reports (with photographs) using new telegraph technology, which revealed the terrible hardships endured by the troops to the home readership.

Charles Darwin

When the English naturalist Charles Darwin (1809–1882) published his famous work *On the Origin of Species by Means of Natural Selection* (1859) he was not the

first to propose the theory of evolution. But his detailed explication of the evolutionary process was revolutionary. Darwin explained that a struggle for existence took place between and within species. Variations gave some organisms advantages in the competition, so only the fittest survived – the process of natural selection. In 1871, in *The Descent of Man*, he argued that humans also evolved by the same principle of natural selection. Darwin's theory caused great controversy; by arguing that the development of organisms was a mechanistic process, Darwin rejected the divine purpose in nature. His theory contradicted the biblical account of creation, a cornerstone of Christian belief.

Garibaldi

Giuseppe Garibaldi (1807–1882) was a Romantic visionary and an Italian patriot. Exiled in 1834 for his part in an earlier nationalist plot, Garibaldi returned to Italy in 1848 to lead the dramatic defense of the newly proclaimed Italian republic. In 1860, Garibaldi embarked on a daring military expedition against the kingdom of the two Sicilies. Evading the Bourbon troops of Napoleon III, he captured Sicily, took Naples and declared a provisional dictatorship over the south. A month later, Garibaldi met King Victor Emmanuel just north of Naples, and – rather than plunging Italy into civil war – relinquished his conquests to the king.

ASIA

1856 Ottoman sultan, Abdul-Medjid, issues a reform edict guaranteeing his Christian subjects security of life and property and the power to exercise freedom of conscience.

Following a Persian invasion of Afghanistan, Britain declares war on Persia.

British annex Oudh, N India.

Chinese officers arrest the entire crew of a British ship, *Arrow*, at Guangzhou, on suspicion of piracy.

Siam (Thailand) signs a treaty with France that guarantees its borders.

1857 British seize the port of Bushire on the Persian Gulf. Persia sues for peace.

Outbreak of Indian Mutiny. Revolt attempts to oust British from India.

1869 ▼

Last Mughal emperor, the puppet Bahadur Shah II, dethroned and exiled by British.

Universities are founded in Calcutta, Madras, and Bombay in India.

France and Britain declare war on China (–1860).

Guangzhou falls to an Anglo-French force after heavy bombardment.

French occupy Da Nang and Saigon (Vietnam).

1858 Queen Victoria is proclaimed ruler of India. The East India Company is abolished.

Treaty of Aigun; China recognizes territory north of the Amur river as Russian.

Treaties of Tianjin provide for aggressive expansion of foreign power in China.

The "White Signal" rebellion is ignited in Guizhou province.

1862 ▼

Japan signs a treaty of commerce and friendship with the US.

1859 Saigon captured by France.

Timor divided between Netherlands and Portugal.

The Taiping rebel army is halted at the gates of Shanghai by British, Indian, and French troops.

Anglo-French forces occupy Beijing.

Sino-French convention ends the war.

AFRICA

1856 Natal is made a British colony.

Western Transvaal Boers adopt a US-style constitution for S African republic, with a capital at Pretoria.

The first rail line in Africa, between Cairo and Alexandria, is inaugurated.

1861 ▼

1857 Al-Hajj 'Umar Tal, the Tukulor Muslim leader, continues his *jihad*, by laying siege to the French fort of Médine on the Senegal river.

French occupy the mountainous region of Kabylie, Algeria.

The bey of Tunisia grants a charter guaranteeing the equal treatment of Muslims and Jews.

1858 English explorers Richard Burton and John Speke reach Lake Tanganyika.

1869 ▼

1859 Livingstone reaches Lake Nyasa.

Work begins on the building of the Suez canal.

EUROPE

1856 Treaty of Paris ends the Crimean War.

Sinn Féin founded in Ireland.

At Neanderthal, near Düsseldorf, the remains of a *homo sapiens*, probably dating from 70,000 years BP, are discovered.

Bessemer invents process for mass production of steel.

1857 Austrians evacuate Moldavia and Wallachia, which remain under Ottoman suzerainty.

Charles Baudelaire begins the Symbolist movement in France with his collection of poems, *Les Fleurs du Mal*.

1858 Count Cavour and Napoleon III sign the agreement of Plombières, an alliance against Austria.

Felice Orsini, an Italian republican, attempts to assassinate Napoleon III. He is captured and guillotined.

Czar Alexander II gives orders for serfs working on the imperial lands to be freed.

Lionel de Rothschild becomes the first Jew to be admitted as an MP to the House of Commons.

Bernadette Soubirous experiences a vision of the Virgin Mary at Lourdes, S France.

1859 Austrian troops invade Piedmont. France declares war on Austria.

French and Piedmontese defeat Austrians at battles of Magenta and Solferino.

France and Austria agree peace terms at Villafranca. Lombardy is ceded to Piedmont.

Nationalist rebellions breakout in Tuscany, Modena, Parma, Ravenna, Ferrara, and Bologna.

The publication of Charles Darwin's *On the Origin of Species by Means of Natural Selection*, which advances the theory of evolution, causes a stir in London.

1860 France signs a treaty with Piedmont at Turin. Piedmont is to annex C Italy, while France is promised Nice and Savoy.

W Garibaldi, the nationalist leader, and his "Thousand" conquer Sicily and Naples.

Margin markers: 1861, 1861, 1871

AMERICAS & AUSTRALASIA

1856 First commercial refrigeration in the US; refined technique developed in Australia by 1859.

1857 In New York City there is panic in the US stock market when the Ohio Life Insurance and Trust Company, one of US's biggest financial houses, collapses.

In New York, the first passenger elevator, invented by Elisha Otis, is installed in a department store.

In Mexico, the adoption of a federal constitution leads to a civil war between conservatives and liberals.

1858 Gold discovered on Fraser river, NW Canada.

King Movement demands Maori state and opposes further land sales in New Zealand.

The liberal government of Mexico, led by Benito Juárez, establishes a capital at Vera Cruz.

The first transatlantic cable, running from the US to Britain via Newfoundland, is laid.

1859 John Brown, a fanatical supporter of the abolition of slavery, is hanged in Virginia for treason, and conspiring with slaves.

First oil well is drilled in Pennsylvania.

Queensland in Australia is established as a separate colony, with its capital at Brisbane.

Naturalist Henry Bates returns to England with 8,000 insects new to science after 11 years in Amazon region.

1860 British government transfers control of Indian affairs to Canada.

Ecuador's president, theocrat Garcia Moreno, launches ambitious program of public works.

American William Walker, the one-time ruler of Nicaragua, is executed by a firing squad.

Thousands of new immigrants have flocked to Victoria, Australia, in the grip of gold fever.

Settler population in New Zealand over 100,000; Europeans outnumber Maori.

Margin markers: 1861, 1861

British troops rush to quell the revolt at Umballa in 1859.

The Revolt of 1857–1859

In India, mounting British arrogance had provoked discontent amongst the troops. In 1857, rumors that rifle cartridges were coated with pork and other animal fat – deeply offensive to both Hindus and Muslims – led to mutiny. The mutineers, joined by disgruntled peasants in revolt against their exploitative local rulers, captured Delhi, "restored" the aging Mughal emperor, and slaughtered British residents of Delhi, Kanpur, and Lucknow.

Although the British lost control of much of the Ganges heartland, the mutiny ultimately failed because it lacked a coordinated command structure. The British retaliations were brutal, and a gulf opened between rulers and ruled, completing the transformation of Britain into an occupying colonial power.

The Exploration of Australia

Over the course of the 19th century, the interior of Australia was revealed to European settlers by a series of hardy intrepid explorers. Newly discovered land answered the colonists' growing need for pastureland, and overland routes were established for drovers, stockmen, and traders

1802	Flinders circummnavigates Australia (–1803).
1813	Gregory Blaxland, William Lawson, and Willliam Wentworth cross the Blue Mountains – the beginning of overland exploration.
1817	Phillip Parker King explores the Australian coast on five voyages (–1822).
1824	Hamilton Hume and William Howell travel south from Lake George to Port Phillip.
1828	Charles Sturt traces sections of the Macquarie, Darling, Murrumbidgee, Lachlan and Murray rivers (–1830).
1841	Edward Eyre crosses the Nullarbor Plain.
1848	Edmund Kennedy follows the Great Divide from Rockingham Bay to Cape York peninsula.
1860	Robert Burke and William Wills cross Australia from south to north. Of the four who set out from Cooper's Creek, only one survives.
1862	In a series of expeditions, starting in 1858, John Stuart achieves a south to north crossing.
1870	Alexander Forrest explores from Port Hedland north to the Fitzroy river.
1872	Ernest Giles explores the desert areas of C and W Australia (–1876).
1873	Peter Warburton crosses the Great Sandy Desert.

Abraham Lincoln

The 16th president of

the US, Abraham Lincoln was born in the Kentucky backwoods of pioneer stock. He had virtually no formal education, but developed an early passion for reading. When his family migrated to Illinois, he studied law, eventually becoming a successful and respected prairie lawyer. After serving in the Illinois state legislature for six years, Lincoln became involved in national politics, rising through the ranks of the newly formed Republican party to become presidential candidate in 1860.

His inauguration as president in 1861 was soon followed by the southern attack on Fort Sumter. As an able and effective war leader, Lincoln put the preservation of the union above abolitionist demands. But in 1863, he issued his Emancipation Proclamation, which abolished slavery in the southern states. Lincoln, a hugely popular and respected president, was elected for a second term in 1864, but he was assassinated by John Wilks Booth, an outspoken advocate of slavery, on April 14, 1865.

Ulysses S. Grant

Commander of the Union forces

in the American Civil War and subsequently president of the US (1868–76), Grant was greatly admired by Lincoln for his fighting qualities. He is remembered especially for his victories along the Mississippi Valley, the bloodbath at Shiloh (April 1862), and the crucial capture of Vicksburg (July 1863). He gained rapid promotion and, when appointed General-in-Chief in 1864, he devised the overall strategy that led to the Confederate surrender the following year.

ASIA

1861 A commercial treaty is signed between Prussia and China.

Following the death of the emperor, Xianfeng and the accession of Tongzhi, the two empresses dowager, Ci'an and Cixi, become regents.

1862 Yunnan Muslims attack the city of Xi'an, China.

Taiping rebels once again attack Shanghai.

In Japan, an imperial decree announces the expulsion of foreigners.

A British merchant named Richardson is killed in a *samurai* attack in Yokohama.

1863 Northwest uprising in Uighur domains of Qing empire; largest Muslim *jihad* in E Asia (–1873).

Satyendra Nath Tagore is the first Indian to enter the Indian Civil Service.

Taiping rebels hand over their stronghold, Suzhou, to the Qing commander, and are executed– against the terms of their surrender.

1867 ▽ French establish protectorate over Cambodia.

A British naval squadron bombards Kagoshima, Japan, in reprisal for the murder of Richardson in 1862.

1864 Taiping ruler, Hong Xiuchuan, kills himself. Nanjing, held by Taiping rebels, falls to imperial forces.

Muslim rebellions break out in Kucha and Urumchi, in Chinese Turkestan.

British, French, Dutch, and US navies bombard Japanese defenses on the straits of Shimonoseki and Kagoshima, forcing Japan to reopen to foreign trade.

1887 ▽ **1865** Cotton boom in India.

1868 ▽ The revolt of the "night-bird bandits" (salt smugglers) breaks out in Gangzhou, Yangshan, Bazhou, and other parts of Zhili province, China.

1867 ▽ Qing troops inflict a decisive defeat on the Miao rebels.

1868 ▽ Muslims forces capture Kashgar. Buzurg Khan declares himself king of Kashgar.

Russians occupy Chinese Turkestan.

Qing forces take Qianxi from the White Signal sect.

The White Signal sect rebels take Guangshun and Dingfan.

AFRICA

1861 British establish a protectorate over the port of Lagos, Nigeria.

Radama II succeeds to the throne of Madagascar, and attempts to impose a policy of westernization. He is opposed by a small governing elite.

Tukulor leader, Al-Hajj 'Umar Tal, destroys and occupies the Bambara kingdom of Segu.

1862 Al-Hajj 'Umar Tal takes the Peul kingdom of Masina, E Africa.

Napoleon III purchases Obock on the African coast of the Gulf of Aden.

1863 Al-Hajj 'Umar Tal clashes with French in Senegal valley. He captures Timbuktu and founds Tukulor empire.

J. H. Speke and J. Grant establish that Lake Victoria is the source of the Nile.

French establish a protectorate over the kingdom of Porto Novo in Dahomey.

1866 ▽ Mohammad Ali's grandson, Isma'il, succeeds to the pashalik of Egypt, and upgrades his title to khedive.

1864 Al-Hajj 'Umar Tal is killed at Masina, W Africa, where he is suppressing a Fulani rebellion.

The Lozi people of the upper Zambezi flood plain revolt against the rule of the Kololo, migrants from the south.

Former slave Samuel Crowther becomes the first black African Anglican bishop of the Niger river area.

1865 Outbreak of war between the Orange Free State and the Basuto (Sotho) (–1866).

1868 ▽ Ethiopian emperor Tewodros II fails to capture the Amharic state of Shoa.

Samory Touré, the leader of the Mandinka of the upper Niger basin, begins to conquer surrounding Dyula states.

c.1865 Chikunda ivory traders of the lower Zambezi are raiding the middle Zambezi valley, taking ivory and slaves by force.

French have established a narrow colony on the Senegal river, extending as far east as Medina.

1870 ▽ Tippu Tip, Swahili trader from C Africa, establishes himself at Nyangwe and Kasongo on the upper Zaire river. He maintains direct contact through Ujiji and Tabora to Zanzibar.

EUROPE

1861 King Victor Emmanuel II of Sardinia is proclaimed king of Italy, following the capture of Gaeta by Piedmontese troops.

 1866

Czar Alexander II emancipates Russia's 20 million serfs.

English philosopher, John Stuart Mill, publishes *Utilitarianism*.

The European powers recognize the principality of Romania (Moldavia and Wallachia).

The vélocipède, a two-wheeled bicycle, is invented in France.

1862 Otto von Bismarck is prime minister of Prussia.

 1867

Garibaldi lands in S Italy, with an army which he hopes will take over the papal states. Pope Pius IX has refused to recognize the new Italian state.

Victor Hugo's novel *Les Misérables* is enthusiastically received in Paris.

1863 King Frederick VII incorporates Schleswig into Denmark.

Following the Danish annexation of Schleswig, Saxon and Hanoverian forces move into Holstein.

Polish nationalists rise up in revolt against Russian rule.

Bismarck signs the convention of Alvensleben with Russia; provision is made for reciprocal military assistance against the Polish rebels.

In Russia, academic freedom is restored to the universities.

Britain cedes the Ionian islands to Greece.

Construction of London Underground begins.

Edouard Manet's painting *Déjeuner sur l'Herbe*, is rejected by the Salon des Refusés in Paris, which claims that it is indecent.

1864 A multilateral agreement on the Red Cross is signed at the Geneva convention.

The peace of Vienna: Denmark gives up Schleswig, Holstein, and Lauenburg.

 1867 **1865** In Ireland, English authorities arrest Fenian leaders who are planning an uprising.

Gregor Mendel, an Austrian monk, formulates the laws of genetic inheritance.

AMERICAS & AUSTRALASIA

1861 Slave states cede from the union, forming the Confederate states of America.

US civil war (–1865).

Abraham Lincoln elected president of the US.

Apache uprisings in SW US (–1863).

British, French, and Spanish troops move in to Vera Cruz following Mexican president Benito Juarez's declaration of a two-year moratorium on the payment of foreign debts.

García Moreno establishes theocratic rule in Ecuador.

At Lambing Flat, Australia, white miners burn camps of 3,000 Chinese miners.

Gold discovered in New Zealand's Otago province.

A truce ends fighting between Maoris and British settlers.

1862 Second Maori War.

 1866 Sioux uprisings in Minnesota and North Dakota (–1864).

1863 Mexican troops are forced to surrender Puebla, following the arrival of French reinforcements.

 1867 Austrian archduke Maximilian is appointed emperor of Mexico.

Navajo War in Arizona and New Mexico (–1866).

President Lincoln declares the last Thursday in November a national holiday of thanksgiving.

1864 Paraguayan War; catastrophic defeat of Paraguay by Brazil, Argentina, and Uruguay (–1870).

End of the American Civil War. Slavery is abolished.

President Lincoln is killed by an assassin's bullet.

Fighting stops between the British and the Kingitanga – a Maori unity movement seeking to prevent individual chiefs from selling land.

The practice of transporting criminals to Australia is abolished.

Wellington is established as the capital of New Zealand.

c.1865 Some 14,000 British troops deployed in New Zealand.

The American Civil War (1861–65)

1861 April 12: Fort Sumter shelled by confederate troops.
April 15: President Lincoln issues call for troops.
April 19: Lincoln proclaims blockade of south.
1862 April 6–7: Battle of Shiloh: heavy casualties on both sides.
April 16: Start of draft in confederate states.
May 1: Union fleet captures New Orleans.
Sept 22: Preliminary Emancipation Proclamation issued.
Dec 13: Severe union defeat at Fredericksburg.
1863 Jan 1: Emancipation Proclamation frees slaves in confederate states in the US.
March 3: Draft law passed in north.
May: Grant's army defeats confederates in Mississippi and starts to besiege Vicksburg.
July 1–3: Confederate defeat at battle of Gettysburg.
July 4: Vicksburg captured by union troops.
19 Nov: Gettysburg Address.
1864 Sept 2: Sherman's troops enter Atlanta.
Nov 5: Sherman begins "march to the sea."
Dec 15–16: Battle of Nashville destroys western confederate army.

Conflict in the US

By 1860, the US was composed of 18 "free" states, mainly in the north, and 15 "slave" states, mainly in the south. The dispute over slavery had brought the US to breaking point. When the southern states decided that their interests were no longer served by the union, seven states seceded, forming the Confederate states of America. On April 12, 1861, they fired the first shots on on Fort Sumter, Virginia, plunging the US into civil war.

The north, with its industrial and demographic superiority and sea power, possessed great advantages, but the Confederates fought with dogged persistence for four years. The northern policy of attrition finally paid off, with General Sherman's "march to the sea" through Georgia in 1864. At the end of the war, the south was devastated, and half its army lay dead. The union was preserved and slavery was abolished.

Battle weary Union soldiers take a break in the trenches following the fighting at Petersburg, Virginia 1865.

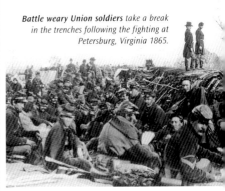

1861–1865 369

Kaiser William I

A professional soldier, William I (1797–1888) was a natural conservative, dedicated to the Prussian army and the tradition of the monarchy. When, shortly after his accession in 1861, he insisted on compulsory military conscription for a three-year term, he precipitated a crisis that would ultimately lead to German unification. The liberal lower chamber rejected his bill, and he enlisted the help of Otto von Bismarck, his newly appointed prime minister.

Bismarck was determined to create a new North German Confederation, which excluded Austria. He achieved this goal through brilliant use of limited war; the Schleswig–Holstein crisis precipitated war with Austria, and Prussia triumphed. Following Prussia's equally decisive victory in the Franco-Prussian war of 1870–71, Bismarck arranged for the German Confederation to admit the southern states. Germany was united, and William I was proclaimed emperor (kaiser).

Sovereign States' Formation (1815–1914)

1829	Kingdom of Greece
1830	Kingdom of Belgium
1860	Kingdom of Italy
1866	Principality of Liechtenstein
1871	Empire of Germany
1877	Kingdom of Romania
1878	Kingdom of Bulgaria
1890	Grand duchy of Luxembourg
1905	Kingdom of Norway
1910	Republic of Portugal (kingdom of Portugal, 1640)
1913	Republic of Albania

ASIA

1867 A group of intellectuals, the Young Turks, form a secret society, with the aim of promoting democracy in the Ottoman Empire.

1874 French protectorate established in Cochin China.

1872 Imperial Qing forces capture a strong-hold of the Miao rebels near Wining.

The last shogun, Tokugawa Keiki, resigns in favor of the Meiji emperor, Mutsuhito.

1871 **1868** Suppression of Muslim states of Bukhara and Samarkand by Russia (–1870).

Ya'qub Beg, leader of the independent Muslim state of Kashgaria, opens relations with Britain and Russia.

British campaigns to control tribes on India's NW frontier.

Eastern Nian rebels are annihilated by imperial forces near Yangzhou.

Western Nian rebels are wiped out by Qing troops in Shandong province.

The revolt of the "night-bird bandits" is put down.

British naval forces capture China's first naval steamship, the Tianji.

Boshin War in Japan; Tokugawa Bakufu defeated by modernizing imperialists (–1869).

Edo is renamed Tokyo, and the new imperial era is named Meiji.

1869 Mirza Asadulla ("Ghalib"), the last poet laureate of the Mughal emperors, dies.

The Japanese emperor moves from Kyoto to Tokyo.

1873 **1870** All the Muslim rebels of N China now fight under Ya'qub Beg's banner.

Tianjin massacre. A Chinese mob attacks a Roman Catholic orphanage in Tianjin; 24 foreigners are killed.

Japan's first telegraph line is laid, between Tokyo and Yokohama.

AFRICA

1866 The Ottoman sultan grants the rights of primogeniture to Isma'il, khedive of Egypt.

Copper trader Msiri establishes trading principality in Central Africa.

1867 Diamonds found at Kimberley, north of Cape Colony, S Africa.

1868 Ethiopian emperor Tewodros II is defeated by the British at the battle of Aroge, which follows a diplomatic dispute, and commits suicide.

In W Africa, the Fante confederation, an alliance of Fante rulers, is established to provide for defense and to create a modern state.

Moshoeshoe, the ruler of the Sotho kingdom, asks for British annexation in order to avoid complete annihilation by the Boers.

King Mswati, the founder of the state of Swaziland, dies.

1871 **1869** Discovery of "Star of South Africa" diamond sets off diamond rush.

The Suez Canal is opened, linking the Mediterranean and the Red Sea.

Gold is found at Tati and Botswana. Thousands of prospectors arrive in S Africa.

1875 **1870** Swahili slave trader, Tippu Tib, sets himself up as ruler west of Lake Tanganyika.

EUROPE

1866 Austro-Prussian War. Prussia annexes Holstein, which came under Austrian rule in 1865. Conflict between Prussia and Austria escalates.

Austria forced to cede Venetia.

Prussia dissolves the German Confederation, and invades Saxony, Hanover, and Hesse.

Prussia's ally, Italy, declares war on Austria, but Italian forces are defeated at the battle of Custoza.

Prussian troops defeat Austrians in Sadowa, Bohemia.

Following an attempt on his life, Czar Alexander II slows down his program of westernization.

Christians on the island of Crete rebel against Ottoman rule.

Fyodor Dostoyevsky publishes *Crime and Punishment*, to instant acclaim.

1867 Dual monarchy of Austria–Hungary established.

Bismarck becomes chancellor of the North German Confederation.

Garibaldi launches a march on Rome. He is defeated by papal and French troops at the battle of Mentana, and captured.

The Great Powers guarantee the independence and neutrality of Luxembourg.

The Fenian brotherhood, an Irish republican movement, launch a bombing campaign in London.

Publication of Marx's *Das Kapital*, an analysis of the economic injustices of the capitalist system.

 1868 Queen Isabella II of Spain is forced to flee to France after a liberal uprising. General Francisco Serrano becomes regent.

1869 The great Russian novelist, Count Leo Tolstoy, completes *War and Peace*.

1870 Italian troops enter Rome and expel the papal troops.

France declares war on Prussia. Paris is besieged.

Following French defeats at Gravelotte and Sedan, Napoleon III capitulates to the Prussians.

In Paris a republic is proclaimed, and a government of national defense formed.

AMERICAS & AUSTRALASIA

1866 First Sioux War (–1876).

Railroad Act permits appropriation of Native American lands by railroad companies.

Peru declares war on Spain; forms an alliance with President José Joaquín Pérez of Chile.

1867 US purchases Alaska from Russia for $7.2 million.

First cattle drives to Kansas.

French troops leave Mexico. The emperor, Maximilian is seized by republican supporters and executed; Benito Juárez becomes president.

Brazilian troops sack the Paraguayan capital of Asunción.

Canada becomes a British dominion.

The first practical typewriter is invented in the US by Christopher Latham Sholes.

 1868 Oglala Sioux Indians sign a peace treaty with General Sherman; this brings two years of conflict between the Sioux and gold miners to an end.

Uprising against Spanish rule in Cuba.

Little Women by Louisa May Alcott is a bestseller.

1869 Women in the US territory of Wyoming are given the vote.

A French–Indian rebellion in W Canada. A provisional government is established at Fort Garry (Winnipeg).

Transcontinental Union-Pacific railroad completed in the US.

15th amendment gives vote to freed slaves in the US.

Last convict ship to arrive in Australia delivers cargo in Fremantle.

Third Maori rebellion ends with the defeat of the guerrilla leader Titokowaru.

1870 First shipload of lepers transported to Kalaupapa peninsula, Molokai, and Hawaii.

c.1870 Germans start to buy up large tracts of W Samoa.

European investment and immigration into Argentina starts to accelerate.

The Suez Canal

In 1859, the French-owned Suez Canal Company began construction of a canal to link the Mediterranean to the Red Sea. In the 1860s, the Egyptian economy was booming, largely because shortages caused by the US civil war created an unprecedented demand for cotton. But decline followed the boom, and Egypt's indebtedness to Europe began to tell. When the Suez Canal opened in 1869, Egypt's trade was dominated by European shipping. In 1876, Ismail, the khedive, admitted that his country was bankrupt and France and Britain took over "dual control" of Egypt's finances.

Victorian London

In the 19th century, London underwent a remarkable population explosion: from one million in 1801 to seven million in 1911. Social researcher Charles Booth estimated that in the 1890s, 30 percent of Londoners were living below the poverty line. Many of the poorest people lived in the pre-Victorian houses of the East End, which had decayed into over-crowded, insanitary slums. London was a city of migrants: from 1841–71 almost a million people migrated there from the countryside. After the 1848 potato famine, Irish migrants flocked to London – by 1861 there were 178,000 Irish in the city and from the 1870s onward, many Jews also arrived, fleeing persecution in Eastern Europe.

In 1872, the French artist Gustav Doré engraved a series of scenes from the everyday life of London. His work was used as evidence in government reports on urban conditions.

Impressionism

Renoir's La Loge. *His interest in the human figure set him apart from the other Impressionists.*

In the late 19th century, several French artists rejected a frozen, accurate rendering of reality in favor of a subjective view, capturing by brushstrokes and pigments the immediate impression of visual surfaces and spaces, bathed in color and light. Claude Monet's painting: *Lever du Soleil* (1873) inspired a hostile critic to name the new style "Impressionism." The Impressionists, including Monet, Renoir, Pissarro, and Manet, were interested in the selectiveness of the human eye, the workings of light, and the complexity of artistic sensibility. At first, their work was universally condemned. Gradually, it came to be accepted that it was their innovative view that had given a vital impetus to modern art.

Art (1848–1890)

1848	William Holman Hunt, John E. Millais, and Dante G. Rossetti found the Pre-Raphaelite brotherhood.
1852	Hunt: *The Light of the World.* Millais: *Ophelia.*
1857	Millet: *The Gleaners.*
1862	Ingres: *Bain Turque.*
1863	Manet: *Le Déjeuner sur l'Herbe.* The Salon de Refusés, Paris.
1866	Degas begins to paint his ballet scenes.
1867	Cézanne: *Rape.* Paris World Fair introduces Japanese art to the west.
1868	Degas: *L'Orchestre.*
1869	Manet: *The Balcony.*
1872	Cézanne and Pissarro at Auvers-sur-Oise. Whistler: *The Artist's Mother.*
1874	First impressionist exhibition, Paris. Renoir: *La Loge.*
1875	Monet: *Boating at Argenteuil.*
1877	Winslow Homer: *The Cotton Pickers.* Rodin: *The Age of Bronze,* sculpture.
1878	William Morris: *The decorative arts.*
1879	Renoir: *Mme. Charpentier and Her Children.*
1880	Cézanne: *Château de Medan.* Pissarro: *The Outer Boulevards.* Renoir: *Place Clichy.* Rodin: *The Thinker,* sculpture.
1881	Monet: *Sunshine and Snow.*
1882	Manet: *Bar aux Folies-Bergère.*
1883	Cézanne: *Rocky Landscape.*
1884	Seurat: *Une Baignade, Asnières.*
1886	John Singer Sargent: *Carnation, Lily, Lily, Rose.* Seurat: *Sunday Afternoon on the Grande Jatte.*
1887	Van Gogh: *Moulin de la Galette.*
1888	Van Gogh: *Yellow Chair.* Toulouse-Lautrec: *Place Clichy.*

1871–1875

ASIA

1871 Russian troops occupy the Ili area of Chinese Turkestan.

London is connected with Shanghai by undersea electric cable.

A new system of Japanese currency is introduced, based on the yen.

1890

Abolition of feudalism in Japan; prefectures are created, education becomes compulsory, and a modern postal system is introduced.

1872 Lord Mayo, the viceroy of India, is murdered by a Muslim nationalist while visiting a penal colony on the Andaman Islands.

The Miao rebellion in China is finally suppressed with the capture of its main leader, Zhang Xiumei.

Du Wenxiu, the leader of the Muslim rebellion in Yunnan, surrenders to Qing troops and is executed.

1873 Russians capture the capital of the khanate of Khiva, Uzbekistan.

Famine in Bengal.

Ya'qub Beg of Kashgaria receives a British envoy.

Massacre of Muslims at Dali, N China, by Qing forces. Muslim rebellions are now effectively defeated.

The Chinese emperor receives ministers from the US, Britain, Russia, Holland, France, and Japan.

The imperial army of Japan is reorganized and modernized on European lines.

Dutch attack on Achin sultanate in Sumatra.

1877

1874 Ya'qub Beg yields to the Russians, who are now masters of all Turkestan.

A treaty acknowledges the French protectorate over Cochin China.

1881

French protectorate established in Annam.

1875 Anglo-Chinese tensions are heightened when a British legation official is murdered near the Burmese border by native bandits.

AFRICA

1871 Cape Colony takes over the government of Basutoland (Lesotho).

Britain annexes the diamond region of Kimberley, S Africa.

Discovery of gold in Transvaal.

US reporter Henry Morton Stanley tracks down Britain's most famous explorer, David Livingstone, at Ujiji, C Africa. He greets him with the famous words "Dr Livingstone, I presume?"

1872 Cape Colony granted full self-government.

British take over the Dutch forts in Gold Coast (Ghana).

1873 Anglo-Ashanti War (–1874). Ashanti forces defeat the British at Assin Nyankumasi in the Gold Coast.

Scottish missionary and explorer, David Livingstone, who discovered Victoria Falls and Lake Nyasa, dies near Lake Bangweulu (Zambia).

British persuade the sultan of Zanzibar to close the island's slave market.

1874 Following a defeat by the British, the king of Ashanti signs a peace treaty.

1884

General Charles Gordon becomes governor-general of Sudan. He conquers Darfur on behalf of the khedive of Egypt.

1887

1875 Tippu Tib establishes trading principality.

Stanley confirms Nile source as Ripon Falls.

Britain buys Suez Canal Company shares.

c.1875 Scottish missionaries are established in the region of modern Malawi, aided by Basotho Christians from S Africa.

1871 King Victor Emmanuel assures the pope that the Vatican remains outside Italian jurisdiction.

The Paris Commune is declared. It is suppressed after two months.

Paris surrenders to Prussian troops. France and Prussia sign a peace treaty at Versailles. France surrenders all of Alsace, and most of Lorraine, to Prussia.

William I of Prussia is declared German emperor (kaiser) at Versailles.

Charles Darwin publishes *The Descent of Man*, which expounds his theory of natural selection.

1880
1872 Prussian *Kulturkampf* against the Catholic church; a law is promulgated banning all religious assemblies.

The League of Three Emperors unites Tsar Alexander, Kaiser William, and Emperor Franz Joseph.

German philosopher, Friedrich Nietzsche publishes *The Birth of Tragedy*.

1873 King Amadeus of Spain abdicates, and the first Spanish republic is proclaimed.

1874 A military coup puts Marshal Francisco Serrano back in power in Spain for 11 months; the infant Don Alfonso is then declared king of Spain.

In Britain, the Factory Act limits the working week to 56.5 hours.

A group of Parisian artists, rejected by the Salon, exhibit their works independently: the "Impressionists" include Claude Monet, Pierre Auguste Renoir, Camille Pissarro, Edgar Degas, and Paul Cézanne.

1875 France adopts a republican constitution.

The peasants of Bosnia and Herzegovina rebel against the Ottomans.

Bulgarian patriots revolt against the Ottomans in Stara Zagora.

The composer Georges Bizet dies after the "failure" of his opera, *Carmen*.

1871 Start of Apache wars in N America.

The National Association of Professional Baseball Players is founded.

1872 Modoc War in Oregon and California.

William "Boss" Tweed, the former head of Tammany Hall, New York City's democratic organization, is jailed for fraud and corruption.

German Wilhelm Reiss scales Cotopaxi, which Humboldt had pronounced unclimbable.

An overland telegraph line links S Australia with Darwin in the north.

1873 A peace treaty is signed at La Paz fixing the frontier between Chile and Argentina along the ridge of the Andes *cordillera*.

Prince William Lunalilo becomes the first elected monarch of Hawaii.

Creation of the Northwest Mounted Police (the Mounties) in Canada.

1874 Red River War in S plains: Comanches, Kiowas, and Cheyennes, led by Quanah Parker, unite against white settlers.

Britain annexes the Fiji Islands. Indian sugarcane workers arrive in Fiji.

1875 New Zealand is brought under one government following the abolition of provincial councils.

The Ruhr

Industrialization came rapidly to Germany. In 1871, it was still largely an agricultural country, but by 1914 there were 30 cities in which the population exceeded 100,000. In the 1840s, Alfred Krupp set up an armaments works in Essen, a small village in the Ruhr valley, west Germany. Demand for his cast steel armaments soon flooded in from Prussia and Russia, and in the 1870s, his factory complex was massively extended.

In 1871, August Thyssen recognized the vast potential of the Ruhr for iron and steel. He established the company Thyssen & Co., and by 1914 was producing 1 million tons of iron and steel a year. In just a generation, the Ruhr region had become the powerhouse of Europe.

Cape Colony mines

The discovery of gold and diamonds in South Africa's interior marked a turning point in the region's history. In 1867, when diamond fields were discovered in British Cape Colony (Kimberley), thousands of people from all over Africa, and miners and speculators from Europe, America, and Australia, converged there. From the outset, whites, who had the resources, capital, and backing of British political power, dominated Africa's mineral wealth. Initially, the mines were exploited by individual "diggers," but by the late 1870s, large companies moved in, with expensive steam machinery. By 1889 one company, De Beers, had established a complete monopoly over the diamond mines.

The pioneer trail

The first settlers in the American West were soon followed by reinforcements, making their arduous way on stagecoaches, covered wagons, and, from 1869, the railroad. Life on the plains of the Midwest was harsh. Settlers built their own houses, often of turf and timber – all that was available. Winters were severe, and cultivating the land with minimal equipment was backbreaking work. But, to the white population of the eastern states, the West was presented as a land of limitless opportunity. As the frontier moved further westward, the struggle between white settlers and native Americans grew more intense. On the plains, the economic base of Indian culture was finally broken when the buffalo herd was cut in two by the railroad; by the 1870s, hunters had wiped out the buffalo.

Indian Wars and Submission (1860–1890)

1860	Paiute war in Nevada.
1861	Apache uprisings in the Southwest.
1862	Homestead Act opens Indian land in Kansas and Nebraska to settlers.
	Sioux uprising in Minnesota and N Dakota.
1863	39 Sioux are hanged; 247 imprisoned in Iowa.
	Navajo war begins in Arizona and New Mexico.
1864	Sand Creek massacre; militiamen kill 300 Cheyenne women and children.
	8,000 Navajos surrender; many forced 300 miles (483 km) east to Bosque Redondo, near Fort Sumner – "the long walk."
1866	1,300 Sioux exiled to Missouri river reservation at Crow Creek.
1868	Red River Métis (part Indian, part Catholic) resist plans to establish a province of Manitoba.
	14th amendment denies Indians the right to vote in the US.
1870	Métis leader, Louis Riel, flees to Ojibwa protection at Red Lake, Minnesota.
1872	Modoc War (–1873) in California and Oregon; ends in the exile of Modocs to a reservation.
1874	Red River Indian War in southern plains. Comanches, Kiowas, and Cheyennes unite.
1876	Sioux, Cheyennes, and Araphoes fight to defend their lands in Black Hills, S Dakota, following arrival of gold prospectors.
	Sioux and Cheyenne victory at battle of Little Bighorn, Montana. Followed by military suppression.
1877	Chief Joseph and the Nez Percé refuse to move to Idaho. Chief Joseph surrenders at Bear Paw Mountain, Montana.
1885	Métis recall Riel, who sets up a provisional government at Batoche. After skirmishes with troops, Riel and 8 Indians are hanged.
1886	Apache chief Geronimo, who has long outwitted the army, is captured in Mexico and imprisoned at St. Augustine, Florida.
1890	US troops massacre 350 Sioux at Wounded Knee

1876–1880

ASIA

1876 Midhat Pasha, the Ottoman grand vizier, introduces a liberal constitution.

Queen Victoria declared empress of India, and a viceroy appointed as her representative.

1882
Japan recognizes Korean independence.

1877 Russians attack and capture the Ottoman fortress of Kars, Caucasus.

Ya'qub Beg, who founded the state of Kashgaria, is murdered. The Chinese embark on the reconquest of Chinese Turkestan.

Famine in N China leaves at least 10 million dead (–1879).

Satsuma rebellion in Japan, led by reformer Saigo Takamori, in defense of traditional values.

1878 Russian forces close in on Istanbul. A British fleet is sent in support of the faltering Ottoman Empire.

Qing conquest of Chinese Turkestan is complete.

Second Afghan War (–1879); British invade Afghanistan, which has come under Russian influence.

1879 By the Treaty of Gandamak, the emir of Afghanistan hands over territories to the British, and agrees to establish diplomatic relations.

The British envoy in Kabul is murdered, disrupting the peace agreement. British force the emir to flee the city.

Japanese invade the kingdom of the Liuqiu (Ryukyu Islands).

1880 British are besieged at Kandahar by Ayub Khan, son of the deposed emir. The garrison is liberated by British troops from Kabul.

The accession of the pro-British Abdur Rahman Khan to the throne of Afghanistan ends the conflict with Britain.

AFRICA

1876 Ethiopians inflict two defeats on the Egyptians near Gura, forcing Egypt to relinquish claims to the whole Nile basin up to Lake Victoria.

Isma'il, khedive of Egypt, is forced to admit that his country is bankrupt.

Stanley travels down the Congo to the Atlantic (–1877).

1877 Britain annexes the S African republic (Transvaal), claiming it is unable to defend itself against its black neighbors.

British at war with the Xhosa, S Africa (–1878). The Xhosa are left with a reserve of land east of the Kei river.

1885
1878 Queen Ranavalona II of Madagascar seizes lands belonging to the French consul and occupies the Sambirano coast, under French protection.

1879 First Zulu War with British, who are crushed at Isandhlwana but win at Ulundi, defeating Zulus.

1882
Britain deposes Isma'il, khedive of Egypt, and puts a puppet ruler, Taufiq, in his place (–1892).

French conquest of Algeria is finally complete.

The White Fathers, a missionary group, arrive in Entebbe, Uganda.

1880 White Boers have appropriated most habitable land in Cape Colony.

1881
Boers declare war on the British and drive them out of the Transvaal.

1904
The Madrid conference guarantees all European powers in Morocco the status of most-favored nation, thus establishing an open-door policy.

Afro-French explorer Pierre de Brazza-Savorgnan makes a treaty with the Kongo kingdom, founding Brazzaville as the basis for a French colony.

c.1880 Mandinka leader Samory extends his conquests to include the Bure goldfields and the upper Niger valley.

EUROPE

1876 Ottomans brutally suppress a rebellion in Bulgaria.

Serbia and Montenegro declare war on the Ottomans.

Ottomans defeat the Serbs at Aleksinac. Under Russian pressure, an armistice is agreed.

The internal-combustion engine constructed by Nikolaus Otto.

1877 When the Ottomans refuse to introduce reforms that will benefit their Christian subjects, Russia declares war on Turkey.

Romania declares its independence, joining Russian troops to lay siege to Ottomans in the Bulgarian town of Plevna.

French inventor, Georges Leclanché makes an electric battery.

1878 Treaty of San Stefano negotiated by Russia and Turkey; independence of Serbia, Montenegro, and Romania recognized.

Congress of Berlin alters terms of San Stefano Treaty; Bulgaria becomes autonomous principality within Ottoman Empire.

Bismarck passes harsh antisocialist laws.

Russians take Adrianople. A British fleet arrives, at the sultan's request, in Istanbul.

Britain is allowed to occupy Cyprus in return for protecting the Ottoman Empire against Russian advances.

The Salvation Army is founded by a former Methodist minister, "General" William Booth.

Gilchrist–Thomas method for steel production.

1879 Following tensions with Russia, Germany forms a dual alliance with Austria.

Tchaikovsky completes his opera *Eugene Onegin*.

1880 Chancellor Bismarck ends his anti-Catholic policy, *Kulturkampf*.

About 4,900,000 Jews living in "Pale of Settlement" in Russian empire.

In Paris, 55,000 copies of Emile Zola's novel *Nana* are sold on the first day of publication.

AMERICAS & AUSTRALASIA

1876 Gold found near Black Hills of Dakota territory, N America (–1878).

War breaks out between the Sioux Indians of the Black Hills of Dakota and white gold prospectors.

Battle of Little Bighorn; Sioux warriors kill 250 US soldiers.

Start of dictatorship of Porfirio Díaz in Mexico. He has US support.

In Queensland, the Goldfields amendment bill imposes a heavy tax on Chinese immigrants to the minefields.

Truganini, said to be the last full-blooded Tasmanian aborigine, dies.

Mark Twain publishes *The Adventures of Tom Sawyer*, a novel based on his own childhood.

Henry J. Heinz begins bottling and marketing tomato ketchup.

Alexander Graham Bell patents telephone.

1877 Chief Joseph's War, between US army and Nez Percé people of the NW plains.

Peak of buffalo slaughter in the US (–1887).

Chief Crazy Horse and his Sioux Indians give themselves up to US troops, abandoning claims to Nebraska.

Apache resistance in southwest US.

Blackfeet Indians cede land to the Canadian government.

First national strike by US railroad employees.

Thomas Alva Edison invents the first phonograph.

1878 Edison invents the electric filament lamp, and founds the Edison Electric Light Company.

1879 War of the Pacific; Chile, Peru, and Bolivia fight for control of nitrate-rich land in the Atacama desert (–1883).

Chilean troops take Lima.

1880 A census shows that the US population is now 50 million.

Spain sends 250,000 troops to suppress renewed Cuban uprising.

Chile moves north and takes the towns of Arica and Tacna.

Communications revolution

Broadway in 1880, its skyline crisscrossed by telegraph and telephone wires.

During the latter half of the 19th century, the application of innovative technology led to the creation of new products, processes, and sources of energy. Electricity was crucial to 19th-century technology: following the conversion of mechanical motion into electrical current by Michael Faraday in 1831, Samuel Morse produced the first telegraph in the 1840s and in 1876 Alexander Graham Bell patented the telephone. Within a few years of his invention, telephones had been installed in many homes in Europe and the US, and a tangle of telephone and telegraph lines was a familiar feature of many city streets.

Industrialization in India

From 1861, when the American Civil War caused international cotton shortages, Britain turned to India for its raw cotton supplies. At this stage, cotton was still produced on a local scale, and British cloth, woven with Indian cotton, was reexported back to India. But this was to change, as India became the first Asian country to experience the impact of western capitalism and industrialization on a large scale. The first machine-made textiles were manufactured in Bombay and Calcutta. Railroads stimulated the commercialization of agriculture, especially in cash crops such as cotton, jute, and indigo. While British investors and traders made money in this vast new market, Indians also became increasingly prominent. By 1900, India had the world's fourth largest textile industry.

In India, locally produced cotton was still traded at local markets in the 1870s.

1876–1880 375

The Exploration of Africa

In 1800, much of Africa's landmass was relatively uncharted. Over the course of the 19th century, a succession of European explorers embarked on arduous and perilous journeys to the African interior. They were motivated by scientific interest, but their governments were acutely aware of the commercial and strategic potential of the vast continent.

1823	Dixon Denham and Hugh Clapperton reach Lake Chad (–1824).
1826	Alexander Laing reaches Timbuktu, but is murdered there.
1828	René Caillié reaches Timbuktu, disguised as an Egyptian Muslim.
1830	Lander brothers discover the mouths of the Niger river.
1849	David Livingstone reaches Lake Ngami
	Heinrich Barth explores, and meticulously maps, the western Sahara (–1855).
1853	David Livingstone crosses Africa (–1856). Discovers Victoria Falls.
1858	Richard Burton and John Speke discover Lake Tanganyika; Speke discovers Lake Victoria.
1859	Livingstone discovers Lake Nyasa.
1862	Speke reaches the source of the Nile.
1869	Gustav Nachtigal travels across the Sahara.
1871	Livingstone meets US journalist Henry M. Stanley at Ujiji.
1873	Verney Cameron makes first European east–west crossing of the African continent.
1875	Stanley circumnavigates Lake Victoria; confirms source of Nile as Ripon Falls.
1876	Stanley travels down the Congo to the Atlantic (–1877).
1883	Joseph Thomson travels from Mombasa to Lake Victoria.
1887	Louis Binger examines countries to the west of the Volta basin.
	Stanley crosses the Ituri Forest to Lake Albert.
1888	Count Samuel Teleki discovers Lake Rudolf.

Bicycles allowed women to enjoy an unprecedented sense of freedom of movement and liberty.

Bicycles

The first effective "vélocipède" was made by the Michaux family in France in the 1860s. Improvements, such as chains, spoked wheels, gears, and pneumatic tyres, were soon introduced, and by the 1880s, bicycles were being mass-produced in Europe and the US. The first cycle race was held at St. Cloud park near Paris in 1868. The Tour de France was inaugurated in 1903. Cycling also became a popular pastime: cycling clubs gave towns-people access to the countryside.

1881–1885

ASIA

1881 Following the Treaty of St. Petersburg, China regains a large strip of territory in Chinese Turkestan.

France declares its sovereignty over Vietnam, and sends troops down the Red river to occupy Tonkin in the north.

1882 Ilbert Bill proposes that Europeans in India should be open to trial by Indian judges.

Commander Henri Rivière seizes the citadel of Hanoi, Vietnam.

A pro-Chinese *coup d'etat* in Korea. The regent, Yi Si-eung, seizes power.

1883 A treaty is signed at Hué recognizing Tonkin, Annam, and Cochin China as French protectorates. China objects, regarding Vietnam as its own vassal.

Vietnamese forces, supported by Chinese "Black Flag" troops, battle with the French near Hanoi.

Over 30,000 people are feared dead after the volcano at Krakatoa, Java, erupts.

1884 Li-Fournier convention; China agrees to recognize Franco-Vietnamese treaties and to open Yunnan and Guangxi to French trade.

Chinese forces break the terms of the Li-Fournier convention, defeating French troops at Bacle, Indochina.

French naval forces respond by bombarding Chilung (Taiwan) and Fuzhou. China declares war on France.

The French government sends an ultimatum, demanding an indemnity and withdrawal of Chinese troops from Indochina. Troops withdraw.

1885 Founding of the Indian National Congress.

Russian troops inflict a crushing defeat on Afghan forces at Ak Tepe.

British seize the Burmese capital, Mandalay, in order to prevent French gaining influence in upper Burma. Third Anglo-Burmese War (–1886).

Qing troops attack and defeat French forces at Langson, Indochina.

Sino-French Treaty of Tianjin reaffirms French protectorate over Indochina.

AFRICA

1881 British troops are defeated by the Boers at Majuba Hill on the border of British Natal.

 1887

At the Pretoria convention, Britain recognizes Transvaal's self-government.

In Sudan, Mohammed Ahmed ibn Abdallah proclaims himself "al-Mahdi" (the Guided One), and calls for a holy war against Egyptians and Europeans.

Mandinka clash with the French, who are extending their control west from the upper Senegal.

Treaty of Bardo makes Tunisia a French protectorate.

Henry Morton Stanley founds Leopoldville on the Congo river.

1882 Nationalist revolt in Egypt prompts occupation by British.

1883 France begins its conquest of Madagascar.

Britain unilaterally abolishes its joint rule with France over Egypt.

Germans settle in port of Angra Pequena, Namibia.

The mahdi of Sudan defeats the Egyptian army, occupying Darfur and Bahr al Ghazal.

The Tembu national church, the first black church in S Africa, is founded.

1884 Germany acquires SW Africa, Togo, and Cameroon.

Berlin conference (–1885), reaches agreement on partition of Africa.

1898

General Gordon is sent by the British government to evacuate Khartoum.

Britain signs a pact with Portugal over control of the Congo estuary.

Henry Morton Stanley has set up 40 trading posts in the Congo area on behalf of a private company founded by King Leopold of the Belgians.

1885 Germany establishes a protectorate over the Tanganyika coast.

King Leopold of Belgium acquires Congo.

Mahdists capture Khartoum, killing General Gordon and the Egyptian soldiers left in the city.

 1896

French acquire the protectorate of Madagascar.

EUROPE

1891 ▼

1881 Assassination of Czar Alexander II provokes first pogroms against Russia's Jews.

The first electric tramway, invented by Werner von Siemens, opens in Berlin.

1882 Germany, Austria-Hungary, and Italy sign a secret defensive alliance directed against France.

In Britain, the Married Women's Property Act allows women to own property in their own right after marriage.

Jews expelled from Moscow, St. Petersburg, and Kharkov.

The composer, Johannes Brahms completes his second piano concerto.

Richard Wagner's new opera *Parsifal* opens at Bayreuth to great acclaim.

1883 The architect Antonio Gaudi begins work on the church of the Holy Family in Barcelona, Spain.

1884 In London, a group of socialists founds the Fabian Society.

Maxim invents a new effective weapon, the machine gun.

1885 The British government passes the Land Act, providing large state loans for Irish peasants to buy lands from English landowners.

1886 ▼

A rebellion in E Rumelia. Prince Alexander of Bulgaria annexes the region. Serbs, supported by Russia, invade Bulgaria, but are defeated at Slivnitsa.

Development of first automobile by Daimler and Benz.

AMERICAS & AUSTRALASIA

1881 US president James Garfield dies of blood poisoning after being shot by an assassin.

Start of migration to US by nearly 400,000 Canadians.

Peak years of German emigration to US (1,300,000).

The outlaw William H Bonney, alias Billy the Kid, is shot dead.

1890 ▼

Sioux chief Sitting Bull, an outlaw for five years, gives himself up to the army.

The geological survey of the Grand Canyon is complete.

Patagonia becomes part of Argentina.

1882 Beginning of major Jewish emigration to the US from Russian empire.

Some 80,000 Scandinavians emigrate to the US.

Chinese immigration into the US is banned.

In Boston, Gilbert and Sullivan's *Iolanthe* becomes the first electrically illuminated theatrical production in the country.

1883 Treaty of Ancón ends the war between Chile, Peru, and Bolivia.

Brooklyn Bridge, designed by John A. Roebling to link New York City and Brooklyn, is opened.

1884 By the Treaty of Valparaíso, Bolivia grants Chile the right to control Antofagasta, including the Atacama desert.

Some 100 suffragists, led by Susan B. Anthony, petition the US president for female suffrage.

Annexation of N New Guinea and Bismarck archipelago by Germany.

1885 The Statue of Liberty arrives in New York City from France.

Suppression of Riel's rebellion in NW Canada.

Completion of Canadian transcontinental railroad.

Cecil Rhodes

Cecil John Rhodes (1853–1902) made a fortune in diamond and gold mining in South Africa. Fiercely proempire, he became an effective political leader. In 1890, as prime minister of Cape Colony, he formulated a scheme to bring more of Africa under British rule; he dreamt of planting the British flag all the way from Cape Town to Cairo. Although he succeeded in bringing much of South Africa into the empire, he failed to topple the Boer government. He supported the Jameson raid of 1895, in which a small British force attempted to overthrow the Boer leader, Paul Kruger. When the raid failed, he was forced to resign.

A lithographic poster of the Illinois Central Railroad. Transcontinental railroads linked the entire North American continent by the 1880s.

US railroads

The earliest railroad to be constructed in the US was the Baltimore and Ohio, begun in 1828. During the first phase of railroad construction, short sections of track were laid down, connecting major cities. By 1852, there were six trans-Appalachian routes, and Chicago had been reached by railroad from the east. In 1854, the Corps of Topographic Engineers began the Pacific Railroad Survey, and the era of transcontinental lines began. The first line to cross the continent was the Union-Pacific, completed in 1869, with initially only one eastbound and one westbound train a week. As more transcontinental lines were laid in the 1880s, starting with the Northern Pacific, the railroads took their place as the mainstay of the US's transportation system.

The Eiffel Tower

In 1889, an international exhibition was held in Paris. The iron tower, erected by engineer Gustave Eiffel, was its crowning glory. At 983 feet (300 m), it was the tallest metal structure in the world. Opened to commemorate the centenary of the 1789 revolution, Eiffel planted a tricolor flag on its summit, illuminated by over 20,000 gas lights. With its modernistic design and glass cage electric elevators, the tower is a monument to the Third Republic's respect for science, modernity, and technology, and an enduring symbol of Paris.

Malaysian rubber

By the end of the 19th century, the British had placed all of Malaya under their colonial administration, primarily on an indirect basis, ruling through local sultans. From 1880 onward, Malaya was rapidly commercialized. Large deposits of tin, in great demand in the industrial west, were discovered there, and by the 1890s Malaya had also become the world's major producer of plantation rubber. Local Malays were subsistence farmers, not interested in these new industries. The British therefore imported Chinese workers, who soon comprised almost half of Malaya's population. The Malays came to resent the Chinese domination of their commercial economy.

The vast rubber plantations of the Malay peninsula provided a secure basis for Britain's economic control of the region.

ASIA

1886 In India, Saiyid Ahmed Khan founds the Muslim Education Conference.

Britain annexes Upper Burma after Third Burmese War.

1887 Riyadh taken by Rashidis, who dominate Nejd.

Baluchistan is declared British territory, and united with India.

Parsi magnate, J. N. Tata, opens his Empress cotton mill at Nagpur – a major step forward for the Indian textile industry.

1888 Britain establishes a protectorate over Sarawak in the Malayan archipelago, and over N Borneo.

The first railroad in China, from Tangshan to Tianjin, is opened.

1889 New Japanese constitution balances imperial authority with parliamentary government.

1892
1890 First general election held in Japan.

AFRICA

1886 Deep seams of gold discovered on the Witwatersrand, S Africa.

The city of Johannesburg, S Africa, is founded.

Germany and Britain divide up E Africa.

1887 Britain establishes its protectorate over Nigeria.

1891
Tippu Tib, the Swahili slave merchant, is made governor of the Stanley Falls district of Congo Free State, on behalf of King Leopold II.

King Lobengula of the Ndebele signs a treaty of friendship with Transvaal Boers.

1893 **1888** King Lobengula grants exclusive mineral rights to a syndicate headed by Cecil Rhodes.

British agree to mount a blockade to help the Germans crush Muslim resistance on the E African coast.

1889 Establishment of first Italian colony in Eritrea.

Cecil Rhodes' British South Africa Company begins colonizing Rhodesia.

1895 **1890** Britain exchanges Heligoland with Germany for Pemba and Zanzibar.

Cecil Rhodes becomes prime minister of the Cape Colony.

EUROPE

1886 Bulgaria and Serbia sign the peace of Bucharest.

The Irish question brings down the government of William Gladstone, when his Irish Home Rule Bill is defeated.

Karl Benz patents the first automobile.

1887 Bulgaria, independent of Ottoman Empire, becomes leading Balkan state.

Russian composer Tchaikovsky completes his ballet *Swan Lake*.

1888 James Keir Hardie founds the Scottish Labour party.

A rail line is opened between Hungary and Istanbul.

Dutch artist Vincent van Gogh moves to Arles, Provence, where he paints *Sunflowers*.

1889 Ottomans suppress a Greek-backed rebellion on the island of Crete.

A strike by 30,000 London dockers begins. It gives rise to a widespread movement of international solidarity.

A strike by 90,000 miners in Germany's Ruhr district.

In Germany, the Social Democrats set up a miners' union.

The Reichstag passes Bismarck's welfare bill, which provides old age pensions and disability insurance.

Eiffel Tower completed for centennial exhibition in Paris.

1890 A growing rift develops between Chancellor Bismarck and the more liberal Kaiser William II. Kaiser William demands Bismarck's resignation.

Universal suffrage is adopted in Spain.

Charles Parnell is forced to resign as leader of the Irish party at Westminster, after he is cited as corespondent in a divorce case.

AMERICAS & AUSTRALASIA

1886 Over 100,000 workers across the US strike for an eight-hour day.

Apache leader Geronimo surrenders to General Nelson A. Miles after a decade of guerrilla warfare.

In Atlanta, a pharmacist, Dr. Pemberton, produces a fizzy drink called Coca-Cola.

1887 New Zealand annexes the Kermadec Islands.

In Hawaii, revolution is threatened after King Kalakaua is identified as the ringleader in an opium bribery case.

1888 Slavery in Brazil at last completely abolished; next decade sees over a million immigrants.

Chile starts colonization of Easter Island.

George Eastman perfects the first Kodak camera.

1889 Two million acres of Native American land in Oklahoma given to white settlers.

Brazil gains republican status as the emperor is forced to leave.

Germany, Britain, and the US sign a treaty guaranteeing the independence and neutrality of the Samoan Islands.

1890 US troops massacre 350 Sioux at the battle of Wounded Knee. Last armed resistance against removal of Indians to reservations.

US frontier declared to exist no longer.

W Australia last state to be granted self-government.

c.1890 Gold discovered at Kalgoorlie, W Australia.

Kauri gum, for varnish, becomes New Zealand's chief export.

The Right to Vote (1848–1922)

Date of universal male suffrage.
(Women's suffrage, where applicable, in brackets).

1848	France – subsequently annulled and reinstated 1852 and 1870 (1944).
	Switzerland – subsequently annulled and reinstated 1874.
1850	Prussia.
1871	German empire (1919).
1884	Great Britain (1928).
1890	Spain.
1893	Belgium (1948).
1896	Netherlands (1946).
1898	Norway (1912).
1907	Austria.
	Hungary.
1908	Ottoman empire (1934).
1909	Sweden (1919).
1910	Portugal.
1915	Denmark.
1921	Yugoslavia (1946).
1922	Ireland (1922).

Louis Pasteur

Louis Pasteur (1822–1895) was an outstanding French scientist, whose skillful experiments revolutionized 19th-century scientific methods. As a professor of chemistry at the university of Lille, he began his studies in fermentation in 1854. He was able to prove that the process of fermentation is caused by the activity of minute organisms. He went on to develop a process which destroyed germs by heat, making it possible to preserve and transport wine, vinegar, beer, and eventually milk (pasteurization). In 1881, he produced an anthrax vaccine for sheep. In 1882, he developed a rabies vaccine and went on to save the life of a nine-year-old boy who had been bitten by a rabid dog.

The modernization of Japan

The Meiji Restoration in Japan (named after the young emperor who succeeded in 1867) marked the beginning of a process of wholesale westernization. Japan's leaders recognized that their power and independence could only be restored by mastering western technology. They had little hesitation in abolishing or transforming traditional institutions. Railroads were quickly built to link cities, and new ports and facilities were constructed. Government and the legal system were reformed along western lines, creating a constitutional monarchy and a parliament. Even western culture, dress, and diet were adopted. By the 1890s, Japan had a modern navy and army, a fast growing industrial base, and a rising share in the Chinese market. Japan now began to emulate the west's colonial ambitions, starting by bringing Korea into its sphere of influence.

From the late 19th century, the newly modernized Japan reopened its doors to foreign trade.

Japanese Modernization 1871–1890

1871	Japanese government mission to the US is convinced of the need for modernization.
	Feudal domains abolished; 250 domains become 72 prefectures and three metropolitan districts.
1871	System of universal education is announced.
1873	National conscription deprives Samurai of monopoly on military service.
	Monetary tax of 3 percent of land value is established.
1884	European style peerage is established.
1885	Cabinet system, with ministers directly appointed by the emperor, is established.
1889	New constitution is promulgated. Elections for the lower house are held.
1890	Diet (*Kokkai*) meets for first time. Imperial Rescript on Education lays out the lines of Confucian and Shinto ideology.

ASIA

1891 British expeditionary forces sent to Manipur, Saminar, and Nagar, N India.

Mob attacks on mission premises in China.

Uprising by the Golden Elixir sect is put down by the Chinese government.

1892 The Indian Councils Act allows for the election of Indians to the provincial and central legislative councils of British India on a limited franchise.

Violence at the polls in Japan, as feudal lords determine to strengthen their representation in parliament.

1893 Siam gives up all its territory east of the Mekong to France and recognizes Laos as a French protectorate.

1894 The Ottoman sultan suppresses a revolutionary movement for Armenian independence. Turkish and Kurdish troops embark on systematic massacres of Armenians.

Following a nationalist rebellion, Chinese and Japanese troops are sent to Korea.

Japanese troops take over the Korean imperial palace. The Japanese sink the British steamer *Kowshing* which is carrying Chinese reinforcements to Korea.

War is declared between China and Japan.

1895 Britain intervenes to stop Armenian massacres.

Japanese impose a humiliating defeat on the Chinese at the battle of Weihaiwei. China and Japan sign the peace treaty of Shimonoseki.

Russia, France, and Germany intervene, forcing Japan to return Liaodong peninsula to China. Japan annexes Taiwan.

Revolutionary leader Sun Yat-sen, who has failed to launch a rebellion in Guangzhou, flees to Hong Kong.

China concludes a secret treaty with Russia, allowing the Russians to build the Trans-Siberian railroad through Manchuria.

Anti-Christian riots erupt in Sichuan province.

AFRICA

1891 Belgian forces attack the Garenganze kingdom in the copper-rich province of Katanga, Zaire.

Britain and Portugal settle their territorial disputes around Lake Nyasa.

Britain declares territories north of the Zambezi, up to the Congo basin, to be within its sphere of influence.

Tippu Tib retires to Zanzibar.

1892 A railroad from Cape Colony through the Orange Free State to Johannesburg is completed.

1893 France destroys the Tukulor empire.

French take Timbuktu, the capital of Mali.

Responsible government is introduced in Natal.

Rabin ibn Fadl Allah, a Sudanese raider and trader, conquers the state of Borno.

Following Ndebele (Matabele) raids, troops of the British South Africa Company invade Matabeleland. The British occupy Bulawayo.

1894 Uganda and Buganda are occupied by Britain.

French conquer Dahomey.

1895 Tananarive, the capital of Madagascar, surrenders to the French.

The Jameson raid; Leander Jameson, an agent of the British South Africa Company, invades the Boer republic of Transvaal.

In British Nyasaland (Malawi) the administrator Harry Johnston faces determined African resistance from the Yao, Swahili, Chewa, and Ngoni.

EUROPE

1891 French troops open fire on striking miners at Fourmies, killing nine people.

France and Russia sign an *entente*.

Russia begins construction of Trans-Siberian railroad (–1916).

Thousands of Jews are forced into Russian ghettoes.

Norwegian playwright, Henrik Ibsen, completes *Hedda Gabler*.

Arthur Conan Doyle publishes *The Adventures of Sherlock Holmes*.

1892 Russia is devastated by a severe famine.

Edvard Munch, the Norwegian painter, is ordered to remove 50 of his paintings by the Berlin Artists' Union.

1893 In Britain, the independent Labour Party holds its first meeting.

A bill is introduced to substantially increase the size of the German army.

The Corinth canal in Greece opens.

The Italian Socialist party is founded in Reggio nell 'Emilia.

1894 Captain Alfred Dreyfus, a Jewish army officer, is arrested for betraying French military secrets to Germany.

1895 Invention of wireless telegraphy (radio) by Guglielmo Marconi.

The Kiel canal, connecting the Baltic with the North Sea, opens.

Louis and Auguste Lumière invent the cinematograph, motion picture camera, and projector.

Irish writer Oscar Wilde, author of *The Importance of Being Earnest*, is sentenced to two years' hard labor in Reading gaol for sodomy.

AMERICAS & AUSTRALASIA

1891 Brazil adopts a constitution similiar to that of the US.

Civil war in Chile. President Manuel Balmaceda commits suicide.

1892 Federal troops are sent in to break up a miners' strike in Idaho.

An office is opened on Ellis Island, New York City, to cope with the huge influx of immigrants, many fleeing persecution in C and E Europe.

Britain proclaims a protectorate over the Gilbert and Ellice Islands, Pacific Ocean.

1893 Following the deposition of the Hawaiian queen, US troops move to annex the islands.

New Zealand is the first country in the world to give women the vote.

The Anti-Saloon League is founded in Ohio to promote the prohibition of alcohol.

Czech composer Antonín Dvořák completes his symphony *From the New World* in New York City.

The Great Northern Railroad between the Mississippi river and the Pacific Ocean is opened.

1894 Judge Sanford B. Dole proclaims the republic of Hawaii.

1895 Nicaragua, Honduras, and El Salvador conclude a treaty of union at Amapala.

Uprising in Cuba against Spanish rule.

More than 50,000 Melanesians indentured to Australia's canefields.

The Trans-Siberian railroad

A brainchild of Czar Alexander III, the construction of the railroad began in 1891. Originally, the Russians received permission from the Chinese to build a line directly across Manchuria, which was completed in 1901. After the Russo-Japanese War of 1904–1905, the Russians, fearing a Japanese takeover of Manchuria, began to build an alternative route, the Amur railroad, completed in 1916. This ensured that the railroad ran entirely through Russian territory. The completion of the railroad marked a turning point in the history of Siberia. It opened up the territory to settlement, enabling its vast mineral wealth to be exploited.

The conquest of Benin

The Yoruba art of Benin, skillfully carved in brass, bronze, and copper, was created to honor and commemorate the *obas* (rulers). Queen Victoria, the ruler of a vast empire, must have been seen as an appropriate subject (*below*). Most of Yorubaland was conquered by the British in 1892–93. The British used African soldiers for the bulk of their frontline troops; these highly disciplined professional battalions were equipped with the latest rifles and artillery.

The traditional lack of unity among the African states in the region helped the British in their piecemeal conquest. The state of Benin City was eventually taken in 1897; the *oba* had resorted to human sacrifices in a desperate attempt to save his ancient kingdom but British forces sacked the city, looting its most valued treasures.

The Boer War (1899–1902)

1899 **Oct 12**: War erupts between Boers and British.
Oct 13: Boers surround Mafeking.
Oct 15: Boers lay siege to Kimberley.
Nov 2: Boers lay siege to Ladysmith.
Dec 11: Boers under Piet Cronje defeat British at Magersfontein.
Dec 15: British forces are defeated by Boers at the battle of Colenso.

1900 **Jan 10**: Lord Roberts becomes commander-in-chief of the British forces, with Herbert Kitchener as his chief-of-staff.

Jan 24: British under General Warren take Spion Kop.

Feb 27: General Piet Cronje surrenders to British at Paardeberg after suffering a defeat.

Feb 28: British forces, who have relieved Kimberley earlier in the month, now relieve Ladysmith.

Mar 13: British forces under Lord Roberts take Bloemfontein.

Apr 9: Boers defeat British at Kroonstadt.

May 20: British relieve Mafeking, defended for 217 days by Colonel Robert Baden-Powell.

May 29: Britain annexes Orange Free State.

Sep 1: Britain annexes the Boer republic of the Transvaal.

1901 **Oct**: Boer commandos invade Cape Colony. British practice a "scorched earth" policy, burning Boer farms and imprisoning their families in "concentration camps."

1902 **May 31**: Boers surrender to the British and sign the peace of Vereeniging, in which they recognize British sovereignty.

Conflict in South Africa

When hundreds of thousands of Englishmen poured into the mining towns of Rhodesia, the Transvaal, and Bechuanaland in the 1880s, they overwhelmed the Boer population, making conflict inevitable. The president of the Transvaal, Paul Kruger, pressurized the foreigners by levying discriminatory taxes on them and curbing their political rights.

Increasingly strident British demands to improve the situation were ignored, and tensions mounted. Kruger declared war in 1899, and Boer commandos stormed across the republic's borders into the Cape and Natal. Although the British suffered some humiliating defeats, they were able to capture the main Boer towns. Boer commandos continued a guerrilla campaign for two years, but were forced to surrender when the British began to burn Boer farms and imprison their women and children in concentration camps.

ASIA

1896 Persian shah, Naser od-Din, is assassinated by an Islamic fundamentalist.

Armenian revolutionaries seize the Ottoman bank in Istanbul; at least 3000 people are massacred in reprisal.

Chinese authorities break up the "Big Sword" society, that has been raiding Catholic homes in Jiangsu.

Britain and France guarantee the independence of Siam, and the French protectorate over Laos is recognized.

1901

1897 Serious uprisings break out in the NW frontier region of India against British rule.

German forces, using the murder of two Catholic missionaries as a pretext, occupy Jiaozhou Bay.

Russian warships enter Port Arthur on the Liaodong peninsula. They intend to force the Germans to withdraw.

1898 In India, the great Muslim lawyer and educational reformer, Saiyid Ahmed Khan, dies.

Germany signs a treaty with China by which it acquires "leased territories."

1905

Emperor Guangxu announces a period of reform. After 100 days, the empress dowager Cixi carries out a *coup d'etat*, crushing the reforms.

The Yellow river causes widespread flooding and devastating famine in China.

Britain obtains the New Territories of Hong Kong under a 99-year lease.

US forces under George Dewey destroy the Spanish fleet in Manila Bay. The Spanish surrender the Philippines to the US.

1902

1899 Philippine rebels proclaim an independent republic. Conflict breaks out with US troops.

1900 Boxer Rebellion (antiwestern revolt in China): Christian missions and western legations attacked.

1901

The allies enter Beijing, ending the siege of their legations.

1904

Russian occupation of Manchuria (–1905).

c.1900 Baku oilfields in Azerbaijan are producing half the world's oil.

AFRICA

1896 Jameson surrenders to the Boers at Doornkop.

Ethiopians decisively defeat the Italians at the battle of Adowa.

Madagascar is proclaimed a French colony.

Sultan Khaled of Zanzibar surrenders to the British.

Commander of the Anglo-Egyptian army, Herbert Kitchener, seizes the town of Dongola, Sudan.

1906

Under the treaty of Addis Ababa, Italy recognizes the independence of Ethiopia, only retaining Eritrea.

British invade and occupy the Ashanti kingdom.

1898 French troops occupy Fashoda on the Nile, causing Anglo-French tensions.

Kitchener leads the British to victory against the Sudanese Mahdists at Omdurman, and takes Khartoum. He forces the French to evacuate Fashoda.

1899 War breaks out between the British and Boers from the Transvaal and Orange Free State (–1902).

Britain and Egypt establish a condominium over Sudan.

Following a victory at Isangi, Germany takes control of Rwanda.

1903 **1900** Nigeria becomes a British protectorate.

Start of copper mining in Katanga.

EUROPE

1896 Revival of Olympic Games at Athens, Greece.

Kaiser William II causes a storm of protest in Britain when he congratulates President Kruger on the Jameson raid.

Christian rebellion against Ottoman rule on Crete.

In Germany, the satirical newspaper *Simplicissimus* is founded by Albert Langen and Thomas Heine.

Anton Chekov's *The Seagull* is hissed at during its premiere in St. Petersburg.

The Lumiére "cinematograph" opens in Paris.

1897 War breaks out between Greece and the Ottoman Empire. After several defeats by the Ottomans, the Greeks withdraw and sign an armistice.

1908

Crete proclaims union with Greece. The Greeks send ships and troops to the island.

Theodor Herzl convenes the first Zionist congress at Basle, Switzerland.

1898 Elizabeth, empress of Austria, is assassinated in Geneva by the Italian anarchist, Luigi Luccheni.

Ottomans evacuate Crete.

An act is passed providing for an expansion of the German navy.

Emile Zola accuses the French war office of anti-Semitism in the Dreyfus affair, writing an open letter entitled *J'Accuse*.

Marie and Pierre Curie discover polonium and radium.

1899 Peace conference at The Hague establishes an international court of arbitration.

Dreyfus is officially pardoned by the French government.

1900 King Umberto of Italy is shot by an anarchist.

Giacomo Puccini's opera *Tosca* is performed in Rome for the first time.

Freud's *The Interpretation of Dreams*, published in Vienna, causes a sensation.

AMERICAS & AUSTRALASIA

1896 In Klondike Gold Rush, more than 100,000 people come to Yukon territory (–1898).

Height of Brazilian rubber boom; Manaus builds opera house.

Simultaneous inventions by Thomas Edison and the Lumiére brothers in France lead to first motion picture shows.

1897 Cuba becomes autonomous but not fully independent from Spain.

An underground railroad system opens in Boston.

1898 Spanish–American War. US occupies Cuba.

The boroughs of Brooklyn, the Bronx, Queen's, Staten Island, and Manhattan unite to form Greater New York.

US seizes Guam from Spain.

First winter camp on Antarctica at Cape Adare.

The US warship *Maine* blows up in Havana harbor. Spanish sabotage is suspected.

The novelist Henry James publishes *The Turn of the Screw*.

1904 **1899** Cession of Cuba and Puerto Rico to US by the Spain.

The US and Germany agree to divide the Pacific Samoan Islands between them.

Liberal revolt in Colombia sparks "War of a Thousand Days" which leaves 100,000 dead.

1900 Start of major Italian emigration to the US and Argentina; by 1910, more than two million have arrived.

Brazil produces 66 percent of the world's coffee; tin supersedes silver as Bolivia's chief export.

Chile and Argentina agree on border protocol.

The photographs of Jacob A Riis, taken in the slums of New York in the 1880s and 1890s, did much to arouse public concern.

The slums of New York City

The influx of immigrants into New York in the latter half of the 19th century precipitated a serious housing crisis. Families lived crowded together in tenements, shoddy buildings usually five stories tall, with four tiny apartments on each floor. In 1864, the first systematic sanitary survey of the city revealed the extent of the problem. Legislation set out to improve the basic tenement design, but reformers were fighting a losing battle. Ramshackle tenement buildings, usually of wood, continued to be erected on the back portion of city lots, making New York's lower East Side one of the most densely populated urban areas in the world.

Pogroms, or riots, against Jews were frequent in the late 1800s. Many fled; others were expelled from designated areas such as St. Petersburg (above).

Migrants

Between 1880 and 1920, two million Jews from eastern Europe arrived in the US; most settled in New York. A great number of the new arrivals worked in the garment industry; adults and children alike labored for long hours at home doing piecework, or in poorly lit, overcrowded sweatshops. Other immigrants sold goods from pushcarts, or opened small shops or restaurants. Despite the depressing conditions, Jewish culture and religion flourished: hundreds of synagogues and religious schools were established, while Yiddish theater companies and Yiddish and Hebrew newspapers provided entertainment.

The World in 1900

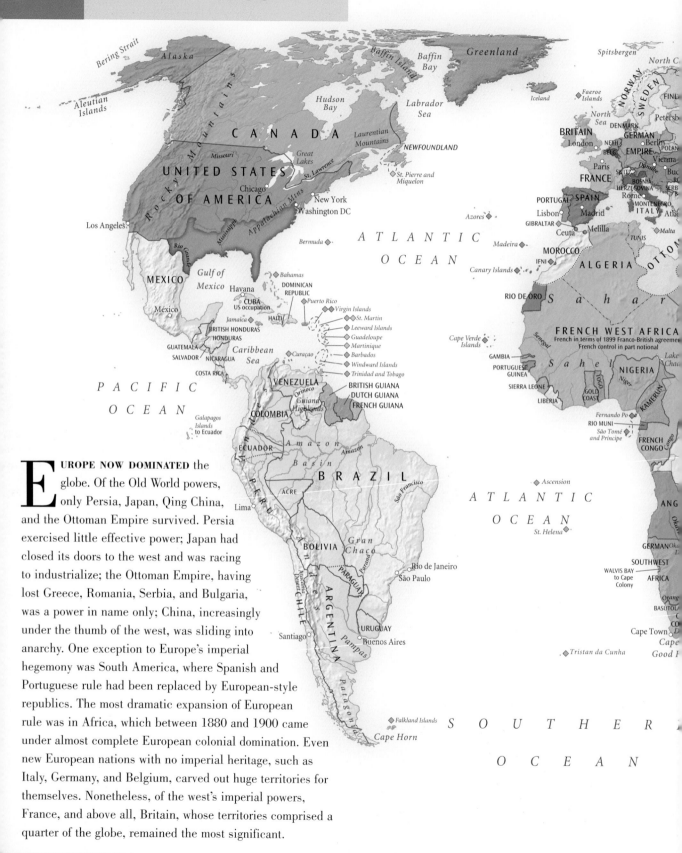

EUROPE NOW DOMINATED the globe. Of the Old World powers, only Persia, Japan, Qing China, and the Ottoman Empire survived. Persia exercised little effective power; Japan had closed its doors to the west and was racing to industrialize; the Ottoman Empire, having lost Greece, Romania, Serbia, and Bulgaria, was a power in name only; China, increasingly under the thumb of the west, was sliding into anarchy. One exception to Europe's imperial hegemony was South America, where Spanish and Portuguese rule had been replaced by European-style republics. The most dramatic expansion of European rule was in Africa, which between 1880 and 1900 came under almost complete European colonial domination. Even new European nations with no imperial heritage, such as Italy, Germany, and Belgium, carved out huge territories for themselves. Nonetheless, of the west's imperial powers, France, and above all, Britain, whose territories comprised a quarter of the globe, remained the most significant.

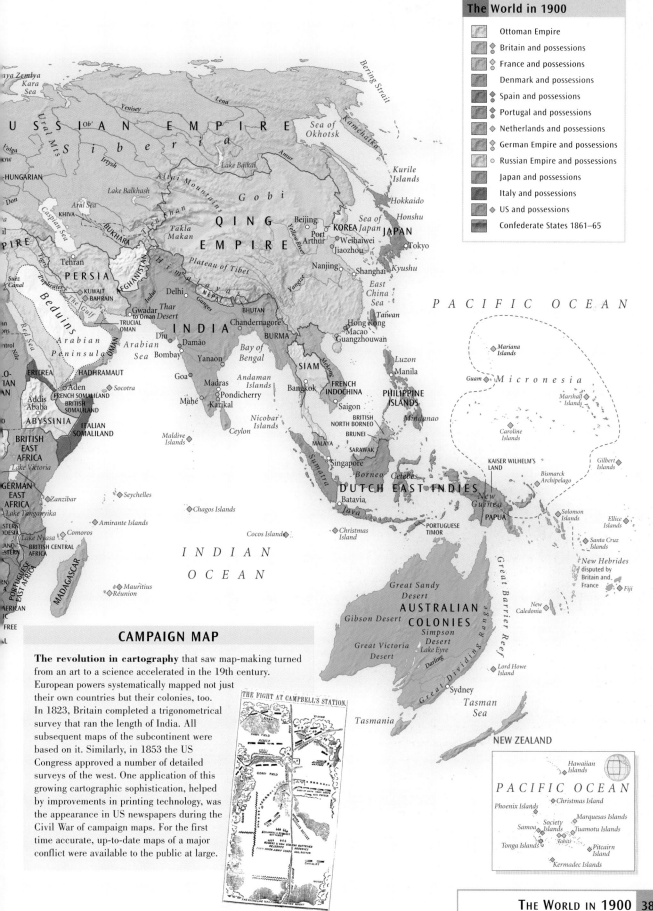

The World in 1900

- Ottoman Empire
- Britain and possessions
- France and possessions
- Denmark and possessions
- Spain and possessions
- Portugal and possessions
- Netherlands and possessions
- German Empire and possessions
- Russian Empire and possessions
- Japan and possessions
- Italy and possessions
- US and possessions
- Confederate States 1861–65

CAMPAIGN MAP

The revolution in cartography that saw map-making turned from an art to a science accelerated in the 19th century. European powers systematically mapped not just their own countries but their colonies, too. In 1823, Britain completed a trigonometrical survey that ran the length of India. All subsequent maps of the subcontinent were based on it. Similarly, in 1853 the US Congress approved a number of detailed surveys of the west. One application of this growing cartographic sophistication, helped by improvements in printing technology, was the appearance in US newspapers during the Civil War of campaign maps. For the first time accurate, up-to-date maps of a major conflict were available to the public at large.

1900 –1925

Clash of Empires

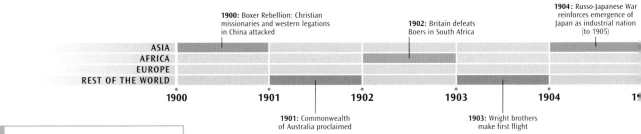

1900: Boxer Rebellion: Christian missionaries and western legations in China attacked

1902: Britain defeats Boers in South Africa

1904: Russo-Japanese War reinforces emergence of Japan as industrial nation (to 1905)

ASIA
AFRICA
EUROPE
REST OF THE WORLD

1900   1901   1902   1903   1904   1

1901: Commonwealth of Australia proclaimed

1903: Wright brothers make first flight

PICTURE ABOVE:
Gassed *by John Singer Sargent is a powerful image of the suffering of World War I. Gas became synonymous with the war's horror, but gas casualties were few compared to the millions killed or maimed by artillery and machine-gun fire.*

A
T LEAST TO WESTERN EYES, the world in 1900 had never seemed more prosperous or stable. The west's empires encircled and dominated the globe; its trade and populations continued to grow spectacularly. As important, there had been no major Europe-wide war since 1815. Even the disintegration of Qing China seemed to favor the west, raising the prospect of further profitable western encroachments. In fact, when the Qing Empire did collapse, in 1911, it began an era of lawlessness that would devastate China until the reimposition of central authority under the communists in 1949. Against a background of instability on this scale, western gains in China inevitably proved short lived.

Paradoxically, the one major setback for European supremacy in the first years of the 20th century – the defeat of Russia in 1905 by an expansionist Japan – in fact tended to highlight western superiority. Russia, whatever its Great Power status, had been defeated by a Japan that had wholeheartedly embraced western industrialization. Japan's aggressive emergence as a world power on the western model was confirmed. Yet Europe was afflicted by an underlying instability that within 14 years would tear it apart. In the process, the military technology that had allowed Europe to dominate the world would be turned on itself. World War I, unleashed on an unsuspecting continent in 1914, was a terrifying demonstration of the destructive capacity of industrially produced weapons.

Rising tensions

In the years before the war, peace in Europe had been preserved by a shifting balance of alliances between the major

Bolshevik "Agitation-Instruction" trains decorated with *revolutionary images traveled the length and breadth of the USSR carrying the gospel of communism to the people.*

powers. By 1914, Germany and Austria-Hungary formed one camp (shortly to be augmented by the Ottomans); Britain, France, and Russia the other. The latent conflict between them had already been heightened by an arms race sparked by the fiercely militaristic Germany. At the same time, Austria and Russia found themselves increasingly at odds over their rival attempts to dominate the Balkans, where fast-ebbing Ottoman control was creating a dangerous power vacuum. Austria-Hungary's annexation of Bosnia-Herzegovina in 1908 was bitterly opposed by Serbia and Russia, but the crisis was averted by the diplomatic intervention of the other major powers. Diplomacy, however, failed to prevent the two Balkan wars of 1912 and 1913, in which Serbia, Greece, Bulgaria, and Turkey fought viciously over the last remnants of the Ottoman Empire in Europe.

It should, therefore, have been no great surprise that, when a European war did come, it was sparked off by yet another incident in the Balkans. On June 28, 1914, the heir to the Habsburg empire, Archduke Franz Ferdinand, and his wife were assassinated by a member of a pro-Slav secret society in the Bosnian capital, Sarajevo. Austria-

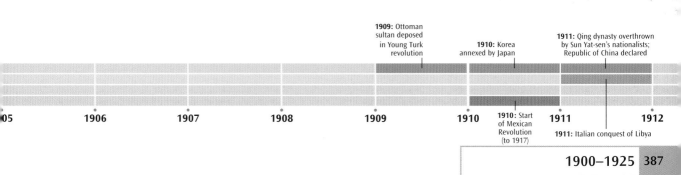

1909: Ottoman sultan deposed in Young Turk revolution

1910: Korea annexed by Japan

1911: Qing dynasty overthrown by Sun Yat-sen's nationalists; Republic of China declared

1910: Start of Mexican Revolution (to 1917)

1911: Italian conquest of Libya

05 1906 1907 1908 1909 1910 1911 1912

Hungary accused Serbia of complicity in the crime, then Russia said it would oppose any Austrian move against Serbia. The two great alliances duly squared up to each other in what was assumed to be no more than a ritual rattling of diplomatic swords. However, Germany, confident of a victory as swift and complete as that of 1870, launched a preemptive strike on Russia's ally, France. When the German assault stalled, Europe was plunged into a four-year war of horrifying proportions.

War of attrition

Though other theaters of war witnessed major battles and appalling slaughter, it was on the Western Front, where the German armies and the French and British faced each other from their opposing lines of trenches and barbed wire, that World War I was decided. Once the front had stabilized in November 1914, the greatest military minds of both sides devoted their energies to one overriding problem: how to achieve a significant breakthrough before the enemy could bring up sufficient reinforcements to plug the gap. They devised new kinds of artillery barrage, employed ingenious inventions such as the tank, and tried to disable the

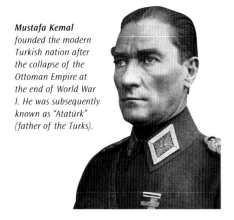

Mustafa Kemal
founded the modern Turkish nation after the collapse of the Ottoman Empire at the end of World War I. He was subsequently known as "Atatürk" (father of the Turks).

enemy with poisonous gas, but the stalemate continued. Each new offensive required hundreds of thousands of shells and millions of rounds of ammunition, and on the home front industry had to be reorganized to produce them. Governments took over the running of the economy, as fuel, foodstuffs, and clothing were rationed in order to concentrate on the war effort. Imports were limited to essentials as German U-boats tried to starve Britain into surrender by sinking merchantmen, while the total British blockade of German shipping gradually had the same effect on Germany. The impact of war on civilian society was far greater than in any previous conflict. There were enormous social consequences in every country, especially for the women who had to take over many of the jobs previously performed by men.

Eventually a breakthrough came, but the German surrender was not the result of a crushing military defeat. In fact, even after the Allied advance in the summer and autumn of 1918, German troops still occupied parts of France and Belgium. But Germany's allies were beginning to desert the Axis cause, food and raw materials were running short, and the German people were simply exhausted, unable to face another winter of cold and starvation. France and Britain, on the other hand, were receiving plentiful supplies from their new ally, the US, whose fresh troops were also now starting to go into action. By the time the armistice came, 9 million soldiers had died, Germany having lost over 2 million, more than any of the other combatant countries.

A new western power

The consequences of World War I were measured not just in casualty figures. At the German and Austrian surrender in

1918, all of Europe's major powers were exhausted and bankrupt. Already, the year before, the Russian empire had collapsed. In February 1917 a liberal revolution had forced the czar to abdicate. Within six months, the revolution had been hijacked by the Bolsheviks under Lenin. After long negotiations, Russia withdrew from the conflict, in the process ceding huge areas of its western territories to Germany. This, however, left the Bolsheviks free to tighten their hold on power. Their ruthless imposition of communist rule led not just to a savage civil war but also, in 1922, to a new Russian empire, the USSR, the world's first communist state.

The one indisputable victor of World War I was the US, which had finally overcome its isolationist instincts to join the Allied side in early 1917. Its military contribution to the Allied victory was more symbolic than real, but its assistance in terms of financial credit, food, and raw materials had been crucial. As the only Allied power whose economy was strengthened rather than shattered by the war, the US became a global superpower. The Treaty of Versailles, the peace settlement that dictated the shape of the postwar world, was presided over by the US president, Woodrow Wilson. The New World had come of age.

Redrawing the world map

The chief results of the settlement were the dismemberment of the German, Austro-Hungarian and Ottoman empires and the creation of a series of new or re-formed countries: the Baltic states of Estonia, Latvia, and Lithuania, Finland, Poland, Hungary, Czechoslovakia, and Yugoslavia. Germany also lost all its overseas colonies and the Ottomans' former Middle Eastern territories were

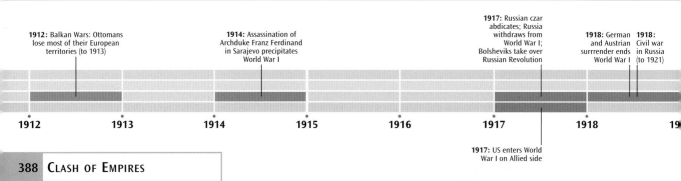

1912: Balkan Wars: Ottomans lose most of their European territories (to 1913)

1914: Assassination of Archduke Franz Ferdinand in Sarajevo precipitates World War I

1917: Russian czar abdicates; Russia withdraws from World War I; Bolsheviks take over Russian Revolution

1918: German and Austrian surrender ends World War I

1918: Civil war in Russia (to 1921)

1912   1913   1914   1915   1916   1917   1918   19

1917: US enters World War I on Allied side

THE LEAGUE OF NATIONS

One of the prime goals of the victorious Allies after World War I was to avoid future carnage on the same terrifying scale. Urged on by the liberal US President, Woodrow Wilson, an international court of arbitration, to which, at least in theory, the whole world could belong, was proposed "to promote international cooperation and to achieve peace and security."

The League of Nations, as it became, was formed in April 1919 by the Treaty of Versailles. It was in trouble from the start, however, when the US Senate, alarmed by the implications of America's new international role, refused to ratify the Treaty or to allow America to join the League. Thereafter, though the other Powers, Britain and France preeminently, were members, it became increasly clear that their support of the League was largely a matter of lip-service.

Its fate as an ineffectual bystander was confirmed in the early 1930s as Japan, Germany, which had only been admitted in 1926, and Italy all withdrew in turn. The ideal lived on, however, and was resurrected in 1945 with the foundation of the United Nations. The League itself was formally dissolved in 1946.

The first session of the Council of the League of Nations on November 15, 1920. Without the US, the League became an organization of limited authority.

The Treaty of Versailles in 1919 created new states from the ruins of the Russian and Austro-Hungarian empires. Despite the tumultuous events of the intervening years, the map of Europe looks remarkably similar today, the major changes being the splitting of Czechoslovakia and the fragmentation of Yugoslavia.

placed under British and French rule "mandated" by the new League of Nations. The creation of the League in 1920, just as much as the creation of new European countries under the doctrine of national "self-determination," highlighted the well-meaning desire to secure the world against future global conflict. Yet the political settlement created more problems than it solved. Overridingly the most important was German resentment at what it saw as the vindictive nature of the Versailles settlement. Already effectively ruined by the war it had started, Germany was further crippled by French insistence on hugely expensive reparations to cover the cost of war damage. It would fall to Hitler in the 1930s to restore German pride.

The consequences of the war were also felt beyond Europe. In the Middle East, Britain had already promised to "facilitate" the creation of a Jewish national homeland. Though the Jewish settlers who arrived were few in number, their presence began an apparently irresoluble conflict that persists to this day. At the same time, western championship of previously oppressed European peoples had the unintended effect of encouraging antiimperialist movements across its empires, above all in India. Europe's seemingly impregnable colonial rule was suddenly under threat.

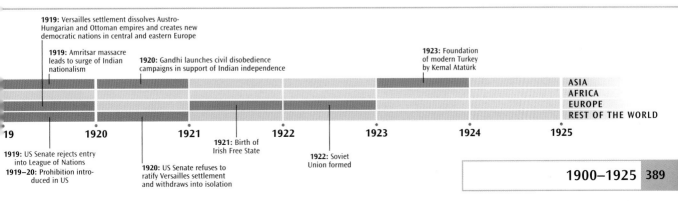

1919: Versailles settlement dissolves Austro-Hungarian and Ottoman empires and creates new democratic nations in central and eastern Europe

1919: Amritsar massacre leads to surge of Indian nationalism

1920: Gandhi launches civil disobedience campaigns in support of Indian independence

1923: Foundation of modern Turkey by Kemal Atatürk

ASIA
AFRICA
EUROPE
REST OF THE WORLD

19   1920   1921   1922   1923   1924   1925

1919: US Senate rejects entry into League of Nations

1919–20: Prohibition introduced in US

1920: US Senate refuses to ratify Versailles settlement and withdraws into isolation

1921: Birth of Irish Free State

1922: Soviet Union formed

The Boxers were just one of the many antigovernment societies that emerged in China at the end of the 19th century.

The Boxer Rebellion

The activities of Christian missionaries in China caused widespread resentment in rural areas and antiwestern riots. By 1900, a group of rebels known as the "Boxers" was on the rampage, burning missions and killing missionaries and Chinese converts. They went on to attack western-built railroads, destroying western-manufactured goods. In June 1900, with covert imperial support, the Boxers besieged the foreign legations in Beijing, which held out until mid-August when they were relieved by a multinational expedition. After brutal reprisals, the western powers, now including Japan, withdrew, and in 1901 the empire was divided into spheres of influence among the foreign powers.

The Flatiron building

Land was at a premium in New York, and from the mid-19th century, the growing demand for commercial real estate was

forcing speculators to look at increasingly tall buildings. From 1848, cast-iron buildings, prefabricated in factories and easily erected by semi-skilled workers, were beginning to dominate the New York skyline. With the introduction of the Otis elevator in 1853, these buildings began to get taller. When William LeBaron Jenney built the world's first skyscraper in Chicago (1883–1884), he introduced a metal cage that supported the entire structure. One of New York's earliest skyscrapers is the 20-story Flatiron (*above*), completed in 1901, which soon became a major cultural icon.

ASIA

1901 The viceroy of India creates the NW Frontier province between Afghanistan and the Punjab.

The Boxer protocol is signed between China and the foreign powers, ending the Boxer Rebellion.

1902 Ibn Saud reclaims his patrimony by capturing Riyadh.

Russia signs a treaty with China over Manchuria, promising to withdraw its troops.

An Anglo-Japanese alliance recognizes the special interests of Britain in China and Japan in Korea.

1903 Coronation durbar for Edward VII, king-emperor, in Delhi.

Negotiations between Russia and China over Manchuria collapse.

Japan lands marines at Mok-Phot to deal with rioting Korean laborers.

1907

1904 Partition of Bengal: nationalist agitation in India.

British forces kill some 300 Tibetans attempting to halt a British mission to Tibet.

British sign a treaty with Tibet, by which Tibet agrees not to cede territory to any foreign power.

Outbreak of Russo-Japanese War. Japanese forces, intent on gaining control of Manchuria, inflict a major defeat on the Russians at Telissu, China.

Japanese destroy the Russian fleet at Port Arthur.

1905 Jewish National Fund established to buy land in Palestine.

In China, the empress dowager announces her commitment to constitutional change.

Japanese defeat the Russians at Mukden and annihilate the Russian fleet in the strait of Tsushima.

AFRICA

1901 Britain annexes the Asante kingdom as part of the Gold coast (Ghana).

Railroad from Mombasa to Lake Victoria completed.

1902 Boers surrender to the British and sign the peace of Vereeniging, recognizing British sovereignty.

British colonial statesman, Cecil Rhodes, dies.

A rail link between Bulawayo and Salisbury (Zimbabwe) is established.

The Nile dam at Aswan, Egypt, is completed.

1906

1903 Troops of the W African Frontier force, led by British officers, take Sokoto, Nigeria. The sultan flees.

1904 French create federation of French W Africa.

France and Spain sign a treaty, recognizing N Morocco as a zone of Spanish influence.

Rebellious Herero massacre 123 German soldiers and settlers near Okahandja, SW Africa.

1907

Hottentot uprising in SW Africa.

France and Britain sign an *entente cordiale* settling their colonial disputes in N Africa.

1905 German soldiers embark on bloodthirsty revenge for the Herero massacre of 1904.

A British officer assassinates the Nandi resistance leader Koitalel in British E Africa (Kenya); part of a drive to suppress native resistance.

1907

Morocco crisis provoked by Kaiser William, who declares that the sultan should be free to deal equally with all foreign powers.

Louis Botha and Het Volk party demand responsible self-government for Transvaal.

EUROPE

1901 Queen Victoria dies and is succeeded by her son, Edward VII.

Anton Chekhov's play *Three Sisters* is performed for the first time, in Moscow.

Marconi sends the first wireless message across the Atlantic.

1902 King Alfonso XIII suspends the Madrid cortes amid growing unrest.

Following political unrest in Dublin, a state of emergency is declared.

More than 30,000 students in Russia strike in protest against government restrictions.

Czar Nicholas II abolishes nominal Finnish autonomy and appoints a Russian governor-general.

1903 Czar Nicholas issues a manifesto conceding important reforms, including religious freedom.

Vladimir Lenin splits the Russian socialists, leading the breakaway Bolsheviks.

Following rebellions in Monastir, the Ottomans massacre 50,000 Bulgarians.

The king and queen of Serbia are assassinated.

1904 Russo-Japanese War; series of Russian defeats halts Russian expansion (–1905).

Puccini's opera *Madam Butterfly*, a tragic love story set in Japan, is premiered in Milan.

1905 Strikes and unrest in Russia. The crew of the *Potemkin*, the most powerful battleship in the Black Sea, mutiny, hoisting the red flag.

Bloody Sunday: the Czar's troops shoot dead more than 500 strikers.

In Russia, the *duma*, a representative assembly, is established.

The Trans-Siberian railroad officially opens.

Norway declares independence from Sweden.

The English suffragettes, Christabel Pankhurst and Annie Kenney, are sent to prison for assaulting a policeman.

1,000 Jews are killed in a pogrom in Odessa.

Einstein's theory of relativity.

AMERICAS & AUSTRALASIA

1901 President William McKinley dies after being shot by an anarchist. Theodore Roosevelt becomes president.

Creek Indian uprising in Oklahoma.

Commonwealth of Australia proclaimed; Australia becomes self-governing federation within British empire.

The Cadillac automobile company is founded in Detroit, US.

George Eastman sets up the Eastman Kodak camera company.

1902 An eruption of Mount Pelée, Martinique, wipes out the whole town of St. Pierre.

The Philippine Government Act, under which Filipinos will be ruled by a US presidential commission, is passed.

The navies of Britain, Germany, and Italy blockade the coastline of Venezuela, after the Venezuelan government refuses to compensate European nationals who have been injured in recent rebellions.

1903 US-backed rebels seize control of the Panama isthmus, proclaiming the republic of Panama.

US and Colombia sign a treaty to allow the construction of the Panama Canal.

Flight of the Wright brothers at Kitty Hawk.

Paul Gauguin, the French artist who made his home in the South Seas, dies in Atuana, Marquesas Island.

1904 The states of Oklahoma and New Mexico are admitted to the union.

US ends its occupation of Cuba.

Border disputes between Brazil and British Guiana.

The New York subway opens.

Exploration of Antarctica and the Arctic

Scott and the Antarctic

Between 1897 and 1917, 16 expeditions from nine countries were sent to explore the Antarctic region. The race to reach the South Pole reached a climax in 1910, when two separate parties, one led by Norwegian Roald Amundsen, the other by Englishman, Robert Scott, set out for the Antarctic. Amundsen's team were experienced in Arctic exploration, and made skillful use of dog sleds. Scott's less experienced party (*above*) resorted to human muscle-power. Amundsen reached the Pole on December 14, 1911, while Scott's party arrived over a month later. His exhausted party perished on their return journey. Scott's stoic acceptance of his fate, as well as his epic endeavors, were recounted in his diary, and, despite his failure, he became a national hero.

1908 ▼
1906 ▼
1908 ▼
1906 ▼

The Transportation Revolution

1876 German engineer, Nikolaus Otto builds an internal-combustion engine.

1881 The first electric tramway, invented by Werner von Siemens, opens in Berlin.

1885 Karl Benz's "horseless carriage" reaches speeds of 8 mph (13 kph).

German engineer, Gottlieb Daimler invents the first motorcycle.

1886 Karl Benz patents the first automobile.

J. B. Dunlop invents the pneumatic tyre.

1892 German engineer, Rudolf Diesel patents the first internal-combustion engine.

1893 Karl Benz constructs a four-wheeled automobile.

1894 The first automobile race takes place, between Paris and Rouen.

1895 Armand Peugeot perfects a gasoline-powered engine and founds the Peugeot automobile company.

1900 Count von Zeppelin's airship makes a maiden flight over Lake Constance, Switzerland.

1901 First Mercedes automobile is built in the US.

Cadillac motorcar company founded in Detroit.

1903 Henry Ford sells his first designs for a low-cost automobile. Wilbur and Orville Wright make the first successful flight from Kitty Hawk, N Carolina, lasting 12 seconds.

First coast-to-coast crossing of the American continent by car: 65 days. A motoring speed limit of 20 mph (32 kph) is set in Britain.

1904 Rolls Royce company founded.

1905 The Wright brothers make the longest flight yet – 28 minutes, 3 seconds.

First motor-driven buses in London.

1906 First Grand Prix sports-car race.

1908 Ford's first Model T is produced in Detroit, "a motor car for the great multitude."

General Motors Corporation formed.

1909 French aviator Louis Blériot makes the first flight across the English Channel (37 minutes).

1915 Ford produces one millionth car.

The first automobiles were patented in the 1880s. Within a decade they had become playthings of the rich, but it was not until mass-production techniques were established, pioneered in the US by Henry Ford in 1908, that motor cars became available for the masses. Ford launched his Model T (above) in 1908. Over the next 20 years, 15 million rolled off the assembly line, making Ford the largest automobile producer in the world. By 1914 there were over a million cars in the US alone.

ASIA

1906 Rebellion in Teheran, following prime minister's attempt to expel two influential preachers.

Foundation of All-India Muslim League.

China grants Britain control of Tibet, following the occupation of Lhasa by British troops.

The world's biggest battleship, *Satsuma*, is launched in Japan.

1907 Nationalist riots rage in Calcutta.

Japan hands Manchuria back to China under the terms of the treaty of Portsmouth.

Crop failure and heavy rains in China lead to famine: 4 million people starve. .

British and Russians sign an agreement defining spheres of influence in Persia, and policies in Afghanistan and Tibet.

1908 In China, the child emperor Puyi succeeds to throne as Xuantong.

1909 Young Turks topple the tyrannical Ottoman sultan, Abdul Hamid II.

Muslim fanatics, backed by the Ottoman sultan, massacre Armenians.

British forces land at Tabriz, Persia, as fear of famine leads to widespread unrest.

Nationalists opposed to the Persian shah take Teheran.

Anglo-Persian Oil Company (later BP) founded in Iran.

"Morley-Minto" reforms in India introduce participation of Indians in government.

Hindus and Muslims riot in Calcutta.

1910 Russians and British decide to intervene in Persia, as political unrest sweeps the country.

Turkish troops battle with Albanian rebels.

The Dalai Lama flees to India as Chinese troops invade Lhasa.

Slavery is abolished in China.

Japanese annexation of Korea.

Russia acknowledges Japan's occupation of Korea in return for a free hand in Manchuria.

AFRICA

1906 British troops arrive in Nigeria to quell protests by the Tiv people against Muslim Hausa rule.

British troops kill 60 Zulus in fierce clashes against the poll tax.

The Transvaal and Orange Free State are given autonomy, with white male suffrage.

Britain, France, and Italy agree on the independence of Ethiopia.

Britain forces Turkey to cede the Sinai peninsula to Egypt.

1907 Germans capture the rebel leader Abdallah Mapanda, who has led *maji-maji* (magic water) uprisings in German E Africa.

In S Africa, white miners strike to preserve a job color bar.

French fleet bombards Casablanca, Morocco.

Nairobi is chosen as the capital of British E Africa.

German defeat of Nama (Hottentots) in SW Africa is complete.

1908 Leopold II transfers sovereignty over Congo Free State to Belgium.

1909 A Franco-German agreement recognizes French hegemony in Morocco.

British and Belgian troops clash over the border of Congo and N Rhodesia.

1910 Formation of union of S Africa with Afrikaners as majority white population. Union becomes a dominion of the British Empire.

France reorganizes French Congo as French Equatorial Africa.

Belgium, Britain, and Germany fix the frontiers of Congo, Uganda, and German E Africa.

France takes the port of Agadir, Morocco.

EUROPE

1906 Russian army officers are massacred in a mutiny at Sebastopol, in the Crimea.

The Russian *duma* is dissolved and martial law is declared.

Launch of HMS *Dreadnought*, the most powerful warship in the world.

1907 France and Russia sign an *entente cordiale*.

In Russia, 20 million people starve in the worst famine on record.

Pablo Picasso's *Les Demoiselles d'Avignon* causes a stir in Paris.

1908 Prince Ferdinand declares Bulgaria independent of the Ottomans.

Crete declares its independence from the Ottomans.

Austria annexes Bosnia-Herzegovina.

Rebellion in Portugal. King Carlos and crown prince Luiz are assassinated.

First radio transmitter built by Marconi.

The English suffragette Emmeline Pankhurst and her daughter are jailed after a sensational trial.

E. M. Forster publishes *A Room with a View*.

1909 The Ottoman Empire accepts Austria's offer of 2.5 million Turkish pounds for Bosnia-Herzegovina.

European powers agree a formula for Serbia to renounce its claims to Bosnia-Herzegovina.

The Ottoman emperor recognizes Bulgarian independence.

Antigovernment revolts in Catalonia, Spain, are suppressed.

1910 Portuguese monarchy overthrown; republic proclaimed.

The *duma* abolishes Finnish autonomy.

Montenegro declares its independence from Ottoman Empire.

Diaghilev's Russian Ballet astonishes Paris with its spectacular production of *The Firebird*.

AMERICAS & AUSTRALASIA

1906 US troops arrive in Cuba at the request of the ousted president to suppress a liberal revolt.

A treaty ends the war between Guatemala and allies, El Salvador and Honduras.

A major earthquake destroys most of the city of San Francisco.

A typhoon in Tahiti kills over 10,000 people.

1907 The record breaking British liner Lusitania crosses the Atlantic in four days, 19 hours, and 52 minutes.

1913

1908 Ford's first Model T car is produced in Detroit.

National Association for the Advancement of Colored People (NAACP) is founded in the US by William E. B. DuBois.

1909 US president William Taft announces that a naval base will be built at Pearl Harbor, Hawaii.

Nicaraguan president is ousted by the US. Dr. José Madriz succeeds him.

1911

1910 Start of the Mexican Revolution.

Thomas Edison demonstrates talking motion pictures.

In this cartoon, Sultan Abdul Hamid II sulks as more Balkan territory is whipped from under his feet by Austria and Bulgaria.

Collapse of the Ottoman Empire

Throughout the 19th century, the unity of the Ottoman Empire was challenged by the nationalist aspirations of its subject peoples. As the government weakened, the territorial aspirations of the Great Powers escalated, and they began to compete over the future of the sultan's domains. In 1875, revolts against Turkish rule in Bosnia led to the Treaty of San Stefano, which recognized the independence of Serbia, Montenegro, and newly created Bulgaria. Bosnia and Herzegovina were placed under Austrian administration.

Over the next 30 years, the European powers stripped Turkey of its remaining possessions in North Africa. As the empire collapsed, the sultan's younger, western-educated subjects became increasingly discontented. In 1909, the tyrannical despot, Sultan Abdul Hamid II, was deposed by these "Young Turks."

A Capitalist Age

In the forty years after 1870, the US national growth rate was 5.3 percent – the world's highest. This sharp increase in productivity was due to a vastly improved transportation infrastructure, new energy sources and more efficient factory machines and assembly line production. For the first time, inexpensive, mass-produced consumer goods were widely available. With the adoption of the gold standard for all major currencies, investment banking grew in importance. The famous US banker, John Pierpont Morgan, financed governments, as well as railroads and steel companies. Captains of industry, such as steel magnate Andrew Carnegie, and the owner of the Standard Oil trust, John D. Rockefeller, amassed great fortunes and wielded unprecedented political power.

Conscription and propaganda

Though World War I began against a background of wild popular enthusiasm in every combatant country, propaganda was a feature from the start. But by 1916, Britain was just one country forced to introduce conscription to meet the demand for fresh troops. Nonetheless, fewer troops were raised by conscription than had volunteered. When the US joined the war in 1917, troops were still drawn from volunteers.

20th Century Art

1904	Cézanne: *La Montagne Sainte Victoire*
1907	Picasso: *Les Demoiselles d'Avignon*
1911	Matisse *The Red Studio*
1913	Balla *Velocity of Cars and Light*
	Marc *The Fate of the Animals*
	Picasso *The Card Player*
	Braque *Young Girl with a Guitar*
1914	Gris *The Sunblind*
1917	Duchamp *The Fountain*; Grosz *Metropolis*
1919	Kockoschka *Woman in Blue*; Leger *City*
1921	Mondrian *Composition with Red, Yellow and Blue*
1924	Miró *Maternity*; Kandinsky *Yellow Accompaniment*
1927	O'Keefe *Oriental Poppies*
1923	Arp *Configuration*
1929	Dufy *The Artist and His Model in the Studio at Le Havre*
1930	Hopper *Early Sunday Morning*
1933	Brancusi *Head of Mademoiselle Pogany III*, sculpture
1931	Dalí *The Persistence of Memory*
1937	Dalí: *The Metamorphosis of Narcissus*
	Picasso *Guernica*
1939	Klee *La Belle Jardinière*
1944	Moore *Madonna*, sculpture
1945	Bacon *Three Studies for Figures at the Base of a Crucifixion*
1949	Pollock *Number 10 1949*
1950	Pollock *Number 1 1950 (Lavender Mist)*
	Rothko *Number 10*
1963	Lichtenstein *In the Car*
1967	Warhol *Marilyn*
1968	Hockney *American Collector*
1972	Christo *Running Fence*
1976	André *Equivalent VIII*, sculpture
1991	Hirst *The Physical Impossibility of Death in the Mind of Someone Living*, sculpture
	Parker *Cold, Dark Matter – An Exploded View*, sculpture
1992	Koon *Puppy*, sculpture
	Whiteread *Untitled* (House), sculpture

ASIA

1911 Chinese Revolution: Qing dynasty overthrown by Sun Yat-sen's nationalist Revolutionary Alliance and Republic of China declared. Flooding in Chang Jiang kills 100,000.

1912 Jan: Sun Yat-sen briefly declared provisional president of Republic of China. Feb: Abdication of last Qing emperor, Hsüan-t'ung; Yüan Shih-k'ai declared new provisional president.

1913 Yüan refuses to endorse new Chinese constitution after Nationalists win over 50 percent of seats in first Chinese parliamentary elections.

1918 ▼

1914 Ottomans ally with Germany and Austria after Britain, France, and Russia declare war.

Japan takes over many German colonies in Pacific and China.

1915 Saminist uprisings against Dutch rule in Dutch East Indies (–1917).

Japan asserts claims to Chinese territory in its "21 Demands."

About one million Armenians massacred or deported by Turks.

Feb: First Turkish attempt to capture Suez.

1918 ▼

Feb: Allied attack on Gallipoli.

1916 ▼

Yüan Shi-K'ai announces plans to become emperor of China.

AFRICA

1911 Italian conquest and occupation of Libya.

Franco-German conflict over French control of Morocco averted when France grants Germany parts of the Congo.

1912 Franco-Spanish protectorate established in Morocco.

African National Congress (ANC) formed in South Africa.

1913 Gandhi arrested in South Africa leading march of miners.

1919 ▼

1914 Egypt made a British protectorate.

South Africa joins World War I on Allied side.

EUROPE

1911 Pierre Prier makes first nonstop flight from London to Paris (3hr, 56min)

1912 First Balkan War: Balkan League (Serbia, Montenegro, Bulgaria, and Greece) capture most Ottoman territories in Europe (–May 1913).

Pravda ("Truth") first published by Russian Communist party.

1913 Second Balkan War: Bulgaria loses most of its gains from First War.

Premiere of Stravinsky's *The Rite of Spring*, Paris.

Greek king, George I, assassinated; succeeded by Constantine I.

1914 Assassination of Archduke Franz Ferndinand in Sarajevo begins renewed Great Power conflict in Balkans leading to Austrian declaration of war against Russia and thereafter general European war: World War I (–1918).

Irish Home Rule Bill passed by British House of Commons.

1915 Nihilistic art movement, Dada, flourishes in Zürich, New York City, Paris, Hannover, and Cologne.

AMERICAS & AUSTRALASIA

1916

1911 Overthrow of Mexican dictator, Porfirio Díaz, and election of radical president, Francisco Madero, prompts civil war. 20,000 US troops sent to Mexican border.

Democratic and social reform launched in Uruguay by José y Ordónez.

Studebaker car company offers world's first deferred-payment plan for car buyers, in US.

1912 US military intervention in Nicaraguan civil war (and at intervals to 1933).

The luxury liner *Titanic* sinks on maiden voyage: 1,523 die, 705 saved.

1918

1913 Woodrow Wilson president of the US (–1921).

Federal Reserve Board (the "Fed") founded, Washington, DC.

1916

Ford Motor Company introduces world's first moving production line, for Model T, in US.

1914 Panama Canal opened, joining Pacific and Atlantic; Canal Zone leased to US.

1918

Canada, Australia, and New Zealand join World War I on Allied side.

1915 US invasion of Haiti and Dominican Republic.

US intervention in Mexico and invasion of Haiti and Dominican Republics.

First traffic lights introduced, Cleveland, US.

First transcontinental telephone link established, US, between New York and San Francisco.

Sun Yat-sen (1886–1925)

Sun Yat-sen was the dominant figure in the early years of the Chinese revolution after 1911, even if ultimately his efforts to unite China under a radical, modernizing, democratic government fell foul of the ambitions of provincial leaders and warlords. His revolutionary instincts were clear from the start. He was also successful in winning overseas support and financing for the cause of Chinese revolution. He was elected provisional president in 1912, when he also established the Kuomintang party, always strongest in south China.

The Mexican Revolution

The Mexican Revolution was just one part of the wider political disturbances which overtook Latin America after about 1900 in which urban radicals, landowners, and peasants took on, and ultimately defeated, the established conservative political elites. In Mexico, though this led first to the overthrow of President Díaz in 1911, the revolutionaries in turn fragmented into numerous splinter groups, the most prominent led by Pancho Villa and Emiliano Zapata, who in 1916 were defeated by forces from north Mexico. But only in 1920, with the election of Plutarco Calles, was a semblance of stability restored.

Mexican revolutionaries used the rail network to conduct campaigns over long distances.

World War I

World War I was one of history's watersheds. It effectively ended the global supremacy of Europe and destroyed the Russian, Austro-Hungarian, German and Ottoman empires. The grim attritional struggle saw 65 million troops mobilized, of whom 9 million died and over one-third were wounded.

The major focus of the conflict was the trench warfare on the Western Front, where French, British, and Belgian troops (joined in 1918 by the US) faced the Germans. The Eastern Front, where Germany and Austria-Hungary confronted Russia, was more mobile. The fighting there was ended by Russia's precipitate collapse into revolution. Subsidiary theaters included the scarcely less bloody conflicts in northeast Italy and the Balkans, as well as the Middle East.

On the Western Front infantry spent long periods in the relative safety of the trenches, but when the generals called for an offensive, they had to go "over the top," often to be met by a hail of machine-gun bullets.

The Western Front

Within three months of the outbreak of war each side was dug in along a 350-mile (563-km) front from Switzerland to the Belgian coast that remained essentially unchanged until 1918. A series of set-piece battles, each preceded by a massive artillery bombardment – at Verdun, on the Somme, at Ypres – were designed to achieve a "decisive" breakthrough, yet neither side could ever follow up its initial successes before the defense plugged the gap with its reserves. The usual result of such offensives was a small amount of ground gained at a cost of slaughter on an unprecedented scale.

1914–1918

WESTERN FRONT

1914 Aug: Germany invades France through Belgium and Luxembourg; British troops land in France; battle of the Frontiers; Germans advance to within 25 miles (40 km) of Paris.

Sep: French government evacuated to Bordeaux (–Dec); Germans advance halted on the Marne; siege of Antwerp (–Oct).

Oct: First battle of Ypres (–Nov).

Nov: Western Front stabilized from Belgian coast to Swiss border.

1915 Jan: Allied offensives in Artois and Champagne (–Mar); first German zeppelin attack on England.

April: Second battle of Ypres; Germans use gas for first time of W Front, but attempted breakthrough fails (–May).

May: Second Battle of Artois. French and British offensives gain little for heavy loss of life (–Jun).

Sep: Allied autumn offensive (–Oct).

Dec: Sir Douglas Haig replaces Sir John French as commander of BEF.

1916 Feb: Massive German attack on Verdun (–Dec).

July: First Battle of the Somme; 60,000 British casualties on first day (–Nov).

Sep: Tanks introduced on Somme battlefield by British.

1917 Feb: Germans withdraw to Hindenburg Line (–Mar).

Aug: Third battle of Ypres (–Nov).

1918 March: Germans launch offensive on the Somme; make rapid gains, but no overall breakthrough; Foch given overall command of Allies on W Front.

April: Second German offensive in Flanders, south of Ypres.

May: US forces in action.

July: Last of the great German offensives of 1918; Second Battle of the Marne; Allied counterattack.

Sep: US forces clear St. Mihiel salient; Franco-American Meuse-Argonne offensive opens.

Nov: Kaiser Wilhelm II abdicates: Nov 11, Armistice day; fighting ceases 11am; Allied troops occupy the Rhineland.

Dec: German fleet scuttled in Scapa Flow.

BALKAN & ITALIAN FRONTS

1914 June: Assassination of Archduke Franz Ferdinand in Sarajevo precipitates start of World War I.

Archduke Franz Ferdinand and his wife in their car shortly before their assassination.

Aug: Austria invades Serbia, but forces are driven back.

Sep: Austria again meets fierce resistance in northern Serbia.

Dec: Third unsuccessful invasion of Serbia.

1915 April: Allies conclude secret Treaty of London with Italy.

May: Italy declares war on Austria-Hungary.

June: First Italian offensive against Austrians on the Isonzo.

Oct: Invasion of Serbia by Germans, Austrians and Bulgarians; third and fourth battles of the Isonzo (–Nov); Anglo-French force lands at Salonica.

1916 March: Fifth battle of the Isonzo.

May: Asiago offensive by Austria (–Jun).

Aug: Sixth and seventh battles of the Isonzo (–Sep); entry of Romania into war.

Oct: Eighth and ninth battles of the Isonzo (–Nov).

Dec: Elimination of Romania by Germans, Austrians, and Bulgarians .

1917 May: Tenth battle of the Isonzo.

Aug: Eleventh battle of the Isonzo (–Sep).

Oct: Italians suffer devastating defeat at Caporetto (–Nov).

Nov: Fall of Monastir to Allied forces.

1918 June: Italians hold back Austrian offensive on the Piave river.

Oct: Italians win decisive victory at Vittorio Veneto (–Nov).

Nov: Armistice agreed and hostilities cease on Nov 3.

EASTERN FRONT

1914 Aug: Russians invade East Prussia: suffer catastrophic defeat at battle of Tannenberg.

Sep: German victory over Russians at first battle of the Masurian Lakes; Austrians retreat in Galicia after series of battles around Lemberg.

Oct: German offensive in Poland halted in front of Warsaw.

Nov: Confused German victory at Lodz; Russians forced onto the defensive.

Dec: Austrians defeat Russians at Limanova.

1915 Jan: Germans use gas at Bolimov on Polish front.

Feb: German defeat Russians at second battle of the Masurian Lakes.

May: German breakthrough at Gorlice-Tarnow.

July: Russian withdrawal (–Sep).

Aug: Germans enter Warsaw.

1916 June: Russian Brusilov offensive severely demoralizes Austro-Hungarians (–Aug).

1917 March: Revolution in Russia; abdication of Czar Nicholas II; Kerensky government takes power.

July: Second Brusilov (Kerensky) offensive; Russian army starts to disintegrate.

Aug: Germans take Riga.

Nov: Bolshevik revolution.

Dec: Armistice betweeen Bolsheviks and Germany.

1918 March: Treaty of Brest-Litovsk; Germans occupy Ukraine.

Russian prisoners *file past their German captors on the Eastern Front.*

WAR IN THE WIDER WORLD

1914 Oct: Turks close Dardanelles. Japan takes over German colonies in n Pacific.

Nov: Turkey declares *jihad*; allies with Germany and Austria against France, Britain, and Russia.

1915 About one million Armenians massacred or deported by Turks.

Feb: Turkish attempt to capture Suez; British and French ships bombard forts on Dardanelles; Germany starts submarine blockade of Britain.

March: Greek premier Venizelos resigns when king refuses to back pro-Allied policy.

April: British and French land forces on Gallipoli peninsula.

May: U-boat sinks British liner *Lusitania* with the loss of American lives, provoking US-German diplomatic crisis

Aug: Further landings on Gallipoli, but Allies remain pinned down on beachheads.

Sep: In response to American pressure Germany halts unrestricted U-Boat activity.

Nov: Battle of Ctesiphon; British retreat in Mesopotamia.

Dec: British force besieged in Kut al Amara by Turks (–Apr 1916); withdrawal of Allied forces from Gallipoli (–Jan).

1916 Feb: Russians take Erzurum in Anatolia.

May: Battle of Jutland in North Sea.

June: Arab revolt; Arabian tribes supported by British rise against Turks (–1918).

1917 March: British take Baghdad.

April: US declares war on Central Powers.

Dec: British take Jerusalem.

1918 Sep: Battle of Megiddo, conclusive Allied victory over Turks in Palestine.

Oct: Turks surrender.

The Sopwith Camel *first saw active service in 1917, becoming one of the most successful fighters of the war. Light, agile, and armed with twin Vickers machine-guns, it was credited with shooting down 1,294 enemy aircraft.*

Mechanized warfare

All the combatants faced the problem of how to penetrate two or three lines of trenches protected by barbed wire and machine-guns. Despite technological advances in gunnery and the development of new weapons such as the tank, breakthrough proved elusive. Terror-weapons such as gas and flame-throwers were used extensively, adding to the appalling toll of casualties.

Aircraft, initially used for reconnaissance and artillery spotting, soon became weapons in themselves: fighters fought duels in the sky, while bombers attacked miltary and civilian targets. At sea the submarine proved a potent weapon in Germany's attempt to deprive Britain of food and raw materials. However, the sinking of merchant and passenger ships was instrumental in bringing the US into the war – a significant factor in Germany's ultimate defeat.

A British Mark I tank crosses a trench during the battle of the Somme in September 1916. This was the first time tanks had seen action. Although they did take the enemy by surprise at first, the tanks were far from reliable and many ended up ditched.

Vladimir Ilyich Lenin

Lenin dominated and drove the Russian Revolution. Despite spending much of his life before the revolution in prison or in exile, he was a leading figure in Russian revolutionary circles from the 1890s. Though a committed Marxist, he also believed that the proletariat needed to be led by a cadre of committed professional revolutionaries, a goal his Bolshevik party, established in 1912, was formed to carry out. Opportunistically sent back to Russia by the Germans in 1917, he rapidly and ruthlessly imposed a "dictatorship of the proletariat."

The Russian Revolution

Weakened by war and riven by glaring class differences, Russia in 1917 was ripe for revolutionary takeover. Within eight months, Lenin's Bolsheviks had seized control.

1917 Mar: Revolution in Russia and abdication of Czar Nicholas II; provisional government set up under Prince Georgii Lvov. Communist-dominated Soviets set up in many cities.

Apr: Germans allow return to Russia of veteran communist agitator Lenin.

July: Socialist Alexander Kerensky made president. Revolution in Petrograd (July Days).

Sept: Russian Republic declared by Kerensky.

Oct: Petrograd Soviet establishes Military Revolutionary Committee under Leon Trotsky.

Nov: Petrograd seized by Military Revolutionary Committee; Bolshevik All-Russian Congress of Soviets, led by Lenin, declared new government of Russia.

Dec: Russia withdraws from World War I.

1918 Mar: German-Russian peace terms agreed to in Treaty of Brest-Litovsk: Poland, Baltic States, Ukraine, and Georgia ceded to Germany.

July: Russian Czar and family murdered by Bolsheviks. Civil war between Bolsheviks and White Russians begins (–1921). Red Army formed.

ASIA

1916 Yüan Shih-k'ai overthrown after attempting to declare himself new emperor of China; fragmented warlord rule follows (–1927).

1917 Balfour Declaration commits Britain to creation of a Jewish state in Palestine.

1918 Oct: Ottomans surrender to Allies ending World War I in Middle East.

Japanese occupation of parts of Manchuria and Siberia during Chinese and Russian civil wars.

1919 Greek forces land in Smyrna, Turkey.

Upswell of nationalism in China – the May 4th Movement – provoked by international support for Japan's territorial claims in China.

Afghanistan granted independence by Britain.

Former-German territories in Pacific "mandated" to Japan by League of Nations.

India and China become founding members of League of Nations; Japan awarded a permanent seat.

1921

1920 Treaty of Sèvres confirms continued rule of Ottoman sultan over a greatly reduced Turkey sparking wave of Turkish nationalism led by Mustafa Kemal (Atatürk).

1925

Former Ottoman territories in Middle East "mandated" to Britain (Palestine and Transjordan and Iraq) and France (Syria).

Chinese Communist Party founded.

Earthquake in Gansu, China, kills 200,000.

AFRICA

1918 First Pan-African Congress held.

1922

1919 Anti-British nationalist uprisings in Egypt.

1920 Former German territories in Africa "mandated" to Britain (Tanganyika, British Cameroons, British Togo), France (French Cameroons, French Togo) and South Africa (Southwest Africa).

1916 Publication of Einstein's *General Theory of Relativity*.

Avalanche in Italian Alps kills 10,000.

1917 Mar: Beginnings of revolution in Russia.

1918 "Spanish" influenza sweeps Europe: over six million die.

Nov: Austria withdraws from World War I. German kaiser flees to Holland; Armistice ends World War I.

Congress of Oppressed Peoples, Rome, calls for breakup of Austro-Hungarian Empire on ethnic lines.

1919 Treaty of Versailles forces Germany to admit war guilt and pay reparations to Allies and establishes new European order with eight new states created, largely in territories belonging to the former Austro-Hungarian and German empires. Other 1919 treaties include those of St. Germain (with Austria) and Neuilly (with Bulgaria).

Communist Spartakist uprising in Germany suppressed.

League of Nations founded.

Short-lived communist regime established by Béla Kun in Hungary.

Russo-Polish war starts (–1920).

1921 Britain concedes dominion status to southern Ireland.

1921 Attempted assassination of Lenin leads to systematic elimination of opposition to Bolsheviks: the Red Terror. Bolsheviks establish Communist International (COMINTERN) to foment revolution abroad (–1943).

International Labor Organization (ILO) founded, Geneva.

Publication of J. M. Keynes's *Economic Consequence of the Peace*.

Bauhaus school of architecture and design in Germany under Walter Gropius; massively influences spread of modernism in architecture.

British airmen Alcock and Brown make first nonstop transatlantic flight (Newfoundland to Ireland).

1920 Treaty of Trianon agrees to dismemberment of Hungary.

1916 Defeat of radical forces under Zapata in Mexican civil war.

Ford in US mass-produces first all-purpose tractor.

1917 US enters World War I on Allied side.

1924 Social protest sweeps across much of Latin America, weakening grip of established rural-based political elites. New constitution restores democracy to Mexico.

US military intervention in Cuba (–1922).

Virgin Islands sold to US by Denmark.

1921 Asian laborers excluded from entering US by Immigration Act.

World's first regular passenger air-service begun, Tampa, Florida.

1918 Jan: President Woodrow Wilson announces his Fourteen Points, affirming the right to national self-determination, as a basis for a future peace settlement in Europe.

1919 US Senate rejects Versailles Settlement and withdraws into isolation, refusing to join the League of Nations.

Federal Bureau of Investigation (FBI) established.

1920 Postwar boom fuels massive economic growth in US, now world's dominant economy, to late 1920s. The "jazz age" epitomizes the new spirit of affluence.

Election of Plutarco Calles ends revolutionary disturbances in Mexico.

Women granted the vote in US.

Prohibition introduced in the US, sparking rise of organized crime.

Submachine gun patented, US.

1923 World's first regularly scheduled radio program broadcast, Pittsburgh.

Revelers mourn the passing of the Volstead Act in 1919, prohibiting the sale of alcohol in the US.

Prohibition

The Volstead Act, or the 18th Amendment, was among the most disastrous social experiments of 20th-century America. Under it, the "manufacture, sale, and transportation of intoxicating liquors" was outlawed across the US. The Act went into effect on January 29, 1920.

The roots of Prohibition sprang from a rural Protestant belief in the harmfulness of alcohol. By World War I movements such as the Prohibition Party of 1869 (which is still in existence), the Woman's Christian Temperance Union of 1874, and the Anti-Saloon League of 1893 had become powerful political forces.

Prohibition did more than underline the divide between rural pro-Prohibition America and urban anti-Prohibition America. It provided a substantial boost to organized crime, which largely met the huge pent-up demand for alcohol. By its peak in the late 1920s, gangs such as Al Capone's in Chicago were generating over $60 million a year from alcohol sales. In the face of such clear evidence that the Act was unenforceable, in February 1933 Prohibition was repealed.

1916–1920 399

Radio transformed popular culture. By the 1930s, audiences for the most successful programs were numbered in millions.

Radio

The explosion in the popularity of radio after World War I was exceptional. From the start of regularly scheduled radio broadcasting in the US in 1920, in only two years nearly 600 radio stations were opened. In 1923, there were an estimated three million radio sets; in 1929, 14 million, and by 1940, there were an estimated 40 million.

For most, radio was foremost a means of entertainment. But it was also a powerful new tool for news broadcasting – in many states, this increasingly meant government propaganda. In the US and Britain, by contrast, the role of radio in spreading impartial, accurate news was crucial.

The Jazz Age

Against a background of undreamed-of levels of economic prosperity and determined to forget the horrors of modern war, the US in the 1920s embarked on a giddy age of pleasure-seeking expansion. Its preeminent symbol – aggressively modern and unmistakably American – was jazz. Its heart was in the speakeasies of Chicago, where performers such as Louis Armstrong (*above*), Duke Ellington, Bix Beiderbecke, and Bessie Smith pioneered a musical style that swept the world.

ASIA

1921 Nationalist government established in Ankara under Atatürk challenges continued rule of the Ottoman sultan.

Mongolia declared independent of China.

1922 Territorial integrity of China and new limits on naval strengths agreed to by US, Britain, and Japan at Washington Conference.

Nationalists drive Greek army from Turkey and overthrow last Ottoman sultan.

Typhoon in Shantou, China, kills 28,000.

British authorities in India sentence Gandhi to six years imprisonment (released after two).

1923 Treaty of Lausanne endorses existence of new, enlarged Turkish state. Turkish Republic proclaimed with Atatürk president.

Nationalist Kuomintang government formed in Canton under Sun Yat-sen.

1924 Muslim caliphate abolished in Turkey by Atatürk. Kurdish schools, publications and association banned

Earthquake in Kanto region, Japan, causes Great Fire of Tokyo and kills 143,000.

1926 ▼ **1925** Civil war breaks out in China. Death of Sun Yat-sen; succeeded by Chiang Kai-shek.

Chinese-Soviet border consolidated.

Nationalist uprising against French rule in Syria.

AFRICA

1921 Spain defeated by Moroccans at Battle of Annual.

1922 Conditional Egyptian independence granted by Britain.

Tomb of Tutankhamun discovered by British archaeologist, Howard Carter, in Egypt's Valley of the Kings.

1926 ▼ **1923** Abyssinia joins League of Nations.

Sahara crossed by car for first time.

1925 French campaigns against Nationalist Moroccan leader, Abd-el Krim, launched.

EUROPE

1921 Bolsheviks triumph in Russian civil war. Lenin attempts to stabilize deteriorating Russian economy by introducing limited forms of capitalism: the New Economic Policy. Major famine (–1923) leads to deaths of six million.

Precise terms of German war reparations agreed to in London: payments scheduled for every year until 1988.

Irish Free State created.

1927 ▼

1922 Union of Soviet Socialist Republics (USSR) created.

1926 ▼

Benito Mussolini becomes prime minister of Italy.

First public radio broadcasts in Britain and France.

Treaty of Rapallo signed between Germany and USSR.

1930 ▼

1923 French and Belgian troops occupy parts of the Ruhr in Germany to ensure delivery of coal as part of war reparations.

Hyperinflation in Germany.

Military coup in Spain: Primo de Rivera becomes dictator.

Italy forced by League of Nations to withdraw from Corfu, Greece.

Communist uprisings in Germany and Bulgaria crushed.

World's first domestic electric refrigerator, Sweden.

1924 Death of Lenin provokes power struggle in USSR.

German reparations reduced by Dawes Plan (and again in 1929).

Winter Olympics first held, Chamonix, France.

1925 General Hindenburg becomes president of Germany.

Release of Russian cinematic masterpiece *Battleship Potemkin*, directed by Sergei Eisenstein.

John Logie Baird transmits first television picture, London.

AMERICAS & AUSTRALASIA

1921 Warren Harding president of US (–1923).

US restricts immigration under "Quota Acts."

Frederick Banting and Charles Best isolate the hormone insulin, used for treatment of diabetes, in Canada.

First two-way mobile radios introduced by police in Detroit.

1922 Five hundred and sixty-four licenced radio stations operating in US. The first commercial is broadcast.

USS *Langley* converted to become world's first aircraft carrier.

Ecuador becomes independent.

1923 Calvin Coolidge president of US (–1929) after death in office of Warren Harding.

1929 ▼

World's first portable radio developed, US.

More than 13 million cars on US roads.

1924 Military coup in Chile.

1926 ▼

Military revolt in Brazil leads to near civil war.

Premier of George Gershwin's *Rhapsody in Blue*, US.

1925 US astronomer Edwin Hubble discovers the existence of galaxies beyond our own and that the Universe is expanding: the foundation of modern cosmology.

"Grand Ole Opry," world's longest-running radio show, first broadcast from Nashville.

In 1923, the mark became essentially worthless. These children are using banknotes as building blocks.

Economic crisis in Germany

With war debts of more than 150 billion marks, Germany's economy was all but wiped out by World War I. However, it suffered a near terminal shock after 1921 when the details of German war reparations were finally agreed upon. Among much else, 90 percent of the German merchant fleet was lost, 75 percent of the country's iron and 70 percent of its zinc ore. The economy disintegrated. By late 1923, hyperinflation had reduced the mark to one-trillionth of its prewar value. The reparations debt was eventually rearranged on easier terms.

Benito Mussolini

Mussolini, leader of the Fascist Party, came to power in Italy in 1922, boosted by popular resentment at the high-handed treatment of Italy by the Allies at the  Versailles Settlement and determined to stamp out Marxist forces within Italy. In 1926 he made Italy a one-party state, styling himself "leader" – *duce*.

His subsequent alliances with Germany and Japan stemmed more from opportunistic efforts to make Italy a world power than from a genuine shared ideology. Fascist Italy, though repressive, never approached the absolute totalitarianism of Nazi Germany.

The World in 1925

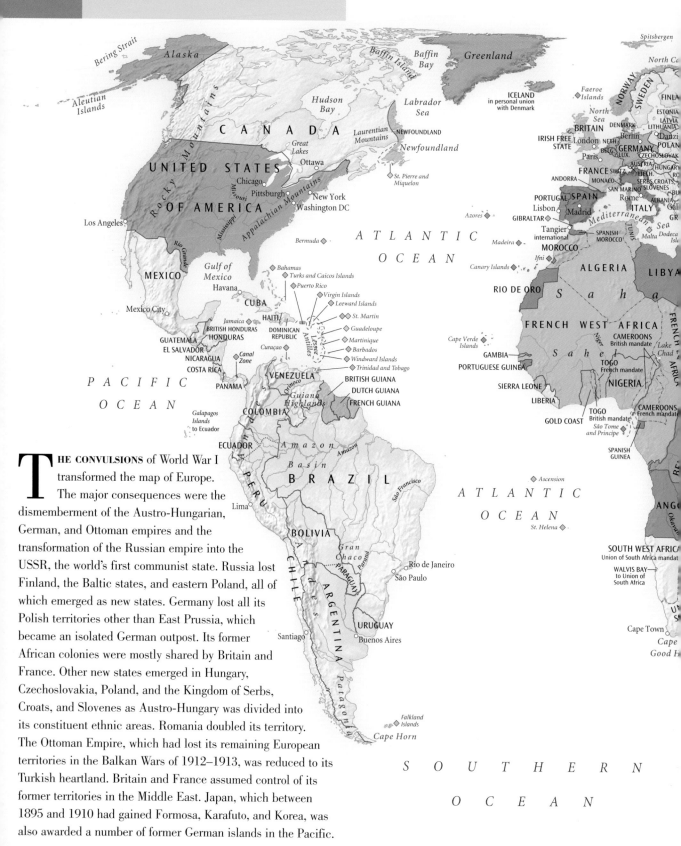

THE CONVULSIONS of World War I transformed the map of Europe. The major consequences were the dismemberment of the Austro-Hungarian, German, and Ottoman empires and the transformation of the Russian empire into the USSR, the world's first communist state. Russia lost Finland, the Baltic states, and eastern Poland, all of which emerged as new states. Germany lost all its Polish territories other than East Prussia, which became an isolated German outpost. Its former African colonies were mostly shared by Britain and France. Other new states emerged in Hungary, Czechoslovakia, Poland, and the Kingdom of Serbs, Croats, and Slovenes as Austro-Hungary was divided into its constituent ethnic areas. Romania doubled its territory. The Ottoman Empire, which had lost its remaining European territories in the Balkan Wars of 1912–1913, was reduced to its Turkish heartland. Britain and France assumed control of its former territories in the Middle East. Japan, which between 1895 and 1910 had gained Formosa, Karafuto, and Korea, was also awarded a number of former German islands in the Pacific.

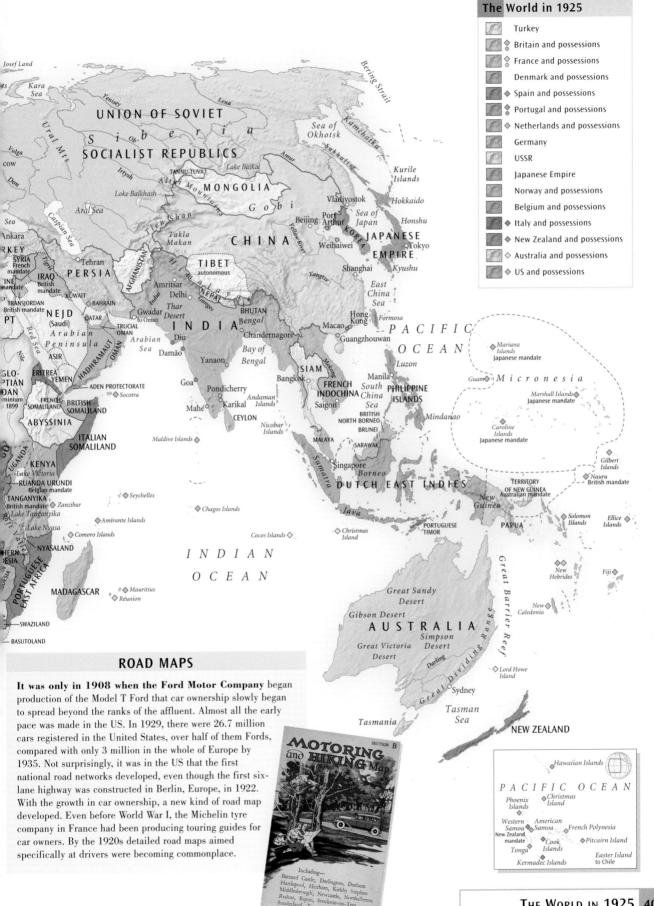

The World in 1925

- Turkey
- Britain and possessions
- France and possessions
- Denmark and possessions
- Spain and possessions
- Portugal and possessions
- Netherlands and possessions
- Germany
- USSR
- Japanese Empire
- Norway and possessions
- Belgium and possessions
- Italy and possessions
- New Zealand and possessions
- Australia and possessions
- US and possessions

ROAD MAPS

It was only in 1908 when the Ford Motor Company began production of the Model T Ford that car ownership slowly began to spread beyond the ranks of the affluent. Almost all the early pace was made in the US. In 1929, there were 26.7 million cars registered in the United States, over half of them Fords, compared with only 3 million in the whole of Europe by 1935. Not surprisingly, it was in the US that the first national road networks developed, even though the first six-lane highway was constructed in Berlin, Europe, in 1922. With the growth in car ownership, a new kind of road map developed. Even before World War I, the Michelin tyre company in France had been producing touring guides for car owners. By the 1920s detailed road maps aimed specifically at drivers were becoming commonplace.

1925–1950
The World between the Wars

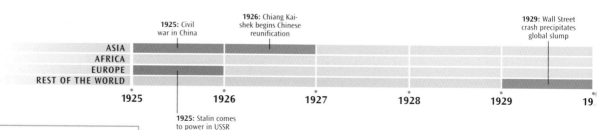

1925: Civil war in China

1926: Chiang Kai-shek begins Chinese reunification

1929: Wall Street crash precipitates global slump

ASIA
AFRICA
EUROPE
REST OF THE WORLD

1925   1926   1927   1928   1929   19

1925: Stalin comes to power in USSR

THE DISRUPTION THAT FOLLOWED the end of World War I led directly to an even greater global conflict just over 20 years later. The era between the wars was marked by political and economic instability almost everywhere, facilitating the rise of authoritarian dictatorships, both of the left and of the right. The world had never seemed more uncertain or dangerous. Even the US, which had ended World War I as the world's most dynamic economic power, was not immune from the mounting crisis. A decade of dizzy economic growth ended abruptly in 1929 with a stock market crash that caused a catastrophic worldwide slump. At the same time, the apparently massive edifice that was European imperialism, the cornerstone of world order before 1914, was being undermined by demands for independence that were increasingly difficult to ignore. The certainties of the pre-1914 world had disappeared for ever.

Above all, however, the world in 1925 was divided along a series of ideological fault lines. By championing national self-determination, the US-inspired Versailles settlement of 1919 had sought to "make the world safe for democracy." But powerful forces were ranged against the fragile new states created after the war just as much as they were against the world's established democracies: an agressively expansionist Japan, determined to dominate China and East Asia militarily as well as economically; a newly expansionist fascist Italy which, under Mussolini from 1922, was determined to assert its "strong rule" on a world stage; and, in the rapidly industrializing Soviet Union, a new communist state no less determined to destabilize its neighbors.

Competing ideologies

By the 1930s, the world's democracies were increasingly beleaguered, struggling to deal with mass unemployment and the the other economic consequences of the Great Crash. Throughout the decade, almost all the new states in Europe created after the war embraced various forms of authoritarian rule. So, too, did Germany, where in 1933 Adolf Hitler was made chancellor. Hitler came to power pledging not just to end the turmoil that had disrupted the country since 1918 but also to overturn what to many Germans were the manifest injustices of the Versailles settlement.

PICTURE ABOVE:
Adolf Hitler speaking at a Nazi rally in Dortmund in 1933, the year he came to power. Hitler's oratory struck a chord in those who thought Germany had been harshly treated after World War I and swallowed his myths of Germany's historic destiny.

The Great Depression, precipitated by the 1929 stock market crash, was the worst ever experienced in the modern industrial era. By 1932, 30 percent of the US workforce was unemployed with hardly any prospect of getting a job.

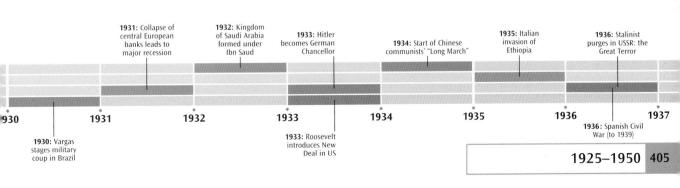

1930: Vargas stages military coup in Brazil

1931: Collapse of central European banks leads to major recession

1932: Kingdom of Saudi Arabia formed under Ibn Saud

1933: Hitler becomes German Chancellor

1933: Roosevelt introduces New Deal in US

1934: Start of Chinese communists' "Long March"

1935: Italian invasion of Ethiopia

1936: Stalinist purges in USSR: the Great Terror

1936: Spanish Civil War (to 1939)

930   1931   1932   1933   1934   1935   1936   1937

JAPANESE PREWAR EXPANSION

Japan's conquests in World War II were no more than the logical extension of a process that had begun at the end of the 19th century. Determined to assert itself on a wider world stage and to secure access to raw materials vital to its continued industrialization, Japan fought wars against China in 1894–1895 and against Russia in 1904–1905, which saw the conquests of Formosa and then Sakhalin. In 1910 the conquest of Korea was completed. In World War I Japan fought on the side of the Allies against Germany and was awarded further holdings in the Pacific in 1919. These were the former German Pacific territories north of the Equator and Tsingtao, the German trading concession in China, which the Japanese had overrun in 1914. However, the Japanese felt that they were never treated as equals by their Western allies, especially in the series of naval limitation treaties that dictated the number of warships Japan could build.

In 1930, a new round of conquest was launched, leading to the capture of Manchuria in northern China. When, in 1933, the League of Nations condemned the invasion, the Japanese delegation simply walked out, and Manchuria was proclaimed the Japanese protectorate – a puppet state in all but name – of Manchukuo. Steady southward expansion into China followed, leading to outright war: Shanghai was invaded in 1937, Nanking, captured in an orgy of looting and destruction in 1938. It was British, American, and Soviet attempts to resist Japan's self-aggrandizing expansion that in 1936 drove the Japanese and the Germans to make common cause together.

Hirohito succeeded to the imperial throne of Japan in 1926. Following Japan's defeat in 1945, he renounced any claim to semidivine status, Japan becoming a constitutional monarchy. He reigned until his death in 1989.

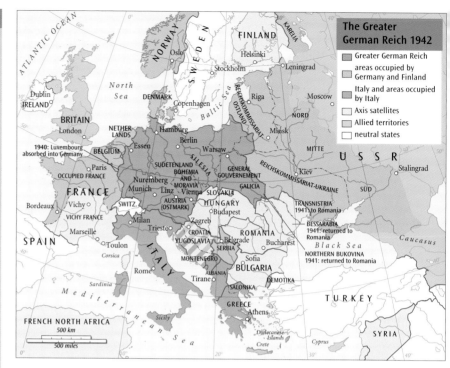

From the states they had conquered, annexed, and occupied, the Nazis created the so-called "Greater German Reich." The conquered areas of the east were ravaged and cleared for German settlement by means of ruthless ethnic cleansing, targeting Jews, Gypsies, political dissidents, and "social deviants."

Nazi Germany rapidly epitomized a new kind of authoritarian state in which the systematic and ruthless persecution of opponents was a central goal of government policy. The Nazis' totalitarian regime was paralleled in the Soviet Union under Josef Stalin, who had come to power in 1925, and where "enemies of the state" were treated equally brutally. Untold millions were executed or allowed to starve to death under Stalin's arbitrary and secretive rule.

However similar in their exercise of power, the Soviet Union and Nazi Germany were nonetheless ideological opposites, the former at least nominally committed to building a workers' state, the latter aggressively nationalistic and militaristic. In 1936, the political tensions between these rival forms of dictatorship came to a head in Spain, where the election of a left-wing Popular Front government precipitated a military revolt by conservative groups. With Germany providing support for the right-wing Nationalists and the USSR support for the left-wing Republicans, the resulting civil war was a foretaste of the wider conflict to come.

The road to war

The Spanish Civil War remained an essentially local conflict; by the late 1930s the eyes of the world were on Hitler's Germany. As Germany rearmed, so it expanded, reoccupying the Rhineland in 1936, marching into neighboring Austria in 1938 and, later

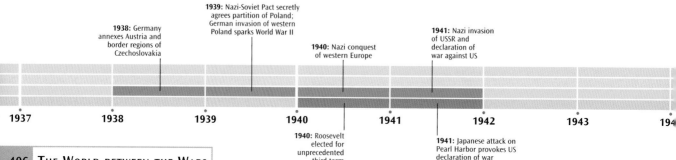

1938: Germany annexes Austria and border regions of Czechoslovakia

1939: Nazi-Soviet Pact secretly agrees partition of Poland; German invasion of western Poland sparks World War II

1940: Nazi conquest of western Europe

1941: Nazi invasion of USSR and declaration of war against US

1940: Roosevelt elected for unprecedented third term

1941: Japanese attack on Pearl Harbor provokes US declaration of war against Japan

1937   1938   1939   1940   1941   1942   1943   194

The Greater German Reich 1942

- Greater German Reich
- areas occupied by Germany and Finland
- Italy and areas occupied by Italy
- Axis satellites
- Allied territories
- neutral states

that year, taking over most of the border regions of Czechoslovakia. Six months later, Germany absorbed the whole of western Czechoslovakia. Hitler's intentions were now obvious to all. However reluctantly, Britain and France committed themselves to oppose further German expansion. It duly came in September 1939 with the German invasion of Poland.

A truly global conflict

Germany's 1936 alliances with Italy and Japan, both already engaged in savage wars of conquest of their own, Japan in China, Italy in Ethiopia, made the conflict a global war from the start.

In Europe, Germany's new, highly mechanized armies at first proved invincible. Poland was crushed in less than a month; in April 1940, Denmark and Norway fell in an even shorter time; and by the end of June, the Netherlands, Belgium, and France had also been overrun. Germany had won control of mainland western Europe and the only state that remained to oppose Hitler's ambitions was Britain. With Italy's declaration of war on Britain and France in June 1940 fighting spread to the Mediterranean and North Africa, where Italian and German troops tried to drive the British out of Egypt. In April 1941, Yugoslavia and Greece were added to Germany's growing list of conquests.

The scope of the war was further extended after the German invasion of the USSR in June 1941 and then six months later by the Japanese attack on Pearl Harbor, which finally brought the US into the war. The scale of the front opened up by the Japanese advances in Southeast Asia and the Pacific was staggering. Nothing like it had ever been witnessed before. By May 1942, they had driven the Americans from the Philippines, the British from the Malayan peninsula, and

the Dutch from Indonesia. Their advance into Burma menaced British India, while troops had also landed on New Guinea and the Solomon Islands, from where they threatened Australia. In June 1942, they even landed on the Aleutian Islands in the far north of the Pacific.

In the end it was the sheer scale of Japanese and German ambition that made their defeat inevitable. Their actions of 1941 brought the world's two most powerful nations into the Allied camp: the US with its unmatched economic and industrial power and the Soviet Union with its seemingly limitless manpower. In spite of this, neither Germany nor Japan was prepared to surrender and both fought on until 1945. Almost no area of the world was untouched by the fighting; many cities and towns, in Japan, in Europe, and especially in the Soviet Union, were completely devastated. The systematic bombing of civilian populations was accepted by both sides as part of the strategy of modern warfare, a way of thinking that culminated in the dropping of atomic bombs on Hiroshima and Nagasaki by the US.

The human cost of World War II was terrifying. Between 50 and 60 million people are estimated to have been killed, among them 21 million Soviet citizens (military and civilians) and six million Jews, the latter systematically exterminated in Hitler's death camps. This was "total war" of a kind and on a scale never seen before.

A perilous future

World War II ended the threats posed by Hitler and Japan but its legacy was further conflict. In part, this was the result of the beginnings of the breakup of Europe's empires. Indian independence

***Jubilant Indians** ride through the streets of Calcutta celebrating Independence Day on August 15, 1947. The darker side of independence was the partition of India and Pakistan, which led to riots and massacres.*

in 1947 and the establishment of a Jewish state in Britain's former Palestinian "mandate" the following year both led to bitter wars, for example. In China, now freed from the threat of the Japanese, the civil war between the Nationalists and the communist forces of Mao Zedong was resumed. Fighting continued until 1949, when the communists emerged triumphant.

The overriding threat to world peace, however, was the hostility between the world's two new superpowers, the US and the USSR. During the war, it had been the imperative of overcoming Germany that brought them together. With Hitler defeated, their latent hostility resurfaced. The eastern European countries that had been liberated from the Germans by the Russians found that they had exchanged one form of totalitarianism for another. Western Europe squared up to eastern Europe across the "Iron Curtain" that ran through the newly divided Germany. It was a hostility made all the more dangerous by a new and terrible threat: nuclear war. The Cold War had dawned.

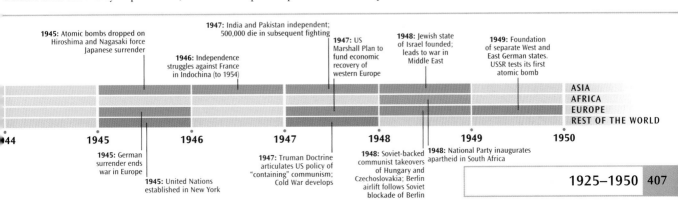

1945: Atomic bombs dropped on Hiroshima and Nagasaki force Japanese surrender

1946: Independence struggles against France in Indochina (to 1954)

1947: India and Pakistan independent; 500,000 die in subsequent fighting

1947: US Marshall Plan to fund economic recovery of western Europe

1948: Jewish state of Israel founded; leads to war in Middle East

1949: Foundation of separate West and East German states. USSR tests its first atomic bomb

| 44 | 1945 | 1946 | 1947 | 1948 | 1949 | 1950 |

ASIA
AFRICA
EUROPE
REST OF THE WORLD

1945: German surrender ends war in Europe

1945: United Nations established in New York

1947: Truman Doctrine articulates US policy of "containing" communism; Cold War develops

1948: Soviet-backed communist takeovers of Hungary and Czechoslovakia; Berlin airlift follows Soviet blockade of Berlin

1948: National Party inaugurates apartheid in South Africa

Hollywood: The Silent Era

The silent era was shortlived but intense. By the arrival of talkies in 1927, Hollywood had become a global business.

1911 First movie studios open in Hollywood.
1914 Release of *The Squaw*, first feature-length Hollywood Western.
1915 D.W. Griffith directs *The Birth of a Nation*.
1917 Charlie Chaplin signs the first $1 million movie contract.
1919 United Artists founded by Charlie Chaplin, Mary Pickford, and Douglas Fairbanks.
1920 Swashbuckling epic comes of age with *The Mask of Zorro*.
1921 *The Four Horsemen of the Apocalypse* produces the first matinee idol: Rudolf Valentino.
1923 First Cecil B. De Mille epic, *The Ten Commandments*. Warner Bros. begins the studio system.
1924 Columbia and MGM studios founded.
1925 King Vidor's antiwar masterpiece: *The Big Parade*.

The USSR: The Five-Year Plan

The USSR's first Five-Year Plan was launched by Stalin in 1929 in an urgent drive not merely toward mass industrialization but also to extend state power over all areas of life in the Soviet Union. In economic terms, it was a success: industry developed faster than at any other time in Russian history and by the late 1930s, the country had become a major industrial power. In human terms, however, it was a catastrophe. The collectivization of agriculture resulted in millions of deaths, many from deliberately engineered famines designed to break peasant resistance.

Collectivization eradicated traditional farming in the USSR. The main targets were land-owning peasants, the "kulaks," who were systematically driven from their farms. The propaganda image of purposeful, contented workers under the benevolent guidance of Stalin was sharply at odds with the reality.

1926–1930

ASIA

1926 Ibn Saud crowns himself king of the Hejaz and sultan of Nejd.

Nationalist Northern Expedition unites Chinese heartland under Chiang Kai-shek (–1928).

1934
Hirohito crowned emperor of Japan.

Communist rebellion against Dutch rule in Java and Sumatra in Indonesia.

1927 Chinese nationalists purge communist supporters.

Oil discovered in Iraq.

Earthquake in Jiangxi, China, kills 200,000.

Major campaigns launched by France against Druze uprising in Syria.

1928 Jawaharalal Nehru formally demands Indian independence from Britain.

1929 Jiangxi Soviet established by Chinese communists in southern China (–1934).

1930 Pu'an Soviet established by Chinese communists in central China (–1935).

AFRICA

1926 S Africa becomes Autonomous Dominion within British Empire.

Italy and Abyssinia sign friendship treaty.

Revolt against French rule in Morocco launched by 'Abd-el Krim.

1928 Muslim Brotherhood founded, Egypt.

EUROPE

1926 Italy becomes one-party state under Mussolini.

Germany admitted to League of Nations

Right-wing dictatorship headed by Antonio Salazar established in Portugal.

Military coup in Poland by General Pilsudski.

Right-wing coup in Latvia.

General Strike in Britain.

1927 Stalin becomes head of state in USSR. Leon Trotsky expelled from Soviet communist party.

Prussia lifts ban on Nazi party.

1928 Penicillin, world's first antibiotic, discovered in UK by Alexander Fleming.

Women first allowed to compete in Olympic Games, Amsterdam.

1929 Europe-wide slump provoked by Wall Street crash; resulting crisis destabilizes political order across Europe for many years.

Stalin introduces first Five-Year Plan in USSR: massive industrialization of industry and wholesale collectivization of agriculture launched.

Lateran Accords end conflict between papacy and state in Italy.

Royal dictatorship established in Yugoslavia.

Stalin engineers expulsion of rival Trotsky from USSR.

German Hans Berger monitors electrical activity in the brain using an electroencephalograph.

1930 Soviet rearmament program launched.

Allied troops withdrawn from Rhineland, Germany.

British engineer Frank Whittle patents the jet engine.

AMERICAS & AUSTRALASIA

1926 Brazil becomes first state to leave League of Nations, protesting at the lack of influence accorded it.

Nicaragua occupied by US (–1933).

Agreement reached on dominion status of Australia and New Zealand.

First dirigible balloon flight over North Pole, by US explorer Byrd.

1927 American Charles Lindbergh makes first non-stop solo transatlantic flight (New York to Paris).

Philo Farnsworth develops first electronic television system, US.

NBC and CBS begin national radio broadcasting, US.

Babe Ruth becomes first man to hit 60 home runs in one baseball season, US.

1928 Trading volumes on Wall Street at all-time high.

Steamboat Willie: Mickey Mouse makes his first appearance on film, US.

1929 Herbert Hoover president of the US (–1933).

Wall Street Crash: collapse of US stock market leads to global Depression; world trade cut by two-thirds in three years.

Motorola introduce world's first car radio.

Byrd makes first flight over South Pole.

First Academy Award ceremony introduces the "Oscar."

1930 Military revolution in Brazil brings Getúlio Vargas to power.

Over 3,000 bank failures in US (–1931).

Introduction of Smoot-Hawley protective tariffs in US lead to worsening of Depression worldwide.

Weekly movie ticket sales in US exceed $100 million.

First soccer World Cup held, Uruguay.

Mahatma Gandhi (1869–1948)

Mohandas Gandhi – Mahatma or "great soul" to his adherents – was the most charismatic figure in the struggle for Indian independence as well as for long periods as its leader. He combined an apparent other-worldliness with an astute political instinct. Trained as a lawyer in London, by 1918 his advocacy of *satyagraha* (nonviolent resistance) had won him nation-wide support which various spells in prison only increased. He further embarrassed the British in World War II by his calls for noncooperation. He played a leading role in the negotiations for independence after the war. Gandhi was assassinated by a Hindu fanatic protesting at the partition of India along religious lines.

Never afraid to defy convention, Gandhi helped inspire anticolonial movements in many parts of the world.

Indian Independence

By the 1930s, it was widely conceded that Indian independence was inevitable. But the eventual breakup of the country into Hindu India and Muslim Pakistan led to massive loss of life.

1919 Massacre of Indian demonstrators by British troops at Amritsar in northern India sparks surge of Indian nationalism.

1920 Mahatma Gandhi leads first Nationalist Congress All-India campaign for self-rule (–1922).

1922 Gandhi imprisoned by British authorities in India.

1924 Gandhi released from prison after being made president of Indian National Congress

1930 Gandhi leads nationalist Indian protests against Salt Tax.

1931 Gandhi re-imprisoned by British authorities.

1937 Burma separated from India and made a British crown colony. Partial self-government conceded to India by Britain.

1939 Indian Congress ministries resign and refuse to help Allied war effort in protest at being allowed no say in Allied declaration of war against Germany. Indian Muslims press for a separate state of Pakistan.

1942 Gandhi and other leaders of Indian Congress interned by British authorities.

1946 Negotiations for Indian and Pakistani independence begun.

1947 Creation of independent India and Pakistan agreed amid wholesale rioting and sectarian violence; estimated 500,000 die. First Indo-Pakistan war fought over control of Kashmir and Jammu (UN cease-fire line agreed to 1949).

Adolf Hitler (1889–1945)

Hitler rose to power on the back of Germany's economic chaos promising to overturn the humiliations of the Versailles Settlement. Chancellor from 1933, he launched a massive program of state spending that by the end of the decade had wiped out unemployment.

He was equally unwavering in his anti-Semitism and hatred of communism. His moves toward military conquest were more tentative. It was more the failure of the Allies to respond to German rearmament than the pursuit of a long-term goal that slowly led him to believe that defeat in World War I could be avenged by victory in a new one.

Rise of the Nazis

1919	Hitler joins Munich-based radical party, the National Socialist German Workers' Party: the Nazis.
1923	Munich putsch: unsuccessful attempt to topple Bavarian government by Nazis under Hitler and right-wing elements of army. Hitler imprisoned; writes personal manifesto, *Mein Kampf* ("My Struggle") in 1925.
1930	Nazis win 18 percent of vote and 107 seats in German elections and hold balance of power.
1932	Unemployment in Germany reaches 6 million. Nazis win 37 percent of vote and 230 seats in German elections.
1933	Hitler Chancellor of Germany. Germany leaves League of Nations.
1934	Hitler assumes presidency of Germany; declares himself *der Führer* – the Leader. One-party rule established, trade unions outlawed, Gestapo formed.
1935	German rearmament begins. Anti-Semitic Nuremberg Laws promulgated.
1936	Rhineland reoccupied.

ASIA

1931 Manchuria invaded and occupied by Japan.

Flooding of Yellow river, China, kills 3,700,000; worst natural disaster of the 20th century.

1932 Iraqi independence granted by Britain.

Kingdom of Saudi Arabia proclaimed under Ibn Saud.

Absolute monarchy abolished in Siam (Thailand).

 1933 Province of Jehol, China, occupied by Japan; Japanese protectorate of Manchukuo (Manchuria) established. Japan leaves League of Nations after general condemnation.

 US company, Standard of California, granted oil concession in Saudi Arabia.

1934 Prince Konoye Fumimaro expounds Amau Doctrine: the creation of a new economic order in Asia free from western influence and dominated by Japan.

Start of Chinese communists' "Long March" (–1935); supremacy of Mao Zedong among Chinese communists established.

AFRICA

1934 Sanusi resistance in Libya put down by Italy.

 1935 Italian invasion of Ethiopia in conscious attempt to create a new Roman Empire.

EUROPE

1931 Collapse of C European banks leads to major recession.

Primo de Rivera overthrown in Spain; socialist republic declared; king flees.

Foundation of British Commonwealth, London.

First electron microscope developed, Germany.

1932 Massive famines in USSR caused by collectivization; estimated five million die.

1933 Major purge of communists in USSR launched by Stalin.

World Economic Conference, London, fails to agree measures to stimulate world trade.

Unemployment in Britain reaches 2.7 million, 25 percent of workforce.

Right-wing groups triumph in Spanish election.

Engelbert Dollfuss establishes authoritarian rule in Austria.

1934 Dollfuss murdered by Nazi supporters.

Rioting in Paris leads to formation of all-party National Solidarity government.

Dictatorships established in Estonia and Latvia.

USSR joins League of Nations (–1939).

1935 Saarland reincorporated into Germany by plebiscite.

"People's Car," the Volkswagen, launched.

Military dictatorship established in Greece.

First experimental radar developed, UK.

AMERICAS & AUSTRALASIA

1931 Golden Age of Hollywood begins as escapist antidote to Depression.

Empire State Building, New York, opened; at 1,250 feet (381 m) the highest building in the world until 1973.

1932 Bolivian claims to northern Paraguay spark Chaco War.

Democracy restored to Argentina.

Commonwealth Conference, Ottawa, sets new tariffs to protect trade within British Empire.

1933 Franklin D. Roosevelt president of the US (–1945): launches "New Deal" to restore US economy and combat unemployment.

US stock market slide that precipitated Great Depression finally ends after total losses of $74 billion.

Prohibition repealed in US.

1934 Vargas becomes effective dictator of Brazil.

Military dictatorship established in Bolivia (–1946).

Mass migration of US farmers from Great Plains to California.

1935 Strikes and riots in many parts of West Indies (–1938).

Chaco War ends with substantial gains by Paraguay (peace treaty signed 1938).

Gate receipts for world heavyweight boxing championship in US exceed $1 million.

The Works Progress Administration (WPA) provided work for 8.5 million Americans. Projects included road building and repair.

The depression and the "New Deal"

The Great Depression precipitated by the Wall Street Crash in October 1929 was catastrophic. Between 1929 and 1932, the US economy shrank by a third and exports fell by 70 percent. By 1935, US unemployment had reached 12.8 million, 25 percent of the workforce.

Under the banner of the National Recovery Administration (NRA), in 1933 the new president, Franklin D. Roosevelt, began a massive program of public works to restart the economy and provide new jobs – the "New Deal." By 1940, more than $10 billion had been spent. The results were never more than patchy, however. It was the boost to US industry generated by the vast US arms program after 1941 that did most to restore the nation's economy.

The Chrysler building

The self-confidence of the US in the 1920s was given tangible form by skyscrapers such as New York's Chrysler Building. Not only was it briefly the tallest building in the world at 1,048 feet (323 m), its uncompromising Art Deco decoration made it an assertive symbol of US modernity. Completed in 1930, it remains one of the most distinctive features of the Manhattan skyline.

Joseph Stalin (1879–1953)

Stalin, born Joseph Vissarionovich Dzhugashvili in Georgia and a Marxist since 1899, was an influential early supporter of revolution in Russia. As People's Commissar for Nationalities, he became a key member of the first Soviet government in 1917. In 1922 he became Secretary-General of the Communist Party. His succession to Lenin after 1924 was never clear-cut but with the enforced exile in 1929 of his most obvious rival, Trotsky (whom he subsequently had murdered), he emerged as the undisputed leader of the USSR.

Industrialization and rearmament after 1929 were as much Stalin's initiative as the purges and show trials of leading communists in the 1930s, in which, largely to consolidate his secretive and vengeful dictatorship, terror became state policy. His political victims were numbered in the tens of millions.

Though caught off guard by the Nazi invasion in 1941, Stalin proved an adroit war leader. The eventual successes of the Red Army in driving the Nazis back into Germany and the creation of a new Soviet empire in eastern Europe confirmed the USSR as a world power.

1936–1940

ASIA

1936 Arab revolt in Palestine in protest at Jewish immigration.

Japan signs anti-Comintern pact with Germany.

1937 July: Sino-Japanese war begins; Chinese communists and nationalists unite to oppose Japanese conquests. Dec: Japanese take Nanjing (Nanking), massacring population.

1938 Mar: Japanese establish puppet Chinese government at Nanjing. Oct: Japanese take Guangzhou (Canton). Japan proclaims its "New Order" in Asia.

Death of Turkish leader, Kemal Atatürk.

First oil exported from Saudi Arabia.

1939 Russia and Japan sign neutrality pact; Japan leaves anti-Comintern pact.

AFRICA

1936 Suez Canal Zone garrisoned by Britain under Anglo-Egyptian alliance.

Addis Ababa capitulates to Italian invaders: Mussolini proclaims the official foundation of the new Roman Empire.

1945

1937 Anti-French uprisings in Tunisia.

1940 Sep: Italians invade Egypt.

Dec: British begin Western Desert Offensive in North Africa against the Italians.

EUROPE

1936 Stalin launches show trials and mass purges in the USSR, including purge of Red Army officers (–1938): the Great Terror.

Election victory in Spain by Republican Popular Front prompts military coup and leads to civil war between republicans and nationalists; Italy and Germany commit themselves to support nationalists.

German forces reoccupy demilitarized Rhineland; Allies fail to respond.

Military dictatorship established in Bulgaria.

BBC in England begins world's first regular television broadcasts.

Single-lens reflex (SLR) camera developed in Germany.

1937 Italy leaves the League of Nations in protest at the imposition of sanctions; joins Germany and Japan in anti-Comintern Pact.

Publication of *On Computable Numbers* by British mathematician Alan Turing; establishes theoretical basis for computer.

1938 Mar: Austria annexed by Germany (Anschluss).

Sep: German annexation of Czech Sudetenland agreed by Britain and France under Munich Agreement.

Royal dictatorship established in Romania.

Otto Hahn and Fritz Strassmann split uranium atoms, Germany.

1939 Mar: Germany annexes remainder of western Czechoslovakia, renaming it Protectorate of Bohemia and Moravia, in defiance of Munich Agreement; Slovakia becomes a German client state.

Nationalists under General Franco capture Madrid, ending Spanish civil war and imposing right-wing dictatorship.

Aug: Nazi-Soviet Non-Aggression Pact allows each a free hand in Poland.

Sep: German invasion of Poland prompts Anglo-French declaration of war against Germany and beginning of World War II in Europe.

First successful jet airplane flown, Germany.

1940 Nazis invade France, Belgium, Luxembourg and Netherlands.

1945 ▼

AMERICAS & AUSTRALASIA

1936 Military dictatorship established in Mexico by General Cárdenas.

Dictatorship established in Peru (–1939).

First flight of revolutionary *Douglas DC3* airliner in US.

1937 Quasi-fascist "New State" in Brazil launched by Vargas (–1945).

1938 NBC broadcasts first feature film on television, US.

American Dupont Company produces nylon, world's first successful synthetic fiber.

1939 Igor Sikorsky develops first single-rotor helicopter, US.

Gone With the Wind released; becomes highest-grossing film in movie history.

1940 Race riots in Harlem, Los Angeles, Detroit, and Chicago.

Commercial FM radio broadcasting begins in US, where an estimated 86 percent of population own radios.

Battery farming introduced, US.

Jarrow March

The plight of the unemployed in Britain during the Great Depression was forcefully underlined by the Jarrow March of October 1936. By 1935, unemployment in Jarrow in northeast England, an area almost entirely dependent on shipbuilding, had reached 73 percent. Prompted by the National Unemployed Workers Movement, 200 Jarrow shipworkers walked the 300 miles (483 km) to London to petition parliament. It was a movingly vivid demonstration of the desperation to which they, and millions of others, had been reduced.

The Spanish Civil War

From the early 1920s, Spain, indisputably in decline, had veered between conservative authoritarian regimes and broadly socialist reformist governments. The election victory in 1936 of the reformist Republican Popular Front then sparked a nationalist military coup which degenerated into a savage three-year civil war. Both sides attracted substantial international support. Germany and Italy committed themselves to the Nationalists, the USSR to the Republicans. The eventual Nationalist victory under General Franco was achieved at the cost of 600,000 dead. Over the next three years, a further 200,000 Republicans were executed.

Many Spanish civilians were killed during the Civil War. This postcard calls for aid for victims of air raids.

World War II

By the end of 1941, what had begun as a series of localized if savage conflicts – between Japan and China from 1937, and between Germany and most of western and central Europe from 1939 – had escalated into a truly global conflict. Germany's invasion of the Soviet Union in June 1941 followed six months later by Japan's attack on the US at Pearl Harbor dramatically widened the scope and scale of the fighting. More than 80 million troops were mobilized, of whom nearly one-third were killed.

There were two main theaters of war: Europe – including North Africa – and the Pacific. Spectacular conquests by Germany and Japan respectively reached their greatest extent by the summer of 1942. The two key factors in the defeat of the Axis were the reorganization and rearmament of Soviet forces after their initial defeats by the Germans in 1941–2 – the Soviets bore the brunt of of the fighting against Germany in Europe – and the massive output of weapons by the US after 1942. American tank production in 1940, for example, was 400; in 1943 it had reached 29,500. At peak production in 1944 American factories were producing one aircraft every five minutes.

A Russian soldier waves a red flag in triumph as the Red Army retakes the city of Stalingrad and the remaining pockets of German troops surrender.

ASIA

1939 March: Burma Road opens, carrying supplies to Chinese Kuomintang forces.

Aug: Japanese defeated in clash with Soviets on Mongolian border.

1940 March: Japan installs puppet regime at Nanjing in China.

Sep: Japan signs Tripartite Pact with Germany and Italy; Japanese forces occupy northern French Indochina.

1941 April: Non-aggression treaty between Japan and Soviet Union.

Dec: Japanese invasion of the Philippines (–May 1942); fall of Hong Kong.

1942 Jan: Japanese overrun Dutch East Indies (–March).

Feb: Fall of Singapore.

1943 Feb: First "Chindit" operation in Burma (–Mar).

1944 March: Japanese launch offensive against northeast India.

Oct: US landings at Leyte in Philippines; naval battle of Leyte Gulf.

1945 Feb: US troops enter Manila.

March: Start of series of US bombing raids on main Japanese cities.

July: 1,000-bomber raid on Japan.

Aug: Atomic bombs dropped on Hiroshima and Nagasaki; war in Pacific ends (Aug 15).

AFRICA

1940 Aug: Italians invade British Somaliland.

Sep: Italian force advances into Egypt from Libya.

Dec: British drive Italians back through Cyrenaica (–Feb 1941)

1941 Jan: British counterattack in E Africa liberates Abyssinia and Eritrea (–May); Australian and British successes against Italians in Libya.

Feb: General Rommel and Afrika Korps sent to N Africa.

April: As they advance toward Egypt, Axis troops isolate and besiege Tobruk.

1942 June: Tobruk falls to Rommel in new Axis offensive.

Nov: British defeat Germans at El Alamein; US troops land at Casablanca, Oran, and Algiers.

1943 Jan: Roosevelt and Churchill meet at conference in Casablanca.

May: Allied forces take Tunis; surrender of Axis troops in N Africa.

British artillery at El Alamein

EUROPE

1939 Aug: Germany and USSR sign non-aggression pact.

Sep: Invasion of Poland by Germany and USSR; Britain and France declare war on Germany (Sep 3).

1940 April: German invasion of Denmark and Norway.

May: Germany invades Netherlands, Belgium, and France (–Jun).

June: Fall of France; Italy declares war on Britain and France.

July: Battle of Britain fought in the air over S England (–Oct).

Oct: Italy invades Albania and Greece.

1941 April: German invasion of Yugoslavia and Greece.

June: Operation Barbarossa: German invasion of USSR.

July: Hitler orders Final Solution (extermination of Europe's Jews).

1942 June: First mass killing by gas at Auschwitz death camp.

Aug: US bombing raids over Europe begin.

Sep: Start of German battle for Stalingrad (–Jan 1943).

1943 April: Jewish uprising in Warsaw.

June: USSR defeats Germans in tank battle at Kursk (–Aug).

July: Allied forces land in Sicily.

Sep: Italians surrender to Allies.

Oct: Italy declares war on Germany.

1944 Jan: End of 900-day siege of Leningrad.

June: D-Day (June 6); Allied forces land in Normandy.

Dec: Battle of the Bulge; Germans halt Allies in the Ardennes (–Jan 1945).

1945 April: Russians reach Berlin: Hitler commits suicide (April 30).

May: Germany surrenders (May 7).

AMERICAS & AUSTRALASIA

American troops land on Makin Atoll in the Gilbert Islands in Nov 1943. The US mounted a succession of amphibious operations against Japanese-held islands in the Pacific.

1941 Dec: US enters war, following Japanese air attack on Pearl Harbor.

1942 Feb: Australia under threat of invasion as Japanese bomb Darwin.

May: Battle of the Coral Sea.

June: Battle of Midway, first major American success in Pacific theater.

Aug: Series of land and naval battles for control of Guadalcanal in the Solomon Islands (–Feb 1943).

1943 Jan: Effective end of Japanese campaign in E New Guinea.

June: Series of landings by US troops in Solomon Islands.

1944 March: US encircle and neutralize Japanese base at Rabaul on New Britain.

June: Battle of the Philippine Sea; US inflicts serious losses on Japanese fleet.

July: US marines land on Guam in the Marianas.

1945 Feb: US landings on Iwo Jima.

April: US land on Okinawa, where fierce fighting lasts till Jun; death of Roosevelt; Truman becomes president.

Oct: United Nations established in New York.

Total war

At least 30 million civilians were killed in the war, more than the combined military losses. The Japanese and Germans alike considered most of their enemies, the Chinese and the Slavs in particular, as inferior peoples, to be worked to death as slave labor or simply exterminated. This policy reached its horrifying conclusion in the "Final Solution," the systematic killing of 6 million European Jews.

At the same time improved weaponry meant that enemy populations could be attacked directly. More than 400,000 Geman civilians, for example, died in Allied bombing raids; one US raid on Tokyo killed 124,711; and a single atomic bomb left at least 70,000 dead at Hiroshima.

A German U-boat under attack from an American naval plane in the Atlantic.

The battle of the Atlantic

Britain's survival after the fall of France in 1940 depended on its ability to keep open the sea lanes to the US. At first German attacks on on British shipping were made mostly by aircraft, but by early 1942, as Germany built up its U-boat fleet, shipping losses started to reach critical levels. Between January and April 1942, two million tons of shipping were lost. In the whole year nearly 5.5 million tons were lost – more than 1,600 ships. The battle was won by a combination of technical advances, chiefly in improved radar on ships and aeroplanes, and doggedness, not least in the painstaking breaking of German naval codes. In 1942 total German U-boat losses were 80; the following year they approached 250 and in May 1943 alone, 41 U-boats were sunk.

Concentration camps

The racial inferiority of the Jews had been a central plank of Nazi policy from the start. But from early 1941, a new, systematic attempt to exterminate the entire Jewish population in German-occupied Europe was enacted: the Final Solution. The program was later expanded to include all groups deemed "asocial," chiefly homosexuals and gypsies. There were eight main extermination camps. Those deemed fit enough were used as slave labor. The remainder – 1.5 million children among them – were killed immediately, normally by gassing. About six million were murdered.

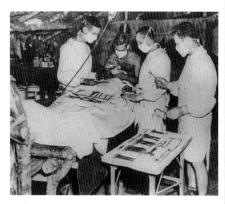

Among the first to benefit from antibiotics were US troops wounded in the Pacific theater of World War II.

Antibiotics

The semi-accidental discovery in 1928 of penicillin by the British doctor Alexander Fleming opened the way to the world's first antibiotics, drugs which help prevent the spread of bacteria. At the time, with its full significance still unrealized, little further research was undertaken. It was only after 1940 when the biochemists Howard Florey and Ernst Chain found a way to process penicillin that the drug became widely available. Its subsequent impact on medicine was as immediate as it was immense.

1941–1945

ASIA

1941 Nationalist guerrilla movement, Viet Minh, formed by Ho Chi Minh in Indo-China.

Japan invades Philippines; fall of Hong Kong.

1942 Cyclone in Bengal (Bangladesh) kills 61,000.

1943 Estimated 1.5 million die in Bengal from famine.

1945 US atomic bombs on Hiroshima and Nagasaki force Japanese surrender ending World War II in the east.

India becomes a UN charter member.

1946 Ho Chi Minh proclaims independent Democratic Republic of Vietnam.

AFRICA

1941 German General Erwin Rommel arrives in Tripoli, North Africa.

1942 Rommel reaches El Alamein near Cairo, Egypt.

British General Bernard Montgomery takes command of Eighth Army in North Africa.

British defeat Germans at El Alamein.

Operation Torch begins U.S. invasion of North Africa.

1943 Allies take Tunisia. German and Italian troops surrender in North Africa.

1945 League of Arab States (Arab League) founded, Cairo.

Nationalist risings in Algeria forcibly put down by France.

1941 US declaration of war against Japan following Japanese attack on Pearl Harbor prompts German declaration of war against US.

Orson Welles's ground-breaking *Citizen Kane* released.

World's first wind-powered turbine generator built, US.

1942 World's first nuclear reactor built, Chicago.

1943 Military takeover in Argentina.

Frank Sinatra's first hit, *All or Nothing at All*, US.

1944 Marxist Enver Hoxha comes to power in Albania (–85).

1944 Avery, Maclyn McCarty, and Colin MacLeod in US discover that DNA carries genetic information.

Term "disc-jockey" first coined, US.

1945

1945 Harry Truman president of the US after Roosevelt dies in office after historic fourth election victory; Truman takes decision to use atomic bomb against Japan after successful test of world's first nuclear device. Presides over buoyant US economy reinvigorated by war-time expansion and set for unprecedented boom.

1948

1945 Berlin capitulates to Red Army, ending World War II in Europe.

Conservatives under Churchill defeated in British General Election by socialist Labour Party campaigning for a Welfare State and the nationalization of most industries.

Potsdam Conference confirms partition of Berlin among Allies.

1946 Stalin begins the mass transfer of ethnic minorities within the USSR to labor camps.

Vargas toppled in Brazil.

International Bank for Reconstruction and Development (IBRD) founded, Washington.

Hiroshima

The dropping of two atomic bombs by the US on the Japanese cities of Hiroshima and Nagasaki on August 6, and 9, 1945 brought a sudden and, for the Japanese, terrifying end to the Pacific war. Both cities were obliterated and over 150,000 people were killed outright or shortly after the blasts. Faced with this overwhelming American military superiority, on August 15 Japan surrendered unconditionally.

A conventional US amphibious invasion of Japan would, it was calculated, have produced over one million casualties and taken well over a year. But however justified the decision to use atomic weapons, the world had entered a new and unprecedentedly dangerous era.

Working women

To a vastly greater extent than in World War I, women almost everywhere were pressed into work during World War II as the economies of all the warring states were turned over to weapons production. Almost two-thirds of all global industrial production in 1944, for example, was devoted to armaments. By the end of the war almost the whole Soviet workforce was female, in Germany about a half, and in the US and Britain about a third.

Women such as these aviation engineers were enormously important to the booming US defense industry.

Not all women worked in factories. Women's contribution to food production was equally significant.

Eva Perón (1919–1952)

Eva Duarte de Perón – Evita – was the
glamorous, charismatic second wife of the
populist Argentine dictator, Juan Perón.
She had an instinctive rapport with
Argentina's dispossessed whom she addressed
as *los descamisados* ("the shirtless ones.")
Her championship of them was crucial to
her husband's hold on office, disguising
much of the corruption and racketeering
of his regime. She died from cancer. After
Perón's overthrow in 1955, her body was sent
to Italy to prevent it from becoming a focus
of opposition to the new regime.

*A poster advertising Marshall Aid forms a backdrop
as a stonemason works on a major reconstruction
project in postwar Berlin.*

The Marshall Plan

Determined to aid the political and
economic recovery of a devastated Europe
after World War II, the US launched a
European Recovery Program in 1947. It
was named after George Marshall, the
secretary of state. The Soviet bloc, fearful
of US influence, rejected the program. But
the whole of western Europe other than
Franco's Spain, benefited. In three years,
$11.8 billion was spent by the US.

ASIA

1946 Civil war breaks out between
nationalists and communists in China
(–1949). Drought and depredations of war
kill estimated five million.

1954 ▼ France launches armed campaign
against nationalists under Ho Ch Minh
in Indochina.

Syrian independence agreed to by France.

Transjordan independence agreed
by Britain.

Philippine independence agreed to by US.

1947 UN partition of Palestine between Jews
and Arabs agreed upon ; sparks widespread
violence before British pull out.

1948 Creation of independent State of
Israel leads directly to first Arab-Israeli
war; cease-fire agreed to in 1949 after
750,000 Palestinians flee Israel.

Gandhi assassinated.

Burma and Ceylon (Sri Lanka) granted
independence; former withdraws from
Commonwealth.

Partition of Korea agreed to by USSR
and US; Kim Il Sung head of state
of communist North Korea (–1994).

US spearheads reconstruction of Japanese
economy and society on capitalist lines.

Communist guerrilla insurgency ("the
Emergency") begins in Malaysia (–1960).

Earthquake in Turkmenistan (USSR)
kills 110,000.

Al-Ghawar oil-field, world's largest,
discovered in Saudi Arabia.

1949 Chinese communists under Mao
Zedong victorious in Chinese civil war.

Indonesia granted independence
by Dutch.

1954 ▼ Laos granted self-government within
French Empire.

1950 Mao launches series of major
initiatives: invasions of Korea, sparking
the Korean War, first major Cold War
confrontation in E Asia, and of Tibet
and huge-scale collectivization of
agriculture in which millions of
peasant landowners are executed.

AFRICA

1948 White supremacist National Party
win election in S Africa.

1949 Apartheid made official policy
of National Party in South Africa.

EUROPE

1946 Stalin confiscates lands and savings of "profiteering" peasants in USSR.

Allied Nuremberg war trials of surviving Nazi leaders begin, Germany.

Civil war in Greece between Soviet-sponsored communists and US-sponsored monarchists begins (–1949).

Democracy restored in Italy.

United Nations Educational, Scientific and Cultural Organization (UNESCO) founded, Paris.

1947 Marshall Plan launched by US.

Christian Dior's "New Look" elegantly ends austerity of wartime fashions, Paris.

1948 Soviet-sponsored Communist regimes established in Poland, Czechoslovakia, and Hungary.

USSR attempts to force Western Allies to abandon Berlin by blockading land routes to the city; West responds with a round-the-clock airlift to bring in essential supplies.

Communist Yugoslavia rejects leadership of USSR.

Communist Albania breaks off relations with Yugoslavia.

Benelux Customs Union founded: Netherlands, Belgium, Luxembourg.

World Health Organization (WHO) founded, Geneva.

1952
1949 Soviets abandon Berlin blockade; Germany partitioned between democratic Federal Republic of Germany and communist German Democratic Republic.

1955
Formation of anti-Soviet defensive alliance, the North Atlantic Treaty Organization (NATO).

Formation by USSR of the Council for Mutual Economic Assistance (COMECON).

USSR tests first atomic bomb.

Council of Europe founded, Strasbourg.

1951
Manchester Mark I computer developed, UK.

AMERICAS & AUSTRALASIA

1951
1946 "Truman Doctrine," under which the United States asserts its determination to "contain" communism worldwide, announced. Winston Churchill, in US, coins phrase "the Iron Curtain." Cold War conflict between US and USSR under way.

US begins nuclear testing at Enewetok and Bikini atolls in Pacific.

Juan Perón launches populist authoritarian rule in Argentina.

1947 General Agreement on Tariffs and Trades (GATT), aimed at liberalizing world trade, signed in US.

Pacific Community founded, New Caledonia.

Sound barrier broken, US.

Polaroid "instant" camera pioneered by Edwin Land in US.

Transistor invented, US.

"Meet the Press," world's longest-running television program, first broadcast, US.

1948 First LPs produced, US.

1953
1949 Truman takes office for second term after surprise election win. Signs Mutual Defense Assistance Act.

National network television introduced in US.

Pan Am introduces first scheduled transatlantic passenger service; flying time 12 hours.

Term "rhythm 'n' blues" first coined, US.

1950 US heads UN forces in Korean War (–1953).

First US involvement in support of French forces in Indochina (Vietnam).

Vargas returned to power in Brazil.

Persecution of communists in US initiated by Senator McCarthy.

Jewish refugees from Nazi Europe arrived in Palestine on crowded ships. The British refused to let some of them land.

The Foundation of Israel

The influx of Jewish settlers to Palestine in the 1930s created a tense conflict between them and the Palestinians which Britain, the "mandated" power, found increasingly hard to control. By 1945, Britain determined to pull out. The issue was turned over to the UN, which agreed by a narrow majority in November 1947 to establish two separate states, Jewish and Arab. On May 14, 1948, they were officially inaugurated. A seven-month war immediately followed, from which Israel emerged victorious. But the fundamental conflict – then as now – remained largely unresolved.

The Chinese Civil War (1946–1949)

Though the Nationalists and Communists had made common cause against the Japanese invaders, the defeat of Japan in 1945 sparked a brutal war between them for control of China.

1945 USSR occupies formerly Japanese-held Manchuria, power base of communist forces under Mao Zedong. US attempts to reconcile Communists and Nationalists under Chiang Kai-shek.

1946 USSR pulls out of Manchuria. Civil war begins with early Nationalist victories.

1948 Nationalists appear close to victory; Chiang Kai-shek appointed president of new Chinese National Assembly. Communist drive in north to recruit peasant support results in victories in Manchuria.

1949 Jan: Communists take Xuzhou; Beijing captured.
Sept: Final Nationalist defeat.
Oct: People's Republic of China established under Mao Zedong.

1950 May: Nationalists flee to Formosa (Taiwan) and establish the Republic of China.

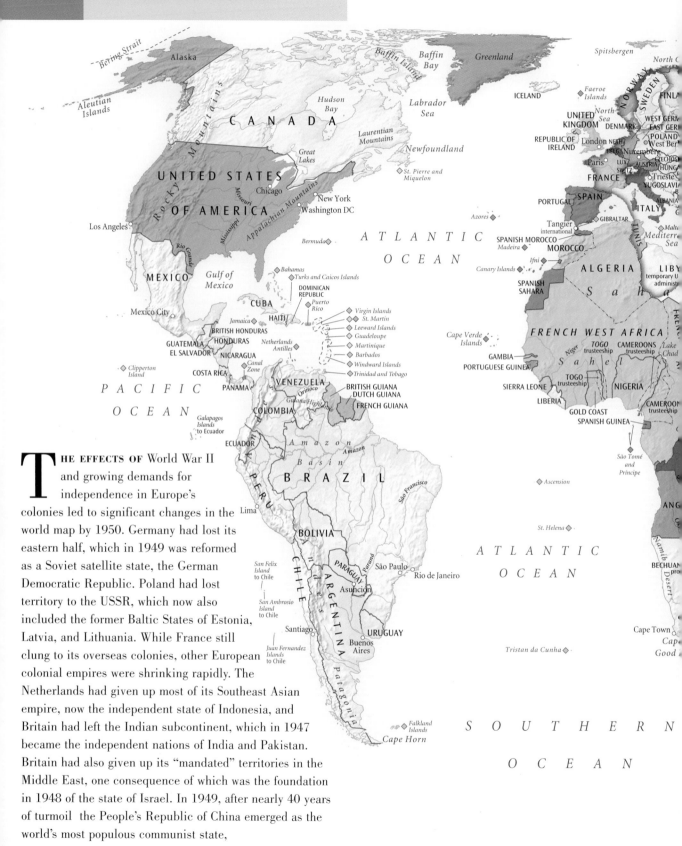

THE EFFECTS OF World War II and growing demands for independence in Europe's colonies led to significant changes in the world map by 1950. Germany had lost its eastern half, which in 1949 was reformed as a Soviet satellite state, the German Democratic Republic. Poland had lost territory to the USSR, which now also included the former Baltic States of Estonia, Latvia, and Lithuania. While France still clung to its overseas colonies, other European colonial empires were shrinking rapidly. The Netherlands had given up most of its Southeast Asian empire, now the independent state of Indonesia, and Britain had left the Indian subcontinent, which in 1947 became the independent nations of India and Pakistan. Britain had also given up its "mandated" territories in the Middle East, one consequence of which was the foundation in 1948 of the state of Israel. In 1949, after nearly 40 years of turmoil the People's Republic of China emerged as the world's most populous communist state,

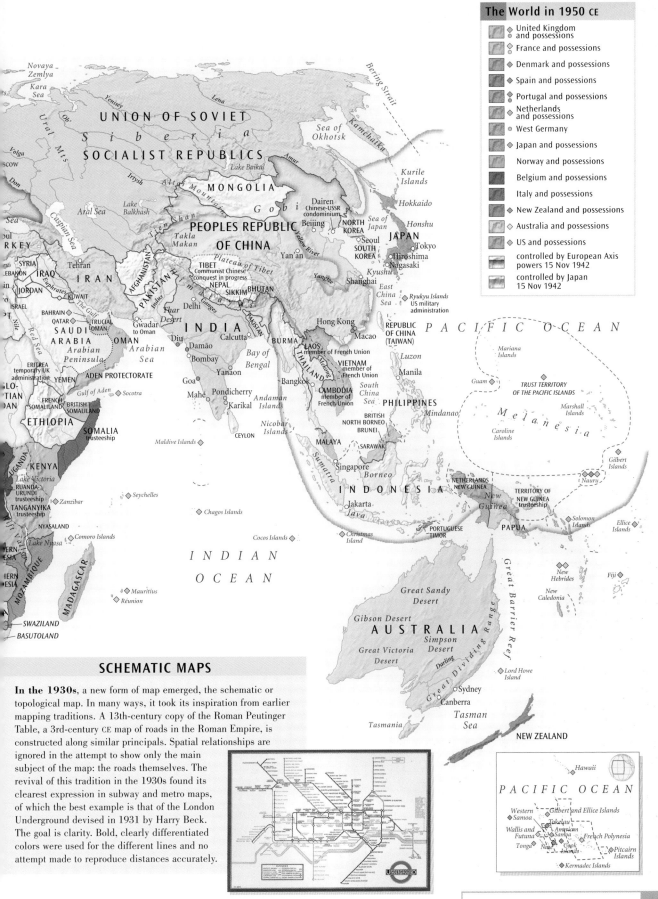

The World in 1950 CE

- United Kingdom and possessions
- France and possessions
- Denmark and possessions
- Spain and possessions
- Portugal and possessions
- Netherlands and possessions
- West Germany
- Japan and possessions
- Norway and possessions
- Belgium and possessions
- Italy and possessions
- New Zealand and possessions
- Australia and possessions
- US and possessions
- controlled by European Axis powers 15 Nov 1942
- controlled by Japan 15 Nov 1942

SCHEMATIC MAPS

In the 1930s, a new form of map emerged, the schematic or topological map. In many ways, it took its inspiration from earlier mapping traditions. A 13th-century copy of the Roman Peutinger Table, a 3rd-century CE map of roads in the Roman Empire, is constructed along similar principals. Spatial relationships are ignored in the attempt to show only the main subject of the map: the roads themselves. The revival of this tradition in the 1930s found its clearest expression in subway and metro maps, of which the best example is that of the London Underground devised in 1931 by Harry Beck. The goal is clarity. Bold, clearly differentiated colors were used for the different lines and no attempt made to reproduce distances accurately.

1950 –1975

The Cold War World

1954: Independence of Laos, Cambodia, and North and South Vietnam end French colonial rule in Indochina

1950: Outbreak of Korean War. China invades Tibet

1953: Anti-Soviet uprising in Berlin suppressed

ASIA
AFRICA
EUROPE
REST OF THE WORLD

1950   1951   1952   1953   1954   19

1954: Algerian uprising against French rule. Nasser takes power in Egypt

By 1950, THE SHAPE of the postwar world was becoming clear. With Europe divided into a Soviet-dominated east and a capitalist west and with the real threat of nuclear holocaust, the Cold War became grim reality. In spite of this, in the west there was a growing optimism. Driven forward by a buoyant US economy, the reconstruction of western Europe gathered increasing momentum. It was to result in an unprecedented consumer-led economic boom that continued until 1974. If the US was the pacesetter, enjoying levels of prosperity unimaginable in the depression of the 1930s, by the early 1960s much of western Europe was not far behind.

Winners and losers

Among the most remarkable of these achievements was the rebuilding of the West German economy. Literally in ruins in 1945, within 20 years West Germany had become the continent's economic giant. The creation of the European Economic Community (EEC) in 1957 further strengthened economic and social revival in western Europe. It not only promoted trade, it reduced the risk of further European conflict. The West's "economic miracle" was only partly shared by eastern Europe. As in the Soviet Union itself, the inherent inefficiencies of a communist command economy made growth sluggish at best. At the same time, dissent was harshly suppressed. The legacy of this economic and social dislocation between eastern and western Europe would be felt for many years to come.

Decolonization

Among the period's most striking developments was the rapid dismantling of Europe's colonial empires. By the mid-1960s, the British Empire, which only 30

In the US boom of the 1950s and '60s, fridges, cars, televisions, and washing machines were sold in their millions to a new generation of "consumers."

years before had occupied almost a quarter of the globe, had effectively been wound up. On the whole, the transition from British rule after 1950 was orderly and peaceful, though there were inevitably some exceptions. In Southern Rhodesia (now Zimbabwe) the white settlers, who controlled the government, refused to accept black majority rule, so in 1965 made a unilateral declaration of independence from Britain. Despite a sustained campaign of guerrilla warfare, the illegal regime, with the support of apartheid South Africa, held on to power until a settlement was reached in 1979.

Other European empires were surrendered less willingly, however. In the 1950s France was engulfed in two bitter and ultimately futile wars to maintain its colonial rule in Indochina and Algeria. By 1958, its increasingly vicious war against separatists in Algeria had provoked a serious political crisis. As in Zimbabwe, the situation was inflamed by the presence of a large

PICTURE ABOVE:
Mao Zedong encouraged *a personality cult portraying him as the caring father of the Chinese nation. In the 1966 Cultural Revolution he encouraged young Red Guards to criticize and abuse elderly intellectuals and "revisionists."*

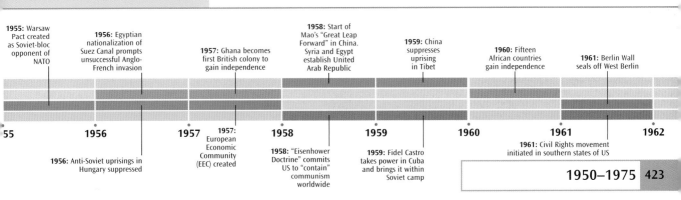

1955: Warsaw Pact created as Soviet-bloc opponent of NATO

1956: Egyptian nationalization of Suez Canal prompts unsuccessful Anglo-French invasion

1957: Ghana becomes first British colony to gain independence

1958: Start of Mao's "Great Leap Forward" in China. Syria and Egypt establish United Arab Republic

1959: China suppresses uprising in Tibet

1960: Fifteen African countries gain independence

1961: Berlin Wall seals off West Berlin

55   1956   1957   1957: European Economic Community (EEC) created   1958   1959   1960   1961   1962

1956: Anti-Soviet uprisings in Hungary suppressed

1958: "Eisenhower Doctrine" commits US to "contain" communism worldwide

1959: Fidel Castro takes power in Cuba and brings it within Soviet camp

1961: Civil Rights movement initiated in southern states of US

ARAB NATIONALISM

As late as 1850, the Arab world could still, just, claim to be the military, economic and cultural equal of the West. By 1900, it had become an impoverished backwater, in thrall to European interests. In 1948, its self-esteem was futher reduced with its defeat by the new Jewish state of Israel in Palestine.

Though the unity of the Arab world had always been fractured by religious and national rivalries, in 1952 Gamel Abdel Nasser attempted to infuse it with a new sense of purpose. Leader of the coup which overthrew the playboy king of Egypt, Farouk, in 1952, two years later he became prime minister of Egypt. His goal was to unify the Arab world, under Egyptian leadership, by making common cause not just against Israel but, by extension, against its western backers.

In 1956, he engineered the nationalization of the Anglo-French-owned Suez Canal. The failure of the cack-handed British-French invasion to liberate the canal the same year enormously increased his prestige. Two years later he masterminded an Egyptian-Syrian union – the portentously name United Arab Republic – that he hoped would prove the forerunner of a united Arab state. His hopes were rapidly dashed, falling foul of inter-Arab tensions and of overwhelming Israeli military superiority alike. By his death in 1970, hopes of revived Arab dominance seemed as distant as ever.

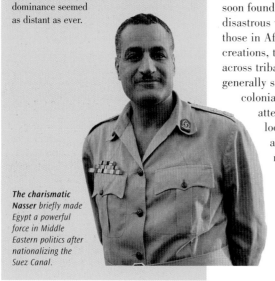

The charismatic Nasser briefly made Egypt a powerful force in Middle Eastern politics after nationalizing the Suez Canal.

number of settlers who were violently opposed to the idea of granting self-government to the Algerians. Charles de Gaulle, who came to power in 1958, decided that the war could not be won and Algeria was finally granted independence in 1962. Portugal's African colonies, Mozambique, Angola, Guinea, and the Cape Verde Islands, were given up even more reluctantly, after years of savage fighting, only in the mid-1970s.

The legacy of colonialism

But whether their transition to independence had been peaceful or violent, Europe's former territories faced formidable difficulties. In part, this was because both the Soviet Union and the US, each determined to outflank the other, saw them as pawns in the wider Cold War struggle. With consequences that were inevitably destabilizing, countries such as Vietnam and Angola became the focus of a global conflict not of their own making.

Even when they did not become proxy battlegrounds for the world's two super-powers, several newly independent states soon found themselves engaged in disastrous wars. Many of them, especially those in Africa, were essentially artificial creations, their frontiers, often cutting across tribal and cultural borders, generally still those imposed by their colonial rulers. In many cases, the attempt to turn what had been loose tribal groupings, lacking all but the most rudimentary mechanisms of government, into modern nation-states on the European pattern resulted in turmoil. Nowhere was this more true than in sub-Saharan Africa. The Congo and Nigeria, for example, were both wracked by vicious civil wars in which dominant

The oil-rich province of Biafra seceded from Nigeria in 1967, provoking a bitter three-year civil war. When Biafra lost its ports to the Nigerian forces, a catastrophic famine ensued, in which more than a million people died.

ethnic groups tried to suppress challenges by smaller tribal peoples. Overall, the result was the emergence of what came to be called the Third World. Unstable, impoverished, and frequently corrupt, large areas of the world slid into seemingly irreversible decline.

Arab-Israeli Wars

Conflict was also endemic in the Middle East. Though partly the result of inter-Arab rivalry, its prime cause was Arab determination to overthrow the Jewish state of Israel, created in 1948 on lands that had been Arab for centuries. The day after the state of Israel had been declared, five Arab armies from neighboring countries invaded. After they had been repulsed, some 725,000 Arabs fled Palestine. There were further Arab-Israeli wars in 1956, 1966, and 1973. Each time, though heavily outnumbered, the Israelis defeated their enemies, in the process dramatically expanding the territories under their rule.

The conflict was much more than just a regional disturbance. US support for Israel inevitably made it a further focus of the Cold War. At the same time, the Middle East's strategic significance as the world's major oil producer gave it a unique leverage over the industrial world, above all the west. The extent of this influence was made clear in 1973 when

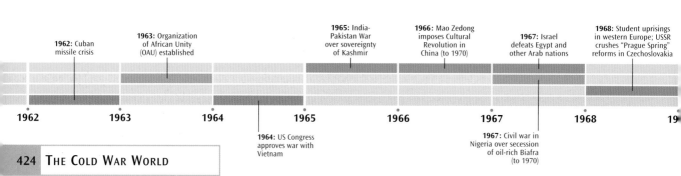

1962: Cuban missile crisis

1963: Organization of African Unity (OAU) established

1965: India-Pakistan War over sovereignty of Kashmir

1966: Mao Zedong imposes Cultural Revolution in China (to 1970)

1967: Israel defeats Egypt and other Arab nations

1968: Student uprisings in western Europe; USSR crushes "Prague Spring" reforms in Czechoslovakia

1962 1963 1964 1965 1966 1967 1968 19

1964: US Congress approves war with Vietnam

1967: Civil war in Nigeria over secession of oil-rich Biafra (to 1970)

the Arab-dominated Organization of Petroleum Exporting Countries (OPEC) engineered a dramatic increase in the price of oil. Its effect was to halt the west's economic boom in its tracks, provoking the most serious economic crisis since the 1930s.

Postwar Japan and China

The most significant developments in East Asia after 1950 were the consolidation of communist rule in China and the dramatic reconstruction of Japan. Like its former ally Germany, Japan in 1945 lay in ruins. Prompted by America, it rebuilt itself as a conservative, capitalist society. Phenomenal economic growth saw Japan emerge by the early 1970s as the world's third largest economy. Developments in China were in stark contrast. The imposition of communism by Mao Zedong in 1949 may have reestablished central authority but the price paid was huge: ruthless elimination of dissent and, under the Great Leap Forward, launched in 1957, a disastrous attempt to modernize industry that resulted in famine and 30 million deaths. The Cultural Revolution of 1966, an ideologically driven attempt to purge the country of counterrevolutionary elements, gave rise to equally widespread misery and disruption.

Korea and Vietnam

Whatever the failures of communist government within China, the Chinese Red Army was the largest in the world and a serious threat to US and western interests in East and Southeast Asia. The two major wars fought by the US during the Cold War period were both undertaken to halt the spread of communism in the region. The first of these, the Korean War (1950–53), was actually conducted in the name of the

United Nations, though the overwhelming majority of the troops engaged were American. When the troops of communist North Korea invaded South Korea in 1950, they were initially pushed back almost to the Chinese border. At this point China entered the war and nearly two more years' savage fighting ensued before a ceasefire was agreed. This restored what was more or less the original prewar border between the two states.

In the 1960s and 1970s the attention of the world was focused on the Vietnam War, where the US again decided to take a stand against the spread of communism. Following the French withdrawal from Indochina in 1954 Vietnam had been partitioned into the communist north and the prowestern South. The US supported the corrupt regime in the South with large

amounts of aid, but from 1965 began to send troops to help South Vietnam fight the Viet Cong guerrillas. Despite their overwhelming technological advantages, the Americans failed miserably and in 1973 withdrew their troops. With the fall of Saigon in 1975, the two Vietnams were united under communist rule.

The war had enormous consequences back home in the US. The level of opposition to the war, especially among students, was unprecedented. This was the start of an age dominated by the media and the effects of American bombing of innocent peasants and other atrocities were shown in graphic detail on television. Demonstrations against American involvement in Vietnam were staged around the world, reflecting a new kind of global counterculture.

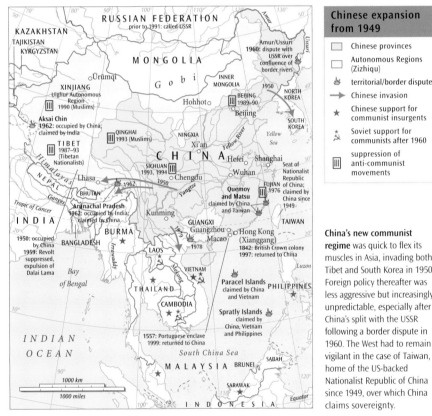

China's new communist regime was quick to flex its muscles in Asia, invading both Tibet and South Korea in 1950. Foreign policy thereafter was less aggressive but increasingly unpredictable, especially after China's split with the USSR following a border dispute in 1960. The West had to remain vigilant in the case of Taiwan, home of the US-backed Nationalist Republic of China since 1949, over which China claims sovereignty.

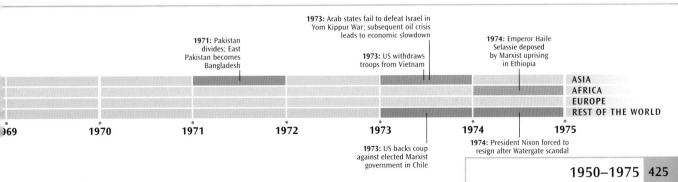

1973: Arab states fail to defeat Israel in Yom Kippur War; subsequent oil crisis leads to economic slowdown

1971: Pakistan divides; East Pakistan becomes Bangladesh

1973: US withdraws troops from Vietnam

1974: Emperor Haile Selassie deposed by Marxist uprising in Ethiopia

ASIA
AFRICA
EUROPE
REST OF THE WORLD

069   1970   1971   1972   1973   1974   1975

1973: US backs coup against elected Marxist government in Chile

1974: President Nixon forced to resign after Watergate scandal

The Korean War 1950–53

The partition of Korea by the US and USSR in 1945 into a Soviet-backed communist North and US-backed capitalist South sowed the seeds for the first major Cold War confrontation in Southeast Asia. The spark was lit by the US pull-out from the South in June 1949.

A year later, the North invaded. A UN force, mostly of US troops, immediately intervened. Four months later, China committed itself to the conflict. With neither side able to gain an advantage, the USSR proposed a cease-fire. The armistice, signed two years later, left the border almost exactly where it had been before the war.

US troops bring in North Korean prisoners of war, 1950. The populations of N and S Korea alike suffered in the Korean War.

The World Cup

From modest beginnings – only 13 countries competed in the first World Cup in 1930 – the World Cup has grown into the world's single largest sporting event, stirring passions around the globe.

	Hosts	Winners
1930	Uruguay	Uruguay
1934	Italy	Italy
1938	France	Italy
1950	Brazil	Uruguay
1954	Switzerland	W Germany
1958	Sweden	Brazil
1962	Chile	Brazil
1966	England	England
1970	Mexico	Brazil
1974	W Germany	W Germany
1978	Argentina	Argentina
1982	Spain	Italy
1986	Mexico	Argentina
1990	Italy	Germany
1994	US	Brazil
1998	France	France
2002	S Korea/Japan	Brazil

ASIA

1951 Mossadeq, prime minister of Iran, nationalizes oil.

Formal end of hostilities between Japan and Allies agreed in San Francisco.

Vatican and China break off diplomatic relations.

1952 First Indian general election won by Congress Party.

Albert Einstein refuses presidency of Israel.

1953 USSR breaks off diplomatic relations with Israel.

17-year-old Prince Hussein becomes king of Jordan.

Death of King Abul Azziz of Saudi Arabia; succeeded by King Saud.

Mount Everest first climbed, by British expedition.

1960 ▼ **1954** France forced to pull out of Indochina after defeat at Dien Bien Phu; Laos, Cambodia, and partitioned Vietnam, as established by Geneva accords, all gain independence.

Sukarno abrogates union with Dutch and declares unitary state of Indonesia.

Bilateral pact signed between Taiwan and US.

Mossadeq ousted in military coup, Iran

1958 ▼ **1955** Afghan government supports movement for separation of Pakhtunistan from Pakistan.

Naga uprising in NE India, the first of numerous tribal insurrections.

Anti-Soviet defensive Baghdad Pact agreed at US urging between Iran, Iraq, Turkey, and Pakistan.

AFRICA

1960 ▼ **1951** Libya independent from Italy.

Algerian National Liberation Front begins guerrilla campaigns against French rule.

1952 Mau Mau uprising begins in Kenya.

Military coup in Egypt.

1953 Rhodesia and Nyasaland brought together by Britain in new administrative unit, the Central African Federation (–1963).

\

1956 ▼ **1954** Deposition of Egyptian king, Farouk; Gamal Abdel Nasser prime minister.

Anglo-Egyptian accord agrees terms for British pull-out of Suez Canal zone.

1955 Soviet military support for Egypt begins.

Anti-French rioting spreads across Morocco and Algeria, killing hundreds.

Civil war begins in Sudan between Christian south and Muslim north.

EUROPE

1957 ▼

1951 European Coal and Steel Authority, partial precursor of EEC, established.

Launch of Ferranti Mark I, world's first commercially produced computer.

1952 Total number of Germans fleeing to the West reaches 985,000.

Nordic Council founded, Stockholm.

De Havilland Comet introduced, world's first jet airliner, UK.

Atom bomb developed by Britain.

1953 Anti-Soviet risings in Poland and East Berlin suppressed.

1956 ▼

Death of Stalin; eventually succeeded by Khrushchev.

Double helix structure of DNA discovered in UK by James Watson and Francis Crick.

Josip Tito elected president of Yugoslavia

1954 Western European Union founded, Brussels.

First sub four-minute mile run by British medical student, Roger Bannister.

1955 Creation of Warsaw Pact, Soviet-bloc military alliance established in opposition to NATO.

West Germany admitted to NATO.

Allied occupation forces pull out of Austria; independence recognized and democracy restored.

AMERICAS & AUSTRALASIA

1951 US commits itself to defend Japan against communism.

ANZUS security pact signed between Australia, New Zealand, and US.

22nd Amendment limits US presidential term of office to eight years (two terms).

Julius and Ethel Rosenberg convicted of espionage charges, US (executed 1953).

1952 Military aid pact agreed between US and Cuba

"Big bang" theory of formation of the universe first propounded.

1953 Dwight D. Eisenhower president of the US (–1961).

F-100 fighter introduced, US, world's first production-line supersonic airplane.

First polio vaccine developed in US by Jonas Salk.

1954 South East Asia Treaty Organization (SEATO) formed under US leadership.

Launch in US of submarine Nautilus, world's first nuclear-powered vessel.

First Burger King opened, Miami.

1955 Argentinian leader, Perón, ousted in military coup.

US military intervention in Iran.

First pocket transistor radios available, US.

First McDonald's opened, California.

US intervention in Iran.

1957 ▼ Bus boycott against segregation in Montgomery, Alabama.

Argentinian leader Juan Perón ousted by military coup. Remains out of power until 1973.

The Discovery of DNA

That the chemical DNA (deoxyribonucleic acid) carries genetic material was discovered in 1944. The double-helix structure of DNA (*right*) was discovered in 1953. In 1973, a technique was developed for the cloning of DNA. In 1990, the Human Genome Project was launched, its aim being to determine the precise sequence of all three billion base DNA pairs and thus to identify every human gene. The project is expected to be completed in 2004. The implications are profound. In theory, it should be possible to eradicate all hereditary diseases.

The Soviet gulag

Though Lenin had never been slow to persecute enemies of the Soviet revolution, it was only under Stalin that terror against its own population became an integral part of the Soviet political system. The initial impetus was provided by the first Five-Year Plan in 1929. Opponents who were not executed or starved to death were sent to special camps – gulags – run by the Interior Commissariat, the NKVD.

In 1930, there were 179,000 prisoners; in 1934, 510,000. The Soviet seizure of eastern Poland and the Baltic States in 1940 increased prisoner numbers by almost one million. By Stalin's death, the camp population was 1.7 million. All were effectively treated as slave labor.

1951–1955

Indpendence day celebrations in Nigeria, 1960.

African independence

Almost all of Europe's African colonies were granted independence in the 15 years after 1951. Libya was the first to be given independence, from Italy, in 1951. Facing nationalist protest, France pulled out of Tunisia and Morocco in 1956. Its retention of Algeria provoked savage civil war followed by inevitable retreat in 1962. Britain gave up all its colonies, generally peacefully, after 1956. In 1960 France and Belgium gave up all their sub-Saharan colonies. Portugal and Spain were the only European colonial powers to resist moves to independence. Nonetheless, they too withdrew in 1975 after costly and futile wars.

The Great Leap Forward

In 1958, China's Mao Zedong initiated a crash three-year program of industrialization and collectivization –

The Great Leap Forward redirected peasant labor to massive public works projects.

the Great Leap Forward. It was an unmitigated catastrophe. By abolishing private land ownership, productive agriculture ended almost overnight. As many as 20 million people died in the resulting famines. The attempts at industrialization, based on 26,000 communes, each given unattainable targets, led to the age of "backyard furnaces" when some 600,000 blast furnaces, all hopelessly inefficient, were set up. Mao came close to being overthrown in the resulting chaos, which provoked a power struggle between Maoists and moderates who wanted China to follow the model provided by the Soviet Union. The experiment was abandoned in 1961.

ASIA

1956 Pakistan becomes independent Islamic Republic within the British Commonwealth.

Japan admitted to UN.

 1957 Malaya granted independence despite continuing communist insurrection.

 S Vietnam attacked by communist Viet Cong guerrillas.

1958 Massive program of forced industrialization launched in China by Mao, "the Great Leap Forward" (–1961); estimated 20 million die in the ensuing chaos.

"Eisenhower Doctrine" commits US to contain communism in the Middle East.

Military coup in Pakistan.

Oil discovered in Trucial States (later the UAE).

Monarchy ousted in Iraqi military coup under General Abdel Karim Kassem.

1959 Start of "Three Hard Years" in China, widespread famine created by the Great Leap Forward.

Tibetan uprising crushed by China; religious institutions banned.

 Lee Kuan Yew president of Singapore (–1993).

1960 Amur-Ussuri border dispute precipitates Sino-Soviet split.

Sporadic civil war between communists and noncommunists in Laos (–1975).

AFRICA

1956 Suez Crisis: Egyptian nationalization of Suez Canal prompts botched Anglo-French invasion, drawing world-wide condemnation, while Israel takes Sinai (and turns it over to UN control).

 France grants independence to Morocco, Tunisia; Britain grants independence to Sudan.

Gold Coast and British Togo unified.

Sudan independent when nominal Anglo-Egyptian condominium ends. It joins the Arab League.

1957 Britain commits itself to the decolonization of its sub-Saharan African colonies: Gold Coast (Ghana) is the first to be granted independence.

1958 United Arab Republic (UAR) established by Egypt and Syria in attempt to create pan-Arab unity; dissolved 1961.

1960 France grants independence to the majority of its African colonies (Chad, Niger, Gabon, French Congo, Cameroon, Central African Republic, Ivory Coast, Togo, Upper Volta, Mali, Mauritania, Dahomey, and Madagascar). Italy grants independence to Somalia. Belgium grants independence to the Congo. Britain grants independence to Nigeria.

Katanga province secedes from Zaire (Congo) prompting civil war and Belgian and later UN intervention.

 Somalia created from former British and Italian colonies in Horn of Africa.

Tidal wave at Agadir, Morocco, kills 12,000.

EUROPE

1956 Hungary withdraws from Warsaw Pact; communist rule restored by large-scale Soviet-led armed invasion prompting widespread unrest, all forcibly suppressed.

Khrushchev emerges as dominant leader in USSR; denounces Stalinist abuses, releases millions from labor camps, and introduces limited economic liberalization.

Terrorist struggle against British rule in Cyprus launched headed by Greek Archbishop Makarios (subsequently deported).

1957 Treaty of Rome: European Economic Community (EEC) founded; goal is full economic union between member states (France, Germany, Italy, Holland, Belgium, Luxembourg).

1961

USSR launches world's first artificial satellite, *Sputnik I*, inaugurating space age. USSR and US both test Intercontinental Ballistic Missiles (ICBMs) to carry nuclear weapons.

Ultrasound scanning pioneered, Scotland.

1958 Fifth Republic declared in France with de Gaulle as president.

International Atomic Energy Agency (IAEA) founded, Vienna.

1959 Christopher Cockerell develops world's first hovercraft, UK.

Release of François Truffaut's *400 Blows* signals emergence of New Wave of intellectual European film-makers.

1960 European Free Trade Association (EFTA) founded, Geneva, as rival to EEC.

Organization of Petroleum Exporting Countries (OPEC) founded, Vienna.

1963

Cyprus granted independence by Britain.

USSR builds world's first solar-powered electricity plant.

AMERICAS & AUSTRALASIA

1956 Alabama bus segregation laws declared illegal by US Supreme Court.

IBM develops means of storing computer data on metal disk.

US atomic testing in the Pacific resumed.

1963

1957 Martin Luther King, Jr. heads nationwide resistance to continuing racial segregation and discrimination in US.

Alarm at apparent Soviet technological supremacy in rocketry fuels fears of a "missile gap" and leads to huge increase in US military spending.

Federal troops ordered to Arkansas to enforce antisegregation laws.

US initiates underground testing of nuclear devices, Nevada.

First nuclear reactor for electricity production opened in US, in Pennsylvania.

John Glenn sets new coast-to-coast air record of 3hr, 23min.

First domestic US jet airliner service begun, New York–Miami.

First electric watch introduced, in the US.

1958 Microchip first developed, US.

First stereo LPs produced, US.

NASA (North American Space Agency) is formed.

First successful US earth satellite, *Explorer I*, launched.

1959 Revolution in Cuba brings communists to power under Fidel Castro; begins imposition of repressive Soviet-style regime and receives substantial Soviet military aid.

Boeing 707 jet airliner enters service; cuts transatlantic flying time to 8 hours.

Hawaii becomes 50th state of the US.

First US weather satellite, *Vanguard*, launched.

John F Kennedy (1917–1963)

At 43, Kennedy was the youngest man elected US president. Domestically, he advocated the extension of civil rights and improved health and education funding. But his brief presidency was dominated by the Cold War, then at its height. His greatest triumph came in facing down the USSR over its deployment of nuclear missiles in Cuba in 1962. He also stepped up US involvement in Vietnam. He was assassinated in Dallas on November 22, 1963.

Castro and Che Guevara

If Fidel Castro, (*above, left*) (born 1926) provided the pragmatism that sustained the Cuban communist revolution of 1959, the Argentine-born Guevara, (*above, right*) (1928–1967), Castro's most trusted lieutenant from 1956, provided the revolutionary fervor. Despite being awarded a succession of high-ranking government jobs by Castro, Guevara's urge to continue the revolutionary struggle elsewhere soon led him to leave Cuba. He was killed in Bolivia by the Bolivian army. Castro meanwhile proved among the most durable communist leaders, surviving both the economic decline of Cuba and the collapse of its chief supporter, the USSR, in 1991.

The Cold War

The world after 1945 was dominated by the two countries that had done most to win World War II: the Soviet Union and the United States. Even during the war their ideological differences had been a source of tension between them; after the Allied victory they came to the fore. When Winston Churchill declared that "From Stettin in the Baltic to Trieste in the Adriatic an iron curtain has descended across the Continent," his poetic metaphor soon became a geopolitical reality, marked on maps for the next 45 years.

That conflict between the world's two new superpowers stopped short of all-out war – became a "Cold War" – was the result of a new factor: fear of nuclear confrontation. With both sides in possession of weapons with the capacity to devastate the world many times over, the consequences of war were too terrible to contemplate. Instead, each sought to outflank and destabilize the other and, by building networks of client states, to increase its spheres of influence.

The Soviet nuclear testing and space center at Baykonur in Kazakhstan. In the end the USSR could not afford to keep up with the US in the arms race.

Though a series of flashpoints erupted – notably in Korea and Vietnam – for the most part the Cold War was played out through local proxy wars and the shadowy world of espionage. By the mid-1980s, the Soviet Union, bogged down in an expensive war in Afghanistan, was under increasing strain. The reforming premier, Mikhail Gorbachev, withdrew Soviet troops from the war and relaxed control over its eastern European satellites. When the Berlin Wall fell in 1989, the Cold War was effectively at an end. In December 1991, the Soviet Union was itself dissolved.

EASTERN HEMISPHERE

1948 Soviet-sponsored regimes established in Poland, Czechoslovakia, and Hungary.

Soviets begin Berlin blockade; Berlin airlift to counter blockade (–1949).

Yugoslavia breaks ties with USSR.

1949 Proclamation of People's Republic of China; land reform and collectivization of agriculture in China; millions of landowners executed (–1956).

Foundation of Council for Mutual Economic Assistance (COMECON), an economic association for communist countries.

USSR tests its first atomic bomb.

1950 Surprise attack by communist N Korea on US-backed S Korea leads to massive American and Chinese military intervention (–1953).

Chinese invasion of Tibet.

1955 Formation of Warsaw Pact; created as Soviet-bloc opponent of NATO.

1956 Anti-communist uprising in Hungary crushed by Soviets.

1957 Soviet Union launches *Sputnik* satellite; start of the "Space Race."

1961 Berlin Wall erected on the night of Aug 12–13, separating E and W Berlin.

1965 US steps up military involvement in Vietnam, backing S Vietnam regime against Viet Cong.

1966 Cultural Revolution in China.

1968 "Prague Spring" reforms in Czechoslovakia crushed by USSR.

US now has 510,000 troops in Vietnam.

1975 American troops leave Vietnam; communists take Saigon; Khmer Rouge seize power in Cambodia.

1978 Communist coup in Afghanistan.

1979 USSR sends troops to Afghanistan.

Vietnamese invade Cambodia. Fall of Khmer Rouge regime.

1985 Mikhail Gorbachev becomes Soviet leader; moves to end Cold War.

1989 Berlin Wall breached; collapse of communism in Poland, Hungary, Czechoslovakia, Romania, E Germany, and Bulgaria (–1990).

USSR withdraws troops from Afghanistan.

WESTERN HEMISPHERE

1948 US Secretary of State announces Marshall Plan.

1949 North Atlantic Treaty signed in Washington.

1955 W Germany admitted to NATO.

Treaty signed in Vienna, reestablishing Austrian republic in pre-1938 borders.

1957 Treaty of Rome; basis of European Economic Community (EEC).

Cold War opponents: Kennedy and Kruschev

1962 Cuban missile crisis; Russia's plan to establish missile bases on Cuba brings world to the brink of nuclear war.

1964 Stanley Kubrick's film *Dr Strangelove* alerts public to dangers of Mutually Assured Destruction (MAD).

1968 Anti-Vietnam War protests in US; Student uprisings throughout Europe.

1969 *Apollo 11* makes first moon landing.

1972 SALT I strategic arms limitation talks.

1973 Salvador Allende's freely elected Marxist government in Chile overthrown by military coup with covert US aid.

1975 Ethiopia becomes socialist state, run increasingly according to Soviet ideology.

1979 SALT II arms limitation agreement.

US deploys Trident I submarine-launched nuclear missiles.

Sandinistas take power in Nicaragua (–1990); US attempts to destabilize regime through secret support for the Contras.

1983 US invades small Caribbean island of Grenada following a Marxist coup.

1987 US and USSR agree to limit intermediate nuclear weapons; Washington Arms Control Treaty decommissions one-fifth of Soviet arms.

1945 Ho Chi Minh proclaims independence of Vietnam.

1946 French try to win back Vietnam in First War of Indo-China (−54).

Philippines become independent republic.

1947 India and Pakistan gain independence from Britain.

1948 Ceylon granted independence by Britain. Name changed to Sri Lanka in 1972.

1949 Following four years of guerrilla warfare, Dutch E Indies granted independence as Indonesia.

1954 French defeated at Dien Bien Phu; Vietnam divided along latitude 17°N.

1957 British protectorate of Malaya gains independence as Malaysia.

1961 India annexes Portuguese enclaves of Goa, Daman, and Diu.

1962 Dutch relinquish West New Guinea, which is absorbed by Indonesia as Irian Jaya the following year.

1965 Singapore leaves federation of Malaysia.

1971 Civil War in E Pakistan, which severs link with Pakistan and becomes independent state of Bangladesh.

1975 Portuguese colony of E Timor occupied by Indonesia (−1999).

1983 Tamil Tigers step up guerrilla war against government of Sri Lanka.

Singapore in 1980, one of the economic success stories of SE Asia's former colonies.

1952 Mau Mau movement in Kenya fights for restoration of African lands (−1956).

1954 Start of Algerian War of Independendence (−1962).

1956 Morocco and Tunisia gain independence from France.

1957 Britain begins process of decolonization in Africa, when Ghana (Gold Coast) becomes first British colony to achieve independence.

1960 Fifteen African countries gain independence; S Africa leaves Commonwealth.

Katanga province secedes from republic of Congo (Zaire); UN intervention follows.

1964 N Rhodesia and Nyasaland become independent as Zambia and Malawi.

1965 Unilateral declaration of independence by S Rhodesia after Ian Smith rejects British demand for majority rule.

1967 Biafra attempts to break away from Nigeria; bitter civil war and extensive famine (−1970).

1974 At least 750,000 settlers return to Portugal as colonial territories are granted independence; independence of Guinea-Bissau.

1975 Angola, Mozambique, and Cape Verde gain independence from Portugal. Angola and Mozambique subsequently torn apart by civil wars.

1980 Black majority comes to power in S Rhodesia, which is renamed Zimbabwe.

1990 ANC legalized in S Africa; Nelson Mandela freed; Namibia gains independence from S Africa.

The End of Colonial Rule

Europe's newly independent former colonies became a prime focus of Cold War rivalry. The major battlegrounds between the communist and capitalist ideologies were the former French colony of Vietnam and Portugal's major African possessions: Angola and Mozambique. After World War II, British, Dutch, and French colonies in SE Asia that had been occupied by the Japanese were determined not to submit to foreign rule again. Decolonization in Africa was a slower process, gaining pace in the late 1950s. Only Portugal refused to accept the inevitable, fighting to crush liberation movements until her own armed forces could take no more and overthrew the government in 1974.

French troops scour the Algerian countryside in an attempt to flush out FLN freedom fighters.

Algerian War of Independence

Some African countries enjoyed a peaceful transition to independence, but others, especially those with a large community of European settlers, achieved it only after bloody wars. In Algeria the war waged by the well-organized FLN (National Liberation Front) lasted from 1954 to 1962. France sent some 500,000 troops to keep Algeria French. The army even erected a barbed-wire fence along the border with Tunisia keep out FLN fighters based there. Within Algeria they used torture and reprisals against people suspected of aiding the FLN.

This only fired the determination of the Algerians to resist and terrible atrocities were committed by both sides. In 1958 the French government fell and De Gaulle was elected in the expectation that he would find a way of defeating the FLN. However, realizing that the war was unwinnable, he ordered a referendum in which Algeria voted for full independence from France.

1945–1990 431

Martin Luther King

Martin Luther King, a Baptist minister from Georgia, was the most charismatic and compelling civil rights advocate in the US. His natural dignity, allied to an unwavering commitment to non-violence and an exceptional talent for public speaking, made him the clear leader of America's oppressed black minority.

Much like his hero Gandhi, repeated prison sentences only reinforced his public standing. His influence was key in the enactment of the Civil Rights Act of 1964 and the Voting Rights Act of 1965. But by the late 1960s, his non-violent approach was being increasingly challenged by the emergent Black Power movement. Nonetheless, his assassination by white supremacist James Earl Ray sparked riots across America's cities.

The rock 'n' roll revolution

The assertive rebelliousness of post-War affluent Western youth culture found its most enduring outlet in rock 'n' roll. By the early 1960s, pop culture had gripped the West.

1955 Bill Hayley's "Rock Around the Clock" reaches number 1 on both sides of the Atlantic: total sales top 22 million. Little Richard releases "Tutti Frutti"; Chuck Berry debuts with "Maybellene".

1956 Elvis Presley releases his first hit, "Heartbreak Hotel" – rock 'n' roll goes mainstream. Presley eventually becomes the biggest-selling singer in pop history.

1957 Jerry Lee Lewis releases "Whole Lotta Shakin" and "Great Balls of Fire"; Buddy Holly's first hit, "Peggy Sue".

1962 Bob Dylan's "Blowin' in the Wind": folk traditions combine with radical protest.

1963 The Beatles have their first hit, "From Me to You": pop music becomes global.

1964 The Beatles take the US by storm, followed by the Rolling Stones: the British invasion.

1965 Bob Dylan pioneers electric folk.

1967 The Summer of Love. The Beatles release "Sgt. Pepper's Lonely Hearts Club Band", pop's first "concept" album.

1968 Woodstock Festival: the alternative music culture goes mainstream.

1969 The Beatles break up.

ASIA

1961 Military coup in S Korea.

Kurds in Iraq renew campaign for independent homeland.

1962 Border dispute over Arunachal Pradesh climaxes in brief Sino-Indian War after years of intermittent clashes. Agreement of Indian border disputes with Myanmar and Nepal and (temporarily) with Pakistan.

Military coup in Myanmar.

US military advisors sent to S Vietnam.

1967 Civil war in Yemen leads to creation of breakaway Yemen Arab Republic.

1963 Creation of Federation of Malaysia (Singapore, Sarawak, Sabah, and Malaya).

West New Guinea ceded to Indonesia by Dutch; Sukarno declared "president for life."

1970 Flooding in East Pakistan (Bangladesh) kills 22,000.

1967 1964 Gulf of Tonkin resolution authorises US air strikes against N Vietnam and Viet Cong; war soons spreads to Laos and Cambodia.

Palestine Liberation Organisation (PLO) established.

High-speed Shinkansen "bullet" train introduced, Japan.

1965 US troops sent to Vietnam to support S Vietnamese regime in Hanoi against continuing communist attacks.

Second inconclusive Indo-Pakistan War over Jammu and Kashmir.

Failed Marxist coup in Indonesia prompts military counter-coup which ends the Sukarno regime.

Singapore secedes from Malaysia and gains independence; rapid economic growth follows.

Ferdinand Marcos takes power in Philippines (–86).

Flooding in East Pakistan (Bangladesh) kills 47,000.

AFRICA

1961 S Africa established as independent republic; leaves the Commonwealth.

Nationalist struggle against Portuguese rule in Angola begins (–74).

Britain grants independence to Sierra Leone.

Italy grants independence to Somalia.

1970 1962 Faced by mounting political crisis at home, France abandons attempts to retain Algeria and grants it full independence.

Belgium grants independence to Rwanda and Burundi.

Britain grants independence to Uganda.

1963 Britain grants independence to Kenya.

1969 Civil war in Sudan (–72).

1964 Nationalist struggle against Portuguese rule in Mozambique begins (–74).

Britain grants independence to Tanzania, Zambia and Malawi.

1965 White minority government in Rhodesia breaks away from British rule by Unilateral Declaration of Independence (UDI).

Britain grants independence to The Gambia.

1969

1961 East German communist regime under Walter Ulbricht builds Berlin Wall, forcibly sealing off E Berlin from W Berlin to prevent continuing migrations of E Germans to the west. E Berlin incorporated into E Germany.

USSR launches first man into space, Yuri Gagarin.

1968

Albania breaks off relations with USSR, switches allegiance to China.

Organisation for Economic Co-operation and Development (OECD) founded, Paris.

1962 Release of first James Bond film, *Dr No*.

1963 US and USSR agree to end atmospheric testing of nuclear weapons.

Turkey and Greece dispute control of Cyprus.

Franco-German "Reconciliation" Treaty signed.

Yugoslavia becomes a socialist republic.

Riots by Turks in Cyprus in protest at anti-Turkish changes to the constitution.

1964 Kruschchev ousted in USSR after failure of economic liberalization; eventually succeeded by Leonid Brezhnev.

Malta granted independence by Britain.

Volga–Baltic Canal, world's longest at 528 miles (850 km) completed, USSR.

British House of Commons votes to abolish the death penalty.

Mass breakout from East Berlin as 57 escape to the West along a 470-foot (133-m) tunnel.

1965 André Courrèges unveils the miniskirt, Paris: birth of pop fashion.

Death of Sir Winston Churchill.

France launches first satellite.

1961 John Kennedy president in US promising "New Frontier" in American life (–63).

US-based Cuban exiles and CIA mount unsuccessful attempt to topple Castro: the Bay of Pigs.

"Freedom Rides" in US organized in defiance of Southern segregation laws, spark major racial riots; continue intermittently throughout decade.

US launches its first man into space, Alan Shepherd.

Oral polio vaccine developed, US.

1962 Cuban missile crisis: US forces USSR to withdraw nuclear missiles from Cuba.

Western Samoa granted independence by US.

Jamaica and Trinidad and Tobago granted independence by Britain.

First transatlantic television pictures transmitted.

1963 John Kennedy assassinated in US; Lyndon Johnson president (–68).

Major march on Washington protesting at continuing racial discrimination in US led by Martin Luther King.

Monetarist economic theory propounded in US by Milton Friedman with *Publication of Inflation: Causes and Consequences*.

1967

1964 US Congress authorizes war against N Vietnam.

President Johnson unveils "Great Society" program; Civil Rights Act forbids segregation in public places in US.

Military coup in Brazil.

Transit satellites, world's first satellite navigation system, launched by US Navy.

1966

1965 Voting Rights Act in US increases numbers of black voters; Watts race riots in Los Angeles.

Australia commits troops to aid US in Vietnam (–72).

1968

American *Mariner 4* space probe reaches Mars.

The *Sound of Music* released, biggest-grossing film musical in history.

Yuri Gagarin (1934–68)

The early lead taken by the USSR after 1957 in what was immediately dubbed the "Space Race" was finally cemented on April 12, 1961 when Soviet cosmonaut Yuri Gagarin became the first man successfully launched into earth orbit. His one-orbit flight of the Earth on board Vostock 1 lasted one hour 48 minutes. The best the US could manage was a 15-minute suborbital flight by Alan Shepherd one month later. Gagarin, immediately proclaimed a hero of the Soviet Union, was later killed on a training flight.

The Space Race

1957 Oct: USSR successfully launches first artificial Earth satellite, *Sputnik 1*.

1961 Apr: Cosmonaut Yuri Gagarin first man in Earth orbit.

May: US sends first man into space, Alan Shepherd, on 15-minute sub-orbital flight; Kennedy announces US intention of landing man on Moon "before the end of this decade."

1962 US sends first man into Earth orbit, John Glenn.

1963 USSR sends first woman into space, Valentina Tereshkova.

1965 US begins two-man *Gemini* program. US aunches first probe to Mars, *Mariner 4*. First space-walk made by cosmonaut Alex Lenonov.

1966 USSR lands first unmanned probe on Moon, *Luna 9*.

1967 Fire on prototype *Apollo* capsule kills three US astronauts: US Moon-landing program delayed by one year. First successful launch of US *Saturn V* rocket.

1968 Oct: First flight of *Apollo* spacecraft, in Earth orbit.

Dec: Second flight of *Apollo* spacecraft, *Apollo 8*, successfully orbits Moon, establishing decisive US lead in space exploration.

1969 July: US lands Neil Armstrong and Buzz Aldrin on Moon and returns them safely to Earth.

1975 New US-USSR rapport in space exploration sealed with successful docking of *Apollo* and *Soyuz* spacecraft.

ASIA

1966 Mao Zedong imposes massive cultural purge of China: the Cultural Revolution (–1970). Revolutionary Red Guards formed (–1968); millions die.

1973

1967 Six-Day War: Arab forces attack Israel and are rapidly repulsed; Israel takes Sinai, Gaza Strip, Golan Heights, West Bank, and Jerusalem. PLO assumes leadership of Palestinian struggle against Israel; begins terrorist attacks.

Britain pulls out of Aden; creation of People's Democratic Republic of Yemen.

Association of Southeast Asia Nations (ASEAN) founded, Jakarta.

1968 Saddam Hussein seizes power in Iraq.

1969 Sino-Russian border clashes resume.

1970 General Hafiz al-Assad seizes power in Syria.

Armed conflicts between Palestinian refugees in Jordan and Jordanian security forces.

Cyclone in East Pakistan (Bangladesh) kills 500,000.

First domestic video cassette players available, Japan.

AFRICA

1966 Britain grants independence to Botswana (Bechuanaland) and Lesotho (Basutoland).

1967 Civil war breaks out in Nigeria after oil-rich eastern province of Biafra attempts to secede; over one million die before famine and superior Nigerian arms force Biafran surrender (–1970).

Egypt closes Gulf of Aqaba to Israeli shipping.

World's first heart transplant operation, South Africa.

1968 Britain grants independence to Swaziland.

1969 Colonel Gaddafi seizes power in Libya.

Military rule imposed in Sudan.

1970 Death of Egyptian leader, Nasser; succeeded by Anwar Sadat.

Military rule imposed in Somalia.

Breakaway republic of Biafra capitulates to famine and superior Nigerian forces.

The Vietnam War

The spread of communist-inspired nationalism in Southeast Asia after World War II presented a clear challenge to US attempts to contain communist influence in the region, above all in its client-state of South Vietnam. By the mid-1960s, the US had committed its full military resources to the struggle. Its efforts were undermined by the inability of its forces to come to terms with guerrilla warfare and by the hostility of US popular opinion to the war. By 1973 the US was forced into a face-saving withdrawal.

The Six-day War

The establishment of the state of Israel in 1948 had created an absolute determination on the part of the wider Arab world to destroy it, which subsequent Israeli military successes had only reinforced. In June 1967 under the leadership of Egypt, a massive pan-Arab attack was launched against Israel. It was comprehensively defeated in under a week. Israel, actively supported by the US, not only repulsed the Arab attacks but also substantially added to the territories under its control, taking the West Bank, the Golan Heights, the Sinai Peninusula, the Gaza Strip, and Jerusalem, which was declared the new capital of Israel.

Israeli military superiority in the Middle East was conclusively underlined in 1967. US arms, unity of purpose, and daring leadership were decisive. Despite overwhelming numerical superiority, the Arab armies were routed.

EUROPE

1966 France withdraws from NATO.

United Nations Industrial Development Organization (UNIDO) founded, Vienna.

World's first vertical takeoff airplane, the Harrier jump jet, introduced, UK.

 1967 Martial law imposed by "Colonels' Regime" in Greece.

CAT scanner pioneered in UK; produces 3-D images of interior of body.

Britain launches Europe's first color television service.

USSR, US, and Britain agree to ban nuclear testing in space.

Attempted royalist coup in Greece is crushed.

1968 Attempted liberalization of communist rule in Czechoslovakia under Alexander Duâek – the "Prague Spring" – crushed by Soviet-led Warsaw Pact invasion.

Widespread student rioting in Paris – Les Évènements – threatens to topple government; student protests spread across much of W Europe.

Albania leaves Warsaw Pact and retreats into self-imposed isolation under Stalinist government.

British presence "east of Suez" formally ended.

Basques launch terror campaign, Spain.

1969 W German chancellor, Willy Brandt, begins rapprochement with E Germany.

French premier, Charles de Gaulle, resigns after defeat in referendum on regional reform.

 Renewed sectarian violence in Northern Ireland; troops sent in to protect Catholics.

1970 Divorce is legalized in Italy.

40,000 square miles (103,600 sq km) of German territory transferred to Poland as relations between the countries are normalized.

AMERICAS & AUSTRALASIA

1966 Race riots in Atlanta: Black Power becomes significant factor in US political life.

France begins testing of nuclear weapons in the Tuamotu Islands.

1967 Student protests against continued US involvement in Vietnam gather pace.

Australian aborigines granted citizenship after referendum.

Super Bowl first played, US.

1968 Assassination of Martin Luther King, Jr. sparks race riots in 124 US cities.

Hundreds of students protesting at high cost of Mexico Olympic games killed by government security forces in Mexico City.

Tupamaros urban guerrilla group founded, Uruguay.

Military junta seize power in Peru.

US launches *Apollo 8*, first manned flight to orbit Moon.

 1969 Richard Nixon president of the US (–1974).

Strategic Arms Limitation Talks (SALT) begun between US and USSR.

250,000 march on Washington in protest against US involvement in Vietnam.

US lands first men on the Moon.

 Arpanet computer network, allowing computers to communicate with each other, launched in US.

Lake Pontchartrain Causeway, Louisiana, opened; at 24 miles (38 km), it is the world's longest bridge.

 1970 Nuclear Nonproliferation Treaty agreed to by US, USSR, and Britain; China and France refuse to ratify it.

Allende elected Marxist president of Chile (–1973).

First jumbo jets enter service, each able to carry almost 500 passengers.

First fiber-optic telephone lines allow direct-dialed transatlantic calls.

Earthquake in Peru kills 67,000.

Young Chinese read from The Thoughts of Chairman Mao *under the watchful guidance of Mao himself. The book was distributed in millions.*

The Cultural Revolution

Determined to maintain the ideological purity and fervor of communist China, in 1966 Mao launched a new revolutionary wave: the Cultural Revolution. Enforced by a hardcore of students and the newly formed Red Guard, and guided by the collected *Thoughts of Chairman Mao*, a vacuous assembly of sayings that later formed the official party line, a relentless and violent revolutionary purge of "counterrevolutionary revisionists" was begun. As with the Great Leap Forward a decade earlier, China was plunged into chaos and millions died.

Under the leadership of Mao's wife, Jiang Qing and Lin Biao, the leader of the army, doctors, teachers, and scientists were forcibly removed from their posts and forced to recant publicly, often wearing dunce's caps. Many of them were summarily executed. Those who survived were forced to undertake peasant labor. By Mao's death in 1976, the Cultural Revolution was still formally in existence.

1966–1970

Japan emerged in the 1960s as a beacon of modernization, all but dominating the world's electronics, automative, and digital industries until the economy faltered in the 1990s.

Economic revival in Japan

At least as much as Germany, Japan at the end of World War II was a country in ruins, its industries devastated, its people impoverished. Forty years later, it had the world's second largest economy. This remarkable reversal was partly the result of American sponsorship of Japan as an Asian bulwark against communism, a policy significantly stepped up after the outbreak of the Korean war in 1950. But it was at least as much a reflection of Japanese discipline and determination. The qualities that had made the country a formidable opponent in the war were now redirected to the reconstruction of its economy.

In the 1950s and 60s, Japan placed most emphasis on heavy industry, shipbuilding, and car production especially. By the 1960s, the economy was growing at almost 11 per cent a year. After the oil crisis of 1973, increasing resources were directed to high-tech electronic industries with the result that Japan consolidated its position as a new global economic giant.

ASIA

1971 Widespread rioting in East Pakistan in support of an independent Bengali state prompts Indian intervention leading to Third Indo-Pakistan War and, with Indian support, the creation of independent Bangladesh.

China admitted to UN; Taiwan expelled.

United Arab Emirates (UAE) created in Gulf from former British Trucial States.

1972 Ferdinand Marcos declares martial law in Philippines (–1981).

Islands surrendered by Japan in World War II are returned to it.

1976 **1973** Yom Kippur War: third Arab attempt to conquer Israel fails. Arab-dominated OPEC responds by restricting flow of crude oil to world markets, raising prices by 200 percent. Global postwar boom brought to sudden halt as recession hits almost everywhere.

Gush Emunim (Bloc of the Faithful) founded, Israel; violently opposes all efforts to restore Israeli-occupied territory to Palestinians.

US troops withdrawn from Vietnam.

US bombing campaign of Cambodia stepped up.

Islamic Mujahedin rebellion in Afghanistan.

1976 **1974** Indonesian invasion of East Timor.

Foundation of Amal, Lebanese terror group committed to the support of Shia Islam.

1975 US-backed regime in S Vietnam falls to Viet Cong, who reunite Vietnam under communist rule.

Communist Pathet Lao movement topples coalition government in Laos.

Chinese-backed Khmer Rouge under Pol Pot seize control of Cambodia and impose savage totalitarian rule (–1979).

Indira Gandhi imposes state of emergency in India after conviction for electoral fraud (–1977).

Martial law imposed in Bangladesh (–1979).

Civil war starts in Lebanon.

US-backed S Vietnam regime falls. End of Vietnam War.

1976 Communist regimes come to power in S Vietnam, Laos, and Cambodia. Khmer Rouge takes over Cambodia; imposes regime of extreme terror.

Indonesia annexes East Timor.

AFRICA

1971 Mogadishu Declaration calls for end of white rule in South Africa; UN declares South African mandate in SW Africa (Namibia) illegal.

Idi Amin seizes power in Uganda and imposes idiosyncratic reign of terror (–1979).

1972 Ugandan Asians expelled by Amin.

1977 **1974** Ethiopian emperor, Haile Selassie, deposed in Marxist military coup under Mengistu Haile Mariam; new regime sustained by USSR.

At least 750,000 colonists leave Angola, Mozambique, and Guinea Bissau return to Portugal after the Portuguese decision to pull out of all its African colonies.

1975 Portugal grants independence to Angola, Mozambique, Guinea Bissau (Portuguese Guinea), and Cape Verde isles. Civil war follows in Angola between Marxist MPLA guerrillas and South African-sponsored UNITA (–1976).

1976 Spain grants independence to Spanish Sahara.

Namibia unilaterally incorporated within South Africa sparking SWAPO resistance struggle.

Substantial Cuban and Soviet military aid made available to many African states.

EUROPE

1971 USSR launches *Salyut I*, first of a series of permanently manned orbiting space stations.

1972 Eleven Israeli athletes murdered by Arab gunmen at Munich Olympics.

1973 Britain, Ireland, and Denmark join the EEC.

Recession begins across Europe after OPEC oil-price rises.

1974 Military coup in Portugal ends prewar right-wing regime.

Colonels' Regime ends in Greece; democracy restored.

Civil war in Cyprus prompts Turkish invasion.

IRA begin bombing campaign in mainland Britain.

Kosovo granted autonomy under revised Yugoslav constitution.

1975 Death of Spanish dictator, Franco. King Juan Carlos new head of state; immediately begins to dismantle totalitarian apparatus and reintroduce democracy.

Helsinki Accords signed promoting "Security and Cooperation in Europe;" Organisation for Security and Cooperation in Europe (OSCE) founded, Vienna.

AMERICAS & AUSTRALASIA

1971 First South Pacific Forum, annual meeting of heads of government.

1972 Sino-American relations partly restored after Nixon's visit to China.

Home Box Office (HBO) launched in US; world's first subscription cable television service.

1973 Right-wing coup, led by General Pinochet, overthrows Allende's Marxist government in Chile.

Juan Perón resumes power in Argentina (dies 1974).

US and USSR sign Agreement on the Prevention of Nuclear War, Washington.

Caribbean Community and Common Market (CARICOM) founded, Guyana.

World Trade Center, New York, new highest building in world at 1,349 feet (411 m).

1974 Richard Nixon becomes the only US president forced to resign after Watergate scandal reveals attempt to sabotage Democratic rivals in 1972 election. Gerald Ford becomes new president (–1977).

First commercial application of Arpanet computer network, US.

Magnetic resonance imaging (MRI) scanner developed, US.

1976 Sears Roebuck Tower, Chicago, new highest building in world at 1,454 feet (443 m).

1975 Restrictions imposed on immigration to Australia.

First personal computers marketed, New Mexico.

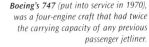

Boeing's 747 (put into service in 1970), was a four-engine craft that had twice the carrying capacity of any previous passenger jetliner.

Mass air travel

Rising incomes, increased leisure, and the development from the late 1950s of wide-bodied jet aircraft capable of carrying hundreds of passengers and crossing continents in hours ushered in the era of mass air travel.

In 1960, 74 billion air passenger miles were flown; in 1979 over 700 billion. In 1999, nearly two billion people were carried on planes and the world's busiest airport, Atlanta, handled 80 million passengers. In the same year, nine million Britons flew to Spain. Numbers on this scale cause increasing problems of pollution, delays, and air-traffic control.

Shining Path

Among the numerous revolutionary movements that swept Latin America in the 20th century, the most extreme was Peru's Shining Path (*Sendero Luminoso*). Though it borrowed from many revolutionary movements, chiefly Maoism, its semi-mystical character was unique.

The movement was begun in 1970 by a former philosophy professor, Abimael Guzmán, also known as Chairman Gonzalo. Guzmán sought to bring about a state of permanent revolution among the bemused indigenous Indians of the Andes, chiefly through a violent guerrilla campaign which in turn sparked a bitter war with security forces. Shining Path largely petered out with the capture and imprisonment of Guzmán in 1992.

Shining Path guerrillas assert their authority in Ayacucho by defiantly parading through the city's streets.

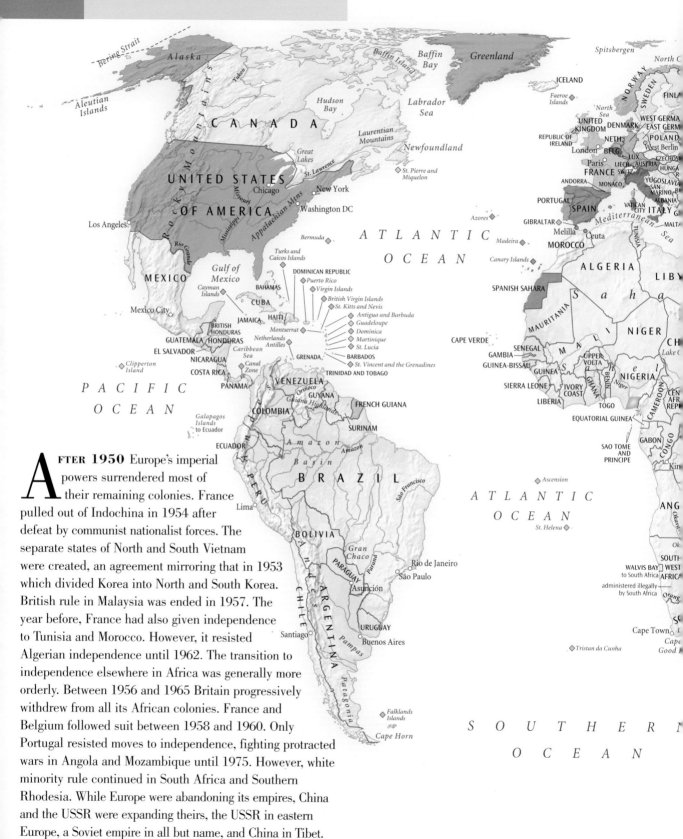

AFTER 1950 Europe's imperial powers surrendered most of their remaining colonies. France pulled out of Indochina in 1954 after defeat by communist nationalist forces. The separate states of North and South Vietnam were created, an agreement mirroring that in 1953 which divided Korea into North and South Korea. British rule in Malaysia was ended in 1957. The year before, France had also given independence to Tunisia and Morocco. However, it resisted Algerian independence until 1962. The transition to independence elsewhere in Africa was generally more orderly. Between 1956 and 1965 Britain progressively withdrew from all its African colonies. France and Belgium followed suit between 1958 and 1960. Only Portugal resisted moves to independence, fighting protracted wars in Angola and Mozambique until 1975. However, white minority rule continued in South Africa and Southern Rhodesia. While Europe were abandoning its empires, China and the USSR were expanding theirs, the USSR in eastern Europe, a Soviet empire in all but name, and China in Tibet.

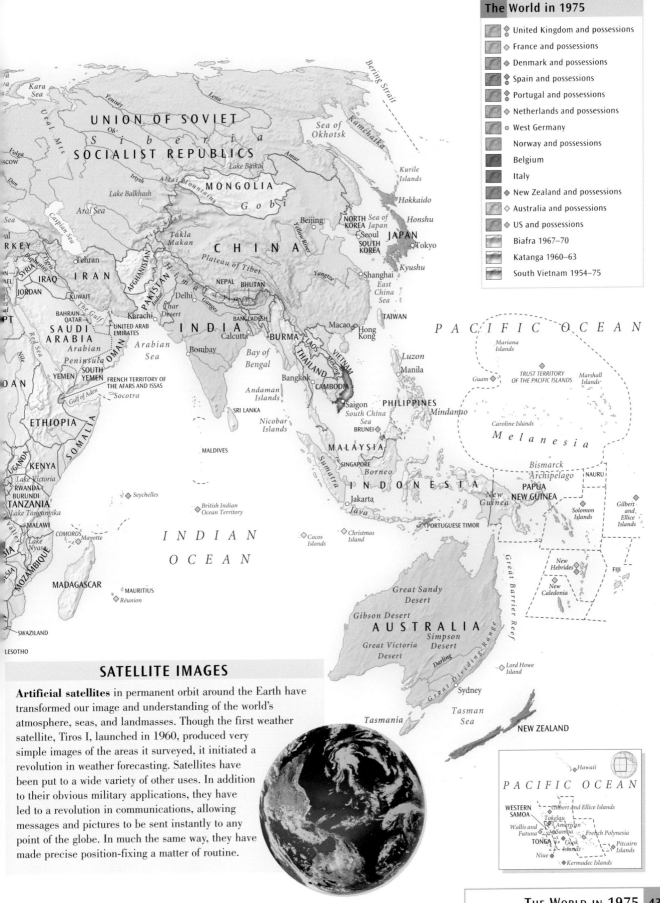

The World in 1975

United Kingdom and possessions
France and possessions
Denmark and possessions
Spain and possessions
Portugal and possessions
Netherlands and possessions
West Germany
Norway and possessions
Belgium
Italy
New Zealand and possessions
Australia and possessions
US and possessions
Biafra 1967–70
Katanga 1960–63
South Vietnam 1954–75

SATELLITE IMAGES

Artificial satellites in permanent orbit around the Earth have transformed our image and understanding of the world's atmosphere, seas, and landmasses. Though the first weather satellite, Tiros I, launched in 1960, produced very simple images of the areas it surveyed, it initiated a revolution in weather forecasting. Satellites have been put to a wide variety of other uses. In addition to their obvious military applications, they have led to a revolution in communications, allowing messages and pictures to be sent instantly to any point of the globe. In much the same way, they have made precise position-fixing a matter of routine.

1975 –2006
The Modern World

1975: Indonesia annexes East Timor. Extremist Khmer Rouge under Pol Pot impose reign of terror on Cambodia (to 1979)

1978: Egypt recognizes existence of Israel under Camp David Treaty. Beginnings of economic liberalization in China

1979: Islamic Revolution in Iran under Ayatollah Khomeini. Invasion of Afghanistan by USSR (to 1989)

1980: Iran-Iraq War (to 1988)

ASIA
AFRICA
EUROPE
REST OF THE WORLD

1975   1976   1977   1978   1979   1980   19

1975: Death of Franco restores democracy to Spain

1975: US-backed South Vietnam regime collapses

1979: Start of Nicaraguan civil war between Marxist Sandinistas and US-backed Contras

By the last quarter of the 20th century the division between the world's rich and poor nations and its stable and unstable regions had never been more obvious. While prosperity and technological progress became more marked in the West, much of the rest of the world, above all Africa and parts of Asia, were scarred by poverty and political turmoil that in some cases descended into anarchy.

As a result, and despite the ending of the Cold War after the collapse of the Soviet Union in 1991, the world grew increasingly dangerous. The military superiority of the west was never in doubt, but the rise of the rogue states – Cambodia, Libya, Iran, Iraq, North Korea, and Serbia among them – often threatened international security. In an age of growing globalization and with the spread of illicit nuclear technology, the capacity of such states to destabilize areas beyond their immediate borders increased dramatically.

The Cold War may have dominated the early part of the period, but its background was one of growing regional instability. In Cambodia, for example, a Marxist regime under Pol Pot took over the country in 1975. Until forcibly halted by a Vietnamese invasion in 1979, Pol Pot's brutal rule saw the murders of upward of one million people. Also in 1975, the Indonesian invasion of the former Portuguese colony of East Timor led to a savage campaign of repression and reprisals that continued until 1999, when the East Timorese people were finally allowed to choose their own destiny and voted for independence.

Other flashpoints in Southeast Asia included Sri Lanka, where Tamil demands for an independent homeland led to an ongoing 20-year civil war, and Kashmir, which in 1989 saw the start of a violent insurrection against Indian rule. At the same time there was no letup in the traditional rivalry between India and Pakistan. Both tested nuclear weapons in 1999 and seemed poised to use them over Kashmir in 2002.

The plight of Africa

In sub-Saharan Africa postcolonial civil wars, often with the participation of outside forces, continued to blight many countries. The Democratic Republic of the Congo (formerly Zaire), Angola, and Rwanda, scene of a terrifying campaign of genocide in 1994, were the countries that suffered most. Others that were reduced lawless anarchy included Somalia, Sierra Leone, and Liberia. In Sudan, conflict between the Arab rulers and the black

PICTURE ABOVE:
A toppled statue of Lenin lies abandoned in a field near Bucharest. After the collapse of communism in 1989, the former Soviet satellites were quick to destroy the symbols of their subjection to an alien and discredited ideology.

The rule of the Khmer Rouge in Cambodia was perhaps the most extreme example of perverted communist idealism. In the name of "reeducation" the largely peasant army killed over a million people.

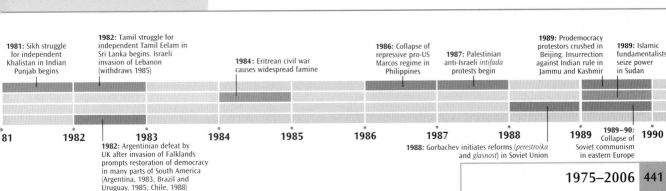

1981: Sikh struggle for independent Khalistan in Indian Punjab begins

1982: Tamil struggle for independent Tamil Eelam in Sri Lanka begins. Israeli invasion of Lebanon (withdraws 1985)

1984: Eritrean civil war causes widespread famine

1986: Collapse of repressive pro-US Marcos regime in Philippines

1987: Palestinian anti-Israeli *intifada* protests begin

1989: Prodemocracy protestors crushed in Beijing. Insurrection against Indian rule in Jammu and Kashmir

1989: Islamic fundamentalists seize power in Sudan

81   1982   1983   1984   1985   1986   1987   1988   1989   1989–90: Collapse of Soviet communism in eastern Europe   1990

1982: Argentinian defeat by UK after invasion of Falklands prompts restoration of democracy in many parts of South America (Argentina, 1983; Brazil and Uruguay, 1985; Chile, 1988)

1988: Gorbachev initiates reforms (*perestroika* and *glasnost*) in Soviet Union

The collapse of communism in Eastern Europe

Soviet Union to 1991	Czechoslovakia to Dec 1992
Soviet-dominated Eastern Europe to 1989	Yugoslavia to 1991
German Democratic Republic, united with Federal Republic of Germany 1990	other communist state before 1991
	1990 date of first free election

African peoples in the south and west led to civil war and brutal "ethnic cleansing." At the same time much of Africa was threatened by the specters of hunger and disease, most alarmingly by the spread of the epidemic of AIDS.

The Islamic world

The problem of Palestine remained the burning issue in the Middle East, where Arab-Israeli hostility continued unchecked. Egypt, the largest Arab state, made peace with Israel in 1978, but much of the Arab world remained implacably opposed to Israel. Israel's response – an invasion of Lebanon in 1982 in an attempt to root out PLO forces – inevitably increased tensions further. There was an apparent improvement in Arab-Israeli relations in the early 1990s under the Oslo Peace Accords, which promised the PLO a measure of self-government. However, a lasting settlement seemed as elusive as ever with no way out of the cycle of Palestinian suicide bombings and Israeli reprisals. In the end, Israel took the drastic measure

of building a wall to divide Israel from the Palestinian Territorities, at the same time withdrawing Israeli settlers from Gaza in 2005.

The late 1970s saw the rise of militant Islam. In 1979, Ayatollah Khomeini overthrew the US-backed government of Iran and imposed a rigorous Islamic rule. But militant Islam was more than just a challenge to a "corrupt" West. It also sparked conflicts within the Arab world itself – not just between the Sunni and Shi'ite branches of Islam, but also between governments committed to modernization and groups determined to assert fundamentalist Muslim values. The bloody Iran-Iraq war (1980–1988) was one manifestation of this rivalry, the no less violent civil war in Algeria after 1992 another. In 1990 the Iraqi invasion of its oil-rich neighbor, Kuwait, provoked a massive US-led military campaign to oust Iraq. Though humiliated militarily, the Iraqi dictator, Saddam Hussein, was allowed to hold on to power.

Relations between the West and the Islamic world took on a completely new complexion in 2001 following the terrorist

attack on New York's World Trade Center. US President George W. Bush declared a "war on terror" and a US-led coalition invaded Afghanistan, where Islamist terrorists were trained under the protection of the fundamentalist regime of the Taliban. In 2003, on the pretext that Iraq possessed "weapons of mass destruction," Bush decided to put an end to the regime of Saddam Hussein. The conquest of Iraq was accomplished swiftly, but attempts to establish a democratically elected Iraqi government were met with sustained violent opposition from Iraqi insurgents aided by foreign terrorists. Attacks on US occupying forces also continued in Afghanistan.

Collapse of the USSR

The Soviet invasion of Afghanistan in 1979 was to prove the Soviet Union's Vietnam. Forced into a humiliating retreat ten years later, the Soviet Union's Afghan debacle had made clear the shortcomings of the world's leading communist state. No longer able to compete in an ever more high-tech Cold

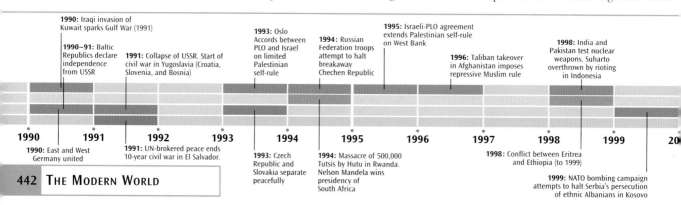

1990: Iraqi invasion of Kuwait sparks Gulf War (1991)

1990–91: Baltic Republics declare independence from USSR

1991: Collapse of USSR. Start of civil war in Yugoslavia (Croatia, Slovenia, and Bosnia)

1993: Oslo Accords between PLO and Israel on limited Palestinian self-rule

1994: Russian Federation troops attempt to halt breakaway Chechen Republic

1995: Israeli-PLO agreement extends Palestinian self-rule on West Bank

1996: Taliban takeover in Afghanistan imposes repressive Muslim rule

1998: India and Pakistan test nuclear weapons. Suharto overthrown by rioting in Indonesia

1990   **1991**   **1992**   **1993**   **1994**   **1995**   **1996**   **1997**   **1998**   **1999**   **20**

1990: East and West Germany united

1991: UN-brokered peace ends 10-year civil war in El Salvador.

1993: Czech Republic and Slovakia separate peacefully

1994: Massacre of 500,000 Tutsis by Hutu in Rwanda. Nelson Mandela wins presidency of South Africa

1998: Conflict between Eritrea and Ethiopia (to 1999)

1999: NATO bombing campaign attempts to halt Serbia's persecution of ethnic Albanians in Kosovo

War struggle, in 1989, under its reforming premier, Mikhail Gorbachev, the USSR effectively abandoned its eastern European empire. When the Berlin Wall was breached in October 1989, the Cold War was over. In a heady burst of liberation, Germany was reunited and Czechoslovakia, Poland, Hungary, Bulgaria, and Romania were welcomed back into the West. By 1991, the Soviet Union itself had been dissolved.

New uncertainties

The legacy of this sudden collapse was mixed. The former territories of the Soviet empire struggled to come to terms with their new freedoms. Moribund industries, the lack of an established political order, and the reappearance of long-suppressed ethnic rivalries created further tensions which were frequently exacerbated by the growth of corruption and organized crime. This was also the pattern of events in the former communist state of Yugoslavia, which in 1991 splintered along ethnic lines, provoking a series of wars in which the dominant Serbs fought Croats, Bosnian Muslims, and Albanians. In 1999 NATO intervened to protect Kosovo's Albanians. Inconclusive in the short term, NATO's action nonetheless paved the way for the overthrow of the Serbian regime.

While Soviet communism had been exposed as a flawed ideology, elsewhere communism was far from dead, particularly in China, the world's most populous state. The country remained harshly totalitarian, as it demonstrated in 1989 with the suppression of a prodemocracy movement in Beijing's Tiananmen Square. However, economic liberalization gave rise to a spectacular boom, making China the fastest-growing economy in the world.

The second hijacked airliner crashes into the World Trade Center in New York on September 11, 2001. The terrorist attack was organized by the shadowy Al-Qaeda movement of Osama bin Laden, which continues to pose a threat to the US and other Western states. The date 9/11 is now indelibly engraved on the minds of the American people.

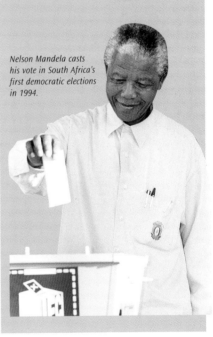

Nelson Mandela casts his vote in South Africa's first democratic elections in 1994.

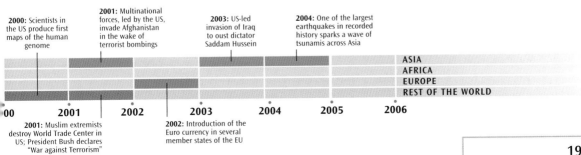

2000: Scientists in the US produce first maps of the human genome

2001: Multinational forces, led by the US, invade Afghanistan in the wake of terrorist bombings

2003: US-led invasion of Iraq to oust dictator Saddam Hussein

2004: One of the largest earthquakes in recorded history sparks a wave of tsunamis across Asia

ASIA
AFRICA
EUROPE
REST OF THE WORLD

00   2001   2002   2003   2004   2005   2006

2001: Muslim extremists destroy World Trade Center in US; President Bush declares "War against Terrorism"

2002: Introduction of the Euro currency in several member states of the EU

James Joyce is portrayed here with a copy of his sprawling masterpiece, Ulysses. The book, as startlingly modern as the works of Picasso or Stravinsky, has suffered an unfair reputation for being "difficult."

1976–1980

ASIA

1976 Death of Chairman Mao of China sparks short-lived coup by "Gang of Four" headed by Mao's wife, Jiang Qing; Hua Guofeng emerges as leader.

Communist consolidation in Vietnam leads to establishment of Socialist Republic of Vietnam.

Indonesia formally annexes East Timor.

Military rule established in Thailand (–1980).

Syria intervenes in Lebanese civil war and imposes Arab peacekeeping force.

Earthquake in Tangshan, China, kills 655,000.

Tidal wave in Philippines kills 5,000.

1977 Peace talks initiated between Egypt and Israel.

Military coup in Pakistan led by devout Sunni Mulism General Zia-ul-Haq alienates Shia population.

1978 Cultural Revolution officially ended in China; beginnings of economic liberalization under Deng Xiaoping.

Backed by USSR, Vietnam begins military intervention in Cambodia to halt despotic Khmer Rouge regime.

Camp David Peace Treaty: Egypt makes peace with Israel earning lasting hostility among Arab nations and expulsion from Arab League.

1979 USSR invades Afghanistan deposing monarchy, sparking civil war, and earning worldwide condemnation.

1981

US-backed Shah of Iran ousted in Islamic revolution; fundamentalist Islamic Republic under Ayatollah Khomeini established. US embassy staff in Tehran taken hostage amid widespread anti-US demonstrations.

Khmer Rouge in Cambodia overthrown by full-scale Vietnamese invasion.

US attempts to reinforce relations with China by severing links with Taiwan.

1980 Iraqi leader Sadam Hussein attempts to exploit revolutionary turmoil in Iran by launching full-scale invasion: resulting Iran-Iraq war lasts eight years and kills estimated 500,000.

1982

First fax machines and domestic camcorders commercially available in Japan.

Start of Iran–Iraq War.

Rapid growth of South Korean economy in this decade.

AFRICA

1976 First black African homelands – bantustans – created by South Africa.

Student race riots in Soweto, South Africa.

Spanish Sahara partitioned between Morocco and Mauritania.

1977 "Islamic socialism" imposed on Libya by maverick ruler Gaddafi.

"Central African Empire" proclaimed by Bokassa.

France grants independence to Djibouti.

1984

Armed conflict between Somalia and Ethiopia over rival claims to Ogaden region (–1988).

1979 Bokassa overthrown.

1985 **1980** Majority black rule established in Zimbabwe (Rhodesia).

EUROPE

1976 Democratic elections in Portugal.

The Concorde, operated by Britain and France and the world's only supersonic airliner, enters service; cuts transatlantic flying time to three and a half hours.

Plans for power-sharing in Northern Ireland abandoned after continued Unionist protests.

New Albanian constitution made country "People's Socialist Republic."

1977 Leonid Brezhnev, General Secretary of the Soviet Communist Party, also named President of the USSR

Declaration by reformist Czechs – Charter 77 – calling for increased political freedoms and respect for human rights in Czechoslovakia; most are subsequently imprisoned.

1978 Prolonged public-service strikes threaten chaos in Britain.

Albania breaks off relations with China; retreats into self-imposed Maoist isolation.

1979 Margaret Thatcher elected prime minister in Britain promising to end trade union abuses.

SALT II arms limitation agreement signed by USSR and US.

Polish-born Pope John Paul II visits Poland, first visit by any pope to a communist country.

1980 Solidarity trade union formed in Poland; rapidly becomes inspirational focus of general opposition to communist government.

Death of Yugoslav ruler, Marshal Tito.

Islamic terrorists seize Iranian embassy in London; subsequently successfully stormed by special forces troops.

Vigdis Finbogadottir becomes world's first nonmonarchical female head of state, Iceland.

AMERICAS & AUSTRALASIA

1976 María Perón deposed by military coup in Argentina.

Military junta in Argentina begins "Dirty Wars" against political opponents: 15,000 enemies of the state are eliminated.

Thirty-two Black African nations boycott Montreal Olympics in protest against continued sporting links between New Zealand and South Africa.

CN Tower, Toronto, becomes world's highest building at 1,815 feet (553 m).

US Supreme Court rules in favor of states' rights to continue the death penalty.

1977 Jimmy Carter president of US (–1981).

Science fiction goes high-tech with release of the movie *Star Wars*.

Apple Computer Company founded, California.

1978 Navstar Global Positioning System (GPS) inaugurated by US Department of Defense; allows instant and precise position-fixing anywhere on earth.

Trans-Amazon Highway completed; runs 3,106 miles (5,000 km) from Recife (Brazil) to Peruvian border.

Illinois Bell Company introduces world's first cellular phone system.

Space Invaders launches craze for computer games.

1979 Civil war in Nicaragua begins between Sandinistas and US-backed Contras.

Diplomatic relations between US and China formally resumed.

US suffers worst-ever nuclear accident after fire at reactor at Three Mile Island, Pennsylvania.

1980 Botched US attempt to free US hostages held in Tehran.

US leads boycott of Moscow Olympics in protest at Soviet invasion of Afghanistan.

Cable News Network (CNN) in US launches world's first 24-hour television news service.

Ronald Reagan (Republican) wins US presidential election. Wins second term in 1984.

Many S American countries return to democracy in this decade.

Civil war in Angola

Civil war was widespread in Angola even before the Portuguese withdrawal in 1975. But with independence the conflict gathered new momentum. Part tribal, part ideological, it rapidly sucked in outside forces, chiefly the USSR and Cuba, which aided the Marxist MPLA government, and South Africa, which supported the rival UNITA forces. Early successes by MPLA could not prevent a full-scale outbreak of further bitter fighting in 1992, which continued through the 1990s.

Conflicts such as that in Angola have led to a complete breakdown in civil order in a number of African countries. Child soldiers have become commonplace.

Pol Pot (1927–1998)

In 1975 the Chinese-backed communist Khmer Rouge guerrilla movement under the veteran revolutionary leader Pol Pot seized power in Cambodia. Pot, determined to create a self-sufficient communist state, immediately imposed a savage rule of terror, partly modeled on the Cultural Revolution. As many as two million, 20 percent of the total population, were executed, among them anyone wearing glasses. The regime was overthrown by a Vietnamese invasion in 1979, though Pot himself continued to lead a Khmer Rouge guerrilla campaign.

Pol Pot's "Killing Fields" in Cambodia produced one of the worst acts of genocide in the 20th century. No one was safe from Pot's arbitrary savagery.

1976–1980 445

Destruction of the rain forest

The world's tropical rain forests are crucial to its delicate ecosystem. Above all, as the emission of "greenhouse gases" increases with the relentless rise of energy consumption, their importance in emitting oxygen has never been greater. Since the 1950s, however, they have been shrinking substantially.

Where once they covered more than 14 percent of the globe, rain forests now account for only 6 percent. The Amazon basin in Brazil, which makes up one-third of the world's total rain forests, has been reduced by 10 percent. The West African and Indian rain forests have been almost entirely destroyed. In Southeast Asia, 50 percent of the rain forest has been destroyed. The consequences of this decline include not just the loss of huge numbers of animal and plant species but soil erosion on a huge scale and severe flooding.

Population growth, land clearance for agriculture, and logging are the prime causes of the shrinking rain forests. Nonetheless, as the implications of their loss have become clearer, the rate of deforestation has been slowed.

ASIA

1981 Iran releases US hostages.

Militant campaign for independent Sikh state of Khalistan in Indian Punjab launched; leads to frequent violent clashes with Indian security forces.

1988 PLO leadership forced to move to Tunis after Israeli invasion of Lebanon; Israel withdraws from Sinai in accordance with Camp David Peace Treaty.

Gulf Cooperation Council established (Saudi Arabia, Bahrain, Kuwait, Oman, Qatar, UAE).

1982 As many as 20,000 militant Islamic opponents of Syrian regime under Assad killed by Syrian security forces at Hama.

Martial law reimposed in Bangladesh (–1986).

First CD player marketed, Japan

1983 Foundation of militant Islamic terror group Hezbollah (Party of God), Lebanon; seeks overthrow of Israel by violent means.

Jordan restores relations with Egypt.

Hindu Tamils in Sri Lanka – the Tamil Tigers – clash with Sinhalese security forces after demanding independent Tamil state – Eelam – in northern Sri Lanka.

1986 Philippine opposition leader, Benigno Aquino, murdered.

1984 Indian prime minister, Indira Gandhi, assassinated by Sikh bodyguard.

1988 First probable use of nerve gas, by Iraq against Iran.

Brunei becomes fully independent from Britain.

1985 Israel withdraws from Lebanon.

AFRICA

1981 Attempted Islamic coup in Egypt foiled after assassination of President Sadat; Mubarak becomes new president.

1989 1983 Islamic law adopted in Sudan; leads to renewed civil war with predominantly Christian south and widespread famine.

1986 1984 Northern Ethiopian province of Eritrea attempts to assert independence; resulting conflict causes severe food shortages, estimated one million Ethiopians die.

1986 1985 State of emergency declared in South Africa in the face of widespread rioting.

Land Acquisition Act: Zimbabwean government begins compulsory purchases of white-owned farms.

EUROPE

1981 Solidarity-inspired popular protests and general strike in Poland lead to imposition of martial law.

Thatcher government in UK begins privatization of nationalized industries, sparking economic revival and providing a model copied in many other parts of the world.

Purge and execution of leading government members in Albania by Enver Hoxha in attempt to ensure continuation of his hard-line rule after his death.

Greece joins the EEC.

1982 Hard-line Soviet leader Leonid Brezhnev dies; succeeded by equally repressive Yuri Andropov.

Spain becomes first new member of NATO since W Germany in 1955.

Solidarity movement outlawed by Polish military government.

Wave of terrorist attacks launched in France by Carlos the Jackal.

1983 Martial Law lifted in Poland.

Miners' strike in Britain decisively broken by Thatcher government heralding final end of trade union stranglehold on British industry.

Mass breakout of nationalist prisoners from Maze Prison, Northern Ireland.

Diplomatic relations between US and Vatican reestablished after 117 years.

1984 Death of Andropov; succeeded by Konstantin Chernenko.

AIDS virus identified by French immunologist Luc Montagnier.

1985 Death of Chernenko; succeeded by reformist Mikhail Gorbachev, who sets about the modernization of Soviet communism, the reform of the moribund Soviet economy and the improvement of tense relations with the West.

Death of Albanian Marxist leader, Enver Hoxha; successor Ramiz Alia begins slow rapprochement with outside world.

AMERICAS & AUSTRALASIA

1981 Ronald Reagan becomes president of US (–1989); immediately increases military spending to confront what he labels the USSR's "evil empire."

First flight of US space shuttle, *Columbia*.

IBM in US launches its first PC; uses Microsoft software.

Agreement reached between Iran and US on release of 52 US hostages being held by Iran.

First meeting of world's leading "G-7" industrial nations, Canada.

US military aid to El Salvador stepped up.

1982 Argentinian junta invades British-held Falklands (Malvinas) and S Georgia; Argentinians expelled by British Task Force. Junta collapses.

Ronald Reagan initiates Strategic Arms Reduction Talks (START) with USSR.

Term "internet" first coined, US.

1983 US announces commitment to build Strategic Defense Initiative (SDI), space-based antimissile defense system.

Marxist coup in Grenada put down by US military intervention.

Democracy restored to Argentina.

Federated states of Micronesia and Marshall Islands enter free association with US.

1984 Soviet-bloc countries other than Romania boycott Los Angeles Olympics in retaliation for US-led boycott of Moscow games in 1980.

1985 Democracy restored to Uruguay.

US and France reject declaration by South Pacific Forum as Pacific as nuclear-free zone.

Volcanic eruption in Colombia kills 25,000.

The computer age

In little more than 20 years, computers have revolutionized working practices, above all in the West. This is much more than a matter of mere computer numbers. The computing capacity of computers is increasing all the time. The *Intel Pentium 4* microchip launched in 2000 was 23 times more powerful than the first Pentium launched in 1993. At the same time, as the uses to which computers are put become increasingly varied, so more and more industries and businesses have become almost entirely dependent on them. The growth of home computers has seen scarcely less dramatic changes: by the late 1990s about 40 percent of all households in the US owned a personal computer.

The Tamil Tigers

In 1972, Sri Lanka committed itself to the creation of a Buddhist-only state. In effect, this amounted to a form of official discrimination against the minority Tamil population of the northeast. Tamil demands for a separate state within a Sri Lankan federation escalated after 1983 into a terrorist campaign, led by the so-called Tamil Tigers, for the creation of a wholly independent Tamil state, Eelam. The crisis deepened with the introduction of an Indian peacekeeping force between 1987 and 1990, leading to the assassination of the former Indian prime minister Rajiv Gandhi in 1991 and the Sri Lankan president Ranasinghe Premadasa in 1993.

A Tamil Tiger guerrilla.

The breaching of the Berlin Wall, the most notorious symbol of communist oppression, in November 1989.

Collapse of communism

After the accession of Mikhail Gorbachev as Soviet leader in 1985, the apparently impregnable monolith of Soviet communism first cracked and then suddenly disintegrated. By Christmas 1991 the Soviet Union itself had been dissolved. In a heady four-month surge of liberation in 1989, communist rule was ended across Eastern Europe. In the face of this complete overthrow of the established system, it was only a matter of time before the Soviet Union gave way to the forces of reform.

Famine in Ethiopia

The imposition of a Marxist regime in 1974 under Mengistu Haile Mariam led to the famines of 1984 and 1985. In 1975, the regime nationalized all land, which it divided into 25-acre (10-ha) plots, causing overcultivation and land degradation. As harvests fell, the government compulsorily bought grain at less than market costs. Combined with drought, the result was famine across northern Ethiopia. The crisis returned in 1994 when a new regime forcibly resettled 600,000 Ethiopians in the south of the country. Over 10 million people were placed at risk.

ASIA

1986 Collapse of pro-US Marcos regime in Philippines. Cory Aquino president.

1987 The intifada: predominantly young Palestinians in Gaza Strip and West Bank repeatedly clash with Israeli security forces.

Most Arab countries restore relations with Egypt.

Sri Lankan government agrees to the use of Indian troops to help in suppression of Tamil separatists.

1988 Iran-Iraq war ends with no clear victor.

PLO acknowledges existence of two states in Palestine, one Arab, one Jewish.

Benazir Bhutto becomes Pakistan leader, first woman to head an Islamic state (–1990).

Hard-line communist regime seizes power in Myanmar.

Earthquake in Armenia kills 60,000.

Completion of Seikan tunnel, Japan, world's longest at 34 miles (55 km).

1989 USSR humiliatingly abandons attempted Afghan conquest and pulls out troops.

Syria restores relations with Egypt.

1991 PLO and Israel begin preliminary talks.

Violent insurrection against Indian rule in Jammu and Kashmir (–1997).

Prodemocracy protestors in Tiananmen Square, Beijing, suppressed by Chinese security forces.

1993 Vietnamese troops pull out of Cambodia.

Democracy restored to Laos.

Tokyo stock market crash ends period of exponential postwar economic growth.

Asia-Pacific Economic Cooperation (APEC) founded, Singapore.

1991 **1990** Bankrupted by Iran-Iraq war, Saddam Hussein orders Iraqi invasion of oil-rich neighbor, Kuwait; UN immediately demands Iraqi withdrawal; US begins to assemble anti-Iraqi military coalition, including many Arab states, under UN auspices.

Opposition victory in Myanmar general election ignored by Marxist ruling junta; opposition leader, Aung San Suu Kyi is imprisoned.

People's Democratic Republic of Yemen and Yemen Arab Republic united.

Earthquake in Iran kills 50,000.

AFRICA

1986 US bombs Libya in protest at alleged Libyan sponsorship of anti-Western terrorism.

1991 Eritrean People's Liberation Front (EPLF) steps up armed independence struggle against Marxist regime in Ethiopia.

US and EEC impose economic sanctions against South Africa.

1988 Tigre People's Liberation Front (TPLF) steps up armed independence struggle against Marxist regime in Ethiopia.

1989 Fundamentalist National Islamic Front seizes power in Sudan; renews attempts to crush non-Muslim majority in south.

Hard-line South African leader P. W. Botha replaced by F. W. de Klerk, who immediately begins moves to dismantle apartheid. Withdraws South African forces from Namibia, which gains independence.

Liberian government toppled; resulting civil war leads to complete breakdown of civil rule.

1990 Opposition parties legalized in South Africa; Nelson Mandela released from prison; becomes leader of ANC.

EUROPE

1986 Breakthrough superpower summit in Reykjavik between Reagan and Gorbachev leads to provisional US-USSR commitment to disarm.

Spain and Portugal join the EEC.

Soviet nuclear reactor at Chernobyl explodes, releasing radioactive material across much of Europe.

USSR launches *Mir* space station; remains in Earth orbit until 2001.

1987 US and USSR agree Intermediate Nuclear Forces (INF) treaty, cutting stockpiles of nuclear weapons by 20 percent.

Slobodan Milošević becomes leader of Serbia.

1988 Gorbachev steps up reform program in Russia, introducing *perestroika* (restructing) and *glasnost* (openness); presses Eastern-bloc allies to follow his lead.

Suspected Libyan terrorist bomb destroys Pan Am jet over Lockerbie, Scotland, killing all 259 on board plus 11 on the ground.

Mass protests in Georgia against Russian ethnic dominance.

1989 Opposition parties legalized in Hungary.

Free elections in Poland bring Solidarity to power.

Partial elections in USSR.

Massive demonstrations on both sides of the Berlin Wall bring about collapse of East German government and (Nov 9) breaching of Berlin Wall. Simultaneous demonstrations end communist rule in Czechoslovakia and Bulgaria.

Despotic Ceaușescu regime in Romania disintegrates; Ceaușescu and wife executed.

1990 Communist party disbanded, Poland. Albania begins moves toward democracy.

Congress of Estonia declares Soviet rule illegal. Free elections held East Germany.

1991 ▼ Boris Yeltsin elected president of Russian Republic; urges Gorbachev to allow greater autonomy to Soviet republics.

Oct: German reunification.

1991 ▼ Serb-dominated Yugoslav government reduces autonomy of Yugoslav provinces in effort to halt secessionist moves; free elections are nonetheless held in Croatia and Slovenia.

Russian troops sent to Azerbaijan as state of emergency declared.

AMERICAS & AUSTRALASIA

1986 Reagan administration rocked by "Iran-Contra" arms revelations.

Two military coups in Fiji threaten to end democracy.

Democracy restored in Brazil.

1987 US stock market crashes.

1988 First fiber-optic transatlantic telephone cable laid; able to carry 40,000 calls simultaneously.

1989 George Bush president of the US (–1993).

Democracy restored in Chile as General Pinochet steps down.

Carlos Menem elected president in Argentina.

US military intervention in Panama leads to overthrow and arrest of Panamanian leader, General Noriega.

1990 US leads diplomatic efforts to isolate Iraq after invasion of Kuwait and spearheads massive buildup of UN coalition forces in Persian Gulf.

Democracy restored in Nicaragua.

1991 ▼ US sends troops to the Persian Gulf in response to Saddam Hussein's invasion of Kuwait.

Tiananmen Square

Tentative moves toward greater freedoms in China had taken place sporadically since the death of Mao in 1976. The death of the former party secretary Hu Yaobang in 1989, sacked three years earlier for his supposed liberalism, then sparked student protests in Beijing. For several weeks, and in the full glare of the West's media, thousands of demonstrators occupied Tiananmen Square, calling for democratic reform. On June 3, the government, fearing its authority was under serious challenge, ordered the army to turn their weapons on the activists.

Between 300 and 400 people were killed. In the aftermath of the demonstrations, the new party secretary, Zhao Ziyang, was dismissed.

The brutal suppression of the protestors effectively crushed China's prodemocracy movement and drove dissent underground.

Aborigines

There have been Aborigines in Australia for at least 40,000 years. European settlers consistently discriminated against them, considering them primitive. The Black War (1804–1830) all but eradicated Aborigines from Tasmania. Later, an official policy of "pacification by force" was adopted.

By 1950, the Aborigines had been assimilated within Australian society but their second-class status was clear. Since then, campaigns have been launched to improve their position. A degree of autonomy has been returned to them by land rights acts; their property rights have been recognized in court decisions.

Aboriginal protestors at the Australian bicentennial celebrations of 1988 display the Aboriginal flag.

1986–1990

449

Rwanda

Ethnic conflict in postindependence Africa came to a head in 1994 when widespread violence flared between the majority Hutu and minority Tutsi populations in Rwanda. In an orgy of brutality, up to 500,000 Tutsis were slaughtered by the Hutu army in revenge for the assassination of President Habyarimana. The conflict destabilized neighboring states, especially Zaire, where up to two million Hutus fled, bringing them into conflict with the Tutsi population of eastern Zaire.

Hussein's tenacious 34-year hold on power has brought poverty, misery, and oppression to the Iraqis.

The Gulf War

Bankrupted by the inconclusive eight-year Iran-Iraq war, in August 1990 Iraq under Saddam Hussein invaded its oil-rich neighbor Kuwait. Though the UN demanded an immediate Iraqi withdrawal, Hussein refused, apparently convinced the UN would be unable to unite sufficiently to back its demands by force. He was wrong. A UN coalition force led by the US was assembled and in January 1991 began an air campaign which it followed a month later by a ground attack. Within four days, the Iraqis were routed. Against the odds, Hussein's regime survived.

ASIA

1991 Massive month-long bombing campaign launched against Iraqi forces in Kuwait – Operation Desert Storm – followed by four-day land campaign: Iraqi forces routed with estimated 200,000 deaths against losses of 150 coalition troops. UN authorizes weapons inspections (–1998); fiercely resisted by Hussein.

PLO-Israeli peace talks in Madrid under US auspices.

Separatists in East Timor massacred by government troops.

N and S Korea sign nonaggression pact; admitted to UN.

Assassination of former Indian premier, Rajiv Gandhi.

Cyclone in Bangladesh kills 200,000.

1992 Yitzhak Rabin comes to power in Israel, promising to pursue peace talks with PLO.

Khmer Rouge launch renewed guerrilla campaign in Cambodia.

1993 Oslo Accords, secret PLO-Israeli peace talks, followed by joint PLO-Israeli Declaration of Principles at White House for limited Palestinian autonomy in West Bank and Gaza Strip.

Sri Lanka president Ranasinghe Premadasa assassinated by Tamil separatists.

King Sihanouk restored in Cambodia; elections held.

Benazir Bhutto restored as prime minister of Pakistan.

Majority of Islamic nations agree Cairo Declaration to curb fundamentalism.

1994 Israel hands control of Jericho and Gaza Strip to Palestinian National Authority.

Death of North Korea's communist dictator, Kim Il Sung; succeeded by his son, Kim Jong Il.

1995 Second stage of Oslo Accords allows further Palestinian self-government in West Bank; Rabin assassinated by Jewish extremist.

Syria agrees to peace talks with Israel

In Myanmar, oppositon leader Aung San Suu Kyi released from prison.

US imposes economic sanctions against Iran.

Fundamentalist Taliban in Afghanistan reignite civil war.

AFRICA

1991 Eritrean and Tigrean attacks on Addis Ababa topple Marxist dictator Mengistu; Eritrea de facto independent.

Fundamentalist Islamic Salvation Front (FIS) posts dramatic gains in Algerian election.

UN sanctions imposed against Libya in response to alleged Libyan involvement in Lockerbie bombing.

Referendum in S Africa overwhelmingly supports creation of new constitution.

Temporary truce in Angolan civil war.

1992 Algerian government annuls results of 1991 election, sparking massive protests and continuing bitter civil war; Algerian president, Boudiaf, assassinated by FIS.

US and UN military intervention to end famine and civil war in Somalia.

Power in S Africa passes to multiracial Executive Council.

General election in Angola unable to halt renewal of civil war.

1993 Eritrean independence declared; first African country to secure independence from another African state.

1994 Intermittent civil war in Rwanda between majority Hutus and ruling minority Tutsis flares into savage conflict with assassination of President Habyarimana; up to 500,000 Tutsis massacred by Hutu while nearly two million Hutus flee to neighboring countries.

ANC triumphs in S Africa's first multiracial elections; Nelson Mandela becomes president (–1999).

1995 The US humiliatingly pulls out of Somalia.

Abuja Accord ends strife in Liberia.

Nigeria expelled from Commonwealth for human rights abuses.

EUROPE

1991 Mar: Baltic Republics assert independence from USSR.

Warsaw Pact (Apr) and COMECON (July) formally scrapped by USSR.

June: Slovenia and Croatia declare independence from Yugoslavia; short-lived Serb-Slovenian war and six-month Serb-Croat war follow.

Aug: Attempted communist coup in Soviet Union suppressed by Russian president, Yeltsin; sparks declarations of independence from all non-Russian republics within USSR.

Dec: USSR dissolved; independence of all non-Russian republics recognized; other than Baltic Republics they become members, under de facto leadership of new Russian Federation, of Commonwealth of Independent States (CIS).

Single European Market lifts trade restrictions within EEC; Maastricht Treaty paves way for closer political union.

1992 War between Christian Armenia and Muslim Azerbaijan over control of Nagorno-Karabakh (–1994).

Civil wars in Georgia and conflicts with Abkhazia and S Ossetia (–1994).

Bosnia-Herzegovina declares independence; three-year war between Muslims, Serbs, and Croats follows, prompting UN intervention.

1993 The "Velvet Divorce": independent Czech Republic and Slovakia formed from former Czechoslovakia.

1996 ▼

1996 ▼ **1994** Chechnian demands for independence prompt Russian invasion; bitter fighting follows.

Further attempted communist overthrow of Yeltsin suppressed.

Channel Tunnel opened between England and France.

1995 NATO military intervention in Bosnian civil war (Aug); Dayton Agreement (Nov) ends fighting.

EEC becomes European Union (EU); Austria, Sweden, and Finland become members.

World Trade Organization (WTO) founded, Geneva.

Cease-fire agreed in Bosnia-Herzegovina. Peace agreement (Dayton Accord) ends the Bosnian War; UN troops remain.

AMERICAS & AUSTRALASIA

1991 US heads UN coalition forces in Gulf War.

US and USSR sign START arms reduction treaty.

US president Bush announces end of Cold War and "New World Order."

USSR ends preferential trade agreement with Cuba; US tightens blockade.

UN-brokered peace ends 10-year civil war in El Salvador.

Internet made available to unrestricted commercial use; number of host computers reaches one million.

1992 Capture of Abimael Guzmán, leader of Maoist "Shining Path" terrorists in Peru.

United Nations Conference on Environment and Development – the Earth Summit – held in Brazil, to reconcile worldwide economic development with protection of the environment.

1993 Bill Clinton president of the US (–2001).

2001 ▼ Islamic fundamentalists bomb World Trade Center.

1994 Haiti invaded by US; democracy restored.

First genetically modified vegetable – tomatoes – available in US.

World's first satellite digital television service launched, US.

Deliberate policies of "ethnic cleansing" by Serbs, especially against Muslims and Albanians, caused huge suffering.

Conflict in Yugoslavia

The dominance of Serbia in Yugoslavia created tensions well before communism collapsed across Europe. From 1990, they dramatically resurfaced, leading to the complete breakup of Yugoslavia. The process was always violent, however, the result chiefly of Serbian attempts to maintain their hegemony. Brief wars after Slovenia and Croatia declared independence in 1991 were followed by prolonged conflict between the Muslim, Serb, and Croat populations in Bosnia-Herzegovina before a fragile peace was imposed in 1995. Bitter fighting also broke out in the Serbian province of Kosovo after 1988. It ended with a Serb climbdown in June 1994 only after NATO military intervention.

This internet cafe in Taiwan offers diners access to the internet while they eat.

The world wide web

The ability of computers to communicate with one another was developed slowly by US academics after 1969, who set up the Arpanet network. By 1990, it had been replaced by the internet, which was made available to commercial use in 1991. Almost at once, it grew dramatically, with users multiplying about 3,500 times a year throughout the 1990s, producing a continuing revolution in communications and business. Internet users in 2000 numbered 295 million; by 2002 there were an estimated 530 million.

A young boy in Colombia inspects some recently harvested coca leaves. Peasant farmers make very little from their crop; the big money is made by cartels that smuggle processed cocaine into the US, usually via Mexico..

The drugs trade

The 1990s saw a steady increase in world drug production, smuggling, and use. The most worrying trend was the growth of the market for crack cocaine, which is far more addictive than ordinary cocaine. In spite of large sums of American aid given to countries such as Peru, Bolivia, and Colombia to clamp down on coca leaf production, the drug continued to be produced in vast quantities. In Colombia this was because most of the production takes place in the south of the country, which is controled by anti-government rebels.

Cloning

In 1997 the Roslin Institute, Edinburgh, announced that it had succeeded in cloning a sheep from a cell taken from the mammary gland of an adult ewe. The nucleus of the cell had been fused with an unfertilized egg cell from which the nucleic DNA had been removed. The resulting offspring was named Dolly, after Dolly Parton, the country and western singer.

1996–2000

ASIA

1996 Taliban forces capture Kabul and declare fundamentalist Islamic State of Afghanistan.

Renewed Chinese military intimidation of Taiwan during Taiwanese elections.

Election of right-winger, Binyamin Netanyahu, as prime minister of Israel threatens to stall Middle East peace processes.

DVDs launched, Japan.

1997 Hong Kong returned to China by UK.

Death of Deng Xiaoping, China.

Israelis pull out of Hebron on West Bank.

 1998 India and Pakistan test nuclear weapons.

Zhu Rongji becomes leader of China; committed to further economic liberalization.

Economic crisis in Indonesia leads to widespread rioting and overthrow of Suharto government.

Financial crisis hits much of SE Asia.

World's biggest airport opens in Hong Kong, with a capacity of up to 87 million passengers a year.

1999 Ehud Barak elected prime minister of Israel; committed to reinvigorate peace process; remaining Israeli troops withdrawn from S Lebanon security zone.

Renewed clashes between Pakistan and India over Kashmir.

General Pervaiz Musharraf seizes power in Pakistan after military coup.

Islamic fundamentalists in Russia declare independence of Dagestan and *jihad* against Russia.

Democracy restored to Indonesia; Sukarnoputri president. East Timor votes for independence from Indonesia.

In Turkey, two devastating earthquakes kill more than 14,000 people.

2000 Controversial visit by Israeli opposition leader Ariel Sharon to Al Aqsa mosque leads to resignation of Barak amid widespread rioting and violence.

USS *Cole* bombed by Islamic fundamentalists during visit to Yemen.

Partial reconciliation between N and S Korea; border reopened.

New strains in China-Taiwanese relations.

AFRICA

1996 F. W. de Klerk steps down as vice-president of South Africa.

 1997 President Mobutu ousted in Zaire; Laurent Kabila takes power; Zaire becomes Democratic Republic of Congo; faces widespread Tutsi revolt.

Seventy people, including 60 foreign tourists, are brually gunned down by Islamic extremists in Egypt's Valley of the Kings.

In Kenya, Daniel Arap Moi is elected for a fifth term as president following an election rumored to have been rigged.

1998 Terrorist bombing attacks at two US Embassies in Nairobi and Dar es Salaam in Tanzania kill 250 people and injure at least 6,000. US authorities suspect involvement of Osama bin Laden's Al-Qaeda network.

1999 Breakdown in civil order in Somalia; northwest breaks away as Somaliland, much of south falls under warlord control.

Much of Congo controlled by anti-Kabila forces supported by Rwanda and Uganda.

ANC win general election in South Africa; Thabo Mbeki becomes new president.

EUROPE

1996 Chechnia de facto independent after Russian forces pull out

Boris Yeltsin narrowly defeats communists in Russian presidential elections; against background of dramatically worsening economy, embarks on erratic term in office, dismissing several governments.

1997 Tony Blair becomes prime minister of UK promising moderate "Third Way" socialism under "New" Labour government.

Diana, Princess of Wales, is killed in a car crash in Paris.

Scientists in Edinburgh reveal the world's first successful cloning of an adult mammal: a sheep named "Dolly."

1998 Sporadic fighting begins between Serbs and ethnic Albanians of Kosovo Liberation Army (KLA); peace talks in Paris only alienate Serbia.

"Good Friday" peace agreement in Northern Ireland.

World's first digital terrestrial television service launched in the UK.

1999 Serbs accelerate "ethnic cleansing" of Kosovo Albanians, leading (Mar) to NATO bombing campaign against Yugoslavia. June: Yugoslavia agrees to NATO demands; NATO troops sent to Kosovo to maintain peace.

Further Russian troops sent to Chechnia as ground war restarts.

Poland, Czech Republic, and Hungary join NATO.

Vladimir Putin made prime minister of Russia by Yeltsin.

New multiparty Northern Ireland Assembly meets, restoring self-rule after 22 years.

2000 Election confirms Putin as Russian president.

Sep: Opposition victory in Serbian election annulled by Slobodan Milošević. Oct: Widespread popular protests topple Milosevic regime; Vojislav Koštunica president, committed to ending Serbian pariah status.

AMERICAS & AUSTRALASIA

1996 France halts nuclear testing in Pacific.

US eases sanctions against Cuba.

Number of internet host computers reaches 10 million.

1997 Microsoft becomes the world's most valuable company, valued at $261 billion

1998 A massive car bomb devastates Oklahoma City's federal building, killing 168 people, including 15 children. US Army Veteran Timothy McVeigh is later found guilty and sentenced to death for his part in the atrocity.

1999 In Venezuela, devastating mudslides caused by torrential rains kill between 20,000 and 50,000 people. It is Latin America's worst natural disaster in the 20th century.

US president, Clinton, acquitted of impeachment by Senate after accusations of lying over sex scandal.

In Canada, Inuit voters elect representatives for the first government of Nunavet, the nation's newly autonomous territory.

2000 Draft of complete human genome produced by US company, Celera Genomics.

Number of internet host computers reaches 95 million; over one billion web pages available; estimated 295 million internet users worldwide.

Kosovan refugees at a camp on the border of Macedonia. Many later returned to find their houses looted and burnt.

Kosovo

In March 1999 the Serbian army stepped up its activities against the KLA (Kosovo Liberation Army) and the campaign rapidly became an exercise in "ethnic cleansing." The start of NATO's retaliatory bombing campaign accelerated the process, which provoked the largest movement of refugees in Europe since World War II. More than 800,000 Kosovo Albanians fled into Albania, Macedonia, and Montenegro. Many had been driven at gunpoint from their homes.

At the end of the millennium the richest man in the world was Bill Gates, chairman of Microsoft.

Bill Gates and Microsoft

Microsoft made its fortune creating operating systems (DOS and Windows) and software programs for personal computers. Windows is used on 80 percent of the world's computers. However, as producer of both the operating system and the applications, the company fell foul of Federal antitrust laws and in 1998 a case was brought against Microsoft. Found guilty of restraint of competition, Gates appealed the decision that Microsoft should be split into two and this has since been reversed, but the final outcome of the case is still unclear.

The intifada ("shaking off") inspired a new era in Palestinian mass mobilization.

Conflict in the Middle East

From 1987, popular Palestinian protest against Israeli occupation – the *intifada* – in the Gaza Strip and West Bank became increasingly militant. As Israel and the PLO began to reach a measure of agreement after 1991 and with the active support of fundamentalist terror groups, there were frequent clashes with Israeli security forces. Though Palestinian police subsequently reduced the level of violence, the *intifada* was reignited in 2000 following Ariel Sharon's visit to a holy site revered by both Muslims and Jews in Jerusalem.

Asylum-seekers in Europe

Economic dislocation in postcommunist eastern Europe and armed conflict, above all in the former Yugoslavia, have created the most serious refugee problem in Europe since World War II. In 1985, there were 700,000 refugees in Europe; in 1998 there were 5.6 million. The problem has given rise to a thriving trade in smuggling displaced peoples into affluent western Europe, as well as prompting growing resentment there, increasing support for right-wing parties.

Asylum-seekers from eastern Europe arrive in Italy by boat.

ASIA

2001 Feb: Ariel Sharon wins overwhelming victory in Israeli election; renewed breakdown in order across Palestinian-held areas; numerous suicide attacks against Israel.

Sept: US demands Taliban surrender of Osama bin Laden following September 11 attacks.

Oct: US and UK begin air campaign against Taliban; supported by ground attacks by anti-Taliban Northern Alliance. US diplomatic effort to secure support of Pakistan in struggle against Taliban; sanctions lifted.

Oct: Further Indian-Pakistan clashes over Kashmir.

Dec: Taliban government overthrown; UN-sponsored agreement on new interim Afghan administration.

Dec: Israel begins bombing and air attacks of Palestinian areas; PLO leader Yasser Arafat effectively becomes Israeli prisoner on West Bank.

2002 Jan: US agreement with Philippines to counter Islamic fundamentalist group, Abu Sayyaf.

Jan: Interim government installed in Afghanistan, headed by an anti-Taliban battlefield commander, Hamid Karzai.

Renewed US-lead attacks against remaining Al-Qaeda forces in Afganhistan.

Musharraf wins Pakistan general election.

Tensions rise and many are killed on both sides as Palestinian militants launch a new wage of suicide bombings and Israel occupies a large part of the West Bank.

Hundreds are killed in western India as the Hindu majority and Muslim minority attack each other over deep-rooted sectarian grievances.

AFRICA

2001 In Democratic Republic of Congo Laurent Kabila is assassinated by bodyguard.

2002 Robert Mugabe wins rigged general election in Zimbabwe; opposition leader Morgan Tsvangirai arrested on treason charges. The country is expelled from the Commonwealth.

The threat of famine looms large in Zambia, Zimbabwe, Angola, Mozambique, Swaziland, and Lesotho as crops fail due to droughts and floods. Attempts to deal with the problem have been hampered by political chaos and the inadequate infrastructure. Some 14 million people are affected.

Sierra Leone holds presidential and parliamentary elections expected to confirm the end of the civil war.

EUROPE

2001 Mar: Ethnic Albanians in Macedonia demand Albanian "Greater Macedonia;" widespread armed clashes between rebels and government begin.

June: Yugoslav government surrenders Slobodan Milošević to UN International Criminal Tribunal in The Hague; remaining UN sanctions against Yugoslavia lifted.

Aug: Peace agreement in Macedonia; British-led NATO operation oversees disarmament.

Oct: IRA begins partial disarmament in Northern Ireland; Northern Ireland Assembly reconstituted.

2002 Single European currency – the Euro – introduced in 11 of the 15 EU Member States.

Pim Fortuyn, a far-right Dutch politician who espoused antiimmigration policies, was murdered by a lone gunman.

AMERICAS & AUSTRALASIA

2001 G.W. Bush becomes president of US; revives National Missile Defense System.

Osama bin Laden coordinates Al-Qaeda terrorist attacks against US; Pentagon hit by hijacked airliner, World Trade Center, NY, destroyed after being hit by two hijacked airliners.

Argentine president, Fernando de la Rue, forced to resign after austerity measures prompt national rioting.

2002 Estimated internet users worldwide 530 million.

Telecommunications giant WorldCom files for bankruptcy in the biggest corporate failure in US history.

New York firemen rise the Stars and Stripes on the shattered site of the World Trade Center: Ground Zero.

September 11

On Tuesday September 11, 2001, fundamentalist Islamic terrorists of the Al-Qaeda network hijacked four US commercial airliners. Two were flown directly into the Twin Towers at the World Trade Center in New York, one was crashed into the Pentagon in Washington DC. The fourth crashed near Shanksville, Pennsylvania, after passengers overpowered the hijackers. Both towers at the World Trade Center collapsed soon afterward, with a final death toll of more than 3,000.

The US response was immediate: an upsurge of patriotic determination to bring the sponsors of the attack, above all the Saudi-born Osama bin Laden, to justice. President Bush announced a "War against Terrorism" and, in his state of the union address in January 2002, designated Iraq, Iran, and North Korea as an "axis of evil" for seeking weapons of mass destruction and harboring and supporting terrorists. In October 2001, air strikes against the fundamentalist Taliban government of Afganhistan, where bin Laden was sheltering, were begun and were followed by ground attacks by US, British, and Afghan opposition forces. By December, the Taliban had fallen. Although bin Laden evaded capture, a US-led coalition continued to hunt down the remnants of Al-Qaeda and Taliban fighters during 2002.

The Modern World

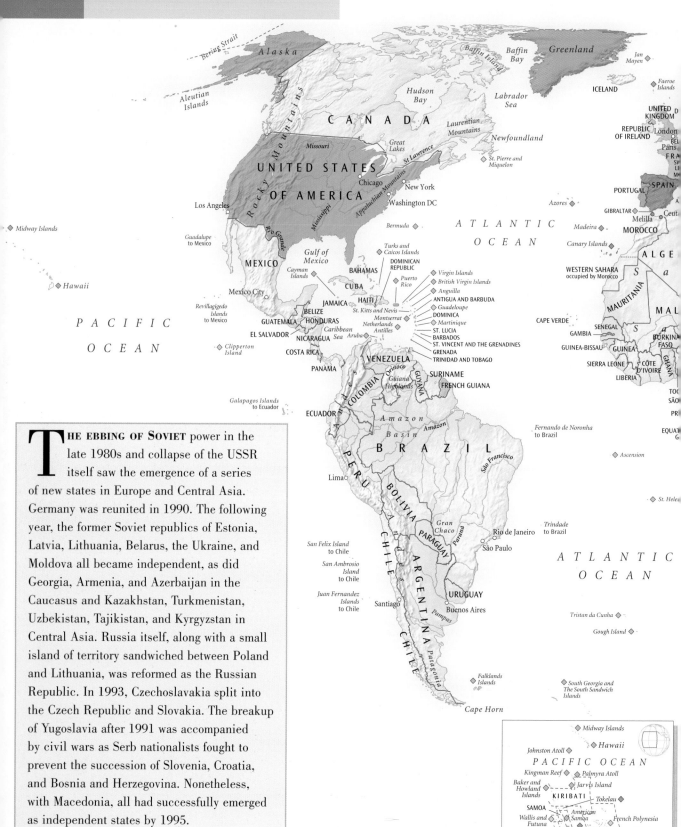

THE EBBING OF SOVIET power in the late 1980s and collapse of the USSR itself saw the emergence of a series of new states in Europe and Central Asia. Germany was reunited in 1990. The following year, the former Soviet republics of Estonia, Latvia, Lithuania, Belarus, the Ukraine, and Moldova all became independent, as did Georgia, Armenia, and Azerbaijan in the Caucasus and Kazakhstan, Turkmenistan, Uzbekistan, Tajikistan, and Kyrgyzstan in Central Asia. Russia itself, along with a small island of territory sandwiched between Poland and Lithuania, was reformed as the Russian Republic. In 1993, Czechoslovakia split into the Czech Republic and Slovakia. The breakup of Yugoslavia after 1991 was accompanied by civil wars as Serb nationalists fought to prevent the succession of Slovenia, Croatia, and Bosnia and Herzegovina. Nonetheless, with Macedonia, all had successfully emerged as independent states by 1995.

The Modern World

- Turkey
- United Kingdom and possessions
- France and possessions
- Denmark and possessions
- Spain and possessions
- Portugal and possessions
- Netherlands and possessions
- Russian Federation
- Japan and possessions
- Norway and possessions
- India and possessions
- Italy
- New Zealand and possessions
- Australia and possessions
- US and possessions
- B-H Bosnia and Herzegovina

Map labels:

North Cape, Novaya Zemlya, Barents Sea, Kara Sea, Bering Strait, FINLAND, ESTONIA, LATVIA, LITHUANIA, BELARUS, RUSSIAN FEDERATION, Moscow, Volga, Don, Ob', Yenisey, Irtysh, Lena, Siberia, Sea of Okhotsk, Kamchatka, Kurile Islands, UKRAINE, MOLDOVA, SLOVAKIA, HUNGARY, ROMANIA, SERB. & MON., BULGARIA, Black Sea, GEORGIA, ARMENIA, AZERBAIJAN, Caspian Sea, Aral Sea, KAZAKHSTAN, Lake Balkhash, Lake Baikal, Altai Mountains, MONGOLIA, Gobi, Amur, Hokkaido, Sea of Japan, NORTH KOREA, SOUTH KOREA, Seoul, JAPAN, Honshu, Tokyo, Kyushu, MACEDONIA, GREECE, ALBANIA, MALTA, ITALY, CYPRUS, LEBANON, ISRAEL, Mediterranean Sea, Istanbul, TURKEY, SYRIA, IRAQ, JORDAN, KUWAIT, Tigris, Euphrates, Tehran, IRAN, UZBEKISTAN, TURKMENISTAN, KYRGYZSTAN, TAJIKISTAN, Takla Makan, AFGHANISTAN, Kabul, AKSAI CHIN claimed by India, controlled by China, CHINA, Beijing, Yellow River, Shanghai, Yangtze, Ryukyu Islands, Hong Kong, Macao, TAIWAN, LIBYA, EGYPT, Cairo, SAUDI ARABIA, Red Sea, Nile, BAHRAIN, QATAR, The Gulf, UNITED ARAB EMIRATES, OMAN, Arabian Sea, PAKISTAN, Indus, Karachi, Thar Desert, Delhi, NEPAL, BHUTAN, Himalayas, Ganges, BANGLADESH, Calcutta (Kolkata), INDIA, Mumbai (Bombay), Bay of Bengal, MYANMAR, LAOS, VIETNAM, Mekong, Paracel Islands disputed, Luzon, Manila, PHILIPPINES, CHAD, SUDAN, ERITREA, YEMEN, Gulf of Aden, DJIBOUTI, Socotra to Yemen, ETHIOPIA, SOMALIA, CENTRAL AFRICAN REPUBLIC, Congo, Congo Basin, RWANDA, UGANDA, KENYA, DEM. REP. CONGO (ZAIRE), BURUNDI, Kinshasa, TANZANIA, Lake Victoria, Lake Tanganyika, MALAWI, Lake Nyasa, ANGOLA, ZAMBIA, Zambezi, Great Rift Valley, COMOROS, Mayotte, MADAGASCAR, MOZAMBIQUE, ZIMBABWE, Okavango, Okavango Delta, Namib Desert, NAMIBIA, BOTSWANA, SOUTH AFRICA, Orange River, SWAZILAND, LESOTHO, Cape of Good Hope, Chennai (Madras), Andaman Islands, Nicobar Islands, SRI LANKA, Laccadive Islands, MALDIVES, SEYCHELLES, British Indian Ocean Territory, Agalega Islands to Mauritius, Tromelin to Réunion, Rodrigues to Mauritius, MAURITIUS, Réunion, THAILAND, Bangkok, CAMBODIA, Spratly Islands disputed, Mindanao, MALAYSIA, SINGAPORE, BRUNEI, Sumatra, Borneo, INDONESIA, Jakarta, Java, EAST TIMOR, Cocos Islands, Christmas Island, Ashmore and Cartier Islands, New Guinea, PAPUA NEW GUINEA, PALAU, MICRONESIA, Guam, Northern Mariana Islands, MARSHALL ISLANDS, Wake Island, KIRIBATI, NAURU, SOLOMON ISLANDS, TUVALU, Coral Sea Islands, VANUATU, FIJI, New Caledonia, Great Sandy Desert, Gibson Desert, Great Victoria Desert, Simpson Desert, Lake Eyre, AUSTRALIA, Darling, Great Dividing Range, Great Barrier Reef, Sydney, Norfolk Island, Lord Howe Island, Tasmania, Tasman Sea, NEW ZEALAND, PACIFIC OCEAN, INDIAN OCEAN

REMOTE-SENSED MAPPING

The development from the 1970s of Color Scanner satellites, able to measure temperature differences anywhere on the Earth, led to a revolution in remote-sensed mapping. As a result, phenomena such as El Niño in the Pacific, which generates significant differences in sea temperatures which in turn have an enormous influence on weather across the globe, could be accurately charted. Today, a ring of geo-synchronous weather satellites produces constantly updated images of the globe. Plant growth can be measured, allowing more precise forecasts of famines, for example. Pollution, environmental degradation, flooding, urban growth, even the presence of new oil and gas fields can also be monitored and mapped by satellites. For the first time a complete picture of the Earth's complex interaction of atmosphere, landmasses and seas is emerging.

CONCORDANCE

A full index to the contents of this book would simply mean the reordering of each Timeline entry alphabetically. Although undoubtedly of use in a conventional date dictionary, this is not the purpose of this book. The reader is, rather, encouraged to examine the presentation of dates on the illustrated pages in terms of their geographical and historical context, especially in relation to other events occurring in a similar time and space. Thus, this Concordance has been designed as a complement to the illustrated pages of the book.

A

Abbas I (*aka* Abbas the Great, c.1571–1629) Safavid shah of Persia (reigned 1588–1629). Crushed the Uzbek rebellions (1597), and recovered Persian territories from the Ottomans, expelling them from Mesopotamia (1603–7). In 1598 he established the Persian capital at Isfahan. *p.288*

ABBASID CALIPHATE

(c.750–1258) The second great Islamic dynasty, replacing the Umayyads in 750 CE. The Abbasid capital from 762 was Baghdad, from where they exercised control over the Islamic world until the 10th century. The last true Abbasid caliph was killed by the Mongols in 1258. Nominally restored (1260), the later Abbasids were puppets of the Mamluks. *p.144*

THE ABBASID CALIPHS

750–754	Abu-I-Abbas al-Saffah
754–775	Al-Mansur
775–785	Al-Mahdi
785–786	Al-Hadi
786–809	Harun al-Rashid
809–813	Al-Amin
813–833	Al-Ma'mun (the Great)
833–842	Al-Mu'tasim
842–847	Al-Wathiq
847–861	Al-Muttawakil
861–862	Al-Muntasir

862–866	Al-Musta'in
866–869	Al-Mu'tazz
869–870	Al-Muqtadi
870–892	Al-Mu'tamid
892–902	Al-Mu'tadid
902–908	Al-Muqtafi
908–932	Al-Muqtadir
932–934	Al-Qahir
934–940	Al-Radi
940–944	Al-Muttaqi
944–946	Al-Mustaqfi
946–974	Al-Muti
974–991	Al-Ta'I
991–1031	Al-Qadir
1031–1075	Al-Qa'im
1075–1094	Al-Muqtadi
1094–1118	Al-Mustazhir
1118–1135	Al-Mustarshid
1135–1136	Al-Rashid
1136–1160	Al-Muqtafi
1160–1170	Al-Mustanjid
1170–1180	Al-Mustadi
1180–1225	Al-Nasir
1225–1226	Al-Zahir
1226–1242	Al-Mustansir
1242–1258	Al-Must'sim

Abd al-Qadir (*aka* Abd el-Kader, Abd al Kadir, 1808–83) Leader of Algerian resistance to French colonial penetration, controlling the Oran region as emir (from 1832), and reaching peace with the French (Treaty of Tafna, 1837). His attempt to further his control to the Moroccan border resulted in warfare (1840–47) after which he was imprisoned (1847–52).

Abd al-Rahman ibn Umar al-Sufi 10th-century Arab astronomer.

Abdul Hamid II (1842–1918) Ottoman sultan (reigned 1876–1909). An autocratic ruler, noted for suppression of revolts in the Balkans, which led to wars with Russia (1877–78), and for the Armenian massacre (1894–96). His failure to modernize his empire led to his deposition in 1909, following a revolt by the Young Turks.

Abdul Majid I (1823–61) Ottoman sultan (reigned 1839–61). Urged by western powers, he issued a series of liberal decrees, known as the Tanzimat (1839–61) to reform the judiciary and administration of the Ottoman Empire.

ABM *see* anti-ballistic missile

Aborigines Native people of Australia, who probably first settled the continent c.60,000 years ago. From c.8000 BCE, when the land bridge to New Guinea was severed by rising sea levels, they lived in more or less complete isolation until the 18th century CE. In the north, there was occasional contact with sailors from the islands of the Torres Strait and Indonesia. *p.449*

Abreu, António de 16th-century Portuguese explorer. Embarked on a voyage to India in 1508. He set out for the Spice Islands in 1511, exploring Amboina, Sumatra, Java, and parts of New Guinea. He was appointed governor of Malacca in 1526.

Abu Bakr (c.573–634 CE) Associate and father-in-law of Muhammad, and first convert to Islam. Accompanied Muhammad on the Hegira to Medina, and became first caliph after Muhammad's death (632 CE) converting Arabia to Islam, and beginning campaign of Islamic expansion into Iraq and Syria.

bushiri Revolt (1888–89) Uprising among Arab coastal population of E Africa upon cession by Sultan of Zanzibar of those regions to Germany (1888), quelled by Anglo-German naval blockade.

byssinia *see* Ethiopia

cademy School of Philosophy where Plato taught in Athens. *p.59*

chaean League Confederation of Greek city-states of the northern Peloponnese, dating back to the 4th-century BCE. The League's traditional enemy was Sparta. was after the League attacked Sparta in 150 BCE, that the Romans destroyed Corinth, the leading city of the League, and made Achaea a Roman province.

chaemenes *see* Achaemenid empire

chaemenid empire (c.550–330 BCE) Greek name for the Persian royal dynasty. From c.550 BCE, Cyrus presided over the expansion of the Persian empire, conquering Lydia, Phrygia, Ionia, and Babylonia. The empire lasted until 330 BCE, when Darius III was killed after his defeat by Alexander at ⚔ Gaugamela. *p.47*

chin (*var.* Atjeh) The Indonesian island of Sumatra became, from the 7th century CE, the center of a powerful Hindu kingdom, established by Indian emigrants. In the 13th century CE, Arabs invaded the Sumatran kingdom of Achin, which converted to Islam. At the end of 16th century, the Dutch attempted to gain supremacy in Achin, a struggle which was to last for the next three centuries.

cheson, Dean (1893–1971) US Secretary of State (1949–53) whose development and implementation of significant US foreign policy initiatives, including the Marshall Plan (1948), the formation of NATO (1949), the rearming of W Germany and recognition of the communist republic of China established USA as a global superpower during the Cold War.

cre ⚔ and siege during Third Crusade (1190); crusader loss during Fifth Crusade (1291); ⚔ and unsuccessful siege by Napoleon (1799).

cropolis Ancient Greek fortified hilltop citadel, the best-known being that of Athens, rebuilt by Pericles after the Persian invasion in the second half of the 5th century BCE. It comprised a complex of buildings including the national treasury and many shrines, mostly devoted to Athene, the city's patron goddess.

Act of Supremacy (1534) British Parliamentary Act which recognized King Henry VIII, and every British sovereign thereafter, as supreme head of the Church of England.

Adams, John (1735–1826) One of the leading political figures of the era of the US struggle for independence from Britain. He was the country's first vice-president under George Washington and its second president (1797–1801).

Adams, Quincy John (1767–1848) Son of John Adans and the sixth US president.

Adena culture (c.700–100 BCE) A series of North American communities, based around what is now southern Ohio, formed the Adena culture. Principally hunter-gatherers, they built circular houses with conical roofs constructed of willow and bark, used stone tools and produced simple pottery. Finds of copper and shell ornaments indicate long-distance trade. *p.45*

Adowa ⚔ of Italian invasion of Abyssinia (1896). Serious Italian defeat put an end to Italian colonial ambitions in Ethiopia. A settlement after the battle acknowledged the full sovereignty and independence of Ethiopia, but preserved Italian rights to Eritrea.

Adrianopolis ⚔ (378) Visigothic victory over Romans.

Aegospotami ⚔ of Peloponnesian Wars (405 BCE). Spartan victory over Athens.

Aelfred *see* Alfred the Great

Aelius Gallus Roman general of the 1st century BCE, who led his troops on an exploratory expedition into Arabia.

Aethelred II *see* Ethelred II

Aetolian League Federal state of Aetolia, in ancient Greece, which by c.340 BCE became a leading military power. Having successfully resisted invasions by Macedonia in 322 BCE and 314–311 BCE, the League grew in strength expanding into Delphi and allying with Boeotia c.300 BCE

Afghani, Jamal ad-Din al- see al-Afghani, Jamal ad-Din

AFGHANISTAN State of C Asia. Its foundations were laid in the mid-18th century, when Ahmad Khan Abdali became paramount chief of the Abdali Pashtun peoples. Landlocked in central Asia, Afghanistan has borders with Iran, Pakistan, China, Tajikistan, Turkmenistan, and Uzbekistan. Three-quarters of its territory is inaccessible terrain. Agriculture is the main activity, but the country has been torn by armed conflict for decades. In the 1980s Islamic Mujahideen factions defeated the communist regime, but rivalries undermined their fragile power-sharing agreement and the hard-line Taliban militia swept to power. Islamic dress codes and behavior were vigorously enforced; women had few rights or opportunities. The Taliban regime was also notorious for harboring extremists. However, in 2001–2002 US-led military operations ousted the Taliban and placed a new coalition in power.

CHRONOLOGY

327 BCE Alexander the Great conquers most of the Afghan satrapies.

997 CE Mahmud of Ghazni comes to the throne and extends his power as far as the Punjab in India.

1219 Genghis Khan invades the eastern part of Afghanistan.

1504 Babur, a descendant of Genghis Khan and Timur, makes Kabul the capital of an independent principality and establishes the Mughal empire in northern India.

1747 Ahmad Khan Abdali is elected king by tribal council and establishes the last great Afghan empire.

1809 Afghanistan signs a treaty of friendship with Britain in which the Afghan ruler Shah Shoja promises to oppose the passage of foreign (Russian) troops through his territory.

1839–42 Following the failure of a British mission to Kabul led by Capt. Alexander Burnes in 1837, Britain invades Afghanistan which eventually leads to the first Anglo-Afghan war.

1878–80 The second Anglo-Afghan war follows the British failure to establish full control over Afghanistan's foreign relations.

1879 Under Treaty of Gandmak signed with Amir Yaqub Ali Khan, various Afghan areas annexed by Britain. Yaqub Ali Khan later exiled. New treaty signed with Amir Abdul Rahman, establishing the Durand line, a contentious boundary between Afghanistan and Pakistan.

1919 Declaration of Afghan independence.

1933 Muhammed Zahir Shar takes power.

▶

1953 Mohammed Daud Khan is named prime minister.

1963 Daud resigns after king rejects his proposals for democratic reforms.

1965 Elections held, but monarchy retains power. Marxist Party of Afghanistan (PDPA) formed and banned. PDPA splits into the Parcham and Khalq factions.

1973 Daud mounts a coup, abolishes monarchy, and declares republic. Mujahideen rebellion begins. Refugees flee to Pakistan.

1978 Opposition to Daud from PDPA culminates in Saur revolution. Revolutionary Council under Mohammad Taraki takes power. Daud assassinated.

1979 Taraki ousted. Hafizullah Amin takes power. Amin killed in December coup backed by USSR. 80,000 Soviet Army troops invade Afghanistan. Mujahideen rebellion stepped up into full-scale guerrilla war, with US backing.

1980 Babrak Karmal, leader of Parcham PDPA, installed as head of Marxist regime.

1986 Najibullah replaces Karmal as head of government.

1989 Soviet Army withdraws. Najibullah remains in office.

1992 Najibullah hands over power to mujahideen factions.

1993 Mujahideen agree on formation of government.

1994 Power struggle between Rabbani and Hekmatyar.

1995 Anti-government taliban militia advance toward Kabul.

1996 Taliban take power and impose strict Islamic regime.

1998 Earthquake in northern regions kills thousands.

1999 Power-sharing agreement between Taliban and Northern Alliance breaks down.

2000 Country suffers worst drought in 30 years. UN imposes sanctions in response to Taliban support for Osama bin Laden.

2001 Taliban government falls after intense US-led air strikes from October – the first campaign in the "war on terrorism." Interim government formed under Hamid Karzai; peacekeepers deployed in Kabul.

2002 Earthquakes kill thousands. Ex-king Zahir Shah returns from exile. Loya Jirga convenes, elects Karzai head of state.

2004 Approval of constitution. 90% of voters registered.

Africa Second largest continent, thought to have been where modern humans originated. *p.10*
Colonized by European powers in the 19th century. *p.343*
Most European colonies granted independence in the course of the 1950s and 1960s. *p.428*
See also individual African countries

African National Congress (ANC) Organization founded in S Africa in 1912 to promote equality for Africans. It was banned by the South African government in 1961, and although its leaders were jailed or forced into exile, became the focus for resistance to the apartheid regime. The ANC signed an agreement with the ruling Nationalists in 1990 and came to power under Nelson Mandela at the election of 1994.

Afrikaner South African of European descent whose first language is Afrikaans, a development of Dutch. *See also* Boers

Aghlabids (*var.* Banu Al-aghlab) Arab Muslim dynasty that ruled Ifriqiyah in present-day Tunisia and eastern Algeria from c.800 CE until their expulsion by the Fatimids in 909. Temporarily invaded Sicily (827) and S Italy. The Aghlabids were nominally subject to the Abbasid caliphs of Baghdad but were in fact independent.

Agincourt ⚔ of Hundred Years' War (1415). French defeat by English.

Agriculture Beginnings of agriculture in Neolithic times *p.14*
Agriculture in medieval Europe. *p.323*
Agricultural revolution: new crops and breeds introduced in 18th century. *p.325*

Agustin I *see* Iturbide

Ahmad ibn Fadi Allan Al-'umari *see* al 'Umari

Ahmad Khan Abdali (*var.* Ahmad Shah, 1724–73) Founder of Afghanistan (1747).

Ahmad Shah *see* Ahmad Khan Abdali

Ahmed Shah *see* Ahmad Khan Abdali

Ahmose *see* Amosis I

Ahuitzotl Aztec ruler (1486–1502).

Ain Jalut ⚔ of Mongol invasions (1260). Mongol defeat by Mamluks, which prevented their advance into Egypt.

Aistulf (died 756) Lombard king, who captured Ravenna from the Byzantines and threatened to take Rome. The pope summoned the Frankish king Pepin to defeat him.

Aix-la-Chapelle, Treaty of (1667) Treaty that ended war between France and Spain over Spanish Netherlands, the French being allowed to keep some of th fortified border towns they had taken.

Akbar (*aka* Akbar the Great, 1542–1605) Mughal emperor (reigned 1556–1605). Became emperor at the age of 14. For the first seven years of his reign, Akbar was engaged in permanent conflict, which left him the undisputed ruler of an empire that stretched from Bengal t Sind, and Kashmir to the Godavari river He evolved a standardized tax system, incorporated the rulers of conquered territory into his own army, and introduced a policy of marriage alliances between the Mughal nobles and the Rajput princely families. He was tolerant towards Hinduism, and encouraged a great florescence in the arts, particularly in miniature painting and architecture, which was remarkable for its synthesis of Western and Islamic styles.

Akhenaton (*var.* Akhenaten, Ikhnaton, Amenhotep, Amenophis IV) 18th-dynasty pharaoh of Egypt (reigned 1353–1336 BCE). A religious and cultural revolutionary who replaced the existing Egyptian pantheon with a monotheistic cult of the solar disc – Aten. He changed his name to reflect his beliefs, replaced the capital at Thebes with his own, El-Amarna (*var.* Akhetaten), and persecuted the older gods, expunging Amon's name from monuments across the country. A significant change in artistic style is representative of his rule, with both royals and commoners portrayed in a naturalistic rather than a formalized way. His unpopular religious reforms, and this artistic tradition, were reversed by Tutankhamun.

Akkad *see* Sargon I of Akkad

al-Afghani, Jamal ad-Din (1838–97) Muslim political agitator and journalist. Born in Persia, he worked in Afghanistan Istanbul and Cairo. Expelled from Egypt (1879) he published *The Firmest Bond* (from 1884), a newspaper critical of British imperialism. Following exile from Persia (1892) he lived in Istanbul, and wa involved in planning the assassination of the Shah of Persia (1896).

al-Hajj Umar Ibn Said Tal *see* 'Umar Tal, Al-Hajj

al-Idrisi, ash Sharif (c.1099–1165) Arab geographer born in Spain. After traveling in Spain, N Africa and Asia Minor, in c.1148 he joined the court of Roger II of

Sicily. There he collated surveys of the known world, incorporating them into *The Book of Roger*, completed in 1154. He also compiled a seventy-part world map. *p.201*

l-Istakhri 10th-century Islamic geographer.

l-Mu'tasim (794–842) Abbasid caliph (reigned 833–842). A son of Harun al-Rashid, al-Mu'tasim moved the Abbasid capital from Baghdad to Samarra. He waged war successfully against the Byzantines in Asia Minor and employed large numbers of Turkish slave soldiers, who subsequently became a powerful force in the Caliphate. (c.836)

l-Qaeda Worldwide Islamic Terrorist organization run by the shadowy Saudi Arabian, Osama bin Laden. It was responsible for the destruction of the World Trade Center towers, in New York on September 11 2001. *p.455*

l-Rashid, Harun (*var.* Harun Ar-rashid, Ibn Muhammad al-Mahdi, Ibn al-mansur al-'Abbasi, 763/766–809). The fifth caliph of the Abbasid dynasty (reigned 786–809), who ruled Islam at the zenith of its empire. *p.137*

l 'Umari (*var.* Shihab Ad-din, Ahmad Ibn Fadl Allah Al-'umari, 1301–1349) Scholar and writer descended from 'Umar, the second Islamic caliph. His works on the administration of the Mamluk dominions of Egypt and Syria became standard sources for Mamluk history.

lamo, The ✘ of Texas Revolution (1836), Mexican victory.

lans People who migrated to Europe from the steppes near the Caspian Sea. They joined the Vandals and Sueves in the Great Migration of 406 from Germany to the Iberian Peninsula. They briefly established a kingdom there, but were ousted by the Visigoths. *p.102*

laric (c.370–410) Chief of the Visigoths from 395 and leader of the army that sacked Rome in 410, an event that came to symbolize the fall of the Western Roman Empire.

laska Purchase (*aka* Seward's Folly). In 1867, US Secretary of State William H. Seward organized the purchase of Alaska from Russia for $7,200,000.

laungpaya (*var.* Alaung Phra, Alompra, Aungzeya) (1714–1760). King (reigned 1752–60) who unified Burma, and founded the Alaungpaya dynasty which held power in Burma until the British annexed the northern part of the region in 1886.

Albanel, Father Charles (1616–96) French Jesuit, who traveled in E Canada (1671–1672), reaching Hudson Bay and traveling along the Saguenay River, in search of fur-trading routes.

ALBANIA Lying at the southeastern end of the Adriatic Sea, opposite the heel of Italy, Albania is a mountainous country which first gained independence in 1912. It became a one-party communist state in 1944. It held multiparty elections in 1991, but economic collapse provoked uprisings in 1997, which were only stabilized by OSCE troops. Still poverty-stricken, Albania has been more stable since the return home of the ethnic Albanian refugees who flooded in from war-torn Kosovo in 1999.

CHRONOLOGY

168 BCE The Romans conquer the territory of the Illyrians along the Adriatic coast, which includes present-day Albania; Greek towns had been established in the area since the 7th century BC.

4th to 7th century CE Successive waves of invasions of the Balkans by Goths (among others) precipitate major population movements; the remaining Illyrians seek refuge in the mountains of Albania.

8th to 14th century Foreign powers (including Byzantium, Bulgaria, Serbia, Epirus, Sicily, and Venice) fight each other for control of Albania and its strategic coastline. The country is divided into feuding principalities. In the late 14th century the Ottoman Turks subject local princes to their rule.

1443–69 Under George Kastrioti, known as Skanderbeg ("Prince Alexander"), the Albanians rebel against Turkish rule. Despite the Turkish reconquest, completed in 1501, which leads to a strong Islamization, Albania remains a relatively unchanged primitive society of tribes and clans.

1760 Mehmed Bushati, the Pasha of Scutari, rallies northern clansmen and throws off Turkish suzerainty. His son Mehmet the Black routs the Turkish armies but with the defeat of his grandson Mustapha in 1831 the power of the Bushatis is broken. In the south Ali

Pasha of Tepelen establishes a virtually independent state, but is overthrown by the Turks in 1822.

1912 After 40 years of nationalist agitation, Albania asserts its independence from Turkish rule in the Balkan Wars (1912–13) but is occupied by various foreign armies for the next nine years.

1921 The major European powers and all neighboring countries recognize the borders of Albania as established in 1913.

1924–1939 Ahmet Zogu, crowned King Zog in 1928, in power.

1939–1943 Occupied by Italy.

1944 Communist state; led by Enver Hoxha until 1985.

1991 First multiparty elections.

1997 Economic chaos as failure of pyramid schemes causes revolt.

1999 Refugee influx from Kosovo.

2001 PSS wins second term. Resurgence of Berber protests.

2002 Berber language Tamazight recognized as national language. FLN victory.

2003 Over 2,000 die in earthquakes. Madani and Belhadj released.

2004 Bouteflika re-elected.

Albert, Prince of Saxe-Coburg-Gotha (1819–61) Consort of Queen Victoria of England.

Albertis, Luigi Maria d' (1841–1901) Italian explorer of New Guinea (1876).

Albigensians *see* Cathars

Alexander I (1777–1825) Czar of Russia (reigned 1801–25). The early years of his reign were marked by attempts to reform Russia, but he failed to abolish serfdom. Initially a member of the coalition against Napoleon, but defeats at Austerlitz and Friedland led to Alexander concluding the Treaty of Tilsit (1807) with France. When Napoleon's invasion of Russia (1812) broke the treaty, Russia joined the Allied pursuit of the French to Paris.

Alexander II (1818–81) Czar of Russia (reigned 1855–81) who emancipated the serfs (1861) and promulgated widespread military, legal, educational, and governmental reforms. During his reign the Russian empire expanded into the Caucasus (1859) and consolidated its control of Central Asia (1865–8) and defeated Turkey (1877–8). He was assassinated by Anarchists.

Alexander the Great (*aka* Alexander III, 356–323 BCE) Greek emperor (reigned 336–323 BCE). Son of Philip II of Macedon, Alexander led one of the most rapid and dramatic military expansions in history, extended Hellenistic culture and conquest as far as India, founding cities and vassal-states throughout West Asia. *p.60, p.61*

Alexandria City on the Mediterranean coast of Egypt founded by Alexander the Great in 331 BCE. It was the seat of the Ptolemies, who ruled Egypt from Alexander's death until the Romans gained control in the first century BCE. It was a major center of Greek culture, famous for its library and the Pharos (lighthouse). *p.63*

Alexius IV (died 1204) Byzantine emperor (reigned 1203–1204). He ascended the throne with the help of the Fourth Crusade but was deposed a year later by a national revolt.

Alfonso VI (*aka* Alfonso the Brave, *Sp.* Alfonso El Bravo, 1040–1109) King of León (reigned 1065–70) and king of reunited Castile and León (1072–1109), who by 1077 had proclaimed himself "emperor of all Spain." His oppression of his Muslim vassals led to the invasion of Spain by an Almoravid army from North Africa in 1086.

Alfred the Great (*var.* Aelfred) King of Wessex (reigned 871–899). Ruler of a Saxon kingdom in SW England. He prevented England from falling to the Danes and promoted learning and literacy. Compilation of the *Anglo-Saxon Chronicle* began during his reign, c.890.

Alfred jewel Anglo-Saxon medallion dating from the reign of Alfred the Great. *p.145*

ALGERIA Africa's second-largest country, Algeria has borders with Morocco, Mauritania, Mali, Niger, Libya, and Tunisia. The conquest of Algeria by France began in 1830. By 1900, French settlers occupied most of the best land. In 1954, war was declared on the colonial administration by the National Liberation Front (FLN), Algeria finally winning independence from France in 1962. The military blocked Islamist militants from taking power after winning elections in 1991, setting up a new civilian regime and throughout the 1990s fighting a bloody terrorist conflict. Algeria has one of the youngest populations, and highest birthrates, in the region.

CHRONOLOGY

100 BCE Algeria, long inhabited by nomadic Berber peoples, becomes the Roman province of Numidia. The area represents a major source of grain for Rome.

429 CE The Vandals invade and end Roman rule.

7th century CE Arab invasions bring Islam to Algeria. A Muslim Ibadite kingdom, which brings together Muslim concepts of government and Berber traditions, is based in Tahert in the central Algerian highlands and flourishes between 760 and 900.

1529 Barbarossa, or Khair-ed-din the "red beard", a Barbary pirate, captures Algiers for the Ottoman Empire and from this base his corsairs attack ships in the Mediterranean.

1830 French troops invade, bringing Ottoman rule to an end, although opposition from the Berbers, led by Abd al-Kadir, is fierce and the region is not fully subjugated until 1848.

1882 The three "departments" of Algiers, Oran and Constantine are incorporated as part of metropolitan France, although from 1900 a governor-general rules with greater local autonomy.

1942 Allied forces seize control of Algeria from the French Vichy administration. Algeria becomes a base for the Free French movement.

1947 An Algerian national assembly is established, although restrictive voting qualifications mean that few Muslims have the vote.

1954 The first of a series of guerrilla attacks marks the start of an independence struggle led by the National Liberation Front (Front de Libération Nationale – FLN). A bitter struggle ensues and French forces numbering 450,000 are deployed in an attempt to retain control of the country.

1958 A military coup by French Algerian generals, who fear that the French government will negotiate with the FLN, precipitates a crisis in metropolitan France. As a result Gen. Charles de Gaulle returns to power and after a referendum in September (in metropolitan France and its colonies including Algeria, where Muslim women were allowed to vote for the first time) the Fifth French Republic is established on October 6 with de Gaulle as President. Meanwhile on Sept. 19 the FLN sets up a "free Algerian" government in Cairo with Ferhat Abbas as Prime Minister.

1959 In the face of continued heavy fighting de Gaulle proposes a referendum on independence for Algeria. French colonists and military personnel opposed to Algerian independence set up the Organization of the Secret Army (Organisation de l'armée secrète – OAS).

1961 The French government and the Algerian provisional government agree to begin negotiations on independence which start on May 20 after an OAS-led coup in Algeria on April 22 collapses after four days.

1962 Negotiations result in signature of a formal ceasefire agreement in Evian, France, and in agreements on the holding of a referendum on independence. The French people approve these agreements in a referendum on April 2.

1962 In a referendum 91.2 percent of the total registered electorate votes in favor of independence, which is declared on July 3 and recognized by France two days later. In September Ahmed Ben Bella is elected Prime Minister and in September 1963, after the approval by referendum of a constitution, he is elected the first President of Algeria.

1965 Military junta topples government of Ahmed Ben Bella. Revolutionary council set up.

1966 Judiciary "Algerianized." Tribunals try "economic crimes."

1971 Oil industry nationalized. President Boumedienne continues with land reform, a national health service, and "socialist" management.

1976 National Charter establishes a socialist state.

1980 Ben Bella released after 15 years' detention. Agreement with France whereby latter gives incentives for return home of 800,000 Algerian immigrants.

1981 Algeria helps to negotiate release of hostages from US embassy in Tehran, Iran.

1985 Two most popular Kabyle (Berber) singers given three-year jail sentences for opposing regime.

1987 Limited economic liberalization. Cooperation agreement with Soviet Union.

1988 Anti-FLN violence; state of emergency. Algeria negotiates release of Kuwaiti hostages from aircraft; Shi'a hijackers escape.

1989 Constitutional reforms diminish power of FLN. New political parties founded, including Islamic Salvation Front (FIS). AMU established.

1990 Political exiles permitted to return. FIS is victorious in municipal elections.

1991 FIS leaders Abassi Madani and Ali Belhadj arrested. FIS wins most seats in National People's Assembly.

1992 President Chadli overthrown by military. President Boudiaf assassinated. Madani and Belhadj given 12 years in jail.

1994 Political violence led by GIA.

1995 Democratic presidential elections won by Liamine Zéroual.

1996 Murders continue, notably of Catholic clergy and GIA leader.

1997 Madani released from jail but debarred from active politics.

1999 Abdelaziz Bouteflika elected president in poll boycotted by opposition candidates.

2000 Economic reforms announced.

2001 Fresh investment in oil and gas benefits economy. Civil strife continues; many thousands have now been killed. Resurgence of Berber protests.

Alhambra Moorish palace in Granada, built by the Nasrid rulers of the last Muslim kingdom in S Spain in the 13th and 14th centuries.

Allies, The *(aka* Allied Powers) General term applied to the victorious Great Powers at the end of World War I (after the US joined the Entente Powers – Britain, France, Russia, Italy – in 1917). More generally used to describe the alliance ranged against the Axis powers during World War II headed by Britain, France, Poland, and the USSR and (from 1941) USA.

Allied Powers *see* Allies, The

Allouez, Father Claude (1622–89) French Jesuit missionary who explored the Great Lakes region of N America (1665–67) as well as the St. Lawrence River, setting up missions in present-day Wisconsin.

Almagro, Diego de (1475–1538) Spanish conquistador. Companion of Pizarro in the conquest of Peru in 1532. In 1535 he set off southward in an attempt to conquer Chile. He later quarreled with Pizarro and civil war broke out between their followers.

Almohad dynasty (1130–1269) Muslim dynasty founded by Ibn Tumart, leader of a puritanical Muslim revival sect. They supplanted the Almoravids (1174), and the Almohads, based at Marrakesh, eventually controlled N Africa as far east as Tripoli, as well as temporarily reclaiming much of the Iberian peninsula from the Christian powers; their power declined from 1228 and they were eventually overthrown in Iberia by the revived Reconquista, following Christian victory at ⚔ of Las Navas de Tolosa (1212) and in N Africa by the Marinids (1269). *p.184*

Almoravid empire (1056–1174) Confederation of Berbers whose religious zeal and military enterprise built an empire in NW Africa based on Marrakesh (founded 1062), eventually extending S to Ghana, and N into Muslim Iberia until defeated by the Almohads (1147).

Alompra *see* Alaungpaya

alphabet, development of *p.23* *See also* writing

Alvarado, Pedro de (c.1485–1541) Spanish conquistador. Took part in the expeditions of Juan de Grijalva and Hernán Cortés in Mexico and C America, later gaining control over highland Guatemala and El Salvador, and becoming governor of Honduras and Guatemala.

Alvare (died 1614) King of Kongo who was restored to his throne with the help of Portuguese troops, largely in order to secure the slave trade, after his country had been invaded in 1568.

Alvarez de Peneda, Alonso 16th-century Spanish explorer of the Yucatan Peninsula (1517–23).

Amadu Lobbo (1775–1844) Fulani leader who established a Muslim state in Masina, W Africa in the 19th century.

Amde Sion (died 1344) Ruler of Ethiopia.

Amenhotep *see* Akhenaton

Amenhotep III *see* Amenophis III

Amenophis III *(var.* Amenhotep) Egyptian pharaoh (reigned 1391–1353 BCE). His reign saw peaceful progress at home and effective diplomacy abroad. 1417 BCE.

Amenophis IV *see* Akhenaton

America Continent of the Western Hemisphere, named after Amerigo Vespucci, one of the early European explorers. Native American cultures were all but destroyed by the colonists in all parts of the continent. *See also* United States of America and other individual countries

American Civil War (1861–65) US Civil war between the northern states (the Union) and the southern Confederate states over the extension of slavery and the rights of individual states to make their own laws. Broke out in Apr 1861 following the secession of seven Confederate states (Mississippi, Florida, Alabama, Georgia, Louisiana, Texas, South Carolina from the Union, shortly followed by Virginia, North Carolina, Tennessee, and Arkansas). The war was won by the Union (1865) and slavery became illegal throughout the US. *p.369*

American War of Independence *(aka* The Revolutionary War, 1775–83) Britain's N American colonies, exasperated at the taxes and restrictions placed on their commercial activities by the government in London, became the first overseas colony of a European state to fight for and win independence. *p.332*

Amphipolis ⚔ of Peloponnesian War (422 BCE). Spartan victory over Athens.

Amritsar massacre (April 13 1919) India. Followed riots on the streets of Amritsar in the Punjab, protesting against the Rowlatt legislation (anti-sedition laws). British troops fired at the demonstrators, killing nearly 400 people, and wounding over 1000. The massacre caused widespread outrage.

Amundsen, Roald (1872–1928) Norwegian explorer. Explored both the N and S Poles, tracing the Northwest Passage (1903–06) and discovering the magnetic North Pole. Led first expedition to reach the S Pole in 1911. Explored the Arctic by air in the 1920s.

An Lushan (703–757) Chinese general, who assembled an army of 160,000 and rebelled against the Tang. He captured Chang'an in 756, but was murdered the following year.

Anasazi culture (200–1500 CE) Ancient culture of the southwestern US. The later period saw the development of complex adobe-built settlements known as pueblos.

Anatolia The Asian part of Turkey. A plateau, largely mountainous, which occupies the peninsula between the Black Sea, the Mediterranean, and the Aegean.

Andersson, Charles (1827–67) Swedish explorer of southwest Africa (1853–59).

ANDORRA A tiny, landlocked principality between France and Spain, Andorra lies high in the eastern Pyrenees. From the 13th century, French and Spanish co-princes (today the President of France and the Bishop of Urgel) have ruled Andorra. In December 1993, the principality held its first full elections. Andorra's spectacular scenery, alpine climate, and duty-free shopping have made tourism, especially skiing, its main source of income.

CHRONOLOGY

742–814 CE The King of the Franks, Emperor Charlemagne, establishes the kingdom as a buffer state against Spanish Muslims.

1278 An agreement is entered into by Pere II, the sovereign Lord of Catalonia, under the terms of which the Roman Catholic Bishop of the Spanish diocese (Seu) of Urgel and the local Count of Foix are designated joint rulers of the co-principality of Andorra. The King of France later inherits the Count's right through marriage.

1866 Building upon earlier administrative statutes of 1748 and 1763, a "Plan of Reform" is passed providing a measure of constitutionality to Andorra's government.

1867 A Franco-Spanish agreement exempts Andorra from the payment of import duties.

1970 Women get the vote.

1982 First constitution enshrines popular sovereignty.

1983 General Council votes in favor of income tax.

1984 Government resigns over attempt to introduce indirect taxes.

1991 EU customs union comes into effect.

1992 Political demonstrations demanding constitutional reform. Government resigns.

1993 Referendum approves new constitution.

1994 Government falls; replaced by center-right Liberal cabinet.

1997, 2001 Liberal cabinet reelected

Angevins Kings of Hungary between 1308 and 1387.

Angevin dynasty (aka Plantagenets) English ruling dynasty established by Henry II, Count of Anjou, in 1154.

Angkor Capital of the Khmer empire (Kambujadesha), located in central Cambodia. Angkor was an extensive city, covering over 25 sq km, of stone temples dedicated to the Khmer god kings. The most impressive temples are Angkor Wat (12th century) and Angkor Thom (13th century). *p.190*

Angkorian dynasty Dynasty that ruled the Khmer empire, founded in 802. *See also* Kambujadesha

Angles Germanic people who invaded England in the 5th century along with the Jutes and Saxons.

Anglo-Burmese wars (1824–26, 1852, 1885) In 1824, after Burmese encroachments on their territory in Assam, NE India, the British declared war on Burma. After two years of intermittent conflict the king of Ava signed the treaty of Yandabo, abandoning all claim to Assam and ceding the coastal provinces of Arakan and Tenasserim. Further conflict in 1852 led to the annexation of the Irrawaddy valley. A third clash in 1885 led to the annexation of Upper Burma and (in 1890) the Shan states.

Anglo-Dutch wars Series of mainly naval conflicts in the second half of the 17th century between England and the Netherlands. The first (1652–53) and second (1664–67) were the result of commercial competition; in the third (1672–74) Charles II of England allied with Louis XIV in an unsuccessful French attempt to crush the Netherlands.

Anglo-French wars Many were fought from the Middle Ages up until the defeat of Napoleon in 1815. In the 18th century Anglo-French rivalry provoked wars not only in Europe but also in India and N America. *p.328*

Anglo-Gurkha War (1814–15) Conflict between the Gurkhas of Nepal and Britain in Sikkim and the Ganges plain.

By the terms in the Treaty of Segauli, the Nepalis were obliged to withdraw from Sikkim and the lower ranges of the western Himalayas.

Anglo-Maratha wars (1775–82, 1803–05, 1817–18) The first Maratha war began when Britain became involved in struggles between Maratha leaders. Though the British were crushed at Wadgaon (1778), they conquered Gujarat and stormed Gwalior, to end the war, which concluded with the Treaty of Salabai (1782). During the Second Maratha War, Maratha artillery was particularly effective at the battles of Assaye and Argaon (1803). British conquest of the three great Maratha powers in the Third War in 1818, allowed Britain to incorporate Maratha territory into her growing S Asian domains.

Anglo-Persian Oil Company (later BP) founded in 1909 to exploit oilfields in Iran

Anglo-Tibetan Convention *see* Anglo-Tibetan Treaty

Anglo-Tibetan Treaty (var. Anglo-Tibetan Convention, September 6 1904). Agreement of mutual support between Britain and Tibet following the opening of commercial relations and establishment of boundaries under the Sikkim Convention (1890, 1893).

ANGOLA An oil- and diamond-rich country in southwest Africa. One of the first European colonies in Africa, the Portuguese having established coastal forts in the region as early as 1482. Angola has suffered almost permanent civil war since independence from Portugal in 1975. For years the West supported UNITA rebels against the Soviet-backed MPLA government. The 1994 UN-backed Lusaka Protocol ultimately failed to resolve matters, but with the death of UNITA leader Jonas Savimbi in 2002, there is at last hope for a peaceful settlement. *p.445*

CHRONOLOGY

1575 Luanda founded by the Portuguese, their first explorers having arrived around 100 years earlier. Portugal subsequently conducts military campaigns to collect slaves and minerals.

1891 The frontiers of Angola are fixed, following the 1884–85 Congress of Berlin which divides the map of Africa among the colonial powers: the process of conquest and settlement accelerates, the Portuguese introduce a system of forced labor, and by 1922 the Portuguese claim that "pacification" is complete. Major settlement by the Portuguese comes only in the quarter-century following the World War II.

1956 Anti-tribal and non-racial Popular Movement for the Liberation of Angola (MPLA) formed with the aim of ending colonial rule. Led by Agostinho Neto, it later receives support from the Soviet bloc; Organization of African Unity assistance is also increasingly channeled in its direction after 1967 as it is established as the most effective of the Angolan liberation movements.

1961 February–March. Rebellions in Luanda and northern Angola, followed by severe repression and the launching by the MPLA of the anti-colonial armed struggle in the rural areas. The northern-based National Front for the Liberation of Angola (FNLA) is formed the following year, under Holden Roberto: it appeals to tribal allegiances and eventually receives support from the USA and Zaire.

1966 Formation of National Union for the Total Independence of Angola (UNITA), the third major nationalist movement, led by Jonas Savimbi. Initially it operates mainly in eastern Angola but by 1990 it controls large parts of the country from its headquarters in Jamba. UNITA enjoys the popular support of the Ovimbundu and receives substantial assistance from the USA and South Africa.

1974 A military coup in Lisbon sweeps away the Caetano regime and leads to the end of the Portuguese colonial wars. Independence is scheduled for November 11, 1975, and a transitional government is formed by the three nationalist movements. However, this soon breaks down and armed conflict ensues between MPLA, FNLA, and UNITA.

1975 November 11. MPLA proclaims the People's Republic of Angola with Neto as President, a South African invasion in support of anti-MPLA forces

having been halted 300 km south of Luanda with the assistance of Soviet materiel support and Cuban troops. Nigeria recognizes the new government later in the month and other African countries soon follow suit. In March 1976 South Africa announces that its troops will be withdrawn from southern Angola.

1979 José Eduardo dos Santos (MPLA) becomes president.

1991 UN-brokered peace.

1992 MPLA election victory provokes UNITA to resume fighting.

1994 Lusaka peace agreement.

1998 Civil war re-erupts.

2000 Fighting spreads as UNITA increases guerrilla activity.

2002 UNITA leader Jonas Savimbi killed.

Annam Historic state of mainland Southeast Asia, in area of modern North Vietnam; under Chinese suzerainty at various times from the 2nd century CE to independence (1428), part of French Indochina from 1880s. *See also* Dai-Viet, Vietnam.

Anne of Bohemia (1366–94) First wife of Richard II of England. She died of plague without producing an heir.

Anschluss (1938) Nazi Germany's annexation of Austria, despite an express prohibition of such a union under the terms of the 1919 Versailles Treaty.

ANTARCTICA The world's fifth-largest continent, Antarctica is almost entirely covered by ice over 2000 m (6560 ft) thick. The area sustains a varied wildlife, including seals, whales, and penguins. The Antarctic Treaty, signed in 1959 and in force in 1961, provides for international governance of Antarctica. To gain Consultative Status, countries have to set up a program of scientific research in the continent. Following a 1994 international agreement, a whale sanctuary was established in the seas around Antarctica.

CHRONOLOGY

The Russian explorer, Thaddeus von Bellingshausen, was the first to sight

Antarctica, in 1820. The South Pole was first reached by the Norwegian, Roald Amundsen, in December 1911. 1773. Captain James Cook crosses the Antarctic Circle, though without sighting land.

1819 The British sealer William Smith finds the South Shetland Islands. Hunters wipe out the fur seal population within a few years.

1820 The Russian explorer, Thaddeus von Bellingshausen, is first to sight Antarctica.

1839–43 Sir James Clark Ross discovers new territory around what is now called the Ross Sea.

1892 The Dundee Whaling expedition arrives in Antarctica.

1909 January. Ernest Shackleton's expedition gets to within 97 miles of the South Pole.

1911 December. The expedition led by Roald Amundsen is the first to reach the South Pole.

1912 January. Robert Falcon Scott reaches the South Pole. He dies two months later, on the return journey.

1929 November. Richard Byrd is the first to fly over the South Pole.

1957–1958 International Geophysical Year launches scientific exploration of Antarctica.

1959 Antarctic Treaty signed by 12 countries. Territorial claims frozen.

1978 Convention limiting seal hunting comes into force.

1985 Ozone depletion disclosed.

1994 Establishment of Antarctic whale sanctuary.

1998 Agreement on 50-year ban on mineral extraction comes into force.

anti-ballistic missile (ABM) Defence system, developed by the US in the late 1960s.

antibiotics Discovered and used in World War II. *p.416*

Anti-Comintern Pact (25 Nov 1936) Joint declaration by Germany and Japan of opposition to Soviet Communism and Communist International; acceded to by Italy (Oct 1937).

Antietam ⚔ of American Civil War (Sep 17 1862) Union victory.

Antigonid Dynasty (c.306–168 BCE) Dynasty of Macedonian monarchs established by one of Alexander's generals Antigonus I Cyclops –

so called because he had lost an eye – after the death of Alexander. They established dominance over the Greek regions of Alexander's empire.

Antigonus I (aka Antigonus Cyclops, c.382–301 BCE) Ruler of part of Alexander the Great's empire after his death.

ANTIGUA & BARBUDA

Located between the Atlantic and the Caribbean, Antigua, one of the Leeward Islands, was in turn a Spanish, French, and British colony. British influence is still strong and most clearly revealed in the Antiguans' passion for cricket. Antigua has two remote dependencies: Barbuda, 50 km (30 miles) to the north, sporting a magnificent beach; and Redonda, 40 km (25 miles) west, an uninhabited rock with its own king.

CHRONOLOGY

1632 After settlement by the Spanish and French in the 16th and early 17th century, a permanent British settlement is established under Sir Thomas Warner.

1666 After a brief interlude of French occupation the Treaty of Breda returns Antigua to Britain.

1860 Barbuda, hitherto owned by the British Codrington family, .. is formally incorporated into the colony.

1951 Universal adult suffrage introduced.

1981 Independence from Britain; union with Antigua opposed by Barbudan secessionist movement.

1983 Supports US invasion of Grenada.

1994 Lester Bird elected prime minister succeeding his father.

1995 New taxes provoke protests.

1999 ALP wins sixth consecutive elections; Lester Bird remains prime minister.

2004 Baldwin Spencer and UPP oust ALP

Antiochus III (died 187 BCE) Seleucid emperor (reigned 223–187 BCE). Ruled over Syria and much of Asia Minor. His interference in Greek affairs brought him into conflict with Rome and he was defeated at Thermopylae in 191.

Anyang Shang capital (1400 BCE).

Anzio (*var.* Anzio Beach) ⚔ of World War II (Jan–May 1944) Allied (US) landings in central Italy established a bridgehead north of German lines of resistance.

Anzio Beach *see* Anzio

Anzus Pact (*var.* Anzus Treaty, 1951). Formerly known as the Pacific Security Treaty, and signed by the US, Australia and New Zealand, it aimed to protect the countries of the Pacific from armed attack.

Anzus Treaty *see* Anzus Pact

Aornos ⚔ and siege of Alexander the Great's expansionist campaigns (327 BCE).

Aotearoa *see* New Zealand

Apache American Indian people of the US southwest. Their remote location meant that they suffered less initial disruption from European expansion. Led by Geronimo, they fought a series of wars (the Apache Wars) against the US army during the mid-19th century before they were eventually forced into reservations in 1887.

apartheid (apartness) Policy in South Africa from the 1960s to 1990, that sanctioned racial segregation and social, political and economic discrimination against the black majority. *See also* South Africa

Appian Way First great Roman road *p.61*

Appomattox (1865) Site of Confederate surrender in American Civil War.

Aquinas, St. Thomas (*var.* Aquinas, Doctor Angelicus, *It.* San Tommaso D'Aquino) (c.1224–74). Italian scholar and Dominican theologian whose doctrinal system became known as Thomism.

Aquitaine Region of SW France. The Roman province of Aquitania, named after the Aquitani, a tribe conquered by Julius Caesar, became the core of the Visigothic kingdom established in 418. This was conquered by the Franks in 507.

Ara Pacis Monument erected in Rome by Augustus in 13 BCE to celebrate the *pax romana* (Roman peace) that he had brought to the Mediterranean world. *p.81*

Arab-Israeli Wars (1948–9, 1956, 1967, 1973, 1982) Series of five wars between Israel and the Arab states over the territorial and strategic consequences of the creation of a Jewish state. *See also* Six-Day War, Suez Crisis, Yom Kippur War, Lebanon, Invasion of, Intifada

Arab League Association of Arab states founded in 1945 with the aim of encouraging Arab unity. The original members were Egypt, Syria, Lebanon, Transjordan, Iraq, Saudi Arabia, and Yemen. By 1994 the League had 22 member states, including Palestine, represented by the Palestine Liberation Organization (PLO).

Arab Revolt (1915–18) Uprising against Turkish rule during World War I by several Arab tribes. Centered on the Hejaz, the revolt subsequently helped the British to capture Palestine and established the Saudi dynasty as rulers of Arabia. *See also* Lawrence, T.E., Faisal, Emir.

Arabia *see* Saudi Arabia

Arabian American Oil Company (ARAMCO) Founded in 1936 by Standard Oil of California and Texaco to exploit petroleum concessions in Saudi Arabia, is now among the most powerful oil groups in the world. In 1979 the Saudi Arabian government took complete control of the company.

Arabs Semitic people originally of the Arabian Peninsula, but now widespread throughout the SW Asia and N Africa after their rapid expansion as they carried the new Islamic faith into all neighboring regions in the 7th century CE. *p.130*

Arafat, Yasser (1929–2004) Palestinian resistance leader, co-founder (1959) of the Palestine Liberation Organization (PLO), and its chairman since 1969. In 1988 he persuaded the majority of his colleagues in the PLO to acknowledge the right of Israel to co-exist with an independent state of Palestine. In 1993, together with the Prime Minister of Israel, Yitzhak Rabin, he negotiated a peace agreement by which Israel agreed to withdraw from Jericho and the Gaza Strip.

ARAMCO *see* Arabian American Oil Company

Araucanians People of central Chile. The Araucanians resisted European conquest for over 300 years. They quickly learnt to ride the horses introduced by the Spanish and proved formidable opponents in war. They were finally subdued by the Chilean army in the 1870s

Arbela ⚔ of wars between Parthia and Rome (216 BCE).

Archimedes (c.287–212 BCE) Greek scientist and mathematican, who made many valuable contributions to theories of mechanics and hydrostatics; among them Archimedes' Principle, which states that a object partially or wholly immersed in a liquid, is buoyed up by a force equal to the weight of the liquid displaced.

rchitecture *see* art and architecture

rcole ⚔ of (1796) Napoleonic Wars, Italian campaign. French victory.

Ardashir I (died 241 CE) Persian king (reigned 208–241 CE). In c.224 Ardashir overcame the Parthian ruler, Artabanus V, and invaded Syria, establishing the Sassanian dynasty and empire. He made Ctesiphon (near modern Baghdad) on the River Tigris his capital and revived Zoroastrianism.

ardennes ⚔ of World War I (Dec 1944–Feb 1945) Final and unsuccessful German counter-offensive in W Europe.

ARGENTINA Occupying most of the southern half of South America, Argentina extends 3460 km (2150 miles) from Bolivia to Cape Horn. The Andes mountains in the west run north– south, forming a natural border with Chile. To the east they slope down to the fertile central pampas, the region known as Entre Ríos. The Spanish first established settlements in the Andean foothills in 1543. The indigenous Amerindians, who had stopped any Inca advance into their territory, also prevented the Spaniards from settling in the east until the 1590s. Agriculture, especially beef, wheat, and fruit, and energy resources are Argentina's main sources of wealth. Politics in Argentina had been characterized in the past by periods of military rule, but in 1983, Argentina returned to a system of multiparty democracy.

CHRONOLOGY

1516 Juan de Solis is killed by the indigenous inhabitants after landing in what is now Argentina.

1526 Sebastian Cabot builds a fort on the estuary of the Rio de la Plata.

1535 Pedro de Mendoza establishes the port of Santa Maria del Buen Aire on the site of the modern-day capital.

1776 Buenos Aires is separated from the Viceroyalty of Peru and becomes the seat of the Viceroyalty of Rio de la Plata.

1816 Independence is achieved as the United Provinces of the River Plate. Conflict ensues between Unitarians advocating a centralized state ruled from Buenos Aires, and the provincial Federalists of the interior who resent domination from the capital.

1827 Bernardino Rivadavia, the republic's first president, resigns after his progressive Unitarian constitution is rejected by the provinces.

1829 Juan Manuel de Rosas, a Federalist caudillo with a broad base of support, is appointed governor of Buenos Aires province. His increasingly authoritarian dictatorship extends the power of Buenos Aires and lays the foundations for national unity.

1835–1852 Dictatorship of Juan Manuel Rosas.

1853 Federal system set up.

1857 Europeans start settling the pampas; six million by 1930.

1877 First refrigerated ship starts frozen beef trade to Europe.

1878–1883 War against pampas Amerindians (almost exterminated).

1916 Hipólito Yrigoyen wins first democratic presidential elections.

1930 Military coup.

1943 New military coup. General Juan Perón organizes trade unions.

1946 Perón elected president, with military and labor backing.

1952 Eva Perón, charismatic wife of Juan Perón, dies of leukemia.

1955 Military coup ousts Perón. Inflation, strikes, unemployment.

1973 Perón returns from exile in Madrid and is reelected president.

1974 Perón dies; succeeded by his third wife "Isabelita," who is unable to exercise control.

1976 Military junta seizes power. Political parties are banned. Brutal repression during "dirty war" sees "disappearance" of over 10,000 "left-wing suspects."

1981 General Galtieri president.

1982 Galtieri orders invasion of Falkland Islands. UK retakes them.

1983 Pro-human rights candidate Raúl Alfonsín (UCR) win presidency in free multiparty elections. Hyperinflation.

1989–1992 Carlos Menem (Peronist) president; inflation down to 18%.

1995 Economy enters recession.

1998–1999 Argentina weathers financial crisis in Brazil.

1999 Fernando de la Rua elected president, leading center-left UCR–FREPASO alliance.

2000 Vice President and FREPASO leader, Carlos "Chaco" Alvarez, resigns over Senate bribes-for-votes scandal. Strikes and protests over fuel tax. Slump in beef exports after outbreak of hoof-and-mouth disease. IMF grants Argentina aid of nearly 40 billion dollars.

2001 Country brought to standstill by strike in protest against proposed government austerity measures. Elections give Peronists control of both houses of parliament. De la Rua resigns after violent protests and riots. Rodriguez Saa named interim president, but resigns after a week.

2002 Peronist Eduardo Duhalde takes over presidency, but economic crisis continues to worsen.

2003 Nestor Kirchner becomes president by default after Menem pulls out of poll.

Arianism Christian doctrine developed by Arius (c.318) which regarded Jesus Christ as a demigod, less divine than God; widely observed by successor states to W Roman Empire (Visigoths, Vandals), but declared heretical at Council of Nicaea (324).

Arica ⚔ of War of the Pacific (1880). Chilean victory.

Aristotle (384–322 bce) Great Greek philosopher who addressed all the major problems of logic, ethics, politics, art, and natural science. His opinions continued to be held in high esteem in the Islamic world and medieval Europe. p.59

ARMENIA Landlocked in the Lesser Caucasus Mountains, Armenia is the smallest of the former Soviet Union's republics and was the first to adopt Christianity as its state religion. It is bordered by Muslim states to the south, east, and west. An ancient people, the Armenians have lost and regained their autonomy many times over the centuries. In 1639, Turkey took the western half of their lands and Persia the east; Persia ceded its part to Russia in 1828. The confrontation with Azerbaijan over the enclave of Nagorno Karabakh has dominated national life since 1988. ▶

◄

CHRONOLOGY

519 BCE The Armenians are conquered by Persia and, in 334 BCE, by Alexander the Great. The country regains its independence in 189 BCE and, under Tigranes II (from 95–56 BCE), becomes one of the most powerful near-east states, before being conquered by Rome.

300 CE Armenia is converted to Christianity.

628 CE Armenia becomes a province of Byzantium, only to be conquered by the Arabs in 652.

866 CE Armenia regains its independence, which it maintains until conquered by the Seljuk tribes in the 12th century.

1609 The Armenian city of Nakhichevan is destroyed by Persia as part of a policy of de-Armenianization, in which populations are deported or forced to convert to Islam. Persia and Turkey continue to dispute power over the region, leading to partition in 1639, in which western Armenia (the larger region) becomes part of Turkey and eastern Armenia is incorporated into the Persian Empire.

1828 Eastern Armenia becomes part of the Russian Empire by the Treaty of Turkmenchai after the Russo-Persian war. Armenian merchants are encouraged by the Czarist regime until 1885, when Armenians become subject to repression and discrimination because of the regime's fear of separatist sentiment.

1877–1878 Massacre of Armenians during Russo-Turkish war.

1894–1896 Some 200,000 Armenians in Turkish Armenia are massacred by the Turks.

1915 Ottomans exile 1.75 million Turkish Armenians; most die.

1920 Independence.

1922 Becomes a Soviet republic.

1988 Earthquake kills 25,000. Conflict with Azerbaijan over Nagorno Karabakh begins.

1991 Independence from USSR.

1994 Cease-fire with Azerbaijan.

1995. First parliamentary elections.

1998 Kocharian elected president.

1999 Shooting of prime minister in attack on parliament.

2003 Kocharian re-elected.

Arms Race General term for the technical development and stockpiling of weapons of mass destruction by the Western and Eastern blocs during the Cold War.

Arnhem ⚔ of World War II (*var.* Operation Market Garden, Sep 1944). Unsuccessful Allied airborne operation intended to secure bridges across the Rhine in advance of land forces.

Arsaces I (died 211 BCE) Founder of the Parthian Empire, which he ruled (c.250–211 BCE), by leading a rebellion against the Seleucids.

Arsacid dynasty Parthian dynasty founded by Arsaces I in 247 bce.

Arsur ⚔ of crusades in the Holy Land. Crusader victory (1191).

art and architecture

Egyptian architecture. *p.32*
Greek art and architecture. *p.43*
Roman architecture. *p.95*
Illuminated manuscripts. *p.129*
Romanesque architecture. *p.166*
Gothic architecture. *p.191, p.209*
Giotto di Bondone. *p.227*
Moorish architecture. *p.240*
Donatello. *p.252*
Renaissance architecture. *p.252*
Russian icons. *p.255*
Masaccio. *p.256*
Duomo, Florence. *p.259*
Sandro Botticelli. *p.262*
Renaissance. *p.272*
Michelangelo. *p.272*
Leonardo da Vinci. *p.273*
The Rococo period. *p.331*
Japanese woodblocks *p.354*
Impressionism *p.372*

Arthur, Gabriel 17th-century explorer of North America. In 1673, Arthur accompanied James Needham southwest across the Blue Ridge Mountains of North America, and into territory occupied by the Cherokee. During his travels he was captured by Indians.

Aryans Nomadic Indo-European-speaking people who migrated into NW India some time after 1500 BCE. Originally cattle pastoralists, they became sedentary farmers, and gradually spread eastward. They were divided into various tribes, often warring amongst themselves. The early Aryan settlers of N India coalesced, by c.600 BCE, into sixteen distinct political units (*see* Magadha), which dominated the Ganges plain.

Asante kingdom Powerful W African state that flourished from the 17th to the late 19th century, when it was conquered by British troops. *p.318*

ASEAN *see* Association of South-East Asia Nations

Ascalon ⚔ of crusades in the Holy Land (1099). City captured by crusaders.

Ashanti *see* Asante

Ashikaga Shogunate (1336–1573) Line of military governors of Japan.

Ashoka (*var.* Asoka, died 232 BCE) Mauryan emperor (reigned 273–232 BCE). The grandson of Chandragupta Maurya, Ashoka established his rule over most of the Indian subcontinent. After his victory in Kalinga by the Bay of Bengal, he became an enthusiastic convert to Buddhism, and published the fundamental principles of the faith on pillars or rock-carved edicts, found throughout India. *p.62*

Ashurbanipal Last of the great kings of Assyria (reigned 668–627 BCE), who assembled the first systematically organized library in the ancient Middle East in Nineveh. *p.42*

Asia Minor (*var.* Anatolia) Roman name for present-day Asian Turkey.

Asiento Slave Agreement Contract in use from the 16th to the mid-18th century, with the Spanish crown, which for an agreed sum of money granted a contractor (*asentista*), a monopoly in supplying African slaves for the Spanish colonies in the Americas.

Asoka *see* Ashoka

Assassins Ismaili Shi'ite sect active in various parts of the Middle East between the 11th and the 13th centuries.

Association of South-East Asian Nations (ASEAN) Established in 1967 to promote economic, social and cultural cooperation.

Assyrian empire (*var.* Neo-Assyrian Empire c.950–612 BCE). State based in Assur on the Tigris in upper Mesopotamia, which conquered its neighbors to establish a vast empire. At its height, between the 9th and 8th centuries BCE, Assyria reached from the Mediterranean in the east to Persia in the west, and from the Persian Gulf northwards to the eastern Anatolian mountains. Invaded Egypt (667 BCE). Overthrown by the Medes and Babylonians in 612 BCE. *p.42*

Astronomy

Egyptian astronomy *p.35*
Arab astronomy *p.155*
Renaissance astronomy. *p.300*

Asylum seekers Asylum seekers in Europe in the earlt 21st century. *p.454*

tacama Desert ⚔ of War of Pacific (1879–83).

tahualpa (1502–1533) Last emperor of the Inca, who emerged victorious from a civil war with his half brother. He was later captured, held for ransom, and then executed by Francisco Pizarro.

tatürk, Mustafa Kemal (*prev.* Mustafa Kemal Pasha, 1881–1938) Founder and first president of the republic of Turkey. Participated in the revolt of the Young Turks (1908). Served with distinction in World War I. In 1919 he broke away from the authority of the Istanbul government and established a provisional government in Ankara. As leader of the Turkish Nationalists he drove the Greeks from W Anatolia (1919–22). In 1922 the Ottoman Sultanate was formally abolished and Turkey became a secular republic, with Kemal as president. He launched a program of social and political reform intended to transform Turkey into a westernized modern republic. In 1934 he took the name Atatürk, "Father of the Turks."

ten (*var.* Aton) Originally the Egyptian sun disc, subsequently the sun god with which pharaoh Akhenaton replaced the existing Middle Kingdom pantheon.

thabascan (*var.* Athapaskan, Athapascan) N American peoples, sub-Arctic nomadic hunters, mainly of western Canada, and the name given to the language group linking a number of peoples from this area.

thaulf Visigothic leader (*fl.* 414).

thens The most celebrated of the city-states of Ancient Greece, both for its unrivalled cultural achievements and for its position under Pericles in the 5th century BCE as the most powerful Greek city-state. In 431 BCE Athens' role as leader of the Delian League provoked the hostility of Sparta, leading to the Peloponnesian War, in which Athens was completely defeated. Under the Romans (from 146 BCE) Athens was more important culturally than politically. In modern times it was chosen as capital of the new kingdom of Greece in 1834. *p.56, p.59*

tjeh *see* Achin

tlanta ⚔ of American Civil War (Jul 20–Sep 2 1864). Union victory.

tlantic, Battle of the Extended naval and air ⚔ of World War II. Protracted German campaign (1939–45) to disrupt Allied shipping and transatlantic convoys, largely through use of U-Boats, gradually defeated by Allied use of air cover and the convoy system. *p.415*

Aton *see* Aten

Atsugashi-yama ⚔ of mdieval Japan (1189) Defeat of Fujiwari clan.

Attalid dynasty (282–133 BCE) Line of rulers, founded by Philetaerus, of a kingdom of Pergamum in NW Asia Minor, in the 3rd and 2nd centuries BCE.

Attila the Hun (c.400–453 BCE) Ruler of the Huns from c.445. Attila devastated much of the East Roman Empire and forced the emperor Theodosius II to pay tribute and grant his people lands in the Balkans. In 451 he invaded Gaul, but was defeated by a Roman and Gothic army at the battle of the Catalaunian Fields. After one more raid – into northern Italy (452) when the Huns destroyed Aquileia – he died and his empire rapidly disintegrated. *See also* Huns

Augusta ⚔ of American Revolutionary War (Jan 29 1779). British victory.

Augustine, St. (St. Augustine of Canterbury, died 604) Italian Christian missionary, who traveled to Britain (597). His mission led to the conversion of many of the southern Anglo-Saxon kingdoms of Britain.

Augustine of Hippo, St. (354–430) Christian bishop and theologian, author of *The City of God*. One of the most influential of the early "Doctors of the Church."

Augustus Caesar (*var.* Octavian, 63 BCE–14 CE) First Roman emperor (27 BCE–14 CE). Octavian was the great nephew and adopted heir of Julius Caesar. On Caesar's death, he gradually won control of the Roman Empire, completing the task with his defeat of Mark Antony and Cleopatra. The Roman senate then granted him the title Augustus and guaranteed his authority for life. *p.81*

Aungzeya *see* Alaungpaya

Aurangzeb (1618–1707) Mughal emperor (reigned 1658–1707). The first Mughal emperor to extend his authority to the extreme south of India, Aurangzeb fought hard to maintain Mughal supremacy in the face of opposition from the Maratha Confederacy. His long reign was harsh and repressive, leading ultimately to the revolt and secession of many provinces. *p.313*

Aurelius, Marcus *see* Marcus Aurelius

Aurignacian tool technology Technology which evolved in the Middle East about 45,000 years ago. Small flint tools were set into wooden or bone handles and spread rapidly throughout S Europe.

Austerlitz D of Napoleonic Wars (1805). Russian/Austrian defeat by French forces. The victory that gave Napoleon virtual control of mainland Europe.

AUSTRALIA The world's sixth-largest country, Australia is an island continent located between the Indian and Pacific Oceans. Dutch, Portuguese, French, and – decisively – British incursions throughout the 17th and 18th centuries signaled the end of a millennia of Aboriginal isolation. Governor Arthur Philip raised the Union Flag at Sydney Cove on January 26 1788. Australia's varied landscapes include tropical rainforests, the deserts of the arid "red center," snow-capped mountains, rolling tracts of pastoral land, and magnificent beaches. Famous natural features include Uluru (Ayers Rock) and the Great Barrier Reef. Most Australians live on the coast, and all the state capitals, including Sydney, host of the 2000 Olympics, are coastal cities. Only Canberra, the national capital, lies inland. The vast interior is dotted with large reserves, sparsely inhabited by communities from the small Aboriginal population.

CHRONOLOGY

45,000 BCE Archaeological evidence suggests Aborigines have lived in Australia since at least this time.

1606 The explorer William Janz goes ashore on the west coast of Cape York.

1642 The Dutch explorer Abel Tasman lands in Van Diemen's Land (now Tasmania).

1688 The first English explorer, William Dampier, lands on Australia's NW coast.

1770 Captain James Cook charts the east coast, landing at Botany Bay. He raises the British flag on an island off Cape York, claiming possession for the United Kingdom.

1788 Eleven ships from Britain land their passengers – which include more than

700 convicts – at Port Jackson (now Sydney) and a penal colony is established.

1790 Free settlers begin arriving in Australia.

1803 A penal colony is established on Tasmania.

1813 Explorers cross the Blue Mountains, part of the Great Dividing Range down the east coast of Australia.

1831 A system of land sales is introduced, replacing the system of land grants by the Governor. It helps finance the passage of immigrants to Australia.

1840 Transportation of convicts to New South Wales is ended.

1850 The British Parliament passes the Australian Colonies Government Act, which allows the colonies to establish legislatures, alter their own constitutions, and fix franchises.

1851 Gold is discovered at Bathurst in New South Wales, and at Ballarat in Victoria. The ensuing gold rush attracts thousands of prospectors.

1853 Transportation to Tasmania is ended.

1853–67 Transportation is temporarily introduced to Western Australia to provide labor.

1863 First of a series of colonial conferences, aimed at creating closer ties between colonies.

1891 The first Australian Federal Convention meets. Delegates draw up a draft constitution.

1901 The Commonwealth of Australia comes into being. A Parliament is created, consisting of a House of Representatives and a Senate. The head of state is the Governor-General, appointed by the crown.

1915 Australian troops suffer heavy casualties at Gallipoli.

1929 Industrial upheaval and financial collapse caused by the Great Depression.

1939 Prime Minister Menzies announces Australia will follow Britain into war with Germany.

1942 Fall of Singapore to Japanese army. Japanese invasion of Australia seems imminent. Government turns to US for help.

1950 Australian troops committed to UN–US Korean War against North Korean communists.

1962 Menzies government commits Australian aid to war in Vietnam.

1966 Adopts decimal currency.

1972 Whitlam government elected. Aid to South Vietnam ceases.

1975 Whitlam government dismissed by Governor-General Sir John Kerr. Malcolm Fraser forms coalition government.

1983 Bob Hawke becomes prime minister at the head of an ALP administration.

1985 Corporate boom followed by deepening recession.

1992 Paul Keating defeats Hawke in leadership vote, becomes prime minister; announces "Turning toward Asia" policy. High Court's "Mabo Judgment" recognizes Aboriginal land rights.

1993 Against most predictions, Keating's ALP government reelected. Native Title Act provides compensation for Aboriginal rights extinguished by existing land title.

1996 Defeat of Keating government. Liberal John Howard becomes prime minister. Shooting of 35 people by gunman in Port Arthur, Tasmania, prompts tightening of gun control laws. First death under Northern Territory's controversial euthanasia legislation; legislation later overruled at federal level.

1998 Elections: Howard's Liberal and National coalition retains power with reduced majority; fears of right-wing One Nation party breakthrough prove unfounded.

1999 Referendum rejects proposals to replace Queen as head of state by indirectly elected president.

2000 Olympic Games in Sydney.

2001 Surprise re-election of Liberal-National coalition.

2002 Bali bombs kills 88 Australians.

2003 Governor-general resigns amid church abuse scandel.

Australoids People who colonized Australia and New Guinea some 60,000 years ago: the ancestors of the Australian Aboriginals and the Papuans.

Australopithecines (meaning "Southern Ape") The genus of ape-like, bipedal hominids which evolved in eastern Africa over 4 million years ago. Several species of *Australopithecus* have been identified, based on variations in skulls and teeth. It is still uncertain whether these hominids are the precursors of fully modern humans, or represent a separate evolutionary line. *p.10*

Australopithecus afarensis Present from c.4 to 3.2 million years ago, *A. afarensis* represented by the virtually complete 3.4–million year-old skeleton of an adult female, known as "Lucy" found in the Hadar region of Ethiopia. *A. Afarensis* has an ape-like body and small brain, but was capable of walking upright like a human. *p.10*

Australopithecus africanus (c.3 to 2 million years ago). Found in cave sites of southern Africa, *A. africanus* is distinguished by higher, rounder braincase than *A. Afarensis*, more powerful teeth and long powerful arms. *p.10*

Australopithecus anamensis Represented by 4.2–million-year-old fossils found near the shores of Lake Rudolf in Kenya. The oldest known member of the Australopithecine genus. *p.10*

Australopithecus boisei (c.2.7 to 1.7 million years ago) A robust species found in eastern Africa, distinguished by a powerful upper body, long upper jaw and the largest molars of any hominid. *p.10*

Australopithecus robustus (c.2 to 1 million years ago) Found in southern Africa, and distinguished by heavy jaws, brow ridge, a bony crest along the top of the skull, and a larger brain capacity than any other Australopithecine. p.10

AUSTRIA Lying in the heart of Europe, Austria is dominated by the Alps in the west of the country, while fertile plains make up the east and north. Austria came under the control of the Habsburgs in 1273. In 1867, the Dual Monarchy of Austria-Hungary was formed under Habsburg rule. Defeat in World War I in 1918 led to the breakup of the Habsburg empire and the formation of the Republic of Austria. Austria was absorbed into Hitler's Germany in 1938. It regained independence in 1955 after the departure of the last Soviet troops from the Allied Occupation Force. Its economy encompasses successful high-tech sectors, a tourist industry which attracts wealthier visitors, and a strong agricultural base. Joining the EU in 1995, in 2002 it was one of the first 12 EU states to adopt the Euro. *See also* Habsburg Empire

Chronology

14 BCE Austria south of the Danube is conquered by the Romans and incorporated within the Roman empire.

790 CE The area becomes the eastern frontier province (Ostmark) of the Frankish empire and later part of Charlemagne's Holy Roman Empire.

976 CE The Babenberg dynasty, which lasts 270 years, is founded by Emperor Otto I, who makes the province a margravate (border county).

1282 The Austrian ducal title is declared hereditary by Count Rudolf of Habsburg, who, in 1273, declares himself King of the Germans and Holy Roman Emperor.

1519–55 Under Charles V (1500–58) the Habsburg empire reaches its zenith, stretching from the Americas to the Low Countries, with Austria acquiring control over Bohemia in 1526 and forming a bulwark of Christian resistance against the Ottoman Turks.

1648 The Treaty of Westphalia, signed at the conclusion of the Thirty Years' War involving Catholic Austria, France, and Spain and Protestant Germany, England, Scandinavia, and Holland, marks the decline of the Holy Roman Empire as a political unit, with German states securing their sovereignty. It heralds the start of the Habsburg's long decline vis-a-vis France and Prussia.

1713 The Treaty of Utrecht, negotiated at the end of the War of Spanish Succession (1702–13), confirms Habsburg claims to the Low Countries (Spanish Netherlands) although a Bourbon becomes King of Spain.

1748 The Treaty of Aix-la-Chapelle, bringing to an end the War of Austrian Succession which broke out in 1740 following the death of Charles VI, the last male Habsburg heir, recognizes his daughter, Maria Theresa, as ruler of the Habsburg lands, although Silesia is ceded to Prussia.

1772–97 Successive partitions of Poland take place. In 1772 Austria gains Galicia in the first partition, confirmed in the 1772 Treaty of St. Petersburg. In 1795 Austria gains "lesser Poland," including Cracow, in the third partition, Austria having not participated in the second. The end of Poland (*Finis Poloniae*) is confirmed in a 1797 treaty.

1805 The Austrians and Russians are defeated at the battle of Austerlitz by Napoleon, who sets up the Confederation of the Rhine a year later, while Franz I of Austria (who had declared himself Emperor the year before) is obliged to renounce his title as Holy Roman Emperor. However, the Congress of Vienna of 1814–15, which seals the defeat of Napoleon, brings territorial gains to Austria, most significantly in northern Italy, and makes Austria titular head of the German Confederation, not least due to the astute diplomacy of Chancellor Metternich.

1848 Popular revolutions within the Habsburg domains lead to the abolition of serfdom, Metternich's resignation, the abdication of Emperor Ferdinand and the succession to the throne of his nephew Franz Josef (reigned 1848–1916).

1867 An Austro-Hungarian "dual monarchy," with independent parliaments for each country, is established by Emperor Franz Josef, a year after Prussia's humiliation of Austria in the Seven Weeks' War.

1908 Austria annexes Bosnia-Herzegovina, leading to the "Bosnian Crisis" which heightens international tension.

1914 The start of World War I is precipitated by assassination of Archduke Franz Ferdinand, heir to the Habsburg throne by a Serbian extremist. Austria-Hungary invades Serbia, but is unsuccessful until the following year when its armies are supported by German troops.

1918 At the end of World War I the Austrian Republic is proclaimed following the abdication of Emperor Charles and the collapse of the Austro-Hungarian empire.

1919 The Treaty of St. Germain between Austria and the Allies reduces Austria to a rump state, as a result of territorial concessions made to Czechoslovakia, Hungary, Italy, Poland, Romania, and Yugoslavia.

1933 Parliamentary government is suspended by the Christian Social Chancellor Engelbert Dollfuss.

1934 Dollfuss starts imprisoning social democrats, communists, and National Socialist (Nazi) Party members. Nazis attempt coup. Dollfuss is assassinated by Austrian Nazis in July and replaced by Kurt von Schuschnigg.

1938 The Anschluss – Austria incorporated into Germany by Hitler.

1945 Austria occupied by Soviet, British, US, and French forces. Elections result in ÖVP–SPÖ coalition.

1950 Attempted coup by Communist Party fails. Marshall Aid helps economic recovery.

1955 Occupying troops withdrawn. Austria recognized as a neutral sovereign state.

1971 SPÖ government formed under Chancellor Bruno Kreisky who dominates Austrian politics for 12 years.

1983 Socialists and the FPÖ form a coalition government under Fred Sinowatz.

1986 Kurt Waldheim, former UN secretary-general, elected president, despite war crimes allegations. Franz Vranitzky replaces Sinowatz as federal chancellor. Nationalist Jörg Haider becomes FPÖ leader, prompting the SPÖ to pull out of government. Elections produce stalemate. Return to "grand coalition" of SPÖ–ÖVP.

1990 ÖVP loses 17 seats in parliamentary elections.

1992 Thomas Klestil (ÖVP) elected president. Elections confirm some traditional ÖVP supporters defecting to FPÖ.

1995 Austria joins EU. Elections after coalition disagreement over budget; SPÖ and ÖVP increase representation; "grand coalition" re-forms in early 1996.

1997 Vranitzky resigns; replaced by Viktor Klima.

1998 Klestil reelected president.

1999 Haider's FPÖ wins 40% of votes in Carinthia regional poll, is equal second with ÖVP in general election in October; SPÖ remains as largest party.

2000 ÖVP accepts FPÖ into coalition, with Wolfgang Schüssel as chancellor; political crisis. EU imposes diplomatic sanctions, lifted after seven months.

2002 Euro fully adopted. FPÖ quits coalition. ÖVP wins fresh elections.

2003 ÖVP–FPÖ coalition re-formed.

2004 Heinz Fischer (SPÖ) president.

Austrian Succession, War of the

(1740–48) On the succession of Maria Theresa to the Austrian throne, Frederick II of Prussia seized Silesia. France allied with Prussia, while Britain formed an alliance with Austria. In Italy, Austria confronted a Bourbon alliance of France and Spain. The war involved conflict in Silesia, Austria, the Austrian Netherlands, southern Germany, Italy, India, and North America. At the end of the war Prussia's seizure of Silesia was recognized.

Austronesians People who spread southeast from Asia through Indonesia c.6000 BCE, reaching New Guinea and the Bismarck Archipelago, from where they set out into the Pacific on voyages of colonization. The Austronesian language group includes most of the languages of Indonesia, all the Polynesian languages, and the language of Madagascar.

Avars Steppe nomads who migrated westwards in the 6th century. In the 7th century they settled on the Danube Plain where they ruled the local Slavic population. Their empire was crushed by Charlemagne in 796.
See also Ruanruan

Averroes (born 1126) Muslim philosopher.

Avidius Cassius Gaius (died 175 CE) Roman military commander. The son of one of Hadrian's civil servants, Avidius Cassius directed Rome's wars with the Parthians (161–165), and became commander of all the military forces in the eastern provinces. He usurped the throne for three months in 175 on hearing a false rumor of Marcus Aurelius' death, but was assassinated by one of his soldiers before Aurelius could arrive to confront him.

Avignon Seven popes reigned in Avignon between 1309 and 1376 during a period of schism in the Catholic church. They were followed by two antipopes. The local bishop's palace was transformed into the magnificent Palace of the Popes. *p.232*

Avila, Pedro Arias *see* Davila, Pedrarias

Axayacatl Aztec ruler (1469–81).

Axis (*var.* Axis Powers) General term for Germany, Japan, and Italy during World War II. Originating with the Pact of Steel (*var.* Axis Pact) between Germany and Italy (May 1939), consolidated by Tripartite Pact between Germany, Italy, and Japan (Sep 1940) assuring mutual military, political and economic assistance in the event of war spreading beyond Europe.

Axum Small Red Sea kingdom (1st century BCE–7th century CE). It grew wealthy through control of the incense trade. Its king and people converted to Christianity in the 4th century CE. This laid the foundations for the later Christian kingdom of Ethiopia. *p.98*

Ayacucho ⚔ of wars of S American liberation (Dec 1824). Victory by Sucre liberated upper Peru (Bolivia).

Ayuthia *see* Ayutthaya

Ayutthaya (*var.* Ayuthia) Capital of Siam founded c.1350.

Ayyubid dynasty (1171–1250) Sunni Muslim dynasty founded by Saladin. The Ayyubids ruled most of the Middle East and Egypt until 1250, when they were defeated by the Mamluks. p.197

AZERBAIJAN Situated on the western coast of the Caspian Sea, Azerbaijan was the first Soviet republic to declare independence. The issue of the disputed enclave of Nagorno Karabakh, which Armenia seeks to annex, led to full-scale war until 1994 and is still a dominant concern. Over 200,000 refugees and more than twice as many internally displaced added to the problems of the troubled economy. Azerbaijan's oil wealth, however, gives it long-term potential.

CHRONOLOGY

3rd century CE The area which is now Azerbaijan falls under the domination of the Persian Sassanian dynasty.

641 Muslims conquer the region and gradually convert Iranian-speaking indigenous population.

11th century Seljuk Turks dominate region until overrun by the Mongols under Genghis Khan in the 13th century, and Tamerlane in the 14th century.

1728 The Treaty of Constantinople affirms Ottoman Turkish control over the region after 300 years of rivalry between Turkey and Persia. Local khanates eventually achieve some independence from both the great powers, but by 1805 growing Russian influence has made several khanates into Russian protectorates.

1828 The Treaty of Turkmenchai divides the region along the river Araks between Persia (to the south) and Russia (to the north).

1918 British forces, fighting against the Bolsheviks in the Civil War which followed the 1917 Russian Revolution, help to install an independent, nationalist government in Azerbaijan. Azerbaijan declares neutrality in the Russian Civil War, but asks for and receives Turkish assistance to remove the Bolshevik Baku Soviet.

1920 Red Army invades. Soviet republic established.

1922 Azerbaijan is incorporated in Transcaucasian Soviet Federative Socialist Republic (TSFSR).

1930 Forced collectivization of agriculture.

1936 TSFSR disbanded; Azerbaijan a full union republic (ASSR).

1945 Attempted annexation of Azeri region of Iran.

1985 Gorbachev tackles corruption in Communist Party of Azerbaijan.

1988 Nagorno Karabakh seeks unification with Armenia.

1990 Nagorno Karabakh attempts secession. Soviet troops move in.

1991 Independence.

1993 Aliyev president; reelected in 1998.

1994 Cease-fire in war with Armenia over Nagorno Karabakh.

1995–2003 General elections. Non-communist NA in power.

2004 Ilham Aliyev, son of Heydar, elected president.

Aztec empire (mid-14th century–1521) Dominant state in Mexico before the Spanish conquest of the 16th century. Centered on the valley of Mexico, the empire grew to include most of central and southern Mexico and was the focus of a sophisticated civilization. *p.261*

B

Babur (*var.* Babar, Baber, 1483–1530) Founder of the Mughal dynasty (reigned 1526–30). At the battle of Panipat (1525) Babur confronted the forces of the Afghan Lodi sultans, and occupied Delhi and Agra. By 1530 his empire stretched from the Oxus to the frontier of Bengal and from the Himalayas to Gwalior.

Babylonian empires (c.1795–1538 BCE, 612–539 BCE) Ancient empires of southern Mesopotamia. The first Babylonian empire was created by Hammurabi (c.1795–1750 BCE), with Babylon on the Euphrates as its capital.

Following a Hittite attack in c.1595, the Empire was ruled by the Kassites for 400 years. The second empire was established following the overthrow of Assyria in 612 BCE. Under its greatest ruler, Nebuchadnezzar II (605–562 BCE) it extended into Mesopotamia, Egypt and Palestine. It was brought to an end by the Persian conquest of 539–538 BCE. *p.39, p.42, p.49*

Bach, Johann Sebastian German composer of the Baroque period (1685–1750). *p.317*

Bacon's Rebellion (1676) N America. Attempt by Nathaniel Bacon, a Virginia planter, to expand into Indian territory. It was denounced by Governor William Berkeley as a rebellion, and Bacon, in response, turned his forces against Berkeley and for a while had control over most of Virginia.

Bactrian Kingdom Hellenistic kingdom in Central Asia, part of the legacy of the conquests of Alexander the Great. It flourished in the third and second centuries BCE.

Baecula ⚔ of Punic Wars (208 BCE). Roman victory over Carthage.

Baffin, William (1584–1622) English navigator who searched for a Northwest Passage to Asia. He discovered Baffin Bay and used the position of the moon to determine longitude at sea.

Baghdad Capital of modern Iraq. The city was founded in 762 CE as the capital of the Abbasid Caliphate.

BAHAMAS Located off the Florida coast in the western Atlantic, the Bahamas comprises some 700 islands and 2400 cays, of which 30 are inhabited. One of the first transatlantic tourist destinations, the Bahamas is also a major offshore financial center. It has one of the world's largest open-registry fleets, although only a tiny fraction is owned by Bahamian nationals.

Chronology
1492 Columbus first sets foot on San Salvador (Watling Island).
1690 The islands are granted to the owners of Carolina.
1717 The British Crown resumes control, and the first British governor arrives the following year.

1781 After being taken by US revolutionaries in 1776 the islands are seized by the Spanish.
1783 The islands are recaptured by the British and confirmed as British territory.
1920–1933 US prohibition laws turn Bahamas into prosperous bootlegging center.
1959–1962 Introduction of male suffrage; women gain the vote.
1973 Independence.
1983 Narcotics-smuggling scandals involving the government.
1997 Elections return Prime Minister Hubert Ingraham to office with increased majority.
2002 PLP returned to power.

Bahia (*var.* Salvador) Capital of Brazil (1549–1763).

Bahmani Kingdom (1347–1583) The earliest Muslim dynasty in the Deccan, founded by Alauddin in 1347, with its capital at Gulbarga. In the 16th century the Bahmani kingdom disintegrated into five independent Deccani kingdoms.

BAHRAIN Bahrain is an archipelago of 33 islands situated between the Qatar peninsula and the Saudi Arabian mainland. Only three of the islands are inhabited. Bahrain Island is connected to Saudi Arabia's eastern province by a causeway opened in 1986. Bahrain was the first Gulf emirate to export oil; its reserves are now almost depleted. Services such as offshore banking, insurance, and tourism are major employment sectors for skilled Bahrainis.

Chronology
1521 The Portuguese assume control of Bahrain.
1782 Bahrain is under Iranian rule.
1783 The Iranians are expelled by the Arabian Utub tribe, whose principal family, the al-Khalifas, are still the ruling dynasty today.
1861 The ruling Sheikh of Bahrain agrees to abstain from war, piracy, and slavery in return for British military support.
1880 Administrative control and foreign relations are granted to Britain.

1933 Oil is discovered in Bahrain.
1971 Independence from Britain.
1981 Founder member of GCC.
1990–1991 Bahrain supports UN action expelling Iraq from Kuwait.
1994–1996 Shi'a unrest.
1999 Accession to throne of Sheikh Hamad bin Isa al-Khalifa.
2001 Referendum approves transition to democracy.
2002 Becomes a constitutional monarchy. Islamists win elections.

Bahram V (died 439) Sassanian king (421–439).

Bajazet *see* Bayazid

Baker, Samuel (1821–93) English explorer who, with John Hanning Speke, helped to locate the source of the Nile (1861–65).

Baku Capital of Azerbaijan. Oil production started in the Baku region c.1900.

Balaton ⚔ of World War II (Mar 1945). Battle in NE Hungary in which a Soviet counter-offensive destroyed German military strength in SE Europe.

Balboa, Vasco Núñez de (c.1475–1519) Spanish conquistador and explorer. On an expedition across the Isthmus of Panama in 1513, he and his men were the first Spaniards to sight the Pacific Ocean.

Baldaya, Alfonso 15th-century Portuguese navigator, who explored the coast of West Africa on behalf of Prince Henry of Portugal (Henry the Navigator).

Baldwin I (*var.* Baldwin of Boulogne, *Fre.* Baudouin, 1058–1118) One of the leaders of the First Crusade, Baldwin captured Edessa in 1098, making the County of Edessa the first Crusader state. He was chosen to be King of Jerusalem on the death of Godfrey of Bouillon and crowned in 1100.

Balfour Declaration (1917) Contained in a letter from Britain's Foreign Secretary, Arthur Balfour, to Lord Rothschild, a prominent Zionist, the declaration stated the British government's support for the establishment of a national home for the Jewish people in Palestine.

Balkan Wars (1912–1913) Two short wars fought for possession of the Ottoman Empire's European territories. In the first, Montenegro, Bulgaria, Greece, and Serbia attacked and defeated Turkey, which was forced to surrender most of her territories in Europe on condition that a new state of Albania was created. The second war was precipitated by disputes among the victors over the division of Macedonia. Romania joined Greece and Serbia against Bulgaria, which was heavily defeated and lost territory to all its enemies.

Balkans *see* Bosnia and Herzegovina, Macedonia, Montegreno, Serbia, Slovenia, Yugoslavia.

Baltic states *see* Estonia, Latvia, Lithuania.

Baltic Wars (1563–70) Naval wars between Sweden and Denmark over which should control shipping through the narrow straits into the Baltic Sea. *p.285*

Bandkeramik pottery Pottery decorated with incised linear decorations by the earliest farming cultures of C Europe (c.5000 BCE), who are named after their pottery style.

BANGLADESH

BANGLADESH (*prev.* East Pakistan) founded (1971). Bangladesh lies at the north of the Bay of Bengal and shares borders with India and Burma. Most of the country is composed of fertile alluvial plains; the north and northeast are mountainous, as is the Chittagong region in the southeast. British rule began in Bengal in 1765, following the defeat of the ruler of Bengal at Plassey by Robert Clive, army head of the East India Company, in 1757. When British India was divided at independence in 1947, present-day Bangladesh was included in the state of Pakistan. After its secession from Pakistan in 1971, Bangladesh had a troubled history of political instability, with periods of emergency rule. Effective democracy was restored in 1991. Bangladesh's major economic sectors are jute production, textiles, and agriculture. Its climate can wreak havoc – in 1991 a massive cyclone killed more than 140,000 people.

CHRONOLOGY

1905 Muslims persuade British rulers to partition state of Bengal, to create a Muslim-dominated East Bengal.

1906 Muslim League established in Dhaka.

1912 Partition of 1905 reversed.

1947 British withdrawal from India. Partition plans establish a largely Muslim state of East (present-day Bangladesh)

and West Pakistan, separated by 1600 km (1000 miles) of Indian, and largely Hindu, territory.

1949 Awami League founded to campaign for autonomy from West Pakistan.

1968 Gen. Yahya Khan heads government in Islamabad.

1970 Elections give Awami League, under Sheikh Mujibur Rahman, clear majority. Rioting and guerrilla warfare following Yahya Khan's refusal to convene assembly. The year ends with the worst recorded storms in Bangladesh's history – between 200,000 and 500,000 dead.

1971 Civil war, as Sheikh Mujib and Awami League declare unilateral independence. Ten million Bangladeshis flee to India. Pakistani troops defeated in 12 days by Mukhti Bahini – the Bengal Liberation Army.

1972 Sheikh Mujib elected prime minister. Nationalization of key industries, including jute and textile. Bangladesh achieves international recognition and joins Commonwealth. Pakistan withdraws in protest.

1974 Severe floods damage rice crop.

1975 Sheikh Mujib assassinated. Military coups end with General Zia ur-Rahman taking power. Single-party state.

1976 Banning of trade union federations.

1977 Gen. Zia assumes presidency. Islam adopted as first principle of the constitution.

1981 Gen. Zia assassinated.

1982 Gen. Ershad takes over.

1983 Democratic elections restored by Ershad. Ershad assumes presidency.

1986 Elections. Awami League and BNP fail to unseat Ershad.

1987 Ershad announces state of emergency.

1988 Islam becomes constitutional state religion.

1990 Ershad resigns following demonstrations.

1991 Elections won by BNP. Khaleda Zia becomes prime minister. Ershad imprisoned. Role of the president reduced to ceremonial functions. Floods kill 150,000 people.

1994 Author Taslima Nasreen, who is accused of blasphemy, escapes to Sweden.

1996 General election returns BNP to power. Opposition parties reject February poll result and force fresh elections. Sheikh Hasina Wajed of the AL takes power.

2001 Supreme Court declares issuing of religious decrees (fatwas) to be a criminal offense. BNP returned to power following violence-marred elections.

2002 Privatization program begins.

Bank of England founded 1694.

Banks, Sir Joseph (1743–1820) British explorer and naturalist. He was a long-time president of the Royal Society and was notable for his promotion of science

Bannockburn ⚔ (1314). Victory by Scots, led by Robert Bruce over English forces.

Banshan culture (*var.* Panshan) Chinese Neolithic culture named after the site of Ban-shan in Gansu province, and known for its distinctive painted pottery, mostly large urns, produced c.2500–2000 BCE.

Bantu Linguistic group occupying much of the southern part of the African continent From their homeland in present-day Nigeria, the Bantu migrated south along eastern and western routes during the 2nd millennium BCE. They had reached present-day Zimbabwe by the 8th century CE.

Banu Al-aghlab *see* Aghlabids

BARBADOS

BARBADOS Situated to the northeast of Trinidad, Barbados is the most easterly of the West Indian Windward Islands. In the 16th century, the Portuguese were the first Europeans to reach the island, then inhabited by Arawak Indians. However, Barbados was not colonized until the 1620s, when British settlers arrived. Popularly referred to by its neighbors as "little England," Barbados now seeks to forge a new national identity for itself.

CHRONOLOGY

1620s The island is settled by Europeans, mainly English.

18th century The island becomes a powerful and prosperous sugar-producing colony with over 80,000 slaves.

1838 The abolition of slavery is a major factor precipitating an economic decline.

1951 Universal adult suffrage introduced.

1961–1966 Full internal self-government. Full independence from Britain.

1983 Supports and provides a base for the US invasion of Grenada.

1994–2003 The BLP wins three successive general elections.

Barbarians Name given by the Greeks to peoples whose language they did not understand. It was applied to many peoples who lived outside the "civilized" Graeco-Roman world, especially the Germanic tribes that ultimately inherited the western half of the Roman Empire in the 5th century CE. *p.102*

Barbarossa Code name for the German invasion of the USSR during World War II (summer–autumn 1941).

Barbarossa, Frederick *see* Frederick I, Holy Roman Emperor

Barents, Willem (c.1550–97) Dutch navigator who searched for a Northeast Passage to Asia. He discovered Bear Island and Spitzbergen and traveled beyond Novaya Zemlya, where he and his crew were the first recorded Europeans to winter in the Arctic.

barrow (*var.* tumulus, cairn) Neolithic and Bronze Age burial traditions included raising an earth mound over single or communal graves (where made of stone, known as a cairn) a practice characteristic of European and central and south Asian communities of the 3rd and 2nd millennia BCE. Barrows marked either inhumation or cremation burials, and sometimes also covered burial structures of wood, stone or megalithic chambers. They vary in shape, but are most commonly round or elongated ovals.

Barth, Heinrich (1821–65) German geographer and explorer of Africa. He traveled the Mediterranean coastal areas that are now part of Tunisia and Libya (1845–47) and published his observations in 1849.

Basil II (*aka* Basil the Bulgar Slayer 958–1025) Byzantine emperor. Sole ruler of the empire (976–1025). He extended Byzantine rule to the Balkans, Georgia, Armenia and Mesopotamia. His 15-year war with Bulgaria culminated in victory and earned him the nickname "Bulgar Slayer." *p.165*

Bass, George (1771–1803) English surgeon and sailor who surveyed coastal Australia with Matthew Flinders. In 1798 they established that a strait existed between Tasmania and the Australian mainland. This was named the Bass Strait.

Bataan ⚔ of World War II in the Pacific (Jan–Apr 1941) Japanese victory over Allied forces.

Batavia (*mod.* Jakarta) Administrative and commercial center of Dutch East Indies, founded in1619.

Bates, Henry (1825–92) English naturalist and scientific explorer, who spent 11 years in S America. On his travels in Brazil, he studied forms of mimicry, in which a defenseless organism bears a close resemblance to a noxious and conspicuous one. This form is called Batesian, in honor of its discoverer.

Baton Rouge ⚔ of American Revolutionary War (Sep 21 1779). Victory by Spanish forces led to Spain controlling the area for the next 20 years.

Batts, Thomas (died 1698) Explorer of N America. Searched for South Sea with Robert Fallam, in 1671, reaching the edge of the Mississippi watershed.

Batu (died 1255) Mongol leader, a grandson of Genghis Khan, who led the invasion of Europe (1236–42).

Bayezid I (*var.* Bayezit, Bajazet, c.1360–1403) Ottoman Sultan (reigned 1389–1403). Known as "the Thunderbolt," he conquered much of Anatolia and the Balkans, besieged Constantinople and invaded Hungary. He was defeated by Timur at the ⚔ of Ankara (1402).

Bayezit *see* Bayezid

Bayinnaung (died 1581) Ruler of the Toungoo Kingdom in Burma (reigned 1551–81). Captured the Siamese capital of Ayutthaya, subdued the Shan states, and ruled over the whole of Burma, except Arakan. His constant warfare, however, reduced his own province to desolation and his son, Nandabayin, completed the ruin of the Toungoo kingdom.

Beaker culture Neolithic culture which may have originated in the lower Rhine region, and spread through western Europe around 2600–2200 BCE. It is named for its distinctive geometrically decorated pottery; one variety, so called Bell Beaker pottery, being shaped like an inverted bell. These pots are often found deposited with weapons as grave goods, and are seen as signaling a move away from earlier traditions of communal burial towards ostentatious statements of individual status and wealth. The burials of this period are frequently single graves covered with an earthen mound or barrow.

Becan Maya fortified site (c.250 BCE).

Becket, Thomas St. (*var.* Thomas à Becket, 1118–70) Archbishop of Canterbury in reign of Henry II of England. Murdered as a result of his opposition to King's attempts to control affairs of the church. *p.192*

Beethoven, Ludwig van (1770–1827) Great German composer of the early Romantic period. *p.349*

Behaim, Martin German geographer, who constructed the oldest known surviving globe (c.1492).

Beijing (*var.* Peking) Capital of China. Several cities have stood on the site, the core of the present city being Genghis Khan's capital Cambaluc. *p.257*

BELARUS Formerly known as Belorussia (literally "white Russia"), Belarus is bordered by Lithuania and Latvia in the northwest, Ukraine in the south, and Poland and Russia in the west and east. Devastated in World War II, and with few resources other than agriculture, Belarus only reluctantly became independent of Moscow in 1991, and President Lukashenka has maintained close links with Russia. The Chernobyl nuclear disaster in Ukraine in 1986 has had lasting effects on the health of Belarussians and the environment.

CHRONOLOGY

1101 The area becomes an independent principality, having previously been part of the Kievan state.

1324 The area is incorporated into the Grand Duchy of Lithuania. Minsk becomes an important commercial and cultural center.

1386 The Grand Duchy of Lithuania unites with Poland. Belorussia becomes part of the Lithuanian-Polish commonwealth, participating in its wars against the Teutonic Order, the Russians, the Tatars, and the Turks.

1772–95 The partition of Poland leads to the region being taken over by Russia. Minsk is destroyed by Napoleon.

1835 Nicholas I decrees that Minsk become one of the few places where Jews can live.

1863 A Polish uprising against Russian rule is echoed in Belorussian lands, where it is led by Kastus Kalinowski. He is executed in 1864. The uprising's failure is followed by increased repression from the Czarist authorities. ▶

1882 Yanka Kupala, Belorussia's national poet, is born. The decade sees the birth of a revival in Belorussian literature and consciousness.

1905 January. The Russian Revolution of 1905 leads to a renewal of the Belorussian national movement. The revolutionary Hromada (community) Party demands autonomy for Belorussia, but wins little support.

1918 Belorussian Bolsheviks stage coup. Independence as Belorussian Soviet Socialist Republic (BSSR).

1919 Invaded by Poland.

1920 Minsk retaken by Red Army. Eastern Belorussia reestablished as Soviet Socialist Republic.

1921 Treaty of Riga – Western Belorussia incorporated into Poland.

1922 BSSR merges with Russian Federation to form USSR.

1929 Stalin implements collectivization of agriculture.

1939 Western Belorussia reincorporated into USSR when Soviet Red Army invades Poland.

1941–1944 Occupied by Germany during World War II.

1945 Founding member of UN (with Ukraine and USSR).

1965 K. T. Mazurau, Communist Party of Belorussia (PKB) leader, becomes first deputy chair of Soviet government.

1986 Radioactive fallout after Chernobyl accident affects 70% of country.

1988 Evidence revealed of mass executions (over 300,000) by Soviet military between 1937 and 1941 near Minsk. Popular outrage fuels formation of nationalist Belorussian Popular Front (BPF), with Zyanon Paznyak as president. PKB authorities crush demonstration.

1989 Belarussian adopted as republic's official language.

1990 PKB prevents BPF participating in elections to Supreme Soviet. BPF members join other opposition groups in Belarussian Democratic Bloc (BDB). BDB wins 25% of seats. PKB bows to opposition pressure and issues Declaration of the State Sovereignty of BSSR.

1991 83% vote in referendum to preserve union with USSR. April: Strikes against PKB and its economic policies. August. Independence declared. Republic of Belarus adopted as official name.

Stanislau Shushkevich elected chair of Supreme Soviet. December. Belarus, Russia, and Ukraine establish CIS.

1992 Supreme Soviet announces that Soviet nuclear weapons must be cleared from Belarus by 1999. Help promised from USA.

1993 Belarussian parliament ratifies START-I and nuclear nonproliferation treaties.

1994 New presidential constitution approved; Aleksandr Lukashenka defeats conservative prime minister Vyacheslav Kebich in elections. Monetary union (reentry into rouble zone) agreed with Russia.

1995 First fully fledged post-Soviet parliament elected.

1996 Union treaty with Russia. Referendum approves constitutional changes, thereby strengthening Lukashenka's powers.

1997 Belarus and Russia ratify union treaty and Charter.

1998 Western ambassadors withdrawn over eviction from embassies.

1999–2001 Further moves on union with Russia.

2000–2001 Disputed parliamentary elections; clampdown on PKB's political opponents.

2001 Lukashenka re-elected; observers label the election seriously flawed.

BELGIUM Located between Germany, France, and the Netherlands, Belgium has a short coastline on the North Sea. The south includes the forested Ardennes region, while the north is crisscrossed by canals. Belgium has been fought over many times in its history; it was occupied by Germany in both world wars. Tensions have existed between the Dutch-speaking Flemings and French-speaking Walloons since the country was created in 1830. These have been somewhat defused by Belgium's move to a federal political structure and the national consensus on the benefits of EU membership.

CHRONOLOGY

51 BCE The Romans complete the conquest of the Celtic and Germanic tribes inhabiting the area covering present-day Belgium; the region becomes part of the province of Gaul.

406–407 CE An invasion by Germanic tribes ends the Roman occupation.

481–511 CE Under Clovis, the Franks establish a kingdom centered in what is now southern Belgium and northern France; under his successors the Frankish kingdom expands to cover most of western Europe, reaching its apogee under Charlemagne (reigned 768–814 CE).

Late 9th century Following several divisions, western Belgium (the county of Flanders) becomes part of the West Frankish kingdom or France, while the rest of the country (the duchy of Lower Lorraine) becomes part of the East Frankish kingdom or Germany (later the Holy Roman Empire).

12th century Feudal fragmentation leads to the rise of six main regional states: the county of Flanders in the west, the duchy of Brabant in the center, the bishopric of Liège in the east, the county of Hainault in the southwest, and the duchy of Luxembourg in the southeast. The towns of Flanders and Brabant are among the most prosperous in Europe.

1384 Philip the Bold, Duke of Burgundy, inherits Flanders; over the next 60 years Burgundy acquires all the other important territories in the region except for Liège, thereby creating an unprecedented degree of unity within the Low Countries.

1477 The Burgundian territories pass to the House of Habsburg.

1555–56 On the abdication of Habsburg Emperor Charles V, the Austrian and Spanish Habsburg lines are separated and the Low Countries become a province of Spain.

1567 Resistance to Spanish rule, fueled in part by the rise of Protestantism, leads to a popular revolt led by sections of the nobility and the powerful merchant class.

1579 The southern provinces (broadly speaking present-day Belgium) form the Union of Arras, reaffirming loyalty to the King and to Catholicism; the northern provinces (the future Netherlands) declare their independence from Spain in 1581.

1585 The Dutch impose a blockade on Antwerp, marking the beginning of a long-term decline of the Southern Netherlands.

1648 The Peace of Westphalia reaffirms Spanish rule over the Southern Netherlands.

1713 Under the Treaty of Utrecht the Southern Netherlands are transferred to Austrian Habsburg rule.

1792–95 French and Austrian troops fight for control of the Austrian Netherlands; despite local demands for independence, the territory is annexed by France.

1814–1815 Congress of Vienna; European powers decide to merge Belgium with the Netherlands under King William I of Orange.

1830 Revolt against Dutch; declaration of independence.

1831 European powers instal Leopold Saxe Coburg as King of the Belgians

1865 Leopold II crowned king.

1885 Berlin Conference gives Leopold Congo basin as colony.

1914 German armies invade. Belgium occupied until 1918.

1921 Belgo-Luxembourg Economic Union formed. Belgian and Luxembourg currencies locked.

1932 Dutch language accorded equal official status with French.

1936 Belgium declares neutrality.

1940 Leopold III capitulates to Hitler. Belgium occupied till 1944.

1948 Customs union with Netherlands and Luxembourg (Benelux) formed.

1950 King wins referendum but rumors over his wartime collaboration persist. Abdicates in favor of his son, Baudouin.

1957 Signs Treaty of Rome as one of six founding members of EEC.

1992 Christian Democrat and Socialist government led by Jean-Luc Dehaene takes over federal government.

1993 Culmination of reforms creating federal state. Death of Baudouin. Succeeded by Albert II.

1995 Allegations of corruption and murder involving French-speaking PS force resignations of Walloon premier, federal deputy premier, and Willy Claes as NATO secretary-general.

1996 The murder and disappearance of young girls arouse fears of an international pedophile ring. Accusations of incompetence, even collusion, of authorities.

1998 Claes and 11 others found guilty of bribery.

1999 Belgium among first 11 countries to introduce euro. June, VLD/PRL wins general election. New coalition formed, including Greens for first time.

2001 Collapse of national airline Sabena.

2002 January, euro fully adopted – withdrawal of Belgian franc. May, legislation of euthanasia.

2003 Government re-elected; Greens lose seats, VB makes gains.

BELIZE Formerly British Honduras, Belize was the last Central American country to gain its independence, in 1981. It lies on the eastern shore of the Yucatan peninsula and shares a border with Mexico along the River Hondo. Belize is Central America's least populous country, and almost half of its land area is still forested. Its swampy coastal plains are protected from flooding by the world's second-largest barrier reef.

Chronology

1670 Spain, the colonial power in Central America, recognizes certain British rights in the uninhabited area then bordered by the Sarstoon river, after unsuccessful attempts to expel timber cutters who settled there with their slaves earlier in the century.

1798 Spain, which continues to claim sovereignty, is defeated at the battle of St. George's Cay.

1802 British sovereignty over the colony is recognized by the Peace of Amiens.

1821 Guatemala claims sovereignty over the territory.

1862 The area becomes a British Crown Colony known as British Honduras.

1919 Demands for more political rights by black Belizeans returning from World War I.

1936 New constitution with limited franchise introduced.

1950 PUP formed. Voting age qualification for women reduced from 30 to 21.

1954 Full adult suffrage.

1972 Guatemala threatens invasion. Britain sends troops.

1981 Full independence.

1998 PUP wins crushing general election victory.

2000 Guatemala revives claim to half of Belize.

2001 Hurricane Iris hits Belize.

2003 PUP wins second term.

Bell, Alexander Graham (1847–1922) US inventor. Patented his design for the telephone in 1876. Later invented the photophone and the gramophone and founded the journal *Science* in 1883. He later concentrated on aeronautical design.

Bellingshausen, Thaddeus (*var.* Faddey Faddeyvich Bellinsgauzen, 1778–1852) Russian naval officer. Made circumnavigation of Antarctica 1820–21 and is credited with the first sighting of the continent. He discovered Peter I and Alexander I islands.

Belorussia *see* Belarus

Bemis Heights ✕ of American Revolutionary War (Oct 7 1777). British victory.

Benalcázar, Sebastián (c.1495–1551) Spanish conquistador. A member of Francisco Pizarro's expedition to Peru, he conquered the northern Inca capital of Quito in 1533.

Benedict, St. (c.480–c.547) Italian founder of Western monasticism. Established the monastery on Monte Cassino near Naples, Italy. The Benedictine Rule served as the basis of Christian monastic organization.

BENIN Benin stretches north from the west African coast, with a 100-km (60-mile) shoreline on the Bight of Benin. Formerly the kingdom of Dahomey, Benin was under French colonial rule, becoming part of French West Africa, until independence in 1960. In 1990 Benin was a pioneer of multipartyism in Africa, ending 17 years of one-party Marxist-Leninist rule. Benin's economy is based on well-diversified agriculture.

Chronology

15th century The north of the country falls under the control of the Songhai empire.

16th century Portuguese seafarers commence trade with coastal rulers.

▶

◄

Porto Novo and Ouidah become the primary commercial ports.

17th century The Dan-Homey kingdom becomes a primary slaving region of West Africa, controlling most sales to European traders.

19th century After the abolition of the slave trade, palm oil becomes the main export.

1863 Porto Novo becomes a French protectorate.

1890–92 Armed conflict between troops of Dan-Homey and France, ending with French victory.

1857 French establish trading post at Grand-Popo.

1889 French defeat King Behanzin.

1892 French protectorate.

1901 Present borders (then known as Dahomey) fixed by France.

1904 Part of French West Africa.

1960 Full independence.

1975 Renamed Benin.

1989 Marxism-Leninism abandoned as official ideology.

1996 Former ruler Kérékou defeats Soglo in controversial election.

2001 Kérékou reelected to presidency amid claims of electoral fraud.

Benin Small forest kingdom at the mouth of the mouth of the Benin river (in present-day Nigeria) established c.1200 CE. It was remarkable for its metalwork, especially bronze statuettes. It was conquered by the British in the 1890s. *p.268, p.381*

Bennington ⚔ of American Revolutionary War (Oct 15 1777). American victory.

Benz, Karl Friedrich (1844–1929) German mechanical engineer who designed and in 1885 built the world's first practical automobile to be powered by an internal-combustion engine.

Berber Pre-Arab inhabitants of North Africa. The Berbers were scattered in tribes across Morocco, Algeria, Tunisia, Libya, and Egypt and tended to be concentrated in the mountain and desert regions. They are still numerous in Algeria and Morocco.

Bering, Vitus (1681–1741) Danish navigator in the service of Czar Peter the Great. Ordered in 1724 to find whether Asia and N America were connected by land or whether there was water between them. He set sail in 1728 and

passed through the strait which bears his name into the Pacific, but bad weather prevented him seeing North America. Given command in 1733 of the Great Northern Expedition during which much of Siberia's Arctic coast was mapped. Died of scurvy on Bering Island. The Bering Sea is also named after him.

Beringia Name given to the land bridge which linked Asia to N America during the last Ice Age.

Berlin Capital of reunited Germany since 1991. It became the seat of the Electors of Brandenburg in the 15th century and capital of the German empire in 1871. However, after World War II the city was divided between E and W Germany, become a potent symbol of the Cold War.

Berlin ⚔ of World War II (May 1945). Scene of final German resistance to invading Soviet forces.

Berlin Airlift (Jun–Sep 1949) Maintenance, under siege conditions, of Western sector of occupied Berlin during Soviet blockade and formal partition of occupied Germany into E and W Germany. *See also* Berlin Blockade

Berlin Blockade (1948–49) International crisis where Soviet forces in eastern Germany began a blockade of transport and communications between Berlin and the West in an attempt to force the Western Allies to abandon their post-World War II jurisdictions in the city.

Berlin Congress (Jun 13–Jul 13 1878). Diplomatic meeting of the major European powers at which the Treaty of San Stefano which concluded the Russo-Turkish War (1877–78) was replaced by the Treaty of Berlin. Officially convened by the Austrian foreign minister, Count Gyula Andrassy, the congress met in Berlin on June 13.

Berlin Conference on Africa (Nov 1884–Feb 1885). Negotiations at Berlin at which the major European nations met to discuss European involvement in Central Africa.

Berlin Wall (*var. Ger.* Berliner Mauer) Barrier that surrounded West Berlin and prevented access to East Berlin and adjacent areas of East Germany from 1961–89. In the years between 1949 and 1961, about 2.5 million East Germans had fled from East to West Germany.

Bernard of Clairvaux, St. (1090–1153) French Cistercian monk and religious

reformer. Became first abbot of new monastery of Clairvaux, in Champagne, and later founded more than 70 monasteries. Drew up the statutes of the Knights Templars in 1128, and secured recognition from Pope Innocent II for the Cistercian order. He was canonized in 1174.

Bessemer, Sir Henry (1813–98) British inventor and engineer, knighted in 1879, who developed the first process for manufacturing steel inexpensively (1856), leading to the development of the Bessemer converter.

BHUTAN Perched in the Himalayas between India and China, Bhutan is 70% forested. The land rises from the low, tropical southern strip, through the fertile central valleys, to the high Himalayas, inhabited by semi-nomadic yak herders. Formally a Buddhist state where power is shared by the king and government, Bhutan began modernizing in the 1960s, but has chosen to do so gradually, and remains largely closed to the outside world.

CHRONOLOGY

1656 Unification of the state by Prince-Abbot Shabdrung Ngawang Namgyal.

1731 Tibet imposes suzerainty on Bhutan and this relationship is passed on in turn to Tibet's own overlord, China.

1770s–80s British involvement in Bhutan begins with missions sent by Warren Hastings after conflict between Bhutan and Cooch Bihar.

1864 British mission led by Ashley Eden results in a border war with Britain which leaves Bhutan without its traditional rights over border areas with Bengal and Assam.

1907 Monarchy established.

1949 Independence.

1953 National Assembly inaugurated.

1968 King forms first cabinet.

1971 Joins UN.

1990 Ethnic Nepalese launch campaign for minority rights.

1998 King proposes to reform government.

1999 First TV service inaugurated.

Biafra Breakaway province of Nigeria, where civil war (1967–70) led to a disastrous famine.

Bible Holy book of the Christian religion. Authoritative Latin version completed by St. Jerome in 404 CE. *p.101*

Bicycle Invention perfected in the late 19th century, a great boon to the working classes in the industrial cities of Europe and N America. *p.376*

Big game hunters The Mesolithic hunters who were probably responsible for the extinction of the megafauna (mammoths and other large mammals) in N America at the end of the last Ice Age. *p.15*

"Big Three" The three major Allied leaders during World War II: Roosevelt (US), Churchill (UK), and Stalin (USSR).

Biological diffusion The exchange of plants, animals, and disease organisms between the Old and New Worlds after European voyages of discovery and conquest in the 15th and 16th centuries. *p.278*

Bismarck Archipelago Group of islands off NE coast of New Guinea. Site of Lapita pottery c.1600 BCE.

Bismarck, Otto von (1815–98) German statesman, chief minister of Prussia (1862–90) and architect of the German empire. Prussia's domination of mainland Europe was achieved by means of three wars: with Denmark (1864) over Schleswig-Holstein; with Austria and other German states (1866); and the Franco-Prussian War (1870–71). With the formation of the German Empire in 1871, he became its first Chancellor. During his years in power, he ruled autocratically – he was known as the "Iron Chancellor" – reforming the Prussian army and carrying out extensive administrative reforms for the new empire.

Black Death Familiar name given to epidemic of bubonic plague that swept across Eurasia in the 14th century, which is estimated to have killed between one-third and one-half of the population of Europe. The name was first used during the 19th century. *p.235*
See also bubonic plague, plague

Black Huns *see* Huns

Black Prince *see* Edward, Prince of Wales

blackbirding Euphemism for slave-raiding in the Pacific in the 19th century. Gangs of Europeans would land on Pacific islands and forcibly "recruit" laborers for the sugar-cane plantations of Queensland.

Blackstock ⚔ of American Revolutionary War (Nov 20 1780). American victory.

Blaeu, William and Joan 17th-century Dutch cartographers

Blanche of Castile (1188–1252) Wife of Louis VIII of France. Ruled France during the minority of her son, Louis IX. *p.210*

Blenheim ⚔ of War of Spanish Succession (1704). French defeated by Marlborough.

Blitz, the Strategic bombing campaign of World War II launched by Germany against London and other industrial centers in Britain, 1940.

Blitzkrieg (*var.* Lightning War) Term used to describe German military strategy during World War II, involving combined operations of fast-moving armoured thrusts supported by tactical air power and reinforced by infantry.

Blunt, Wilfred Scawen (1840–1922) British author, poet, diplomat, and explorer. In 1879, accompanied by his wife Anne, he traveled across the Arabian Peninsula.

Boer (*var.* Dut. Husbandman, or farmer). South African of Dutch or Huguenot descent, especially one of the early settlers of the Transvaal and the Orange Free State.

Boer War (1899–1902) Conflict in S Africa between Britain and the settlers of Dutch origin who had set up the independent republics of Transvaal and Orange Free State. The Boer guerrillas proved very effective in their campaigns against the British and Imperial forces sent to crush them, but were finally forced to surrender and their lands, along with their considerable mineral wealth, were incorporated in the British Empire. *p.382*

Bohemia Historic region, now part of the Czech Republic. In the late Middle Ages Bohemia was a powerful independent kingdom, especially under Charles I of the Luxembourg dynasty, who was elected Holy Roman Emperor (as Charles IV) and made Prague the center of the empire. *p.237*

Bojador, Cape Rounded by Gil Eanes, Portuguese explorer in 1434.

Bolívar, Simón (1783–1830) The most celebrated of the liberators of Spanish S America. Having liberated Venezuela in 1813, Bolívar had to fight against an army sent from Spain under General Morillo. He fled the country, but returned to liberate Venezuela again in 1818. *p.355*

BOLIVIA Bolivia lies landlocked high in central South America and is one of the continent's poorest nations. The Aymara civilization was conquered by the Incas in the late 1400s. Fifty years later, the Incas were defeated by the conquistadors and Upper Peru, as it became, was governed by Spain from Lima. Today over half the population lives on the altiplano, the windswept plateau between two ranges of the Andes, 3500 m (11,500 feet) above sea level. La Paz, the highest capital in the world, has spawned a neighboring large twin, El Alto. Bolivia has the world's highest golf course, ski run, and soccer stadium. The eastern lowland regions are tropical and underdeveloped but are rapidly being colonized.

CHRONOLOGY

1545 Cerro Rico, the Silver Mountain, discovered at Potosí. Provides Spain with vast wealth.

1776 Upper Peru becomes part of Viceroyalty of Río de la Plata centered on Buenos Aires.

1809 Simón Bolívar inspires first revolutionary uprisings in Latin America at Chuquisaca (Sucre), La Paz, and Cochabamba, but they fail.

1824 Spaniards suffer final defeat by Bolívar's general, José de Sucre.

1825 Independence.

1836–1839 Union with Peru fails. Internal disorder.

1864–1871 Ruthless rule of Mariano Melgarejo. Three Amerindian revolts over seizure of ancestral lands.

1879–1883 War of the Pacific, won by Chile. Bolivia left landlocked.

1880–1930 Period of stable governments. Exports from revived mining industry bring prosperity.

1903 Acre province ceded to Brazil.

1914 Republican Party founded.

1920 Amerindian rebellion.

1923 Miners bloodily suppressed.

1932–1935 Chaco War with Paraguay. Bolivia loses three-quarters of Chaco. Rise of radicalism and labor movement.

1951 Víctor Paz Estenssoro of MNR elected president. Military coup.

1952 Revolution. Paz Estenssoro and MNR brought back. Land reforms improve Amerindians' status.

▶

Education reforms, universal suffrage, tin mines nationalized.

1964 Military takes over in coup.

1967 Che Guevara killed while trying to mobilize Bolivian workers.

1969–1979 Military regimes rule with increasing severity. 1979 coup fails. Interim civilian rule.

1980 Military takes over again.

1982 President-elect Siles Zuazo finally heads leftist civilian MIR government. Inflation 24,000%.

1985 Paz Estenssoro's MNR wins elections. Austerity measures. Annual inflation down to 20%.

1986 Tin market collapses. 21,000 miners sacked.

1989 MIR takes power after close-run elections. President Paz Zamora makes pact with 1970s dictator General Hugo Banzer, leader of ADN.

1990 1.6 million hectares (4 million acres) of rainforest recognized as Amerindian territory.

1993 MNR voted back to power.

1997 Banzer wins largest proportion of vote in presidential elections.

1999 Opposition demands inquiry into Banzer's role in regional military repression in 1970s.

2000 Government's water supply privatization plans and coca eradication provoke uprisings by peasants and coca growers.

2002 MNR wins elections. Sánchez de Lozda returns as president.

2003 Violent popular demonstrations. Sánchez de Lozada oustedL Carlos Mesa president.

Bologna University Considered Europe's first university, founded in 1088. *p.211*

Bolsheviks Members of the more radical wing of the Russian Social Democratic Workers' Party who seized power in Russia in the October revolution of 1917. In 1918 they adopted the name "communists."

Bonpland, Aimé (1773–1858). French botanist who traveled in South America (1799–1804), discovering 6000 new species of plants.

Boone, Daniel (1735–1820) US frontiersman. Traveled to Kentucky through the Cumberland Gap in the Appalachian Mountains in 1767. Later

traced the Wilderness Road and founded the town of Boonesboro on the Kentucky river. His explorations were instrumental in encouraging settlement west of the eastern mountains of the US. Booneville ⚔ of American Civil War (17 Jun 1861). Union victory. *p.330*

Bornu empire Kingdom and emirate of north eastern Nigeria. Originally a province of the Kanem Empire until the latter's territory was reduced to that of Bornu by c.1380. By the early 16th century Bornu had recaptured Kanem and made it a protectorate. The re-amalgamated Kanem-Bornu reached its height in the reign of Mai Idris Alawma (reigned 1571–1603).

Borobudur Buddhist temple on Java built c.778–850 CE. *p.136*

Borodino ⚔ of Napoleonic Wars (Sep 7 1812). Defeated Russians lose 50,000 troops.

Boshin War (1868–69) Restored the Meiji ("enlightened rule") emperor of Japan, inaugurating a period of political and social reform.

Bosnia *see* Bosnia & Herzegovina

BOSNIA & HERZEGOVINA

Bosnia is a mountainous country bordered by Croatia and Yugoslavia. A corridor south of Mostar provides access to the Adriatic Sea at Neum. Between 1945 and 1990, the Yugoslavian regime promoted coexistence between Muslims, Croats, and Serbs, but, with the dissolution of Yugoslavia, the ethnic populations fought over Bosnia. Around 250,000 died, more than two million were displaced, and cities were destroyed before the 1995 Dayton peace accord was signed.

CHRONOLOGY

168 BCE The Romans subjugate Illyria, including territory of modern-day Bosnia-Herzegovina. After the decline of the Western Roman Empire the area is conquered, in turn, by the Eastern Roman Empire (the Byzantines), the Huns and Bulgars, and the Avars who bring Slavs to the area as vassals.

1180 Kulin, a member of the heretical Christian Bogomils, rules a prosperous Bosnia, despite a Catholic crusade, waged

by Hungary on the Church's behalf, against Bogomilism in the Balkans.

1254 Bela IV asserts the authority of the Hungaro-Croatian kings over Bosnia's rulers.

1322 Stephen Kotromanic becomes ruler of a Bosnia subject to Hungary. He extends the territory into what is now Herzegovina and had hitherto been independent.

1353 Kotromanic's nephew Tvrtko succeeds his uncle and, with Serbia in decline, increases Bosnia's territory and in 1390 is crowned King of Serbia, Bosnia, Croatia and the coast, despite failing to prevent an Ottoman Turkish victory over the Serbs at Kosovo in 1389.

1482 Ottomans conquer Bosnia and Herzegovina (which takes its name from the title *herceg* (duke) assumed by its ruler Stevan Vukcic in 1448). Significant sections of the population convert to Islam. Bosnia becomes a key outpost for the Turks in their European wars.

1697 The Hungarian prince Eugene captures Sarajevo from Turks. Under the Treaty of Karlowitz in 1699 Bosnia is divided between the Ottoman and Habsburg empires.

1831 Hussein Kapetan, the "Dragon of Bosnia," launches a holy war against Turks. After occupying territory in Macedonia and Bulgaria, he is defeated and exiled.

1875 An insurrection against Turkish rule in Herzegovina spreads to Bosnia and is supported by Serbs and Montenegrins. Serbia, which has long aspired to unification with Bosnia, declares war on Turks, but is swiftly defeated. Austria-Hungary occupies Bosnia-Herzegovina and the Sandzak of Novy Pazar, land separating Serbia from Montenegro, "in the name of the Sultan" after Turkey's defeat in the Russo-Turkish war of 1877 and 1878. The new rulers prove unable to reduce tensions between Bosnia's Catholic, Orthodox, and Muslim communities.

1908 Austria-Hungary annexes Bosnia-Herzegovina, with tacit agreement from Russia, weakened by the 1905 Revolution and war with Japan. The Sandzak is restored to the Ottoman Empire. Serbia protests but, without Russian support, can do nothing and the annexation is recognized by major powers in April 1909.

1914 June 28. Gavrilo Princip, a Bosnian Serbian revolutionary of the Black Hand secret society, assassinates the Austrian Archduke Franz Ferdinand, heir to the Emperor Franz-Josef, and his wife in Sarajevo. An Austrian ultimatum is rejected by Serbia and the war between them spreads across Europe.

1918 National committee is formed in Sarajevo after the defeat of the Central Powers and Bosnia is unites with Serbia in Kingdom of Serbs, Croats, and Slovenes. A period of democracy follows, marred by ethnic disputes.

1929 Dictatorship imposed by King Alexander in attempt to end nationalism. The country is renamed Yugoslavia.

1941 Germany invades Yugoslavia. Bosnia and Herzegovina assigned to the State of Croatia, under the rule of the fascist Pavelic. Rival partisan groups form to offer resistance; the Serbian royalist Chetniks and the communist partisans under Josef Broz Tito, leader of the Communist Party of Yugoslavia, who forms a provisional government in 1943.

1945 Tito's provisional government abolishes the monarchy and proclaims the Federative People's Republic of Yugoslavia, in which Bosnia and Herzegovina is a constituent republic. In the 1960s, the Muslim population is deemed to constitute a "nation."

1972 Trials of nationalists begin in Sarajevo in the wake of an increase in ethnic tension throughout Yugoslavia.

1980 Tito dies and is replaced by collective leaderships of the government and party who are unable to halt economic decline. In Bosnia-Herzegovina the local regime is characterized by corruption and authoritarianism.

1990 Nationalists defeat communists in multiparty elections.

1991 Parliament announces republican sovereignty.

1992 EU and USA recognize Bosnia. Serbs declare "Serbian Republic." Civil war begins.

1995 NATO air strikes on Serbs; US-brokered Dayton peace accord.

1996 NATO-led implementation of peace accord. First international war crimes trial since 1945 opens in The Hague. Elections held under Dayton accord.

1998–2000 Elections; dwindling support for nationalist parties.

2001 Ethnic Croats briefly establish autonomy in Herzegovina (in south).

2002 Elections: renewed support for nationalist parties.

Boston Massacre (Mar 5 1770) The culmination of a series of confrontations between British troops and American colonists in Boston, Massachusetts: five people killed when troops open fire on a crowd. The incident becomes a focus for British unpopularity and was depicted by the propagandist, Samuel Adams as a battle for American liberty.

Botany Bay British settlement in Australia (1788).

BOTSWANA Arid and landlocked, Botswana's central plateau separates the populous eastern grasslands from the Kalahari desert and the swamps of the Okavango delta in the west. From 1600, Tswana migrations slowly displaced the original San people. In 1895, at local request, the UK set up the Bechuanaland Protectorate to preempt annexation by South Africa. Although Botswana is a multiparty democracy, the Botswana Democratic Party has won every election since independence. Diamonds provide Botswana with a prosperous economy, but rain is an even more precious resource, honored in the name of the currency, the pula.

CHRONOLOGY

1813 The London Missionary Society establish a mission, the first permanent settlements having been established by the Kwena (a Tswana people), who had come from South Africa around one hundred years earlier.

1885 January 27. Britain establishes the Bechuanaland Protectorate.

1900 The administration passes to the High Commissioner for Basutoland, Bechuanaland, and Swaziland. There is minimal interference in tribal affairs and only limited sales of land to white settlers and companies.

1920 An elected European advisory council and a separate nominated African advisory council are formed. The latter serves as a forum for African opposition to South African pressure for incorporation.

1950 A joint advisory council is formed.

1958 A legislative council is conceded.

1948 Incorporation into South Africa is effectively ruled out when the National Party comes to power there. However, South Africa by now dominates the economy, which is little more than a labour reserve for South African mines and farms.

1950 As a result of South African pressure, Seretse Khama is exiled by the UK colonial administration following his marriage to a white Englishwoman. He is only allowed to return six years later on condition that he renounces the chieftainship of the Bamangwato. However, no other chief is appointed.

1965 BDP, led by Sir Seretse Khama, wins first general election and all subsequent general elections.

1966 Independence declared

1980 Vice President Quett (later Ketumile) Masire succeeds the late Sir Seretse as president.

1985–1986 South African raids.

1992–1993 Strikes and corruption scandals prompt resignations of senior BDP figures.

1994 BDP support eroded in general election.

1998 Vice President Festus Mogae succeeds Masire as president.

2001–2002 Botswana has world's highest rate of adult AIDS sufferers.

Bottego, Vittorio 19th-century Italian explorer of Ethiopia (1892–97).

Botticelli, Sandro (f/n Alessandro di Mariano Filipepi, 1444–1510) Leading painter of the Italian Renaissance. *p.262*

Bougainville, Louis Antoine de (1729–1811) French soldier and explorer. Bougainville's expedition of 1776–79 was the first French circumnavigation of the globe. His most important discoveries were in the Pacific and his glowing descriptions of Tahiti inspired French (and other European) interest in this Polynesian "Garden of Eden."

Boulton, Matthew (1728–1809) English manufacturer and engineer who financed and introduced James Watt's steam engine.

Bourbon dynasty (1589–1830) French royal dynasty which began with the accession of Henry of Bourbon, king of Navarre and a Calvinist. In the face of opposition by French Catholics, he renounced Calvinism in 1593, and became King Henry IV. The Bourbon dynasty reached its zenith with Louis XIV (1638–1715), who reigned for over 50 years as the personification of absolute power. The Bourbons continued to hold the throne of France until the French Revolution (1791) and again from 1814–30. *See also* France

Boxer Rebellion (1900–01) Chinese popular uprising aimed at driving out all foreign traders, diplomats and missionaries. *p.390*

Boyacá ⚔ of wars of S American liberation. Colombia liberated by Bolívár.

Braddock, General Edward (1675–1755) Led British attack against France in French Indian Wars in America. He was mortally wounded in 1755 on the way to Fort Duquesne (Pittsburgh).

Braganza, House of (*var. Port.* Bragança) Ruling dynasty of Portugal (1640–1910) and of the empire of Brazil (1822–89).

Brahmans Hindus of the higher caste, traditionally assigned to the priesthood.

Brandenburg Brandenburg was a margravate (border county) of the Holy Roman Empire. The margraves of Brandenburg became electors in 1415. Their territory expanded over the centuries to include Prussia and in 1701, the Elector of Brandenburg was granted the title king of Prussia. *p.329*

Brandywine ⚔ of American Revolutionary War (Sep 11 1777) British victory.

BRAZIL The largest country in South America, Brazil became independent of Portugal in 1822. Today, it is renowned as the site of the world's largest tropical rainforest, the threat to which led to the UN's first international environment conference, held in Rio de Janeiro in 1992. Covering one-third of Brazil's total land area, the rainforest grows around the massive Amazon River and its delta. Apart from the basin of the River Plate to the south, the rest of the country consists of highlands. The mountainous northeast is part forested and part desert. Brazil is the world's leading coffee producer and also has rich reserves of gold, diamonds, oil, and iron ore. Cattle-ranching is an expanding industry. The city of São Paulo is the world's fourth-biggest conurbation, with 18 million inhabitants. *p.317*

CHRONOLOGY

1494 The Treaty of Tordesillas between Portugal and Spain grants Portugal roughly the eastern half of South America.

1500 Pedro Alvares Cabral reaches the Brazilian coast.

1549 A Captain-General is sent out to establish a centralized government at Bahia. He is accompanied by Jesuits who play a key role in the unification of the colony and the exploration of the interior.

1630–54 The Dutch control a large sugar-growing region in the northeast.

1630–95 Free slave settlements are established which oppose the colonialists, particularly at Palmares in the north under African leader Zumbi.

1763 Rio de Janeiro becomes capital.

1788 Inconfidência rebellion, led by Tiradentes, fails.

1807 French invade Portugal. King João VI flees to Brazil with British naval escort. In return, Brazil's ports opened to foreign trade.

1821 King returns to Portugal. Son Pedro made regent of Brazil.

1822 Pedro I declares independence and is made Emperor of Brazil.

1828 Brazil loses Uruguay.

1831 Military revolt after war with Argentina (1825–1828). Emperor abdicates. Five-year-old son succeeds him as Pedro II.

1835–1845 Rio Grande secedes.

1865–1870 Brazil wins war of Triple Alliance with Argentina and Uruguay against Paraguay.

1888 Pedro II abolishes slavery; landowners and military turn against him.

1889 First Republic established. Emperor goes into exile in Paris. Increasing prosperity as result of international demand for coffee.

1891 Federal constitution established.

1914–1918 World War I causes coffee exports to slump.

1920s Working-class and intellectual movements call for end to oligarchic rule.

1930 Coffee prices collapse. Revolt led by Dr. Getúlio Vargas, the "Father of the Poor," who becomes president. Fast industrial growth.

1937 Vargas's position as benevolent dictator formalized in "New State," based on fascist model.

1942 Declares war on Germany.

1945 Vargas forced out by military.

1950 Vargas reelected president.

1954 US opposes Vargas's socialist policies. The right, backed by the military, demand his resignation. Commits suicide.

1956–1960 President Juscelino Kubitschek, backed by Brazilian Labor Party (PTB), attracts foreign investment for new industries, especially from USA.

1960–1961 Conservative Jânio da Silva Quadros president. Tries to break dependence on US trade.

1961 Brasília, built in three years, becomes new capital. PTB leader, João Goulart, elected president.

1961–1964 President's powers briefly curtailed as right wing reacts to presidential policies.

1964 Bloodless military coup under army chief Gen. Castelo Branco.

1965 Branco assumes dictatorship; bans existing political parties, but creates two official new ones. He is followed by a succession of military rulers. Fast-track economic development, the Brazilian Miracle, is counterbalanced by ruthless suppression of left-wing activists.

1974 World oil crisis marks end of economic boom. Brazil's foreign debt now largest in world.

1979 More political parties allowed.

1980 Huge migrations into Rondônia state begin.

1985 Civilian senator Tancredo Neves wins presidential elections as candidate of new liberal alliance, but dies before taking office. Illiterate adults get the vote.

1987 Gold found on Yanomami lands in Roraima state; illegal diggers rush in by the thousand.

1988 New constitution promises massive social spending but fails to address land reform. Chico Mendes, union leader and environmentalist, murdered.

1989 Brazil's first environmental protection plan drawn up. Yearly inflation reaches

1000%. Fernando Collor de Mello wins first fully democratic presidential elections.

1992 Earth Summit in Rio. Collor de Mello resigns and is impeached for corruption.

1994–1995 Plan Real ends hyperinflation. Congress resists constitutional reforms, but passes key privatizations of state monopolies.

1998–1999 Fernando Henrique Cardoso, in power since 1995, reelected president. Real devalued in economic crisis.

2000 Economy recovers. Ruling parties divide over elections of heads of Congress.

2003 Lula da Silva takes office as president.

Brazza, Pierre Savorgnan de (1852–1905) Italian-born French explorer and colonial administrator who founded the French Congo, and explored Gabon. He also founded the city of Brazzaville.

Breda ⚔ of Dutch Revolt (1590). Dutch victory over Spain.

Breitenfeld ⚔ of Thirty Years' War (1631). Swedish protestant forces defeat of Habsburg emperor Frederick II and the Catholic League.

Brest Litovsk, Treaty of (Mar 1918). The peace treaty which ended conflict between Russia and the Central Powers in World War I. The independence of Poland, Finland, Georgia, the Baltic states, and Ukraine was recognized by Russia. The treaty was voided by the Armistice later that year.

Brétigny, Treaty of (1360). Treaty signed by England and France at Brétigny which concluded the first phase of the Hundred Years' War. Territory, including Aquitaine, was granted to Edward III of England, with the understanding that he renounced his claim to the French throne.

Briar Creek ⚔ of American Revolutionary War (Mar 3 1779). British victory.

Britain *see* Great Britain, England, Wales, Scotland, Ireland, United Kingdom

Britain, Battle of Air ⚔ of World War II (Jul–Oct 1940) Prolonged struggle for air superiority over English Channel and southern England in which the RAF halted German Luftwaffe bombing raids on Britain (the Blitz) and averted a planned German invasion of Britain.

British East India Company *see* English East India Company

British South Africa Company Mercantile company, based in London, that was incorporated in 1889 under a royal charter at the instigation of Cecil Rhodes, with the object of acquiring and exercising commercial and administrative rights in south-central Africa.

Bronze Age Following the Paleolithic and Neolithic ages the Bronze Age was the third phase in the development of material culture among the ancient peoples of Europe, Asia, and the Middle East. The term also denotes the first period in which metal was used. The date at which the age began varied with regions; in Greece and China, for example, the Bronze Age began before 3000 BCE, whereas in Britain it did not start until about 1900 BCE. *p.29*

Broz, Josip *see* Tito, Marshall

Bruce, James (1730–94) Scottish explorer who whilst traveling in Ethiopia, reached the headstream of the Blue Nile in 1772, which was then thought to be the source of the Nile.

Bruce, Robert *see* Robert I "the Bruce"

BRUNEI Lying on the northwestern coast of the island of Borneo, Brunei is divided in two by a strip of the surrounding Malaysian state of Sarawak. The interior is mostly rainforest. Independent from the UK since 1984, Brunei is ruled by decree of the sultan. It is undergoing increasing Islamicization. Oil and gas reserves have brought one of the world's highest standards of living.

CHRONOLOGY

6th century CE Extensive trade links develop between Brunei and China.

13th century Islam arrives in Brunei.

13th–15th century Brunei is brought under the control of the Javanese Majapahit empire.

1521 At the time of the Magellan expedition's visit to Brunei Sultan Bolkiah controls most of Borneo and the Sulu Archipelago.

1841 After a revolt against the Sultan he cedes Sarawak to the British soldier who had helped to crush the uprising, the "white raja" James Brooke.

1877 The Sultan allows British merchants to take control of Sabah, later to come under the rule of the North Borneo Company.

1888 Brunei is declared a British protectorate.

1929 Oil extraction begins.

1959 First constitution enshrines Islam as state religion. Internal self-government.

1962 Prodemocracy rebellion. State of emergency; sultan rules by decree.

1984 Independence from Britain. Brunei joins ASEAN.

1990 Ideology of "Malay Muslim Monarchy" introduced.

1991 Imports of alcohol banned.

1992 Joins Non-Aligned Movement.

1998 Sultan's son, Prince Al-Muhtadee Billah, made crown prince.

2004 Legislature reconvened.

Brunel, Isambard Kingdom (1806–59) British civil and mechanical engineer who designed the *Great Western*, the first transatlantic steamer in 1838.

Brusilov Offensive (Jun–Aug 1916) Major Russian offensive against Austria-Hungary during World War I, led by General Aleksey Alekseyevich Brusilov (1853–1926).

Brutus, Lucius Junius Legendary figure of the 6th century BCE, believed to have ousted the despotic Etruscan king Lucius Tarquinius Superbus from Rome in 509 and then to have founded the Roman Republic.

bubonic plague Bacterial disease spread to humans via rat fleas, and still endemic in parts of Asia. Infection results in delirium, fever, and the formation of large buboes. There were several major plague epidemics during the Middle Ages; the most devastating was the Black Death of the mid-14th century. *See also* Black Death

Bucephala ⚔ of Alexander the Great's campaigns in Asia (326 BCE). Alexander's troops refused to go any further east.

Buckland, Revd William (1784–1856) English geologist and clergyman who attempted to relate geology to the biblical description of the creation. In 1845 he became Dean of Westminster.

Buddha (*aka* Siddartha Gautama, "The Enlightened One," c.563–c.483 BCE) Founder of the world religion of Buddhism. Born the son of a nobleman of the Hindu Kshatriya castle. When aged about 30, he abandoned earthly ambitions to pursue self-enlightenment.

Traditionally, he attained this sat under a tree at Bodh Gaya. He spent the next 40 years teaching and gaining disciples and followers. Died at Kushinagara.

Buddhism Major religion of S and E Asia founded by Siddhartha Gautama. Maintains that sorrow and suffering are inherent in life and one can be released from them by ridding oneself of desire and self-delusion.
Bronze statue of Buddha, Thailand *p.122*
Buddhism in Japan *p.135*

Buena Vista ⚔ of US-Mexican War (1847). US victory.

Buenos Aires Capital of Argentina. The Spanish made a first attempt at settlement on the River Plate in 1535 but were driven away by the local Indians. The city was refounded in 1580 and in 1776 became the capital of the newly founded Viceroyalty of Río de la Plata.

BULGARIA Located in southeastern Europe, Bulgaria is a mainly mountainous country. The River Danube forms the northern border, while the popular resorts of the Black Sea lie to the east. The most populated areas are around Sofia in the west, Plovdiv in the south, and along the Danube plain. Bulgaria was ruled by the Turks from 1396 until 1878. In 1908, it became an independent kingdom and was under communist rule from 1947, with Todor Zhivkov in power from 1954 to 1989. The 1990s brought political instability as the country adjusted to democracy and economic reconstruction.

CHRONOLOGY

681 CE Byzantium cedes the territories north of the Balkan ridge to Khan Asparuh and the first Bulgarian state, with its capital at Pliska, emerges, peopled by Bulgars, tribes of Slavic and Turkic origin who have settled in the region over the preceding 200 years.

865 CE During the reign of Boris I Bulgaria accepts Christianity; the church follows the Slavonic liturgy, introduced by disciples of Cyril and Methodius. An expansion of the kingdom under Boris's son Simeon, crowned in 913, is accompanied by a flourishing in the arts.

1242 A new golden age during which the Bulgarian state again expands to the dimensions of Simeon's empire (with its capital at Tarnovo) is ended by the Mongol invasion, and the Bulgarian state splinters.

1393–96 Bulgaria is conquered by the Turks. The Bulgarian Patriarchate is suppressed, and the Church turns towards the Greek Orthodox Church. Turkish domination lasts almost 500 years, and Turks settle in several regions of Bulgaria.

1876 An uprising against the Turks, originating in Bosnia in 1875, is suppressed, attracting sympathy for the Bulgarian cause from the Great Powers.

1878 After the defeat of the Ottoman Empire in the Russo-Turkish War of 1877–78, the Treaty of San Stefano is signed which would have created a new Bulgarian state stretching from the Danube to the Aegean. Austria-Hungary and Britain force Russia to reconsider, and the new Bulgaria is divided into three parts by the Treaty of Berlin concluded a few months later: a Bulgarian principality, north of the Balkan mountains; Eastern Rumelia south of the Balkan mountains and under Turkish rule; and Macedonia.

1885 Eastern Rumelia is added to the Bulgarian principality by force. A dispute between Bulgaria and Russia results in the abdication of the Bulgarian ruler Alexander of Battenburg (elected in 1879), and the election in 1887 by the National Assembly of the pro-Austrian Ferdinand of Saxe-Coburg to the throne.

1908 After Austria-Hungary annexes Bosnia-Herzegovina, Bulgaria declares itself an independent kingdom, and Ferdinand proclaims himself Czar.

1912 Bulgaria, Serbia, Greece, and Montenegro defeat Turkey in the First Balkan War, resulting in Bulgarian expansion, opposed especially by Serbia. The following year Bulgaria attacks its former allies, who are joined by Romania and Turkey, and is defeated, losing to Romania and Turkey much of Macedonia in addition to other lands.

1915 Bulgaria enters World War I on the side of the Central Powers, and declares war on Serbia.

1919 By the Treaty of Neuilly the defeated Bulgaria loses Thrace to Greece and Southern Dobrudja to Romania – lands ceded in 1913 and briefly retaken during the war.

1920 The left-wing Agrarian Party wins power. The Communist Party, also strong in the country's first parliament, refuses to participate in government.

1923 Prime Minister Aleksandur Stambolski is killed in a coup. Insurrections by the agrarians and communists fail. Terrorist organizations become active. A succession of coalition governments lasts until a military government seizes power in a coup in May.

1934 King Boris III establishes his personal dictatorship.

1941 Officially neutral but pro-fascist in reality in World War II, Bulgaria permits the German army to occupy its territory. Bulgaria joins the Axis powers the following month and takes part in the occupation of Yugoslavia in April, for which it is granted much of Macedonia. Boris III dies suddenly in August 1943.

1943 Child king Simeon II accedes.

1944 Allies firebomb Sofia. Soviet army invades. Antifascist Fatherland Front coalition, including Agrarian Party and Bulgarian Communist Party (BCP), takes power in bloodless coup. Kimon Georgiev prime minister.

1946 September, referendum abolishes monarchy. Republic proclaimed. October, general election results in BCP majority.

1947 Prime Minister Georgi Dmitrov discredits Agrarian Party leader Nikola Petkov. Petkov arrested and sentenced to death. International recognition of Dmitrov government. Soviet-style constitution adopted; one-party state established. Country renamed People's Republic of Bulgaria. Nationalization of economy begins.

1949 Dmitrov dies, succeeded as prime minister by Vasil Kolarov.

1950 Kolarov dies. "Little Stalin" Vulko Chervenkov replaces him and begins BCP purge and collectivization.

1953 Stalin dies; Chervenkov's power begins to wane.

1954 Chervenkov yields power to Todor Zhivkov. Zhivkov sets out to make Bulgaria an inseparable part of the Soviet system.

1955–1960 Zhivkov exonerates victims of Chervenkov's purges.

1965 Plot to overthrow Zhivkov discovered by Soviet agents.

1968 Bulgarian troops aid Soviet army in invasion of Czechoslovakia.

1971 New constitution. Zhivkov becomes president of State Council and resigns as premier.

1978 Purge of BCP: 30,000 members expelled.

1984 Turkish minority forced to take Slavic names.

1989 June–August. Exodus of 300,000 Bulgarian Turks. November, Zhivkov ousted as BCP leader and head of state. Replaced by Petur Mladenov. Mass protest in Sofia for democratic reform. December, Union of Democratic Forces (UDF) formed.

1990 Economic collapse. Zhivkov arrested. BCP loses constitutional role as leading political party, changes name to Bulgarian Socialist Party (BSP). June, election produces no overall result. August, Zhelyu Zhelev, UDF leader, becomes president. BSP in government. Country renamed Republic of Bulgaria; communist symbols removed from national flag.

1991 February, price controls abolished; steep price rises. July, new constitution adopted. October, UDF wins elections.

1992 Continued political and social unrest. October, UDF resigns after losing vote of confidence. December, Movement for Rights and Freedoms (MRF) forms government. Zhivkov convicted of corruption and human rights abuses.

1993 Ambitious privatization program begins.

1994 General elections return BSP to power.

1995 BSP leader, Zhan Videnov, heads coalition government.

1996 Financial crisis and collapse of lev. Presidential elections won by opposition UDF candidate, Peter Stoyanov.

1997 General election won by UDF, whose leader Ivan Kostov becomes prime minister.

2001 Despite economic upturn, voters turn to new party headed by ex-king, who becomes prime minister under name of Simeon Saxecoburggotski. November, BSP leader Georgi Purvanov elected president.

2004 Joins Nato.

Bulgarians *see* Bulgars

Bulgars (*var.* Bulgarians) People known in eastern European history during the Middle Ages. One branch of this people was ancestral to the modern Bulgarians. The Bulgars may have originated as a Turkic tribe of Central Asia and arrived in the European steppe west of the Volga River with the Huns about 370 CE; retreating with the Huns, they resettled about 460 CE in an arc of country north and east of the Sea of Azov.

Bull Run (*aka* Manassas) ⚔ of American Civil War (two battles, Jul 21 and Aug 29–30 1862). Confederate victories.

Bunker Hill (Boston) ⚔ of American Revolutionary War (Jun 16 1775). British victory. *p.332*

Burckhardt, Johann Ludwig (1784–1817) Swiss explorer of the Middle East. He was the first European to visit Petra in Jordan and the Egyptian temple of Abu Simbel on the Nile. In 1814 he crossed the Red Sea from the Sudan and visited Mecca disguised as a Muslim.

Burebista Ruler of Dacia, a kingdom in the Carpathian Mountains and Transylvania, in present north-central and western Romania. The Roman province of Dacia eventually included wider territories both to the north and east. In about 60–50 BCE King Burebista unified and extended the kingdom, which, however, split into four parts after his death (45 BCE).

Burgundians Germanic tribes who occupied the lands of western Switzerland from the 5th century CE onward. Although they retained political control, they lost contact with their former homelands and were assimilated into the Roman Celtic population.

Burgundy Powerful medieval duchy at its height in the 14th and 15th centuries. In 1384 Philip the Bold inherited the Low Countries and the duchy continued to expand until a disastrous defeat at the hands of the Swiss in 1477. Duke Charles the Bold was killed and the Burgundy lands passed to the House of Habsburg.

Burke, Robert O'Hara (1821–61) Irish-born explorer of Australia. In 1853 he emigrated to Melbourne, where he joined the police. In 1860 he was chosen to lead an expedition crossing Australia from south to north. Coastal swamps prevented his party reaching the sea at the Gulf of Carpentaria. The journey ended in tragedy. Burke died of starvation with two of his companions; one of the party survived thanks to the assistance of local Aborigines.

BURKINA Landlocked in West Africa, Burkina (formerly Upper Volta) gained independence from France in 1960. The majority of Burkina lies in the arid fringe of the Sahara known as the Sahel. Ruled by military dictators for much of its postindependence history, Burkina became a multiparty state in 1991. However, much power still rests with President Blaise Compaoré. Burkina's economy remains largely based on agriculture.

CHRONOLOGY

11th century Rise of the Mossi kingdom.

14th century Arrival of Islam.

1890s French conquest overcomes the armed resistance of the Mossi (led by the emperor, the Moro Naba).

1920 Upper Volta is created as a colony separate from French Soudan.

1932 The region is divided between Ivory Coast, Soudan, and Niger.

1947 Upper Volta is recreated by the French. The first political party to emerge is Maurice Yameogo's Volta Democratic Union (UDV).

1958 Upper Volta is granted self-governing status within the French Community.

1960 Maurice Yameogo, elected December 11 1959, becomes the first President of the fully independent state, and bans opposition parties.

1966 After demonstrations and threatened strikes, the military intervene to depose President Yameogo, with Lt.-Col. (later Gen.) Sangoule Lamizana taking his place at the head of a government dominated by the military.

1970 A new Constitution allowing for power-sharing between politicians and the army is approved by referendum.

1974 President Lamizana restores full military rule, dissolves the national assembly and suspends the Constitution.

1977 Another constitution is approved by referendum. Lamizana retains the presidency.

1980 Ousting of Lamizana; Col. Saye Zerbo becomes president.

1982 Capt. Thomas Sankara takes power. People's Salvation Council (PSC) begins radical reforms.

1984 Renamed Burkina.

1987 Sankara assassinated, Capt. Blaise Compaoré takes power.

1991 New constitution. Compaoré elected president.

1997 CDP landslide election victory.

1999 General strike.

2001 Ex-presidential guard head accused of 1998 killing of journalist Norbert Zongo.

2001–2003 Meningitis outbreak kills thousands.

2002 CDP narrowly wins elections.

BURMA Forming the eastern shores of the Bay of Bengal and the Andaman Sea in southeast Asia, Burma is mountainous in the north, while the once-forested, fertile Irrawaddy basin occupies most of the country. Burma gained independence from British colonial control in 1948 and has recently suffered widespread political repression and ethnic conflict. In 1990, the National League for Democracy (NLD) gained a majority in free elections but was prevented from taking power by the military. Rich in natural resources, which include fisheries and teak forests, Burma's economy remains mostly agricultural. *See also* Myanmar

Chronology

11th century Burma is first united under King Anarutha (1044–77), the founder of the Pagan dynasty.

1287 Burma is overrun by the Kublai Khan.

1530s Burma is reunited under King Tabinshweti, the founder of the Toungoo dynasty.

18th century At its height the Burmese kingdom stretches to include parts of Thailand and India.

1824–85 Burma fights three separate wars against the British as the two countries come into conflict over the boundaries of Britain's Indian empire.

1886 Burma becomes a province of British India.

1930–1931 Economic depression triggers unrest.

1937 Separation from India.

1942 Japan invades.

1945 Antifascist People's Freedom League (AFPFL), led by Aung San, helps Allies reoccupy country.

1947 UK agrees to Burmese independence. Aung San wins elections, but is assassinated.

1948 Independence under new prime minister, U Nu, who initiates socialist policies. Revolts by ethnic separatists, notably Karen liberation struggle.

1958 Ruling AFPFL splits into two. Shan liberation struggle begins.

1960 U Nu's faction wins elections.

1961 Kachin rebellion begins.

1962 Gen. Ne Win stages military coup. "New Order" policy of "Buddhist Socialism" deepens international isolation. Mining and other industries nationalized. Free trade prohibited.

1964 Socialist Program Party declared sole legal party.

1976 Social unrest. Attempted military coup. Ethnic liberation groups gain control of 40% of country.

1982 Nonindigenous people barred from public office.

1988 Thousands die in student riots. Ne Win resigns. Martial law. Aung San Suu Kyi, daughter of Aung San, and others form NLD. Gen. Saw Maung leads military coup. State Law and Order Restoration Council (SLORC) takes power. Ethnic resistance groups form Democratic Alliance of Burma.

1989 Army arrests NLD leaders and steps up antirebel activity. Officially renamed Union of Myanmar.

1990 Elections permitted. NLD wins landslide. SLORC remains in power, however. More NLD leaders arrested.

1991 Aung San Suu Kyi awarded Nobel Peace Prize.

1992 Gen. Than Shwe takes over as SLORC leader.

1995 Aung San Suu Kyi released from house arrest.

1996 Demonstrations against approval of Burma's membership of ASEAN.

1997 Ruling SLORC renamed State Peace and Development Council (SPDC). US imposes sanctions and bans further investment in Burma.

1998 NLD sets deadline for convening parliament; junta refuses.

1999 Aung San Suu Kyi rejects conditions set by SPDC for visiting the UK to see her husband, Michael Aris, who dies of cancer.

2000 Negotiations between junta and NLD begin.

2003 Aung San Suu Kyi detained once more, after a year's freedom. US bans imports from Burma.

Bursa Byzantine city in Anatolia which became the first Ottoman capital in 1326

Burton, Sir Richard Francis (1821–90) British linguist, diplomat, writer, and explorer. His extensive knowledge of Far Eastern customs and languages enabled him in 1853 to travel, disguised as a Muslim, to Medina and Mecca. He Explored E Africa with John Speke, in 1858 The author of over 50 books, he is best known for his translation of *The Thousand Nights and a Night (The Arabian Nights)*.

Bush, George (1924–) 41st President of the US (Republican, 1988–92). Led US in Gulf War (1990–91) and signed arms limitation treaties with USSR and later, Russian Federation. Established NAFTA (North American Free Trade Agreement) with Canada and Mexico (1992).

Bushi *see* Bushido

Bushido (*Eng.* Way of the warrior) Of or pertaining to *bushi, bushidan*, Japanese chivalric code based on feudal loyalty to lord, associated with samurai caste.

BURUNDI Landlocked Burundi lies just south of the equator on the Nile-Congo watershed. Lake Tanganyika forms part of its border with Congo (former Zaire). Tension between the Hutu majority and the dominant Tutsi minority remains the main factor in politics. The current political unrest dates from the assassination of the first-ever Hutu president in a coup by the Tutsi-dominated army in October 1993, which sparked terrible violence.

Chronology

5th Century Beginnings of settlement of Hutu agriculturalists followed 1,000 years later by Tutsi settlement.

1899 Traditional Burundi kingdom absorbed into German East Africa.

1916 Belgium takes over, under League of Nations Mandate, after Germany's defeat in World War I.

1946 UN trust territory.

1959 Split from Rwanda.

1962 Independence.

1966 Army overthrows monarchy.

1972 150,000 Hutu massacred.

1993 Ndadaye wins first free elections; killed four months later.

1996 Buyoya retakes power.

1999 Talks between warring groups.

2000 Renewed violence.

2001 Power-sharing agreement between Tutsis and Hutus.

2003 Domitien Ndayizeye becomes president in peaceful transfer.

Buwayhid dynasty (945–1055) Islamic dynasty of Iranian and Shi'a character that provided native rule in western Iran and Iraq in the period between the Arab and Turkish conquests.

Byrd, Richard Evelyn (1888–1957) US naval officer. Made the first flight over N Pole in 1926, and in 1929 flew over the S Pole. Explored Antarctica, leading expeditions in 1933–34, 1939–41 and 1955–56.

BYZANTINE EMPIRE

(*var.* Eastern Roman empire, 395–1453) The Roman Empire in the west fell in 476, but the eastern empire with its capital at Constantinople (Byzantium) survived until it was conquered by the Ottoman Turks in 1453. The empire was essentially Greek Orthodox and Christianity was the state religion. The empire expanded under emperors such as Justinian I and Basil II, but for most of its history was on the defensive, losing much territory to the Arabs in the 7th century, and for the first half of the 13th century being ousted from Constantinople by the Venetians and crusading knights from western Europe.

BYZANTINE EMPERORS

474–491	Zeno
491–518	Anastasius I
518–527	Justin I (Flavius Justinus)
527 (518)–565	Justinian the Great (Flavius Justinianus)
565–578	Justin II (Flavius Justinus)
578 (574)–582	Tiberius (Flavius Constantinus Tiberius)
582–602	Maurice (Mauritius)
602–610	Phocas I
610–641	Heraclius I
641	Constantine III (Constantinus)
641	Heracleon (Heracleonas)
641–668	Constans II
668–685	Constantine IV (Pogonatus)
685–695	Justinian II (Rhinotmetus)
695–698	Leontius II
698–705	Tiberius III (Apsimar)
705–711	Justinian II (Rhinotmetus)
711–713	Philippicus
713–715	Anastasius II
715–717	Theodosius III
717–741	Leo III (the Isaurian)
741–775	Constantine V (Kopronymus)
775–780	Leo IV
780–797	Constantine VI (Porphyrogenetus)
797–802	Irene (empress)
802–811	Nicephorus I
811	Stauracius (Staurakius)
811–813	Michael I (Rhangabé)
813–820	Leo V (the Armenian)
820–829	Michael II (Balbus)
829 (820)–842	Theophilus I
842–867	Michael III
842–866	Bardas
867	Theophilus II
867 (866)–886	Basil I (the Macedonian)
886–912	Leo VI (the Wise)
912–913	Alexander III
913–959	Constantine VII (Porphyrogenetus)
919–944	Romanus I (Lecapenus)
959–963	Romanus II
963 (976)–1025	Basil II (Bulgaroctonus, the Bulgar Slayer)
963–969	Nicephorus II (Phocas)
969–976	John I (Tzimisces)
1025 (976)–1028	Constantine VIII
1028–1050	Zoë (empress)
1028–1034	Romanus III (Argyropolus)
1034–1041	Michael IV (the Paphlagonian)
1041–1042	Michael V (Kalaphates)
1042–1054	Constantine IX (Monomachus)
1054–1056	Theodora (empress)
1056–1057	Michael VI (Stratioticus)
1057–1059	Isaac I (Comnenus)
1059–1067	Constantine X (Dukas)
1067	Andronicus
1067–1071	Romanus IV (Diogenes)
1071–1078	Michael VII (Parapinakes)
1078–1081	Nicephorus III (Botaniates)
1081–1118	Alexius I (Comnenus)
1118–1143	John II (Calus)
1143–1180	Manuel I
1180–1183	Alexius II
1182–1185	Andronicus I
1185–1195	Isaac II (Angelus-Comnenus)
1195–1203	Alexius III (Angelus)
1203–1204	Isaac II (restored)
1203–1204	Alexius IV
1204	Alexius V (Dukas)

Latin emperors

1204–1205	Baldwin I
1205–1216	Henry
1216–1217	Peter de Courtenay
1218–1228	Robert de Courtenay
1228–1261	Baldwin II

Nicaean emperors

1206–1222	Theodore I (Lascaris)
1222–1254	John Dukas Vatatzes
1254–1259	Theodore II (Lascaris)
1258–1261	John IV (Lascaris)
1259–1261 (1282)	Michael VIII (Paleologus)

The Paleologi

1261 (1259)–1282	Michael VIII
1282–1328	Andronicus II (the Elder)
1295–1320	Michael IX (co-emperor)
1328–1341	Andronicus III (the Younger)
1341–1347	John V (Paleologus)
1347 (1341)–1354	John VI (Cantacuzene)
1355–1376	John V (restored)
1376–1379	Andronicus IV
1379–1391	John V (restored)
1390	John VII
1391–1425	Manuel II
1425–1448	John VII
1448–1453	Constantine XI

C

Cabeza de Vaca, Álvar Núñez
(c.1490–1560) Ill-fated Spanish explorer of N and S America. On an expedition of 1528 to colonize lands on the north coast of the Gulf of Mexico, he was one of only four survivors, who wandered the region for eight years. He later explored S America, and was appointed governor of the Río de la Plata province, but was replaced in 1545, after his men mutinied.

Cabot, John (c.1450–1499) Navigator, born in Genoa. In 1497, sponsored by Henry VII of England, he led the first recorded European expedition to the coast of N America since the Norwegian voyages of the 10th century, although he believed he had discovered China.

Cabot, Sebastian (1474–1557) Son of John Cabot, he was a cartographer, navigator, and explorer who first traveled to N America in 1508, possibly reaching Hudson Bay and traveling down the eastern coast. In 1526, under the auspices of Spain, he led an expedition to S America to find a western route to the Pacific Ocean. He made a number of later voyages to find the Northeast Passage to China.

Cabral, Gonçalo Velho Early 15th-century Portuguese navigator, among the first Portuguese to sail to the Azores.

Cabral, Pedro Álvares (1467–1520) Portuguese navigator, discoverer of Brazil. After Vasco da Gama's successful voyage to India in 1498, King Manuel of Portugal sponsored a second expedition, captained by Cabral. In 1500, while following da Gama's course, sailing out into the Atlantic to use the prevailing winds, Cabral made an accidental landfall in S America, which he claimed for Portugal.

Cadamosto, Alvise (var. Ca'da Mosto, 1432–88) Venetian explorer and trader retained by Henry the Navigator, believed to be the first European to reach the Cape Verde Islands in 1456.

Caesar, Gaius Julius (102–44 BCE) Roman statesman and general. Caesar's conquest of Gaul (58–51 BCE) and his victory in a civil war against his rival Pompey (48) raised Caesar to a position of complete dominance of the Roman world. In 46 he was named dictator for 10 years, but was assassinated by enemies, who feared his power would bring the Roman republic to an end. *p.73*

Cahokia Major center of Mississippian moundbuilding culture in the 11th century CE. At its peak its population may have reached 15,000. *p.169*

Caillé, René (1799–1839) French traveler who was the first European to reach the legendary city of Timbuktu and to survive and tell the tale of his experiences there.

Cairo Capital of modern Egypt, founded in 969 by the Fatimids near the earlier Arab settlement of Al Fustat. The al-Azhar university, established in 970, is the most respected center of Koranic studies and Islamic jurisprudence in the world. *p.144, p.151*

Calabozo ⚔ of wars of S American liberation (Feb 1818) in Venezuela.

Calama ⚔ of War of the Pacific (1879). Chilean victory.

Çaldiran (var. Chaldiron) ⚔ between the Ottomans and the Safavids (1514). Ottoman victory enabled them to gain control of most of eastern Anatolia.

Caliphate, the The caliph, seen as the successor to the Prophet Muhammad, was the leader of the Islamic world. Early caliphates, under the Ummayad dynasty (661–750), were based at Medina and Damascus. Under the Abbasid dynasty (756–1258), the caliphate was based at the new city of Baghdad (founded 766), which was to become a potent symbol of Arab power. A breakaway Ummayad caliphate was estrablished at Cordoba in Spain (756–1031). Various regioal Muslim powers claimed caliphate staus, including the Fatimids in Cairo. The last Abbasid caliph was killed by the Mongols (1258), but the title was revived by the Ottomans in the 19th century, and abvolished with Turkish reformation (1924).

Calvin, John (1509–64) French theologian. A leader of the Protestant Reformation in France and Switzerland, he established the first presbyterian government in Geneva. His *Institutes of the Christian Religion* (1546) presented the basis of what came to be known as Calvinism.

Cambaluc (var. Khanbaliq, later Beijing, Peking) Kublai Khan's capital when he became first Mongol emperor of China.

CAMBODIA Located in the Indo-chinese peninsula in Asia, Cambodia has a coastline on the Gulf of Thailand and shares borders with Thailand, Laos, and Vietnam. Its main topographical feature is the Tônlé Sap, or Great Lake, which drains into the Mekong River. Over three-quarters of Cambodia are forested, with mangroves lining the coast. Rice is the principal crop. A former French protectorate, Cambodia gained independence in 1953 as a constitutional monarchy with Norodom Sihanouk as king. Cambodia has since emerged from two decades of civil war and an invasion from Vietnam. The UN's biggest peacekeeping operation since its creation culminated in elections in 1993. *p.126*

CHRONOLOGY

5th-6th century CE An important trading state, Funan, which linked the Chinese and Indian states, developed and prospered.

800 The Angkor empire is captured by the neighboring Javanese kingdom of Ayutthaya, resulting in the royal court moving to Phnom Penh.

1863 The French force King Norodom into signing French protectorate status over Cambodia.

1887 After two years of fighting the Cambodians are forced into accepting incorporation into the French Union Indochinoise.

1955 Sihanouk abdicates to pursue political career; takes title "Prince." 1970 Right-wing coup led by Prime Minister Lon Nol deposes Sihanouk. Exiled Sihanouk forms Royal Government of National Union of Cambodia (GRUNC), backed by communist Khmer Rouge. Lon Nol proclaims Khmer Republic.

1975 GRUNC troops capture Phnom Penh. Prince Sihanouk head of state, Khmer Rouge assumes power. Huge numbers die under radical extremist regime.

1976 Country renamed Democratic Kampuchea. Elections. Sihanouk resigns; GRUNC dissolved. Khieu Samphan head of state; Pol Pot prime minister.

1978 December, Vietnam invades, supported by Cambodian communists opposed to Pol Pot.

1979 Vietnamese capture Phnom Penh. Khmer Rouge ousted by Kampuchean

People's Revolutionary Party (KPRP), led by Pen Sovan. Khmer Rouge starts guerrilla war. Pol Pot held responsible for genocide and sentenced to death in absentia.

1982 Government-in-exile including Khmer Rouge and Khmer People's National Liberation Front, headed by Prince Sihanouk, is recognized by UN.

1989 Withdrawal of Vietnamese troops.

1990 UN Security Council approves plan for UN-monitored cease-fire and elections.

1991 Signing of Paris peace accords. Sihanouk reinstated as head of state of Cambodia.

1993 UN-supervised elections won by royalist Funcinpec. Sihanouk takes title of "King."

1994 Khmer Rouge refuses to join peace process.

1995 Former finance minister Sam Rainsy forms opposition party.

1996 Leading Khmer Rouge member Ieng Sary defects.

1997 Joint prime minister Hun Sen mounts coup against royalist co-premier Prince Ranariddh.

1998 April, death of Pol Pot; June, Khmer Rouge surrender; July, parliamentary elections; November, Hun Sen heads coalition government including Funcinpec.

1999 Cambodia admitted to ASEAN.

2001 Law approved on trials of Khmer Rouge leaders for atrocities committed by regime.

2003 Relatively peaceful elections won by CPP; coalition talks begin.

2004 CPP–Funcinpec coalition re-formed after 11-month stalemate.

Cambyses II (reigned 529–522 BCE) Achaemenid king of Persia, son of Cyrus the Great.

Camden ⚔ of American Revolutionary War (16 Jan 1781). British victory

camels Introduced to the Sahara by the Romans c.100 BCE.

CAMEROON Located on the central west African coast, over half of Cameroon is forested, with equatorial rainforest to the south, and evergreen forest and wooded savanna north of the Sanaga river. Most cities are located in the south, although there are densely populated areas around Mount Cameroon, a dormant volcano. For 30 years Cameroon was effectively a one-party state. Democratic elections in 1992 returned the former ruling party to power.

CHRONOLOGY

11th century Expansion of the Kanem-Bornu empire to include the northern regions.

1472 Arrival of Portuguese explorers. 16th-18th centuries. Expansion of slave trade by Europeans.

1884 Germany declares Kamerun protectorate and begins to lay infrastructure.

1916 February. French and British forces depose the last German governor.

1922 August. Four-fifths of the territory is mandated by the League of Nations to France, with the remainder mandated to Britain.

1946 The formation of political parties begins.

1955 Revolt; French kill 10,000.

1960 French sector independent.

1961 British south joins Cameroon (north joins Nigeria). Federal system established – abolished in 1972.

1982 Ahidjo dies; Paul Biya president.

1983–1984 Coup attempts. Heavy casualties; 50 plotters executed.

1990 Demonstrations and strikes; declaration of multiparty state.

1992 Multiparty elections.

1997 President and ruling RDPC returned in disputed elections.

2000 World Bank funds pipeline project, despite environmental fears.

2001 Over 80% of indigenous forests allocated for logging.

2002 RDPC increases its majority.

Camp David Accords (1978) Named after the official country house compound of the US President, Camp David, in Maryland, the accords were a framework for a settlement intended to end the Middle East conflict between Israel and the Arab world. Brokered in 1978 by US President Jimmy Carter between President Sadat of Egypt and Prime Minister Begin of Israel, the Accords laid the foundation for the 1979 peace treaty between the two nations.

Canaanites Canaan was the ancient name for Palestine around 2000 BCE, and its people occupied the area between the Mediterranean coast eastwards possibly to the River Jordan and the Dead Sea. After the exodus of the Israelites from Egypt in the 13th century BCE they were confined to the coastal strip, and were condemned by the Hebrews for their worship of local deities, and their tradition of sacrifice and sacred prostitution. They developed the first truly alphabetic script.

CANADA Canada is the world's third-largest country, stretching north to Cape Columbia on Ellesmere Island, south to Lake Erie, and across five time zones from Newfoundland to the Pacific seaboard. The interior lowlands around Hudson Bay make up 80% of Canada's land area and include the vast Canadian Shield, with the plains of Saskatchewan and Manitoba and the Rocky Mountains to the west. The St. Lawrence, Yukon, Mackenzie, and Fraser Rivers are among the world's 40 largest. The St. Lawrence river and Great Lakes lowlands are the most populous areas. An Inuit homeland, Nunavut, was created in 1999, covering nearly a quarter of Canada's land area, formerly the eastern part of Northwest Territories. French-speaking Québec's relationship with the rest of the country causes recurring constitutional arguments.

CHRONOLOGY

10th and 11th centuries The eastern coast of present-day Canada is explored and briefly settled by Norse explorers from Greenland.

1497–98 John Cabot explores the coast between Labrador and Chesapeake Bay.

16th century The exploration and settlement of Newfoundland and Québec is carried out.

1608 Québec city is founded.

1610 Henry Hudson discovers Hudson Bay.

1629 English forces occupy the French stronghold of Québec city.

1632 Control of New France (the area around present-day Québec) and of Acadia (present-day Nova Scotia and New Brunswick) is granted to France by King Charles I of England.

▶

1663 New France becomes a French Royal colony.

1713 Newfoundland and mainland Acadia are awarded to the United Kingdom under the terms of the Peace of Utrecht.

1756–63 The Seven Years War, fought in North America as well as Europe, is concluded by the Treaty of Paris which awards to Britain all French possessions in North America except the islands of Saint Pierre and Miquelon.

1758 The first elected legislative assembly in British North America meets at Halifax.

1754 British fight French and Indian War. France forced to relinquish St. Lawrence and Québec settlements to Britain.

1774 Act of Québec recognizes Roman Catholicism, French language, culture, and traditions.

1775–1783 American War of Independence. Canada becomes refuge for loyalists to British Crown.

1867 Federation of Canada created under British North America Act.

1885 Transcontinental railroad completed.

1897 Klondike gold rush begins.

1914–1918, 1939–1945 Canada supports Allies in both world wars.

1931 Autonomy within Commonwealth.

1949 Founder member of NATO. Newfoundland joins Federation.

1968 Liberal Party under Pierre Trudeau in power. Separatist Parti Québécois (PQ) formed to demand complete separation from federation.

1970s Québec secessionist movement grows, accompanied by terrorist attacks.

1976 In Québec, PQ wins elections

1977 French made official language.

1980 Separation of Québec rejected at referendum. Trudeau prime minister again.

1982 UK transfers all powers relating to Canada in British law.

1984 Trudeau resigns. Elections won by PCP. Brian Mulroney prime minister until 1993.

1987 Meech Lake Accord.

1989 Canadian–USA Free Trade Agreement.

1992 Charlottetown Agreement on provincial–federal issues rejected at referendum. Canada, Mexico, and USA finalize terms for NAFTA.

1993 Crushing election defeat of PCP, rise of regional parties.

1994 PQ regains power in Québec. NAFTA takes effect.

1995 Narrow "no" vote in second Québec sovereignty referendum.

1995 Fishing dispute with EU.

1997 Regional considerations again dominate federal election; Liberals retain power; election victory based on support in Ontario.

1998 PQ only narrowly holds power in Québec.

2000 November, early elections. Liberals retain power.

2003 PQ ousted by Liberals in Québec after nine years in power. Chrértien stands down in favor of Paul Martin.

2004 Early elections. Liberals again retain power.

CANADIAN PREMIERS (FROM 1867)

1867–1873	John Alexander MacDonald
1873–1878	Alexander Mackenzie
1878–1891	John Alexander MacDonald
1891–1892	John Joseph Caldwell Abbott
1892–1894	John Sparrow David Thompson
1894–1896	Mackenzie Bowell
1896	Charles Tupper
1896)–1911	Wilfrid Laurier
1911–1920	Robert Laird Borden
1920–1921	Arthur Meighen
1921–1926	William Lyon Mackenzie King
1926	Arthur Meighen
1926–1930	William Lyon Mackenzie King
1930–1935	Richard Bedford Bennett
1935–1948	William Lyon Mackenzie King
1948–1957	Louis Stephen Saint-Laurent
1957–1963	John George Diefenbaker
1963–1968	Lester Bowles Pearson
1968–1979	Pierre Elliott Trudeau
1979–1980	Charles Joseph (Joe) Clark
1980–1984	Pierre Elliott Trudeau
1984	John Napier Turner
1984–1993	Martin Brian Mulroney
1993	Kim Campbell
1993–2003	Jean Joseph Jacques Chrétien
2003	Paul Martin

Candra Gupta *see* Chandragupta Maurya

Cannae ⚔ of Second Punic War (216 BCE). Hannibal's greatest victory over the Romans.

cannon Developed in the 13th century, following the arrival of gunpowder in Europe from China, it began to make its mark in siege warfare in the 14th century. *p.229*

Cantino, Alberto Agent of the Duke of Ferrara in Lisbon, who in 1502 obtained a Portuguese world map, showing the latest discoveries of Portuguese sailors, including the coast of Brazil and Madagascar. The famous map is known as the Cantino Planisphere.

Canton *see* Guangzhou

Canterbury The city in Kent, SE England, became the see of the Primate of all England following the mission from Rome of St. Augustine in 597. St. Augustine was himself the first archbishop. After 1533, when Henry VIII split from Rome, appointing himself Defender of the Faith in his own kingdom, the archbishop of Canterbury became the spiritual head of the newly established Church of England.

ARCHBISHOPS OF CANTERBURY (SINCE 1533)

1533–1556	Thomas Cranmer
1556–1558	Reginald Pole
1559–1575	Matthew Parker
1575–1583	Edmund Grindal
1583–1604	John Whitgift
1604–1610	Richard Bancroft
1611–1633	George Abbot
1633–1645	William Laud
1645–1660	see vacant under the Catholic Queen Mary I
1660–1663	William Juxon
1663–1677	Gilbert Sheldon
1678–1691	William Sancroft
1691–1694	John Tillotson
1694–1715	Thomas Tenison
1716–1737	William Wake
1737–1747	John Potter
1747–1757	Thomas Herring
1757–1758	Matthew Hutton
1758–1768	Thomas Secker
1768–1783	Hon. Frederick Cornwallis
1783–1805	John Moore
1805–1828	Charles Manners-Sutton
1828–1848	William Howley
1848–1862	John Bird Sumner
1862–1868	Charles Thomas Longley
1868–1882	Archibald Campbell Tait
1882–1896	Edward White Benson
1896–1902	Frederick Temple
1903–1928	Randall Thomas Davidson
1928–1942	Cosmo Gordon Lang
1942–1945	William Temple
1945–1961	Geoffrey Francis Fisher

1961–1974	Arthur Michael Ramsey
1974–1980	Frederick Donald Coggan
1980–1991	Robert Alexander Kennedy Runcie
1991–2002	George Leonard Carey
2002–	Rowan Williams

Canute (*var.* Canute the Great, Knut, Knud, Knutden Mektige) Danish king of England (reigned 1016–35), of Denmark (as Canute II, reigned 1019–35), and of Norway (reigned 1028–35), who was a power in the politics of Europe in the 11th century. *p.163*

Cão, Diogo (*fl.*1480–86). Portuguese navigator who in 1482, became the first European to discover the mouth of the Congo.

Cape Colony A settlement was established at the southern tip of Africa in 1652 by the Dutch East India Company, which brought settlers to raise cattle – the original Boers (farmers). The colony was seized by the British in 1795 and formally ceded to Britain in 1806. The 19th century was dominated by conflict between the British and the Boers, many of whom migrated north to found their own republics, Transvaal and the Orange Free State. When gold and diamonds were discovered in South Africa, the conflict intensified, leading to the Boer War. *p.309, p.373*
See also South Africa, Boer War

CAPE VERDE The Cape Verde archipelago off the west coast of Africa became independent of Portugal in 1975. Most islands are mountainous and volcanic; the low-lying islands of Sal, Boa Vista, and Maio have agricultural potential, though they are prone to debilitating droughts. Around 50% of the population lives on São Tiago. A period of single-party socialist rule followed independence. Cape Verde held its first multiparty elections in 1991.

CHRONOLOGY
1455 Antonio da Noli, a Genoese navigator working for the Portuguese, makes the first recorded mention of São Tiago and four other islands.
1462 Portuguese seafarers begin the process of settlement of the uninhabited islands. Slaves were brought from mainland Africa to work the small parcels of arable land.
1600–1760 Ribeira Grande (on Santo Antão) becomes an important entrepot for the trans-Atlantic slave trade, with many slaves sold for transportation to the Spanish West Indies and Colombia, and later to Brazil.
1774 Praia becomes the seat of government.
1869 Emancipation of slaves begins.
1956 The African Party for the Independence of Guinea-Bissau and Cape Verde (PAIGC) is established by Amilcar Cabral and Aristides Pereira.
1961 Joint struggle for independence of Cape Verde and Guinea-Bissau begins.
1974 Guinea-Bissau independent.
1975 Independence.
1981 Final split from Guinea-Bissau.
1991 MPD wins first multiparty poll.
2001 General election returns PAICV to power.

Capetian Dynasty (987–1328) Ruling dynasty of France founded by Hugh Capet who replaced the previous Carolingian line. *See also* France

Capitalism Investment banking and economic growth in the US in the late 19th century. *p.393*

Carabobo ⚔ of wars of S American independence. Last battle on Venezuelan soil won by Simon Bolívar.

caravel Light sailing ship of the 15–17th centuries in Europe, developed by the Portuguese for exploring the coast of Africa.

cardial pottery (*var.* cardium) Pottery decorated with impressions of cockle shells (cardium), made by the earliest communities to adopt farming along the shores of the Mediterranean (c.6200–5000 BCE).

Carlist Wars (1834–49) Regional opposition to the liberal Spanish regime led to war in support of the claims of Don Carlos (1788–1855) and his descendants to the throne of Spain.

Carlowitz, Peace of *see* Karlowitz, Peace of

Carnac Site of stone avenues in Brittany, striking Megalithic structures created by one of the farming and fishing communities of Neolithic Europe. *p.23*

Carolingian Dynasty (751–987) Frankish dynasty, named after Charlemagne (Carolus Magnus). The first Carolingian ruler of France was Pepin, father of Charlemagne, who was crowned in 751.

Carpini, John of Plano (c.1182–1252) Italian Franciscan monk and traveler sent by Pope Innocent IV to meet the emperor of the Mongols.

Carranza, Venustiano (1859–1920) Mexican political leader. In 1910 led revolution against the government of Porfirio Diaz, and in 1913 led the overthrow of General Victoriano Huerta. He became president in 1915 following a power struggle. Carranza tried to establish a progressive constitution approved in 1917 but was overthrown in 1920, forced to flee and assassinated.

Carrhae ⚔ (53 BCE) Stopped the Roman invasion of Parthian Mesopotamia.

cars *see* automobiles

Carter, James Earl (Jimmy) (1924–) 39th President of the US (Democrat 1977–81). During Carter's presidency the Panama Canal Treaty and Camp David Accords were signed. The greatest crisis of his presidency was the seizure of the US embassy in Iran in 1979 following the overthrow of the Shah.

Carthage North African city founded by Phoenician merchants, possibly in 814 BCE. It began as a harbour on the Phoenicians' route to the valuable tin and silver mines of southern Iberia. Between 550 BCE and c.500 BCE, Carthaginian soldiers conquered most of eastern Sicily, defeated the Phoenicians and Massaliotes on the coast of Corsica, and subdued Sardinia and the Balearic islands. However, conflict with the Roman Empire during the Punic Wars ended with the defeat and destruction of the empire in 146 BCE. *See also* Punic Wars

Cartier, Jacques (1491–1557) French explorer and navigator. Sent to America by Francis I in 1534 in search of gold, he explored the Gulf of St. Lawrence, returning in 1535 to reach the site of present-day Montreal, and again in 1541. His explorations proved important in the establishment of French claims on N America.

cartography Babylonian map. *p.49*
world view (1–500 CE). *p.79*
mosaic map of Jerusalem. *p.109*
Catalan Atlas (c.1375). *p.247*
American Civil War campaign map. *p.385*
road map (1925). *p.410*
London underground schematic map. *p.421*
remote-sensed mapping. *p.457*
See also exploration and mapping

Casablanca Conference (Jan 12–14 1943) Allied summit conference of World War II between US President Roosevelt and British Premier Churchill which agreed basis for Allied landings in Europe, the anti-U-Boat offensive, the Combined Bombing Offensive and supply of the Soviet Union.

Casimir III (*var.* Casimir the Great, 1309–70) Ruler of Poland (1333–70). Casimir restored Polish power in the region, strengthened administrative institutions, and founded a university at Cracow. In 1386, his daughter married the Lithuanian ruler Jagiello, uniting the two crowns.

Cassander (358–297 BCE) Ruler of one of the Greek successor states after the death of Alexander the Great.

Cassini, César François (1714–84) French astronomer and cartographer. Succeeded his father Jacques Cassini and director of the Paris observatory and began a detailed topographical map of France using the triangulation method.

Cassini, Jacques Dominique, Comte de (1748–1845) French astronomer and cartographer. Son of C.F. Cassini, and his successor as director of the Paris observatory. Completed the topographical map of France begun sby his father.

Cassino (*var.* Monte Cassino) ⚔ of World War II (Jan–May 1943). Site of prolonged German resistance to Allied advance in central Italy.

caste system Form of social hierarchy unique to Hinduism, which is based on ideas of spiritual purity, and influences all social and physical contact. In this system, people are "ordered" according to their religious purity, lineage, and occupational group, the Brahman or priest caste being the highest. Contact between castes is thought to be polluting and is avoided.

Castile, Council of Spanish bureaucratic body established in the late 15th century, for the execution of royal policy. The Catholic monarchs set up a Council of Finance in 1480, the Council of the Hermandad in 1476, the Council of the Inquisition 1483, and the Council of the Orders of Knighthood and they reorganized the Council of Aragon. Charles I and Philip II were later to continue this work adding further councils, notably those of the Indies (1524) and of Italy (1558).

Castro, Fidel (1926–) Leader of a guerrilla campaign (1954–58) waged against the right wing US puppet government of Fulgencio Batista in Cuba. In 1958 Castro's army captured Havana and Castro became prime minister the following year. Under Castro's rule the Communist Party of Cuba became the sole legal party and a new constitution was introduced (1976). Castro continued to reject any moves towards economic liberalization, leading to increasing international isolation. *p.429*

Catalan Atlas Magnificent medieval world map produced in Majorca c.1375. *p.247*

Çatal Hüyük Well-preserved settlement in S Turkey, dating from c.6000 BCE. *p.20*

Catalaunian Fields ⚔ (451) Attila the Hun defeated by Roman and mercenary Goth forces.

Cathars (*aka* Albigensians) Heretical sect which flourished in southern France in the 12th century. It had little to do with Christianity; its most extreme followers believed in the evil of matter and aspired to reach the state of the "perfect," those who had forsaken the material world. The Albigensian Crusade (1210–26) not only stamped out the heretics but also placed Toulouse and much of southern France under the control of the French crown. *p.189*

Cathay Medieval European name for China.

Cathedrals Romanesque cathedrals. *p.166* Gothic cathedrals. *p.191*

Catherine II (*aka* Catherine the Great, 1729–96) Czarina of Russia (reigned 1762–96). Born a German princess, she was an intelligent and enlightened monarch, but her attempts at reform achieved little for the Russian people. Pursuing an active foreign policy, her reign was marked by territorial expansion south to the Black Sea, and territorial gains in the partition of Poland.

Catholic Reformation *see* Counter-Reformation

Catholicism *see* Roman Catholicism *See also* Vatican, Jesuits, Papacy, individual popes

Cavour, Camillo, Benso Count (1810–61) Piedmontese statesman who masterminded the unification of northern Italy under Victor Emmanuel II in 1859, and secretly encouraged the 1860 expedition of Garibaldi to Sicily and Naples which brought the south into a united Italy. *See also* Risorgimento

Celts Identified by their common language and cultural features, the Celts probably originated in France and S Germany in the Bronze Age, and identifiably Celtic artifacts first appear in the upper Danube in the 13th century BCE. They expanded around 800 BCE, sacked Rome in 390 BCE and Delphi a century later, eventually covering Asia Minor, Gaul (France), Italy, Galicia, Spain, and Britain. The Celts were gifted craftsmen and warriors, but their lack of political stability led to their demise in the 1st century BCE when the Romans and Germanic tribes marginalized them. Celtic dialects survive in several parts of Europe; including Wales, Brittany, and Ireland. *p.69*

CENTO Pact *see* Central Treaty Organization ▸

CENTRAL AFRICAN REPUBLIC

(*aka* CAR) Landlocked at the western end of the Sahel, the Central African Republic (CAR) is a low plateau stretching north from one of Africa's great rivers, the Ubangi, which forms its border with Dem. Rep. Congo (formerly Zaire). Almost all the population lives in the equatorial, rainforested south. "Emperor" Bokassa's eccentric rule from 1965 to 1979 was followed by military dictatorship. Democracy was restored in 1993.

CHRONOLOGY

18th century-early 19th century Slave raids from Chad and Sudan are common.

1889 France establishes a base at Bangui.

1905 May. The Oubangui-Chari colony is founded. Later revolts by the plantation forced-labour workers are brutally suppressed.

1950 September 28. The territory's first parliamentary deputy, Barthelemy Boganda, founds the Movement for Social Evolution in Black Africa (Mesan).

1958 Internal self-government is granted with Boganda as Prime Minister.

1960 August 13. Independence is achieved under President David Dacko (Boganda having died in an air crash).

1960 One-party state.

1965 Coup by Jean-Bédel Bokassa.

1977 Bokassa crowned "Emperor." State known as Central African Empire.

1979 French help reinstate Dacko.

1981 Gen. Kolingba ousts Dacko.
1996 Government of national unity formed following army rebellion.
2001–2003 Coup attempts.
2003 Gen. Bozizé leads coup.

Central Intelligence Agency (CIA) Established in 1947 in the US to gather intelligence information abroad and report to the President and National Security Council.

Central Powers The belligerents opposed to the Entente Powers in World War I: Germany and Austria-Hungary, together with their allies Turkey and Bulgaria.

Central Treaty Organization (CENTO Pact, 1955) Defence alliance originally known as Baghdad Pact, between Iran, Iraq, Pakistan, Turkey, and the United Kingdom.

ceramics *see* pottery

Ceylon *see* Sri Lanka

Chacabuco ⚔ of wars of S American independence (Feb 1817). Spanish forces defeated by San Martin.

Chaco War (1932–35) Conflict between Bolivia and Paraguay over the Chaco Boreal, a wilderness region that forms part of the Gran Chaco. A peace treaty was arranged by the Chaco Peace Conference and was signed in Buenos Aires on July 21 1938. Paraguay gained clear title to most of the disputed region, but Bolivia was given a corridor to the Paraguay River.

CHAD Landlocked in north central Africa, Chad has had a turbulent history since independence from France in 1960. Intermittent periods of civil war, involving French and Libyan troops, followed a military coup in 1975. Following a coup in 1990, an interim government commenced the transition to multipartyism, now enshrined in a new constitution. The discovery of large oil reserves could eventually have a dramatic impact on the economy. The tropical, cotton-producing south is the most populous region.

CHRONOLOGY

9th century The Kanem-Bornu empire is founded in the north of what is now Chad. By the end of the 11th century its kings or "mais" convert to Islam.

16th–17th centuries The Baguirmi and Ouaddai kingdoms hold sway over the region.

1878 Rabah Zobeir begins the conquest of Chad from Sudan and over the next 20 years comes to head the most powerful state in the region, but he is defeated in 1900 by the French at Kasseri after which they begin to establish control over Chad.

1958 Chad becomes an autonomous republic within the French African Community.

1959 Pre-independence elections result in victory for Francois (later Ngarta) Tombalbaye, who is confirmed as Prime Minister (a post he has held since March).

1960 Independence. One-party state.

1973 Libyans seize Aozou strip.

1975 Coup by Gen. Félix Malloum.

1979–1982 North-south civil war.

1980 Goukouni Oueddei in power.

1982 Hissène Habré (northerner) defeats Oueddei.

1990 Idriss Déby overthrows Habré, who flees to Senegal.

1994 Libya relinquishes Aozou strip.

1996 National cease-fire; new constitution.

1997 Déby's MPS largest party in new parliament.

1999 Rebellion in north.

2001 Heavy fighting continues. Déby reelected.

2002 MPS increases its majority

2003 Oil production begins.

Chaeronea ⚔ of Philip II's campaigns against Athens and allied Greek city-states (338 BCE). Decisive confrontation which left the Macedonians in effective control of all Greece.

Chagatai (*var.* Jagatai, died 1241) Mongol ruler, the second son of Genghis Khan. On the death of Genghis in 1227, Chagatai was granted a large vassal khanate in Central Asia, centered on Transoxania. Despite its eclipse by Timur at the end of the 14th century, the Chagatai Khanate survived into the 16th century.

Chaka Zulu *see* Shaka Zulu

Chaldean dynasty (626–539 BCE) Originating in the area at the head of the Persian Gulf, the Chaldeans established a Babylonian dynasty in 626 BCE. After their overthrow in 539 BCE the Babylonian and Chaldean dynasties became synonymous.

Chaldiron *see* Çaldiran

Chalukya dynasty (550–750 BCE) Deccan-based dynasty, founded in about 550 CE. The Chalukyas were eventually superseded by the Rashtrakutas in 750 CE. The Rashtrakutas were overthrown in 973 CE by Taila II, a scion of the Chalukyas dynasty, who founded a second dynasty known as the Chalukyas of Kalyani, which went into decline during the 11th century.

chamber tombs (*var.* dolmens) Megalithic monuments constructed of upright stones (orthostats) and capstones, beneath an earth mound. Often used for collective burials they comprise a series of chambers which can contain collections of different skeletal parts. Evidence suggests they were used over successive generations, during the Neolithic period in Europe, from c.5000 BCE. *p.23*

Champa South Vietnamese Hindu-Buddhist kingdom with its capital at Vijaya (modern Binh Dinh). The capital was annexed by the expanding north Vietnamese kingdom of Dai-Viet in 1471.

Champlain, Samuel de (1567–1635) French explorer of N America. Founded colony of New France, later to become Canada. Explored the St. Lawrence River, establishing a colony at Port Royal in 1604, founding Québec in 1608, and discovering Lake Champlain in 1609.

Chan Chan Chimú capital (11th century).

Chancellor, Richard (died 1556) British navigator and pioneer of Anglo-Russian trade. Appointed pilot-general in 1553 to Sir Hugh Willoughby's expedition seeking a Northeast passage to China. Separated from them by bad weather, he continued into the White Sea and went overland to Moscow. The Muscovy Company was founded in London to carry out the trade.

Chancellorsville ⚔ of American Civil War (May 1–4 1863). Confederate victory.

Chandragupta II (380–415) Gupta dynasty king (reigned c.375–415). Famous for long campaign he waged against invading Shakas (Scythians), from 388 to 409. He extended the Gupta domains, both by military conquest and marriage alliance.

Chandragupta Maurya (*var.* Candra Gupta) Founder of the Mauryan dynasty (reigned c.321–297 BCE) and the first ruler to unify most of India under one administration. Having seized the Magadhan throne in 327 BCE, he annexed all the lands east of the Indus, occupied much of north-central

India and captured much of Afghanistan from Seleucus Nicator, the successor of Alexander the Great.

Chang'an (*var.* Xi'an) Great capital of Tang China (618–904) and for a long period the most populous city in the world.

Chang Ch'ien *see* Zhang Qian

Chang Yuan 13th-century Chinese explorer of Central Asia.

Chang Zhun (Ch'iu Ch'ang-ch'un, 1148–1227). Chinese Taoist sage summoned to attend the court of Genghis Khan and sent on a mission from Beijing, via the Altai Mountains, Samarkand and the Tien Shan to just south of Kabul.

Chao dynasty *see* Zhao dynasty.

Chao Ju-kua *see* Zhao Ju-kua

Chaplin, Charlie (Sir Charles Spencer Chaplin, 1889–1977) English film actor and director, who won international fame in American-made silent comedy films.

Charlemagne (*var. Lat.* Carolus Magnus, c.742–814) King of the Franks and Holy Roman Emperor. Charlemagne's kingdom comprised France, much of Germany, and northern Italy, and became the first medieval Holy Roman Empire. The pope crowned him as emperor on Christmas day, 800. *p.137*

Charles I (1600–49) King of England, Scotland and Ireland (reigned 1625–49). His marriage to the Catholic Henrietta Maria aroused public hostility. He dissolved three parliaments in the first four years of his reign, and then ruled without one for 11 years until rebellion in Scotland forced him to recall it. Conflict with the Long Parliaments led to the English Civil War (1642–46). He was defeated at ⚔ Naseby in 1645 by Parliamentarian forces. He escaped briefly, but was recaptured, tried for treason, and beheaded. *p.306*

Charles II (1630–85) King of England (reigned 1660–85). Restored to the English throne after the Commonwealth collapsed following the death of `Oliver Cromwell in 1658.

Charles IV (1316–78) Holy Roman Emperor (reigned 1347–78) and King of Bohemia (as Charles I). The greatest of the Luxembourg rulers of Bohemia. He briefly made Prague center of the Empire. *p.237*

Charles Martel (c.688–741) Frankish leader, Mayor of the Palace to the late Merovingian kings (reigned 719–741). He

was the effective ruler of the Frankish kingdoms and defeated Muslim invaders at Poitiers in 732. *p.133*

Charles the Bold (1433–77) Last reigning duke of Burgundy (reigned 1467–77). Continually at war with Louis XI, he almost succeeded in creating a kingdom independent of France. His death while fighting the Swiss ended Burgundy's resistance to France.

Charles V (1500–58) Holy Roman Emperor. Charles inherited the Netherlands from his father, Spain (which he ruled as Charles I) from his mother, and the German Habsburg territories from his grandfather, all before he was 20. Elected Emperor in 1520, to protect his lands he had to fight numerous wars against France and the Ottoman Turks, while his reign also saw Germany torn apart by the wars of the Reformation. He abdicated in 1555, leaving his Spanish possessions and the Netherlands to his son Philip II and his Austrian and German lands to his brother Ferdinand.

Charles VII (1403–61) King of France (reigned 1422–61). Not actually crowned until 1429 when Joan of Arc raised the siege of Orléans. By 1453 he had expelled the English from all France except Calais, thus ending the Hundred Years' War.

Charles VIII (1470–1498) King of France (reigned 1483–1498), remembered for beginning the French expeditions into Italy that lasted until the middle of the 16th century.

Charles X (1622–60) King of Sweden (reigned 1654–60). Invaded Poland in 1655. In a successful war with Denmark (1657–58), Sweden reached the limit of its territorial expansion.

Charleston ⚔ of American Revolutionary War (Jun 28 1776). British victory.

Chartres One of the finest of France's Gothic cathedrals, famous for its magnificent stained glass. Construction began in 1154.

Chateau-Thierry ⚔ of Napoleon's defence of France (Feb 12 1814).

Chattanooga ⚔ of American Civil War (Nov 23–25 1863). Union victory.

Chaucer, Geoffrey (c.1340–1400) English poet and author of *The Canterbury Tales*. *p.243*

Chavín culture (c.850–200 BCE) From its origins around 1000 BCE this culture united around 800 sq km of Peruvian coast from

its base at Chavín de Huantar in the eastern Andes. This unity was religious rather than political, and was at its height around 400–200 BCE. Their sites are noted for stone carvings of the Occulate Being, a deity with with projecting fangs and a snarling mouth. Elements of this iconography spread throughout the Andean region and permeated the art and religion of later Andean cultures. The Chavín also made improvements in maize cultivation, metallurgy, and weaving. *p.42*

Cheng Ho *see* Zheng He.

Ch'eng Tsu *see* Chengzu

Chengzu (aka Yonglo, 1360–1424, reigned 1402–24) Son of Zhu Yuanzhang, the founder of the Ming dynasty in China. Ruled China in the early 15th century.

Cherokee Native people of N America. Formerly ranged across much of the southern US. Removed to reservations in Oklahoma and N Carolina in the late 19th century. Chesapeake Bay

Chiang Kai-shek *see* Jiang Jieshi.

Chibcha *see* Muisca

Chichén Itzá Mayan site on the Yucatan peninsula, which flourished for most of the first millennium CE. Many of its later monuments show Toltec influence.

Chichimec People of NW Mexico (c.12th century CE). They created small city-states and were in constant conflict with each other. In the 1170s, as their homeland became increasingly desiccated and famine-struck, they sacked the Toltec city of Tula.

Chickamauga ⚔ of American Civil War (Sep 19–20 1863). Confederate victory.

Children's Crusade (1212) Possibly legendary event. Many thousands of children from France and Germany are supposed to have marched to Marseille and other Mediterranean ports in order to sail to the Holy Land.

CHILE Chile extends in a narrow ribbon 4350 km (2700 miles) down the Pacific coast of South America. The plains of the central pampa lie between a coastal range and the Andes; most of the population lives in the fertile heartland around Santiago. Glaciers are a prominent feature of the southern Andes, as are fjords, lakes, and deep sea channels. In 1989, Chile returned to elected civilian rule, following a popular rejection of the Pinochet dictatorship. A collapse in copper prices, coupled with weaker export markets, has interrupted the high growth seen in the 1990s.

CHRONOLOGY

1541 Spanish expedition led by Pedro de Valdivia crosses the Andes from Peru and founds several cities including Santiago. Lautaro, leader of the Araucanian Indians who offer fierce resistance, is killed in 1557. Valdivia is killed by the Araucanians in 1554.

1817 San Martin's army crosses the Andes and routs the Spaniards at the Battle of Chacabuco.

1817–1818 Bernardo O'Higgins leads republican Army of the Andes in victories against royalist forces.

1818 April 5. The Battle of Maipu pits the independence army, assisted by San Martin's liberation forces, against the remaining Spanish forces and sets the seal on Chilean independence.

1817–23 As autocratic leader of the new republic Bernardo O'Higgins, formerly the Viceroy of Peru and known as the Liberator in the Chilean fight for independence, lays the foundations of an oligarchic state which are later consolidated in the 1833 Constitution, establishing a strong presidency and a centralized administration.

1829–30 After a civil war between liberals and conservatives, a conservative alliance led by Diego Portales seizes power.

1833 A coup installs the 100-day "Socialist republic" of Carlos Davila.

1836–39 During a war against Peru which Chile wins, Portales is assassinated.

1879–84 Chile emerges enriched from the Pacific War, waged against Bolivia and Peru over control of strategic nitrate areas and the port of Antofagasta.

1886–91 The presidency of Jose Manuel Balmaceda, a Liberal, which is characterized by a struggle between presidential and congressional authority, ends in a bloody civil war in 1891.

1920 December. Election of President Arturo Alessandri ("The Lion"), who introduces social reforms and seeks to extend participation in political life.

1936–1946 Communist, Radical, and Socialist parties form influential Popular Front coalition.

1943 Chile backs USA in World War II.

1946–1964 Right-wing Chilean presidents follow US McCarthy policy and marginalize the left.

1970 Salvador Allende elected. Reforms provoke strong reaction from the right.

1973 Allende dies in army coup. Brutal dictatorship of General Pinochet.

1988 Referendum votes "no" to Pinochet staying in power.

1989 Democracy peacefully restored; Pinochet steps down after Aylwin election victory.

1998 Pinochet detained while on visit to the UK pending extradition to Spain on human rights charges.

2000 Ricardo Lagos (PS) sworn in as president. Pinochet, deemed unfit to face trial, returns to Chile. Charges there are suspended in 2001.

Chimú culture (c.700–1476). Civilization of N Peru. Flourished for over 700 years until its defeat by the Incas in 1476. The Chimú empire was built around military conquest, efficient communications, and social control. Chimú craftsmen were noted for their metalwork, pottery, and textiles. *p.199*

Ch'i dynasty *see* Qi dynasty
Ch'in dynasty *see* Qin dynasty
Chin dynasty *see* Jin dynasty

CHINA Covering a vast area of eastern Asia, China is bordered by 14 countries; to the east it has a long Pacific coastline. Two-thirds of China is uplands. The southwestern mountains include the Tibetan Plateau; in the northwest, the Tien Shan Mountains separate the Tarim and Dzungarian basins. The low-lying east is home to two-thirds of the population. China has the world's oldest continuous civilization. Its recorded history begins 4000 years ago with the Shang dynasty, founded in the north c.1800 BCE. Succeeding dynasties expanded China's boundaries; it reached its greatest extent under the Manchu (Qing) dynasty in the 18th century. Chinese isolationism frustrated Europe's attempts to expand into the empire until the 19th century, when China had

fallen behind the industrializing West. For much of the previous 3000 years, it had been the world's most advanced nation. From the founding of the Communist People's Republic in 1949 until his death in 1976, China was dominated by Mao Zedong. Despite the major disasters of the 1950s Great Leap Forward and the 1960s Cultural Revolution, it became an industrial and nuclear power. Today, China is rapidly developing a market-oriented economy, but political liberalization is not on the agenda. The current leadership remains set on enforcing single-party rule, as were veterans such as "elder statesman" Deng Xiaoping, who died in 1997.

CHRONOLOGY

6th–5th century BCE Schools of philosophy flourish: Confucius (c.551–c.479 BCE) passes his teachings down to his disciples to be recorded in the *Analects*; Confucian thought is supplemented by the teachings of Mencius in the 4th century BC; Lao Zu (possibly mythical) creates the philosophy later set down in the Dao De Jing as Taoist thought; Han Fei Zi establishes the legalist school.

221 BCE China is unified for the first time under an imperial dynasty, the Qin, with its capital in Chang'an (present day Xi'an). The first emperor, Shi Huangdi, infamous for his hardline suppression of subversion and mass execution of intellectuals, is also credited with the instigation of the "Great Wall." Script and weights and measures are standardized.

206 BCE Liu Bang leads a peasant uprising to overthrow the Qin Dynasty and establish the Han, under which dynasty China was to be unified almost continually for over four centuries. Stability allows major advances to be

▶

made in political thought, economics, invention, and administration, and Chinese territory expands through several successful military campaigns.

6 CE The declining Han dynasty is usurped by Wang Mang who establishes the short-lived Xin Dynasty.

25 CE The Han dynasty is restored with its capital further East in Luoyang; the second phase is known as the Eastern Han.

220 CE The Eastern Han fails to produce the stability and achievements of the earlier Western Han due to a succession of young and weak emperors, and the country splits into three warring kingdoms: Shu, Wei, and Wu.

265 CE The Northern and Southern dynasties period begins; during this period the North of China is ruled by six different dynasties and the South by three.

589 CE Yang Jian, regent of the Northern Zhou dynasty conquers the Southern Chen dynasty and establishes the Sui, building a new capital in Luoyang. The Sui dynasty instigates many of the institutions developed to great success in the Tang: the administration, tax, forced labor, penal and examination systems. The Grand Canal is constructed. Excessive demands on the peasants for forced labor under the second emperor of the Sui bring about a peasant revolt in 611 CE which heralds the end of the dynasty.

618 CE Li Yuan leads an army revolt and captures Chang'an, hereafter capital of the Tang, but in 626 CE passes the throne to his second son Li Shimin, who becomes the famous Emperor Tai Zong of the Tang. The political institutions of the Sui are reformed along less repressive lines and the empire consolidated. "Land equalization" is carried out. The Tang is referred to in Chinese history as a "Golden Age," mostly for its arts (especially poetry and painting) which flourish under imperial patronage, and for unprecedented territorial expansion, but also for its political and religious tolerance.

755 CE Poor government leads to social disorder; An Lushan leads a rebellion which takes eight years to quell. The Tang recovers for nearly another century of stability (mid-Tang), but social order declines due to power struggles within the court throughout the late Tang period (820–907 CE).

906 CE The collapse of the Tang produces 54 years of disunity when rule passes between five separate dynasties (Later Liang, Later Tang, Later Jin, Later Han, and Later Zhou). Parts of North China come under the rule of ten non-Chinese kingdoms.

960 CE Zhou Kuangyin, commander of the Later Zhou's imperial army, leads a revolt to seize power, founds the Song dynasty, creating the capital in Kaifeng, and conquers the other Chinese states over a period of 15 years. In spite of rigorous attempts at centralizing control and defending itself against external attack, the Song never achieves the unity of the Tang. Political and military instability breeds philosophical and religious ferment, including the development of neo-Confucian thought.

1127 The Jurchen conquest of Northern China combines with factional struggle and peasant rebellion to produce the collapse of the Northern Song dynasty which re-establishes itself in Hangzhou as the Southern Song, the North of China lying under the control of the Jurchen Jin dynasty. Military conflict continues between the two regimes. The writing of Ci poetry reaches its peak in the South. Mongol armies under Ghengis Khan begin their gradual conquest of China.

1275 Marco Polo arrives in China.

1279 The Mongol conquest of China is completed under Kublai Khan, and the Yuan dynasty established, bringing the capital to the site of present day Beijing for the first time. Under the Mongols, agriculture, communications, and local administration are strengthened, drama flourishes and advances are made in science and technology. A policy of tolerance is adopted towards religion. Like many dynasties before it, the Mongol dynasty deteriorates through corruption and is overthrown by peasant rebellions.

1368 Zhu Yuanzhang establishes the Ming dynasty, moving the capital to Nanjing, then back to Beijing in 1421.

1421 Policies are adopted to restore order in the countryside: land is allocated to refugees and taxation eased. The bureaucracy is reorganized. Indiscriminate executions and a secret service ensure the unopposed rule of the emperor, and heavy censorship is instigated. The novel is introduced as a new form of literature and *The Water Margin* and *Journey to the West* (*"Monkey"*) achieve particular acclaim. The

dynasty is consistently shaken by peasant uprisings, and weakened by the power of eunuchs in the court. It is, however, Manchu invaders who bring about the fall of the Ming Dynasty.

1582 Portuguese traders arrive at Guangzhou.

1644 The Manchus conquer China, expand the region to an unprecedented extent and modify the Qing institutions. They allow the Han to participate in government, while holding onto power. Neo-Confucianism is the order of the day, though most of the emperors are also Buddhist adherents. While Czarist Russia encroaches on Chinese territory in the north, as well as establishing trade links, European merchants and later, Americans, begin to arrive by sea and stake out trading areas along the south coast.

1736 Emperor Qianlong comes to power, a patron of Buddhism under whose reign huge amounts of resources are spent on imperial leisure.

1839–1860 Opium Wars with Britain. China defeated; forced to open ports to foreigners.

1850–1873 Internal rebellions against Manchu empire.

1895 Defeat by Japan in war over control of Korean peninsula.

1900 Boxer Rebellion, an attempt to expel all foreigners, is suppressed.

1911 Manchu empire overthrown by nationalists led by Sun Yat-sen. Republic of China declared.

1912 Sun Yat-sen forms National People's Party (Guomindang).

1916 Nationalists factionalize. Sun Yat-sen sets up government in Guangdong. Rest of China under control of rival warlords.

1921 CCP founded in Shanghai.

1923 CCP joins Soviet-backed Guomindang to fight warlords.

1925 Chiang Kai-shek becomes Guomindang leader on death of Sun Yat-sen.

1927 Chiang turns on CCP. CCP leaders escape to rural south.

1930–1934 Mao Zedong formulates strategy of peasant-led revolution.

1931 Japan invades Manchuria.

1934 Chiang forces CCP out of its southern bases. Start of the Long March.

1935 Long March ends in Yanan, Shaanxi province. Mao becomes CCP leader.

1937–1945 War against Japan: CCP Red Army in north, Guomindang in south. Japan defeated.

1945–1949 War between Red Army and Guomindang. US-backed Guomindang retreats to Taiwan.

1949 October 1. Mao proclaims People's Republic of China.

1950 Invasion of Tibet. Mutual assistance treaty with USSR.

1950–1958 Land reform; culminates in setting up of communes. First Five-Year Plan (1953–1958) fails.

1958 "Great Leap Forward" to boost production fails; contributes to millions of deaths during 1959–1961 famine. Mao resigns as CCP chairman; succeeded by Liu Shaoqi.

1960 Sino-Soviet split.

1961–1965 More pragmatic economic approach led by Liu and Deng Xiaoping.

1966 Cultural Revolution initiated by Mao to restore his supreme power. Youthful Red Guards attack all authority. Mao rules, with Military Commission under Lin Biao and State Council under Zhou Enlai.

1967 Army intervenes to restore order amid countrywide chaos. Liu and Deng purged from party.

1969 Mao regains chair of CCP. Lin Biao designated his successor, but quickly attacked by Mao.

1971 Lin dies in plane crash.

1972 US President Nixon visits. More open foreign policy initiated by Zhou Enlai.

1973 Mao's wife Jiang Qing and other "Gang of Four" members elected to CCP politburo. Deng Xiaoping rehabilitated.

1976 Death of Zhou Enlai. Mao strips Deng of posts. September, Mao dies. October. Gang of Four arrested.

1977 Deng regains party posts, begins to extend power base.

1978 Decade of economic modernization launched. Open door policy to foreign investment and farmers are allowed to farm for profit.

1980 Deng emerges as China's paramount leader. Economic reform gathers pace, but hopes for political change suppressed.

1983–1984 Conservative elderly leaders attempt to slow reform.

1984 Industrial reforms announced.

1989 Prodemocracy demonstrations in Tiananmen Square. Crushed by army; 1000–5000 dead. Beijing under martial law.

1992–1995 Trials of prodemocracy activists continue. Plans for market economy accelerated.

1993 Jiang Zemin president.

1997 Deng Xiaoping dies at 92. July. UK hands back Hong Kong. September. Five-yearly party congress confirms Jiang's leadership and backs his reformist policies.

1999 China develops neutron bomb. Portugal hands back Macao. Friction over Taiwanese claim of statehood. Clampdown on Falun Gong sect.

2000 Taiwanese presidential election causes tension. USA normalizes trade relations.

2001 Major diplomatic incident with US when Chinese pilot is killed and US spy-plane is forced down on Hainan Island. Beijing awarded 2008 Olympic Games.

2002 Crackdown on Uyghur separatism.

2003 Hu Jintao president. SARS outbreak. June, Three Gorges Dam flooded. October, first manned aircraft launched.

CHINESE DYNASTIES

c.2000–1800 BCE	Hsia dynasty (legendary)
c.1800–1000 BCE	Shang dynasty
c.1000–256 BCE	Zhou dynasty
c.1000–771 BCE	Former (Western) Zhou
771–256 BCE	Later (Eastern) Zhou
771–481 BCE	"Spring and Autumn" Period
403–221 BCE	"Warring States" Period
221–206 BCE	Qin dynasty
206 BCE–220 CE	Han dynasty
206 BCE–9 CE	Former Han
9 CE–23 CE	Wang Mang interregnum; Xin dynasty
25–220	Later Han
220–80	Three kingdoms:
220–65	Wei
221–65	Shu Han
222–80	Wu
265–420	Jin dynasty
265–317	Western Jin
317–420	Eastern Jin
420–481	Southern and Northern dynasties
386–543	Wei dynasty
581–618	Sui dynasty
618–906	Tang dynasty
907–960	Five dynasties
937–1125	Liao dynasty
960–1279	Song dynasty
960–1126	Northern Song
1127–1279	Southern Song
960–1227	Hsi-Hsia
1115–1234	Jin dynasty
1260–1367	Yuan dynasty
1368–1644	Ming dynasty
1644–1912	Qing dynasty

CHINESE LEADERS (1912–)

Presidents (Republic of China)

1912	Dr Sun Yat-sen (Sun Zhongshan)
1912–1916	Yuan Shikai
1916–1917	Li Yuan-hung
1917–1918	Feng Kuo-chang
1918–1922	Hsu Shih-ch'ang
1922–1923	Li Yuan-hung (second term)
1923–1924	T'sao Kun
1924–1926	Tuan Chi-jui
1927–1928	Chang Tso-lin
1928–1931	Chiang Kai-shek (Jiang Jieshi)
1932–1943	Lin Sen
1943–1949	Chiang Kai-shek (Jiang Jieshi)
1949–1950	Li Tsung-jen

PEOPLE'S REPUBLIC OF CHINA (founded, 1949)

Presidents

1949–1959	Mao Zedong
1959–1968	Liu Shaoqi
1968–1975	Tung Pi Wu
1975–1976	Chu Te
1976–1983	Yeh Chien-ying
1983–1988	Li Xiannian
1988–1993	Yang Shangkun
1993–2003	Jiang Zemin
2003–	Hu Jintao

Prime Ministers

1949–1976	Zhou Enlai
1976–1980	Hua Guofeng
1980–1987	Zhao Ziyang
1987–1998	Li Peng
1998–2003	Zhu Rongji
2003–	Wen Jiabao

LEADERS OF THE COMMUNIST PARTY OF CHINA

Chairmen

1943–1976	Mao Zedong
1976–1981	Hua Guofeng
1981–1982	Hu Yaobang

General secretaries

1956–1957	Deng Xiaoping
1980–1987	Hu Yaobang
1987–1989	Zhao Ziyang
1989–2003	Jiang Zemin
2003–	Hu Jintao

chinampas Artificial islands, used by peoples of Central America (especially the Aztecs) for raising crops.

Ch'in dynasty *see* Qin dynasty

Ching dynasty *see* Qing dynasty

Ching empire *see* Qing empire

Ching-Ghis Khan *see* Genghis Khan

Chingis Khan *see* Genghis Khan

Chola dynasty (*var.* Cola dynasty, c.860–1279). The Chola kingdom, mentioned in the inscriptions of Ashoka, came into prominence in southern India in c.860 CE. Under Rajaraja the Great, who came to the throne in 985, Chola control extended to Ceylon, which was conquered in 1018, and parts of the Malay Peninsula. Chola power gradually declined after the 11th century. *p.162*

Chou Dynasty *see* Zhou dynasty

Chou En-lai *see* Zhou Enlai

Christianity One of the world's great religions, an offshoot of Judaism that emerged in Palestine in the 1st century CE, based on the life and teachings of Jesus of Nazareth. The early Christian faith diverged into many sects, but by the 8th century CE there were two main branches: the Eastern Orthodox and the Roman Catholic Churches. In 16th-century Europe, a reaction to the Roman Church, known as the Reformation, led to the foundation of many breakaway Protestant churches which refused to recognize the authority of the pope in Rome.
Early Christianity. *p.86, p.90, p.99*
Christianity in Europe (400–850). *p.129*
Northern Christianity. *p.132*
Major Christian Missionaries. *p.143*
Norwegian Christianity. *p.189*
Reformation. *p.275*
See also Roman Catholicism, Judaism, Reformation, Protestantism

Christ, Jesus *see* Jesus of Nazareth

Chrysler Building New York skyscraper completed in 1930. *p.411*

Chu-ssu-pen *see* Zhu Siben

Chu Yuan-chang *see* Zhu Yuanzhang

Chucuito culture Andean culture that flourished in the 13th century CE.

Church of England (*var.* Anglican Church) Protestant episcopalian church founded by Henry VIII in 1534. The Act of Supremacy made the king or queen of England head of the English church in place of the pope. *See also* Canterbury, Archbishops of

Churchill, Sir Winston Leonard Spencer (1874–1965) British statesman. Service in Omdurman campaign (1897–98) and as a journalist during the Boer War (1899–1900) preceded his entry to Parliament (1900). Became Home Secretary (1910) and First Lord of the Admiralty (1911–15), bearing responsibility for the Dardanelles campaign, thereafter serving in the trenches and entering political "wilderness." Formed coalition government (1940) and oversaw Britain's policy and strategy during World War II. Lost election upon Allied victory (1945), but returned as Prime Minister (1951–55).

CIA *see* Central Intelligence Agency

cinema Hollwood: the silent era. *p.408*

CIS *see* Commonwealth of Independent States, Russia, USSR

Cistercians Roman Catholic monastic order that was founded in 1098 and named after the original establishment at Cîteaux, France. The order's founding fathers, led by St. Robert of Molesmes, were a group of Benedictine monks who wished to a live a solitary life under the strictest interpretation of the Rule of St. Benedict. *p.181*

city-state A single urban center and its hinterland. Although politically autonomous, city-states, in Ancient Greece and pre-Colombian America for example, usually shared cultural traits – such as language and religion – with their neighbors.

Civil Rights Movement US mass movement to combat segregation and discriminatory practices against Black people. Arose in the US in the 1950s and 1960s. The movement began with the Montgomery bus boycott of 1956, following the arrest of a black woman, Rosa Parks, for refusing to move to the "Negro" section of the bus. The movement gained momentum with the involvement of Martin Luther King who advocated the principle of non-violent protest, culminating in the 1963 March on Washington by more than a million people. The Civil Rights Act of 1964 and the Voting Rights Act of 1965 were legal responses to the pressure generated by the movement.

Cixi, Dowager Empress (*var.* Tz'u-Hsi, 1835–1908) Manchu empress (reigned 1861–1908). Became regent in China and opposed all modernization. Helped foment the Boxer Rebellion in 1900 and organized the murder of her successor, the emperor Guangxu, in 1908.

Clapperton, Hugh (1788–1827) The first European explorer in W Africa to return with a first-hand account of the region around present-day N Nigeria. He journeyed with explorers Dixon Denham and Walter Oudney (1821–26).

Clark, William (1770–1838) US explorer. With Meriwether Lewis he was sent by President Thomas Jefferson to explore the lands acquired in the Louisiana Purchase of 1803, and to find a land route to the Pacific Ocean.

Classical Age Greece (5th–3rd centuries BCE) An era of city-states characterized by stone or marble monumental architecture – the zenith of architecture, art and sculpture, which set the standards of beauty and proportion for figurative art for the next 2500 years. This era also saw the flowering of literature, philosophy and science.

Classis The port of Ravenna, the late Roman, Ostrogothic and Byzantine capital of Italy. *p.106*

Claudius Ptolemaeus *see* Ptolemy

Clavus 15th-century Danish mapmaker. Added detail of northern Europe to the Ptolemaic map of the world (1425).

Cleopatra VII (*var.* Thea Philopator) (69–3C BCE) Queen of Egypt (reigned 51–30 BCE) The last of the Ptolemaic dynasty which ruled Egypt after Alexander the Great's death. Cleopatra was a Macedonian, and ruled alongside her brothers, Ptolemy XIII Ptolemy XIV, and subsequently, her son Ptolemy XV Caesar, and alone amongst her dynasty learned to speak Egyptian. She used her famed charm and beauty to delay Egypt's annexation by Rome, bearing children by two of its statesmen, Julius Caesar and Mark Antony. The latter restored much of the old Ptolemaic empire to her, and awarded areas of Rome's eastern provinces to their children a policy which led to their defeat by Octavian at Actium in 31 BCE. Soon after, both she and Antony committed suicide.

Clermont (*mod.* Clermont-Ferrand) French city where Pope Urban II preached the First Crusade (1095).

Clinton, William Jefferson (Bill) (1946–) 42nd President of the US. (Democrat, 1992– 2000). The youngest-ever governor of Arkansas, in 1992 he defeated George Bush to become the first Democrat president since Jimmy Carter. Despite a number of scandals, remained enormousl popular at home due to the buoyant US economy, and was re-elected in 1996. Became first 20th-century president to undergo an impeachment trial in 1999.

live, Sir Robert (1725–74). Commanded British troops at the defence of Arcot (1751), and defeated a combined French and Mughal force at the battle of Plassey (1757), which laid the foundations of the British empire in India. He became the Governor of the East India Company's settlements in Bengal (1757–60, 1765–67), and instituted major reforms of the Company's administration.

loning The first mammal cloned from a single cell of an adult animal: the celebrated Dolly the sheep. *p.452*

lovis I (c.465–511). King of the Franks and founder of the Merovingian dynasty, Clovis was responsible for creating the kingdom of France from the old Roman province of Gaul. He defeated the Visigoths in Aquitaine.

lovis point Heavy projectile point, usually in the shape of a leaf, dating from the 10th millennium BCE, specifically in eastern New Mexico. They are often found close to finds of mammoth bones.

ocaine White crystalline alkaloid obtained from the leaves of the coca plant, cultivated in Africa, northern S America, SE Asia, and Taiwan. An increasingly popular recreational drug. The drugs trade in the 1990s. *p.452*

oclé culture Culture that flourished in Panama in the second half of the first millennium CE. *p.167*

odomannus *see* Darius III

oins The first coins. *p.46*
Coin of Emper Honorius. *p.100*

oke, Thomas William (1752–1842) (created Earl of Leicester of Holkham in 1837). English agriculturalist who developed new and more robust strains of cattle, pigs and sheep, on his experimental farm. He also helped to initiate the switch from rye to wheat-growing in NW Norfolk.

ola Dynasty *see* Chola dynasty

old Harbor ⚔ of American Civil War (Jun 3 1864). Inconclusive result.

old War (c.1947–1991). Period of ideological, political, economic, and military confrontation between the Communist bloc, dominated by the Soviet Union and China, and the Western free market economy nations bound to US by NATO. Effectively ended by the dissolution of the Soviet Union in 1991. *p.430*

COLOMBIA Lying in northwest South America, Colombia has coastlines on both the Caribbean and the Pacific. The east of the country is densely forested and sparsely populated, and separated from the western coastal plains by the Andes mountains. The Andes divide into three ranges *(cordilleras)* in Colombia. The eastern range is divided from the two western ranges by the densely populated Magdalena river valley. The Colombian lowlands are very wet, hot, and fertile, supporting two harvests and allowing many crops to be planted at any time of year. A multiparty democracy since 1957, Colombia is noted for its coffee, emeralds, gold, and narcotics trafficking.

CHRONOLOGY

1525 Spain began the conquest of Colombia, which became its chief source of gold.

1530s Gonzalo Jimenez de Quesada explores what is now Colombia.

1718 Santa Fé de Bogota becomes capital of the new Viceroyalty of New Granada, established in 1717.

1813 Independence is declared in Cundinamarca.

1819 Simón Bolívar defeats the Spanish at Boyacá. Republic of Gran Colombia formed with Venezuela, Ecuador, and Panama.

1830 Venezuela and Ecuador split away during revolts and civil wars.

1849 The Centralist Conservative and federalist Liberal parties are established.

1861–1886 Period in which Liberals hold monopoly on power.

1886–1930 Conservative rule.

1899–1903 Liberal "War of 1000 Days" revolt fails; 120,000 die.

1903 Panama secedes, but is not recognized by Colombia until 1921.

1930 Liberal President Olaya Herrera elected by coalition in first peaceful change of power.

1946 Conservatives take over.

1948 Shooting of Liberal mayor of Bogotá and riot known as El Bogotazo spark civil war, La Violencia, to 1957; 300,000 killed.

1953–1957 Military dictatorship of Rojas Pinilla.

1958 Conservatives and Liberals agree to alternate government in a National Front until 1974. Other parties banned.

1965 Left-wing guerrilla movements, the National Liberation Army and the Maoist Popular Liberation Army, founded.

1966 Pro-Soviet FARC guerrilla group formed.

1968 Constitutional reform allows new parties, but two-party parity continues. Guerrilla groups proliferate from now on.

1984 Minister of justice assassinated for attempting to enforce antidrugs campaign.

1985 M-19 guerrillas blast way into Ministry of Justice; 11 judges and 90 others killed. Patriotic Union (UP) party formed.

1986 Liberal Virgilio Barco Vargas wins presidential elections, ending power-sharing. UP wins ten seats in parliament. Right-wing paramilitary start murder campaign against UP politicians. Violence by both left-wing groups and death squads run by drugs cartels continues.

1989 M-19 reaches a peace agreement with the government, including the granting of a full pardon. M-19 becomes legal party.

1990 UP and PL presidential candidates are murdered during the general election. Liberal César Gaviria is elected on an antidrugs platform.

1991 New constitution legalizes divorce, prohibits extradition of Colombian nationals. Indigenous peoples' democratic rights guaranteed, but territorial claims are not addressed.

1992–1993 Medellín drugs cartel leader, Pablo Escobar, captured. He escapes and is shot dead by police.

1995–1996 President Samper cleared of charges of receiving Cali cartel drug funds for elections.

1998 Andres Pastrana Arango elected to succeed Samper.

1999 Earthquake kills thousands.

2001 USA-backed spraying of illegal coca plantations begins in south; destruction of food crops by herbicides provokes resentment among peasant farmers.

2002 Peace talks abandoned. Renewed military offensive. Independent candidate Alvaro Uribe Velez elected president.

2004 ELN offered cease-fire.

Colonization European colonization 1466–1600. *p.289*

Columba, St. (c.521–597) Irish missionary to Scotland. *p.119*

Columbus, Christopher (*var. It.* Cristoforo Colombo, c.1451–1506) Genoese explorer. In 1492, having been financed by Ferdinand and Isabella of Spain, Columbus crossed the Atlantic in search of China and Japan, but made a landfall, probably in the Bahamas, sailed on to Cuba, and then founded a colony on Hispaniola. He made three more voyages which greatly increased European knowledge of the Caribbean, but his governorship of the expanding colonies was never successful and once, in 1500, he was arrested and sent back to Spain in chains. *p.270*

Combined Bombing Offensive Joint strategic bombing campaign by US and RAF against Nazi-occupied Europe during World War II; inaugurated in 1942, it reached a climax with the destruction of Dresden (Feb 13–15 1945).

COMECON *see* Council for Economic Assistance

Comintern (*aka* Communist International) International socialist organization established 1919, promulgated by the leadership of Bolshevik Russia, envisioning export of Soviet Communism worldwide. Split the world socialist movement and led to uprisings in Europe and elsewhere. Dissolved in 1943.

Committee of Correspondence Set up by legislatures in Britain's 13 American colonies to provide leadership to the Colonial cause and aid cooperation. The first group was organized by Samuel Adams at Boston in Nov 1772.

Commodus, Caesar Marcus Aurelius (161–92 CE) Commodus' tenure as Roman emperor between 180–92 CE ended 84 years of stability and prosperity in Rome. As he lapsed into insanity, he renamed Rome "Colonia Commodiana," and believed himself to be the god Hercules. When he took to appearing in gladiatorial garb his advisors in desperation had him strangled by a champion wrestler.

Common Market *see* European Union.

Commonwealth of Independent States (CIS) (*var. Rus.* Sodruzhestvo Nezavisimykh Gosudarstv). Free association of sovereign states formed in 1991, and comprising Russia and 11 other republics that were formerly part of the Soviet Union. *See also* Russian Federation

communications The 19th century saw a complete revolution in long-distance communications thanks to the invention of the the electric telegraph, the telephone, and – at the end of the century – the wireless. *p.375*

Communism Political and social ideology developed by Karl Marx (1818–83) and Friedrich Engels (1820–95) whereby all property and goods are owned communally and distributed according to need. Implemented under socialist revolutionary conditions with escalating degrees of failure by Lenin and Stalin in Russia, and by Mao Zedong in China.

Communist Bloc (*var.* Eastern Bloc, the East). General geo-political term for the group of socialist (Communist states in military and economic alliance following World War II, led by USSR and China. Soviet hegemony was formalized by COMECON (1949) and the Warsaw Pact (1955) binding the Soviet-dominated nations of central and eastern Europe into a military grouping, although the Communist bloc was weakened by the Sino-Soviet dispute (1960). The Soviet alliance collapsed in 1989–90, and was partly replaced by the Commonwealth of Independent States (CIS, 1991). Collapse of Communism. *p.448 See also* Warsaw Pact

COMOROS The archipelago Republic of the Comoros lies off the east African coast, between Mozambique and Madagascar. It consists of three main islands and a number of islets. Most of the population are subsistence farmers. In 1975, the Comoros Islands, except for Mayotte, became independent of France. Since then instability has plagued this poor region, with several coups and counter-coups, and repeated attempts at secession by smaller islands.

CHRONOLOGY

1886 Comoros becomes a French protectorate. Previous to this it had strong cultural and trading ties with the Arab world and mainland East Africa.
1947 The islands acquire the status of a French overseas territory.
1961 Internal self-government.
1975 Independence.
1978 Mercenaries restore Ahmed Abdallah to power.
1989 Abdallah assassinated.
1992 Chaotic first multiparty polls.
1996 Mohammed Taki Abdoulkarim elected president.
1997 Anjouan separatists beat off government troops.
1999 Col. Azzali seizes power. Anjouan militias clash.
2000 Fomboni declaration signed with Anjouan.
2001 President Azzali promises return to civilian government by early 2002.
2002 New constitution. Azali returned to office.
2004 Regional parties win majority in legislative elections.

Compass Invention of the magnetic compass. *p.220*

Computers The Computer Age. *p.447*

Comstoke Lode Site of gold find in Nevada (1849–50).

Concentration camps The notorious camps in which Jews and other civilians were interned by the Nazis were not an invention of World War II. They were first used in South Africa in the Boer War (1899–1902) when the British rounded up women and children to cut off all possible aid to the Boer guerrillas. *p.416*

Concepción ⚔ of wars of S American independence in Chile (May 1817).

Concord ⚔ of American Revolutionary War (Apr 19 1775). American victory.

Confederacy (Confederate states) The 11 Southern states which seceded from the United States in 1860–61 to form a separate government, so leading to Civil War. The states were Alabama, Arkansas, Florida, Georgia, Louisiana, Mississippi, N Carolina, S Carolina, Tennessee, Texas and Virginia. These were reincorporated into the Union in 1865 following the Confederate surrender.

Confucius (*var.* K'ung-fu-tzu, Kongzi) 551–479 BCE) Chinese accountant, administrator, and philosopher whose teachings and writings (Analects) espoused the inherent common good in correct conduct, morality, ethics, education, and respect, which codified the Chinese social and political system, acquiring the status of a religion.

CONGO Straddling the equator in west central Africa, Congo achieved independence from France in 1960. It fell under a Marxist-Leninist regime with a one-party form of government which discouraged much foreign investment. Multiparty democracy was achieved in 1991, but has since been overtaken by years of feuding and violence.

CHRONOLOGY

15th century–18th century Two kingdoms occupy the territory of what is today Congo: Loango in the south, Makoko further inland. Northern forest regions are the territory of the Binga pygmies. Loango eventually falls under the domination of the Kongo kingdom, whose capital is in present day Angola. Portuguese traders establish Europe's first regular contacts with the region.

1875 The French explorer Count Savorgnan de Brazza visits the region. He agrees a treaty with Makoko, chief of the Teke, which he claims gives rights to the entire Bateke plateau.

1891 France founds the Congo colony, on the north bank of Stanley Pool on the Zaire river.

1910 French Congo is integrated into French Equatorial Africa, whose capital is Brazzaville, on Stanley Pool.

1926–1942 Unrest, associated with Andre Matswa's "matswatisme" movement.

1940 The French governor, Gen. Felix Eboue, chooses to support de Gaulle and reject France"s Vichy government, which has agreed to collaborate with the Germans.

1944 January-February. de Gaulle holds the Brazzaville conference to reorganize France's African colonies.

1956 Abbot Fulbert Youlou founds the Democratic Union for the Defence of African Interests (UDDIA).

1958 Admission of Congo to the Franco-African Community as an autonomous state.

1958 Proclamation of the republic.

1959 Youlou is elected President.

1960 August 15. Congo gains full independence from France. It is known as Congo-Brazzaville, to distinguish it from the much larger Congo-Kinshasa (former Belgian Congo) until the latter changes its name to Zaire in 1971.

1964 Marxist-Leninist National Revolution Movement (MNR) becomes sole legal party.

1977 Yhompi-Opango head of state after President Ngoumbi's murder.

1979 Col. Denis Sassou-Nguesso president.

1992 Pascal Lissouba elected president.

1993 Elections: Lissouba's UPADS party gains majority.

1997 Lissouba ousted by Sassou-Nguesso. December, cease-fire signed.

2001 Draft constitution approved by parliament, subject to popular referendum.

2002 New constitution approved. Sassou-Nguesso wins elections.

CONGO, DEMOCRATIC REPUBLIC

Lying in east central Africa, the Democratic Republic of Congo (DRC), known as Zaire from 1971 to 1997, is one of Africa's largest countries. The rainforested basin of the Congo River occupies 60% of the land area. The modern Congo was the site of the Kongo and other powerful African kingdoms and a focus of the slave trade. Belgium's King Leopold II claimed most of the Congo basin after 1876 as his personal possession. The treatment of the Africans in the Congo Free State, especially those forced to pick rubber at gunpoint, provoked an international outcry – the so-called "Red Rubber" scandal. In 1908 Leopold handed over control of the colony to the Belgian government. On independence in 1960, civil war broke out. The notoriously corrupt Genertal Mobutu ruled from 1965 until his overthrow in 1997 by rebel forces under Laurent-Désiré Kabila. A rebellion launched in 1998 plunged the countryinto renewed chaos. Peace initiatives were revitalized by Joseph Kabila's succession in January 2001. *See also* Zaire

CHRONOLOGY

1885 Brutal colonization of Congo Free State (CFS) as King Leopold's private fief.

1908 Belgium takes over CFS after international outcry.

1960 Independence of Republic of Congo. Katanga province secedes. UN intervenes.

1963 Katanga secession collapses.

1965 General Mobutu seizes power.

1970 Mobutu elected president; his MPR becomes sole legal party.

1971 Country renamed Zaire.

1977–1978 Two invasions by former Katanga separatists repulsed .

1982 Opposition parties set up Union for Democracy and Social Progress (UDPS).

1986–1990 Civil unrest and foreign criticism of human rights abuses.

1990 Belgium suspends aid after security forces kill prodemocracy demonstrators. Mobutu announces transition to multiparty rule.

1991 Opposition leader Etienne Tshisekedi heads short-lived "crisis government" formed by Mobutu.

1992–1993 Rival governments claim legitimacy.

1994 Combined High Council of the Republic–Transitional Parliament established, elects Kengo wa Dondo as prime minister.

1995 Regime demands international assistance to support a million Rwandan Hutu refugees.

1996 Major insurgency launched in east by Alliance of Democratic forces for the Liberation of the Congo (AFDL) including Laurent Kabila's Popular Revolutionary Party (PRP), with disaffected ethnic Tutsi Banyamulunge.

1997 Forces led by Kabila sweep south and west. Mobutu flees and dies in exile. Kabila takes power. Country renamed DRC.

1998 Banyamulunge join Kabila's opponents and launch rebellion in the east, backed by Rwanda and Uganda. Southern African states, give military backing to Kabila.

2000 UN approves peacekeeping mission; arrival stalled by Kabila.

2001 January, Laurent Kabila assassinated; succeeded by son Joseph. Peace talks start, with troop withdrawals from front line, but progress slow.

2003 April, Final Act peace accord signed. Hundreds massacred at Drodro in northeast during tribal conflict.

conquistador (conqueror) Name given to any leader of the Spanish conquest of America, especially of Mexico and Peru, in the 16th century. *See also* individual entries on explorers of N and S America

Conrad III (1093–1152) German king (reigned 1138–1152) who was the first sovereign of the Hohenstaufen family.

Constantine I (Constantine the Great, c.280–337) Roman emperor (reigned 307–337). Constantine eliminated various rivals and co-emperors to emerge as sole ruler in 324. His reign was remarkable for his conversion to Christianity and the Edict of Milan (313), which granted toleration of Christianity throughout the empire. His creation of a new capital at Constantinople in 330 also had momentous consequences for the later development of the Roman Empire. *p.93*

Constantinople (*var.* Bysantion, Byzantium, mod. Istanbul). Ancient Greek city rebuilt by Constantine (c.324–330) as new capital of his empire. It remained the capital of the Byzantine Empire until 1453 when it fell to the Ottoman Turks. *p.263*

Conti, Niccolo di (c.1395–1469) Venetian merchant who embarked on journeys through Arabia, Persia, India, Burma and the East Indies. He was forced to convert to Islam on his travels, but on his return to Europe embraced Christianity.

Contras Nicaraguan counter-revolutionaries, supported by the US in the 1980s. From bases in Honduras, they mounted guerrilla actions against the ruling left-wing Sandinistas.

Cook, Captain James (1728–79) English explorer of the Pacific. Cook's three epic voyages to the Pacific added immeasurably to European knowledge of the region. The ostensible purpose of the first (1768–71) was to observe the transit of Venus across the face of the sun from Tahiti, but Cook also mapped the whole of New Zealand and the uncharted east coast of Australia. The second (1772–75) included the circumnavigation of Antarctica, and the third (1776–79) took him north to the Bering Strait. On the way, he discovered the Hawaiian Islands. Returning there, he was killed in an argument between islanders and his crew. *p.333*

Coolidge, (John) Calvin (1872–1933) 30th President of the US (Republican, 1923–28). Became president on death of Warren Harding. His laissez faire policies, including tax cuts and business deregulation were later thought to have been responsible for the stock market crash of 1929. His administration presided over the Dawes Plan, reducing German reparations after World War I, and the Kellogg-Briand Pact.

Copper Age Name given to the period in European history – the 5th and 4th millennia BCE – before the Bronze Age, when many societies started to work metal first by hammering, then by smelting. The metals used were chiefly copper and gold, the objects made being generally ornamental rather than practical.

Copts Members of the Coptic Church, an ancient Monophysite branch of Christianity well established in Egypt by the 5th century, which has survived to the present day. *p.106*

Coral Sea Naval ⚔ of World War II (May 1942). US forces halted Japanese advance in southwest Pacific

Córdoba, Hernández de 16th-century Spanish explorer of N America (1517–24).

Cordoba, Caliphate of (756–1031) After the Umayyad caliphate fell to the Abbasids in 749, one branch of the Umayyad dynasty won control of the Muslim territories in the Iberian Peninsula. In 928 Abd al-Rahman III proclaimed himself Caliph. The rule of the Umayyads ended in the 11th century, as the Caliphate splintered into many small kingdoms. The Great Mosque of Cordoba. *p.153*

cord scoring Method of decoration created by imprinting unfired ceramic objects with a length of cord.

Corinth Greek city totally destroyed by the Romans in 146 BCE. It was later rebuilt under Roman rule.

Cornwallis, General Charles,1st Marquis (1738–1805) English soldier. Despite opposing the taxation of American colonists, he led British forces against the Americans in the American Revolution, winning at Camden (1780) but was forced to surrender after the siege of Yorktown (1781) paving the way for British defeat in the war. He later held senior government and military posts in France, Ireland and India where he twice held the post of Governor-General.

Coronado, Francisco Vásquez de (1510–54) Spanish explorer of N America. Appointed governor of New Galicia province in Mexico. In 1540 he set out to find the "seven treasure cities of the north" on the orders of the viceroy. In 1541 he traveled north of the Arkansas River.

Corregidor ⚔ of World War II (May 1942) Took place on island in Manila Bay, marking last defeat of US forces in Philippines by Japan.

Cortenuova ⚔ (1237) Italian communes defeated by Emperor Frederick II.

Cortés, Hernán (*var.* Cortéz) (1485–1547). Spanish conquistador who overthrew the Aztec empire (1519–21) and won Mexico for the Spanish crown. *p.277*

Cortéz, Hernán *see* Cortés, Hernán

Corte-Real, Gaspar and Miguel (died 1501 and 1502) Portuguese explorers. Gaspar traveled down the N American coast from Greenland c.1500 but his ship was lost on a subsequent expedition. On a later expedition in 1502, Miguel's ship was also lost. Spanish recognition of the lands they discovered allowed Portuguese exploitation of the rich fisheries in the Newfoundland banks.

Corupedium ⚔ of (281 BCE) Lysimachus defeated by Seleucus.

Cosa, Juan de la (died 1509) Spanish cartographer and navigator who accompanied Columbus on his second expedition in 1493. In 1500 he compiled a world map which recorded all Columbus's recent discoveries.

Cosa Nostra *see* Mafia

Cossacks Inhabitants of the northern hinterlands of the Black and Caspian seas. They had a tradition of independence and finally received privileges from the Russian government in return for military services.

COSTA RICA Located in Central America between Nicaragua and Panama, Costa Rica was under Spanish rule until 1821 and gained full independence in 1838. From 1948 until the end of the 1980s, it had the most developed welfare state in Central America. Costa Rica is nominally a multiparty democracy, but two parties dominate. Coffee and bananas are the major exports. Its army was abolished in 1948; the 1949 constitution then forbade national armies.

CHRONOLOGY

1502 Columbus lands during the course of his last voyage. In the second half of the century the territory is annexed to the

Captaincy-General of Guatemala and becomes a European-oriented society of small landowners.

1821–40 Upon independence Costa Rica forms part of the United Provinces of Central America until the dissolution of the federation.

1948 Disputed elections lead to civil war; ended by Social Democratic Party (later the PLN) forming provisional government under José Ferrer. Army abolished.

1949 New constitution promulgated.

1987 Central American Peace Plan initiated by President Arias.

1998 PUSC returns to power.

Côte d'Ivoire *See* Ivory Coast

Cotopaxi Volcano in Ecuador scaled by Wilhelm Reiss (1872).

Cotton The cotton plantations of the southern United States in the 19th century. *p.360*

Council for Economic Assistance (COMECON) Communist organization, established (1949), under auspices of Soviet Union, to create sphere of economic and trade links within Eastern Bloc countries. *See also* Communist bloc.

Counter-Reformation (*var.* Catholic Reformation, Catholic Revival) Efforts directed, in the 16th and early 17th centuries, both against the Protestant Reformation and toward internal renewal of the Roman Catholic Church.

Courland (*var.* Courland Pocket) ✂ of World War II (Feb–May 1945) between Germans and Soviets for control of the Baltic region.

Covilhã, Pero de (*var.* Pedro de Covilham, Covilhão) (c.1460–1526). Portuguese explorer. In 1487 he went in search of the mythical "Prester John," sailing down the Red Sea and exploring the west coast of India and E Africa. Established relations between Portugal and Ethiopia.

Cowpens ✂ of American Revolutionary War (Jan 17 1781). American victory.

Crécy ✂ of Hundred Years' War (1346). English defeat French.

Creole Name given to descendants of European settlers in Central and S America and the Caribbean. Also language which is a mixture of a European and another, especially African language.

Cresques, Abraham 14th-century Majorcan cartographer to King Peter IV of Aragon, creator of the so-called "Catalan Atlas." *p.247*

Crete Mediterranean island, cradle of the spectacular Minoan civilization which arose c.2000 BCE. The island experienced periods of Greek, Roman, Byzantine, and Arab rule, before passing to Venice in the 13th century. The Ottomans finaly ousted the Venetians from the island in 1669. It became part of Greece in 1913.

Crimea Peninsula on N coast of Black Sea, formerly a vassal state of the Ottomans, conquered and annexed by Russia (1783).

Crimean War (1853–56) War fought by France, Britain, and Turkey against Russia. The origins of the war lay in Russia's claim to be the protector of all Greek Christians in the Turkish Empire and from British and French distrust of Russia's ambitions in the Black Sea area, which posed a threat to their overland routes to India. Following a series of battles in the Crimean peninsula and a prolonged siege of the Russian fortress at Sebastapol, the Russians withdrew forces from the peninsula. Peace negotiations at Paris checked Russian influence in southeast Europe. *p.365*

Cristoforo Colombo *see* Columbus, Christopher

CROATIA Located to the south of Slovenia and west of Yugoslavia, Croatia includes the historic regions of Istria, Dalmatia, and Slavonia. Its Adriatic coastline is vital for tourism and shipping. During the breakup of the former Yugoslavia, Croatia fought to defend its own territory and was involved in the Bosnian war. Military offensives in 1995 ended Serb control over several enclaves, while Eastern Slavonia was administered by the UN until its return to Croatia in 1998.

CHRONOLOGY

640 CE Croats conquer the Avars who had controlled the area which is now Croatia after the decline of the Roman Empire. A Croat duchy is formed, the Croats accepting rule by the Franks in the following century. The Croats formally convert to Roman Catholicism at the Council of Split in 1060, which bans services in Church Slavonic (the language of the Eastern Orthodox church).

925 CE Duke Tomislav assumes the title of King of Croatia, which is recognized by the Papacy. A truce in the conflicts with Byzantium and their successors in the region, the Venetians, is followed by expansion in Dalmatia.

1060 The Croats formally convert to Roman Catholicism at the Council of Split, which bans services in Church Slavonic (the language of the Eastern Orthodox church).

1089 The assassination of King Demetrius Zvonimir leads to anarchy. Croatia is conquered by Hungary, Zvonimir's widow being sister to the Hungarian king. In 1102 Croatia unites with Hungary, although it retains some measure of autonomy.

1526 The Turks defeat the Hungarians at Mohács, and occupy most of Croatia. In 1527 Croatian nobles elect Ferdinand of Austria as their king. Croatia is thus split between the Austro-Hungarian and the Ottoman empires.

1699 The Ottoman Empire is forced to cede Croatia to Austria-Hungary under the Treaty of Karlowitz, after failing to capture Vienna in 1683. Recolonization takes place, establishing pockets of Serbian population in Croatia.

1809 Napoleon captures the Croatian territory held by Austria-Hungary and reorganizes it into an Illyrian Province, along French lines, giving an impetus to Croatian national sentiment. Austria-Hungary regains control in 1813.

1843 Hungary imposes a language law making Magyar the official language in Croatia amid increased Croatian nationalism. The Croatian parliament makes Croat the official language in 1847. In 1849 Croatia becomes an Austrian crown land after a revolt in Austrian-controlled Hungary in 1848 is crushed, with the assistance of Croatian troops.

1867 Croatia becomes an autonomous land under Hungarian control once more, after Austria and Hungary divide their Slav lands after the Habsburgs' defeat by Prussia. In 1868 the Hungarians recognize the existence of the Croatian nation, albeit subordinate to Hungary, with its official language, parliament and ruler, invoking the 12th century agreement to this effect.

1875 An insurrection against Turkish rule in Herzegovina spreads to Bosnia and provokes a crisis in the region which spreads to Croatia, where there is

▶

agitation for Bosnia to be incorporated into Croatia, anti-Hungarian rioting (in 1883), and a rise in anti-Serb feeling.

1912 December. After nearly a decade of nationalist disturbances and the emergence of a majority Serbo-Croat coalition for Yugoslav unity, which takes power in Croatia in 1906, the Hungarian government suspends the Croatian constitution and imposes a dictatorship.

1914 The First World War breaks out, triggered by the murder of the Austrian archduke Ferdinand, heir to the Emperor, in Sarajevo, the Bosnian capital on June 28. Austria-Hungary clamps down on Croatian nationalism. A group of Croatian exiles in London helps to form the Yugoslav Committee and continues to demand union with Serbia.

1918 October 29. The Croatian Diet, with the Central Powers on the verge of collapse, declares independence from Hungary and appeals for help from the Serbian army. On December 1 Serbian Prince Alexander proclaims the united Kingdom of Serbs, Croats, and Slovenes.

1920 Elections to a Constituent Assembly result in a centrist government led by the Serb Nikola Pasic. A unitary constitution, promulgated in 1921, is consistently opposed by Croat parliamentarians.

1929 Alexander imposes a dictatorship to end Serbian, Croatian, and Slovene nationalism and renames the country Yugoslavia. He is assassinated on October 9 1934 by a Macedonian extremist. Yugoslavia, ruled by regents on behalf of the child King Peter, is threatened by the rise of Nazi Germany and Soviet hostility.

1941 Germany invades Yugoslavia after the overthrow of a Yugoslav government which signed a pact with the Axis powers. The country is partitioned. Croatia is ruled by the fascist Pavelic, a protege of Mussolini, and annexes Bosnia-Herzegovina. Fascist Croats (Ustashi) undertake the extermination of Orthodox Serbs, Jews, and Gypsies. Rival partisan groups begin resistance – the Serbian royalist Chetniks and the communist partisans under Josip Broz Tito, leader of the Communist Party of Yugoslavia, who forms a provisional government in 1943.

1945 Tito's provisional government abolishes the monarchy and proclaims the Federative People's Republic of Yugoslavia.

1953 The bicameral National Assembly adopts a new constitution guaranteeing sovereignty to the Yugoslav republics. The relationship of each republic with the federal state is "between two essentially equal and mutually independent and interlinked social and political communities."

1971 Strike by students at the University of Zagreb heralds a wave of pro-Croatian demonstrations. A mass movement for greater political autonomy, is suppressed. Four prominent communists, including Prof. Dabcevich-Kucar, Chairman of the League of Communists of Croatia, resign their posts.

1972 January 26. Croatian separatist terrorists, amid a sharp growth of nationalist feeling, blow up a Yugoslav Airlines DC-9, killing 28 people. An express train is blown up on the same day.

1972 Dabcevich-Kucar and her three colleagues are expelled from the LCC over their responsibility for the "infiltration of nationalist forces into the party." On July 26 an armed group of extreme Croat separatists, known as Ustashi after the war-time fighters, enter Yugoslavia. A pitched battle with Yugoslav security forces leaves 17 of the 19 dead. Ustashi terrorists hijack a Swedish DC-9 aircraft in September. Trials of Croatian nationalists continue throughout the year.

1980 May 4. Tito dies and is replaced by collective leaderships of the government and party. Efforts to revitalize the Yugoslav economy fail to halt decline.

1987 A workers' revolt spreads from its center in Croatia.

1988 December. The federal government falls when its budget proposals are defeated in the National Assembly. Meanwhile pressure from Croatia and Slovenia over greater republican autonomy is opposed by hardliners in Serbia who demand a strong centralized state.

1990 The League of Communists of Yugoslavia votes to abolish its leading role at a party congress as democratization sweeps across the communist world. However the Communist parties of the various republics differ sharply over the means to achieve reform.

1990 The nationalist Croatian Democratic Union (HDZ), led by Franjo Tudjman, wins multiparty elections in Croatia.

Nationalist parties win elections in Slovenia, Macedonia, and Bosnia-Herzegovina, while communists retain control of Serbia and Montenegro.

1991 Serbia and its allies refuse to support the normally automatic election of the Vice-President of Croatia, Croatian nationalist Stjepan Mesic, as President of the collective state Presidency. On May 29 Croatia declares its sovereignty.

1992 Tudjman president. Involvement in Bosnian civil war.

1995 Krajina and Western Slavonia recaptured.

1997 Tudjman reelected.

1998 Eastern Slavonia reintegrated.

1999 Death of Tudjman.

2000 Center-left wins elections.

2003 HDZ regains primacy in polls.

cromlechs *see* megaliths

Cromwell, Oliver (1599–1658) English soldier and statesman. A sincere Puritan he was an effective leader of the anti-royalist forces in the English Civil War. After the battle of Naseby (1645) he led the demand for the execution of Charles I. After the king's execution, he quelled the Royalists in Scotland and Ireland. In 1653 he dissolved the "Rump" Parliament and established the Protectorate, which he ruled as Lord Protector (1653–58). *p.306*

Crusades The Series of campaigns by western European armies to recapture the Holy Land from the Muslims. The success of the First Crusade in 1099 led to the foundation of the Kingdom of Jerusalem and other "Latin" (i.e. western European, not Greek) states. Subsequent expeditions to defend these territories or reconquer land lost to the Muslims were less successful. The name crusade was given to campaigns in other parts of Europe, notably Spain and the Baltic.
First Crusade. *p.179*
Crusader States. *p.185*
The Crusades (1050–1350). *p.195*
Fourth Crusade .*p.206*
Crusades of Louis IX. *p.215*

Crystal Palace Glass structure erected in London for Great Exhibition of 1851. *p.364*

Ctesiphon Ancient city on the Tigris, capital of the Sassanian Persian empire after defeat of the Parthians in 226 CE.

CUBA The Caribbean's largest island, Cuba has widely cultivated lowlands which fall between three mountainous areas. The fertile soil of the lowlands supports the sugar cane, rice, and coffee plantations. Sugar, the country's major export, suffers from underinvestment, low yields, and fluctuating world prices. A former Spanish colony, Cuba is the only communist state in the Caribbean. Since the collapse of communism in the Soviet Union, the USA sees Cuba as less of a threat, in marked contrast to 1962, when the deployment of Soviet nuclear missiles on the island brought the two superpowers close to war. Veteran president Fidel Castro is still very much in control.

CHRONOLOGY

1492 First Europeans arrive with Christopher Columbus and claim the island for Spain.

1511 Cuba is settled and colonized by Spaniards.

1762 The British occupy Havana, returning it to Spain later the same year under the Treaty of Havana. Cuba prospers under a slave labor economy with access to North American markets. The presence of a strong Spanish garrison inhibits moves towards independence.

1868 A major rebellion against Spanish rule initiates a 10-year guerrilla war.

1868 End of the slave trade.

1868–1878 Ten Years' War for independence from Spain ends in defeat.

1895 Second war of independence. Thousands of Cubans die in Spanish concentration camps.

1898 In support of Cuban rebels US declares war on Spain to protect strong American financial interests in Cuba.

1899 US takes Cuba and installs military interim government.

1901 US is granted intervention rights and military bases, including Guantánamo Bay naval base.

1902 Tomás Estrada Palma takes over as first Cuban president. US leaves Cuba, but intervenes in 1906–1909 and 1919–1924.

1909 Liberal presidency of José Miguel Goméz. Economy prospers; US investment in tourism, gambling, and sugar.

1925–1933 Dictatorship of President Gerardo Machado.

1933 Years of guerrilla activity end in revolution. Sgt. Fulgencio Batista takes over; military dictatorship.

1955 Fidel Castro exiled after two years' imprisonment for subversion.

1956–1958 Castro returns to lead a guerrilla war in the Sierra Maestra.

1959 Batista flees. Castro takes over; brother, Raúl, is deputy; Che Guevara third in rank. Wholesale nationalizations; Cuba reorganized on Soviet model.

1961 USA breaks off relations. US-backed invasion of Bay of Pigs by anti-Castro Cubans fails. Cuba declares itself Marxist-Leninist.

1962 US economic and political blockade. Missile crisis: Soviet deployment of nuclear weapons in Cuba leads to extreme Soviet-US tension; war averted by Khrushchev ordering withdrawal of weapons.

1965 Che Guevara resigns to pursue foreign liberation wars. One-party state formalized.

1972 Cuba joins COMECON (communist economic bloc).

1976 New socialist constitution. Cuban troops in Angola until 1991.

1977 Sends troops to Ethiopia.

1980 125,000 Cubans, including "undesirables" (criminals or people with learning disabilities), flee to the USA.

1982 USA tightens sanctions and bans flights and tourism to Cuba.

1983 US invasion of Grenada. Cuba involved in clashes with US forces.

1984 Agreement with USA on Cuban emigration and repatriation of "undesirables" is short-lived.

1986 Soviet-style glasnost rejected.

1988 UN's second veto of US attempt to accuse Cuba of human rights violations. Diplomatic relations established with EU.

1989 Senior military executed for arms and narcotics smuggling.

1991 Preferential trade agreement with USSR ends. Severe rationing.

1992–1993 USA tightens blockade. All former Soviet military leave.

1994–1995 Economic reforms to boost foreign trade and investment.

1996 US Helms-Burton Act tightens sanctions.

1998 Visit of Pope John Paul II.

1999 Leading moderate dissidents put on trial.

2001 Hurrican Michelle hits Cuba.

2002 Guanánamo Bay used as high-security prinson for captives from US "war on terrorism."

2003 Major crackdown on dissidents.

Cúcuta ⚔ of wars of S American independence in Colombia (Feb 1813).

Cucuteni-Tripolye culture Civilization noted for its distinctive pottery which flourished in the region between the Carpathians and the Dniester c.4000 BCE.

Cultural Revolution, the (*aka* "Great Proletarian Cultural Revolution") Movement to reaffirm core ideological values of Chinese communism launched by Mao Zedong in 1966. It was fervently implemented by student groups organized into the Red Guard. They revived extreme collectivism and attacked revisionists, intellectuals and any suspected of ideological weakness. This resulted in thousands of executions, and the purge of many of Mao's original coterie. After losing control of the movement, Mao disbanded the Red Guard in 1968, but depradations continued under, initially, the military control of Lin Biao, and then under the "Gang of Four" (led by Mao's wife, Jiang Qing) until Mao's death in 1976. *p.435*

Cumberland Gap Strategic route through the Cumberland Mountains close to the borders of Virginia, Kentucky, and Tennessee in the eastern US. Daniel Boone's Wilderness Road ran through the Gap, which had been named in 1750 by Thomas Walker.

Cuneiform Form of writing developed by the Sumerians and used in south west Asia for over 3000 years from the end of the 4th millennium BCE. It originally used pictographs which became stylized to represent words, syllables and phonetic elements. The earliest cuneiform was written from top to bottom.

Curzon, Lord (*full name* George Nathaniel Curzon, Marquis of Kedleston, 1898–1905) Viceroy of India (1898–1905). An energetic reformer of the civil service, education system, and police force, he created the new Northwest Frontier Province (1898) and partitioned the province of Bengal (1905).

Cush (*var.* Kush) Nubian kingdom founded c.900 BCE. In the 8th century BCE its rule extended over much of Egypt.

Cuzco Ancient capital of the Inca empire, captured by Pizarro in 1533.

Cynoscephalae ⚔ (197 BCE) Roman victory over Greeks.

CYPRUS The island of Cyprus, which rises from a central plateau to a high point at Mount Olympus, lies south of Turkey in the eastern Mediterranean. Cyprus was partitioned in 1974, following an invasion by Turkish troops. The south of the island is the Greek Cypriot Republic of Cyprus (Cyprus); the self-proclaimed Turkish Republic of Northern Cyprus (TRNC) is recognized only by Turkey.

CHRONOLOGY

4th century BCE Alexander the Great captures the island.

58 BCE Cyprus passes into Roman hands and is incorporated into the Byzantine Empire at the end of the 4th century CE.

1189–92 A brief period of English rule under Richard the Lionheart at the end of the Third Crusade is followed by French domination.

1489 The Venetians annex the island.

1571 The Ottoman invasion marks the beginning of 300 years of Muslim Turkish rule.

1878 At the Congress of Berlin it is agreed that Britain should take over the administration of Cyprus under continued Turkish sovereignty in return for a British pledge of support for Turkey against any aggression from Russia.

1915 Britain annexes Cyprus when Turkey joins the Central Powers in World War I.

1923 Greece and Turkey acknowledge British sovereignty over Cyprus under the Treaty of Lausanne.

1925 Cyprus becomes British Crown Colony.

1931 Greek Cypriot demands for union with Greece culminate in rioting and the suspension of constitutional government, but Britain maintains its rule until after World War II.

1955 The National Organization of Cypriot Struggle (EOKA) comprising Greek Cypriots seeking political unity with Greece (enosis) begins a guerrilla war which lasts until December 1958. Its political leader is Archbishop Makarios III.

1959 The Zurich and London agreements provide for Cyprus to become independent under a power-sharing agreement between the Greek and Turkish communities, with trilateral guarantees (from Greece, Turkey and the UK) and the retention of two UK military bases. Makarios is elected President in December 1959.

1960 Independence from UK.

1963 Turkish Cypriots abandon parliament.

1974 President Makarios deposed by Greek military junta. Turkey invades. Partition.

1983 Self-proclamation of TRNC.

1993 Glafcos Clerides becomes president.

1998 Talks on EU membership start, following 1990 application to join.

2003 Tassos Papadopoulos elected president. Green Line opened.

2004 Referendum rejects plan for reunifications. Cyprus joins EU.

Cyril, St. (826–69) Christian missionary, originally called Constantine, who, with his brother Methodius (825–884), took the Orthodox faith from Constantinople to the Slavs of Moravia. Cyril invented an alphabet, based on Greek characters, to translate the Bible into Slavonic languages. A later version of the alphabet, called Cyrillic, is used in modern Russian and Bulgarian. *p.143 See also* Methodius, St.

Cyrus II (*aka* Cyrus the Great, c.580/590 BCE–529 BCE) Cyrus created the Persian Achaemenid empire, named after his ancestor Achaemenes, by defeating the Medes, Lydians and Babylonians. His empire extended from the Mediterranean to the Hindu Kush, and he was known for his enlightened and tolerant policies of religious conciliation.

CZECH REPUBLIC Landlocked in central Europe, the Czech Republic comprises the territories of Bohemia and Moravia, and for most of the 20th century it was part of Czechoslovakia. In 1989, the "Velvet Revolution" ended four decades of communist rule, and free elections followed in 1990. In 1993 the Czech Republic and Slovakia peacefully dissolved their federal union to become two independent states.

CHRONOLOGY

962 CE The coronation of Otto I marks the beginning of the Holy Roman Empire, of which Bohemia is a founding member.

973 CE The bishopric of Prague is created.

Early 13th century. Under Ottakar I, Bohemia becomes a kingdom, the only one within the Holy Roman Empire.

1222 Ottakar I annexes Moravia from Poland.

1310 John of Luxembourg is elected King of Bohemia and marries Elisabeth, the sister of Wenceslas III.

1344 Prague becomes an archbishopric four years before the founding of the Charles University in Prague. Around this time Prague is considered the third most important city of Europe after Constantinople and Paris.

1346 The Czech King Charles (son of John of Luxembourg) is crowned Charles IV Holy Roman Emperor, marking the apogee of the Bohemian kingdom.

1415 The Czech priest and scholar Jan Hus is burnt at the stake after leading a religious reformation which came to have nationalist overtones. The execution sparks nearly 20 years of religious and civil war.

1419 Hussites seeking to reform Czech society throw prominent Catholic nobles from a Prague castle window in the first "defenestration of Prague."

1526 Bohemia comes under the rule of the Austrian Habsburgs.

1618 Rising tensions between Catholics and Protestants result in another defenestration which marks the beginning of the Thirty Years' war.

1620 Protestant nobles seeking to break Habsburg rule are beaten at the Battle of the White Mountain outside Prague.

1740 Prussia invades Silesia, which has belonged to Bohemia since the 14th century. The 1745 Treaty of Dresden confirms Prussian control over Silesia except for a small part in the east known as Austrian Silesia.

1781 Under the reign of Habsburg King Joseph II, an edict of tolerance benefits both Protestants and Jews. Serfdom is also abolished, although the feudal system is not. German is decreed the sole administrative language of Bohemia and Moravia.

1848 Czech nationalist Frantisek Palacky and the Czech authorities refuse to participate in the elections held by universal suffrage within the German Confederation (of which Bohemia forms a part) in contrast to the Germans in Bohemia and Moravia who wish to be part of a unified Germany. Simultaneously elections are held by universal suffrage throughout the Austrian Habsburg lands, with the exception of Hungary, to a parliament in Vienna.

1918 Czechoslovakia is established as a democratic state comprising the Czech Lands of Bohemia and Moravia, and Slovakia. Tomas Masaryk becomes President.

1938 The Sudetenland is ceded to Adolf Hitler and incorporated into German Reich after a Munich meeting between Hitler and British Prime Minister Neville Chamberlain.

1939 Hitler annexes the rest of Czechoslovakia and creates a German "protectorate" of Bohemia and Moravia. The Diet (legislative assembly) of Bratislava declares Slovakian independence under protection of the German Reich and the leadership of Maj. Josef Tiso.

1942 The assassination of Nazi "protector" Reinhard Heydrich prompts reprisals, including the murder of the male population of Lidice.

1945 Edvard Benes, the pre-war President, who has maintained a government-in-exile in London, reaches agreement in Moscow with the exiled communist leader Klement Gottwald on the formation of a multiparty National Front.

1946 The communists poll 38 percent of the vote in general election. Gottwald is invited to lead an all-party coalition government.

1948 President Benes swears in a new communist-dominated cabinet led by Gottwald which takes power in the "Prague coup" after intimidation by the Communist Party (CPCz) leads those who are not communists to resign from the coalition government.

1948 The Social Democratic Party is merged with the CPCz.

1948 A new constitution declares Czechoslovakia a people's democracy.

1950 The start of a wave of political show trials ushers in a period of purges and executions of party members and officials.

1968 The "Prague Spring" begins when the Slovak Alexander Dubcek takes over as CPCz leader and, in April, announces far-reaching political reforms and economic liberalization measures. "Prague Spring" comes to an end with nvasion by Warsaw Pact countries.

1989 "Velvet Revolution."

1990 Elections; Vaclav Havel president.

1993 Division of Czechoslovakia into Czech Republic and Slovakia.

1998 Start of EU membership negotiations

1999 Joins NATO.

2002 CSSD reelected. Serious floods.

2003 Vaclav Kaus elected as president.

2004 Joins EU.

D

D-Day *see* Normandy Landings

Dagobert I (reigned 623–63) Merovingian king of the Franks, who briefly reunited the Frankish empire and made Paris his capital. *p.125*

Dahomey Kingdom of W Africa, active in the slave trade in the 18th century. Defeated by the French in 1892–3, becoming a French protectorate and part of French West Africa. Gained full independence in 1960, but early years of independence were marked by almost continuous civil unrest and fierce rivalry between north and south. In 1975 the state changed its name to the People's Republic of Benin. *See also* Benin

Dai-Viet After northern Vietnam won independence from China, which had dominated it for ten centuries, in 946, the kingdom was named Dai-Viet (Greater Viet) in 1009. Dai-Viet repelled a Chinese invasion in 1076. When the Ming invaded in 1406, their oppressive rule led to a Vietnamese national resistance movement, and the Chinese armies were routed in 1426. Vietnamese independence was recognized in 1427, and a new capital was established at Hanoi. *See also* Annam, Vietnam

Daimler, Gottlieb Wilhelm (1834–1900) German engineer who developed an early automobile, a tricycle powered by gasoline.

Daimyo (10th–19th centuries CE) Medieval Japanese provincial feudal lordships.

Damascus Capital of modern Syria. An ancient city that became a provincial capital of the East Roman Empire, it fell to the Arabs in 635. The Umayyad caliphs made it their capital (661–750) and the Christian church was rebuilt in 705 as the Great Mosque. *p.131*

Dalai Lama (*var.* Tenzin Gyatso, 1935–) Spiritual and titular leader of Tibet, regarded as reincarnation of Compassionate Buddha. Designated 14th Dalai Lama in 1937, installed in 1940 but ruled under regency until 1950, and negotiated autonomy agreement after communist Chinese invasion of Tibet (1950). Following suppression of Tibetan uprising (1959) has ruled in exile.

Dampier, William (c.1651–1715) English adventurer and explorer. Dampier gained notoriety as a buccaneer, raiding Spanish colonies in the Caribbean and S America. The first Englishman to land in Australia in 1688, he was later sent by the Admiralty on an official voyage of exploration around Australia and New Guinea (1699–1701).

Darius I (*aka* Darius the Great, 550–486 BCE) King of Persia (522–486 BCE) Noted for his administrative reforms and religious toleration. Darius's military conquests consolidated the frontiers of the Achaemenid empire, and his division of land into administrative provinces, or satrapies, outlasted the empire itself. His famed building projects included a renowned road system and a palace at Persepolis, later destroyed by Alexander the Great.

Darius III (*var.* Codomannus) (381–331 BCE) Persian king (reigned 336–331 BCE). Distant relative of Artaxerxes III who successfully fought against the Cadusians, Darius ascended to the Persian throne in 336 BCE. He was defeated by Alexander the Great at the battles of Issus and Gaugamela (331 BCE), and, as Alexander pursued him across his empire, was murdered by the Bactrian satrap Bessus.

Darwin, Charles Robert (1809–82) The first scientist to put forward a viable theory of evolution in his great work *On the Origin of Species by Means of Natural Selection* published in 1859. *p.366*

David (reigned c.1000–966 BCE) The second king of Israel, David was the first of the dynasty that ruled Judaea and Israel together, uniting the Jewish tribes into a settled nation. He moved the capital from Hebron to Jerusalem (Zion, the "City of David"), where he brought the Ark of the Covenant, said to contain the Ten Commandments. David defeated the Philistines when he slew their giant warrior Goliath.

Davis, John (c.1550–1605) English navigator. Explored Davis Strait, Baffin Island and the Cumberland Sound in Canada in search of Northwest Passage to India between 1585 and 1587. In 1591 he traveled as far south as the Falkland Islands. He also published works on navigation and developed navigational instruments including the double quadrant.

Dawes Plan The report which outlined German reparations as compensation for World War I. Starting at 1,000,000,000 gold marks in 1924, payments were to rise to 2,500,000,000 by 1928, but no total amount was fixed. An initial loan of 800,000,000 marks was given to Germany.

DDR *see* East Germany

Deccan First cities appear on Deccan plateau (c.200 CE).

Declaration of Independence Document drawn up by the Congressional representatives of the original 13 states of the US, declaring independence from Britain. It was signed on Jul 4 1776.

Decolonization The granting of independence to the colonies of the major European imperial powers, chiefly in Asia and Africa, after World War II. *p.431*

Del Cano, Juan Sebastián (c.1476–1526) Basque navigator who sailed with Magellan. Captain of the one ship that completed the circumnavigation of the world on Magellan's voyage of 1519–21. After Magellan was killed in the Philippine Islands in 1521, Del Cano sailed the *Victoria* back to Spain with a valuable cargo of cloves from the East Indies, thus becoming the first man to complete the circumnavigation of the globe.

Delhi sultanate (1206–1398) Turkish-Afghan dynasty, based at Delhi. Its control over northern India fluctuated along with its various rulers' fortunes; in 1294, under Alauddin Khalji, conquering armies invaded Gujarat, Rajputana, and the southernmost tip of the subcontinent. Under the sultanate, Muslims were appointed to high office, and Hindus became vassals. *p.198*

Delian League Confederacy of ancient Greek states under the leadership of

Athens, with headquarters at Delos, founded in 478 BCE during the Graeco-Persian wars.

democracy From the Greek, meaning rule by the people, although in the Greek city-states suffrage was far from universal. The ideal of democracy was revived in Europe the 18th century, notably in the French Revolution. Since then, in most of the world's states, the granting of the vote to all members of society has led to the widely accepted modern ideal of democratic government

Democratic Party Major US political party. Originally founded by Thomas Jefferson as the Democratic Republican party, the modern name was first used c.1828. Until the 1930s, support for the Democrats was drawn mainly from the Southern US, but the New Deal policies of Franklin D. Roosevelt in the 1930s, and the passage of social reform and civil rights legislation in the 1960s drew a wider base of support.

Denham, Dixon (1786–1828) English soldier who became one of the early explorers of western Africa. He accompanied Walter Oudney and Hugh Clapperton on an expedition across the Sahara to the Lake Chad basin (1821–25).

DENMARK The most southerly country in Scandinavia, Denmark occupies the Jutland (Jylland) peninsula, the islands of Sjælland, Fyn, Lolland, and Falster, and more than 400 smaller islands. Its terrain is among the flattest in the world. The Faeroe Islands and Greenland in the North Atlantic are self-governing associated territories. Politically, Denmark is a very stable country, despite a preponderance of minority governments since 1945. It possesses a long liberal tradition and was one of the first countries to establish a welfare system, in the 1930s.

Chronology

Early 9th century CE The Dan people or Danes, who originally came from southern Sweden, join other Viking groups in waves of seaborne migrations and conquest across Europe and beyond, lasting until the 11th century.

950 CE Present-day Denmark and southern Sweden are united under the sovereignty of Gorm the Old who died in 950.

11th century Christianity becomes the dominant religion.

1014–53 Canute the Great unites all of Scandinavia and much of England under his rule, but his empire rapidly disintegrates after his death.

1157–82 Denmark's ascendancy within Scandinavia is reasserted during the reign of Valdemar the Great.

1397 Under the Union of Kalmar Denmark, Norway, and Sweden (including Finland) are united in personal union under Queen Margrethe I of Denmark; Sweden secedes from the union in 1523.

1448 Christian I ascends the throne as the first monarch of the Oldenburg royal house.

1533–36 A civil war precedes the implementation of the Lutheran reformation, and Evangelical Lutheranism is established as the state church.

1660 A new Constitution sponsored by King Frederick III breaks the privileges of the nobility and establishes an absolute monarchy, initially supported by the middle classes.

1721 The end of the Great Northern war (1700–21) marks the end of Denmark as a regional power.

1814 Denmark, which had been an ally of Napoleonic France, loses its remaining German possessions and (under the Treaty of Kiel) cedes Norway to Sweden.

1849 Creation of first democratic constitution.

1864 Denmark forced to cede provinces of Schleswig and Holstein after losing war with Prussia.

1914–1918 Denmark neutral in World War I.

1915 Universal adult suffrage introduced. Rise of Social Democrat party (SD).

1920 Northern Schleswig votes to return to Danish rule.

1929 First full SD government takes power under prime minister Thorvald Stauning.

1930s Implementation of advanced social welfare legislation and other liberal reforms.

1939 Outbreak of World War II; Denmark reaffirms neutrality.

1940 Nazi occupation. National coalition government formed.

1943 Danish Resistance successes lead Nazis to take full control.

1944 Iceland declares independence from Denmark.

1945 Denmark recognizes Icelandic independence. After defeat of Nazi

Germany, SD leads postwar coalition governments.

1948 Faeroes granted home rule.

1952 Denmark is founder member of the Nordic Council.

1953 Constitution reformed; single-chamber, proportionally elected parliament created.

1959 Denmark joins the European Free Trade Association (EFTA).

1973 Denmark joins European Communities.

1979 Greenland granted home rule.

1975–1982 SD's Anker Jorgensen heads series of coalitions; elections in 1977, 1979, and 1981. Final coalition collapses over economic policy differences.

1982 Poul Schlüter first Conservative prime minister since 1894.

1992 Referendum rejects Maastricht Treaty on European Union.

1993 Schlüter resigns over "Tamilgate" scandal. Center-left government led by Poul Nyrup Rasmussen. Danish voters ratify revised Maastricht Treaty.

1994, 1998 General elections; Rasmussen heads SD-led minority coalition.

2000 Referendum rejects joining euro single currency.

2001 Elections: Liberals regain power. Anders Fogh Rasmussen appointed prime minister.

Desert Storm (1991) Allied campaign against Iraqi forces which ended Gulf War. *See also* Gulf War

Deventer, Jacob van 16th-century Dutch cartographer.

Devolution, War of (1667) French invasion of the Spanish Netherlands.

Diamond Sutra The Earliest documented printed work (868 CE)

Dias, Bartolomeu (1450–1500) Portuguese navigator and explorer who led the first European expedition round the Cape of Good Hope in 1488, opening the sea route to Asia via the Atlantic and Indian oceans.

Dias, Diogo Portuguese navigator, a member of Cabral's expedition to India in 1500. On the outward journey he became separated from the main fleet and discovered Madagascar.

Díaz de Solís, Juan (c.1470–1516) Spanish explorer of the Atlantic coast of S America. He sailed with Vicente Yáñez Pinzón and Amerigo Vespucci. Killed by indigenous

people while exploring the Plate river in search of a route to the Pacific.

Díaz, Porfirio (1830–1915) Mexican statesman and soldier. A hero of the war of the Reform (1857–60) and the French intervention (1861–67). Became president in 1876, after rebelling against the fourth re-election of Benito Juárez. Elected again in 1884, he ruled uninterrupted until he was deposed in 1911 at the start of the Mexican Revolution.

Diderot, Denis (1713–84) French philosopher and writer. Chief editor of the *Encyclopédie* (1751–72) which attempted to encompass the full breadth of Enlightenment thought.

Dien Bien Phu ⚔ (Feb 3– May 7 1954) Attempting to regain control in Vietnam, the French were surrounded by Viet-Minh forces. Subsequently they withdrew from Vietnam.

Diocletian (245–316) Roman emperor (reigned 284–305). Responsible for reorganizing the administration of the Roman Empire, dividing it into four regions to be ruled by two senior and two junior emperors. His reign also saw widespread persecution of Christians.

dioxyribonucleic acid *see* DNA

Directory (*var. Fr.* Directoire) Name given to the revolutionary executive power in France between Nov 1795 and Nov 1799. It came to an end when Napoleon staged a coup d'état and made himself First Consul.

Disney, Walter Elias (Walt, 1901–69) US animator and film producer. Set up a studio producing cartoons in the 1920s. Creator of Mickey Mouse, and producer of some of the most technically advanced animated films, his company grew to become a huge entertainment empire.

DJIBOUTI A city state with a desert hinterland, Djibouti lies in northeast Africa on the strait linking the Red Sea and the Indian Ocean. Known from 1967 as the French Territory of the Afars and Issas, Djibouti became independent in 1977. Its economy relies on the main port, the railroad to Addis Ababa, and French aid. A guerrilla war which erupted in 1991 as a result of tension between the Issas in the south and the Afars in the north has largely been resolved.

CHRONOLOGY

1861 France gains control of the trading port of Obock in northern Djibouti.

1897 In a treaty signed between the emperor of Ethiopia and France, Djibouti is designated "the official outlet for Ethiopian commerce."

1909 The Franco-Ethiopian Railway Company (CFE) begins construction of a railway from Djibouti to Addis Ababa, providing further impetus for the development of Djibouti as a port and trading center for the region. The railway is completed by 1917.

1917 Railroad from Addis Ababa reaches Djibouti port.

1977 Independence.

1981–1992 One-party state.

1989 Eruption of violence between the Afars and the Issas.

1991 FRUD (Front for the Restoration of Unity and Democracy), an Afar guerrilla group, launches armed insurrection.

1994 Peace agreement with FRUD.

1999 Ismael Omar Guelleh becomes president.

2000 Coup attempt by police officers fails.

Djoser *see* Zoser

DNA (dioxyribonucleic acid) Main constituent of genetic material in chromosomes of living organisms. Its structure (a double helix) was worked out by Crick and Watson in 1953. *p.427*

Doge Title of the elected ruler of Venice, from the Latin *dux*, from c.697 to the end of the Venetian Republic in 1797.

Domesday Book Comprehensive survey of land ownership in England, commissioned by William I (1086). *p.177*

Dominic, St. (c.1170–1221) Spanish founder of the Dominicans, the Order of Friars Preachers. He was canonized in 1234.

DOMINICA Dominica is renowned as the Caribbean island that resisted European colonization until the 18th century, when it was controlled first by the French then, from 1759, by the British. Known as the "Nature Island" due to its spectacular, lush, and abundant flora and fauna, which are protected by extensive national parks, Dominica is the most mountainous of

▶

the Lesser Antilles. Located between Guadeloupe and Martinique in the West Indian Windward Islands group, its volcanic origin has given it very fertile soils and the second-largest boiling lake in the world.

CHRONOLOGY

1493 Columbus lands on Dominica.

1759 The island is seized by the British after control had been fiercely contested by British, French, and Caribs in the 17th and 18th centuries. The production of sugar cane is established using slave labor, followed by cotton and coffee.

1805 Dominica becomes a British colony.

1951 Universal suffrage is introduced.

1958-62 Dominica is a member of the West Indies Federation.

1960 January. A new Constitution is introduced as Dominica and other Windward islands achieve separate status.

1967 Full internal autonomy is achieved as a West Indies Associated State, with Edward Le Blanc as Premier. the UK retains responsibility for defence and foreign relations.

1974 On his retirement as DLP leader and Prime Minister LeBlanc is succeeded by Patrick John who conducts independence negotiations.

1975 Morne Trois Pitons national park established.

1978 Independence from UK. Patrick John first prime minister.

1980 Eugenia Charles, the Caribbean's first woman prime minister, elected.

1981 Two coup attempts, backed by Patrick John, foiled.

1995 Opposition DUWP defeats DFP. Dame Eugenia Charles retires after 27 years in politics.

2000 DLP wins elections.

DOMINICAN REPUBLIC

The largest tourist destination in the Caribbean, the Dominican Republic lies 970 km (600 miles) southeast of Florida. Once ruled by Spain, it occupies the eastern two-thirds of the island of Hispaniola and boasts both the highest point (Pico Duarte, 3175 m – 10,420 ft)

and the lowest point (Lake Enriquillo, 44 m – 144 ft – below sea level) in the West Indies. Spanish-speaking, it seeks closer ties with the anglophone Caribbean.

CHRONOLOGY

1492 Columbus reaches the island of Hispaniola which the present-day Dominican Republic shares with Haiti. The first soil actually to be settled by Spaniards, it becomes the center of Spanish activity and rule in the region, producing gold, sugar, and finally cattle.

1697 The island is divided between Spain and France.

1795 French domination is extended to the Spanish section of Hispaniola, but this is occupied by native Haitian forces under Toussaint L'Ouverture. Between 1809 and 1844 French troops are ejected, but years of fighting ensue between French and Spanish troops and L'Ouverture's forces.

1844 The Dominican Republic achieves independence with the formal but arbitrary division of the two parts of the island.

1861 Spanish colonial rule is reestablished at the request of President Pedro Santana as a bulwark against Haitian attempts to take back the Dominican Republic.

1865 The Dominican Republic finally becomes independent from Spain but further years of instability ensue.

1916–24. The Dominican Republic is occupied by US troops; the USA retains customs control until September 1940.

1930 Gen. Rafael Trujillo is elected President and establishes a brutal and repressive dictatorship, dominating political life directly or indirectly until his assassination in May 1961.

1930–1961 Gen. Molina dictator.

1965 Civil war. US intervention.

1966 Joaquín Balaguer's first of seven presidential terms over next 30 years.

1996 Center-left PRD candidate succeeds Balaguer.

1998 Major hurricane damage.

2000 Hipolito Mejia of PRD wins presidency.

2004 Fernández reelected.

Domino effect (*aka* Domino theory) Theory that, in the event of a communist victory in the Vietnam War (1954–75), the adjacent states of SE Asia would fall successively under communist control.

Dom Pérignon (1639–1715) French Benedictine monk, the inventor of Champagne.

Donatello (1386–1466) Florentine sculptor, one of the leading artists of the early Renaissance. *p.252*

Dong Son Prehistoric Indo-Chinese culture of the 1st millennium BCE named after the northern Vietnamese village where many remains have been found. The Dong Son used iron and built stone monuments, but are best known for their highly skilled bronze-working, especially the ritual kettle drums found at the site.

Dorylaeum ⚔ of crusades (1147). Turkish victory over emperor Conrad.

Doughty, Charles Montagu (1843–1926) British explorer, writer and poet. From 1876–78 he traveled from Damascus to Mecca, recording his journey in his acclaimed *Travels in Arabia Deserta*, published in 1888.

Dr Strangelove Film directed by Stanley Kubrick (1964) mocking the absurdity of the nuclear arms race.

Drake, Sir Francis (c.1540–1596) English privateer. Regarded in Spain as a dangerous pirate, Drake made a career of attacking Spanish ships and ports in search of bullion. He played an important role in the defeat of the Spanish Armada in 1588. His greatest feat of navigation was his circumnavigation 1577–80 in the *Golden Hind*.

Dred Scott Decision (Mar 6 1857) Landmark decision about the spread of slavery in the US. Scott, a slave who had been taken by his master into the West argued that he should be free as slavery was not legal in the new territory. The Supreme Court ruled that Congress had no power to exclude slavery from the territories, thus making slavery legal in all US territories.

drugs trade Scourge of the modern world. Despite vasts sums of money spent on attempts to limit trade in illegal drugs, especially by the US, the trade continues to grow. *p.452*

Dubcek, Alexander (1921–92) First secretary of the Communist Party of Czechoslovakia (Jan 5 1968–Apr 17 1969), whose liberal reforms led to the Soviet invasion and occupation of Czechoslovakia in Aug 1968.

Dublin Capital of the Republic of Ireland. The city was founded by the Vikings in 841 CE.

Dumont d'Urville, Jules Sébastien-César (1790–1842) French naval officer. Acted as naturalist on a series of expeditions to the Pacific in 1826–29. In 1837–40 he traveled to Antarctica where he discovered Terre Adélie and Joinville Island.

Dusan, Stefan (c.1308–55) Ruler of Serbia. Through campaigns in the Balkans, Stefan carved out a large Serbian Empire.

Dust Bowl Name given to the prairie states of the US which suffered from serious soil erosion during the 1930s following a long period of drought. Thousands of farmers were forced to abandon their ruined land.

Dutch East India Company (*var.* United East India Company) Company founded by the Dutch in 1602 to protect their trade in the Indian Ocean and to assist in their war of independence from Spain. Dissolved in 1799.

Dutch East Indies General historic term for Dutch colonial holdings in SE Asia, 17th–20th centuries. *See also* Indonesia

Dutch Revolt Name usually given to the long struggle by the United Provinces to gain independence from Spain from 1565 until their independence was finally recognized by the Spanish in 1648. *p.284 See also* Netherlands

Dzungaria (*aka* Xiankiang) Steppe and semi-desert region of NW China. Formerly under control of a Mongol federation, it was annexed by China in 1751.

E

Eanes, Gil 15th-century Portuguese explorer credited with rounding Cape Bojador, Africa, in 1434.

East Asia Geographic term for traditional regions of China, Mongolia, Manchuria, Korea and the Japanese archipelago.

East Germany (*var.* German Democratic Republic, DDR) Communist state formed (1949) by Soviet Union following postwar occupation of Germany, dissolved upon German reunification (1990). *See also* Germany

East India Company *see* English East India Company, Dutch East India Company, French East India Company

East Indies General geographic term for the archipelagos of maritime SE Asia.

East Pakistan *see* Bangladesh

EAST TIMOR This new nation occupies the eastern half of the island of Timor, colonized from 1520 by the Portuguese. Invaded by Indonesia in 1975, it declared independence in 1999.

CHRONOLOGY

13–15th century The Javanese based Majapahit empire extends its control over the Indonesian archipelago, including Timor.

1520 The Portuguese first arrive and settle on the island of Timor.

1613 Dutch colonists gain increasing control of the island and claim possession over its western half. From this date on the political fate of West Timor correlates with that of the Netherlands East Indies, and its Indonesian successor state.

1860 A treaty between the Dutch and the Portuguese codifies the relationship between the two colonial powers of Timor. However, the final boundaries are not delineated until after an arbitration committee makes a ruling in 1914.

1942–45 The Japanese occupy Timor. At the end of the war the Portuguese regain sovereignty.

1974 The Portuguese Revolution results in collapse of their overseas empire and unrest in all their colonies, including East Timor.

1975 The moderate Democratic Union of Timor (UDT) stages a coup in East Timor, demanding complete and immediate independence from Portugal and the imprisonment of all members of Fretilin, the recently-formed anti-Indonesian revolutionary movement; civil war breaks out between the UDT and Fretilin.

1975 Fretilin proclaims the independence of the Democratic Republic of East Timor. ndonesian forces invade East Timor, swiftly establishing their authority. The Portuguese authorities break off diplomatic relations with Indonesia.

1976 UN Security Council adopts a resolution calling on Indonesia to withdraw all its forces from East Timor without delay.

1976 President Suharto of Indonesia signs a decree making East Timor the 27th province of Indonesia.

1986 After years of resistance against the Indonesians throughout the 1980s, Fretilin and UDT agree to coordinate diplomatic and military ventures.

1988 Indonesian government, in the belief that they have gained full control over resistance activities, declare East Timor an "open territory," thus giving foreign access to East Timor for the first time in 13 years.

1991 Indonesia agrees to allow parliamentary delegation from Portugal to visit East Timor, after mounting criticisms of Indonesia's human rights record. However, proposed trip is canceled after Indonesia objects to presence of an Australian journalist as part of the delegation.

1991 Indonesian troops open fire on a crowd of funeral mourners in Dili, killing at least 50 people and placing the issue of East Timor back on the international agenda. Australia and Indonesia conclude an agreement over the Timor Gap, an area of rich oil deposits.

1992 Fretilin leader Jose Xanana Gusmao captured near Dili.

1993 Xanana Gusmao sentenced to life imprisonment.

1994 Indonesian military hold talks with the imprisoned Gusmao on possibility of UN referendum on East Timor.

1998 Indonesian President Suharto resigns.

1999 People of East Timor allowed to vote to decide their fate. Elections preceded by violent attacks by pro-Indonesian militias, but result is overwhelming vote for independence. In September UN peacekeeping force takes over.

2001 Elections to new Constituent Assembly; Fretlin wins majority.

2002 May. East Timor fully independent with Xanana Gusmao as president.

Easter Island (*var.* Rapa Nui) Remote Pacific island colonized by Polynesians c.300 CE. Famous for its enormous stone statues of heads with elongated ears and red topknots. *p.226*

Eastern Bloc *see* Communist Bloc

Eastern Front General term for the eastern theater of war during World War I and World War II, including eastern Germany, Austria-Hungary, Poland, Romania, the Baltic States, and Russia.

Eastern Han *see* Han dynasty

Eastern Zhou *see* Zhou dynasty

East, the *see* Communist Bloc

EC *see* European Union

ECSC *see* European Coal and Steel Community

ECUADOR Once part of the Inca heartland, Ecuador lies on the western coast of South America. It was ruled by Spain from 1533, when the last Inca emperor was executed, until independence achieved in 1822. Most Ecuadorians live either in the coastal region or in the Andean Sierra. The Amazonian Amerindians are now pressing for their land rights to be recognized. Massive depreciation of the sucre forced the government to dollarize the currency in 2000.

CHRONOLOGY

1528 Francisco Pizarro sails along the coast as far as the border of present-day Ecuador and Peru.

1534 Sebastian de Benalcazar, one of Pizarro's lieutenants, leads expedition to the region and founds Quito.

1563 The Audiencia of Quito is established within the Viceroyalty of Peru and is later transferred to the jurisdiction of the Vicroyalty of New Granada in 1739.

1822 Quito is liberated by Gen. Sucre at the Battle of Pichincha. Ecuador is made part of Gran Colombia which also embraces Colombia, Panama, and Venezuela.

1830 Gran Colombia dissolves, and Ecuador becomes an independent state under Gen. Juan Jose Flores, a Conservative.

1941–1942 Loss of mineral-rich El Oro region to Peru.

1948–1960 Prosperity from bananas.

1972 Oil production starts.

1979 Return to democracy.

1992 Amerindians win land in Amazonia.

1996–1997 Abdalá Bucarám Ortíz removed from presidency on grounds of mental incapacity.

1998–1999 Jamil Mahuad of DP wins elections; forms new majority alliance. Economic crisis.

2000 Army sides with Amerindian protestors. Vice president Gustavo Noboa replaces Mahuad.

2002 Lucio Gutiérrez, leader of 2000 coup, elected president.

Edessa Crusader state established in 1096. It fell to Zangi, governor of Mosul in 1144.

Edo Old name for Tokyo. It was made the imperial capital of Tokugawa Japan in 1603.

Edward I (1239–1307) King of England (reigned 1272–1307). Eldest son of Henry III. He supported Simon de Montfort in the Barons' War (1264–67), later joining his father to defeat de Montfort at the battle of Evesham (1265). Constant campaigning led to the annexation of north and west Wales, and much of the rest of his reign was spent attempting to unite England and Scotland against fierce Scottish opposition. Though he defeated William Wallace's armies at Falkirk in 1298, he was unable to control Scotland and died at Carlisle on the way to confront the newly-crowned Robert Bruce. His reorganization of both local and central government and judicial reforms won him comparisons with the emperor Justinian.

Edward III (1312–77) King of England (reigned 1327–77). Son of Edward II, in 1330 he overthrew his French mother Isabella who had governed during his minority. In the early years of his reign he became involved in wars with Scotland. In 1337 his claim to the French throne provoked the Hundred Years' War, during which he fought in the battle of Crécy and at the siege of Calais.

Edward, Prince of Wales (*aka* the Black Prince, 1330–76) The son of Edward III, he was an outstanding English military commander in the Hundred Years' War, fighting with distinction at Crécy and winning a great victory at Poitiers (1356). Said to have gained his title because he appeared in battle wearing black armour.

Edward the Confessor (c.1003–66) King of England (reigned 1042–66). Edward is remembered for his piety – he was canonized in 1611 – and as founder of Westminster Abbey in London. His reign, however, was marked by feuds that would erupt on his death into a battle for succession to the throne between Harold, son of Earl Godwin of Wessex and William of Normandy. *p.169*

EEC European Economic Community, created in 1957. *See also* European Union

---

EGYPT Occupying the northeast corner of Africa, Egypt is bisected by the highly fertile Nile valley separating the arid western desert from the smaller semiarid eastern desert. The annual flooding of the Nile valley created astonishingly fertile agricultural land. This led to a food surplus that allowed the civilization of Ancient Egypt to flourish throughout the first three millennia BCE. Since then Egypt has been ruled by Greeks, Romans, various Arab dynasties, the Mamluks, the Ottoman Turks, and the British, until it became fully independent in 1936. Since World War II its politics have been dominated by relations with neighboring Israel. Egypt's 1979 peace treaty with Israel brought security, the return of the Sinai, and large injections of US aid. Its essentially pro-Western military-backed regime is now being challenged by an increasingly influential Islamic fundamentalist movement.

CHRONOLOGY

c. 3000 BCE With the foundation of the Old Kingdom the fertile lands along the Nile are united under a single ruler for the first time. Previously there have been two kingdoms, one on the Nile delta and one in the lower Nile valley.

c.2060–1785 BCE The Middle Kingdom expands trade with Asia and develops more complex administrative systems but Egyptian expansion up the Nile into Nubia (in contemporary Sudan) is then stalled by nomadic Hyksos invaders from the east in 1730 BCE.

c.1580–1050 BCE The New Kingdom resumes expansion of Egypt's frontiers to the south and into Mesopotamia. By the 11th century BCE Egyptian control of Nubia is weakened and a separate kingdom is established in Kush further to the south which between 770 BCE and 716 BCE conquers Egypt.

671–666 BCE Following Assyrian invasions iron working becomes an important activity. The Persians in turn conquer Egypt in 525 BCE.

525 BCE Egypt conquered by Persians under Cambyses II, who rule until 404 bce.

343–332 BCE Second period of Persian rule.

332 BCE Alexander of Macedon (Alexander the Great) conquers Egypt. His general, Ptolemy, establishes the Ptolemaic dynasty and moves the capital from the Nile to new city of Alexandria on the Mediterranean.

331 BCE Foundation of city and port of Alexandria.

304 BCE After Alexander's death in 323 BCE, Egypt eventually passes to one of his generals who rules as Ptolemy I.

51 BCE Last of the Greek Ptolemaic dynasty, Cleopatra, becomes ruler of Egypt. Her reign is dominated by attempts to resist the power of Rome.

31 BCE Naval battle of Actium. Fleet of Antony and Cleopatra defeated by Romans of Augustus. Suicide of Antony and Cleopatra the following year. Egypt becomes part of the Roman Empire. Its rich harvests are an impoprtant part of the Roman economy.

30 BCE Rome defeats the forces of Cleopatra, the last Ptolemaic ruler, and Egypt becomes a Roman colony.

c.100 CE Alexandria an important early Christian bishopric.

616 CE Persians conquer Egypt.

632 CE Islam is brought to Egypt. By the 8th century Arabic is established as the official language and in 969 CE Cairo is founded.

641–642 CE Byzantine Empire loses Egypt to Muslim invaders from Arabia.

868–905 CE Tulunid dynasty wrests control of Egypt from the Abbasid Caliphate.

969 CE The Shi'ite Fatimids make Cairo their capital.

1171 Saladin, scourge of the crusaders, takes Egypt and founds short-lived Ayyubid dynasty.

1250 Mamluks, slave soldiers, mainly of Circassian origin, take power.

1517 Cairo is captured by Turkish forces. Egypt becomes part of the Ottoman Empire.

1798 Napoleon invades Egypt but his fleet is destroyed by the British at the battle of the Nile at Aboukir Bay.

1804 Mohammed Ali, an Albanian officer in the Turkish army, seizes power and is recognized by Constantinople as Viceroy of Egypt.

1869 The Suez Canal is opened. In 1875 Britain and France take control of the Suez Canal.

1882 British forces occupy Cairo following the defeat of the "Egypt for the Egyptians" movement. Egypt comes effectively under British rule, although it is formally still part of the Ottoman Empire.

1914 Britain declares Egypt a protectorate.

1922 Faced with growing nationalist unrest, Britain grants Egypt limited independence.

1923 Constitutional monarchy is established. Sultan Ahmed Fuad becomes King Fuad and rules until his death on April 28, 1936, when he is succeeded by his son King Farouk.

1924 The first democratic election held under the 1923 constitution brings Wafd Party leader Saad Zaghlul to power.

1936 The Anglo-Egyptian treaty ends the British military presence in Egypt (which began in 1882), while permitting continued British military control of the canal zone. During the Second World War Britain defends Egypt and the canal under this agreement and German and Italian forces are repulsed at El Alamein in November 1942.

1948 The first Arab-Israeli war ends in defeat for Egypt.

1952 The Free Officers' Movement, led by Gen. Mohammed Neguib, forces King Farouk to abdicate. The constitution is suspended.

1953 Political parties dissolved and their funds confiscated. Republic proclaimed with General Mohammed Neguib as president. He announces a "transitional period" of three years before democracy will be restored.

1954 Nasser deposes Neguib to become president.

1956 Suez Crisis over nationalization of Suez Canal. Israeli, British, and French forces invade, but withdraw after pressure from UN and US.

1957 Suez Canal reopens after UN salvage fleet clears blockade.

1958 Egypt merges with Syria as United Arab Republic.

1960–1970 Building of Aswan Dam.

1961 Syria breaks away from union with Egypt.

1967 Six Day War with Israel; loss of Sinai.

1970 Nasser dies of heart attack. Succeeded by Anwar Sadat.

1971 Readopts the name Egypt. Islam becomes state religion.

1972 Soviet military advisers dismissed from Egypt.

1974–1975 US brokers partial Israeli withdrawal from Sinai.

1977 Sadat visits Jerusalem for first-ever meeting with Israeli prime minister.

1978 Camp David accords, brokered by US, signed by Egypt and Israel.

1979 Egypt and Israel sign peace treaty, alienating most Arab states.

1981 Sadat assassinated by Islamist extremists. Succeeded by Hosni Mubarak.

1982 Last Israeli troops leave Sinai.

1986 President Mubarak meets Israeli Prime Minister Shimon Peres to discuss Middle East peace.

1988 Novelist Naguib Mahfuz wins Nobel Prize for Literature.

1989 After 12-year rift, Egypt and Syria resume diplomatic relations.

1990–1991 Egypt participates in UN operation to liberate Kuwait.

1991 Damascus Declaration provides for a defense pact among Egypt, Syria, and GCC countries against Iraq.

1994–1998 Islamist extremist terror campaign, killing civilians and tourists. Government steps up counter-measures.

1999 Banned Gamaat Islamiya ends campaign to overthrow government.

2000 Egypt recalls ambassador to Israel because of escalating Israeli aggression against Palestinians.

2001 Heavy decline in tourist numbers following September 2001 attack on US.

2003 State of emergency extended for further three years.

EGYPT, ANCIENT

KINGS OF EGYPT

Late Predynastic Period (c.3000)

Zekhen; Narmer

Early Dynastic Period (2920–2575)

2920–2770	**1st dynasty**
	Menes
2770–2649	**2nd dynasty**
	Hetepsekhemwy; Reneb;
	Ninetjer; Peribsen;
	Khasekhem(wy)
2649–2575	**3rd dynasty**
2649–2630	Zanakht
2630–2611	Djoser
2611–2603	Sekhemkhet
2603–2599	Khaba
2599–2575	Huni

Old Kingdom (2575–2134)

2575–2465	**4th dynasty**
2575–2551	Snofru
2551–2528	Khufu Cheops
2528–2520	Radjedef
2520–2494	Khephren
2490–2472	Menkaure
2472–2467	Shepseskaf

2465–2323	**5th dynasty**
2465–2458	Userkaf
2458–2446	Sahure
2446–2426	Neferirkare/Kakai
2426–2419	Shepseskare/Ini
2419–2416	Raneferef
2416–2392	Neuserre/Izi
2396–2388	Menkauhor
2388–2356	Djedkare/Izezi
2356–2323	Wenis
2323–2150	**6th dynasty**
2323–2291	Teti
2289–2255	Pepy I
2255–2246	Merenre/Nemtyemzaf
2246–2152	Pepy II/Neferkare'
2150–2134	**7th/8th dynasty**
	Numerous ephemeral kings, including Neferkare

1st Intermediate Period (2134–2040)

2134–2040	**9th/10th dynasty (Herakleopolitan)**
	Several kings called Khety; Merykare; Ity
2134–2040	**11th dynasty (Theban)**
2134–2118	Inyotef I Sehertawy
2118–2069	Inyotef II Wah'ankh
2069–2061	Inyotef III
2061–2010	Nakhtnebtepnufer/ Mentuhotpe

Middle Kingdom (all Egypt: 2040–1640)

2040–1991	**11th dynasty**
2061–2010	Nebhepetre/Mentuhotpe
2010–1998	Sankhare/Mentuhotpe
1998–1991	Nebtawyre Mentuhotpe
1991–1783	**12th dynasty**
1991–1962	Amenemhet I
1971–1926	Senwosret I
1929–1892	Amenemhet II
1897–1878	Senwosret II
1878–1841?	Senwosret III
1844–1797	Amenemhet III
1799–1787	Amenemhet IV
1787–1783	Nefrusobk
1783–after 1640	**13th dynasty**
	About 70 kings, including:
1783–1779	Wegaf; Amenemhet V; Harnedjheriotef; Amenyqemau

c.1750	Sebekhotpe I; Hor; Amenemhet VII; Sebekhotpe II; Khendjer
c.1745	Sebekhotpe III
c.1741–1730	Neferhotep I
c.1730–1720	Sebekhotpe IV
c.1720–1715	Sebekhotpe V
c.1704–1690	Aya; Mentuemzaf; Dedumose II; Neferhotep III

14th dynasty
A group of minor kings who were probably all contemporary with the 13th or 15th dynasty

2nd Intermediate Period (1640–1532)

1640–1532	**15th dynasty (Hyksos)**
	Salitis; Sheshi; Khian
c.1585–1542	Apophis
c.1542–1532	Khamudi

16th dynasty
Minor Hyksos rulers, contemporary with the 15th dynasty

1640–1550	**17th dynasty**
	Numerous Theban kings, including:
c.1640–1635	Inyotef V Sebekemzaf I; Nebireyeraw; Sebekamzaf II; Tao I; Tao II
c.1555–1550	Kamose

New Kingdom (1550–1070)

1550–1307	**18th dynasty**
1550–1525	Ahmose
1525–1504	Amenophis I
1504–1492	Tuthmosis I
1492–1479	Tuthmosis II
1479–1425	Tuthmosis III
1473–1458	Hatshepsut
1427–1401	Amenophis II
1401–1391	Tuthmosis IV
1391–1353	Amenophis III
1353–1335	Akhenaton/AmenophisIV/ Akhenaten
1335–1333	Smenkhkare (Ankhkheprure) (= Nefertiti)
1333–1323	Tutankhamun (Nebkheprure)
1323–1319	Aya (Kheperkheprure)
1319–1307	Haremhab (Djeserkheprure)

1307–1196	**19th dynasty**
1307–1306	Ramses I
1306–1290	Seti I
1290–1224	Ramses II
1224–1214	Merneptah
1214–1204	Seti II Amenmesse (usurper during reign of Seti II)
1204–1198	Siptah
1198–1196	Twosre
1196–1070	**20th dynasty**
1196–1194	Sethnakhte
1194–1163	Ramses III
1163–1156	Ramses IV
1156–1151	Ramses V
1151–1143	Ramses VI
1143–1136	Ramses VII
1136–1131	Ramses VIII
1131–1112	Ramses IX
1112–1100	Ramses X
1100–1070	Ramses XI

3rd Intermediate Period (1070–712)

1070–945	**21st dynasty**
1070–1044	Smendes
1044–1040	Amenemnisu
1040–992	Psusennes I
993–984	Amenemope
984–978	Osorkon I
978–959	Siamun
959–945	Psusennes II
945–712	**22nd dynasty**
945–924	Shoshenq I
924–909	Osorkon II
909	Takelot I
883	Shoshenq II
883–855	Osorkon III
860–835	Takelot II
835–783	Shoshenq III
783–773	Pami
773–735	Shoshenq V
735–712	Osorkon V
c.828–712	**23rd dynasty**
	Various lines of kings recognized in Thebes, Hermopolis, Herakleopolis, Leontopolis, and Tanis, including:
828–803	Pedubaste I
777–749	Osorkon IV
740–725	Peftjauawybast
724–712	**24th dynasty (Sais)**
724–717	Tefnakhte
717–712	Bocchoris

770–712	25th dynasty (Nubia and Thebes)
770–750	Kashta
750–712	Piye

Late Period (712–332)

712–657	25th dynasty (Nubia and all Egypt)
712–698	Shabaka
698–690	Shebitku
690–664	Taharqa
664–657	Tantamani

664–525	26th dynasty
664–610	Psammetichus I
610–595	Necho II
595–589	Psammetichus II
589–570	Apries
570–526	Amasis
526–525	Psammetichus III

525–404	27th dynasty (Persian)
525–522	Cambyses
521–486	Darius I
486–466	Xerxes I
465–424	Artaxerxes I
424–404	Darius II

404–399	28th dynasty
404–399	Amyrtaios

399–380	29th dynasty
399–393	Nepherites I
393	Psammuthis
393–380	Hakoris
380	Nepherites II

380–343	30th dynasty
380–362	Nectanebo I
365–360	Teos
360–343	Nectanebo II

343–332	2nd Persian Period
343–338	Artaxerxes III Ochus
338–336	Arses
335–332	Darius III Codoman

Graeco-Roman Period (332 BCE–395 CE)

332–304	Macedonian dynasty
332–323	Alexander III the Great
323–316	Philip Arrhidaeus
316–304	Alexander IV

304–330	Ptolemaic dynasty
304–284	Ptolemy I Soter I
285–246	Ptolemy II Philadelphus

246–221	Ptolemy III Euergetes I
221–205	Ptolemy IV Philopator
205–180	Ptolemy V Epiphanes
180–164; 163–145	Ptolemy VI Philometor
170–163; 145–116	Ptolemy VIII Euergetes II (Physkon)
145	Ptolemy VII Neos Philopator
116–107	Cleopatra III and Ptolemy IX Soter II (Lathyros)
107–88	Cleopatra III and Ptolemy X Alexander I
88–81	Ptolemy IX Soter II
81–80	Cleopatra Berenice
80	Ptolemy XI Alexander II
80–58	Ptolemy XII Neos Dionysos (Auletes)
55–51	
58–55	Berenice IV
51–30	Cleopatra VII
51–47	Ptolemy XIII
47–44	Ptolemy XIV
44–30	Ptolemy XV Caesarion

Egyptian-Israeli Peace Treaty
see Camp David Agreement

Eiffel Tower Paris landmark, built in 1889 by Gustave Eiffel (1832–1923). *p.378*

Einsatzgruppen German or Axis security police, controlled by SS, operating as extermination squads in eastern Europe in the wake of conventional armed forces.

Eisenhower Doctrine (1957). US foreign-policy declaration by President Eisenhower which promised aid to any Middle Eastern country in combating aggression from Communist countries. Like the Truman Doctrine, it aimed at total resistance to any extension of Soviet influence.

Eisenhower, Dwight David (1890–1969) US general and 34th President of the US (Republican 1952–60). During World War II he commanded US forces in N Africa and Operation Overlord, the allied invasion of Normandy. In 1944 he became Supreme Commander of the Allied forces. After the war he was Supreme Commander of NATO land forces until his election President in 1952. He oversaw the end of the Korean War (1953) and setting up of SEATO, and his presidency witnessed the emergence as a major political force of the Civil Rights Movement. He was re-elected in 1956.

El Alamein ⚔ of World War II (Oct–Nov 1942). Allied victory marking start of the Allied conquest of N Africa by British and Commonwealth forces.

El-Amarna (*var.* Akhetaton) City built by unorthodox Egyptian pharaoh Akhenaton c.1350 BCE.

El Cid (died 1099) Spanish hero who fought both for the Christian kingdoms of the north and the Moorish leaders of the south. For a time he ruled over Valencia and Murcia. *p.178*

El Dorado Myth among Spanish conquistadores in S America of a golden man or a golden city. *p.283*

EL SALVADOR

EL SALVADOR The smallest and most densely populated Central American republic, El Salvador won full independence in 1841. Located on the Pacific coast, it lies within a zone of seismic activity. Between 1979 and 1991, El Salvador was ravaged by a civil war between US-backed right-wing government forces and left-wing FMLN guerrillas. Since the UN-brokered peace agreement, the country has been rebuilding its shattered economy.

CHRONOLOGY

1522 A Spanish expeditionary force disembarks in the Gulf of Fonseca and calls the territory Cuscatlan.

1528 San Salvador is founded by Diego de Alvarado before being transferred to its present location in 1541.

1821 The territory, which forms part of the Captaincy-General of Guatemala, proclaims its independence from Spain as part of a federation of Central American states. Years of internal conflict ensue.

1839 The Act of Independence is signed in Guatemala.

1841 El Salvador leaves the federation of Central American states.

1849 El Salvador is confirmed as an independent sovereign republic.

1932 Army crushes popular insurrection led by Farabundo Martí.

1944–1979 Army rules through PCN.

1979 Reformist officers overthrow PCN government.

1981 Left-wing Farabundo Martí National Liberation Movement launches civil war.

1991 UN-brokered peace. FMLN recognized as a political party.

1997 Leftist wins San Salvador mayoralty.

2001 Devastating earthquakes kill hundreds; dollarization of economy.

2004 Arena retains presidency.

Elam State of SW Mesopotamia. The Elamites made Susa their capital and flourished in the 13th century BCE, when their empire stretched from Babylon to Persepolis. They gained control of the great Sumerian city of Ur c.2000 BCE.

Eleanor of Aquitaine (c.1122–1204) Married first to Louis VII of France, Eleanor became the wife of Henry II of England, when that marriage was annulled. Active in the management of her own lands in political life, Eleanor supported her sons, Richard and John in a rebellion against their father and was imprisoned for 15 years. Later she acted as regent for Richard I while he was crusading abroad, and led an army to crush a rebellion in Anjou against her son John in 1200. *p.190*

Elizabeth I (1533–1603) Queen of England (reigned 1558–1603). Daughter of Henry VIII and Anne Boleyn, she ascended the throne on the death of her half-sister Mary I. She established the Church of England and put an end to Catholic plots, notably by executing Mary, Queen of Scots (1587) and defeating the Spanish Armada (1588). An intelligent and industrious monarch, under her rule the nation achieved prestige, stability and prosperity, and a great flourishing of the arts. *p.284*

Elmina (*var.* São Jorge da Mina) Portuguese fortified trading post on coast of W Africa. Built in 1482, it had a long history as an entrepôt for the Atlantic slave trade.

Emancipation Proclamation US President Abraham Lincoln's announcement of 22 Sept 1862, that all slaves in rebellion against the Confederate states were free from the start of 1863. The Civil War thus became a fight against slavery, and the Union was able to recruit thousands of black troops to its cause.

Emory, Lt. William 19th-century explorer of the western US.

Empty Quarter *see* Rub' al Khali

Encyclopédie *see* Diderot

Endlösung *see* Final Solution

England *see* United Kingdom

English Civil Wars (*aka* the Great Rebellion, 1640–51) Conflict in the British Isles between Parliamentarians and supporters of the monarchy. It was precipitated by the Bishops' War (1639–1640) with Scotland. The civil wars caused comparatively little loss of life or destruction of property, but led to the execution of King Charles I and his replacement by the Protectorate of Oliver Cromwell. p.306

English East India Company (*aka* British East India Company) The "Governor and Company of Merchants of London trading into the East Indies" was founded in 1600 by Queen Elizabeth I. Initially, British expeditions to the East were confronted by the Portuguese, but the building of a factory at Surat (1612) began the British settlement of India. The Company gained concessions under the Mughals, and won control of Bengal in 1757. But its political activities were gradually curtailed and, after the Mutiny of 1857, it ceased to be the British government's agency in India. It was dissolved in 1873. *p.291*

Enigma Code name for German telecommunications encryption during World War II.

Enlightenment Name given to philosophical and scientific movents of the 18th century in Europe, characterized by a radical scepticism towards existing forms of government and the teachings of the church. *p.326*

Enlil Chief deity of the Sumerian pantheon, Enlil embodied energy and force. His Akkadian counterpart, Bel, was the Mesopotamian god of the atmosphere.

Entente powers Collective name given to the European nations in alliance against Germany, Austria-Hungary, and their allies (the Central Powers) during World War I. Also used to denote the foreign powers in alliance against the Bolsheviks during the Russian Civil War. *See also* Allied forces

EQUATORIAL GUINEA

EQUATORIAL GUINEA Comprising five islands and the territory of Río Muni on the west coast of Africa, Equatorial Guinea lies just north of the equator. Mangrove swamps border the mainland coast. The republic gained its independence in 1968 after 190 years of Spanish rule. Multipartyism was accepted in 1991, but the fairness of subsequent general elections has been questioned.

CHRONOLOGY

1778 Portugal hands over the islands of Fernando Poo and Annobon to Spain under the Treaty of El Pardo. 1840s. Spain develops a trading post on islands off the coast of Rio Muni.

1858 Spain permanently occupies Bioko, developing cocoa plantations.

1900 Treaty of Paris confirms Spanish rule over Rio Muni (within present-day borders). 1920s. Forestry concessions and oil palm plantations are developed in Rio Muni, with smallholder cocoa and coffee plantations later. Spain provides some social services, but the oppressive colonial system allows Africans few rights.

1959 Fernando Poo and Rio Muni are incorporated into metropolitan Spain; the inhabitants gain full Spanish citizenship.

1963 Spain grants autonomy, with moderate nationalists holding power locally.

1968 Independence, with Francisco Macias Nguema, from the Esangui Fang clan as President. Macias abandons democracy, and installs a repressive regime.

1979 Coup puts nephew in power.

1991 Multiparty constitution.

1999 Ruling party wins majority in election condemned as fraudulent.

2001 Government resigns en masse following allegations of mismanagement and corruption.

2002 Obiang Nguema reelected in disputed vote.

2004 PDGE wins denounced poll. Coup attempt failed.

Eratosthenes of Cyrene (c.276–194 BCE) Greek geographer, astronomer, and mathematician. Among a range of achievements he measured the circumference of the earth and invented a system for identifying prime numbers, as well as writing on geography, literary criticism, and chronology.

Erik the Red 10th-century Norwegian navigator and explorer. Having sighted Greenland in about 983, he returned to Iceland to persuade Viking settlers to follow him. He set out in 986 with 25 ships and founded two settlements. The early settlers of Greenland followed an Icelandic model of government; Erik the Red acted as the "Law Speaker." At its peak, the Norse population of Greenland numbered c.4000.

Eriksson, Leif ("the Lucky," born c.970 CE) Viking explorer. He may have been first European to land in N America. In search of grazing and timber he founded settlements in Greenland, and was later based at l'Anse-aux-Meadows in present-day Newfoundland.

Eriksson, Thorvald Viking explorer of N America (1003) and brother of Leif Eriksson.

ERITREA Lying on the shores of the Red Sea, Eritrea's landscape is one of rugged mountains, bush, and desert. A former Italian colony later annexed by Ethiopia, Eritrea fought a long war to win independence in 1993. Like its southern neighbor, Eritrea is prone to recurring droughts and the threat of famine. War with Ethiopia in 1998–2000 brought heavy losses on both sides, until the signing of a comprehensive peace agreement in December 2000.

CHRONOLOGY

1885 Italy occupies Massawa and begins colonization of Eritrea. In the centuries before this Eritrea passed under the control of Arabs, Ottomans, and Egyptians.

1895 Italy launches an abortive invasion of Ethiopia from Eritrea.

1896 Italian forces are defeated at the battle of Adowa.

1941 Administration is taken over by the UK after the defeat of Italian forces in Ethiopia. New administration permits political activity.

1950 The UN General Assembly gives Eritrea self-government within a federal union with Ethiopia, whose government had demanded the incorporation of Eritrea.

1952 Eritrea absorbed by Ethiopia.

1961 Beginning of armed struggle.

1987 EPLF refuses offer of autonomy; fighting intensifies.

1991 EPLF takes Asmara.

1993 Formal independence.

1998 Border war with Ethiopia.

2000 OAU peace treaty signed.

2001 Ethiopia completes troop withdrawal.

2002 Border demarcation begins.

Erlitou Earliest known city of Shang China, founded c.1900 BCE.

Eskimo see Aleut, Inuit

Esquival, Juan de 16th-century Spanish explorer of N America.

Estado Novo see New State

ESTONIA Traditionally the most Western-oriented of the Baltic states, Estonia is bordered by Latvia and the Russian Federation. Its terrain is flat, boggy, and partly wooded, and includes more than 1500 islands. After Swedish and then Russian rule, Estonia briefly enjoyed independence from 1921 until its incorporation into the Soviet Union in 1940. Estonia formally regained its independence as a multiparty democracy in 1991. In contrast to the peoples of Latvia and Lithuania, Estonians are Finno-Ugric and their language is related to Finnish.

CHRONOLOGY

1219 Reval (now Tallinn) founded by Danish invaders. The Danish and German invaders conquer and convert to Catholicism the pagan Estonians. Sweden takes control of Estonia in 1561, as Russia, under Ivan the Terrible, conquers nearby regions.

1721 By the Treaty of Nystadt, Russia acquires Estonia and Livonia (now southern Estonia and Latvia) from Sweden, under whose rule Estonia has become Lutheran.

1881 A policy of Russification in public life serves only to strengthen Estonian national consciousness.

1905 The Russian Revolution is echoed in Estonia by demands for greater national self-determination. A social democratic party is formed in 1906.

1917 The Russian provisional government allows the creation of a unified Estonian district and the calling in June of elections to an Estonian National Council. The Council moves to secede from Russia after the October Revolution. A Bolshevik government is imposed.

1918 Estonia declares independence after the Bolsheviks retreat from advancing German forces but its new government falls. The German surrender in November 1918 is followed by the return of the government and a new Soviet invasion.

1919 Assisted by British fleet and Finnish volunteer forces, Estonia forces the Red Army out of the country, its independence being confirmed by the Treaty of Tartu in February, 1920, and a period of unstable coalition governments begins.

1933 President Konstantin Paets declares a state of emergency in the face of the rise of an anti-communist movement and rules by decree until 1938.

1940 Soviet forces annex Estonia, Lithuania, and Latvia as provided for in the Nazi-Soviet pact of August

1939 In July, after the election victory of the Union of Workers, a socialist republic is proclaimed in Estonia and in August 1940 all three countries are admitted to the Soviet Union. More than 60,000 people are deported by June 1941.

1941 Germany invades the Soviet Union, capturing Estonia. Thousands are killed and thousands more are drafted into forced labor until the Red Army reconquers Estonia in November.

1944 Thousands of Estonians fight for the Finns against the Soviet forces.

1949 Estonia claims that some 95,000 people are arrested and deported to Soviet labor camps in a third wave of purges. A policy of Sovietization and Russification begins.

1985 Mikhail Gorbachev becomes CPSU General Secretary, but his policies of reform bring little change to Estonia's hardline communist leadership.

1987 The anniversary of the 1939 Molotov-Ribbentrop Pact is marked by demonstrations. Environmental protests in the republic also sparks a new rise in national consciousness.

1988 The Estonian Supreme Soviet declares sovereignty, after the formation of the Estonian Popular Front (EPF) and other nationalist movements earlier in the year, and a shift towards them by the Communist Party of Estonia.

1990 Elections to the Estonian Supreme Soviet result in a nationalist majority. On March 30 it declares the continued existence of the Republic of Estonia (the formal name change is adopted on May 8 1990) and the illegality of Soviet rule. Pressure mounts against independence from the republic's Russian minority.

1991 Attempted coup by communists in Moscow is declared illegal by Estonia. Soviet troops move toward Tallinn. The renamed Estonian Supreme Council declares Estonia independent on Aug. 20. Soviet paratroops seize the Tallinn TV tower on Aug. 21, before the coup collapses. Estonia is recognized as independent by the USSR on September 6.

1992 First multiparty elections: election of center-right government.

1996 President Meri wins 2nd term of office.

1997 EU opens membership negotiations.

1999 Elections result in new center-right government.

2001 Communist-era leader Arnold Ruutel elected president.

2003 Centre party and Union for the Republic tie in elections.

2004 Estonia joins NATO and EU.

Ethelbald (died 757) Anglo-Saxon Mercian king.

Ethelred II (*var.* Aethelred II, Ethelred the Unready, died 1016, reigned 978–1013) King of Wessex (England), during whose reign Danish incursions and influence increased, leading to his retreat to Normandy, The English thereafter recognizing Sven Forkbeard as king.

ETHIOPIA (var. Abyssinia) Located in northeast Africa, the former empire of Ethiopia is the cradle of an ancient civilization, which adopted Orthodox Christianity in the 4th century. It has been landlocked since 1993, when Eritrea, on the Red Sea, seceded. Ethiopia is mountainous except for desert lowlands in the northeast and southeast, and is prone to devastating drought and famine. A long civil war ended in 1991 with the defeat of the Stalinist military dictatorship that had ruled since 1974. A free-market, multiparty democratic system now provides substantial regional autonomy. War with Eritrea in 1998–2000 brought heavy losses on both sides, before a peace agreement was signed in December 2000 and arbitrators were brought in to redefine the border.

Christianity in Ethiopia. *p.305*
Famine in Ethiopia. *p.448*.

CHRONOLOGY

500 BCE Foundation of kingdom of Axum, the nucleus of later Ethiopia.

330 CE Christianity adopted as state religion.

1270 Overthrow of Zagwe dynasty by Amhara princes. Foundation of Solomid dynasty.

1523 Muslim invasion, later repelled with Portuguese assistance.

1632 Gondar becomes capital.

1855 Amhara chief overthrows Gondar dynasty and proclaims himself Emperor Tewodoros (Theodore) II, with his capital at Magdala.

1868 Tewodoros commits suicide rather than surrender to British expeditionary force.

1889 Menelik II becomes emperor and begins expansion of empire in east and south, eventually doubling the size of his empire.

1896 Italian invasion of Tigre defeated. Europeans recognize Ethiopia's independence.

1913 Menelik II dies.

1916 His son, Lij Iyasu, is deposed for his conversion to Islam and proposed alliance with Turkey. Menelik's daughter, Zauditu, becomes empress with Ras Tafari as regent.

1923 Joins League of Nations.

1930 Zauditu dies. Ras Tafari crowned Emperor Haile Selassie.

1936 Italians occupy Ethiopia. League of Nations fails to react.

1941 British oust Italians and restore Haile Selassie, who sets up a constitution, parliament, and cabinet, but retains personal power and the feudal system.

1952 Eritrea, ruled by Italy until 1941, then under British mandate, federated with Ethiopia.

1962 Unitary state created; Eritrea loses its autonomy within the Ethiopian state despite the demands of secessionists.

1972–1974 Famine kills 200,000.

1974 Strikes and army mutinies at Haile Selassie's autocratic rule and country's economic decline. Dergue (Military Committee) stages coup.

1975 Ethiopia becomes socialist state: nationalizations, worker cooperatives, and health reforms.

1977 Colonel Mengistu Haile Mariam takes over. Somali invasion of Ogaden defeated with Soviet and Cuban help.

1978–1979 Thousands of political opponents killed or imprisoned.

1984 Workers' Party of Ethiopia (WPE) set up on Soviet model. One million die in famine after drought and years of war. Live Aid concert raises funds for relief.

1986 Eritrean rebels now control the whole northeastern coast.

1987 Serious drought threatens famine.

1988 Eritrean and Tigrean People's Liberation Fronts (EPLF and TPLF) begin new offensives. Mengistu's budget is for "Everything to the War Front." Diplomatic relations with Somalia restored.

1989 Military coup attempt fails. TPLF in control of most of Tigre. TPLF and Ethiopian People's Revolutionary Movement form alliance – EPRDF.

1990 Military gains by opponents of Mengistu regime. Moves toward market economy and restructuring of ruling party to include non-Marxists. Distribution of food aid for victims of new famine is hampered by government and rebel forces.

1991 Mengistu accepts military defeat and flees country. EPRDF enters Addis Ababa, sets up provisional government, promising representation for all ethnic groups. Outbreaks of fighting continue, between Tigrean EPRDF and opposing groups.

1993 Eritrean independence recognized following referendum.

1995 Transitional rule ends. EPRDF wins landslide in multiparty elections, sets up first democratic government. New nine-state federation is formed.

1998–2000 Tensions with Eritrea escalate into a border war.

2000 OAU peace treaty signed. Haile Selassie's remains buried in Trinity Cathedral, Addis Ababa.

2001 Ethiopia completes troop withdrawal from Eritrea.

2002 Over 120 human rights demonstrators killed by police.

Etruscans Ancient, pre-Roman people who flourished in west and central Italy from the 8th century BCE. The last Etruscan king, Tarquin II, was overthrown in 509 BCE, and in 283 BCE they succumbed completely to the Romans, but their cultural influence endured; skilled engineers and urban planners, they were also accomplished metal workers and traded with Greece. *p.44*

EU *see* European Union

Eudoxus of Cyzicus (born c.135 BCE) Greek explorer, who made trading journeys to India on behalf of Ptolemaic kings of Egypt.

Eugénie (1826–1920) Empress of France. Born in Spain, she was consort of the French emperor, Napoleon III. After his deposition in 1871, she fled to England, where he joined her after a period of imprisonment in Germany.

Eurasia Geopolitical term for combined continents of Europe and Asia, historically often including Egypt and Graeco-Roman tracts of N Africa.

EURATOM *see* European Atomic Energy Community

Euripides (484–406 BCE) Athenian tragic dramatist, originally an artist, who took up literature and wrote 80 dramas, 19 of which survive.

European Atomic Energy Community (EURATOM) International organization founded in 1957 by the Treaty of Rome to promote and develop the peaceful use of atomic energy in Europe. D214

European Coal and Steel Community (ECSC) Body established in 1952 to co-ordinate the production of coal and steel in France, Italy, W Germany, and the Benelux countries.

European Economic Community (EEC) *see* European Union

European Recovery Program *see* Marshall Plan

European Union (EU) Organization formed (1993) to integrate the economies of 15 member states and promote cooperation and coordination of policies. Originated in Treaty of Rome (1957) and the formation of the EEC (France, Germany, Italy, Belgium, Netherlands, and Luxembourg), admitting the UK, Irish Republic, and Denmark in 1973 (EC). Greece joined in 1981, followed by Spain and Portugal in 1986 and Austria, Finland, and Sweden in 1995. The organization developed in 1990s towards greater and fuller integration.

European Union Treaty *see* Maastricht Treaty

Eutaw Springs ⚔ of American Revolutionary War (Sep 8 1781). British victory.

Everest, Sir George (1790–1866). Army officer with British East India Company, who instituted the great Trigonometrical Survey of India. From 1823, he was responsible for triangulating the entire subcontinent. Mount Everest was named after him.

exploration and discovery explorers of the oceans (500–1000 CE). *p.113*
European discovery of N America. *p.251*
European voyages of discovery. *p.271*
exploration of S America. *p.281*
exploration of N America. *p.330*
exploration of Australia. *p.367*
European exploration of Africa. *p.376*
exploration of the Arctic. *p.391*
exploration of Antarctica. *p.391*

Eylau ⚔ of Napoleonic Wars – the War of the 3rd Coalition (1807). French victory.

Eyre, Edward (1815–1901) British-born explorer of Australia. Eyre's journeys were inspired by the search for new pasturelands for cattle. His greatest journey was his crossing of the Nullarbor Plain in 1840–41. It would have failed without the local Aborigines who helped the expedition find water.

Ezana Axumite king (c.350.)

F

Fa Xian (*var.* Fa Hsien, *fl.* c.400 CE) Chinese Buddhist monk and traveler. Made the first recorded journey overland from China to India and back by sea between 399 and 414 CE. The purpose of his travels was the gathering of religious texts; his experiences greatly enriched Chinese geography.

FAEROE ISLANDS The Faeroe Islands gained internal self-government in 1948. The Danish Constitution of 1953 declares the islands to be an integral part of the Danish kingdom.

CHRONOLOGY

8th century Irish monks first settle the Faeroes; they are followed by Norwegian Vikings in 800 CE.

1035 The Faeroes formally become a Norwegian possession.

1274 The original Faeroese Althing, which has origins in the 9th century and in which all yeomen have a right to contribute to policy making, becomes a Loegting which has judicial powers and contact with the king and his officials, including the Futin, the king's high commissioner in the Faeroes.

1380 Along with Norway proper, the Faeroes become part of Denmark. This is confirmed in the 1397 Union of Kalmar.

1814 Under the Treaty of Kiel Norway is transferred to the Swedish crown; Faeroes remain Danish possession. Two years later the Loegting is abolished, and Faeroes are made administrative district of Denmark.

1852 The regional parliament, the Loegting, is restored but only as a consultative body.

1940–45 After metropolitan Denmark is occupied by Nazi Germany during the Second World War, the Faeroes are occupied by British troops.

1946 A referendum narrowly favors independence from Denmark rather than limited home rule but differences as to whether the referendum binding or merely consultative lead to general election in which parties favoring home rule are successful. Resulting home rule act of 1948 grants the Faeroes internal self-government

but leaves the Danish government in control of foreign and defence policy.

1968 Faeroes join the European Free Trade Association eight years after Denmark joined as a founder member, but leave the organization in 1972 because of adverse effects membership has on local economy.

1972 In a national referendum the Faeroese opt to remain outside the European Communities (EC), while metropolitan Denmark votes to join (formally acceding on Jan 1 1973). The islands are granted special external associate status which gives them a relationship to the EC similar to that of the EFTA countries. EC policies including the common fisheries policy do not apply to the Faeroes.

1983 The Loegting unanimously declares the islands to be a "nuclear free zone."

1988 The Faeroese Social Democratic Party loses its relative majority to the People's Party in a general election.

1989 The People's Party and three other parties form a center-right coalition under Jogvan Sundstein.

1990 In early elections, caused by the government's collapse over disagreements on economic policy, the Social Democrats return as the largest single party and form a center-left coalition under Atli Dam.

1993 Marita Petersen succeeds Dam as Prime Minister, who resigned due to health concerns.

1993 The coalition falls over fisheries policy and is replaced by a coalition of the Social Democratic, Republican and Home Rule parties; Petersen remains Prime Minister.

1994 Social Democrats lose support in general election and Union Party leader Edmund Joensen forms a new broad-based coalition comprising the Unionist Party, the Social Democrats, the Home Rule Party, and the newly-formed Workers' Party of trade unionists.

2004 Coalition formed between the Unionist Party, the People's Party and the Social Democratic Party. Jóannes Eidesgaard appointed as Prime Minister.

Faisal I (*var.* Feisal, 1885–1933) Fought in Arab Revolt (1916–18) against Turkey during World War I. Became King of Iraq (1921–33). In 1930 he negotiated a treaty with the British, who held mandate in Iraq, that gave Iraq independence.

FALKLAND ISLANDS (var. Las Malvinas)

Island group in the S Atlantic, comprising two main islands and some 200 smaller islands and islets. The bleak rocky landscape supports sheep, but little else. A British colony since 1833, the islands are claimed by Argentina, which in 1982 sent an invasion force to occupy them. A British expeditionary force was sent and the Falklands recaptured in the space of six weeks.

Chronology

1592 First visited by English sailors in the ship *Desire* and given their name after the Naval Treasurer Viscount Falkland by Capt. Strong of the *Welfare* who made the first recorded landing in 1690.

1764 French settlers land and name the islands Les Malouines, but relinquish their rights to Spain in 1766.

1765–66 A British settlement is established which Spain recognizes in 1771 but which is withdrawn in 1774 for economic reasons. A Spanish garrison is also withdrawn in 1811, leaving the islands uninhabited.

1820 Buenos Aires sends a ship to the islands, now a base for UK and US whaling industries, to proclaim its sovereignty as successor to the former colonial power. In 1829 the United Provinces of La Plata appoints a governor to the islands.

1833 UK sovereignty is established after US and UK warships expel Argentinians in 1831–32.

1955 The UK submits the dispute over the Falkland Islands Dependencies – South Georgia and the South Sandwich Islands (formally claimed by Argentina respectively in 1927 and in 1948) – to the International Court of Justice after an Argentinian naval expedition establishes bases in "British Antarctica."

1962 The British Antarctic Territory is established, comprising mainly the South Shetland and South Orkney Islands.

1966 A group of Argentinian nationalists stage a symbolic invasion. Negotiations begin between the UK and Argentina.

1976 A group of Argentinian scientists occupy and remain on Southern Thule, one of the South Sandwich Islands.

1982 March 19. A party of Argentinian scrap merchants land on South Georgia.

1982 April 2. Argentinian forces invade and occupy the Falklands and install an Argentinian governor. The UK despatches a large task force arriving late April.

1982 June 14. Argentinian forces surrender after six weeks of fighting in which about 1,000 people are killed.

1989 In election to the Legislative Council all eight seats are won by independent candidates opposed to links with Argentina.

1990 United Kingdom and Argentina agree to restore diplomatic relations.

1995 Agreement reached on division of revenues from oil and gas exploration in offshore waters.

2002 Howard Pearce elected as governer.

Falklands War (1982) Conflict between Argentina and the UK over disputed sovereignty of islands in S Atlantic.

Fallam, Robert 17th-century explorer of eastern N America. Accompanied Thomas Batts in 1671 in search of a South Sea.

Fallen Timbers ⚔ (Aug 20 1794) US victory over the Northwest Indian Confederation which enabled the extension of white settlement of their former territory.

Fashoda ⚔ (1898) British and French clash in N Africa.

Fasiladas (died 1667) Ethiopian emperor (reigned 1632–67). Severed links between his country and Europe, instigating a policy of isolation that lasted for more than two centuries.

Fatimid dynasty (909–1171) Muslim dynasty, founded in Tunisia, the Fatimids claimed descent from Fatima, Muhammad's daughter. In 969 the fourth Fatimid Caliph, Muizz, conquered Egypt and established his capital at Cairo, from where the Fatimids ruled until the 12th century. *p.151*

Federal Bureau of Investigation (FBI) US government agency first established in 1908 to deal with matters of internal security, counter-intelligence, and federal law-enforcement. *See also* Hoover, Edgar

Federal Republic of Germany *see* Germany, West Germany

Federmann, Nikolaus (died 1542) German explorer of S America. Federmann was a representative of the Welsers, Charles V's bankers, who were granted lands in present-day Venezuela. Federmann led expeditions into the interior in 1530 and 1537. On the second, he scaled Cordillera Oriental of the Andes to reach Bogotá in 1539. He was recalled to Spain, accused of misappropriation of royal funds.

Feisal I *see* Faisal I

Ferdinand II (1578–1637) Holy Roman Emperor (reigned 1619–37). A devout Catholic, his deposition as king of Bohemia by Bohemian Protestants led to the Thirty Years' War. After his victory at ⚔ The White Mountain (1620) he reimposed Catholicism on Bohemia.

Ferdinand III of Naples *see* Ferdinand of Aragon

Ferdinand V of Castile *see* Ferdinand of Aragon

Ferdinand of Aragon (1452–1516) The first monarch of all Spain, Ferdinand ruled as Ferdinand V of Castile (from 1474), Ferdinand II of Aragon and Sicily (from 1479) and Ferdinand III of Naples (from 1503). His marriage to Isabella of Castile (1451–1504) in 1469 led to the union of Aragon and Castile. His reconquest of Granada from the Moors (1492) completed the unification of Spain. He expelled the Jews from Spain and financed Columbus's voyage to the New World.

Ferghana Region of C Asia famed for its cavalry horses.

fertility cult Set of beliefs and practices associated with promulgating the fertility of the land. Finds of apparently pregnant female figures are often thought to have been associated with these kinds of beliefs.

Fezzan *see* Garamantes

Field of Blood ⚔ (1119) of crusades. Muslim victory.

FIJI

FIJI is a volcanic archipelago in the southern Pacific Ocean, comprising two main islands and nearly 900 smaller islands and islets. The introduction of ethnic Indian workers by the British in 1879–1916 had dramatic consequences. Between 1946 and 1997 Indo-Fijians outnumbered Melanesian Fijians. A series of coups led by Fijian supremacists between 1987 and 2000 led to a mass exodus of ethnic Indians, the most recent seriously damaging the economy.

Chronology

1290 BCE Artifacts dating back to this time indicate that the Fijian islands had a resident population.

50 BCE Migratory groups from Melanesia begin to arrive (to 1100 CE).

1643 Abel Tasman, the Dutch explorer, sights the Fijian islands.

1800 The first Europeans begin to settle in Fiji: a handful of sailors, escaped convicts from Australia, sandalwood traders and by the 1830s, missionaries.

1874 Fiji becomes a British colony.

1875 A measles epidemic wipes out a third of the Fijian population.

1879 The first Indian laborers arrive to work on the copra and sugarcane plantations.

1937 Fiji's Legislative Council becomes partly elected, partly nominated.

1970 Independence from Britain.

1987 Election win for Indo-Fijian coalition. Sitiveni Rabuka's coups secure minority ethnic Fijian rule. Ejected from Commonwealth.

1989 Mass Indo-Fijian emigration.

1990 Constitution discriminating against Indo-Fijians introduced.

1992 Rabuka wins legislative polls.

1997 Census shows ethnic Fijians outnumber Indo-Fijians. Fiji rejoins Commonwealth. New constitution.

1999 General election won by FLP. First Indo-Fijian prime minister.

2000 Civilian-led coup; new ethnic Fijian government.

2001 Nationalists win elections.

Final Solution Nazi policy to exterminate European Jewry, implicit in Nazi anti-semitism from the 1930s, but formalized (verbally) by Hitler in July 1941. The first death camp at Chelmno was opened in Dec 1941, detailed plans for implementation of the policy agreed at the Wannsee conference, Jan 1942. The policy was in operation until the liberation of the death camps by Allied forces in 1945.

Finley, John 18th-century explorer of the eastern US, who realized the importance of Cumberland Gap in 1752.

FINLAND Bordered to the north and west by Norway and Sweden, and to the east by Russia, Finland is a low-lying country of forests and 187, 888 lakes. Politics are based on consensus, and the country has been stable despite successive short-lived coalitions. Russia annexed Finland in 1809, ruling it until 1917, and subsequently Finland accepted a close relationship with the USSR as the price of maintaining its

independence. It joined the European Union in 1995 and, despite popular suspicion of Brussels bureaucracy, Finland was among the 11 EU states to introduce the euro from 1999.

CHRONOLOGY

1323 Treaty of Pähkinäsaari. Finland part of Swedish Kingdom.

1581 Finland is made a grand duchy under the Swedish crown.

1700–21 Sweden is defeated by Russia in the Great Northern War and is obliged to cede Finnish Karelia and territory on the Gulf of Finland to Russia.

1809 Treaty of Fredrikshamn, Sweden cedes Finland to Russia. Finland becomes Grand Duchy enjoying considerable autonomy.

1812 Helsinki becomes capital.

1863 Finnish becomes an official language alongside Swedish.

1865 Grand Duchy acquires its own monetary system.

1879 Conscription law lays the foundation for a Finnish army.

1899 Czar Nicholas II begins process of Russification. Labor Party founded.

1900 Gradual imposition of Russian as the official language begins.

1901 Finnish army disbanded, men ordered into Russian units. Disobedience campaign prevents men being drafted into the army.

1903 Labor Party becomes SDP.

1905 National strike forces restoration of 1899 status quo.

1906 Parliamentary reform. Universal suffrage introduced.

1910 Responsibility for important legislation passed to Russian Duma.

1917 Russian revolution allows Finland to declare independence.

1918 Civil war between Bolsheviks and right-wing government. General Gustav Mannerheim leads government to victory at Battle of Tampere.

1919 Finland becomes republic. Kaarlo Ståhlberg elected president with wide political powers.

1920 Treaty of Tartu: USSR recognizes Finland's borders.

1921 London Convention. Åland Islands become part of Finland.

1939 August, Hitler-Stalin nonaggression pact gives USSR a free hand in Finland. November. Soviet invasion; strong Finnish resistance in ensuing Winter War.

1940 Treaty of Moscow. Finland cedes a tenth of national territory.

1941 Finnish troops join Germany in its invasion of USSR.

1944 Red Army invades. August. President Risto Ryti resigns. September. Finland, led by Marshal Mannerheim, signs armistice.

1946 President Mannerheim resigns, Juho Paasikivi president.

1948 Signs friendship treaty with USSR. Agrees to resist any attack on USSR made through Finland by Germany or its allies.

1952 Payment of $570 million in war reparations completed.

1956 Uhro Kekkonen, leader of the Agrarian Party, becomes president.

1956–1991 A series of coalition governments involving SDP and Agrarians, renamed KESK in 1965, hold power.

1981 President Kekkonen resigns.

1982 Mauno Koivisto president.

1989 USSR recognizes Finnish neutrality for first time.

1991 Non-SDP government elected. Austerity measures.

1992 January, signs ten-year agreement with Russia which, for first time since World War II, involves no military agreement.

1994 SDP candidate Martti Ahtisaari elected president.

1995 Finland joins EU. Election returns SDP-led coalition under Paavo Lipponen.

1999 Finland among first 11 countries to introduce euro. General election returns Lipponen's coalition to power.

2000 Tarja Halonen elected as first female president.

2002 Euro fully adopted.

2003 KESK wins elections. Prime Minister Anneli Jäätteenmäki resigns.

First Emperor *see* Qin dynasty, Shi Huangdi

First Fleet The name given to the convict ships that landed at Botany Bay in 1788 to found the first British colony in Australia. The fleet consisted of eleven ships under the command of Captain Arthur Phillip, the first governor of New South Wales. *p.335*

First Intermediate Period Period of almost 100 years in Egypt from c.2134 BCE, where the balance of power and governmental responsibility shifted from the court to the provinces.

First World War *see* World War I

Fitch, Ralph (c.1550–1611) British merchant who was among the first Englishmen to travel through India and Southeast Asia.

Five Dynasties and Ten Kingdoms (907–960) Period of Chinese history that followed the Tang dynasty when China fragmented into regional states.

Flatiron building Landmark skyscraper of New York, completed in 1901. *p.390*

Fleurus ⚔ of Napoleonic Wars during the War of the 1st Coalition (1794). French victory.

Flinders, Matthew (1774–1814) English naval officer. In 1798–99, with George Bass, he circumnavigated Tasmania, proving it was an island. Then appointed Commander of HMS Investigator, the British ship that undertook a thorough survey of the entire coastline of Australia.

Florida Claimed for Spain by Ponce de León in 1513. *p.285*

Flying Fortress Nickname for US B17 heavy bomber first used for high-level daylight raids on Nazi Germany in World War II.

FNLA *see* National Front for the Liberation of Angola

Ford, Gerald Rudolf (1913–) 38th President of the US (Republican, 1974–76). Became President following the resignation of Richard Nixon in 1974, but failed to retain the Presidency at the next election.

Ford, Henry (1863–1947) US engineer and car manufacturer. Founded the Ford Motor Company in 1903, where he pioneered the assembly-line method of mass production for the first "people's automobile," the Model-T Ford.

Former Han *see* Han dynasty

Formosa *see* Taiwan

Forrest, Alexander 19th-century explorer of Australia.

Forrest, John (1847–1918) Australian explorer and politician. Forrest's first expedition in 1869 was in search of the lost party of Ludwig Leichhardt. He made several more journeys into the interior of Western Australia. His brother Alexander was also an explorer. In 1883 John Forrest became the colony's surveyor-general, and later Western Australia's first state premier.

Fort Donelson ⚔ of American Civil War (Feb 16 1862). Union victory.

Fort Henry ⚔ of American Civil War (Feb 6 1862). Union victory.

Fort Jesus Fort founded by the Portuguese in 1593 at Mombasa on the E coast of Africa. It was taken by Omani Arabs in 1698. *p.290*

Fort St. George Fortified trading post founded by the English East India Company in 1693 in SE India. It grew to become the modern city of Madras (Chennai). *p.305*

Fort Sumter Attack on the fort starts US Civil War (1861).

Fortress Europe General term for Nazi-occupied Europe during World War II, after the Soviet Union's entry to the war and the full Allied blockade was enforced.

FRANCE Straddling western Europe from the English Channel to the Mediterranean, France was Europe's first modern republic, and possessed a colonial empire second only to that of the UK. Today, it is one of the world's major industrial powers and its fourth-largest exporter. Industry is the leading economic sector, but the agricultural lobby remains powerful – French farmers will mount the barricades in defense of their interests. France's focus is very much on Europe. Together with Germany it was a founder member of the European Economic Community (EEC), and has supported successive steps to build a more closely integrated European Union. Paris, the French capital, is generally considered one of the world's most beautiful cities. It has been home to some of the most influential artists, writers, and film-makers of the modern era.

Chronology

57–52 BCE The Romans, under Julius Caesar, conquer and subjugate Gaul, an area roughly equivalent to modern France.

486 CE The Romans are ousted from Gaul ("Francia") by King Clovis I (c.466–511 CE), the first of the Merovingians, who rule until 751 CE, when they are succeeded by the Carolingians. Clovis's reign also marks the foundation of a Frankish empire.

800 CE King Charlemagne (ruled 768–814), after conducting a series of military campaigns which extend and unify his empire, is crowned Emperor of the West by Pope Leo III and establishes the Carolingian empire, although in 843 the German-speaking lands of Franconia are lost.

987 CE The Capetian dynasty, which lasts from 987 until 1328 and succeeds that of the Carolingians, is founded by Hugh Capet (ruled 987–996 CE), though it is not until the late 12th century that the Capetian realm attains its greatest territorial extent.

1309 The Papacy is moved from Rome to Avignon in France by Pope Clement V. From 1378, during the period of the schism, there are two rival Popes, until the Roman party achieves sole recognition in 1417.

1337 The Hundred Years" War, between France and England, begins. English kings seek to dominate France. After winning the battle of Agincourt in 1415, they then lose control over Normandy by 1450, over Gascony by 1450, and over Aquitaine by 1453. Only Calais remains under English control and is not lost to France until 1558.

1562 In the French Wars of Religion, which begin in 1562, Protestant Huguenot and Catholic nobles fight for supremacy following the sudden death of the last Valois King, Henry II in 1559.

1572 4,000 Huguenots are killed in the St. Bartholomew's Day massacre.

1594 Henry IV, who has converted to Catholicism in 1593 on the grounds that "Paris is worth a mass," is crowned the first of the Bourbon kings. The Huguenots are granted freedom of worship in the 1598 Edict of Nantes.

1610 Henry IV is assassinated. Succeeded by Louis XIII, whose first minister Cardinal Richelieu consolidates the monarchy's standing both at home and abroad, notably in the Thirty Years' War (1618–48).

1643 Louis XIV (1638–1715), the "Sun King," ascends the throne. During his long reign the absolutism of the ancient regime is consolidated and reaches it peak. At home the arts flourish at Versailles under his patronage. In 1685 he revokes the Edict of Nantes. Abroad he establishes French hegemony over much of western Europe in a series of victorious military campaigns. However, from 1700, as Europe unites in resistance, his position begins to be undermined.

1715 Death of Louis XIV. His successor and great-grandson, Louis XV (ruled 1715–74), though well-intentioned, lacks interest in government and politics and is less successful in campaigns abroad and in countering growing opposition at home.

1740 The War of the Austrian Succession begins following the death of the last male Habsburg Emperor, Charles VI. France and Prussia unsuccessfully support the claim of the Elector of Bavaria to the Habsburg throne against that of Charles's daughter Maria Theresa, who is supported by Britain and whose claim is vindicated at the 1748 Treaty of Aix-la-Chapelle.

1756–63 The Seven Years' War continues disputes left unresolved by the Treaty of Aix-la-Chapelle as Britain and France seek to win maritime and colonial supremacy in North America, the West Indies, and India. As a result France is obliged to cede American possessions in Canada, east of the Mississippi, and in the West Indies. French support for the Americans in their War of Independence (1776–83) is costly and helps undermine the Ancien Régime.

1789 For the first time since 1614, Louis XVI (reigned 1774–92) summons the advisory Estates-General in May in an attempt to secure revenue and administrative reforms which have been resisted by the nobles and "parlements." As the nobles and clergy (the first and second estates) lose control to the "third estate" (the commoners) and as early repression backfires, a National Assembly is formed by the third estate and demands reform of the monarchy. The indecisive response of Louis XVI sparks the storming of the Bastille on July 14 and on August 26 the National Assembly issues a Declaration of the Rights of Man. Further hesitation on Louis XVI's part prompts women of Paris to march to Versailles in October to demand bread, and they take the royal family to Paris as hostages.

1790 A new Constitution is proclaimed on July 14, and in June 1791 the King and his family attempt to flee in disguise but are brought back as prisoners; Louis XVI is forced to accept a new Constitution in September.

1792 Royalist emigrés begin to muster support abroad and war begins in April. On August 10 the Paris mob storms the royal palace of the Tuileries. The Paris Commune led by Georges Jacques Danton seizes power and a National Convention replaces the National Assembly and abolishes the monarchy on September 21.

1793 Louis XVI is convicted of treason on January 15 and executed on January 21. From June control of the country passes from the moderate Girondins to the extremist Jacobins, led by Maximilien François Robespierre (1758–94) and the "Reign of Terror" begins with a series of mass executions on September 5.

1794 Robespierre's Committee of Public Safety is overthrown in the coup of 9 Thermidor (July 27); Robespierre is executed. A new constitution in August 1795 establishes the more moderate Directory which, however, becomes increasingly corrupt.

1799 Napoleon Bonaparte (1769–1821), a general from the Revolutionary Wars (1792–1802), overthrows the Directory and assumes dictatorial powers in the coup of 18 Brumaire (November 9).

1804 At a ceremony in December Napoleon seizes the crown from the Pope and proclaims himself Emperor of the French. At home he introduces reforms including the legal "Code Napoléon" and abroad he defeats the Austrians and Russians at Austerlitz in December 1805 and the Prussians at Jena in October 1806.

1812 Napoleon's invasion of Russia leads to defeat due to the Russian winter and to the Austro-Prussian capture of Paris on March 31 1814. He is deposed on April 3 and the Bourbon monarchy is reinstalled, with Louis XVIII as king.

1815 Napoleon returns from exile on the island of Elba for a final "hundred days" which end in defeat by British and Prussian forces at the battle of Waterloo on June 18.

1830 Louis XVIII's brother King Charles X, who ascended the throne in 1824, is forced to abdicate in the "July Revolution" and Louis Philippe I of Orléans is installed as the "citizen king."

1848 At a time of food shortage, Louis Philippe is toppled by popular riots in a revolution on Feb. 24–25 and a Second Republic is proclaimed.

1852 Louis Napoleon (1808–73), nephew of Napoleon Bonaparte, having seized power in a 1851 coup d'état, takes the title of Emperor Napoleon III. On December 2, 1852, he proclaims a Second Empire based on plebiscitary autocracy and becomes involved in wars with Russia in the Crimea in 1854–56 and with Austria in 1859 and in imperial expansion in Indochina.

1870–71 Napoleon III is defeated in the Franco-Prussian war and a new liberal-democratic Third Republic is proclaimed on September 4 1870. Prussian, Russian, and Austrian forces enter Paris in January 1871, and France is obliged to cede Alsace and Lorraine to Germany. In Paris, a revolutionary Commune holds power from March 28 until May 28 1871, but is brutally suppressed at the cost of 20,000 lives by Louis Adolphe Thiers (1797–1877) who serves as President from 1871 until 1873 when Patrice MacMahon is elected to the post. Governmental instability is endemic and over the next 70 years there are 109 separate governments.

1881 Tunisia becomes a French protectorate, and in 1883 a French protectorate is established in Indochina.

1899 France and England reach agreement over spheres of influence in Africa, enabling France to consolidate its position in northwestern and Saharan Africa.

1905 December. The Church and State are separated in the wake of the Dreyfus affair in which the Alsatian Jew, Captain Alfred Dreyfus, is unjustly convicted of treason in 1894 and only acquitted in 1906.

1914 Germany declares war on France, an ally of Russia since 1894. During four years of fighting, 1,363,000 French soldiers are killed, with 550,000 lives lost during the Battle of Verdun (from Feb 21 1915 to Dec 18 1916) and 200,000 during the second Battle of the Aisne (from April 16 to May 9 1917), before the tide is reversed at the 2nd Battle of the Marne (July 15–Aug 4 1918).

1914–1918 1.4 million Frenchmen killed in World War I.

1918–1939 Economic recession and political instability; 20 prime ministers and 44 governments.

1940 Capitulation to Germany. Puppet Vichy regime. General de Gaulle leads "Free French" abroad.

1944 Liberation of France.

1946–1958 Fourth Republic. Political instability with 26 governments. Nationalizations. France takes leading role in EEC formation.

1958 Fifth Republic. De Gaulle becomes president with strong executive powers.

1960 Most French colonies gain independence.

▶

CONCORDANCE

1962 Algerian independence after bitter war with France.

1966 France withdraws from NATO military command.

1968 General strike and riots over education policy and low wages. National Assembly dissolved; Gaullist victory in June elections.

1969 De Gaulle resigns after defeat in referendum on regional reform; replaced by Georges Pompidou.

1974 Valéry Giscard d'Estaing president. Center-right coalition.

1981 Left wins elections; François Mitterrand president.

1983–1986 Government U-turn on economic policy.

1986 "Cohabitation" between socialist president and new right-wing government led by Jacques Chirac.

1988 Mitterrand wins second term. PS-led coalition returns.

1991 Edith Cresson becomes first woman prime minister.

1993 Center-right wins elections. Second period of cohabitation.

1995 Jacques Chirac president.

1995–1996 Controversial series of Pacific nuclear tests.

1996 Unpopular austerity measures to prepare economy for European monetary union.

1997 Center-right loses elections. PS-led government takes office in reversed "cohabitation." Lionel Jospin prime minister.

1998–1999 Extensive privatization program initiated.

2000 35-hour week becomes law.

2002 January. Euro replaces Franc. April–June, centre-right victory in presidential and legislative elections.

2003 Strikes over pension reform. Heatwave kills 15,000 people.

2004 Regional polls dent centre-right ascendancy.

FRENCH RULERS (from 987)

CAPETIAN DYNASTY

987–996	Hugh Capet (Hugues Capet)
996–1031	Robert II the Pious
1031–1060	Henry I (Henri)
1060–1108	Philip I (Philippe)
1108–1137	Louis VI the Fat
1137–1180	Louis VII the Young
1180–1223	Philip II Augustus (Philippe Auguste)

1223–1226	Louis VIII the Lion
1226–1270	Louis IX (St. Louis)
1270–1285	Philip III the Bold (Philippe)
1285–1314	Philip IV the Fair
1314–1316	Louis X the Stubborn
1316	John I (Jean)
1316–1322	Philip V the Tall
1322–1328	Charles IV the Fair

VALOIS DYNASTY

1328–1350	Philip VI (Philippe)
1350–1364	John II the Good
1364–1380	Charles V the Wise
1380–1422	Charles VI the Mad, Well-Beloved, or Foolish
1422–1461	Charles VII the Well-Served or Victorious
1461–1483	Louis XI the Spider
1483–1498	Charles VIII (Father of his People)
1498–1515	Louis XII
1515–1547	Francis I (François)
1547–1559	Henry II
1559–1560	Francis II (François)
1560–1574	Charles IX
1574–1589	Henry III (Henri)

BOURBON DYNASTY

1589–1610	Henry IV (Henri)
1610–1643	Louis XIII
1643–1715	Louis XIV the Sun King
1715–1774	Louis XV
1774–1792	Louis XVI
1793–1795	Louis XVII (uncrowned, died in captivity during Revolution)

FIRST REPUBLIC

1792–1795	National Convention
1795–1799	Directory (Directoire)

Directors

Group of five "directors," chosen by the legislature, who held executive power under the constitution of 1795.

1795–1799	Paul François Jean Nicolas de Barras
1795–1799	Jean-François Reubell
1795–1799	Louis Marie La Revellíere-Lépeaux
1795–1797	Lazare Nicolas Marguerite Carnot
1795–1797	Etienne Le Tourneur
1797	François Marquis de Barthélemy
1797–1799	Philippe Antoine Merlin de Douai

1797–1798	François de Neufchâteau
1798–1799	Jean Baptiste Comte de Treilhard
1799	Emmanuel Joseph Comte de Sieyés
1799	Roger Comte de Ducos
1799	Jean François Auguste Moulins
1799	Louis Gohier

CONSULATE

First consul

1799–1804	Napoleon Bonaparte

Second consul

1799	Emmanuel Joseph Comte de Sieyés
1799–1804	Jean-Jacques Régis Cambacérès

Third consul

1799	Pierre-Roger Ducos
1799–1804	Charles François Lebrun

FIRST EMPIRE

1804–1814	Napoleon I
1814–1815	Louis XVIII (king)
1815	Napoleon I (second time)

BOURBON DYNASTY (restored)

1814–1824	Louis XVIII
1824–1830	Charles X

HOUSE OF ORLÉANS

1830–1848	Louis Philippe

SECOND REPUBLIC

Presidents

1848	Louis Eugéne Cavaignac
1848–1852	Louis-Napoleon (later Napoleon III)

SECOND EMPIRE

1852–1870	Napoleon III

THIRD REPUBLIC

Presidents and Prime Ministers

Presidency of Adolphe Thiers 1871–1873

1871–1873	Jules Dufaure

Presidency of Marshal Macmahon 1873–1879

1873–1874	Duke of Broglie
1874–1875	Courtot de Cissey
1875–1876	Louis Buffet
1876	Jules Dufaure
1876	Jules Dufaure

1876–1877	Jules Simon
1877	Duke of Broglie
1877	Grimaudet de Rochebouët
1877–1879	Jules Dufaure

First Presidency of Jules Grévy 1879–1885

1879	William Waddington
1879–1880	Charles de Freycinet
1880–1881	Jules Ferry
1881–1882	Léon Gambetta
1882	Charles de Freycinet
1882–1883	Charles Duclerc
1883	Armand Fallières
1883–1885	Jules Ferry
1885–1886	Henri Brisson

Second Presidency of Jules Grévy 1885–1887

1886	Charles de Freycinet
1886–1887	René Goblet
1887	Maurice Rouvier

Presidency of Marie François Sadi-Carnot 1887–1894

1887–1888	Pierre Tirard
1888–1889)	Charles Floquet
1889–1890	Pierre Tirard
1890–1892	Charles de Freycinet
1892	Émile Loubet
1892–1893	Alexandre Ribot
1893	Alexandre Ribot
1893	Charles Dupuy
1893–1894	Jean Casimir-Périer
1894	Charles Dupuy

Presidency of Jean Casimir-Périer 1894–1895

1894–1895	Charles Dupuy

Presidency of Félix Faure 1895–1899

1895	Alexandre Ribot
1895–1896	Léon Bourgeois
1896–1898	Jules Méline
1898	Henri Brisson
1898–1899	Charles Dupuy

Presidency of Émile Loubert 1899–1906

1899	Charles Dupuy
1899–1902	René Waldeck-Rousseau
1902–1905	Émile Combes
1905–1906	Maurice Rouvier

Presidency of Armand Falliéres 1906–1913

1906	Maurice Rouvier
1906	Jean Sarrien
1906–1909	Georges Clemenceau
1909–1911	Aristide Briand
1911	Joseph Caillaux

1912–1913	Raymond Poincaré
1913	Aristide Briand

Presidency of Raymond Poincaré 1913–1920

1913	Aristide Briand
1913	Louis Barthou
1913–1914	Gaston Doumergue
1914	Alexandre Ribot
1914–1915	René Viviani
1915–1917	Aristide Briand
1917	Alexandre Ribot
1917	Paul Painlevé
1917–1920	Georges Clemenceau
1920	Alexandre Millerand

Presidency of Paul Deschanel 1920

1920	Alexandre Millerand

Presidency of Alexandre Millerand 1920–1924

1920–1921	Georges Leygues
1921–1922	Aristide Briand
1922–1924	Raymond Poincaré
1924	Frédéric François-Marsal

Presidency of Gaston Doumergue 1924–1931

1924–1925	Édouard Herriot
1925	Paul Painlevé
1925–1926	Aristide Briand
1926	Édouard Herriot
1926–1929	Raymond Poincaré
1929	Aristide Briand
1929–1930	André Tardieu
1930	Camille Chautemps
1930	André Tardieu
1930–1931	Theodore Steeg
1931	Pierre Laval

Presidency of Paul Doumer 1931–1932

1931–1932	Pierre Laval
1932	André Tardieu

First Presidency of Albert Lebrun 1932–1939

1932	Edouard Herriot
1932–1933	Joseph Paul-Boncour
1933	Edouard Daladier
1933	Albert Sarraut
1933–1934	Camille Chautemps
1934	Édouard Daladier
1934	Gaston Doumergue
1934–1935	Pierre Flandin
1935	Fernand Bouisson
1935–1936	Pierre Laval
1936	Albert Sarraut
1936–1937	Léon Blum
1937–1938	Camille Chautemps

1938	Camille Chautemps
1938	Léon Blum
1938–1940	Édouard Daladier

Second Presidency of Albert Lebrun 1939–1940

1940	Paul Reynaud
1940	Marshal Philippe Pétain

VICHY RÉGIME
Chief of State

1940–1944	Marshal Philippe Pétain

Presidents of the Government of the French Republic 1945–1947

1945–1946	General Charles de Gaulle
1946	Felix Gouin
1946–1947	Georges Bidault

FOURTH REPUBLIC
Presidents

1947–1954	Vincent Auriol
1954–1959	René Coty

FIFTH REPUBLIC
Presidents

1959–1969	General Charles de Gaulle
1969–1969	Alain Poher
1969–1974	Georges Pompidou
1974–1974	Alain Poher
1974–1981	Valéry Giscard d'Estaing
1981–1995	François Mitterand
1995–	Jacques Chirac

France Antarctique (*var.* Ilha de Villegagnon) Island off south eastern Brazil which was colonized by French Huguenots under Nicolas Durand de Villegaigon in 1555. A Portuguese invasion in 1560 forced the Huguenots to abandon the island.

Francis I (*Fre.* François I, 1491–1547) King of France (reigned 1515–47) whose reign was dominated by his rivalry with Emperor Charles V for the control of Italy. He was a notable patron of the Renaissance and created the Palace of Fontainebleau.

Francis of Assisi, St. (c.1181–1226) Italian founder of the Franciscan Order, and later the "Poor Clares," a Franciscan order for women. He was canonized in 1228. The members of the order strove to cultivate the ideals of the order's founder who insisted on "holy poverty" as his guiding principle. *p.207*

Francis Xavier, St. 16th-century Spanish missionary to China.

Franco, General Francisco (*full name* Francisco Paulino Hermenegildo Teódulo Franco Bahamonde, 1892–1975) Spanish general and dictator and leader of the Nationalist rebel forces in the Spanish Civil War (1936–1939). He seized power at the end of the war and in 1947 he announced that Spain was to become a monarchy again. This occurred, but only after Franco's death in 1975.

Franco-Prussian War (1870–71) Prussian support for the accession of Hohenzollern prince to the Spanish throne prompted Napoleon III of France, alarmed at the growth of their power, to declare war on Prussia. The defeat of the French at Sedan (Sep 1 1870) and Prussian annexation of Alsace-Lorraine, persuaded the southern German states to join the new German Reich. Jan 1871, King William I of Prussia declared German emperor at Versailles.

Frankish empire A Germanic people based in the area of present-day France and western Germany, the Franks came to dominate the region after the collapse of the Western Roman Empire, c.493 CE. Under Clovis I (481–511) and his successors the Franks became the most important successors to the Roman empire, dominating much of western Europe for next three centuries. Under Charlemagne, their realm extended to cover most of Germany. *See also* Charlemagne

Franklin ⚔ of American Civil War (Nov 30 1864). Inconclusive result.

Franklin, Sir John (1786–1847) British naval officer and explorer. Made first expedition to Arctic in 1818. Later led two overland expeditions to chart the Arctic coast of N America, in 1819–22 and 1825–27. In 1845 he sailed in search of a Northwest Passage. The entire crew of 129 perished, and a number of voyages were made in search of the lost party.

Franz Ferdinand, Archduke Heir to the Austrian throne, whose assassination in Sarajevo was a catalyst for World War I.

Frederick I (*var.* Frederick Barbarossa, 1123–90) Holy Roman Emperor (reigned 1152–90) and king of Germany and Italy. Established German predominance over much of western Europe. Gained authority over Italy, Poland, Hungary, Denmark, and Burgundy. Led the Third Crusade in 1189, with victories at Philomelium and Iconium; drowned before reaching Holy Land. *p.193*

Frederick II (*var.* Lat. Stupor Mundi, 1194–1250) Holy Roman Emperor (reigned 1220–1250) and king of Germany. Grandson of Frederick I, Barbarossa and the last great Hohenstaufen ruler. *p.212*

Frederick II (*var.* Frederick the Great, 1712–86) King of Prussia (reigned 1740–86). He ruled Prussia as an enlightened despot, introducing religious toleration, and reforming the army and agriculture. In 1740 he occupied Silesia, fighting to retain it in the War of the Austrian Succession (1740–48) and the Seven Years' War (1756–63). In the first partition of Poland (1772) he gained W Prussia. Under him, Prussia became a leading European power.

Frederick Barbarossa *see* Frederick I

Frederick William I (*var.* the Great Elector, 1620–88) Elector of Brandenburg (reigned 1640–88). Under his rule, the state of Brandenburg gained full sovereignty in Prussia, and Brandenburg-Prussia became powerful state with a large army. *p.320*

Fredericksburg ⚔ of American Civil War (Dec 13 1862). Confederate victory.

Freeman's Farm ⚔ of American Revolutionary War (Sep 19 1777). American victory.

Freetown British freed slave settlement in W Africa, established in 1787.

Fremont, Lt. John Charles (1813–90) American explorer. During the early 1840s he explored much of the southwestern US and the map he produced helped to popularize westward migration across the continent. He traveled to California and took part in the Bear Flag Revolt; was court-martialed and forced to resign his commission. Having made a fortune in the California Gold Rush of 1848 he ran as an unsuccessful presidential candidate in 1856.

FRENCH GUIANA
Chronology

1568 Frenchman Gaspar de Sostelle and 126 families attempt to settle but are driven out by the indigenous population.

1596 A shortlived French settlement is established.

17th century There are several French and Dutch attempts to settle the area.

1676 Territory is recaptured by France from the Dutch.

1808 Cayenne becomes an Anglo-Portuguese possession.

1816 Under the Treaty of Paris the territory becomes a French colony.

1946 The French Constituent Assembly agrees to confer on the territory the status of a department of France.

1974 The territory achieves the status of a region of France.

FRENCH POLYNESIA
Chronology

1521 Ferdinand Magellan discovers Pukapuka in the Tuamotu Archipelago, which are already inhabited by Polynesian people. Spanish, Portuguese, Dutch, and English explorers follow.

1767 Captain Samuel Wallis of the British frigate HMS *Dolphin* visits Tahiti.

1769 Captain James Cook arrives in Tahiti, aboard the *Endeavour*.

1842 France makes Tahiti a Protectorate.

1880 Tahiti and its dependants become a French colony. The rest of the island groups are annexed by 1900.

1946 French Polynesia becomes an Overseas Territory, with a Governor, Council of Government and Territorial Assembly.

1963 The French government announces plans for a nuclear testing program in French Polynesia.

1966 The first nuclear test takes place at Mururoa Atoll.

1984 An autonomy statute for French Polynesia is passed by the French Senate, though it gives few additional powers to the Territorial government.

1984 Gaston Flosse is elected to the new position of President of French Polynesia.

1991 Flosse is re-elected President of French Polynesia, following elections in March.

1993 July French President declares that the 1992 decision to suspend nuclear testing would be maintained for the immediate future.

1994 A second court of appeal overturns a 1992 corruption conviction against Flosse on a technicality. His six-month 0suspended prison sentence is thereby quashed.

1995 French conduct nuclear tests on the Fangataufa and Mururoa Atoll despite a barrage of international criticism. Last of five Greenpeace vessels accused of entering the 20-km exclusion zone around atolls was seized by French commandos.

G

Tahiti's Territorial Assembly reported to have approved an autonomy bill designed to give the territory greater powers which would require the approval of the French National Assembly to be enacted.
2004 Becomes an "overseas country."

French Revolution (1789) Political uprising which ended in the downfall of the Bourbon monarchy in France and profoundly affected every aspect of French government and society. In spring 1789, with the state heavily in debt and the peasantry crippled by taxes, Louis XVI was forced to convene the Estates-General. From it emerged the National Assembly which responded to public unrest, such as the storming of the Bastille (July 14), with sweeping political, economic and social reforms. These included the abolition of feudal and aristocratic privileges; the nationalization of church lands; and a Declaration of the Rights of Man. The royal family was removed from Versailles to Paris. In 1792, following an attempt to flee the country, they were imprisoned and executed, the monarchy abolished and France declared a republic. *p.337 See also* France, Bourbons, Directory, Jacobins

FRG *see* West Germany

Friedland ⚔ of Napoleonic Wars during the War of the 3rd Coalition (1807). French victory.

Frisius, Gemma 16th-century Flemish theoretical mathematician, physician, and astronomer who served as a mentor to Flemish cartographer Gerardus Mercator.

Frobisher, Sir Martin (c.1535–94) English navigator who traveled in search of the Northwest Passage in 1576, discovering Frobisher Bay in Canada.

Fujiwara family Dynastic family that, by shrewd intermarriage and diplomacy, dominated the Japanese imperial government from the 9th to the 12th century.

Fulani *see* Fulbe

Fulbe (*var.* Peul, Fulani) Primarily Muslim people who inhabit many parts of W Africa, from Lake Chad in the east, to the Atlantic coast. *p.323*

Fur trade Fur trade in N America in the 17th century. *p.311*

Futa Jallon Fulbe confederation established in W Africa c.1730.

GABON An equatorial country on the west coast of Africa, Gabon's major economic activity is the production of oil. Only a small area of Gabon is cultivated, and more than two-thirds of it constitute one of the world's finest virgin rainforests. Gabon became independent of France in 1960. A single-party state from 1968, it returned to multiparty democracy in 1990. Gabon's population is small, and the government is encouraging its increase.

CHRONOLOGY

1472 Portuguese trading ships make the first European contact with Gabon's earliest inhabitants, who were pygmies.
17th–19th century European merchants trade tobacco, cloth, and arms for ivory, slaves, and rubber. The Fang, moving south from the savannah lands of Cameroon, expel the indigenous peoples.
1849 Libreville is founded by Vili slaves freed by the French, who had established a permanent presence.
1878 Count Savorgnan de Brazza signs a treaty with King Makoko of the Teke. This claims to give France rights over a vast tract of central Africa, including present-day Gabon, although most of this area was not in fact under the control of Makoko.
1960 Independence. Léon M'ba president.
1964 Military coup. French intervene to reinstate M'ba.
1967 Albert-Bernard (later Omar) Bongo president.
1968 Single-party state instituted.
1990 Multiparty democracy.
1998 Bongo reelected president.
2001 Elections: ruling PDG retains majority.

Gadsden Purchase (1853) Purchase by US from Mexico of 77,700 sq km (30,000 sq miles) of land in New Mexico and Arizona by James Gadsden, in order to establish a southern railroad to the Pacific.

Gagarin, Yuri (1934–68) Soviet cosmonaut, who made the first manned space flight in 1961. *p.433*

Gai-Long (*var.* Nguyen Phuc Anh, 1762–1820) Emperor and founder of the last dynasty of Vietnam before conquest by France.

Gaiseric (*var.* Genseric, died 477) King of the Vandals and the Alani (reigned 428–477) who conquered a large part of Roman Africa and in 455 sacked Rome.

Galerius (*var.* Gaius Galerius Valerius Maximianus, died 311) Roman emperor (reigned 305–311), notorious for his persecution of Christians.

Galileo (*var.* Galileo Galilei, 1564–1642) Italian philosopher, astronomer, and mathematician who made fundamental contributions to the sciences of motion, astronomy, and strength of materials, and to the development of scientific method.

galleon Full-rigged sailing ship that was built primarily for war, and which developed in the 15th and 16th centuries. The largest galleons were built by the Spanish and the Portuguese for their profitable overseas trade.

Gallipoli Campaign of World War I (Feb–Dec 1915) between Allied forces and Turkey. Attempt by Allies to force a passage through the Dardanelles channel and occupy Constantinople.

Gama, Vasco da (c.1460–1524) Portuguese navigator who, in 1497, was commissioned by the Portuguese king to establish trading links with the East Indies. He stopped at coastal trading centers of eastern Africa, sailing northeast across the Indian Ocean, and reaching Calicut on May 20 1498. He made a second voyage to India in 1502.

GAMBIA A narrow country on the western coast of Africa, the Gambia was renowned as a stable democracy until an army coup in 1994. Agriculture accounts for 65% of GDP, yet many Gambians are leaving rural areas for the towns, where average incomes are four times higher. Its position as a semi-enclave within Senegal seems likely to endure, following the failure of an experiment in federation in the 1980s.

CHRONOLOGY

13th century First southward migration of significant numbers of Fula.
1661 British capture James Island.
1816 Britain acquires Bathurst (now Banjul) after a struggle for control among European seafaring countries.

▶

◄
1888 British possession.
1959 Dawda Jawara founds PPP.
1965 Independence from Britain.
1970 Republic; Jawara president.
1981 Senegalese troops help crush
  army coup attempt.
1982–1989 Federation with Senegal.
1994 Jawara ousted in army coup.
1996 Yahya Jammeh wins presidential
  election.
2000 Military coup foiled.
2001 $2 million anti-poverty program
  launched by government.
2002 Jammeh's party sweeps
  parliamentary elections.

Gandhara (*var.* Kandahar) Indo-Greek state of S Central Asia (3rd century BCE–5th century CE). Located in the Punjab, Gandhara was one of several Indo-Greek kingdoms which were the successors of the Greek colony of Bactria, founded by Alexander the Great. With the decline of the Mauryan empire, the Bactrian Greeks crossed into the Kabul valley and Punjab and founded independent kingdoms there. The Buddhist art of Gandhara is famous for its eclectic mixture of western and Indian styles. Gandhara, with its capital at Taxila, fell to invading Asian nomads (the Scythians) in c.90 BCE. *p.85*

Gandhi, Indira (1917–84) Daughter of Nehru, Indian prime minister (1966–77). Confronted by a growing anti-government protest movement, she declared a national emergency in 1975, and returned to power as leader of Congress I party, in 1980. She was assassinated by Sikh extremists.

Gandhi, Mohandas K. (*aka* Mahatma Gandhi, 1869–1948) Indian independence leader. Worked as a lawyer in South Africa, and became the leader of a movement for Indian civil rights there. On his return to India in 1915 he transformed the Indian National Congress into a powerful force, utilizing the techniques of passive resistance and mass non-cooperation. His attacks on the Salt Tax and March to the Sea (1930) and major civil disobedience campaigns (1920–22, 1930–34, 1940–42) were important catalysts in India's progress towards independence. He was assassinated by a Hindu fanatic. *p.409*

Gandhi, Rajiv (*var.* Rajiv Ratna Gandhi, 1944–1991) Leading general secretary of India's Congress Party from 1981, Gandhi became prime minister of India (1984–89) after the assassination of his mother, Indira Gandhi. He was himself assassinated by Tamil separatists.

Gang of Four *see* Cultural Revolution

Gao Zu (*var.* Kao Tsu, *aka* Liu Chi, Liu Pang, 256–195 BCE) Founder and first emperor of the Han dynasty in 206 BCE, after emerging victorious from the civil war following the death of Shi Huangdi. He was a violent but pragmatic and flexible ruler.

Garamantes (*var.* Fezzan, Fazzan, *Lat.* Phazania) Saharan kingdom, now the SW part of Libya. It was annexed by Rome in 19 BCE who called it Phazania.

Garay, Francisco de 16th-century Spanish explorer of N America.

Garibaldi, Giuseppe (1807–82) Italian revolutionary, soldier, and the greatest figure of the Risorgimento. When Italy's war of liberation broke out in 1859, he and his thousand "Redshirts" captured Sicily and Naples, handing them over to Victor Emmanuel II. *p.366*

Gates, Bill Founder of Microsoft computer software company. *p.453*

Gaugamela ⚔ of Alexander's campaigns (331 BCE). Decisive Greek victory against the Persians.

Gaul (*Lat.* Gallia) Roman name for the lands of the Galli (Celts): Cisalpine Gaul in N Italy and Transalpine Gaul, roughly equivalent to modern France. The Roman conquest of Gaul was completed by Julius Caesar in 58–51 BCE. *See also* France

Gaulle, Charles de (*f/n* Charles-André-Marie-Joseph de Gaulle, 1890–1970) French soldier, writer, and statesman who orchestrated France's Fifth Republic. He played an active role in the French Resistance during World War II and became French president in 1947, relinquishing leadership in 1953. In 1958 he took office as the first president of the Fifth Republic. During the period 1959–60 he granted self-government to French African colonies.

Gedymin (c.1275–1341) Grand Duke of Lithuania (c.1315–41). His conquests laid the foundations of the great Lithuanian state (in personal union with Poland) of the late Middle Ages.

Geheime Staatspolizei *see* Gestapo

Genghis Khan (*full name* Temujin, *var.* Ching-Gis, Chingis, Jenghiz, or Jinghis, died 1227). Mongolian warrior-ruler, who unified tribes and then extended his empire across Asia to the Adriatic Sea through military conquest. *p.209*

Genoa (*Ital.* Genoa) Italy's principal port. In the 10th century Genoa emerged as a powerful independent city-state. In the Middle Ages it rivalled Venice as the leading maritme power in the Mediterranean, with trading routes reaching to the Black Sea.

Genseric *see* Gaiseric

GEORGIA Situated on the eastern coast of the Black Sea, Georgia is largely mountainous. Its coastline stretches from Abkhazia in the north to Ajaria in the south. Georgia was one of the first republics to demand independence from Moscow, but has been plagued over recent years by civil war and ethnic disputes in Abkhazia and South Ossetia. Birthplace of Stalin, Georgia is primarily agricultural and is famous for its wine.

CHRONOLOGY

4th century BCE First records of a Georgian kingdom following Alexander the Great's conquest of the Persian Empire.

318 CE Georgia is converted to Christianity. The following 300 years see a conflict between Byzantium and Persia which leads to the division of the country.

1014 King Bagrat III dies after uniting eastern and western Georgia. A golden age follows during the reign of Queen Tamara (1184 to 1213).

1236 The Mongols conquer eastern Georgia, although the western territory of Imeretia remains independent.

1453 The fall of the Byzantine empire leaves Georgia isolated from western Christianity. Muslim invaders partition the country.

1586 Threatened by Muslims, Georgia's Orthodox Christian rulers invite Russian rule.

1783 Russia guarantees Georgian independence, but fails to protect it against a Persian invasion in 1795.

1801 Russia annexes Persian-ruled provinces of Kartlia and Kakhetia in eastern Georgia after appeals for protection; in 1810 western Georgia, which had been occupied by the Turks, is also annexed by Russia.

1826–28 Russia again defeats Persia in a war over Georgia.

1864 Peasants receive limited freedoms after emancipation of serfs in Russia. A policy of Russification and racial assimilation pursued after 1881 leads to an increase in radicalism and national consciousness.

1918 Georgia proclaims its independence under a Menshevik government and is briefly occupied by British forces after the surrender of the Central Powers at the end of World War I.

1920 Recognized by Soviet Russia as an independent state.

1921 The Red Army invades Georgia, ordered in by Josef Stalin (himself a native Georgian) despite a treaty of recognition between the two countries signed in May.

1922–1936 Incorporated into Transcaucasian Soviet Federative Socialist Republic (TSFSR).

1989 Pro-independence riots in Tbilisi put down by Soviet troops.

1990 Declares sovereignty.

1991 Independence. Zviad Gamsakhurdia elected president.

1992 Gamsakhurdia flees Tbilisi. Shevardnadze elected chair of Supreme Soviet and State Council.

1992–1993 Abkhazia conflict.

1995 Shevardnadze narrowly survives assassination attempt, subsequently elected president.

1999 Opening of pipeline from Caspian to Black Sea.

2000 Shevardnadze reelected. Russian troop withdrawal begins.

2003 Shevardnadze ousted in "velvet revolution."

2004 Mikhail Saakashvili president.

German Confederation (1815–66) Alliance of German sovereign states. At the Congress of Vienna the 39 states formed a loose grouping to protect themselves against French ambitions following Napoleon's destruction of the Holy Roman Empire (1806).

Germantown ⚔ American Revolutionary War (Oct 4 1777). British victory.

GERMANY With coastlines on both the Baltic and North Seas, Germany is bordered by nine countries. Plains and rolling hills in the north give way to more mountainous terrain in the south. Europe's foremost industrial power, and its most populous country apart from Russia, Germany is the world's second-biggest exporter. Unified in the 1870s, it was divided after the defeat of the Nazi regime in 1945. The communist-ruled east was part of the Soviet bloc until the collapse of the East German regime in 1989, which paved the way for reunification in 1990. Tensions created by wealth differences between east and west were then exacerbated by record levels of unemployment. The government committed itself to European union and adopted the single currency, the euro, even though the stable Deutsche mark had been a symbol of German pride.

Brandenburg-Prussia. *p.320, p.329*
Industrialization. *p.373*
World War I. *p.396*
Economic crisis in 1920s. *p.401*
World War II. *p.414*
See also Holy Roman Empire; East Germany; West Germany

CHRONOLOGY

9 CE The extension of the Roman empire north of the Rhineland is thwarted by a Germanic tribe, the Cherusci.

800 The Frankish empire, founded in the fifth century, reaches its apogee when King Charlemagne is crowned Emperor of the West by Pope Leo III, although in 843 the German-speaking lands of Franconia are separated from what later becomes France in the Partition of Verdun.

911 Duke Conrad, successor to Louis the Child, the last of the German Carolingians, is elected the first King of the Germans.

962 Otto I (ruled 936–73) of the Saxon dynasty, having defeated the independent dukes of south Germany and destroyed the Magyars at the Battle of Lechfeld (955), is crowned Holy Roman Emperor by the Pope. Otto controls much of Germany and neighboring areas.

1152 Frederick I Barbarossa (ruled 1152–90) of the Hohenstaufen dynasty, briefly revives German and Holy Roman Imperial power but, although the Teutonic Knights continue to expand the Empire eastwards, the area covered by modern Germany becomes a patchwork of nominally independent states.

1241 A number of north German cities form a trading alliance, the Hanseatic League, which during the later Middle Ages functions as an independent political power with its own army and navy.

1273 Count Rudolf of Habsburg (1218–91) establishes himself as King of the Germans and Holy Roman Emperor. This marks the start of the Habsburg dynasty's domination of Austria and Germany.

1517 The German theologian Martin Luther (1483–1546) nails the *95 theses* on the door of a Wittenberg church, challenging the established Catholic hierarchies and especially the practice of selling indulgences to raise funds. This act marks the start of the Protestant Reformation.

1524–26 Influenced by radical Protestant preachers and frustrated by economic hardship, Germany's lower classes rise up in the Peasants' Revolt. However, they are crushed by the army of Philip of Hesse (1504–67), a Protestant who enjoys Luther's support, and 100,000 are slaughtered.

1555 Under the terms of the Peace of Augsburg, it is agreed by the Holy Roman Emperor that each German prince should be left free to impose the faith of his choice within his territories.

1618 The Thirty Years' War begins. Fought mainly between Catholic and Protestant states within Germany, the conflict escalates into a Franco-Habsburg confrontation from 1635 and results in the area's splintering into small principalities and kingdoms. In the 1648 Treaty of Westphalia the Holy Roman Emperor recognizes the full religious and political sovereignty of the German states; territory is ceded to Sweden in the north and to France in the west.

1740 Frederick II "the Great" (1712–86) of the Hohenzollern dynasty becomes king of Prussia. During his reign he establishes Prussia as a major power, gaining Silesia during the Austrian War of Succession in 1740–48 (which Austria fails to regain in the Seven Years" War in 1756–63) and gaining Pomerania and East Prussia in the first partition of Poland in 1772 (as laid down in the Treaty of St. Petersburg of July 1772). A benevolent despot at home, Frederick II concedes full religious tolerance, abolishes torture, and liberates state serfs.

1793 and 1795 In the second partition of Poland in 1793 Prussia, now ruled by Frederick William II, gains "greater Poland" which includes Posen (Poznan), Lodz, and Danzig (Gdansk), as confirmed in the Treaty of Grodno, and in 1795 in the third partition gains Warsaw. The end of Poland is confirmed in a 1797 treaty.

1806 Following the defeat of the Habsburg monarch Francis I (1768–1835) at

Austerlitz in December 1805 Napoleon Bonaparte of France declares the Holy Roman Empire (First German Reich) dissolved and creates new Rhenish League under his protectorship. This comprises 16 princedoms and cities including Bavaria, Hesse and Württemberg. The Prussian army is defeated at Jena in October 1806.

1813 The Rhenish League breaks up after Napoleon is defeated at Leipzig in October 1813 following his retreat from Russia. It is replaced at the Congress of Vienna in 1814–15 by a new German Confederation comprising 39 substantially independent states and with a diet under the nominal presidency of Austria.

1833 To increase its relative authority Prussia founds a Zollverein (or customs union) by merging the North German Zollverein with smaller customs unions.

1848 Popular revolutions break out in many German states, temporarily overthrowing the monarchies. In Frankfurt a constituent assembly is elected and discusses the drafting of a constitution for a united Germany. However, its proposals are rejected by Emperor Ferdinand of Austria and Frederick William IV of Prussia. By 1849 the revolutions have been suppressed and the old order restored.

1862 Otto von Bismarck (1815–98) becomes Chancellor of Prussia, a post he holds until 1890. First he gains Schleswig-Holstein from Denmark in 1864 and then in Seven Weeks' war of 1866 defeats Austria at the Battle of Sadowa. This results in the 1866 Peace of Prague which gives Prussia control of most of Germany north of the river Main. In 1867 a North German Confederation is formed which unites most German states excluding notably Saxony, Thuringia, Bavaria, Württemberg, Baden, and Hesse-Darmstadt.

1864–1870 Prussia defeats Austrians, Danes, and French; north German states under Prussian control.

1871 Southern states join Prussian-led unified German Empire under Wilhelm I.

1870s Rapid industrialization.

1890 Kaiser Wilhelm II accedes, with hopes for German world role. Bismarck sacked.

1914 August. Germany enters World War I on the side of Austria-Hungary (an ally since 1879) and Ottoman Turkey as one of the Central Powers, fighting against the Allied Powers of Britain, France, Russia, Japan, and Serbia. Hopes of a quick victory on the Western Front are not fulfilled when Germany is obliged to retreat after the first Battle of the Marne in September 1914 and troops become bogged down in trench warfare with great loss of life. In April 1917 the United States joins the war on the Allied side. There is greater success for Germany in the east where defeats for Russia precipitate a revolution after which the new Bolshevik government withdraws from the war and accepts the degrading Peace of Brest-Litovsk in March 1918.

1918 Despite thereafter being able to concentrate its forces on the western front, Germany is beaten back and forced to concede defeat in an armistice signed on November 11 1918, after 1,774,000 German soldiers' lives have been sacrificed. Facing a mutiny by military and naval forces and popular disillusionment with the war, Kaiser Wilhelm II abdicates on November 9 and flees to Holland. Later that day a republic is proclaimed in Berlin with a government headed by Friedrich Ebert (1871–1925), leader of the German Socialist Workers' Party (which was established in 1875 and is the precursor to the contemporary Social Democratic Party of Germany – SPD).

1919 Ebert crushes a "Spartakist" revolt in Berlin, led by the German Communist Party (KPD) founded by Karl Liebknecht and Rosa Luxemburg at the end of 1918. In February Ebert is elected President and the Constitution of a liberal democratic Weimar Republic is approved later in the year. June. Germany agrees at the Versailles Peace Conference both to cede territory and pay substantial war reparations. Alsace-Lorraine goes to France, West Prussia and Poznan to Poland, and part of Schleswig to Denmark; the Rhineland is demilitarized and occupied, and all Germany's overseas colonies are lost.

1923 In retaliation for Germany's non-payment of reparations, French and Belgian troops occupy the Ruhr, withdrawing in 1924 after Germany accepts the Dawes Plan on reparations.

1923 Adolf Hitler, leader of the nationalist, anti-Semitic National Socialist German Workers' Party (NSDAP or Nazis) stages an abortive putsch in Munich, as hyper-inflation rages. He is imprisoned for eight months in 1924 during which time he writes *Mein Kampf*.

1925 Field Marshal Paul von Hindenburg becomes President ushering in a period of greater political stability. The arts flourish in Berlin, and Germany is admitted to the League of Nations in 1926 (of which it remains a member until Hitler's withdrawal in October 1933). However, the Weimar Republic proves too weak to weather the global recession after 1929.

1930 In a general election support for the NSDAP increases eightfold (to 18.3 percent) as compared with the last election.

1932 In a general election in July the NSDAP wins 37.4 pe cent of the vote and replaces the SPD as the largest single party, although in a further election in November its share of the vote falls to 33.2 per cent. The Reichstag (parliament) finds itself increasingly unable to retain control of the situation as street violence escalates and Nazi supporters clash with their opponents.

1933 President Hindenburg appoints Hitler Chancellor at the head of a minority government. In March, after blaming the communists for an arson attack on Feb. 27–28 on the Reichstag, Hitler secures passage of an enabling law granting him dictatorial powers for four years. In July Germany becomes a one-party state.

1934 June. In the "Night of the Long Knives," Nazis liquidate thousands of opponents within and outside the party. When Hindenburg dies in August 1934 Hitler assumes the presidency, though retaining the title "Führer" (leader).

1935 The Saar, under League of Nations control since the end of World War I, again becomes part of Germany after a plebiscite reveals great support for reintegration. In March the following year, in violation of the 1919 Treaty of Versailles, German troops reoccupy the demilitarized Rhineland.

1938 In what is known as the "Anschluss", German troops enter Austria and incorporate it into the Third Reich. Britain and France at the Munich conference agree to Hitler's occupation of the Sudetenland and by March 1939 the whole of Czechoslovakia is under Nazi control.

1938 November 9–10. Already stripped of German citizenship by the Nuremberg decrees of 1935, Jews and their property are attacked throughout Germany in the "Kristallnacht" (crystal night) pogrom.

1939 September. After secretly signing the Molotov-Ribbentrop non-aggression pact with the Soviet Union on Aug 23, Germany invades Poland on Sep 1. Britain and France, treaty-bound to defend Poland, declare war on Germany on Sep 3, thus beginning World War II.

1940–42 Having launched successful "Blitzkrieg" invasions of Norway, Denmark, Holland, France, and Belgium by June 1940, Germany opens a new eastern front, first invading Yugoslavia and Greece in April 1941 and then in June launching an offensive against the Soviet Union. By end of the year both Leningrad and Moscow are under siege. In North Africa the army of Field Marshal Erwin Rommel is gradually beaten back during 1942 and defeated at El Alamein in October. On the eastern front 300,000 German soldiers die defending Stalingrad but Field Marshal Paulus is forced to surrender on Feb. 2, 1943. The Japanese attack on Pearl Harbor in December 1941 which brings the United States into the war. The addition of US forces on the allied side eventually turns the tide in the Allies' favor.

1943 In mid-1943 British and US air forces launch successive bombing raids on German cities and in June 1944 allied forces land in Normandy, France, liberating Paris in August, Brussels in September and crossing the Rhine in March 1945 while in the east Soviet forces march on Berlin.

1945 April 30. Faced with military defeat on both the eastern and western fronts, Hitler commits suicide in his Berlin bunker.May 2. Berlin falls to Soviet forces. May 7. German army capitulates to the allies. June 5. Allied Control Commission assumes control of Germany, which is divided into four (British, French, Soviet. and US) occupation zones, with four-power control over Berlin. In all, 3,250,000 German soldiers and 500,000 German civilians die during World War II. Around 6,000,000 Jews (half of whom die at the Auschwitz-Birkenau concentration camp in Poland) are also massacred in the associated holocaust. Nov 20. Trial of Nazi war criminals commences at Nuremberg.

1949 Germany divided: communist East led by Walter Ulbricht 1951– 71, Erich Honecker 1971–89; liberal democratic West led by CDU's Konrad Adenauer 1949–1963.

1955 West Germany joins NATO.

1961 Berlin Wall built.

1966–1969 West German grand coalition of CDU and SPD.

1969–1982 SPD-led West German governments under Willy Brandt (1969–1974), Helmut Schmidt (1974–1982).

1973 Both Germanies join UN.

1982 Helmut Kohl West German chancellor, CDU–FDP coalition.

1989 Fall of Berlin Wall.

1990 Reunification of Germany. First all-German elections since 1933; Kohl heads government.

1996 Rising concern over jobs.

1998 Gerhard Schröder heads coalition of SPD and Greens.

1999 Euro introduced.

2000 Disgrace of Kohl in party funding scandal.

2001 Coalition of SPD and former communist PDS in city of Berlin

2002 Euro fully adopted.

2004 Horst Köler of CDU elected president.

GERMAN CHANCELLORS

West German (Federal Republic) Chancellors (1945–1990)

1949–1963	Konrad Adenauer
1963–1966	Ludwig Erhard
1966–1969	Kurt Georg Kiesinger
1969–1974	Willy Brandt
1974	Walter Scheel
1974–1982	Helmut Schmidt
1982–1990	Helmut Kohl

Chancellors of reunited Germany (1990–)

1990–1998	Helmut Kohl
1998–	Gerhard Schröder

German Democratic Republic
see East Germany

Gestapo (*var.* Ger. Geheime Staatspolizei). The secret police of Nazi Germany, originally part of the Prussian State Police, moulded by Goering and Himmler.

Gettysburg ⚔ of American Civil War (Jul 1–3 1863). Union victory. Often considered to be the turning point in the Civil War.

Gettysburg Address (Nov 19 1863) Speech made by US President Abraham Lincoln at the dedication of the National Cemetery at Gettysburg. It ends with the hope that: "This nation, under God, shall have a new birth of freedom – and that government of the people, by the people, for the people, shall not perish from the earth."

GHANA The heartland of the ancient Asante kingdom, modern Ghana is a union of the former British colony of the Gold Coast and the British-administered part of the UN Trust Territory of Togoland. Ghana gained independence in 1957, the first British colony to do so. Multiparty democracy was embraced in 1992, and the handover of power to the main opposition party in 2000 confirmed the shift away from Ghana's recent history of intermittent military rule.

CHRONOLOGY

12th century Akan peoples begin to settle the northern forest lands of the present-day Asante region.

1482 Portuguese seafarers ask for permission to build a castle at the spot now known as Elmina. 16th century. Akan peoples develop the export of gold by land and sea routes.

18th century The Akwamu empire reaches its fullest expansion; its power is gradually replaced by the Asante kingdom and its allies, with Kumasi at the center.

1806–14 The Asante assert their military superiority over the coastal Fanti people and demand recognition of their authority by British and other European traders.

1874 UK forces devastate Kumasi in the first of the Asante Wars; others follow in 1896 and 1900.

1947 J.B. Danquah sets up the United Gold Coast Convention (UGCC) to campaign for increased self-government.

1948 Kwame Nkrumah breaks from the UGCC to form his own Convention People's Party (CPP).

1952 After electoral victories for his CPP, Nkrumah becomes Prime Minister.

1957 Independence under Kwame Nkrumah.

1964 Single-party state.

1966 Army coup.

1972–1979 "Kleptocracy" of General Acheampong. Executed 1979.

1979 Flight Lieutenant Jerry Rawlings' coup. Civilian Hilla Limann wins elections.

1981 Rawlings takes power again.

1992, 1996 Rawlings and NDC win multiparty elections.

2000 Opposition NPP wins elections; John Kufuor wins presidency.

Ghaznavid dynasty
see Mahmud of Ghazni
Ghiyas al-Din *see* Muhammad of Ghur

GIBRALTAR Tiny British enclave at southern tip of Spain facing Morocco. It has been in British hands since 1704 and in recent times has been the subject of protracted negotiations over sovereignty between the governments of Spain and the UK. The landscape is dominated by the famous Rock of Gibraltar (Jebel-al-Tariq, the Mountain of Tariq, leader of the Muslim army that crossed into Spain in 711).

Chronology

1502 After Spanish forces expel the last of the Moors, Gibraltar is annexed to Spain.

1704 During the war of the Spanish succession Gibraltar is taken by British and Dutch forces.

1713 The Treaty of Utrecht formally cedes the territory to Britain.

1830 Gibraltar becomes a British Crown Colony.

1963 Spain revives its claim to Gibraltar, using the UN decolonization committee.

1964 Under a new constitution incorporating provisions agreed in April, the UK grants Gibraltar limited self-government. In October 1964 Spain enforces new border restrictions.

1967 In a referendum Gibraltarians vote overwhelmingly to maintain links with UK.

1969 New Constitution enters into force allowing for full internal self-government and guaranteeing that sovereignty over Gibraltar will not be relinquished to Spain against the freely, democratically expressed wishes of the Gibraltarian people. In protest the Spanish authorities close the border.

1977 Talks between the UK and Spain include, for the first time, Gibraltarian representatives.

1980 Under Lisbon agreement the UK and Spain declare their intent to resolve the Gibraltar question in a spirit of friendship.

1984 The Brussels agreement, under which the UK agrees to discuss the question of sovereignty, brings significant improvement in Spanish-UK relations.

1985 Spain-Gibraltar border fully reopened.

1988 An election success for the Gibraltar Socialist Labour Party (GSLP) under Joe Bossano ends nearly 20 years of rule by the Gibraltar Labour Party/Association for the Advancement of Civil Rights. The GSLP election manifesto rejects the 1984 Brussels agreement and a UK-Spanish accord of Dec 1987 on joint Spanish-Gibraltarian administration of Gibraltar's airport.

1992 The GSLP is reelected with 73.3 percent of the vote on a platform calling for greater self-determination without hostility towards Spain.

1995 In response to talks between the UK and Spanish governments, Chief Minister Bossano calls on the Spanish government to recognize that the people of Gibraltar would not accept any agreement on their future without a direct say in negotiations.

1995 The UK threatens to impose direct rule when Bossano resists bringing Gibraltar's banking and customs practices into line with European Union (EU) regulations.

2002 Talks between Spain and UK result in plan for shared sovereignty of Gibraltar. Population of Gibraltar bitterly opposed. Unofficial referendum rejects joint sovereignty.

Giles, Ernest (1835–97) British-born Australian who explored western Australia between 1872 and 1876.

Gilgamesh Legendary Sumerian king (c.3rd millennium BCE).

Giotto di Bondone (c.1267–1337) Italian painter, precursor of the Renaissance. Works include cycle of frescoes on the life of St. Francis in Assisi. *p.227*

Gist, Christopher (c.1705–59). American explorer. Surveyed the Ohio River Valley in 1750–51, and was part of George Washington's expedition to remove the French from the Ohio valley in 1753–54.

Giza Site of Egypt's most celebrated pyramids built 2530–2470 BCE. *p.22*

Gnosticism System of religious beliefs, especially of cults of late pre-Christian and early Christian centuries, characterized by the belief that matter is evil and that emancipation comes through gnosis (knowledge).

Godfrey of Bouillon (c.1060–1100) One of the leaders of the First Crusade, chosen to become the first king of Jerusalem (reigned 1099–1100).

Gold Rush Phenomenon at its peak in 19th century as gold is discovered in various remote parts of the globe, such as California, Australia, South Africa, and the Yukon. *p.363*

Golden Bull (1356) Imperial edict of Charle IV, which established clear rules as to which rulers qualified as Electors with the right to choose Holy Roman Emperor. *p.23*

Golden Horde Mongol Khanate of central Asia, with its capital at Saray. Founded by Batu, grandson of Genghis Khan in 1242, the khanate flourished from the 13th to the 15th century, exacting tribute from the Russian principalities to the northwest.

Golden Triangle Name given to the border areas between Thailand, Burma, Vietnam and Laos which is a major cente for the production and distribution of narcotics, primarily heroin.

Gomes, Diogo (1440–84) Portuguese explorer sent by Henry the Navigator to investigate the W African coast in 1458.

Gomez, Estaban (*var.* Estevão Gomes, c.1484–1538) Portuguese pilot in the service of Spain. Refused to explore the southern part of the Strait of Magellan in 1520 and deserted, but in 1524–25 he traced the N American coast from Nova Scotia to Florida, charting the coast in great detail. He was killed by Indians while accompanying Pedro de Mendoza's expedition to the Plate river.

Gonzalez Davila, Gil 16th-century Spanish conquistador who explored the Lake Nicaragua region and made the first, but failed, attempt to conquer what is now Nicaragua in 1522.

Good Hope, Cape of Most southerly point of the African continent, rounded by Portuguese navigator Bartolomeu Dia in 1488. A Dutch colony was established at the cape in 1652, but this was seized by the British in 1795.

Gorbachev, Mikhail Sergeyevich (1931– Soviet official, the general secretary of the Communist Party of the Soviet Union (CPSU) from 1985 to 1991 and president of the Soviet Union in 1990–91. During his time in office he was responsible for introducing the policy of *glasnost* which encouraged more friendly relations between the Soviet Union and the West and for brokering reductions in the number of nuclear weapons held.

Gorée Island off Senegal. Settlement founded by Dutch in 1621 became important center of the slave trade. *p.301*

Gordillo, Francisco 16th-century Spanish navigator who in 1521 made landfall near Cape Fear, North Carolina, initiating thorough exploration of the area.

Gorlice-Tarnow ⚔ of World War I (May 1915). Russian forces driven back by the Central Powers (Austria-Hungary and Germany).

Gothic architecture Term given to the spectacular style of architecture that evolved in the 12th century in N Europe, starting in northern France. *p.209*

Goths General term for Germanic peoples whose incursions into the Roman Empire during the 4th century CE hastened its decline. *See also* Avars, Ostrogoths, Visigoths.

Granada Last Moorish kingdom on the Iberian Peninsula; fell to Spain in 1492.

Gran Colombia *see* Greater Colombia

Granicus ⚔ of (334 BCE) Alexander the Great's first major engagement with the Persians occurred at a river-crossing formerly known as the "Gates of Asia, "where he launched a famously audacious attack at dusk, tricking, surprising, and overwhelming the various enemy forces ranged against him."

Grant, Ulysses Simpson (*prev.* Hiram Ulysses Grant, 1822–85) US general and 18th President of the US (Republican, 1869–77). Appointed supreme commander of the Union forces in 1864 during the Civil War, his strategy of operating several armies at once against the less numerous Confederate forces headed by Robert E. Lee, led to the Confederacy's complete surrender in April 1865. *p.368*

Great Britain The largest of the British Isles, comprising England, Scotland, and Wales. The term is often used to indicate the United Kingdom of Great Britain and Northern Ireland. After centuries of warfare, the English and Scottish crowns were united in 1601 with the accession of James I (James VI of Scotland). Wales had been subdued by England in the 13th century. Hostility to England, both in Wales and Scotland, has flared up sporadically, and is still alive among separatists today. *See also* United Kingdom

Great Depression, the (c.1929–34) World-wide economic crisis sparked off by the Wall Street Crash of 1929. It resulted in the collapse of banking confidence and the calling-in of European loans, creating massive unemployment in America and Europe, and other industrialized areas of the world until the start of World War II.

Great Leap Forward, the (1958) Attempt to increase production in China by the creation of huge rural communes and urban associations. Resulted in famine and 30 million deaths and was abandoned in 1961. *p.428*

Great Migration, the Name given to the movements of peoples across Europe in the 5th century CE. The Vandals, Alans, and Sueves crossed the Rhine into the Roman Empire, then moved through Gaul to Iberia, the Vandals continuing to N Africa.

Great Northern Expedition, the (1733–42) Russian expedition commissioned by Czar Peter the Great, commanded by Vitus Bering, to explore and map the Siberian coast and Kurile Islands.

Great Northern War, the (1700–21) Long drawn out struggle between Sweden and Russia for control of the Baltic region. After initial Swedish successes under Charles XII, Russia under Peter the Great emerged the dominant power in the region.

Great Rebellion, the *see* English Civil War

Great Schism, the Name given to two schisms within the Christian church. The first, the definitive schism between the Eastern Orthodox Church and the Roman Catholic Church took place in 1054. *p.171* The second was a more local affair affecting only the papacy. Following the Avignon Papacy (1309–77), when the papacy was under French control, a Roman pope, Urban VI, was elected, only to be deposed by the cardinals. They elected a new pope, antipope Clement VII, who returned the papacy to Avignon. This schism (1378–1417) divided western Christendom until the Council of Constance (1414–18) when a new pope, Martin V was elected and universally recognized.

Great Seljuk empire *see* Seljuk Turks

Great Trek (*var. Af.* Groot Trek) The emigration of over 12,000 Afrikaner from Cape Colony, in South Africa, between 1835 and the early 1840s, in protest against the policies of the British government and in search of fresh pasturelands. *p.357*

Great Wall of China General name for defensive barrier system across northern China, stretching from Pacific coast to the Takla Makan Desert, erected to protect the China from the Xiongnu and northern and Central Asian peoples. First conceived as a system during the Qin period (c.220 CE), which linked earlier defensive barriers, and extended far to the west under the Han. In the Ming period the present continuous masonry wall was created, punctuated by watchtowers from which warning beacon signals could be transmitted.

Great War *see* World War I

Great Zimbabwe Complex of stone enclosures in southern Africa, built by the Shona people from the 3rd century CE to the 15th century. The name is also applied to the kingdom centered on the site, which flourished in the 13th and 14th centuries. The kingdom fell to the Mutapa empire c.1450. *p.238*

Greater Colombia (*var.* Gran Colombia, Republic of Colombia, 1822–30) Republic comprising the modern nations of Ecuador, Colombia, Panama, and Venezuela (formerly the Viceroyalty of New Granada), set up as a result of the independence campaigns led by Simón Bolívar. The secession of Venezuela and Ecuador, and the death of Bolívar in 1930, led to the collapse of the Republic.

Greater East Asia Co-Prosperity Sphere Term used by Japan to describe the empire they established in E Asia from the 1930s onward. It collapsed in 1945 with the defeat of Japan.

Greater German Reich (*var. Ger.* Grossdeutschland) Core German state proclaimed by Nazis in 1939 following the acquisition of Saarland, Austria, Bohemia-Moravia, and Memelland, divided into *Gaue* (regions), each with its *Gauleiter*.

GREECE The southernmost country of the Balkans, Greece is surrounded by the Aegean, Ionian, and Cretan seas. Its mainly mountainous territory includes more than 2000 islands. Only one-third of the land is cultivated. The flourishing of the arts, philosophy, and political theory in Ancient Greece – especially in 5th-century bce Athens – shaped the future development of Europe. Greek values were adopted by Rome and survived, albeit in a highly Christianized form, throughout the long history of the Byzantine Empire. Thereafter Greece was rather cut off from its glorious past by its subjection to the Ottoman Empire.

Modern Greece is a young country that only came into existence in 1830 after a war of independence against the Turks. There is a strong seafaring tradition, and some of the world's biggest ship-owners are Greek. Greece is rich in minerals – including chromium, whose ▶

◄

occurrence is rare. Relations with Turkey, marked by conflict and territorial disputes, have improved in recent years. To the north, however, upheavals in Albania and the conflicts in former Yugoslavia have made for greater instability.

Greek art. *p.43*
Olympic Games. *p.45*
Athens. *p.56*
Greek philosophy. *p.59*
Alexander the Great. *p.60, p.61*
Greek independence struggle. *p.352*

CHRONOLOGY

2300–1400 BCE Minoan culture flourishes on Crete and extends to Mycenae on the mainland.

491 BCE The military defeat of the Persian forces of King Darius by the Athenians at the battle of Marathon marks the rise of the city-state of Athens and the golden age of Classical Greece.

356–23 BCE Philip of Macedon and his son Alexander the Great complete the conquest of the whole country; Alexander overthrows the Persian Empire and extends Greek rule as far as India. On his death the Greek Empire is divided into four parts.

146 BCE The destruction of Corinth by Roman forces precipitates the inclusion of the whole country in the Roman Empire.

4th century CE Greece becomes part of the East Roman, or Byzantine, Empire.

1071–1453 The gradual defeat of the Byzantine Empire by Muslim forces begins with the battle of Manzikert (1071) and ends with the fall of Constantinople (1453), leaving Greece as part of Ottoman Empire.

1821 A Greek nationalist movement declares independence and the country's first national assembly is convened. When a Turkish expeditionary force attempts to restore Turkish rule, the Greeks appeal for help from France, Britain and Russia.

1829 The Treaty of Adrianople, concluding the Russo-Turkish war, includes a protocol demarcating Greek territory.

1832 France, Britain and Russia install Otto, the son of King Ludwig of Bavaria, as king of Greece; he is deposed in 1862 in favor of Prince George of Denmark (Georgios I).

1911–13 In Balkan Wars, Greece extends its territory to include Macedonia, southern Epirus, eastern Aegean Islands, and Crete.

1913 Georgios I is assassinated and succeeded by Constantine XII. His pro-German sympathies bring him into conflict with Prime Minister Eleftherios Venizelos, who takes Greece into World War I on the side of the Allies. Constantine abdicates in favor of his son Alexander, regains the throne on Alexander's death in 1920, but abdicates in 1922; succeeded by Georgios II.

1921–22 Greece attempts to regain territory in Asia Minor in war with Turkey but is defeated, and recognizes Turkish sovereignty over most of the disputed territory under the 1923 Treaty of Lausanne.

1924 A republic is declared and a period of political instability ensues, characterized by the influence of Venizelos and by military intervention.

1935 A plebiscite following Venizelos's electoral defeat in June results in a vote for the restoration of the monarchy. Georgios II returns to the throne and after an inconclusive election in 1936 creates a right-wing dictatorship under Gen. Joannis Metaxas known as the "Third Civilization."

1941 Greece is overrun by German forces, the government goes into exile, and in September an organized resistance is formed - the National Liberation Front (EAM). The German army retreats in October 1944 and the government returns, headed by Georgios Papandreou.

1946–49 Conflicts between royalist forces and guerrillas of the communist Greek People's Liberation Army (ELAS) erupt into full scale civil war, which leaves up to 80,000 dead by the time ELAS surrenders in Oct 1949. The victorious royalist forces led by Marshall Alexander Papagos, who, after a period of government by unstable liberal centrist and left-wing parties, forms the Greek Rally and wins the election of Nov 1952 (under a Constitution giving women the vote for the first time).

1955 Papagos dies, and leadership of Greek Rally, reformed as the National Radical Union, passes to Konstantine Karamanlis, who remains in power until 1963.

1963 The opposition Center Union led by Georgios Papandreou wins a general election and in a further election in February 1964 achieves an overall majority.

1964 King Constantine succeeds his father, King Paul.

1967 Military coup. King in exile. Colonel Giorgios Papadopoulos becomes premier.

1973 Greece declared a republic, with Papadopoulos as president. Papadopoulos overthrown in military coup. Lieutenant General Ghizikis president. Adamantios Androutsopoulos prime minister.

1974 Greece leaves NATO in protest at Turkish occupation of northern Cyprus. "Colonels' regime" falls. Constantinos Karamanlis becomes premier and his ND party wins subsequent elections.

1975 Konstantinos Tsatsou becomes president.

1977 Elections: ND reelected.

1980 Karamanlis president. Georgios Rallis prime minister. Greece rejoins NATO.

1981 PASOK wins elections. Andreas Papandreou first-ever socialist premier. Greece joins European Communities.

1985 Proposals to limit power of president. Karamanlis resigns. Christos Sartzetakis president. Greece and Albania reopen borders, closed since 1940.

1985–1989 Civil unrest caused by economic austerity program.

1988 Cabinet implicated in financial scandal. Leading members resign.

1989 Defense agreement with USA. Two inconclusive elections lead to formation of all-party coalition.

1990 Coalition government collapses. ND wins elections. Konstantinos Mitsotakis prime minister; Karamanlis president.

1990–1992 Strikes against economic reform.

1992 EU persuaded to withhold recognition of Former Yugoslav Republic of Macedonia.

1993 PASOK wins election, Andreas Papandreou premier.

1995 Stephanopoulos elected president; recognition of sovereignty of FYRM.

1996 Andreas Papandreou resigns as prime minister; succeeded by Kostas Simitis.

2000 PASOK led by Simitis wins general election.

2001 January, introduction of euro.

2004 New Democracy wins general election. Athens hosts centennial Olympics.

Greek Independence, War of (1821–30) The revolt by Greek subjects against Turkish domination. Greece fought alone until 1825, but thereafter her cause was taken up by Britain, Russia, and France. Following the destruction of Turkey's fleet at Navarino (1827) and Treaty of Adrianople (1829), in 1830 Greek independence was confirmed by her allies. *p.352*

GREENLAND The world's largest island, an autonomous territory under Danish protection. It was settled by Eric the Red in 989 ce and became home to a sizable Norse community. However, climate change meant that in the 14th and 15th centuries the colonists were completely abandoned. They either died out or were assimilated by the native Inuit population.

Chronology

3000 bce Begins to be settled by Eskimo (Inuit) peoples. 10th century. Norwegian Vikings establish settlements in south.

1262 Greenland formally becomes a Norwegian possession.

1380 Along with Norway proper, Greenland becomes part of Denmark. This is confirmed in the 1397 Union of Kalmar.

16th century European whalers arrive in; some settle and intermarry with local Inuit.

1953 A referendum approves major changes to the Danish Constitution which include the abolition of Greenland's colonial status and its full integration as part of the Kingdom of Denmark.

1972 National referendum on Danish membership of the EC, Greenlanders vote against by 71 to 29 percent, but they are bound by the "yes" vote in Denmark and join the EC with effect from Jan 1 1973.

1979 By 73 percent to 27 percent voters approve the terms of an autonomy statute under which only foreign policy and defence remain under Danish control; home rule takes effect on May 1.

1979 The center-left Forward party (Siumut) wins the first elections for the new autonomous legislature; Jonathan Motzfeldt becomes the island's first chief minister.

Gregory VII, St. (c.1020–1085) Great reforming pope of the Middle Ages (reigned 1073–85). He criticized abuses in the church. From 1075 he contested Emperor Henry IV over lay investiture.

GRENADA The most southerly of the Windward Islands, Grenada also includes the islands of Carriacou and Petite Martinique. A French colony from 1650, Grenada was captured by the British in 1762. It is the world's second-largest producer of nutmeg. Grenada became a focus of international attention in 1983 when the US, with backing from several Caribbean states, mounted an invasion to sever its growing links with Castro's Cuba. Grenada is one of the seven members of the OECS (Organization of Eastern Caribbean States).

Chronology

1498 Columbus visits the island which he names Concepcion.

1650 The island is occupied by the forces of the governor of the French possession of Martinique.

1674 French control is imposed against resistance from the native population. Sugar mills are established, supported by slave labor.

18th century The British take control and introduce a slave labor economy producing cotton, cocoa and nutmeg.

1958–62 Grenada forms part of the West Indies Federation.

1951 Universal suffrage introduced.

1967–1974 Internal self-government. Full independence from the UK.

1979 Coup. Maurice Bishop prime minister. Growing links with Cuba.

1983 US invasion establishes pro-US administration.

1999 NNP (New National Party) reelected, taking all 15 seats in House of Representatives.

2000–2002 Blacklisted as tax haven.

2003 NNP reelected.

2004 Hurrican Ivan damages 90% of buildings.

Griffith, D.W. (David Llewelyn Wark, 1875–1948) Pioneering US film-maker and director of *Birth of a Nation*.

Grijalva, Juan de (c.1480–1527) Spanish conquistador. Took part in conquest of Cuba in 1508. In 1518 while reconnoitering Yucatan, became first European to receive information about the existence of the Aztec Empire. Later served in Central America under Pedrarias Dávila.

Groot Trek *see* Great Trek

Grossdeutschland *see* Greater German Reich

Groseilliers, Medart Chouart des 17th-century French explorer of N America (1659–60).

Guadalcanal Series of naval and land ✕ during World War II (Aug 1942–Feb 1943). Fought on and around Guadalcanal in the Solomon Islands, the battles marked the halt by Allied forces of Japanese advance in the southwest Pacific.

Guangala Coastal culture of western S America (c.250 bce).

Guaraní Tupian-speaking South American people. The aboriginal Guaraní inhabited eastern Paraguay and adjacent areas in Brazil and Argentina. In the 14th and 15th centuries some Tupian speakers migrated inland to the Río de la Plata, where they became the Guaraní of Paraguay.

Guarmani, Carlo 19th–century Italian explorer of the Arabian Peninsula. He was an enterprising Italian horse dealer who made an extensive journey from Jerusalem to the heart of Arabia to buy Arab stallions for the French government and for the King of Italy.

GUATEMALA The largest and most populous of the states of the Central American isthmus, Guatemala was home to the ancient Maya civilization. Its fertile Pacific and Caribbean coastal lowlands give way to the highlands which dominate the country. Independent since 1838, Guatemala's history since 1954 has been one of military rule. Civilian rule was restored in 1986, but 90 percent of the population live below the poverty line.

Chronology

1524 The Spaniards set foot in Guatemala and in 1526 incorporate it into the Viceroyalty of New Spain which embraces the five "provinces" of Central America.

1821 As a regional capital of the Viceroyalty of New Spain Guatemala proclaims its independence.

1823 Guatemala, along with El Salvador, Honduras, Nicaragua, and Costa Rica reaffirm their independence as the United Provinces of Central America.

1838 Guatemala becomes an independent republic.

1944 Gen. Jorge Ubico Castaneda, who took power in 1931, is overthrown in a popular uprising. Liberal reformer Juan Jose Arevalo wins subsequent 1945 election.

1952 Col. Jacobo Arbenz Guzman, elected in 1950, introduces land and social reforms.

▶

1954 US-backed coup topples reformist government.

1966–1984 Counterinsurgency war; highlands "pacification."

1986–1993 Return of civilian rule; President Serrano elected. Flees country after abortive "self-coup."

1996 President Arzú elected; peace deal with URNG guerrillas ends 36 years of civil war.

1998 Bishop Juan Gerardi, human rights campaigner, murdered.

1999 "Truth Commission" blames army for most human rights abuses. Portillo and FRG win elections.

2004 Oscar Berger takes office as president.

Guerra de Guatemala 1847 *see* Mexican-American War

Guiana *see* Guyana

Guilford Court House ⚔ of American Revolutionary War (Mar 5 1781). Inconclusive result.

GUINEA Guinea lies on the western coast of Africa. The central densely forested or savanna highlands slope down to coastal plains and swamps in the west and to the semidesert of the north. Military rule, established in 1984, ended with legislative elections in 1995; however, the results were disputed.

CHRONOLOGY

10th-15th centuries Gold-producing area of Wangara becomes an important center in development of Islamic Mali Empire.

17th-18th centuries Revival of Islam under the Fula people of the Futa Jallon region.

19th century Almamy Samori Toure consolidates his Mandinka empire of Wassulu which becomes a symbol of resistance to the French colonization of the region. From his capital at Bisandugu, Samori captures Kankan in about 1870.

1881 France signs a treaty with Futa Jallon.

1890 War breaks out between Samori's forces and the French. Samori's offer to cede his empire to the UK.

1896 The French invade Futa Djallon.

1898 The French defeat Samori. Colonization begins.

1947 Ahmed Sekou Touré and others form the Democratic Party of Guinea (PDG).

1958 Guinea is the only French colony to vote "no" to President de Gaulle's offer of a French community; the French immediately withdraw. October. Guinea becomes independent with Sekou Touré as President and the Democratic Party of Guinea (PDG) as the sole legal party.

1984 Sekou Touré dies. Army coup.

1993–1995 Disputed elections.

1998 Conté reelected president.

2000 Cross-border attacks from Sierra Leone and Liberia place Guinea in a state of civil war.

2002 PUP wins delayed elections.

2003 Conté reelected president.

GUINEA-BISSAU Lying on Africa's west coast, impoverished Guinea-Bissau, a former Portuguese territory, is bordered by Senegal to the north and Guinea to the south and east. Apart from savanna highlands in the northeast, the country is low-lying. The PAIGC initiated a process of change to multiparty democracy in 1990, and elections were held in 1994. A military coup in 1999 followed army rebellion the previous year, but legislative and presidential elections have since been held.

CHRONOLOGY

1456 First Portuguese sailors visit the area.

1616 Portugal installs a military garrison at Cacheu to control the slave trade.

1879 Portugal claims Portuguese Guinea, with a capital at Geba.

1936 Portugal declares the "pacification" of the territory.

1956 Amilcar Cabral forms the African Party for the Independence of Guinea-Bissau and Cape Verde (PAIGC).

1959 Striking dockers are massacred in Bissau. PAIGC sets up its headquarters in Conakry, Guinea.

1960s PAIGC occupies large areas of the country.

1970 Conakry is invaded by Portuguese-backed mercenaries.

1973 Amilcar Cabral is assassinated.

1973 PAIGC declares the country independent, with Luiz Cabral as

---

President of the State Council; international recognition follows a year later, including by Portugal.

1974 Independence. PAIGC takes power.

1980 Military coup.

1990 Multiparty politics accepted.

1994 Multiparty elections.

1998 Army rebellion led by General Mane.

1999 Transitional government. May, army seizes power. November, PRS defeats PAIGC in elections.

2000 Kumba Yalla president. Mane killed in failed coup attempt.

2003 President Kumba Yalla overthrown in military coup.

2004 PAIGC returns to power.

Guevara, Che (*f/n* Ernesto Guevara, 1928–67) Latin American revolutionary, born in Argentina, who fought with Fidel Castro for the independence of Cuba. *p.429*

Gulag Soviet authority responsible for running prisons and labor camps. *p.427*

Gulf War (1990–91) War precipitated by Iraq's invasion of Kuwait (Aug 1990). The UN condemned the invasion and demanded Iraq's withdrawal. When Iraq, led by President Saddam Hussein, refused to comply, a US-led coalition of 29 states launched Operation Desert Storm. Saddam's forces surrendered in Feb 1991. Kuwait was liberated and harsh economic sanctions imposed on Iraq by UN. *p.450*

Guomindang *see* Kuomintang

Gupta dynasty (c.300–500 CE) During this period, India was ruled by five great monarchs from the city of Pataliputra, and subsequently Ayodhya. At its greatest extent, Gupta rule extended from the Punjab in the west to northern Bengal. Gupta administration was enlightened and tolerant, and arts, music, sculpture, and painting flourished. Trade extended in all directions. Buddhism was the state religion, but reviving Hinduism absorbed many Buddhist tenets. The invasions of the Huns in the 5th and 6th centuries brought about the political collapse of the empire. *p.94*

Gurjara-Pratiharas (8th–11th century) Indian kingdom which originated in Rajasthan and, from 836 CE, controlled the area between eastern Punjab and northern Bengal, before disintegrating into smaller warring kingdoms in the 10th century.

Gustavus II (Gustavus Adolphus, 1594–1632) King of Sweden (reigned 1611–32). Recovered the Baltic provinces from Denmark, and ended the wars with Russia (1617) and Poland (1629). He championed the Protestant cause in the Thirty Years' War, winning a series of victories campaigning in Germany. *p.303*

Gustavus Adolphus *see* Gustavus II

Gutenberg, Johannes (*var.* Johann Gensfleisch zur Laden zum Gutenberg, died 1468) German craftsman and inventor who originated a method of printing from movable type that was used without real change until the 20th century.

GUYANA Guyana lies on the northeast coast of South America, bordered by Venezuela, Brazil, and Suriname. Dense interior rainforest covers some three-quarters of its territory, but this is diminishing at a worrying rate as a result of logging. Independence from the UK came in 1966. Exports of sugar, bauxite, rice, gold, and timber sustain the economy. The vast majority of Guyana's population lives on the narrow coastal plain partially reclaimed from the sea.

Chronology

1499 Guyana coast is discovered by Alonso de Ojeda on Columbus's third voyage.

1530s onwards Search for El Dorado centers on Amazon and Orinoco areas.

1616 A Dutch expedition under Adrian Groenewegen establishes a fort at Kykoveral; Dutch settlers arrive in 1624.

1648 Under the Treaty of Munster Spain recognizes Berbice and Essequibo, including Demerara, as Dutch colonies.

1831 The territory becomes a British colony with the name of British Guiana.

1953 First universal elections won by PPP under Cheddi Jagan; parliament later suspended by UK.

1964 PNC dominates ruling coalition parties.

1966 Independence from UK.

1973 PPP boycotts parliament, accusing PNC of electoral fraud.

1992 Elections won by PPP. Jagan president.

1997–1998 Jagan dies in office; PNC rejects his widow Janet's election victory. Political crisis.

1999 Caricom-brokered peace deal. Janet Jagan resigns; Bharrat Jagdeo takes over.

2001 Jagdeo and PPP reelected.

Güyük (1206–1248) Grandson of Ghengis Khan, he reigned as Great Khan of the Mongols from 1246–48.

Guzmán, Nuño de 16th-century Spanish conquistador, who took part in the conquest of Mexico.

Gyogi 8th-century Japanese Buddhist priest who began to compile maps of Japan's provinces.

H

Haarlem ⚔ of Dutch Revolt (1572–73) Spanish victory over Dutch.

Habsburg dynasty (*var.* Hapsburg) Major European royal and imperial family. From 1438 to 1806 all Holy Roman Emperors but one belonged to Habsburg house. Reached its peak as a world power under Charles V who brought Spain into the Habsburg dominions. After Charles' death, the house split into the Spanish line, which died out in 1700, and the Austrian line which remained in power until 1918. Habsburg-Ottoman conflict. *p.314*
See also Charles V, Holy Roman Empire, Austria

Habyarimana Juvénal (1937–94) President of Rwanda (1973–94).

Hadrian (*var.* Publius Aelius Hadrianus, 76–138 CE) Roman Emperor (reigned 117–138 CE), under whom the Roman Empire consolidated its defenses and enjoyed a period of peace and prosperity. Hadrian traveled extensively round the empire, not as a soldier, but as an administrator and connoisseur of the arts. He commissioned many new buildings, notably in Athens and Rome, and new cities, such as Aelia Capitolina, built on the ruins of Jerusalem.

Hadrian's Wall 117-km-long wall built by emperor Hadrian (reigned 117–138 CE) to consolidate the northern frontier of the Roman Empire. Constructed between 122–28 CE, it straddles northern England from the Solway Firth to the River Tyne, and was defended by 16 forts, 80 milecastles, and numerous signal turrets and stretches of ditch. Despite attacks by northern tribes it survived until c.400 CE.

Hafsid dynasty Berber dynasty of the 13th–16th century in Ifriqiya (Tunisia and eastern Algeria), founded by the Almohad governor Abu Zakriyya' Yahya about 1229.

Hagia Sophia *see* Santa Sophia

Haile Selassie I (1892–1975, reigned 1930–74) Emperor of Ethiopia, formerly Prince Ras Tafari. Driven out of Ethiopia by the Italian occupation of 1936–41, but led the reconquest, helped by Britain, and began to modernize Ethiopia. A revolution provoked by famine in 1974 deposed him; died under house arrest. He is still revered by certain groups, notably the Rastafarians.

HAITI Haiti occupies the western third of the Caribbean island of Hispaniola. A former Spanish colony, in 1804 it was the first Caribbean state to become independent, and has been in a state of political chaos virtually ever since. Democracy did not materialize with the exile of the dictator Jean-Claude Duvalier in 1986. Elections were held in 1990, but by 1991 the military were back in power and were ousted in 1994 only through US intervention.

Chronology

1492 During his first voyage to the Americas Columbus reaches the island of Hispaniola.

1697 The buccaneer-based French community of Saint-Domingue is recognized by Spain under the Treaty of Ryswick and flourishes as a rich French plantation colony with an estimated 500,000 slaves by 1789.

1791 A massacre of French by slaves signals the beginning of a bitter 13–year civil war under native Haitian leader Toussaint L'Ouverture. The Haitians strongly resist French, Dutch, and English troops.

1804 Jean Jacques Dessalines proclaims the independence of Haiti as the first black republic in the Americas and subsequently appoints himself Emperor.

1806 Henri Christophe cuts down Dessalines and is appointed president in 1807, becoming King Henri I in 1911 until his suicide in 1829.

1822–44 Haitians invade the neighboring Spanish colony of Santo Domingo and rule repressively.

1915–1934 US occupation.

1957–1971 François "Papa Doc" Duvalier's brutal dictatorship.

1971–1986 His son Jean-Claude, "Baby Doc," rules; eventually flees.

▶

1986–1988 Military rule.
1990 Jean-Bertrand Aristide of left-wing Lavalas party elected; exiled in 1991 coup.
1994–1995 US forces oust military. Aristide reinstated; elections.
1997–1999 Political deadlock.
2000 Lavalas coalition and Aristide reelected.
2004 Aristide resigns and flees.

Haj (*var.* Hajj) Pilgrimage to Mecca. Every adult Muslim is required to make the journey to the Islamic holy city of Mecca in Saudi Arabia at least once in his or her lifetime. The object of the pilgrimage is the Kaaba, the sacred shrine of Islam containing the "black stone" in the middle of the Great Mosque.

Hajj *see* Haj

Halley, Edmund (1656–1742) English astronomer, who correctly calculated the return of the comet that bears his name after 76 years. *p.172*

Hallstatt Culture Name given to Iron Age culture that flourished in Europe c.800 BCE.

Hammurabi Babylonian king (1790–1750 BCE), famous for his code of laws that has survived since first drafted. *p.30*

Han dynasty Ruling dynasty of China, successors to the Qin. The Former or Western Han (206 BCE–9 CE), with their capital at Chang'an, greatly expanded Chinese realms under emperor Wudi (140–87 BCE) The Later, or Eastern Han (25–220 CE), made their capital at Luoyang, during which Buddhism was introduced, and extended their domains into Central Asia; their empire collapsed under pressure from northern peoples. *p.87*

Hannibal (247–183 BCE) Carthaginian general who, in 218, invaded Roman Italy by marching his army (including elephants and cavalry) over the Alps. His initial campaigns were all successful, but he became pinned down in the south of Italy. He was eventually summoned to return to Africa, where he was defeated at Zama in 202. Hannibal fled to the court of Antiochus III, the Seleucid king of Syria. *p.65*

Hanseatic League Trading association of north German and Baltic towns, which flourished between the13th and 15th centuries. Important members of the league included Lübeck, Cologne, Danzig, and Brunswick. *p.236*

Hapsburg dynasty/empire
see Habsburg dynasty

Harald Hardrada (*var.* Haardraade, 1015–66) King of Norway. After fleeing Norway, he commanded the Varangian Guard in Constantinople, where he won a reputation as a fearsome warrior (Hardrada meant ruthless). On his return home, he first shared the kingdom with his nephew, then became sole ruler in 1048. In 1066, he claimed the throne of England but was defeated by Harold Godwinson, and killed at the battle of Stamford Bridge.

Harappan culture The first urban communities of the Indian subcontinent developed c.2500 BCE in the Indus plain, with two major cities at Harappa and Mohenjo-Daro. Over 100 urban settlements are known, most of them major towns of baked brick buildings, dominated by citadels containing religious and ceremonial buildings. The Harappan cities had extensive trade links, reaching as far as southern Mesopotamia. The urban civilization ended c.2000 BCE; the reasons for its demise could be connected to Aryan invasion, or to changed environmental conditions disrupting Indus agriculture.

Harding, Warren Gamaliel (1865–1923) 29th President of the US (Republican, 1921–23). On his election, Harding promised a return to normal life after World War I. His administration oversaw the completion of peace treaties with Germany, Austria, and Hungary. However, the exposure of serious corruption by his Cabinet colleagues in 1923 (which became the so-called "Teapot Dome" scandal) is thought to have contributed to his death.

Hargreaves, James (c.1720–78) English inventor of the spinning jenny (c.1764), the first practical application of multiple spinning by a machine, one of the major innovations of the Industrial Revolution.

Harold II (*var.* Harold Godwinson, c.1022–66). Claimed the throne of England on the death of Edward the Confessor in 1066, but later that year was defeated by William of Normandy and killed at the battle of Hastings.

Harris, Richard T. 19th-century explorer, made the first gold strike in Alaska (1880).

Harrison, John (1693–1776) British clockmaker who made a clock accurate and reliable enough to be used to calculate longitude.

Harun al-Rashid *see* al-Rashid, Harun

Hastings ⚔ of Norman invasion of England (1066). Victory of William, Duke of Normandy, over Harold, King of England.

Hastings, Warren (1732–1818). First Governor-General of India (1774–85). He instituted reforms in the system of revenue collection and civil courts. He was impeached on corruption charges, but finally acquitted in 1795.

Hatshepsut (*aka* Hatshopitu, reigned 1472–1458 BCE) Female pharaoh of Egypt.

Hattin ⚔ of the Crusades (1187), where Saladin defeated Christians of the Crusader States.

Hawaiian Islands Group of islands in the central Pacific, settled by Polynesians c.400 CE. The islands were first visited by Europeans when Captin Cook sailed there on his third voyage in 1778. The US annexed the islands during 1898, and in 1959 they became a state of the Union.

Hawkins, Sir John (1532–95) English admiral who made three voyages to the New World (1562, 1564 and 1567), during which he made attacks on Portuguese slavers, and forced the Spanish colonies to trade with him. From 1573 he became the administrative officer of the English navy. In 1588 he served as rear-admiral against the Spanish Armada and was knighted. He died, on an expedition with Sir Francis Drake, off the coast of Puerto Rico in 1595.

Hebrews *see* Jews

Hedin, Sven Anders von (1865–1952). Swedish explorer and geographer of uncharted regions of Central Asia, Tibet, and China.

Hegira (*var.* Hijra) Muhammad's flight from Mecca to Medina (622). Year of the Hegira marks beginning of the Muslim calendar.

Heian Period (794–1185) Period of Japanese history that began with the transfer of the capital to Heian-kyo.

Heijn, Piet *see* Heyn, Piet

Hejaz Mountainous plateau in western Saudi Arabia covering an area of some 388,500 sq km. It contains the holy cities of Islam: Mecca and Medina.

henge Ritual monument, normally a circular space defined by an earthen bank with one or more entrances, with an internal ditch providing a symbolic separation between activities inside and outside the henge. Henges are sometimes further defined by arrangements of standing stones or menhirs, often precisely located along astronomical alignments.

Hennepin, Father Louis (1640–c.1701) Belgian explorer. Sailed to Canada in

1675 as a Franciscan missionary. Explored the upper course of the Mississippi River with the Frenchman La Salle, but did not, as he claimed in a memoir of his travels, discover the river's mouth.

Henry II (1133–89) King of England (reigned 1154–89). French-born, he inherited the Duchy of Normandy from his mother and became Duke of Anjou on the death of his father, gaining Poitou and Guyenne on his marriage to Eleanor of Aquitaine. When he succeeded Stephen in 1154, he added England to his possessions. He extended the judicial and administrative power of the crown, but clashed with Thomas Becket over his attempts to restrict church authority, and later with members of his own family.

Henry V (1387–1422) King of England (reigned 1413–22). A skilful military leader, in 1415 he invaded France and defeated the French at Agincourt. By 1419 he had conquered Normandy, and was recognized as heir to the French throne.

Henry VIII (1491–1547) King of England (reigned 1509–1547). The Pope's refusal to annul his marriage to his first wife, Catherine of Aragon, led to England's break with the Roman Catholic Church, and to Henry becoming supreme head of the Church in England. The dissolution of the monasteries followed. In 1536 he executed his second wife, Anne Boleyn for infidelity. Successive marriages were to Jane Seymour (died), Anne of Cleves (divorced), Catherine Howard (beheaded), and Catherine Parr (survived after Henry's death). *p.280*

Henry II (1519–59) King of France (reigned 1547–59). His marriage to Catherine de Médicis produced three future kings of France. Dominated by his mistresses, Diane de Poitiers and Anne de Montmorency. Through the influence of the de Guise family he formed an alliance with Scotland, and declared war on England, which ended with the seizure of Calais in 1558. Continued wars against Emperor Charles V and Spain.

Henry I (*aka* Henry the Fowler) King of Saxony (reigned 876–936). Henry was elected King of Germany, which he transformed into a viable state. His imperial ambitions were realized by his son Otto.

Henry II (972–1024) Bavarian king of Germany and Holy Roman Emperor, noted for his piety and canonized in 1146. *p.163*

Henry IV (1050–1106) German Emperor, who inherited the kingdoms of Germany, Italy, and Burgundy in 1056 under his mother's regency. His conflict with Pope Gregory VII over the investiture question led to his excommunication in 1075; in 1077, his public abasement at Canossa restored him to the Church. He appointed Clement III as antipope in 1084 and was crowned emperor. Repeated conflict with the German nobles, eventually led by his younger son (Henry V), forced his abdication in 1105. *p.174*

Henry the Navigator (*aka* Prince Henry of Portugal, 1394–1460) Son of João I of Portugal, Henry founded a school of navigation in the Algarve in 1416, from where he sponsered a series of journeys of exploration along the coast of Africa.

Hephthalites *see* White Huns

Heraclius (c.572–642) East Roman Emperor. Proclaimed emperor in 610, He defeated the Persian armies that were threatening his empire and victory in the Tigris plain in 627 forced the Persians to make peace. In 629 Arab armies made their first incursion into Syria and, by 637, they had occupied Syria, Palestine, and Egypt. Heraclius did little to confront the new threat.

Herat Ancient city of Afghanistan, frequently conquered owing to its position on the trade route between the Islamic world and China. It was sacked by Genghis Khan in 1221.Herati metalwork. *p.194*

Herbert, Sir Thomas (1602–82) English traveler and author. In 1627 he embarked on a voyage to the Cape, Madagascar, Goa, and Surat, and made extensive journeys throughout Persia. He returned via Sri Lanka, the Coromandel coast, and St. Helena. His service to the king in the Civil War was rewarded with a baronetcy at the Restoration (1660). He described his journeys, which included an account of the ruins of Persepolis, in his *Description of the Persian Monarchy* (1634).

Herjölfsson, Bjarni 10th-century Viking explorer, the first European to sight the New World. Icelandic sagas relate how, in c.985 CE, Herjolfsson was blown off course from Greenland and sighted land to the west, the coast of Labrador. Some 15 years later, Leif Eriksson set sail from Greenland to investigate Herjolfsson's sightings.

Herod the Great (c.73–4 BCE) Herod's father served under Caesar in Egypt and appointed him ruler of Galilee. In 40 BCE Herod led the Roman army's expulsion of

the Parthians from Jerusalem, became King of a Judaea loyal to Rome.

Herodotus (c.484–420 BCE) Greek historian, writer and geographer, known as the "Father of History." He made extensive journeys throughout the ancient world, but is best known for his history of the Persian Wars.

Heyn, Piet (*var.* Heijn, 1577–1629) Dutch naval commander. As vice-admiral of the Dutch East India Company in 1624, he defeated the Spanish near San Salvador, Brazil and in 1626 off Bahia. His 1626 capture of the Spanish silver fleet let to his appointment as Admiral of Holland.

Hezbollah (*var.* Hizbullah, Hizbollah, "Party of God") The largest of the Shi'ite Islamic political groups in Lebanon. Under Iranian sponsorship, they have been associated with the kidnapping of Westerners and terrorist attacks to further political aims, and have been in conflict with Israeli forces since Israel's invasion of Lebanon in 1982.

Hidalgo, Father Miguel y Costilla (1753–1811) Mexican priest, celebrated as beginning the revolution against Spain which resulted in Mexican independence. He led a force of 80,000 against the Spanish before turning back at Mexico City in 1811. He was later executed.

hieroglyphics Ancient system of writing using symbols, named from the Greek "sacred carving." They were originally pictographs, usually written right to left and giving three kinds of information: an object or concept in the real world; a consonant or sequence of consonants; or an explanation of an otherwise ambiguous associated symbol. The first evidence for hieroglyphs comes from c.3250 BCE and they continue in use into the late 3rd century CE. They mainly appear in religious and monumental contexts.

Hijra *see* Hegira

hillforts Earthwork monuments located on hilltops or high ground and comprising a central occupation area accessed through often complex "gates" through the surrounding series of one or more banks and ditches. Built by Iron Age populations across western Europe, they acted as defensive centers when communities were under threat, and the scale of the earthworks was a declaration of the power and prestige of their builders.

Hindenburg Line (*var.* the Siegfried Line) German fortified line of defence (named for Field Marshal Hindenburg) on the

Western Front during World War I, to which German forces retreated early in 1917. The line remained unbroken until 1918.

Hinduism The dominant religion in India that involves belief in destiny (Karma) and cycles of reincarnation (Samsara) and adheres to a particular moral law (Sharma). It is associated with a class system of social organization (caste) and includes ritual ceremonies, mystical contemplation and self-denying practices. All-embracing in its forms, capable of including extreme polytheism and high monotheism, animal sacrifice and refusal to take any form of life. Unique among world religions in having no single founder, but has grown over a period of 4000 years. The Vedas are accepted as the most sacred scriptures.

Hippalus First-century CE Greek merchant who was the first to recognize the regularity of the monsoon winds, harnessing them for his voyage through the Red Sea to the Indus from 14–37 CE.

Hipparchus (*var.* Hipparchos, c.180–125 BCE) Greek astronomer and mathematician. First to use latitude and longitude to define the position of places on the earth.

Hiroshima Japanese city on which the US dropped the first atomic bomb in August 1945. *p.417*

Hitler, Adolf (1889–1945) German dictator. Following service in the trenches in World War I, he became a political agitator during the Weimar period, building support for his National Socialist (Nazi) party, based on extreme nationalism, anti-communism, and racism. He became chancellor in 1933, rapidly disposing of parliamentary constraints, and establishing dictatorship (as Führer, through the Enabling Law of 1933). Hitler transformed the German economy, by placing it on a war footing, and recovered pre-World War I territories, annexing Austria, and invading Poland (1939), to precipitate World War II. He adopted personal responsibility for the conduct of the war, and inaugurated the Final Solution extermination program against the Jews (1942). He committed suicide as Soviet forces entered Berlin. *p.410*

Hittite empire (fl.1450–1200 BCE) Indo-Europeans, who probably came from north of the Black Sea to settle in Anatolia and northern Syria, establishing their capital Hattushash near modern Boêazköy. After the indecisive battle of Kadesh against the Egyptians (c.1285 BCE) they established peace, but were overthrown c.1200.

Hizbollah *see* Hezbollah
Hizbullah *see* Hezbollah
Ho Chi Minh (1890–1969) Vietnamese statesman. In 1930 founded the Indochina Communist Party. He became the leader of the Viet Minh guerrillas and at the end of World War II established a government in Hanoi. When the French tried to regain control of their former colony, he proclaimed Vietnam's independence (1945) and led the resistance that forced French forces to withdraw from the north. President of North Vietnam from 1954, he countered American intervention in Vietnam in the 1960s. When the Vietnam war ended with fall of Saigon in 1975, the city was renamed Ho Chi Minh in his honor.

Hobkirk's Hill ⚔ of American Revolutionary War (Apr 25 1781). American victory.

Hogarth, William (1697–1764) English painter and engraver, an acute satirist of the follies of his age. *p.324*

Hohenlinden ⚔ of Napoleonic Wars – the War of the 2nd Coalition (1800). French victory forced Austrians to sue for peace.

Hohenstaufen dynasty (*var.* Staufen dynasty) German dynasty that ruled the Holy Roman Empire from 1138 to 1208 and from 1212 to 1254. *p.212*

Hohokam Native-American people of the US southwest. Their society flourished in the 11th century CE.

Hojo Japanese family of warrior regents which dominated Japan in the 13th century, especially during the Mongol invasions of Japan in 1274 and 1281.

Hollywood Home of the major movie studios in Los Angeles, California. The silent era. *p.408*

Holocaust Name given to persecution of the Europe's Jews by Nazi Germany from 1933–45, which led ultimately to the deaths of about six million Jews.

HOLY ROMAN EMPIRE Complex of European territories under the rule of the Frankish or German king who bore the title of Holy Roman Emperor, founded by Charlemagne in 800 CE. After Charlemagne, imperial power was at its greatest under the Hohenstaufens in the 12th–13th centuries. The empire, by then a ridiculous anachronism, was dissolved by Napoleon in 1806. *p.187, p.212*

Holy Roman Emperors

800–814	Charlemagne
814–840	Louis I (the Pious; crowned 816)
840–855	Lothair I
855–875	Louis II (in Italy)
875–877	Charles II the Bald (West Frankish)
877–887	Charles III the Fat (East Frankish); crowned 881
887–891	Interregnum during the war between Guido of Spoleto and Berengar of Friuli
891–894	Guido
892–899	Lambert (coregent-emperor with Guido)
896–901	Arnluf (rival of Lambert; crowned by the pope)
901–905	Louis III of Provence
905–924	Berengar

Italian Line

924–926	Rudolf of Burgundy
926–945	Hugh of Provence
945–950	Lothair III
952–962	Berengar

German Line

911–918	Conrad I (Franconian); never crowned at Rome
918–936	Henry I the Fowler (Saxon); never crowned at Rome
936–973	Otto I the Great; crowned 962
973–983	Otto II
983–1002	Otto III; crowned 996
1002–1024	Henry II the Saint (Bavarian); crowned 1014
1024–1039	Conrad II the Salian (Franconian); crowned 1027
1039–1056	Henry III the Black; crowned 1046
1056–1106	Henry IV; crowned 1084
Rivals of Henry IV:	
1077–1080	Rudolf of Swabia
1081–1093	Hermann of Luxembourg
1093–1101	Conrad of Franconia

1106–1125 Henry V; crowned 1111
1125–1137 Lothair II (Saxon);
           crowned 1133
1138–1152 Conrad III (Swabian);
           never crowned at Rome
1152–1190 Frederick I, Barbarossa;
           crowned 1155
1190–1197 Henry VI; crowned 1191
1198–1212 Otto IV (Brunswick);
           crowned 1209.
Rival of Otto IV:
   1198–1208 Philip II of Swabia;
           never crowned

1212–1250 Frederick II; crowned 1220.
Rivals:
   1246–1247 Henry Raspe;
           never crowned
   1247–1256 William of Holland;
           never crowned
   1250–1254 Conrad IV;
           never crowned

1254–1273 The Great Interregnum
Competitors:
   1257–1273 Richard of Cornwall;
           never crowned
   1257–1272 Alfonso X of Castile;
           never crowned

1273–1291 Rudolf I (Habsburg);
           recognized by pope 1274,
           but not crowned
1292–1298 Adolf I (Nassau);
           never crowned
1298–1308 Albert I (Habsburg);
           never crowned
1308–1313 Henry VII (Luxembourg);
           crowned 1312
1314–1347 Louis IV (Bavaria);
           crowned 1328.
Rival of Louis IV:
   1325–1330 Frederick of Habsburg,
           co-regent

1347–1378 Charles IV (Luxembourg);
           crowned 1355.
Rival of Charles IV:
   1347–1349 Günther of Schwarzburg

1378–1400 Wenzel or Wenceslas
           (Luxembourg);
           crowned 1376
1400–1410 Rupert or Rupprecht
           (Palatinate);
           never crowned

1410–1437 Sigismund (Luxembourg);
           crowned 1433.
Rival of Sigismund:
   1410–1411 Jobst of Moravia

1438–1439 Albert II (Habsburg);
           never crowned
1440–1493 Frederick III; last emperor
           crowned in Rome
1493–1519 Maximilian I;
           never crowned
1519–1556 Charles V; last emperor
           crowned by the pope
           (at Bologna)
1558–1564 Ferdinand I
1564–1576 Maximilian II
1576–1612 Rudolf II
1612–1619 Matthias
1619–1637 Ferdinand II
1637–1657 Ferdinand III
1658–1705 Leopold I
1705–1711 Joseph I
1711–1740 Charles VI
1742–1745 Charles VII (Bavaria)
1745–1765 Francis I (Lorraine)
1765–1790 Joseph II
1790–1792 Leopold II
1792–1806 Francis II

Homer (*var. Gk.* Homeros) 9th-century BCE Greek poet, credited with writing the greatest early Greek poems, including *The Iliad* and *The Odyssey*. His work formalized the long oral traditions of recounting the stories and legends of ancient Greece.

Homo Term used for creatures belonging to the same genetic group as modern humans. The earliest known homo is *Homo habilis*, which evolved about 2.5 million years ago.

Homo erectus ("upright man," c.1.7 million to 100,000 years ago) Diverse species found throughout Asia and Africa, distinguished by relatively large brain size, tall, long-legged physique, tool-making skills, and ability to colonize marginal environments. They invented the hand-axe, and also mastered the use of fire. *p.10*

Homo habilis ("handy man," c.2.5 to 1.6 million years ago), so called because of its stone tool-making abilities. *H. habilis* was the earliest member of the genus *Homo*, with a brain capacity about half the size of modern humans, but about 50% larger than any Australopithecine species. *p.10*

Homo sapiens sapiens (c.100,000 years ago) First appearing in Africa, the earliest anatomically modern human species used their hunting skills, adaptability and innovative tool-making abilities to colonize the rest of the globe, reaching the southern tip of S America by c.12,000 BCE. They demonstrate the capacity for abstract thought, revealed in evidence of rituals and finds of rock art, dating back 45,000 years. *p.10*

HONDURAS Straddling the Central American isthmus, Honduras has only a short Pacific coast. Its long Caribbean shoreline includes the virtually uninhabited Mosquito Coast, while most of the rest of the country is mountainous. After a succession of military governments in the 19th and early 20th centuries, it returned to full civilian rule in 1984. In 1998 Honduras was devastated by Hurricane Mitch, which resulted in the death of t least 5600 people and damage estimated at some $3 billion.

CHRONOLOGY

1821 After forming part of the Captaincy-General of Guatemala, Honduras becomes independent from Spain, as part of Mexico until 1823, and then as part of the Central American Federation of States until 1838.

1838 Declares full independence.

1890s US banana plantations set up.

1932–1949 Dictatorship of General Tiburcio Carías Andino of PNH.

1954–1957 Elected PLH president Villeda Morales deposed, reelected.

1963 Military coup.

1969 13-day Football War with El Salvador sparked by World Cup.

1980–1983 PLH wins elections but General Gustavo Alvarez holds real power. Military maneuvers with USA. Trades unionists arrested; death squads operate.

1984 Return to democracy.

1988 12,000 Contra rebels forced out of Nicaragua into Honduras.

1995 Military defies human rights charges.

1998 Hurricane Mitch wreaks havoc.

1999 Appointment of first civilian defense minister.

2002 Ricardo Maduro takes office as president.

HONG KONG Island off the Chinese ceded to Britain in 1842. Further territory on the mainland was aquired in 1860 (the Kowloon peninsula) and 1898 (the New Territories). Hong Kong was returned to Chinese rule in 1997.

CHRONOLOGY

1842 China's defeat by the UK in the Opium war of 1839–42 results in the cession of Hong Kong to the UK under the Treaty of Nanjing.

1860 Defeat in the second Opium war (1856–60) leads to the further cession of Kowloon under the terms of the Peking Convention.

1898 Continued aggression and threats pressure the Qing government to sign the second Peking Convention, granting the 99-year lease of Hong Kong Island, Kowloon, and the New Territories to the UK.

1941–45 The Japanese invade and occupy Hong Kong.

1949 The communist takeover of mainland China halts British plans (begun in 1946) to allow greater autonomy to Hong Kong.

1967 Hong Kong trade is disrupted by civil disturbances created by the influence of the Cultural Revolution in China.

1981 The British Nationality Act, granting British Nationality (Overseas) but not right of abode in the UK to Hong Kong Chinese creates great controversy.

1984 The Sino-British Joint Declaration, produced after two years of negotiations, is signed; grants China sovereignty over Hong Kong after 1997 and control of Hong Kong's foreign and defence policies, while guaranteeing high degree of autonomy in economic affairs and continuation of the present social and legal systems, capitalist economic system and freedom of speech.

1997 Hong Kong handed back to China; as Special Administrative Region of China.

Hong Xiuquan (*var.* Hung Hsui-ch'uan, 1814–64) *see* Taiping Rebellion

Hoover, Herbert Clark (1874–1964) 31st President of the US (Republican, 1929–33). Rose to prominence during World War I for his successful administration of relief activities. His presidency was immediately struck by the Wall Street Crash and the subsequent Great Depression. Though he did institute some relief efforts, he lacked a "common touch" and rapidly lost public support, resulting in his defeat by Franklin D. Roosevelt in his 1933 re-election bid.

Hopewell Culture based in the Scioto River Valley in present-day Ohio, between c.500 BCE and 400 CE. The Hopewell had a rich burial tradition and are known for their conical burial mounds and associated geometric ceremonial earthworks which include the largest burial mound in the US. The best known is the Great Serpent Mound in Ohio, which is 213 m long. The Hopewell are also renowned for their sculptures, often of animals and birds. *p.88*

Hospital of St. John of Jerusalem *see* Knights Hospitaller

Hsia dynasty *see* Xia dynasty

Hsin dynasty *see* Xin dynasty.

Hsuan-tsang *see* Xuan Zang

Hsiung-nu *see* Xiongnu

Huari (c.500–800) Andean state, based in the Ayacucho basin. Militaristic expansion facilitated by the construction of major trunk roads, interspersed with military barracks. The general populace labored on public works as a form of taxation.

Huayna Capac (reigned 1493–1525) Sapa Inca who ascended to the royal throne in 1493 after dynastic struggle for succession. He extended the northern boundary of the Inca Empire to the Ancasmayo River, before dying in an epidemic (which may have been spread by Spanish colonists). His death was followed by another struggle for succession, which was still unresolved when the Spanish arrived in 1532; within three years the Inca empire was lost.

Hudson, Henry (c.1565–1611) English navigator. Appointed by Muscovy Company to find Northwest Passage to Asia, in 1608 he sailed along the coast of Greenland as far as Spitzbergen. In 1609, sponsored by the Dutch East India Company, he attempted to find an eastern route but changed course and sailed to N America where he explored Chesapeake and Delaware Bays. On his last expedition, in 1610, he sailed into the great bay which bears his name and south into James Bay.

Hudson's Bay Company Set up in 1670 to occupy the land around Hudson Bay, and engage in trade. Controlled the fur trade in Canada for nearly two centuries until it lost its charter in 1869. *p.311*

Huerta, Victoriano (1854–1916) Mexican dictator. A general in the Mexican army, Huerta was allied with the liberal president Francisco Madero at the start of the Mexican Revolution in 1910, successfully suppressing armed dissent by Zapata and others. In 1913 he overthrew Madero's regime, violently suppressing dissent. He was forced into exile when the US government withdrew its support.

Hülegü (c.1217–65) Mongol leader. Founder of the Il-Khanate (1258) after he sacked Baghdad and toppled the Abbasid Caliphate, killing the last caliph. Invaded Syria (1260). *p.216*

Humanism Name given to the philosophy of the Renaissance which stressed the value of human reason in the manner of the Ancient Greeks and began to challenge the authority of the traditional teachings of the church. *p.273*

Humboldt, Alexander von (1769–1859) Prussian natural scientist, made a notable journey to S America in 1799–1804.

Huna *see* Huns

Hundred Years' War (1337–1453) Struggle between England and France in the 14th–15th centuries over a series of disputes, stemming from Edward III's claim to the French throne. Notable English victories at Crécy (1346), Poitiers (1356) and Agincourt (1415), amounted to nothing and by 1455 the English crown had lost all its French possessions except Calais. *p.234*

Hungarian Revolt (1956) Demands by students for the withdrawal of Soviet troops led to mass demonstrations. When the deposed Imre Nagy was reinstated as premier, he announced that Hungary was leaving the Warsaw Pact. Soviet forces moved in to crush the revolt, killing 25,000 people. Nagy was executed following a show trial in 1958.

HUNGARY Lying at the heart of central Europe, Hungary is landlocked and has borders with seven states. On several occasions since their arrival in Europe in the 9th century CE, the Magyars have controlled much larger areas of land, but Hungary was unfortunate in the redistribution of Habsburg lands after World War I. Historically, Hungary has been a cosmopolitan cultural center, and during its years of market socialism was more prosperous than the other Eastern Bloc countries. Economic and political reforms have brought it closer to the EU, which it expects to join in the first "wave" of eastward enlargement; Hungary has also become a member of the NATO alliance. In foreign policy it is particularly sensitive about the treatment of Hungarian minorities in neighboring states.

CHRONOLOGY

4th to 6th century CE The central Carpathian basin is successively invaded by Huns and Avars who are then conquered by Charlemagne.

9th century CE The Magyars, a Finno-Ugric people from somewhere beyond the Urals conquer the region.

904 Semi-legendary prince Árpád, leader of the Magyars, founds a dynasty which lasts until 1301.

1001 August 15. Saint Stephen, who unifies the Magyars and completes Hungary's conversion to Christianity, is crowned the first King of Hungary and rules until 1038.

1458–90 The reign of Matthias Hunyadi or Corvinus (after the raven on the family crest) marks the golden age of Hungarian history. Mining of the country's gold, silver and copper deposits makes it one of the richest countries in Europe, while the Italian Renaissance fuels a cultural flowering which results in the foundation of Buda university and the Corvinus library.

1514 A peasant revolt allows the Turks to take control of central Hungary, while the west of the country submits to the Austrian Habsburg Ferdinand and in the east Transylvania is ruled by the elected John Szapolyai who rules until 1540. There are tensions between Catholic "royal Hungary" and Transylvania, where freedom of worship for both Catholics and Lutherans is guaranteed by the 1558 Diet of Torda. These are especially great at the time of the Thirty Years' War (1618–48).

1699 The Treaty of Karlowitz confirms the expulsion of the Turks, whom the Austrians and allies have progressively beaten back following the unsuccessful siege of Vienna in 1683 and the unification of Hungary under the Habsburgs.

1703 In Transylvania Ferenc II Rakoczi leads a revolt, but this is crushed by the Austrians, whose rule is confirmed in the Peace of Szatmar of 1711.

1780 Emperor Joseph II, who rules until 1790, attempts reforms, including the abolition of serfdom, but is thwarted by the Hungarian aristocracy. The Hungarian language becomes officially recognized, first in education (instead of Latin) in 1792 and by 1844 as the official language for administrative purposes. Hungarian literature and sciences contribute to the flowering of Romanticism in Europe and to a growing Hungarian nationalism.

1848 A revolution, one of a wave that sweeps across Europe in 1848, forces Emperor Ferdinand to make government accountable to parliament. Nationalist grievances lead to civil war.

1849 A new King, Franz-Joseph, is deposed and Lajos Kossuth, one of the leaders of the revolution, is declared provisional governor. Austria appeals to Russia for assistance. Some 200,000 Russian troops crush the revolt. Kossuth flees the country.

1861 The Hungarian Diet demands equality between Austria and Hungary.

1867 A dual monarchy of Austria-Hungary is created after Austria's defeat the previous year in a war against Prussia. Count Gyula Andrassy becomes the first Hungarian Prime Minister.

1914 Austria-Hungary joins the Central Powers after the murder of the Austrian Archduke Franz Ferdinand in Sarajevo.

1918 Hungarian Republic created as successor state to Austria-Hungary.

1919 Béla Kún leads short-lived communist government. Romania intervenes militarily and hands power to Admiral Horthy.

1938–1941 Hungary gains territory from Czechoslovakia, Yugoslavia, and Romania in return for supporting Nazi Germany.

1941 Hungary drawn into World War II on Axis side when Hitler attacks Soviet Union.

1944 Nazi Germany preempts Soviet advance on Hungary by invading. Deportation of Hungarian Jews and Roma to extermination camps begins. Soviet Red Army enters in October. Horthy forced to resign.

1945 Liberated by Red Army. Soviet-formed provisional government installed. Imre Nagy introduces land reform.

1947 Communists emerge as largest party in second postwar election.

1949 New constitution; formally becomes People's Republic.

1950–1951 First Secretary Mátyás Rákosi uses authoritarian powers to collectivize agriculture and industrialize the economy.

1953 Imre Nagy, Rákosi's rival, becomes premier and reduces political terror.

1955 Nagy deposed by Rákosi.

1956 Rákosi out. Student demonstrations, demanding withdrawal of Soviet troops, become popular uprising. Nagy appointed premier and János Kádár First Secretary. Nagy announces Hungary will leave Warsaw Pact. Soviet forces suppress protests; 25,000 killed. Kádár becomes premier.

1958 Nagy executed.

1968 Kádár introduces "New Economic Mechanism" to bring market elements to socialism.

1986 Police suppress commemoration of 1956 uprising. Democratic opposition demands Kádár resign.

1987 Party reformers establish MDF as a political movement.

1988 Kádár ousted. Protests force suspension of plans for Nagymaros Dam on the Danube.

1989 End of one-party state as parliament votes to allow independent parties. Posthumous rehabilitation of Nagy, who is given state funeral. Round table talks between HSWP and opposition.

1990 József Antall's MDF wins multiparty elections. Speed of economic reform hotly debated. Árpád Göncz president.

1991 Warsaw Pact dissolved. Last Soviet troops leave Hungary.

1994 Hungary joins NATO's Partnership for Peace program. Former communist MSzP wins general election. Austerity program prompts protests.

1998 EU entry negotiations open. Elections; Viktor Orbán (Fidesz-MPP) forms right-of-center coalition.

1999 Joins NATO. Airspace used in NATO bombing of Yugoslavia.

2000 Ferenc Mádl succeeds Göncz as president.

2002 Socialist and free democrat alliance win elections. Medgyessy prime minister.

2004 Joins EU. Medgyessy resigns.

Hung Hsui-ch'uan *see* Taiping Rebellion

Hung-wu *see* Zhu Yuanzhang

Huns Coalition of steppe cavalry who moved east across C Asia in the late 4th century CE. The Black Huns under Attila invaded the Roman Empire in mid-5th century; defeated at the Catalaunian Fields in Gaul (451), thereafter breaking up. The Huna (White Huns or Hephthalites) invaded Gupta India (480 CE) and Sassanian Persia (484 CE). *See also* Xiongnu. *p.96*

hunter-gatherers (*aka* foragers or band societies) Communities living on a combination of hunting animals and gathering food. At the start of the Mesolithic period the global population lived this way; amongst the tiny percentage of the world's population who do so today, men hunt exclusively and women gather.

Hunyadi, János (c.1387–1456) Hungarian national hero. Won a series of victories against the Turks, but was defeated at Varna (1444). Regent of Hungary (1446–52). His victory at Belgrade (1456) stemmed the Turkish invasion of Hungary for 70 years.

Huron North American Indian people from the St. Lawrence River region, who gave French expeditions, led by Cartier and Champlain (1543, 1603), a friendly reception. At the end of the 16th century, the Iroquois drove many Huron westward into Ontario, where they formed a confederacy with a number of other tribes. In 1648–50 Iroquois invasions broke up the confederacy, leading to the death of many thousands of Hurons.

Hus, Jan (*var.* John Huss, c.1369–1415) Bohemian religious reformer. His preaching against clerical privilege led to his excommunication (1411). In 1413 he published his main work, *e Ecclesia*. Tried and condemned for heresy. His death by burning provoked the Hussite Wars. *p.255*

Husaynid dynasty Ruling dynasty of Tunisia from 1705 until the foundation of the Republic of Tunisia in 1957.

Husky Code name for the Allied invasion of Sicily in July 1943 during World War II.

Huss, John *see* Hus, Jan

Hussein, Saddam (1937–) Iraqi dictator. Joined the Arab Ba'ath Socialist Party in 1957. He played a leading role in the 1968 revolution which ousted the civilian government and established a Revolutionary Command Council (RCC). In 1979 he became President of Iraq. His attack on Iran in 1980 led to a war of attrition which lasted eight years. His invasion of Kuwait in Aug 1990 plunged Iraq into another full-scale war. Though Iraq lost the war, was forced to retreat from Kuwait, and is suffering from heavy economic sanctions imposed by the UN, Saddam continues to hold power. *See* Iran-Iraq War; Gulf War

Hussites Followers of the Bohemian religious reformer Jan Hus.

Hutu (*var.* Bahutu, Wahutu) Bantu-speaking people of Rwanda and Burundi. Hutu extremists were responsible for a terrifying massacre of rival Tutsis in Rwanda in 1994.

Hyksos After the Middle Kingdom in Egypt the Hyksos, or "Shepherd Kings" founded the 15th dynasty c.1670 BCE. They were nomads from the deserts of Palestine, who ruled Lower and parts of Upper Egypt until c.1550 BCE. Although credited with the introduction of the horse and chariot, in most other areas they appear to have deferred to native Egyptian culture.

I dynasty *see* Yi dynasty

Ibarro, Francisco de 16th-century Spanish governor of the Mexican province of Nuevo Viscaya. The city of Durango, founded under his direction in 1563, was named after a city in his native province of Spain.

Iberia *see* Spain, Portugal

Ibn Al-mansur Al-'Abbas *see* al-Rashid, Harun

Ibn Battuta (*var.* Muhammad Ibn Abdullah, 1304–68) Muslim traveler and writer. Leaving Tangier in 1325 he traveled along the north coast of Africa to Egypt, then north to Damascus. After a pilgrimage to Mecca, he undertook several journeys in Africa and W Asia, then traveled east along the Silk Road to Delhi, and from there to Sumatra and China.

Ibn Muhammad al-Mahdi *see* Harun al-Rashid

Ibn Saud *see* Saud, Abd al-Aziz ibn

Ibn Tughluq, Muhammad *see* Tughluqs

Ibn Tulun, Ahmad (reigned 868–883) The stepson of a Turkish general, who was given the fiefdom of Egypt in 868, was sent to Egypt by his stepfather as lieutenant. Between 868 and 875 he built up a substantial power base in Egypt, founding a new city outside Cairo, embarking on a massive building program and, in 875, refusing to send tribute to Baghdad. In 878 Ibn Tulun obtained the submission of the chief cities of Syria, leading to open rupture with the Caliph of Baghdad and the founding of the Tulunid dynasty. *p.144*

ICBM *see* intercontinental ballistic missile

Ice Ages Periods of extreme cold in the earth's history. Effects of the last Ice Age include falls in sea levels, which occurred when water was locked in glaciers and the creation of land bridges, which helped humans and animals to colonize new parts of the globe. The last Ice Age reached its peak about 20,000 years ago, and ended about 10,000 years ago.

ICELAND Europe's westernmost country, Iceland has a strategic location in the North Atlantic, just south of the Arctic Circle. Its position, on the rift where the North American and European continental plates are pulling apart, accounts for its 200 volcanoes and its many geysers and solfataras. Previously a Danish possession, Iceland became fully independent in 1944. Most settlements are along the coast, where ports remain ice-free in winter.

CHRONOLOGY

874 CE Iceland is settled by Vikings of Norwegian origin.

930 CE The Althing, the world's oldest sovereign parliament, is founded.

12th and 13th centuries The great Icelandic sagas are written commemorating the exploits of the island's warriors.

1262 Iceland, until then an independent commonwealth, declares allegiance to Norway.

1380 Iceland comes under Danish rule when the Norwegian crown is united with that of Denmark. The union is confirmed in the 1397 Union of Kalmar.

1662 Iceland accepts the authority of the absolutist monarchy in Denmark.

1800 The Althing, which has faded into insignificance under the Danish monarchy, ceases to exist.

1814 In the Treaty of Kiel at the end of the Napoleonic wars Iceland is confirmed as under control of the Danish crown although Norway is ceded to Sweden.

1843 The Althing is reconstituted as a consultative assembly and, once constitutional monarchy is introduced in Denmark in 1849, pressure grows for the introduction of a constitution for Iceland.

1874 King Christian IX promulgates an Icelandic constitution, granting limited home rule.

1915 Universal suffrage is introduced.

1918 The Act of Union establishes internal home rule under the Danish crown, which continues to control defense and foreign policy matters.

1940–1945 Occupied by UK and USA.

1944 Independence as republic.

1949 Founder member of NATO.

1951 US air base built at Keflavík despite strong local opposition.

1972–1976 Extends fishing limits to 50 miles; two "cod wars" with UK.

1975 Sets 200–mile fishing limit.

1980 Vigdís Finnbogadóttir world's first elected woman head of state.

1985 Declares nuclear-free status.

1995–1999 Formation of center-right coalition under David Oddsson after general election; reelected in 1999.

I-ching *see* Yijing

Icons Russian religious icons of the Middle Ages. *p.255*

Idrisi, ash Sharif al- (*var.* Abu Abd Allah Muhammad al, c.1099–1165) Arab geographer born in Spain. After traveling in Spain, N Africa and Asia Minor, in c.1148 he joined the court of Roger II of Sicily. There he collated surveys of the known world, incorporating them into *The Book of Roger*, completed in 1154. He also compiled a seventy-part world map.

Ieyasu *see* Tokugawa Ieyasu

Ife Yoruba culture that flourished in SW Nigeria (11th–15th centuries CE). Noted for its terra-cotta and bronze heads. *p.194*

Igbo-Ukwu A small kingdom in the forests of southern Nigeria (8th–9th centuries CE). Evidence from burials indicate that the peoples of Igbo-Ukwu were connected with the long-distance trade networks of the Sahara and Sahel. Carnelian, found in the burial of a dignitary, may even have come from Persia or India. Bronzes, believed to be the burial objects of a religious leader or ruler, indicate that metal-working had developed to a fine art.

Ignatius Loyola, St. (1491–1556) Spanish-born founder of Jesuits. *See also* Jesuits

Il-Khanate (1256–1353) Mongol dynasty founded by Hülegü, who seized Persia in 1258 and captured Baghdad. Contact with the Mongol rulers of China was lost after the Il-Khan Ghazan (1255–1304) converted to Sunni Islam; conflict between Sunnis and Shi'a fatally weakened the dynasty.

Ikhnaton *see* Akhenaton

Illinois River River of North America, explored by Jolliet and Marquette in 1673.

Imhotep (*fl.* 2680 BCE) Egyptian chancellor, architect, writer, physician, and high priest of the sun god in Heliopolis during the reign of Zoser (3rd dynasty). He was the architect of the Step pyramid at Saqqara; his innovative genius was to translate building techniques which had hitherto only been used on wooden structures into quarried stone. He was deified during Ptolemaic times.

Impressionism Dominant artistic movement, especially in France, in the late 19th century. *p.372*

Inca empire (c.1470–1532) Empire which became the preeminent state in S America from c.1470, when it began to conquer neighboring peoples, to 1532 when it fell into the hands of Spanish *conquistadores*. Following Andean tradition, the Inca Empire was expanded by military conquest, ruled by the Sapa Inca (believed to descend from the Sun God). It was a strictly hierarchical society, dependent on the mass organization of labor, for the construction of roads, towns, mining, and agriculture. It had no writing system, and its administration was entirely dependent on an arithmetic system. *p.244, p.268*

Inca Yupanqui *see* Topa

INDIA Separated from the rest of Asia by the Himalaya mountain range, India forms a subcontinent. As well as the Himalayas, there are two other main geographical regions, the Indo-Gangetic plain, which lies between the foothills of the Himalayas and the Vindhya Mountains, and the central-southern plateau. The fertility of India, due to regular annual rainfall of the monsoon, has attracted many foreign invaders over the centuries. Many Islamic invaders from C Asia were drawn to the riches of N India: from Mahmud of Ghazni in the late 10th century to Babur, founder of the Mughal empire, in 1526. The most recent invaders were the British who gradually took over the whole of India in the 19th century, ruling until independence in 1947.

Today India is the world's largest democracy and second most populous country after China. The birthrate has recently been falling, but even at its current level India's population will probably overtake China's by 2030. After years of protectionism, India is opening up its economy to the outside world. The hope is that the free market will go some way to alleviating one of the country's major problems, poverty.

CHRONOLOGY

2500 BCE Emergence of Indus civilization.

1500 BCE Aryan invaders destroy Indus civilization and introduce Hinduism. Vedic age develops Brahmanic caste system.

320–185 BCE The Mauryan empire unifies most of India and establishes Buddhism as the state religion.

320 CE Foundation of the Gupta dynasty and the institution of the "classical age."

500 CE The arrival of the Huns and the overthrow of the Guptas.

674 CE Muslim conquest reaches river Indus.

1192–1398 The Muslim Delhi Sultanate is established in the Indo-Gangetic plain of north India.

1526 The establishment of the Mughal empire which reaches its peak during the reign of the Emperor Akbar (1556–1605).

1707 The death of the Mughal emperor Aurangzeb and the onset of Mughal decline.

1757 British victory in Bengal heralds consolidation of British power in India.

1857 Indian revolt or "Sepoy Mutiny" seeks to resist British rule.

1858 Formal dissolution of Mughal empire and the assumption of direct control by Britain.

1876 Queen Victoria is proclaimed Empress of India.

1885 Formation of Indian National Congress.

1919 Act of parliament introduces "responsible government."

◄

1920–1922 Mahatma Gandhi's first civil disobedience campaign.

1935 Government of India Act grants autonomy to provinces.

1936 First elections under new constitution.

1942–1943 "Quit India" movement.

1947 August. Independence and partition into India and Pakistan. Jawarhalal Nehru becomes first prime minister.

1948 Assassination of Mahatma Gandhi. War with Pakistan over Kashmir. India becomes a republic.

1951–1952 First general election won by Congress party.

1957 Congress party reelected. First elected communist state government installed in Kerala.

1960 Bombay divided into states of Gujarat and Maharashtra.

1962 Congress party reelected. Border war with China.

1964 Death of Nehru. Lal Bahadur Shastri becomes prime minister.

1965 Second war with Pakistan over Kashmir.

1966 Shastri dies; Indira Gandhi (daughter of Nehru) becomes prime minister.

1969 Congress party splits into two factions; larger faction led by Indira Gandhi.

1971 Indira Gandhi's Congress party wins elections. Third war with Pakistan, over creation of Bangladesh.

1972 Simla (peace) Agreement signed with Pakistan.

1974 Explosion of first nuclear device in underground test.

1975–1977 Imposition of state of emergency.

1977 Congress loses general election. People's Party (JD) takes power.

1978 New political group, Congress (Indira) – C(I) – formally established.

1980 Indira Gandhi's C(I) wins general election.

1984 Indian troops storm Sikh Golden Temple in Amritsar. Assassination of Indira Gandhi by Sikh bodyguard; her son Rajiv becomes prime minister and C(I) leader. Gas explosion at US-owned Union Carbide Corporation plant in Bhopal kills 2000 people in India's worst industrial disaster.

1985 Peace accords with militant separatists in Assam and Punjab.

1987 Deployment of Indian peacekeeping force in Sri Lanka to combat Tamil Tigers.

1989 General election; National Front forms minority government with BJP support. Congress (Indira) party implicated in Bofors scandal.

1990 Withdrawal of peacekeeping force from Sri Lanka. BJP leader Lal Advani arrested.

1991 C(I) withdraws from coalition government. Rajiv Gandhi assassinated during ensuing election campaign; Narasimha Rao becomes prime minister of a C(I) minority government. Program of economic liberalization initiated.

1992 Demolition of Babri Masjid mosque at Ayodhya by Hindu extremists triggers widespread violence; 1200 people die.

1993 Resurgence of Hindu-Muslim riots. Bomb explosions in Bombay (Mumbai). Border troop agreement with China.

1994 Rupee made fully convertible. C(I) routed in key state elections amid increasing allegations of corruption in ruling party. Outbreak of pneumonic plague.

1995 Punjab chief minister assassinated by Sikh extremists.

1996 Corruption scandal triggers political crisis. C(I) suffers its worst electoral defeat. Hindu nationalist BJP fails to win vote of confidence; leftist United Front coalition government takes office.

1997 Successive governments fall as C(I) withdraws support.

1998 General election; BJP led by Atal Bihari Vajpayee forms coalition government. Sonia Gandhi, widow of Rajiv Gandhi, becomes president of C(I). India detonates nuclear bomb.

1999 Vajpayee travels to Pakistan to inaugurate bus service between India and Pakistan. India and Pakistan test nuclear missiles, and engage in violent confrontation in Kashmir. BJP returned to power after elections triggered by vote of no confidence.

2001 Earthquake kills more than 25,000 people in Gujarat. BJP government implicated in major bribery scandal centering on illegal arms sales. July. Talks in Agra between Vajpayee and President Musharraf of Pakistan.

2002 Fresh crisis over Kashmir, as Indian government accuses Pakistan of direct responsibilty for terrorist attacks by Kashmiri separatists.

2003 Heatwave kills over 1400.

2004 C(I) wins elections; Manmohan Singh appointed prime minister.

BRITISH GOVERNORS-GENERAL OF INDIA (1774–1858)

1774–1785	Warren Hastings
1785–1786	Sir John MacPherson (acting)
1786–1793	Lord Cornwallis (General Charles Mann Cornwallis, Marquis of Cornwallis)
1793–1798	Sir John Shore (Baron Teignmouth)
1798–1805	Lord Wellesley (Richard Colley Wellesley, Baron Wellesley; later Marquess Wellesley)
1805	Lord Cornwallis
1805–1807	Sir George Hilario Barlow acting)
1807–1813	Lord Minto (Baron Gilbert Elliot-Murray-Kynynmound Minto)
1813–1823	Francis Rawdon-Hastings (Earl of Moira; later, marquess of Hastings)
1823	John Adam (acting)
1823–1828	Baron William Pitt Amherst (later, Earl Amherst
1828	William Butterworth Bayley (acting)
1828–1835	Lord Bentinck (William Henry Cavendish-Bentinck)
1835–1836	Sir Charles Theophilus Metcalfe (acting)
1836–1842	George Eden, Earl of Auckland
1842–1844	Edward Law, Earl of Ellenborough
1844	William W Bird (acting)
1844–1848	Henry Hardinge, Viscount Hardinge
1848–1856	James Andrew Broun Ramsay, Earl of Dalhousie
1856–1858	Charles John Canning, Viscount Canning

BRITISH VICEROYS OF INDIA (1858–1950)

1858–1862	Charles John Canning, Viscount Canning
1862–1863	James Bruce, Earl of Elgin
1863	Sir Robert Cornelius Napier (acting)
1863–1864	Sir William Thomas Denison (acting)
1864–1869	Sir John Laird Mair Lawrence
1869–1872	Richard Southwell Bourke, Earl of Mayo
1872	Sir John Strachey (acting)

1872	Francis Napier, Baron of Ettrick (acting)
1872–1876	Thomas George Baring, Viscount Baring of Lee (Earl Northbrook)
1876–1880	Robert Bulwer-Lytton, Baron of Lytton
1880–1884	George Frederick Samuel Robinson, Marquess of Rippon
1884–1888	Frederick Hamilton-Temple-Blackwood, Earl of Dufferin
1888–1894	Henry Petty-Fitzmaurice, Marquess of Lansdowne
1894–1899	Victor Alexander Bruce, Earl of Elgin
1899–1905	George Nathaniel Curzon
1905–1910	Gilbert Elliot-Murray-Kynynmound, Earl of Minto
1910–1916	Charles Hardinge, Baron Hardinge of Penhurst
1916–1921	Frederic John Napier Thesiger, Baron Chelmsford
1921–1925	Rufus Daniel Isaacs, Baron Reading of Erleigh
1925–1926	Victor Alexander George Robert Bulwer-Lytton, Earl of Lytton
1926–1929	Edward Frederick Lindley Wood, Baron Irwin (Lord Halifax)
1929–1931	George Joachim Goschen, Viscount Goschen of Hawkhurst
1931–1936	George Freeman Freeman-Thomas, Earl of Willingdon
1936–1943	Victor Alexander John Hope, Marquess of Linlithgow
1943–1947	Archibald Percival Wavell, Viscount Wavell
1947	Louis Francis Mountbatten, Viscount Mountbatten of Burma
	Governors-General of India (after Independence)
1947–1948	Louis Francis Mountbatten, Earl Mountbatten of Burma
1948–1950	Chakravarthi Rajagopalachari

PRESIDENTS OF INDIA (from 1950)

1950–1962	Rajendra Prasad
1962–1967	Sarvepalli Radhakrishnan
1967–1969	Zakir Husain
1969	V. V. Giri (acting)
1969	Mohammed Hidayatullah (acting)
1969–1974	V. V. Giri
1974–1977	Fakhruddin Ali Ahmed
1977	B. D. Jatti (acting)
1977–1982	N. Sanjeeva Reddy
1982–1987	Zail Singh
1987–1992	R. Venkataraman
1992–1997	Shankar Dayal Sharma
1997–	K. R. Narayanan

PRIME MINISTERS OF INDIA (from 1947)

1947–1964	Jawaharlal Nehru
1964	Gulzari Lal Nanda (interim)
1964–1966	Lal Bahadur Shastri
1966	Gulzari Lal Nanda (interim)
1966–1977	Indira Gandhi
1977–1979	Morarji Desai
1979–1980	Charan Singh
1980–1984	Indira Gandhi
1984–1989	Rajiv Gandhi
1989–1990	Vishwanath Pratap Singh
1990–1991	Chandra Shekhar
1991–1996	P. V. Narasimha Rao
1996	Atal Bihari Vajpayee
1996–1997	H. D. Deve Gowda
1997–1998	Inder Kumar Gujral
1998–	Atal Bihari Vajpayee
2004	Manmohan Singh

Indian Mutiny *See* Indian Revolt

Indian National Congress Founded in 1885, the party was transformed into a mass movement for Indian independence by Mahatma Gandhi who instituted mass non-cooperations during the 1930s.

Indian Removal Act (May 28 1830) Act authorizing the granting of western territory to Indian tribes of E and SE USA in exchange for their lands which fell within state borders, in order to provide new lands for white settlers. Though a number of northern tribes relocated peacefully, a number of the SE groups put up substantial resistance to their removal from their settled farms to unknown western territory.

Indian Revolt (*var.* the Indian Mutiny, 1857–59) The revolt of 1857–59 was the result of disaffection within the ranks of the East India Company's Bengal army, combined with an attempt by nobles and landowners to throw off the imperial yoke. The revolt started with the seizure of Delhi by rebels (May 1857). The city was subsequently recaptured in September. The massacre of British evacuees at Cawnpore (Jun 27 1857) raised a storm of anger. The British re-taking of Lucknow (Mar 22 1858) after a siege was a decisive turning-point. A campaign in central India (Feb–Jun 1858) effectively put an end to the revolt, although it smouldered for many months. In 1858, the government of India was transferred from the East India Company to the British crown.

Indian Wars Name given to the series of conflicts (1860–90) in the US that crushed native American resistance to the juggernaut of industrial progress. *p.374*

Indies, Council of (*var.* Consejo de Indias) Supreme governing body of Spain's territories in America (1524–1834) which was responsible for all legislation governing the colonies in the king's name.

Indo-Pakistan wars In 1948, war broke out between India and Pakistan over the Muslim-majority state of Kashmir, whose Hindu ruler had ceded to India. In 1949 the UN negotiated a ceasefire which effectively divided Kashmir between the two countries, but left the issue unresolved. In Aug 1965 war once again broke out, when the Indian army repelled Pakistan's forces and launched a counterattack. Soviet mediation led to the conclusion of a peace treaty at Tashkent (Jan 1966). Kashmir remains a major flashpoint between India and Pakistan.

INDONESIA The world's largest archipelago, Indonesia's islands stretch 5000 km (3100 miles) eastward across the Pacific, from the Malay Peninsula to New Guinea. Sumatra, Java, Kalimantan, Irian Jaya, and Sulawesi are mountainous, volcanic, and forested. Indonesia, formerly the Dutch East Indies, achieved independence in 1949. Politics was dominated by the military for over three decades, until the fall of the Suharto regime in 1998, when a partial "civilianization" began. In outlying regions, the forcibly suppressed demands for greater autonomy have flared up, bringing renewed violence. Indonesian militias ravaged East Timor after its independence vote in 1999.

CHRONOLOGY

1st century CE The peoples of the Indonesian archipelago first come into contact with the Hindu-Buddhist culture of India.

7th century CE The Buddhist, Sumatra-based Sri-Vijaya empire emerges as the earliest known Indonesian kingdom; it subsequently extends from Sumatra over Malaya and southern Thailand.

12th century Islam begins its penetration of Indonesia.

1293 The Sri-Vijaya empire is succeeded by the Hindu-Buddhist Java-based Majapahit empire, which controls much of the archipelago until the mid-15th century.

14th century Small Islamic principalities begin to emerge along the sea-lanes and coastal areas.

16th century The first European intrusion occurs in the early 16th century when Portuguese traders gain control of the Moluccan clove trade.

1602 The Dutch United East India Company (VOC) is formed under a charter issued by the Dutch parliament and quickly establishes a monopoly over the regional spice trade.

1799 The VOC charter expires and the Dutch government takes control of the archipelago.

1825–30 The "Java Wars" are the first unsuccessful indigenous rebellion against Dutch rule.

1830 The Dutch implement the notorious "Culture System" which entailed the forced cultivation of commercial crops for export, seriously distorting indigenous economies.

1901 The Dutch introduce a new "Ethical Policy" aimed at providing limited educational and administrative opportunities for indigenous population.

1910 Dutch expansion to the Outer Islands is completed; all of present-day Indonesia is under Dutch control.

1930s Dutch repress nationalists.

1942–1945 Japanese occupation. Sukarno works with Japanese while promoting independence.

1945 Declaration of independence.

1945–1949 Nationalist guerrilla war.

1949 Dutch grant independence under President Sukarno.

1957–1959 Sukarno introduces authoritarian "Guided Democracy."

1962 Dutch relinquish Irian Jaya.

1965 Communist PKI alliance with military ends. Army led by General Suharto crushes abortive coup and acts to eliminate PKI.

1966 Sukarno hands over power to General Suharto.

1968 Suharto becomes president.

1975 Invasion of East Timor; becomes 27th province in 1976.

1984 Muslim protests in Jakarta trigger Islamic movement.

1989 Unrest in Java and Sumbawa.

1991 Indonesian troops massacre pro-independence demonstrators in East Timor.

1996 Anti-government demonstrations in Jakarta.

1997 Economic recession. Smog across region from forest fires.

1998 Suharto resigns amid unrest.

1999 Election victory for opposition led by Megawati Sukarnoputri. East Timor referendum backing independence triggers violent backlash. UN appoints transitional authority. Abdurrahman Wahid elected president, Megawati named vice president.

2001 Wahid removed, replaced by Megawati.

2002 Autonomy officially granted to Ppua. Attack in Bali kills over 200 holidaymakers.

2003 Offensive against Aceh separatists.

2004 Gen. Yudhoyono elected president.

Indus Valley civilization
see Harappan culture

Industrial Revolution The transition from a primarily agricultural to an industrial economy, which had begun in Great Britain by 1750, with the striking expansion and greater efficiency of certain key industries: textiles and mining. In the late 18th century, a series of inventions and innovations, notably the steam engine, greatly increased output, and small workshops began to be replaced by large factories. Industrialization soon spread to other parts of Europe, especially areas, such as northern France, Belgium, and the Ruhr valley, with extensive coal deposits, and to the US, which by 1890, thanks to rich natural resources, a growing population, and technological innovations had become the world's leading industrial nation. *p.334, p.351*

Innocent III (*prev. It.* Lotario de'Conti di Segni, 1160–1216) Pope (reigned 1198–1216) whose pontificate saw the apogee of medieval papal power, the Latin conquest of Constantinople in the Fourth Crusade, and the legitimization of itinerant preaching and apostolic poverty. *p.206*

Intercontinental ballistic missile (ICBM) Key land and/or submarine-launched deterrent weapon initially developed by the Western Allies during the Cold War, but built in proliferation by both Western and Eastern bloc superpowers by 1970s.

Internet International computer network. Initially set up to link universities and other educational institutions, in the 1980s it became a world-wide information network, used increasingly in business as both a sales and a communications channel. *p.451*

Inuit Inupiaq-speaking peoples native to the far north of Canada, with an ancient hunting and gathering culture stretching back to perhaps 30,000 years ago.

Ipsus ⚔ (301 BCE) between successors to the empire of Alexander the Great. Antigonus defeated by allied forces of Seleucus and Lysimachus.

Iran-Iraq War (1980–88) Conflict between Iran and Iraq caused by a dispute over territory, and Iraq's fear of Iranian provocation of its own Shi'ite population following Iran's Islamic Revolution in 1979. In 1980, Iraq invaded Iran. By the time the war reached an inconclusive end, an estimated half a million lives had been lost on both sides.

IRAN Iran is surrounded by turbulent neighbors, with republics of the former Soviet Union to the north, Afghanistan and Pakistan to the east, and Iraq and Turkey to the west. The south faces the Persian Gulf and the Gulf of Oman. Since 1979, when a revolution led by Ayatollah Khomeini deposed the shah, Iran has become the world's largest theocracy and the leading center for militant Shi'a Islam. Iran's active support for Islamic fundamentalist movements has led to strained relations with central Asian, Middle Eastern, and north African states, as well as the US and western Europe.

CHRONOLOGY

533 BCE Cyrus the Great unites the Medes and Persians to form the first great Persian empire, which is ruled by the Achaemenid dynasty and is conquered by Alexander of Macedon (Alexander the Great) in 331 BCE.

637–641 CE The Sassanian Empire, founded in 22 CE, is conquered by Muslim Arabs and divided up.

1502 The Safavid Empire is founded by Ismail Safavi, and Persia again becomes a political entity.

1779 Rise of the Qajar dynasty which remains in control until 1926.

1814 The Treaty of Tehran is concluded with Great Britain to protect Persian territories from unprovoked aggression.

1890 A tobacco monopoly is granted to a British subject and this causes widespread strikes and riots.

1906 After demands for reform a constitution is approved and a Constituent National Assembly (or Majlis) created.

1908 The Anglo-Persian Oil Company is founded.

1920 Bolshevik forces enter the Caspian province of Gilan, in support of a rebellion. Separatist movements emerge in various parts of Persia.

1921 Reza Khan, leader of the Persian Cossack Brigade, seizes power and a treaty is signed with Soviet Russia. This paves way for the withdrawal of the Bolshevik forces.

1922 Four major regions (Gilan, Khurasan, Azerbaijan and Kurdistan) are restored to central control.

1926 Reza Khan becomes shah and establishes the Pahlavi dynasty. He embarks on a major reform program of modernization and Westernization, but becomes increasingly reliant on Germany for support. In 1935 he changes the country's name from Persia to Iran.

1941 The United Kingdom and the Soviet Union invade Iran and in September the Shah is forced to abdicate in favor of his son, Muhammad Reza Shah.

1957 SAVAK, shah's secret police, established to control opposition.

1964 Ayatollah Khomeini is exiled to Iraq for criticizing secular state.

1971 Shah celebrates 2500th anniversary of Persian monarchy.

1975 Agreement with Iraq over Shatt al 'Arab waterway.

1977 Khomeini's son dies. Anti-shah demonstrations during mourning.

1978 Riots; Khomeini settles in Paris.

1979 Shah goes into exile. Ayatollah Khomeini returns from exile in France and declares an Islamic republic. Students seize 63 hostages at US embassy in Tehran.

1980 Shah dies in exile. Start of eight-year Iran-Iraq war.

1981 US hostages released. Hojatoleslam Ali Khamenei elected president.

1985 Khamenei reelected.

1987 275 pilgrims killed in riots in Mecca.

1988 USS *Vincennes* shoots down Iranian airliner; 290 killed. End of Iran–Iraq war.

1989 Khomeini issues *fatwa* condemning Salman Rushdie to death for blasphemy. Khomeini dies. President Ali Khamenei appointed Supreme Religious Leader. Hashemi Rafsanjani elected president.

1990 Earthquake in northern Iran kills 45,000 people.

1992 Majlis elections.

1993 Rafsanjani reelected president.

1995 Imposition of US sanctions.

1996 Majlis elections. Society for Combatant Clergy loses ground to more liberal Servants of Iran's Construction.

1997 Earthquake south of Mashhad kills 1500 people. Mohammad Khatami elected president.

1998 Khatami government dissociates itself from *fatwa* against Salman Rushdie.

1999 First nationwide local elections since 1979. President Khatami visits Italy – first Iranian leader to be welcomed by a Western government since 1979.

2000 Election victory for reformists. Crackdown on reformist newspapers.

2001 Khatami reelected, winning 77 percent of vote.

2003 Bam earthquake kills over 40,000.

2004 Conservatives win election.

IRAQ Oil-rich Iraq, divided by the Euphrates and Tigris rivers, shares borders with Iran, Turkey, Syria, Jordan, Saudi Arabia, and Kuwait. The Euphrates valley is fertile, but most of the country is desert or mountains. Iraq was the site of the ancient civilization of Babylon. Its capital Baghdad was the center of the the Arab world under the Abbasid Caliphate from the 8th century CE, but the great city was razed to the ground by the Mongols in 1257.

The modern state of Iraq was created after World War I when the old Ottoman empire was broken up. Iraq was first placed under a British mandate, then became an independent kingdom in 1932. After the removal of the monarchy in 1958, it experienced domestic political turmoil. Despite Iraq's defeat in the 1991 Gulf War, the current regime (in place since 1979) retains power – through repression.

CHRONOLOGY

539–538 BCE The Persians seize Babylon.

334–327 BCE Alexander the Great conquers Iraq.

637 CE The Arab Muslims take over Iraq at the battle of Jalula.

10th-11th century Baghdad falls to the Shi'ite Buwaihids.

11th century The Seljuks dominate Iraq.

1534 The Ottoman Sultan Suleyman conquers Baghdad.

1914 Basra is captured by British troops.

1917 British troops capture Baghdad.

1920 Arabs revolt against British Mandate.

1921 Amir Faisal Ibn Hussein accedes to the throne as King of Baghdad.

1922 An Anglo-Iraqi Treaty is signed. It guarantees the UK special interests in exchange for the establishment of a constituent assembly.

1930 The Anglo-Iraqi Treaty grants Iraq independence from the United Kingdom.

1932 The King formally proclaims Iraq an independent and sovereign state.

1948 Iraqi troops are sent to Israel to fight in the Arab-Israeli war.

1958 King Faisal II and the Crown Prince of Iraq are killed in a coup and Brig. Abd-Al-Karim Kassem becomes president.

1961 Start of Kurdish rebellion. Iraq claims sovereignty over Kuwait on the eve of Kuwait's independence.

1963 Kassem overthrown. Colonel Abd as-Salem Muhammad Aref takes power. Kuwait's sovereignty recognized.

1966 Aref is succeeded by his brother, Abd ar-Rahman.

1968 Ba'athists under Ahmad Hassan al-Bakr take power.

1970 Revolutionary Command Council agrees manifesto on Kurdish autonomy.

1972 Nationalization of Western-controlled Iraq Petroleum Company.

1978 Iraq and Syria form economic and political union.

1979 Saddam Hussein replaces al-Bakr as president.

▶

1980 Outbreak of Iraq-Iran war.

1982 Shi'a leader Mohammed Baqir al-Hakim, exiled in Tehran, forms Supreme Council of the Islamic Revolution in Iraq.

1988 Iraq and Iran agree cease-fire. Iraqi chemical weapons attack on Kurdish village.

1990 Iraq and Iran restore diplomatic relations. Iraq invades Kuwait. UN imposes trade sanctions.

1991 Gulf War. US-led military coalition defeats Iraq and liberates Kuwait. Iraqi regime suppresses Shi'a rebellion.

1992 Western powers proclaim air exclusion zone over southern Iraq.

1993 Attempts to recover equipment from Kuwait provoke Western air attacks.

1994 Outbreak of Kurdish civil war. Iraq recognizes Kuwaiti sovereignty.

1995 Government minister Gen. Hussein Kamil defects to Jordan, and is murdered on his return to Iraq in January 1996.

1996 Elections won by ruling Ba'ath Party. UN supervises limited sales of Iraq oil to purchase humanitarian supplies.

1998–1999 UN weapons inspection teams refused reentry into Iraq; US and UK mount punitive air strikes.

2003 Coalition forces invade. Saddam Hussein overthrown.

2004 Transitional constitution.

IRELAND, REPUBLIC OF Lying in the Atlantic Ocean, off the west coast of Britain, the Irish Republic occupies about 85 percent of the island of Ireland. Low coastal mountain ranges surround a central basin with lakes, hills, and peat bogs. Centuries of struggle against English colonialism led to the formation of the Irish Free State in 1922 and full sovereignty in 1937. Hopes for the resolution of the Northern Ireland conflict center on the 1998 Good Friday accord, to which Ireland is a party.

Chronology

c. 300 BCE Ireland is invaded by Gaelic-speaking Celts.

432 CE Christianity is introduced to Ireland by the missionary St. Patrick (389–461), who became the country's patron saint.

1014 At the battle of Clontarf, Viking power (concentrated since the late 8th century in coastal areas) is broken and the five traditional Irish kingdoms of Ulster, Leinster, Munster, Meath, and Connaught are briefly united.

1171 During the reign of the English King Henry II (ruled 1154–89) Anglo-Norman adventurers conquer parts of Ireland, having received authorization from Pope Adrian IV (an Englishman) to subjugate Ireland. By the 1175 Treaty of Windsor the High King of Ireland recognizes the English King as his overlord.

1494 Under the terms of Poynings' Law, English laws henceforward apply to Ireland.

1541 Having broken the power of Ireland's feudal lords, England's King Henry VIII (reigned 1509–47) adopts the title of King of Ireland.

1559–1603 Against the backcloth of attempts by Elizabeth I (reigned 1558–1603) to impose Protestantism, a succession of unsuccessful rebellions against the English is launched in Ulster (1559–66 and 1593–1603) and Munster (1569–72). Despite support from Catholic Spain, they are suppressed, and from 1607 over 100,000 Scottish Presbyterian settlers move to Ulster in the northeast, where land is confiscated from Irish Catholics.

1641 Taking advantage of the developing civil war in England, Ulster Catholics launch a rebellion against English rule which is eventually crushed at Drogheda in 1649 by Oliver Cromwell (1599–1658).

1690 Irish Catholics, who have flocked to the colors of the deposed English Catholic King James II (reigned 1685–88), are defeated by the forces of William of Orange (reigned 1688–1702) at the Battle of the Boyne. Under the terms of a new penal code (relaxed in 1782), Catholics are deprived of citizenship and the right to own property.

1739–41 Perhaps 300,000 die in famine caused by failure of potato crop.

1801 The Act of Union between Great Britain and Ireland comes into force. The Irish parliament is abolished after further rebellions (May–July 1798 and July 1803) are suppressed. Ireland obtains representation at Westminster but it is not until 1829, after a campaign by Daniel O'Connell (1775–1847), that Catholics are allowed to sit in the House of Commons.

1845–1851 Famine. One million die; more than one million emigrate.

1916 Easter Rising in Dublin soon crushed. Executions of leaders by the British have effect of increasing support and sympathy for the Republican cause.

1919–1921 Anglo-Irish war after republican Sinn Féin proclaims Irish independence.

1921 Anglo-Irish treaties divides country in two – with six counties in the north remaining in the UK.

1922 Irish Free State established. Civil war between pro-Treaty and anti-Treaty factions.

1932 Eamonn De Valera and Fianna Fail come to power

1937 Full sovereignty as Eire.

1949 Eire becomes the Republic of Ireland and leaves the British Commonwealth.

1973 Fine Gael/Labour Party alliance wins elections ending Fianna Fail's ascendancy since 1932.

1990 Mary Robinson elected first woman president.

1995 Referendum favors divorce.

1998 Good Friday accord on Northern Ireland.

2002 Euro fully adopted.

Irish famine (1845–51) Period of famine and unrest in Ireland caused by the failure in 1845 of the potato crop, Ireland's staple food. Estimated one million people died of starvation and another 1.5 million emigrated as a result. *p.360*

Irish Free State From 1921, when Ireland was partitioned and the south gained dominion status, it was known as the Irish Free State. In 1937 it became a sovereign state as Eire and gained full independence in 1949 as the Republic of Ireland.

Iron Age The final archaeological period in the Old World, used to denote (from c.1000 BCE) societies which used iron, not only for luxury goods, but also for household and agricultural implements and weapons. In general, the Iron Age followed the Bronze Age, but in some parts of the Old World, for example, Africa, the transition was made from Stone Age to Iron Age, without the intervening Copper and Bronze Ages.

Iron Curtain Political, military, and ideological barrier, of the post World War II period, between the Soviet Union and its eastern European allies; and the West and other non-Communist areas.

Iroquois In 1570, five nations of Native American peoples, the Mohawk, Oneida, Seneca, Onondaga, and Cayuga, joined to form a confederacy know as the Iroquois. They were later joined by the Tuscarora. The Iroquois were an important influence in early colonial America, and the French, in particular, made alliances with them. The confederacy was split after the American Revolutionary War, when those groups which had supported the loyalist cause (the Cayugas, Senecas, and Mohawks) migrated to Canada.

Isabella of Castile (1451–1504) *see* Ferdinand of Aragon

Isandhlwana ⚔ of Zulu wars (1879). Zulus inflicted severe defeat on British.

Isfahan Ancient city of Iran. Shah Abbas I made Isfahan the capital of Safavid Persia when he came to the throne in 1587. *p.303*

Islam The religion of the Muslims, founded by the Prophet Muhammad (c.570–632). It teaches that there is only one God (Allah), and that Muhammad is his prophet. The Koran (Qu'ran) is the sacred book of Islam, believed to be the words of God dictated to Muhammad, through the medium of the angel Gabriel. The spread of Islam. *p.124, p.130*
Abbasid Caliphate. *p.144*
Islamic trade. *p.213*
Islam in Africa. *p.233*
See also individual Muslim countries

Ismail I (c.1487–1524) Shah of Persia and founder of the Shi'ite Safavid dynasty (1499). A revered national figure, regarded as both saint and shah, he was a formidable warrior. In 1510, he defeated the Uzbeks who had been making regular incursions into Khurasan. In 1514, he was confronted by the forces of the Turkish sultan, Selim, who annexed Tabriz.

Isidore of Seville (c.570–536) Spanish historian and encylopedist. He became archbishop of Seville in 609. Confronted by barbarian invasions, he dedicated himself to the preservation of Greek and Roman culture. His great work, the *Originum sive etymologiarum libri* (622–633) is a tribute to his scholarship in the liberal arts, theology, the sciences and political theory.

Isonzo ⚔ of World War I (1915–17) Series of 12 battles which took place between Austria and Italy along the Isonzo river on the eastern Italian Front. The final battle, in Oct 1917, saw the Italians defeated after a heavy Austro-German bombardment.

ISRAEL Created as a new state in 1948 with the backing of the US and other Allied powers, Israel is bordered by Egypt, Jordan, Syria, and Lebanon. The Dead Sea on the Israel-Jordan border is the lowest point on the Earth's land surface. After wars with its Arab neighbors, Israel has unilaterally extended its boundaries. Resolving the Israeli-Palestinian conflict hinges on the future of the West Bank and East Jerusalem, under a "land for peace" deal. *p.419*

CHRONOLOGY

1897 At the Basle Congress in Switzerland, Theodor Herzl defines aim of Zionism as "striving to create for the Jewish people a home in Palestine secured by public law."

1916 The Sykes-Picot Agreement is signed between Britain and France. It establishes their respective spheres of influence, and Palestine is promised to Britain.

1917 In the Balfour Declaration, the British government agrees to the establishment of a national home for the Jewish people, "it being clearly understood that nothing is done which may prejudice the existing civil and religious rights of existing non-Jewish communities in Palestine."

1920 The San Remo Conference gives the Mandate for Palestine to Britain.

1921 King Abdallah is proclaimed ruler of Transjordan.

1929 Violent protests and clashes between Arabs and Jews take place in Palestine.

1936 The Arab population of Palestine go on a six-month strike. It is followed by a large-scale rebellion.

1939 The British government issues White Paper which envisages future independence of Palestine as a state in which Arabs and Jews share government in such a way as to ensure that the essential interests of each community are safeguarded.

1942 At the Extraordinary Zionist Congress in New York, David Ben Gurion, Chairman of the Jewish Agency Executive, calls for the immigration of Jews to Palestine and the establishment of a Jewish State.

1947 The UN General Assembly adopts a plan for Palestine which divides the country into six parts, with three of the larger parts allocated to the Jews. The Arabs refuse to accept it; clashes follow, and 1,700 people are killed.

1948 Clashes between Arabs and Jews turn into a full-scale war. Provisional Jewish government is established with Ben Gurion as prime minister. The Mandate is terminated and 400,000 Arabs flee. State of Israel is officially declared, and is recognized by the United States of America and the Union of Soviet Socialist Republics.

1949 The first general election is held for a single-chamber Knesset (parliament) elected by proportional representation.

1956 President Nasser of Egypt nationalizes the Suez Canal.

1956 Israel invades Sinai and Anglo-French forces invade Port Said in Egypt.

1957 Following an agreement, Israeli forces withdraw from the territories invaded in the Suez conflict.

1967 Six-Day War; Israel takes West Bank, Gaza, Sinai, Golan Heights.

1973 Egypt and Syria attack Israel. Yom Kippur War.

1978 Camp David accords with Egypt.

1978 Formal peace treaty, Sinai returned to Egypt.

1982 Israel invades Lebanon.

1987 Palestinians launch *intifada*.

1993 Oslo Accords.

1994 Palestinian autonomy begins in Gaza and Jericho.

1995 Prime minister Yitzhak Rabin assassinated: replaced by Peres.

1996 Palestinian elections. Benjamin Netanyahu (Likud) first directly elected Israeli prime minister.

1998 Israel stalls on US-backed plan to revive peace process.

1999 Ehud Barak (Labor) elected prime minister. Renewed peace process with Palestinians and Syria.

2000 Israeli forces withdraw from southern Lebanon. Large-scale violent Israeli-Palestinian clashes.

2001 Ariel Sharon (Likud) elected prime minister; forms unity government. Conflict worsens.

2002 Intifada and reprisals intensify. Untiy government collapses.

2003 Likud wins elections. US peace "roadmap" published.

2004 Gaza withdrawal agreed.

Issus ⚔ (333 BCE) Major battle of Alexander the Great's invasion of Asia in Anatolia (modern-day Turkey). The Greeks were victorious.

ITALY The boot-shaped Italian peninsula stretches 800 km (496 miles) southwards into the Mediterranean, while the Alps form a natural boundary to the north. Italy also includes Sicily, Sardinia, and several smaller islands. The south is an area of seismic activity, with two famous volcanoes, Vesuvius and Etna. Rival city-states flourished in Renaissance Italy, a unified country only in Roman times and since 1870 following the Risorgimento, the Italian nationalist movement. Fascist rule under Mussolini from 1922 ended with Italy's defeat in World War II. The Christian Democrats (CD) then dominated Italy's notoriously short-lived governments for decades, until in the 1990s the established parties and patronage systems were shaken up by corruption investigations.

CHRONOLOGY

753 BCE At this time, traditional date of the foundation of Rome, the Romans are one of several peoples inhabiting Italy. Others include Etruscans in Tuscany, Sabines in central Italy, Greeks in colonies in the south and Sicily, and Gauls in the north.

510 BCE Rome becomes a republic after the expulsion of king Tarquinius Superbus; over next two centuries the military might of Rome conquers the surrounding peoples.

272 BCE After the conquest of Taranto in the south, all of central and southern Italy is united under Roman rule.

264–146 BCE Rome defeats Carthage in the three Punic Wars (264–241 BCE, 218–201 BCE and 149–146 BCE); Rome proceeds to conquer Greece and most of the Mediterranean region.

12 BCE Octavian proclaimed Pontifex Maximus, thereby inaugurating imperial rule.

117–138 CE During reign of Emperor Hadrian, Roman Empire includes the Iberian peninsula, Gaul (France), Britannia (England), Greece, all of central Europe south of the Rhine and Danube rivers, Asia Minor, Armenia, Syria (including Palestine), Egypt and North Africa.

313 CE Religious freedom is guaranteed throughout empire by the Edict of Milan; Christianity becomes the dominant religion and Rome becomes the seat of the papacy.

476 CE Roman Empire collapses in west.

492 Italy falls to the Ostrogoths. Theodoric founds Kingdom of Italy; capital at Ravenna.

533–555 Byzantine emperor Justinian I achieves reconquest of Italy.

568 Italy invaded by the Lombards. They never conquer the whole peninsula: Byzantines retain control of parts of Italy.

774 Franks under Charlemagne conquer the Lombard kingdom in northern Italy; Charlemagne is crowned Emperor in 800.

962 The coronation by Pope John XII of Otto I of Germany as emperor marks beginning of the Holy Roman Empire.

1030–1137 The Normans conquer Sicily and southern Italy. The Kingdom of Sicily, later known as Naples or the Two Sicilies, is established in 1130.

14th century Following the withdrawal of the German emperors, northern Italy fragments into a number of small but increasingly powerful states, notably Venice, Florence, and Genoa and the duchy of Milan; these cities, among the great trading and industrial centers of Europe, are in the vanguard of the Renaissance, the great cultural revival of the 15th century.

1494–1525 In a series of wars France and Spain vie for domination of Italy. The wars end in defeat for France and also mark the decline of the city states, which suffer major devastation and are adversely affected by the new economic conditions created by the severance of traditional land trade routes to the East and the opening of the new Atlantic and Cape routes.

1700 The Spanish domination of Italy ends. After the War of the Spanish Succession (1701–14) its position is usurped by Austria.

1796–97 French revolutionary forces under Napoleon conquer most of Italy. Napoleon re-draws the country's map and creates the Kingdom of Italy in the north (1805), but after the defeat of France the Congress of Vienna (1814–15) restores the old order.

1831 Giuseppe Mazzini forms the Young Italy movement and becomes one of the intellectual fathers of the Risorgimento, the national movement aiming for unification of all the Italian states.

1848–49 Nationalists rise against Austrian rulers in north and against the papacy. Defeated by Austrian troops at Novara and French troops called in by Pope Pius IX.

1859–70 Unification of Italy is achieved under leadership of King Victor Emmanuel II of Sardinia-Piedmont, his chief minister, Count Camillo Cavour, and the forces of Giuseppe Garibaldi. Most of northern Italy united with Sardinia-Piedmont after the War of Unification against Austria in 1859, Garibaldi conquers Sicily and Naples in 1860–61, Venice is ceded by Austria after war in 1866, and Rome is occupied by Italian troops (and proclaimed the capital) in 1870.

1882 Italy joins Austria-Hungary and Germany in the Triple Alliance.

1889–1912 Italy conquers Eritrea and Somalia, but is defeated by Ethiopia at the battle of Adowa in 1896; Libya conquered in war against Ottomans in 1911–12.

1915 Having abandoned Triple Alliance, Italy joins World War I on side of the Entente powers. Under Treaty of Paris (1919) Italy is awarded South Tyrol and Trieste.

1928 One-party rule by Fascists.

1929 Lateran Treaties with Vatican recognize sovereignty of Holy See.

1936–1937 Axis formed with Nazi Germany. Abyssinia (Ethiopia) conquered.

1939 Albania annexed.

1940 Italy enters World War II on German side.

1943 Italy invaded by Allies. Armistice with Allies. Mussolini imprisoned, but escapes to north. Italy declares war on Germany, but Germans continue to fight Allies in Italy.

1944 Germans put up fierce resistance, especially at Monte Cassino. Allied landings at Anzio. Allies enter Rome in June.

1945 Mussolini and his mistress executed by Italian partisans.

1946 Referendum votes in favor of Italy becoming a republic.

1947 Italy signs peace treaty, ceding border areas to France and Yugoslavia, Dodecanese to Greece, and giving up colonies.

1948 Elections: DC heads coalition.

1949 Founder member of NATO.

1950 Agreement with USA on bases in Italy.

1957 Founder member of European Economic Community.

1964 DC government under Aldo Moro forms coalition with Socialist Party (PSI).

1972 Support for extreme right reaches postwar peak (9 percent). Rise in urban terrorism by both extreme left and right.

1976 Communist Party (PCI) support reaches 34 percent under Berlinguer, proponent of moderate Eurocommunist policies.

1980 Extreme right bombing of Bologna station kills 84, wounds 200.

1983–1987 Center-left coalition formed.

1992 Corruption scandal, uncovered in Milan. Government members accused.

1994 General election: coalition government formed between Silvio Berlusconi's Forza Italia, Northern League, and neo-fascists.
1996 Center-left Olive Tree alliance wins election; Romano Prodi prime minister.
1998 Italy qualifies to join euro currency. Massimo D'Alema prime minister.
2000 D'Alema replaced by Giuliano Amato.
2001 Berlusconi victory in general election.
2002 Euro fully adopted.

ITALIAN MINISTRIES (since 1860)

Italian prime ministers

1860–1861	Count Camillo Benso di Cavour
1861–1862	Baron Bettino Ricasoli
1862	Urbano Ratazzi
1862–1864	Marco Minghetti
1864 –1866	General Alfonso La Marmora
1866–1867	Baron Bettino Ricasoli
1867	Urbano Ratazzi
1867–1869	Luigi Federico Menabrea
1869–1873	Domenico Lanza
1873–1876	Marco Minghetti
1876–1878	Agostino Depretis
1878	Benedetto Cairoli
1878–1879	Agostino Depretis
1879–1881	Benedetto Cairoli
1881–1887	Agostino Depretis
1887–1891	Francesco Crispi
1891–1892	Marquis di Rudini
1892–1893	Giovanni Giolitti
1893–1896	Francesco Crispi
1896–1898	Marchese di Rudini
1898–1900	General Luigi Pelloux
1900–1901	Giuseppe Saracco
1901–1903	Giuseppe Zanardelli
1903–1906	Giovanni Giolitti
1906	Baron Sidney Sonnino
1906–1909	Giovanni Giolitti
1909–1910	Baron Sidney Sonnino
1910–1911	Luigi Luzzatti
1911–1914	Giovanni Giolitti
1914–1916	Antonio Salandra
1916–1917	Paolo Boselli
1917–1919	Vittorio Orlando
1919–1920	Francesco Nitti
1920–1921	Giovanni Giolitti
1921–1922	Ivanoe Bonomi
1922	Luigi Facta
1922–1943	Benito Mussolini
1943–1944	Marshal Pietro Badoglio
1944–1945	Ivanoe Bonomi
1945	Ferruccio Parri
1945–1946	Alcide de Gasperi

Italian prime ministers (since 1946)

1946–1953	Alcide de Gasperi
1953–1954	Giuseppe Pella
1954	Amintore Fanfani
1954 –1955	Mario Scelba
1955–1957	Antonio Segni
1957–1958	Adone Zoli
1958–1959	Amintore Fanfani
1959	Antonio Segni
1960–1960	Fernando Tambroni
1960–1963	Amintore Fanfani
1963–1963	Giovanni Leone
1963–1968	Aldo Moro
1968–1968	Giovanni Leone
1968–1970	Mariano Rumor
1970–1972	Emilio Colombo
1972–1973	Giulio Andreotti
1973–1974	Mariano Rumor
1974–1976	Aldo Moro
1976–1979	Giulio Andreotti
1979–1980	Francesco Cossiga
1980–1981	Arnaldo Forlani
1981–1982	Giovanni Spadolini
1982–1983	Amintore Fanfani
1983–1987	Bettino Craxi
1987	Amintore Fanfani
1987–1988	Giovanni Goria
1988–1989	Ciriaco De Mita
1989–1992	Giulio Andreotti
1992–1993	Giuliano Amato
1993–1995	Carlo Azeglio Ciampi
1994–	Silvio Berlusconi
1995–1996	Lamberto Dini
1996–1998	Romano Prodi
1998–1999	Massimo D'Alema
1999–2001	Giuliano Amato
2001–	Silvio Berlusconi

Italian presidents

1946–1948	Enrico De Nicola (Interim head of state and president of republic)
1948–1955	Luigi Einaudi
1955–1962	Giovanni Gronchi
1964	Cesare Merzagora
1962–1964	Antonio Segni
1964–1971	Giuseppe Saragat
1971–1978	Giovanni Leone
1978	Amintore Fanfani
1978–1985	Alessandro Pertini
1985–1992	Francesco Cossiga
1992	Giovanni Spadolini
1992–1999	Oscar Luigi Scalfaro
1999–	Carlo Azeglio Ciampi

Itzcoatl (died 1440) Ruler of Aztec empire (1427–40).

Ivan III (*var.* Ivan Vasilyevich, *aka* Ivan the Great, 1440–1505) Grand Prince of Moscow (reigned 1462–1505), he freed the city from the Tatars and extended the territories of Muscovite Russia. In 1472 he assumed the title "Sovereign of all Russia."

Ivan IV (*aka* Ivan the Terrible, 1530–84) First czar of Russia (reigned 1533–84). He created a centrally administered Russian state and began the eastward expansion of Russia into non-Slavic lands. He gave Russia its first national assembly in 1549. He killed his son Ivan, and embarked on a reign of terror against the Boyars. *p.283*

IVORY COAST One of the larger west African coastal countries, Ivory Coast – officially Côte d'Ivoire – is the world's biggest cocoa producer. The forested interior, apart from the capital, is more sparsely populated than the coastal strip. Pro-Western President Houphouët-Boigny ruled from independence in 1960 until 1993. Military rule in 1999 gave way in 2000 to an elected president after a chaotic poll.

CHRONOLOGY

14th century The Mandinka population arrive in the area.
16th century European slaving activities along the coast.
1840s French forces build forts at Assinie, Bassam and Dabou.
1893 A French colony is declared, with a capital at Grand Bassam.
1910 A rebellion by the southern Abe people is harshly suppressed.
1934 Abidjan becomes the capital.
1903–1935 Plantations developed.
1960 Félix Houphouët-Boigny declares independence.
1970 Oil production starts.
1990 First contested polls: Houphouët-Boigny and PDCI win.
1993 Houphouët-Boigny dies.
1998 Power of president increased, Ouattara apparently barred from standing in presidential elections.
1999 Military coup by General Guei.
2000 Guei ousted after falsely claiming election victory. Laurent Gbagbo president.
2003 Peace agreement signed.
2004 Power-sharing deal falters.

J

Jackson, Andrew (*aka* "Old Hickory", 1767–1845) 7th President of the US (Democrat, 1828–36). A hero of the war of 1812 following his defeat of the British at New Orleans. As President he was resolute in his defence of the Union, and encouraged Indian removals to free new lands for settlement on the frontier.

Jacobins Members of the most famous of the political clubs of the French Revolution, exercising great influence in the National Assembly. Became increasingly radical and, under Robespierre, instituted the Reign of Terror. *See also* French Revolution, Robespierre, the Terror.

Jacobite Church Christian church of Syria, Iraq and India, founded in the 6th century as a Monophysite church in Syria. Regarded as heretical by Roman Catholics and the Eastern Orthodox Church.

Jacquerie Peasant rebellion against the nobility in NE France in 1358, during the Hundred Years' War.

Jagatai *see* Chagatai

Jagiello (c.1351–1434) Grand duke of Lithuania (reigned 1377–1401) and king of Poland (reigned 1386–1434) who founded Poland's Jagiellon dynasty (1386–1572).

Jahan *see* Shah Jahan

Jahangir (reigned 1605–27) Mughal emperor. The son of Akbar, Jahangir moved the capital to Lahore. He was strongly influenced by his favorite wife, Nur Jahan, and the currency was struck in her name. During his reign, the English established themselves at Surat and sent an embassy to the Mughal court.

Jainism Sect of Hindu dissenters which, according to Jain tradition, was founded as early as the 7th century BCE. Jain theology centers on the quest for liberation from the transmigration of souls, through monastic discipline, abstinence, and chastity. Great stress is placed on the vow to preserve all living things.

JAMAICA First colonized by the Spanish and then, from 1655, by the English, Jamaica is located in the Caribbean, 145 km (90 miles) south of Cuba. It was the first of the Caribbean island countries to become independent in the postwar years, and remains an active force in Caribbean politics. Jamaica is also influential on the world music scene; reggae and ragga (or dancehall) developed in the tough conditions of Kingston's poor districts.

CHRONOLOGY

1494 Columbus lands at Dry Harbour, now Discovery Bay, on his second voyage.
1509 Columbus's son Diego Colon takes the island and appoints Juan de Esquivel as the first governor.
1655 A British expedition under Admiral Penn lands. Spain capitulates. The island becomes a haven for buccaneers. Sugar cane, cotton, and cattle are established in a slave labor economy.
1660 The Spanish are finally expelled.
1670 Jamaica is ceded to England by the Treaty of Madrid.
1866 The island becomes a British Crown Colony.
1942 The discovery of bauxite and its subsequent development displaces sugar as the main industry.
1957 Internal self-government is achieved.
1958–1961 West Indies Federation.
1962 Independence under JLP.
1972 PNP elected. Reforms fail; street violence begins.
1980 Unpopular IMF austerity measures lead to JLP election win.
1991–2002 PNP returned and austerity continues.
1999 Violent protests over fuel tax increases.

Jamestown ⚔ of American Revolutionary War (Jul 6 1781). British victory.

Jammu and Kashmir Muslim majority province contested between India and Pakistan since 1947, when control was left unresolved following the partition of India. Two wars have been fought over the province (1947–48 and 1965).

Janapadas Series of states or realms, formed by Aryan settlers in India during the first millennium BCE. *See also* Magadha

Janissary corps Military force which constituted the standing army of the Ottoman Empire. From 1330, a number of Christian boys were taken from their parents in the Ottoman provinces, apprenticed, and enrolled into the new corps. By 1582, this strict mode of admission had been relaxed and the privileges of membership of the corps were much sought after. In 1591 the whole corps numbered 48,688 men. Janissaries were not allowed to marry or leave their barracks, but were to spend their time practising the arts of war. The first recorded revolt of the Janissaries in 1443; repeated revolts and disorder culminated in the disbanding of the corps in 1826. *p.241*

JAPAN A constitutional monarchy, with an emperor as ceremonial head of state, Japan is located off the east Asian coast in the north Pacific. It comprises four principal islands and more than 3000 smaller islands. Sovereignty over the most southerly islands in the Kurile chain is disputed with the Russian Federation. The terrain is mostly mountainous, with fertile coastal plains; over two-thirds is woodland. The Pacific coast is vulnerable to tsunamis – tidal waves triggered by submarine earthquakes. Most cities are located by the sea; Tokyo, Kawasaki, and Yokohama together constitute the most populous and heavily industrialized area. Hokkaido is the most rural of the main islands. Japan's power in the global economy, with annual trade surpluses exceeding $100 billion and massive overseas investments, has been shaken since the early 1990s by a series of bad debt crises, bankruptcies in the financial sector, and prolonged recession since 1997.

CHRONOLOGY

c.350 CE Japan is unified under the rule of the Yamato clan.

538 CE Buddhism is introduced to Japan, through China and Korea.

604 CE Prince Shotoku issues the so-called "Constitution of Seventeen Articles," setting out ethical maxims of government, which shows Buddhist and Confucian influence.

645 CE Fujiwara Kamatari institutes a reformed system of government following the Chinese model of a complex, centralized administration.

794 CE The Heian period begins, during which the power of the Emperors declines and falls into hands of the Fujiwara clan.

1185 A military government is consolidated under the leader of the Minamoto clan, Minamoto Yorimoto, after his defeat of the rival Taira clan.

1274 The first Mongol invasion is defeated.

1281 The second Mongol invasion is repulsed after a typhoon wipes out the Mongol armada.

1339 The Muromachi period, which lasts until 1573, begins; it is a period of devastating civil wars and the breakdown of central government, but also of growth in the arts and commerce.

1542 or 1543 The Portuguese land in Japan, probably the first Europeans to do so. They introduce the musket.

1592 The Japanese invade Korea and are defeated.

1597 A second Japanese invasion of Korea also ends in failure.

1637 A decree is issued forbidding Japanese citizens to leave the country. Japan effectively isolates itself from the rest of the world.

1853 Commodore Matthew Perry of the United States Navy enters Yedo (now Tokyo) harbour, and demands the opening of trade relations.

1854 A trade treaty is signed with the US. Treaties with the United Kingdom, Russia, France and others follow.

1859 The Shogun is assassinated by nationalists in reaction against treaties with foreigners.

1863 Japanese fire on foreign vessels, in an attempt to expel foreigners.

1864 British, US, French, and Dutch naval fleets force Japan to abide by the treaties.

1868 Meiji Restoration; overthrow of Tokugawa regime and restoration of imperial power.

1872 Modernization along Western lines. Japan's strong military tradition becomes state-directed.

1889 Constitution modeled on Bismarck's Germany adopted.

1894–1895 War with China; ends in Japanese victory.

1904–1905 War with Russia; ends in Japanese victory. Formosa (Taiwan) and Korea annexed.

1914 Joins World War I on Allied side. Sees limited naval action.

1919 Versailles peace conference gives Japan limited territorial gains in the Pacific.

1923 Yokohama earthquake kills 140,000.

1927 Japan enters period of radical nationalism, and introduces the notion of a "coprosperity sphere" in southeast Asia under Japanese control. Interpreted in the US as a threat to its Pacific interests.

1931 Chinese Manchuria invaded and renamed Manchukuo.

1937 Japan launches full-scale invasion of China proper.

1938 All political parties placed under one common banner; Japan effectively ruled by militarists.

1939 Undeclared border war with Soviet Union; Japan defeated.

1940 Fall of France in Europe; Japan occupies French Indochina.

1941 USA imposes total trade embargo, including oil, on Japan thereby threatening to stifle its military machine. Japan responds in December by launching attack on US fleet at Pearl Harbor and invading US, British, and Dutch possessions in the Pacific.

1942 Japan loses decisive naval battle of Midway.

1945 Huge US bombing campaign culminates in dropping of atomic bombs on Hiroshima and Nagasaki. Soviet Union declares war on Japan. Emperor Hirohito surrenders, gives up divine status. Japan placed under US military government with General MacArthur installed as supreme commander of Allied Powers in Japan.

1947 New Japanese constitution: modeled on USA's, but retains emperor in ceremonial role.

1950 Korean War. US army contracts lead to quick expansion of Japanese economy.

1952 Treaty of San Francisco. Japan regains independence. Industrial production recovers to 15 percent above 1936 levels.

1955 Merger of conservative parties to form LDP which governs for next 38 years.

1964 Tokyo Olympics. Shinkansen (bullet train) inaugurated. Japan admitted to OECD.

1973 Oil crisis. Economic growth cut. Government-led economic reassessment decides to concentrate on high-tech industries.

1976 LDP shaken by Lockheed bribery scandal; in subsequent election it remains in power but loses outright majority for first time.

1979 Second oil crisis. Growth continues at 6 percent per year.

1980 Elections: restoration of LDP overall majority.

1982 Honda establishes its first car factory in US.

1988 Japan becomes world's largest aid donor and overseas investor.

1989 Death of Emperor Hirohito. Recruit–Cosmos bribery scandal leads to resignation of Prime Minister Noburo Takeshita; replaced by Sosuke Uno, who is in turn forced to resign over sexual scandal. Tokyo stock market crash.

1991–1992 LDP torn by factional disputes, further financial scandals, and the issue of electoral reform.

1993 Reformists split from LDP and create new parties. Elections; LDP loses power. Morihiro Hosokawa becomes prime minister at head of seven-party coalition.

1994 Hosokawa resigns. Withdrawal of SDPJ causes collapse of coalition. New three-party coalition includes LDP and SDPJ. Opposition parties unified by creation of Shinshinto. Implementation of far-reaching political and electoral reforms designed to eradicate "money politics."

1995 Kobe earthquake kills more than 5000 people.

1996 Elections: LDP minority government. Copper trader Yasuo Yamanaka sentenced to eight years in prison for incurring losses of $2.6 billion while acting for the Sumitomo Corporation.

1997 Severe economic recession.

1998 Crisis over reform of banking and financial system.

2000 Prime Minister Keizo Obuchi falls into coma, replaced by Yoshiro Mori. June. LDP loses overall majority in general election.

2001 LDP turns to populist right-winger Junichiro Koizumi as prime minister; five women appointed to cabinet.

2002 Japan cohosts soccer World Cup with South Korea.
2003 LDP reelected.
2004 Non-combat soldiers arrive in Iraq in first Japanese deployment in a combat zone since World War II.

THE RULERS OF JAPAN

Legendary emperors
1 Jimmu
2 Suizei
3 Annei
4 Itoku
5 Kosho
6 Koan
7 Korei
8 Kogen
9 Kaika
10 Sujin
11 Suinin
12 Keiko
13 Seimu
14 Chuai

Recorded emperors
Late 4th–5th century
        Ojin
5th century (first half)
        Nintoku
        Richu
        Hanzei
Mid-5th century
        Ingyo
        Anko
5th century (latter half)
        Yuryaku
        Seinei
        Kenzo
        Ninken
        Buretsu
6th century (first half)
        Keitai
        Ankan
        Senka
531/539–571 Kimmei
572–585 Bidatsu
585–587 Yomei
587–592 Sushun
593–628 Suiko (empress)
629–641 Jomei
642–645 Kogyoku (empress)
645–654 Kotoku
655–661 Saimei (empress)
661–672 Tenji
672 Kobun

672–686 Temmu
686–697 Jito (empress)
697–707 Mommu
707–715 Gemmei (empress)
715–724 Gensho (empress)
724–749 Shomu
749–758 Koken (empress)
758–764 Junnin
764–770 Shotoku (empress)
770–781 Konin
781–806 Kammu
806–809 Heizei
809–823 Saga
823–833 Junna
833–850 Nimmyo
850–858 Montoku
858–876 Seiwa
876–884 Yozei
884–887 Koko
887–897 Uda
897–930 Daigo
930–946 Suzaku
946–967 Murakami
967–969 Reizei
969–984 Enyu
984–986 Kazan
986–1011 Ichijo
1011–1016 Sanjo
1016–1036 Go-Ichijo
1036–1045 Go-Suzaku
1045–1068 Go-Reizei
1068–1073 Go-Sanjo
1073–1087 Shirakawa
1087–1107 Horikawa
1107–1123 Toba
1123–1142 Sutoku
1142–1155 Konoe
1155–1158 Go-Shirakawa
1158–1165 Nijo
1165–1168 Rokujo
1168–1180 Takakura
1180–1185 Antoku
1183–1198 Go-Toba
1198–1210 Tsuchimikado
1210–1221 Juntoku
1221 Chukyo
1221–1232 Go-Horikawa
1232–1242 Shijo
1242–1246 Go-Saga
1246–1260 Go-Fukakusa
1260–1274 Kameyama
1274–1287 Go-Uda
1287–1298 Fushimi
1298–1301 Go-Fushimi
1301–1308 Go-Nijo
1308–1318 Hanazono

1318–1339 Go-Daigo
1339–1368 Go-Murakami
1368–1383 Chokei
1383–1392 Go-Kameyama
1331–1333 Kogon
1336–1348 Komyo
1348–1351 Suko
1351–1371 Go-Kogon
1371–1382 Go-Enyu
1382–1412 Go-Komatsu
1412–1428 Shoko
1428–1464 Go-Hanazono
1464–1500 Go-Tsuchimikado
1500–1526 Go-Kashiwabara
1526–1557 Go-Nara
1557–1586 Ogimachi
1586–1611 Go-Yozei
1611–1629 Go-Mizunoo
1629–1643 Meisho (empress)
1643–1654 Go-Komyo
1655–1663 Gosai
1663–1687 Reigen
1687–1709 Higashiyama
1709–1735 Nakamikado
1735–1747 Sakuramachi
1747–1762 Momozono
1762–1771 Go-Sakuramachi (empress)
1771–1779 Go-Momozono
1780–1817 Kokaku
1817–1846 Ninko
1846–1867 Komei
1867–1912 Meiji
1912–1926 Taisho
1926–1989 Hirohito
1989– Akihito

Kamakura Shoguns
1192–1199 Minamoto no Yoritomo
1202–1203 Minamoto no Yoriie
1203–1219 Minamoto no Sanetomo
1226–1244 Kujo Yoritsune
1244–1252 Kujo Yoritsugu
1252–1266 Prince Munetaka
1266–1289 Prince Koreyasu
1289–1308 Prince Hisaaki
1308–1333 Prince Morikuni

Regents of the Kamakura Shogunate
1203–1205 Hojo Tokimasa
1205–1224 Hojo Yoshitoki
1224–1242 Hojo Yasutoki
1242–1246 Hojo Tsunetoki
1246–1256 Hojo Tokiyori
1256–1264 Hojo Nagatoki
1264–1268 Hojo Masamura

1268–1284	Hojo Tokimune
1284–1301	Hojo Sadatoki
1301–1311	Hojo Morotoki
1311–1312	Hojo Munenobu
1312–1315	Hojo Hirotoki
1315	Hojo Mototoki
1316–1326	Hojo Takatoki
1326	Hojo Sadaaki
1327–1333	Hojo Moritoki

Ashikaga Shoguns

1338–1358	Takauji
1359–1368	Yoshiakira
1368–1394	Yoshimitsu
1395–1423	Yoshimochi
1423–1425	Yoshikazu
1429–1441	Yoshinori
1442–1443	Yoshikatsu
1449–1473	Yoshimasa
1474–1489	Yoshihisa
1490–1493	Yoshitane
1495–1508	Yoshizumi
1508–1521	Yoshitane
1522–1547	Yoshiharu
1547–1565	Yoshiteru
1568	Yoshihide
1568–1573	Yoshiaki
1568–1582	Oda Nobunaga
1582–1598	Toyotomi Hideyoshi

Tokugawa Shoguns

1603–1605	Ieyasu
1605–1623	Hidetada
1623–1651	Iemitsu
1651–1680	Ietsuna
1680–1709	Tsunayoshi
1709–1712	Ienobu
1713–1716	Ietsugu
1716–1745	Yoshimune
1745–1760	Ieshige
1760–1786	Ieharu
1787–1837	Ienari
1837–1853	Ieyoshi
1853–1858	Iesada
1858–1866	Iemochi
1867	Yoshinobu

Prime Ministers

1885–1888	Ito Hirobumi
1888–1889	Kuroda Kiyotaka
1889–1891	Yamagata Aritomo
1891–1892	Matsukata Masayoshi
1892–1896	Ito Hirobumi
1896–1898	Matsukata Masayoshi
1898	Ito Hirobumi
1898	Okuma Shigenobu

1898–1900	Yamagata Aritomo
1900–1901	Ito Hirobumi
1901–1906	Katsura Taro
1906–1908	Saionji Kimmochi
1908–1911	Katsura Taro
1911–1912	Saionji Kimmochi
1912–1913	Katsura Taro
1913–1914	Yamamoto Gonnohyoe
1914–1916	Okuma Shigenobu
1916–1918	Terauchi Masatake
1918–1921	Hara Takashi
1921–1922	Takahashi Korekiyo
1922–1923	Kato Tomosaburo
1923–1924	Yamamoto Gonnohyoe
1924	Kiyoura Keigo
1924–1925	Kato Takaaki
1926–1927	Wakatsuki Reijiro
1927–1929	Tanaka Giichi
1929–1931	Hamaguchi Osachi
1931	Wakatsuki Reijiro
1931–1932	Inukai Tsuyoshi
1932–1934	Saito Makoto
1934–1936	Okada Keisuke
1936–1937	Hirota Koki
1937	Hayashi Senjuro
1937–1939	Konoe Fumimaro
1939	Hiranuma Kiichiro
1939–1940	Abe Nobuyuki
1940	Yonai Mitsumasa
1940–1941	Konoe Fumimaro
1941–1944	Tojo Hideki
1944–1945	Koiso Kuniaki
1945	Suzuki Kantaro
1945	Higashikuni Naruhiko
1945–1946	Shidehara Kijuro
1946–1947	Yoshida Shigeru
1947–1948	Katayama Tetsu
1948	Ashida Hitoshi
1948–1954	Yoshida Shigeru
1954–1956	Hatoyama Ichiro
1956–1957	Ishibashi Tanzan
1957–1960	Kishi Nobusuke
1960–1964	Ikedo Hayato
1964–1972	Sato Eisaku
1972–1974	Tanaka Kakuei
1974–1976	Miki Takeo
1976–1978	Fukuda Takeo
1978–1980	Ohira Masayoshi
1980–1982	Suzuki Zenko
1982–1987	Nakasone Yasuhiro
1987–1989	Takeshita Noboru
1989	Uno Sosuke
1989–1991	Kaifu Toshiki
1991–1993	Miyazawa Kiichi
1993–1994	Hosokawa Morihiro
1994	Hata Tsutomu

1994–1996	Murayama Tomiichi
1996–1998	Hashimoto Ryutaro
1998–2000	Obuchi Keizo
2000–2001	Mori Yoshiro
2001–	Koizumi Junichiro

Jarrow March Protest march of unemployed shipworkers from Jarrow in NE England to London at the height of the depression in 1936. *p.413*

Jayavarman II (reigned 802–869) Founder of the Angkorian dynasty, which ruled the Khmer state in Cambodia (9th–12th centuries). He was worshiped as a deity. During his rule the Khmer capital was at Roulos; his great nephew, Yasovarman, began the construction of the magnificent temple of Angkor Thom c.900.

Jazz Age The heyday of jazz in the US in the 1920s. *p.400*

Jazz Singer, The First film with sound (1927).

Jeanne d'Arc *see* Joan of Arc

Jefferson, Thomas (1743–1826) 3rd President of the US (Republican Democrat, 1801–09). Drafted the Declaration of Independence and helped to form the Virginia state constitution acting as governor from 1779–81. In 1789, appointed Secretary of State by George Washington. Became Vice-President under John Adams (1797–1801). Presided over the war with Tripoli, and the Louisiana Purchase of 1803 which opened up much of the West to American expansion and the Embargo Act of 1807.

Jena Auerstädt ⚔ of Napoleonic Wars – the War of the 3rd Coalition (1806). French victory.

Jenghiz Khan *see* Genghis Khan

Jenkin's Ear, War of Naval war between Britain and Spain (1739–42).

Jenkinson, Anthony (died 1611) English merchant who traveled from Moscow down the Volga to Astrakhan and crossed the Caspian Sea into Persia, to the Mongol city of Bukhara. He wrote the first account of the Tatars in the English language.

Jenne (var. Djenné) City of Mali, once a great market for trade in gold, salt, and slaves. It also became the most important center of Islamic learning in the region. The Great Mosque is a spectacular example of baked mud architecture. *p.233*

Jerusalem Capital of modern Israel. The city is sacred to the three great monotheistic religions: Judaism, Christianity, and Islam. Its origins date back to the 4th millennium BCE. King David supposedly made the city his capital c.1000 BCE, but archeological remains from this period are lacking. The city prospered under the rule of Herod the Great (c.73–4 BCE), who rebuilt the Temple. Herod's city, however, was destroyed by the Romans after the Jewish revolts of 66–70 and 132–135 CE and completely rebuilt under Hadrian as the city of Aelia Capitolina. Mosaic map of Jerusalem (500 CE). *p.108*

Jesuits Religious order founded by St. Ignatius Loyola in 1534, properly known as the Society of Jesus. The most vigorous defenders of the Catholic faith in the Counter-Reformation, the Jesuits specialized in education and missionary work. Dedicated Jesuit missionaries even carried Catholicism to China and Japan. In S America, their missions among the Indians became virtually autonomous states within the Spanish Empire. Their political power became so great that they were expelled from Portugal and its territories in 1759 and suppressed by the pope in 1773, though the order was restored in 1814. *p.279* Jesuits in Japan. *p.299* Jesuits in China. *p.327*

Jesus of Nazareth (*aka* Jesus Christ, c.4 BCE–29 CE) During the Roman occupation of Palestine, he became the inspiration of the Christian religion, believed by his followers to be the Son of God. Jesus was crucified as a troublemaker in Jerusalem c.29 CE. The Greek *Khristos* means "anointed one," a translation of the Hebrew Messiah. His life, preaching, and miracles are recounted in the New Testament.

Jewish diaspora Term used today to describe the Jewish communities living outside the Holy Land. Originally used to designate the dispersal of the Jews outside Palestine after the Babylonian exile in 586 BCE, and following the Jewish revolts of 66–74 CE and 132–35 CE.

Jewish revolts Series of rebellions in Judaea following its conquest by the Romans in 63 CE. The first revolt began in 66 CE, was put down by Vespasian and his son Titus, and led to the legendary Jewish martyrdom at Masada in 73 CE. The second revolt of 132–135 led by Simon Bar Cochba. Suppression led to dispersal of Jews (diaspora) throughout southwest Asia and the Roman Empire.

Jews People of southwest Asia, originally descendants of Judah, the fourth son of Jacob. Later came to designate followers of the religion of Judaism.

Jiang Jieshi (*var.* Chiang Kai-shek, 1887–1975) Chinese general and political leader. Leader of the Kuomintang from 1926, president of the republic 1928–31. Opposed the Chinese Communist Party until defeated in 1949 when he withdrew to Taiwan.

Jiang Qing *see* Cultural Revolution
jihad Holy war of the Muslims.

Jin dynasty (*var.* Chin dynasty, reigned 1115–1234) Northern Chinese dynasty of the Sixteen Kingdoms period.

Jin empire *see* Jin dynasty

Jinghis Khan *see* Genghis Khan

Joan of Arc (*var.* Fr. Jeanne d'Arc, *aka* the Maid of Orleans, Fr. La Pucelle, c.1412–31). French national heroine. Claiming to hear voices urging her to rid France of English domination, she led an army which raised the siege of Orléans (1429), enabling the dauphin to be crowned Charles VII at Rheims. Captured and sold to the English, she was convicted of heresy and burnt at the stake. She was canonized in 1920. *p.258*

João I (1357–1433) King of Portugal (reigned 1385–1433). Founder of the House of Avis, he saved his country from the threat of union with Spain by his victory at ⚔ Aljubarotta (1385).

João V (1689–1750) King of Portugal (1707–50). A supporter of the Triple Alliance (between Britain, Austria, and the Netherlands), he embarked on a series of unsuccessful campaigns in Castile during the War of the Spanish Succession. Though his treasury benefited from the recent discovery of gold in Brazil, João V was entirely under the influence of the clergy and the administration suffered from his neglect.

John (1167–1216) King of England (reigned 1199–1216). His reign saw the renewal of war with Philip II Augustus of France, to whom he had lost several continental possessions. Tensions between John and Pope Innocent III led to the imposition of an interdict over England in 1208 and the king's excommunication in 1212. He was also forced to grant the Magna Carta at Runnymede. *p.208*

Johnson, Lyndon Baines (1908–73) 36th President of the US (Democrat, 1963–68). Became President following the assassination of John F. Kennedy in 1963. His administration passed the Civil Rights Act (1964), the Voting Rights Act (1965) aimed at improving the position of African Americans, and introduced a series of economic and social reforms under the slogan the "Great Society," but his personal standing was severely weakened by public protests against the escalation of the Vietnam War.

Jolliet, Father Louis (1645–1700) Explorer of N America. Born in Canada, Jolliet discovered the source of the Mississippi River with Jacques Marquette. In 1672–73 they traveled along the river to within 640 km of the Gulf of Mexico.

Jolson, Al (prev. Asa Yoelson, 1886–1950) Russian-born American actor and singer. He toured with various stage and minstrel shows, making his Broadway debut in 1911. In 1928, he made screen history when he starred in the first full-length "talkie," *The Jazz Singer*. In 1928, his first big record hit "Sonny boy/there's a rainbow round my shoulder" sold over three million copies.

Jomon culture Hunters, fishers, and gatherers who lived in Japan from c.7500 to 250 BCE. They fully exploited an abundance of fish, animal, and plant resources and, in the densely populated east, lived in permanent villages, but there is no evidence of plant cultivation. Jomon pottery dates back to c.10,000 BCE, the earliest known anywhere in the world. The culture is named from the cord-decorated pottery found at the Omori shell mounds near Tokyo. c.6500 BCE.

JORDAN Sharing borders with Iraq, Syria, Israel, and Saudi Arabia, Jordan has just 26 km (16 miles) of coastline on the Gulf of Aqaba. Jordan formally includes the West Bank of the Jordan river and East Jerusalem in its territory, but Israel has occupied these areas since 1967. Jordan ceded its claim to the West Bank to the PLO in 1988. Phosphates, and tourism associated with important historical sites such as Petra, are the mainstays of the economy.

CHRONOLOGY

1918 King Faisal,after playing leading role in Arab Revolt against Turks establishes an autonomous Arab government in Damascus.

1920 The Palestine Mandate is awarded to the United Kingdom and King Faisal is forced out of Damascus.

1921 King Abdallah is proclaimed ruler of Transjordan.

1948 King Abdallah is declared King of all Palestine.

1949 The remaining part of Palestine becomes the "Hashemite Kingdom of Jordan."

1953 Hussein appointed king.

1967 Israel seizes West Bank territories.

1970 Massive crackdown on PLO in Jordan.

1988 Jordan cedes claims to West Bank to PLO.

1994 Peace treaty with Israel.

1999 Death of King Hussein; succession of King Abdullah II.

Juan Carlos I (1938–) King of Spain (reigned 1978–). The grandson of Alfonso XIII (who abdicated in 1931), he was named as his successor to the dictator, General Franco in 1969, and proclaimed king in 1975. Juan Carlos presided over a rapid, and peaceful, transition to democracy; by 1978 Spain was declared a parliamentary monarchy. In 1981 King Juan Carlos foiled a Francoist military coup by taking preventative action and winning pledges of loyalty from military commanders.

Juan-juan *see* Ruanruan

Juárez, Benito (1806–72) Mexican statesman (reigned 1861–72). As part of the Liberal government which replaced the Conservative Santa Anna, Juárez helped pass the anti-clerical and liberal constitution of 1857. In 1861 he assumed the role of president of Mexico, a post he held until his death. A French invasion under Maximilian forced him to retreat to the north, but after the French were defeated in 1867 he was able to restore Republican rule.

Judaism Religion of the Jewish people, developed among the ancient Hebrews and characterized by a belief in one God, its ethical system and its ritual practices, based on the Pentateuch as interpreted by the rabbis of the Talmudic period in the first five centuries CE and their successors up to the present day. *p.41*

Jugurtha (died 104 BCE) King of Numidia (reigned 118–105 BCE), who struggled to free his N African kingdom from Roman rule.

Julio-Claudian dynasty The four successors of the Roman Emperor Augustus (reigned 31 BCE–14 CE), all indirectly descended from Julius Caesar. The Emperor Augustus, who had extended the frontiers of the empire and introduced stable and efficient government, was succeeded by Tiberius (14–37 CE), the most able of the dynasty. Caligula (37–41 CE), was famous for his excesses and capricious behaviour. He was succeeded by Claudius (41–54 CE), who devoted himself to public works and administrative reforms, although he never gained the respect of his subjects. The tyrannical Nero (54–68) was notorious for his ruthless murders, and the revenge he took on the Christians for the great fire of Rome (64 CE) which, it was rumored, he had started himself.

Juneau, Joe 19th-century French explorer of Alaska. Founded town of Juneau and made important gold strike in Alaska in 1880.

Jupiter (*var.* Gr. Zeus) Most powerful god in the Greco-Roman pantheon.

Jurchen People originating in the mountains of eastern Manchuria, Central Asia. Established the Jin state and seized northern China 1126, restricting Song rule to the south of China. *See also* Jin dynasty

Justinian I (483–565) Byzantine emperor. Born in what is now Yugoslavia, he was adopted by his uncle Justin I, who ascended the throne in 518, and succeeded him in 527. He is famous for his reforms of the Roman law codes and imperial constitutions, and the publication of the *Codex Justinianus* (534). His program of costly public works included the building of the church of Santa Sophia in Constantinople. He attempted to win back large areas of the Roman Empire that had been lost in the previous century, engaging in major campaigns against the Vandals in Spain and North Africa and the Ostrogoths in Italy, but his victories proved fragile. *p.117*

Jutes Germanic people who, with the Angles and Saxons, invaded Britain in the 5th century CE.

Jutland Naval ⚔ of World War I (May 31 1916) between the British and German fleets in the North Sea. Though the result was inconclusive, the Allies thereafter retained control of the North Sea.

K

K'ang-hsi *see* Kangxi

Kabuki theater Form of highly stylized Japanese theater that dramatizes popular legends, using only male actors. *p.315*

Kadesh ⚔ between the Egyptians and Hittites (c.1285 BCE). First recorded battle in world history.

Kadphises I (*var.* Kujula Kadphises, Chiu-Chiu-Chueh) Kushan ruler who achieved political unity of the Yuezhi tribes in the 1st century CE, and ruled over northern India, Afghanistan and parts of central Asia.

Kalewa ⚔ of World War II (May 1942). Marked furthest point of Japanese advance in Burma.

Kalmar, Union of (Jun 1397) Scandinavian union that brought the kingdoms of Norway, Sweden, and Denmark together under a single monarch until 1523.

Kalmyks Buddhist Mongolian people of C Asia who came under pressure from Qing China 1758–59.

Kamakura shogunate Military rulers of Japan (1185–1333). *p.218*

Kamehameha I (1782–1819) The king of one of the four kingdoms of Hawaii who, with superior vessels and firearms, as well as foreign aid, succeeded in conquering all the islands, with the exception of Kauai and Niihau, by 1795. He reorganized government, encouraged industry, while withstanding foreign cultural influence and adhering to traditional Hawaiian religious practices (abolished after his death by his favorite queen, Kaahumanu). *p.347*

kamikaze Japanese term for "divine wind", a typhoon which halted second Mongol invasion attempt (1281); adopted as name by Japanese suicide fighter-bomber squadrons during final campaigns of World War II.

Kaminalijuyú (*fl.* 500 BCE) Central American civilization.

Kangxi (*var.* K'ang-his, 1654–1722) Emperor of the Manchu (Qing) dynasty of China (reigned 1661–1722).

Kanishka (*var.* Kaniska, reigned c.78–96 CE) Ruler of the Kushan, or Kushana, empire of south central Asia whose adoption of (Mahayana) Buddhism was instrumental in the spread of the faith to Central Asia and along the Silk Road to China.

Kansas Nebraska Act (1854) The third of the critical decisions regarding the extension of slavery in the US, the Kansas-Nebraska Act applied the principle of popular sovereignty to the territorial organization of Kansas and Nebraska. The passage of the act led to the formation of the Republican Party to oppose the expansion of slavery into new territories.

Kao Tsu *see* Gao Zhu

Kara Khitai Muslim empire in central Asia which rose to prominence in the 12th century. In 1141 the Kara Khitai defeated the Seljuk Turks at Samarkand.

Karlowitz, Peace of (*var.* Carlowitz, 1699) Peace settlement that ended hostilities (1683–99) between the Ottoman Empire and the Holy League (Austria, Poland, Venice, and Russia) which significantly diminished Turkish influence in east-central Europe, making Austria the dominant power there.

Kashmir Region of south Asia on the border between India and Pakistan, bittery disputed since partition in 1947. *See also* Jammu and Kashmir

Kasyapa (447–495) Ruler of Sigiriya in Sri Lanka, who usurped power and believed he was a god-king. *p.107*

Katanga Province that secedes from the newly independent Congo in 1960. The UN tried to broker a reconciliation, but their own troops were caught up in the fighting. A settlement was reached in 1963.

Kay, John Inventor of flying shuttle (1733).

Kazakhs People of Central Asia. Traditionally pastoral nomads; incorporated into the Russian Empire in the mid-19th century, now mainly settled in Kazakhstan.

KAZAKHSTAN The second-largest of the former Soviet republics, Kazakhstan extends almost 2000 km (1240 miles) from the Caspian Sea in the west to the Altai Mountains in the east and 1300 km (806 miles) north to south. It borders Russia to the north and China to the east. Kazakhstan was the last Soviet republic to declare its independence, in 1991. In 1999, elections confirmed the former communist Nursultan Nazarbayev and his supporters in power. Kazakhstan has considerable economic potential, and many Western companies seek to exploit its mineral resources.

CHRONOLOGY

16th century Kypachs and other Turkic, Mongol, and Iranian groups break away from the Golden Horde and migrate to the territory now known as Kazakhstan, forming three nomadic states: the Senior Zhouz (Horde) in the southeast, the Middle Zhouz in the northern and central areas, and the Junior Zhouz in the northwest.

1846 The Senior Zhouz joins the Russian Empire.

1889 Russian eastward expansion leads to a law on designated areas for state-aided settlement, including regions of present-day Kazakhstan.

1916 Rebellion against Russian rule brutally suppressed.

1917 Russian Revolution inspires civil war in Kazakhstan between Bolsheviks, anti-Bolsheviks, and Kazakh nationalists. Russian settlement intensified after the 1917 Revolution and Kazakhstan was subjected to intensive industrial and agricultural development.

1918 Kazakh nationalists set up autonomous republic.

1920 Bolsheviks take control. Kirghiz Autonomous Soviet Socialist Republic (ASSR) set up within Russian Soviet Federative Socialist Republic.

1925 Kirghiz ASSR renamed Kazakh ASSR.

1936 Kazakhstan becomes full union republic of the USSR as Kazakh SSR.

1930s Stalin's collectivization program leads to increase in Russian settlement and the deaths of an estimated million Kazakhs.

1941–1945 Large-scale deportations of Germans, Jews, Crimean Tatars, and others to Kazakhstan.

1950s Nuclear test site set up at Semipalatinsk; 500 nuclear explosions follow before testing ends in 1991.

1954–1960 Khrushchev's policy to plow "Virgin Lands" for grain most vigorously followed in Kazakhstan. Russian settlement reaches a peak.

1986 Riots in Almaty after an ethnic Russian, Gennadi Kolbin, appointed head of Kazakhstan Communist Party (CPK) to replace Kazakh, Dinmukhamed Kunyev.

1989 Kolbin replaced by Nursultan Nazarbayev, an ethnic Kazakh and chair of Council of Ministers. Reform of political and administrative system.

1990 CPK wins elections to Supreme Soviet by overwhelming majority. Nazarbayev appointed first president of Kazakhstan. Kazakhstan declares sovereignty.

1991 Kazakhstan votes to preserve USSR as union of sovereign states. USSR authorities hand control of enterprises in Kazakhstan to Kazakh government. CPK restructures itself as Socialist Party of Kazakhstan (SPK). Independent Republic of Kazakhstan declared; joins CIS.

1992 Opposition demonstrations against dominance of reformed communists in Supreme Soviet, now Supreme Kenges. Nationalists form Republican Party, Azat.

1993 Adoption of new constitution. Introduction of new currency, the tenge.

1994 Legislative elections annulled after proof of widespread voting irregularities.

1995 Adoption of new constitution broadening presidential powers; referendum extends Nazarbayev's term until 2000; legislative elections.

1998 Legislature approves constitutional amendments, including the holding of early presidential election.

1999 Nazarbayev reelected president for a further seven-year term.

2003 Sale of farmland legalized.

Kemal Pasha, Mustafa *see* Atatürk

Kennedy, Edmund (1818–48) Born in the Channel Islands, he migrated to New South Wales in 1840. Trained as a surveyor he joined Sir Thomas Mitchell's expedition into central Queensland in 1847. In 1848 he led an expedition up the eastern coast of Queensland to Cape York. During the course of the journey all his party perished – Kennedy was speared by Aborigines while within sight of his supply ship.

Kennedy, John Fitzgerald (1917–1963) 35th President of the US (Democrat, 1960–63). Following service in US navy during World War II, became the youngest elected US president at the age of 43. He aimed to introduce legislation for the improvement of civil rights and for the extension of funding for healthcare and education. Foreign policy issues included the unsuccessful invasion of the Bay of Pigs in Cuba, the division of Europe, the Cuban Missile Crisis which brought the world to the brink of nuclear war, and the continuing involvement of the US in Vietnam. He was assassinated in Dallas, Texas on Nov 22 1963. *p.429*

Kennesaw Mountain ⚔ of American Civil War (Jun 27 1864). Confederate victory.

KENYA
Kenya straddles the equator on Africa's east coast. Its central plateau is bisected by the Great Rift Valley. The land to the north is desert, while to the east lies a fertile coastal belt. From the 10th century, Arab coastal settlers mixed with indigenous peoples in the region. Britain's need for a route to landlocked Uganda led to the formation in 1895 of the British East African Protectorate in the coastal region. After independence from the UK in 1963, politics was dominated by Jomo Kenyatta, who was succeeded in 1978 by President Daniel arap Moi, whose divide-and-rule policies have drawn accusations of favoritism and of fomenting ethnic hatreds. His KANU won elections easily in 1992 and 1997, amid accusations of electoral fraud. Economic mainstays are tourism and agriculture, but high population growth is a major problem.

CHRONOLOGY
1900–1918 White settlement.
1920 Interior becomes British colony.
1930 Jomo Kenyatta goes to UK; stays 14 years.
1944 Kenyan African Union (KAU) formed; Kenyatta returns to lead it.
1952–1956 Mau Mau, Kikuyu-led violent campaign to restore African lands. State of emergency; 13,000 people killed.
1953 KAU banned. Kenyatta jailed.

1960 State of emergency ends. Tom Mboya and Oginga Odinga form KANU.
1961 Kenyatta freed; takes up presidency of KANU.
1963 KANU wins elections. Kenyatta prime minister. Full independence declared.
1964 Republic of Kenya formed with Kenyatta as president and Odinga as vice president.
1966 Odinga defects to form Kenya People's Union (KPU).
1969 KANU sole party to contest elections (also 1974). Tom Mboya of KANU assassinated. Unrest. KPU banned and Odinga arrested.
1978 Kenyatta dies. Vice President Daniel arap Moi succeeds him.
1982 Kenya declared a one-party state. Opposition to Moi. Abortive air force coup. Odinga rearrested.
1986 Open "queue-voting" replaces secret ballot in first stage of general elections. Other measures to extend Moi's powers incite opposition.
1988 Moi wins third term and extends his control over judiciary.
1990 Government implicated in deaths of foreign minister Robert Ouko and Anglican archbishop. Riots. Odinga and others form FORD, outlawed by government.
1991 Arrest of FORD leaders and attempts to stop prodemocracy demonstrations. Donors suspend aid. Moi agrees to introduce multiparty system. Ethnic violence on increase.
1992 FORD splits into factions led by ex-minister Kenneth Matiba and Odinga. Opposition weakness helps Moi win December elections.
1994 Odinga dies.
1997 December, Moi wins further term in widely criticized elections.
1998 Bomb explodes at US embassy in Nairobi, killing 230 and wounding thousands.
1999 Moi appoints paleontologist Richard Leakey to lead government drive against corruption.
2000 Worst drought since 1947.
2001 Leakey resigns. Drought threatens starvation for millions.
2002 Thousands displaced by recurrence of major floods. Israeli tourists targeted in terrorist attacks. KANU defeated by NARC and Mwai Kibaki elected president.

Khanbaliq *see* Beijing, Cambaluc
Khedive of Egypt The title, granted by the Sultan of Turkey in 1867, to his viceroy in Egypt, Ismail. "Khedive" is a Persian word meaning prince, or sovereign. The title was abandoned in 1914 when the title "Sultan" was adopted.
Khitans (*var.* Liao) People of Mongolia who established the Liao Empire in Manchuria (907–1125).
Khmer Rouge A Marxist party in Cambodia, led by Pol Pot, organized to oppose the right-wing government of Lon Nol, 1970–75. They overthrew the government in 1975 and instituted a reign of terror which led to the death of over two million Cambodians. They were overthrown in 1979 following a Vietnamese invasion.
Khmer state In the 12th and 13th cenuries, the Khmer kingdom controlled most of SE Asia from the magnificent city of Angkor in southern Cambodia. Although Hinduism was the state religion, it combined many elements of Buddhism, as can be seen in the magnificent monumental architecture of Angkor, which reached its zenith under the rule of Jayavarman VII (c.1200).
Khomeini, Ayatollah Ruhollah (1900–1989) Iranian religious and political leader. A Shi'ite Muslim whose bitter opposition to the pro-Western regime of Muhammad Reza Shah Pahlavi led to his exile from Iran in 1964. Following a popular revolution and the overthrow of the Shah's government in 1979, he returned to Iran and was proclaimed religious leader of the Islamic Revolution. Islamic law was once more imposed, and a return to strict fundamentalist Islamic tradition enforced.
Khosrau I (*var.* Khosrow I, *aka* Khosrau the Just, reigned 531–579) Sassanian Persian shah who quelled the Mazdakite rebellion and successfully resisted the Byzantines.
Khosrau II (*var.* Khosrow II, *aka* Khosrau the Victorious) (reigned 591–628). Persian shah at the apogee of the Sassanian era. In 601 he attacked Byzantium, capturing Antioch, Jerusalem, and Alexandria.
Khrushchev, Nikita Sergeyevich (1894–1971) Soviet statesman and successor to Stalin. First Secretary of the Communist Party (1953–64). Deposed in a coup and replaced by Leonid Brezhnev.

Khufu (c.2575–2465 BCE) Egyptian pharaoh of the 4th dynasty who initiated the building of the largest pyramid at Giza: 147 m high, consisting of c.2.3 million blocks, each weighing c.2.5 tonnes.

Khwarizm empire (*aka* Empire of the Khwarizm Shah, Uzbek Empire) State of Turkic origin, broadly corresponding with ancient Chorasmia, N Persia, based around Samarkand from the 12th century. Overrun by Mongols, then forming part of Khanate of the Golden Horde, and subsequently conquered by Timur (1378), the state fragmented into a number of Muslim khanates based around Bukhara and Samarkand which were finally absorbed into the Russian Empire during the 19th century.

Kiev ⚔ of World War II (Sep–Nov 1943) Soviet forces defeat of German counter-offensive in Ukraine.

Kievan Rus State established in 840 by Vikings from Sweden who were trading along the rivers between the Baltic and the Black seas. Kiev became a flourishing capital; through trading links with Byzantium the Christian faith became established there at the end of the 10th century. Repeated sackings by nomads from the east reduced Kiev to a number of independent and warring principalities from the middle of the 11th century. Monastery of the Caves (1051). *p.167*

Kilwa Island off the coast of present-day Tanzania. An important trading center was founded there in the 10th century by merchants from the Gulf. *p.196*

Kimberley South Africa, site of important gold finds in 1867.

King, Clarence (1842–1901) American explorer and geologist. In 1867, as director in charge of the United States Geological Exploration of the Fortieth Parallel he began extensive ten-year survey of a 160-km-wide strip of land running from Cheyenne, Wyoming to the eastern Sierra Nevada.

King, Martin Luther (1929–1968) US civil rights leader. A baptist minister in Alabama, Martin Luther King founded the Southern Christian Leadership Conference in 1957 to organize activities for the promotion of black civil rights throughout the US. He advocated a policy of non-violence and passive resistance, an effective strategy which undoubtedly helped the passage of the Civil Rights Act of 1964 and the Voting Rights Act of 1965. He was awarded the Kennedy Peace Prize and the Nobel Prize. In 1969 he was assassinated in Memphis, Tennessee by James Earl Ray. The third Monday in January is now celebrated as Martin Luther King Day in the US. *p.432*

King Movement A Maori movement of the late 1850s that opposed land sales to European settlers and demanded a Maori state. It was led by chief "King" Te Wherowhero.

King Philip's War (1675–76) Conflict between English colonists and Indians in New England following the rapid expansion of European settlement into Indian territory from 1640 onwards. The conflict involved most of the tribes of New England including the Wapanoag and the Narragansett, and may have led to the loss of perhaps 600 settlers and 3000 Indians, who thereafter fled north and west.

King's Mountain ⚔ of American Revolutionary War, Oct 7 1780, American victory.

Kingsley, Mary (1862–1900) English traveler who journeyed through western and equatorial Africa and became the first European to enter parts of present-day Gabon.

KIRIBATI Formerly part of the colony of the Gilbert and Ellice Islands, the Gilberts became independent from Britain in 1979 and took the name Kiribati (pronounced "Kir-ee-bahs"). British interest in the Gilbert Islands rested solely on the exploitation of the phosphate deposits on Banaba; these ran out in 1980. In 1981, Kiribati won damages (but not the costs of litigation) from the British for decades of phosphate exploitation.

CHRONOLOGY

1606 The Spanish explorer, Quiros, sights one of the islands in Kiribati, already inhabited by Micronesian people. European exploration continues during the 18th and 19th centuries.

1857 Christianity is introduced.

1892 The British establish protectorate over the phosphate-producing Gilbert and Ellice Islands.

1916 The Gilbert and Ellice Islands are declared a British colony.

1942–3 The Gilbert Islands are occupied by the Japanese. Tarawa Atoll is the site of a fierce battle between United States and Japanese troops.

1957 First British nuclear tests take place near Kiritimati.

1979 Independence as two states, Kiribati and Tuvalu.

1981 Kiribati wins damages for phosphate mining from UK.

1986 Kiribati-US fishing deal.

1994 NPP loses election.

1998 Elections confirm Teburoro Tito in power.

1999 National drought emergency.

Klerk, Frederik Willem de (1936–) South African politician who as president of South Africa (1989–94), brought the apartheid system of racial segregation to an end. Both he and Nelson Mandela received the Nobel Peace Prize in 1993, in recognition of their efforts to establish non-racial democracy in South Africa.

Klondike Region of Canada close to Alaska. The discovery of gold there in 1896 prompted the gold rush of 1897–8.

Knights Hospitaller (*var.* Knights of St. John) Military/religious order established at Jerusalem in the early 12th century following the success of the First Crusade. Its purpose was to care for pilgrims to the Holy Land, but the Knights also played an important role in the defence of the Crusader states. In 1310, the Hospitallers took Rhodes, which remained their base until 1522, when it was taken by the Ottomans. They were then granted the island of Malta by Charles V.

Knights of St. John *see* Knights Hospitaller

Knights Templar Military/religious order founded c.1118 to protect pilgrim routes to Jerusalem. In the 12th and 13th centuries, knights of the order fought in all the major campaigns against Islam. They acquired estates all over Christian Europe, but their wealth and influence made them enemies. In 1307, Philip IV of France had the order accused of heresy and other crimes and it was suppressed in 1312.

Knossos Bronze Age city on Crete, a focus of the Minoan civilization, and known for the artistic and architectural brilliance of its palace, built c.2000 BCE, which dominated the city's mansions, houses, and paved roads. Knossos flourished for some 1500 years, despite its palace being destroyed several times (once by the erupton of Thera), and invasion by the Mycenaeans c.1450. It was finally destroyed by the Romans 68–67 BCE. *See also* Minoan civilization

Knut *see* Canute

Koguryo North Korean clan destroyed by the Tang in 668. *See also* Korea

Kök Türk (Blue Turk) Empire of Central Asia (551–72).

Kongo (14th–17th century) Kingdom of C Africa, which came increasingly under Portuguese influence after 1483. *p.291*

Kongzi *see* Confucius

Königsberg ⚔ of World War II (Feb–Apr 1945) Prolonged siege of German forces by Soviet troops.

Koran (*var.* Qu'ran) The holy book of Islam. *p.125 See also* Islam

Korea Peninsula of E Asia, frequently under Chinese and Japanese influence and control; early states included Koguryo (c.150–668 CE), Paekche (c.250–663 CE), and Silla (from 313 CE). The Silla Period lasted from 676 to 935, the Koryo Period from 936 to 1392. The Yi dynasty (1392–1910), with its capital at Kyongsang, was often ruled as a vassal of the Ming or Qing. Korea was annexed to Japan during the period 1910–1945, then partitioned into the separate states of N and S Korea (1948). Yi royal tombs. *p.265 See also* Korea, North; Korea, South

KOREA, NORTH

Comprising the northern half of the Korean peninsula, North Korea is separated from the US-dominated South by an armistice line straddling the 38th parallel. Much of the country is mountainous; the Chaeryong and Pyongyang plains in the southwest are the most fertile regions. An independent communist republic from 1948, it remains largely isolated. With its economy starved of capital, it now faces a food crisis requiring large-scale international assistance. *See also* Korea; Korea, South; Korean War

Chronology

1946 KWP (Korean Workers' Party) founded. One of leaders is Kim Il Sung, who has received training in Red Army.

1948 Democratic People's Republic of Korea created with Kim Il Sung as leader.

1950–1953 Korean War. Kim Il Sung invades South Korea with idea of uniting country. N Koreans take much of the south, before American intervention drives them back.

1950s Kim Il Sung starts to develop personality cult.

1991 North and South Korea join the United Nations.

1994 Kim Il Sung dies; declared "Eternal President" four years later. Kim Il Sung's son Kim Jong Il succeeds him, but does not take presidential title.

1996 Famine follows widespread floods. N Korea troops enter demilitarized zone.

1997 Threat of famine worsens. Kim Jong Il becomes party leader.

1998 N Korean mini-submarine captured in S Korean waters.

2000 Historic North-South summit.

KOREA, SOUTH

South Korea occupies the southern half of the Korean peninsula in East Asia. Over 80% of its terrain is mountainous and two-thirds is forested. Rice is the major agricultural product, grown by over 85% of South Korea's three million farmers. The whole peninsula was annexed by Japan from 1910 to 1945. The split between South Korea and the communist North originated with the arrival of rival US and Soviet armies in 1945. Although the two states have discussed reunification, the legacy of hostility arising from the 1950–1953 Korean War remains a major obstacle.

Chronology

676 CE The Korean peninsula is unified under the Silla kingdom.

936 CE A soldier of one of the warring kingdoms into which the Silla regime has disintegrated rebels, becomes king and succeeds in unifying Korea, calling the kingdom Koryo, whence the name Korea.

1392 Yi Song-gye, general under the increasingly bankrupt Koryo regime, leads a revolt to depose the king, founding Korea's longest-reigning and best-known dynasty, the Yi dynasty.

1644 After conquering China, the Manchus invade Korea, and it becomes a vassal state of China under the Qing Dynasty.

1894–95 Japan defeats the Chinese in Korea, beginning the Sino-Japanese War.

1904–1905 Russo-Japanese War. Japan conquers Korea.

1910 Japan annexes Korea.

1919 Independence protests violently suppressed.

1945 US and Soviet armies arrive. Korea split at 38°N. South under de facto US rule.

1948 Republic of South Korea created; Syngman Rhee becomes president of an increasingly authoritarian regime.

1950 Hostilities between North and South, each aspiring to rule a united Korea. North invades, sparking Korean War. US, with UN backing, enters on South's side; China unofficially assists North.

1951 Fighting stabilizes near 38th parallel.

1953 Armistice; de facto border at cease-fire line, close to the 38th parallel.

1960 Syngman Rhee resigns in face of popular revolt.

1961 Military coup leads to authoritarian junta led by Park Chung Hee.

1963 Pressure for civilian government. Park reelected as president (also in 1967 and 1971). Strong manufacturing base and exports drive massive economic development program.

1965 Links restored with Japan.

1966 45,000 troops engaged in South Vietnam.

1972 Martial law stifles political opposition. New constitution with greater presidential powers.

1979 Park assassinated. Gen. Chun Doo Hwan, intelligence chief, leads coup.

1980 Chun chosen as president. Kim Dae Jung and other opposition leaders arrested.

1986 Car exports start.

1987 Emergence of prodemocracy movement. Roh Tae Woo, Chun's chosen successor, elected president.

1988 Inauguration of Sixth Republic which includes genuine multiparty democracy. Restrictions on foreign travel lifted.

1991 South Korea joins UN.

1992 Diplomatic links established with China. Kim Young Sam elected president.

1996 Chun sentenced to death on charges of organizing 1979–1980 overthrow of civilian government; Roh given prison term. Both sentences rescinded.

▶

1997 Violent protests against new labor laws. Steel scandal brings down government. Economic crisis.
1998 Kim Dae Jung president.
2000 Historic North-South summit in Pyongyang. Lee Han Dong appointed premier.
2002 Roh Moo Hyun president.
2003 182 die in subway arson attack.
2004 Roh suspended for two months. UP wins elections. Loudspeakers in DMZ cease propaganda broadcasts.

Korean War Conflict (1950–53) between newly created (1948) states of N and S Korea, precipitated when the communist north invaded the south, escalating to involve Chinese, UN, and US troops. *p.426*

Koryo Kingdom of medieval Korea, founded in 935.

Köse Dagh ⚔ (1243) Seljuks of Rum defeated by Mongols.

Kosovo (*var.* Kosovo Polje, "Field of the Blackbirds") ⚔ (1389) Defeat of Christian Serbs and Bosnians by Muslim Ottomans under Murad I, who died in the battle.

Kosovo Province within the republic of Yugoslavia with ethnic Albanian majority population. Serb ethnic cleansing directed at Albanians led to NATO intervention in 1999. *p.453*

Krak des Chevaliers Crusader castle in present-day Syria. *p.186*

Kristallnacht (*var.* Eng. 'The night of the broken glass') (Nov 9 1938). 91 Jews were killed and many synagogues burned down in coordinated attacks by Nazis against Jews and Jewish property in Germany and Austria.

K'ung-fu-tzu *see* Confucius

Ku Klux Klan Extreme right-wing organization, founded in the southern US after the American Civil War to oppose the new rights granted to Blacks. Though the original Klan was outlawed in 1871, a new version appeared in about 1915, reaching the height of its membership during the 1920s and carrying out acts of terrorism and murder agains Blacks and other minority groups including Jews, Catholics, and other immigrants.

Kublai Khan (*var.* Kubilai Khan, 1215–94) Great Khan of the Mongols from 1260. Founder of the Yuan dynasty which united China, and first foreigner ever to rule a united China.

Kuomintang (*var.* Guomindang). Chinese Nationalist Party. Political party that ruled China from 1928 until the Communist victory in 1949.

Kurds Sunni Muslim people, numbering some 9–10 million, who occupy a mountainous region divided between Turkey, Iran, Iraq, and Syria which the Kurds themselves call Kurdistan. They are politically oppressed in Turkey, and subject to religious persecution in Iraq. In 1988 the support given by Kurdish insurgents to Iran during the Iran-Iraq war led to the use of chemical weapons against them by Saddam Hussein. When Iraq was defeated in the Gulf War, the Kurds staged a revolt in northern Iraq.

Kursk ⚔ of World War II (Jul–Aug 1943). Major tank engagement in which Soviet forces destroyed much of Germany's armoured capacity in Russia; largest tank battle in history.

Kushan empire (*var.* Kushana) State of south Central Asia created in 1st century CE, capital Peshawar, which grew to straddle the Hindu Kush and the Pamirs, incorporating Punjab, Afghanistan, and Sogdiana. The founder of the second Kushana dynasty, Kanishka (reigned c.78–96 CE) adopted Buddhism, and aided its dissemination along the Silk Road to China.

Kushana *see* Kushan empire

Kutuzov, Mikhail Ilarionovich (1745–1813) Russian soldier. Commander-in-Chief of Russian forces which defeated Napoleon at Borodino (1812) and pursued the French army during its retreat from Moscow.

KUWAIT At the northwest extreme of the Gulf, Kuwait is dwarfed by its neighbors Iraq, Iran, and Saudi Arabia. The flat, almost featureless landscape conceals huge oil and gas reserves, which put Kuwait among the world's first oil-rich states. Kuwait traces its independence to 1710, but was under British rule from the late 18th century until 1961. The government denies any historical link with Iraq. In 1990 Iraq invaded, claiming Kuwait as its 19th province. A US-led alliance, under the aegis of the UN, expelled Iraqi forces following a short war in 1991. Since its liberation, Kuwait has built a wall separating its territory from Iraq.

CHRONOLOGY
750–1258 The Abbasid Caliphate of Baghdad controls Kuwait.
1258–1546 Kuwait is under Mongol rule.
1546–1918 The Ottomans govern Kuwait.
1756 The Sabah ruling dynasty is founded.
1899 Shaikh Mubarak the Great, the ruler of Kuwait, grants the UK control of the country's foreign relations.
1934 Shaikh Ahmad al-Jabir grants a concession to the Gulf Oil Corporation of the United States and the Anglo-Persian Oil Company, later the Kuwait Oil Company.
1961 Independence from UK. Iraq claims Kuwait.
1976 Amir suspends National Assembly.
1990 Iraqi invasion.
1991 Liberation following Gulf War.
1992 National Assembly elections.
1999, 2003 Elections; Islamists and liberals win most seats.

Kyoto The cultural and spiritual heart of Japan, the city became the Japanese capital in 794.

KYRGYZSTAN Kyrgyzstan is a small and very mountainous state in central Asia. It is the least urbanized of the former Soviet republics (the rural population is growing faster than the towns) and was among the last to develop its own cultural nationalism. Its moderate government is treading uncertainly between Kyrgyz nationalist pressures and ensuring that the minority Russians are not alienated, since they tend to possess the skills necessary to run a market-based economy.

CHRONOLOGY
8th to 12th centuries Kyrgyz people settle and trade in the valley of the river Chu, site of the present-day capital Bishkek (known as Frunze during Soviet period).
18th century The Kyrgyz develop a recognizable ethnic consciousnes.
1855 Borombei Bekmuratov, chief of the nomad Bugu tribe east of Issyk Kul, accepts dependence on the Russian empire, while other tribes are ruled by the Kokand Khanate.
1860s Expansion of Russian empire into Kyrgyz lands.

1924 Incorporated in USSR.
1991 Independence from USSR under President Akayev, who was already in power under Soviets.
1995 New constitution adopted.
2000 Legislative and presidential elections; Akayev reelected for third term.
2002 Government resigns after police shoot demonstrators.

L

a Pérouse, J.F. Galaup de *see* Pérouse, Jean François Galaup de la

a Salle, René-Robert Cavelier Sieur de (1643–87) French explorer of N America. Between 1679 and 1681 he explored the Great Lakes before traveling the length of the Mississippi and reaching its mouth in 1682. He took over the Mississippi Valley for France, naming the region Louisiana.

ake Regillus ⚔ (496 BCE) Roman victory over an alliance of surrounding Latin cities. The battle ensured Rome's dominance over neighboring cities

alibela An important center of christian pilgrimage in northern Ethiopia, famous for its rock-cut churches build in the 12th century. *p.198*

ander, Richard (1804–34) British explorer of W Africa who traced course of the lower Niger river to its delta.

angobardi *see* Lombards

ao-Tzu (*var.* Laozi) 6th-century BCE Chinese philosopher and sage. Regarded as the inspiration for Taoism and for one of its principal works, the *Tao-te Ching*, compiled c.300 years after his death. This teaches self-sufficiency, simplicity, and respect for nature and ancestors.

LAOS Laos is a landlocked country bordered by Vietnam, Cambodia, Thailand, Burma, and China. The Mekong river forms its main thoroughfare and feeds the fertile lowlands of the Mekong valley. In the late 19th century, France established control over the three small kingdoms of Champasak, Louangphrabang, and Vientiane. Independence from France in 1953 was followed by two decades of civil war, and heavy bombing by US forces during the Vietnam War. The communist Lao People's Revolutionary Party (LPRP) has held power since 1975. The government began to introduce market-oriented reforms in 1986. A transfer of power to a younger generation within the LPRP took place during the 1990s.

CHRONOLOGY

1893 Franco-Siamese treaty establishes French control over all territory east of the Mekong.
1899 Creation of a unified Laos under the French.
1941 Japanese seize power from Vichy French in Indochina.
1946 French rule resumed.
1950 Lao Patriotic Front (LPF) set up to oppose French rule. Gains support of newly formed communist Lao People's Party (LPP).
1953 Independence as a constitutional monarchy backed by France and the US.
1963 LPF begins armed struggle against royal government through its armed wing, the Pathet Lao.
1964 US bombing of North Vietnamese sanctuaries in Laos.
1973 LPRP (formerly the LPF) and royal government form a coalition after withdrawal of US forces from Indochina.
1975 LPRP seizes power, abolishes monarchy, and proclaims Lao People's Democratic Republic. Premier Kaysone Phomvihane adopts policies for "socialist transformation" of economy.
1977 The Treaty of Friendship and Cooperation, providing for mutual security, signed with Vietnam. Relations cool with China.
1978 Popular unrest and resistance to collectivization. Former king and crown prince are arrested and die in captivity. Almost 50,000 Laotians flee to Thailand.
1979 Softer economic line adopted and speed of "socialist transformation" slows.
1986 Fourth Party Congress introduces market-oriented economic reforms.
1988 Brief border war with Thailand. Restoration of diplomatic relations with China.

1989 National elections held. All candidates approved by LPRP. Rapprochement with Thailand.
1990 Counteroffensives against right-wing, largely Hmong, guerrilla bases located in the outer provinces. Most agricultural collectives and state farms disbanded. Arrest of three former officials for promoting multiparty democracy.
1991 A constitution providing for a National Assembly, confirming the leading role of the LPRP, and enshrining the right of private ownership, is promulgated. Kaysone steps down as prime minister and takes up post of president. Khamtay Siphandone becomes prime minister.
1992 Death of President Kaysone; Khamtay becomes LPRP leader.
1994 Thailand-Laos bridge opens over Mekong – first direct road link between the two countries.
1997 Laos becomes a member of ASEAN.
1998 Former prime minister Khamtay becomes president.
1999 October. Student-led demonstration in Vientiane demanding greater political freedom.
2001 Prime Minister Sisavat Keobounphan resigns over economic mismanagement.

Laozi *see* Lao-Tzu

Lapita Austronesian speakers, ancestors of modern Polynesians. Their distinctive style of pottery provides evidence for their migrations in the western Pacific. Remains of their pottery have been found in the Bismarck Archipelago, Fiji, Samoa, and New Caledonia, all dating from the first millennium bce. *p.31*

Lascaux Celebrated cave paintings in southern France, dating from c.17,000 BP.

Lashio ⚔ of World War II (April 1942). Japanese take control of central Burma.

Later Han *see* Han dynasty

Latin colony Dependency of ancient Rome in Italy, where inhabitants had limited rights compared to full Roman citizens.

Latin League Confederacy of small city-states established in the 5th century BCE. The supremacy of Rome gradually made the principles of the league obsolete and it was formally abandoned in 338.

Latins People of central Italy whose lands were annexed by Rome in the 4th century BCE. Their language was carried by the Romans throughout their empire.

LATVIA

LATVIA Lying between Estonia and Lithuania, Latvia is situated on the eastern coast of the Baltic Sea. To the east it borders the Russian Federation and Belarus. The whole country is a low-lying plain, which nowhere rises above 300 meters (975 ft). The Letts (as Latvians were once called) were conquered and christianized by the Livonian Knights (Sword Brothers) in the 13th century. Up until the 20th century their lands were always ruled by their more powerful neighbors. A brief spell of independence after World War I came to an end in 1940. Latvia's independence was recognized by Moscow in 1991. Defense-related industries and agriculture play an important role in the economy. Only just over half of the population are ethnic Latvians.

CHRONOLOGY

1237 The Livonian and Teutonic knights merge after the territory of modern-day Latvia is subjugated by Germans.

1558 Russia, under Ivan the Terrible, declares war on the Livonian Order over access to the Baltic, capturing 20 Livonian strongholds.

1561 Russia, Poland, and Sweden continue to fight over the area.

1609 Livonia is ceded to Sweden by the Russian Basil Shuisky in return for troops during the Russian Time of Troubles.

1700 Sweden attacks Livonia during the Great Northern war against Russia, which acquires Livonia and Estonia from Sweden under Treaty of Nystadt in 1721.

1772 On the first partition of Poland, the Polish part of current-day Latvia becomes part of the Russian Empire. Russia obtains Courland in 1795.

1917 Opposes Russian Bolshevik revolution. Declares independence.

1918–1920 Invaded by Bolsheviks and Germany.

1920 Gains independence.

1944 Incorporated into USSR.

1989 Popular Front (PLF) wins elections; declares independence.

1991 Independence recognized.

1995 TP (People's Party)-led coalition formed.

1998 Elections; LC (Latvia's Way)-led coalition. Naturalization procedure eased.

1999 First woman president. Andris Skele of TP returns as premier.

2000 Skele resigns; replaced by Andris Berzins.

2004 Indulis Emsis becomes world's first Green prime minister. Latvia joins NATO and EU.

Lausanne, Treaty of (1922–23) Peace treaty between World War I Allies and Turkey resolving problems caused by Treaty of Sèvres, which had been rejected by the new Turkish government led by Atatürk. Turkey recovered eastern Thrace and the Dardanelles were opened to all shipping. *See also* Sèvres, Treaty of

Lawrence, Thomas Edward (*aka* "Lawrence of Arabia," 1888–1935) British scholar, soldier, and author. In 1916 he joined the Arab Revolt against the Turks led by Emir Faisal, and participated in the capture of Damascus (1918). He was an adviser to Faisal at the Paris Peace Conference, but later withdrew from public life. His account of the Arab Revolt (1926), has become one of the classics of English literature.

Léry, Chaussegros de 18th-century French explorer of N America.

Le Maire, Jacob (died 1616) Dutch explorer. Commander of voyage round Cape Horn and across the Pacific in 1615–16 with Willem Schouten as pilot. The expedition failed in its aim of finding a practicable route to the Indies in order to break the Dutch East India Company's monopoly of the spice trade. Le Maire died in the Indian Ocean on the homeward journey.

League of Nations Established by the Allied Powers at the Paris Peace Conference (1919) after World War I, the League aimed, by arms reduction, international arbitration and diplomacy, to reduce the threat of further conflict. The League was weakened from the outset by the refusal of US Congress to ratify the Treaty of Versailles, and during the 1930s it proved unable to contain the expansionism of Germany, Japan, and Italy. It was replaced in 1946 by the United Nations. *p.389*

LEBANON

LEBANON Lebanon is dwarfed by its two powerful neighbors, Syria and Israel. The country's coastal strip is fertile and the hinterland mountainous. Although in the minority, Maronite Christians have traditionally ruled Lebanon. A civil war between Muslim and Christian factional groups which began in 1975 threatened to lead to the breakup of the state. However, Saudi Arabia brokered a peace agreement in 1989; politics became more stable and reconstruction began.

CHRONOLOGY

10th century Muslim sects begin their penetration of the Lebanese mountains, until then a predominantly Christian territory.

1516–17 The Ottomans conquer Lebanon.

1608 Fakhr al-Din establishes an autonomous power with the help of the Grand Duchy of Tuscany.

1632 Sultan Murad IV takes control of Lebanon.

1860 The Druzes and Maronites clash and massacres are carried out by both parties in the conflict.

1920 September. France creates the State of Greater Lebanon which includes Tripoli, Tyre, and Beirut.

1941 The Free French proclaim Lebanon free and independent, achieving full autonomy in 1946.

1958 Following a political crisis over Lebanese foreign policy towards the United Arab Republic, President Chamoun requests the presence of US troops to help solve the political crisis.

1975 Civil war erupts.

1982 Israeli invasion.

1989 Taif Agreement ends civil war.

1992 First election in 20 years. Rafiq al-Hariri prime minister.

1996 Israeli attack kills over 100 civilians at UN base in Qana.

1998 Émile Lahoud president.

2000 Israeli forces withdraw.

Lechfeld ⚔ (955). Magyars defeated by Otto I.

Leipzig ⚔ of Napoleonic Wars (Oct 14–16 1813). Allies won great victory over Napoleon but he was able to escape with a remnant of his army.

Legnano ⚔ (1176) Defeat of Frederick Barbarossa by Lombard League.

Leichhardt, Ludwig (1813–48) Prussian-born explorer of the Australian interior. His party vanished without trace on his attempt to cross Australia from east to west in 1848.

Lenin, Vladimir Ilyich (*prev.* Ulyanov, 1870–1924) Russian revolutionary leader. The prime architect of the Bolshevik revolution in Russia, Lenin advocated the creation of a core of professional activists to spearhead a Marxist revolution. In October 1917, following the deposing of Czar Nicholas II, Lenin's Bolsheviks overthrew the provisional government to inaugurate the "dictatorship of the proletariat." *p.398*

Leningrad (*hist. and mod.* St. Petersburg, *temp.* Petrograd, 1914–23) City and port of W Russia, founded by Peter the Great.

Leningrad ⚔ of World War II. Soviets besieged by Germans 1941–43.

Leo I, Pope (*aka* St. Leo I, Leo the Great, died 461 CE, reigned 440–61 CE) In 452 CE went personally to entreat Attila and his Huns not to march on Rome.

Leo III, Pope (reigned 795–816) Leo called on Charlemagne to secure his papal throne and in return created him Holy Roman Emperor, thus beginning the medieval interdependence and rivalry between popes and emperors.

Leopold II (1835–1909) The second king of the Belgians (reigned 1865–1909). He was the prime mover behind the establishment of the Congo Free State, which gradually became his own private African business venture. The administration of the state was severely criticized for the brutal methods used to force native people to pick rubber. In 1908 Leopold handed the Congo over to the Belgian government and it was then administered as a colony.

Lepanto ⚔ of (1571) Decisive naval engagement at which the Ottoman fleet was destroyed by the Venetian-led Holy League. *p.287*

Lepenski Vir Important early European settlement c.6000 BCE.

Léry, Chaussegros de 18th-century French explorer of North America. In his capacity as Chief Engineer of Canada, de Léry conducted a thorough survey of the upper Ohio river in 1729.

LESOTHO A mountainous and landlocked country entirely surrounded by South Africa, Lesotho is economically dependent on its larger neighbor. However, Lesotho is beginning to benefit from the export of energy from the recently completed Highlands Water Scheme. Elections in 1993 ended a period of military rule, but South Africa had to send in its troops when serious political unrest erupted in 1998.

CHRONOLOGY

1868 British protectorate established after King Moshoeshoe I, who had successfully united various Sotho speaking groups earlier in the century, is forced to cede fertile areas to the Boers. After a period of administration by Cape Colony between 1871–83, the UK resumes direct responsibility. Under the system of indirect rule traditional rulers maintain their power but economic development is neglected, with the result that by the end of the century the system of large scale migration of labor to South Africa is firmly established. Throughout the period of UK rule the traditional leaders strongly oppose incorporation into South Africa.

1884 As Basutoland, Lesotho became a British Crown colony.

1966 Independent kingdom.

1986 Military coup.

1990 King Moshoeshoe II exiled. Son installed as Letsie III.

1993 Free elections.

1994 Return of Moshoeshoe II.

1996 Letsie III succeeds to throne.

1998 New LCD (Lesotho Congress for Democracy) wins polls. South Africa intervenes after coup attempt, and reconciles king and parties.

2000 Elections postponed.

2002 Food emergency after successive poor harvests. LCD wins long-postponed elections.

Lesseps, Ferdinand, Vicomte de (1805–94) French diplomat and engineer. In 1854 he began to plan the Suez Canal, supervising its construction until its opening in 1869. In 1881 work began on his scheme for a Panama Canal, but this had to be abandoned in 1888 and was not completed until 1914. *See also* Suez Canal

Levant Name formerly given to the countries bordering the E Mediterranean from Egypt to Turkey, and later more particularly to Lebanon and Syria.

Lewis, Meriwether (1774–1809) US explorer. With Clark, led the famous expedition (1803–06), sponsored by President Jefferson, to explore the land acquired in the Louisiana Purchase and find a land route to the Pacific.

Lexington ⚔ of American Revolutionary War (Apr 19 1775). British victory.

Leyte Gulf Naval ⚔ of World War II (Oct 1944). Major US victory over Japan, facilitating US invasion of Philippines.

Li dynasty *see* Yi dynasty

Li Tzu-cheng *see* Li Zicheng

Li Zicheng (*var.* Li Tzu-cheng, c.1605–45) Chinese rebel leader whose entry in 1644 into Beijing precipitated the suicide of the last Ming emperor.

Liao *see* Khitans

Liao empire Extensive state established by the nomadic Khitan people in Manchuria, Mongolia, and northeastern China in the early 10th century. The empire coexisted with the Chinese Song dynasty, becoming its tributary in 1005 but, in 1125, fell to the Jurchen people, who founded the Jin dynasty of northern China.

LIBERIA Founded in 1847 by freed slaves from the USA, Liberia today is struggling to recover from a civil war which reduced it to anarchy between 1990 and 1996. Facing the Atlantic in equatorial west Africa, most of its coastline is characterized by lagoons and mangrove swamps. Inland, a grassland plateau supports the limited agriculture (just 1 percent of land is arable). Liberia has the world's largest flag of convenience merchant fleet.

CHRONOLOGY

1822 American Colonization Society begins settling freed slaves along the coast.

1847 Foundation as an independent state.

1890s Government asserts the present boundaries in response to UK and French colonial expansion.

1944 William Tubman becomes President and introduces vote for property-owners.

1971 William Tolbert succeeds Tubman.

1980 Coup. President assassinated by Samuel Doe.

▶

1990 Outbreak of civil war. Peace-keeping force backed by Nigeria and Ghana sent to restore order.

1991 Doe assassinated.

1996 Second peace agreement.

1997 Charles Taylor president.

1999 Withdrawal of ECOMOG peace-keeping force.

2001 Borders with Guinea and Sierra Leone closed. Conflict with rebels escalates.

2002 State of emergency declared.

2003 Rebels reach Monrovia. Taylor ousted. Transitional government in place.

LIBYA Libya is situated between Egypt and Algeria on the south Mediterranean coast of north Africa, with Chad and Niger on its southern borders. Apart from the coastal strip and the mountains in the south, it is desert or semidesert. Libya's strategic position in north Africa and its abundant oil and gas resources made it an important trading partner for European states. It has for many years been politically marginalized by the West for its links with terrorist groups, but UN sanctions were suspended in 1999, when it handed over the two men suspected of the 1988 Lockerbie plane bombing over Scotland.

CHRONOLOGY

c. 700 BCE Phoenician traders establish settlements in Tripolitania, in the northwest, while Cyrenaica in the northeast is settled by Greeks.

1st century BCE Coastal region becomes part of Roman Empire. Roman rule is subsequently extended inland to Fezzan.

642 CE Arab invasions end Byzantine rule.

1158 Almohads from Morocco establish control over Tripolitania and rule for the next 350 years. Cyrenaica comes under Egyptian control.

1510 Tripoli is captured by Spanish King Ferdinand.

1551 Sinan Pasha recaptures Tripoli, establishing Ottoman rule. Turkish pashas rule from Tripoli.

1711 Ahmad Karamanli kills Ottoman pasha. Governorship of Tripoli becomes hereditary office of Karamanli family.

1835 Ottoman forces are despatched to Tripoli as a result of a disputed succession within the Karamanli family. Karamanli leader is deposed. Within a few years a militant Muslim sect known as the Sanusi or Senussi is founded.

1911 Italy attacks Tripoli and other Libyan ports.

1912 The Ottoman empire yields control of Libya to Italy in the Treaty of Ouchy.

1914 Although Italian military supremacy is established in most of the country there are continuing attacks from rebel Senussi in the south.

1932 The Italians re-establish control after the defeat of Senussi forces seeking self-government. Italian colonists begin to arrive.

1945 British forces capture Tripoli and set up a military administration.

1951 The United Republic of Libya (comprising Tripolitania, Cyrenaica and Fezzan) is proclaimed with Mohammed Sayed Idris el-Senussi, the Emir of Cyrenaica, as king.

1969 King Idris deposed in coup by Revolutionary Command Council led by Colonel Gaddafi. Tripoli Charter sets up revolutionary alliance with Egypt and Sudan.

1970 UK and US military ordered out. Property of Italians and Jews confiscated. Western oil company assets nationalized, a process completed in 1973.

1973 Libya forms abortive union with Egypt. Gaddafi launches "Cultural Revolution." Occupies Aozou Strip in Chad.

1974 Libya forms union of Libya and Tunisia.

1977 Official name changed to the Great Socialist People's Libyan Arab Jamahiriyah.

1979 Members of Revolution Command Council replaced by elected officials. Gaddafi remains Leader of the Revolution.

1981 USA shoots down two Libyan aircraft over Gulf of Sirte.

1984 Gunman at Libyan embassy in London kills British policewoman; UK severs diplomatic relations with Libya (until 1999). Libya signs Oudja Accord with Morocco for an Arab Africa Federation.

1985 Libya expels 30,000 foreign workers. Tunisia cuts diplomatic links.

1986 US aircraft bomb Libya, killing 101 people and destroying Gaddafi's residence.

1988 Army and police abolished. Pan-Am airliner explodes over Lockerbie, Scotland; allegations of Libyan complicity.

1989 Arab Maghreb Union established with Algeria, Morocco, Mauritania, and Tunisia. Libya and Chad cease-fire in Aozou Strip.

1990 Libya expels Palestinian splinter group led by Abu Abbas.

1991 Opening of first branch of Great Man-Made River project.

1992–1993 UN sanctions imposed as Libya fails to hand over Lockerbie suspects; sanctions made stricter.

1994 Religious leaders obtain right to issue religious decrees (fatwas) for first time since 1969. Return of Aozou strip to Chad.

1996 US legislation imposes penalties on foreign companies investing in Libya's energy sector.

1999 Lockerbie suspects handed over for trial in the Netherlands under Scottish law; UN sanctions eased.

2000 Gaddafi announces plans to form United States of Africa.

2001 Lockerbie trial verdict: one suspect convicted on apparently flimsy evidence; one is released. Sanctions eased further.

2002 US–Libya talks, but Libya added to "axis of evil".

2003 Compensation agreed for 1980s terrorism; UN sanctions lifted.

2004 Relations restored with US.

LIECHTENSTEIN Perched in the Alps between Switzerland and Austria, the principality of Liechtenstein is rare among small states in having both a thriving banking sector and a well-diversified manufacturing economy. It is closely allied to Switzerland, which handles its foreign relations and defense. Life in Liechtenstein is stable and conservative. Its banking secrecy laws and low taxes make it home to many overseas trusts, banks, and investment companies.

CHRONOLOGY

1342 Graf Hartmann von Montfort becomes owner of the Castle of Vaduz and in 1396, still under the control of the Montfort family, Vaduz is confirmed as a fief of the Holy Roman Empire.

1416 The last Montfort count bequeaths Vaduz to Baron von Brandis from Emmental, who in 1434 also gains control of the domain of Schellenberg, which lies to the north of Vaduz.

1712 While Schellenberg comes under the control of the Liechtenstein family from 1608, Vaduz is not purchased by Prince Johann Adam Andreas von Liechtenstein until 1712, within months of his death. The territory is now large enough to become a (demilitarized) principality and in 1719 Emperor Charles VI raises status of Vaduz and Schellenberg to that of a principality under the name of Liechtenstein.

1806 Liechtenstein declares its full sovereignty on July 12 and achieves it on August 6 when the Holy Roman Empire is dissolved. A Rheinbund league of German princes, which is formed at the suggestion of Napoleon Bonaparte, does not outlast Napoleon and in 1815 Liechtenstein joins the German Confederation, remaining a member until its dissolution in 1866.

1852 A customs union is formed with Austria and the Austrian currency becomes the legal tender. This lasts until the dismemberment of the Austro-Hungarian Empire in 1918.

1866 Liechtenstein formally achieves independence following the dissolution of the German Confederation.

1868 Standing army abolished.

1921 October. A constitution is approved under which authority is jointly exercised by an hereditary prince (females do not have the right of succession) and by a Landtag (parliament), although the Prince has the last word.

1924 Customs union with Switzerland.

1990 Joins UN.

1995 Joins EEA.

1997 End of VU-FBP coalition in power since 1938. Mario Frick heads VU government.

2001 FBP wins majority in elections; Otmar Hasler premier.

2003 Prince wins greater powers.

2004 Prince hands control to son.

Liegnitz ⚔ (1241) Polish army defeated by Mongols.

Lima Capital of modern Peru, founded by Pizarro in 1535.

limes Defensive lines built by the Romans to protect the borders of their empire. The limes could consist of a continuous wall, as in northern Britain and parts of the German frontier, or a string of isolated forts, as in Syria.

Limited War Doctrine Strategic policy of limited military commitment and geographic containment, developed by the Western Allies during Korean War, in an attempt to contain spread of Cold War confrontations into intercontinental conflict.

Lincoln, Abraham (1809–65) 16th President of the US (Republican, 1861–65). The setting up of the Republican party in 1856, to oppose the extension of slavery in the US, brought Abraham Lincoln, a self-educated lawyer, who had sat in Congress since 1846, to national prominence. In 1860 he won a comfortable majority in the presidential election but was unable to prevent the secession of seven of the southern states from the Union, and the resultant Civil War between the Union and Confederate states. While defining the preservation of the Union as the primary issue of the war, most famously in the Gettysburg Address of 1863, his Emancipation Proclamation of the same year freed the slaves in the southern states. Re-elected for a second term in 1865, he was assassinated barely a month after his inaugural address. *p.368*

Literature
Roman literature. *p.83*
Romanticism. *p.346*
The 19th-century novel. *p.356*
20th-century literature. *p.444*

LITHUANIA Lying on the eastern coast of the Baltic Sea, Lithuania is bordered by Latvia, Belarus, Poland, and the Kaliningrad area of the Russian Federation. Its terrain is mostly flat with many lakes, moors, and bogs. Now a multiparty democracy, Lithuania achieved independence from the former USSR in 1991. Industrial production and agriculture are the mainstays of the economy. Russia finally withdrew all its troops from Lithuania in 1993.

CHRONOLOGY

1322 Gediminas establishes the capital at Vilnius, and conquers areas of present-day Belarus, having completed the unification of the Lithuanian tribes begun by his brother Vytenis in 1295. His son Algirdas expands Lithuania into present-day Ukraine.

1386 Poland and Lithuania are united with the marriage of Queen Jadwiga of Poland and Grand Prince Jagiello of Lithuania. Jagiello, a pagan, converts to Catholicism. At the height of their power in the 15th century the domains of the Jagiellonian kings stretch from the Baltic to the Black Sea.

1569 The Union of Lublin binds Lithuania and Poland with a common Diet and single capital city, Warsaw, supplanting Vilnius and Cracow. The Vilnius region subsequently becomes Polonized.

1795 The three partitions of Poland result in Lithuania becoming Russian territory. Poles and Lithuanians participate in the uprisings against Russian rule in 1831 and 1863.

1915 Occupied by German troops.

1918 Independence declared.

1926 Military coup; one-party rule.

1940 Annexed by Soviet Union.

1941–1944 Nazi occupation.

1945 Incorporated into USSR.

1991 Achieves full independence.

1992 First multiparty elections.

1993 Russian troops withdraw.

1996 Prime minister forced from office by banking scandal. General election; conservative TS(LK) wins.

1998 Valdas Adamkus president.

2000 Brief center-left coalition.

2001 Ex-president Brazauskas becomes prime minister.

2004 Joins NATO. President Paksas impeached. Joins EU.

Little Bighorn (*aka* Greasy Grass) ⚔ (1876). American forces, led by General Custer, destroyed by Sioux and Cheyenne

Livingstone, David (1813–73) Scottish missionary who, during his three visits to Africa in the period 1841–73, undertook journeys of exploration throughout the southern half of the continent. He was the first European to reach Lake Ngami in 1849 and the first to *see* the Victoria Falls in 1855. Appalled by the treatment of African slaves, he dedicated much of his life to fighting the trade, clashing frequently with the Boers and Portuguese. Between 1866 and 1871 no news was heard of Livingstone until he was tracked down by Henry Morton Stanley, who had been sent by a New York newspaper to find him.

Livonian Order *see* Sword Brothers

Lodi ⚔ of Napoleon's Italian campaign (1896). French victory.

Lodi, Peace of (1454) Ended wars in Italy between Milan, Venice, Florence, and the Papal States.

Lodz ⚔ of World War I (Nov 11–25 1914)

Lollards Reforming religious group, influential in Europe during the 14th–15th centuries, famous for their attacks on church corruption and emphasis on the Biblical scriptures.

Lombard League Alliance of cities of northern Italy formed in 1167, to oppose the German Emperor Frederick I (Barbarossa).

Lombards (*var.* Langobardi). Germanic people settled along the Danube in the 5th century. In 568 they invaded northern Italy, swiftly overrunning the region now known as Lombardy, and establishing two southern duchies, Benevento and Spoleto. They never controlled the whole of Italy and conflict with the Byzantine empire and the Papacy continued for 200 years, until their defeat by Charlemagne in 774. *p.118, p.134*

London Capital of the UK. Did not become capital city of England officially until 14th century. Since then has grown and prospered, despite setbacks such as the great plague of 1665 and the Great Fire of 1666. After the fire it was extensively rebuilt with many fine churches by Sir Christopher Wren and others. At its zenith in the 19th century as center of the British Empire. *p.371*
Great Fire of London. *p.311*
St.Paul's Cathedral. *p.321*

Long Island ⚔ of American Revolutionary War (Aug 27 1776). British victory.

Long, Major Stephen H. (1784–1864) US army engineer and explorer. Led expeditions along the Missouri (1819–20) and the Platte and South Platte Rivers in the Rocky Mountains, south to the Red River (1821). Produced a map which named the region as the Great American Desert. Later explored the 49th parallel.

Long March, the (Oct 1934–Oct 1935) Withdrawal of the Communist forces during the Chinese Civil War from their bases in southern China to the northwest, led by Mao Zedong.

Longshan culture Named after Long Shan (Dragon Mountain) in NE China's Shandong province. This Neolithic culture developed from the Yangshao culture as bronze was coming into use, and flourished between c.3000–1700 BCE in the Yellow River valley. Their economy was based on millet, pigs, cows, and goats, and is characterized by polished stone tools and distinctive pottery, the first in the Far East made on a fast wheel, and kiln – fired to a uniform black color.

López de Cárdenas, Garcia 16th-century Spanish explorer of the Americas, a member of Coronado's expedition north from Mexico in 1540–42.

Lothair I (795–855) Ruler of the Middle Kingdom of the Franks after the division of Charlemagne's empire by the Treaty of Verdun (843). The region became known as Lotharingia (*mod.* Lorraine). *p.141*

Louis I (*aka* Louis the Great, 1326–82) King of Hungary. A member of the Anjou dynasty that became kings of Naples in the 13th century, Louis frequently intervened in Neapolitan politics after the murder of his brother, the Queen's consort, in 1345. He also fought three wars with Venice for control of the Dalmatian coast. In 1370 he inherited the crown of Poland, but could not really impose his authority there.

Louis the Pious (778–840) Frankish king, son of Charlemagne. Crowned by his father in 813, Louis attempted to hold the Carolingian Empire together, but the last decade of his reign was marked by civil wars between him and his four sons.

Louis VII (1120–80) King of France. In 1152 Louis divorced Eleanor of Aquitaine, who then married Henry of Anjou, who became king of England as Henry II in 1154. This weakened the position of the French crown, as large tracts of France came under English control. Led a crusade t the Holy Land (1147–49)

Louis IX (*aka* St. Louis, 1214–70) King of France. Famed for his piety, for which he was canonized in 1297, Louis was also an enthusiastic crusader and organized and led two crusades. On the first in 1248, he was captured and ransomed in Egypt. On the second in 1270, he died while besieging Tunis.

Louis XIV (*aka* "the Sun King", 1638–1715) King of France (reigned 1643–1715). Effective ruler after 1661, he established an absolute monarchy. For the next 50 years he was the most powerful monarch

in Europe, but his ambition to establish French supremacy in Europe led to numerous wars, especially with Spain, Holland, and England. His attempt to forge a union between France and Spain led to the War of the Spanish Succession (1701–14), which left France virtually bankrupt. His long reign was marked by a flourishing of the French arts, symbolized by the Palace of Versailles. *p.310*

Louis XVI (1754–93) King of France. In 1788 Louis' financial problems forced him to summon the Estates-General (the French parliament that had not met since 1614). This became the National Assembly and precipitated the French Revolution. Louis became virtually a prisoner of the state. His unsuccessful attempt to flee France in 1791 led to his trial the following year and in 1793 he was guillotined for treason.

Louis-Napoleon *see* Napoleon III

Louis-Philippe (1773–1850) King of France (reigned 1830–48). Son of the Duke of Orléans, cousin of Louis XVI, Louis-Philippe, like his father, who was known as Philippe Égalité, at first supported the Revolution. But after Louis-Philippe fled the country, his father was executed in 1793. Louis-Philippe was invited to become king in 1830 after the July Revolution of that year, but abdicated during the 1848 revolution and died in exile in England.

Louisiana Purchase French territory added to the US in 1803 following its purchase from France for less than 3 cents an acre by Thomas Jefferson. It more than doubled the area of the US at the time, adding more than 2,144,520 sq km (828,000 sq miles) of territory. Much of the new territory were explored by Lewis and Clarke (1805–06).

Lucius Tarquinius Priscus *see* Tarquin I

Lucius Tarquinius Superbus *see* Tarquin II

Luddite riots Protests by English textile workers, chiefly in the Midlands, alarmed at the introduction of industrial machinery and fearful for their jobs. The first such riots, accompanied by widespread machine-wrecking, occurred in 1811.

Ludwig, Daniel Keith (1897–1992) American entrepreneur who began a billion-dollar development of the Jari River valley in Brazil, but in 1982 he abandoned the costly project, which had led to the destruction of large tracts of tropical rain forest.

Luther, Martin (1483–1546) German scholar and priest whose questioning of certain church practices led to the Protestant Reformation. He first clashed with the Catholic authorities in 1517 after his *95 Theses* attacking the sale of indulgences denied that the pope and clergy could forgive sins. He inspired a movement that revolutionized religious thought, incidentally provoking much social and political upheaval in northern Europe. *p.274*

LUXEMBOURG Luxembourg shares borders with the industrial regions of Germany, France, and Belgium, and has the highest per capita income in the EU. Making up part of the plateau of the Ardennes, its countryside is undulating and forested. Its prosperity was once based on steel; before World War II it produced more per capita than the USA. Today, it is known as a tax haven and banking center, and as the headquarters of key EU institutions.

CHRONOLOGY

406–07 CE An invasion by Germanic tribes ends the Roman occupation; the region of Luxembourg becomes part of the Frankish kingdom.

963 Luxembourg becomes an autonomous county within the Holy Roman Empire and a Duchy within the Empire from 1354.

1308–1437 The House of Luxembourg provides four Holy Roman Emperors.

1443 Luxembourg becomes one of the Burgundian lands in the Low Countries.

1482 Along with the other Burgundian territories, Luxembourg passes to the Habsburgs. As part of the southern Netherlands it is ruled by the Spanish Habsburgs from 1555–56 until 1713.

1713 Under the Treaty of Utrecht the southern Netherlands pass to Austrian Habsburg rule.

1795 French troops secure control over Luxembourg and the Duchy is annexed by France.

1815 In the post-Napoleonic reorganization of Europe, the Congress of Vienna makes Luxembourg into an independent Grand Duchy within the German Confederation, with the King of the Netherlands as head of state; in 1852 Luxembourg joins the German Customs Union.

1831 After the French-speaking western part of the Grand Duchy supports the demand for Belgian independence from the Netherlands, Luxembourg is divided; the western half becomes the Belgian province of Luxembourg and is still known by that name.

1839 The Treaty of London reaffirms Luxembourg's independent status.

1867 A congress in London confirms Luxembourg's perpetual neutrality, a Prussian garrison is withdrawn and King William III of the Netherlands is obliged to keep the Grand Duchy (after rumours that he wished to sell it to the French had caused the so-called "Luxembourg crisis" and threatened renewed war between France and Prussia).

1890 Link with Dutch throne ends.

1921 Economic union with Belgium. End of German ties.

1940–1944 German occupation.

1948 Benelux treaty (1944) creating a customs union comes into effect.

1957 Signs Treaty of Rome as one of six founding members of EEC.

1995 Premier Jacques Santer is president of European Commission.

1999 Euro introduced. Santer resigns amid corruption allegations. Socialist losses in general election.

2000 Grand Duke Jean abdicates in favor of his son, Henri.

2002 Euro fully adopted.

Luxembourg dynasty The counts of Luxembourg were a powerful dynasty in the late Middle Ages. They were also kings of Bohemia and four of their number were elected emperor, the most famous being Charles IV.

Luxor *see* Thebes

Lydenburg heads Early examples of ironworking in southern Africa found in Transvaal, dating from c.500 CE. *p.115*

Lysimachus (*var. Gre.* Lysimachos, 360–281 BCE) Macedonian general of Alexander the Great. Following Alexander's death in 323, Lysimachus became ruler of Thrace. He extended his territories in the wars between Alexander's successors, but was killed in the battle of Corupedium against Seleucus, the Syrian king with whom he had formerly been allied.

M

Maastricht Treaty (*var.* European Union Treaty, Dec 1991) International agreement between the states of the European Community (EC) in Maastricht, Netherlands which established the European Union (EU), with Union citizenship for every person holding the nationality of a member state. It provided for the establishment of a central banking system and the implementation of a common foreign and security policy.

Macao Portuguese colony in China since 1557, it was returned to China in 1999.

Macedon Kingdom of northern Greece (5th century BCE–167 BCE). Under Philip II (reigned 359–336 BCE) it became the dominant power in Greece, and under his son, Alexander the Great (reigned 336–323 BCE) the nucleus of a vast empire that stretched as far as India.

MACEDONIA The former Yugoslav Republic of Macedonia (FYRM) is landlocked in southeastern Europe. Despite the signing of an accord in 1995, Greece remains suspicious that it harbors ambitions about absorbing northern Greece – also called Macedonia – in a "Greater Macedonia." A militant movement among ethnic Albanians erupted into violent conflict in 2001, threatening the survival of the multi-ethnic governing coalition.

CHRONOLOGY

4th century BCE The first Macedonian state covers the territory now occupied by northern Greece and southern Albania, former Yugoslavia, and Bulgaria. Under Philip II of Macedon and his son Alexander the Great, Macedonia expands into Asia Minor and the Middle East, but disintegrates after Alexander's death, becoming a Roman province in 146 BCE

5th century CE Slavs occupy Macedonia.

9th century Region becomes part of the Bulgarian empire following two centuries of dispute with Byzantium.

963 CE Macedonia achieves independence under Shishman I after the Bulgarian empire's decline. A short-lived expansion ends in 1018 when Macedonia becomes part of Byzantine empire.

1380 The Turks occupy Macedonia, which has an ethnic mix of Slavs, Greeks, and Albanians. Turkish rule leads to a decline in the Christian population through emigration; the Serbian and Bulgarian patriarchates are abolished in 1766 and 1777.

1893 Russia's victory over Turkey and the subsequent independence of Bulgaria leads to Bulgarian, Serb, and Greek claims to Macedonia, in anticipation of its liberation from Turkey. The secret Internal Macedonian Revolutionary Organization (VMRO) is formed and calls for "Macedonia for the Macedonians" and a Balkan federation.

1895 A Supreme Committee for Macedonia and Adrianople is formed in Sofia to prepare Macedonia for incorporation into Bulgaria. Greece sends guerrillas into Macedonia, provoking a war with Turkey in 1897, which ends in a Greek defeat. Bulgaria and Serbia also send guerrilla fighters.

1903 August. Bulgarian insurgents spark an uprising in Macedonia which lasts ten days and is brutally suppressed. Some 1,700 noncombatant Macedonian Slavs are shot by the Turks. Thousands flee to Bulgaria.

1912 October. Bulgaria, Serbia, and Greece attack and defeat Turkey over its failure to deliver promised reforms in Macedonia. The victors fail to agree on the division of lands taken from Turkey and the consequent Balkan Wars lead to the partitioning of Macedonia. Greece takes the southern half, Bulgaria receives the Strumitsa district and the Pirin massif, with the remainder going to Serbia.

1915 Bulgaria enters World War I on the side of the Central Powers and occupies all of Serbian Macedonia. The 1919 post-war settlement after the defeat of the Central Powers transfers Strumitsa to the new Yugoslavia, leaving Pirin in Bulgarian hands.

1924 The publication of a VMRO manifesto for an autonomous Macedonia within a communist Balkan federation leads to a wave of assassinations of opposing federalists by the VMRO, and to government repression. A new Yugoslav government crushes the VMRO in 1934.

1941 Germany invades Yugoslavia after a the overthrow of a Yugoslav government which signed a pact with Axis powers. The country is partitioned and most of Macedonia (with the exception of Albanian lands ceded to Italy) is occupied by Bulgaria. In July 1943 the Bulgarian and Greek communist leaders agree that after the war Macedonia should be independent within a communist Balkan federation. Meanwhile the partisan leader Josip Broz Tito begins organizing a Macedonian liberation movement.

1944 Tito establishes republic, stressing Macedonian identity.

1945 Adoption of standardized Macedonian language.

1989–1990 Multiparty elections.

1991 Independence declared. EU recognition delayed by Greeks.

1995 Accord with Greece.

1998–1999 Right-wing VMRO–DPMNE coalition wins elections.

1999 Upheaval over Kosovo conflict.

2001 Conflict with ethnic Albanian militants.

2002 Left-of-center ZMZ alliance wins general election.

2004 Prime Minister Branko Crvenkovski elected president.

MacKenzie, Colin (c.1753–1821) Officer in the British East India Company, whose accurate mapping led to his appointment as Surveyor-general of India in 1819.

Mackenzie, Sir Alexander (c.1755–1820) Explorer and fur-trader. In 1789, on behalf of the Northwestern Company, he ventured to Great Slave Lake and down what was to become the Mackenzie River to the Arctic Ocean. His next expedition, starting from Lake Athabasca in 1792, eventually reached the Pacific Ocean, making him the first white man to cross N America north of Mexico.

MADAGASCAR Lying in the Indian Ocean, Madagascar is the world's fourth-largest island. Its isolation means that there is a host of unique wildlife and plants. To the east, the large central plateau drops precipitously through forested cliffs to the coast; in the west, gentler gradients give way to fertile plains. It became independent from France in 1960, and after 18 years of radical socialism under Didier Ratsiraka, became a multiparty democracy. It is dependent on the IMF as it tries to rebuild its agriculture-based economy.

CHRONOLOGY

5th century CE First settlers arrive from Indonesia and Africa.

1506 Portuguese explorers first visit.

1883–85 The first Franco-Malagasy war leads to the establishment of a French protectorate.

1895 The French invade and capture Antananarivo.

1896 Madagascar becomes a French colony. The Merina monarchy is abolished.

1898–1904 A revolt against French rule is suppressed with great brutality.

1947–1948 French troops kill thousands in nationalist uprisings.

1960 Independence from France.

1975 Radical socialist Didier Ratsiraka takes power.

1990 Multiparty political reforms.

1991 Opposition Forces Vives (CFV) coalition set up; led by Albert Zafy. Mass strikes against regime.

1992 Civilian rule restored.

1993 Zafy's CFV defeats Ratsiraka's coalition, the MFM, in free elections.

1996 Zafy impeached.

1997 Ratsiraka elected president.

1998 New constitution adopted.

2002 Country divided after opposition leader Marc Ravalomanana claims victory in 2001 presidential election.

Madero, Francisco Indalecio (1873–1913) Mexican revolutionary and statesman. In 1908, Madero launched a presidential campaign against the dictator, Porfirio Díaz. Imprisoned by Díaz, he then fled to the US and launched a military campaign, capturing Ciudad Juárez, which he made his capital in May 1911. He made moderate reforms as President, but was increasingly faced by revolts demanding land reform. He was murdered in Feb 1913 following a military coup by Victoriano Huerta, assisted by the US ambassador.

Mafia (*aka* Cosa Nostra) International criminal organization, originally based in Sicily and dating from the 13th century. In the US, the Mafia became one of the major forces in the development of organized crime, especially during the Prohibition era.

Magadha One of the 16 mahajanapadas (great realms) which dominated the Ganges plain from c.600 BCE. Gradually all the other kingdoms were absorbed into Magadha, with its capital at Pataliputra (Patna), which dominated the lucrative Ganges trade routes. Magadha became the nucleus of the first Indian empire, the Mauryan Empire when its throne was seized by Chandragupta Maurya in 327 BCE. Magadha was the scene of many of the incidents in the life of Gautama Buddha. Later the center of the Gupta dynasty.

Magellan, Ferdinand (c.1480–1521) Portuguese navigator, who undertook his most famous voyage in the service of the Spanish crown. In 1519 he sailed with five ships to discover a westward route to the Indies. This he achieved, sailing through the Strait of Magellan (1520), then crossing the Pacific to the Philippines. There, Magellan was killed after intervening in a local war. One of his ships, captained by Sebastián del Cano, made the journey back to Spain, thus completing the first circumnavigation of the globe. *p.277*

Magna Carta Historic document signed by King John of England in 1215, guaranteeing feudal privileges to his barons after a long period of rebellion and anarchy. *p.208*

Magnesia ⚔ (190 BCE) Roman victory over Seleucid king Antiochus III.

Magyars People of the steppes, the ancestors of today's Hungarians, who migrated into present-day Hungary in the late 9th century. Their raids at first struck fear into western European states, but following their defeat by Otto I at Lechfeld in 955, the Magyars started to lead a more settled existence and in the 11th century Hungary became a Christian kingdom.

Mahabharata Sanskrit epic which, along with the Ramayana, was composed c.400 BCE. It tells the story of an epic struggle for supremacy between two groups of cousins, the Kauravas and the Pandavas. The battle was fought in northwestern India, and is probably an account of Mauryan expansion. *p.58*

Mahavira (c.540–468 BCE) Brought up as a pious Jain near Patna, Mahavira became a monk, who instructed 11 disciples, and became the foremost preceptor of the Jain religion.

Mahayana Buddhism (*aka* Greater Vehicle) Interpretation of Buddhism developed from 1st century CE which spread from NW India into China, Korea, Japan, and Tibet; focusing on the concept of the Bodhisattva, who would postpone entry into nirvana until all others are similarly enlightened, Mahayana regards the historical Buddha as a temporary manifestation of the eternal and innate nature of the Buddha. *See also* Buddhism

Mahmud of Ghazni (*var.* Muhammad of Ghazni, 971–1030) Ruler of an empire, consisting of Afghanistan, northeastern Persia, and northwest India (reigned 997–1030). Mahmud was the son of a Turkish ruler of Khurasan, a vassal of the Samanids. His reign was notable for the frequent raids he made on northern India. The Ghaznavid dynasty continued to rule until the late 12th century when they were overthrown by the Ghurids.

Majapahit empire Javanese empire from the late 13th to the 16th century. Although Majapahit probably exercised direct rule only over Java and nearby small islands, in its heyday in the 14th century, its powerful fleets controled trade over a far wider area, including the Moluccan Spice Islands.

Majuba Hill ⚔ (190 BCE) Roman victory over Greece.

Malacca (*var.* Melaka) Important trading center on the Malay Peninsula, founded c.1400. Its inhabitants converted to Islam through contact with merchants from central and south Asia. It was captured by the Portuguese in 1510, then by the Dutch in 1641, passing into British hands in the 19th century.

MALAWI Landlocked in southeast Africa, Malawi borders the Great Rift Valley. One-fifth of the country is submerged under Africa's third-largest expanse of water, Lake Nyasa. After strong Scottish missionary activity, Malawi came under British rule as Nyasaland in 1891. Part of the Federation of Rhodesia and Nyasaland rom 1953, before being granted independence in 1964. In the 1980s Malawi hosted large numbers of Mozambican refugees, at some cost to its fragile economy. Malawi established democracy in 1994 after three decades of one-party rule under Dr. Hastings Banda. Bakili Muluzi was reelected president in June 1999.

CHRONOLOGY
1891 Malawi becomes British colony of Nyasaland.
1953 Malawi Incorporated in Federation of Rhodesia and Nyasaland.
1964 Independence under Hastings Banda.
1966 One-party state.
1992 Antigovernment riots. Illegal prodemocracy groups unite.
1993 Referendum for multipartyism.
1994 Muluzi's UDF wins elections.
1999 Muluzi reelected president.
2001 Floods leave many homeless.
2002 Severe cholera epidemic, exacerbated by food shortages.

Malaya *see* Malaysia

MALAYSIA Comprising the three territories of Peninsular Malaysia, Sarawak, and Sabah, Malaysia stretches over 2000 km (1240 miles) from the Malay Peninsula to the northeastern end of the island of Borneo. It shares borders with Thailand, Indonesia, and the enclave states of Singapore and Brunei. A central mountain chain divides Peninsular Malaysia, separating fertile western plains from an eastern coastal belt. Sarawak and Sabah have swampy coastal plains rising to mountains on the Indonesian border. The former British protectorate of Malaya, made up of 11 states, gained independence in 1957. The federation of Malaysia, incorporating Singapore, Sarawak, and Sabah, was founded in 1963. Putrajaya, just south of Kuala Lumpur, is a high-tech development intended as the future capital. *p.378*

CHRONOLOGY
1965 Singapore leaves federation, reducing Malaysian states to 13.
1970 Malay-Chinese ethnic tension forces resignation of Prime Minister Tunku ▶

Abdul Rahman. New prime minister, Tun Abdul Razak, creates the BN coalition.

1976–1978 Guerrilla attacks by banned Communist Party of Malaya (CPM), based in southern Thailand.

1976 Tun Abdul Razak dies. Succeeded by his deputy.

1977 Unrest in Kelantan following expulsion of its chief minister from Pan-Malaysian Islamic Party (PAS). National emergency declared. PAS expelled from BN.

1978 Elections consolidate BN power. PAS marginalized. Government rejects plans for Chinese university.

1978–1989 Unrestricted asylum given to Vietnamese refugees.

1981 Mahathir Mohamed becomes prime minister.

1982 General election returns BN with increased majority.

1985 BN defeated by PBS in Sabah state elections.

1986 PBS joins BN coalition. Dispute between Mahathir and his deputy, Dakuk Musa, triggers general election, won by BN.

1987 Detention without trial of 106 politicians from all parties suspected of Chinese sympathies. Media censored.

1989 Disaffected UMNO members join PAS. Screening of Vietnamese refugees introduced. CPM signs peace agreement with Malaysian and Thai governments.

1990 General election. BN returned to power with reduced majority.

1993 Sultans lose powers, including legal immunity.

1995 BN wins landslide victory in the country's ninth general election.

1997 A major financial crisis ends a decade of spectacular economic growth.

1998–1999 Deputy Prime Minister Anwar Ibrahim dismissed from office. Launches Reformasi (reform) movement. Found guilty of corruption, later convicted of sodomy and six-year sentence extended to 15 years; his wife, Wan Azizah, forms Keadilan (later renamed as PKR) to continue democracy campaign. UMNO loses ground in November 1999 general election.

2003 Mahathir steps down after 22 years: Abdullah Badawi succeeds.

2004 BN wins landslide victory. Anwar Ibrahim released.

MALDIVES The Maldives is an archipelago of 1190 small coral islands set in the Indian Ocean southwest of India. The islands, none of which rise above 1.8 m (6 feet), are protected by encircling reefs or faros. Only 200 are inhabited. Tourism has grown in recent years, though vacation islands are separate from settled islands. In 1998, President Maumoon Abdul Gayoom, who has survived three coup attempts, was elected for a fifth term in office.

Chronology

1155 According to legend, the Maldive king is converted to Islam by a holy man.

1558–73 The islands are occupied by the Portuguese, who are eventually evicted by Bidu Muhammad Takurufana al Alam, founder of a new dynasty and hero of Maldivian history.

1887 British protectorate over the islands formalizes control dating back to 1796 when Britain took possession of Sri Lanka.

1932 First written constitution.

1965 gained its independence.

1968 Sultanate abolished; republic declared. Ibrahim Nasir elected as first president.

1978 Gayoom becomes president.

1994 Nonparty legislative elections.

1998 New constitution; Gayoom reelected for fifth five-year term.

1998 Gayoom wins sixth term.

MALI Mali is landlocked in the heart of west Africa. Its mostly flat terrain comprises virtually uninhabited Saharan plains in the north and more fertile savanna land in the south, where most of the population live. The Niger river irrigates the central and southwestern regions. Mali achieved independence from France in 1960. Multiparty democratic elections under a new constitution, in 1992 and then in 1997, provoked accusations of severe irregularities.

Chronology

8th–11th centuries Empire of Ghana.

12th–15th centuries Empire of Mali in the western regions.

11th–16th centuries Empire of Songhay in the eastern regions. 18th century. Kingdom of Segou flourished.

19th century Fula and Tukulor jihads spread from east and west.

1881–1895 The French colonize the area.

1898 The French destroy Samori Toure's Mandinka state.

1960 Independence.

1968 Coup by Gen. Moussa Traoré.

1990 Prodemocracy demonstrations.

1991 Traoré arrested.

1992 Free multiparty elections.

1997 President Konaré and ADEMA party reelected in disputed polls.

1999 Traoré's death sentence commuted to life imprisonment.

2002 Elections; Col. Touré president; ADEMA loses majority.

Mali empire West African state at its most powerful in the 13th and 14th centuries. The empire was founded by Sundiata c.1235, though a small state had existed there for some two centuries before. It reached the height of its power under the fabulously wealthy Mansa Musa (reigned c.1312–1337). Conquered by neighboring Songhay in1546, Mali finally collapsed c.1660.

Malinke West African people, the most influential of the Mali empire, famous as traveling merchants.

MALTA The Maltese archipelago is strategically located, lying between Europe and north Africa. Controlled throughout its history by successive colonial powers, Malta finally gained independence from the UK in 1964. The islands are mainly low-lying, with rocky coastlines; only Malta, Gozo (Ghawdex), and Kemmuna are inhabited. Tourism is Malta's chief source of income, with an influx of tourists each year of over three times the islands' population.

Chronology

870 CE Saracens seize Malta, which has been successively ruled by Phoenicians, Carthaginians, Greeks, and Romans.

1090 Malta is conquered by the Norman-ruled kingdom of Sicily.

1282 Malta comes under Spanish rule.

1530 Malta is entrusted to the Knights of St John of the Hospital (the Hospitallers) by the Habsburg Emperor.

1800 The British take control of Malta after two years under rule of Napoleon, who drives out the Knights. British possession is confirmed by the 1814 Treaty of Paris at the Congress of Vienna.

1921 Malta is granted a representative assembly, although this autonomy is revoked at the beginning of World War II.

1929 Tension grows between the United Kingdom, the Roman Catholic Church, and Italy under Mussolini, who lays claim to the island.

1939–1945 Malta comes under sustained attack by the Axis powers throughout World War II. In 1942 Britain awards Malta the George Cross for its resistance.

1947 Internal self-government.

1964 Full independence from UK.

1971 Dom Mintoff's MLP in power.

1987–1996 Edward Fenech Adami (NP) is premier.

1998 Early elections bring Fenech Adami back to power after brief MLP interlude.

2004 Lawrence Gonzi takes over as prime minister. Malta joins EU.

Mamluks (*var.* Mamelukes) Slave soldiers in many medieval Islamic states, frequently of Turkish origin, noted for their skill and bravery. Mamluks often rose to occupy positions of great power. In Egypt they ruled the country from 1250 until 1517, when it was conquered by the Ottomans. *p.219*

Manassas *see* Bull Run

Manchuria Region of northeast China. The Manchu army toppled the Ming dynasty in 1644, founding the Qing dynasty, which ruled China until 1911. In 1918–20 Manchuria was occupied by Japan.

Manchu dynasty *see* Qing dynasty

Mandela, Nelson (*full name* Nelson Rolihlahla Mandela, 1918–) South African Black nationalist and statesman, imprisoned for 28 years (1962–90) but subsequently elected president in 1994.

Manichaeism Dualist religion founded in Persia in the 3rd century CE by Mani, who tried to integrate the messages of Zoroaster, Jesus, and Buddha into one universal creed. Often regarded as a Christian heresy.

Manila galleon Every year, from the late16th century, the Spanish sent a galleon laden with silver from Acapulco to Manila in the Philippines to pay for silk and other luxury goods from China. The galleon returned to Mexico, laden with silks and oriental luxury goods that were then shipped on to Spain.

Mansa Musa Ruler of Mali Empire (reigned c.1312–1337) Under Mansa Musa, the Mali Empire reached the height of its power, largely through its control of the West African gold trade. He demonstrated his country's great wealth on the pilgrimage he made to Mecca in 1324. *p.230*

Mansurah ⚔ of the Crusades (1250) Defeat of the crusader army of Louis IX as it advanced into Egypt.

Manzikert ⚔ of 1071. Decisive victory of the Seljuk Turks over the Byzantines which resulted in the collapse of Byzantine power in Asia Minor.

Mao Tse-tung *see* Mao Zedong

Mao Zedong (*var.* Mao Tse-tung, 1893–1976) Chinese Communist leader and first Chairman of the People's Republic of China (1949).

Maori Indigenous people of New Zealand of Polynesian origin. They reached New Zealand (Aotearoa) c.700 BCE, making it one of the last Pacific island groups to be colonized.

Maratha Confederacy Hindu state, based in the rock forts of the Western Ghats, the Maratha Confederacy was founded by Sivaji. Although the Mughal emperor Aurangzeb checked the advance of the Marathas during his lifetime, after his death in 1707 the Confederacy gained control over much of India. In 1761 the Marathas confronted invading Afghans and were routed at ⚔ Panipat. Yet the Marathas continued to present a formidable military obstacle to the growing power of the British. The three Anglo-Maratha wars, which took place from 1775–1818 ultimately led to Maratha defeat.

Marathon ⚔ (490 BCE) Athenian defeat of Persians.

Marcel, Étienne French rebel. Provost of the merchants of Paris, who briefly took over the running of the city in 1356. *p.236*

Marchand, Jean-Baptiste (1863–1934) French soldier and explorer who in 1898 occupied Fashoda in the Sudan.

Marco Polo *see* Polo. Marco

Marconi, Guglielmo (1874–1937) Italian physicist and inventor of wireless telegraphy (1895).

Marcos, Ferdinand (1917–89) US-sponsored President of the Philippines (reigned 1965–86), accused of repression, fraud and corruption. Died in exile in Hawaii following electoral defeat.

Marcus Antonius *see* Mark Antony

Marcus Ulpius Traianus *see* Trajan

Mari Ancient Mari was the most important city on the middle Euphrates in the 3rd and 2nd millennia BCE, until its destruction by the Babylonians in 1759 BCE. Its importance as the center of a vast trading network covering northwest Mesopotamia is evidenced by around 20,000 cuneiform tablets which were found there.

Mariana Islands ⚔ of World War II (Jun–Aug 1944) Scene of a series of major US amphibious assaults during the "island-hopping" campaign in central Pacific.

Marie Antoinette (1755–93) Queen of France. The daughter of Maria Theresa of Austria, she married the future Louis XVI of France in 1770. As an Austrian, she was never popular with the French. Her reputation sank even lower with the Revolution and she was tried and executed in 1793.

Marienburg (*var. Pol.* Malbork) Headquarters ot the Teutonic Knights, becoming the seat of their grand master in 1309. It passed to Poland in 1457 and to Prussia in 1792. Since 1945 has been in modern Poland.

Marignano ⚔ (1515) Swiss defeated by Francis I of France.

Marin, Luis 16th-century Spanish colonizer of Mexico.

Marinids Berber dynasty that ruled Morocco from the 13th to the 15th century.

Marius, Gaius (157–86 BCE) Roman general and politician, who married into the aristocracy and achieved high position due to his military talents, including his role in suppressing the rebellious Numidian king, Jugurtha. Ruthlessly ambitious, he held an unprecedented seven consulships, and reformed the army by recruiting men of no property to create a professional fighting force, with the legions divided for the first time into cohorts and centuries.

Mark Antony (*var.* Marcus Antonius, 83 BCE–30 BCE) A relative and staunch supporter of Julius Caesar. After Caesar's death in 44 BCE, he almost assumed absolute power in Rome, laying the foundations of future power struggles with Caesar's heir Octavian. While reorganizing the government of the eastern provinces he met Cleopatra, by whom he had several children. When he started giving large areas of Rome's eastern territories to his children, declaring Cleopatra's son by Julius Caesar heir in Octavian's place, Octavian rallied Rome against him. Antony was defeated at Actium in 31 BCE, and committed suicide soon after.

Market Garden, Operation *see* Arnhem

Marne ⚔ of World War I (Sep 1914) Saw the Allied halting of the German advance on Paris.

Marne ⚔ of World War I (Jul 1918). The second battle of the Marne ended the great German offensive on the Western Front in 1918.

Marquette, Father Jacques (1637–75) French Jesuit missionary, who accompanied Louis Jolliet down the Mississippi River in 1673, coming to within 640 km of its mouth.

MARSHALL ISLANDS The Marshall Islands comprise a group of 34 widely scattered atolls in the central Pacific Ocean. After a period under Spanish rule, the Marshall Islands became a German protectorate in 1885; Japan took possession at the start of World War I. The islands were transferred to US control in 1945, becoming part of the UN Trust Territory of the Pacific Islands. An agreement which granted internal sovereignty in free association with the USA became operational in 1986, and the Trust was formally dissolved in 1990. The economy is almost entirely dependent on US aid and rent for the US missile base on Kwajalein atoll.

CHRONOLOGY

1946 US nuclear testing begins.

1947 UN Trust Territory of the Pacific established.

1961 Kwajalein becomes US army missile range.

1979 Constitution approved in referendum. Government set up.

1986 Compact of Free Association with US operational.

1990 Trust terminated by UN.

1997 Imata Kabua elected president after death in office of Amata Kabua, his cousin.

2000 Kessai Note president after opposition election victory.

2003 New compact agreed.

Marshall Plan (*aka* European Recovery Program) (Apr 1948–Dec 1951). US-sponsored program designed to rehabilitate the economies of 17 European nations in order to create stable conditions in which democratic institutions could survive. *p.418*

Martínez de Irala, Domingo (c.1512–56) Commander of the precarious Spanish colony at Asunción in the 1540s and 1550s. He explored the Gran Chaco region and discovered a route across the continent to Peru.

Marx, Karl (1818–83) German political theorist, author of *Das Kapital*, whose ideas formed the basis of modern communism. *p.362*

Masaccio (*f/n* Tommaso Guidi, 1401–28) Early Renaissance Florentine painter. One of the first artists to make use of the principles of perspective in his work. *p.256*

Masada Mass suicide of Jewish Zealots in 74 CE after failure of Jewish revolt against Roman rule. *p.83*

Masinissa (c.240–148 BCE) Ruler of the N African kingdom of Numidia who assisted Rome conquer Carthaginian territory.

Massachusetts Bay English colony founded in 1630.

Massalia (*var.* Lat. Massilia, *mod.* Marseille) Greek colony in the south of France that was a significant political and economic power in the 3rd and 2nd centuries BCE. It was gradually absorbed by Rome.

Mataram Sultanate of Java, founded in the 16th century. In the course of expansion in 17th century, it clashed frequently with the Dutch East India Company.

Matthias Corvinus *see* Matthias I Hunyadi

Matthias I Hunyadi (*aka* Matthias Corvinus, 1443–90) King of Hungary (reigned 1458–90). During his reign, Hungary was almost continually at war against Bohemia and the Turks. In 1477 his armies invaded Austria, besieging and capturing Vienna. Patron of learning and science and founder of the Corvina Library at Buda.

Mauri Berber inhabitants of the Roman province of Mauretania.

MAURITANIA Located in northwest Africa, Mauritania is a member of the OAU and the Arab League. Once part of the Almoravid empire, Mauritania became a French colony in 1814. The country has taken a strongly Arab direction since 1964; today, the Maures control political life and dominate the minority black population. The Sahara covers two-thirds of Mauritania's territory; the only productive land is that drained by the Senegal river in the south and southwest.

CHRONOLOGY

1960 Independence; one-party state.

1972 Peace with Polisario in war waged over Western Sahara.

1984 Colonel Moaouia Taya takes power in bloodless coup.

1992 First multiparty elections.

1997 Taya reelected as president.

2003 Apparent coup fails.

MAURITIUS The islands that make up Mauritius lie in the Indian Ocean east of Madagascar. The main island, from which the country takes its name, is of volcanic origin and surrounded by coral reefs. Along with Rodrigues to the east, the country includes the Agalega Islands and the Cargados Carajos Shoals to the north. Mauritius was ruled by the Dutch in the 17th century, the French (1710–1810), and the British. Mauritius has enjoyed economic success following industrial diversification and the expansion of tourism.

CHRONOLOGY

1959 First full elections.

1968 Independence. Riots between Creoles and Muslims.

1982–1995 Sir Anerood Jugnauth prime minister; forms MSM.

1992 Becomes a republic.

1995 Elections won by PTr–MMM.

2000 Return of Jugnauth.

2000 Paul Bérenger of MMM takes over as prime minister.

Maurits of Nassau (1604–79). Sent by his cousin, the stadholder, Frederick Henry, to govern the colony in Brazil which the Dutch had taken from the Portuguese. After his successful governorship (1836–44) he returned to Europe and fought in wars against Britain and France.

Mauryan dynasty (321–180 BCE) Ancient Indian dynasty and the first to establish control over all India. Founded by Chandragupta Maurya in 321 BCE and extended by his son Bindusara and his grandson Ashoka. The dynasty's power declined under Ashoka's successors and finally ended c.180 BCE. *p.53*

Mawson, Sir Douglas (1882–1958) Australian explorer and geologist. Accompanied Shackleton to the Antarctic in 1907–09 and reached the Magnetic S Pole. Led the Australasian Antarctic Expedition 1911–14, and a joint British, Australasian and New Zealand Antarctic expedition in 1929–31.

Maya People of Central American and the dominant culture of Central America, between 250 and 900 CE, in present-day southern Mexico, Guatemala, northern Belize, and western Honduras. The Maya are famed for their skills in astronomy, including developing solar and sacred calendars, hieroglyphic writing, and ceremonial architecture. An elite of priests and nobles ruled the agricultural population from political centers, characterized by plazas and vast palaces and pyramid temples. *p.92*
Maya calendar. *p.120*
Maya temple at Edzná. *p.145*

Mecca Capital of the Hejaz region of western Saudi Arabia. The birthplace of the Prophet Muhammad, it is Islam's holiest city and the center of pilgrimage. *See also* Haj

Medes Ancient people who lived to the south-west of the Caspian Sea. They were at their peak during the 7th century BCE when, alongside the Babylonians, they conquered the Assyrians and extended their power westwards to central Anatolia and eastward through most of Persia. Their empire was overwhelmed by the Persians in the mid-6th century BCE.

Medieval Europe Medieval knights. *p.183*. Medieval fairs and commerce. *p.225*. Medieval chronicles. *p.253*.

Medina Muhammad's capital from 622 CE.

megaliths (*var.* cromlechs, *Gr.* mega lithas: large stones) European prehistoric structures, often tombs, were constructed of massive, roughly dressed stone slabs and were built across Europe during the Neolithic period, from c.5000 BCE. They are comparable, although unrelated, to megalithic monuments found in S India, Tibet, and SE Asia. *p.23*

Mehmet Ali *see* Mohammad Ali

Megiddo ⚔ of World War I (Sep 18–23 1918). Final battle of the Palestine campaign fought by British and Commonwealth troops against Turkey. A British and Commonwealth victory, it also marked the last use of massed cavalry in warfare.

Mehmet II "the Conqueror" (1432–1481) Ottoman sultan (reigned 1451–81) who in 1453 captured Constantinople (Istanbul) and pursued the rapid expansion of the empire into Greece, the Balkans, and Hungary.

Mehmet VI (1861–1926) Ottoman Sultan (reigned 1918–22). His failure to suppress the Turkish Nationalists, led by Mustafa Kemal (Atatürk), resulted in the abolition of the sultanate, and his subsequent exile.

Meiji Japanese term meaning "enlightened rule". The restoration of the Meiji emperor in 1868 ended Japan's two centuries of isolationism under the Tokugawa Shogunate and initiated a period of political and economic reform.

Melanesia One of three broad geographical divisions of the Pacific, the others being Micronesia and Polynesia. Melanesia includes New Guinea, New Caledonia, the Solomons, and Vanuatu.

Memphis ⚔ of American Civil War (Jun 5 1862). Union victory.

Memphis The capital of Old Kingdom Egypt, founded c.3100 BCE.

Mena *see* Narmer

Mencius (*var.* Meng-tzu) (c.371–c.289 BCE) Chinese philosopher who continued the teachings of Confucius. Developed a school to promote Confucian ideas, and from the age of 40 traveled China for 20 years searching for a ruler to implement Confucian morals and ideals. Believed that man was by nature good, but required the proper conditions for moral growth.

Mendaña, Álvaro de (c.1542–95) Spanish explorer of the Pacific. On Mendaña's first Pacific voyage in 1568, he discovered the Solomon Islands. He was attempting to return there and establish a colony in 1595, but he could not find the islands. He died on Santa Cruz Island.

Mendoza, Hurtado de 16th-century Spanish explorer of Lower California.

Menéndez de Avilés, Pedro 16th-century Spanish conquistador and explorer of N America. Founded San Agustín in Florida (1565).

Menes *see* Narmer

Meneses, Jorge de 16th-century Portuguese traveler in the East Indies. Sighted New Guinea (1526).

Meng-tzu *see* Mencius

Meni *see* Narmer

Mercator, Gerardus (prev. Gerhard Kremer, 1512–94) Flemish cartographer. Originator of the Mercator projection and publisher of the first book to use the world "Atlas" to describe a set of maps.

Meroë Capital of Nubian kingdom of Cush from 6th century BCE.

Merovingians (c.448–751) The first dynasty of Frankish kings of Gaul, named after Merovech, grandfather of Clovis I.

Mesa Verde Major Anasazi site in southwestern US, dating from the 11th century CE. *p.178*

Mesolithic Literally the "middle stone age", this is a term applied to the transitional period between the Palaeolithic (old stone age) and Neolithic (new stone age) in western Europe. The Mesolithic covers around five millennia from the end of the last Ice Age, c.10,000 BCE and the adoption of farming, c.5000 years ago. The Mesolithic is a transitional period, when Ice Age hunters gradually adapted to climatic changes and new environments and resources. It is characterized in the archaeological record by chipped stone tools, in particular microliths, very small stone tools intended for mounting on a shaft. These, as well as tools made of bone, antler, and wood, were used by hunter-gatherer communities, roughly contemporary with Neolithic farming groups further east. *p.13*

Mesopotamia The area between the Tigris and Euphrates, literally "land between the rivers." Lower Mesopotamia covered Baghdad to the Persian Gulf, and was home to the world's first urban civilizations in the 4th millennium BCE. Upper Mesopotamia extended from Baghdad north-west to the foothills of eastern Anatolia. *p.30*

metallurgy The range of techniques associated with metal-working: extracting metals from their ores, converting them into useful forms such as alloys, and fabricating objects. *p.21, p.27*
See also bronze; copper; gold; silver

Metaurus River ⚔ of Punic Wars (207 BCE). Roman victory.

Metternich, Clemens Fürst von (1773–1859) Austrian statesman. In 1809 he became Austrian foreign minister and was instrumental in the fall of Napoleon. He was the architect of the "Vienna system" in 1814–15, and the major force in European politics from 1814 until he was forced from office by the Viennese revolution of 1848.

Mexican Civil War (1858–67) Broke out between conservatives and liberals in 1858. The liberal leader Benito Juárez became president. His defeat of the conservative forces in 1860 was dependent on loans from western powers. France, Spain, and Britain invaded Mexico to enforce loan repayments; in 1863 a French army occupied Mexico city. The French appointed Archduke Maximilian of Austria as Mexican emperor. He was ousted in 1867 by Juárez's forces, and Juárez was reelected president (1867–72).

Mexican Revolution (1910–20) Beginning in 1910 with a revolt against the incumbent dictator Porfirio Díaz, and the entrenched interests of landowners and industrialists, the Mexican Revolution drew in a range of different factions in a protracted struggle which eventually led to the creation of Mexico as a constitutional republic. *p.395*
See also Victoriano Huerta, Francisco Madero, Pancho Villa, Emiliano Zapata

Mexican-American War (*var. Sp.* Guerra de 1847, Guerra de Estados Unidos) (Apr 1846–Feb 1848). The result of the US annexation of Texas in 1845 and a subsequent dispute over the territorial extent of Texas. A series of battles on land and sea resulted in US victory, and the military phase of the war ended with the fall of Mexico City. Via the Treaty of Guadalupe Hidalgo, the US gained the territory that would become the states of New Mexico, Utah, Nevada, Arizona, California, Texas, and western Colorado for $15,000,000.

MEXICO Increasingly considered a part of North rather than Central America, Mexico straddles the southern end of the continent. Coastal plains along its Pacific and Caribbean seaboards rise into an arid central plateau, which includes one of the world's biggest conurbations, Mexico City, built on the site of the Aztec capital, Tenochtitlán. Colonized by the Spanish for its silver mines, Mexico achieved independence in 1836. In the "Epic Revolution" of 1910–1920, in which 250,000 died, much of modern Mexico's structure was established. In 1994, Mexico signed the North American Free Trade Agreement (NAFTA).

CHRONOLOGY

1519–21 Hernán Cortés lands in Mexico and takes control of the Aztec empire ruled by Emperor Montezuma.

1522 Cortés is named governor and captain-general of New Spain.

1535 The Viceroyalty of New Spain, incorporating the captaincy-general, is established. By 1546 the Spaniards have discovered large silver mines at Zacatecas. Mexico, then known as New Spain, becomes a key part of the Spanish colonial empire.

1808 The Viceroy of New Spain is ousted and the territory remains in royalist hands (supporting Ferdinand VII of Spain whom Napoleon had deposed) until 1821.

1810 Fr. Miguel Hidalgo leads abortive rising against Spanish.

1821 Spanish viceroy forced to leave by Agustín de Iturbide.

1822 Federal Republic established.

1823 Texas opened to US immigration.

1829 Spanish military expedition fails to regain control.

1836 US is first country to recognize Mexico's independence. Spain follows suit. Texas declares its independence from Mexico.

1846 War breaks out with US.

1848 Loses modern-day New Mexico, Arizona, Nevada, Utah, California, and part of Colorado.

1858–1861 War of Reform won by anticlerical Liberals.

1862 France, Britain, and Spain launch military expedition.

1863 French troops capture Mexico City. Maximilian of Austria established as Mexican emperor.

1867 Mexico recaptured by Benito Juárez. Maximilian shot.

1876 Porfirio Díaz president. Economic growth; rail system built.

1901 First year of oil production.

1910–1920 Epic Revolution provoked by excessive exploitation by foreign companies and desire for land reform. 250,000 killed.

1911 Díaz overthrown by Francisco Madero. Guerrilla war breaks out in north. Emilio Zapata leads peasant revolt in the south.

1913 Madero murdered.

1917 New constitution limits power of Church. Minerals and subsoil rights reserved for the nation.

1926–1929 Cristero rebellion led by militant Catholic priests.

1929 National Revolutionary Party (later PRI) formed.

1934 General Cárdenas president. Land reform accelerated, cooperative farms established, railroads nationalized, and US and UK oil companies expelled.

1940s US war effort helps Mexican economy to grow.

1970 Accelerating population growth reaches 3 percent a year.

1982 Mexico declares it cannot repay its foreign debt of over $800 billion. IMF insists on economic reforms to reschedule the debt.

1984 Government contravenes constitution by relaxing laws on foreign investment.

1985 Earthquake in Mexico City. Official death toll 7000. Economic cost estimated at $425 million.

1988 Carlos Salinas de Gortari, minister of planning during the earthquake, elected president.

1990 Privatization program begun.

1994–1995 Guerrilla rebellion in southern Chiapas state brutally suppressed by army. 100 dead. Mexico joins NAFTA. PRI presidential candidate Luis Colosio murdered. Ernesto Zedillo replaces him and is elected. Economic crisis.

1997 Watershed elections; end of PRI's monopoly on power in Congress.

1999 Austerity budget and controversial bail-out of the banking system approved with PAN support.

2000 July, PAN wins presidency and elections, ending 70 years of PRI rule. President Vicente Fox takes office.
2001 EZLN guerrillas and supporters make 16-day motorcade from Chiapas to Mexico City to push for an indigenous rights law.
2002 Hard-liner Roberto Madrazo elected PRI leader.
2003 PRI gain in midterm elections.

MEXICAN LEADERS (since 1884)

1884–1911	Porfirio Díaz (second time)
1911	Francisco León de la Barra (interim)
1911–1913	Francisco Ignacio Madero
1913	Pedro Lascuráin (interim)
1913–1914	Victoriano Huerta (interim)
1914	Francisco S Carbajal (interim)
1914	Venustiano Carranza
1914	Antonio I Villarreal González
1914–1915	Eulalio Martin Gutiérrez Ortiz (interim, named by convention of Aguascalientes)
1915	Roque González Garza
1915	Francisco Lagos Chazáro
1915–1920	Venustiano Carranza
1920	Adolfo de la Huerta (interim)
1920–1924	Alvaro Obregón
1924–1928	Plutarco Elías Calles
1928–1930	Emilio Portes Gil (interim)
1930–1932	Pascual Ortíz Rubio
1932–1934	Abelardo Luján Rodríguez (interim)
1934–1940	Lázaro Cárdenas
1940–1946	Manuel Avila Camacho
1946–1952	Miguel Alemán Valdés
1952–1958	Adolfo Ruíz Cortines
1958–1964	Adolfo López Mateos
1964–1970	Gustavo Díaz Ordaz Balanos
1970–1976	Luis Echeverría Alvarez
1976–1982	José López Portillo y Pacheca
1982–1988	Miguel de la Madrid Hurtado
1988–1994	Carlos Salinas de Gortari
1994–2000	Ernesto Zedillo Ponce de León
2000–	Vincente Fox

Mfecane (*var.* Difaqane, "the Crushing") A series of Zulu and other Nguni wars and forced migrations in southern Africa during the first half of the 19th century which were set in motion by the rise of the Zulu military kingdom under Shaka.

Michelangelo (Michelangelo Buonarroti, 1475–1564) Florentine painter, sculptor, architect, and poet, one of the great geniuses of the Renaissance. *p.272*
Michael Palaeologus (c.1277–1320). Byzantine co-emperor with his father, Andronicus II, from 1295, who failed to stem the decline of the empire, despite his efforts in fighting the Turks and in resisting the invasions of Catalan mercenaries.
microliths Tool technology developed in Africa c.30,000 years ago, and some time after the peak of the last Ice Age, c.16,000 years ago, in Europe. Small (microlithic) flints were mounted in a range of bone or wooden hafts, to make "composite" tools, which could be used to exploit the much wider range of food resources becoming available as the last Ice Age ended.
Micronesia Region of the western Pacific, dotted with tiny archipelagos, including the Marianas and the Marshall Islands. The peoples of Micronesia are of more mixed ancestry than those of Polynesia to the east, having had more frequent contact with mainland E Asia. Micronesian shell map. *p.134*

MICRONESIA The Federated States of Micronesia (FSM), situated in the Pacific Ocean, encompasses all the Caroline Islands except Palau. It is composed of four island cluster states: Pohnpei, Kosrae, Chuuk, and Yap. The Caroline Islands were first visited by the Spanish as early as 1526, but were not formally colonized until 1886. Sold to Germany in 1899, the islands were occupied by Japan from 1914 and served as an important base in World War II. US control began in 1945, the islands becoming part of the UN Trust Territory of the Pacific Islands. An agreement which granted internal sovereignty in free association with the USA became operational in 1986, and the Trust was formally dissolved in 1990. The islands continue to receive considerable aid from the US.

CHRONOLOGY
1947 UN Trust Territory of the Pacific Islands established.
1979 Becomes independent.
1986 Compact of Free Association with USA operational.

1990 Official termination of trusteeship agreement.
1991 Joins UN.
1995 President Bailey Olter reelected.
1997 Jacob Nena formally succeeds Olter as president after the latter is incapacitated by a stroke.
2001 Submerged remains of *USS Mississinewa* causes oil leak in Yap.
2003 Joseph Urusemal elected president. New Compact agreed.

Microsoft US computer software firm, founded in 1975. In the 1990s it ran into trouble with US antitrust laws because of its domination of the market. *p.453*
Middendorff, Alexander von 19th-century Russian explorer of Siberia.
Middleburg ✕ of Dutch Revolt (1574). Dutch victory over Spain.
Middle East *see* individual countries Conflict in the Middle East. *p.454*
Middle Kingdom Division of ancient Egyptian history, c.2050–1750 BCE, which saw some expansion into Palestine, and fortification of the Nubian frontier.
Midway Naval ✕ of World War II (Jun 1942). Defeat of Japanese by US forces in mid-Pacific Ocean, marking turning point in Pacific War.
Migration Migration to the US from Europe (1880–1920) *p.383*
Milan, Edict of (313 CE) Proclamation that permanently established religious toleration for Christianity within the Roman Empire. It was the outcome of a political agreement concluded in Milan between the Roman emperors Constantine I and Licinius in Feb 313 CE.
Milne Bay ✕ of World War II (Aug 1942). Defeat of Japanese landing force in southeastern New Guinea.
Milošević, Slobodan (1941–) Politician and administrator who, as leader of the League of Communists of Serbia (from 1987) and president (1989–97), pursued Serb nationalist policies that led to the breakup of Yugoslavia.
Milvian Bridge ✕ (312) Constantine defeated his rival Maxentius just north of Rome to become master of the western half of the Roman Empire. He attributed his victory to a vision of the cross of Christ he had seen on the eve of the battle.
Min *see* Narmer

Minamoto Yoritomo (1147–99) Founder of the Kamakura Shogunate in Japan, who crushed the Taira clan.

Minas Gerais The rich gold-mining area of Brazil, which helped prop up the Portuguese economy in the 18th century. Gold was first discovered there in 1695.

minerals *see* metallurgy

Mines Act (1842) Act passed by British parliament, forbidding employment of women and children underground.

Ming dynasty (1368–1644) Ruling dynasty of China, which drove out the Mongols, founded by Zhu Yuanzhang. It was eventually toppled by the Manchus in 1644. *p.245*

Ming empire *see* Ming dynasty

Minoan civilization Named after the legendary King Minos of Crete, the Minoans were the first great European civilization, c.2000 BCE, whose main cities were Knossos and Phaestus. They had strong trade links with Egypt, and flourished due to their control of sea routes c.2200–1450 BCE. Evidence from their complex palaces attests their high standards of art, metal-working, and jewelry-making. Early Minoan pictorial writing has been found, dating to around 1880 BCE, which was superseded by the still undeciphered Linear A and then early Greek writing known as Linear B. *p.31*

Minos The first king of Crete, according to legend, the son of Zeus and Europa, and husband of Pasiphae. Knossos was said to have been his capital from where he ruled a powerful seafaring empire. The ancient civilization of Crete, Minoan civilization, is named after him. His palace at Knossos was built c.2000 BCE.

Minsk ⚔ of World War II (Jun–Aug 1943). Encirclement of German forces by Soviets in Belorussia.

MIRV *see* Multiple Independently Targeted Warhead Re-entry Vehicle

Mississippian culture (c.800–1500 CE). Based in the river valleys of the present-day states of Mississippi, Alabama, Georgia, Arkansas, Missouri, Kentucky, Illinois, Indiana, and Ohio, with scattered populations in Wisconsin and Minnesota and on the Great Plains. A settled agricultural culture, it was distinctive for the oval earthworks which dominated most settlements.

Missouri Compromise (1820) The measure which allowed for the admission of Missouri as the 24th US state in 1821.

James Tallmadge's attempt to add an anti-slavery amendment legislation for the admission of new states to the US led to a major debate over the right of the government to restrict slavery in new states. The issue remained unresolved in 1819 when the northern state of Maine applied for statehood. The Senate passed a bill allowing Maine to enter the Union as a free state and Missouri to be admitted with no restriction on slavery. A further amendment was then added that allowed Missouri to become a slave state but banned slavery in the rest of the Louisiana Purchase north of latitude 36°30'.

Mitanni Indo-Persian people whose empire in northern Mesopotamia flourished c.1500–1360 BCE. Their capital, Wahshukanni, was probably in the Khabur River region, and at their height they ruled over lands from the Zagros Mountains west to the Mediterranean.

Mitchell, Thomas (1792–1855) Scottish-born soldier and explorer. Surveyor-General of New South Wales from 1827, he led several important expeditions into the Australian interior.

Mithraism Worship of Mithras, an Indian and Persian god of justice and law. Spread as a mystery cult in the Roman Empire, with Mithras as a divine savior. Ousted by Christianity in the 4th century CE.

Mithras *see* Mithraism

Mithridates II (*var.* Mithradates, died 88 BCE). After recovering the eastern provinces that had been overrun during his father's reign, Mithridates was one of the most successful Parthian kings, concluding the first treaty between Parthia and Rome in 92 BCE.

Mobile Bay ⚔ of American Civil War (Aug 5 1864). Union victory.

Mobuto, Sese Seko Koko Ngbendu wa za Banga (Joseph-Désiré) (1930–97) President of Zaire. Mobutu staged a coup to become president in 1965 and held on to power for over 30 years despite the flagrant corruption of his regime. He finally lost control Zaire, while in Europe for medical treatment in 1997 and never returned.

Moche culture (*var.* Mohica) The earliest major civilization on the north coast of Peru, based in the ancient city of Moche around 200 BCE–550 CE. It is best known for the twin brick pyramids of the Sun and Moon, Huaca del Sol and Huaca de la Luna, which were

richly decorated with multi-colored murals. The Moche people also carried out extensive irrigation, fortified their ceremonial centers, and produced cast, alloyed and gilded metalwork. *p.80*

Mogollon Native American culture of the US Southwest that flourished c.600–1300 CE. The Mogollon constructed pueblos that altered considerably in style over the centuries, as did their pottery.

Mogul dynasty *see* Mughal dynasty

Mohács ⚔ (1526) The Ottomans under Suleyman the Magnificent crushed the Hungarian army, subsequently advancing to the gates of Vienna.

Mohammed *see* Muhammad

Mohammed Ali (*var.* Mehmet Ali, Muhammad Ali, c.1769–1849) Viceroy of Egypt (1805–48), who made Egypt the leading power in the eastern Mediterranean. An Albanian military officer, he went to Egypt (1801) in command of an Ottoman army sent to face Napoleon. After many successful military campaigns, he turned against the Ottomans, defeating them in Asia Minor (1839), but European intervention prevented the overthrow of the sultan. *p.348*

Mohenjo-Daro Major city of the Harappan culture, which flourished along the Indus valley c.2500–1500 BCE. *p.28*

Mohica see Moche culture

Moldavia see Moldova

MOLDOVA (*prev.* Moldavia, Bessarabia) Mostly undulating steppe country, Moldova is the smallest and most densely populated of the former Soviet republics. Once a part of Romania, it was incorporated into the Soviet Union in 1940. Independence in 1991 brought with it the expectation that Moldova would be reunited with Romania. In a 1994 plebiscite, however, Moldovans voted against the proposal. Most of its population is engaged in intensive agriculture.

CHRONOLOGY

7th century BCE A Greek colony exists on Moldova's Black Sea coast.

2nd century CE The territory forms part of the kingdom of Dacia.

6th century CE Slavs migrate to the area.

1300 Dragos becomes the first prince of Moldavia, having migrated to the territory with his followers from the northern Carpathians. In 1349 the first independent Moldavian state emerges, but it soon becomes subject to Poland.

1475 Stephen the Great, whose reign is characterized by his championing of Christendom, defeats a Turkish army at Rahova, but in 1484, with no support from Poland or Hungary, his army is defeated and by 1513 Stephen's son Bogdan III pays tribute to Turkey; by the end of the 16th century Bessarabia (Eastern Moldavia) is under Turkish control. Western Moldavia eventually became part of Romania.

1812 Russia annexes Bessarabia. Despite a relatively liberal Russian regime, many Moldavians flee, fearing serfdom.

1917 A Moldavian National Committee, formed after the February Revolution, demands autonomy, land reform, and the use of the Romanian language. December. A national council declares Bessarabia an autonomous constituent republic of the Federation of Russian Socialist Republics. Fighting breaks out between Russian revolutionary forces and Moldavians, who appeal to Romania for assistance. Romanian troops drive out the Russians in January 1918.

1918 Bessarabia joins Romania.

1924 Moldavian Autonomous Soviet Republic formed within USSR.

1940 Romania cedes Bessarabia to Ukrainian and Moldavian SSRs.

1941–1945 Bessarabia again under Romanian control.

1945 Returns to Soviet control.

1990 Declares sovereignty.

1991 Independence as Moldova.

1993–1994 Pro-unification parties' election defeat; referendum rejects Romanian unification. Rejoins CIS.

1996 Lucinschi elected president.

1998 Communist revival at general election.

2001 CPM wins big majority. Voronin becomes president.

2002 Mass protests over education plans.

Moluccas The fabled Spice Islands of the East Indies. The Portuguese established a trading center at Ternate, from which they shipped back the islands' precious cloves and nutmeg. In the 17th century they were ousted by the Dutch.

MONACO Monaco is a tiny enclave on the Côte d'Azur in southeastern France. Its destiny changed radically in 1863, when Prince Charles III, after whom Monte Carlo is named, opened the casino. Today, Monaco is a lucrative banking and services center, as well as a tourist destination. Prince Rainier's marriage to film star Grace Kelly, and some astute management of the economy, successfully transformed Monaco into a center for the international jet set. In 1962, the prince's absolute authority was abolished by a new constitution.

CHRONOLOGY

1191 The ancient port of Monaco is ceded by Henry VI, Holy Roman Emperor, to the Republic of Genoa, and a fortress is built.

1297 The Grimaldis, one of Genoa's most ancient families, establish themselves as the Principality's hereditary rulers after suppressing a local uprising.

1641 Monaco becomes a protectorate of France.

1793 At the time of the French revolution Monaco is temporarily annexed and the Grimaldis are imprisoned.

1814 Under the Treaty of Paris the Grimaldis regain power, but a year later Monaco is placed under the protectorate of Sardinia.

1861 Independent under French protection.

1911 Constitution promulgated.

1949 Rainier III accedes to throne.

1962 Constitution rewritten: end of absolute authority of the prince.

1963 Democratic legislative elections held for first time.

1982 Princess Grace dies following a car accident.

2002 Euro introduced.

Monasteries Monastic foundations of the early Middle Ages. *p.147*
See also Cistercians, Benedict, St

Money The first coins. *p.46*
Paper money. *p.196*
Money and banking. *p.269*

Möngke (died 1259) Mongol leader, a grandson of Genghis Khan, elected Great Khan in 1251. Möngke's rule saw the start of the so-called "Mongol Peace", when travel and trade across Central Asia flourished.

MONGOLIA Landlocked between Russia and China, Mongolia rises from the semiarid Gobi Desert to mountainous steppe. The traditionally nomadic Mongols were first unified by Genghis Khan in 1206. In the 17th century, the Manchus took control of Mongolia. It stayed in Chinese hands until 1911. Mongolia finally achieved independence from China as a communist state in 1924 and was officially aligned with the USSR from 1936. In 1990, it abandoned communist rule and widespread poverty ensued. Particularly harsh winters in 1999–2001 devastated the rural economy.

CHRONOLOGY

1919 China reoccupies Mongolia.

1924 Independent communist state.

1989–1990 Prodemocracy protests; communist election defeat.

1992 Former communists, renamed MPRP, returned to power.

1996 Democratic Union coalition wins general election.

1997 MPRP wins presidency.

1999–2001 Severe winters.

2000 Landslide electoral victory for MPRP.

2004 Election leaves both MPRP and MDC just short of a majority.

Mongols Pastoralist, nomadic people of Central Asia. Their conquests from the 13th century onwards were the last assault by nomadic armies inflicted upon the settled peoples of western Asia. Under the eadership of Ghengis Khan (1206–27) they conquered northern China and much of central Asia, with raiding parties reaching as far west as the Crimea. Under his descendants Mongol armies penetrated Europe, reaching Poland and the Adriatic. They also conquered much of Russia, the lands of the Caliphate, and eventually the whole of China, where Kublai Khan ruled as the first emperor of the Yuan dynasty. Two attempted invasions of Japan (1274, 1281) and an expedition to Java (1293), were however, unsuccessful. By 1300 the Mongols ruled over four great empires: China (the empire of the Great Khan), the Chagatai Khanate, the Il-Khanate, and the Khanate of the Golden Horde.
Genghis Khan. *p.209*
Mongol invasions. *p.216*

Hülegü Khan. *p.216*
Mongol military tactics. *p.217*
Siege of Hezhou. *p.217*
Mongol peace. *p.221*
Mongol invasion of Japan. *p.222*
Conquests of Timur. *p.239*

Monmouth Court House ⚔ of American Revolutionary War (June 28 1778). Inconclusive result.

monsoon Wind system involving seasonal reversal of prevailing wind direction. Occurs mainly in the Indian Ocean, the western Pacific, and off the W African coast. The term also applies to the rainy seasons of much of southern and eastern Asia, and of E and W Africa.

Montcalm, Louis Joseph, Marquis de (1712–59) Commander of the French troops in Canada in the Seven Years' War. He was mortally wounded defending Quebec.

Monte Albán Important ceremonial center in central America from c.500 BCE. It was founded by the Zapotecs and dominated the three valleys of the Oaxaca until c.600 CE. *p.120*

Monte Cassino *see* Cassino

Montezuma I Aztec ruler (1440–68).

Montezuma II (*aka* Montezuma Xocoyotl, Moteuczoma II, 1466–1520) Ninth emperor of the Aztecs (reigned 1502–20). During the Spanish conquest of Mexico by Hernán Cortés and his conquistadors, he was deposed as ruler and imprisoned.

Montgomery Montgomery, Alabama was the scene of a historic boycott against segregation in the US South (1955).

Montmirail ⚔ of Napoleon's defense of France (Feb 11 1814). French victory.

Montoya, Father Ruiz de 17th-century Jesuit missionary in South America.

Montreal The chief city of French-speaking Canada, second only to Toronto as an economic center. It was captured by the British in 1760.

Moors Name given to the Islamic conquerors of the Iberian peninsula in the 8th century CE.
Moorish architecture. *p.240*

Morgan, Sir Henry (c.1635–88) Welsh buccaneer who operated in the West Indies, preying primarily on Spanish ships and territories including Panama, which he captured in 1671. Though arrested and transported to London to placate the Spanish, he returned to the West Indies and became a wealthy planter.

MOROCCO Morocco is situated in northern Africa, but at its northernmost point lies only 12 km (8 miles) from mainland Europe, across the Strait of Gibraltar. Morocco's northern regions have a Mediterranean climate, while the south comprises semiarid desert. The late King Hassan's international prestige gave Morocco status out of proportion to its wealth. The main issues the country faces are the internal threat of Islamic militancy and the unresolved fate of Western Sahara, the former Spanish colony occupied by Morocco since 1975. The key economic strengths are tourism, phosphate production, and agriculture.

CHRONOLOGY

6th century BCE Originally inhabited by Berbers, the region along the north African coast as far as Lixus (now called Larache) was first colonized by the Phoenicians. By the sixth century BCE their descendants, the Carthaginians, controlled most of the coastal trading ports from Leptis (in contemporary Libya) to Lixus and Mogador (now called Essaouira) in Morocco.

264–146 BCE Rome's Punic Wars against Carthage (in modern Tunisia) eventually results in the sacking of Carthage in 146 BCE and the extension of the Roman Empire along the north African coast.

429 CE Vandals occupy the area from Tangier to Carthage.

8th century CE Idris brings Islam to the region and establishes the Idrissid kingdom which lasts until 920.

1062 Sultan Ibn Tachfin establishes the Almoravid dynasty in Morocco and W Algeria. By time of his death in 1106 he also holds sway over Muslim Spain.

1147 The Almohads replace Almoravids and are in turn conquered by the Zenatas from the Sahara in the 13th century.

Mid-17th century The Alaouite dynasty is founded by Moulay Rashid. When he dies in 1672 disorder reigns and it is only in 1677 that his son Moulay Ismail regains control of the region. A 150,000-strong slave army wins back all the Spanish coastal enclaves except Ceuta and Melilla. Moulay Ismail establishes a new palace and capital at Meknes.

1904 France and Spain conclude a secret agreement to partition Morocco.

1906 At the Algeciras conference France and Spain promise to respect Morocco's independence but are given the power to police the country.

1911 In the Agadir incident Germany sends a gunboat to the Moroccan port of Agadir, officially to protect German interests against French expansion. Negotiations lead to Germany recognizing France's rights in Morocco in return for ceding territory in Congo.

1912 A French protectorate is established under the Treaty of Fez after Sultan Abd ul-Hafiz uses French troops to quash his rivals.

1927 Sidi Mohammed Yousif becomes Sultan of Morocco.

1953 Sultan Mohammed Yousif is forced to abdicate by the French because of his support for independence.

1955 Sultan Mohammed returns from exile in Madagascar to conclude an independence agreement with France.

1956 France recognizes Moroccan independence under Sultan Mohammed Ibn Yousif. Morocco joins UN. Spain renounces control over most of its territories.

1957 Sultan Mohammed king.

1961 Hassan succeeds his father.

1967 Morocco backs Arab cause in Six-Day War with Israel.

1969 Spain returns Ifni to Morocco.

1975 International Court of Justice grants right of self-determination to Western Saharan people. King Hassan orders Moroccan forces to seize Saharan capital.

1976 Morocco and Mauritania partition Western Sahara.

1979 Mauritania renounces claim to part of Western Sahara, which is added to Morocco's territory.

1984 King Hassan signs Oujda Treaty with Col. Gaddafi of Libya as first step toward a Maghreb union. Morocco leaves OAU after criticism of its role in Western Sahara.

1986 Morocco abrogates Oujda Treaty.

1987 Defensive wall around Western Sahara.

1989 Arab Maghreb Union (AMU) creates no-tariff zone between Morocco, Algeria, Tunisia, Libya, and Mauritania.

1990 Morocco condemns Iraq's invasion of Kuwait.

1991 Morocco accepts UN plan for referendum in Western Sahara.

1992 New constitution grants majority party in parliament right to choose the government.

1993 First general election for nine years. After major parties refuse his invitation, king appoints nonparty government.

1994 King Hassan replaces veteran prime minister Karim Lamrani with Abdellatif Filali.

1995 Islamist opposition leader Mohamed Basri returns after 28 years of exile.

1998 Socialists enter government with Abderrahmane el Youssoufi as prime minister.

1999 Death of King Hassan. Mohammed VI enthroned. Liberalization program announced.

2000–2001 UN plan for Western Sahara founders; UN special representative proposes a ten-year trial period as part of Morocco.

2002 Islamists gain in elections.

2003 Polisario accepts UN plan to grant Western Sahara autonomy within Morocco, though Moroccan government rejects it.

2004 Over 500 killed in earthquake.

Morse, Samuel (1791–1872) American painter and inventor who devised a code using dots and dashes for use with the electric telegraph.

Moscow Capital city of the Russian Federation (formerly the USSR), Moscow first emerged as an important center in the 14th century, when it was the chief city of the principality of Muscovy. It gained supremacy of the other Russian principalities, first by allying with the Mongol overloads of the Golden Horde, then by leading the fight against them. Although a new Russian capital was created at St. Petersburg, Moscow retained its importance and became the capital once more under the Soviets. The Kremlin. *p.267*

Moscow ⚔ of World War II (Dec 1941). Soviet forces halted German advance during Operation Barbarossa.

Moteuczoma Xocoyotl *see* Montezuma II

Moslem *see* Muslim

Moundbuilders Name given especially to the Mississippian culture of eastern north America.

Mount Olympus Cult center of the Ancient Greeks.

MOZAMBIQUE

MOZAMBIQUE Situated on the southeast African coast, Mozambique is bisected by the Zambezi River. South of the Zambezi lies a semiarid savanna lowland. The more fertile north-central delta provinces around Tete are home to most of Mozambique's ethnically diverse population. Following independence from Portugal in 1975, Mozambique was torn apart by civil war between the (then Marxist) FRELIMO government and the South African-backed Mozambique National Resistance (RENAMO). The conflict finally ended in 1992 after UN arbitration. Multiparty elections in 1994 returned FRELIMO to power. Devastating floods in 2000 and 2001 have created a desperate situation for this impoverished country.

CHRONOLOGY

16th century The establishment of the first Portuguese trading center at Quelimane, which becomes a center for slave trading.

1684 The Mwene Matapa kingdom recognizes Portuguese sovereignty. Later in the 17th century the Changamire of the Rozvi kingdom conquer the Mwene Matapa and push the Portuguese south of the River Zambezi. Only after the Portuguese re-establish control north of the Zambezi do they appoint a colonial governor (in 1752). From the late 17th to the 19th century the slave trade becomes a major factor in the Mozambican economy. The Portuguese introduce a system of forced labor when slavery is ended in the late 19th century.

1951 Mozambique becomes an overseas province of Portugal, the Portuguese government having, in the decade prior to the Second World War, taken control of those parts of Mozambique previously administered by private Portuguese companies. In the next 20 years Lisbon introduces ambitious settlement schemes.

1964 FRELIMO starts war of liberation.

1975 Independence. FRELIMO leader Samora Machel is president.

1976 Resistance movement RENAMO set up inside Mozambique by Rhodesians.

1976–1980 Mozambique closes Rhodesian border and supports Zimbabwean freedom fighters. Reprisals by RENAMO.

1977 FRELIMO constitutes itself as Marxist–Leninist party.

1980 South Africa takes over backing of RENAMO.

1984 South Africa agrees to stop support for RENAMO, and Mozambique for ANC, but fighting continues.

1986 RENAMO declares war on Zimbabwe. Tanzanian troops reinforce FRELIMO. Machel dies in air crash in South Africa. Joaquim Chissano replaces him.

1988 Nkomati Accord reactivated. Mozambicans allowed back to work in South African mines.

1989 War and malnutrition said to claim one million lives. FRELIMO drops Marxist–Leninism.

1990 Multipartyism and free-market economy in new constitution. RENAMO breaches ceasefire.

1992 Chissano signs peace agreement with RENAMO.

1994 Democratic elections return FRELIMO to power.

1995 Joins Commonwealth. Economic reforms begun.

1999 G7 chooses Mozambique as flagship for international debt relief initiative. RENAMO disputes results of elections.

2000–2001 Thousands displaced by devastating floods.

MPLA *see* People's Movement for the Liberation of Angola

MRV *see* Multiple Re-entry Vehicle

Msiri 19th-century trader who settled with his Nyamwezi followers in southern Katanga, central Africa in 1856. Msiri dominated the region by about 1870.

MUGHAL EMPIRE

MUGHAL EMPIRE (*var.* Mogul Empire, 1526–1857) The victory of Babur, an Afghan Muslim, at Panipat in 1525, was the beginning of the Mughal empire, which dominated India until 1739. The empire reached its peak during the reign of Akbar, when it extended from Bengal to Sind and Gujarat, and from Kashmir to the Godavari river. From the 1670s, confrontation with the Marathas depleted the power of the Mughals and decline soon set in. In 1739 Nadir Shah of Persia swept into India, and sacked Delhi, and from this point the Mughals were merely puppet emperors. *p.282*

▶

MUGHAL DYNASTY (1526–1858)	
1526–1530	Babur
1530–1540	Humayun
1556–1605	Akbar
1605–1627	Jahangir
1627–1628	Dawar Baksh
1628–1658	Shah Jahan
1658–1707	Aurangzeb Alamgir
1707–1712	Bahadur Shah I (Shah Alam I)
1712–1713	Jahandar Muizzuddin Shah
1713–1719	Farrukh-siyar
1719	Shamsuddin Rafi-ud-Darajat
1719	Shah Jahan II (Rafi-ud-Dawlah)
1719	Nikusiyar Muhammed
1719–1748	Muhammed Shah
1748–1754	Ahmad Bahadur Shah
1754–1759	Azizuddin Alamgir II
1759	Shah Jahan III
1759–1788	Shah Alam II
1788	Bedar Bakht
1806–1837	Muinuddin Akbar II
1837–1857	Sirajuddin Bahadur Shah Zafar II

Muhammad (var. Mohammed, c.570–632) Founder of Islamic religion, born in Mecca (Saudi Arabia). In 610 a vision of the Angel Gabriel revealed messages from God. These messages, written down as the Koran (meaning "Reading" or "Recitation"), are revered as the Holy Book of Islam. In 622 Muhammad and his followers were forced to move to Medina, a migration (Hegira) which marks the beginning of the Islamic calendar. As a religious leader, he conquered Mecca in 630, destroyed the pagan idols and unified much of Arabia. His legacy passed to his father-in-law, Abu Bakr, the first caliph.

Muhammad III Sultan of Morocco (reigned 1757–90) who introduced administrative reforms and reopened trade with Europe after a long embargo.

Muhammad al Ghur (var. Ghiyas al-Din, died 1202, reigned 1173–1202) Leader of an Afghan army, in 1191 he defeated the Rajput clans of northern India, and in 1206 his general, Qutb al-Din Aybak, established the Ghurid dynasty, the first Turko-Afghan dynasty in Delhi, ruling it as sultan.

Muhammad Ali see Mohammed Ali
Muhammad Ibn Adullah see Ibn Battuta
Muhammad of Ghazni
see Mahmud of Ghazni

Muisca (var. Chibcha). Native people of the highlands around Bogotá. It was in Muisca lands that the legend of El Dorado caught the imagination of Spanish conquistadores.

Mujahedin (var. Mujahideen) Islamic nationalist forces during Afghan civil war (from 1973) who spearheaded resistance to Soviet invasion (1979–89) with Pakistani backing, forming a government (1983), but opposed by Taliban from 1995.

Mujahideen see Mujahedin

Multiple Re-entry Vehicle (MRV) ICBM developed by US in the early 1960s that could deliver a "footprint" of warheads in a selected area, greatly increasing US nuclear potential during the Cold War.

Multiple Independently Targeted Warhead Re-entry Vehicle (MIRV) ICBM developed by US in late 1960s, that could select several targets, greatly increasing US nuclear potential during the Cold War.

Mumbai see Bombay

Mummification Preservation of human and animal bodies by embalming and wrapping in lengths of cloth, after removal of the internal organs. Mummification is associated with belief in life after death, and was practiced by the ancient Egyptians amongst others. p.40

Mungo, Lake Site of first known cremation in Australia (26,000 BP).

Murad I (c.1326–89) Third Ottoman Sultan, who pursued the expansion of the empire in the Balkans, annexing Bulgaria and much of Serbia. He was killed at the battle of Kosovo Polje.

Murasaki Shikibu (died c.1014) Japanese writer, author of the Tale of Genji. p.161

Muret ⚔ of Albigensian Crusade (1213). Peter II of Aragon killed by crusading army.

Murfreesboro (aka Stones River). ⚔ of American Civil War (Dec 31 1862–Jan 2 1863). Union victory.

Muscovy State created by the Grand Princes of Moscow in the 13th century. Though isolated, Muscovy became increasingly powerful through the annexation of Novgorod and the proclamation of independence from the Mongols in 1480. By 1556 Muscovy had annexed the Khanate of Astrakhan, controlling the Volga down to the Caspian Sea. In 1571 Moscow was sacked by Crimean Tatars.

Muscovy Company Formed in 1555 by the navigator and explorer Sebastian Cabot and various London merchants in order to trade with Russia, the company was granted a monopoly of Anglo-Russian trade. Sponsored much Arctic exploration.

Musket Wars A series of conflicts between Maori tribes in the 1820s, sparked by the introduction of firearms into New Zealand.

Muslim (var. Moslem, Mussulman) Of or pertaining to the Islamic faith. See Islam

Muslim League Formed in 1906, as a result of the conflicts created within Bengal by Lord Curzon's 1905 partition of the province. The League's original aim was to promote separate electorates for Muslim minorities within Hindu majority areas, but by the 1940s it had started to demand a separate Muslim state. It was pressure from the League that led to the creation of Pakistan in 1947.

Mussolini, Benito Amilcare Andrea (1883–1945) Italian dictator (1925–43). Expelled from the socialist party for pressing for support of the Allies during World War I; after the war Mussolini founded the Fasci di Combattimento (Fascist movement). Aided by Blackshirt supporters, he attacked Communism, and in 1922 marched on Rome. He was appointed Prime Minister by King Victor Emmanuel III, and by 1925 had declared himself Il Duce (the leader) and swiftly established a totalitarian regime within Italy. In 1935 he invaded Ethiopia as part of a plan to form an Italian empire, and by 1936 had formed the Rome-Berlin axis with Hitler, declaring war on the Allies in 1940. Dependence on Hitler broke support for Mussolini and he was deposed and executed in 1945. p.401

Mutapa empire (var. Muwenutapa) Kingdom of southern Africa that flourished between the 15th and 18th centuries, absorbing great Zimbabwe c.1450.

Mustafa Kemal Pasha see Atatürk

Mutually Assured Destruction (MAD) Term coined by US Secretary of State John Foster Dulles (1953–59) to describe Cold War intercontinental arms stalemate between US and Soviet Union.

Mwenemutapa see Mutapa empire

Myanmar Forming the eastern shores of the Bay of Bengal and the Andaman Sea in Southeast Asia, Myanmar has recently suffered extensive political repression and ethnic conflict. See also Burma

Mycale (var. Gre. Mykale) ⚔ (479 BCE) when the Greeks defeated the Persian navy off the coast of Asia Minor.

Mycenaean Greece Named after its capital Mycenae, Bronze Age Greek culture which dominated mainland Greece between 1580–1120 BCE. The Mycenaeans appear to have conquered Knossos in Crete around 1450 BCE, and they traded widely in Asia Minor, Cyprus, and Syria. Their sacking of Troy c.1200 BCE was later mythologized in Homer's *Iliad*. Archaeological evidence points to great wealth and skill, with palaces at Mycenae, Tiryns, and Pylos at the center of a system of government by a warrior class overseeing a redistributive economy. The final destruction or abandonment of these palaces is now thought to be due to internal unrest rather than external conquest.

N

Naddod 9th-century Viking explorer who visited Iceland (c.870).

Nadir Shah (1688–1747) A bandit chieftain of Turkish origin, in 1736 he seized the Safavid throne of Persia, immediately embarking on campaigns against neighboring states. In 1739 he attacked Delhi, capital of Mughal India, slaughtered its citizens and stole the Koh-i-noor diamond. Cruel and ruthless, he was eventually assassinated by his own troops.

NAFTA *see* North American Free Trade Agreement

Nagasaki Japanese city, where the second atomic bomb was dropped by US in 1945.

Nain Singh 19th-century Indian surveyor, who made a journey in disguise through Tibet on behalf of the Survey of India.

NAMIBIA Located in southwestern Africa, Namibia has an arid coastal strip formed by the Namib Desert. After many years of guerrilla warfare, Namibia won independence from South Africa in 1990. Despite the move away from apartheid, Namibia's economy remains reliant on the expertise of the small white population, a legacy of the previously poor education for blacks. Namibia is Africa's fourth-largest minerals producer.

CHRONOLOGY

1890 An Anglo-German agreement acknowledges German control of South West Africa and Britain's annexation of Walvis Bay four years earlier for Cape Colony. The German colonists take the best farming land and displace the indigenous people, ruthlessly suppress a rising by the Hereros in 1904, kill an estimated 80,000 Hereros in over a year of open genocide and introduce a harsh forced labor regime.

1915 German forces surrender to South African troops. Five years of military occupation follow and in 1920 the League of Nations award to South Africa the mandate to administer the territory "as an integral part of the Union of South Africa." South Africa is also charged with promoting the "material and moral well-being and the social progress of the inhabitants" and preparing the territory for eventual self-determination. South Africa extends the German policy of reserves for the indigenous population, 17 of which are established by 1939.

1946 The UN General Assembly rejects a South African request to incorporate South West Africa into its own territory. South Africa, which argues that the mandate system has lapsed with the dissolution of the League, refuses to enter into a trusteeship agreement. In 1949 it refuses to submit to the UN any further annual reports on the administration of the territory and gives whites there representation in the South African parliament. Five years later South Africa transfers the administration of "native affairs" in South West Africa to the Union Government.

1950 The International Court of Justice rules that South Africa has no right to change the international status of the territory. Two further ICJ rulings, in 1955 and 1956, uphold the UN's right to supervise the administration.

1960 The South West Africa People's Organisation (SWAPO) is formed under the leadership of Sam Nujoma and Herman Toivo ja Toivo. Based on the Ovamboland People's Organisation, which had been formed earlier with the objective of ending the contract labor system, SWAPO has broader objectives and national scope; it will seek to mobilize all the people of Namibia

against South African rule. From 1963 its meetings are effectively banned, although technically it remains legal.

1966 Apartheid laws imposed. SWAPO begins armed struggle.

1968 Renamed Namibia.

1973 UN recognizes SWAPO.

1990 Independence.

1994 South Africa relinquishes Walvis Bay.

1999 President Sam Nujoma wins third term.

Nanjing Capital of the Chinese, which ruled northern China before the Mongol invasions of the 13th century. It was again briefly capital of China under the Ming from 1368. The Treaty of Nanjing in 1842 brought an end to the Opium War and opened up China to foreign trade.

Nanjing, Treaty of *see* Opium War

Nansen, Fridjof (1861–1930) Norwegian scientist, explorer, and statesman. Crossed Greenland icecap in 1888 on foot. In his specially-designed ship, the Fram, he explored the Arctic from 1893–96, stopping to take part in a bid for the North Pole. In 1918 he became a commissioner to the League of Nations and was awarded the Nobel Peace Prize in 1923 for his work in assisting famine-struck regions of the Soviet Union.

Nantes, Edict of (1598) Order signed by Henry IV of France granting the Protestant Huguenots the right to practice their own religion. It was revoked in 1685 by Louis XIV, and as a result many non-Catholics fled the country.

Napoleon I, Bonaparte (1769–1821) French military and political leader, and Emperor of France (1804–1815). Following successful Italian campaign (1796–7) and invasion of Egypt (1798), he assumed power as First Consul in 1799. A brilliant general, he defeated every European coalition which fought against him over the next decade. Decline set in with failure of Peninsular War in Spain and disastrous invasion of Russia (1812). Defeated at Leipzig (1813) by a new European alliance, he abdicated in 1814 and went into exile, but escaped and ruled as emperor during the Hundred Days. Finally defeated at Waterloo (1815) and exiled to St. Helena. As an administrator, his achievements were of lasting significance and include the Code Napoléon, which remains the basis for French law. *p.344*

Napoleon III (*var.* Charles Louis Napoléon Bonaparte, 1808–1873) Nephew of Napoleon I, he became president of the Second Republic (1848), and was elected emperor of France (1852–71). Involved France in the Crimean War (1853–6) and the Franco-Prussian War (1870–71), which ended in France's defeat and Napoleon's exile to Britain. *See also* Crimean War, Franco-Prussian War.

Nara period (710–784) Period of Japanese history that began with the establishment of a capital at Heijo-kyo (to the west of the modern city of Nara).

Narbo (Narbonne) Visigothic state founded in 414 CE.

Narmer (*var.* Menes, Mena, Meni, Min) The first king or pharaoh of the New Kingdom in Egypt (the height of his rule was c.2925 BCE), Narmer unified the formerly discrete fortified towns of Upper and Lower Egypt into a powerful state, and is credited with founding the capital at Memphis near Cairo. According to the 3rd century BCE historian Manetho, Narmer ruled for 62 years and was killed by a hippo.

Narváez, Panfilo de (c.1478–1528) Spanish conquistador. Took part in conquest of Cuba and Cortés's conquest of Mexico. Commissioned to conquer Florida in 1526. The journey took ten months and decimated the crew. Narváez himself died on the Texas coast, although survivors of the party did go on to complete the map of the northern Gulf coast.

NASA *see* National Aeronautics and Space Administration

Nashville ⚔ of American Civil War (Dec 15–16 1864). Union victory.

National Aeronautics and Space Administration (NASA) Founded in US in 1958 to compete with USSR in the "Space Race".

National Front for the Liberation of Angola (FNLA) Political party of Angola.

National Recovery Administration (NRA) US government agency set up as part of Roosevelt's New Deal program. The National Industrial Recovery Act authorized the introduction of industry-wide codes to reduce unfair trade practices and cut down unemployment, establish minimum wages and maximum hours, and guarantee right of collective bargaining. The NRA ended when it was invalidated by the Supreme Court in 1935, but many of its provisions were included in subsequent legislation.

Nationalism Desire for independence of a people, based on cultural, ethnic, and linguistic grounds. In 19th century Europe this led both to the unification of small states, as in the case of Germany and Italy, and the fragmentation of large empires, for example in the Balkan territories of the Ottoman Empire. *p.370*

NATO *see* North Atlantic Treaty Organization

Natufian peoples Levantine people, named after the site of Wadi en-Natuf in Israel. From c.13,000 BCE, Natufian peoples intensively harvested wild cereals, using grindstones to crush the grains. They were the precursors of the first farmers.

NAURU Nauru, the world's smallest republic, lies in the Pacific Ocean, 4000 km (2480 miles) northeast of Australia. A former British colony, Nauru was exploited for its phosphates by the UK, Australia, and New Zealand. After independence in 1968, the phosphates industry made Nauruans among the wealthiest people in the world. Economic mismanagement and the approaching end of phosphate reserves have left Nauru facing financial ruin, prompting economic reform.

CHRONOLOGY

1888 Nauru is annexed by Germany.
1914 Nauru is captured by Australian forces in World War I.
1920 A League of Nations mandate places Nauru under the control of Australia, New Zealand, and the UK with the island's administration conducted by Australia.
1942 The Japanese occupy Nauru (to Sep 1945). More than a thousand islanders deported to Truk (Micronesia) where 500 die from bombing and starvation.
1947 Australia, New Zealand, and the UK administer Nauru under a UN trusteeship.
1968 Independence.
1970 Gains phosphate control.
1992 Australia agrees compensation for phosphate extraction.

Navas de Tolosa, Las ⚔ of Reconquest of Spain (1212). Defeat of Almohads.

Navigation Means of navigation available to the European explorers of the 15th and 16th centuries. *p.270*

Nazca culture Coastal culture of southern Peru which flourished between c.350 BCE and 500 CE. The Nazca are noted for their ceramic human and animal figures but are best known for the "Nazca lines" large abstract designs and animal shapes which they laid out on a huge scale by clearing and aligning stones, and which are best seen from the air. *p.67*

Nazi Party (*var.* National-Sozialistische Deutsche Arbeiterpartei) *see* Nazism

Nazi-Soviet Non-Aggression Pact Treaty signed Aug 1939 arranging for division of Poland. Paved way for outbreak of World War II in Europe.

Nazism Political creed developed by Adolf Hitler in the 1920s and implemented by his National Socialist (Nazi) party after Hitler became Chancellor of Germany in 1933. Based on extreme nationalism, anti-Communism, and racism (especially anti-semitism), Nazi policies of social and economic mobilization led to the dramatic recovery of Germany in the 1930s, but also led the nation into a program of territorial aggression which plunged Europe into World War II. Rise of Nazis. *p.410*

Neanderthals (c.120,000 to 35,000 years ago) Variety of early humans. Named after the Neander Valley in Germany, where the first skull of their type was recognized, the Neanderthals lived in Europe and the Middle East. Distinguished by their strong, heavy skeleton, projecting face, broad nose and large teeth, their brain capacity was at least the size of modern humans. They were accomplished tool-makers, and were the first type of human known to bury their dead. They demonstrated, in their cultural behavior and social organization, many of the characteristics of modern humans. Appear to have become extinct, rather than interbreed with modern humans. *p.10*

Nearchus (died 312 BCE) Admiral of Alexander the Great's fleet. In 325 BCE he was instructed to sail west along the coast from the mouth of the Indus to the mouth of the Euphrates. His voyage opened a coastal trading route to India for Greek merchants.

Nebuchadnezzar II (c.630–562 BCE) Babylon's most famous king and founder of the new Babylonian empire (reigned 605–562 BCE), during whose reign the Babylonian civilization reached its peak. Nebuchadnezzar instituted many major building projects including the Hanging Gardens, one of the Seven Wonders of the ancient world. He led his father's army to victory over the Egyptians at Carchemish, and famously exiled the Jews after capturing Jerusalem in 586 BCE.

Needham, James (died 1673) 17th-century explorer of N America. Gained experience of the frontier with Henry Woodward and then accompanied Gabriel Arthur on the journey to find a route to the "South Sea".

Nehru, Jawaharlal (1889–1964) First prime minister of independent India (reigned 1947–64). He joined the nationalist movement in 1920, and was President of the Indian National Congress Party 1920–30, 1936–7, 1946, 1951–4.

Nelson, Horatio, Viscount (1758–1805) British admiral. On the outbreak of war with France in 1793, he achieved a series of brilliant and decisive victories at the Nile (1798) and at Copenhagen (1801). His defeat of a united Spanish and French fleet at Trafalgar (1805) saved Britain from the threat of invasion by Napoleon. He was mortally wounded in the battle.

Neo-Assyrian empire see Assyrian empire
Neolithic The last period of the Stone Age, encompassing the period in human history when crops and animals were domesticated, pottery was manufactured, and efficient stone tools were made by grinding and polishing.

NEPAL

On the shoulder of the southern Himalayas, Nepal is surrounded by India and China. It was ruled by an absolute monarchy until 1990; since then its politics have become increasingly turbulent. The mainly agricultural economy is heavily dependent on the prompt arrival of the monsoon. Hopes for development have been invested in hydroelectric power, despite the adverse impact of large dams. Backpackers, a major source of tourist income, also cause environmental problems.

CHRONOLOGY
1769 Formation of the Nepali state by King Prithvinarayan Shah, Raja of Gorkha, following his conquest of three Nepal Valley kingdoms.

1775 Death of King Prithvinarayan Shah, founder of the state of Nepal.
1816–1923 Establishment of quasi-British protectorate.
1959 First multiparty constitution.
1960 Constitution suspended.
1962–1990 Panchayat non-party system.
1972 Birendra succeeds to throne.
1991 NCP victory in elections.
1994 First communist government.
1995–1998 Succession of weak coalition governments.
1999 NCP election victory. Maoist insurgency in rural areas.
2001 June, Birendra and family killed in palace shootings. Gyanendra crowned amid unrest.
2002 Gyanendra dismisses Sher Bahadur Deuba's government.
2004 Deuba reinstated.

Nerchinsk, Treaty of (1689) Peace agreement between Russia and China, in which Russia withdrew from the area north of the Amur river. First treaty between China and a European power.
Nero (37–68 CE) Roman emperor. The last of the family of Augustus Caesar to rule Rome (reigned 54–68). Palace intrigues and murders (including that of his mother) gave Nero's reign a notoriety unmatched by that of any previous emperor. He committed suicide as provincial governors joined in revolt against him.
Nestorian Church Followers of Nestorius, whose Christian teachings, condemned by the councils of Ephesus (431) and Chalcedon (451), emphasized the independence of the divine and human natures of Christ. Represented today by the Syrian Orthodox Church.

NETHERLANDS

The Netherlands is located at the delta of four major rivers in northwest Europe. The few hills in the eastern and southern part of the country fall into a flat coastal area, bordered by the North Sea to the north and west. This is protected by a giant infrastructure of dunes, dikes, and canals, as 27 percent of the coast is below sea level. The Netherlands became one of the world's first confederative republics after Spain

recognized its independence in 1648. Its highly successful economy has a long trading tradition, and Rotterdam is the world's largest port.

CHRONOLOGY
6th century CE After the departure of the Romans, three Germanic tribes (Franks in the south, Frisians in the north, Saxons in the east) assert control.
768–814 CE During Charlemagne's reign, the Franks conquer the whole of the Netherlands; after his death the region becomes part of the Middle Frankish kingdom and then of the East Frankish kingdom, later the Holy Roman Empire.
11th century Decline of central authority leads to a feudal fragmentation and the formation of autonomous states; the county of Holland, in the west, becomes the dominant power in the region.
1433 Holland becomes a Burgundian possession by inheritance, and becomes part of the Habsburg Empire in 1482.
1515–1555 During the reign of Charles V, all the remaining autonomous territories become Habsburg possessions; the Netherlands is thus united for the first time; on Charles's abdication they come under Spanish Habsburg rule.
1567 Resistance to Philip II of Spain, fuelled in part by the rise of Protestantism, leads to a popular revolt led by William (the Silent) of Orange, sections of the nobility, and the powerful merchant class.
1581 The northern provinces formally declare their independence from Spain and form the Republic of the Seven United Provinces of the Netherlands.
1609 Spain accepts the reality of Dutch independence; by this stage the Dutch republic has become one of the world's main trading powers.
1648 The Peace of Munster confirms Dutch independence, bringing to an end the so-called Eighty Years' war.
1713 The Treaty of Utrecht, ending the War of the Spanish Succession, effectively marks end of direct Dutch involvement in European power struggles.
1795 French forces invade the Netherlands; local groups proclaim Batavian Republic, modeled on revolutionary France.
1806 Holland again becomes a kingdom under Louis Bonaparte, but is annexed by France four years later.

▶

◄

1813 Dutch oust French after 18 years of French rule and choose to become a constitutional monarchy.

1815 Congress of Vienna. United Kingdom of Netherlands formed. It includes Belgium and Luxembourg.

1839 Recognition of 1830 secession of Catholic southern provinces as Belgium.

1848 New constitution – ministers to be accountable to parliament.

1897–1901 Wide-ranging social legislation enacted. Development of trade unions.

1898 Wilhelmina succeeds to throne, ending Luxembourg union, where male hereditary Salic Law is in force.

1914–1918 Dutch neutrality respected in World War I.

1922 Women fully enfranchised.

1940 Dutch assert neutrality in World War II, but Germany invades. Fierce resistance.

1942 Japan invades Dutch East Indies.

1944–1945 "Winter of starvation" in German-occupied western provinces.

1945 Liberation. International Court of Justice set up in The Hague.

1946–1958 PvdA leads center-left coalitions. Marshall Aid from USA speeds reconstruction.

1948 Juliana becomes queen.

1949 Joins NATO. Most of East Indies colonies gain independence as Indonesia.

1957 Founder member of EEC.

1960 Economic union with Belgium and Luxembourg comes into effect.

1973 PvdA wins power after 15 years spent mainly in opposition. Center-left coalition.

1977–1981 CDA/VVD coalition.

1980 CDA alliance of the "confessional" parties forms a single party. Beatrix becomes queen.

1982 PvdA rejects deployment of US cruise missiles in Netherlands. CDA/VVD center-right coalition under Ruud Lubbers.

1989 VVD refuses to support finance for 20–year National Environment Policy (NEP). Elections. Lubbers forms CDA/PvdA center-left coalition.

1990 NEP introduced.

1992 Licensed brothels legalized.

1994 Elections. Wim Kok of PvdA heads coalition with VVD and D66.

1999 Netherlands among 11 EU countries to introduce euro.

2001 Euthanasia and gay marriage are legalized.

2002 Euro fully adopted. Government resigns after report blames Dutch military in Bosnia for failing to prevent Srebrenica massacre in 1995. Populist politician Pim Fortuyn assassinated. In elections, the CDA-led coalition collapses.

2003 CDA reelected; forms coalition with VVD and D66.

Netjerykhet *see* Zoser

Nevsky, Alexander (c.1220–1263) Prince of Novgorod. One of Russia's greatest heroes on account of his victories over the Swedes on the Neva river in 1240 and over the Teutonic Knights at Lake Peipus in 1242. *p.215*

New Amsterdam Town established by the Dutch on Manhattan in the 1620s as the capital of the colony of New Netherland. It was seized by the English and renamed New York in 1664. *See also* New York

New Deal Policy of Franklin D. Roosevelt, designed to help US out of the Great Depression in the 1930s. *p.411* *See also* Roosevelt, Franklin Delano

New England Region of the US, comprising Maine, New Hampshire, Vermont, Rhode Island, and Connecticut. It was explored by Captain John Smith c.1614, and was settled by English Puritans, including the Pilgrim Fathers in the 1620s.

New France Name given to the French colonies in North America in the 17th century. *p.299*

New Granada Spanish viceroyalty, comprising Colombia, Venezuela, Ecuador, and Panama, first established in 1717, but then reconstituted in 1739.

New Guinea The world's second-largest island, New Guinea has been inhabited by Papuan peoples for at least 50,000 years. Time and the island's mountainous terrain have spawned the richest variety of languages and dialects anywhere on earth. Europeans had hardly any contact before 1825 when the Dutch claimed the western half of the island. *See also* Papua New Guinea

New Holland Dutch colony in Brazil, established in 1630. Recife and other settlements captured from the Portuguese. It lasted until 1654.

New Kingdom (c.1550–1050 BCE) Period of ancient Egyptian history marked by strong central government control in ancient Egypt, and one which saw the height of Egyptian power. Punctuated by the El-Amarna period of Akhenaton.

New Spain (*var. Sp.* Virreinato de Nueva España) Spanish Viceroyalty established in 1535 to govern Spain's conquered lands north of the Isthmus of Panama and regions in present-day Lower California.

New State (*var.* Port. Estado Novo) Dictatorship (1937–45) of President Getúlio Vargas of Brazil, initiated by a new constitution issued in Nov 1937. Vargas himself wrote it with the assistance of his minister of justice, Francisco Campos.

New York Seized by the English from the Dutch in 1664, New York expanded rapidly in the 18th century and was briefly the first capital of US after the American War of Independence. The most populous city in the US, it rapidly became its most important port and the dominant commercial center. Slums of New York City. *p.383* *See also* New Amsterdam

NEW ZEALAND
Lying in the South Pacific, 1600 km (992 miles) southeast of Australia, New Zealand comprises the main North and South Islands, separated by the Cook Strait, and a number of smaller islands. South Island is the more mountainous; North Island contains hot springs and geysers, and the bulk of the population. The political tradition is liberal and egalitarian, and has been dominated by the National and Labour Parties. Radical, and often unpopular, reforms since 1984 have restored economic growth, speeded up economic diversification, and strengthened New Zealand's position within the Pacific Rim countries. *p.347*

CHRONOLOGY

c.700 CE The Maori arrive in New Zealand from eastern Polynesia.

1642 The Dutch explorer Abel Tasman sights the west coast of the South Island.

1769 Captain James Cook makes the first of three visits to New Zealand.

1840 British sovereignty is proclaimed in the Treaty of Waitangi by leaders of some Maori tribes and a British representative. Settlers brought from the United Kingdom by the New Zealand Company arrive at Port Nicholson (now Wellington).

1852 The British Parliament passes a Constitution Act which creates a House of Representatives and Legislative Council in New Zealand.

1860 The Taranaki war begins, when British troops try to remove Maori people from land allegedly bought by the Crown.

1863 A war between the Maori people and British troops breaks out over land in Waikato. The colonial government eventually confiscates the land.

1867 Four Maori seats are established in the House of Representatives.

1890 A Liberal government is elected, with John Ballance as premier.

1893 Women are given the vote.

1894 The Liberal government, now under the leadership of Richard John Seddon, passes legislation providing for industrial arbitration and conciliation and better factory conditions.

1907 New Zealand became a dominion, self-governing from 1926

1947 Gains full independence.

1962 Western Samoa (now Samoa) gains independence.

1965 Cook Islands become self-governing.

1975 Conservative NP wins elections. Economic austerity program introduced.

1976 Immigration cut by over 80%.

1984 LP elected; David Lange prime minister. Auckland harbor headland restored to Maoris.

1985 New Zealand prohibits nuclear vessels. French agents sink Greenpeace ship Rainbow Warrior in Auckland harbor.

1986 USA suspends military obligations under ANZUS Treaty.

1987 LP wins elections. Introduction of controversial privatization plan. Nuclear ban enshrined in legislation.

1989 Cabinet split. Lange resigns. Succeeded by Geoffrey Palmer.

1990 Palmer resigns. LP defeated by NP in elections. James Bolger prime minister.

1992 Maoris win South Island fishing rights. Majority vote for electoral reform in referendum.

1993 Docking of first French naval ship for eight years. NP returned with single-seat majority in election. Proportional representation introduced by referendum.

1994 US agrees not to send nuclear-armed ships to New Zealand ports. Maoris reject government ten-year land claims settlement of NZ$1 billion.

1995 Waitangi Day celebrations abandoned following Maori protests. Crown apologizes to Maoris and signs Waikato Raupatu Claims Act. UK warship visits resume.

1996 NP forms coalition to preserve overall legislative majority. First general election under new proportional representation system.

1997 NP forms coalition with New Zealand First (NZF) party. Bolger resigns. Jenny Shipley becomes first woman prime minister.

1998 Shipley sacks NZF leader Winston Peters as deputy prime minister, and forms minority government when coalition splits. Waitangi Tribunal orders government to return to Maoris NZ$6.1 million of confiscated land.

1999 November, LP led by Helen Clark wins general election.

2001 Air New Zealand renationalized.

2002 Combat wing of air force taken out of service. LP reelected in elections.

Newbery, John 16th-century English explorer and merchant. Traveling to Hormuz in 1581–83 to survey its commercial prospects, he became the first Englishman to sail down the Euphrates and visit Hormuz, Shiraz, and Isfahan. He returned overland through Persia to Constantinople.

Newcomen, Thomas (1663–1729) English inventor of a steam engine. *p.321*

Newfoundland The island off the eastern coast of Canada was reached by the Vikings c.1000 and probably rediscovered by John Cabot in 1497, though the site of his landfall is uncertain.

Newton, Sir Isaac (1642–1727) English mathematician and physicist. His work on calculus, the laws of motion, gravity, and light made him the most celebrated scientist of his age.

Nez Percé War (1877) Conflict which broke out between the Nez Percé Indians of the NW plains and the US army. It was the result of a long-running dispute over the drastic reduction of the Nez Percé reservation in 1863 after gold was discovered on their lands, and incursions by European settlers. Led by Chief Joseph, a band of 250 Nez Percé kept US forces at bay for more than five months. They were subsequently forced to relocate to Oklahoma.

Nguni Bantu people of the Eastern Cape. They clashed many times with European settlers, the first of many frontier wars being fought against the Dutch in 1779.

Nguyen Puc Anh *see* Gai Long

Nian Rebellion (*var.* Nien, 1853–68) Chinese peasant rebellion of the mid-19th century.

Nicaea Council of Early Christian doctrinal assembly under the auspices of Constantine (325).

NICARAGUA Bounded by the Pacific Ocean to the west and the Caribbean Sea to the east, Nicaragua lies at the heart of Central America. After more than 40 years of dictatorship, the Sandinista revolution in 1978 led to 11 years of civil war, which almost destroyed the economy. The Sandinistas unexpectedly lost the elections in 1990, and right-wing parties have held power since then. Despite a party split, the Sandinistas remain the main opposition on the left.

CHRONOLOGY

1544 Nicaragua is incorporated into the Captaincy-General of Guatemala.

1821 Nicaragua becomes independent from Spain and is incorporated into the federation of Central American states.

1838 After a period of annexation to Mexico, Nicaragua becomes a republic.

1858 Walker proclaims himself President as part of a move to establish a slave republic in Central America.

1905 The Altamirano-Harrison treaty between the United Kingdom and Nicaragua recognizes full Nicaraguan sovereignty over the Atlantic coast, where the UK had a protectorate until 1894.

1909 United States Marines land in Bluefields and bring Juan Estrada to power, who signs pacts placing Nicaragua effectively under US administration. The Marines intervene in Nicaragua again in 1912–25 and in 1926–33.

1936 Anastasio Somoza takes power after the National Guard forces President Sacasa's resignation, instituting a 50–year family dictatorship.

1956 On Somoza's assassination he is succeeded by his son Luis.

1962 Foundation of the Sandinista National Liberation Front (FSLN).

◄

1967 Luis Somoza is succeeded by his brother Anastasio.

1974 The FSLN offensive against the Somoza government gathers force, intensifying into civil war by 1978.

1978–1990 FSLN ends Somoza dictatorship; civil war between FSLN and Contras.

1998 Hurricane Mitch devastates country.

2002 Bolaños becomes president.

Nicaraguan civil war (1978–89) After 40 years of dictatorship, a revolution in 1978 by the left-wing Sandinistas, who drew on the support of a rural peasant base, began 11 years of civil war. The right-wing Contras received covert US support during the period of Sandinista government. Despite losing the first free elections of 1990, the Sandinistas remain a potent force in the country.

Niebuhr, Carsten (1733–1815) German-born surveyor who took part in an international scientific expedition in 1761, financed by the King of Denmark, to explore the Arabian Peninsula. Niebuhr was the only survivor. His systematic accounts of the expedition, containing maps and illustrations, were published in 1772 and 1774.

Nieuwpoort ⚔ of Dutch Revolt (1600). Dutch victory over Spain.

NIGER Landlocked in the west of Africa, Niger is linked to the sea by the Niger river. Saharan conditions prevail in the northern regions, in the area around the Aïr mountains, and, particularly, in the vast uninhabited northeast. Niger was ruled by one-party or military regimes until 1992 when a multiparty constitution was introduced, but a much-troubled democratic process was disrupted by military coups in 1996 and 1999.

CHRONOLOGY

11th–16th centuries The Songhay Empire is at its height.

14th century Agadez becomes an important center of trans-Sahara trade.

19th century The first contact is made with European explorers, with France establishing a military post at Niamey in the 1890s.

1916–17 The Tuareg occupy Agadez and control the Air Mountains.

1950s Two political movements emerge, the radical Sawaba party of Djibo Bakary and the conservative Niger Progressive Party (PPN) of Hamani Diori. Sawaba is banned in 1959, a year before independence at which time Diori becomes president.

1960 Independence.

1968 French open uranium mines.

1973 Drought; 60 percent of livestock die.

1974 Military coup. General Kountché bans political parties.

1984 New drought; Niger river dries up. Uranium boom ends.

1987 Kountché dies. General Ali Saibou eases transition to democracy.

1990–1995 Tuareg rebellion.

1992 Multiparty constitution.

1993 Democratic elections.

1996 Military coup. Staged elections.

1999 New constitution. General Mainassara assassinated. Multiparty elections won by Mamadou Tandja.

2001 Hunting banned in effort to save wildlife.

NIGERIA Africa's most populous state, Nigeria gained its independence from Britain in 1960. Bordered by Benin, Niger, Chad, and Cameroon, its terrain varies from tropical rainforest and swamps in the south to savanna in the north. Nigeria has been dominated by military governments since 1966. After many delays, a promised return to civilian rule came about in 1999, with the election as president of Olusegun Obasanjo, a former general who had been head of state from 1976 to 1979. Nigeria is OPEC's fourth-largest oil producer, but it has experienced a fall in living standards since the oil boom of the 1970s.

CHRONOLOGY

15th century European contacts begin with Portuguese landings. With Britain taking the lead, the slave trade develops to the point where in the 18th century 15,000 slaves are being exported annually from the Bight of Benin and a further 15,000 from the Bight of Biafra.

1861 The British annex Lagos and the process of formal colonization begins. Their interest has now shifted from slaves to the export of raw materials.

1885 Royal Niger Company given official responsibility for British sphere of influence along Niger and Benue rivers. British armed forces coerce local rulers into accepting British rule.

1897 West Africa Frontier Force (WAFF) established; subjugation of the north of the region begins.

1898 The Royal Niger Company's charter revoked.

1900 British Protectorate of Northern Nigeria established.

1906 Lagos incorporated into the Protectorate of Southern Nigeria.

1914 Protectorates of Northern and Southern Nigeria joined to form colony of Nigeria.

1960 Independence. Nigeria established as a federation.

1961 Northern part of UK-administered UN Trust Territory of the Cameroons incorporated as part of Nigeria's Northern Region.

1966 First military coup, led by Major General Ironsi. Counter-coup mounted by group of northern army officers. Ironsi murdered. Thousands of Ibo in Northern Region massacred. General Gowon in control of north and west.

1967–1970 Civil war. Lieutenant Colonel Ojukwu calls for secession of oil-rich east under the new name Biafra. Over one million Nigerians die before secessionists defeated by federal forces.

1970 General Gowon in power.

1975 Gowon toppled in bloodless coup. Brig. Mohammed takes power.

1976 Murtala Mohammed murdered in abortive coup. Succeeded by General Olusegun Obasanjo.

1978 Political parties legalized, on condition they represent national, not tribal, interests.

1979 Elections won by Alhaji Shehu Shagari and the National Party of Nigeria (NPN); return to civilian government.

1983 Military coup. Major General Mohammed Buhari heads Supreme Military Council.

1985 Major General Ibrahim Babangida heads bloodless coup, promising a return to democracy.

1993 Elections annulled; Babangida resigns; military sets up Interim National Government (ING). November, ING dissolved. Military, headed by General Sani Abacha, takes over.

1994 Moshood Abiola arrested, opposition harassed.

1995 Ban on parties lifted. Military tribunal convicts former head of state General Olusegun Obasanjo and 39 others for plotting coup. Execution of Ken Saro-Wiwa and eight other Ogoni activists; EU imposes sanctions, Commonwealth suspends Nigeria's membership.

1998 Abacha dies; Abiola dies; Abacha's successor announces timetable for restoring civilian rule by 1999.

1999 Elections for state governors, legislature, and presidency, won by Olusegun Obasanjo. Commonwealth membership restored; sanctions lifted.

2000 Ethnic violence escalates, threatens national unity.

2001 March, Bauchi becomes tenth state to introduce sharia.

2002 1000 killed in Lagos munitions dump explosion and ensuing chaos.

2003 PDP majority and Obasanjo reelected in disputed elections.

2004 57,000 flee religious violence in Kano and Plateau State. Shell admits that its activities fueled corruption and poverty.

Ninety-five Theses (1517) Document demanding ecclesiastical reforms, especially with regard to the sale of indulgences, nailed to a church door in Wittenberg by Martin Luther. *See also* Martin Luther.

Niño, Andreas 16th-century Spanish explorer of Central America.

Nintoku Fifth-century emperor of Japan. Keyhole tomb of Nintoku. *p.105*

Nixon, Richard Milhous (1913–94) 37th President of the US. (Republican, 1969–74). Came to political prominence as a member of HUAC (the House Committee on Un-American Activities) investigating the Alger Hiss case. He served as Vice-President under Dwight D. Eisenhower from 1952–59, but lost the 1960 Presidential election to John F. Kennedy. He was eventually elected President in 1968 and won a second term in 1972 by a narrow margin. Nixon's term of office saw the invasion of Cambodia in

1970, the ending of the Vietnam War, the initiation of arms limitation talks with the Soviet Union and the reestablishment of US relations with China. His involvement in the Watergate scandal led to his resignation in 1974, although he was granted a full pardon by his successor Gerald Ford.

Njinga Queen of the Ndongo kingdom in southwest Africa (reigned 1624–63). She resisted Portuguese attempts to expand their control of the Angola region.

Nkrumah, Dr. Kwame (1909–72) Ghanaian nationalist leader who led the Gold Coast's drive for independence from Britain and presided over its emergence as the new nation of Ghana. He headed the country from independence in 1957 until he was overthrown by a coup in 1966.

No theater Form of classical Japanese theater, performed by masked actors, involving music and dance. *p.230*

Nobile, Umberto (1885–1978) Italian aviator. Crossed the N Pole in his dirigible balloon in 1926, along with Amundsen and 14 others. A second expedition ended in disaster with the loss of seven lives.

Nok culture Ancient Iron Age culture that existed on the Benue plateau of Nigeria between about 500 BCE and 200 CE. They produced the earliest known iron-working south of the Sahara, and distinctive terra-cotta figurines. *p.54*

Nordenskjöld, Baron Nils Adolf Erik (1832–1901) Swedish explorer and scientist. Made several expeditions to Spitzbergen. In 1870 led expedition to explore Greenland ice cap. In 1878–79, he sailed through the Northeast Passage on the ship Vega.

Noriega, Gen. Manuel Antonio Morena (1940–) Panamanian politician and soldier. As Commander of the National Guard and de facto ruler of Panama (1982–89), Noriega enjoyed US support until 1987. In 1988 he was indicted by a US grand jury on charges of drug trafficking, and in 1989 he was arrested during a US military operation in Panama, and deported to the US.

Normandy Duchy in northern France founded by Vikings in 911.

Normandy Landings (*var.* D-Day, Operation Overlord) ⚔ of World War II (Jun–Jul 1944). Allied combined operation, the largest amphibious landing in history, which initiated the Allied invasion of Nazi Europe.

Normans Name given to the Vikings, chiefly of Danish origin, who, under their leader Rollo, settled in northern France from the early 10th century. Originally the word meant Northmen or Norsemen. The Viking settlers of Normandy soon became French speakers, well integrated with the local population, but their adventurous spirit showed itself in the 10th century in their conquests of England (1066) and of Southern Italy and Sicily (1091). *p.173*

Norsemen *see* Vikings

North American Free Trade Agreement (NAFTA). Agreement betwen the US, Canada and Mexico to remove trade barriers between the three nations for a ten-year period. It came into force in Jan 1994. *See also* USA, Canada

North Atlantic Treaty Organization (NATO). Established in 1949 as security coalition among Western Allies, dominated by US. Frequently deployed troops from member states as peace-keeping forces, but played a large role in Gulf War (1991) and Yugoslav conflict (1999).

North Korea *see* Korea, North

North Vietnam *see* Vietnam

Northeast Passage Maritime route along the northern coast of Europe and Asia between the Atlantic and Pacific oceans, not fully navigated until 20th century.

Northern Chou *see* Northern Zhou

Northern Expedition (1926–28) An attempt by the Kuomintang (Guomindang) to unify China, led by Jiang Jieshi (Chiang Kai-shek).

Northern Song *see* Song dynasty

Northern Wei *see* Toba Wei

Northern Zhou (*var.* Northern Chou) Ruling dynasty of northern China (557–581) who overthrew the Northern Qi.

NORWAY Occupying the western part of Scandinavia, Norway's western coastline is characterized by numerous fjords and islands. Large oil and gas revenues have brought prosperity. Gro Harlem Brundtland, Norway's first woman prime minister, went on to take top UN posts. Despite the Europe-wide recession in the early 1990s, Norway contained rising unemployment, which peaked at 6 percent in 1993. A constitutional requirement is that government creates conditions that enable every person to find work. Christianity in Norway. *p.189*

▶

CHRONOLOGY

Early 9th century Norwegians join other Viking groups in waves of seaborne migrations and conquests across Europe and westward to Iceland, Greenland and N America lasting until the 11th century.

c.900 CE Harald I Fairhair unifies the small kingdoms covering present-day Norway and proclaims himself King of the Norwegians.

Early 11th century Christianity becomes the dominant religion.

1397 Under Union of Kalmar, Margrethe I of Denmark becomes Queen of Norway. The union with Denmark lasts until 1814.

1536 Norway is proclaimed a province of Denmark, although it is allowed to retain some of its traditional political and legal institutions. Evangelical Lutheranism is declared the established church.

1814 Under the Treaty of Kiel Norway is transferred to the Swedish crown. A national assembly approves a new Norwegian constitution, which provides for a strong parliament or Storting with two chambers (the Odelsting and the Lagting), and elects the Danish Prince Christian Frederik as King. A brief rebellion led by Christian Frederik against Swedish rule ends with a cease-fire on August 14. On November 4 , the elderly Carl XIII of Sweden is elected king of Norway and accepts the Norwegian constitution. He is succeeded later in the year by Carl Johann who was born Jean-Baptiste Bernadotte in the south of France and was a successful soldier, appointed Marshall of France in 1804. In 1810 was elected heir to Carl XIII.

1905 As tension with Sweden grows, the Storting declares a plebiscite and obtains overwhelming support for independence; Sweden agrees to dissolve the union. Prince Carl of Denmark becomes King Håkon VII of Norway.

1935 DNA forms government.

1940–1945 Nazi occupation. Puppet regime led by Vidkun Quisling.

1945 DNA resumes power.

1949 Founder member of NATO.

1957 King Håkon dies. Succeeded by son, Olaf V.

1960 Becomes member of EFTA.

1962 Unsuccessfully applies to join the European Communities (EC).

1965 DNA electoral defeat by SP coalition led by Per Borten.

1967 Second bid for EC membership.

1971 Prime minister Per Borten resigns following disclosure of secret negotiations to join EC. DNA government, led by Trygve Bratteli.

1972 EC membership rejected in popular referendum by 3 percent majority. Bratteli resigns. Center coalition government takes power with Lars Korvald as prime minister.

1973 Elections. Bratteli returns to power as prime minister.

1976 Bratteli succeeded by Odvar Nordli.

1981 Nordli resigns owing to ill health. Gro Harlem Brundtland becomes first woman prime minister. Elections bring to power Norway's first Conservative Party (H) government for 53 years. Kare Willoch prime minister.

1983 Conservatives form coalition with SP and KrF.

1985 Election. Willoch's H–SP–KrF coalition returned. Norway agrees to suspend commercial whaling.

1986 100,000 demonstrate for better working conditions. Brundtland forms minority DNA government. Currency devalued by 12 percent.

1989 Brundtland resigns. H–KrF coalition in power. Soviet Union agrees exchange of information after fires on Soviet nuclear submarines off Norwegian coast.

1990 H–KrF coalition breaks up over closer ties with EU (formerly EC). Brundtland and DNA in power.

1991 Olaf V dies; succeeded by son, King Harald V.

1994 EEA comes into effect. Referendum rejects EU membership.

1996 Brundtland resigns; replaced by Thorbjørn Jagland (also DNA).

1997 DNA loses ground in general election; Kjell Magne Bondevik forms center-right coalition.

2000 Jens Stoltenberg (DNA) prime minister at head of three-party coalition.

2001 Right-wing victory in elections. Bondevik heads coalition government.

Novgorod Powerful Russian state in the Middle Ages from 1136, when it gained independance from Kievan Rus. According to legend the town Novgorod was where Rurik the Viking was invited to rule by the local people in 862 CE, an event that led to the establishment of Kievan Rus.

NRA *see* National Recovery Administration

Nubia The name given by the Egyptians to the area extending from the First Cataract of the Nile south to the Sudan. Its capital was first at Napata then at Meroë. In the 2nd millennium BCE the Nubians were under Egyptian rule, but themselves ruled Egypt in the 1st millennium, making Napata briefly the center of the ancient world. Egypt's 25th dynasty, 751–668 BCE, came from Cush and 300 of their pyramids remain. Christianity reached Nubia in the 5th century CE, when the cathedral of St. Anne at Faras was first built. *Fresco from Cathedral of St. Anne. p.131*

Nuclear Age General term for the period since the end of World War II when nuclear fission technology, used for power generation and weapons of mass destruction, was developed by a coterie of powerful nations.

Numidia Roman province north of the Sahara, occupying most of coastal region of present-day Algeria. In the 3rd century BCE the Numidian king Masinissa allied with Rome against Carthage (c.210 BCE). His grandson Jugurtha (reigned 113–104 BCE) fought a war against Rome, was captured, and died in captivity.

Nur al-Din (died 1174) Turkish leader of Muslim resistance to the crusader states from his territories in Syria. He sent his general Saladin to Egypt, where he brought the Fatimid Caliphate to an end in 1169. *p.192*

Nyasaland *see* Malawi

Nyerere, Julius (1922–99) The first prime minister of independent Tanganyika (1961), who became the first president of the new state of Tanzania (1964). Nyerere was also the major force behind the Organization of African Unity (OAU).

O'Higgins, Bernardo (1778–1842) Liberator of Chile. Son of an Irish-born soldier who emigrated to Chile, O'Higgins rose to be leader of the patriotic forces that fought for liberation from Spain from 1810. Defeated and driven from Chile in 1814, he received support from the newly-independent Republic of Río de la Plata, crossed the Andes with José de San Martín and won the battle of Chacabuco in 1817. He became the first president of Chile, but his authoritarian rule was unpopular and he was driven from office in 1823. He died in exile in Peru.

Oaxaca Region of southern Mexico which was the site for the some of the earliest civilizations of Central America including the Zapotec.

Ocampo, Sebastián de Early 16th-century Spanish conquistador, leader of expedition from Hispaniola to Cuba.

Oceania General geographic term for the island groups of the Pacific Ocean, sometimes including Australia and New Zealand.

Octavian *see* Augustus Caesar

Oda Nobunaga (1534–82) Provincial leader who initiated the unification of Japan (reigned 1568–82).

Odda's Chapel Tiny Saxon chapel, built by Odda, Earl of Hwicce in reign of Edward the Confessor. It is dedicated to the memory of Odda's half-brother, Elfric, who died in 1053. *p.171*

Odoacer 5th-century barbarian chieftain, who in 476 deposed the last Roman emperor, Romulus Augustulus, to become ruler of Italy with his capital at Ravenna. He was killed in 493 after surrendering to Theodoric the Ostrogoth.

Offa (reigned 757–96). King of Mercia, which during Offa's reign became the most powerful of the Anglo-Saxon kingdoms of Britain.

Offa's Dyke Rampart and ditch built c.785 by Offa of Mercia to define the border between the English and the Welsh.

Ogedei *see* Ögödei

Ögödei (*var.* Ogedei, died 1241) Mongol leader, son of Genghis Khan, elected Great Khan in 1229. He led successful campaigns against the Khwarizm Shah and the Jin of northern China.

Oirats Nomadic people descended from the western group of Mongols who migrated westward to the Volga in the 17th century.

Okinawa ⚔ of World War II (Mar–Jun 1945) Major US amphibious assault which, with Iwo Jima, secured an island base for strategic bombing campaign against Japan.

Old Kingdom (2575–2134 BCE) Period of Egyptian history encompassing the 4th to the 8th dynasties which was especially notable for the building of the pyramids.

Old World General geo-historic term for Africa and Eurasia, prior to European discovery of Americas and Australasia.

Olid, Cristóbal de Early 16th-century Spanish conquistador, leader of expedition from Mexico to Honduras.

Oligarchy In the ancient Greek city-states an oligarchy was in place when power was in the hands of a minority of male citizens, as contrasted with democracy when power was held by the majority.

Olmec culture Elaborate Central American Indian culture based on the Mexican Gulf coast, which flourished between 1200 and 800 BCE. The Olmecs influenced the rise and development of other great civilizations and are credited with having the first planned religious centers, with monumental sculptures and temples, and with devising the 260-day Mesoamerican calendar. *p.33*

Olustee ⚔ of American Civil War (Feb 20 1864). Union victory.

Olympia Sanctuary sacred to Zeus in Ancient Greece. In 776 BCE the first Olympic Games were held there, a tradition that lasted over 1000 years. *p.45*

Olympic Games The idea of holding an international athletics meeting every four years, modeled on the Ancient Greek Olympiads, was revived at Athens in 1896.

Omagua People of the Upper Amazon region of S America.

OMAN Sharing borders with Yemen, the United Arab Emirates and Saudi Arabia, Oman occupies a strategic position at the entrance to the Gulf. It is the least developed of the Gulf states. The most densely populated areas are the northern coast and the southern Salalah plain. Oil exports have given Oman modest prosperity under a paternalistic sultan, who defeated a Marxist-led insurgency in the 1970s.

CHRONOLOGY

8th Century CE The tribe of Al-Azd establish their own independent Imamate in Oman.
1507 The Portuguese take control of Oman.
1650 Imam Nasir Ibn Murshid of the Yaariba dynasty expels the Portuguese.
1730 The Omanis conquer Portuguese settlements on the East Coast of Africa.
1749 Ahmad Ibn Said is elected Imam and founds the Al-Said dynasty.

1932 Sultan bin Taimur in power.
1970 Sultan Qaboos bin Said seizes power from his father.
1975 Suppression of Dhofar revolt.
1991 Consultative Council set up.
1993 Limits on oil production lifted.
2000 Consultative Council members elected for first time.
2003 Universal suffrage introduced for Consultative Council elections.

Oñate, Cristóbal de 16th-century Spanish explorer, leader of an expedition from Mexico to New Mexico and Arizona.

Oñate, Juan de (c.1550–1630) Spanish conquistador. Led colonizing expedition into New Mexico in 1598 establishing settlements north of the Rio Grande. Reached mouth of Colorado River in 1605. Governor of New Mexico from 1605–08.

Onin War (1467–77) Struggle between Japanese warlords.

OPEC *see* Organization of Petroleum Exporting Countries

Opera The Age of Grand Opera. *p.361*

Operation Market Garden *see* Arnhem

Operation Overlord *see* D-Day, Normandy Landings

Opium Wars Confrontations (1839–42, 1850–60) arising from Chinese (Qing) attempts to limit the profitable British opium trade in S and E China. British naval forces attacked or blockaded several Chinese ports (Guangzhou, Xiamen, Fuzhou, Ningbo, Tianjin, Shanghai) wresting the first of many territorial trading cessions (Treaty Ports) in the peace settlement, the Treaty of Nanjing (1842). *p.359*

Orange Free State Boer republic founded in 1854.

Orbigny, Alcide Dessalines d' (1802–57) French palaeontologist, who spent eight years (1826–34) traveling in South America, producing a 10–volume account of his travels and the first detailed map of the whole continent. His observations on fossils in sedimentary rocks gave rise to the science of micropalaeontology.

Orellana, Francisco de (c.1490–1546) Spanish conquistador. Orellana was a member of an expedition to the eastern slopes of the Andes led by Gonzalo Pizarro, brother of Francisco. He and companions became separated from the main party and sailed the length of the Amazon.

Organization of African Unity (OAU)

Organization founded in 1963 by independent African statesto strengthen the continent of africa and nake it less vulnerable to outside influences.

Organization of Petroleum

Exporting Countries (OPEC). International organization seeking to regulate the price of oil. Founded in 1960, it consists of thirteen oil-producing countries which include Saudi Arabia, Iran, Iraq, Kuwait, Venezuela, Libya and Algeria.

Oriskany ⚔ of American Revolutionary War (Aug 6 1777). American victory.

Orléans, Siege of (1429) Turning point in Hundred Years' War. The city, under siege from the English, was relieved by the French, inspired by Joan of Arc.

Oromo People of East Africa who migrated north into Ethiopia in large numbers in the 16th and 17th centuries.

Orozco, Francisco 16th-century Spanish explorer of N America.

Orozco, Pascual (1882–1915) Mexican revolutionary leader

Ortelius, Abraham (1527–98) Dutch cartographer and publisher. Publisher of the first "modern" atlas, the *Theatrum Orbis Terrarum* in 1570. *p.293*

Osei Tutu (died 1712) Founder and first ruler of the Asante nation.

Osman I (c.1258–1324) Founder of the Ottoman dynasty, which grew powerful in the regions of northwest Anatolia bordering Byzantium. By the time of his death the Ottomans controled most of Bithynia. *See also* Ottoman empire

Ostrogoths The "Eastern Goths" first emerged as a threat to Rome in 453, after the death of Attila and the dispersal of the Huns. Under their leader Theodoric the Great, they conquered Italy in 493, establishing a kingdom that lasted until 553. *See also* Goths.

Otto I (*aka* Otto the Great, 912–73). He was elected King of the Germans in 936 and crowned Holy Roman Emperor in 962. His defeat of the Magyars at Lechfeld in 955 put an end to their raids on western Europe. Made Germany the most powerful political entity in western Europe.

Otto II (955–83) Holy Roman Emperor. Joint emperor with his father Otto I from 967. *p.152*

Ottokar II (1230–78). King of Bohemia, who extended Bohemian rule almost to the Adriatic. Defeated by the emperor Rudolf of Habsburg at the battle of Marchfeld.

OTTOMAN EMPIRE

OTTOMAN EMPIRE Islamic empire founded in Anatolia (1299) by Turkish tribes who established their capital at Bursa (1326), reaching its peak in the 16th century when it stretched from the Persian Gulf to Morocco in the south, and from the Crimea to the gates of Vienna in the north. After the unsuccessful siege of Vienna (1683), the empire began a protracted decline, gradually losing territory in SE Europe collapsing altogether when Turkey, one of the Central Powers was defeated in World War I.
Capture of Constantinople. *p.263*
Ottoman campaigns. *p.263*
Ottoman in Europe. *p.314*
Collapse of the Ottoman empire. *p.393*
See also Turkey, Osman I, Suleyman the Magnificent

CHRONOLOGY

1071 Muslim Seljuk Turks defeat the Byzantines at the battle of Manzikert, and in 1098 they establish a Sultanate.

c. 1300 Foundation of Ottoman dynasty by Osman I.

1396 Ottoman rule is established over much of Anatolia under Sultan Bayezid.

1402 Bayezid defeated by Timur at battle of Ankara.

1453 Turkish forces under Mehmet II ("the Conqueror") regain Constantinople and make it the capital of the empire, renaming it Istanbul.

1451–1520 Under sultans Mehmet II, Bayezid II, and Selim I, the Ottoman Empire is extended into the Balkans, the Crimea, and the Middle East.

1520–61 The Empire reaches its peak under Suleyman the Magnificent, who conquers the eastern shore of the Black Sea and the Greek islands and makes an unsuccessful assault on Vienna in 1529.

1571 The defeat of the Ottoman fleet at the battle of Lepanto marks the beginning of the Empire's decline.

1699 Under the Treaty of Karlowitz Ottomans lose Hungary and other eastern European lands to the Habsburg Empire.

1774 Under the Treaty of Kutchuk-Kainardji Ottomans lose the Crimea and other lands to Russia.

1812–98 The Empire disintegrates and Turkey becomes known as the "sick man of Europe", losing Bessarabia in 1812,

Serbia in 1817, Greece in 1829, Algeria in 1830, Bosnia, Bulgaria and Cyprus in 1878 (under the Congress of Berlin), Tunisia in 1881, and Crete in 1898.

1894–96 A nationalist revolt in Armenia is put down ruthlessly.

1908 The Young Turks radical nationalist movement forces the Sultan to restore the brief constitutional rule of 1876–77.

1911–13 The Empire faces defeat in the First and Second Balkan Wars and loses nearly all of its territory in Europe.

1914–18 Turkey enters World War I on the side of the Central Powers.

1915 Turkish forces massacre some 1,500,000 Armenians.

1919 Greek forces enter Izmir (May); Mustapha Kemal "Atatürk" convenes the first Nationalist Congress (July).

1920 Atatürk sets up a provisional government; the Sultan signs the Treaty of Sèvres (August), conceding Izmir to Greece, relinquishing all Turkey's Arab territories and allowing the establishment of both an independent Armenia in eastern Anatolia and an independent Kurdistan in the east. The provisional government repudiates the treaty, and it never comes into effect.

1922 Atatürk's forces drive the Greeks out of Izmir and crush the Armenian republic. In October the Sultan is deposed and the sultanate abolished.

OTTOMAN SULTANS (c.1300–1924)

c.1300–1324	Osman I
1324–1360	Orkhan
1360–1389	Murad I
1389–1402	Yildirim Bayezid I (the Thunderbolt)
1402–1421	Mehmet I
1421–1444	Murad II (first reign)
1444–1446	Mehmet II (the Conqueror) (first reign)
1446–1451	Murad II (second reign)
1451–1481	Mehmet II (the Conqueror) (second reign)
1481–1512	Bayezid II
1512–1520	Selim I (the Grim)
1520–1566	Suleyman I (the Magnificent)
1566–1574	Selim II
1574–1595	Murad III
1595–1603	Mehmet III
1603–1617	Ahmed I
1617–1618	Mustafa I
1618–1622	Osman II

1622–1623	Mustafa I (restored)
1623–1640	Murad IV
1640–1648	Ibrahim I
1648–1687	Mehmet IV
1687–1691	Suleyman II
1691–1695	Ahmed II
1695–1703	Mustafa II
1703–1730	Ahmed III
1730–1754	Mahmud I
1754–1757	Osman III
1757–1774	Mustafa III
1774–1789	Abdul-Hamid I
1789–1807	Selim III
1807–1808	Mustafa IV
1808–1839	Mahmud II
1839–1861	Abdul-Mejid I
1861–1876	Abdul-Aziz
1876	Murad V
1876–1909	Abdul-Hamid II (the Damned)
1909–1918	Mehmet V
1918–1922	Mehmet VI
1922–1924	Abdul-Mejid II (caliph only)

Ottonian dynasty Saxon dynasty, named after Otto I, who assumed the Holy Roman Empire in the 10th and 11th centuries.

Oudney, Walter (died 1824) British naval officer and explorer. He accompanied Denham and Clapperton across the Sahara to Lake Chad in 1822, but died during the journey.

Oxford, siege of (1646) Turning point in English Civil War. *p.307*

Oyo West African state established c.1500. Gained control of the Niger Delta in 1747, and dominated the region between the Volta and the Niger in the 18th century. Profited by trading with European slavers.

P

Pachacuti Inca (*var.* Pachacutec) The ruler in whose reign (reigned 1438–71) the Inca empire expanded from its heartlands around Cuzco to dominate the Andean region as far north as Quito.

Pacific Rim Geopolitical term for those countries of E Asia, Australasia, and the Americas with Pacific shorelines, used in relation to trans-Pacific trade agreements and associated with the region's economic boom during the 1980s and 1990s. *See also* Tiger Economies

Pacific War (1937–45) General term for the war in the eastern theater of operations during World War II.

Pacific, War of the (1879–83) War between Chile, Peru, and Bolivia, fought over the valuable nitrate deposits in the Atacama Desert. Chile made substantial territorial gains from both Bolivia and Peru; Bolivia lost its access to the Pacific coast for ever.

padrão Mariner's milestone placed by Portuguese navigators along the coast of Africa during the 14th–15th centuries.

Paekche Ancient kingdom of the Korean peninsula. It flourished from the 3rd to the 7th centuries CE. *See also* Korea

Páez, Jose Antonio (1790–1873) Venezuelan revolutionary who fought against the Spanish with Simón Bolívar, and Venezuela's first president. In 1829 he led the movement to separate Venezuela from Gran Colombia and controlled the new country from his election as president in 1831 until 1846 when he was forced into exile. Returned as dictator 1861–63 and died in exile in New York.

Pagan (c.1050–1287) Burmese empire. The capital was at the predominantly Buddhist temple-city of Pagan (founded 847) on the Irrawaddy river. Went on to form the first major Burmese state (1044). Sacked by Mongol invaders in 1287. *p.170*

PAKISTAN Once a part of British India, Pakistan was created in 1947 in response to the demand for an independent and predominantly Muslim Indian state. Initially the new nation included East Pakistan, present-day Bangladesh, which seceded from Pakistan in 1971. Eastern and southern Pakistan, the flood plain of the Indus river, is highly fertile and produces cotton, the basis of the large textile industry. *See also* India, Bangladesh

CHRONOLOGY

8th–16th centuries Islamic rule extended to northwest and northeast India. Punjab and Sindh, annexed by the British East India Company in the 1850s, were ceded to the British Raj in 1857.

1906 Muslim League founded as organ of Indian Muslim separatism.

1947 Partition of India. Muhammad Ali Jinnah first governor-general of Pakistan, divided by 1600 km (994 miles) of Indian territory into East and West Pakistan. Millions displaced by large-scale migration.

1948 First Indo-Pakistan war over Kashmir.

1949 New Awami League (AL) demands East Pakistan's autonomy.

1956 Constitution establishes Pakistan as an Islamic republic.

1958 Martial law. General Muhammad Ayub Khan takes over; elected president two years later.

1965 Second Indo-Pakistan war over Kashmir.

1970 Ayub Khan resigns. General Agha Yahya Khan takes over. First direct elections won by AL; West Pakistani parties reject results. Military crackdown in East Pakistan. War with India over East Pakistan.

1971 East Pakistan secedes as Bangladesh. PPP leader Zulfikar Ali Bhutto becomes Pakistan's president.

1972 Simla (peace) agreement with India.

1973 Bhutto, now prime minister, initiates Islamic socialism.

1977 General election. Riots over allegations of vote rigging. General Zia ul-Haq stages military coup.

1979 Bhutto executed.

1986 Bhutto's daughter Benazir returns from exile to lead PPP.

1988 Zia killed in air crash. Benazir Bhutto wins general election.

1990 Ethnic violence in Sindh. President dismisses Benazir Bhutto. Nawaz Sharif becomes premier.

1991 Muslim sharia law incorporated in legal code.

1992 Violence between Sindhis and Mohajirs escalates in Sindh.

1993 President Khan and prime minister Sharif resign. Elections; Benazir Bhutto returned to power.

1996 President dismisses Benazir Bhutto.

1997 PML wins election; Nawaz Sharif elected prime minister. President's power to dismiss prime minister removed.

1998 Nuclear tests.

1999–2000 Military coup. Sharif found guilty of treason; exiled to Saudi Arabia.

2001 National Assembly suspended, Gen. Musharraf appoints himself president. July. Talks between Musharraf and Indian Prime Minister Vajpayee.

▶

2002 US and French nationals killed in terrorist attacks. Threat of war with India over Kashmir.

2004 Musharraf chooses Shaukat Aziz to become prime minister.

2005 Earthquake in Kashmir kills tens of thousands; even more are left homeless.

Palaeolithic Period of human prehistory (Old Stone Age) from c.850,000 BCE (Lower Palaeolithic), when the first hominids reached Europe from Africa, to the Middle Palaeolithic (c.200,000 BCE), and ending with the Upper Palaeolithic (c.35,000–10,000 BCE). The Upper Palaeolithic in Europe is associated with evidence of complex social structures, organized settlements, technological innovation and the florescence of rock art and carving.

Palas Late 8th-century Indian dynasty which maintained power in NE India, with strong Buddhist ties with Tibet.

PALAU The Republic of Palau (locally known as Belau) is situated in the western Pacific and comprises more than 300 islands in the Caroline Islands archipelago, only nine of which are inhabited. The Caroline Islands were colonized in turn by Spain, Germany, and Japan before being transferred to US control in 1945. They then became part of the US-administered Trust Territory of the Pacific Islands. Palau became independent in association with the US in 1994, but continues to be heavily dependent on US aid.

CHRONOLOGY

1947 UN Trust Territory of the Pacific Islands established.

1982 Palau signs Compact of Free Association with US.

1993 Compact approved.

1994 Palau becomes independent in free association with the US on October 1.

Palenque Maya city built (c.300). *p.128*
Pale, the Area in Ireland around Dublin which was under direct English rule. The concept was first mentioned in the 14th century.

Pale of Settlement (*var. Rus.* Cherta Osedlosti) Area within the Russian empire where Jews were permitted to live. Arose following the partitions of Poland in the late 18th century. Between 1783 and 1794, Catherine the Great issued a series of decrees restricting the rights of Jews to operate commercially within the newly-annexed areas. By the 19th century, the Pale included Russian Poland, Lithuania, Belorussia, most of Ukraine, the Crimea, and Bessarabia, and with few exceptions, Jews were increasingly restricted to this area with further restriction occurring towards the end of the 19th century, when a census revealed a population of nearly 5 million Jews within the Pale, with about 200,000 elsewhere in Russia.

PALESTINE Originally the land inhabited by the Philistines, the name has since been used in many different ways. The Romans adopted the name to describe one of its Middle Eastern Provinces and the British used it for the mandated territory they acquired after World War I. Today a Palestinian state is the unrealized dream of the Arabs of Israel's Occupied Territories. *See also* Holy Land, Israel

CHRONOLOGY

7th century, Palestine is conquered by the Arabs.

16th century, Palestine comes under Ottoman tutelage.

1916 The area is included in the zone of influence allocated to the United Kingdom under the Sykes-Picot Treaty.

1917 November. Palestine is included in the area designated as a Jewish National Home.

1920 Syrian National Congress proclaims Faisal King of Syria and Palestine.

1920 The Palestine Mandate is awarded to the UK at the San Remo Conference.

1948 British troops begin their withdrawal and the State of Israel is proclaimed. Arab armies enter the former Palestinian territories and following defeat, the Arab population flees.

1964 The Palestine Liberation Organization (PLO) and the Palestine Liberation Army are formed in Jerusalem.

1967 Israel captures all territory west of the Jordan river.

1982 Israeli forces invade Lebanon to drive the PLO out of Lebanon.

1987 Riots and violent protests lead to clashes between Israeli forces and Palestinians in the West Bank and Gaza. They mark the beginning of the *Intifada*.

1988 The Palestine National Council declares the establishment of the independent state of Palestine with Jerusalem as its capital.

1993 An Israeli-PLO "declaration of principles" – providing for self-rule in the Gaza Strip and Jericho and more limited autonomy for the rest of the West Bank – is signed in Washington.

1998 Government stalls on US-backed peace plan to revive peace process.

2000 Israel withdraws from Lebanon. *Intifada* relaunched.

2002 I*Intifada* and reprisals intensify. Unity government collapses.

2003 US peace roadmap established.

2004 Gaza withdrawal agreed.

Palestine Liberation Organizaton (PLO) Organization to restore the Palestinian people to their homeland. In 1974 it was recognized by the Arab nations as the "sole legitimate representative of the Palestinian people." In 1993 the PLO signed an agreement with Israel formally recognizing the state of Palestine and Israel. *See also* Israel, Arafat, Yasser

Palgrave, William Gifford (1826–88) British Jesuit explorer. Working as a spy for Napoleon III of France, he was the first European to make the west-east crossing of the Arabian Peninsula in 1862–63.

Palliser, Lt. John 19th-century Irish explorer of Canada, who conducted a major survey of the prairies and the Rocky Mountains in the 1850s.

PANAMA The southernmost of the seven countries occupying the isthmus that joins North and South America. The rainforests of the southeastern Darien Peninsula are some of the wildest areas in the Americas. Elected governments have held power since the US invasion of 1989. Panama's economic strength is its banking sector. The US returned control of the Canal Zone to Panama on December 31 1999.

CHRONOLOGY

1513 Vasco Nunez de Balboa sights the Pacific from Panama which due to its position becomes a commercial center of geopolitical importance until the end of the 18th century.

1717 As a province of Colombia, Panama is transferred from the Viceroyalty of Peru to the Viceroyalty of Granada.

1821 On independence from Spain, Panama becomes part of Gran Colombia.

1830 On breakup of Gran Colombia, Panama remains part of Colombia.

1903 With US support Panama revolts against Colombia and declares independence, immediately granting the US rights over an Atlantic-Pacific corridor through its territory.

1914 The Panama Canal is completed.

1968 Accession of Brig-Gen. Omar Torrijos Herrera to power in a coup.

1977 Torrijos and US President Carter sign new Panama Canal treaties transferring control of the canal to Panama on December 31 1999.

1979 Treaties officially ending US control over the Panama Canal Zone enter into force.

1987 A state of emergency is imposed after anti-government protests over the alleged rigging of the 1984 elections by the power behind the civilian government, Gen. Manuel Noriega.

1989 Three days after presidential elections are held, Noriega annuls the results.

1989 Noriega formally assumes power as head of state with wide powers.

1989 The US installs the apparent victor in the 1989 election, Guillermo Endara Gallimany, as head of state and invades with 23,000 troops to depose Noriega whom it accuses of drug-related activities.

1990 Noriega surrenders to the US authorities and is taken to the USA for trial on drug charges.

Panama Canal Shipping canal across the Isthmus of Panama (64.85 km wide), linking the Atlantic and Pacific Oceans. In 1903 a strip of territory was granted to the US by Panama; construction of the canal began early in 1904. It was opened to traffic on Aug 15 1914. Further work to deepen and widen the canal was begun in 1959.

Panda Zulu king (reigned 1840–72).

Panipat ⚔ (Apr 20 1526) A victory by the Mughal leader, Babur, who confronted the Afghan Lodi Sultanate. Babur's use of artillery was decisive, the Sultan was routed, and control of the entire Ganges valley passed to the Mughals. *p.331*

Pannonia Roman province including territory now mostly in Hungary and the former states of Yugoslavia.

Paoli ⚔ of American Revolutionary War (Sep 20 1777). British victory.

Papacy *see* Roman Catholic Church, Catholicism, Papal States, Vatican

Papal States (*var.* Patrimony of St. Peter) The territory in central Italy under papal rule. The Papal States became political reality under Renaissance popes such as Alexander VI and Julius II. The Papal States ceased to exist in 1870, when Rome fell to the troops of the recently united Kingdom of Italy.

PAPUA NEW GUINEA The most linguistically diverse country in the world, with around 750 languages, Papua New Guinea (PNG) achieved independence from Australia in 1975. The country occupies the eastern end of New Guinea, the world's second-largest island, and several other groups of islands. Much of the country is still isolated, with the rural population experiencing basic living conditions.

CHRONOLOGY

1526 The Portuguese explorer Jorge de Meneses lands on the northwest coast of the island of New Guinea.

1884 Britain lays claim to the southeast coast of New Guinea island, and to the islands to the east, while Germany claims the northeast coast and nearby islands.

1904 Australia takes over British sector; renamed Papua in 1906.

1914 German sector occupied by Australia.

1942–1945 Japanese occupation.

1964 National Parliament created.

1971 Renamed Papua New Guinea.

1975 Independence under Michael Somare, leader since 1972.

1988 Bougainville Revolutionary Army begins guerrilla campaign.

1997 El Niño effect causes severe drought and tsunamis. Sir Julius Chan resigns as prime minister over the use of Western-led mercenaries in Bougainville.

2000 Loloata Understanding promises autonomy for Bougainville.

2001 PDM claims parliamentary majority. Final peace agreement with Bougainville ratified after three-year cease-fire.

Paracas culture Centered on a barren Peruvian peninsula, and renowned for its ornate prehistoric pottery and colorful textiles. Many artifacts have been found in mummified burials dating from about 600–100 BCE. *p.55*

PARAGUAY Landlocked in South America and a Spanish possession until 1811, Paraguay gained large tracts of land from Bolivia in 1938. Until the overthrow in 1989 of General Alfredo Stroessner, it experienced periods of anarchy and military rule. The Paraguay river divides the eastern hills and fertile plains, where 90 percent of people live, from the Chaco in the west. Paraguay's economy is largely agricultural.

CHRONOLOGY

1537 Sailing up the Parana in search of silver, the Spaniards establish a fort at Asunción which becomes the capital of La Plata province.

1767 The Jesuits who had arrived in 1588 and organized the Indians into mission communities are expelled.

1811 Spanish administration is deposed. Over the next 50 years, ruled by dictatorships and cut off from the outside world, Paraguay is protected from the unrest affecting its neighbors and becomes an economic power.

1864–1870 Loses War of the Triple Alliance against Argentina, Brazil, and Uruguay.

1928–1935 Two Chaco Wars against Bolivia over disputed territory.

1938 Boundary with Bolivia fixed; Paraguay awarded large tracts.

1954–1989 Rule of Gen. Stroessner; repressive military regime.

1993 First democratic elections.

1996 Coup attempt by General Lino Oviedo.

1998–1999 Raúl Cubas elected president; resigns after assassination of vice president; Cubas and Oviedo leave country.

2000 Further failed coup attempt by Oviedo.

Paraguayan War (1864–70) Boundary disputes led Paraguay to go to war with Brazil in 1864, resulting in an invasion of Paraguay by an alliance of Argentina, Brazil, and Uruguay early in 1865. An intense five-year struggle followed, involving every able-bodied citizen and only ending with the complete defeat of the Paraguayan forces. The total population of 1,337,439 was reduced to less than 250,000.

Parhae *see* Pohai empire

Paris, Matthew (c.1200–1259) Benedictine monk and chronicler. Produced the *Chronica Majora*, acknowledged to be the finest chronicle of the 13th century.

Paris The capital of France, named after the Parisii tribe. Under the Romans , it was known as Lutetia Parisiorum. From the small fishing village conquered by Julius Caesar it grew to a sizable town and one of the capitals used by Clovis and other Merovingian kings of France. Under the Capetians (987–1328) it became firmly established as capital, and with the foundation of the Sorbonne University, the most important center of theological scholarship in Europe.

Park, Mungo (1771–1806) Scottish explorer and author of *Travels in the Interior of Africa*. He worked as chief medical officer with East India Company before carrying out two explorations of the Niger river system (1795–96, 1805–06) sponsored by the African Associaton.

Parry, Sir William Edward (1790–1855) British navigator and explorer. Traveled to the Arctic on behalf of Royal Navy to protect whales from over-hunting. Led four expeditions to the Arctic between 1818 and 1827, navigating more than half of the Northeast Passage, and attempting to reach the N Pole on foot from Spitzbergen.

Parthenon The greatest temple of Athens, situated on the summit of the Acropolis, replacing an earlier Temple of Athena destroyed by the Persians in 480 BCE. Constructed during the rule of Pericles, it is built entirely from marble and decorated with a remarkable frieze, part of which is to be found in the British Museum in London (the Elgin Marbles). It was finally completed in 432 BCE. *p.56*

Parthians Iranian nomads from Central Asia who in c.240 BCE rebelled against Seleucid rule, formed their own state, and came to dominate Asia Minor and Persia from about 140 BCE. In 53 BCE they defeated the Romans at the battle of Carrhae, and in 40 BCE they captured Jerusalem. The Parthians were attacked by the Romans in 216 CE, and finally crushed by the Sassanians in 224 CE. *p.68*

pastoralism The practice of herding animals, which is common in climates which are too dry, mountainous, or cold for agriculture. Pastoralists tend to be nomadic to varying degrees, and as a result may be long-distance traders.

Pasteur, Louis (1822–95) French chemist, remembered chiefly for his discovery that microorganisms could be killed off by the process of "pasteurization." *p.379*

Patna ⚔ (1759) Challenge by Mughal crown prince repulsed by British army under Clive.

Paul, St. Jewish convert to Christianity who became the leading missionary of the early Church, undertaking great journeys to Greece and Asia Minor. Probably martyred in Rome between 62 and 68 CE.

Paulistas In the 17th and 18th centuries, bands of adventurers from São Paulo, who went on raids into the jungles of Brazil in search of Indians to enslave. In the 17th century they came into conflict with the Jesuits of Paraguay. *See also* São Paulo

Pavia ⚔ (1525) in N Italy. Francis I of France was defeated and captured by Emperor Charles V. *p.276*

Pearl Harbor (1941) Japanese air attack on the US naval base in Hawaii which led to US entry into World War II.

Peary, Robert Edwin (1856–1920) US explorer of the Arctic. Reputedly the first man to reach the N Pole (Apr 6 1909).

Peasants' Revolt (1381) Uprising in England led by Wat Tyler to protest against the Poll Tax.

Pedro I Emperor of Brazil (*aka* Pedro IV, King of Portugal, 1798–1834, reigned 1822–31 in Brazil) When Brazil and Portugal split in 1822, Pedro, son of King João VI, remained in Brazil as its first emperor. His father returned to Portugal, but died in 1826. This made Pedro king of Portugal, but he abdicated in favor of his daughter, Maria. In 1831 Pedro returned to Portugal to fight his brother Miguel, who was trying to usurp the throne.

Peipus, Lake ⚔ (1142) Russian defeat of Teutonic Knights.

Peking *see* Beijing

Peloponnesian War (431–404 BCE) Series of land and sea battles between Athens and Sparta. Caused by the threat of Athenian imperialism, the conflict only ended when the Persians intervened on the Spartans' side, leading to the dismantling of the Athenian Empire.

Peninsular War (1808–14) Campaign during the Napoleon Wars fought out in the Iberian Peninsula between France and an alliance of Britain, Spain, and Portugal. Napoleon's invasion of Portugal (1807) and installation of his brother Joseph on the Spanish throne, sparked off a long guerrilla struggle. The initial British intervention ended in retreat. When Napoleon withdrew French troops to Russia, the future Duke of Wellington, Arthur Wellesley, invaded Spain from Portugal, winning a decisive battle at Vitoria in 1813.

People's Movement for the Liberation of Angola (MPLA) Political party of Angola founded in 1956 and backed during the civil war (1975–91) by Cuba and the Soviet Union.

Pepin (*aka* Pepin the Short, *var. Fre.* Pépin le Bref, c.714–68) Frankish king. Mayor of the Palace of the last Merovingian king of the Franks, Childeric III. He forced Childeric to abdicate and was crowned in his place, becoming founder of the Carolingian dynasty. In 753 he won Ravenna from the Lombards for the Papacy.

Pequot War (1637) Indian uprising against European encroachment in New England (N America).

Pergamum (*var. Gr.* Pergamon) Ancient city of Asia Minor. It became the capital of a Hellenistic kingdom that flourished in the second century BCE. Its last king, Attalus III, who died in 133 BCE, willed his kingdom to Rome. *p.66*

Pericles (c.495–429 BCE) Athenian general who became the uncrowned king of Athens' Golden Age (reigned 443–429). He was responsible for establishing full democracy in Athens, and his opposition to Sparta was instrumental in provoking the Peloponnesian Wars. *p.56*

Periplus of the Erythraean Sea Greek trading manual of the 1st century CE.

Perón, Eva (1919–52) Wife of president Juan Perón, adored by many of the Argentinian people. *p.418*

Perón, Juan Domingo (1895–1974) Army colonel who became president of Argentina (1946–55, 1973–74), founder and leader of the Peronist movement.

Pérouse, Jean François Galaup de la (1741–88) French explorer of the Pacific. His voyage of 1785–88 was financed by

King Louis XVI. It was the most far-ranging voyage to the Pacific yet attempted, although it failed in its prime aim: to find the Northwest Passage. La Pérouse and his two ships were last seen by members of the First Fleet at Botany Bay in Mar 1788. It was later established that they sank off Vanikoro in the Santa Cruz Islands.

Perry, Commodore Matthew (1794–1858) US naval commander. Led the expedition to Japan 1853–54 which forced Japan to end its isolation of two centuries and open relations with the world.

Perryville ⚔ of American Civil War (Oct 8 1862). Union victory.

Persepolis Capital of Achaemenid Persia, founded by Darius I c.151 BCE.

Persia see Achaemenid dynasty; Iran; Parthians; Safavid empire; Sassanian empire; Seleucid empire

Persian Royal Road see Royal Road

PERU

PERU Lying just south of the equator, on the Pacific coast of South America, Peru became independent of Spain in 1824. It rises from an arid coastal strip to the Andes, dominated in the south by volcanoes; about half of Peru's population live in mountain regions. Peru's border with Bolivia to the south runs through Lake Titicaca, the highest navigable lake in the world. In 1995, Peru was involved in a brief border war with Ecuador, its northern neighbor, and the issue was finally settled in 1998.

CHRONOLOGY

1528 Francisco Pizarro sails along the coast as far as the frontier of present-day Peru-Ecuador.

1532 Pizarro lands and captures the Inca ruler Atahualpa. The Indians are massacred at Cajamarca. Atahualpa is executed in 1533 and the invaders advance to Cuzco and strip it of gold.

1544 Viceroyalty of Peru is established.

1780–81 Tupac Amaru II leads Indian revolt.

1821 Independence proclaimed in Lima after its capture by Argentine liberator, José de San Martín, who had just freed Chile.

1824 Spain suffers final defeats at battles of Junín and Ayacucho by Simon Bolívar and General Sucre.

1836–1839 Peru and Bolivia joined in short-lived confederation.

1866 Peruvian-Spanish War.

1879–1884 War of the Pacific. Chile defeats Peru and Bolivia. Peru loses territory in south.

1908 Augusto Leguía y Salcedo's dictatorial rule begins.

1924 Dr. Víctor Raúl Haya de la Torre founds nationalist APRA in exile in Mexico.

1930 Leguía ousted. APRA moves to Peru as first political party.

1931–1945 APRA banned.

1939–1945 Moderate, pro-US civilian government.

1948 Gen. Manuel Odría takes power. APRA banned again.

1956 Civilian government restored.

1962–1963 Two military coups.

1963 Election of Fernando Belaúnde Terry. Land reform, but military used to suppress communist-inspired insurgency.

1968 Military junta takes over. Attempts to alleviate poverty. Adopts policy of widespread nationalization.

1975–1978 New right-wing junta.

1980 Belaúnde reelected. Maoist Sendero Luminoso (Shining Path) begins armed struggle.

1981–98 War with Ecuador over Cordillera del Cóndor, given to Peru by a 1942 protocol. Ecuador wants access to Amazon.

1982 Deaths and "disappearances" start to escalate as army cracks down on guerrillas and drugs trade.

1985 Electoral win for left-wing APRA under Alán García Pérez.

1987 Peru goes bankrupt. Plans to nationalize banks are blocked by new Libertad movement led by writer Mario Vargas Llosa.

1990 Over 3000 political murders. Alberto Fujimori, an independent, elected president on anticorruption platform. Severe austerity program.

1992–95 Fujimori "self-coup." New constitution. Fujimori reelected.

1996–1997 Left-wing Tupac Amarú guerrillas seize hundreds of hostages at Japanese ambassador's residence in four-month siege.

2000 November. Fujimori resigns amid corruption scandal despite having won controversial third term in May; seeks refuge in Japan.

2001 Fresh presidential elections, won by Alejandro Toledo in run-off against García.

2003 Beatriz Merino appointed first female prime minister.

Peruzzi Powerful banking family of Florence with branches across Europe from c.1275. The Peruzzi went bankrupt in the 1340s after Edward III of England had defaulted on repayment of large loans.

Peter the Great (Peter I, 1672–1725) Czar of Russia. He succeeded to the throne in 1682, taking full control in 1689. Following an extensive tour of Europe (1697–8), he set about the westernization of Russia, building a new capital, St. Petersburg (1703). He reformed government and the military, founding the Russian navy. He fought major wars with the Ottoman empire, Persia, and Sweden, defeating the latter in the Great Northern War (1700–1721), which gained for Russia secure access to the Baltic coast. *p.316*

Petersburg, Siege of ⚔ of American Civil War (Jun 20 1864–Apr 2 1865). Union victory.

Petra Capital of the Nabataeans from 4th century BCE–2nd century CE, it derived its prosperity from its position on the caravan trade route from southern Arabia, especially during the height of the frankincense trade. Petra was annexed by the Romans in 106 CE. The remains of the city include temples and tombs carved into the pink rock of the surrounding hills. Revealed as a major site by Burckhardt (1812). *p.70*

petroglyph Prehistoric rock carving, often taken to be some of the earliest examples of writing.

Petrograd see St. Petersburg

Peutinger Table Copy (1265) of a Roman map showing road systems and routes within the Roman Empire.

Pharaonic Egypt During the New Kingdom from c.1500 BCE onwards Egypt was ruled by the pharaohs or god-kings, who wielded immense religious, military, and civil power and were believed to be the sons of the god Osiris. They were the mediators between their mortal subjects and the gods and under their rule Egypt's power and territory greatly increased. The term was only used by the Egyptians themselves from 950 BCE onwards.

Pharos Lighthouse at Alexandria, one of the Seven Wonders of the Ancient World. *p.63*

Phidias (var. Pheidias, c.490–430 BCE) Greece's greatest sculptor, Phidias was commissioned by Pericles to carry out Athens' major works and ultimately became superintendent of public works.

His legacy includes the gold and ivory work at the Parthenon. When accused of stealing the gold from his statue of Zeus at Olympia, Phidias fled from Athens.

Philby, Harry St. John (1885–1960) English explorer and Arabist. In 1932 he crossed the Rub' al Khali, or 'Empty Quarter', of Arabia. *See also* Rub' al Khali

Philip II (*var.* Philip Augustus, *Fr.* Philippe Auguste, 1165–1223). The great Capetian king of France (reigned 1179–1223), who gradually reclaimed French territories held by the kings of England and also extended the royal sphere into Flanders and Languedoc. He was a major figure in the Third Crusade to the Holy Land in 1191.

Philip II (c.382–336 BCE) Rose to the Macedonian throne in 359 BCE. After the battle of Chaeronea (338 BCE), he assumed control of the Greek forces and planned an expedition to reverse the expansion of the Persian Empire, but was murdered in Aegeae before he could fulfil it. Father of Alexander the Great.

Philip II (1527–98) King of Spain (reigned 1556–98) and king of Portugal as Philip I (reigned 1580–98) who championed the Roman Catholic Counter-Reformation. His reign saw the apogee of the Spanish empire, though he failed to suppress the revolt of the Netherlands (1566–1609) and lost the Armada in his attempted invasion of England in 1588.

PHILIPPINES

PHILIPPINES Lying in the western Pacific Ocean, the Philippines is the world's second-largest archipelago after Indonesia. It comprises 7107 islands, of which 4600 are named and 1000 inhabited. There are three main island groupings: Luzon, Visayan, and the Mindanao and Sulu islands. Located on the Pacific "ring of fire," the country is subject to frequent earthquakes and volcanic activity. Economic growth outstripped population increase in the 1990s, until the 1997–1998 "Asian crisis," but efforts to build a stable democracy have been compromised by high-level corruption.

Chronology

1521 A Spanish expedition led by the Portuguese explorer Ferdinand Magellan lands in the Philippines. Magellan himself is later killed in the Philippines.

1565 Miguel Lopez de Legazpi founds first Spanish settlement in the Philippines.
1892 The Katipunan ("Sons of the People") movement is founded under the leadership of Andres Bonifacio.
1896 Katipunan launches the Philippine revolution. Influential pro-independence writer, Jose Rizal, executed by the Spanish.
1897 Bonifacio is executed on the orders of a military court appointed by a rival rebel leader, Emilio Aguinaldo. Later that year Aguinaldo is exiled to Hong Kong.
1898 Spanish-American War: US forces destroy the Spanish fleet in Manila Bay. Spain cedes the Philippines to the USA.
1901 Aguinaldo, who had returned from exile, is captured. Having first been an ally of the US he later fights against the occupying forces.
1935 The Sakdalistas (a movement formed to combat inequitable land distribution and excessive taxes) begins an uprising which is quickly put down.
1935 The Commonwealth of the Philippines is created, in preparation for complete independence. Manuel Quezon is its president.
1941 The Philippines is invaded by Japanese forces.
1944 US forces land on the Philippines.
1946 Philippine Republic is inaugurated, giving the country independence from the US. Manuel A. Roxas is its first president.
1965 Ferdinand Marcos president.
1972 Marcos declares martial law. Opposition leaders arrested, National Assembly suspended, press censored.
1977 Ex-Liberal Party leader Benigno Aquino sentenced to death. Criticism forces Marcos to delay execution.
1978 Elections won by New Society (KBL). Marcos president and prime minister.
1981 Martial law ends. Marcos reelected president by referendum.
1983 Aquino shot dead on return from US. Inquiry blames military conspiracy.
1986 US compels presidential election. Result disputed. Army rebels led by General Fidel Ramos, and public demonstrations, bring Aquino's widow, Corazon, to power. Marcos exiled to US.
1987 New constitution. Aquino-led coalition wins Congress elections.
1988 Marcos and wife Imelda indicted for massive racketeering.
1989 Marcos dies in US.

1990 Imelda Marcos acquitted of fraud charges in US. Earthquake in Baguio City leaves 1600 dead.
1991 Mt. Pinatubo erupts..
1992 General Fidel Ramos wins the presidential election. US withdraws from Subic Bay base.
1998 Joseph Estrada president.
1999 First execution in 22 years.
2000 Death penalty suspended.
2001 Estrada overthrown. Gloria Macapagal Arroyo assumes presidency. Muslim MILF joins peace process.
2002 Local elections described as "peaceful" despite 86 deaths.

Philistines An ancient people of the southeast Mediterranean; originally a seafaring people who settled in south Palestine in the 12th century BCE. They gained control of land and sea routes and were long-standing enemies of the Israelites until their defeat by King David.

Phoenicians Decendents of the Canaanites, the Phoenicians dominated the coastal strip of the eastern Mediterranean at the end of the 2nd millennium BCE. They expanded across the whole of the Mediterranean, establishing trading posts in the western Mediterranean and N Africa. The Phoenicians are noted for developing one of the first alphabets, which consisted purely of consonants.

Photography Development by Daguerre and Niepce in early 19th century. *p.358*

Phrygians Originating in Europe around 1200 BCE, the Phrygians occupied the central plateau and western edge of Asia Minor, reaching their widest extent at the start of the 1st millennium BCE. Their power declined in the 6th century BCE with the arrival of the Lydians.

Piankhi (reigned c.741–715 BCE) King of ancient Nubia (Cush). Subdued Upper Egypt c.721 BCE and defeated Tefnakhte of Lower Egypt, but returned to Nubian capital at Napata c.718 BCE.

pictograph (*var.* pictogram) The earliest forms of writing were based on these stylized outline representations of objects. The earliest examples come from c.3250 BCE Egypt, but they occur across the world; because they represent objects rather than linguistic elements, pictograms cross conventional language boundaries. *See also* hieroglyphics

Picts Group of tribes who occupied N Scotland in early Christian times, known for their fierce raiding. Connections between the kings of the Picts and the Scots of SW Scotland grew closer in the 9th century, leading to the creation of the medieval kingdom of Scotland.

Pike, Lt. Zebulon Montgomery (1779–1813) US soldier and explorer. In 1805–06, he led an expedition in search of the source of the Mississippi. In 1806–07, he traveled up the Arkansas River to the Colorado Mountains and attempted to climb Pike's Peak. His party was captured by the Spanish, but later released.

Pinochet, General Augusto Ugarte (1915–) Leader of the military junta that overthrew the Marxist government of President Salvador Allende of Chile on Sep 11 1973. He subsequently headed Chile's military government (1974–90).

Pinzón, Vicente Yáñez (*fl.* 1492–1509) Spanish navigator who sailed with Columbus. Discovered the mouth of the Amazon (1500) and was made governor of Puerto Rico. Also explored (1508–09) the coasts of Honduras and Venezuela.

Pioneers The pioneer trail to the American West. *p.374*

Pisa Powerful maritime republic from the 10th to the 13th century – a rival of Genoa and Venice for the carrying trade in the Mediterranean. Vied with Genoa for control of the island of Corsica. Suffered heavy defeat by a Genoese fleet at the battle of Meloria (1284). Pisa cathedral is a magnificent example of Romanesque architecture. *p.172*

Pizarro, Francisco (c.1475–1541) Spanish conquistador. Pizarro first sailed to the New World in 1502. He took part in several expeditions around the Caribbean, before turning his attention to Peru. In 1531 he set off from Panama with 185 men and 27 horses. By exploiting a recent civil war among the Incas, and treacherously killing their leader Atahualpa, Pizarro was able to conquer the great Inca empire and seize large quantities of gold ornaments that were melted down to be shipped to Spain. The early years of the colony were marked by rivalry between the conquistadores and Pizarro was killed by supporters of one of his lieutenants, Diego de Almagro, in 1541. *p.278*

plagues Many killer diseases have been dubbed "plagues" in the course of human history, but the word is usually reserved for bubonic plague. Famous outbreaks include the Plague of Justinian (542 CE) and the Black Death (1347). *See also* Black Death

plantation System for the farming of cash crops such as rubber and cotton on a large scale in European colonies. This system was often reliant on slave labor.

Plantagenets *see* Angevin dynasty

Plassey ⚔ of Anglo-French war in India (Jun 23 1757). Defeat of a large Indian army under the command of the Nawab of Bengal by British forces under the command of Robert Clive, at the village of Plassey on the Hooghly river. *p.328*

Plataea ⚔ of the Persian Wars (480 BCE). The decisive defeat of the Persians by the Greeks.

Plato (c.427–347 BCE). An Athenian aristocrat and disciple of the philosopher Socrates, Plato traveled widely before founding his own academy of philosophy in Athens. His 35 dialogues, many of which feature Socrates, are concerned with defining moral concepts, and developing Plato's own doctrines and self criticisms. Plato distinguished between the transient and finite objects experienced by the senses and that of the timeless universal forms which he called the true objects of knowledge. His ideas influenced the Romans and shaped Christian theology and Western philosophy. *p.59*

PLO *see* Palestine Liberation Organization

pogrom An organized massacre or riot. Originally used with reference to the murder of Russian Jews in the late 19th and early 20th centuries.

Pohai empire (*var.* Parhae) Empire of Manchuria formed by Koguryo refugees in 696. Destroyed by Khitans in 926.

POLAND Located in the heart of Europe, Poland's low-lying plains extend from the Baltic shore in the north to the Tatra Mountains on its southern border with the Czech Republic and Slovakia. Since the collapse of communism, Poland has undergone massive social, economic, and political change. Opting for a radical form of economic "shock therapy" in the early 1990s to kick-start the switch to a market economy, it has experienced rapid growth, is one of the front runners in negotiations to join the EU, and has already been accepted as a member of NATO.

CHRONOLOGY

966 King Mieszko, who had united three Slavonic tribes and founded the Polish Piast dynasty, converts to Christianity.

1386 Poland and Lithuania are united by the marriage of Queen Jadwiga of Poland and Grand Prince Jagiello of Lithuania. At the height of their power in the 15th century the domains of the Jagiellonian kings are the largest in Europe, stretching from the Baltic to the Black Sea.

1572 Sigisumund August, the last of the Jagiellonian dynasty, dies, after having concluded in 1569 the Union of Lublin, strengthening the common state of Poland and Lithuania. The two capitals of Cracow and Vilnius are replaced by a single capital city, Warsaw, in 1596.

1764 Stanislas August Poniatowski is appointed to the Polish throne through the influence of Russian Czarina Catherine II after nearly two centuries of intermittent war between Poland and its neighbors – Russia, Sweden, and the Ottoman Empire.

1772 The first partition of Poland takes place between Prussia, Austria, and Russia at the Treaty of St. Petersburg.

1791 A new liberal constitution, forced through by Stanislas, reduces the traditional powers of the nobility. The nobles call on Russia for aid.

1793 Second partition of Poland: the Treaty of Grodno divides more Polish territory between Russia and Prussia.

1795 Austria, Prussia, and Russia negotiate the third partition of Poland, despite a brief Polish insurrection the previous year, and in 1797 proclaim the abolition of Poland *(Finis Poloniae)*, following Stanislas August's abdication in 1795.

1807–13 Following the Treaty of Tilsit between Napoleon and Tsar Aleksandr I, Poland is partially resurrected as the French vassal state of the Grand Duchy of Warsaw during the Napoleonic Wars.

1815 The Treaty of Vienna allocates to Russia a large portion of the Grand Duchy including Warsaw.

1830 Insurrection in Warsaw, inspired by the French and Belgian revolutions.

1831 Czar Nicholas I is deposed by the Polish Diet, which creates a national government. However, Russian troops invade and take Warsaw in September, and direct rule from Russia is imposed.

▶

◄

1846 Austria annexes Cracow, established as a republic by the Treaty of Vienna, allowing some self-government, and Cracow becomes a center of Polish nationalist aspirations.

1863 An uprising against Russian rule is suppressed with Prussian help and puts an end to liberal reforms of 1861–62.

1918 Polish state recreated.

1921 Democratic constitution.

1926–1935 Pilsudski heads military coup. Nine years of authoritarian rule.

1939 Germany invades and divides Poland with Russia.

1941 First concentration camps builtl.

1944 Warsaw Uprising.

1945 Potsdam and Yalta Conferences set present borders and determine political allegiance to Soviet Union.

1947 Communists manipulate elections to gain power.

1970 Food price increases lead to strikes and riots in the Baltic port cities. Hundreds are killed.

1979 Cardinal Karol Wojtyla of Cracow is elected pope and takes the name of John Paul II.

1980 Strikes force the government to negotiate with the Solidarity union. Resulting Gdansk Accords grant the right to strike and to form free trade unions.

1981 Gen. Wojciech Jaruzelski becomes prime minister.

1981–83 Martial law. Solidarity movement forced underground. Many of its leaders, including Lech Walesa, are interned.

1983 Walesa awarded Nobel Peace Prize.

1986 Amnesty for political prisoners.

1987 Referendum rejects government austerity program.

1989 Ruling party holds talks with Solidarity, which is relegalized. Partially free elections are held. First postwar noncommunist government formed.

1990 Launch of market reforms. Walesa elected president.

1991 Free elections lead to fragmented parliament.

1992 Last Russian troops leave.

1993 Elections. Reformed communists head coalition government.

1994 Launch of mass privatization.

1995 Leader of reformed communists Aleksander Kwasniewski elected president.

1996 Historic Gdansk shipyard declared bankrupt and closed down.

1997 Parliament finally adopts new postcommunist constitution. Legislative elections end former communist majority with big swing to AWS coalition. EU agrees to open membership negotiations.

1999 Joins NATO.

2000 AWS in minority government.

2004 Joins EU. Marek Belka appointed prime minister.

polis The Greek city-state, that of Athens being one of several which characterize the Classical Age.

Polo, Marco (1254–1324) Venetian merchant and traveler. In 1271 he accompanied his father, Nicolò, and his uncle, Maffeo, on their second journey to the court of Kublai Khan, the Mongol ruler of China. He spent almost 17 years in the Khan's service, traveling widely in China before returning to Venice in 1295. His account of his travels has remained a bestseller ever since, although many have questioned its veracity. *p.221*

Pol Pot (*aka* Saloth Sar, 1926–1998) Cambodian communist leader. He led the pro-Chinese communist Khmer Rouge guerrillas from the 1960s and seized power in 1975. He attempted to create a self-sufficient socialist state using brutal methods, resulting in a death toll of over 2 million, one-fifth of the population of Cambodia. Once overthrown in 1979 by the Vietnamese, he remained in the Khmer Rouge during a renewed guerrilla campaign. *p.445*

Polynesians Pacific people, who share close genetic and linguistic heritage with the peoples of the Philippines and central and eastern Indonesia. Early Lapita colonists spread from the islands of SE Asia as far east as Tonga and Samoa. Polynesian culture had its origins in the Fiji-Samoa region c.1000 BCE. From c.200 BCE, colonists settled all of the islands of the Pacific, reaching New Zealand by 700 CE. Chiefdom societies developed throughout the region from c.1200 CE.

Pombal, Marquis of (1699–1782) Portuguese chief minister under King José I. Won respect for his efficiency and speed in planning the rebuilding of Lisbon after the terrible earthquake of 1755. He was subsequently responsible for the expulsion of the Jesuits from Portugal and its colonies (1759). *p.327*

Pompeii Town near Naples, destroyed by eruption of Vesuvius in 79 CE. *p.82*

Pompey the Great (Gnaeus Pompeius Magnus, 106–48 BCE) Roman general and rival of Julius Caesar. He was defeated by the Caesar at ✕ Pharsalus (48 BCE). *p.71*

Ponce de León, Juan (1460–1521) Spanish explorer who discovered Florida in 1513 and was made governor. Failing to subdue his new subjects, he retired to Cuba.

Pontus Kingdom of Asia Minor. It reached its greatest extent under Mithridates VI Eupator (reigned 120–63 BCE) who clashed frequently with the armies of the expanding Romans.

Poor Men of Lyons *see* Waldensians

Popular Front International alliance of left-wing elements which gained some prominence during the 1930s, especially in Spain, where the Popular Front governed from 1936–39, and opposed General Franco and his supporters during the Spanish Civil War.

Port Hudson ✕ of American Civil War (Jul 9 1863). Inconclusive result.

portolan chart Navigational chart of a kind produced from c.1300–1500, mainly in Italy and Spain. They used a series of rhumb lines radiating out from a central point in the direction of the wind or the compass points. They were used primarily to enable pilots to find their way from harbor to harbor.

PORTUGAL Portugal, with its long Atlantic coast, lies on the western side of the Iberian peninsula. The river Tagus divides the more mountainous north from the lower, undulating terrain to the south. In 1974, a bloodless military coup overthrew a long-standing conservative dictatorship. A constituent assembly was elected in 1975 and the armed forces withdrew from politics thereafter. Portugal then began a substantial program of economic modernization and accompanying social change. Membership of the EU has helped underpin this process.

CHRONOLOGY

2nd century BCE Portugal becomes part of the Roman Empire. When the Roman Empire collapses, what is now Portugal falls to the Visigoths and subsequently to the Moors.

1139 Afonso Henriques declares himself king of Portugal, formerly a small country of the kingdom of León and Castile.

1147 Lisbon falls to Christian forces.

1249 Afonso III expels the last of the Moors from the Algarve.

1418 Prince Henry the Navigator, son of João I made governor of the Algarve. Sponsors series of voyages of exporation out into the Atlantic and south along the coast of Africa.

1494 Under the Treaty of Tordesillas, Pope Alexander VI divides the "New World" between Portugal and Spain.

1497–99 Vasco da Gama voyages around the Cape of Good Hope to India.

1500 Pedro Álvares Cabral accidentally discovers Brazil on journey to India.

1580 Philip II of Spain claims Portuguese crown and invades.

1580–1640 Portugal is united with Spain

1598–1663 Many overseas territorial possessions lost to the Dutch.

1640–1668 War with Spain. Portugal regains independence after uprising led by Duke of Braganza.

1755 Earthquake destroys Lisbon.

1793 Joins coalition against revolutionary France.

1807 France invades; royal family flees to Brazil.

1808 British troops arrive under Wellington. Start of Peninsular War.

1820 Liberal revolution.

1822 King João VI returns and accepts first Portuguese constitution. His son Dom Pedro declares independence of Brazil.

1834 Dom Pedro returns to Portugal to end civil war and installs his daughter as Queen Mary II.

1875–1876 Republican and Socialist parties founded.

1890 Planned land connection between colonies of Angola and Mozambique thwarted by the British.

1891 Republican uprising in Porto.

1908 Assassination of King Carlos I and heir to the throne.

1910 Abdication of Manuel II and proclamation of the Republic. Church and state separated.

1916 Portugal joins Allies in World War I.

1917–18 New Republic led by Sidónio Pais.

1926 Army overturns republic.

1928 António Salazar joins government as finance minister. Economy improves.

1932 Salazar prime minister.

1933 Promulgation of the constitution of the "New State," instituting right-wing dictatorship.

1936–1939 Salazar assists Franco in Spanish Civil War.

1939–1945 Portugal neutral during World War II, but lets UK use air bases in Azores.

1949 Founder member of NATO.

1955 Joins UN.

1961 India annexes Goa. Guerrilla warfare in Angola, Mozambique, and Guinea.

1970 Death of Salazar, incapacitated since 1968. Succeeded by Marcelo Caetano.

1971 Caetano attempts liberalization.

1974 Carnation Revolution – left-wing Armed Forces Movement overthrows Caetano in bloodless revolution.

1974–1975 Portuguese possessions in Africa attain independence. Some 750,000 Portuguese expatriates return to Portugal.

1975 Communist takeover foiled by moderates and Mário Soares' PS.

1975–1976 Indonesia seizes former Portuguese East Timor unopposed.

1976 General António Eanes elected president. Adoption of new constitution. Soares appointed prime minister.

1978 Period of non-party technocratic government instituted.

1980 Center-right wins elections. General Eanes reelected.

1982 Full civilian government formally restored.

1983 Soares becomes caretaker prime minister; PS is majority party.

1985 Anibal Cavaco Silva becomes prime minister. Minority PSD government.

1986 Soares elected president. Portugal joins EU, which funds major infrastructure and construction projects.

1987 Cavaco Silva wins absolute majority in parliament.

1991 Soares reelected president.

1995 PS wins elections; António Guterres becomes prime minister.

1996 Former PS leader Jorge Sampaio elected president.

1999 Portugal among first 11 EU countries to adopt euro. In general election ruling PS strengthens its position. December. Macao returned to China.

2001 Guterres resigns as prime minister.

2002 José Manuel Durão Barroso forms center-right coalition government.

2004 Hosts Euro 2004

Potosí Silver mine discovered by the Spanish in 1545, high in the Andes in present-day Bolivia. For 50 years it was the richest source of silver in the world and grew to become the largest city in the Americas. *p.281*

Potsdam Conference (Jul 17–Aug 2 1945) Allied conference of World War II held at Potsdam, Berlin. The conferees, including US President Harry Truman, British Prime Minister Winston Churchill or Clement Attlee, who became prime minister during the conference and Soviet Premier Joseph Stalin, discussed the substance and procedures of the peace settlements. The chief concerns of the three powers were the immediate administration of defeated Germany, the demarcation of the boundaries of Poland, the occupation of Austria, the definition of the Soviet Union's role in eastern Europe, the determination of reparations, and the further prosecution of the war against Japan.

pottery and ceramics
Invention of pottery *p.15*
Song ceramics *p.161*
Ming porcelain *p.245*
Transporting Chinese porcelain *p.266*
Chinese ceramics *p.312*
Iznik pottery *p.274*
Meissen porcelain *p.319*

Prague ⚔ of World War II (May 1945). Final reduction of German troops by Soviet forces in Central Europe.

Prague, Defenestrations of Prague has witnessed two historic defenestrations. In the first (1419) the magistrates of the king were thrown out of the windows of the town hall, which heralded the start of the Hussite Wars. The second (1618), when representatives of the Emperor were thrown from the windows of the Royal Palace, sparked off the Thirty Years' War.

Prague Spring Czechoslovakian reforms crushed by Soviet troops (1968). *See also* Dubcek, Alexander

Prambanan Site of spectacular group of 9th-century Hindu temples on Java. *p.146*

Preveza ⚔ of 1538. Defeat by the Ottomans of a combined Venetian and Spanish papal fleet.

Princeton ⚔ of American Revolutionary War (Jan 3 1777). British victory.

printing Originally a Chinese invention, printing was well advanced in China by the 9th century, the date of the oldest surviving printed book, the *Diamond Sutra*. The Chinese also invented movable type

(c. 1045), but this was not of great practical value as Chinese contains so many different characters. The use of movable metal type, introduced to Europe in the mid-15th century, was a far more influential invention, permitting fast, cheap diffusion of written information for the first time in history. *p.142, p.168, p.260*

Prohibition Era The prohibition of the sale or manufacture of alcohol in the US, from 1919–33. Added to the US Constitution as the 18th Amendment, enforced by the Volstead Act of 1919, and repealed via the 33rd Amendment in 1933. *p.399*

Protestantism The form of western Christianity which grew up following Martin Luther and his supporters' split from the Roman Catholic church in 1529. Protestants rejected the authority of the pope, and used the Bible (in a vernacular translation) as their principal source of spiritual authority. *See also* Reformation

Prussia (*Ger.* Preussen) Baltic region conquered by the Teutonic Knights in 1283. The original Prussians spoke a Baltic language, but the area was rapidly populated by German-speakers. With the demise of the Teutonic Knights in the 15th century, Prussia came under Polish rule, then passed to the Electors of Brandenburg in the 17th century. In 1701 Prussia became a kingdom, and in 1871 King Wilhelm I was crowned Kaiser of a united Germany. *See also* Germany, Brandenburg, Franco-Prussian War

Przhevalsky, Nikolai Mikhailovich (1839–88) Russian soldier and explorer of Central Asia. Collected large number of botanical and zoological specimens, including *Equus przevalskii*, the last breed of wild horse to be discovered.

Ptolemaic dynasty Dynasty of Macedonian kings founded by Alexander the Great's general Ptolemy I. After Alexander's death in 323 BCE the Ptolemies emerged as rulers of Egypt and the Hellenistic maritime empire in the Aegean and eastern Mediterranean.

Ptolemy (*var.* Lat. Claudius Ptolemaeus, c.90–168 CE) Greek astronomer and geographer of Alexandria, Egypt. Author of *The Geography*, he considered the earth the center of the universe.

Ptolemy I (*var.* Ptolemy Soter ("Saviour"), c.366–283 BCE) Ptolemy was one of Alexander the Great's generals, who ruled Egypt when the Macedonian Empire was dismantled after Alexander's death. In 304 he adopted a royal title and founded the Ptolemaic dynasty. An able military and administrative leader, he secured Palestine, Cyprus, and parts of Asia Minor.

Ptolemy V (reigned 205–180 BCE) King of ancient Egypt of the Ptolemaic dynasty. Under his rule Egypt lost all of Palestine and possessions in Asia Minor. Peace was gained by his marriage to Cleopatra, daughter of Antiochus III of Syria.

Publius Cornelius Scipio
see Scipio Africanus

pueblo American Indians living in New Mexico and Arizona who are descended from the Anasazi culture (*see* Anasazi). The term is also used to describe the settlements they built.

Pueblo Bonito Spectacular pueblo settlement in Chaco Canyon. *p.148*

PUERTO RICO A US territory since its invasion in 1898, Puerto Rico is the easternmost of the Greater Antilles chain in the Caribbean. The population density, highest around San Juan, is higher than in any US state. The tropical climate attracts growing numbers of tourists, 80 percent from the US, and there have been major efforts to expand hotel and resort facilities. Puerto Rico was granted its current commonwealth status in 1952, four years after an abortive pro-independence uprising. The inhabitants have US citizenship but only limited self-government. In 1967, 1993, and 1998, the islanders endorsed continued commonwealth status rather than opting for either US statehood or independence.

CHRONOLOGY

15th century Puerto Rico is discovered by Columbus and colonized by Spain.

1812–40 A struggle for administrative reform is suppressed by the Spaniards.

1868 An armed revolt against colonial rule leads to an unsuccessful proclamation of independence in Lares.

1897 Negotiations begin with Spain on limited autonomy.

1898 During the Spanish-American war US troops land in Puerto Rico; the island is ceded by Spain to the US, and assumes a key role in US global strategy.

1917 Puerto Ricans are granted US citizenship.

1947 Limited self-government is granted.

1948 Luis Marin becomes the first elected governor.

1952 Puerto Rico is granted commonwealth association with the US.

1967 A plebiscite on relations with the US results in a 60 percent vote for the continuation of autonomous commonwealth status.

1968 The pro-statehood New Progressive Party (NPP) under Carlos Romero Barcelo wins the governorship election.

1972 The Popular Democratic Party (PPD), which supports the enhancement of the present commonwealth status, gains control of both houses of the legislature.

1991 A referendum on the island's future relationship with the US results in a majority in favor of closer integration.

1992 Elections for the governorship result in the victory of Pedro Rossello, whose NPP (advocating US statehood rather than continuing commonwealth status) also wins legislative elections,.

1993 A non-binding referendum produces a result narrowly in favor of retaining commonwealth status.

2001 Pro-statehood Pedro Rossello eplaced by the anti-statehood Sila Calderón – the first female governor of Puerto Rico.

Punic Wars Three wars fought between Rome and Carthage for domination of the western Mediterranean. The first war (264–241 BCE) saw Rome build a navy powerful enough to compete with Carthage, but unable to conquer the Carthaginan homeland. In the second (218–201) Rome was threatened by the invasion of Italy by Hannibal, but fought back to impose a humiliating peace settlement on Carthage. The third (149–146) ended in the complete destruction of Carthage. *p.65*

Puranas Collection of encyclopedic works, rich in geographic content, belonging to the sacred texts of Hinduism, which record the Creation and the early history of humanity. The Puranas relate to the expansion of the Aryan tribes and their formation into small kingdoms and republics during the first millennium BCE.

Pydna ⚔ (168 BCE). Roman victory over Greece.

pyramid Structure not unique to the Egyptians – many Central and South American cultures built pyramids – but none can rival the Great Pyramid of Giza, built c.2540. *p.22*

Pytheas of Massalia (born c.300 BCE) Greek navigator and geographer. Probably traveled around coast of Britain and northern Europe. He was one of the first people to fix the position of places using latitudes.

Pythian games Pan-Hellenic festival held every four years in the Sanctuary of Apollo at Delphi. The name Pythios meaning "python slayer", was the name by which Apollo was known there.

Q

QATAR Projecting north from the Arabian peninsula into the Gulf, Qatar has land borders with Saudi Arabia and the United Arab Emirates, and a sea border with Bahrain. Most of the country is flat, semi-arid desert. Qatar is a founder member of OPEC, and plentiful oil and natural gas reserves make it one of the wealthiest states in the region. The country enjoys political stability under the al-Thani clan, related to the Khalifa family of Bahrain. Their rule dates back to the 18th century.

CHRONOLOGY

1971 Independence from the UK.
1972 Accession of Amir Khalifa.
1995 Shaikh Hamad overthrows Shaikh Khalifa.
1999 First ever polls, to elect new municipal council.

Qi dynasty (*var.* Ch'i) One of the southern dynasties of China (420–589).

Qin dynasty (*var.* Ch'in dynasty) Ruling dynasty of China (221–206 BCE), founded by King Zheng, later the self-styled First Emperor (Shi Huangdi, 259–210 CE, reigned 247–210 CE) who ruled from Xianyang and from 230 unified China, imposing territorial reorganization,

central bureaucracy, built first Great Wall, proscribed books and introduced universal weights and measures.

Qin empire *see* Qin dynasty

Qing dynasty (*var.* Ching, *aka* Manchu dynasty, 1644–1911) Ruling dynasty of China established by the Manchus. By the 19th century China controlled vast territories in inner Asia, treating as tributary states Korea, Indochina, Siam, Burma, and Nepal.

Qing empire *see* Qing dynasty

Quebec ⚔ of American Revolutionary War (Dec 30–31 1775). French victory.

Quebec ⚔ of Seven Years' War in N America (1759). British victory over France. Britain subsequently gained control over much of N America.

Quetzalcoatl The serpent god of both the Toltec and Aztec civilizations. The symbol of death and resurrection, he was also known as the patron of priests, inventor of books and calendars.

Quexos, Pedro de 16th-century Spanish explorer of N America (1521).

Quirós, Pedro Fernandez de (c.1560–1614) Spanish explorer of the Pacific. After serving on several trans-Pacific sailings, in 1605 he realized his ambition of mounting an expedition of his own to find the mythical "Great South Land." He discovered a number of small islands, including Espiritu Santo, the principal island of Vanuatu, which he announced was the east coast of the Terra Australis Incognita.

Qutb ud-Din Aibak (*var.* Aybeg) General of Muhammad al Ghur; founded the Delhi Sultanate in 1206.

R

Ra In ancient Egyptian religion, the sun god, one of the most important gods of ancient Egypt. Early Egyptian kings alleged descent from Ra. Ra had several manifestations, the most common being the hawk and the lion.

Radio The growth in radio listening in the 1920s and 1930s. *p.400*

Radisson, Pierre-Esprit (c.1636–1710) Fur-trader and explorer. Established Fort Nelson in Hudson Bay, (his brother-in-law, Groseilliers had previously

established Fort Rupert). Their efforts led effectively to the founding of the Hudson's Bay Company in 1670.

Raffles, Sir Thomas Stamford (1760–1841) The founder of Singapore. In 1819, in his capacity as Lieutenant-Governor of Benkulen (the East India Company's principal station in Sumatra) he persuaded the sultan of Johore to cede the uninhabited island to him. It was incorporated into the British colony of the Straits Settlement in 1826. *p.351*

railroads The first passenger railroad was the Stockton-Darlington line in northern England, opened in 1825.
US railroads. *p.377*
Trans-Siberian Railroad. *p.381*

Railroad Act (1866) Act passed by US Congress allowing Railroad Companies to take over Indian lands in the west.

rainforest The destruction of the world's rainforests in the late 20th century. *p.446*

Rajaraja the Great (reigned 985–1014) King who extended Chola control into the eastern Deccan, Ceylon, and the Malay Peninsula. By the time he died, he was the paramount ruler of southern India.

Rajendra I (reigned 1014–44) King of the Chola dynasty of southern India. Under his rule the Chola navy took control of the eastern sea route between Arabia and China and conquered Ceylon (1018). He ruled from the city of Tanjore.

Rajput clans People of Rajputana, N India. Defeated in 1191 by the Afghan leader Muhammad of Ghur.

Raleigh, Sir Walter (c.1554–1618) English adventurer. He found favor under Elizabeth I and named the colony he founded at Roanoke Island in 1584 Virginia after the "virgin queen." Fell out of favor with Elizabeth and under James I was imprisoned. Released in 1616 to undertake a voyage to Guiana in search of El Dorado. This ended in disaster and Raleigh was executed on his return to England.

Ramayana Classical Sanskrit epic of India relating the adventures of Rama, probably composed in the 3rd century BCE. Based on numerous legends, the epic was revised and set down in its best-known form by the poet Tulsi Das (1532–1623).

Ramesses III *see* Ramses III

Ramses III (*var.* Ramesses, reigned c.1184–53 BCE) Second king of the 20th dynasty of Egypt. Went to war with the Philistines and the "Sea Peoples."

Rapa Nui *see* Easter Island

Rashtrakutas Kingdom established in 753 CE in the northern Deccan. At its peak, Rashtrakuta control extended from southern Gujarat to Tanjore.

Ravenna Capital of Italy under the Ostrogoths and Byzantines. It was captured by the Lombards in 752, but they were subsequently driven out by the Franks.

Reagan, Ronald Wilson (1911–) 40th president of the United States (1981–89). A former movie actor, Reagan cooperated with efforts to combat alleged Communist influences in the American film industry. He was governor of California from 1967–74. In 1980 he won the Presidential elections in a landslide victory. During his tenure he introduced the controversial SDI (Strategic Defense Initiative) and signed the INF treaty with the Soviet Union which limited intermediate range missiles. His administration was damaged by revelations that profits from arms deals with Iran had been used to support the Contra rebels against the Sandinista government of Nicaragua.

Recceswinth Seventh-century Visigothic ruler of Spain. His crown is a magnificent example of Visigothic jewelry. *p.127*

Reconquest (*var. Sp.* Reconquista) The reconquest of Muslim Spain by the Christian states, from the 11th to the 15th century.

Reconquista *see* Reconquest

Reconstruction (1865–77) Period following the US Civil War in which the southern states were controlled by a Federal government which introduced new social legislation, including new rights for Blacks.

Red River Indian War (1874–75) Major uprising by members of the Arapaho, Cheyenne, Comanche, Kiowa, and Kataka tribes from reservations in Oklahoma and Texas against white settlers in the area. US forces led by General William Sherman were forced to fight 14 battles against the Indians in the Red River Valley, before their eventual surrender.

Red Scare Name given to the fear of Communist subversion in the US which arose in the late 1940s, leading to the setting up of schemes such as the Federal Employee Loyalty Program, and Senator Joseph McCarthy's list of government employees whom he claimed had Soviet sympathies. The scare led to a significant degree of persecution (the McCarthy Witchhunt) of those suspected of Communist sympathies, and many people – especially in the government, schools, universities, and the mass media – found themselves unable to work because of their suspected beliefs.

reducciones Jesuit frontier settlements in Spanish S America.

Reformation Religious revolution of the 16th century which took place in the Roman Catholic church, led by Martin Luther and John Calvin. The Reformation had long-term political, economic, and social effects, and laid the groundwork for the foundation of Protestantism. *p.275* *See also* Martin Luther, John Calvin, Counter-Reformation

Religious orders New religious orders of the Counter-Reformation. *p.279* *See also* Jesuits

Remojadas Early Mexican civilization (c.600–900 CE).

Renaissance (*var.* Renascence, c.1300–1550) Period of cultural, economic, and political revival in medieval Europe, characterized by the rediscovery of classical Greek and Roman culture, which found expression, initially in Italy, in the growth of Humanist studies and writing, and in a revitalization of architecture, painting, sculpture, and the arts in general. *p.272*

Renascence *see* Renaissance

Rennell, James (1742–1830) British naval officer who became the Surveyor-General of Bengal in 1764. He was responsible for the first consistent mapping of the Indian subcontinent, the *Survey of India*.

Republican Party One of the two major political parties of the US. Formed in 1854 to support anti-slavery policies prior to the Civil War, Abraham Lincoln was its first president. Today, it favors limited government and interventionist foreign policy and is considered to be more right-wing than the Democratic Party.

Réunions Lands occupied by France during the reign of Louis XIV following the decisions of a special court convened for the purpose, the Chambre des Réunions. Important annexations included Luxembourg (1679) and Strasbourg (1684). Most of the territories had to be returned by the Treaty of Ryswijk (1697).

Revolutions, Year of (1848) Year in which the old political order of Europe established at the Congress of Vienna in 1815 was challenged throughout much of Italy, Germany, Central Europe, and France. *p.362*

Rhodes, Cecil (1853–1902) Financier, statesman, and empire builder of British South Africa. He was prime minister of Cape Colony (1890–96) and founder of the diamond mining company De Beers Consolidated Mines Limited (1888). *p.377*

Rhodesia British colony named after Cecil Rhodes. Southern Rhodesia was a self-governing colony from 1922, while northern Rhodesia was a British Protectorate. The two were joined along with Nyasaland to form the Federation of Rhodesia and Nyasaland. Northern Rhodesia was granted independence as Zambia in 1963, but southern Rhodesia refused to hand over political power to the black majority and declared UDI (Unilateral Declaration of Independence). Minority rule continued until 1980 when the country became Zimbabwe. *See also* Zimbabwe; Zambia

Ri dynasty *see* Yi dynasty

Ricci, Matteo (1552–1610) Italian Jesuit missionary and cartographer. Joined Jesuit mission in Macao in 1582, and then established mission on Chinese territory, eventually settling in Beijing in 1601. His maps and other data, gave the Western world unprecedented access to information about China.

Richard I of England (*aka* Richard the Lion-Heart, Lion-Hearted, *Fr.* Richard Coeur de Lion, 1157–1199) Duke of Aquitaine from 1168 and of Poitiers from 1172 and King of England, Duke of Normandy, and Count of Anjou (reigned 1189–99). His prowess in the Third Crusade (1189–92) made him a popular king in his own time.

Richard II (1367–1400) King of England (reigned 1377–99). Son of Edward the Black Prince. Deposed in 1399 by his cousin, Henry of Lancaster, later crowned Henry IV. He died in prison, possibly murdered.

Richelieu, Cardinal (Armand Jean du Plessis, 1585–1642) Chief minister of Louis XIII with whom he collaborated to make France a leading European power.

Riel Rebellions (1869, 1885) Rebellions by the Metis (mixed-blood descendants of Cree Indians and French fur traders) and their Indian allies against incursions of European settlers into their lands.

Rig Veda Completed c.900 BCE, this is the great literary monument of Aryan settlers of the Punjab. A collection of sacred hymns, it traces the religious development of Aryan India and depicts the Aryan settlers as chariot-driving warriors who gradually adapt to a more sedentary life. It is rich in geographical references.

Rio de Janeiro Rio replaced Bahia as Brazilian capital in 1763, but was in turn replaced by Brasilia in 1960. *See also* Brazil

Río de la Plata Spanish viceroyalty established in 1776. *See also* Argentina

Robert I "the Bruce" (1274–1329) King of Scotland (reigned 1306–29). Defeated the English at the battle of Bannockburn (1314). English acknowledgement of Scottish independence and Robert's right to the throne came in 1328.

Robert of Normandy (c.1054–1134) Duke of Normandy (reigned 1087–1106). Eldest son of William I of England. Inherited Normandy upon the death of his father. Took part in the First Crusade (1096–1100).

Robespierre, Maximilien François Marie-Isidore de (1758–94) French revolutionary and Jacobin leader, who had a key role in the overthrow of the Girondins. A member of the Committee for Public Safety which instituted the Reign of Terror (1793–4). Overthrown by the Convention, he was tried and guillotined. *See also* French Revolution, Jacobins, Terror, Reign of

rock art The oldest known art form, dating back to c.30,000 BCE in W Europe, usually depicting hunting scenes, and found in caves or, commonly in African examples, rock shelters and exposed rock faces. The images are either painted or etched into the rock surface, and are not purely decorative: some occur in recesses so difficult to access that they are thought to have played a part in ritual activities. Rock art is more abundant in the Saharan region than anywhere else in the world.

rock 'n' roll The evolution of popular music in the 1950s and 1960s. *p.432*

Rococo Architectural style of the 18th century: a light, playful development of the Baroque. *p.331*

Roerich, Nicolas (1874–1947) Russian traveler and painter in Central Asia.

Roger II of Sicily (1095–1154, reigned 1101–54) First Norman king of Sicily whose court at Palermo was a meeting place for Christian and Arab scholars. Commissioned the *Book of Roger*, a medieval book of maps. *p.186*

Roggeveen, Jacob (1659–1729) Dutch explorer. His voyage across the Pacific in 1722 established the first European contact with a number of islands, including Easter Island and Samoa.

Roman Catholic Church The largest and most powerful branch of the Christian church, governed by the proclamations of the pope in Rome. The once extensive territory governed by the pope has shrunk to the Vatican City, a tiny walled enclave within the City of Rome, but still independent. The church claims that the popes represent an unbroken line of apostolic succession from St. Peter, supposedly martyred in Rome in the reign of Nero, to the present day. *See also* Vatican City, Papacy

---

ROMAN EMPIRE The largest empire ever established in Europe, stretching from northern Britain to Egypt. From its apogee in the 2nd century ce, the Empire became increasingly difficult to govern and in 395, it was divided into two. The Western Empire fell in 476 to successive waves of Germanic invaders, but the East Roman (or Byzantine) Empire, with its capital at Constantinople, survived until 1453.
Early Rome. *p.44*
Roman roads. *p.61*
Roman revolts. *p.69*
Roman conquests (250–50 BCE). *p.70*
Luxury in Rome. *p.72*
Roman surveying. *p.75*
Roman literature. *p.83*
Roman conquests (50 BCE–117 CE). *p.84*
The Roman imprint. *p.88*
Roman emperors. *p.89*
Imperial Rome. *p.93*
Roman buildings. *p.95*
See also Rome, Byzantine Empire

ROMAN EMPERORS

27 BCE–14 CE	Augustus (Gaius Julius Caesar Octavianus)
14–37	Tiberius (Tiberius Claudius Nero Caesar)
37–41	Caligula (Gaius Claudius Nero Caesar Germanicus)
41–54	Claudius (Tiberius Claudius Nero Caesar Drusus)
54–68	Nero (Lucius Domitius Ahenobarbus Claudius Drusus)
68–69	Galba (Servius Sulpicius Galba)
69	Otho (Marcus Salvius Otho)
69	Vitellius (Aulus Vitellius Germanicus)
69–79	Vespasian (Titus Flavius Vespasianus)
79–81	Titus (Titus Flavius Vespasianus)
81–96	Domitian (Titus Flavius Domitianus)
96–98	Nerva (Marcus Cocceius Nerva)
98–117	Trajan (Marcus Ulpius Nerva Traianus)
117–138	Hadrian (Publius Aelius Traianus Hadrianus)
138–161	Antoninus Pius (Titus Aurelius Fulvius Boionius Arrius Antoninus Pius)
161(147)–180	Marcus Aurelius (Marcus Annius Aurelius Verus)
161–169	Lucius Aurelius Verus (Lucius Ceionius Commodus Verus)
180(172)–192	Commodus (Lucius Aelius Marcus Aurelius Antoninus Commodus)
193	Pertinax (Publius Helvius Pertinax)
193	Didius Julian (Marcus Didius Salvius Julianus Severus)
193–211	Septimius Severus (Lucius Septimius Severus)
211(198)–217	Caracalla (Marcus Aurelius Antoninus Bassianus Caracallus)
209–211	Geta (Publius Septimius Geta)
217–218	Macrinus (Marcus Opellius Severus Macrinus)
218–222	Elagabulus (Marcus Varius Avitus Bassianus Aurelius Antoninus Heliogabalus)
222–235	Alexander Severus (Marcus Alexianus Bassianus Aurelius Severus Alexander)
235–238	Maximin (Gaius Julius Verus Maximinus "Thrax")
237–238	Gordian I (Marcus Antonius Gordianus)
238	Pupienus (Marcus Clodius Pupienus Maximus)
238	Balbinus (Decimus Caelius Balbinus)
238–244	Gordian III (Marcus Antonius Gordianus)
244–249	Philipp the Arab (Marcus Julius Philippus "Arabus")
249–251	Decius (Gaius Messius Quintus Traianus Decius)
251–253	Gallus (Gaius Vibius Trebonianus Gallus)
252–253	Aemilian (Marcus Julius Aemilius Aemilianus)
253–259	Valerian (Gaius Publius Licinius Valerianus)

259(255)–268	Gallien (Publius Licinius Egnatius Gallienus)
268–270	Claudius II (Marcus Aurelius Claudius Gothicus)
270–275	Aurelian (Lucius Domitius Aurelianus)
275–276	Tacitus (Marcus Claudius Tacitus)
276–282	Probus (Marcus Aurelius Probus)
281–283	Carus (Marcus Aurelius Carus)
284–305	Diocletian (Gaius Aurelius Valerius Diocles Jovius)
286–305	Maximian (Marcus Aurelius Valerius Maximianus Herculius)
305(293)–306	Constantius I (Flavius Valerius Constantius Chlorus)
305(293)–311	Galerius (Gaius Galerius Valerius Maximianus)
306–307	Severus (Flavius Valerius Severus)
306–312	Maxentius (Marcus Aurelius Valerius Maxentius)
311(307)–324	Licinius (Gaius Flavius Valerius Licinianus Licinius)
311(306)–337	Constantine I the Great (Flavius Valerius Constantinus)
337–340	Constantine II (Flavius Valerius Claudius Constantinus)
337–361	Constantius II (Flavius Valerius Julius Constantius)
337–350	Constans (Flavius Valerius Julius Constans)
361–363	Julian the Apostate (Flavius Claudius Julianus)
363–364	Jovian (Flavius Jovianus)
364–375	Valentinian I (Flavius Valentinianus, in the West)
364–378	Valens (in the East)
375(367)–383	Gratian (Flavius Gratianus Augustus, in the West)
375–392	Valentinian II (Flavius Valentinianus, in the West)
379–395	Theodosius the Great (Flavius Theodosius, in the East, and, after 392, in the West)
383–388	Maximus (Magnus Clemens Maximus)
392–394	Eugenius
395(383)–408	Arcadius (in the East)
395(393)–423	Honorius (Flavius Honorius, in the West)
408(402)–450	Theodosius II (in the East)
425–454	Valentinian III (Flavius Placidius Valentinianus, in the West)
450–457	Marcian (Marcianus, in the East)
455	Petronius (Flavius Ancius Petronius Maximus, in the West)
455–457	Avitus (Flavius Maecilius Eparchus Avitus, in the West)
457–461	Majorian (Julius Valerius Maioranus, in the West)
457–474	Leo I (Leo Thrax, Magnus, in the East)
461–465	Severus (Libius Severianus Severus, in the West)
467–472	Anthemius (Procopius Anthemius, in the West)
472	Olybrius (Anicius Olybrius, in the West)
473–474	Glycerius (in the West)
473–475	Julius Nepos (in the West)
473–474	Leo II (in the East)
474–491	Zeno (in the East)
475–476	Romulus Augustulus (Flavius Momyllus Romulus Augustus, in the West)

ROMANIA

ROMANIA Romania lies on the Black Sea coast, with the Danube as its southern border. The Carpathian Mountains curve around the upland basin of Transylvania. Long dominated by the Ottoman, Russian, and Habsburg empires, Romania became an independent monarchy in 1878. After World War II, this was supplanted by a communist People's Republic, headed from 1965 by Nicolae Ceaucescu. A coup in 1989 resulted in his execution and a limited democracy under Ion Iliescu. Although defeated in elections in 1996, Iliescu was returned to office in 2000.

CHRONOLOGY

106 CE The Roman Emperor Trajan conquers the area now forming Romania, and establishes the province of Dacia. Roman rule lasts until 272. The Latin-derived language and the country's name are hallmarks of Roman influence.

7th–11th century, Invasions first of Slavs and later of Magyars, who occupy and settle in Transylvania.

11th–15th century Hungary conquers Transylvania. Separate Romanian principalities emerge in Wallachia and Moldavia but are conquered by the Turks; Wallachia pays tribute to the Ottomans from 1396, Moldavia from 1456, and Transylvania from 1526.

1699 Habsburgs win control of Transylvania under Treaty of Karlowitz. Wallachia and Moldavia remain vassals of the Turks.

1848 Demands from the various Romanian provinces for independence are swiftly crushed by the imperial authorities.

1858 The Paris Convention, after the Crimean War, recognizes Wallachia's and Moldavia's independence within the Ottoman Empire; the notion of Romanian unity and independence gains strength.

1859 Unification of Moldova and Wallachia forms basis of future Romania.

1878 Independence, but at cost of losing Bessarabia to Russia.

1916–1918 Enters World War I on the Allied side. Gains substantial territory at end of war, including Transylvania from Hungary.

1924 Communists banned in unstable political arena. Rise of fascist "Iron Guard."

1938 King Carol establishes royal autocracy.

1940 Territory forcibly ceded to Soviet Union, Bulgaria, and Hungary. Coup by Iron Guard. King Carol abdicates in favor of son, Michael. Tripartite Pact with Germany. Enters war on Axis side, hoping to recover Bessarabia.

1944 Romania switches sides as Soviet troops reach border.

1945 Soviet-backed regime installed. Romanian Communist Party plays an increasing role.

1946 Romania regains Transylvania. Bessarabia goes to Soviet Union, which also demands huge reparations. Communist-led National Democratic Front wins majority in disputed elections.

1947 Michael forced to abdicate.

1948–1953 Centrally planned economy put in place.

1953 Leaders of Jewish community prosecuted for Zionism.

1958 Soviet troops withdraw.

1964 Prime Minister Gheorghiu-Dej declares national sovereignty. Proposes joint planning by all communist countries to lessen Soviet economic control.

1965 Ceaucescu becomes party secretary after death of Gheorghiu-Dej.

1968–1980 Ceaucescu condemns Soviet invasion of Czechoslovakia; courts US and European Community.

1982 Ceaucescu vows to pay foreign debt.

1989 Demonstrations; many killed by military. Armed forces join with opposition in National Salvation Front (NSF) to form government. Ion Iliescu declared president. Ceaucescu summarily tried and shot.

1990 NSF election victory. Political prisoners freed but many later reinterned.

1991 New constitution, providing for market reform, approved.

1992 Second free elections. NSF splits into factions. Nicolae Vacaroiu forms minority government.

1994 General strike demands faster economic reform.

1996 Reconciliation treaty with Hungary. Center-right wins elections; Emil Constantinescu president.

1997 Treaty recognizes Ukraine's sovereignty over territory ruled by Romania in 1919–1940.

1998 Coalition differences; prime minister Victor Ciorbea resigns.

2000 Ion Iliescu and PDSR win elections.

2004 Joins NATO.

Romanticism Artistic movement of the late 18th and early 19th century. *p.346*

Rome Rome began as a small city-state which, through military might combined with skilful use of threats and alliances, conquered first the Italian peninsula, then, by the 1st century BCE, the entire Mediterranean world. Rome's importance declined from the 4th century CE. From the 7th century, it regained prestige as the seat of the pope and headquarters of the Roman Catholic Church. It was ruled by the Papacy until it became the capital of the newly-united kingdom of Italy in 1871. *See also* Roman Empire

Rome, Treaty of *see* European Union

Romulus Augustus Roman Emperor, deposed (476.)

Roosevelt, Franklin Delano (*aka* FDR, 1882–1945) 32nd President of the US (Democrat, 1932–45). Roosevelt became president in 1932, on the cusp of the worst years of the Great Depression. He immediately launched a series of reforms collectively known as the "New Deal" to combat the depression; these included the abandonment of the gold standard and agricultural price support, as well as programs such as the Works Progress Administration, aimed at providing work for the unemployed and the creation of a Social Security Act. His "common touch" and immense personal popularity saw him elected for an unprecedented four terms. Though initially opposed to involvement in conflict in Europe, by the outbreak of World War II, he broke with neutrality to support the Allied position, bringing the US fully into the war following the bombing of Pearl Harbor in Dec 1941.

Roosevelt, Theodore (Teddy, 1858–1919) 26th President of the US. Republican. (1901–09). After commanding the "Roughriders" in the Spanish-American War (1898), Roosevelt returned as Governor of New York from 1898–1900, and was subsequently elected Vice-President. He became president following the assassination of William McKinley. He initiated the building of the Panama Canal, strengthened the US navy, and won the Nobel Peace Prize in 1906 for his part in ending the Russo-Japanese war. He formed a "progressive" movement in the Republican party but was defeated on the Progressive ticket in the elections of 1910.

Rosas, Juan Manuel de (1793–1877) Argentinian dictator. Although his official title was only Governor of Buenos Aires province, Rosas was the effective ruler of Argentina from 1829–52. He owed his position to his loyal force of gauchos, and his wars of conquest against the Patagonian Indians.

Rosebloom, Johannes 17th-century explorer in N America. Employed by Governor Thomas Dongan to discover new fur trade routes. Reached Michilimackinac between Lakes Huron and Michigan in 1685 after traveling for three months.

Rosenberg, Ethel and Julius (1915–53; 1918–53) American communists and part of a transatlantic spy ring. Convicted of passing on atomic secrets to the Soviet Union and executed. They were the first US citizens to be executed for espionage.

Roses, Wars of the (1452–85) Bloody civil war between two noble houses – York and Lancaster – contending for the English throne. The last king of the House of York, Richard III, was defeated and killed at Bosworth Field in 1485. *p.265*

Rosetta stone Basalt slab inscribed by priests of Ptolemy V of Egypt in hieroglyphic, demotic and Greek. Found near the city of Rosetta in Egypt in 1799 and taken by the British in 1801; now in the British Museum in London. Served as the key to understanding Egyptian hieroglyphic. *p.66*

Ross, Sir James Clark (1800–62) British naval officer and explorer of the Poles. Accompanied both Edward Parry and his uncle John Ross on expeditions in the Arctic. In 1839–43 he led the navy's first major Antarctic expedition. He discovered the Ross Sea, the Ross Ice Shelf, Ross Island and Victoria Land.

Rousseau, Jean Jacques (1712–78) French philosopher and writer. Believed in the original goodness of human nature and that it was society that created inequality and misery. His most famous work, *Du Contrat Social* (1762), profoundly influenced French revolutionary thought.

Royal Road Road constructed under the Persian Achaemenid Empire in the 6th century BCE from Susa, the ancient capital of Persia, to Sardis, on the Aegean Sea.

Rozwi empire Empire of southern Africa (c.1684–early 19th-century).

Ruanruan (*var.* Juan-juan, Avars). Nomadic steppe peoples whose expulsion from Mongolia by the Blue (Celestial) Turks in the 4th century CE impelled them westwards, entering Europe in the mid-6th century. *See also* Avars

Rub' al Khali (*var.* the "Empty Quarter") Area of waterless desert covering some 777,000 sq km (3,000,000 sq miles) of the southern Arabian peninsula.

Rudolf I (1218–91) Count of Habsburg and Holy Roman Emperor. The first Habsburg to be elected Emperor, Rudolf secured Austria as the center of the Habsburg domains through his defeat of Ottokar II of Bohemia in 1278.

Ruhr valley Center of the German steel industry in 19th and 20th centuries. *p.373*

Rukh (1377–1447) Mongol shah, son of Timur.

Rum Seljuk sultanate in Anatolia in the 12th and 13th centuries, with its capital at Konya (Iconium). Its name is derived from Rome, because its lands had been captured from the Byzantine (East Roman) Empire.

Rurik the Viking (reigned c.862–79) Semi-legendary Swedish ruler of the merchant town of Novgorod, seen as the founder of the Russian state (named after "Rus," the Finnish word for Swede).

RUSSIA (Russian Federation) Russia's territory extends over 17 million sq km (6.6 million sq miles). This makes it by far the world's largest state, almost twice as big as either the US or China. Bounded by the Arctic and Pacific Oceans on its northern and eastern coasts, it also has land boundaries with 13 countries. The present-day state has it origins in the rise of Muscovy in 16th century under Ivan IV, who defeated the Tatars and united neighboring principalities, proclaiming himself czar. Russia consolidated its power in eastern Europe and expanded beyond the Urals in 17th century (notably under Peter the Great), to dominate northern and central Asia by the 18th century. Czarist rule was toppled by Bolshevik (Communist) revolution in 1917. With the formal dissolution of the USSR in 1991, Russia became an independent sovereign state. Within the CIS, it maintains a traditionally dominant role in central Asia and Eurasia. Ethnic Russians make up 82 percent of the population, but there are around 150 smaller ethnic groups, many with their own national territories within Russia's borders. Regionalism and separatism are major political issues. The situation is complicated by the fact that many of these territories are rich in key resources such as oil, gas, gold, and diamonds. *See also* USSR

CHRONOLOGY

862 Rurik the Viking establishes order among quarrelling Slav tribes in Novgorod. Varangians (the Swedish Vikings) use the Dnieper river to trade with Constantinople.

882 Oleg, Rurik's successor, occupies Kiev, and further descendants of Rurik unite the Kievan and Novgorod states.

988 Prince Vladimir is baptized and converts the Kievan lands (Rus) to Eastern Orthodox Christianity. He marries Anne, sister of the Byzantine Emperor Basil II.

1240 The Mongols (Tatars) conquer Rus, and rule for nearly 250 years. The polity of Rus, centered on Kiev, has disintegrated since its golden age under Prince Yaroslav the Wise into quarrelling princedoms.

1328 The Tatar Khan gives Ivan Kalita, prince of Moscow, the right of seniority over the other Russian princes and Moscow

emerges as the most powerful Russian princedom. In 1326 the Metropolitan of Russia moves his seat to Moscow, after residing in Vladimir since the fall of Kiev.

1453 Constantinople, the center of eastern Christianity, falls to the Turks. Moscow comes to regard itself as Constantinople's successor, "the third Rome," to emphasize which Ivan III of Muscovy marries the niece of the last Byzantine Emperor and calls himself Czar (a corruption of the Latin Caesar). When Novgorod falls to Moscow in 1471, the Russian princedoms are united.

1480 Ivan ceases to pay tribute to Tatars.

1533 Ivan Grozny (Ivan IV "the Terrible"), grandson of Ivan III, ascends to the throne aged three. His reign effectively begins in 1547, when he becomes the first ruler to be crowned Czar. He conquers the Khanate of Kazan in 1552 and of Astrakhan in 1554. The second half of his rule is marked by repression of the boyars (noblemen), many of whom he executes for treason.

1598 Election of Boris Godunov, brother-in-law of Fedor I, Ivan's son, as czar. On his death in 1605, the "Time of Troubles" begins – a turbulent period, the result of a lack of a natural successor to the throne, a rise in social discontent, and war in Russia sparked by Swedish and Polish aggression.

1613 Mikhail Romanov, first of the dynasty which will rule until 1917, is elected czar after the Poles are driven out of Moscow. He is succeeded in 1645 by his son Alexis.

1689 Peter I (Peter the Great) becomes czar, after a confused period of palace coups and struggles for the succession. Peter introduces, sometimes by force, western culture, customs, education, economy, and government to Russia. In 1703 he founds St. Petersburg, which in 1712 becomes the Russian capital. War with Sweden prompts Peter to create Russia's first navy and its first modern army. He dies in 1725, having had his son executed and established the right of the sovereign to leave the throne to whomever he or she wishes. Palace coups establish and terminate the next eight reigns until 1801.

1762 The German-born Catherine II (Catherine the Great) becomes empress after leading a palace coup against her husband, Peter III. Her reign extends Russian territory at the expense of Poland and Turkey, and although initially the ideas of the Enlightenment are welcomed

in the Russian state, they are curtailed by the French Revolution of 1789. Catherine dies in 1796.

1773 The Don Cossack Emelian Pugachev leads rebellion against the injustices of the Russian feudal system, takes control of a large part of eastern Russia and threatens Moscow, before being defeated in 1774.

1812 Napoleon invades Russia and within three months has entered Moscow, but the same night a terrible fire razes the city. Czar Alexander I, Catherine's grandson, who acceded in 1801 on the murder of his father Paul I, refuses to surrender; the French, cut off from their supply lines, are forced to retreat through the Russian winter, pursued by the Russian army.

1814 Alexander I leads Russian, Austrian, and Prussian armies into Paris. The Congress of Vienna of 1815 redraws the political map of Europe, establishing Russia as a major force in European affairs. Anti-autocratic ideas gain currency among the young nobility during the military campaigns in the west.

1825 On Alexander's unexpected death, young army officers (the "Decembrists") stage a revolt in favor of the abolition of serfdom and constitutional reform, including a constitutional monarchy. The uprising is suppressed and the new czar, Alexander's brother, Nicholas I, begins a 30-year reign of reactionary policies, characterized by militarism and bureaucracy, which earns him the soubriquet "the gendarme of Europe."

1848 Revolutions elsewhere in Europe prompt Nicholas to impose new censorship, new restrictions on academic freedom in Russia's universities and a prohibition on foreign travel.

1854–55 The Crimean war against Turkey, France and Britain ends in humiliating defeat for Russia. Nicholas dies in March 1855 and is succeeded by his son, Alexander II.

1861 Alexander orders the emancipation of the serfs and begins a period of reform of local government (creating the zemstva or rural councils), the judiciary. and financial institutions, although the reforms are limited by remaining within an autocratic framework.

1860 Russian revolutionary movements emerge, including the influential Narodniki (Populists), who preach that intellectuals could inspire "the people" with revolutionary ideas because the peasantry embody socialism in their communally arranged households. However, in 1874–77 the failure of a Populists' crusade to win the hearts of Russia's peasants leads some factions to turn to terrorism.

1881 Alexander II is assassinated by the terrorist group Narodnaya Volya (The People's Will), an offshoot of the Populist movement. Alexander III establishes a period of reaction, Russification and militant Orthodoxy. Pogroms against Jewish communities begin.

1894 The last Russian czar, Nicholas II, accedes to the throne. In the 1890s, Russian industry grows by an average of 8 percent a year, creating a significant and highly localized working class, for which the social infrastructure is inadequate. Marxism begins to attract considerable strength among intellectuals and radicals.

1904–1905 Russian war against Japan; ends in defeat for Russia.

1905 Revolution.

1909–1914 Rapid economic expansion.

1914 Enters World War I against Germany.

1917 February Revolution; abdication of Nicholas II. October Revolution; Bolsheviks take over with Lenin as leader.

1918 July. Nicholas II and family shot.

1918–1920 Civil war.

1922 USSR established.

1924 Lenin dies. Leadership struggle eventually won by Stalin.

1928 First Five-Year Plan: forced industrialization and collectivization.

1929 Trotsky deported.

1936–1938 Show trials and campaigns against actual and suspected members of opposition. Millions sent to gulags in Siberia and elsewhere. Purges widespread.

1939 Hitler-Stalin pact gives USSR Baltic states, eastern Poland, and Bessarabia.

1941 Germany attacks USSR and armies advance rapidly. Stalin unprepared.

1943 February. Great Soviet victory at Stalingrad halts Germans. Besieged German army surrenders.

1944–1945 Soviet offensive penetrates Balkans.

1945 Germany defeated. Eastern and southeastern Europe become Soviet zone of influence.

1947 Stalin on defensive and fears penetration of Western capitalist values.

1953 Stalin dies.

1957 Krushchev consolidates power. Sputnik launched.

1961 Yuri Gagarin first man in space.

1962 Cuban missile crisis.

1964 Krushchev ousted in coup, replaced by Leonid Brezhnev.

1975 Helsinki Final Act; confirms European frontiers as at end of World War II. Soviets agree human rights are concern of international community.

1979 Invades Afghanistan. Beginning of new intensification of Cold War.

1982 Brezhnev dies.

1985 Gorbachev in power. Start of perestroika, "restructuring." First of three US-USSR summits resulting in arms reduction. Nationality conflicts surface.

1988 Law of State Enterprises gives more power to enterprises; inflation and dislocation of economy.

1990 Gorbachev becomes Soviet president. First partly freely elected parliament.

1991 Boris Yeltsin elected president of Russia. Yeltsin and Muscovites resist hard-line communist coup. Gorbachev sidelined. CIS established; demise of USSR.

1992 Economic shock therapy.

1993 Yeltsin decrees dissolution of Supreme Soviet and uses force to disband parliament. Elections return conservative state Duma (parliament).

1994 Russian military offensive against Chechnya.

1995 Communists win elections.

1996 Yeltsin reelected despite strong communist challenge; undergoes extensive heart surgery. Peace accord in Chechnya.

1998 Economic turmoil forces devaluation of rouble. Severe recession, rampant inflation.

1998–1999 Yeltsin repeatedly changes prime minister in a succession of crises.

1999 December. Parliamentary elections; Yeltsin resigns; Prime Minister Putin is acting president.

1999–2000 Terrorist violence blamed on Islamic separatists in Dagestan and Chechnya. Offensive against Chechnya; fall of capital Grozny to Russian forces.

2000 Putin wins presidential election, consolidates power. Attack on "oligarchs" in big business. Improvement in the Russian economy. Kursk nuclear submarine disaster. Submarine sinks in the Barents Sea with loss of entire crew.

2001 Party mergers make Putin's Unity Party the largest grouping in parliament.

2002 Agreement with US on strategic nuclear weapons reduction. Russia and NATO establish council to cooperate on countering terrorism.

2004 Militants seize hostages in Beslan school; hundreds killed, mainly children.

RUSSIAN CZARS AND EMPRESSES
(FROM 1325)

1325–1340	Ivan I (Moneybags)
1340–1353	Semyon (Simeon) the Proud
1353–1359	Ivan II the Meek
1359–1389	Dmitry Donskoy
1389–1425	Vasily I
1425–1462	Vasily II

House of Rurik

1462–1505	Ivan III the Great
1505–1533	Vasily III
1533–1584	Ivan IV the Terrible
1584–1598	Fyodor I

House of Godunov

1598–1605	Boris Godunov
1605	Fyodor II

Usurpers

1605–1606	(False) Dmitry
1606–1610	Vasily IV

Interregnum

1610–1612	Wladyslaw

House of Romanov

1613–1645	Mikhail (Michael III) Fyodorovich
1645–1676	Aleksej (Alexis) Mikhailovich
1676–1682	Fyodor III
1682–1725	Peter I, The Great (Ivan V co-ruler, 1682–1689)
1725–1727	Catherine I
1727–1730	Peter II
1730–1740	Anna Ioannovna
1740–1741	Ivan VI; Anna Leopoldovna (regency)
1741–1761	Elizaveta (Elizabeth) Petrovna
1761–1762	Peter III
1762–1796	Catherine II, the Great
1796–1801	Pavel (Paul) I
1801–1825	Alexander I
1825–1855	Nikolai (Nicholas) I
1855–1881	Alexander II
1881–1894	Alexander III
1894–1917	Nikolai (Nicholas) II

RUSSIAN PRESIDENTS

Chairmen of the Central Executive Committee of the All-Russian Congress of the Soviets

1917	Lev Borisovic Kamenev
1917–1919	Yakov Mikhailovic Sverdlov
1919	Mikhail Fyodorovich Vladimirsky
1919–1938	Mikhail Ivanovic Kalinin

Chairman of the Central Executive Committee of the Union of Soviet Socialist Republics

1922–1938	Mikhail Ivanovic Kalinin

Chairmen of the Presidium of the Supreme Soviet

1938–1946	Mikhail Ivanovich Kalinin
1946–1953	Nikolay Mikhailovich Shvernik
1953–1960	Kliment Yefremovich Voroshilov
1960–1964	Leonid Ilyich Brezhnev
1964–1965	Anastas Ivanovich Mikoyan
1965–1977	Nikolay Viktorovich Podgorny
1977–1982	Leonid Ilyich Brezhnev
1982–1983	Vasiliy Vasilyevich Kuznetsov
1983–1984	Yuri Vladimirovich Andropov
1984	Vasily Vasilyevich Kuznetsov
1984–1985	Konstantin Ustinovich Chernenko
1985	Vasily Vasilyevich Kuznetsov
1985–1988	Andrei Andreyevich Gromyko
1988–1989	Mikhail Sergeyevich Gorbachev

Chairman of the Supreme Soviet

1989–1990	Mikhail Sergeyevich Gorbachev

President of the USSR

1990–1991	Mikhail Sergeyevich Gorbachev

Presidents of the Russian Republic

1991–1999	Boris Nikolayevich Yeltsin
1999–	Vladimir Vladimirovich Putin

Russian Revolution (1917) Two revolutions took place in 1917. The first, at the beginning of March, was a bourgeois revolution which saw the abdication of Czar Nicholas II. The second (the October Revolution – although it happened in early November by the western calendar) was a coup staged by the Bolsheviks led by Lenin. They took over the Winter Palace in Petrograd and swiftly established strongholds in towns throughout European Russia. Bolsheviks then began negotiations with the Germans, withdrawing from World War I, as the old Russian empire was plunged into chaotic civil war. *p.398*

Russo-Japanese War (1904–05) Territorial war culminating in Japanese victory over the Russians in the Tsushima Strait.

RWANDA Landlocked Rwanda lies just south of the equator in east central Africa. Since independence in 1962, ethnic tensions have dominated politics. In 1994, the violent death of the president led to appalling political and ethnic violence. Over half of the surviving population were displaced. The perpetrators of the genocide held sway in overcrowded refugee camps in adjacent countries, greatly complicating the process of eventual repatriation and reintegration. *p.450*

CHRONOLOGY

11th century Arrival of the Hutu.

15th century Hamitic Tutsi arrive as cattle-rearing overlords.

1899 The traditional kingdom is absorbed into German East Africa.

1919 Belgium takes over Rwanda from Germany, under a League of Nations mandate.

1952 Under UN trusteeship terms, Belgium begins moves towards democracy and independence.

1959 King Mutara III dies in unexplained circumstances. His death is followed by the seizure of power by a Tutsi clan who attempt to eliminate Hutu leaders. Hutus stage a bloody rebellion. Belgium introduces democracy, allowing Hutus to overthrow the minority Tutsi overlord class.

1960 Hutus win the communal elections; Joseph Habyarimana is elected President and Gregoire Kayibanda prime minister.

1962 Independence. Hutu-led government.

1960s Tutsi revolt; massacres by Hutu; thousands of Tutsi in exile.

1973 Coup by General Habyarimana.

1994 Habyarimana dies in plane crash. Genocidal violence unleashed by Hutu extremist regime, ousted by Tutsi-led FPR. Hutu refugee exodus.

1995 Start of war crimes tribunal.

1997 Refugees forcibly repatriated.

2001 Limited troop withdrawal from Congo (former Zaire) begins.

S

Sadat, Anwar (1918–81) President of Egypt (1970–81). Launched the unsuccessful invasion of Israel in 1973. In 1979 he signed the Camp David Accord with Israel, but in revenge for his "betrayal" was assassinated by Muslim fundamentalists in 1981.

Sadlier, George 19th-century British army officer and explorer of the Arabian Peninsula. On a diplomatic mission to the Egyptian forces operating against the Wahhabi tribesmen in Arabia, he was the first European to cross the Arabian peninsula from east to west.

Safavid dynasty Persian dynasty which arose around 1500 under Shah Ismail I, who united the country and converted it from Sunni to Shi'ite Islam. The Safavids brought a halt to the Ottomans' eastward expansion.

ST. KITTS & NEVIS One of the Caribbean's most popular tourist destinations, St. Kitts and Nevis, a former British colony, lies at the northern end of the Leeward Islands chain. St. Kitts is of volcanic origin; Mount Liamuiga, a dormant volcano with a crater 227 m (745 feet) deep, is the highest point on the island. Nevis, separated from St. Kitts by a channel 3 km (2 miles) wide, is the lusher but less developed of the two islands. A British colony since 1783 and part of the Leeward Islands Federation until 1956, St. Kitts and Nevis achieved independence in 1983. In the 18th century, its famed hot and cold springs gained Nevis the title "the Spa of the Caribbean."

CHRONOLOGY

1932 Pro-independence St. Kitts-Nevis-Anguilla Labour Party set up.

1967 Internal self-government.

1980 Anguilla formally separates from St. Kitts and Nevis.

1983 Independence from UK.

1995 Opposition SKLP wins election.

1998 Nevis referendum narrowly rejects secession.

ST. LUCIA

St. Lucia is one of the most beautiful islands of the Windward group of the Antilles. The twin Pitons, south of Soufrière, are one of the most striking natural features in the Caribbean. An excellent naval raiding base in the Caribbean in the 17th and 18th centuries, St. Lucia was fought over by France and Britain. Ownership alternated before it was finally ceded to Britain in 1814. French influence survives in St. Lucian patois and the local cuisine. A multiparty democracy, it lives by banana-growing and tourism, with enticing beaches and a rich variety of wildlife in the rainforest.

CHRONOLOGY

1958 Joins West Indies Federation.
1964 Sugar-growing ceases.
1979 Gains independence and joins Commonwealth.
1990 Establishes body with Dominica, Grenada, and St. Vincent to discuss forming a Windward Islands Federation.
1997 Hitherto ruling UWP reduced to one seat in general election.
2000 Blacklisted by the OECD as an international tax haven.

ST. VINCENT & THE GRENADINES

Among the most attractive of the Windward Islands group, St. Vincent and the Grenadines is renowned as the Caribbean playground of the international jet set. Tourism and bananas are the economic mainstays, and St. Vincent is also the world's largest arrowroot producer. St. Vincent is mostly volcanic; the one remaining active volcano, La Soufrière, last erupted in 1979. The Grenadines are flat, mainly bare, coral reefs.

CHRONOLOGY

1951 Universal suffrage.
1969 Internal self-government.
1972 James Mitchell premier; holds balance of power between People's Political Party (PPP) and St. Vincent Labour Party (SVLP).
1974 PPP–SVLP coalition.
1979 Full independence under Milton Cato of SVLP. La Soufrière volcano erupts.

1984 NDP, founded by Mitchell in 1975, wins first of four terms.
2000 Mitchell resigns premiership.
2001 ULP wins landslide victory. Ralph Gonsalves prime minister.

St. Petersburg (*var.* Petrograd, Leningrad) City founded by Peter the Great in 1703.

Saite dynasty The 26th dynasty of ancient Egypt which ruled from Sais (662–525 BCE). Pharaoh Samtik I asserted independence from the retreating Nubian Cushites and by gaining the trust of other princes was able to keep Egypt under a firm rule which allowed it to recover its material and cultural prosperity.

Saladin (1138–93) Kurdish Muslim general in the army of Nur al-Din who defeated the Crusaders at Aleppo, Hattin, and Acre, and in 1187 drove them from Jerusalem. A widely respected leader, he became ruler of Egypt, founded the Ayyubid dynasty (1174) and restored Jerusalem's Muslim shrine the Dome of the Rock. *p.197*

Salamis ⚔ of Graeco-Persian Wars (480 BCE). Greek victory.

SALT *see* Strategic Arms Limitation Treaty

Salvador *see* Bahia

Samanid dynasty (874–1005) Muslim dynasty of Persia.

Samarra Islamic city, Abbasid capital founded by al-Mu'tasim (c.836). *p.140*

Samnites People of south central Italy, the most powerful of the tribes that opposed Rome's expansion in Italy in the 4th and 3rd centuries BCE. It took three wars (the last ending in 290 BCE) to defeat them.

SAMOA

Samoa lies in the heart of the South Pacific, 2400 km (1490 miles) north of New Zealand. Four of its nine volcanic islands are inhabited – Apolima, Manono, Sava'ai (the largest), and Upolu). Rainforests cloak the mountains; vegetable gardens and coconut plantations thrive around the coasts. Polynesians settled Samoa in about 1000 BCE. Western rivalry after 1830 led to the 1899 division of the islands into German Western and American Eastern Samoa. High unemployment and low wages have made Samoa one of the world's least developed countries.

CHRONOLOGY

1914 New Zealand occupies Western Samoa.
1962 Becomes first independent Polynesian nation.
1990 Cyclone Ofa leaves 10,000 people homeless.
1991 HRPP retains power in first election under universal adult suffrage.
1996 and 2001 HRPP returned to power in elections.
1997 The country's name is changed from Western Samoa to Samoa.

samurai Knightly warrior or retainer of Japanese feudal lord or emperor. *p.180*

San Francisco, Treaty of (1952) Peace treaty between Japan and most of its World War II adversaries (excluding Soviet Union), by which Japan regained its independence.

San Ildefonso, Treaty of (1777). Treaty between Spain and Portugal that defined boundaries between their respective colonies in S America, especially in the Uruguay region.

SAN MARINO

Perched on the slopes of Mount Titano in the Italian Appennines, tiny San Marino is the world's oldest republic. Founded in the 4th century, the Republic of San Marino became one of the many small medieval Italian city-states. It refused to join the unified Italian state created between 1860 and 1871 and has maintained its independence ever since. The territory is divided into nine castles, or districts. One-third of Sammarinesi live in the northern town of Serravalle. Today San Marino makes its living through agriculture, tourism, and limited industry. Italy effectively controls most of its affairs.

CHRONOLOGY

1862 San Marino signs friendship treaty with Italy.
1914–1918 San Marino fights for Italy in World War I.
1940 Supports Axis powers and declares war on the Allies.
1943 Declares neutrality shortly before Italy surrenders.

1960 Women obtain vote.
1978 Coalition of San Marino Communist Party (PCS) and PSS – sole communist-led government in Western Europe.
1986 Financial scandals lead to a new PDCS/PCS government.
1988 Joins Council of Europe.
1990 PCS renames itself the PPDS.
1992 Joins UN. Collapse of communism in Europe sees PDCS/PPDS alliance replaced by a PDCS/PSS coalition government.
2002 Introduction of euro.

San Martín, José de (1778–1850) Argentinian general and liberator of Chile and Peru from Spanish rule. Resigned as Protector of Peru in 1822 after differences with Simón Bolívar. Died in exile in France.

Sandinistas Members of the Sandinista National Liberation Front (FSLN), founded in 1962 in Nicaragua as a left-wing, anti-US guerrilla group. The guerrilla campaign ended in full-scale civil war, resulting in the overthrow of the pro-US Somoza regime (1979).

Sandoval, Gonzalo de 16th-century Spanish explorer of N America (1521).

Santa Sofia (*var.* Hagia Sofia) Originally a Christian church at Constantinople (Istanbul) and later (1453) a mosque. Its present structure was built in 532–37 under the emperor Justinian.

Santiago de Compostela City in NW Spain. Its cathedral, which supposedly houses the remains of St. James the Apostle, was a major destination for pilgrimages in the Middle Ages. *p.188*

São Jorge da Mina *see* Elmina

SÃO TOMÉ & PRÍNCIPE Composed of the main islands of São Tomé and Príncipe and surrounding islets, the republic is situated off the western coast of Africa. The preindependence history of the islands was as a Portuguese colony exploited by plantation owners. In 1975, a classic Marxist single-party regime was established following independence from Portugal, but a referendum in 1990 resulted in a 72 percent vote in favor of democracy. São Tomé's main concerns are to rebuild relations with Portugal and to seek closer ties with the EU and the US.

CHRONOLOGY
1972–1973 Strikes by plantation workers.
1975 Independence as Marxist state. Plantations nationalized.
1978 Abortive coup.
1990 New democratic constitution.
1991–2000 Miguel Trovoada president for two terms.
1995 Príncipe granted autonomy.
2001 De Menezes wins presidency.
2003 Brief military takeover.

Saracens Greek and Roman term for the Arabs, hence used in medieval Europe for all Muslims.

Sarajevo Capital of Bosnia and Herzegovina. Scene of the assassination of Franz Ferdinand (1914).

Saratoga ⚔ of American Revolutionary War (Oct 17 1777). American victory.

Sargon I (reigned c.2334–2279 BCE) Ruler of the Akkad area of central Mesopotamia, who founded the city of Agade in c.2350 BCE. In the south he conquered the Sumerians and expanded his lands to Syria and eastern Asia Minor. He ruled for 56 years, and despite revolts toward the end of his reign his conquests ensured Akkadian supremacy for the next hundred years. Although Akkad subsequently became simply the name of a region, Akkadian remained the major spoken language in Mesopotamia.

Sassanian empire (*aka* Sasanid empire/dynasty) Persian ruling dynasty founded in 224 CE by Ardashir I (reigned 208–241). At its peak in the 6th century under Khosrau I, the Sassanian empire stretched from Roman Anatolia in the west to Taxila (now Pakistan) in the east although their westward expansion was checked by the Byzantine emperor Heraclius in 628. The empire fell to Muslim Arabs with their capture in 637 of the Sassanian capital Ctesiphon and their victory in 642 at Nehavend. *p.91, p.100*

Satavahanas Dynasty of central India from the 1st to the 2nd century CE. Displaced by the Vakataka dynasty.

satrapy Persian province under the Achaemenids and Alexander the Great.

Saud, Abd al-Aziz ibn (*var.* Ibn Saud, 1880–1953) The founder of the kingdom of Saudi Arabia. Born at Riyadh, his father was the youngest son of the Sultan of Nejd. Following civil wars (1875–91)

between the sultan's successors, Ibn Saud recaptured Riyadh and was once again proclaimed ruler of Nejd in 1901. He laid the foundations of a non-tribal, nationalist Arab state, underpinned by an agricultural economy, and ruled by Sharia Islamic law. From 1918, Ibn Saud began to extend his kingdom and by 1926 had captured the kingdom of Hejaz and the ultimate prize, Mecca.

SAUDI ARABIA Occupying most of the Arabian peninsula, Saudi Arabia covers an area as large as western Europe. Over 95 percent of its land is desert, with the most arid part, known as the "Empty Quarter" or Rub al Khali, being in the southeast. Saudi Arabia has the world's largest oil and gas reserves and major refining and petrochemicals industries. It includes Islam's holiest cities, Medina and Mecca, visited each year by two million Muslims performing the pilgrimage known as the haj. The al-Sa'ud family have been Saudi Arabia's absolutist rulers since 1932. It is the only state in the modern world to be named after its royal family

CHRONOLOGY
1932 The unification of Saudi Arabia under King Abd al-Aziz (ibn-Sa'ud).
1937 Oil reserves discovered near Riyadh.
1939 Ceremonial start of oil production at Az Zahran.
1953 King Sa'ud succeeds on the death of his father Abd al-Aziz.
1964 King Sa'ud abdicates in favor of his brother Faisal.
1967 Saudi Arabia joins Jordan and Iraq against Israel in Six-Day War.
1973 Saudi Arabia imposes oil embargo on Western supporters of Israel.
1975 King Faisal assassinated by a deranged nephew; succeeded by his brother Khalid.
1979 Muslim fundamentalists led by Juhaiman ibn Seif al-Otaibi seize Grand Mosque in Mecca, proclaim a mahdi (messiah) on first day of Islamic year 1400.
1981 Formation of Gulf Cooperation Council, with its secretariat in Riyadh.
1982 King Fahd succeeds on the death of his brother King Khalid. Promises to create consultative assembly.
1986 Opening of King Fahd Causeway to Bahrain. Oil minster Sheikh Yamani sacked.

1987 Diplomatic relations with Iran deteriorate after 402 people die in riots involving Islamic fundamentalists at Mecca during the haj (pilgrimage).

1989 Saudi Arabia signs nonaggression pact with Iraq. Saudi Arabia brokers political settlement to Lebanese civil war.

1990 Kuwaiti royal family seeks sanctuary in Taif after Iraqi invasion.

1990–1991 US, UK, French, Egyptian, and Syrian forces assemble in Saudi Arabia for Operation Desert Storm. Public executions are halted.

1991 Iraqis seize border town of Al Khafji, but are repulsed by Saudi, US, and Qatari forces.

1993 King Fahd appoints 60-man Consultative Council (Majlis ash-Shoura).

1996 King Fahd briefly relinquishes control to Crown Prince Abdullah. Bomb attack at US military complex in Az Zahran kills 19 US citizens.

1997, 2001 Consultative Council expanded, first to 90 then to 120 members.

2002 Crown Prince Abdullah unveils Middle East peace plan.

Savannah ⚔ of American Revolutionary War (Dec 29 1778). British victory.

Savorgnan de Brazza, Pierre *see* Brazza, Pierre Savorgnan de

Sawahili *see* Swahili

Saxons Germanic people who, upon the decline of the Roman Empire, began campaigns of colonization, notably in England in the 5th century CE.

Schism, Great *see* Great Schism

Schomburgk, Sir Robert Hermann (1804–65) Prussian-born British traveler and official. Sent by the Royal Geographical Society to explore British Guiana (1831–35) and employed to draw the controversial "Schomburgk-line" as a provisional boundary with Venezuela and Brazil.

Schouten, Willem (c.1567–1625) Dutch navigator and explorer. Completed circumnavigation of the world in 1616, rounding Cape Horn, which he named after his home town of Hoorn in Holland.

Schutzstaffel (SS, *Eng.* Security Troops) Elite troops of the Nazi Party, established 1925, and from 1929 developed by Heinrich Himmler into a security squad. Combat troops (Waffen SS) operated on the front line, while others implemented the Final Solution against the Jews.

Science and technology

Science and Technology (1500–1630) *p.300*
Optical instruments *p.310*
Science and Technology (1831–1870) *p.358*

Scipio Africanus (*var.* Publius Cornelius Scipio, 236–183 BCE) Roman general. His campaigns in the Iberian Peninsula against the Carthaginians (210–206 BCE) were the key to Rome's victory in the Second Punic War. In 204 he sailed to N Africa to confront the Carthaginians in their homeland. Carthage's greatest general, Hannibal, was recalled from Italy to counter the threat, but was defeated by Scipio at Zama in 202. On his triumphal return to Rome, Scipio received the honorary surname Africanus.

Scopes "Monkey Trial" (Jul 10–21, 1925) Trial of John T. Scopes, a teacher in Dayton, Tennessee, for teaching pupils the theory of evolution. This was in violation of a state law which prohibited the teaching of any theory which denied the Biblical story of creation.

SCOTLAND Now part of the United Kingdom, Scotland was an independent kindom until 1603, when the two crowns were united.
See also United Kingdom

KINGS AND QUEENS OF SCOTLAND (843–1603)

The House of Alpin 843–943

843–858	Kenneth MacAlpin
858–862	Donald I
863–877	Constantine I
877–878	Aed (Aodh)
878–889	Eochaid (Eocha) and Giric (Ciric)
889–900	Donald II
900–943	Constantine II

The House of Dunkeld 943–1058

943–954	Malcolm I
954–962	Indulf
962–967	Dubh the Black
967–971	Cuilean (Culen)
971–995	Kenneth II
995–997	Constantine III
997–1005	Kenneth III
1005–1034	Malcolm II
1034–1040	Duncan I
1040–1057	Macbeth
1057–1058	Lulach the Fool

The House of Canmore 1058–1290

1058–1093	Malcolm Canmore III
1093–1094	Donalbane
1094	Duncan II
1094–1097	Donalbane (restored) and Edmund
1097–1107	Edgar the Peacable
1107–1124	Alexander I the Fierce
1124–1153	David I
1153–1165	Malcolm IV the Maiden
1165–1214	William I the Lion
1214–1249	Alexander II
1249–1286	Alexander III
1286–1290	Margaret (Maid of Norway)

The House of Balliol 1292–1296

1292–1296	John Balliol

The House of Bruce 1306–1371

1306–1329	Robert I the Bruce
1329–1371	David II

The House of Stuart 1371–1603

1371–1390	Robert II
1390–1406	Robert III
1406–1437	James I
1437–1460	James II
1460–1488	James III
1488–1513	James IV
1513–1542	James V
1542–1567	Mary, Queen of Scots
1567–1603	James VI (James I of England after the union of Scottish and English crowns)

Scott, Robert Falcon (1868–1912) British naval officer and polar explorer. In 1900, led expedition to the Antarctic on behalf of the Royal Geographical Society with Edmund Wilson and Ernest Shackleton. In 1910 he led a second expedition, reaching the South Pole on Jan 17 1912, one month after the Norwegian, Roald Amundsen. The whole party later perished before reaching their base camp. *p.391*

Scramble for Africa Name given to the race between the major European powers to colonize Africa at the end of the 19th century. *p.343*

Scylax of Caryander 6th-century BCE Greek navigator who reached the Indus Valley, sailed down the river, then back along the Persian and Arabian coast to the Red Sea.

Scythians An Indo-European, nomadic people of the Russian steppes, who migrated in the 8th century BCE to the area north of the Black Sea. They traded corn with the Greeks for luxury goods, and were driven out by the Medes.

SDI *see* Strategic Defense Initiative

Second Republic (1848–52). Republican government of France from the deposition of Louis Philippe (1848) until the Second Empire (1852).

Second World War *see* World War II

Sekigahara ⚔ (1600) whereby Japanese Tokugawa Shogunate decisively established hegemony over rival warlord clans.

Seleucid empire The dynasty of Macedonian kings, founded by one of Alexander's generals Seleucus, which after Alexander's death in 323 BCE ruled Babylonia (Syria and Persia) until 129 BCE, when it fell to the Parthians and the Romans. Under Antiochus III (242–187 BCE), the Seleucid Empire extended from Bactria in the east to Egypt and Greece in the west.

Seleucus I (c.358–281 BCE) One of Alexander's generals, who after Alexander's death in 323 BCE, ruled Babylonia, founding a dynasty and an empire. *See also* Seleucid empire

Selim I (1470–1520) Ottoman Sultan (reigned 1512–1520). Massacred the followers of the Safavid Shah Ismail, and occupied Tabriz. In 1516–17 he overcame the Mamluks in Egypt and Syria, and by his death had established Ottoman rule in Jerusalem, Mecca, and Medina.

Selim II (1524–74) Ottoman Sultan (reigned 1566–74). Defeated at the battle of Lepanto (1571) by Don John of Austria.

Seljuk Turks Nomadic Turkish people from Central Asia who in the 11th century began to spread southwards. They took Baghdad in 1055, conquered Armenia, expelled the Byzantines from Asia Minor after the battle of Manzikert (1071), and seized Syria and Palestine from the Fatimids. By the 12th century they had reunited all of the old Abbasid territories, but in 1243 were routed by the Mongols at Köse Dagh. The Seljuks established a heritage of magnificent architecture. A Seljuk descendant, Osman, founded the Ottoman state in 1299. *p.174, p.176*

Seminole American Indian groups of the Creek Confederacy, originally based in Florida and the far South of the US. Fought a fierce series of wars against forced relocation from 1816–58.

Semites Speakers of the Semitic group of languages, of which Arabic, Hebrew and Amharic are still current.

Sendero Luminoso, Partido Comunista de Peru *see* Shining Path

SENEGAL Senegal's capital, Dakar, lies on the westernmost cape of Africa. The country is mostly low, with open savanna and semidesert in the north and thicker savanna in the south. France colonized Senegal, a major entrepôt from the 15th century, in 1890. Dakar was the capital of French West Africa. After independence from France in 1960, Senegal was ruled until 1981 by President Léopold Senghor. He was succeeded by his prime minister, Abdou Diouf, who held power for almost 20 years until his election defeat in 2000.

CHRONOLOGY
1960 Independence under Senghor.
1966–1976 One-party state.
1981 Full multipartyism restored.
2000 Presidency won by Abdoulaye Wade in first ever defeat for PS.
2001 Referendum approves new constitution.
2002 1800 die in ferry disaster.

September 11 Date of attacks in 2001 by Al-Qaeda terrorists on New York and Washington. *p.455*

Septimius Severus (*var.* Lucius Septimius Severus, 146–211 CE) Emperor of Rome (reigned 193–211 CE). A professional soldier who was proclaimed emperor by his troops, upon which he founded the Severan dynasty and adopted a militaristic style of government. He disbanded the elite Praetorian Guard, whose support was essential to achieving high office, and replaced them with his own men. He died at Eburacum (York, in England).

Sera Metropolis *see* Chang'an

SERBIA AND MONTENEGRO
Union of Formerly the Federal Republic of Yugoslavia, the union consists of Serbia and Montenegro, two of the six republics of pre-1991 Yugoslavia. Slobodan Milosevic whipped up Serbian nationalist feeling in rising to power as the socialist federation disintegrated. His regime was condemned internationally over the Bosnian war (1992–1995), and for backing "ethnic cleansing" in the majority-Albanian province of Kosovo, until NATO bombing in 1999 forced it to withdraw. Within two years of this debacle, Milosevic was ousted and handed over to face trial in The Hague for war crimes. The country adopted the new name of Union of Serbia and Montenagro in 2002.

CHRONOLOGY
168 BCE The Romans subjugate the Illyrians, who populated the territory of modern-day Yugoslavia since around 2000 bce By 9 ce the territory is divided and renamed Illyricum and Moesia. The Western Roman Empire declines in the 4th century and the territory is conquered, in turn, by the Eastern Roman Empire (the Byzantines), the Huns and Bulgars, and the Avars who bring Slavs to the area as vassals.

626 CE The Byzantine Empire defeats the Avars.

879 CE Croats in the north and west break away from Byzantium and turn to Catholic Rome, but are invaded, at Rome's invitation, by Hungary in 1089 Eastern Orthodox Serbs in the south and west become part of the Bulgarian Empire at the beginning of the 10th century but later gain some autonomy under the expansionist Stephen Vojislav.

1101 Civil war breaks out in Serbia after the death of King Constantin Bodin.

1165 The Nemanjic dynasty establishes a Serbian Empire which lasts until the death of King Stefan Dusan in 1355.

1389 The Battle of Kosovo Polje points to the end of Serbian independence, as Prince Lazar Hrebljanovic is defeated by the Ottoman Turks.

1463 The Turks complete the conquest of the former Serbian Empire, leaving only tiny Montenegro independent, under Ivan IV. A new statute adopted in 1516 places Montenegro under the suzerainty of the Ottoman Empire.

1699 The Ottoman Empire is forced to cede Croatia and most of northern Serbia to Austria-Hungary under the Treaty of Karlowitz, after failing to capture Vienna. Turkey recaptures Serbia in 1739.

1804 Anti-Turkish revolts, led by Karageorge break out in Serbia, and last until 1813 when they are crushed.

1829 Serbian autonomy is established by the Treaty of Adrianople, which ends a Russo-Turkish war. Milos Obrenovic, leader of an insurrection in 1815, is recognized as hereditary Prince and attempts to expand Serbia, before abdicating in 1839 in the face of opposition. A period of faction fighting is followed by a coup in 1842 which brings Alexander Karageorgevic (son of Karageorge) to power.

1858 Milos returns to power after Alexander Karageorgevic is deposed. His son Michael succeeds him in attempting to modernize the Serbian government, before being assassinated in 1868.

1876 Serbia and Montenegro declare war on Turkey in support of Bosnian insurrectionists. Russia declares war in 1877 and, after the Turkish defeat, Serbia becomes an independent principality under the Treaty of San Stefano. Bosnia-Herzegovina is occupied by Austria, and Macedonia remains under Turkish control under the Treaty of Berlin (1878) while Montenegro receives independence. Bulgaria loses territory to Serbia and Montenegro. A period of nationalist and international conflict follows.

1903 June. Serbian King Alexander is brutally murdered by officers in his Belgrade palace after years of factionalism and corruption in government which began during the reign of his father, King Milan.

1908 October. Austria-Hungary annexes Bosnia, with tacit Russian agreement. Serbia protests but, without Russian support, can do nothing and the annexation is recognised by the major powers in April 1909.

1912 The First Balkan War begins after Greece and Montenegro declares war on Turkey. Turkey is defeated by the Balkan League – a Serbian-Bulgarian-Greek military alliance. Montenegro and Serbia increase their territory under the Treaty of Bucharest, including the award of central and southern Macedonia to Serbia from Bulgaria.

1914 World War I is triggered by the assassination by Gavrilo Princip, a Serbian revolutionary, of the Austrian archduke Franz Ferdinand, heir to the Austrian Emperor, in Sarajevo. An Austrian ultimatum is rejected by Serbia and the war between them spreads across Europe.

1918 Serbian Prince Alexander Karageorgevic unites the weakened Serbia, Montenegro, and Slovenia into the Kingdom of Serbs, Croats, and Slovenes, after the defeat of the Central Powers. Alexander becomes King in August 1921.

1920 Elections to a Constituent Assembly result in a centrist government led by the Serbian Nikola Pasic. A unitary constitution, promulgated in 1921, is consistently opposed by Croat parliamentarians.

1929 Alexander imposes a dictatorship to end Serbian, Croatian, and Slovene nationalism and renames the country Yugoslavia. However his rule merely increases Serbian domination, bureaucracy and repression by the police.

1934 Alexander assassinated in France. Yugoslavia, ruled by regents on behalf of the child King Peter, is threatened by the rise of Nazi Germany and Soviet hostility.

1941 Germany invades Yugoslavia after the overthrow of a Yugoslav government which signed a pact with the Axis powers. The country is partitioned. Rival partisan groups resist – the Serbian royalist Cetniks and the communist partisans under Josip Broz Tito, leader of the Communist Party of Yugoslavia.

1942 The communists set up an Anti-Fascist National Liberation Council which becomes a provisional government in 1943 and takes power after the defeat of the Nazis.

1945 Tito's provisional government abolishes the monarchy and proclaims the Federative People's Republic of Yugoslavia. Nationalization of industry, transport, and banking begins, as does the collectivization of agriculture. The majority Albanian region of Kosovo is given status of an autonomous region within Serbia.

1948 Tito takes Yugoslavia out of the Soviet bloc after the Cominform accuses him of "nationalist deviationism" over his reluctance to allow Yugoslavia to become merely a Moscow satellite. A Soviet economic blockade is imposed. Tito seeks help from the US and Western Europe.

1953 The National Assembly adopts a new constitution guaranteeing sovereignty to the Yugoslav republics. The relationship of each republic with the federal state is "between two essentially equal and mutually independent and interlinked social and political communities."

1972 Croatian terrorists blow up a Yugoslav Airlines DC-9, killing 28 people. An express train is blown up on the same day. On July 26 an armed group of extreme Croat separatists, known as Ustashi, enter Yugoslavia. A pitched battle with Yugoslav security forces leaves 17 of the 19 dead. Ustashi terrorists hijack an Swedish DC-9 in September.

1988 The federal government falls when its budget proposals are defeated in the National Assembly. Meanwhile pressure from Croatia and Slovenia over greater republican autonomy is opposed by hardliners in Serbia who demand a strong centralized state.

1990 SPS wins elections in Serbia. Communists win presidency and dominate Montenegro elections.

1992 EU recognizes breakaway republics of Croatia, Slovenia, and Bosnia and Herzegovina. Bosnian war begins. UN sanctions imposed. Ibrahim Rugova elected president of self-declared republic of Kosovo. Milosevic reelected president of Serbia, but SPS loses majority.

1995 Bosnian peace accord.

1996 UN sanctions formally lifted.

1997 Milosevic becomes federal president.

1998 Conflict in Kosovo escalates.

1999 Kosovo talks break down; "ethnic cleansing" precipitates mass exodus. NATO aerial bombing of FRY. Withdrawal of Serbian forces and police from Kosovo, and entry of international force, KFOR.

2000 Defeat of Milosevic in first round of presidential election. Opposition candidate Vojislav Kostunica swept to power. Democratic Opposition dominates Serbian elections.

2001 Arrest of Milosevic, who is subsequently extradited to face war crimes tribunal in The Hague.

2002 Country adopts Union of Serbia and Montenegro as official title.

2003 Serbian Prime Minister Zoran Djindjic shot. Far-right SRS wins polls in Serbia.

2004 Kostunica becomes Serbian prime minister. Resurgence of ethnic violence in Kosovo.

serfs Peasant class with no personal property or freedom of movement, obligated to the lord on whose land they worked and to whom they contributed part of their own produce.

Serpa Pinto, Alexandre (1846–1900). Portuguese explorer and colonial administrator who crossed southern and central Africa and mapped the interior of the continent. In 1887 he was named consul-general to Zanzibar and, in 1889, governor-general of Mozambique.

Serrão, Francisco (died c.1516) Portuguese explorer. He accompanied de Abreu on his exploration of the East Indies, was captured by pirates and taken to Ternate – the first Portuguese to reach the Spice Islands.

Seven Days ⚔ of American Civil War (Jun 25–Jul 1 1862). Confederate victory.

Seven Years' War (1756–63). Wide-ranging conflict between Prussia and Britain, and a coalition of Russia, Austria and France. It was both a struggle for maritime and colonial supremacy between Britain and France, and an attempt by Austria to regain Silesia which it had lost to Prussia in 1748. Prussia retained Silesia while, overseas, Britain destroyed French power in N America, the Caribbean and India.

Sèvres, Treaty of (1920) Part of the Versailles Peace Settlement, signed between the Allies and Turkey, which forced Turkey to give up all her non-Turkish lands. Syria became a French mandate, and Britain accepted the mandate for Iraq, Palestine and Transjordan. The treaty was rejected by Atatürk, who obtained a redefinition of Turkey's borders in the Treaty of Lausanne (1923). *See also* Ataturk, and Lausanne, Treaty of

Seward's Folly *see* Alaska Purchase

SEYCHELLES The 115 islands of the Seychelles, lying in the Indian Ocean, support unique flora and fauna, including the giant tortoise and the world's largest seed, the coco-de-mer. Formerly a UK colony and then under one-party rule for 16 years, the country became a multiparty democracy in 1993. The economy relies on tourism.

CHRONOLOGY

1741 The islands are explored by France, which claims possession of them in 1750.
1770 The first settlers arrive to exploit the abundant supplies of tortoises and timber; they later introduce slavery.
1814 The Treaty of Paris transfers control of the islands from France to Britain.
1872 A resident administrator is appointed to the Seychelles (previously governed from Mauritius).
1903 Seychelles becomes a crown colony.
1952 Political parties formed, led by F. A. René (pro-independence) and James Mancham (pro-UK rule).
1965 UK returns Desroches, Aldabra, and Farquhar islands, which are leased to USA to 1976.
1976 Independence. Coalition with Mancham president, René premier.
1977 René takes over in coup.
1979 One-party socialist state.
1979–1987 Several coup attempts.
1992 Politicians in exile return.
1993 Democratic elections.
2001 René reelected in early presidential elections.

Shackleton, Sir Ernest Henry (1874–1922) British merchant naval officer and Antarctic explorer. After accompanying the Scott expedition of 1901–04, Shackleton explored the Antarctic on the ship Nimrod from 1907–09, reaching to within 150 km of the Pole. In 1914–17 he took the ship Endurance to the Weddell Sea, but the ship was crushed by ice.

Shakespeare, William (1564–1616) English playwright and poet, whose plays have exerted a lasting influence over English literature. *p.298*

Shah Jahan (*var.* Jehan, 1592–1666) Mughal emperor (reigned 1627–58). The grandson of Akbar, Shah Jahan presided over the most magnificent period of the Mughal empire. He founded the city of Delhi, and created the Taj Mahal at Agra, the mausoleum of his favorite wife, Mumtaz. He had four sons; his third son, Aurangzeb, overthrew his brothers, proclaiming himself emperor while his father was still alive. *p.304*

Shaka Zulu (*var.* Chaka, Tshaka, c.1787–1828) Zulu chief (reigned 1816–28) who founded southern Africa's Zulu empire and created a fighting force that dominated the entire region.

Shang dynasty (11th–6th centuries BCE) The first Chinese dynasty identified from both archaeological and documentary evidence. Shang kings consulted diviners and the culture is named after Anyang where oracle bones were found, incised with the earliest known Chinese characters.

The Shang were hunters and warriors of the north China plain, and their rule gradually extended over the Yellow River valley where they developed complex agriculture and the beginnings of bronze casting. The latter part of this dynasty is also known as the Yin dynasty, which was succeeded by the Zhou dynasty. *p.41*

Shangdu (*var.* Xanadu) Kublai Khan's summer palace.

Shapur I (c.242–272) Son of Ardashir, founder of the Sassanian Empire, Shapur inflicted a series of major defeats on the Romans, including the victory at Edessa in 260, and completed the conquest of Kushan.

Shapur II (*aka* Shapur the Great, 309–79) Declared king of Persia at birth. Campaigned against the Romans, forcing them to cede five provinces (363), and established Persian control over Armenia.

Sharia The Holy Law of Islam, which was compiled and codified by the great Muslim jurists of the 8th and 9th centuries. It describes in minute detail the Islamic way of life, and prescribes the way for a Muslim to fulfil the commands of God and reach heaven. *See also* Islam

Shaybanids *see* Uzbeks

shell midden Large rubbish heap consisting of the discarded shells of edible shellfish, representing many years of accumulation. Shell middens can reveal the role played by marine resources in the prehistoric diet.

Sherley, Sir Robert (c.1581–1628) With his brother, Anthony, traveled through Syria and Persia in 1598, and reached Isfahan, the Persian capital. Both brothers were sent by the Persian ruler, Shah Abbas "the Great", as ambassadors to Europe.

Sherman, William Tecumseh (1820–91) Union soldier in the American Civil War, promoted to general after the first battle of Bull Run. He destroyed the Confederate forces on his famous march through Georgia (1864). Appointed head of the army in 1869 by President Grant.

Shiah i-Ali *see* Shi'ites

Shi Huangdi (*var.* Shi Huang-ti, King Zheng, First Emperor) First Qin Emperor (reigned 221-206 BCE) who assumed the title Shi Huangdi (First August Emperor). He unified China by means of a radical series of political reforms, also building roads and canals and creating the Great Wall of China. He is now remembered cheifly for the vast array of terra-cotta soldiers with which he is buried. *See also* Qin dynasty.

Shi Huang-ti *see* Shi Huangdi

Shi'ites (*var.* Ar. Shiah i-Ali, "the partisans of Ali"). Shi'ites comprise the largest minority group of Muslims. Although they have different devotions and religious practices from the Sunni Muslims, there is no difference in the essentials of the faith in the two traditions. *See also* Sunnis.

Shiloh ⚔ of American Civil War, Tennessee (Apr 6–7 1862). Union victory.

Shining Path (*var. Sp.* Sendero Luminoso, Partido Comunista de Peru). Revolutionary movement founded in 1970 which employed guerrilla tactics and violent terrorism in the name of Maoism. *p.437*

Shinto Ancient religion of Japan characterized by ancestor worship, devotion to the gods of natural forces, and belief in the divinity of the Emperor. *p.164*

Shiva Hindu god combining apparently contradictory qualities of destruction and restoration, revenge and benevolence, asceticism and sensuality.

Shogun Japanese military governor or warlord, effective ruler of Japan prior to the Meiji Restoration (1868).

Shu, Wu and Wei kingdoms When the Han dynasty ended, several of its generals fought for supremacy in China. The period 220–280 CE saw the country divided into three kingdoms, a period known as "San-kuo." the Shu kingdom controlled what is now Sichuan, the Wei controlled the north, while the Wu kingdom comprised present-day Nanjing, south of the Yangtze River.

Siam *see* Thailand

Sicilian Vespers (1282) Uprising in Sicily against Charles of Anjou. The Sicilian crown was given to Peter III of Aragon.

Sicily Island off southern tip of Italy, the largest island in the Mediterranean. Throughout history its position has made it an inviting prize for invaders and colonists. The Greeks, Carthaginians, Romans, Arabs, and Normans all played a part in creating a distinctive culture, very different from that of mainland Italy.

Siddhartha Gautama *see* Buddha

Siegfried Line *see* Hindenburg Line

SIERRA LEONE The west African state of Sierra Leone was founded by the British in 1787 for Africans freed from slavery. The terrain rises from coastal lowlands to mountains in the northeast. A democratic government took office in 1996 during a bloody rebellion. Sierra Leone soon plunged into a savage civil war. Although a 1999 peace agreement was short-lived, an ECOWAS-brokered accord signed in late 2000 seemed to be holding.

CHRONOLOGY

12th–14th centuries Waves of settlers move into the country.

15th century First contact is made by Portuguese seafarers.

1787 British administer the coastal colony around Freetown, which is settled by freed slaves.

1896 A UK protectorate is declared.

1961 Independence.

1978 Single-party republic.

1991 RUF rebellion starts.

1996 Civilian rule restored after 1992 army coup; Kabbah president.

1998 Kabbah restored following coup in 1997; fighting continues.

1999 Power-sharing agreement.

2000 November, new cease-fire after renewed fighting.

2001 RUF ends insurgency.

Sigirya Palace fortress built by Kassapa (447–495) in Sri Lanka. This rock citadel was surmounted by the royal palace, while other residences and courts were arranged on descending levels. The palace was reached by a walkway which clung precariously to the side of the rock. *p.107*

Sikhism Indian religious order founded by Guru Nanak (1469–1539), who preached a devotion to God that was neither Hindu nor Muslim. Sikhs emerged as a militant movement in the Punjab in the 18th and 19th centuries, especially under the leadership of Ranjit Singh. They confronted and were defeated by the British in the Anglo-Sikh Wars.

Sikh Wars In 1845, a Sikh army numbering 60,000 men invaded British territory. Four pitched battles were fought at Mudki, Frerozeshah, Aliwal, and Sobraon, and the Sikhs were driven back across the Sutlej River and surrendered to the British, who annexed the tract between the Sutlej and Ravi rivers. In 1848, a general Sikh uprising broke out. After disastrous losses at Chillianwalla, the British destroyed the Sikh army at Gujarat, and annexed the Punjab.

Silk Road System of trade routes across Central Asia linking Southwest Asia and the Mediterranean with China (traditional termini at Merv in Bactria and Anxi or Luoyang in China) which developed during the Han period (from c.110 BCE). Split into seasonal routes running north and south of the Takla Makan Desert (summer and winter respectively) the system operated at the mercy of Central Asian tribes. A major conduit not only for east–west trade, it also provided passage for ideas such as Buddhism and Islam, and was revived during the "Mongol Peace" c.1250–1350. *p.87*

Silla Ancient state of Korea established in the 3rd century CE and gaining control of Korean peninsula in 220 CE. *p.127* *See also* Korea.

Sinai Taken by Israel in Six Day War (1967).

Singapore ⚔ of World War II (Feb 1942). Defeat of British garrison by Japanese.

SINGAPORE An island state linked to the southernmost tip of the Malay Peninsula by a causeway, Singapore was largely uninhabited between the 14th and 18th centuries. In 1819, an official of the British East India Company, Stamford Raffles, recognized the island's strategic position on key trade routes, and established Singapore as a trading settlement. Today, Singapore remains one of the most important entrepôts in Asia.

CHRONOLOGY

1819 Sir Stamford Raffles, a British East India Company official, gains permission from the Malay Sultan of Riau-Johor and the local chief to establish a trading station on Singapore, largely uninhabited since the fourteenth century.

1824 The Malays cede the whole island to the East India Company in perpetuity.

1826 The Company merges Singapore with its two neighboring West Malay peninsular territories, Malacca and Penang, to form the Straits Settlement.

1867 The Settlements become a British Crown Colony.

1869 The opening of the Suez Canal places Singapore at the heart of the new trade route between Europe and East Asia.

1942 February, Singapore falls to a Japanese land attack.

▶

1945 September, The British return to Singapore after the Japanese surrender.
1946 The Straits Settlements are dissolved and Singapore becomes a separate Crown Colony.
1954 The People's Action Party (PAP) is formed under the leadership of Lee Kuan Yew.
1959 PAP becomes ruling party.
1965 Independence.
1990 Lee Kuan Yew resigns as prime minister.
1993 Ong Teng Cheong first directly elected president

Sino-Indian War Conflict (1962) between India and China over border territory of Arunachal Pradesh; Chinese victory resulted in withdrawal of troops, and Chinese occupation of various other border territories including Aksai Chin.

Sino-Japanese War (1894–95) War between China and Japan arising from disputes in Korea. The Treaty of Shimonoseki in 1895 granted Taiwan to Japan.

Sioux (*var.* Dakota) American Indian groups of the upper Mississippi and Missouri basins. Nomadic warrior people with a livelihood based on hunting buffalo, the Sioux resisted European attempts to remove them from their lands, especially at ⚔ Little Bighorn, where, led by Sitting Bull and Crazy Horse, they destroyed General Custer's forces. The Sioux were among the last of the American Indian peoples to be forced onto reservations, their resistance ending following ⚔ Wounded Knee in 1890 when more than 200 Sioux were killed by the US army.

Sitting Bull (*var.* Tatanka Iyotake, c.1834–90) Chief of the Teton Dakota Sioux, he was a determined opponent of the displacement of Indian peoples from their ancestral lands. He led the massacre of Custer and his troops at ⚔ Little Bighorn (1881), but was subsequently forced to live on the Sioux reservation at Standing Rock.

Sivaji (1627–80) The charismatic founder of the Maratha kingdom, Sivaji operated from his heavily fortified base in the Western Ghats. Leading a force of highly mobile, armored horsemen, he relentlessly harried Mughal forces, carving out a kingdom which was ultimately to emasculate Mughal power.

Six Day War (June 5–10 1967) Arab-Israeli War caused by Egypt's closure of the Gulf of Aqaba to Israeli shipping. Israel defeated the combined forces of Egypt, Jordan, and Syria, and occupied the Gaza Strip, the Sinai, Jerusalem, the West Bank of the Jordan, and the Golan Heights. *p.434*

Sixteen Kingdoms, the Period of Chinese history (304–439 CE) when northern China was partitioned among Chinese, Xiongnu, and Tibetan rulers.

Sixtus IV (prev. Francesco della Rovere, 1414–84) Pope from 1471 and a famous Franciscan preacher. He built the Sistine Chapel and was a patron of artists, but lowered the moral authority of the papacy.

slavery
The Atlantic Slave Trade. *p.322*
Slavery in the Americas. *p.322*

Slavs Largest ethnic group of Europe, linguistically derived from the Indo-European family. Traditionally divided into West Slavs (*aka* Lusatians, including Poles, Czechs, Slovaks, and Wends), the South Slavs (including Slovenes, Serbs, Croats, Montenegrins, Macedonians, Bosnians, and Bulgars) and the largest subgroup, the East Slavs (comprising Russians, Belorussians or White Russians, and Ukrainians).

SLOVAKIA Slovakia is bordered by the Czech Republic, Austria, Poland, Hungary, and Ukraine. Southern lowlands contrast with the Carpathian mountain range, which extends along the Polish border. Once part of the Austro-Hungarian empire, Slovakia and the Czech provinces of Bohemia and Moravias were united to form the Republic of Czechoslovakia in 1918. An independent democracy since 1993, Slovakia is the less developed half of the former Czechoslovakia. It is facing difficulties in making its heavy industry-based economy efficient.

Chronology
1939–1945 Separate Slovak state under pro-Nazi Jozef Tiso.
1945 Czechoslovak state restored.
1947 Communists seize power.
1968 "Prague Spring" ended by Warsaw pact invasion.
1989 "Velvet Revolution."

1990 Free multiparty elections.
1993 Jan 1. Separate Slovak and Czech states established.
1994 HZDS election victory.
1998 Broad-based coalition wins general election.
1999 Rudolf Schuster defeats Meciar in direct presidential poll.
2004 Slovakia joins NATO and EU.

SLOVENIA Of all the former Yugoslav republics, Slovenia has the closest links with western Europe. Located at the northeastern end of the Adriatic Sea, this small, Alpine country controls some of Europe's major transit routes. Slovenia's transition to independence in 1991 avoided the violence of the breakup of Yugoslavia. The most prosperous of the former communist European states, it is the only former Yugoslav republic on the "fast track" to EU membership.

Chronology
34 BCE The Roman general Gaius Octavius (later the Emperor Augustus) founds a city on the site of Ljubljana.
451 CE The area is devastated by the Huns.
900 CE The Magyars take Ljubljana, which passes into the hands of the dukes of Carinthia in the 12th century.
1277 The Habsburgs control the region and while under Austrian rule Ljubljana becomes a center for a Slovenian national movement.
1809 Napoleon captures the territories held by Austria and reorganizes them into the Illyrian Provinces, along French lines, with Ljubljana as the seat of government. Among other reforms, serfdom is abolished and the peasants are given their lands during a period regarded as the first Yugoslav state. Austria-Hungary regains control in 1813.
1867 Austria-Hungary reorganizes the Slav peoples under its control after its defeat by Prussia. The Slovenes are linked to Austria.
1855 Slovenian nationalists develop a co-operative movement to strengthen Slovenian consciousness in the countryside by providing credit and other services to help Slovenes break free of

Germanic institutions. A co-operative federation is formed in 1883 and a second one becomes the economic wing of the Slovene People's Party in 1895.

1918 Serbian Prince Alexander unites Serbia, Montenegro and Slovenia into the Kingdom of Serbs, Croats and Slovenes, after the defeat of the Central Powers. Alexander becomes King in August 1921.

1920 Elections to a Constituent Assembly result in a centrist government. A unitary constitution, promulgated in 1921, is opposed by Croat parliamentarians.

1929 Alexander imposes a dictatorship to end Serbian, Croatian and Slovene nationalism and renames the country Yugoslavia. However his rule merely increases Serbian domination, bureaucracy and repression by the police. Alexander is assassinated in 1934.

1949 Tito's break with Moscow.

1989 Parliament confirms right to secede. Calls multiparty elections.

1990 Control over army asserted, referendum approves secession.

1991 Independence declared; first republic to secede. Yugoslav federal army repelled.

1992 First multiparty elections. Milan Kuâan president, Janez Drnovsek prime minister.

1993 Joins IMF and IBRD.

1998 EU membership talks begin.

2000 Drnovsek ousted; returns to office after elections.

2004 Joins EU and NATO.

Sluis ⚔ of Dutch Revolt (1604). Dutch victory over Spain.

Smith, John (c.1580–1631) British soldier, colonist and explorer in N America. First traveled to Virginia in 1605, hoping to find a river route to the Pacific. In 1608 he was elected leader of the Virginia colony.

Smoot–Hawley Tariff (Jun 17 1930) Protective tariff imposed on imports to the US following the 1929 Wall Street Crash which set an average level of duty of 50% against a previous average of 26 percent, causing serious disruption to US-European trade.

Snell, Willebrod van Roijen (var. Lat. Snellius, 1580–1626) Dutch mathematician who discovered the law of refraction known as Snell's law. He was also instrumental in the development of triangulation in surveying.

Snellius see Snell, Willebrod van Rijen

Sokoto Fulani Kingdom of western Africa established in 1820.

Solomon (c.1015–977 BCE) King of Israel and second son of David and Bathsheba. The kingdom under Solomon attained its widest limit, and splendid temples and palaces were constructed. He was credited with transcendent wisdom.

SOLOMON ISLANDS Scattered over 645,000 sq km (250,000 sq miles), the Solomons archipelago has several hundred islands, but most people live on the six largest – Guadalcanal, Malaita, New Georgia, Makira, Santa Isabel, and Choiseul. The islands have been settled since at least 1000 bce. The Spanish arrived in 1568 and a British colony was established in 1893. Ethnic conflict between rival islanders ravaged the country from 1998 to 2000. Most of the Solomons are coral reefs. Just 1 percent of the land area is cultivable.

CHRONOLOGY

1900 Britain acquires northern Solomons from Germany.

1942–1943 Japanese occupation.

1978 Independence from UK.

1983 Diplomatic relations with Taiwan established.

1998–2000 Civil conflict between Guadalcanal and Malaita islanders.

2003 International peacekeeping forces arrive.

SOMALIA Occupying the horn of Africa, Italian Somaliland and British Somaliland were united in 1960 to form an independent Somalia. Except in the fertile south, the land is semiarid. Years of clan-based civil war have resulted in the collapse of central government, the frustration of US and UN intervention initiatives aimed at easing a huge refugee crisis, and mass starvation.

CHRONOLOGY

1880s The lands of the Somalis became British and Italian colonies.

1960 Unification at independence.

1964–1987 Conflict with Ethiopia over Ogaden region.

1969 Gen. Siad Barre takes power.

1991 Siad Barre ousted. Civil war and clan chaos. Mass starvation. Somaliland declares secession.

1992 Abortive US intervention.

1995 UN force withdrawn.

1997 Accord signed by 26 clan factions.

2000 National reconciliation conference appoints government; warlords dispute its authority.

2001 Somali Reconciliation and Restoration Council set up, with support from southern clan leaders.

2004 New transitional assembly sworn in.

Somme ⚔ of World War I (Jul–Nov 1916). Major battle on the Western Front, incurring massive casualties for Britain, France, and Germany; over one million died over the course of four months.

Song dynasty (var. Sung dynasty, 960–1279) Dynasty of China, divided into Northern Song (960–1126), destroyed by the Jin, and Southern Song (1127–1279), overrun by the Mongol (Yuan) dynasty. *p.161, p.176*

Song Taizu Founder of the Song dynasty (reigned 960–76). *p.150*

Songgye see Yi dynasty

Songhay 15th–16th century empire of west Africa.

Soter see Ptolemy I

Soto, Hernando de (c.1499–1542) Spanish conquistador and explorer. Fought in Panama and Nicaragua before joining the conquest of Peru. In 1535 he received a commission from Spain for the conquest of Florida. His expedition reached Tampa Bay in May 1539 but then became lost for three years.

SOUTH AFRICA Rich in natural resources, South Africa comprises a central plateau, or veld, bordered to the south and east by the Drakensberg Mountains. After eight decades of white minority rule, with racial segregation under the apartheid policy since 1948, South Africa held its first multiracial elections in 1994. The revolution in South Africa's politics began in 1990, when black freedom groups were legalized and the dismantling of apartheid began. The ▶

African National Congress (ANC), under Nelson Mandela and his successor Thabo Mbeki, is now the leading political movement. *p.382, p.443*

CHRONOLOGY

15th century After migrating from the north, African peoples are settled in today's Transvaal, Natal and Eastern Cape.

1652 The Dutch East India Company establishes a provisioning station at Table Bay in the Cape – the first white pioneer settlement. The "Afrikaner" or "Boer" colonists who settle subsequently venture inland from the Cape taking more and more land from the indigenous San and Khoikhoi peoples, who either become farm workers or move further into the interior.

18th century In the late 18th century competition for grazing and arable land between the Boers and the Xhosa develops into a series of frontier wars. The first takes place in 1779 and conflict continues for the next hundred years. There is also tension between the frontier farmers and successive governments in the Cape, which is captured by the British in 1795. After a further three-year period of Dutch rule from 1803–06 the British regain control and in the early 19th century bring out immigrants from Britain.

1834 Land-hungry Boer settlers, frustrated by Xhosa resistance and resenting British domination, begin their Great Trek north. Despite fierce battles with the Zulus and other African peoples, they steadily expand the area of white occupation into what is now the Transvaal, Natal and the Orange Free State.

1850s The Transvaal and the Orange Free State both gain their independence, the early British policy of annexing the new areas of white settlement having given way to a policy of withdrawal. Natal (proclaimed a colony in 1843) remains under British rule and is populated by British settlers.

1872 Three years after the discovery of diamonds the British annex the diamond fields. This is followed in 1877 by the annexation of the Transvaal with its gold fields. The exploitation of diamonds and gold leads to an economic boom in the later 19th century and the development of the migrant labor system, with African areas becoming "labor reservoirs."

1880–81 In the First South African (Boer) War, the Boers rise in revolt and British forces are defeated at Majuba Hill in 1881. The British are also fighting the Zulus, and finally defeat them, though only after suffering a massive defeat at Isandlwana in 1879 when more British officers die than at the Battle of Waterloo.

1896 January. The "Jameson Raid" ends in fiasco when a mounted column of British South Africa Company troops from Bechuanaland are captured by Boer forces. The Transvaal rebellion which Cecil Rhodes had sent the column to support fails to materialize when the European "uitlander" mineworkers refuse to rise, despite Rhodes' efforts to stimulate anti-Boer sentiment.

1899–1902 The Second South African (Boer) War is launched by Boer leader Paul Kruger in October 1899 with attacks on the British-controlled Natal and Cape Colony. After initial Boer successes the Boer capital, Pretoria, is captured in June 1900 and Boer guerrilla resistance is broken down. Under the 1902 Treaty of Vereeniging the Transvaal and Orange Free State are again incorporated within the British Empire.

1910 Union of South Africa set up as British dominion; white monopoly of power formalized.

1912 ANC formed.

1934 Independence.

1948 NP takes power; apartheid segregationist policy introduced.

1958–1966 Hendrik Verwoerd prime minister. "Grand Apartheid" policy implemented.

1959 Pan African Congress (PAC) formed.

1960 Sharpeville massacre. ANC, PAC banned.

1961 South Africa becomes republic; leaves Commonwealth.

1964 Senior ANC leader Nelson Mandela jailed.

1976 Soweto uprisings by black students; hundreds killed.

1978 P. W. Botha in office.

1984 New constitution: Indians and Coloreds get some representation. Growing black opposition.

1985 State of emergency introduced. International sanctions.

1989 F. W. De Klerk replaces Botha as president. Elections underline white conservative hostility to change.

1990 De Klerk legalizes ANC and PAC; frees Nelson Mandela.

1990–1993 International sanctions gradually withdrawn.

1991 Convention for a Democratic South Africa (CODESA) starts work.

1992 De Klerk wins whites-only referendum.

1993 Mandela and De Klerk win Nobel Peace Prize.

1994 Multiracial elections won by ANC; Mandela president.

1996 TRC begins work.

1997 New constitution takes effect.

1998 TRC report condemns both apartheid crimes and ANC excesses.

1999 ANC election victory; Thabo Mbeki succeeds Mandela as president.

2000 DA wins nearly 25 percent of votes in local elections.

South African Prime Ministers (from 1908)

1910–1919	Louis Botha
1919–1924	Jan Christiaan Smuts
1924–1939	James Barry Munnik Hertzog
1939–1948	Jan Christiaan Smuts
1948)–1954	Daniël François Malan
1954–1958)	Johannes Gerhardus Strijdom
1958–1966	Henrik Frensch Verwoerd
1966–1978	Balthazar Johannes Vorster
1978–1984	Pieter Willem Botha

South African Presidents (from 1961)

1961–1967	Charles Roberts Swarts
1967–1968	Theophilus E Dönges
1968–1975	Jacobus Johannes Fouché
1975	Johannes de Klerk (acting)
1975–1978	Nicolaas Johannes Diederichs
1978	Marais Viljoen (acting)
1978–1979	Balthazar Johannes Vorster
1979–1984	Marais Viljoen
1984–1989	Pieter Willem Botha
1989	J. Christian Heunis (acting)
1989–1994	Frederik Willem De Klerk
1994–1999	Nelson Rolihlahla Mandela
1999–	Thabo Mvuyelwa Mbeki

South America Populated by peoples migrating from N America at least 12,000 years ago, South America was then isolated for a long time. Many local cultures developed in Amazonia and in the Andes. At a later date some had limited contact with the civilizations of

C America. In the 16th century the arrival of the Spanish in Peru and the Portuguese in Brazil had a catastrophic impact with the introduction of lethal European diseases such as smallpox. In Brazil, once the Portuguese could find no more indigenous people to work on the sugar plantations, they began to import African slaves in huge numbers. South American Independence. *p.353 See also* Chavín, Huari, Incas, Moche, Nazca, Tiahuanaco, and individual countries

Southern Cult Widespread set of religious beliefs in southern N America in 12th-13th centuries CE. *p.241*

Southern Song *see* Song dynasty

Space Race Cold War competition between the US and the USSR in the exploration of space, sparked off by launching of the *Sputnik 1* satellite in 1957. *p.433*

SPAIN Occupying the major part of the Iberian peninsula in southwest Europe, Spain has both an Atlantic and a Mediterranean coast, and is dominated by a central plateau. Spain evolved from a number of small Christian kingdoms in the north of the peninsula which gradually drove out the Islamic Moors from the south. Once the kingdom had been united by the marriage of Isabella of Castile and Ferdinand of Aragon in 1469, Spain became a major European power and the possessor of the greatest empire in the world. However, the country went into a decline from the 17th century onward. Its South and Central American empires were lost by 1830. The 19th century saw the start of a long series of struggles between liberal progressive forces and reactionaries, which culminated in the Spanish Civil War of the 1930s. With the help of Nazi Germany, General Franco overcame the forces of the left and instituted a repressive dictatorship. After the death of Franco in 1975, Spain managed a rapid and relatively peaceful transition to democracy. Since EU membership in 1986, there has been an increasing devolution of power to the regions. For just over 13 years from 1982, Spain had a center-left government, but the right-of-center Popular Party has dominated since 1996.

CHRONOLOGY

2nd century BCE Spain conquered by the Romans after they have driven out the Carthaginians.

419 CE A Visigothic kingdom is established.

587 CE King Recared I is converted to Christianity.

711 CE Visigoths defeated by the Moors.

962 CE The Christian reconquest of Spain is launched.

1212 The extent of Moorish rule is reduced to Granada.

1469 The Kingdom is united by the marriage of Isabella of Castile and Ferdinand of Aragon.

1478 The Spanish Inquisition is formed to test the sincerity of Jewish converts to Christianity. It is not officially abolished until 1834.

1492 Spanish forces expel the Moors from Granada. Christopher Columbus reaches the "New World."

1516–1555 Holy Roman Emperor Charles of Habsburg becomes Carlos I of Spain, but Austrian Habsburg lands and the Spanish Crown are divided again in 1555 with the accession of Philip II.

1580 Portugal comes under the control of the Spanish Crown.

1618–48 The Thirty Years' War, with the loss of Portugal and the United Provinces (Netherlands), marks the beginning of the decline of imperial Spain.

1702–13 The War of the Spanish Succession ends with the Treaty of Utrecht, which deprives Spain of large amounts of territory and leaves the Spanish throne in the hands of the French house of Bourbon.

1808–13 Napoleon invades Spain, provoking the Peninsular War.

1810–30 Spain loses most of its American colonies.

1868–86 Disputed succession leads to a series of Carlist revolts and counter-coups.

1873–74 A republic is briefly declared.

1874 Constitutional monarchy restored under Alfonso XII.

1885 Death of Alfonso XII.

1898 Defeat in war with US results in loss of Cuba, Puerto Rico, and the Philippines.

1914–1918 Spain neutral in World War I.

1921 Spanish army routed by Berbers in Spanish Morocco.

1923 Coup by General Primo de Rivera accepted by King Alfonso XIII. Military dictatorship.

1930 Primo de Rivera dismissed by monarchy.

1931 Second Republic proclaimed. Alfonso XIII flees Spain.

1933 Center-right coalition wins general election.

1934 Asturias uprising quashed by army. Failure of attempt to form Catalan state.

1936 Popular Front wins elections. Right-wing military uprising against Republic. General Francisco Franco subsequently appointed leader.

1939 Nationalists under Franco's command win the civil war, which claims perhaps 500,000 lives.

1940 Franco meets Hitler, but does not enter World War II.

1946 UN condemns Franco regime.

1948 Spain is excluded from the Marshall Plan.

1950 UN lifts veto.

1953 Concordat with Vatican. Spain grants US military bases.

1955 Spain joins UN.

1959 Stabilization Plan is basis for 1960s rapid economic growth.

1962 Franco government applies for eventual membership of EEC.

1969 Gen. Franco names Juan Carlos, grandson of Alfonso XIII, his successor.

1970 Spain signs preferential trade agreement with EEC.

1973 Basque separatists assassinate Prime Minister Carrero Blanco; replaced by Arias Navarro.

1975 Death of Franco. Proclamation of King Juan Carlos I.

1976 King appoints Adolfo Suárez as prime minister.

1977 First democratic elections since 1936 won by Suárez's Democratic Center Union.

1978 New constitution declares Spain a parliamentary monarchy.

1981 Leopoldo Calvo Sotelo replaces Suárez. King foils military coup. Calvo takes Spain into NATO.

1982 Felipe González wins landslide victory for PSOE.

1986 Joins European Community. González wins referendum on keeping Spain in NATO.

1992 Olympic Games held in Barcelona, Expo '92 in Seville.

1996 PSOE loses election; José María Aznar of PP prime minister.

▶

1998 Former PSOE minister found guilty of involvement in Basque kidnappings.
1999 December. ETA ends cease-fire.
2000 Aznar and PP win elections.
2002 Euro introduced. Sunken oil tanker *Prestige* pollutes Galicia.
2004 Madrid train bombings kill 201 people. PSOE wins elections; José Luis Rodriguez Zapatero becomes prime minister.

SPANISH RULERS (SINCE 1300)

Castile (including León)

1296–1312	Ferdinand IV (Fernando)
1312–1350	Alfonso XI
1350–1366	Peter I (Pedro)
1366–1367	Henry II (Enrique)
1367–1369	Peter I (second time)
1369–1379	Henry II (second time)
1379–1390	John I (Juan)
1390–1406	Henry III (Enrique)
1406–1454	John II (Juan)
1454–1474	Henry IV (Enrique)
1474–1504	Isabella I and Ferdinand V
1504–1506	Joan and Philip I
1506–1516	Ferdinand V

Aragón

1291–1327	James II (Jaime)
1327–1336	Alfonso IV
1336–1387	Peter IV (Pedro)
1387–1395	John I (Juan)
1395–1412	Martin
1412–1416	Ferdinand I (Fernando)
1416–1458	Alfonso V
1458–1479	John II (Juan)
1479–1516	Ferdinand II and Isabella I

House of Habsburg

1516–1556	Charles I (Carlos)
1556–1598	Philip II (Felipe)
1598–1621	Philip III (Felipe)
1621–1665	Philip IV (Felipe)
1665–1700	Charles II (Carlos)

House of Bourbon

1700–1724	Philip V
1724	Louis I (Luis)
1724–1746	Philip V (restored)
1746–1759	Ferdinand VI
1759–1788	Charles III (Carlos)
1788–1808	Charles IV (Carlos)
1808	Ferdinand VII (Fernando)

House of Bonaparte

1808–1813	Joseph (José) Bonaparte

House of Bourbon

1814–1833	Ferdinand VII (second time)
1833–1868	Isabella II
1869–1870	Francisco Semano y Dominguez, regent

House of Savoy

1870–1873	Amadeo

1873–1874	**First Republic**

House of Bourbon

1874–1885	Alfonso XII
1886–1931	Alfonso XIII

1931–1939	**Second Republic**

Nationalist regime

1939–1975	Francisco Franco, dictator

House of Bourbon (restored)

1975–	Juan Carlos

Spanish-American War (1898) US intervention in a Cuban insurrection led to war with Spain. The Spanish fleet in the Far East was defeated by Admiral Dewey, although resistance to the invasion was sustained by Filipino partisans. The Spanish garrison at Santiago de Cuba surrendered after a fortnight's resistance. By the peace agreement of Aug 9 1898, Spain renounced her rights of sovereignty over Cuba and Puerto Rico and ceded the Philippines and the island of Guam to the US.

Spanish Civil War (1936–39) Civil war between the elected Republican government of Spain and the conservative Nationalist opposition, supported by the military and receiving aid from Italy and Germany (both under fascist control at the time). The Republicans also received support from around 60,000 volunteer International Brigades from other European nations and the US, and from the Soviet Union. From the end of 1936, the Civil War became a war of attrition, with the Nationalists gradually gaining ground at the expense of the Republicans who eventually surrendered in March 1939. The Spanish Civil war is thought to have claimed at least 500,000 casualties. *p.413*

Spanish Succession, War of the (1701–14) In 1701, Leopold of Austria, supported by England and the Dutch Republic, invaded Italy in opposition to the will of Carlos II of Spain, which bequeathed Spain's possessions in Europe and overseas to Philip, grandson of Louis XIV of France. Portugal, Savoy, and the Holy Roman Empire also declared war on France. A compromise was eventually reached at the Peace of Utrecht (1714); Philip retained Spain but the Spanish Netherlands and Italian territories went to the Austrian Habsburgs and Savoy.

Sparta One of the leading Greek city-states, Sparta was forced to institute a series of military and social reforms in response to territorial revolts. As a result it remained inward-looking and militaristic in contrast to Athens' developing democracy and imperial acquisitions. *p.57*

Special Economic Zones Regions of eastern and southern China (Beijing, Shanghai, Xiamen, Shantou, Shenzhen, Guangzhou, and since 1997, Hong Kong) established after 1978, under Deng Xiaoping, designed to attract foreign investment and develop Chinese economic strengths and relations with free market economies.

Speke, John Hanning (1827–94) English soldier and explorer of Africa. Accompanied Richard Burton on a voyage to Somaliland in 1854; three years later they were sent by the Royal Geographical Society to search for the great African lakes. Speke, exploring alone, came across the headwaters of the Nile, later confirming the location with James Grant in 1860.

Spice Islands *see* Moluccas

Spion Kop ✕ of 2nd Boer War (1900). Boer victory over British.

"Springtime of Nations" Name given to the nationalist uprisings that broke out across Europe in 1848–49. *p.363*

Spotsylvania Court House ✕ of American Civil War (May 8–19 1864). Inconclusive result.

Sputnik First artificial space satellite, launched in Oct 1957 by the Soviet Union.

SRI LANKA Separated from India by the Palk Strait, Sri Lanka comprises one large island and several coral islets to the northwest in the Palk Strait. The main island is dominated by rugged central uplands. The fertile plains to the north are crisscrossed by rivers and bordered to the southeast by the Mahaweli River. Sri Lankan affairs are dominated by the long-standing conflict between the government and the Tamils, who are fighting for an independent state.

CHRONOLOGY

1505 Portuguese fleet lands in Ceylon.
1658–1796 Period of Dutch control.
1802 Ceylon becomes a British Crown Colony, formalizing British control over the island established in 1796.
1931 Constitutional reforms are introduced on the recommendation of the Donoughmore Commission, amounting in effect to an assurance of self-government in the near future and including universal suffrage.
1948 February 4. The island is granted independence following the appointment of the Soulbury Commission in 1944 to prepare the way for self-government.
1948 Indian Tamil workers stripped of suffrage and citizenship rights.
1956 SLFP wins election, promotes Sinhalese language.
1972 Name changed to Sri Lanka.
1983 Tamil Tigers begin civil war.
1993 President Premadasa killed.
1994 Left-wing PA wins election; Chandrika Kumaratunga president.
1995–1996 Collapse of peace talks, civil war resumes.
1999 Kumaratunga survives assassination attempt; reelected.
2000 Sirimavo Bandaranaike, world's first woman prime minister, dies.

Srivijaya Maritime empire which emerged in western Indonesia in the 7th century CE, with a capital at Palembang in southern Sumatra. For seven centuries, Srivijaya controlled the lucrative trade passing through the straits of Malacca and Sunda Strait and across the Isthmus of Kra.

SS *see* Schutzstaffel

Stalin, Josef (*var.* Iosif Vissarionovich Stalin, Georg. Ioseb Dzhugashvili, 1879–1953) Secretary-general of the Communist Party of the Soviet Union (1922–53) and premier of the Soviet state (1941–53), who for a quarter of a century dictatorially ruled the Soviet Union and transformed it into a major world power. *p.412*

Stalingrad ⚔ of World War II (Sep 1942–Feb 1943) marking the halt by Soviet forces of the German advance into Russia; following a prolonged siege, Soviet forces secured the first surrender of German troops in the war.

Stamford Bridge ⚔ for the throne of England (Sep 25 1066). Victory of Harold over his brother Tostig and Harald Hardrada of Norway.

Stamp Act (1765) Act, passed by British government, imposing direct taxes on all printed papers in the American colonies, including legal documents, newspapers and pamphlets, in order to raise revenue for the defence of the colonies. It was met by vigorous protest from the colonists who refused to use the stamps, as well as refusing to import British goods. They defended their right to be taxed only by their own consent. Though the Act was quickly repealed, the Declaratory Act, issued at the same time, asserted the British government's right to tax directly anywhere within its empire.

Standard Oil of California (ESSO) The company started to extract oil in Saudi Arabia (1933).

Stanley, Henry Morton (prev. John Rowlands, 1841–1904) British-American explorer of central Africa, famous for his rescue of the Scottish missionary and explorer David Livingstone and for his discoveries in and development of the Congo region. He was knighted in 1899.

START *see* Strategic Arms Reduction Talks

Star Wars *see* Strategic Defense Initiative

Staufen dynasty *see* Hohenstaufen dynasty

Staunton ⚔ of American Civil War (Jun 8–9 1862). Confederate victory.

Steam The power that drove the Industrial Revolution.
Newcomen's steam engine. *p.321*
The Age of Steam. *p.352*
See also Industrial Revolution, Railroads

Stefan Dusan (1114–1200) Ruler of medieval Kingdom of Serbia *p.237*

Stefansson, Vilhjalmur (1879–1962) Explorer of the Canadian Arctic. From 1906–12 he studied the culture of the Inuit people of the Arctic. From 1913–18 he explored huge areas of the Arctic north of Canada and Alaska.

Stephen I (977–1038) King of Hungary. Stephen founded the kingdom of Hungary and helped establish the Roman church in his country. In recognition of this, he was made a saint in 1083.

Stephenson, Robert (1803–59) English engineer, son of George Stephenson (1781–1848). They worked together on the Stockton to Darlington Railway (1825) and the Liverpool–Manchester Railway (1829), for which they built the famous steam engine *Rocket*.

steppe nomads General term for the various groups of pastoral nomads of the Eurasian Steppes, historically extending from S Ukraine to Manchuria. Often referred to by Greek and Roman writers as Scythians. *p.57, p.90 See also* Huns, Kazakhs, Uzbeks, Turks, Xiongnu

Stilicho, Flavius (365–408, reigned 394–408) Half-Vandal general who acted as regent to the late Roman emperor Honorius.

stirrup Chinese inventiion c.350 CE. *p.97*

Stockton to Darlington railroad, first passenger service (1825).

Stoicism A philosophical movement which flourished in Greece and Rome between 300 BCE and 180 CE, named after the Stoa Poikile, the painted colonnade in Athens where its founder Zeno of Citium taught. Its central premise was that reason is the governing principle of nature, thus an ideal life would see individuals living in harmony with nature and valuing equanimity in the face of life's uncertainties.

Stone Age The first known period of prehistoric human culture, characterized by the use of stone tools and conventionally divided into Paleolithic, Mesolithic, and Neolithic. *p.13, p.14*

Stonehenge Group of standing stones near Salisbury in England, originally in two concentric circles enclosing two rows of smaller stones. Construction is thought to have begun as a wooden structure c.3000 BCE. The great stone structure was erected c.2000 BCE. Its exact origin and purpose remain a mystery, but may have been connected with rituals of consecration and some kind of sacrifice. On midsummer day the rising sun aligns with the axis of Stonehenge. *p.25*

Strabo (c.64 BCE–23 CE) Roman historian and geographer. He traveled widely in Greece and Egypt, collecting material for his *Historical Studies* (47 vols), most of which have been lost, but his *Geographica* (17 vols) survived almost intact and contained valuable information on countries in Europe, Asia and Africa.

Strategic Arms Limitation Talks (SALT) SALT I (signed 1972) was the outcome of tentative negotiations between US and Soviet Union to reduce their nuclear arsenals, begun in 1969; SALT II (signed 1979) remained unratified by the US.

Strategic Arms Reduction Talks (START) Initiated in 1982 in an attempt to control arms proliferation in US and Soviet Union during Cold War. A treaty was eventually signed in 1991.

Strategic Defense Initiative (SDI *aka* Star Wars). Satellite-based defence system initiated by US in mid-1980s in response to increased Soviet arms budget.

Stuart, John McDouall (1815–66) English-born explorer of Australia. In 1861–62 he crossed the continent from south to north, reaching the Indian Ocean just to the east of Darwin.

Sturt, Charles (1795–1869) British soldier and explorer of the Australian interior. He completed a survey of the Murray-Darling river system in 1830. Sturt's expedition of 1844–46 to the center of Australia failed to find the inland sea he believed lay there.

Sübedei Mongol general, one of Genghis Khan's most trusted commanders. He led a raid deep into Russia in 1222.

Sucre, Antonio José de (1790–1830) Colleague of Simón Bolívar, general of armies of liberation in Colombia, Ecuador, Peru, and Bolivia.

SUDAM (*full name* Superintendancy for the Development of the Amazon Region, *Port.* Superintendencia para o Desenvolvimento de Amazonia). A Brazilian agency founded in 1953 to funnel federal funds into development projects in Amazonia, and oversee tax incentives which were intended to stimulate investments of private capital.

SUDAN Bordered by the Red Sea, Sudan is the largest country in Africa. Its landscape changes from desert in the north to lush tropical in the south, with grassy plains and swamps in the center. Tensions between the Arab north and African south have led to two civil wars since independence from British and Egyptian rule in 1956. The second of these conflicts remains unresolved. In 1989, an army coup installed a military Islamic fundamentalist regime.

CHRONOLOGY

c. 1580–1050 BCE The New Kingdom in Egypt expands its frontiers up the river Nile to the south into Nubia (in the north of contemporary Sudan). By the 11th century bce Egyptian control of Nubia is weakened and a separate kingdom is established in Kush, further to the south, which between 770 and 716 bce conquers Egypt.

641 CE Muslim Arabs conquer what is now Sudan. (At this time the term "Sudan" is generally used to refer to the whole belt of territory immediately south of the Sahara which is known in Arabic as "bilad al-Sudan" or the "land of the black men" and roughly corresponds to what is today called the Sahel.)

1821 Northern Sudan is conquered by the Viceroy of Egypt, Mohammed Ali. Trade routes are opened up through the southern Sudd swamps. The slave trade annihilates much of the southern population.

1874–80 The Sudan is administered for the Egyptian viceroy by the British General Gordon.

1881 Muhammad Ahmed el-Mahdi declares a holy war against the Egyptian administration in Khartoum.

1882 British invade Egypt.

1883 Muslim revolt in Sudan led by Muhammad Ahmed, the Mahdi.

1898 Mahdists defeated. Anglo-Egyptian condominium set up.

1954 Becomes self-governing.

1955 Rebellion in south starts 17 years of civil war.

1956 Independence as republic.

1958–1964 Military rule.

1965 Civilian revolution, elections.

1969 Coup led by Col. Jaafar Nimeiri.

1972 South gets limited autonomy.

1973 Sudanese Socialist Union is sole political party.

1983 Southern rebellion resumes. Sharia law imposed.

1984 Devastating drought.

1986 Army coup.

1989 Gen. Omar Bashir takes over.

1991 Sharia penal code instituted. Pro-Iraq stance in Gulf War.

2000 Bashir ousts fundamentalist al-Turabi from leadership of NC. New attempts to make peace with southern rebels.

2002 SPLA signs cease-fire. Fighting increases between rival factions over southern oil reserves.

2004 Ethnic violence in Darfur escalates into humanitarian crisis.

Suebi *see* Sueves

Sueves (*var.* Suevi, Suebi, Swabians) Roman name for group of German tribes. One group took part in the Great Migration of 406, eventually founding a kingdom in Galicia and northern Portugal.

Suevi *see* Sueves

Suez Canal Shipping canal 170 km long linking the Mediterranean to the Red Sea. Built to a plan by Ferdinand de Lesseps, who supervised its construction, it opened in 1869 and soon became one of the world's most heavily used waterways. In 1875 Britain paid the bankrupt Khedive of Egypt four million pounds for a substantial shareholding in the Canal. In 1956 Egypt nationalized the Suez Canal Company, precipitating the Suez War which temporarily closed the Canal. *p.371*

Suez Crisis (1956) Military conflict involving British, French, Israeli, and Egyptian forces. Caused by Egypt nationalizing the Suez Canal. In a combined operation, Israel invaded Sinai and French and British troops occupied the Canal area. Under US pressure, invading forces withdrew and were replaced by a UN peace-keeping force.

Sugar Act (1764) Act passed by British government, designed via strict customs enforcement to end the smuggling of sugar and molasses from the French and Dutch West Indies into the American colonies, and give additional funding for British military responsibilities in America. It was deeply unpopular in the American colonies.

Sui dynasty (581–618) Ruling Chinese dynasty which united China in 589 after three centuries of disorder following the collapse of the Han dynasty. Replaced by the Tang dynasty in 619.

Sukarno, Ahmed (*aka* Bung Karno, 1902–70) Indonesian statesman, responsible for forming the Indonesian National Party in 1927. After suffering imprisonment by the Dutch authorities, he cooperated with the occupying Japanese authorities (1942–45). In Aug 1945 he declared independence from the

Netherlands. In 1949, after four years of nationalist guerrilla war with the Dutch, Indonesia became independent under President Sukarno. In 1959, he assumed dictatorial powers, but was deposed by a military coup in 1965.

Sukhothai Medieval Thai kingdom. *p.214*

Suleyman I (*aka* Suleyman the Magnificent, c.1495–1566) The son of Selim I, Suleyman became Ottoman Sultan in 1520 and presided over the period of the empire's greatest expansion and consolidation. In 1521 the Ottomans captured Belgrade and in 1526 defeated the Hungarians at Mohács. Suleyman was celebrated for his lawmaking and was an enthusiastic patron of architecture and the arts.

Sulla (Lucius Cornelius Sulla Felix, 138–78 BCE) Successful Roman general and dictator. *p.71*

Sumer Term used to designate the southern part of ancient Mesopotamia, and area of Sumerian civilization. Sumerians are credited with the creation of the first cities and the invention of cuneiform writing. Excavations show a flourishing civilization by 3000 BCE.

Sun Yat-sen *see* Sun Zhongshan

Sun Zhongshan (*var.* Sun Yat-sen, 1866–1925) Elected provisional head of state in China in 1911 during the anti-Qing revolution, but resigned a few months later. Gained full control of the country in 1923 and reorganized the Kuomintang (Guomindang) to resemble the Soviet Communist Party. Inspired both Nationalists and Communists. His efforts to unify China were continued by Jiang Jieshi. *p.395*

Sundiata (died 1255) West African monarch who founded the empire of Mali.

Sung dynasty *see* Song dynasty

Sunna *see* Sunni

Sunni (*var. Ar.* Sunna "the way"). The Sunna is the way of the Prophet Muhammad and includes everything he did, said, caused, ordered or allowed to happen. A Sunni is a Muslim who follows this way. The word is most commonly used to distinguish the majority of Muslims from the Shi'ite minority. *See also* Islam, Muhammad, Shi'ites.

Sunni Ali (reigned 1464–92) Emperor of Songhay in W Africa. He reduced many former Mali provinces to Songhay dependencies, created a professional army and river-navy and introduced many administrative reforms.

SURINAME Located on the north coast of South America, Suriname is bordered by Guyana, French Guiana, and Brazil. The interior is rainforested highlands; most people live near the coast. Dutch rule began in 1667, after an Anglo-Dutch treaty whose terms included Britain ceding its colony in Suriname to the Dutch but gaining New Amsterdam (New York). In 1975, after almost 300 years of Dutch rule, Suriname became independent. The Netherlands is still its main aid supplier, and is home to a third of Surinamese. Democracy was restored in 1991, after almost 11 years of military rule.

CHRONOLOGY

1975 Independence.
1980 Coup. Rule by Lieutenant Colonel Desi Bouterse.
1982 Opponents executed. Dutch suspend aid for six years.
1986–1992 Bosneger rebel war.
1988–1991 Elections, coup, and new elections.
1992 Bouterse quits as army head.
1998–1999 President Wijdenbosch refuses to extradite Bouterse to the Netherlands on drug charges.

Survey of India The appointment of James Rennell as Surveyor-General to Bengal was the beginning of Britain's systematic mapping of the Indian subcontinent. From the late 18th century, army officers such as Colin Mackenzie and William Lambton pioneered trigonometrical surveys from 1800, and their work was continued, from 1823, by George Everest.

Suryavarman II Khmer warrior king (reigned c.1113–50).

Susa Ancient city of Persia, the summer residence of the Achaemenid rules. The Royal Road ran from Susa to Sardis on the Aegean Sea.

Sutter's Mill Site in eastern California that saw the start of the 1848 gold rush.

Sutton Hoo Burial site of Anglo-Saxon chieftain in eastern England. *p.122*

Swabians *see* Sueves

Swahili (*var. Ar.* Sawahili) Bantu language which in its vocabulary shows evidence of the contact between Arabian traders and the inhabitants of the east coast of Africa over many centuries.

SWAZILAND The tiny southern African kingdom of Swaziland, bordered on three sides by South Africa and to the east by Mozambique, comprises mainly upland plateaus and mountains. Governed by a strong hereditary monarchy, Swaziland is a country in which tradition is being challenged by demands for modern multiparty government. Swaziland became a British protectorate in 1903. King Mswati III, crowned in 1986, has overhauled the electoral process, but has still to legalize party politics.

CHRONOLOGY

1968 Independence.
1973 King bans political activity and repeals constitution.
1978 New constitution confirms king's executive, legislative control.
1982 King Sobhuza dies. Queen Mother becomes regent for Prince Makhosetive. Power struggle between modernists and traditionalists in royal Dlamini clan.
1986 Makhosetive crowned King Mswati III at the age of 18.
1992 Limited electoral reforms; parties still banned.
1993 Elections under new system.
1996 Review of political system.
1998 Poor turnout at elections.
2000 Mass prodemocracy protests.
2003 New constitution offers human rights but parties still banned.

SWEDEN Situated on the Scandinavian peninsula with Norway to its west, Sweden is a densely forested country with numerous lakes. The north of Sweden falls within the Arctic Circle; much of the south is fertile and widely cultivated. Sweden has one of the most extensive welfare systems in the world, and is among the world's leading proponents of equal rights for women. Its economic strengths include high-tech industries, such as Ericsson, and car production, most notably Volvo and Saab. Unlike neighboring Norway, it joined the EU in January 1995. The Swedish empire (1600–1800). p.297

▶

CHRONOLOGY

7th century The Svear (from which "Sweden" is derived) extend their rule over much of central Sweden.

Early 9th century The Svear and Gota ("Goths") join other Viking groups in waves of seaborne migrations and conquest which extend across Europe and beyond and last until the 11th century.

Late 12th century Christianity becomes the dominant religion throughout Sweden; Erik IX (reigned 1150–60) and his successors incorporate Gotland into the kingdom, which by this stage covers most of present-day Sweden.

1319–65 Under Magnus II Sweden establishes control over Finland and Norway.

1397 Under the Union of Kalmar Sweden and Denmark are joined in personal union under Queen Margrethe I of Denmark.

1523 With tension between Sweden and Denmark growing, the Swedish estates elect a local noble, Gustav Vasa, as King, thus dissolving the Union of Kalmar.

1527 Evangelical Lutheranism is established as the state religion.

1611 During the reign of Gustavus II Adolphus, which begins in 1611, Sweden takes an active part in the Thirty Years' War (1618–48) and becomes the dominant regional power and a major European power. In 1632 Gustavus II Adolphus is mortally wounded at the battle of Lützen, near Leipzig, although Sweden is victorious.

1632 He is succeeded by his six-year-old daughter Kristina, while his Chancellor, Axel Oxenstierna, continues to manage affairs of state during her minority. She rules until 1654, during which time she is an enthusiastic patron of the arts and the Swedish court attracts some of the best minds in Europe. Having secretly converted to Catholicism, she abdicates in 1654 and dies in Rome in 1689.

1660 The Peace of Copenhagen confirms Sweden's empire, which includes Finland, Estonia, Ingria, Livonia and Pomerania, and several other possessions in Germany.

1679 Under the "reduction" King Charles XI (reigned 1660–97) breaks the power of the nobility and establishes an absolute monarchy with the support of the parliament (Riksdag).

1721 The Treaty of Nystad, at the end of the Great Northern war (1700–21), marks the end of Sweden as a major power; it loses its Baltic empire to Russia.

1723 A constitution is adopted which subordinates the crown to parliament (although absolute rule is partially reasserted under Gustav III, who rules from 1771 until 1792).

1809 Sweden is obliged to cede Finland to Russia; a new parliamentary Constitution is adopted later in the year.

1814–1815 Congress of Vienna. Sweden cedes territory to Russia and Denmark. Period of unbroken peace begins.

1865–1866 Riksdag (parliament) reformed into a bicameral structure.

1905 Norway gains independence from Sweden.

1911 First Liberal government comes to power.

1914 Government resigns over defense policy.

1914–1917 Sweden remains neutral during World War I but supplies Germany. Allied blockade.

1917 Food shortages. Conservative government falls. Nils Edén forms a Liberal government: limits exports contributing to German war effort.

1919 Universal adult suffrage.

1921 Finland gains Åland Islands as retribution for Sweden's war role.

1932 Severe recession. Social Democrat government under Per Albin Hansson elected.

1939–1945 Sweden neutral. Grants transit rights to German forces.

1945–1976 Continuing Social Democratic rule under Tage Erlander establishes Sweden as world's most advanced welfare state, and one of the most affluent.

1950 Gustav VI Adolf becomes king.

1953 Nordic Council member.

1959 Founder member of EFTA.

1969 Erlander succeeded by Olof Palme as prime minister.

1973 Carl XVI Gustaf on throne.

1975 Major constitutional reform. Riksdag (parliament) becomes unicameral with a three-year term. Role of monarchy reduced to ceremonial functions.

1976 SAP loses power. Nonsocialist coalition led by Thorbjörn Fälldin in government.

1978 Fälldin resigns over issue of nuclear power. Ola Ullsten prime minister.

1979 Fälldin prime minister again.

1982 Elections. SAP forms minority government. Palme returns as prime minister.

1986 Palme shot dead. His deputy, Ingvar Carlsson, succeeds him as prime minister. Police fail to find the killer.

1990 Carlsson introduces moderate austerity package, cuts government spending, raises indirect taxes.

1991 Sweden applies to join EU. SAP remains largest party after general election but is unable to form government; Carlsson resigns. Carl Bildt, leader of Moderate Party (MS), forms coalition of nonsocialist parties in middle of serious recession.

1992 Austerity measures succeed in reducing inflation but SAP refuses to support further spending cuts.

1994 Terms of EU membership settled. Elections return SAP to power. Referendum favors joining EU.

1995 Joins EU.

1996 Carlsson resigns; replaced by Göran Persson.

1998 Persson remains in office, despite SAP losses in elections; dependent on Left and Greens for parliamentary majority.

2001 Defense reform program.

2003 Foreign Minister Anna Lindh stabbed to death. Euro rejected in referendum.

Swift, Jonathan (1667–1745) Anglo-Irish cleric and satirical writer. Dean of St. Patrick's Cathedral in Dublin and author of *Gulliver's Travels*. p.323

SWITZERLAND Switzerland lies at the center of western Europe geographically, but outside it politically. Sometimes called Europe's water tower, it is the source of all four of the region's major river systems: the Po, the Rhine, the Rhône, and the Inn-Danube. In 1291, the three cantons of Unterwalden, Schwyz, and Uri set up the Perpetual League to pursue Swiss liberty. Joined by other cantons, they succeeded in 1499 in gaining virtual independence from historic feudal allegiance to the Habsburg empire. Switzerland has built one of the world's most prosperous economies, aided by the fact that it has retained its neutral status through every major European conflict since 1815. The process of European integration has been the latest and strongest challenge to Swiss neutralism, but it remains outside the EU.

CHRONOLOGY

1648 Peace of Westphalia ending Thirty Years' War, in which Switzerland played no active part, recognizes full Swiss independence.

1798 Invaded by French.

1815 Congress of Vienna after Napoleon's defeat confirms Swiss independence and establishes its neutrality. Geneva and Valais join Swiss Confederation.

1848 New constitution – central government given more powers, but cantons' powers guaranteed.

1857 Neuchâtel joins confederation.

1863 Henri Dunant founds ICRC in Geneva.

1874 Referendum established as important decision-making tool.

1914–1918 Plays humanitarian role in World War I.

1919 Proportional representation ensures future political stability.

1920 Joins League of Nations.

1939–1945 Neutral again. Refuses to join UN in 1945.

1959 Founder member of EFTA. Present four-party coalition comes to power, taking over FDP/PRD dominance of government.

1967 Right-wing groups make electoral gains, campaigning to restrict entry of foreign workers.

1971 Most women granted right to vote in federal elections.

1984 Parliament approves application for UN membership. Elisabeth Kopp is first woman minister (justice minister).

1986 Referendum opposes joining UN. Immigrant numbers restricted.

1988 Kopp resigns over allegedly violating secrecy of information laws.

1990 Kopp acquitted. Case revealed Public Prosecutor's office held secret files on 200,000 people. Violent protests. State security laws amended.

1991 Large increase in attacks on asylum-seekers' hostels.

1992 Joins IMF and World Bank. Referendum vetoes joining European Economic Area.

1994 Referendum approves new antiracism law and tighter laws against narcotics traffickers and illegal immigrants.

1998 $1.25 billion compensation for Holocaust victims whose funds were deposited in Swiss banks.

1999 Ruth Dreifuss first woman president.

2000 Referendum endorses close trade links with EU.

2001 EU membership again rejected in referendum.

2002 Referendum on joining UN gives approval. Legalization of abortions as currently carried out also approved.

Sword Brothers (*var.* Livonian Order) Crusading order, which conquered Livonia in the Baltic region in the early 13th century. After their defeat by Lithuanians in 1236, their activities were taken over by the Teutonic Knights.

SYRIA Syria shares borders with Lebanon, Israel, Jordan, Iraq, and Turkey. Many Syrians identify their country with a Greater Syria encompassing Lebanon, Jordan, and Palestine. Since independence, Syria's foreign relations have been turbulent, although President Hafez al-Assad's authoritarian Ba'athist regime brought a measure of internal stability.

CHRONOLOGY

634 CE Muslim forces conquer Syria, defeating the Byzantines.

997 CE Northern Syria falls to the Byzantines and the south is ruled by the Egyptian Fatimid Dynasty.

1098 The First crusade takes Antioch.

1303–1516 The Mamluks control Syria.

1516 Syria falls to the Ottomans.

1963 Ba'athist military junta seizes power. Major General Amin al-Hafez president.

1966 Hafez ousted by coup supported by members of the radical Ba'ath Party.

1967 Israel overruns Syrian positions above Lake Tiberias, seizes Golan Heights, and occupies Quneitra. Syria boycotts Arab summit and rejects compromise with Israel.

1970 Hafez al-Assad seizes power in "corrective coup."

1971 Assad elected president for a seven-year term.

1973 New constitution approved confirming Ba'ath Party as dominant force. War launched with Egypt against Israel to regain territory lost in 1967. Further territory temporarily lost to Israel.

1976 With peacekeeping mandate from Arab League, Syria intervenes to quell fighting in Lebanon.

1977 Relations broken off with Egypt after President Sadat's visit to Jerusalem.

1978 National charter signed with Iraq for union. Assad returned for second term.

1980 Membership of Muslim Brotherhood made capital offense. Treaty of Friendship with USSR.

1981 Israel formally annexes Golan Heights. Charter with Iraq collapses.

1982 Islamic extremist uprising in Hama crushed; thousands killed. Israel invades Lebanon; Syrian missiles in Bekaa Valley destroyed.

1985 Assad reelected president. US claims Syrian links to airport bombings at Rome and Vienna.

1986 Syrian complicity alleged in planting of bomb aboard Israeli airliner in London. EU states, with exception of Greece, impose sanctions.

1989 Diplomatic relations reestablished with Egypt.

1991 Troops take part in Operation Desert Storm. Aid and defense pact signed with Egypt, Saudi Arabia, Kuwait, UAE, Qatar, Bahrain, and Oman.

1999 Assad reconfirmed as president.

2000 Forced resignation after 13 years and subsequent suicide of prime minister, Mahmoud az-Zoubi. Death of Hafez al-Assad. Succession of his son Bashar.

2003 Israel bombs "terrorist camps" in Syria.

T

Tahiti *see* French Polynesia

Taika Reform Social and political reform of Japan initiated in 645 CE.

Taiping Rebellion (1850–64) Major peasant uprising during late Qing dynasty China, led by quasi-Christian charismatic and ascetic, Hong Xiuquan. Originating in

S China, around Guangxi, Hong proclaimed Taiping (the Heavenly Kingdom of Great Peace), and identified the Qing as satanic oppressors. By the mid-1850s the rebellion had gained massive support and their armies moved north to Wuchang and Nanjing where they established a separate government (and where over 40,000 defenders were slaughtered). They failed to take Shanghai (1860, 1862) and were finally defeated by Qing forces with enormous loss of life. *p.364*

Taira Clan Japanese warrior family ascendant in the 12th century.

TAIWAN The island of Taiwan, formerly known as Formosa, lies off the southeast coast of mainland China. Mountains run north to south, covering two-thirds of the island. The lowlands are highly fertile, cultivated mostly with rice, and densely populated. In 1949, when the Chinese communists ousted Chiang Kai-shek's Kuomintang (KMT) from power on the mainland, he established the Republic of China government on the island. De facto military rule has been democratized progressively since 1986. The KMT's grip on power was shaken by defeat in the 2000 presidential election. Mainland China still considers Taiwan a renegade province, and only a few countries now give official recognition to the regime there.

CHRONOLOGY

1590 Portuguese reach the island and name it Formosa (beautiful).
1641 Dutch take control of the island.
1683 Manchus take the island and it becomes part of Qing China.
1895 After Sino-Japanese War, island passes to Japan.
1945 After World War II Taiwan is returned to China.
1949 Chiang Kai-shek's army, defeated by the communists on the mainland, take refuge on Taiwan. Establishment of the Republic of China government.
1971 People's Republic of China replaces Taiwan at UN and on UN Security Council.
1973 Taipei's KMT regime rejects Beijing's offer of secret talks on reunification of China.

1975 President Chiang Kai-shek dies. His son General Chiang Ching-kuo becomes KMT leader. Yen Chia-kan succeeds as president.
1978 Chiang Ching-kuo elected president.
1979 US severs relations with Taiwan and formally recognizes People's Republic of China.
1984 President Chiang reelected.
1986 Political reforms: KMT allows multiparty democracy, ends martial law, and permits visits to Chinese mainland for "humanitarian" purposes for first time in 38 years. In 1988, mainland Chinese are allowed to visit Taiwan on same basis.
1988 Lee Teng-hui president.
1990 KMT formally ends state of war with People's Republic of China.
1991 DPP draft constitution for Taiwan independence opposed by ruling KMT and Beijing. KMT reelected with large majority.
1995–1996 Legislative elections. KMT majority reduced.
1996 Lee Teng-hui wins first direct presidential elections.
1998 KMT secures absolute majority in elections to Legislative Yuan.
1999 Chinese threats over reference to "separate states" status. September. Thousands die in earthquake.
2000 March. Chen Shui-bian of DPP wins presidency; overturns KMT dominance.
2004 Chen narrowly reelected.

Taizu *see* Zhu Yuanzhang

TAJIKISTAN Tajikistan lies on the western slopes of the Pamirs in central Asia. Language and traditions are similar to those of Iran rather than those of Turkic Uzbekistan. In the 19th century, Tajikistan was a collection of semi-independent principalities, some under Russian control, others under the influence of the Emirate of Bukhara. Tajikistan decided on independence only when neighboring Soviet republics declared theirs in late 1991. Fighting between communist government forces and Islamist rebels, which erupted shortly afterwards, has been contained since 1997 by a tenuous peace agreement.

CHRONOLOGY

1925 Soviets take over Tajikistan.
1940 Cyrillic script introduced.
1989 Tajik becomes official language.
1991 Independence from Moscow.
1994, 1999 Imomali Rakhmanov reelected president.
1995 Legislative elections. Tajik currency introduced.
1997–1998 Peace accord with rebels.
2000 Pro-Rakhmanov PDPT wins legislative elections.

Talas River ⚔ (751) Between victorious Arab (Muslim) and Tang armies in Central Asia, marking for a time the furthest expansion of each empire.

Taleban *see* Taliban

Taliban (*var.* Talibaan, Taleban) Extreme Sunni Muslim fundamentalist militia group which emerged in Afghanistan in the wake of the 1979–89 war. They took effective control of the capital and southern areas of the country from 1995. Driven from power by the US-led offensive of 2001–02.

Tamerlane *see* Timur

Tamil Eelam The aspiration of the minority Tamils in Sri Lanka is to break away from the Sinhalese and form an independent state (Tamil Eelam) in the north and east of the country. Civil war broke out in 1984 and the Sri Lankan government has always refused to to countenance federalism.

Tamil Tigers Force of Tamil guerrilla fighters that control much of the northeast of Sri Lanka and demands the creation of an independent state (Tamil Eelam).

Tang dynasty (618–907) Chinese ruling dynasty, which unified China after a long period of instability. The Tang Empire extended into Central Asia, with a population of c.60 million people. It established trade links, both maritime and overland, with the West. *p.123, p.130*

Tanganyika *see* Tanzania

Tanguts People of southern Mongolia. Established a state in northwest China, the Xixia empire (1038).

Tannenberg ⚔ of World War I (Aug 26–30 1914). German victory over Russia which sustained the loss of almost an entire army, and massive quantities of weapons. The early Russian invasion of East Prussia meant that the Germans had to divert troops from their attack on France at a crucial moment of that campaign.

Tantric Buddhism (*var.* Tibetan Buddhism) School of Buddhism developed in Tibet from 8th century CE, and also practiced in Mongolia, centered on monasticism and headed by the Dalai Lama as the reincarnation of the Compassionate Buddha and titular head of the Tibetan state. *See also* Buddhism, Dalai Lama

---

TANZANIA Tanzania lies between Kenya and Mozambique on the east African coast. Formed by the union of Tanganyika and Zanzibar and other islands, Tanzania comprises a coastal lowland, volcanic highlands, and the Great Rift Valley. It includes Mount Kilimanjaro, Africa's highest peak. The island of Zanzibar had always played an important role in Arab trade with E Africa, especially the trade in slaves and ivory. In 1841 the Omani sultan Sayyid Said transferred his capital there. The mainland became the German colony of Tanganyika in 1884, while the Sultanate of Zanzibar became a British protectorate in 1890. After World War I Germany lost Tanganyika and it became a British mandated territory and part of British East Africa. Tanganyika gained independence in 1961, Zanzibar in 1963, the two states merging to form Tanzania in 1964. The country was led by the socialist Julius Nyerere from 1962 until 1985. His Revolutionary Party of Tanzania (CCM) won multiparty elections held in 1995 and 2000.

CHRONOLOGY

1918 Tanganyika British mandate.
1961 Tanganyika independent.
1962 Nyerere becomes president.
1963 Zanzibar independent.
1964 Zanzibar signs union with Tanganyika to form Tanzania.
1985 President Mwinyi begins relaxation of socialist policies.
1992 Political parties allowed.
1995 Multiparty elections. Benjamin Mkapa becomes president.
1999 Death of Nyerere.
2000 Mkapa elected for second term.
2001 Increasing unrest among Zanzibar separatists.

Taoism Major Chinese religion, founded by Lao Tzu, based on the "Way," living in selfless accord with nature and natural forces, and respecting the example of ancestors. *See also* Lao Tzu

Tapajós A chiefdom centered on Santarém in Brazil, which dominated the region in the 16th and 17th centuries. The warlike people extracted tribute and labor from those they controlled.

Taprobane *see* Sri Lanka

Tarquin I (*var. Lat.* Lucius Tarquinius Priscus, reigned 616–578 BCE) The first Etruscan king of Rome.

Tarquin II (*var.* Lat. Lucius Tarquinus Superbus, c.534–509 BCE). Tyrannical Etruscan king of Rome, traditionally the seventh and last of his line whose expulsion in 509 BCE is seen as marking the start of the Roman Republic. There is some debate over whether he is a historical or legendary figure.

Tasman, Abel Janszoon (c.1603–59) Dutch explorer, employed by the Dutch East India Company. He made two voyages of exploration to New Holland (Australia). On the first (1642–43), he sailed from Mauritius, missed the Australian mainland altogether, but made a landfall on Tasmania, which he named Van Diemen's Land after the governor-general of Batavia. He also visited New Zealand, Tonga, and Fiji. The aim of his second, less successful, journey (1644) was to determine whether New Guinea and Australia were separate islands or parts of the same land mass. This he failed to do.

Tasmania (*prev.* Van Diemen's land) Island off southeast coast of Australia, sighted by Dutch navigator Abel Tasman. When the British colonized the island in 19th century it was used as a penal colony. By the beginning of the 20th century the native aborigines were completely exterminated.

Tatanka Iyotake *see* Sitting Bull

Tavernier, Jean Baptiste (1605–89) French traveler and explorer in Asia.

Tehran Capital of modern Iran. American diplomats were held hostage in the US embassy in Tehran after the Islamic revolution of 1979 until 1981.

Tehran Conference (Nov 1943–Jan 1944) Meeting at which the Allied leaders (Roosevelt, Churchill and Stalin) drew up plans for the Anglo-American invasion of France and a Russian offensive against eastern Germany.

Tell, William Legendary figure of the Swiss struggle for independence from the Habsburgs in the Middle Ages. *p.228*

Temujin *see* Genghis Khan

Tenochtitlán The magnificent capital city of the Aztecs, founded in 1325 on an island in Laxe Texcoco. The city fell to the Spanish conquistador Hernán Cortés in 1521. *p.277*

Tenzin Gyatzo *see* Dalai Lama

Teotihuacán The most important trading and religious center in central America in the first half of the first millennium CE. In the 6th century the city started to decline and in 750 CE was devastated by fire.

Terror, Reign of (1793–94) Final phase of the French Revolution. The Committee of Public Safety, led by Robespierre, carried out a ruthless elimination of political opponents of the Jacobins and anyone considered sympathetic to the counter-revolutionaries. Some 40,000 are thought to have been executed in France. *See also* French Revolution, Jacobins, Robespierre

Tetrarchy Literally "government of four." The name was given to the system of rule by two emperors (Augusti), assisted by two Caesars, introduced by Diocletian to govern the Roman Empire in the late 3rd century.

Teutonic Knights Crusading order of knights, established during the Siege of Acre in 1190. The Knights subsequently subdued the pagan peoples of the Baltic in the 13th and 14th centuries, establishing their own state in Prussia, Livonia, and Estonia. *p.226*

Texas Revolution (1835–36) Originally part of Mexico, Texas declared independence in 1836, becoming (briefly) a republic. In 1845 it became the 28th state of the US.

textiles Textile industry in 12th century Flanders. *p.184*

THAILAND (*prev.* Siam) Thailand lies in southeast Asia, between the Indian and Pacific Oceans. The north, the western border with Burma, and the long Isthmus of Kra are mountainous. The central plain is the most fertile and densely populated area, while the low northeastern plateau is the poorest region. Siam emerged as a kingdom in the 13th century, and by the late 17th century its then capital, Ayutthya, was the largest city in southeast Asia. In 1782, the present Chakri dynasty and a new capital, Bangkok, were founded. ▶

Since 1932, Thailand has been a constitutional monarchy with both military and civilian governments. Rapid industrialization is resulting in massive congestion in Bangkok and a serious depletion of natural resources. Buddhism in Thailand. *p.122* Expansion in 15th century. *p.264*

CHRONOLOGY

1855 King Mongut signs Bowring trade treaty with British – Thailand never colonized by Europeans.
1868–1910 King Chulalongkorn westernizes Thailand.
1907 Thailand cedes western Khmer (Cambodia) to France.
1925 King Prajadhipok begins absolute rule.
1932 Bloodless military-civilian coup. Constitutional monarchy.
1933 Military takes control.
1941 Japanese invade. Government collaborates.
1944 Pro-Japanese prime minister Phibun voted out of office.
1945 Exiled King Ananda returns.
1946 Ananda assassinated. King Bhumibol accedes.
1947 Military coup. Phibun back.
1957 Military coup. Constitution abolished.
1965 Thailand allows US to use Thai bases in Vietnam War.
1969 New constitution endorses elected parliament.
1971 Army suspends constitution.
1973–1976 Student riots lead to interlude of democracy.
1976 Military takeover.
1980–1988 General Prem Tinsulanond prime minister. Partial democracy.
1988 General Chatichai Choonhaven, right-wing CT leader, named prime minister.
1991 Military coup. Civilian Anand Panyarachun caretaker premier.
1992 Elections. General Suchinda named premier. Demonstrations. King forces Suchinda to step down and reinstalls Anand. Moderates win new elections.
1995 CT wins general election.
1996 Early elections; Chaovalit Yongchaiyuth of NAP becomes prime minister.
1997 Financial and economic crisis; Chaovalit government falls; DP's Chuan Leekpai prime minister.
2001 TRT, led by Thaksin Shinawatra, wins elections.

Thea Philopator *see* Cleopatra VII
Thebes (*mod.* Luxor and Karnak) One of the capitals of Ancient Egypt. It rose to prominence under the 11th dynasty (2134–2040 BCE). Site of Valley of the Kings.
Theodoric (c.445–526) Ostrogothic leader and king of Italy. After various wars against the East Roman Empire, Theodoric invaded Italy in 489 and defeated Odoacer. In 492 he took Ravenna, making it his capital. He preserved many of the traditions of Roman rule. *p.117*
Theodosius I (*aka* Theodosius the Great) (c.346–395, reigned 379–95) Roman emperor. Appointed to rule the Eastern Empire upon the death of Valens, and administered the Western Empire after the death of Maximus in 388. He established Christianity as the official Roman religion in 380. After his death the Empire was finally divided into two halves.
Theravada Buddhism (*aka* Lesser Vehicle) Traditional interpretation of Buddhism, based on the personal experience and teachings of the Buddha, Siddhartha Gautama, and practiced widely in Sri Lanka, Burma, and SE Asia. *See also* Buddhism
Thermopylae ⚔ of (191 BCE) Roman victory over Seleucid king Antiochus III.
Thesiger, Wilfred (1910–) British soldier, explorer and writer. Having explored in Ethiopia and the Sudan, in 1946–47 and 1947–49 he twice crossed the Rub' al Khali ("Empty Quarter") of Arabia, recording his journeys in the book *Arabian Sands* (1959).
Thirty Years' War (1618–48) Conflict between rival dynastic and religious interests in the Holy Roman Empire. The struggle began with a Protestant revolt in Bohemia against the Counter-Reformation policies of the imperial government at Prague. The war was divided into four periods: the Bohemian Period (1618–25), the Danish Period (1625–29), the Swedish Period (1630–35), and the Swedish-French Period (1635–48). *p.302, p.307*
Thomas, Bertram (1892–1950) A British political officer in the service of the Sultan of Muscat and Oman, he was the first European to cross the Rub' al Khali (the "Empty Quarter") of southern Arabia, and the first to systematically record the topography of the region.
Three Feudatories Rebellion (1674–83) Pro-Ming rebellion in China eventually crushed by the Qing.

Three Hard Years Period of modern Chinese history (1959–62) following the failure of the Great Leap Forward initiative when agrarian decline, drought and crop failure resulted in widespread famine and up to 30 million deaths.
Three Kingdoms *see* Shu, Wei, and Wu
Thule culture Inuit (Eskimo) culture of the Canadian Arctic and Greenland. Partially sedentary, they hunted the rich wildlife of the Arctic. They expanded westwards between from c.1000 CE to become the dominant culture of the region.
Thutmosis III (*var.* Thutmose, reigned c.1479–c.1425) Egyptian pharaoh of the 18th dynasty, and one of the greatest rulers. He extended Egyptian territories and built and restored many temples. He erected the obelisk "Cleopatra's Needle," which was brought to London in 1878 by Sir Erasmus Wilson.
Tiahuanaco culture Culture of the Andes established c.500–1000 CE. Its stone architecture included temple complexes, and large-scale land reclamation schemes were undertaken to feed its citizens. *p.121*
Tiananmen Square massacre (1989) Pro-democracy protests in Beijing in May and June by thousands of Chinese finally ended in the massacre of many demonstrators by the army. Between 400 and 800 are thought to have been killed. *p.449*
Tibbu Tib (*var.* Tippu Tip, 1837–1905) 19th-century Arab trader in Africa who in the 1860s built a state in central Africa based on the ivory trade.
Tibet Himalayan nation of south central Asia, unified by introduction of Buddhism in 7th century CE, center of empire 7th–9th centuries CE, under Chinese (Qing) control from c.1720; closed to foreign visitors until late 19th century; entered British sphere of influence with Anglo-Tibetan Treaty (1904); invaded by Communist China 1950, and uprising crushed (1959) when titular head of state, Dalai Lama, forced into exile. Became nominally a Chinese Autonomous Region, 1965. *See also* China
Tibetan Buddhism *see* Tantric Buddhism
Tiger economies Name given to the states in Southeast Asia, such as Singapore, Indonesia, Malaysia, that enjoyed an export-led boom and spectacular growth in the 1980s and early 1990s.
Timbuktu Center of the salt trade in the Sahara. The caravans of camels that came to trade linked sub-Saharan Africa with the states of N Africa. *p.259*

Timur (*aka* Timur the Lame, *var.* Tamerlane, 1336–1405) The Mongol (though ethnically Turkish) leader who in the 14th century embarked from his capital Samarkand upon a whirlwind of campaigns against the Persians, the Khanate of the Golden Horde, the Sultanate of Delhi, the Mamluks, and the Ottomans. *p.239, p.244*

Tippu Tip *see* Tibbu Tib

Tito, Marshal (*prev.* Josip Broz, 1892–1980) Yugoslav president. Tito led the communist partisans who waged a successful guerrilla war against the occupying German forces in World War II. In 1945 he became head of a communist government, and in 1948 split with Stalin and turned Yugoslavia into a non-aligned communist state, which traded more with the West than the USSR. He was first elected president in 1953 and remained in power till his death.

Titus Flavius Sabinus Vespasianus *see* Vespasian

Tlaxcaltecs Native American peoples of Central Mexico. During Cortés's conquest of the Aztec Empire (1519–21), they acted as allies to the Spanish conquistadors.

Toba Wei (*var.* Northern Wei) Ruling dynasty of northern China (c.380–524). They unified northern China in 386.

TOGO Togo is sandwiched between Ghana and Benin in west Africa. A central forested region is bounded by savanna lands to the north and south. The port of Lomé is an important entrepôt for west African trade. After colonization by Germany in 1894, Togoland was divided between France and the UK in 1922. The president, General Gnassingbé Eyadéma, has held power since 1967.

Chronology

1960 French sector independent as Togo (UK part joined to Ghana).
1967 Eyadéma takes power.
1991–1992 General strike; repression.
1993 Eyadéma elected president.
1998, 1999 Eyadéma claims victory in disputed elections.

Tokugawa Ieyasu (1543–1616) Shogun (reigned 1603–05) who won ⚔ Sekigahara in 1600 in the war to unify Japan. Founder of the Tokugawa shogunate.

Tokugawa shogunate (1603–1868) Dynasty of hereditary shoguns or military dictators ruling Japan, founded by Tokugawa Ieyasu.

Toltec empire The dominant culture in central Mexico c.900–1200 CE. The Toltecs founded the city of Tula (*var.* Tikal) c.968, and destroyed the city of Teotihuacan, but the empire's later years were marked by famine, combined with fragmentation of the surrounding city-states. *p.160*

TONGA Located in the south Pacific northeast of New Zealand, Tonga is an archipelago of 170 islands. These are divided into three main groups, Vava'u, Ha'apai, and Tongatapu. Tonga's easterly islands are generally low and fertile. Those in the west are higher and volcanic in origin. Tonga was visited by the Dutch in the 17th century and Captain Cook in the 18th century. In the latter half of the 19th century, during the reign of King George Tupou I, the islands became a unified state after a period of civil war. Tonga's economy is based on agriculture, especially coconut, cassava, and passion fruit production. Politics is effectively controlled by the king.

Chronology

1875 First constitution established.
1900 Concern over German ambitions in region; Treaty of Friendship and Protection with UK.
1918–1965 Reign of Queen Salote Tupou III.
1958 Greater autonomy from UK enshrined in Friendship Treaty.
1965 King Taufa'ahau Tupou IV accedes on his mother's death.
1970 Full independence within British Commonwealth.
1988 Treaty allows US nuclear warships right of transit through Tongan waters.
1999 General election sees strong showing by prodemocracy candidates for the few directly elected seats.
2000 King appoints third son as prime minister.
2001 Court jester steals US$20 million of state funds.

Tonghak Revolt (1894) Populist nationalist, quasi-religious rebellion in Korea which was the catalyst for the Sino-Japanese War.

tools Technology of early man. *p.10*

Topa (*var.* Inca Yupanqui, reigned 1471–93) Inca ruler who extended the territory of the empire to its southernmost point, in present-day central Chile, and eliminated resistance to Inca rule in southern Peru.

Topkapi Palace of the Ottoman sultans in Constantinople. *p.262*

Tordesillas, Treaty of Papal decree of 1494, which divided new discoveries of the world between the two Catholic kingdoms of Spain and Portugal.

Torres, Luís Váez de 17th-century Spanish navigator on the Quirós expedition of 1605–07. In 1606 he found himself on the Pacific island of Espiritu Santo, separated from the leader of the expedition and in command of two ships. These he sailed west between Australia and New Guinea, through the strait that now bears his name. However, the Torres Strait did not appear on any map before the 18th century, because his surveys remained unpublished for nearly 100 years.

Totonacs Native American peoples of Central Mexico. During Cortés, conquest of the Aztec Empire (1519–21), they acted as allies to the Spanish conquistadors.

Toussaint l'Ouverture, Pierre Dominique (1743–1803) Leader of independence movement in Haiti. A former slave, Toussaint rose to prominence in the slave revolt in the French colony of St. Domingue in 1791. He then sided with the French Revolutionary authorities, becoming commander of the French forces on the island. However, when Napoleon came to power, he was determined to crush the slave revolt. Toussaint invaded Spanish Santo Domingo in 1801, but the following year was defeated and captured by French troops and taken to France, where he died in prison. *p.345*

Towns Appearance of the first towns. *p.21*

Townshend Acts (Jun 15–Jul 2 1767) Four acts passed by Britain in order to assert colonial authority via the suspension of the uncooperative colonial assembly, and the imposition of strict new taxes, and methods for their collection. The acts were met with hostility, and on March 5 1770, most of the acts' provisions were lifted.

Toyotomi Hideyoshi (1536–98, reigned 1585–98) Unifier of 16th-century Japan who carried on the struggle initiated by Oda Nobunaga. *p.289*

Trade The supply of Rome. *p.53*
Trade in the Islamic world. *p.181*
European trade with Asia. *p.312*

Trafalgar ⚔ of Napoleonic Wars (Jun 18 1815) Victory of British fleet under Nelson over French and Spanish fleets. *p.345*

Trail of Tears (1838–39) The forcible removal of the Cherokee people from their lands in Georgia, despite the finding of the Supreme Court that the Treaty of New Echota of 1835 which ceded Cherokee lands east of the Mississippi to the US, was not binding. More than 15,000 Cherokee were sent west to NE Oklahoma, accompanied by 7000 US troops. More than 4000 Indians died en route.

Trailok (1448–88) King of Siam. *p.264*

Trajan (*var.* Marcus Ulpius Traianus) (53–117) Spanish-born Roman emperor. Trajan was adopted by the emperor Nerva and, in turn, adopted his successor, Hadrian. Trajan's reign (98–117) was the last period of significant expansion. He added Dacia to the empire, his campaigns there being immortalized on the column he had erected in Rome. His victories against the Parthians were less conclusive and many of his gains were given up on his death. Trajan's column. *p.85*

Trans-Amazon Highway 3400 mile (5470 km) highway running from the Atlantic port of Recife in Brazil to Cruzeiro do Sul on the Peruvian border.

Trans-Siberian Railroad Transportation link spanning the Russian Empire from Moscow to Vladivostok – 5778 miles (9198 km). Built between 1891 and 1917.

Transjordan *see* Jordan

Transportation Transportation in Ancient Egypt and Mesopotamia. *p.19*
Transportation revolution (late 19th and early 20th century). *p.392*
Mass air travel. *p.437*
See also railroads

Trasimenus, Lake (*var.* Lat. Lacus Trasimenus) ⚔ of Punic Wars (217 BCE). Victory of Hannibal and invading Carthaginian army over Romans.

Trebia ⚔ of Punic Wars (218 BCE). Carthaginian victory.

Trent, Council of Ecumenical council of the Roman Catholic church (1545–63), which played a vital role in revitalizing the Roman Catholic church and setting the agenda of the Counter-Reformation.

Trenton ⚔ of American Revolutionary War (Dec 25 1776). American victory.

Tri-Partite Pact Agreement signed on Sep 27 1940 between Italy, Germany, and Japan to support one another in the event of a spread of World War II to the Far East.

Trident Long range nuclear ballistic missile system, designed for delivery from submarines, developed by US during 1980s.

TRINIDAD & TOBAGO

The two islands of Trinidad and Tobago are the most southerly of the Caribbean Windward Islands and lie just 15 km (9 miles) off the Venezuelan coast. Britain seized Trinidad from Spain in 1797 and Tobago from France in 1802. They were unified in 1888. They gained joint independence from Britain in 1962, and Tobago was given internal autonomy in 1987. The spectacular mountain ranges and large swamps are rich in tropical flora and fauna. Pitch Lake in Trinidad is the world's largest natural reservoir of asphalt.

CHRONOLOGY

1956 Eric Williams founds PNM and wins general election: main support from blacks. The large Asian population supports opposition.

1958–1961 Member of West Indian Federation.

1962 Independence.

1970 Black Power demonstrations.

1980 Tobago gets own House of Assembly; internal autonomy 1987.

1990–1991 Premier taken hostage in failed fundamentalist coup. PNM returned to power.

1995 UNC's Basdeo Panday is first Asian-origin prime minister.

1998–1999 Trinidad withdraws from international human rights bodies over death sentences.

2001 UNC reelected.

Truman Doctrine (Mar 12 1947) US foreign policy promulgated by President Harry S. Truman (1945–52), guaranteeing US support for peoples and nations threatened by international communism.

Truman, Harry S. (1884–1972) 33rd President of the US (Democrat, 1945–52). Born in Missouri, Truman served on the judiciary of the state from 1922–34 when he was elected to the US Senate. He became Vice-President in 1944 and President following the death of Roosevelt in 1945, and was re-elected in a surprise vote in 1948. During his Presidency, he authorized the dropping of the atom bombs, the Marshall Plan, the Truman Doctrine, the Berlin Airlift (1948–49), the establishment of NATO (1949), the deployment of US troops to combat Communism in South Korea, and the setting up of the CIA, as well as the introduction of the "Fair Deal" program of economic reform.

Tshaka Zulu *see* Shaka Zulu

Tsybikov, Gombozhab (1873–1930) Russian scholar and traveler in Tibet.

Tughluqs Dynasty of the Delhi Sultanate headed by Muhammad ibn Tughluq (1325–51). Under his rule, the Sultanate reached its greatest extent, incorporating 23 provinces and all the southern kingdoms. But administrative inefficiency, high taxation, and an ill-advised attempt to move the capital to Daulatabad hastened the decline of the Sultanate, which, by 1398, had split into many warring kingdoms.

Tukulor empire Muslim theocracy that flourished in the 19th century in western Africa from Senegal eastward to Timbuktu.

Tula Toltec capital, founded by Topiltzin (c.900). *p.160*

Tunis ⚔ of World War II (Apr–May 1943). Marked the surrender of the German Afrika Korps and final conquest of northern Africa by Allied forces.

TUNISIA

Tunisia lies sandwiched between Libya and Algeria. The populous north is mountainous, fertile in places and has a long Mediterranean coastline. The south is largely desert. Habib Bourguiba ruled the country from independence in 1956 until a bloodless coup in 1987. Under President Ben Ali, the government has moved toward multiparty democracy, but faces a challenge from Islamic fundamentalists. Closer ties with the EU, Tunisia's main trading partner, were strengthened through the first Euro-Mediterranean conference held in 1995.

CHRONOLOGY

1100 BCE Phoenician traders establish a port at Utica and gain control of the coastal region from the Berber inhabitants.

814 BCE The Phoenician Queen Elyssa (also known as Dido) founds Carthage. By the sixth century BCE Carthage has a population of 400,000 and Carthaginians control most of the coastal trading ports from Leptis (in Tripolitania in contemporary Libya) to Lixus and also Mogador (now called Essaouira) in Morocco.

264 BCE The start of the First Punic War marks the beginning of a Roman campaign against Carthage which culminates in the sacking of Carthage in 146 BCE.

439 CE Roman occupation is ended by the Vandals.

534 CE Byzantine rule is established over what becomes known as Ifriqiya. This lasts until the late seventh century when Arab invaders from the east bring Islam to the region. Growing maritime strength allows the Arabs to seize Carthage and establish a new Arab city at Tunis.

1230 The Hafsid dynasty is founded and rules over the territory from Tripolitania to eastern Algeria. Tunis becomes the capital and an important trading center.

1574 Tunisia becomes a province of the Ottoman Empire. By the early 18th century those controlling the region have won considerable autonomy and established an hereditary pasha (rather than one appointed from Constantinople), who is known as the Bey.

1883 Tunisia is made a French protectorate, ending semi-independence. Bey of Tunis remains monarch.

1900 Influx of French and Italians.

1920 Destour (Constitution) Party formed; calls for self-government.

1935 Habib Bourguiba forms Neo-Destour (New Constitution) Party.

1943 Defeat of Axis powers by British troops restores French rule.

1955 Internal autonomy. Bourguiba returns from exile.

1956 Independence. Bourguiba elected prime minister. Personal Statutes Code gives rights to women. Family planning introduced.

1957 Bey is deposed. Tunisia becomes republic with Bourguiba as president.

1964 Neo-Destour made sole legal party; renamed Destour Socialist Party (PSD). A moderate socialist economic program is introduced.

1969 Agricultural collectivization program, begun 1964, abandoned.

1974 Bourguiba elected president-for-life by National Assembly.

1974–1976 Hundreds imprisoned for belonging to "illegal organizations."

1978 Trade union movement, UGTT, holds strike; more than 50 killed in clashes. UGTT leadership replaced with PSD loyalists.

1980 New prime minister Muhammed Mazli ushers in greater political tolerance.

1981 Elections. Opposition groups allege electoral malpractice.

1984 Widespread riots after food price increases.

1986 Gen. Zine al-Abidine Ben Ali becomes interior minister. Four Muslim fundamentalists sentenced to death.

1987 Fundamentalist leader Rachid Ghannouchi arrested. Ben Ali becomes prime minister; takes over presidency after doctors certify Bourguiba senile. PSD renamed RCD.

1988 Most political prisoners released. Constitutional reforms introduce multiparty system and abolish life presidency. Two of Tunisia's opposition parties legalized.

1989 Elections: RCD wins all seats; Ben Ali president. Fundamentalists take 13 percent of vote.

1990 Tunisia backs Iraq in Gulf War.

1991 Abortive coup blamed on Al-Nahda; over 500 arrests.

1993 Multiparty agreement on electoral reform.

1994 Presidential and legislative elections. Ben Ali, sole candidate, is reelected. Ruling RCD wins all elected seats; opposition parties gain 19 reserved seats.

1996 Opposition MDS leader Mohammed Moada imprisoned for dealings with foreign agents.

1999 Ben Ali and RCD dominate elections.

2002 Suicide bomb attack in Jerba kills 14 German tourists.

Tupac Amaru Old Inca name assumed by Bolivian who led rebellion against Spanish rule in 1780. *p.335*

Tupamaros (*var. Sp.* Movimiento De Liberación Nacional) Uruguayan leftist urban guerrilla organization founded c.1963.

TURKEY Turkey, mainly in western Asia, also includes the region of Eastern Thrace in Europe. It thus controls the entrance to the Black Sea, which is straddled by Turkey's largest city, Istanbul. Most Turks live in the western half of the country. The eastern and southeastern reaches of the Anatolia Plateau are Kurdish regions. Turkey's strategic location gives it great influence in the Black Sea, the Mediterranean, and the Middle East. Lying on a major earthquake fault line, many Turkish towns are vulnerable to earthquakes such as the one which devastated Izmit in 1999. Following the collapse of the Ottoman Empire and Turkey's defeat in World War I, nationalist Mustafa Kemal Atatürk deposed the ruling sultan in 1922, declaring Turkey a republic in 1923. *See also* Ottoman Empire; Atatürk; World War I

CHRONOLOGY

1924 Religious courts abolished.

1928 Islam no longer state religion.

1934 Women given the vote.

1938 President Atatürk dies. Succeeded by Ismet Inonu.

1945 Turkey declares war on Germany. Joins UN.

1952 Joins NATO.

1960 Army stages coup against ruling Democratic Party and suspends National Assembly.

1961 New constitution.

1963 Association agreement with European Economic Community.

1974 Invades northern Cyprus.

1980 Military coup; martial law.

1982 New constitution.

1983 General election won by Turgut Özal's ANAP (Motherland Party).

1984 Turkey recognizes "Turkish Republic of Northern Cyprus." Kurdish separatist PKK (Kurdistan Workers' Party) launches guerrilla war in southeast.

1987 Turkey applies to join European Communities.

1990 US-led coalition launches air strikes on Iraq from Turkish bases.

1991 Elections won by DYP (True Path Party. Süleyman Demirel premier.

1992 Joins Black Sea alliance.

1993 Demirel elected president. Tansu Çiller becomes DYP leader and heads coalition.

1995 Major anti-Kurdish offensive. Reforms lower voting age to 18. Çiller coalition collapses. Pro-Islamic RP wins election, but center-right DYP-ANAP coalition takes office. Customs union with EU.

1996–1997 RP (Welfare Party) leader Necmettin Erbakan heads first pro-Islamic government since 1923.

1997 Mesut Yilmaz reappointed to head minority ANAP government.

1998 RP banned; many of its MPs join Virtue Party. Yilmaz resigns amid corruption allegations; replaced by Bulent Ecevit of DSP (Democratic Left Party).

1999 DSP wins most seats in election; Ecevit heads right-wing coalition. Captured Kurdish leader Abdullah Ocalan sentenced to death. Izmit earthquake kills 14,000.

2000 National Assembly refuses to endorse Demirel's reelection. He is replaced by Ahmet Necdet Sezer.

2001 Acute financial crisis. Prisoners and their relatives die staging hunger strikes against conditions and discrimination in high-security prisons. Virtue Party banned.

TURKMENISTAN Originally the poorest state among the former Soviet republics, Turkmenistan has adjusted better than most to independence, exploiting the market value of its abundant natural gas supplies. A largely Sunni Muslim area, Turkmenistan is part of the former Turkestan, the last expanse of central Asia incorporated into czarist Russia. Much of life is still based on tribal relationships. Turkmenistan remains isolated – telephones are rare and other communications limited.

CHRONOLOGY

13th century Genghis Khan conquers the region.

17th–19th centuries The territory, occupied by Turkoman tribes, is fought for by Persia, Khiva, Bukhara, and Afghanistan.

1881 Russian forces, led by Gen. Skobelev, attack and conquer the Turkoman stronghold of Geok-Teppeh despite resistance from the Takkesh tribes, killing over 14,000 people. Ashkhabad is founded by the Russians in the Akhal-Teke oasis in 1881 and becomes first a military stronghold and then a trading center.

1884 The oasis city of Mari is conquered by Russia. The invasion results in Turkoman tribes fleeing to Persia.

1918 After the Russian revolution, Soviet-backed troops defeat a Turkmen socialist movement and establish Soviet authority.

1924 Creation of Turkmen Soviet Socialist Republic.

1991 Independence from USSR. Niyazov retains power, becoming president.

1994 Former communists win first elections.

1999 Niyazov's term extended indefinitely by parliament.

Turks General name for Central Asian peoples of nomadic pastoral origin who came to dominate the Steppes during the 1st millennium CE.

Tuscarora War (1711) War between the Tuscarora Indians of N Carolina and European colonists, following the seizure of Tuscarora lands and the kidnapping of their people by colonists. The Tuscarora thereafter moved north, becoming the 6th nation of the Iroquois confederacy, and settling in New York state and SE Canada.

Tutankhamun (reigned 1333–1323 BCE) 18th dynasty Egyptian pharaoh. Known mostly because the riches of his tomb survived undisturbed until their discovery by Howard Carter. A successor and son-in-law of the monotheist Akhenaton, he became pharaoh as a young boy and reinstated the gods his predecessor had replaced. Unlike Akhenaton, however, he did not persecute followers of the previous religion, but simply changed his name from Tutankhaten and moved his capital from El-Amarna to Memphis.

Tutsi (*var.* Batusi, Tussi, Watusi) Ethnic group whose members live within Rwanda and Burundi. Suffered a terrifying massacre in 1994.

TUVALU One of the world's smallest, most isolated states, Tuvalu lies 1050 km (650 miles) north of Fiji in the central Pacific. A chain of nine coral atolls, it has a land area of just 26 square km (10 sq miles). The former Ellice Islands, together with the Gilbert Islands, were annexed by the UK in 1892. The two groups remained linked as a British colony until independence in 1978. Politically and socially conservative, Tuvaluans live by subsistence farming and fishing.

CHRONOLOGY

1974 Ellice Islanders vote to separate from Gilbertese.

1978 Independence as Tuvalu.

1987 Tuvalu Trust Fund set up.

1996–98 Bikenibeu Paeniu prime minister.

2000 Joins UN as 189th member. Sudden death of Prime Minister Ionatana.

Tyler, Wat (*var.* Walter Tyler) Leader of Peasants' Revolt in England (1381). *p.242*

Tz'u-Hsi *see* Cixi, Dowager Empress.

U

U-Boat (*var. Ger.* Unterseeboot). German naval submarine of World War I and World War II.

Ubaid culture These first settlers of Sumer, who arrived between 4500–4000 BCE, were non-Semitic peoples, now called proto-Euphrateans or Ubaidians after the village al-Ubaid where their remains were first found. They began to develop trade and industry in the area; the progenitors of the Sumerian civilization although they were not Sumerian speakers.

UGANDA An east African country of fertile upland plateaus and mountains, Uganda has outlets to the sea through Kenya and Tanzania. Uganda's ancient kingdoms were ruled under a British protectorate from 1893 until independence in 1962.Its history from independence until 1986 was one of ethnic strife. Since 1986, under President Museveni, peace has been restored and steps have been taken to rebuild the economy and democracy.

CHRONOLOGY

1894 A British protectorate is established over Buganda. Bunyoro, Toro, Ankole, and Busoga follow in 1896.

1953 The Kabaka of Buganda, Mutesa II, is exiled to the UK until 1955 for opposing UK plans for a unitary state after independence.

1962 Benedicto Kiwanuka is first prime minister when Uganda attains self-government in March 1962. However, after elections in April Milton Obote becomes Prime Minister, his UPC having won 37 seats to the Democratic Party's 24.

1962–1971 Milton Obote in power.

1971–1986 Ethnic strife, economic collapse under Idi Amin and Obote.

1986 President Museveni in power.

1996 Museveni wins first presidential elections.

2000 Referendum endorses "no-party" system.

2004 Commitment to multipartyism.

Uighurs Turkic people of Central Asia. Established empire on the steppe northwest of China. Latterly formed the largest Muslim ethnic group in China.

UKRAINE Ukraine is bordered by seven states; to the south it lies on the Black Sea and the Sea of Azov. An independent Ukrainian state was established in 1918, but was overrun in the same year by Soviet forces from the east and Polish forces from the west. In 1991, Ukraine again became an independent state. The country has historically been divided between the nationally conscious and Ukrainian-speaking west (including areas which were part of Poland until World War II) and the east, which has a large ethnic Russian population.

Chronology

1918 Independent Ukrainian state after collapse of Russian and Austrian empires. Brest-Litovsk Treaty signed with Germany.

1919 Red Army invades. Ukrainian Soviet Socialist Republic proclaimed.

1920 Poland invades; western Ukraine under Polish occupation.

1922 USSR founded; Ukrainian SSR is one of founder members.

1922–1930 Cultural revival under Lenin's "Ukrainianization" policy to pacify national sentiment.

1932–1933 "Ukrainianization" policy reversed. Stalin induces famine to eliminate Ukraine as source of opposition; seven million die.

1939 Soviet Union invades Poland and incorporates its ethnic Ukrainian territories into the Ukrainian SSR.

1941 Germany invades USSR. 7.5 million Ukrainians die by 1945.

1942 Nationalists form Ukrainian Insurgent Army, which wages war against both Germans and Soviets.

1954 Crimea ceded to Ukrainian SSR.

1972 Widespread arrests of intellectuals and dissidents by Soviet state. Vladimir Shcherbitsky, a Brezhnevite, replaces moderate reformer Petr Shelest as head of Communist Party of Ukraine (CPU).

1986 World's worst nuclear disaster at Chernobyl power station.

1989 First major coalminers' strike in Donbass. Pro-Gorbachev Volodymyr Ivashko heads CPU.

1990 Ukrainian parliament declares Ukrainian SSR a sovereign state. Leonid Kravchuk replaces Ivashko.

1991 Government declares full independence, conditional on approval by referendum, supported by 90 percent of voters. CPU banned. Crimea declared an autonomous republic within Ukrainian SSR.

1993 Sstrike in Donbass results in costly settlement, which exacerbates budget deficit and stimulates hyperinflation. CPU reestablished at Donetsk congress.

1994 Crimea elects Yuri Meshkov as its first president. Leonid Kuchma defeats Kravchuk to become first democratically elected president of Ukraine.

1996 Hryvna replaces karbovanets as national currency. New constitution comes into force.

1997 Friendship treaty signed with Russia. Accord on Black Sea fleet.

1998 Ten-year cooperation agreement with Russia. CPU secures largest number of seats in general election.

1999 Reelection of Kuchma. Opposition claims of fraud. Kuchma appoints pro-reform government.

2000 Chernobyl site closed.

2001 Growing protests linking Kuchma with murder of journalist. May, Kuchma replaces reformist premier after parliamentary defeat.

Ulloa, Francisco de (died c.1540) Spanish explorer sent by Hernán Cortés to explore the Gulf of California. He sailed to the head of the Gulf, thus proving that lower California was a peninsula.

Ultra Code name for Allied decryptions of German Enigma intelligence during World War II.

'Umar Tal, Al-Hajj (*var.* Al-Hajj Umar Ibn Said Tal, c.1797–1864) W African Tukulor leader who launched a jihad in 1854 which led to the foundation of the Muslim Tukulor empire (1863), between the upper Senegal and Niger rivers.

Umayyad Caliphate Muslim dynasty of caliphs founded in 661. They were deposed in 750 by the Abbasids, but a branch continued to rule Muslim Spain (756–1031). *See also* Caliphate of Cordoba

UN *see* United Nations

Union of Soviet Socialist Republics (USSR) Centralized Bolshevik (communist) regime in Russia, emerging fom the Bolshevik revolution (1917), and formally organized in 1922, substantially expanded during World War II, and the principal communist state, dominating Eastern Europe, during the Cold War. Dissolved under pressure for *glasnost* (openness), *perestroika* (reform) and devolution in 1991; the rump state formed the Russian Federation, the Union was replaced by a Commonwealth of Independent States (CIS). *See also* Russia

UNITA (National Union for the Total Independence of Angola) Movement engaged in civil war (1975–2002) against the ruling MPLA.

UNITED ARAB EMIRATES The Arab world's only working federation, the United Arab Emirates (UAE) shares borders with Oman, Saudi Arabia, and Qatar, as well as a disputed maritime boundary with Iran. The UAE is mostly semiarid desert relieved by occasional oases. The cities, watered by extensive irrigation systems, have lavish greenery. The UAE was influenced by the Portuguese and the Ottomans, but British control became dominant in the 19th century. The UAE's economic prosperity once relied on pearls, but it is now a sizable gas and oil exporter, and has a growing services sector.

Chronology

1959 Significant oil strikes in the region.

1971 The UK withdraws as protecting power and the UAE federation is formed.

1991 UAE offers bases to Western forces after Kuwait is invaded.

UNITED KINGDOM Lying in northwestern Europe, the United Kingdom (UK) occupies the major portion of the British Isles. It includes the countries of England, Scotland, and Wales, the constitutionally distinct region of Northern Ireland, and several outlying islands. Its only land border is with the Republic of Ireland. The UK is separated from the European mainland by the English Channel and the North Sea. To the west lies the Atlantic Ocean. Most of the population live in towns and cities and, in England, is fairly well scattered. The most densely populated region is the southeast. Scotland is the wildest region, with the Highlands less populated today than in the 18th century. The UK joined the European Communities (EC – later the EU) in 1973, and most of its trade is now with its European partners. Membership of the UN Security Council also gives the UK a prominent role in international diplomacy. *See also* Britain, Great Britain England, Scotland, Wales

CHRONOLOGY

43 CE Britain (Britannia) is invaded and conquered by the Romans

60 CE Revolt by Boadicea, queen of the Iceni in East Anglia, is suppressed.

450 CE Anglo-Saxon conquest of Britain commences with the departure of the Roman legions.

790 CE Viking raids on Britain from Denmark and Norway begin.

871 Vikings suffer defeats by king of Wessex, Alfred the Great (ruled 871–99).

1066 Norman conquest of England following the defeat of King Harold II (ruled 1053–66) at Hastings by the army of Duke William of Normandy. As King William I, or "William the Conqueror" (ruled 1066–87), he crushes a series of rebellions and builds more than 5,000 castles.

1189 Richard I, "the Lionheart," ascends the throne and spends much of his 10-year reign abroad fighting to regain Jerusalem during the Crusades. Killed fighting in France, he is succeeded by his brother John (reigned 1199–1216).

1215 A charter, the Magna Carta, is signed at Runnymede by King John and English barons. This protects human rights against the excessive use of royal power.

1314 Robert the Bruce (ruled Scotland 1306–29) confirms the independence of the Scottish at the battle of Bannockburn.

1338 The Hundred Years" War, between England and France, begins. English Kings attempt to dominate France and gain control over Normandy between 1419 and 1450, Gascony between 1360 and 1450 and Aquitaine between 1152 and 1453. Although Henry V (ruled 1413–22) secures a major victory at Agincourt in October 1415, by 1453 England holds only Calais (which reverts to France in 1558).

1348–50 The Black Death sweeps across Europe and kills between one third and one half of the English population.

1381 Sparked by the imposition of a poll tax in 1380, serfs in many parts of England rebel in a Peasants' Revolt led by Wat Tyler.

1399 Richard II is deposed by his cousin, Henry of Lancaster (Henry IV), at the start of a period of conflict between the houses of Lancaster and York (the Wars of the Roses), which lasts until 1485.

1485 King Richard III is defeated and killed at Bosworth Field by the Lancastrian Henry Tudor, who becomes Henry VII (reigned 1485–1509).

1534 Following the pope's refusal to annul his marriage to Catherine of Aragon, King Henry VIII breaks with Rome and the Catholic Church, and becomes Supreme Head of the Anglican Church.

1536 Although earlier subjugated in 1284, a political union of Wales with England is forged, formally conferring Welsh representation in parliament.

1541 Having broken the power of Ireland's feudal lords, King Henry VIII adopts the title of King of Ireland.

1553 Mary, daughter of Catherine of Aragon and Henry VIII, becomes Queen Mary I, upon the death of Henry's only son, Edward VI. She attempts to bring England back into the Catholic fold.

1558 Mary is succeeded by her Protestant sister, Elizabeth (reigned 1558–1603). Attempts to restore a Catholic to the throne founder when Mary Queen of Scots is executed in February 1587 after three plots to bring her to the throne are unmasked.

1588 The English navy defeats the naval and military Spanish Armada, which is sent by Philip II (ruled 1556–98) of Spain with the purpose of invading Britain.

1603 Upon Elizabeth's death, James VI of Scotland becomes James I of England from 1603 to 1625, thus uniting the crowns, though not the governments, of England and Scotland.

1642 The English Civil War, fought between supporters of the king ("cavaliers") and parliamentarians ("roundheads"), breaks out over religious differences. At Preston in 1648 the army of King Charles I is decisively defeated by the roundheads led by the Puritan Oliver Cromwell.

1649 Charles is executed in January; a Commonwealth is established from May, and Catholic opposition in Ireland is brutally quashed at the battle of Drogheda in September. Cromwell acts as Lord Protector from 1653 till his death in 1658.

1660 The monarchy is restored with Charles II as king.

1688 In the bloodless "Glorious Revolution" Catholic James II is succeeded as monarch by his daughter Mary II, who is married to the Dutch Protestant William III. The following year, Catholics are debarred from the throne and a constitutional form of government is established, with parliamentary consent becoming necessary for the King to levy taxes, suspend laws, or raise a peacetime army.

1690 In Ireland a Catholic uprising led by James II is defeated.

1707 Act of Union between England and Scotland, creating Great Britain. Scotland retains its legal system and church, but the Scottish parliament is abolished.

1745 Rebellion by Scottish Jacobites (supporters of the exiled royal house of Stuart). Led by "Bonnie Prince Charlie," they invade England but are routed at battle of Culloden in 1746.

1775–83 Britain loses its North American colonies in the American War of Independence.

1801 Great Britain (England, Scotland, and Wales) is formally united with Ireland to form the United Kingdom.

1832 The Great Reform Act is passed, conferring voting rights on middle class men. Working class men are enfranchised by the Reform Acts of 1867 and 1884.

1846 Home Secretary Robert Peel repeals the Corn Laws, imposed from 1815 to control the import and export of grain. A significant victory for the free-trade lobby over landed protectionists.

1877 Queen Victoria is declared Empress of India, as Britain approaches its zenith as an imperial power.

1906 Reformist Liberal government.

1914 World War I begins.

1918 Armistice signals end of war. Cost to Britain: 750,000 dead.

1921 Irish Free State agreed.

1926 General Strike.

1929 World stock market crash. Widespread unemployment.

1931 UK leaves gold standard and devalues pound.

1936 Edward VIII abdicates over marriage to Mrs. Simpson.

1938 Prime Minister Neville Chamberlain meets Hitler in Munich over Czech crisis, says threat of war with Germany averted.

1939 Germany invades Poland. UK declares war on Germany. Start of World War II.

1940 Winston Churchill prime minister. Battle of Britain.

1944 June 6. D-Day: invasion of German-occupied France.

1945 End of World War II. War costs 330,000 British lives. Labour government comes to power on social welfare platform.

1946 Nationalization of Bank of England, railroads, coal, utilities.

1947 Indian independence.

1948 National Health Service established.

1949 Founder member of NATO.

1956 Suez crisis. UK intervenes in Canal Zone. Withdraws under US pressure.

1961 UK application to EC rejected by French President de Gaulle.

1968 Abortion and homosexuality are legalized.

1969 British troops sent into N Ireland.

1970 Conservatives in power under Edward Heath.

1973 Joins EC. Oil crisis. Industry on three-day week following strikes by power workers and miners.

1974 Labour government, under Harold Wilson, concedes miners' demands; strikes end. High inflation.

1975 Margaret Thatcher leads Conservatives. Referendum ratifies EC membership. First North Sea oil pipeline in operation.

1979–1997 Conservative rule.

1980 Anti-US Cruise missiles protests. Rising unemployment. Inner-city riots.

1981 Privatization program begun.

1982 Argentina invades Falklands. Islands retaken by UK task force.

1983 Tax-cutting policies.

1986 Financial services market deregularized ("Big Bang").

1990 John Major Conservative leader. UK joins Gulf War.

1992 Conservatives win fourth consecutive election.

1994 Tony Blair Labour leader.

1996 Health crisis linking "mad cow" disease (BSE) with fatal variant Creutzfeldt-Jakob disease (vCJD).

1997 Landslide election victory for Labour. Diana, Princess of Wales, killed in car crash in Paris. Scottish and Welsh referendums approve creation of own assemblies.

1998–1999 "Good Friday" agreement on political settlement in Northern Ireland, endorsed by referendum but held up by disputes over decommissioning weapons.

1999 Involvement in NATO air war with Yugoslavia over Kosovo crisis. May. New Scottish Parliament and Welsh Assembly elected. December. Devolution to power-sharing executive in Northern Ireland.

2001 Foot-and-mouth epidemic and mass livestock culling. June. Labour wins second term in office with huge majority.

2002 50th anniversary of accession to throne of Queen Elizabeth II.

2003 UK troops invade Iraq alongside US forces.

KINGS AND QUEENS OF ENGLAND
(from 924)

Sovereigns of England (after Mercia merges with Kingdom of Wessex 919)

924–939	Athelstan
939–946	Edmund I, the Magnificent
946–955	Eadred (Edred)
955–959	Eadwig (Edwy) All-Fair
959–975	Edgar the Peaceable
975–978	Edward the Martyr
978–1016	Ethelred (Aethelred), the Unready
1016	Edmund II Ironside

Danish line

1013–1014	Svein (Sweyn) Forkbeard
1016–1035	Canute (Knut), the Great
1035–1040	Harold I Harefoot
1040–1042	Hardicanute

House of Wessex, restored

1042–1066	Edward the Confessor
1066	Harold II

The Normans

1066–1087	William I, the Conqueror
1087–1100	William II, Rufus or Redhead
1100–1135	Henry I Beauclerc
1135–1154	Stephen
1141	Empress Matilda

The Angevins or Plantagenets

1154–1189	Henry II, Curtmantle
1189–1199	Richard I, the Lionheart
1199–1216	John, Lackland
1216–1272	Henry III
1272–1307	Edward I, Longshanks
1307–1327	Edward II
1327–1377	Edward III
1377–1399	Richard II

The Plantagenets: House of Lancaster

1399–1413	Henry IV Bolingbroke
1413–1422	Henry V
1422–1461; 1470–1471	Henry VI

The Plantagenets: House of York

1461–1470; 1471–1483	Edward IV
1483	Edward V
1483–1485	Richard III, Crookback

The Tudors

1485–1509	Henry VII Tudor
1509–1547	Henry VIII
1547–1553	Edward VI
1553	Lady Jane Grey
1553–1558	Mary I Tudor
1558–1603	Elizabeth I

Rulers of Great Britain and the United Kingdom

The Stuarts

1603–1625	James I (VI of Scotland)
1625–1649	Charles I

The Commonwealth

1653–1658	Oliver Cromwell, Lord Protector
1658–1659	Richard Cromwell, Lord Protector

House of Stuart, restored

1660–1685	Charles II
1685–1688	James II (VII of Scotland)

House of Orange and Stuart

1689–1702	William III and Mary II

House of Stuart

1702–1714	Anne

House of Hanover

1714–1727	George I
1727–1760	George II
1760–1820	George III
1820–1830	George IV
1830–1837	William IV
1837–1901	Victoria

House of Saxe-Coburg-Gotha

1901–1910	Edward VII

House of Windsor

1910–1936	George V
1936	Edward VIII
1936–1952	George VI
1952–	Elizabeth II

BRITISH PRIME MINISTERS (from 1721)

1721–1742	Sir Robert Walpole
1742–1743	Lord John Carteret
1743–1754	Henry Pelham
1754–1756	Duke of Newcastle
1756–1757	Duke of Devonshire (William Pitt the Elder, secretary of state)
1757–1761	Duke of Newcastle
1761–1763	Earl of Bute
1763–1765	George Grenville
1765–1766	Marquis of Rockingham
1766–1770	Duke of Grafton
1770–1782	Lord Frederick North
1782	Marquis of Rockingham
1782–1783	Earl of Shelburne
1783	Duke of Portland
1783–1801	William Pitt the Younger
1801–1804	Henry Addington
1804–1806	William Pitt the Younger
1806–1807	Lord William Grenville
1807–1809	Duke of Portland
1809–1812	Spencer Perceval
1812–1827	Earl of Liverpool
1827	George Canning
1827–1828	Viscount Goderich
1828–1830	Duke of Wellington
1830–1834	Earl Grey
1834	Viscount Melbourne
1834–1835	Sir Robert Peel
1835–1841	Viscount Melbourne
1841–1846	Sir Robert Peel
1846–1852	Lord John Russell
1852	Earl of Derby
1852–1855	Earl of Aberdeen

1855–1858	Viscount Palmerston
1858–1859	Earl of Derby
1859–1865	Viscount Palmerston
1865–1866	Lord John Russell
1866–1868	Earl of Derby
1868	Benjamin Disraeli
1868–1874	William E Gladstone
1874–1880	Benjamin Disraeli
1880–1885	William E Gladstone
1885–1886	Marquis of Salisbury
1886	William E Gladstone
1886–1892	Marquis of Salisbury
1892–1894	William E Gladstone
1894–1895	Earl of Rosebery
1895–1902	Marquis of Salisbury
1902–1905	Arthur J Balfour
1905–1908	Sir Henry Campbell-Bannerman
1908–1916	Herbert H Asquith
1916–1922	David Lloyd George
1922–1923	Bonar Law
1923–1924	Stanley Baldwin
1924	James Ramsay MacDonald
1924–1929	Stanley Baldwin
1929–1935	James Ramsay MacDonald
1935–1937	Stanley Baldwin
1937–1940	Neville Chamberlain
1940–1945	Winston S Churchill
1945–1951	Clement R Attlee
1951–1955	Winston S Churchill
1955–1957	Anthony Eden
1957–1963	Harold Macmillan
1963–1964	Sir Alec Douglas-Home
1964–1970	Harold Wilson
1970–1974	Edward Heath
1974–1976	Harold Wilson
1976–1979	James Callaghan
1979–1990	Margaret Thatcher
1990–1997	John Major
1997–	Tony Blair

United Nations (UN) Established in 1945 with aim of maintaining international peace and security and promoting cooperation over economic, social, cultural and humanitarian problems. In 1999, there were 184 members, with the Security Council consisting of China, France, Russia, UK, and US.

United Provinces The name taken by the seven provinces of the Low Countries that declared their independence from Spain from 1581. It was in use until the Napoleonic era. *See also* Netherlands

UNITED STATES OF AMERICA

(USA) The world's fourth-largest country, the United States is neither overpopulated (like China) nor in the main subject to extremes of climate (like much of Russia and Canada). Its main landmass, bounded by Canada and Mexico, contains 48 of its 50 states. The two others, Alaska at the northwest tip of the Americas and Hawaii in the Pacific, became states in 1959. The US was not built on ethnic identity but on a concept of nationhood intimately bound up with the 18th-century Founding Fathers' ideas of democracy and liberty – still powerful touchstones in both a political and an economic sense. Since the breakup of the Soviet Union, the US holds a unique position – but arouses extreme hatreds – as the sole global superpower.

CHRONOLOGY

1565–1626 Following the arrival of Columbus in 1492, Spanish and English settlers establish the first European settlements at St Augustine (Florida), and Jamestown (Virginia). "New Netherlands" is established by Dutch settlers in present-day Albany and New York City.

1665 Following the second Anglo-Dutch naval war, control of "New Netherlands" passes to the British crown. The colony and the city of New Amsterdam are both renamed New York.

1756–63 The Seven Years' War is concluded by the Treaty of Paris which grants Britain control over French Canada and a portion of Louisiana lying east of the Mississippi. Spain surrenders Florida to the British.

1773 Massachusetts citizens board three ships in Boston harbour and throw their cargoes overboard protesting against the imposition of a tea tax, an event known as the "Boston tea party."

1775783 War of Independence. Forces of the 13 colonies defeat the British army.

1776 The Declaration of Independence is written by Thomas Jefferson.

1783 The Treaty of Paris recognizes the independence of the United States. Florida is restored to Spain.

1787 A Constitutional Convention revises the Articles of Confederation, originally agreed in 1777, by drafting a new constitution for the federation of the 13 states.

1787–90 The new constitution is ratified by the 13 states; it is officially accepted on June 21, 1788, after the number of states to ratify it reaches nine, thereby giving it the required two-thirds level of approval.

1789 George Washington is elected first President of the US in February, and the first Congress meets in New York City, the designated seat of federal government. The Supreme Court is established.

1791 Ten amendments to the constitution guaranteeing freedom of speech, assembly, and other rights, come into effect as the Bill of Rights.

1803 The Louisiana purchase is made; France sells land from the Gulf of Mexico to the Canadian border to the US.

1812–14 The war of 1812 between Britain and the US fails to dislodge the British from Canada.

1819 Spain sells Florida to the US.

1820 The Missouri compromise bill allows slavery in Missouri but outlaws it in territory west of the Missouri river and north of a line extending from the southern boundary of Missouri.

1823 The Monroe Doctrine asserts US supremacy in the Western hemisphere and warns European powers against any further attempts at colonization in the Americas.

1828 The Democrat-Republican party becomes the Democratic party as Andrew Jackson is elected president.

1836 Texas declares independence from Mexico; a Texan army defeats a Mexican army at San Jacinto.

1845 Texas is annexed to the US.

1846–48 Mexico is defeated in the US-Mexican war and forced to renounce claim to Texas and to cede New Mexico and California to the US.

1853 Under the terms of the Gadsen purchase the US acquires parts of Southern New Mexico and Arizona.

1854 The Republican party is formed to opposing the extension of slavery.

1860 Abraham Lincoln is elected as first Republican President. South Carolina becomes the first state to secede from the Union over the issue of slavery.

1861–1865 The Civil War is fought. The conflict begins when eleven secessionist states form the Confederate States of America. The Confederate States eventually surrender on April 9 1865, at Appomattox following the fall of Charleston and Richmond. In the same month Abraham Lincoln is assassinated. Slavery is abolished by the Thirteenth Amendment to the Constitution.

1867 Russia sells Alaska to the US.

1890 The massacre at Wounded Knee, South Dakota, is the last major military engagement between Indian and US forces.

1896 The Supreme Court affirms the "separate but equal" doctrine allowing racial segregation.

1898 The Spanish-American war ends with the US gaining control over Guam, the Philippines, Puerto Rico, and Cuba.

1917 Enters World War I.

1929 New York stock market collapse; economic depression.

1941 Japanese attack on Pearl Harbor; US enters World War II.

1950–1953 Korean War.

1954 Supreme Court rules racial segregation in schools is unconstitutional. Blacks start campaign of civil disobedience.

1959 Alaska, Hawaii become states.

1961 John F. Kennedy president. Promises aid to South Vietnam. US-backed invasion of Cuba defeated at Bay of Pigs.

1962 Soviet missile bases found on Cuba; threat of nuclear war averted.

1963 November. Kennedy assassinated. Lyndon Baines Johnson president.

1964 US involvement in Vietnam stepped up. Civil Rights Act gives blacks constitutional equality.

1968 Martin Luther King is assassinated.

1969 Republican Richard Nixon president. Growing public opposition to Vietnam War.

1972 Nixon reelected. Makes historic visit to China.

1973 Withdrawal of troops from Vietnam; 58,000 US troops dead by end of war.

1974 Nixon resigns following "Watergate" scandal over break-in to Democrat headquarters. Gerald Ford president.

1976 Democrat Jimmy Carter president.

1978 US-sponsored "Camp David" accord between Egypt and Israel.

1979 Seizure of US hostages in Tehran, Iran.

1980 Ronald Reagan wins elections for Republicans. Adopts tough anticommunist foreign policy.

1983 Military invasion of Grenada.

1985 Air strikes against Libyan cities. Relations with USSR improve; first of three summits held.

1986 Iran-Contra affair revealed.

1987 Intermediate Nuclear Forces Treaty signed by USA and USSR.

1988 George Bush Sr. wins presidency.

1989 US overthrows General Noriega of Panama, arrested on drug charges.

1991 Gulf War against Iraq. USA and USSR sign START arms reduction treaty.

1992 Black youths riot in Los Angeles and other cities. Bush-Yeltsin summit agrees further arms reductions. Democrat Bill Clinton defeats Bush in election.

1994 Health care reform legislation defeated in Congress. Special counsel investigation of Whitewater scandal begins, over Clintons' financial dealings in Arkansas. Sexual harassment charges filed against Clinton. Midterm elections, Republican majorities in both houses of Congress.

1995 Oklahoma bombing by Timothy McVeigh; over 160 die. Clinton in conflict with Congress over budget.

1996 Clinton reelected.

1997 Madeleine Albright first woman to head State Department.

1998 Scandal over Clinton's affair with White House intern leads to impeachment trial. Bombing of US embassies in Kenya and Tanzania; revenge air strikes on Sudan and Afghanistan. Air strikes against Iraq.

1999 Clinton acquitted in Senate impeachment trial. Columbine High School shootings by two students. NATO involvement to end Kosovo conflict, bombardment of Yugoslavia.

2000 Al Gore concedes tightest presidential election ever to George W. Bush.

2001 President Bush takes office. World's worst terrorist attack kills thousands as hijacked planes destroy World Trade Center, damage Pentagon on September 11. US-led "war on terrorism" begins with extensive aerial bombing campaign in Afghanistan.

2002 WorldCom bankruptcy is the world's biggest ever corporate collapse.

2003 Bush launches war on Iraq, despite lack of UN backing.

2004 Bush defeats Democrat John Kerry in presidential election.

PRESIDENTS OF THE UNITED STATES

1789–1797	George Washington
1797–1801	John Adams
1801–1809	Thomas Jefferson
1809–1817	James Madison
1817–1825	James Monroe
1825–1829	John Quincy Adams
1829–1837	Andrew Jackson

◄

1837–1841	Martin Van Buren
1841	William Henry Harrison
1841–1845	John Tyler
1845–1849	James Knox Polk
1849–1850	Zachary Taylor
1850–1853	Millard Fillmore
1853–1857	Franklin Pierce
1857–1861	James Buchanan
1861–1865	Abraham Lincoln
1865–1869	Andrew Johnson
1869–1877	Ulysses Simpson Grant
1877–1881	Rutherford Birchard Hayes
1881	James Abram Garfield
1881–1885	Chester Alan Arthur
1885–1889	Grover Cleveland
1889–1893	Benjamin Harrison
1893–1897	Grover Cleveland
1897–1901	William McKinley
1901–1909	Theodore Roosevelt
1909–1913	William Howard Taft
1913–1921	Woodrow Wilson
1921–1923	Warren Gamaliel Harding
1923–1929	John Calvin Coolidge
1929–1933	Herbert Clark Hoover
1933–1945	Franklin Delano Roosevelt
1945–1953	Harry S Truman
1953–1961	Dwight D Eisenhower
1961–1963	John Fitzgerald Kennedy
1963–1969	Lyndon Baines Johnson
1969–1974	Richard Milhous Nixon
1974–1977	Gerald Rudolph Ford
1977–1981	James (Jimmy) Earl Carter
1981–1989	Ronald Reagan
1989–1993	George Herbert Walker Bush
1993–2001	William Jefferson Clinton
2001–	George Walker Bush, Jr.

Unterseeboot *see* U-boat

Upanishads Prose and verse reflections which, with the Vedas, form the central corpus of Hindu literature. They were composed between 800 BCE and 300 CE.

Ur Ancient city of Sumeria. It was already an important center of trade by 2500 BCE. It fell to Sargon of Akkad c.2340 BCE, but a new Sumerian dynasty was founded by Ur-Namma c.2100 BCE.

Ur-Nammu Founder of the 3rd dynasty of Sumeria, who made Ur the capital of a new empire c.2150 BCE. He constructed the ziggurat at Nippur to confirm his position as earthly representative of Enlil.

Urartu Ancient kingdom of the Near East around Lake Van (c.1270–612 BCE), repeatedly attacked by Assyrian kings and invaded by the Scythians and Medes.

Urban II (c.1035–99, reigned 1088–99). Pope who believed in the freedom of the Church from state interference. He preached the First Crusade in 1095.

URUGUAY Uruguay is situated in southeastern South America. Its capital, Montevideo, is an Atlantic port on the River Plate, lying across the river from Buenos Aires, Argentina's capital. The Spaniards were the first to colonize the area north of the River Plate. In 1680, the Portuguese also founded a colony there, at Colonia del Sacramento, so starting 150 years of rivalry between the colonial powers for control of the territory. Uruguay finally became independent in 1828. Decades of liberal government ended in 1973 with a military coup that was to result in 12 years of dictatorship, during which 400,000 people emigrated. Most have since returned. Almost the entire low-lying landscape is devoted to the rearing of livestock, especially cattle and sheep. Uruguay is the world's second-largest wool exporter. Tourism and offshore banking now bring in substantial foreign earnings.

CHRONOLOGY

1726 Spaniards found Montevideo. By end of the century, whole country is divided into large cattle ranches.

1808 Montevideo declares independence from Buenos Aires.

1811 Rancher and local caudillo, José Gervasio Artigas, fends off Brazilian attack.

1812–1820 Uruguayans, known as Orientales ("Easterners," from the eastern side of the River Plate), fight wars against Argentinian and Brazilian invaders. Brazil finally takes Montevideo.

1827 General Lavalleja defeats Brazilians with Argentine help.

1828 Seeing trade benefits that an independent Uruguay would bring as a buffer state between Argentina and Brazil, Britain mediates and secures Uruguayan independence.

1836 Start of large-scale European immigration.

1838–1865 La Guerra Grande civil war between Blancos (Whites, future conservative party) and Colorados (Reds, future liberals).

1865–1870 Colorado president, General Venancio Flores, takes Uruguay into War of the Triple Alliance against Paraguay.

1872 Peace under military rule. Blancos strong in country, Colorados in cities.

1890s Violent strikes by immigrant trade unionists against landed elite enriched by massive European investment in ranching.

1903–1907 Reformist Colorado, José Batllé y Ordóñez, president.

1911–1915 Batllé serves second term in office. Batllismo creates the only welfare state in Latin America with pensions, social security, and free education and health service; also nationalizations, disestablishment of Church, abolition of death penalty.

1933 Military coup. Opposition groups excluded from politics.

1942 President Alfredo Baldomir dismisses government and tries to bring back proper representation.

1939–1945 Neutral in World War II.

1951 New constitution replaces president with nine-member council. Decade of great prosperity follows until world agricultural prices plummet. Drop in foreign investment.

1958 Blancos win elections for first time in 93 years.

1962 Tupamaros urban guerrillas founded. Its guerrilla campaign lasts until 1973.

1966 Presidency reinstated. Colorados back in power.

1967 Jorge Pacheco president. Tries to stifle opposition to tough anti-inflation policies.

1973 Military coup. Promises to encourage foreign investment counteracted by denial of political freedom and brutal repression of the left; 400,000 emigrate.

1984–1985 Military step down. Elections. Julio Sanguinetti (Colorado) president.

1986 Those guilty of human rights abuse granted amnesty.

1989 Referendum endorses amnesty in interests of stability. Elections won by Lacalle Herrera and Blancos.

1994–1995 Sanguinetti reelected, forms coalition government.

1999 Presidential election won by Colorado Jorge Batlle.

2000 Foot-and-mouth disease forces temporary suspension of beef exports.

2002 Uruguay loses investment grade status due to impact of Argentine crisis.

Uruk Mesopotamian city-state (c.3500 BCE).

US, USA *see* United States of America

Usman dan Fodio (*var.* Uthman, *Ar.* Uthman ibn Fudio, 1754–1817) Fulani philosopher and reformer who, in a *jihad* between 1804 and 1808, conquered the Hausa city-states, created a new Muslim state, and established a Sokoto Fulani empire, in present-day Nigeria.

USSR *see* Union of Soviet Socialist Republics

Uthman ibn Fodio *see* Usman dan Fodio

Utrecht, Union of (1579) During the Dutch Revolt (1565–1609) an anti-Spanish alliance of provinces. Their independence was effectively conceded by Spain in 1609 and formally recognized in 1648.

Uzbek empire *see* Khwarizm empire

UZBEKISTAN Sharing the Aral sea coastline with its northern neighbor, Kazakhstan, Uzbekistan has common borders with five countries. It is the most populous central Asian republic and has considerable natural resources. Uzbekistan contains the ancient cities of Samarkand, Bukhara (Bukhoro), Khiva, and Tashkent. The dictatorship of President Karimov has prevented the spread of Islamic fundamentalism.

CHRONOLOGY

6th century BCE Cyrus the Great, founder of the Persian empire, conquers Central Asia.

4th century BCE Alexander the Great conquers Central Asia.

6th century CE The Turks control Central Asia but are driven out by the Arabs, returning in the 10th century.

14th century Bukhara and Samarkand emerge as major centers of Islamic culture.

1500 The Shaybani Uzbeks rule from Bukhara and Samarkand until 1599.

1876 Expansionist Russia annexes the Khanates of Kokand and Bukhara.

1916 An armed uprising against Russian domination in Samarkand is crushed.

1917 The Russian revolution leads to demands for an independent Bukhara.

1917 Soviet power established in Tashkent.

1918 Turkestan Autonomous Soviet Socialist Republic (ASSR), incorporating present-day Uzbekistan, proclaimed.

1923–1941 Language changed from Arabic alphabet to Latin, then based on Iranized Tashkent, and finally replaced by Cyrillic.

1924 Basmachi rebels who resisted Soviet rule crushed. Uzbek SSR founded (which, until 1929, includes the Tajik ASSR).

1925 Anti-Islamic campaign bans schools and closes mosques.

1936 Karakalpak ASSR (formerly part of the Russian Soviet Federative Socialist Republic) incorporated into the Uzbek SSR.

1937 Uzbek communist leadership is purged by Stalin.

1941–1945 Industrial boom.

1959 Sharaf Rashidov first secretary of Communist Party of Uzbekistan (CPUz). Retains position until 1983.

1982–1983 Yuri Andropov becomes leader in Moscow. His anticorruption purge results in emergence of a new generation of central Asian officials.

1989 First noncommunist political movement, Unity Party (Birlik), formed but not officially registered. Birlik campaign leads to Uzbek being declared the official language.

1990 Islam Karimov becomes executive president of the new Uzbek Supreme Soviet. Interethnic fighting in Fergana Valley; 320 killed.

1991 Independence is proclaimed and Republic of Uzbekistan is adopted as official name. Uzbekistan signs treaty establishing economic community with seven other former Soviet republics. November. CPUz restructured as the People's Democratic Party of Uzbekistan (PDP); Karimov remains its leader. December. Karimov confirmed in post of president. Uzbekistan joins the CIS.

1992 Price liberalization provokes student riots in Tashkent. New constitution adopted along Western democratic lines. All religious parties banned. Uzbekistan sends troops to Tajikistan to suppress violence and strengthen border controls.

1993 Growing harassment of opposition political parties, Erk and Birlik.

1994 Introduction of new currency, the som, which becomes sole legal tender.

1995 Karimov's PDP wins legislative elections. Referendum extends Karimov's presidential term until 2000. Utkur Sultanov replaces Abdulashim Mutalov as prime minister.

1999 Bomb attacks by Islamic terrorists lead to crackdown and arrests of hundreds of opposition activists. Legislative elections.

2000 Karimov reelected as president.

V

Valdivia, Pedro de (1497–1554). Spanish conquistador, who crossed the Atacama desert (1540) and founded Santiago (1541), then led a series of expeditions from Peru to Chile (1548–53). His campaigns were successful until confronted by the warlike Araucanians. It was in a battle against them that Valdivia was killed.

Valens (c.328–378) Eastern Roman emperor (reigned 364–378), appointed co-emperor by his brother Valentinian. Defeated and killed by the Visigoths at the battle of Adrianopolis.

Valerian (c.190–260). Roman emperor (reigned 253–260) who led campaigns against the Goths and the Persians. Defeated at Edessa (259) by the Persians and died in captivity.

Valois dynasty King of France 1328–1589.

Vandals Germanic people, who played a prominent role in the affairs of the later Roman empire. After migrating through Gaul (406) and Iberia, in 429 they crossed into N Africa, capturing Carthage (439) and founding a kingdom that lasted until they were conquered by the Byzantines in 534. The Vandals gained their reputation for destructiveness after they sacked Rome in 455. *p.105*

VANUATU An archipelago strung out over 1300 km (800 miles) of the South Pacific, Vanuatu lies 1000 km (620 miles) west of Fiji. Mountainous and volcanic in origin, only 12 of the 82 islands are of significant size – Espiritu Santo and Malekula are the largest. Formerly the New Hebrides – ruled jointly by France and Britain from 1906 – Vanuatu became independent in 1980. Politics since independence have been democratic but volatile.

CHRONOLOGY

1980 Independence; Walter Lini of VP prime minister. Secession bid by Espiritu Santo.

1991 UMP coalition with NUP set up by Lini after his expulsion from VP.

1999 Tidal wave causes extensive damage.

2001 Prime Minister Sope ousted in no-confidence vote.

Varangians Name given to the Vikings of Sweden famous for their navigation of the rivers of Russia. They reached Constantinople where the Byzantine emperors employed them as an elite fighting force, the Varangian Guard. *See also* Vikings

Vardhamana *see* Mahavira

Vargas, Getúlio Dornelles (1883–1954) President of Brazil (1930–45, 1951–54), who brought social and economic changes that helped modernize the country. In 1937 he introduced the corporate-style dictatorship of the "New State."

Varthema, Ludovico di (c.1468–1517) Italian adventurer. He traveled widely in the Middle East and Asia, and was the first Christian to make the pilgrimage to Mecca, disguised as a Muslim.

Vasa Swedish and Polish dynasty founded by Gustav Eriksson Vasa, who became regent of Sweden in 1521 and King Gustavus I Vasa in 1523. His descendants reigned until 1818.

Vasilievich, Ivan *see* Ivan IV

VATICAN CITY

The Vatican, or Holy See, is the seat of the Roman Catholic Church and residence of the pope. The Vatican Palace is located in Rome behind St. Peter's Basilica, where according to tradition St. Peter lies buried. Constantine had a basilica built over the site of the tomb in 324. This was pulled down in the Renaissance to make way for a new St. Peter's, the work of Michelangelo, Bernini, and others. The Vatican has been the pope's usual residence since 1417, when the pontiffs returned from Avignon in France at the end of the 39 years of Great Schism. Vatican City is the world's smallest independent state. It consists of the walled city around St. Peter's, ten other buildings in Rome, and the pope's summer residence at Castel Gandolfo, south of Rome.

CHRONOLOGY

1870 Italian forces enter Rome and annex Papal States in central Italy.
1929 Lateran Treaty – Italy accepts Vatican City as independent state.
1978 Cardinal Karol Wojtyla pope.
1981–1982 Attempts on pope's life.

1984 Catholicism disestablished as Italian state religion.
1985 Catholic Catechism revised for first time since 1566.
1994–1995 Opposition to abortion and contraception reiterated at UN conferences in Cairo and Beijing.
1998 Statement repenting Catholic passivity during Nazi Holocaust.
2000 Jubilee Year. Papal apology for Catholic violence and oppression over two millennia.
2001 John Paul II becomes first pope to enter a mosque.
2005 John Paul II dies. Cardinal Joseph Ratzenberger becomes Pope Benedict XVI.

Vauban, Sébastien le Prestre de (1633–1707) French military engineer who revolutionized the art of siege craft.

Vedas Collection of ancient Hindu hymns and sacred verses composed from 1800 BCE onwards.

Veii Etruscan city taken by Rome (396 CE).

Velasquez, Diego 16th-century Spanish explorer of N America.

Venetian Republic Immensely wealthy Italian city-state of the medieval period. In 1204 the Venetians contrived to sack Constantinople and establish a number of Latin states in place of the Byzantine Empire. *p.205*

VENEZUELA

Located on the northern coast of South America, Venezuela's vast central plain is drained by the Orinoco, while the Guiana Highlands dominate the southwest of the country. A Spanish colony until 1811, Venezuela was lauded as Latin America's most stable democracy. Recent political upheavals have, however, led to fears of instability. Despite having one of the largest known oil deposits outside the Middle East, much of Venezuela's population still lives in shanty-town squalor.

CHRONOLOGY

1498–1500 Columbus sails along the Venezuelan coast on his third voyage.
1777 Venezuela becomes a Captaincy-General within the Viceroyalty of New Granada.

1806–21 War of Liberation, spearheaded by Simón Bolívar, in which 25 percent of the Venezuelan population die.
1811 Independence is formally declared under a republican constitution, but Venezuela again falls under Spanish rule in 1812.
1813 Bolívar sets up a government in Caracas but is driven out by Spanish the following year.
1816 Bolívar returns from exile with an expeditionary force and establishes a capital at Angostura (now Ciudad Bolívar).
1819 A congress at Angostura establishes Gran Colombia incorporating Venezuela, New Granada (Panama and Colombia) and Ecuador.
1821 Battle of Carabobo finally overthrows Spanish rule and leads to consolidation of independence within Gran Colombia (Venezuela, Colombia, and Ecuador).
1830 Gran Colombia collapses. José Antonio Páez rules Venezuela; coffee planters effectively in control.
1870 Guzmán Blanco in power. Rail system constructed.
1908 General Juan Vicente Gómez dictator; oil industry developed.
1935 Gómez falls from power. Increasing mass participation in political process.
1945 Military coup. Rómulo Betancourt takes power as leader of a civilian-military junta.
1948 AD (Democratic Action party) wins elections. Military coup. Marcos Pérez Jiménez forms government, with US and military backing.
1958 General strike. Admiral Larrázabal leads military coup. Free elections. Betancourt, newly returned from exile, wins presidential election for AD. Anticommunist campaign mounted. A few state welfare programs introduced.
1960 Movement of the Revolutionary Left (MIR) splits from AD, begins antigovernment activities.
1961 Founder member of OPEC.
1962 Communist-backed guerrilla warfare attempts repetition of Cuban revolution in Venezuela, but fails to gain sufficient popular support.
1963 Raúl Leoni (AD) elected president – first democratic transference of power. Antiguerrilla campaign continues.
1966 Failed coup attempt by supporters of former president, Pérez Jiménez.

1969 Rafael Caldera Rodríguez of COPEI president. Continues Leoni policies.

1973 Oil and steel industries nationalized. World oil crisis. Venezuelan currency peaks in value against the US dollar.

1978 Elections won by COPEI's Luis Herrera Campíns. Disastrous economic programs.

1983 Election victory under Jaime Lusinchi. Fall in world oil prices leads to unrest and cuts in state welfare.

1988–1989 Carlos Andrés Pérez wins elections for AD. Caracas food riots; 1500 dead.

1993–1995 Andrés Pérez ousted on charges of corruption; Caldera Rodríguez reelected. More social unrest.

1998–1999 Hugo Chávez's Patriotic Front coalition defeats COPEI-led coalition in elections; Chávez embarks on political reform.

1999 Controversial Constituent Assembly elected. It approves new constitution, subsequently endorsed by referendum. December. Thousands killed in floods and mud slides.

2000 Chávez's mandate confirmed by presidential elections. New National Assembly convenes.

2002 April, Chávez ousted in military coup. Reinstated a day later, after foreign and domestic protests. December, mass strike cripples economy (ends early 2003).

2004 Chávez wins approval in referendum.

Venice *see* Venetian Republic

Venus figurines Form of portable art, dating to c.35,000 BCE, found in Europe and Russia. These stylized carvings of female figures, with exaggerated breasts and buttocks, may have been representations of the mother goddess, or were perhaps associated with fertility rituals.

Veracruz Landing site of Cortés in Mexico (1519).

Verdun ⚔ of World War I (1916) French forces eventually repulsed a sustained German attack on the town of Verdun in northeastern France.

Verdun, Treaty of (843) Treaty that divided the Frankish realms between three sons of Louis the Pious: Charles the Bald, who took France, Louis the German who took lands east of the Rhine, and the Emperor Lothar, who took a broad strip of land between the other two kingdoms, as well as northern Italy.

Vereenigde Oost-Indische Compagnie *see* Dutch East India Company

Vereeniging, Peace of (May 31 1902) Treaty signed in Pretoria that ended the Boer War after initial Boer approval in Vereeniging, between representatives of the British and ex-republican Boer governments. Transvaal and the Orange Free State came under British military administration.

Verrazano, Giovanni da (c.1480–1527) Italian navigator and explorer. Traveled to N America on behalf of Francis I of France in 1524, exploring the coast from Cape Fear to Cape Breton, and later traveling to Brazil and the West Indies.

Versailles, Treaty of (Jun 28 1919) Agreement signed between Germany and the Allies at the end of World War I. Germany lost territory to France, Belgium, Denmark, Poland, and Japan; the Rhineland became a demilitarized zone and Danzig became a free city under the control of the newly-formed League of Nations. In addition Germany agreed to pay heavy war reparations. *See also* Dawes Plan, League of Nations.

Vespasian (*var. Lat.* Titus Flavius Sabinus Vespasianus, 9–79 CE). Roman emperor and founder of the Flavian dynasty (69–79 CE). The civil wars which erupted after Nero's overthrow came to an end when Vespasian was declared emperor by his troops and invaded Italy. He restored Rome to a sound financial footing, re-established army discipline and embarked on a lavish building program which included the construction of Rome's Colosseum.

Vesconte, Pietro (*fl.*1311–27) Italian cartographer who drew portolan charts 1311–27, his *Carta Nautica* (1311) being the oldest extant example, and his *Mappamundi* the most famous.

Vespucci, Amerigo (1451–1512). Italian-born Spanish explorer after whom the American continent is named. He provisioned one or two of Christopher Columbus' expeditions. He discovered and explored the mouths of the Amazon and sailed as far south as the Rio de la Plata. He evolved an ingenious system for computing longitude, and accepted South America as a new continent, not part of Asia.

Vesuvius Volcano in S Italy whose eruption destroyed Pompeii (79 CE). *p.82*

Vichy Sector of southern France administered by French government in collaboration with Germany during World War II, 1940–42. Also administered French overseas territories.

Vicksburg ⚔ of American Civil War (May 19–Jul 4 1863). Union victory.

Victor Emmanuel II (1820–78, reigned 1861–78) The first king of a united Italy.

Victoria (1819–1901) Queen of Great Britain and Ireland (reigned 1837–1901) and Empress of India (from 1876), she succeeded her uncle, Wlliam IV. Married (1840) to Prince Albert of Saxe-Coburg-Gotha (1819–61, *aka* the Prince Consort), her long reign was marked by an active British foreign policy, notably in the development of the British empire (Victoria being proclaimed Empress of india in 1876), by the growth of Britain as a global industrial and military power, and by an assertion of middle-class family values. Her Diamond Jubilee (1897) marked a high point in British aspirations as a world power.

Viele, Arnout (1640–c.1704) Dutch explorer and interpreter in N America. From 1692–94 he led an expedition north of the Great Lakes into Canada and then down to the upper Ohio river and present-day Indiana.

Vienna City on the Danube, capital of present-day Austria, up until 1918 the seat of the Habsburg emperors. In 1529 and 1683 the city withstood sieges by invading Ottoman armies. In the 18th century it expanded rapidly to become one of Europe's finest cities, renowned for its art and music. Siege of Vienna (1529). *p.276*

Vienna ⚔ of World War II (Apr 1945). Soviet reduction of final German resistance in Austria.

Vienna, Congress of (1814–15). International peace conference that settled the affairs of Europe after the defeat of Napoleon. The dominant powers were Austria, Britain, Prussia and Russia. Its guiding principle was the restoration of legitimate rulers. *p.348*

VIETNAM (*aka* Annam, Dai-Viet) Located on the eastern coast of the Indochinese peninsula, over half of Vietnam is dominated by the heavily forested mountain range, the Chaîne ▶

Annamitique. The most populated areas, which are also the most intensively cultivated, are along the Red and Mekong rivers. Partitioned after World War II, the country was reunited when the communist north won the world's longest modern-day conflict, the 1962–1975 Vietnam War. Vietnam is now a single-party state ruled by the Communist Party. Since 1986, the regime has pursued a liberal economic policy known as *doi moi* (renovation).

CHRONOLOGY

939 CE After almost a 1,000 years of Chinese domination a semi-independent Vietnamese state is created around the Red River Delta by Ngo Quyen.

1516 A group of Portuguese adventurers are first Europeans to reach in Vietnam.

1867 Southern Vietnam (Cochin China) becomes a French colony, followed by central and northern Vietnam (Annam and Tonkin) 16 years later.

1920 Quoc ngu (Roman script) replaces Chinese script.

1930 Ho Chi Minh founds Indochina Communist Party.

1940 Japanese invasion.

1941 Viet Minh resistance founded in exile in China.

1945 Viet Minh take Saigon and Hanoi. Emperor abdicates. Republic proclaimed with Ho Chi Minh as president.

1946 French reenter. First Indochina War.

1954 French defeated at Dien Bien Phu. Vietnam divided at 17°N. USSR supports North; US arms South.

1960 Groups opposed to Diem's regime in South unite as Viet Cong.

1961 US pours in military advisers.

1964 US Congress approves war.

1965 Gen. Nguyen Van Thieu takes over military government of South. First US combat troops arrive.

1965–1968 Operation Rolling Thunder – intense bombing of North by US.

1967 Antiwar protests start in US and elsewhere.

1968 Tet (New Year) Offensive – 105 towns attacked simultaneously in South with infiltrated arms. Viet Cong suffer serious losses. Peace talks begin. US eases bombing and starts withdrawing troops.

1969 Ho Chi Minh dies. Succeeded by Le Duan. War intensifies in spite of talks.

1970 US begins secret attacks in Laos and Cambodia and new mass bombing of North to stop arms reaching Viet Cong.

1972 11-day Christmas Campaign is heaviest US bombing of war.

1973 Paris Peace Agreements signed, but fighting continues.

1975 Fall of Saigon to combined forces of North and Provisional Revolutionary (Viet Cong) Government of South. One million flee after end of war.

1976 Vietnam united as Socialist Republic of Vietnam. Saigon renamed Ho Chi Minh City.

1978 Invasion of Cambodia to oust Pol Pot regime (by January 1979).

1979 Nine-Day War with China. Chinese troops pushed back after destroying everything for 40 km (25 miles) inside Vietnam. "Boat people" crisis. At UN conference, Vietnam agrees to allow legal emigration, but exodus continues.

1986 Death of Le Duan. Nguyen Van Linh, new Communist Party general secretary, initiates liberal economic policy of *doi moi* (renovation).

1987 Fighting in Thailand as Vietnam pursues Kampuchean resistance fighters across border.

1989 Troops leave Cambodia.

1991 Open anticommunist dissent made a criminal offense.

1992 Revised constitution allows foreign investment, but essential role of Communist Party is unchanged.

1995 US-Vietnamese relations normalized. Vietnam joins ASEAN.

1996 Eighth Communist Party congress.

1997 Legislative elections. Tran Duc Luong president, Phan Van Khai prime minister.

1998 Asian financial crisis dampens economic boom.

1999 Signing of border treaty with China.

2000 Visit by US president Clinton.

2001 March, visit by Russian president Putin. April. Ninth party congress. Nong Duc Manh becomes general secretary.

2003 An outbreak of acute pneumonia

Vietnam War The First and Second Indo-China Wars (1946–54) ended with French defeat at Dien Bien Phu, and the division of Vietnam at 17°N. From the late 1950s, conflict developed between north and south, supported by the USSR and USA respectively. US advisors became involved in S Vietnam in 1962, and active US military involvement began in 1965, and a series of aerial bombing campaigns over N Vietnam began. In 1973 the Paris Peace Accords were signed, and US troops began to be withdrawn, but fighting continued until 1975 when Saigon fell to the N Vietnamese and the Americans were evacuated. In 1976 Vietnam was reunited as the Socialist Republic of Vietnam. *p.434*

Vijayanagara A powerful Hindu kingdom (1345–1570), based on the Krishna valley. It exercised an ill-defined sovereignty over the whole of southern India from the 14th to 16th centuries, and was based at the magnificent city of Vijayanagara (modern Hampi). In 1565 the Muslim Sultanates of the Deccan (the successors of the Bahmani kingdom) united against the Hindu raja of Vijayanagara, who was defeated and slain in the battle of Talikota, which decisively ended Hindu supremacy in the south. *p.238*

Vikings (*var.* Norsemen, Northmen, Varangians). Term used to describe Scandinavian voyagers and warriors of the 8th–12th centuries. Norwegian, Danish, and Swedish raiders, traders, and settlers mounted expeditions that eventually took them as far as the Caspian Sea and N America. They colonized Iceland and Greenland, were established as dukes of Normandy, and ruled England under Canute. *p.138, p.139, p.149, p.150*

Vilgerdarsson, Floki Viking navigator of the 9th century whose ice-locked overwintering in the western bays of Iceland encouraged Viking colonization of the island. He coined the name Iceland.

Villa, Francisco (Pancho) (*var.* Doroteo Arangol, 1877–1923) Mexican revolutionary leader. Originally allied with Venustiano Carranza against the dictatorship of Victoriano Huerta, Villa and Zapata were defeated by Carranza in 1915 in a struggle for control of the military. He withdrew to northern Mexico where he continued guerrilla activity both in Mexico and along the US border. His attacks on towns in the southern US led to punitive US intervention.

Vinci, Leonardo da (1452–1519) Italian painter, sculptor, and engineer. One of the leading figures of the Renaissance, he was summoned to France by King Francis I. Leonardo's notebooks display a bewildering range of interests. *p.273*

Virginia State of the US. In 107 Jamestown was the site of the first permanent English settlement in America.

Virginia Capes ⚔ of American Revolutionary War (Sep 5 1781). French victory.

Vishnu Hindu god and the object of special or exclusive worship to Vaishnavas, a major Hindu sect. Traditionally Vishnu manifested himself in nine incarnations (including Buddha) to save men from evil. His tenth and final incarnation is yet to come. *p.149*

Visigoths *(aka* Western Goths) The name was first used to describe the Goths who settled in Moesia in the late 4th century. Under their ruler Alaric, they raided the Balkans, then Italy, where they sacked Rome in 410. They came to an agreement with the Romans and settled in southwest France, their kingdom also extending south into Iberia. Pushed southward by the Franks, they made Toledo their capital, controlling most of the Iberian Peninsula until the Muslim invasion of 711. *p.118 See also* Goths

Vittorio Veneto ⚔ of World War I (Oct 1918) Final battle of the Italian Front, resulted in victory for the Italians against Austrian forces, who obtained an armistice in Nov 1918.

Vizcaino, Sebastián 16th–17th century Spanish navigator. Sailed regularly on the Manila treasure galleon from 1586. In the early 17th century made expeditions to trace the Pacific coast of N America, identifying a useful harbour at Monterey and making a detailed survey of the coast. Later commissioned to search the north Pacific for the islands of Rica de Oro and Rica de Plata and to establish diplomatic relations with Japan.

Vladimir I (956–1015) Ruler of Kiev, who converted to christianity and is regarded as father of Russian Orthodox Church. *p.152*

Volstead Act (Oct 28 1919) Law to enforce the 18th Amendment, which prohibited the sale and manufacture of alcoholic drinks in the US.

Voltaire Pseudonym of François-Marie Arouet (1694–1778). Wit, poet, dramatist. His outspoken belief in political, social and religious freedom made him the embodiment of the 18th-century Enlightenment. His major works include *Lettres Philosophiques* (1734) and his satirical novel *Candide* (1759).

Voortrekker *see* Boers

Voting Rights Act (1965)

Vouillé ⚔ (517). Visigoths defeated by Clovis I.

Vulgate Latin version of bible completed (404). *p.101*

W

Wahhabis Followers of Muhammad ibn 'Abd al-Wahhab (1703–92), who founded an orthodox sect in Nejd, to preserve the "purity of Islam." An alliance between the Wahhabis and the Saud family led in the 18th century to the unification of most of the Arabian Peninsula in 1802 they took Mecca, but were driven out in 1812. In 1902 Abd al-Aziz ibn Saud began to reform and expand the modern kingdom of Saudi Arabia. The Wahhabi form of Islam remains Saudi Arabia's official faith. *See also* Abd al-Aziz ibn Saud

Waitangi, Treaty of (Feb 6 1840) Treaty drawn up to facilitate British annexation of New Zealand. The Maori acknowledged British sovereignty in return for ownership of their lands, which could only be purchased from them by crown agents. The initial ceremony at Waitangi was followed by further signings at sites all over N Island and the treaty was eventually signed by over 500 Maori chiefs. The Maori translation of the English text led them to believe that they would retain authority over their lands and peoples. *p.359*

Waldenses *see* Waldensians

Waldensians *(var.* Waldenses, *aka* Poor Men of Lyons) Reformist Christian sect founded c.1170, based on teachings of Peter Waldo/Valdez (c.1140–1217), based on simplicity, poverty, and evangelical zeal. Highly critical of clerical behavior, Waldo was condemned by the Council of Verona (1184), and his followers were subject to persecution during the period of the Albigensian Crusade (1209)

Waldseemüller, Martin (1470–1521) Cartographer from Lorraine. Famous as the man who coined the word "America" after the Italian explorer Amerigo Vespucci for his world map of 1507. He also published an edition of Ptolemy's *Geography* in 1513.

Wales Part of the UK, Wales put up stern resistance to English rule in the Middle Ages. When the Normans conquered England, they made only limited progress into the Welsh borders. In the 13th century Edward I set about completing the conquest and in 1301 had his son crowned Prince of Wales. *p.220 See also* United Kingdom

Wall Street Crash (1929) Collapse in the price of stocks and shares on the New York stock exchange which created panic in financial markets across the world and was a major contributory factor in the Great Depression of the 1930s.

Wallace, Alfred Russel (1823–1913) English naturalist who traveled to the Amazon (1848–52) and Malay archipelago (1854–62). He developed theories of natural selection which had a profound influence on Charles Darwin. The Wallace Line, which divides the different types of fauna found to the east and west of the archipelago, was named after him.

Wallace, William (c.1270–1305) Scottish national hero who led Scottish resistance forces during the first years of the long struggle against English rule.

Wandiwash ⚔ of Seven Years' War in India (1760). French defeated by British.

Wang Mang *see* Xin dynasty

Wang Yangming *(var.* Wang Yang-ming, 1472–1529) Chinese Neo-Confucian philosopher of Ming dynasty, who taught that Confucian ethics of behaviour and morality were innate, and could be discovered and promoted through contemplation and self-awareness rather than the study of classical texts and tradition. His teachings are frequently compared to tenets of Zen Buddhism.

Wang Yang-min *see* Wang Yangming

Warburton, Peter (1813–89) English-born explorer of Australia. After emigrating in 1853, he set out N from Adelaide, exploring the Simpson Desert and S Queensland; in 1872 he traveled W from Alice Springs across the Great Sandy Desert to the W coast.

Warring States period (403–221 BCE) A time of civil war in China when the Zhou confederation collapsed into rival factions: the Qi in the northeast, Chu in the south, and Qin in the northwest. Brought to an end by the Qin dynasty.

Wars of Liberation *see* South America

Wars of the Roses *see* Roses, Wars of the

Warsaw Pact (*var.* Warsaw Treaty Organization1955). Cold War political and military alliance formed in 1955, dominated by USSR, including Poland, E Germany, Czechoslovakia, Hungary, Romania, Bulgaria, and (to1968) Albania.

Warsaw Treaty Organization *see* Warsaw Pact

Washington, George (1732–99) First president of the US (1789–97). Born in Virginia, Washington served with distinction on the British side during the Seven Years' War against France (1754–61). He later represented Virginia in the House of Burgesses, and in the Continental Congresses of 1774 and 1775. When war broke out between Britain and the American colonists, Washington was the first choice to lead the colonial army. Important successes included the battles of Trenton and Princeton, and the key battle of Yorktown in 1781 which virtually ended the American Revolution. From 1783, Washington sought to establish a constitutional government for the new nation. In 1789 the first government under the new constitution was assembled, with Washington at its President. He was elected to a second term, retiring in 1797 in the face of increasing disputes between the Democratic Republicans of Thomas Jefferson and the Federalists, led by Alexander Hamilton.

Washington Naval Agreement (1922) After the concession of various Pacific territories to Japan at the Treaty of Versailles, this agreement was designed to limit and balance the level of naval power in the region, assuring predominance to the Western Powers.

Watergate (*aka* Watergate Affair) Scandal sparked off by involvement of US Republican President Richard M. Nixon's administration in a break-in at the Democratic Party national headquarters (the Watergate building, Washington) during the presidential elections (June 1972). The televised hearings of a special Senate committee revealed escalating degrees of White House involvement and attempted cover-up. This ultimately led to a House Judiciary Committee investigation, the release and publication of sensitive tapes, and the erosion of confidence in Nixon's administration (and Washington practices in general). The imprisonment of three of Nixon's senior aides preceded the adoption of three articles of impeachment against the president, resulting in Nixon's resignation (Aug 9 1974), although he was pardoned by his successor, Gerald R Ford.

Waterloo ⚔ of Napoleonic Wars (Jun 18 1815) Final defeat of Napoleonic forces.

Watt, James (1736–1819) Scottish inventor whose improvements to the steam engine (1765) accelerated the spread of the Industrial Revolution in Britain.

wavy line pottery The first pottery to be made in Africa (c.7000 BCE) by the hunters and fishers of the southern Sahara, who lived in a broad swathe stretching from Mali to the Nile Valley. The pottery was decorated by parallel wavy-lines; these could be made by dragging the spine of a fish across the clay while it was still wet, or using bone or wooden points.

Weddell, James (1787–1834) English navigator whose claim to have sailed into the vast bay in W Antarctica (1823), bounded by the Antarctic Peninsula, Coats Land and the Ronne Ice Shelf, led to it being named after him.

Wei kingdom *see* Shu

Wellington, Arthur Wellesley, 1st Duke of (1769–1852) British general and statesman; Prime Minister (1828–30). Campaigned in India, then commanded the British forces in the Peninsular War (1808–14), driving the French out of Portugal and Spain. After Napoleon's escape from Elba, he defeated the French at Waterloo.

Wells cathedral clock (c.1386) Medieval mechanical clock preserved in London's science museum. *p.242*

West, the Geopolitical term relating to the free market economies and countries of US/NATO alliance during the Cold War.

West Bank Lands on the west bank of Jordan taken by Israel in Six Day War. They constitute the area that by the Oslo Accords ought to become a self-governing Palestinian state.

West Germany (*var.* Federal Republic of Germany, FRG or BRG) Established 1949 following Soviet partition of post-war occupied Germany. Joined NATO (1955), and founder member of EEC enjoying huge economic growth until dissolution upon German reunification (1990).

Western Front The western theater of war during World War I, based primarily in N France and southern Belgium.

Western Goths *see* Visigoths

Western Han *see* Han dynasty

Western Jin Ruling dynasty of China (265–304 ce) who overthrew the Wei and briefly established Chinese unity.

Western Samoa *see* Samoa

Western Zhou *see* Zhou dynasty

Westphalia, Peace of (1648) General name for the 11 separate treaties, negotiated 1643–48, between the Habsburgs and their adversaries, bringing to an end the Thirty Years' War, which recognized religious tolerance and secularization of Church lands in much of Germany, and the independence of the United Provinces and the Swiss Confederation.

Wheeler, George Montague (1842–1905) US army officer and explorer. After completing a survey for the military of the area east of the Sierras in 1869, he set up his own organization: the United States Geographical Surveys West of the One-Hundredth Meridian, and surveyed thousands of miles of the West.

Whirling dervishes Mystical Islamic sect probably founded by Sufi poet Jalal ad-Din in the 13th century. *p.219*

Whitby, Synod of (664) Ecclesiastical council which led to Britain's Christian communities adopting the practices and doctrines of Rome rather than those of Celtic Christianity.

White Huns (*var.* Hephthalites) *see* Huns

White Mountain ⚔ of Thirty Years' War (1620). Bohemians defeated by Habsburg imperial armies.

White Plains ⚔ of American Revolutionary War (Oct 28 1776). British victory.

Whitney, Eli (1765–1825) US inventor, whose development of the cotton gin, to separate cotton fibre from cotton seed in 1793, transformed the efficiency of the Southern cotton industry and the conditions of its slave work force. Never properly patented, his invention was widely copied. He later manufactured firearms using a prototype production line system.

Wilderness, The ⚔ of American Civil War (May 5–7 1864). Inconclusive result.

Wilhelm I (1797–1888) King of Prussia (reigned 1861–88) and first German Emperor (reigned 1871–88). Dominated by chancellor Bismarck, whose policies led to creation of German empire. *p.370*

Wilhelm II (1859–1941) German emperor and king of Prussia (reigned 1888–1918). He dismissed Bismarck (1890) and in a long period of personal rule, asserted Germany's claim to world leadership. Forced to abdicate at the end of World War I.

Wilkes, Charles (1798–1877) US explorer of Antarctica. After appointment as head of Depot of Charts and Instruments (1834) he commanded the US Exploring Expedition (1838–42) in the Southern Ocean, surveying the part of Antarctica now known as Wilkes Land. Court-martialled for cruelty, he served during the American Civil War, retiring as rear-admiral.

William I (*aka* William, Duke of Normandy, William the Conqueror, c.1028–87) First Norman king of England (reigned 1066–87), who inherited the dukedom of Normandy in 1035. In 1066 he invaded England, defeating Harold Godwinson at the battle of Hastings (1066), ending the era of Saxon rule. His victory was recorded, and claims to the English throne justified, in the Bayeux Tapestry. He introduced religious, political and social reform, and began the process of English unification. Although largely based in Normandy, he commissioned the first systematic survey of English property, the Domesday Book (1085), the foundation of the English feudal system. *p.173*

William I, Prince of Orange (*aka* William of Nassau, William the Silent, 1533–84) Dutch statesman who marshalled resistance to Spanish Catholic rule in the Netherlands during the Dutch Revolt (1565–1609).

William, Duke of Normandy *see* William I

William of Nassau *see* Nassau

William the Conqueror *see* William I

William of Rubruck (c.1215–1295) Franciscan friar, in 1253–55 he was sent on a religious mission to the Mongols by Louis IX of France. His description of his travels and his meeting with the Great Khan Möngke were contained in his Itinerary, one of the best-known works of travel of the medieval period.

Willoughby, Sir Hugh (died 1554) British military officer and explorer. Appointed captain-general of a fleet of three ships sent by London merchants to seek a Northeast Passage. One of the ships, commanded by Richard Chancellor, reached the White Sea.

Wills, William (1834–61) English explorer of Australia, who accompanied Robert Burke on his journey across Australia from south to north. Died of starvation at base camp, Cooper's Creek, after reaching swamps at the Gulf of Carpentaria. *See also* Burke, Robert O'Hara.

Wilson (Thomas) Woodrow (1856–1924) 28th President of the US (Democrat, 1912–21). Under Wilson's administration, women's right to vote was added to the Constitution, along with the prohibition of the sale of alcohol. Wilson took the US into World War I in 1917 and intervened in the Mexican Revolution following Pancho Villa's attacks on US territory and citizens. He laid out the "fourteen point" plan for peace which led to the Armistice in November 1918, and gave vigorous support to the League of Nations. His health was broken by the Senate's refusal to ratify the Treaty of Versailles.

Wilson's Creek ⚔ of American Civil War (Aug 10 1861). Confederate victory.

Windmills Introduced into Europe c.1200. *p.213*

Witchcraft Trials for witchcraft increased dramatically in protestant Europe (and North America) in the 16th and 17th centuries. *p.308*

Witwatersrand Gold finds (1886).

Women The vast increase in the number of women workers during World War II. *p.417*

Wolfe, General James (1727–59) English general. Led British forces during the Seven Years' War against France in N America. He was instrumental in the capture of Louisburg in 1758, but was killed during the Battle of Quebec in 1759 which resulted in British victory.

Woodward, Dr Henry (died c.1686) 17th-century explorer of N America. From 1668 he explored much of the Carolinas, including the Savannah river.

World Cup Soccer championship inaugurated in 1930. *p.426*

World Trade Organization (WTO) Organization for the regulation and liberalization of world trade, set up in January 1995 as a successor to GATT (the General Agreement on Tariffs and Trade) established in 1947. 104 countries were founding members of the WTO, which is responsible for making sure that GATT agreements are adhered to, as well as setting up new trade agreements.

World War I (*var.* First World War, The Great War, 1914–18) Major conflict in which expansionist aggression by Germany, Austria-Hungary, and the Ottoman Empire, in Europe and their colonial holdings (the Central Powers), was countered by an Allied coalition led by France, Britain, Russia, Italy, and (from 1917) US. The first war to be fought on a truly industrial scale, involving mass mobilization of population and industry, and the innovative use of airplanes, gas, and tanks on the battlefield, it was also a war of attrition on a massive scale. It heralded the end of European imperialism, the Russian Revolution, the redrafting of the map of Europe, and the dismemberment of the Ottoman empire. *p.394, p.396*

World War II (*var.* Second World War) Major conflict (1939–45) arising from territorial expansion and aggressive racist policies of Germany, Italy and Japan (the Axis), who were countered by an Allied coalition led by Britain and the Commonwealth, forces from Axis-occupied nations, USSR and US (from 1941). Mass mobilization of the population and industry by all belligerents, the gradual involvement of most countries in the world, the prosecution of the war on land, sea and air, the widespread involvement of partisans, technological innovation, and the impact of the war on civilian populations led to its characterization as a "Total War." The insistence by the Allies on unconditional surrender, and their deployment of nuclear weapons over Japan proved decisive. The final stages saw the destruction and partition of Europe, the occupation of Japan and the emergence of USSR and US as ideologically opposed superpowers during the Cold War. *p.414*

World Wide Web International computer network offering a huge interface for the storage, retrieval, and exchange of information. *p.451*

Wounded Knee (1890). More than 200 Sioux were massacred by US army troops in last major confrontation between Indians and the US army.

Wrangel, Baron Ferdinand von (1797–1870) Russian vice-admiral and explorer of Arctic coastline of Siberia.

writing The origin of writing and alphabets. *p.23*

WTO *see* World Trade Organization

Wu kingdom *see* Shu, Wu, and Wei Kingdoms

Würtzburg cathedral Fine example of Romanesque architecture of the 11th and 12th centuries. *p.166*

Wudi (*var.* Wu-ti, 156–87 BCE). Most powerful of Former Han rulers (reigned 140–87 BCE), whose campaigns in S and SW China, Vietnam and against the Xiongnu of Central Asia greatly extended Chinese realms. He established the role of emperor and Confucianism as state religion, and revived central bureaucracy.

X

Xanadu *see* Shangdu

Xenophon (c.431–350 BCE) Greek historian and disciple of Socrates. A skilled soldier, he fought with 10,000 Greek mercenaries under the Persian prince, Cyrus, in the 401 BCE campaign against Cyrus's brother, the King of Persia. Cyrus's death left the Greeks stranded 930 miles (1500 km) from home. Elected leader, Xenophon led them safely to the Black Sea.

Xerxes I (*var.* Xerxes the Great, 519–465 BCE) The son of Darius I, Achaemenid king of Persia, Xerxes (reigned 486–465 BCE) is known mainly for his massive and unsuccessful invasion of Greece from the Hellespont in 480 BCE.

Xhosa Bantu-speaking people of southern Africa, inhabitants of S African homeland of Transkei during late 20th century

Xia dynasty (*var.* Hsia, c.2000–1800 BCE) Ruling dynasty of first Chinese proto-state, forerunners of the Shang.

Xiankiang *see* Dzungaria

Xin dynasty (*var.* Hsin dynasty) Ruling dynasty of China (9–23 CE) under sole emperor Wang Mang (former Han regent 1–8 CE) who introduced major reforms, including taxation, money lending, nationalization of estates, and government monopolies on main industries (salt, coinage, iron, wine) during his brief interregnum before accession of Later Han.

Xiongnu (*var.* Hsiung-nu) Chinese name for federation of largely nomadic steppe peoples that dominated central Asia from c.3rd century BCE to the 4th century CE, constantly threatening China's northern borders. Disrupted by campaigns of Former Han (55 BCE), they split into eastern and western hordes; after decline of Han dynasty, Xiongnu generals established dynastic kingdoms in N China during the Sixteen Kingdoms period. Sometimes associated with the Huns.

Xixia empire (*var.* Hsihsia) *See also* Tanguts

Xuan Zang (*var.* Hsuan-tsang, 596–664) Chinese pilgrim and traveler whose search for original Buddhist texts took him across the Gobi and Takla Makan deserts, to Bactria and the Punjab to the Gangetic Plain, returning overland. His account of his 16-year journey, and its geographical descriptions, were published by imperial command.

Y

Yalta Conference (Feb 4–11 1945) Meeting of Allied World War II leaders led by Roosevelt, Churchill, and Stalin (the "Big Three"). Reaffirmed the decision to demand unconditional Axis surrender and planned a four-power occupation of Germany. Also discussed the plans for the United Nations.

Yamasee War (1715–16) Conflict between British colonists and the Yamasee Indians and their allies in SE South Carolina, a result of European incursions into Indian lands and the fur trade.

Yamato state Ancient Japanese clan on island of Honshu, which founded a state that started to expand c.300 CE.

Yan'an (*var.* Yenan) End of Chinese Communists "Long March."

Yangshao culture (c.5000–3000 BCE) Early agricultural culture of China centered on the Yellow River basin, later replaced by Longshan culture. The Yangshao is characterized by square and round timber and thatch houses and handmade red burnished pottery, finished on a slow wheel. Yangshao communities grew millet and had domesticated pigs and dogs.

Yanomani Hunter-gatherer tribal people of Amazonian rainforest, whose traditional lifestyle was threatened by commercial concerns developing in the region in the late 20th century.

Yayoi culture (c.300 BCE–300 CE). Period in Japanese history when rice, pottery and metals were introduced. *p.91*

Yellow Turbans (*var.* Zhang Yue) Religious sectarian revolt of Later Han (184 CE). The Yellow Turbans communal lifestyle and vision of a forthcoming age of "Great Wellbeing" made theirs the most significant of the peasant revolts which attended Han decline.

Yeltsin, Boris (1931–) First president of the Russian Federation after the breakup of the old USSR. Shortly after his election in 1991 he succeeds in foiling hard-line communist coup, appearing in armored car in front of parliament building. Tenure of presidency marked by erratic behavior, poor health, and clashes with parliament. He fires four prime ministers before he retires from presidency in 1999.

YEMEN Yemen is located in southern Arabia neighboring Saudi Arabia and Oman. The north is mountainous, with a fertile strip along the Red Sea. The south is largely arid mountains and desert. From the 9th century, the Zaydi dynasty ruled Yemen until their defeat by the Ottoman Turks in 1517. The Turks were expelled by the Zaydi imams in 1636. Until 1990 Yemen was two countries, the Yemen Arab Republic in the north and the People's Democratic Republic of Yemen in the south. The north was run by successive military regimes; the poorer south was the Arab world's only Marxist state. Postunification conflict between the two ruling hierarchies, nominally in coalition, led to full-scale civil war in 1994 and the ousting of the southern-based former Marxists.

CHRONOLOGY

1839 Britain occupies Aden.

1918 Yemen gains independence.

1937 Aden made a Crown Colony, hinterland a Protectorate.

1962 Army coup. Imam deposed, Yemen Arab Republic (YAR) declared in north.

1962–1970 Northern civil war between royalists and republicans.

1963 Aden and Protectorate united to form Federation of South Arabia.

1967 British troops leave Aden.

1970 South Yemen renamed People's Democratic Republic of Yemen (PDRY). Republicans victorious in the north.

1971 Civilian elections in YAR.

1972 War between YAR and PDRY ends in peace settlement.

1974 Army coup in YAR.

1978 Lieutenant-Colonel Ali Saleh YAR president. Coup in PDRY. Radical Abdalfattah Ismail in power.

1980 Ismail replaced by moderate Ali Muhammed.

1982 PDRY signs peace treaty with Sultan of Oman.

1986 Coup attempt in PDRY leads to civil war. Rebels take control of Aden. New PDRY president meets YAR counterpart.

1987 Oil production starts in YAR.

1988 YAR elections for consultative council; Muslim brotherhood gains influence.

1989 Speeding-up of unification process. Constitution of unified Yemen published.

1990 May. Formal unification amid protests from pro-Islamic groups opposed to secular constitution. Ali Saleh becomes president of Republic of Yemen.

1991 Yemeni guest workers expelled by Saudi Arabia in retaliation for Yemen's position over the Iraqi invasion of Kuwait.

1994 Southern secessionists defeated in civil war.

1997 President Saleh's GPC wins an absolute majority in general election.

1998–1999 Violent border dispute with Saudi Arabia. Kidnapping of tourists, four killed; three members of Islamic Army of Aden (IAA) sentenced to death.

1999 Saleh reelected.

2000 Yemen agrees border with Saudi Arabia after 66–year dispute.

2001 Referendum approves extension of presidential term to seven years.

2003 Government targets suspected al-Qaeda allies in tribal areas, expels 100 foreign "scholars."

Yenan *see* Yan'an

Yermak, Timofeyevich (died 1585) Russian Cossack whose campaign against the Tatar khanate across the central Urals (1581) led to the first Russian settlement of Siberia.

Yi dynasty (*var.* I, Li, Ri, 1392–1910) Ruling dynasty of Korea, founded by Yi Songgye with Ming support.

Yijing (*var.* I-ching) Chinese Buddhist pilgrim of late 7th century CE who visited the hearth of Buddhism by sea.

Yi Songgye *see* Yi dynasty

Yom Kippur War War in which Egypt and Syria launched a joint surprise attack on Israel on the Jewish festival of Yom Kippur (Oct 6 1973). The war ended three weeks later when Israel had repulsed Syria, and crossed the Suez Canal, encircling an Egyptian army. Following UN cease-fire, Israel withdrew from Egyptian side of Canal and, after 1979 treaty, from Sinai.

Yorktown, Siege of ⚔ of American Revolutionary War (Sep 28–Oct 19 1781). American victory.

Yoruba People of W Africa, noted for urban cultures on lower reaches of Niger, whose kingdom of Oyo emerged as one of the most powerful in the region until the early 18th century.

Young Turks The failure of the Ottoman sultan, Abdul Hamid II, to modernize the empire led in 1908 to a revolution by the Young Turks, an association of army officers and reformers. The sultan was forced to restore the suspended constitution before his deposition in 1909. The Young Turks subsequently became the empire's dominant political party. *See also* Atatürk

Younghusband, Francis (1863–1942) British explorer of Central Asia. In 1902 led the expedition which opened up Tibet to the western world, leading to Anglo-Tibetan Treaty (1904).

Yuan dynasty (1206–1367) Ruling Mongol dynasty of China.

Yuan Shih-k'ai *see* Yuan Shikai

Yuan Shikai (*var.* Yuan Shih-k'ai) (1859–1916) First president of the Republic of China in 1912 after the 1911 revolution. Precipitated civil war in 1913 by murdering the revolutionary party chairman and trying to create a new imperial dynasty.

Yucatán Peninsula Site of many of the major Maya cities and temples.

Yuezhi Tribal people of SC Asia who were unified under the Kushanas (c.60 CE).

Yugoslavia Conflict in Yugoslavia. *p.451* *See also* Croatia, Macedonia, Slovenia, Serbia and Montenegro

Yungang Cave (5th century CE) Datong, north central China, site of colossal Buddhist rock-carvings. *p.104*

Z

Zagwe dynasty (1137–1270) Ruling dynasty of Ethiopia, whose interregnum in the Solomonian line was marked by fragmentation and a move away from the ancient capital of Axum.

Zaire Name given to Congo in 1971, but following fall of President Mobutu in 1997, country is renamed Democratic Republic of Congo. *See also* Congo, Democratic Republic

Zama ⚔ of Punic Wars (202 BCE). Decisive Roman victory.

ZAMBIA Lying in the heart of southern Africa, Zambia is a country of upland plateaus, bordered to the south by the Zambezi river. Its economic fortunes are tied to the copper industry. Falling copper prices in the late 1970s, and then the growing inaccessibility of remaining reserves, have led to a severe decline in the economy. The United National Independence Party (UNIP), led by Kenneth Kaunda, took power at Zambian independence in 1964. In 1991 there was a peaceful transition from single-party rule to multiparty democracy.

CHRONOLOGY

1972 UNIP one-party government.

1982–1991 Austerity measures and corruption: pressure for democracy.

1991 MMD government elected; Frederick Chiluba defeats Kaunda.

1996 Controversial elections return Chiluba and MMD to power.

2002 Levy Mwanawasa president.

Zangi (*aka* Imad al-Din Zangi, 1084–1146). Seljuk governor of Mosul (1126), who carved out an independent state around Aleppo, and whose capture of Edessa from the Franks (1144) led to the Second Crusade. Assassinated by associates whilst campaigning to capture Damascus. Succeeded by his son, Nur al-Din (1144)

Zanzibar Arab sultanate island off the east coast of Africa, which became a British protectorate in 1890. Granted independence in 1963, it merged with Tanganyika to form Tanzania the following year. *See also* Tanzania

Zapata, Emiliano (1879–1919) Mexican revolutionary. Following the outbreak of the Mexican Revolution (1910–17), Zapata organized the occupation of large estates, demanding the return of land to the people. His forces were mainly responsible for bringing down the dictatorship of Porfirio Diaz, and he later opposed the government of Venustiano Carranza. He continued agrarian reform in the south, setting up the Rural Loan Bank.

Zapotecs Pre-Columbian Mesoamerican people that flourished in southern Mexico between 300 BCE–300 CE. They were centered on Monte Albán and produced the earliest hieroglyphic inscriptions in the Americas. *p.54*

Zen Buddhism Sectarian form of Buddhism developed and practiced in China, Korea and Japan, based on intense meditation, austere discipline, and monasticism, seeking to achieve enlightenment through non-rational forms of thought. Frequently associated with martial arts and intense aestheticism.

Zhang Qian (*var.* Chang Ch'ien, died c.114 BCE) Han diplomat and ambassador whose travels in Central Asia seeking Han allies against the Xiongnu make him the earliest recorded explorer. Imprisoned by the Xiongnu for ten years (139–129 BCE), he escaped and traveled to Ferghana and Bactria, returning to China in 126 BCE. Reports of his journeys, which marked out the Silk Road, including a second trip to Parthia (115), encouraged Han expansion in Central Asia.

Zhang Yue *see* Yellow Turbans

Zheng He (*var.* Cheng Ho, 1371–1435) Chinese admiral and emissary of the emperor Chengzu. Undertook expeditions to SE Asia, India, Arabia and Africa. *p.253*

Zhengzhou Capital of Shang China (2nd millennium BCE).

Zhongdu Capital of Jin China (1115–1234).

Zhou dynasty (*var.* Chou, 1111–256 BCE) Chinese dynasty that overthrew the Shang dynasty in 1027 BCE. The Western Zhou developed political unity until 771 BCE, when the Eastern Zhou established a new capital at Luoyang and rivalry and dissent between the states eroded centralized power. The Zhou confederation collapsed into civil war (the Warring States period, 403–221 BCE) and was brought to an end by the Qin dynasty.

Zhou Enlai (*var.* Chou en-lai, 1898–1976) Chinese statesman, founder member of the Chinese Communist Party, and loyal supporter of Mao Zedong. Active during Japanese and Civil wars, became prime minister upon Communist victory (1949) until his death, also serving as foreign minister (1949–58). Generally moderate, in favor of detente, he established the Four Modernizations program (1975).

Zhu Siben (*var.* Chu-ssu-pen, 1273–1337) Chinese map-maker of Yuan (Mongol) dynasty, whose Atlas comprised a single-scale map of China and its neighbors, with details extending to the Indian Ocean, and most of the African coastline.

Zhu Yuanzhang (*var.* Taizu, Hung-wu [mightily martial] emperor, Chu Yuan-chang, 1328–98) Founder and first emperor of Chinese Ming dynasty (reigned 1366–98). Born into poverty, he became a monk in 1344, before joining a bandit gang. Rose to become leader of a rebel army which seized Nanjing (1356) and over the next 12 years overthrew the Mongol (Yuan) rulers, proclaiming the Ming imperial dynasty in 1366. *p.239*

ziggurat Tower structure built in ancient Sumeria and adjacent Elam, these are temples constructed on a high pyramidal mound with external stairways on all sides leading to a surmounting shrine.

ZIMBABWE Situated in southern Africa, Zimbabwe is bordered by South Africa, Botswana, Zambia, and Mozambique. The upland center is crisscrossed by rivers, which flow into Lake Kariba and the Zambezi River. The Zambezi possesses Zimbabwe's most spectacular natural feature, the Victoria Falls. Formerly the British colony of Southern Rhodesia,

Zimbabwe achieved independence in 1980, after a struggle between the white minority, led by the prime minister, Ian Smith, and the black majority, represented by Robert Mugabe and Joshua Nkomo's Patriotic Front (PF). *See also* Great Zimbabwe, Rhodesia

CHRONOLOGY

1953 British colony of Southern Rhodesia became part of the Federation of Rhodesia and Nyasaland with Northern Rhodesia (now Zambia) and Nyasaland (now Malawi).

1961 Joshua Nkomo forms ZAPU.

1962 ZAPU banned. Segregationist Rhodesian Front (RF) wins elections.

1963 African nationalists in Northern Rhodesia and Nyasaland demand dissolution of Federation. ZANU, offshoot of ZAPU, formed by Rev. Sithole and Robert Mugabe.

1964 New RF prime minister Ian Smith rejects British demands for majority rule. ZANU banned.

1965 RF reelected. State of emergency declared (renewed until 1990). Smith's unilateral declaration of independence. UK imposes economic sanctions. ANC, ZANU, and ZAPU begin guerrilla war.

1974 RF regime agrees cease-fire terms with African nationalists.

1976 ZANU and ZAPU unite as Patriotic Front (PF).

1979 After four years, eventual agreement on constitution.

1980 Independence as Zimbabwe. Following violent election campaign, Mugabe becomes prime minister. Relations severed with South Africa.

1983–1984 Unrest in Matabeleland, ZAPU–PF's power base.

1985 Elections return ZANU–PF, with manifesto to create one-party state. Many ZAPU–PF members arrested.

1987 ZAPU–PF banned. Provision for white seats in parliament abolished. ZANU–PF and ZAPU–PF sign unity agreement. Mugabe elected president.

1990 Elections won by ZANU–PF. Mugabe reelected president.

1998 Nationwide strikes, student protests and talk of attempted military coup.

1999 Death of Vice President Nkomo. Opposition forms MDC.

2000 Referendum on new constitution: government defeated. Expropriations of white-owned farmland by squatters. June. Strong MDC performance in general election. ZANU–PF accused of using intimidation to retain majority.
2002 Mugabe reelected in flawed poll. Commonwealth membership suspended. Threat of mass starvation and economic collapse.
2003 Zimbabwe leaves Commonwealth.

Zimbabwe, Great *see* Great Zimbabwe
Zollverein The customs union of German states organized in 1834 under Prussian auspices. It marked an important step towards German unification.
Zoroastrianism A monotheistic religion dating back to the Achaemenid era founded by Zoroaster (Zarathustra, Zardushi), a Persian or Bactrian prophet who lived from about 628–551 BCE. The roots of Zoroastrianism lay in the ancient polytheistic folk-myths of India, from which Zoroaster abstracted a single Wise God, Ahura Mazda, opposed by the evil spirit Angra Mainyu. After the Greek and Roman eras, the Sassanians restored Zoroastrianism as Persia's state religion. Its modern adherents are the Parsees.
Zoser (*var.* Djoser, Netjerykhet, c.2650–c.2575 BCE) Egyptian ruler of the 3rd dynasty. He was the first to make Memphis his exclusive residence and his reign was a period of technical innovation and cultural flowering, including the construction of Egypt's first stone buildings; formerly they were made of bricks and mud. He initiated the building of the first step pyramid, at Saqqara, the first structure of its size in the world.
Zulu kingdom Nation of Nbguni-speaking in southern Africa which arose under Zulu leader Shaka (reigned 1816–28), who with a well-disciplined and efficient fighting force, conquered most of present-day Natal. *p.350*

ACKNOWLEDGMENTS

The publisher would like to thank the following for their kind permission to reproduce their photographs:

Abbreviations key:
b=bottom; c=centre; l=left; r=right; t=top

9 **Natural History Museum, London**: b; 10 **The Natural History Museum, London**: cl, cr, t;

13 **Professor Joseph E. Schwartzberg**; 14 **Museum of London**;

15 **American Museum of Natural History**: t; **Simon Kaner**: Kokugakuin University Archaeological Museum b; 18 © **The British Museum**; 19 © **The British Museum**;

20 © **Michael Holford**: Ankara Museum t; 21 **AKG London**: Erich Lessing;

23 © **The British Museum**: t; 25 **John Woodcock**; 26 © **The British Museum**;

27 **The Art Archive**: National Museum, Copenhagen;

28 © **The British Museum**: t; **Robert Harding Picture Library**: Karachi Museum, Pakistan c;

29 **Museum of London**; 30 © **Michael Holford**: Musée du Louvre, Paris b;

31 **Ancient Art & Architecture Collection**: Ronald Sheridan t; **The University Of Auckland**: Department of Anthropology/Excavated by Prof. R.C. Green b;

33 **Werner Forman Archive**: N. J. Saunders; 34 **Werner Forman Archive**;

37-38 **AKG London**: Erich Lessing;

38 **AKG London**: Erich Lessing c; **Werner Forman Archive**: The British Museum t;

39 **Bridgeman Art Library, London/New York**: The British Museum tc; **The Art Archive**: Historical Museum of Armenia, Erevn tr;

40 © **The British Museum**: (AES 48971 - 2);

41 **AKG London**: The Israel Museum, Jerusalem t; **The Art Archive**: The British Museum b;

42 **The Art Archive**: The British Museum/Dagli Orti (A) t; **South American Pictures**: Kathy Jarvis b;

43 **Bridgeman Art Library, London/New York**: National Archaeological Museum, Athens, Greece;

44 **AKG London**: t; **The Art Archive**: Museo di Villa Giulia Rome/Dagli Orti (A) b;

45 **AKG London**: t; **Ohio Historical Society**: b;

46 © **The British Museum**: t; © **Michael Holford**: The British Museum b;

47 **The Art Archive**: Dagli Orti (A);

48 **Heritage Image Partnership**: The British Museum (ANE, 92687);

51-52 **TAP Service Archaeological Receipts Fund Hellenic Republic Ministry of Culture**;

52 **Eye Ubiquitous**: Nick Bonetti t; 53 **AKG London**: bl; **The Art Archive**: br;

54 **Werner Forman Archive**: Courtesy Entwistle Gallery, London b; **INAH**: t;

55 **Werner Forman Archive**: David Bernstein Fine Art, New York;

56 **Ancient Art & Architecture Collection**: Ronald Sheridan t;

57 **Ancient Art & Architecture Collection**: Ronald Sheridan b; **The Art Archive**: The Hermitage, Leningrad t;

58 **Bridgeman Art Library, London/New York**: Oriental Museum, Durham University, UK;

59 **The Art Archive**: Museo Nazionale Romano Rome/Dagli Orti (A) b; **Bridgeman Art Library, London/New York**: Museo Archeologico Nazionale, Naples, Italy t;

60 **Ancient Art & Architecture Collection**: Ronald Sheridan t; **Robert Harding Picture Library**: Archaeological Museum, Istanbul t; 61 **Corbis**: Archivo Iconografico, S.A. b;

62 **Hutchison Library**: Jenny Pate; 64 **The Art Archive**: Dagli Orti;

66 **AKG London**: Erich Lessing b; **The British Museum**: t;

67 **Ancient Art & Architecture Collection**: Mike Andrews t; **Royal Museum of Scotland**: b;

68 **Bridgeman Art Library, London/New York**: Louvre, Paris, France t; **Novosti (London)**: b;

69 **Werner Forman Archive**: The British Museum t; 70 **Alistair Duncan** t;

71 **Bridgeman Art Library, London/New York**: Louvre, France b; © **The British Museum**: (CM Sicily BMC 21) t; 72 © **The British Museum**: (GR); 73 **Corbis**: Bettmann;

74 **Scala Group S.p.A.**: Museo della Civilta' Romana, Rome;

77-78 **The Art Archive**: Musée du Louvre Paris/Dagli Orti;

78 **Robert Harding Picture Library**: t; **Réunion Des Musées Nationaux Agence Photographique**: Musée des arts Asiatiques-Guimet, Paris/Richard Lambert br;

79 **INAH**: b; 80 **Royal Museum of Scotland**; 81 **AKG London**: t;

83 **Corbis**: Richard T. Nowitz t; 84 **Ancient Art & Architecture Collection**: Ronald Sheridan t;

85 **Bridgeman Art Library, London/New York**: t; **Scala Group S.p.A.**: Victoria and Albert Museum b;

86 **AKG London**: Erich Lessing b; **Ancient Art & Architecture Collection**: t;

87 **Scala Group S.p.A.**: Museo Kabul; 88 © **The British Museum**: b; **Werner Forman Archive**: Ohio State Museum t; 90 **Bridgeman Art Library, London/New York**: Bonhams, London t; **Ashmolean Museum**: b; 91 **Bibliothèque Nationale De France, Paris**: b; **Kyoto National Museum**: t; 92 **Werner Forman Archive**: Private Collection, New York t; **INAH**: b;

93 **Capitoline Museums**: b; 94 **Scala Group S.p.A.**; 95 **The Art Archive**: Dagli Orti b;

96 **AKG London**: National Museum, Budapest/Erich Lessing b;

97 **Robert Harding Picture Library**: Chinese Exhibition; 98 **Werner Forman Archive**;

99 **The Art Archive**: Archaeological Museum Syracuse/Dagli Orti;

100 **Bridgeman Art Library, London/New York**: Private Collection b; © **The British Museum**: t; 101 **Sonia Halliday Photographs**: Laura Lushington;

103 **Bridgeman Art Library, London/New York**: Biblioteca Medicea-Laurenziana, Florence, Italy t; Huntington Library and Art Gallery, San Marino, California b; 104 **Corbis**: Dean Conger;

105 © **Michael Holford**: The British Museum b; **Network Photographers Ltd.**: George Gerster t;

106 **Ancient Art & Architecture Collection**: Ronald Sheridan b; **Bridgeman Art Library, London/New York**: Sant Apollinare Nuovo, Ravenna, Italy t;

107 **The Art Archive**: Dagli Orti (A); 108 **Sonia Halliday Photographs**;

111-112 **Eye Ubiquitous**: Kevin Nicol; 112 **AKG London**: Erich Lessing c;

113 **Peter Crawford**: cr; **Werner Forman Archive**: Statens Historiska Museum, Stockholm tl;

114 **The Art Archive**; 115 **South African Museum Iziko Museums of Cape Town**: Herschel Mair; 116 **Werner Forman Archive**: b; 117 **Ancient Art & Architecture Collection**: Ronald Sheridan t; **Bridgeman Art Library, London/New York**: San Vitale, Ravenna b;

118 **Ancient Art & Architecture Collection**: Ronald Sheridan t; **Heritage Image Partnership** © The British Museum b; 119 **Alan Williams**;

120 **James Davis Travel Photography**: b; **Werner Forman Archive**: National Musuem of Anthropology, Mexico t; 121 **Royal Museum of Scotland**: b; **The Art Archive**: Dagli Orti t; 122 © **The British Museum**: (OA 1963.10-16.1) b; © **Michael Holford**: The British Museum t; 123 **Royal Museum of Scotland**; 124 **The Art Archive**: Topkapi Museum Istanbul/Dagli Orti b; 125 **Bibliothèque Nationale De France, Paris**: t; **Werner Forman Archive**: Mrs Bashir Mohamed Collection b; 126 **Museum Rietberg Zürich**: Wettstein & Kauf;

127 **The Art Archive**: Archaeological Museum, Madrid t; **Heritage Image Partnership**: The British Museum b; 128 **Werner Forman Archive**: National Museum of Anthropology b;

129 **AKG London**: British Library t; **Ashmolean Museum**: b;

130 **British Library**: (Add. 25900 f.121v) t; **David Gower**: b; 131 **Corbis**: Paul Almasy b, t;

132 **AKG London**: British Library t; **Bridgeman Art Library, London/New York**: National Museum of Ireland t; 133 **The Art Archive**: Bibliothèque Nationale Paris;

134 **Heritage Image Partnership**: © The British Museum t; **Scala Group S.p.A.**: b;

135 **Corbis**: Paul A. Berry; 136 **Werner Forman Archive**; 137 **Bridgeman Art Library, London/New York**: British Library b; Musée Goya, Castres/Giraudon t;

138 **University Museum of Cultural Heritage - University of Oslo, Norway**: b; **Viking Ship Museum, Norway**: t;

139 **University Museum of Cultural Heritage - University of Oslo, Norway**: Ove Holst t; 140 **The Art Archive**: Dagli Orti; 141 **The Art Archive**: British Library;

142 **Bridgeman Art Library, London/New York**: British Library; 143 **Corbis**: Gianni Dagli t;

145 **Ancient Art & Architecture Collection**: Ronald Sheridan b; **Corbis**: Macduff Everton t;

146 **Werner Forman Archive**; 148 **Corbis**: David Muench;

149 **AKG London**: Irmgard Wagner b; 150 **Danish National Museum**: b; **Collection of the National Palace Museum, Taiwan, Republic Of China**: t; 151 **Corbis**: Angelo Hornak t;

152 **Bridgeman Art Library, London/New York**: Musée Conde, Chantilly t; **Novosti (London)**: b;

154 **Bodleian Library, University of Oxford**: (Ms. Marsh 144 P.167);

157-158 **Bridgeman Art Library, London/New York**: British Library;

158 **Werner Forman Archive**: Beijing Museum, Beijing c;

159 **AKG London**: National Museum, Tokyo cr; **The Art Archive**: Dagli Orti c;

160 **Bridgeman Art Library, London/New York**: t; **INAH**: b;

161 **The Art Archive**: Private Collection Paris/Dagli Orti t; **Corbis**: Asian Art & Archaeology, Inc. b;

162 **Ancient Art & Architecture Collection**: Chantal Boulanger b; **Ashmolean Museum**: t;

163 **AKG London**: Erich Lessing b; © **The British Museum**: (CM 1915-5-7-1201) t;

164 **Robert Harding Picture Library**: Nigel Blythe;

165 **Werner Forman Archive**: Biblioteca Nazionale, Venice b; **Gables Travels**: t;

166 **Corbis**: Adam Woolfitt; 167 **AKG London**: b; **Werner Forman Archive**: David Berstein Fine Art, New York t; 169 **Corbis**: Michael S. Lewis t; **Dean and Chapter of Westminster**: b;

170 **Ancient Art & Architecture Collection**: Crisp t; **Bibliothèque Nationale De France, Paris**:

(Ms. Grec. 74, folio 143) b; **171 Biblioteca Nacional, Madrid**: t; **RJL Smith, Much Wenlock, Shropshire**: b; **172 AKG London**: Erich Lessing t; **The Art Archive**: Dagli Orti b;

173 Ancient Art & Architecture Collection: Ronald Sheridan;

174 AKG London: t; **Werner Forman Archive**: Biblioteca Nacional, Madrid b;

175 AKG London: Erich Lessing; **176 Ancient Art & Architecture Collection**: t; **Robert Harding Picture Library**: b; **177 Public Record Office**;

178 Ancient Art & Architecture Collection: Ronald Sheridan b; **Werner Forman Archive**: t;

179 Bridgeman Art Library, London/New York: Bibliotheque Nationale, France;

180 The Art Archive; **181 AKG London**: b; **Ancient Art & Architecture Collection**: Cheryl Hogue t;

182 Ghent University Library: (Ms.92 Folio 241r); **183 The Art Archive**: British Library;

184 Bridgeman Art Library, London/New York: Bibliothèque Nationale de France, Paris t; Institut Amatller D'art Hispànic (Arxiu MAS): b;

185 The Art Archive: Uppsala University Library Sweden/Dagli Orti;

186 AKG London: Erich Lessing b; **Robert Harding Picture Library**: t;

187 Berlin, Staatsbibliothek zu Berlin - Pressischer Kulturbesitz - Handschriftenabteilung: (Ms. 92, fol. 241r); **188 Bridgeman Art Library, London/New York**: Cathedral of St. James, Santiago da Compostela, Spain; **189 Werner Forman Archive**: b; **190 The Art Archive**: Dagli Orti t;

191 Sonia Halliday Photographs: b; **192 AKG London**: British Library; **193 AKG London**;

194 Werner Forman Archive: The British Museum b; **Heritage Image Partnership**: The British Museum t; **196** © **The British Museum**: b; **Werner Forman Archive**: t; **197 AKG London**;

198 AKG London: Jean-Louis Nou b; **Werner Forman Archive**: t;

199 Bridgeman Art Library, London/New York: Museo del Oro, Lima, Peru;

200 Bodleian Library, University of Oxford: (Ms Pococke 375, fols 3v-4r);

203-204 Bridgeman Art Library, London/New York: British Library;

204 Bridgeman Art Library, London/New York: Bibliothèque Nationale de France, Paris c;

205 Sonia Halliday Photographs: Topkapi Palace Museum, Istanbul (Ms. 3109) tl; **Robert Harding Picture Library**: cr; **206 AKG London**: San Benedetto Monastery, Subiaco (Sacro Speco) b; **Photo Josse**: Bibliotheque de l'Arsenal, Paris t; **207 The Art Archive**: Musée du Louvre Paris/Dagli Orti (A); **208 Bridgeman Art Library, London/New York**: Dept. of the Environment, London, UK; **209 Bridgeman Art Library, London/New York**: British Library b;

210 AKG London: b; **Mary Evans Picture Library**: t; **211 Musée Marmottan**: b;

212 AKG London; **213 Sonia Halliday Photographs**: t; **Hulton Archive/Getty Images**: b;

215 Bridgeman Art Library, London/New York: Château Roux, France b; **Hulton Archive/Getty Images**: t; **216** © **The British Museum**: (OA 1920-9-17.0130) t;

217 Bridgeman Art Library, London/New York: Victoria & Albert Museum, London b; **Werner Forman Archive**: Gulistan Imperial Library, Teheran t;

218 Ancient Art & Architecture Collection: Ronald Sheridan;

219 AKG London: Bibliothèque Nationale de France, Paris (Add. 18866, fol.140) t;

220 National Maritime Museum, London: b;

221 Bridgeman Art Library, London/New York: Bibliotheque Nationale, Paris, France t;

222 Ancient Art & Architecture Collection;

223 Bridgeman Art Library, London/New York: Corpus Christi College, Oxford, UK;

224 Collection of the National Palace Museum, Taiwan, Republic Of China;

225 Bridgeman Art Library, London/New York: Bibliotheque Nationale, Paris;

226 AKG London: t; **Bridgeman Art Library, London/New York**: b;

227 Bridgeman Art Library, London/New York; **228 Bridgeman Art Library, London/New York**: National Library of Scotland t; **Mary Evans Picture Library**: b;

229 Bridgeman Art Library, London/New York: British Library;

230 Bridgeman Art Library, London/New York: The British Museum t;

231 Bodleian Library; **233 Eye Ubiquitous**: Thelma Sanders b;

234 Bridgeman Art Library, London/New York: Bibliotheque Nationale, Paris b;

235 The Art Archive: Biblioteca Nazionale Marciana Venice/Dagli Orti b;

236 AKG London: t; **Bridgeman Art Library, London/New York**: Staatsarchiv, Hamburg, Germany b;

237 AKG London: b; **Serbian Unity Congress (www.serbianunity.net)**: t;

238 Robert Aberman: t; **Robert Harding Picture Library**:

239 Collection of the National Palace Museum, Taiwan, Republic Of China: b;

240 Werner Forman Archive; **241 Ancient Art & Architecture Collection**: Ronald Sheridan b; **Werner Forman Archive**: National Museum of the American Indian, New York t;

242 Bridgeman Art Library, London/New York: British Library t; **Heritage Image Partnership**: Science Museum, London b; **243 Bridgeman Art Library, London/New York**: Private Collection;

244 The Art Archive: Victoria & Albert Museum, London t; **Werner Forman Archive**: Barbara Heller/Nick Saunders b; **245** © **The British Museum**;

246 Bridgeman Art Library, London/New York: The British Museum;

249-250 AKG London: Erich Lessing t; **250 Werner Forman Archive**: b; **Sonia Halliday Photographs**: Topkapi Palace Museum, Istanbul t; **251 AKG London**;

252 Bridgeman Art Library, London/New York: Bargello, Florence, Italy t;

253 Bridgeman Art Library, London/New York: British Library; **254 AKG London**;

255 Bridgeman Art Library, London/New York: Tretyakov Gallery, Moscow t; **Corbis**: Archivo Iconografico, S.A. b; **256 AKG London**: Erich Lessing;

257 Bridgeman Art Library, London/New York: British Library t; **James Davis Travel Photography**: b; **258 Bridgeman Art Library, London/New York**: Archives Nationales, Paris, France; **259 Corbis**: Roger Antrobus b; **The Art Archive**: Musée des Arts Africains et Océaniens/Dagli Orti t; **260 AKG London**;

261 Bridgeman Art Library, London/New York: Biblioteca Nazionale Centrale, Florence, Italy;

262 AKG London: Erich Lessing t; **Corbis**: Michael Nicholson b; **263 AKG London**: Visioars;

264 Robert Harding Picture Library; **265 Robert Harding Picture Library**: Sybil Sassoon;

266 The Art Archive: Topkapi Museum Istanbul/Dagli Orti; **267 AKG London**;

268 Bridgeman Art Library, London/New York: t; The British Museum b;

269 AKG London; **270 Bridgeman Art Library, London/New York**: Bibliothèque Nationale de France b; Private Collection t; **271 Bridgeman Art Library, London/New York**: British Library b;

272 Bridgeman Art Library, London/New York: Vatican Museum and Galleries, Vatican City, Italy t;

273 Bridgeman Art Library, London/New York: Private Collection t; **Musée de Louvre**: b;

274 Bridgeman Art Library, London/New York: Bristol City Museum and Art Gallery, UK t; **Ashmolean Museum**: b; **276 Bridgeman Art Library, London/New York**: British Library, t; Nationalmuseum, Stockholm, Sweden b; **277 AKG London**: t; **The Art Archive**: b;

278 AKG London: b; **Institut Amatller D'art Hispànic (Arxiu MAS)**: t;

279 Bridgeman Art Library, London/New York: Musee de Sibiu, Rumania/Giraudon b; **Ashmolean Museum**: t; **280 AKG London**: t;

281 The Art Archive: Science Academy Lisbon/Dagli Orti b; **Robert Harding Picture Library**: Cartes et Plans, Bibliothèque Nationale de France, Paris t;

282 Bridgeman Art Library, London/New York: Private Collection;

283 Bridgeman Art Library, London/New York: The British Museum t; Nationalmuseet, Copenhagen, Denmark b; **284 Bridgeman Art Library, London/New York**: Walker Art Gallery, Liverpool, UK b; **285 The Art Archive**: Maritime Museum Stockholm Sweden/Dagli Orti (A) t; **Peter Newark's Pictures**: b; **286 Bridgeman Art Library, London/New York**: Lauros-Giraudon;

287 AKG London: t; **Wallace Collection**: b; **288 The Art Archive**: b; **Louvre, Paris, France**: t;

289 Bridgeman Art Library, London/New York: Private Collection b;

290 Bridgeman Art Library, London/New York: British Library t; **Eye Ubiquitous**: Adina Tovy Amsel b; **291 AKG London**: t; **292 British Library**;

295-296 Bridgeman Art Library, London/New York: Victoria & Albert Museum, London, UK;

296 Bridgeman Art Library, London/New York: Archives Charmet, Bibliothèque de L'Arsenal, Paris t; **National Maritime Museum, London**: c;

297 Bridgeman Art Library, London/New York: Trinity College, Cambridge;

299 The Art Archive: Navy Historical Service Vincennes France/Dagli Orti t; **Werner Forman Archive**: H M De Young Memorial Museum, San Francisco, USA b;

300 Bridgeman Art Library, London/New York: Private Collection b;

301 AKG London: t; **Netherlands Maritime Museum, Amsterdam**: b;

302 AKG London: b; **Wallace Collection**: t; **303 Bridgeman Art Library, London/New York**: Madrasa-yi Madar-i Shah, Isfahan, Iran b; Private Collection t;

304 Bridgeman Art Library, London/New York: Metropolitan Museum of Art, New York, USA;

305 Bridgeman Art Library, London/New York: Private Collection b; **Eye Ubiquitous**: Julia Bayne t;

306 Bridgeman Art Library, London/New York: Private Collection b; **Wallace Collection**: t;

307 The Art Archive: Private Collection t; **Bridgeman Art Library, London/New York**: Grosjean Collection, Paris, France b; **308 Mary Evans Picture Library**: t; **Williamson Collection**: b;

309 Fotomas Index: t; **310 Bridgeman Art Library, London/New York**: Giraudon/Chateau de Versaille, France t; Royal Society, London b; **311 Heritage Image Partnership**: Museum of London b; **Peter Newark's Pictures**: t; **312 British Library**: (Harl. 4379, f. 83v) b; **Mary Evans Picture Library**: t; **313 Bridgeman Art Library, London/New York**: Bibliotheque Nationale, France; **314 AKG London**: Erich Lessing; **315 Bridgeman Art Library, London/New York**: The British Museum; **316 Bridgeman Art Library, London/New York**: Hermitage, St. Petersburg;

317 AKG London: t; **Bridgeman Art Library, London/New York**: Royal Geographical Society b;

318 The Art Archive: Eileen Tweedy t;

319 AKG London: t; **Bridgeman Art Library, London/New York**: Maidstone Museum and Art Gallery b; **320 Bildarchiv Preußischer Kulturbesitz**: Berlin;

321 **Bridgeman Art Library, London/New York**: Private Collection t;

323 **Heritage Image Partnership**: British Library b; 324 **AKG London**: t; **Ancient Art & Architecture Collection**: Ronald Sheridan b; 325 **Bridgeman Art Library, London/New York**: Private Collection; 326 **Bridgeman Art Library, London/New York**: Stapleton Collection t;

327 **Bridgeman Art Library, London/New York**: Joseph & Earle Vanderar t;

328 **National Army Museum**: Courtesy of the Director t; **Peter Newark's Pictures**: b;

329 **Bildarchiv Preußischer Kulturbesitz**: Kunstbibliothek Preußischer Kulturbesitz, Berlin;

330 **Peter Newark's Pictures**; 331 **The Art Archive**: British Library b;

332 **Peter Newark's Pictures**; 333 **Bridgeman Art Library, London/New York**: Mitchell Library, State Library of New South Wales b; **Peter Newark's Pictures**: t; 334 **Science Museum**: t;

335 **The Art Archive**: American Museum of Art Cuzco/Mireille Vautier t; **Bridgeman Art Library, London/New York**: Royal Geographical Society, London b; 336 **AKG London**;

337 **Bridgeman Art Library, London/New York**: Musee Carnavalet, Paris t;

338 **National Maritime Museum, London**; 341-342 **AKG London**;

342 **Peter Newark's Pictures**: b, t; 343 **Bridgeman Art Library, London/New York**: The British Museum, London; 344 **Bridgeman Art Library, London/New York**: Louvre, Paris, France t; **National Army Museum**: b; 345 **The Art Archive**: Eileen Tweedy b; **Mary Evans Picture Library**: t;

346 **AKG London**; 347 **The Art Archive**: British Library b; **Robert Harding Picture Library**: Adina Tovy t; 348 **AKG London**: t; **The Art Archive**: Eileen Tweedy b; 349 **AKG London**;

350 **Bridgeman Art Library, London/New York**: Stapleton Collection;

351 **The Art Archive**: Eileen Tweedy b; 352 **Public Record Office**: t;

353 **The Art Archive**: Museo Historico Nacional Buenos Aires/Dagli Orti;

354 **AKG London**: b; **Bridgeman Art Library, London/New York**: Victoria & Albert Museum, London t; 355 **AKG London**; 356 **Mary Evans Picture Library**: b;

357 **Bridgeman Art Library, London/New York**: Taylor Gallery, London t; **Peter Newark's Pictures**: b; 358 **Hulton Archive/Getty Images**: Louis Jacques Daguerre b;

359 **Bridgeman Art Library, London/New York**: Alexander Turnbull Library, National Library of New Zealand, Te Puna Mātauranga o Aotearoa b; **National Maritime Museum, London**: t;

360 **Bridgeman Art Library, London/New York**: Private Collection b; **Peter Newark's Pictures**: t; 361 **Mary Evans Picture Library**: b; 362 **AKG London**: b; **Mary Evans Picture Library**: t;

363 **Peter Newark's Pictures**: b; 364 **The Art Archive**: School of Oriental & African Studies/Eileen Tweedy t; **Bridgeman Art Library, London/New York**: Guildhall Library, Corporation of London b; 365 **Peter Newark's Pictures**;

366 **The Art Archive**: Museo del Risorgimento Brescia/Dagli Orti b; **Mary Evans Picture Library**: t; 367 **Bridgeman Art Library, London/New York**: British Library, London t;

368 **Mary Evans Picture Library**: t; **Peter Newark's Pictures**: b;

369 **TRH Pictures**: USNA b; 370 **AKG London**; 371 **Mary Evans Picture Library**: b, t;

372 **Bridgeman Art Library, London/New York**: Courtauld Gallery, London t;

373 **AKG London**: b, t; 374 **Corbis**: Bettmann t; **Museum of Mankind**: b;

375 **Mary Evans Picture Library**: b; **Peter Newark's Pictures**: t;

376 **Royal Geographical Society**: t; **Hulton Archive/Getty Images**: b;

377 **Mary Evans Picture Library**: t; **Library Of Congress, Washington, D.C.**: b;

378 **Mary Evans Picture Library**: b; **Musee Gauguin, Tahiti**: t;

379 **The Art Archive**: Musée d'Orsay Paris/Dagli Orti; 380 **Werner Forman Archive**: C.D. Wertheim Collection; 381 **Katz/FSP**: Roger Viollet t; **Pitt Rivers Museum**: b;

382 **The Art Archive**: Eileen Tweedy; 383 **Corbis**: Hulton-Deutsch Collection t; **Mary Evans Picture Library**: b; 384 **William L. Clements Library, The University Of Michigan**;

387-388 **Imperial War Museum**; 388 **David King Collection**:;

389 **Corbis**: Bettmann/Underwood c; **Hulton Archive/Getty Images**: br;

390 **AKG London**: b; **Corbis**: t; 391 **Corbis**: Bettmann b; 392 **Corbis**: Hulton-Deutsch Collection b;

393 **Mary Evans Picture Library**: t; **Peter Newark's Pictures**: b;

394 **Hulton Archive/Getty Images**: t; 395 **Hulton Archive/Getty Images**: t; **Peter Newark's Pictures**: b; 396 **Corbis**: cl; Bettmann tr; 397 **Hulton Archive/Getty Images**: bl, br; **Imperial War Museum**: Reeve Photography t; 398 **Hulton Archive/Getty Images**: t;

399 **The Art Archive**: Domenica del Corriere/Dagli Orti (A);

400 **Advertising Archives**: t; **Corbis**: Bettmann b; 401 **Corbis**: b; **Hulton Archive/Getty Images**: t; 402 **National Motor Museum, Beaulieu**; 405-406 **Peter Newark's Pictures**;

406 **AKG London**: c; 407 **Hulton Archive/Getty Images**: tl; **Peter Newark's Pictures**: br;

408 **David King Collection**: b; 409 **Hulton Archive/Getty Images**: t;

410 **Michael Butler Collection**: b; **Mary Evans Picture Library**: t; 411 **Corbis**: t;

412 **Hulton Archive/Getty Images**; 413 **AKG London**: b; **Hulton Archive/Getty Images**: t;

414 **Peter Newark's Pictures**: bl, br; 415 **Corbis**: cr; Bettmann t; 416 **Corbis**: Hulton-Deutsch

Collection b; **Rex Features**: t; 417 **Corbis**: UPI/Bettmann b; **Hulton Archive/Getty Images**: t;

418 **Corbis**: Bettmann b; **Hulton Archive/Getty Images**: t; 419 **Hulton Archive/Getty Images**: t;

420 **London Transport Museum**; 423-424 **Peter Newark's Pictures**;

424 **Advertising Archives**: c; 425 **AKG London**: Tony Vaccaro b; **Corbis**: Hulton-Deutsch Collection t; 426 **Hulton Archive/Getty Images**: t; 427 **David King Collection**: b; **Science Photo Library**: Dr Tim Evans t; 428 **David King Collection**: b; **Popperfoto**: t;

429 **Hulton Archive/Getty Images**: b; **Popperfoto**: t;

430 **Rex Features**: Sipa Press /East News cl; **Topham Picturepoint**: © 2002 AP cr;

431 **Corbis**: Bettmann cr; Dean Conger bl;

432 **Katz/FSP**: Getty Hulton Liaison t; 433 **Peter Newark's Pictures**: t;

434 **Hulton Archive/Getty Images**: b; **Rex Features**: Tim Page t;

435 **Hulton Archive/Getty Images**; 436 **Rex Features**: Ben Simmons;

437 **Austin Brown/Aviation Picture Library**: The Boeing Company t; **Corbis Sygma**: A Balaguer b; 438 **Getty Images**; 441-442 **Corbis**: Barry Lewis; 442 **Katz/FSP**: Diffidenti t;

443 **Corbis**: Philippe Wojazer/Reuter c; **Rex Features**: Christiana Laruffa t;

445 **Rex Features**: Mark Brewer t; **SIPA-Press** t; 446 **Panos Pictures**: Michael Harvey;

447 **Rex Features**: Andre Camara t; **Katz/FSP**: Gamma t; 448 **Panos Pictures**: David Dahmen b; **Rex Features**: Jacques Witt t; 449 **Magnum**: Stuart Franklin t; **Panos Pictures**: Penny Tweedie b;

450 **Peter Newark's Pictures**: b; **Panos Pictures**: Betty Press t; 451 **Panos Pictures**: Chris Stowers b; **Katz/FSP**: Noel Quidu t; 452 **Rex Features**: James Fraser b; Sipa t;

453 **Corbis**: Ethan Miller b; **Rex Features**: Vladimir Sichov/Sipa Press t;

454 **Katz/FSP**: Wendy Sue Lamm/Gamma t; Anticoli Livio b;

455 **Network Photographers Ltd.**: SABA/Thomas Franklin;

457 **Science Photo Library**: CNES, 1986 Distribution Spot Image;

JACKET: *Front, row 1 from left to right:* **DK Picture Library**; **AKG London**: Erich Lessing; **Werner Forman Archive**: Courtesy Entwistle Gallery, London; **AKG London**.
Front, row 2 from left to right: **Bridgeman Art Library, London/New York**: Private Collection; **Ashmolean Museum**; **Werner Forman Archive**: National Museum of Arthropology, Mexico; **Robert Harding Picture Library**: Bildagentur Schuster/Krauskopf; **Bridgeman Art Library, London/New York**: Private Collection.
Front, row 3 from left to right: **Bridgeman Art Library, London/New York**: Private Collection; **Bridgeman Art Library, London/New York**: Archives Charmet, Bibliotheque de L'Arsenal, Paris; **Public Record Office**; **The Art Archive**: National Archives Washington DC; **Mary Evans Picture Library**.
Front, row 4 from left to right: **Rex Features**; **NASA**; **Rex Features**: Tim Page; **Popperfoto**: Ulli Michel/Reuters; **Network Photographers Ltd.**: SABA/Thomas Franklin.
Back, from left to right: **Bridgeman Art Library, London/New York**: Private Collection; **Ashmolean Museum**; **Werner Forman Archive**: National Museum of Arthropology, Mexico; **Robert Harding Picture Library**: Bildagentur Schuster/Krauskopf; **Bridgeman Art Library, London/New York**: Private Collection.
Spine: **Werner Forman Archive**: Courtesy Entwistle Gallery, London.
Back flap: **Ashmolean Museum**.

All other images © Dorling Kindersley; For further information see: www.dkimages.com

AUTHOR'S ACKNOWLEDGMENTS

These people read portions of the original manuscript in area of their speciality.
All of the following were on the faculty at Colgate University in Hamilton, N. Y.

Dr. Harold Stone: Egypt, Rome, and Great Britain

Dr. Philippe Uninsky: France

Dr. Padma Kaimal: India

Dr. Andy Rotter: United States

Dr. Luis Martinez-Fernandez: Latin America

Dr. Kira Stevens: Russia/Soviet Union

Dr. Tia Kolbaba: Byzantine Empire

Dr. Po-shek-Fu: China